Information Systems Today

Managing in the Digital World

Fourth Edition

Joe Valacich
Washington State University

Christoph Schneider
City University of Hong Kong

Prentice Hall
Upper Saddle River, New Jersey 07458

Library of Congress Cataloging-in-Publication Data

Valacich, Joseph S.

  Information systems today : managing in the digital world / Joseph S. Valacich,
Christoph Schneider.—4th ed.

    p. cm.

  Previous eds. by Leonard M. Jessup.

  Includes bibliographical references and index.

  ISBN 0-13-607840-0

  1. Information technology. 2. Information storage and retrieval systems—
Business. I. Schneider, Christoph. II. Jessup, Leonard M., 1961–Information
systems today. III. Title.

T58.5.J47 2009

658.4'038011—dc22

                                            2009000291

Executive Editor: Bob Horan
Editorial Director: Sally Yagan
Editor in Chief: Eric Svendsen
Assistant Editor: Kelly Loftus
Editorial Assistant: Valerie Patruno
Senior Marketing Manager: Anne Fahlgren
Permissions Project Manager: Charles Morris
Senior Managing Editor: Judy Leale
Production Project Manager: Clara Bartunek
Senior Operations Specialist: Arnold Vila
Cover & Interior Art Director: Mike Fruhbeis
Cover & Interior Designer: Frubilicious Design Co.
Cover Illustration/Photos: AP Photo/Ben Margot,
  AP Photo/Joerg Sarbach, AP Photo/Paul Sakuma,
  AP Photo/Jason DeCrow

Manager, Rights and Permissions: Zina Arabia
Manager, Visual Research: Beth Brenzel
Image Permission Coordinator: Craig Jones
Photo Researcher: Rachel Lucas
Manager, Cover Visual Research & Permissions:
  Karen Sanatar
Composition: GGS Higher Education Resources,
  A Divison of Premedia Global, Inc.
Full-Service Project Management: Ann Courtney/
  GGS Higher Education Resources, A Divison of
  Premedia Global, Inc.
Interior Printer/Binder: Webcrafters Inc.
Cover Printer: Lehigh - Phoenix Color
  Corp./Hagerstown
Typeface: 10/12 Times

Credits and acknowledgments borrowed from other sources and reproduced, with permission,
in this textbook appear on appropriate page within text (or on page 598).

Microsoft® and Windows® are registered trademarks of the Microsoft Corporation in the
U.S.A. and other countries. Screen shots and icons reprinted with permission from the
Microsoft Corporation. This book is not sponsored or endorsed by or affiliated with the
Microsoft Corporation.

Pearson Education Ltd., London
Pearson Education Singapore, Pte. Ltd
Pearson Education, Canada, Inc.
Pearson Education–Japan
Pearson Education Australia PTY, Limited

Pearson Education North Asia, Ltd., Hong Kong
Pearson Educación de Mexico, S.A. de C.V.
Pearson Education Malaysia, Pte. Ltd
Pearson Education Upper Saddle River,
  New Jersey

Prentice Hall
is an imprint of

www.pearsonhighered.com

10 9 8 7 6 5 4 3 2 1
ISBN-13: 978-0-13-607840-1
ISBN-10:   0-13-607840-0

Dedication

To Jackie, Jordan, and James for your sacrifices, love, and support.
—**Joe**

To Birgit for your love and support.
—**Christoph**

About the Authors

Joe Valacich is the George and Carolyn Hubman Distinguished Professor of Management Information Systems and was the inaugural Marian E. Smith Presidential Endowed Chair at Washington State University. He was previously an associate professor with tenure (early) at Indiana University, Bloomington, and was named the Sanjay Subhedar Faculty Fellow. He has had visiting faculty appointments at the University of Arizona, City University of Hong Kong, Buskerud College (Norway), Norwegian University of Life Sciences, Riga Technical University (Latvia), and Helsinki School of Economics and Business. He received his PhD degree from the University of Arizona (MIS) and his MBA and BS (computer science) degrees from the University of Montana. His teaching interests include systems analysis and design, collaborative computing, project management, and the management of information systems. Professor Valacich served on the national task forces to design *IS '97* and *2002: The Model Curriculum and Guidelines for Undergraduate Degree Programs in Information Systems* as well as *MSIS 2000* and *2006: The Master of Science in Information Systems Model Curriculum.* He is currently cochairing the task force designing *IS 2008.* He also served on the executive committee, funded by the National Science Foundation, to define the *IS Program Accreditation Standards* and on the board of directors for CSAB (formally, the Computing Sciences Accreditation Board) representing the Association for Information Systems (AIS). He was the general conference cochair for the 2003 International Conference on Information Systems (ICIS) in Seattle and was the vice chair of ICIS 1999 in Charlotte, NC.

Dr. Valacich has conducted numerous corporate training and executive development programs for organizations, including AT&T, Boeing, Dow Chemical, EDS, Exxon, FedEx, General Motors, Microsoft, and Xerox. He is currently a senior editor at *MIS Quarterly* and is on the editorial boards at *Decision Sciences* and *Small Group Research.* He was previously an associate editor at *Information Systems Research.* His primary research interests include technology-mediated collaboration, human-computer interaction, mobile and emerging technologies, e-business, and distance education. His work has appeared in numerous prestigious journals, including *MIS Quarterly, Information Systems Research, Management Science, Academy of Management Journal, Journal of MIS, Decision Sciences, Journal of the AIS, Communications of the ACM, Organizational Behavior and Human Decision Processes, Journal of Applied Psychology,* and many others. He is a coauthor of the best-selling textbook *Modern Systems Analysis and Design* (5th Edition), as well as *Essentials of Systems Analysis and Design* (4th Edition), *Object-Oriented Systems Analysis and Design* (2nd Edition), and *Information Systems Project Management* (1st Edition); all are published by Prentice Hall.

Christoph Schneider is an assistant professor in the Department of Information Systems at City University of Hong Kong and previously held a visiting faculty appointment at Boise State University. He earned a Swiss Higher Diploma in hotel management at the University Centre César Ritz in Brig, Switzerland, and a BA in hotel and restaurant administration at Washington State University. Following extensive experience in the international hospitality industry, he studied information systems at the Martin Luther University in Halle, Germany, before joining the information systems department at Washington State University to earn his PhD degree. His teaching interests include the management of information systems, business intelligence, and enterprise-wide information systems.

Dr. Schneider is an active researcher. His primary research interests include human-computer interaction, electronic commerce and computer-mediated collaboration. His research has appeared in peer reviewed journals, such as *Information Systems Research, Management Information Systems Quarterly,* and *IEEE Transactions on Professional Communication;* further, he has presented his research at various national and international conferences, such as the International Conference on Information Systems, the European Conference on Information Systems, and the Hawaii International Conference on System Sciences.

Brief Contents

Preface xvii

Chapter 1   Managing in the Digital World   2

Chapter 2   Fueling Globalization through Information Systems   38

Chapter 3   Valuing Information Systems Investments   82

Chapter 4   Managing the Information Systems Infrastructure   130

Chapter 5   Enabling Commerce Using the Internet   186

Chapter 6   Enhancing Collaboration Using Web 2.0   232

Chapter 7   Securing Information Systems   268

Chapter 8   Enhancing Business Intelligence Using Information Systems   310

Chapter 9   Building Organizational Partnerships Using Enterprise Information Systems   358

Chapter 10   Developing and Acquiring Information Systems   406

Chapter 11   Managing Information Systems Ethics and Crime   452

Technology Briefing   Advanced Topics and Trends in Managing the Information Systems Infrastructure   498

Contents

Preface xvii

Chapter 1 Managing in the Digital World 2

MANAGING IN THE DIGITAL WORLD: Apple Computer 3

What You Will Find in This Book 5

Information Systems Today 5

Characteristics of the Digital World 7

Information Systems Defined 8

Data: The Root and Purpose of Information Systems 8

■ WHEN THINGS GO WRONG: Failure: The Path to Success? 9

Information Technology: The Components of Information Systems 11

■ COMING ATTRACTIONS: How to Build a Bionic Contact Lens 12

People: The Builders and Managers of Information Systems 13

■ POWERFUL PARTNERSHIPS: The Two Steves—Jobs & Wozniak 19

Organizations: The Context of Information Systems 20

■ NET STATS: Worldwide Internet Usage 25

The Dual Nature of Information Systems 26

Case in Point: An Information System Gone Awry: London-Heathrow International Airport 25

Case in Point: An Information System That Works: FedEx 27

Information Systems for Competitive Advantage 27

■ ETHICAL DILEMMA: Online Rights Not Always Universal 28

Why Information Systems Matter 29

■ BRIEF CASE: Guerilla Wi-Fi 29

■ INDUSTRY ANALYSIS: Business Career Outlook 30

Key Points Review 32 • Key Terms 32 • Review Questions 32 • Self-Study Questions 33 • Problems and Exercises 33 • Application Exercises 34 • Team Work Exercise: How to Find Out What Is Current in IS 35 • Answers to the Self-Study Questions 35

■ CLICK CLIQUE–FACEBOOK.COM 36

■ ARE WE THERE YET?–ONLINE MAP SERVICES 37

Chapter 2 Fueling Globalization Through Information Systems 38

MANAGING IN THE DIGITAL WORLD: Infosys Technologies Ltd. 39

Evolution of Globalization 40

Globalization 1.0 40

Globalization 2.0 41

Globalization 3.0 41

■ POWERFUL PARTNERSHIPS: Netscape's James H. Clark and Marc Andreessen 44

■ NET STATS: Online Searching 51

The Rise of Outsourcing 52

Opportunities for Operating in the Digital World 54

■ BRIEF CASE: IT Globalization: Accenture in India 55

Opportunities for Reaching New Markets 55

Opportunities of a Global Workforce 55

Challenges of Operating in the Digital World 57

Governmental Challenges 57

Geoeconomic Challenges 60

■ ETHICAL DILEMMA: Underground Gaming Economy   61

Demographic Challenges   63

Cultural Challenges   64

■ COMING ATTRACTIONS: Learning Languages in Context   66

■ WHEN THINGS GO WRONG: e-Waste   68

Going Global: International Business Strategies in the Digital World   69

Home Replication Strategy   70

Global Business Strategy   71

Transnational Business Strategy   73

■ INDUSTRY ANALYSIS: The Automobile Industry   74

Key Points Review   75   •   Key Terms   76   •   Review Questions   76   •
Self-Study Questions   76   •   Problems and Exercises   77   •   Application
Exercises   78   •   Team Work Exercise: Becoming a Global Leader   79   •
Answers to the Self-Study Questions   79

■ GLOBAL PICTURE SHARING: FLICKR   79

■ ENABLING GLOBAL PAYMENTS AT PAYPAL   80

Chapter 3   Valuing Information Systems Investments   82

MANAGING IN THE DIGITAL WORLD: TiVo   83

Valuing Information Systems   84

Information Systems for Automating: Doing Things Faster   85

Information Systems for Organizational Learning: Doing Things Better   86

Information Systems for Supporting Strategy: Doing Things Smarter   87

Sources of Competitive Advantage   88

■ ETHICAL DILEMMA: The IT Department Often *Knows*   89

Information Systems and Value Chain Analysis   90

The Role of Information Systems in Value Chain Analysis   90

The Technology/Strategy Fit   91

Making the Business Case for an Information System   91

Business Case Objectives   91

■ WHEN THINGS GO WRONG: Rootkits: Sony's Secret   92

The Productivity Paradox   93

■ POWERFUL PARTNERSHIPS: Microsoft's Bill Gates and Paul Allen   96

Making a Successful Business Case   97

Presenting the Business Case   103

■ NET STATS: Who is Sharing Files?   104

Assessing Value for the Information Systems Infrastructure   106

Changing Mind-sets About Information Systems   107

Valuing Innovations   107

The Need for Constant IS Innovation   107

■ BRIEF CASE: For Sale by Owner: Your Company's Name.com   108

Successful Innovation is Difficult   109

Organizational Requirements for Innovation   111

Predicting the Next New Thing   112

■ COMING ATTRACTIONS: What Were You Thinking? Brain Sensor
for Market Research   112

The Innovator's Dilemma   113

**Freeconomics: Why Free Products are the Future of the Digital
World   118**

How Freeconomics Works   118

The Freeconomics Value Proposition   118

Applying Freecomonics in the Digital World   119

■ INDUSTRY ANALYSIS: Photo Industry   121

Key Points Review   122   •   Key Terms   123   •   Review Questions   123   •
Self-Study Questions   124   •   Problems and Exercises   125   •   Application
Exercises   126   •   Team Work Exercise: Pizza, Anyone?   126   •   Answers to
the Self-Study Questions   126

■ NETFLIX   127

■ LINKEDIN   128

Chapter 4   Managing the Information Systems Infrastructure   130

MANAGING IN THE DIGITAL WORLD: "I Googled You!"   131

The Information Systems Infrastructure   132

Information Systems Hardware Infrastructure   134

Input Technologies   134

Processing Technologies   135

■ ETHICAL DILEMMA: Cookies: Harmless Identifiers or Privacy
Violations?   137

■ WHEN THINGS GO WRONG: BlackBerry   141

Output Technologies   142

Types of Computers   142

Hardware Infrastructure Trends   142

Information Systems Software Infrastructure   146

Systems Software/Operating System   146

■ POWERFUL PARTNERSHIPS: Google's Larry Page and Sergey Brin   147

Application Software   150

Software Infrastructure Trends   150

Communications and Collaboration Infrastructure   152

Human Communication and Computer Networking   152

■ NET STATS: Broadband Access Increases   152

Computer Networks   154

Networking Fundamentals   155

How Did the Internet Get Started?   158

■ BRIEF CASE: Autonomic Computing   159

The Internet Uses Packet-Switching Technology   160

Transmission Control Protocol/Internet Protocol   160

World Wide Web   161

Managing the Communication and Collaboration Infrastructure   163

■ COMING ATTRACTIONS: TV for the Visually Impaired   166

Data and Knowledge Infrastructure   166

The Database Approach: Foundation Concepts   167

Advantages of the Database Approach   167

Effective Management of Databases   168

Key Database Activities   171

How Organizations Get the Most from Their Data   172

■ INDUSTRY ANALYSIS: Movie Industry   177

Key Points Review   178   •   Key Terms   179   •   Review Questions   180   •
Self-Study Questions   181   •   Problems and Exercises   181   •   Application
Exercises   182   •   Team Work Exercise: Your Personal Communication
Infrastructure Assessment   183   •   Answers to the Self-Study Questions   183

■ DATABASE AS A SERVICE: AMAZON'S SIMPLEDB   183

■ BROADBAND SERVICE ON AIRPLANES: WIFI IN THE SKY   184

Chapter 5   Enabling Commerce Using the Internet   186

DOING VIRTUAL BUSINESS: Second Life   187

Electronic Commerce Defined   188

Internet and World Wide Web Capabilities   189

Electronic Commerce Business Strategies   193

■ WHEN THINGS GO WRONG: Virtual Crime   194

Business-to-Business Electronic Commerce: Extranets   196

■ NET STATS: E-Business is BIG Business   197

The Need for Organizations to Exchange Data   198

Exchanging Organizational Data Using Extranets   198

Benefits of Extranets   198

Extranet System Architecture   199

Extranet Applications   199

■ ETHICAL DILEMMA: Monitoring Productive Employees   200

Business-to-Employee Electronic Commerce: Intranets   201

Intranet System Architecture   201

Intranet Applications   201

■ BRIEF CASE: Human Powered Search Engines: ChaCha   204

Business-to-Consumer Electronic Commerce   204

Stages of Business-to-Consumer Electronic Commerce   204

E-Tailing: Selling Goods and Services in the Digital World   205

E-Commerce Web Sites: Attracting and Retaining Online Customers   208

E-Business Strategy   210

Search Marketing   210

Securing Payments in the Digital World   212

■ POWERFUL PARTNERSHIPS: YouTube's Steve Chen and Chad Hurley   214

Managing Financial Transactions in the Digital World   215

Consumer-to-Consumer E-Commerce   215

E-Auctions   215

Emerging Topics in Electronic Commerce   216

The Rise in M-Commerce   217

Mobile Entertainment   219

E-Government   219

■ COMING ATTRACTIONS: Transforming Communication: Ribbit   220

Issues in E-Commerce   221

■ INDUSTRY ANALYSIS: Retailing   224

Key Points Review   225   •   Key Terms   226   •   Review Questions   226   •
Self-Study Questions   227   •   Problems and Exercises   227   •   Application
Exercises   228   •   Team Work Exercise: So Many Books, So Little Time   229   •
Answers to the Self-Study Questions 229

■ CROWDSOURCING   229

■ YOUTUBE   230

Chapter 6   Enhancing Collaboration Using Web 2.0   232

MANAGING IN A DIGITAL WORLD: Digg.com: Changing How News
Is Delivered   233

Defining Web 2.0   234

Pillars of Web 2.0   235

Key Web 2.0 Capabilities   236

Tools for Collaboration   238

Content Management Systems   242

The Web of the Future   243

■ ETHICAL DILEMMA: Virtual Reality People   244

■ POWERFUL PARTNERSHIPS: Digg's Kevin Rose and Jay Adelson   245

■ WHEN THINGS GO WRONG: False Stories Receive Attention: Madness of the Crowds 246

Empowering Individuals with Web 2.0 247

Wikis 247

Tagging 248

Blogging 249

Netcasts 251

Printing-On-Demand 252

■ NET STATS: Top Web 2.0 Sites 253

Enhancing Collaboration with Web 2.0 254

Virtual Teams 255

Social Online Communities 255

■ COMING ATTRACTIONS: Virtual Extras 256

Viral Marketing 258

■ BRIEF CASE: The Internet Movie Database (IMDb) 259

Crowdsourcing 260

■ INDUSTRY ANALYSIS: Online Travel 261

Key Points Review 261 • Key Terms 262 • Review Questions 262 •
Self-Study Questions 263 • Problems and Exercises 263 • Application
Exercises 264 • Team Work Exercise: Online Social Communities 265 •
Answers to the Self-Study Questions 265

■ GOOGLE'S OPENSOCIAL API 265

■ WIKIPEDIA: WHO IS EDITING? 266

Chapter 7 Securing Information Systems 268

MANAGING IN THE DIGITAL WORLD: Drive-by Hacking 269

Information Systems Security 270

Primary Threats to Information Systems Security 270

■ WHEN THINGS GO WRONG: Backhoe Cyberthreat 272

■ NET STATS: Adware/Spyware Lurks on Most PCs 275

Safeguarding Information Systems Resources 279

■ BRIEF CASE: Hacking an Airplane 280

Technological Safeguards 281

■ ETHICAL DILEMMA: Stealing WiFi 285

■ POWERFUL PARTNERSHIPS: The Disruptive Duo, Niklas Zennström
and Janus Friis 290

Human Safeguards 294

Managing Information Systems Security 295

Developing an Information Systems Security Plan 295

The State of Systems Security Management 298

■ COMING ATTRACTIONS: Recharging Gadgets Wirelessly 299

**Information Systems Controls, Auditing and the Sarbanes-Oxley
Act 299**

Information Systems Auditing 301

The Sarbanes-Oxley Act 301

■ INDUSTRY ANALYSIS: Banking Industry 302

Key Points Review 303 • Key Terms 303 • Review Questions 304 •
Self-Study Questions 304 • Problems and Exercises 305 • Application
Exercises 306 • Team Work Exercise: Should Security Upgrades Be Made
Available for Pirated Software? 307 • Answers to the Self-Study
Questions 307

■ UNDER ATTACK 307

■ CHINA'S GREAT (FIRE)WALL 308

Chapter 8   Enhancing Business Intelligence Using Information Systems   310

MANAGING IN THE DIGITAL WORLD: Providing Business Intelligence to eBay Customers   311

Business Intelligence   312

Why Organizations Need Business Intelligence   312

Business Intelligence and Organizational Decision-Making Levels   314

Providing Inputs into Business Intelligence Applications   317

Transaction Processing Systems   317

■ WHEN THINGS GO WRONG: Bad Intelligence—Anonymous Hackers Punish the Wrong Person   318

■ NET STATS: The Demise of Broadcast TV   321

Business Intelligence Components   321

Information and Knowledge Discovery   321

Business Analytics to Support Decision Making   325

■ ETHICAL DILEMMA: Too Much Intelligence? RFID and Privacy   328

■ BRIEF CASE: Instant Messaging at Work   333

■ COMING ATTRACTIONS: Very Smart Phones   341

■ POWERFUL PARTNERSHIPS: Adobe's Jack Warnock and Chuck Geschke   345

Information Visualization   346

■ INDUSTRY ANALYSIS: Healthcare   349

Key Points Review   350   •   Key Terms   351   •   Review Questions   352   •   Self-Study Questions   352   •   Problems and Exercises   353   •   Application Exercises   354   •   Team Work Exercise: What's the Hot Topic?   355   •   Answers to the Self-Study Questions   355

■ THE NETFLIX PRIZE   355

■ APPLICATIONS TO MAKE YOU SMARTER   356

Chapter 9   Building Organizational Partnerships Using Enterprise Information Systems   358

MANAGING IN THE DIGITAL WORLD: Amazon.com   359

Enterprise Systems   360

Supporting Business Processes   362

■ COMING ATTRACTIONS: Three-Dimensional Fabrication   364

Internally Focused Applications   364

Externally Focused Applications   367

The Rise of Enterprise Systems   367

■ BRIEF CASE: Outsourcing Your McDonald's Order   368

■ POWERFUL PARTNERSHIPS: SAP—Dietmar Hopp, Hans-Werner Hector, Hasso Plattner, Klaus Tschira, and Claus Wellenreuther   374

Enterprise Resource Planning   374

Integrating Data to Integrate Applications   375

Choosing an ERP System   376

■ WHEN THINGS GO WRONG: Census Computers   377

ERP Limitations   377

Customer Relationship Management   378

Developing a CRM Strategy   380

Architecture of a CRM   381

Ethical Concerns with CRM   386

■ ETHICAL DILEMMA: Customer Relationship Management (CRM)—Targeting or Discriminating?   386

Supply Chain Management   387

What Is Supply Chain Management?   387

SCM Architecture   389

Developing an SCM Strategy   390

Emerging SCM Trends   391

Trading Exchanges   392

■ NET STATS: RFID on the Rise   395

The Formula for Enterprise System Success   396

Secure Executive Sponsorship   396

Get Help from Outside Experts   396

Thoroughly Train Users   397

Take a Multidisciplinary Approach to Implementations   397

Look Beyond ERP   397

■ INDUSTRY ANALYSIS: Manufacturing   399

Key Points Review   400   •   Key Terms   401   •   Review Questions   401   •
Self-Study Questions   401   •   Problems and Exercises   402   •   Application
Exercises   403   •   Team Work Exercise: ERP, CRM, and SCM   404   •   Answers
to the Self-Study Questions   404

■ THE BATTLE FOR THE DASHBOARD   404

■ REAL OR FAKE? TECH MAY TELL   405

Chapter 10   Developing and Acquiring Information Systems   406

MANAGING IN THE DIGITAL WORLD: Casual Gaming: You, Me,
and Wii   407

Customized Versus Off-the-Shelf Software   408

Customized Software   408

Off-the-Shelf Software   409

Combining Customized and Off-the-Shelf Software   409

■ COMING ATTRACTIONS: Microsoft's Surface   410

The Need for Structured Systems Development   411

The Evolution of Information Systems Development   411

Information Systems Development in Action   411

The Role of Users in the Systems Development Process   412

Steps in the Systems Development Process   414

■ WHEN THINGS GO WRONG: Conquering Computer Contagion   413

Phase 1: Systems Planning and Selection   414

Phase 2: Systems Analysis   415

■ POWERFUL PARTNERSHIPS: MySpace: Tom Anderson and Chris
DeWolfe   420

Phase 3: Systems Design   421

Phase 4: Systems Implementation and Operation   423

Ongoing Systems Maintenance   425

■ BRIEF CASE: Hackers, Patches, and Reverse Engineering   427

Other Approaches to Designing and Building Systems   428

Prototyping   428

Rapid Application Development   429

Object-Oriented Analysis and Design   429

Need for Alternatives to Building Systems Yourself   430

Situation 1: Limited IS Staff   431

Situation 2: IS Staff Has Limited Skill Set   431

Situation 3: IS Staff Is Overworked   431

Situation 4: Problems with Performance of IS Staff   431

Common Alternatives to In-House Systems Development   432

External Acquisition   432

■ NET STATS: Adopting New Technology   432

Outsourcing Systems Development 437

■ ETHICAL DILEMMA: Genetic Testing 439

End-User Development 440

■ INDUSTRY ANALYSIS: Broadcasting 444

Key Points Review 444 • Key Terms 446 • Review Questions 446 •
Self-Study Questions 446 • Problems and Exercises 447 • Application
Exercises 448 • Team Work Exercise: Determining a Development
Approach 449 • Answers to the Self-Study Questions 449

■ THE EMERGENCE OF OPEN SOURCE SOFTWARE 449

■ FBI DATABASE TO EXPAND 450

Chapter 11 Managing Information Systems Ethics and Crime 452

MANAGING IN THE DIGITAL WORLD: BitTorrent 453

Information Systems Ethics 454

The Information Age Arrives 455

Computer Literacy and the Digital Divide 455

Information Privacy 459

Information Accuracy 461

Information Property 463

Information Accessibility 466

The Need for a Code of Ethical Conduct 468

■ POWERFUL PARTNERSHIPS: Flickr's Caterina Fake and Stewart
Butterfield 469

Computer Crime 470

The Computer Access Debate 470

Unauthorized Computer Access 471

Federal and State Laws 472

Computer Forensics 473

■ NET STATS: Top Cyber Threats 474

Hacking and Cracking 474

■ ETHICAL DILEMMA: Ethical Hacking 475

Types of Computer Criminals and Crimes 476

Software Piracy 477

Computer Viruses and Other Destructive Code 480

■ BRIEF CASE: The Vulnerabilities of Online Banking 481

Internet Hoaxes 482

Cyber Harassment, Stalking, and Bullying 482

■ COMING ATTRACTIONS: Invisibility on the Horizon? 483

Cyberwar and Cyberterrorism 483

Cyberwar 484

■ WHEN THINGS GO WRONG: War and the Value of Networks 486

Cyberterrorism 486

■ INDUSTRY ANALYSIS: Cybercops Track Cybercriminals 490

Key Points Review 490 • Key Terms 491 • Review Questions 492 •
Self-Study Questions 492 • Problems and Exercises 493 • Application
Exercises 494 • Team Work Exercise: Making Copies or Programs, Games,
Music, and Videos 495 • Answers to the Self-Study Questions 495

■ BRIDGING THE DIGITAL DIVIDE 495

■ TERRORISTS INVADE GAMING 496

**Technology Briefing Advanced Topics and Trends in Managing
the Information Systems Infrastructure 498**

Advanced Topics in Information Systems Hardware 499

Input Technologies 499

Processing: Transforming Inputs into Outputs   502

Output Technologies   506

Types of Computers   507

Advanced Topics in Information Systems Software   513

Systems Software   513

Application Software   514

Programming Language and Development Environments   514

Advanced Topics in Networking   523

Evolution of Computer Networking   523

Types of Networks   525

Networking Fundamentals   527

Network Standards and Technologies   535

The Internet   540

Advanced Topics in Database Management   546

Database Design   547

Key Points Review   552   •   Key Terms   554   •   Review Questions   555   •
Self-Study Questions   555   •   Problems and Exercises   556   •   Answers to
the Self-Study Questions   557

Acronyms   559

Glossary   561

References   583

Name Index   529

Organization Index   591

Subject Index   593

Preface

Approach

The world is *flat*. Companies are focusing on the *long tails*. New business models based on concepts of *freeconomics* are flourishing. Change is the norm in the digital world. Globalization, downsizing, outsourcing, and off-shoring are a way of life for today's organizations and tomorrow's managers. What does all this mean? What are the catalysts of these concepts and of all this change? More important, how can organizations thrive in this dynamic and highly competitive marketplace? The answer to these and many similar questions is that information systems and related information technologies are driving globalization, new business models, and hyper-competition. It is little wonder that teaching an introductory course on information systems has never been more crucial, or more challenging.

One of the greatest challenges that we face in teaching information systems courses is how to keep pace in the class with what is happening out in the real world. Being relevant to students while at the same time providing the necessary foundation for understanding the breadth, depth, and complexity of information systems has never been more difficult. We wrote *Information Systems Today,* Fourth Edition, with this overarching goal in mind, to be both rigorous *and* relevant. To accomplish this, we want students to not only learn about information systems, but to clearly understand the importance of information systems for individuals, organizations, and society. Additionally, we do not want to simply spoon-feed students with technical terms and the history of information systems. Instead, students must understand exactly what innovative organizations are doing with contemporary information systems and, more important, where things are heading. Finally, we want to empower students with the essential knowledge needed to be successful in the use and understanding of information technology in their careers.

To this end, we wrote *Information Systems Today,* Fourth Edition, so that it is contemporary, fun to read, and useful, focusing on what business students need to know about information systems to survive and thrive in the digital world.

Audience

Information Systems Today, Fourth Edition, is primarily for the undergraduate introductory information systems course required of all business students. The introductory information systems course typically has a diverse audience of students majoring in many different areas, such as accounting, economics, finance, marketing, general management, human resource management, production and operations, international business, entrepreneurship, and information systems. Given the range of students taking this type of course, we have written this book so that it is a valuable guide to all business students and provides them with the essential information they need to know. Students majoring in areas outside of business may also attend the introductory information systems course. Therefore, this book has been written to appeal to a diverse audience.

Information Systems Today, Fourth Edition, can also be used for the introductory course offered at the graduate level—for example, in the first year of an MBA program. Such usage would be especially appropriate if the course focused on the diverse set of cases provided in each chapter.

What's New to the Fourth Edition

Our primary goal for *Information Systems Today*, Fourth Edition, was to emphasize the importance of information systems to all business students as the role of information technology and systems continues to expand within organizations and society. Most notably, we extensively examine how information systems are fueling globalization—making the world smaller and more competitive—in virtually every industry and at an ever-increasing pace. Given this clear focus, we are better able to identify those topics most critical to students and future business professionals. Consequently, we have made substantial revisions to the basic content of the chapters and pedagogical elements, as well as the inclusion of several new elements that we believe achieve this goal. A sample of the new or expanded chapter topics include:

- A new chapter, Chapter 6—Enhancing Collaboration Using Web 2.0—examining the evolution of Internet technologies, specifically how Web 2.0 technologies—blogging, tagging, wikis, podcasting, and so on—are enabling new forms of collaboration including virtual teams, social networking, and crowdsourcing.
- In Chapter 3—Valuing Information Systems Investments—we provide expanded coverage on the complexities related to assessing information systems investment decisions, including a new section examining Chris Anderson's concept of "freeconomics," the concept of making massive profits by *giving things away*, as used by many companies such as Yahoo!, Google, or Comcast.
- An updated chapter, Chapter 4—Managing the Information Systems Infrastructure— covers essential infrastructure concepts related to hardware, software, networking and the Internet, and databases. These updates allow the instructor to better introduce the basic concepts necessary for understanding why and how information systems function and how these collective components serve as a foundation for an organization's information systems infrastructure.
- In Chapter 5—Enabling Commerce Using the Internet—we update our coverage on various topics on how the Internet is transforming commerce and society. For example, we sharpen our discussion on the "Long Tails" of consumer demand as a strategy for better competing in the digital world.
- In Chapter 7—Securing Information Systems—we provide expanded coverage on information systems security, control, auditing, and disaster recovery planning, including a discussion of the implications of the Sarbanes-Oxley Act on securing information systems and the creation of an information systems security plan.
- In Chapter 8—Enhancing Business Intelligence Using Information Systems—we sharpen our focus on various topics related to business intelligence, including how BI is used at the operational, managerial, and executive levels of an organization to enhance and streamline organizational business processes.
- In Chapter 11—Managing Information Systems Ethics and Crime—we provide updates to our coverage of cyberwar and cyberterrorism, particularly focusing on the new *cyber cold war* as well as how the "business processes" of global terrorism are being transformed in the digital world. We also introduce recent ethical issues such as cyber bullying, cyber harassment, and cyber stalking.
- An updated and expanded technology briefing covers advanced concepts related to various information technologies. The technology briefing further expands the concepts introduced in Chapter 4 and is intended for use in more technically oriented courses.

In addition to the changes within the main chapter content, we have also added two new features to each chapter—"Powerful Partnerships" and "Coming Attractions." "Powerful Partnerships" briefly introduces some of the important collaborations that have forever shaped the IT industry and society. For example, in Chapter 5, we introduce Steven Chen and Chad Hurley, the founders of YouTube. "Coming Attractions" presents a description of a new technology that has the potential to have a significant impact on organizations or society. For example, in Chapter 4, we discuss how software developed by researchers at the Schepens Eye Research Institute, an affiliate of Harvard Medical School, can enhance the experience of watching television for the visually impaired.

Beyond the chapter content and features, we have also made substantial changes and refinements to the end of each chapter. First, we carefully revised the end-of-chapter problems and exercises to reflect content change and new material. Second, we have introduced all new end-of-chapter cases about real, contemporary organizations to illustrate the issues businesses face when operating in the digital world. Each case mirrors the primary content of its chapter to better emphasize its relevancy within the context of a real organization. All these elements are discussed more thoroughly next.

Our goal has always been to provide only the information that is relevant to all business students, nothing more and nothing less. We believe that we have again achieved this goal with *Information Systems Today*, Fourth Edition. We hope you agree.

Key Features

As authors, teachers, developers, and managers of information systems, we understand that in order for students to best learn about information systems with this book, they must be motivated to learn. To this end we have included a number of unique features to help students quickly and easily assess the true value of information systems and their impact on everyday life. We show how today's professionals are using information systems to help modern organizations become more efficient and competitive. Our focus is on the application of technology to real-world, contemporary situations. Next, we describe each of the features that contribute to that focus.

A Multitiered Approach

Each chapter utilizes cases in a variety of ways to emphasize and highlight how contemporary organizations are utilizing information systems to gain competitive advantage, streamline organizational processes, or improve customer relationships.

Opening Case—Managing in the Digital World   All chapters begin with an opening case describing a real-world company, technology, and/or issue to spark students' interest in the chapter topic. We have chosen engaging cases that relate to students' interests and concerns by highlighting why information systems have become central for managing in the digital world. Each opening case includes a series of associated questions the students will be able to answer after reading the chapter contents. The organizations, technologies, or issues highlighted in these cases include:

- Apple Computer's rise, fall, and reemergence as a global technology giant.
- InfoSys, India's growing IT consulting juggernaut.
- How TiVo has changed the television industry, laying the foundation for video on demand and other entertainment services.
- Google's meteoric rise and the challenges associated with maintaining its success.
- How Second Life and other virtual worlds are blurring the distinction between the real and virtual worlds.
- How the Web 2.0 phenomenon Digg is influencing news and information dissemination.
- The vulnerability of your information systems and networks to hacker attacks via wireless networks.
- eBay's use of business intelligence to battle its ongoing struggles with counterfeit products and fraudulent buyers and sellers.
- Amazon.com's use of its sophisticated infrastructure to automate the supply chain for both large and small customers.
- How the Nintendo Wii created tremendous demand by purposefully being different than the Sony PlayStation or Microsoft X-Box.
- How technologies such as BitTorrent are staying one step ahead of illegal file sharing legislation.

Brief Case   Each chapter also includes a brief case that discusses important issues related to companies, technologies, or society. These are embedded in the text of the chapter and highlight concepts from the surrounding chapter material. Discussion

Brief Case

questions are provided to seed critical thinking assignments or class discussions. Some of the organizations, trends, and products highlighted in these cases include:

- How some are sharing their Internet connection to help others.
- How consulting giant Accenture has grown to dominate India's massive IT services industry.
- How domainers—those who buy and sell lucrative domain names on the Internet—have grown into a multibillion-dollar industry.
- How self-managing autonomic computing systems may be a key element in an organization's IT infrastructure of the future.
- How the human powered search engine ChaCha makes any mobile phone smarter.
- How the Internet Movie Database (IMDb) provides comprehensive information on films, television, and video games to enhance and change the entertainment industry.
- How it may now be possible to hack into airplanes that rely more and more on internal computers and networks.
- How organizations can best utilize instant messaging to aid the collaboration of an increasingly distributed workforce.
- How McDonald's is outsourcing drive-through order placement.
- How Microsoft aids hackers by releasing security update patches.
- How online banking is being targeted by hackers.

End-of-Chapter Case   To test and reinforce chapter content, we present two current real-world cases at the end of each chapter. Sources for these cases include *InformationWeek*, *Business Week*, *CIO* Magazine, and various Web sites. Like the Brief Cases within the chapter, these are taken from the news and are contemporary. However, these are longer and more substantive than the Brief Cases. They too are followed by discussion questions that help the student apply and master the chapter. The organizations and products highlighted in these cases include:

- How social networking sites like Facebook have become big business on the Internet.
- How online mapping services like Google maps are enabling many innovative products and services.
- How picture exchange site Flickr aids in the globalization movement.
- How PayPal created a global currency to enable worldwide collaboration and commerce.
- How NetFlix is transforming the movie and gaming industries.
- How LinkedIn, a social networking site for professionals, can help people find jobs, useful business contacts, and business opportunities.
- How Amazon's SimpleDB provides a low-cost database infrastructure for individuals and organizations.
- How broadband Internet access in airplanes has evolved and will soon become commonplace.
- How the Internet is fueling crowdsourcing, the phenomenon of having everyday people perform tasks traditionally performed by employees.
- How YouTube has grown into a mainstream Web marvel.
- How Google is helping developers create innovative applications for social networking sites with its OpenSocial programming tools.
- How Wikipedia has become both a useful and sometimes controversial Web resource.
- How and why cybercriminals target eBay, PayPal, and other popular Web sites and resources.
- How China limits information exchange within its society through its "great firewall."
- How Netflix is utilizing crowdsourcing to improve its ability to make movie recommendations to customers.
- How the use of SuperMemo, a software application, can actually make you smarter.
- How the automobile industry is expanding their supply chains as cars become more reliant on information technologies for information services, navigation, and communication.

- How technologies are providing the intelligence to quickly identify and track counterfeit products.
- How the advent of open source software systems, such as the Linux operating system, Apache Web server, and Firefox Web browser, are transforming the software industry.
- How the FBI is developing a comprehensive database of biometric information to better track and apprehend criminals.
- How the One Laptop per Child (OLPC) program is attempting to bridge the digital divide.
- How terrorists are now visiting virtual worlds like Second Life and World of Warcraft to test the reactions of citizens to different types of attacks.

MyMISLab

MyMISLab is now available to bring a greater software applications emphasis to your class. Included is MyITLab, a Microsoft Office simulation currently used by thousands of students allowing them to gain practical skills in the use of spreadsheet and database software. End-of Chapter applications are tied to this unique tutorial.

A turn-key collaboration application in the form of **Microsoft's SharePoint** is ready for your class. No need to worry about coordinating through your school's computer lab and server. Monitor your students' activities as they work through their teamwork assignments—all from within **MyMISLab**.

Please visit www.mymislab.com and contact your local rep for more details.

Common Chapter Features

Throughout every chapter, a variety of short pedagogical elements are presented to highlight key information systems issues and concepts in a variety of contexts. These elements help to show students the broader organizational and societal implications of various topics.

Industry Analysis

Every industry is being transformed by the Internet and the increasing use of information systems by individuals and organizations. To give you a feel for just how pervasive and profound these changes are, each chapter presents an analysis of a specific industry to highlight the new rules for operating in the digital world. Given that no industry or profession is immune from these changes, each Industry Analysis highlights the importance of understanding information systems for *every* business student, not only for information systems majors. Discussion questions help students better understand the rapidly changing opportunities and risks of operating in the digital world. Chapter 1 examines how the digital world is transforming the opportunities for virtually all business professions. Subsequent chapters examine how globalization and the digital world have eliminated or forever transformed various industries, including automobile, photo, movie, retail, travel, banking, health care, manufacturing, broadcasting, and law enforcement. Clearly, we are in a time of tremendous change, and understanding this evolution will better equip students to not only survive but thrive in the digital world.

Coming Attractions

We worked to ensure that this book is contemporary. We cover literally hundreds of different current and emerging technologies throughout the book. This feature, however, focuses on an innovation that is likely to soon have an impact on organizations or society. Topics include:

- Bionic contact lenses
- Language learning through social networking
- Brain sensors to improve market research
- Television for the visually impaired
- Merging and managing multiple phones
- Virtual extras in animated films and games
- Wirelessly recharging your gadgets

- Very smart phones and services
- High-speed 3-D fabrication
- Microsoft's Surface computerized table
- Nanowires and invisibility

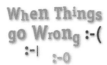

When Things Go Wrong

Textbooks don't usually describe what not to do, but this can be very helpful to students. This feature enables students to learn about a real-world situation in which information systems did not work or were not built or used well. Topics include:

- Apple Computer's numerous product and strategy failures.
- eWaste and what to do with all our old computers and gadgets.
- Sony's "rootkit" spyware used to track customers' listening behavior and prevent illegal copying.
- Blackberry's copyright infringement that nearly shut down its network for millions of customers.
- The rise of crime within virtual worlds like Second Life.
- How the Internet can quickly disseminate false information with unforeseen consequences.
- Unusual cyberthreats, such as accidentally (or purposely) digging up largely unprotected fiber optic networks.
- The consequences of anonymous hackers sometimes punishing the "wrong" person.
- How the government is failing in its attempts to design a handheld computer for future census takers.
- How spam and spyware are creating traffic jams on the information superhighway.
- How the overreliance on technology-based networks is hindering the war on terror.

Net Stats

The Internet is now a significant part of every organization as well as our personal lives. Net Stats provide interesting, important trends and forecasts related to Internet usage within a variety of contexts. These insights help students better understand the Internet's role in fueling globalization and transforming the digital world. Topics include:

- Global Internet usage
- Online search market share
- File sharing
- Broadband access
- E-business growth
- Top Web 2.0 sites
- Adware and Spyware
- Demise of broadcast television
- RFID growth
- Lagging IT Adopters
- Top Cyber Threats

Ethical Dilemma

Ethical business practices are now a predominant part of contemporary management education and practice. This feature examines contemporary dilemmas related to the chapter content and highlights the implications of these dilemmas for managers, organizations, and society. Topics include:

- Differences in online rights throughout the world
- Underground gaming industry selling virtual goods for "real" money

- Reporting work colleagues who use IT resources for illegal or unethical practices
- Cookies to "enhance" your Web surfing
- Crime in virtual worlds
- Growth of virtual versus real experiences
- Stealing WiFi
- RFID privacy
- Using CRM systems to target or discriminate
- Genetic testing and discrimination
- Ethical hacking

Powerful Partnerships

A variety of key collaborations have shaped the IT industry. While there are countless people who have contributed to today's digital world, this feature presents some of the more prominent teams that have significantly advanced technologies or lead important companies. These partnerships include:

- Apple's Steve Jobs and Steve Wozniak
- Netscape's James H. Clark and Marc Andreessen
- Microsoft's Bill Gates and Paul Allen
- Google's Sergey Brin and Larry Page
- YouTube's Steve Chen and Chad Hurley
- Digg's Kevin Rose and Jay Adelson
- Skype's Niklas Zennström and Janus Friis
- Adobe's John Warnock and Chuck Geschke
- SAP's Dietmar Hopp, Hans-Werner Hector, Hasso Plattner, Klaus Tschira, and Claus Wellenreuther
- MySpace's Tom Anderson and Chris DeWolfe
- Flickr's Caterina Fake and Stewart Butterfield

End-of-Chapter Material

Our end-of-chapter material is designed to accommodate various teaching and learning styles. It promotes learning beyond the book and the classroom. Elements include the following:

- Key Terms—Highlight key concepts within the chapter.
- Review Questions—Test students' understanding of basic content.
- Self-Study Questions—Enable students to assess whether they are ready for a test.
- Matching Questions—Check quickly to see if students understand basic terms.
- Problems and Exercises—Push students deeper into the material and encourage them to synthesize and apply it.
- Application Exercises—Challenge students to solve two real-world management problems using spreadsheet and database applications from a running case centered on a university travel agency. Student data files referenced within the exercises are available on the companion Web site: www.pearsonhighered.com/valacich.
- Team Work Exercise—Enable students to work in teams to solve a problem and/or address an issue related to the chapter material.

We have extensively updated these elements to reflect new chapter content and the natural evolution of the material.

Pedagogy

In addition to the features described above, we provide a list of learning objectives to lay the foundation for each chapter. At the end of the chapter, the Key Points Review repeats these learning objectives and describes how each objective was achieved. A list of references is located at the end of the text, organized by chapter.

Organization

The content and organization of this book are based on our own teaching, as well as on feedback from reviewers and colleagues throughout the field. Each chapter builds on the others to reinforce key concepts and allow for a seamless learning experience. Essentially, the book has been structured to answer three fundamental questions:

1. What are contemporary information systems, and how are they being used in innovative ways?
2. Why are information systems so important and interesting?
3. How best can we build, acquire, manage, and safeguard information systems?

The ordering and content of our chapters was also significantly influenced by a recent article, "What Every Business Student Needs to Know about Information Systems."[1] This article was written by forty prominent information systems scholars to define the information systems core body of knowledge for all business students. By design, the content of *Information Systems Today*, Fourth Edition, carefully follows the guidance of this article. We are, therefore, very confident that our book provides a solid and widely agreed upon foundation for any introductory information systems course.

The chapters are organized as follows:

- **Chapter 1: Managing in the Digital World**—This chapter helps the student understand what information systems are and how they have become a vital part of modern organizations. We walk the student through the technology, people, and organizational components of an information system, and we lay out types of jobs and career opportunities in information systems and in related fields. We use a number of cases and examples, such as that of Apple Computers, to show the student the types of systems being used and to point out common "best practices" in systems use and management.

- **Chapter 2: Fueling Globalization through Information Systems**—In this chapter, which draws heavily on Thomas Friedman's best seller *The World is Flat*, we provide a discussion of how globalization evolved and what opportunities globalization presents for organizations. Using examples, such as Infosys, we highlight the factors organizations have to consider when operating in the digital world. We also present different business and information systems strategies for companies operating in the digital world.

- **Chapter 3: Valuing Information Systems Investments**—Here, we discuss how companies, such as TiVo, can use information systems for automation, organizational learning, and strategic advantage. Further, we describe how to formulate and present the business case for an information system. Given the rapid advancement of new technologies, we also explain why and how companies are continually looking for innovative ways to use information systems for competitive advantage.

- **Chapter 4: Managing the Information Systems Infrastructure**—In this chapter, we provide an overview of the essential information systems infrastructure components and describe why they are necessary for satisfying an organization's informational needs. With the ever-increasing complexity of maintaining a solid information systems infrastructure, it becomes increasingly important for organizations, such as Google, to design a reliable, robust, and secure infrastructure. We discuss foundational concepts, as well as recent trends to support an information systems infrastructure.

---

[1]Ives, B., Valacich, J., Watson, R., Zmud, R. (2002). "What Every Business Student Needs to Know about Information Systems." *Communications of the Association for Information Systems*, 9(30). Other contributing scholars to this article include: Maryam Alavi, Richard Baskerville, Jack J Baroudi, Cynthia Beath, Thomas Clark, Eric K. Clemons, Gordon B. Davis, Fred Davis, Alan R. Dennis, Omar A. El Sawy, Jane Fedorowicz, Robert D. Galliers, Joey George, Michael Ginzberg, Paul Gray, Rudy Hirschheim, Sirkka Jarvenpaa, Len Jessup, Chris F. Kemerer, John L. King, Benn Konsynski, Ken Kraemer, Jerry N. Luftman, Salvatore T. March, M. Lynne Markus, Richard O. Mason, F. Warren McFarlan, Ephraim R. McLean, Lorne Olfman, Margrethe H. Olson, John Rockart, V. Sambamurthy, Peter Todd, Michael Vitale, Ron Weber, and Andrew B. Whinston.

- **Chapter 5: Enabling Commerce Using the Internet**—Perhaps nothing has changed the landscape of business more than the use of the Internet for electronic commerce. In this extensively updated chapter, we describe how a number of firms, such as Alaska Air, Timbuk2, or the Boeing Company, use the Internet to conduct commerce in cyberspace. Further, we explain how organizations build intranets to support internal processes and build extranets to interact with other firms. We then describe the stages of business-to-consumer electronic commerce and discuss emerging trends in consumer-to-consumer e-commerce and mobile commerce. Finally, we explain different forms of e-government and show how governmental regulations can become a threat to e-commerce.

- **Chapter 6: Enhancing Collaboration Using Web 2.0**—With the collapse of the dot-com bubble, many EC-based businesses failed, but others continued to be very successful using a variety of innovative business models. In this new chapter, we examine the business models and information systems that contributed to the success of these survivors and discuss where these technologies are heading. Further, using examples, such as Digg.com, we discuss the emergence and importance of user-generated content and the emergence of wikis, blogs, netcasts, tagging, and so on. Finally, we describe how Web 2.0 technologies have helped new forms of collaboration, such as virtual teams, social networking, and crowdsourcing.

- **Chapter 7: Securing Information Systems**—With the pervasive use of information systems, new dangers have arisen for organizations, and information security has become a paramount issue within the context of global information management. In this chapter, we examine the primary threats to information systems security and how systems are compromised. Using examples of organizations, such as PayPal, we show how companies can implement both technological and human-based safeguards to better manage information systems. We also discuss the role of auditing, IS controls, and the Sarbanes-Oxley Act.

- **Chapter 8: Enhancing Business Intelligence Using Information Systems**—Given how many different types of information systems organizations use to run their business and gain business intelligence, in this chapter we use examples from eBay.com and other firms to describe the various types of systems. In this extensively updated chapter, we describe how business intelligence is used at the operational, managerial, and executive levels of an organization. Further, we discuss three components of business intelligence: information and knowledge discovery, business analytics, and information visualization.

- **Chapter 9: Building Organizational Partnerships Using Enterprise Information Systems**—In this chapter, we focus on enterprise systems, which are a popular type of information system used to integrate information and span organizations' boundaries to better connect a firm with customers, suppliers, and other partners. We show the student how Amazon.com and other firms use enterprise resource planning, customer relationship management, and supply chain management to compete in the digital world.

- **Chapter 10: Developing and Acquiring Information Systems**—How are all these systems built or acquired? In this chapter, we examine how Nintendo, Southwest Airlines, and other firms build and acquire new information systems. We walk the student through the traditional systems development approach, as well as more contemporary approaches, such as prototyping, rapid application development, and object-oriented analysis and design. Finally, we examine the steps followed to request and acquire an information system from an outside vendor.

- **Chapter 11: Managing Information Systems Ethics and Crime**—In this extensively updated chapter, we describe the ethical dilemmas associated with information systems, as well as common forms of computer crime. We examine the ethical concerns BitTorrent and other firms deal with in the information age and how computer ethics influences the use of information systems. We also define computer crime and list several types of computer crime. Lastly, given its growing relevance to managing and living in the digital world, we significantly updated and expanded our discussion of cyberwar and cyberterrorism.

In addition to these eleven chapters, we include a Technology Briefing focusing on advanced concepts regarding hardware, software, networking and the Internet, and databases. While Chapter 4—Managing the Information Systems Infrastructure—provides a basic understanding of these technological building blocks, this material is intended to allow for a more in-depth discussion of these topics. By delivering this material as a Technology Briefing, we provide instructors the greatest flexibility in how and when they can apply it.

Supplement Support

Instructor's Resource Center Online and on CD-ROM

The convenient Instructor's Resource Center is available both online and on CD-ROM. The online center is accessible from www.pearsonhighered.com/valacich by choosing the "Instructor Resources" link from the catalog page. Both the online center and CD-ROM include the following supplements: Instructor's Manual, Test Item File, PowerPoint presentations, and Image Library (text art). The online center also contains TestGen and TestGen conversions in WebCT and BlackBoard-ready files.

The Instructor's Manual includes answers to all review and discussion questions, exercises, and case questions. The Test Item File (Test Bank) includes multiple-choice, true-false, and essay questions for each chapter. The Test Bank is delivered in MS Word, as well as in the form of TestGen. The PowerPoint presentations highlight text learning objectives and key topics. Finally, the Image Library is a collection of the figures and tables from the text for instructor use in PowerPoint slides and class lectures.

CourseSmart eTextbooks Online

CourseSmart is an exciting new choice for students looking to save money. As an alternative to purchasing the print textbook, students can purchase an electronic version of the same content and save up to 50 percent off the suggested list price of the print text. With a CourseSmart eTextbook, students can search the text, make notes online, print out reading assignments that incorporate lecture notes, and bookmark important passages for later review. For more information or to purchase access to the CourseSmart eTextbook, visit www.coursesmart.com.

MyMISLab

MyMISLab is now available to bring a greater software applications emphasis to your class. Included is MyITLab, a Microsoft Office simulation currently used by thousands of students allowing them to gain practical skills in the use of spreadsheet and database software. End-of Chapter applications are tied to this unique tutorial.

A turn-key collaboration application in the form of **Microsoft's SharePoint** is ready for your class. No need to worry about coordinating through your school's computer lab and server. Monitor your students' activities as they work through their teamwork assignments—all from within **MyMISLab**.

Please visit www.mymislab.com and contact your local rep for more details.

Reviewers

We wish to thank the following faculty who participated in reviews for this and previous editions:

Lawrence L. Andrew, Western Illinois University
Karin A. Bast, University of Wisconsin–La Crosse
Rochelle Brooks, Viterbo University
Brian Carpani, Southwestern College
Amita Chin, Virginia Commonwealth University
Jon D. Clark, Colorado State University
Thomas Engler, Florida Institute of Technology
Roy H. Farmer, California Lutheran University

David Firth, University of Montana
Frederick Fisher, Florida State University
James Frost, Idaho State University
Frederick Gallegos, California State Polytechnic University–Pomona
Dale Gust, Central Michigan University
Albert Harris, Appalachian State University
Traci Hess, Washington State University

Bruce Hunt, California State University–Fullerton
Carol Jensen, Southwestern College
Bhushan Kapoor, California State University–Fullerton
Elizabeth Kemm, Central Michigan University
Beth Kiggins, University of Indianapolis
Chang E. Koh, University of North Texas
Brian R. Kovar, Kansas State University
Kapil Ladha, Drexel University
Linda K. Lau, Longwood University
Cameron Lawrence, University of Montana
Martha Leva, Penn State University–Abington
Weiqi Li, University of Michigan–Flint
Dana L. McCann, Central Michigan University
Richard McCarthy, Quinnipiac University
Patricia McQuaid, California State Polytechnic University
Michael Newby, California State University–Fullerton

Kathleen Noce, Penn State University–Eerie
Timothy Peterson, University of Minnesota–Duluth
Eugene Rathswohl, University of San Diego
Rene F. Reitsma, Oregon State University
Kenneth Rowe, Purdue University
G. Shankaranarayanan, Boston University
James Sneeringer, St. Edward's University
Cheri Speier, Michigan State University
Bill Turnquist, Central Washington University
Craig K. Tyran, Western Washington University
William Wagner, Villanova University
Minhua Wang, State University of New York–Canton
John Wells, Washington State University
Nilmini Wickramasinghe, Cleveland State University
Yue Zhang, California State University–Northridge

Acknowledgments

Although only our two names are listed as the authors for this book, this was truly a team effort that went well beyond the two of us. Prentice Hall has been an outstanding publishing company to work with. They are innovative, have high standards, and are as competitive as we are.

Among the many amazingly helpful people at Prentice Hall, there are a handful of people we wish to thank specifically. First, Kelly Loftus, our assistant editor, helped to whip us and this book into shape and get it finished on time. Additionally, Clara Bartunek, our production editor, and Ann Courtney of GGS Higher Education Resources helped in getting approval for photos, figures, Web sites, and other graphics as well as coordinating refinements as the book moved through the stages of production. Finally, our executive editor, Bob Horan, guided the book and us from its inception, and he dared us to dream of and to write the best introductory information systems textbook ever.

In addition to our colleagues at Prentice Hall, two individuals were particularly instrumental in making the fourth edition the best ever. First, Karen Judson did an outstanding job drafting our new case elements. Likewise, Ryan Wright, a former PhD student at WSU, now an assistant professor at the University of San Francisco, provided many innovative ideas for chapter updates, end-of-chapter problems, and chapter elements as well as drafting key parts of the new Web 2.0 chapter. Thanks, team! We could not have done it without you.

Most important, we thank our families for their patience and assistance in helping us to complete this book. Joe's wife Jackie, daughter Jordan, and son James were a constant inspiration, as was Christoph's wife Birgit. This one is for you all.

1

Managing in the Digital World

After reading this chapter, you will be able to do the following:

1 Explain what an information system is, contrasting its data, technology, people, and organizational components.

2 Describe types of jobs and career opportunities in information systems and in related fields.

3 Describe the dual nature of information systems in the success and failure of modern organizations.

Preview

Today, organizations from Apple Computer to Zales Jewelers use computer-based information systems to better manage their organizations in the digital world. These organizations use information systems to provide high-quality goods and services as well as to gain or sustain competitive advantage over rivals. Our objective for Chapter 1 is to help you understand what information systems are, how they have evolved to become a vital part of modern organizations, and why this understanding is necessary for you to become an effective manager in the digital world.

The next section provides a brief overview of the book. Then, we explain what information systems are and how they have evolved. We conclude by illustrating how information systems can be utilized to improve organizational performance.

Managing in the Digital World: Apple Computer

It happened on April Fools' Day, 1976, but history has shown it was no joke. On that date, Stephen "Woz" Wozniak and Steven Paul Jobs officially formed the Apple Computer Company. The two friends had been fascinated with computers since their days as students at Homestead High School in Cupertino, California. Wozniak graduated first, in 1967, because he is five years older than Jobs, but their shared interest in anything digital kept bringing the two together, both before Jobs graduated from high school and after he graduated in 1972.

The two Steves both dropped out of college to work on building computers—first in Jobs' bedroom, then in his garage when the bedroom got too crowded. (Wozniak later returned to school at the University of California in Berkeley and graduated with a degree in engineering in 1986.) At first they were interested just in building circuit boards but later decided to build entire computers and sell them to home users. The Apple I debuted shortly after the company was formed and sold for $666.66.

Before the Apple I came the Altair 8800—the first home computer. Buyers had to assemble the machine themselves, there was no monitor, and switches had to be tripped manually and in proper sequence for the machine to function at all. The machine was a fun tool for geeks but not practical for the average computer user (in fact, there were no "average computer users" as we know them today).

However, the introduction of the Apple I computer paved the way for profound changes in the way everyday people would use computers. Shortly after the introduction of the Apple I, Wozniak and Jobs developed the Apple II, which included a keyboard, a floppy disk drive, and color graphics. Because of its jazzy appearance and ease of use (which can't be compared with today's personal computers), consumers liked the Apple II, and the Apple Company eventually sold 50,000 units. It continued to be Apple's dominant product until 1993. To date, the Apple II's seventeen-year life span is a record within the computer industry.

Wozniak and Jobs' working relationship was key to Apple's success. Wozniak, the engineer, was concerned primarily with a computer's function, while Jobs focused on ease of use and design. Thanks to the two-Steves team, the Apple II was an attractive and functional addition to a family's living room. Apple continues to offer products that are a blend of engineering and aesthetics, and many consumers are devoted to the products. The history of Apple Computers, however, includes a series of high highs and low lows. For example, the Lisa, introduced in 1983, was a commercial disaster, and the Apple III, introduced shortly after the Apple II, was discontinued after only a year on the market when it failed to entice consumers. In 1984, Apple once again had a hit when it introduced the popular Macintosh 128K, featuring the AppleMouse II (the first computer mouse introduced to the mass market) and the first true graphical user interface. When Apple introduced the Macintosh Portable (an early laptop), it had only limited success, but after is was redesigned and renamed, the PowerBook proved a marketplace success. Other near failures for Apple included the Apple Newton (an early PDA) and the G3 enterprise server computer (for more on Apple's failures, see *When Things Go Wrong* later in the chapter).

Jobs left Apple in 1985 amid employee complaints that he was an erratic and tempestuous manager; Wozniak left Apple for good in 1986. Jobs was so disgruntled when he left Apple that he sold all but one share of his stock in the company. Jobs then started another computer company, NeXT Computer, which designed and marketed a technologically advanced computer that did not sell well because of its high price. Apple's leadership foundered for a while,

FIGURE 1.1

Apple has been an innovative leader in the computer and consumer electronics industries.

but the company purchased NeXT for $402 million in 1996, and Jobs again took over the helm. Jobs brought Apple back to profitability by revamping its product line. The iMac, a PowerBook featuring a fourteen-inch display, and Mac OS X—a new operating system—were the most successful units in the 1998 product line.

Jobs has remained Apple's chief executive officer (CEO), seeing the company through additional product successes with the introduction of the iPod, the iPhone, and the MacBook Air.

The iPod is the universally familiar hard drive–based MP3 music player, which debuted in November 2001 (selling for $250, and offering 4 GB of storage for music files) and went mainstream in 2003. The simple user interface and small size made the iPod one of the most sought after digital music players. What is so attractive to consumers is the fact that the iPod is offered with several customizable features, such as connectability to a car's stereo system or to external speakers, a camera, and choices of outer skin color. Apple soon improved on the original iPod design, offering the iPod mini, iPod color, iPod shuffle, iPod nano, and so on. Although competitors have released their own digital music players, none have achieved Apple's market share.

To add to the iPod's success, Apple created an online music store called iTunes, where users could download digital music for 99 cents per track. The combination of product (the iPod) and service (online iTunes store) resulted in massive profits for Apple. Although initially the music from the online store could only be downloaded using an Apple computer, later the downloads could be made from any machine (though they still can only be played on iPods). Recently, iTunes has expanded into the video market, providing videos—television shows as well as new releases of Hollywood blockbusters—for video-capable iPods.

The most recent addition to the iTunes Store is iTunes U, a selection of educational material from various universities. Apple says iTunes U puts "the power of the iTunes Store to work for colleges and universities, so users can easily search, download, and play course content just like they do music, movies, and TV shows." Apple continued its success with new products in 2007 when it introduced the iPhone—a smart phone with Internet access and a touch-screen interface (see Figure 1.1)—and again in 2008 with the MacBook Air. The iPhone sold 1.4 million units the first ninety days after its introduction and has continued to outsell other smart phones on the market.

Barely as thick as your index finger and weighing a mere three pounds, the MacBook Air, introduced in 2008, also proved popular with consumers. The lightweight laptop boasted 2 GB of built-in RAM, an 80 GB hard drive, and a 1.6 to 1.8 GHz Intel Core 2 dual processor.

While Apple Computers has a long list of successful products, in 2005, environmentalists criticized the company for its lack of an e-waste recycling policy. Jobs was at first defiant, dismissing such complaints as trivial, but shortly after Apple's annual meeting in April 2005, he announced that Apple would take back used iPods for free. In 2006, he further expanded Apple's recycling programs to any customer who buys a new Mac. This program includes shipping and "environmentally friendly disposal" of customers' old systems. In late 2007, Apple once again came under scrutiny from Greenpeace, this time for the use of toxic chemicals in the iPhone. Only a few days later, Apple announced that in addition to recycling its old products, toxic chemicals would be removed from new products.

Thanks to innovative product design, clever marketing tactics, and swift response to environmental concerns, Apple Computers' profits have consistently risen over the past several years, and financial analysts see more of the same in the company's future.

After reading this chapter, you will be able to answer the following:

1. Given the pace at which technology is converging (e.g., phones, music players, cameras, and so on), what do you think is next for Apple?
2. Apple has had many "near death" experiences throughout its history. Is Apple now here to stay?
3. Jobs has been the catalyst for many of Apple's successes (and failures). Can Apple survive without Jobs?

Based on:

Anonymous (n.d.). Apple education—iTunes U. Retrieved May 17, 2008, from www.apple.com/itunesu.

Anonymous (n.d.). Apple—Environment. Retrieved May 17, 2008, from http://www.apple.com/environment.

Anonymous (n.d.). Apple-history.com: Recent changes. Retrieved May 17, 2008, from http://www.apple-history.com.

Anonymous (n.d.). Apple MacBook Air—Design. Retrieved May 17, 2008, from http://www.apple.com/macbookair/design.html.

Borland, J. (2006, January 12). Apple's iTunes raises privacy concerns. *ZDNet*. Retrieved May 17, 2008, from http://news.zdnet.com/2100-1009_22-6026542.html.

Flynn, L. J. (2003, April 17). Profits at Apple computer are down 65% in quarter. *New York Times*. Retrieved May 17, 2008, from http://query.nytimes.com/gst/fullpage.html?res=9A05E3DD163AF934A25757C0A9659C8B63.

Kim, R. (2007, November 5). IPhone's success spawns generations of imitators—and challengers. *SFGate*. Retrieved May 17, 2008, from http://www.sfgate.com:80/cgi-bin/article.cgi?f=/c/a/2007/11/05/BU0GT5310.DTL.

McElhearn, K. (2006, January 11). iTunes: Apple's new spyware and adware application? Retrieved May 17, 2008, from http://www.mcelhearn.com/article.php?story=20060111150127268.

Oswald, E. (2007, January 17). Apple posts $1 billion holiday profit. *Betanews*. Retrieved May 17, 2008, from http://www.betanews.com/article/Apple_Posts_1_Billion_Holiday_Profit/1169072684.

Thomas, O. (2006, January 19). iTunes video boosts TV ratings: Downloads of *The Office* and *Lost* are on the rise, and so are their ratings. *CNNMoney.com*. Retrieved May 17, 2008, from http://money.cnn.com/2006/01/17/technology/browser0117/index.htm.

Weyhrich, S. (2008, April 8). Apple II history chap 1. Retrieved May 17, 2008, from http://apple2history.org/history/ah01.html.

Weyhrich, S. (2008, April 15). Apple II history appendix C. Retrieved May 17, 2008, from http://apple2history.org/history/appy/ahc.html.

What You Will Find in This Book

This book provides a comprehensive presentation of the information systems body of knowledge and is organized as follows:

- ■ *Chapter 1—Managing in the Digital World.* Here we provide an overview of what information systems are and how they are being used in modern organizations.
- ■ *Chapter 2—Fueling Globalization Through Information Systems.* Here we provide an overview of how the pervasive use of information systems is fueling globalization and rapid change in the world.
- ■ *Chapter 3—Valuing Information Systems Investments.* Here we examine how information systems can be utilized to improve organizational performance as well as provide a return on investment.
- ■ *Chapter 4—Managing the Information Systems Infrastructure.* Here we provide an overview of the various components of a comprehensive infrastructure and how organizations are managing this infrastructure to best utilize their information systems investments.
- ■ *Chapter 5—Enabling Commerce Using the Internet.* Here we focus on how organizations are utilizing the Internet to create business opportunities and sustain competitive advantage.
- ■ *Chapter 6—Enhancing Collaboration Using Web 2.0.* Here we examine various emerging Web technologies that are expanding the capabilities of individuals and organizations.
- ■ *Chapter 7—Securing Information Systems.* Here we examine how organizations can best secure their information systems.
- ■ *Chapter 8—Enhancing Business Intelligence Using Information Systems.* Here we describe various kinds of information systems that firms use to improve business decision making.
- ■ *Chapter 9—Building Organizational Partnerships Using Enterprise Information Systems.* Here we examine how information systems can be used to help integrate the entire organization and help connect the firm to customers, suppliers, and partners.
- ■ *Chapter 10—Developing and Acquiring Information Systems.* Here we describe how information systems and services are developed and/or acquired.
- ■ *Chapter 11—Managing Information Systems Ethics and Crime.* Here we discuss key legal and ethical issues for successfully managing information systems.

In addition to these chapters, an optional technology briefing provides a foundation for better understanding how these various technologies function and can be configured to create the power of modern information systems.

Our primary objective when designing this book was to focus on the big picture, trying not to bog you down with unnecessary technological jargon. Nevertheless, to effectively manage in the digital world, you need a comprehensive understanding of what information systems are, the necessary vocabulary to understand and explain these technologies, what factors are shaping the digital world, the categories and types of information systems, and how organizations are deploying these systems to create value and competitive advantage. We hope that you agree after reading the book that we have achieved this objective.

Information Systems Today

In 1959, Peter Drucker predicted this rise in the importance of information and of information technology, and at that point, over four decades ago, he coined the term **knowledge worker**. Knowledge workers are typically professionals who are relatively well educated and who create, modify, and/or synthesize knowledge as a fundamental part of their jobs.

Drucker's predictions about knowledge workers were very accurate. As he predicted, they are generally paid better than their prior agricultural and industrial counterparts; they rely on and are empowered by formal education, yet they often also possess valuable real-world skills; they are continually learning how to do their jobs better; they have much better career opportunities and far more bargaining power than workers ever had before; they make up about a quarter of the workforce in the United States and in other developed nations; and their numbers are rising quickly.

Drucker also predicted that, with the growth in the number of knowledge workers and with their rise in importance and leadership, a **knowledge society** would emerge. He reasoned that, given the importance of education and learning to knowledge workers and the firms that need them, education would become the cornerstone of the knowledge society. Possessing knowledge, he argued, would be as important as possessing land, labor, or capital (if not more so) (see Figure 1.2). Indeed, research shows that people equipped to prosper in the knowledge society, such as those with a college education, earn far more on average than people without a college education, and that gap is increasing. In fact, information from the U.S. Census Bureau (2007 data) reinforces the value of a college education: workers eighteen and over with a bachelor's degree earn an average of $56,788 a year, while those with a high school diploma earn $31,071. Workers with an advanced degree make an average of $82,320, and those without a high school diploma average $20,873. Additionally, getting a college degree will qualify you for many jobs that would not be available to you otherwise and will distinguish you from other job candidates. Finally, a college degree is often a requirement to qualify for career advancement and promotion opportunities once you do get that job.

People generally agree that Drucker was accurate about knowledge workers and the evolution of society. While people have settled on Drucker's term "knowledge worker," there are many alternatives to the term "knowledge society." For example, Manuel Castell has written that we now live in a network society. *Wired* magazine has published that we now live in a **new economy** and described it as follows:

> So what is the new economy? When we talk about the new economy, we're talking about a world in which people work with their brains instead of their hands. A world in which communications technology creates global competition—not just for running shoes and laptop computers, but also for bank loans and other services that can't be packed into a crate and shipped. A world in which innovation is more important than mass production. A world in which investment buys new concepts or the means to create them, rather than new machines. A world in which rapid change is a

FIGURE 1.2

In the knowledge society, information has become as important as—and many feel *more important than*—land, labor, and capital resources.

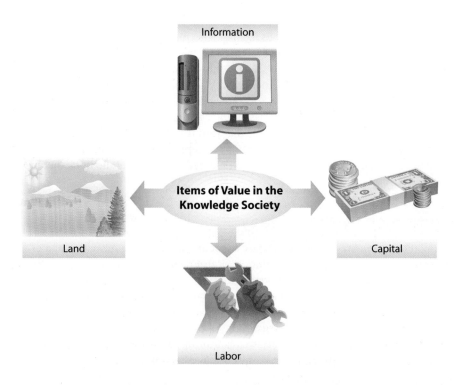

constant. A world at least as different from what came before it as the industrial age was from its agricultural predecessor. A world so different its emergence can only be described as a revolution (Browning and Reiss, 1998).

Others have referred to this phenomenon as the knowledge economy, the digital society, the network era, the Internet era, and other names. We simply refer to this as the *digital world*. All of these ideas have in common the premise that information and related technologies and systems have become very important to us and that knowledge workers are vital.

Some have argued, however, that there is a downside to being a knowledge worker and to living in the digital world. For example, Kit Sims-Taylor has argued that knowledge workers will be the first to be replaced by automation with information technology. Jeremy Rifkin has argued that our overreliance on information technology has caused us to think and act hastily and to lose our perspective. Others have argued that in the new economy there is a *digital divide,* where those with access to information technology have great advantages over those without access to information technology (for more, see Chapter 11).

To be sure, there is a downside to overreliance on knowledge workers and information technology, but one thing is for certain: knowledge workers and information technologies are now critical to the success of modern organizations, economies, and societies. What are some of the characteristics of the digital world? This is examined next.

Characteristics of the Digital World

Computers are the core component of information systems. Over the past decade, the advent of powerful, relatively inexpensive, easy-to-use computers has had a major impact on business. To see this impact, look around your school or place of work. At your school, you may register for classes online, use e-mail to communicate with fellow students and your instructors, and complete or submit assignments on networked personal computers. At work, you may use a personal computer for e-mail and other tasks. Your paychecks are probably generated by computer and automatically deposited in your checking account via high-speed networks. Chances are that each year you see more information technology than you did the year before, and this technology is a more fundamental and important part of your learning and work than ever before.

When you stop and think about it, it is easy to see why information technology is important. Increasing global competitiveness has forced companies to find ways to be better and to do things less expensively. The answer for many firms continues to be to use information systems to do things better, faster, and cheaper. Using global telecommunications networks, companies can more easily integrate their operations to access new markets for their products and services as well as access a large pool of talented labor in countries with lower wages.

This integration of economies throughout the world, enabled by technological progress, is called *globalization* (see Chapter 2). You can see the effects of globalization in many ways, such as the greater international movement of commodities, money, information, and labor, as well as the development of technologies, standards, and processes to facilitate this movement (see Figure 1.3). Specifically, a more global and competitive world includes visible economic, cultural, and technological changes, including the following:

- ■ *Economic Changes.* Increases in international trade, in the development of global financial systems and currency, and in the outsourcing of labor.
- ■ *Cultural Changes.* Increases in the availability of multiculturalism through television and movies; the frequency of international travel, tourism, and immigration; the availability of ethnic foods and restaurants; and the frequency of worldwide fads and phenomena such as Pokémon, Sudoku, *Idol* television, and MySpace.
- ■ *Technological Changes.* The development of low-cost computing platforms and communication technologies; the availability of low-cost communication systems such as e-mail, Skype, and instant messaging; the ubiquitous nature of a low-cost global telecommunications infrastructure like the Internet; and the enforcement of global patent and copyright laws to spur further innovation.

FIGURE 1.3

Globalization can be seen in
visible economic, cultural, and
technological changes.

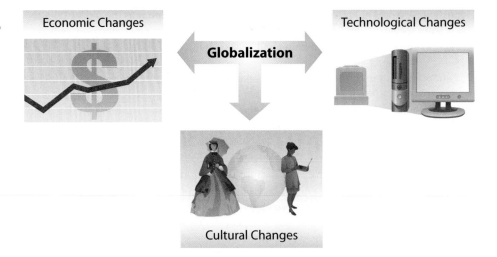

Through the convergence of economics and culture, fueled by a robust global technology
infrastructure, the world has forever changed. Given their central role in this ongoing
global revolution, information systems are defined next.

Information Systems Defined

Information systems (IS) are combinations of **hardware**, **software**, and **telecommunications networks** that *people* build and use to collect, create, and distribute useful
data, typically in organizational settings. Hardware refers to physical computer equipment,
such as the computer monitor, central processing unit, or keyboard. Software refers to a
program or set of programs that tell the computer to perform certain tasks. Telecommunications networks refer to a group of two or more computer systems linked together with
communications equipment. Although we discuss the design, implementation, use, and
implications of hardware, software, and telecommunications throughout the chapters, the
specifics on hardware, software, and telecommunications are discussed in detail in Chapter
4 and the Technology Briefing. In Figure 1.5, we show the relationships among these IS
components.

People in organizations use information systems to process sales transactions, manage
loan applications, or help financial analysts decide where, when, and how to invest. Product
managers also use them to help decide where, when, and how to market their products and
related services, and production managers use them to help decide when and how to manufacture products. Information systems also enable us to get cash from ATMs, communicate
by live video with people in other parts of the world, and buy concert or airline tickets.
(Note that the term "information systems" is also used to describe the field comprising people who develop, use, manage, and study information systems in organizations.)

It is important to note that people use various terms to describe the field of information
systems, such as management information systems, data processing management, systems
management, business computer systems, computer information systems, and simply "systems." Since the term "information systems" is most common, we will stick with this term
and its acronym, IS. Next, we more thoroughly examine each of the key components of the
information systems definition.

Data: The Root and Purpose of Information Systems

Earlier, we defined IS as combinations of hardware, software, and telecommunications
networks that people build and use to collect, create, and distribute useful data, typically in
organizational settings. We will begin by talking about data, the most basic element of any
information system.

Data Before you can understand how information systems work, it is important to distinguish between data and information, terms that are often erroneously used interchangeably.
Data is raw material—recorded, unformatted information, such as words and numbers.

Failure: The Path to Success?

Management consultant Tom Peters, author or coauthor of ten international best-sellers, including *In Search of Excellence, Thriving on Chaos, The Pursuit of Wow!,* and his latest, *Re-Imagine! Business Excellence in a Disruptive Age,* often tells business managers that a company's survival may depend upon those employees who fail over and over again as they try new ideas. There's little that is more important to tomorrow's managers than failure, Peters maintains.

Apparently Apple Computers lives by Peters' philosophy. In January 2008, to help celebrate twenty-five years of the Mac, first introduced to consumers in 1984, *Wired* magazine recalled some of Apple's more infamous failures.

One of Apple's most visible flops was the Newton, actually the name of a newly conceived operating system that stuck to the product as a whole. The Newton, which Apple promised would "reinvent personal computing," fell far short of its hype when it was introduced in 1993 as a not-so-revolutionary PDA. The Newton was on the market for six years—a relatively long time for an unsuccessful product—but one of Steve Jobs' first acts when he returned to Apple's helm in 1997 was to cut the Newton Systems Group.

Other Apple product failures include:

- The Pippin, introduced in 1993, an inexpensive game player/network computer that couldn't compete with Nintendo's 64 or the Sony PlayStation.

FIGURE 1.4

The Apple Newton was not a commercial success.

- The TAM (Twentieth Anniversary Macintosh), which debuted in 1997 and lasted only a year. The sleek design was contemporary and attractive, but the machine was panned as overpriced and underpowered.
- The Macintosh television, of which only ten thousand units were produced, from 1993 to 1994. It tanked because it was incapable of showing television feeds in a desktop window.
- The PowerMac G4 Cube, an 8" × 8" × 8" designer machine that needed a separate monitor (as opposed to the popular iMac series) and was never popular with consumers.
- The Apple IIc (the "c" is for compact), which was meant to be the world's first portable computer and came complete with carrying case. It lacked internal expansion slots and direct access to the motherboard, however, and thus was less popular than other Apple II models that allowed users to upgrade.
- The puck mouse that came with the iMac G3. Apple made the mouse popular, but miscued when it expected consumers to adapt to this too-small, awkward-to-control device that users often mistakenly used upside down. The puck was soon replaced with the Mighty Mouse—a consumer favorite.
- The Lisa, introduced in 1983, was intended for business use, but its whopping $9,995 price tag (more than $20,000 in current dollars) made it too rich for most businesses, which could buy PCs at much lower prices. The Lisa was retired in 1986, after the Mac had captured consumers' attention.

Apple's failures are often cited by its competitors, but the company has proved Peters right time and time again: Any company without an interesting list of failures probably isn't trying hard enough.

Based on:

Gardiner, B. (2008, January 24). Learning from failure: Apple's most notorious flops. *Wired.* Retrieved May 17, 2008, from http://www.wired.com/gadgets/mac/multimedia/2008/01/gallery_apple_flops.

FIGURE 1.5

An information system is a combination of five key elements: people, hardware, software, data, and telecommunications networks.

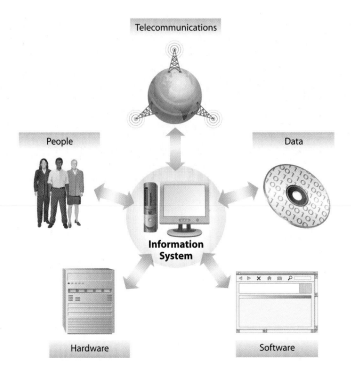

Data has no meaning in and of itself. For example, if we asked you what 465889727 meant or stood for, you could not tell us (see Figure 1.6). However, if we presented the same data as 465-88-9727 and told you it was located in a certain database, in John Doe's file, in a field labeled "SSN," you might rightly surmise that the number was actually the Social Security number of someone named John Doe.

Information   Data formatted with dashes or labels is more useful than unformatted data. By adding context, it is transformed into **information**, which can be defined as a representation of reality. In the previous example, 465-88-9727 was used to represent and identify an individual person, John Doe (see Figure 1.6). Contextual cues, such as a label, are needed to turn data into information that is familiar to the reader. Think about your experience with ATMs. A list of all the transactions at a bank's ATMs over the course of a month would be fairly useless data. However, a table that divided ATM users into two categories, bank customers and non–bank customers, and compared the two groups' use of the machine—their purpose for using the ATMs and the times and days on which they use them—would be incredibly useful information. A bank manager could use this information to create marketing mailings to attract new customers. Without information systems, it would be difficult to make data useful by turning it into information.

FIGURE 1.6

Data, information, knowledge, and wisdom.

Data	Information	Knowledge	Wisdom		
465889727	465-88-9727	465-88-9727 → John Doe	465-88-9727 → John Doe	School Records — Employment Records — Medical Records	
Unformatted Data	Formatted Data	Data Relationships	Data Relationships for Multiple Domains		
Meaning: ----------- ???	Meaning: ----------- SSN	Meaning: ----------- SSN → Unique Person	Meaning: ----------- SSN → Uniqe Person → Any Information About the person		

Knowledge In addition to data and information, knowledge and wisdom are also important. **Knowledge** is needed to understand relationships between different pieces of information. For example, you must have knowledge to be aware that only one Social Security number can uniquely identify each individual (see Figure 1.6). Knowledge is a body of governing procedures, such as guidelines or rules, that are used to organize or manipulate data to make it suitable for a given task.

Wisdom Finally, **wisdom** is accumulated knowledge. Wisdom goes beyond knowledge in that it represents broader, more generalized rules and schemas for understanding a specific domain or domains. Wisdom allows you to understand how to apply concepts from one domain to new situations or problems. Understanding that a unique individual identifier, such as a Social Security number, can be applied in certain programming situations to single out an individual record in a database is the result of accumulated knowledge (see Figure 1.6). Wisdom can be gained through a combination of academic study and personal experience.

Understanding the distinctions between data, information, knowledge, and wisdom is important because all are used in the study, development, and use of information systems.

Information Technology: The Components of Information Systems

When we use the term "information system," we are talking about **computer-based information systems**. Computer-based information systems are a type of technology. Here we briefly distinguish between technology, information technology (IT), and information systems.

Technology Versus Information Technology **Technology** is any mechanical and/or electrical means to supplement, extend, or replace human, manual operations, or devices. Sample technologies include the heating and cooling system for a building, the braking system for an automobile, and a laser used for surgery. In Figure 1.7, we show the relationship between technologies and computer-based information systems.

The term **information technology (IT)** refers to machine technology that is controlled by or uses information. One type of information technology is a programmable robot on the shop floor of a manufacturing firm that receives component specifications and operational instructions from a computer-based database. Throughout this book, when we speak of technology, we are typically referring to IT unless noted.

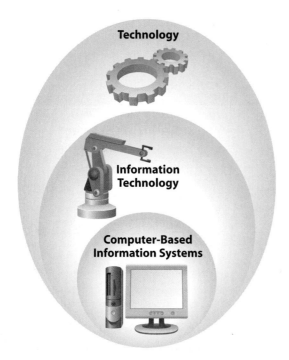

FIGURE 1.7

Computer-based information systems are a subset of information technologies and of technologies in general.

We could argue that any technology makes use of information in some fundamental way, as does each of the three examples of basic technology listed earlier (heating system, braking system, and a laser). However, information technologies, such as programmable manufacturing robots, use more information and in a more sophisticated way. It may appear that we are splitting hairs by distinguishing among technologies and information technologies. While the distinction is subtle, it is important. Information technologies use machine technologies as building blocks and then combine them with computing and networking technologies. A technology such as a mechanical drill press is useful, but it is more useful when combined with a computer database that instructs that drill press when and how to act.

Information Technology Versus Information Systems Information technologies and information systems are similar but also different. Remember that we defined an information system as a combination of hardware, software, and telecommunications networks that people build and use to collect, create, and distribute data. The goal of an information system is to provide useful data to people. An example of an information system is the use of specialized software on a computer-controlled, mechanical machine

Coming Attractions

How to Build a Bionic Contact Lens

Harbingers of the future see individuals wearing computers, rather than sitting in front of them. Maybe your clothing is wired to send and receive messages, your eyeglasses can connect to the Internet from any location, or a bionic contact lens for your eye constantly monitors body systems and alerts you to disease or other harmful physiological conditions. Is it possible? Scientists say "absolutely" and, in an attempt to extend "personal computer" to its ultimate definition, are at work on all of these concepts.

Bionic eyes for implant into the eyes of blind or partially blind individuals are currently in development, but a less intrusive bionic contact lens that a sighted individual would wear is also in the works at the University of Washington in Seattle. There, computer scientists and engineers are working on implanting electronics into polymers that can ultimately be worn like contact lenses. The purpose of the electronic lens research is twofold: (1) to determine if it is possible to create a contact lens that superimposes a display over the wearer's field of vision, without interfering with real-world vision; and (2) to build the lenses for practical applications, such as displaying text messages from cell phones, monitoring body chemistry, or even sensing environmental changes for soldiers in the field.

Construction problems must be solved, however, before any practical applications are feasible. For instance:

- Plastics used as a substrate for the electronics must be biocompatible.
- Electronic components containing light-emitting diodes (LEDs) must be small enough to fit over the eye without causing discomfort and yet must be functional.
- The high heat necessary to bond electronics to plastics can melt the plastic, so an extra step is needed to place the electronics on the plastic lens.
- Where will the power come from to run the electronics? (Scientists designing the lens are exploring coils that harvest radio frequency energy.)

Furthermore, the bionic lens has yet to be tested on the human eye. To date, the lens was tested on a rabbit's eye for twenty minutes with no ill effects, but the LEDs were not turned on. Scientists have yet to determine that the device is safe and operational when LEDs are working.

Clearly, the concept of wearable computers is no longer a science fiction dream, but is becoming reality.

Based on:

Greene, K. (2008, January 25). How to build a bionic eye: Researchers have created an electronic contact lens that could be used as a display or a medical sensor. *Technology Review.* Retrieved May 17, 2008, from http://www.technologyreview.com/Infotech/20113.

Penland, J. (2008, February 22). Bionic contact lenses. *Sciencentral News.* Retrieved May 17, 2008, from http://www.sciencentral.com/articles/view.php3?type=article&article_id=218393067.

used to produce compact discs (CDs), combined with other shop-floor equipment that allows a person to monitor and control the production of each CD from a separate, possibly remote, computer.

Other examples of information systems include a series of integrated electronic spreadsheets used for creating a budget, an order-fulfillment system for managing customers' purchases, and a set of linked pages on the Web to display company and product information. You may be asking, "Does my PC at work or school count as part of the company's or university's overall information system?" Our answer is yes. Information systems include personal, group, organizational, interorganizational, and even global computing systems.

People: The Builders and Managers of Information Systems

The information systems field includes a vast collection of people who develop, maintain, manage, and study information systems. The career opportunities for a person with IS training continue to be strong, and they are expected to continue to improve over the next ten years. For example, in 2008, the U.S. Bureau of Labor Statistics predicted that employment for computer and information systems managers will grow faster than the average for all occupations through 2016. This boost in employment will occur in nearly every industry, not just computer hardware and software companies, as more and more organizations rely more heavily on IS professionals. Likewise, *Money* magazine (http://money.cnn.com/magazines/moneymag/bestjobs) ranked "Computer/IT Analyst" as one of its top ten best jobs for the next decade (see Table 1.1); also, *FastCompany Magazine* (http://www.fastcompany.com/articles/2006/01/top-jobs-main.html) rated "Computer and Information Systems Managers" as its fifth-best job over the coming decade. Finally, in 2008, *US News & World Report* selected being a systems analyst as one of its thirty-one best careers.

In addition to an ample supply of jobs, earnings for information systems professionals will remain strong. According to the U.S. Bureau of Labor Statistics, median annual earnings of these managers in May 2006 were $101,580. The middle 50 percent earned between $79,240 and $129,250. Also, according to Salary.com, average salaries in 2008 for high-level information technology managers ranged from $89,864 to $119,900. According to a 2007 survey by the National Association of Colleges and Employers, starting salary offers for information systems majors, with one year or less of experience, averaged $49,966. Finally, computer and information systems managers, especially those at higher levels, often receive more employment-related benefits—such as expense accounts, stock option plans, and bonuses—than do nonmanagerial workers in their organizations.

Even with lower-level, highly technical jobs, such as systems programmers, being *outsourced* to organizations in other countries (in order to reduce labor costs; outsourcing will be discussed later in this chapter), there continues to be a very strong need for people with information systems knowledge, skills, and abilities—in particular, people with advanced information systems capabilities, as we will describe here. In fact, information systems careers are regularly selected as not only one of the fastest growing, but a career with far above average opportunities for greater personal growth, stability, and advancement.

TABLE 1.1 Best Jobs for the Next Decade

Rank	Career	Job Growth (10-year forecast)	Average Pay (salary and bonus)
1	Software engineer	46.07%	$80,427
2	College professor	31.39%	$81,491
3	Financial adviser	25.92%	$122,462
4	Human resources manager	23.47%	$73,731
5	Physician assistant	49.65%	$75,117
6	Market research analyst	20.19%	$82,317
7	**Computer/IT analyst**	**36.10%**	**$83,427**
8	Real estate appraiser	22.78%	$66,216
9	Pharmacist	24.57%	$91,998
10	Psychologist	19.14%	$66,359

Based on: http://money.cnn.com/magazines/moneymag/bestjobs.

Careers in IS The field of IS includes those people in organizations who design and build systems, those who use these systems, and those responsible for managing these systems. In Table 1.2, we list careers in IS and the salaries you might earn in those positions. The people who help develop and manage systems in organizations include systems analysts, systems programmers, systems operators, network administrators, database administrators, systems designers, systems managers, and chief information officers.

Another significant part of the IS field is the group of people who work in IS consulting firms, such as IBM, EDS, and Accenture. Experts in these consulting firms advise organizations on how to build and manage their systems and sometimes actually build and run those systems. Companies that have traditionally been hardware/software companies (such as IBM) are now doing a lot of systems consulting and related work. Similarly, companies such as Accenture that specialize in systems consulting are very successful—hiring more people, opening new offices, taking on new business, and generating lots of revenue.

University professors are another group of people in IS. These professors conduct research on the development, use, and management of information systems. Nonacademic researchers who conduct research for agencies such as the Department of Defense or for large corporations such as IBM, Xerox, Hewlett-Packard, and AT&T face almost unlimited opportunities. These professionals generally conduct more applied research and development than academic researchers. For example, a researcher for a major computer manufacturer might be developing a new computer product or examining ways to extend the life of a current product by integrating leading-edge components with the older architecture.

The Advent of the Chief Information Officer A number of important indications show that organizations are trying hard to manage information systems better. But perhaps nothing better demonstrates the growing importance of information systems in organizations than the advent of the **chief information officer (CIO)** and related positions in contemporary organizations.

EVOLUTION OF THE CIO. In the early 1980s, the CIO position became popular as the new title given to executive-level individuals who were responsible for the information systems component within their organizations. The CIO was charged with integrating new technologies into the organization's business strategy. Traditionally, the responsibility for integrating technology and strategy had not officially rested with any one manager. Responsibility for managing the day-to-day information systems function had previously rested with a mid-level operations manager or, in some cases, with a vice president of information systems. Ultimate responsibility for these activities would now rest with a high-level executive, the CIO. People began to realize that the information systems department was not simply a cost center—a necessary evil that simply consumed resources. They realized that information systems could be of tremendous strategic value to the organiza-

TABLE 1.2 Careers and Salaries in the Information Systems Field (National Average)

IS Activities	Typical Careers	Salary Ranges in Percentiles (25%–75%)
Develop	Systems analyst	$50,000–$85,000
	Systems programmer	$50,000–$80,000
	Systems consultant	$80,000–$120,000
Maintain	Information systems auditor	$45,000–$75,000
	Database administrator	$75,000–$100,000
	Webmaster	$55,000–$80,000
Manage	IS manager	$60,000–$90,000
	IS director	$85,000–$120,000
	Chief information officer (CIO)	$150,000–$250,000
Study	University professor	$70,000–$180,000
	Government scientist	$60,000–$200,000

Based on: http://www.salary.com; http://cnnmoney.com.

tion. As a result, this new IS executive would work much like other executives, sitting at the strategy table, working right alongside the chief executive officer, chief financial officer, chief operating officer, and other chief executives and key people in the organization. When strategic decisions were to be made, technology would play a major role, and the CIO needed to participate in the strategic decision-making process.

Not surprisingly, many organizations jumped on the CIO bandwagon and either hired or named a CIO. As a result, many people thought that the CIO boom was a fad that would soon end, as do many other popular management trends. In fact, in early 1990, *BusinessWeek* printed a story titled "CIO Is Starting to Stand for 'Career Is Over': Once Deemed Indispensable, the Chief Information Officer Has Become an Endangered Species" (Rothfeder and Driscoll, 1990). In this story, the authors reported statistics showing that in 1989 the CIO dismissal rate had doubled to 13 percent, which was noticeably higher than the 9 percent for all top executives. They explained that the primary reasons for CIO dismissals included tightening budgets for technology and management's overblown expectations of CIO functions. Apparently, many organizations had been caught up in the rush to have a CIO without thinking enough about why they needed a CIO in the first place. The authors countered, however, that given the growing trend toward using information systems to achieve a competitive advantage, the CIO could become relevant and important again. How right they were.

THE CIO TODAY. Today, most large organizations have a CIO or an equivalent position. It is also now common for midsized and smaller organizations to have a CIO-like position within their organizations, although they may give this person a title such as director of information systems. In 2007, *InformationWeek* named Tim Stanley of Harrah's Entertainment its CIO of the year. Harrah's, the largest casino gaming company in the world, is the envy of its industry due to its ability to anticipate and exceed customer needs and wants. Over the past year, for example, Stanley has led efforts to consolidate and leverage a massive customer data warehouse to better predict and react to customer needs. Additionally, he has led efforts to deploy wireless technologies such as RFID (see Chapter 9) to track customer movement and the rate at which chips are played as well as deploying new virtual games that can be accessed throughout Harrah's properties. Being a business innovation leader is an ongoing process for most CIOs. We will talk much more about gaining, and sustaining, competitive advantage using information systems in Chapter 3.

IS MANAGERIAL PERSONNEL. In large organizations, there typically are many other different management positions in addition to the CIO position within the IS function. In Table 1.3, we describe several such positions. This list is not exhaustive; rather, it is intended to provide a sampling of IS management positions. Furthermore, many firms will use the same job title, but each is likely to define it in a different way, or companies will have different titles for the same basic function. As you can see from Table 1.3, the range of career opportunities for IS managers is very broad.

What Makes IS Personnel So Valuable? In addition to the growing importance of people in the IS field, there have been changes in the nature of this type of work. No longer are IS departments in organizations filled only with nerdy men with pocket protectors (Figure 1.8). Many more women are in IS positions now. Also, it is now more common for an IS professional to be a polished, professional systems analyst who can talk fluently about both business and technology. IS personnel are now well-trained, highly skilled, valuable professionals who garner high wages and prestige and who play a pivotal role in helping firms be successful.

Many studies have been aimed at helping us understand what knowledge and skills are necessary for a person in the IS area to be successful (see, e.g., Todd, McKeen, and Gallupe, 1995). Interestingly, these studies also point out just what it is about IS personnel that makes them so valuable to their organizations. In a nutshell, good IS personnel possess valuable, integrated knowledge and skills in three areas—technical, business, and systems—as outlined in Table 1.4.

TECHNICAL COMPETENCY. The technical competency area includes knowledge and skills in hardware, software, networking, and security. In a sense, this is the "nuts and bolts" of IS. This is not to say that the IS professional must be a high-level technical expert in these

TABLE 1.3 Some IS Management Job Titles and Brief Job Descriptions

Job Title	Job Description
CIO	Highest-ranking IS manager. Responsible for strategic planning and IS use throughout the firm
IS director	Responsible for managing all systems throughout the firm and the day-to-day operations of the entire IS unit
Division or account executive	Responsible for managing the day-to-day operations of all aspects of IS within one particular division, plant, functional business area, or product unit
Information center manager	Responsible for managing IS services, such as help desks, hotlines, training, consulting, and so on
Development manager	Responsible for coordinating and managing all new systems projects
Project manager	Responsible for managing a particular new systems project
Maintenance manager	Responsible for coordinating and managing all systems maintenance projects
Systems manager	Responsible for managing a particular existing system
IS planning manager	Responsible for developing an enterprise-wide hardware, software, and networking architecture and for planning for systems growth and change
Operations manager	Responsible for supervising the day-to-day operations of the data and/or computer center
Programming manager	Responsible for coordinating all application programming efforts
Systems programming manager	Responsible for coordinating support for maintenance of all systems software (e.g., operating systems, utilities, programming languages, and so on)
Manager of emerging technologies	Responsible for forecasting technology trends and for evaluating and experimenting with new technologies
Telecommunications manager	Responsible for coordinating and managing the entire voice and data network
Network manager	Responsible for managing one piece of the enterprise-wide network
Database administrator	Responsible for managing database and database management software use
Audit or computer security manager	Responsible for managing ethical and legal use of information systems within the firm
Quality assurance manager	Responsible for developing and monitoring standards and procedures to ensure that systems within the firm are accurate and of good quality
Webmaster	Responsible for managing the firm's Web site

areas. On the contrary, the IS professional must know just enough about these areas to understand how they work and how they can and should be applied. Typically, the IS professional manages or directs those who have deeper, more detailed technical knowledge.

The technical area of competency is, perhaps, the most difficult to maintain because the popularity of individual technologies is so fleeting. However, according to industry analysts, many programming jobs or support jobs will have been outsourced to third-party providers in the United States or abroad by 2010, so there is a shift in the hot skills the market will demand (Collett, 2006). While there is the need for a diverse set of technical skills such as network design or data warehousing, other easier-to-codify jobs will be automated or outsourced (see Table 1.5). In fact, many of the hot skills listed in Table 1.5 are focused on the business domain, which will be discussed next.

FIGURE 1.8

Information systems personnel are no longer nerds.

Past   Present

TABLE 1.4 IS Professional Core Competencies

Domain	Description
Technical Knowledge and Skills	
Hardware	Hardware platforms, peripherals
Software	Operating systems, application software, drivers
Networking	Network operating systems, cabling and network interface cards, LANs, WANs, wireless, Internet, security
Business Knowledge and Skills	
Business integration, industry	Business processes, functional areas of business and their integration, industry characteristics
Managing people and projects	Planning, organizing, leading, controlling, managing people and projects
Social	Interpersonal, group dynamics, political
Communication	Verbal, written, and technological communication and presentation
Systems Knowledge and Skills	
Systems integration	Connectivity, compatibility, integrating subsystems and systems
Development methodologies	Steps in systems analysis and design, systems development life cycle, alternative development methodologies
Critical thinking	Challenging one's and others' assumptions and ideas
Problem solving	Information gathering and synthesis, problem identification, solution formulation, comparison, and choice

TABLE 1.5 Hot Skills for 2010 and Beyond

Domain	Hot	Cold
Business Domain	• Enterprise architecture • Project leadership • Business process modeling • Project planning, budgeting, and scheduling • Third-party provider management	
Technology Infrastructure and Services	• Systems analysis • Systems design • Network design • Systems auditing	• Programming • Routine coding • Systems testing • Support and help desk • Operations—server hosting, telecommunications, operating systems
Security	• IT security planning and management	• Continuity and recovery
Storage	• Storage administration	
Application	• Customer-facing application development	• Legacy systems development
Internet	• Customer-facing Web application systems • Artificial intelligence • Web mining • Data warehousing	
Business Intelligence	• Business intelligence • Data warehousing • Data mining	

Based on: Collett, 2006.

BUSINESS COMPETENCY. The business competency area is one that sets the IS professional apart from others who have only technical knowledge and skills, and in an era of increased outsourcing it may well save a person's job. For example, even though low-level technology jobs may be outsourced, MSNBC.com recently reported (http://www.msnbc.msn.com/id/5077435) that information systems management is one of ten professions that is not likely to be outsourced. As a result, it is absolutely vital for IS professionals to understand the technical areas *and* the nature of the business as well. IS professionals must also be able to understand and manage people and projects, not just the technology. These business skills propel IS professionals into project management and, ultimately, high-paying middle- and upper-level management positions.

SYSTEMS COMPETENCY. Systems competency is another area that sets the IS professional apart from others with only technical knowledge and skills. Those who understand how to build and integrate systems and how to solve problems will ultimately manage large, complex systems projects as well as manage those in the firm who have only technical knowledge and skills.

Perhaps now you can see why IS professionals are so valuable to their organizations. These individuals have a solid, integrated foundation in technical, business, and systems knowledge and skills. Perhaps most important, they also have the social skills to understand how to work well with and motivate others. It is these core competencies that continue to make IS professionals valuable employees.

Given how important technology is, what does this mean for your career? Technology is being used to radically change how business is conducted—from the way products and services are produced, distributed, and accounted for to the ways they are marketed and sold. Whether you are majoring in information systems, finance, accounting, operations management, human resource management, business law, or marketing, knowledge of technology is critical to a successful career in business.

Finding Qualified Personnel To effectively utilize information systems, organizations must have a highly trained workforce. Unfortunately, given the increased sophistication of modern information systems, organizations can often have a difficult time finding qualified personnel. In fact, finding the right people with the right skills is not possible in some areas. Consequently, over time, certain areas have become known for the availability of talented staff in a certain sector or with a certain set of skills, and thus organizations operating in that sector or relying on those skills tend to locate operations in such areas. Such areas are often characterized by a high quality of life for the people living there, and it is no surprise that many companies in the information technology sector within the United States are headquartered in Silicon Valley, California; Boston, Massachusetts; Austin, Texas; or Seattle, Washington. In other areas, organizations may have to find creative ways to attract and retain people from other areas.

One way to attract talented personnel is through creative human resource policies. For example, many organizations provide educational grants or expense-matching programs to encourage employees to improve their education and skills. Typically, after receiving continuing education benefits, employees must agree to remain with the organization for some specified period of time or be forced to repay the employer. Other human resource policies, such as telecommuting, flextime, and creative benefit packages, can also help to attract and retain the best employees.

With increasing globalization, other regions throughout the world are boasting about their highly skilled personnel. One such example is the Indian city of Bangalore, where, over a century ago, Maharajas started to lure talented technology-oriented people to the region, building a world-class human resource infrastructure that attracted companies from around the world. Although this has certainly helped to attract top Indian companies and multinational corporations alike, many companies have recently started complaining about other infrastructure issues, such as bad roads, power outages, housing conditions, traffic jams, and heavy rains. Clearly, for an area, just having a good human resource infrastructure is not sufficient, as organizations have to balance all their infrastructure needs when deciding where to move their headquarters or where to set up a new local subsidiary.

Powerful Partnerships

The Two Steves—Jobs & Wozniak

Steve Jobs, born in 1955, and Steve Wozniak, born in 1950—one of the most famous partnerships in the history of computing—combined their separate talents to form one of the most successful companies in IT—Apple Computers (see Figure 1.9). The two actually knew each other in high school, but renewed the friendship while Wozniak was working at Hewlett-Packard and Jobs took a summer job there. They visualized and designed the first marketable Apple computer (the Apple I), working first out of Jobs' bedroom, then out of a garage, and founded a company to sell their invention in 1976. The partners realized early on that they could probably sell one thousand computers a month, but as Wozniak recently wrote on his Web site, "That took a lot of money. We had none, so we went looking. We met Mark Markkula, and he launched us. I had to leave Hewlett Packard and that was tough."

The infusion of much-needed capital came just in time for Jobs and Wozniak to enter their product in the first West Coast Computer Faire. They rented a prime booth location and even managed to rent a video projector, a feat that Wozniak describes as follows: "This was such an early year that such projectors were virtually unknown. It was a BIG deal." The partners' professional business presentation at the Faire—far above other amateur efforts at the time—earned them several contracts for orders, and Apple Computers was off and running.

Both men left the company in 1985, less than ten years after founding it. Wozniak left to return to college, where he finally received his engineering degree under the pseudonym Rocky Clark. Steve Jobs, who stayed with Apple, persuaded John Sculley, the former CEO of Pepsi, to come aboard as captain. Ironically, Jobs and Sculley did not get along, and Sculley fired Jobs. Disillusioned, Jobs started his own company, called NeXT, which Apple eventually purchased, and in 1996, a wiser and less erratic Jobs again became Apple's chief executive. (Jobs was also the CEO and major shareholder of Pixar Animation Studios until Walt Disney Studios acquired the company in 2006.)

While Jobs and Wozniak differed widely in personality type and management style, the partners' abilities complemented each other and were an asset to the company they founded. Jobs, somewhat flamboyant and intuitive in anticipating which new concepts will capture consumers' imaginations, is still Apple Computer's CEO. Wozniak, a talented engineer, is more introverted and less willing than Jobs to assume center stage. "Woz" has founded several companies since leaving Apple, has taught children, and sponsors music festivals and charitable events. Furthermore, Wozniak is actually still on the payroll as an Apple employee. (He appreciates the 10 percent discount he gets when he buys Apple products.)

Many biographies have been written about the two Steves (*Inside Steve's Brain* by Leander Kahney is the latest about Jobs), and Wozniak has written his autobiography, *iWoz*. The books offer first-hand accounts of the fabled partnership and glimpses into the creation of one of the world's most successful computer companies.

FIGURE 1.9

Steve Jobs (left) and Steve Wozniak (right) of Apple Computer in the 1980s.

Based on:

Anonymous (n.d.). Woz.org . . . Everyone is welcome. Retrieved May 17, 2008, from http://www.woz.org.

Bellis, M. (n.d.). Inventors of the modern computer: The invention of the Apple Macintosh—Apple Computers—Steve Jobs and Steve Wozniak. *About.com*. Retrieved May 17, 2008, from http://inventors.about.com/library/weekly/aa051599.htm.

Hoyer, S. (2007, May 14). Interview: Steve Wozniak. *Macnotes.de*. Retrieved May 17, 2008, from http://www.macnotes.de/2007/05/14/interview-steve-wozniak-english-version.

Organizations: The Context of Information Systems

We have talked about data versus information, the technology side of IS, and the people side of IS. The last part of our IS definition is the term "organization." People use information systems to help their organization to be more productive and profitable, to help their firm gain competitive advantage, to help their firm reach more customers, or to improve service to their customers. This holds true for all types of organizations—professional, social, religious, educational, and governmental. In fact, not too long ago, the U.S. Internal Revenue Service launched its own site on the Web for the reasons just described (see Figure 1.10). The IRS Web site was so popular that approximately 220,000 users visited it during the first twenty-four hours and more than a million visited it in its first week—even before the Web address for the site was officially announced. Today, popular Web sites like MySpace.com and Yahoo.com receive millions of visitors every day.

Types of Information Systems Throughout this book, we will explore various types of information systems commonly used in organizations. It makes sense, however, for us to describe briefly here the various types of systems used so that you will better understand what we mean by the term "information system" as we use it throughout the rest of the book. Table 1.6 provides a list of the major types of information systems used in organizations.

Topping the list in the table are some of the more traditional, major categories that are used to describe information systems. These include *transaction processing systems, management information systems, executive information systems, decision support systems, intelligent systems, data mining and visualization systems, knowledge management systems, geographic information systems,* and *functional area information systems.* Five to ten years ago, it would have been typical to see systems that fell cleanly into one of these categories. Today, with **internetworking**—connecting host computers and their networks together to form even larger networks like the Internet—and **systems integration**—connecting separate information systems and data to improve business processes and decision making—it is difficult to say that any given information system fits into only one of these categories (e.g., that a system is a management information system only and nothing else). Modern-day information systems tend to span several of these categories of information systems, helping not only to collect data from throughout the firm and from customers, but also to integrate all that diverse data and present it to busy decision makers, along with tools to manipulate and

FIGURE 1.10

Web site of the U.S. Department of the Treasury, Internal Revenue Service, http://www.irs.gov.

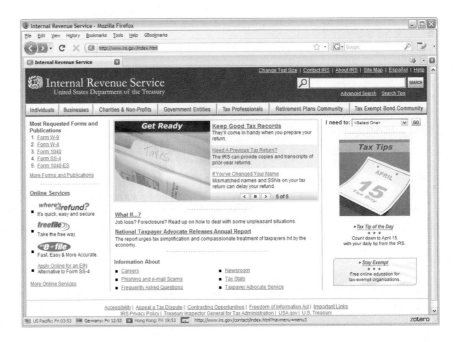

TABLE 1.6 **Types of Information Systems Used in Organizations**

Type of System	Purpose	Sample Application
Transaction processing system	Process day-to-day business event data at the operational level of the organization	Grocery store checkout cash register with connection to network
Management information system	Produce detailed information to help manage a firm or a part of the firm	Inventory management and planning system
Executive information system	Provide very high-level, aggregate information to support executive-level decision making	News retrieval and stock update information system
Decision support system	Provide analysis tools and access to databases in order to support quantitative decision making	Product demand forecasting system
Intelligent system	Emulate or enhance human capabilities	Automated system for analyzing bank loan applications
Data mining and visualization system	Methods and systems for analyzing data warehouses to better understand various aspects of a business	Market analysis
Office automation system (aka personal productivity software)	Support a wide range of predefined day-to-day work activities of individuals and small groups	Word processor
Collaboration system	Enable people to communicate, collaborate, and coordinate with each other	Electronic mail system with automated, shared calendar
Knowledge management system	Collection of technology-based tools to enable the generation, storage, sharing, and management of knowledge assets	Knowledge portal
Geographical information system (GIS)	Create, store, analyze, and manage spatial data	Site selection for new shopping mall
Functional area information system	Support the activities within a specific functional area of the firm	System for planning for personnel training and work assignments
Customer relationship management (CRM) system	Support interaction between the firm and its customers	Sales force automation
Enterprise resource planning (ERP) system	Support and integrate all facets of the business, including planning, manufacturing, sales, marketing, and so on	Financial, operations, and human resource management
Supply chain management (SCM) system	Support the coordination of suppliers, product or service production, and distribution	Procurement planning
Electronic commerce system	Enable customers to buy goods and services from a firm's Web site	Amazon.com

analyze those data. *Customer relationship management, supply chain management,* and *enterprise resource planning* systems are good examples of these types of systems that encompass many features and types of data and cannot easily be categorized.

Office automation systems and **collaboration systems** are typically bought "off the shelf" and enable people to (1) perform their own work and (2) work with others. A handful of software packages dominate this sector of the software industry and are commonly found on personal computers in people's homes and offices. Microsoft Office and the OpenOffice.org Productivity Suite are examples of popular office automation systems that provide word processing, spreadsheet, and other personal productivity tools. Microsoft's Exchange/Outlook and Lotus Notes are good examples of very popular collaboration systems that provide people with e-mail, automated calendaring, and online, threaded discussions.

Systems for electronic commerce, such as corporate Web sites, are also very popular and important. These systems are typically Internet-based and enable (1) consumers to find information about and to purchase goods and services from each other and from business firms and (2) business firms to electronically exchange products, services, and information. Given the pervasive use of the Internet to support electronic commerce, we devote a great deal of time to this topic in subsequent chapters. In Chapter 4, we talk about the nuts and bolts of how the Internet works, and in Chapter 5, we talk about how people are using the Internet to conduct electronic commerce.

While many modern-day information systems span several of these IS categories, it is still useful to understand these categories. Doing so enables you to better understand the myriad approaches, goals, features, and functions of modern information systems.

We have talked about each of the parts of our definition of IS, and we have talked about different types of information systems. In the next section, we focus on how information systems can be managed within organizations.

Organizing the Information Systems Function The current emphasis on the use of technology within businesses is not a fad. Indeed, all indicators point to the increased use of technology and to organizations' continued awareness of the importance of technology, both as a tool for productivity and as a vehicle for achieving competitive advantage and organizational change. Just as information systems have evolved over the past several years, so too has the IS function. Next, we briefly review the evolution of the IS function within organizations.

EARLY HISTORY: POOR SERVICE AND WORSE ATTITUDES. Early IS departments typically had huge project backlogs, and IS personnel would often deliver systems that were over budget, were completed much too late, were difficult to use, and did not always work well. In addition, many of these old-school IS personnel believed they owned and controlled the computing resources, that they knew better than users did, and that they should tell users what they could and could not do with the computing resources. Needless to say, this was not a recipe for success and good relationships. Indeed, relations between IS personnel and users within a firm were often sour and were sometimes bitter.

THE RISE AND FALL OF END-USER DEVELOPMENT. In the early years of information systems within organizations, users were often forced to put up with the poor service and the poor attitude. Then technology started to become significantly better—faster, easier to build and use, and cheaper—with the advent of the personal computer (PC) and standard software packages (see Figure 1.11). As a result, end users began to develop their own computing applications using PC-based spreadsheet packages (e.g., Visicalc), database management systems (e.g., dBase), and programming languages (e.g., BASIC). Disgruntled users simply said, "If the IS staff cannot or will not do this for us, then we will

FIGURE 1.11

The advent of the IBM PC and early applications packages led to end-user development.

Source: http://www-03.ibm.com/ ibm/history/exhibits/pc25/images/ 6705PH04.jpg

build our own systems." In many cases, they did just that, and they did it well, much to the dismay of some of the IS managers. Although end-user development clearly has strengths and still exists in some organizations, it also has serious weaknesses (see Chapter 10); thus, today, most organizations leave the systems development to the professionals.

THE MODERN INFORMATION SYSTEMS ORGANIZATION.   Business managers soon became more savvy about technology and the possibilities and opportunities that it offered, and they reasoned that the possibilities and opportunities were too great to let the IS function simply wither away as end-user development took over. In addition, smart, concerned IS personnel realized that they needed an attitude adjustment. Some people believe that the changes in the nature of technology forced people to cooperate more. For example, the shift from large "mainframe" computers to a "server-centric" model (i.e., relatively power- ful personal computers spread throughout the organization that share data, applications, or peripherals that are hosted by more powerful server computers—see Chapter 4) may have forced people within the IS function to improve their operations and their relationships with people in other units of the firm. The client-server model required a new kind of rela- tionship between IS and other people throughout the firm (Stevens, 1994). As a result of these forces, in modern IS units that do a good job, the atmosphere, attitude, and culture are very different and much more sensitive and responsive than they used to be.

In these more responsive IS units, the personnel have taken on more of a consulting relationship with their users. The IS personnel believe that, fundamentally, they are there to help the users solve problems and be more productive. Indeed, in many cases, the IS per- sonnel do not even refer to the users as "users." They are "clients" or "customers," or, even better, they are "colleagues" within the organization. This new attitude is a major change from the old days, when IS personnel did not want to be bothered by users and thought that the techies knew better than users. It is unfortunate that this old-school mentality still exists in some organizations.

The new IS culture is much like that found in successful service organizations. Think of how customers are treated in service organizations, such as Citigroup's Smith Barney or Ernst & Young, or in product-based organizations where service is also important, such as McDonald's or Nordstrom. Great service to the customer is absolutely critical, and employees do everything they can to please customers. They often live by the credo that "the customer is always right."

The same holds for IS units that have taken on this new **service mentality**. The IS per- sonnel do everything they can to ensure that they are satisfying their systems customers within the firm. They reach out to customers and proactively seek their input and needs rather than waiting for customers to come in with systems complaints. They modify the systems at a moment's notice just to meet customer needs quickly and effectively. They celebrate the customer's new systems ideas rather than putting up roadblocks and giving reasons that the new ideas cannot or will not work. They fundamentally believe that the customers own the technology and the information and that the technology and informa- tion are there for the customers, not for the systems personnel. They create help desks, hot- lines, information centers, and training centers to support customers. These service- oriented IS units structure the IS function so that it can better serve the customer.

The implications of this new service mentality for the IS function are staggering. It is simply amazing how unproductive a company can be when the IS personnel and other peo- ple within the firm are at odds with one another. On the other hand, it is even more amaz- ing how productive and enjoyable work can be when people in the IS function work hand- in-hand with people throughout the organization. Technology is, potentially, the great lever, but it works best when people work together, not against each other, to use it.

The Spread of Technology in Organizations   Another phenomenon that shows how integral and vital information systems and their proper management have become to orga- nizations is the extent to which the technology is firmly integrated and entrenched within the various business units (such as accounting, sales, and marketing).

In many organizations today, you will find that the builders and managers of a partic- ular information system or subsystem spend most of their time out in the business unit, along with the users of that particular system. Many times, these systems personnel are permanently placed—with an office, desk, phone, and personal computer—in the business unit along with the users.

In addition, it is not uncommon for systems personnel to have formal education, training, and work experience in information systems as well as in the functional area that the system supports, such as finance. It is becoming increasingly more difficult to separate the technology from the business or the systems staff from the other people in the organization. For this reason, how information systems are managed is important to you, no matter what career option you pursue.

As information systems are used more broadly throughout organizations, IS personnel often have dual-reporting relationships—reporting to both the central IS group and the business function they serve. Therefore, at least some need for centralized IS planning, deployment, and management continues—particularly with respect to achieving economies of scale in systems acquisition and development and in optimizing systems integration, enterprise networking, and the like. Even in organizations that are decentralizing technology and related decisions, a need for technology and related decisions to be coordinated across the firm still persists. This coordination is likely to continue to happen through some form of a centralized (or, at least, centrally coordinated) IS staff. Organizations are likely to continue to want to reap the benefits of IS decentralization (flexibility, adaptability, and systems responsiveness), but it is equally likely that they will not want to—and will not be able to—forgo the benefits of IS centralization (coordination, economies of scale, compatibility, and connectivity).

Given the trend toward pushing people from the IS staff out into the various business units of the firm and given the need for people within each of the functional areas of the business to have technology skills, there is clearly a need for people who know the technology side *and* the business side of the business. We suspect that the need for people to play these boundary-spanning roles will continue.

Downsizing and Outsourcing Many organizations that are **downsizing**, or rightsizing as some call it, are looking for ways to streamline business functions and, in some cases, to slash costs and replace people. Often, these organizations try to use the IS function and technology as the lever for simultaneously shrinking the organization by reducing personnel headcount and making the organization more productive (i.e., doing more with less). Although this approach may not be fair for the people who lose their jobs, many firms are forced to do this to remain competitive and, in some cases, to continue to exist. Such uses of information systems have interesting implications for the size and structure of organizations and for the size and structure of the IS function.

Similarly, **outsourcing** is on the rise for all aspects of business. In outsourcing, many of the more routine jobs are "outsourced": these jobs and/or tasks are being conducted by people in another firm, in another part of the country, or on another continent at less cost (referred to as *offshore outsourcing*—see Chapter 2). Some of these outsourced jobs are within the information systems function. For example, many computer programming tasks are now being completed by firms in India and China. *CIO* magazine reported that although the United States leads the world when it comes to the number and quality of IS-related workers, outsourcing to low-wage countries has become a large and key component of managing most IS organizations. In 2006, the global market for outsourcing was $930 billion. By the end of 2009, the global market is projected to be worth more than $1.43 trillion. The outsourcing market for IT services alone was $233 billion in 2006. Additionally, by 2006, nearly 90 percent of all large organizations used some type of offshore outsourcing of business functions. What implications does that have for people considering careers in business or, in particular, in information systems?

Career Prospects and Opportunities Although technology continues to become easier to use, there is still and is likely to continue to be an acute need for people within the organization to have the responsibility of planning for, designing, developing, maintaining, and managing technologies. Much of this will happen within the business units and will be done by those with primarily business duties and tasks as opposed to systems duties and tasks. However, we are a long way from the day when technology is so easy to deploy that a need no longer exists for people with advanced information systems knowledge and skills. In fact, many people believe that this day may never come. Although increasing numbers of people will incorporate systems responsibilities within their nonsystems jobs, there will continue to be a need for people with primarily systems responsibilities. In short, IS staffs and departments will likely continue to exist and play an important role in the foreseeable future.

While many organizations are downsizing and while some are shrinking their IS staffs and/or sending the more routine jobs abroad, overall hiring within IS is back again and is expected to grow. Given that information systems continue to be a critical tool for business success, it is not likely that IS departments will go away or even shrink significantly. Indeed, all projections are for long-term growth of IS in both scale and scope. Also, as is the case in any area of business, those people who are continually learning, continuing to grow, and continuing to find new ways to add value and who have advanced and/or unique skills will always be sought after, whether in information systems or in any area of the firm.

The future opportunities in the IS field are likely to be found in a variety of areas, which is good news for everyone. Diversity in the technology area can embrace us all. It really does not matter much which area of IS you choose to pursue—there will likely be a promising future there for you. Even if your career interests are outside IS, being a well-informed and capable user of information technologies will greatly enhance your career prospects.

 Net Stats

Worldwide Internet Usage

In March 2008, 17.5 percent of the world's active Internet users were located in North America. This is down 2 percent from 2006 and down from about half in 2004. Overall, it was estimated that there were over 1.4 billion active Internet users worldwide: over 578 million users in Asia, 384 million in Europe, and 248 million in North America (about 215 million active users in the United States alone) (see Table 1.7). The Internet is most heavily used in North America, with 73.1 percent of the total population going online; Africa has the lowest penetration (percentage of a region's population using the Internet) with 5.3 percent. China has the most users with 253 million, followed by the United States. As the world continues to embrace the Internet, it is inevitable that the U.S. proportion will continue to get smaller. What do you think these statistics will look like in ten years? In twenty years?

Based on:

Anonymous (n.d.). World Internet usage statistics. Retrieved September 14, 2008, from http://www.internetworldstats.com/stats.htm.

TABLE 1.7 World Internet Usage and Population Statistics

World Regions	Population (2008 estimates)	Population (% of world)	Internet Usage, Latest Data	% Population (penetration)	Usage (% of world)	Usage Growth (2000–2008)
Africa	955,206,348	14.3%	51,065,630	5.3%	3.5%	1031.2%
Asia	3,776,181,949	56.6%	578,538,257	15.3%	39.5%	406.1%
Europe	800,401,065	12.0%	384,633,765	48.1%	26.3%	266.0%
Middle East	197,090,443	3.0%	41,939,200	21.3%	2.9%	1176.8%
North America	337,167,248	5.1%	248,241,969	73.6%	17.0%	129.6%
Latin America/ Caribbean	576,091,673	8.6%	139,009,209	24.1%	9.5%	669.3%
Oceania/Australia	33,981,562	0.5%	20,204,331	59.5%	1.4%	165.1%
World Total	6,676,120,288	100.0%	1,463,632,351	21.9%	100.0%	305.5%

Note: Internet usage and world population statistics were updated for June 30, 2008. ©Copyright 2008, Miniwatts Marketing Group. All rights reserved.

The Dual Nature of Information Systems

Given how important and expensive information systems have become, information technology is like a sword—you can use it effectively as a competitive weapon, but, as the old saying goes, those who live by the sword sometimes die by the sword. The two following cases illustrate this dual nature of information systems.

Case in Point: An Information System Gone Awry: London-Heathrow International Airport

What happens when an information system is implemented poorly? An example of an information system gone wrong that made the news in early 2008 is the automated baggage-handling system for the $8.5 billion Terminal 5 of London's Heathrow Airport, England's largest international airport (see Figure 1.12). Terminal 5, built for the exclusive use of British Airways, was built to handle up to 35 million passengers annually and was optimized for large airplanes flying long-haul international routes, such as the new Airbus A380.

Like the newly constructed terminal, the new automated baggage-handling system was intended to be amazing. Although management was aware that they could not afford the new terminal to be a proving ground, they also wanted to ensure that the system was state of the art. Due to the enormous complexity, it took 400,000 man-hours to develop the software for the baggage-handling system. In order to ensure performance, the manufacturer extensively used simulation and modeling even before the actual system was built. The system, which cost $500 million, included the following features:

- 11 miles of conveyor belts
- 8,500 electric motors
- Ability to handle up to 6,000 bags per hour
- 132 check-in stations
- Bag storage warehouse for 4,000 bags, each of which can be individually retrieved at any time
- 11 baggage claim belts

On the opening day of the terminal, the problems started. Due to problems in the software, the system misrouted cargo or reported that planes for which luggage was on the way had already left, so that luggage was stored for later flights, and many planes eventually left without luggage. Flights were cancelled, and only passengers traveling without checked luggage were checked in. After the first week of operation, 500 flights had been canceled and 28,000 misrouted bags had accumulated. In order to clear the chaos, several thousands of these bags were trucked to Milan, Italy, where they would be sorted and then delivered to the passengers. Analysts estimate the overall costs of the disaster to be up to $50 million.

FIGURE 1.12

Travelers waiting for their luggage at London's Heathrow Airport.

The story has a happy ending, or beginning, as it were. They fixed the software and the automated baggage system is now operational. Indeed, the baggage-handling system is one of many ways that this organization is attempting to be innovative and to outdo the competition. However, the airport is still useful as an example of how a problematic information system can adversely affect the performance of an organization.

Case in Point: An Information System That Works: FedEx

Just as there are examples of information systems gone wrong, there are many examples of information systems gone right. FedEx, now a $38 billion family of companies (2008 data), is the world's largest express transportation company and delivers millions of packages and millions of pounds of freight to 220 countries and territories each business day (see Figure 1.13). FedEx uses extensive, interconnected information systems to coordinate more than 290,000 employees, hundreds of aircraft, and tens of thousands of ground vehicles worldwide.

To improve its services and sustain a competitive advantage, FedEx offers extensive services on the Internet. FedEx.com has more than 15 million unique visitors per month and over 3 million tracking requests per day. FedEx.com has become the information hub for a business where managing information *is the business*. In addition to shipment tracking, customers use the site for finding out about delivery options and costs, use tools to prepare their own packages, verify them online, and print bar-coded shipping documents. These and other information systems have positioned FedEx as the global leader in express transportation.

Information Systems for Competitive Advantage

Heathrow's baggage-handling system and FedEx's Web site are typical of those used in large, complex organizations. These systems are so large in scale and scope that they are difficult to build. It is important to handle the development of such systems the right way the first time around. These examples also show that as we rely more and more on information systems, the capabilities of these systems are paramount to business success.

Not only were these systems large and complicated, but they were—and continue to be—critical to the success of the firms that built them. The choices made in developing the new systems at both London's Heathrow airport and FedEx were **strategic** in their intent. These systems were not developed solely because managers in these organizations wanted to do things faster or because they wanted to have the latest, greatest technology. These organizations developed these systems strategically to help gain or sustain some **competitive advantage** (Porter, 1985; Porter and Millar, 1985) over their rivals. Let us not let this notion slip by us—while the use of technology can enable efficiency and while information systems must provide a return on investment, technology use can also be strategic and can be a powerful enabler of competitive advantage.

FedEx is an innovator in successfully using information systems.

Ethical Dilemma

Online Rights Not Always Universal

American Internet users have been fortunate in that online content is not censored, and U.S.-based bloggers, journalists, and e-mailers are generally not subject to government intrusion or harassment. As the world becomes flatter, however, and the Internet becomes available to users in diverse countries, the question of who owns and/or controls Web-published data becomes an issue.

China has often been in the news for alleged violations of human rights. Since American companies have provided software and hardware for China's Internet infrastructure, the question arises, When China restricts online rights for its citizens, should U.S. companies providing services be cooperative? Consider the following:

- U.S.-based Cisco built the entire Chinese Internet infrastructure and allegedly agreed to supply equipment that allows the Chinese government to monitor Internet users.
- Chinese Internet users use Microsoft's blog tool, MSN Spaces. Microsoft censors the Chinese version of its software using a blacklist supplied by Beijing. Among words that will be automatically rejected by the Chinese system are "democracy" and "capitalism."
- In order to do business in China, in 2004 Google agreed to censor "subversive" articles from Google News China or from their search results.
- In 2005, Yahoo! was said to have aided the conviction of a Chinese journalist, Shi Tao, when employees of Yahoo!'s China office supplied details about Shi's e-mail address to local authorities. Mr. Shi, one of five journalists whose convictions for "revealing state secrets" Yahoo! allegedly aided, is currently serving a ten-year prison term in China.
- During the 2008 Olympic Games in Beijing, journalists were initially unable to access Web sites such as www.amnesty.org (the restrictions were later lessened after international protests).

Similar to Mr. Shi's situation, a Chinese journalist in Beijing recently posted content that, although probably factually correct, was deemed inappropriate by the Chinese government. The government then requested that Microsoft shut down the blog, and Microsoft complied. The Chinese government monitors all online activity, shutting down "dissident" Web sites and deleting "subversive" postings. Since Chinese bloggers often write under pseudonyms, the Chinese government has recently asked Internet access provider firms to reveal the identities of bloggers who post "inappropriate" content. As a result, several Chinese bloggers have been arrested and sentenced to lengthy jail terms after their identities were revealed.

Reporters Without Borders and other critics have called such censorship agreements unethical. Cisco, Microsoft, Google, and Yahoo! have replied that they are simply following local laws. Opponents argue, however, that online product and service providers based outside of China should not assist the Chinese government in its campaign against Internet users' online rights.

In reference to the company's involvement in Shi Tao's conviction and sentencing, Yahoo! twice faced congressional hearings and was denounced by human rights organizations and others in support of Shi Tao. Consequently, in 2007 Yahoo! settled a legal complaint filed by Shi's family for an undisclosed amount, and Yahoo! CEO Jerry Yang made a public apology to Shi's mother at a congressional hearing. In addition, Yahoo! established a Human Rights Fund to "provide humanitarian and legal assistance to persons in the People's Republic of China who have been imprisoned or persecuted for expressing their views using the Internet."

For human rights activists, the major issue is that American companies, such as Microsoft, Google, and Yahoo!, that profess to value free speech, are acting unethically when they cooperate with governments that curtail Internet users' rights to freedom of expression. The fact that Article 19 of the Universal Declaration of Human Rights supports freedom of expression lends legitimacy to this argument.

Another question that arises in such situations is, "Who owns Web-posted data?" Since the data is often not physically present in the local country supplying Internet access, do the local authorities have the right to censor the data? (Local authorities would probably argue that the impact of the content posted online is felt locally.) Do local authorities have a right to regulate online content when Internet access is hosted by companies located outside a country?

Most important, is the online environment independent of the digital world we live in, or is it subject to all the rules and regulations of countries the Internet passes through? Should the Internet adapt its own laws that all hosting companies must follow?

These are questions that will need to be answered in the twenty-first century as the world gets smaller and the Internet becomes an integral service in all countries.

Based on:

Barboza, D., & T. Zellar, Jr. (2006, January 8). Microsoft's shutdown of Chinese blog is condemned. *International Herald Tribune.* Retrieved May 17, 2008, from http://www.iht.com/articles/2006/01/06/technology/web.0107msft.php.

McKinnon, R. (2008, April). Asia's fight for web rights. *Far Eastern Economic Review.* Retrieved May 17, 2008, from http://feer.com/essays/2008/april/asias-fight-for-web-rights.

Pain, J. (2005, December 1). Perspective: A cyber blind spot on human rights. *CNET News.com.* Retrieved May 17, 2008, from http://news.com.com/A+cyber+blind+spot+on+human+rights/2010-1028_3-5977410.html.

Although we described information systems' uses at two relatively large organizations, firms of all types and sizes can use information systems to gain or sustain a competitive advantage over their rivals. Whether it is a small mom-and-pop boutique or a large government agency, every organization can find a way to use information technology to beat its rivals. In Chapter 3, we will talk more about this opportunity to use information systems strategically.

Why Information Systems Matter

On May 1, 2003, Nicholas Carr published an article titled "IT Doesn't Matter" in *Harvard Business Review* that created quite a stir. He argued that as IT becomes more pervasive, it will become more standardized and ubiquitous, more of a commodity that is absolutely necessary for every company. He reasoned then that companies should focus IT strictly on

Brief Case ◆

Guerilla Wi-Fi

The digital divide refers to the "haves" and "have-nots" in the IT world. One Laptop per Child (OLPC), a nonprofit organization formed in 2005, attempts to overcome the digital divide, in part by providing low-cost computers to children who could otherwise not afford to buy them. However, just having a computer is not enough to join the club of the "haves," and even households that have computers do not always have access to affordable Internet connection services. One start-up company is addressing this problem: Meraki Networks, Inc., a three-year-old enterprise headed by Sanjit Biswas, an MIT student taking time off from working on his doctoral degree in computer science. (*Meraki* is a Greek word, meaning "inserting yourself into something you create.")

It has been determined that at least one billion people now connect to the Internet. Biswas' goal is to help the next billion, and the next after that, connect. The device the company sells to accomplish this is the $50 Mini—a wireless router about the size of two iPhones stacked up. The Mini can act like a "typical" wireless router, but the key to its individuality is its atypical software that allows Minis to "piggy-back," so that one Mini connected to the Internet can relay the connection through other Minis, thus forming a large network for Internet users. According to Biswas, Minis within line-of-sight (approximately 700 feet) allow a single DSL connection to accommodate up to fifty Internet users. In this way, a Mini network administrator can provide Internet connection service at nominal cost—perhaps as low as $1 per month. The drawback is that some Internet connection providers, such as Verizon and Time Warner, forbid subscribers from sharing connections. Less well-known providers, such as Speakeasy and bway.net, have no such restrictions.

Thanks to Biswas's Mini, the so-called "Guerilla Wi-Fi" phenomenon is spreading and helping former Internet connection have-nots to become connected—and part of the Internet community.

Questions

1. Should Internet providers be pressured to allow customers to share their connections with "non-paying" customers?
2. Would you share your connection with a total stranger even if it meant that you would sometimes experience a slowdown to your connection speed?

Based on:

Mims, C. (2007, August 6). Meraki's guerilla Wi-Fi to put a billion more people online. *Scientific American.* Retrieved May 17, 2008, from http://www.sciam.com/article.cfm?id=merakis-guerilla-wi-fi-to-put-billion-people-online.

cost reduction and risk mitigation and that investing in IT for differentiation or for competitive advantage is futile. Many experts in academia, in the popular press, and within technology companies not only disagreed with that argument but also felt that, if taken literally, such a line of thinking could hurt companies' competitiveness.

Given the debate that this article caused, on May 1, 2004, *CIO* magazine's editor in chief, Abbie Lundberg, published an interview with Carr on the subject, along with an invited counterpoint essay titled "The Engine That Drives Success: The Best Companies Have the Best Business Models Because They Have the Best IT Strategies" by noted technology and business strategy author Don Tapscott. Tapscott argued that companies with bad business models tend to fail regardless of whether they use information technology or not. On the other hand, companies that have good business models and use information technology successfully to carry out those business models tend to be very successful. He described many examples, across a variety of industries, where firms dominate their respective markets; have superior customer relationships, business designs, and differentiated offerings; and are well known for their superior use of IT in supporting a unique business strategy. His examples included Amazon.com, Best Buy, Citigroup, PepsiCo, Herman Miller, Cisco, Progressive Casualty Insurance, Marriott, FedEx, GE, Southwest Airlines, and Starbucks.

We tend to side with Tapscott on this one. We believe that information systems are a necessary part of doing business, that they can be used to create efficiencies, and that they can also be used as an enabler of competitive advantage. We do agree with Carr, however, that the competitive advantage from the use of information systems can be fleeting, as competitors can eventually do the same thing. Also, given how expensive information systems projects have become and given how cost conscious and competitive businesses now are, nearly every information system project today must show a clear return on investment. Again, we'll talk more about the role of information systems in competitive advantage and return on investment in Chapter 3 and throughout the book.

Industry Analysis

Business Career Outlook

In Chapter 2, we carefully examine how information systems are fueling globalization and tremendous changes throughout the world. Today, organizations are increasingly moving away from focusing exclusively on local markets. For example, PriceWaterhouseCoopers is focusing on forming overseas partnerships to increase its client base and to better serve the regions located away from its U.S. home. This means that it is not only more likely that you will need to travel overseas in your career or even take an overseas assignment, but it is also extremely likely that you will have to work with customers, suppliers, or colleagues from other parts of the world. Given this globalization trend, there is a shortage of business professionals with the necessary "global skills" for operating in the digital world. Three strategies for improving your skills include the following:

1. **Gain International Experience.** The first strategy is very straightforward. Simply put, by gaining international experiences, you will more likely possess the necessary cultural sensitivity to empathize with other cultures and, more important, you will be a valuable asset to any global organization.

2. **Learn More Than One Language.** A second strategy is to learn more than your native language. Language problems within global organizations are often hidden beneath the surface. Many people are embarrassed to admit when they don't completely understand a foreign colleague. Unfortunately, the miscommunication of important information can have disastrous effects on the business.

3. **Sensitize Yourself to Global Cultural and Political Issues.** A third strategy focuses on developing greater sensitivity to the various cultural and political differences within the world. Such sensitivity and awareness can be developed through coursework, seminars, and international travel. Understanding current events and the political climate of international colleagues will enhance communication, cohesiveness, and job performance.

In addition to these strategies, prior to making an international visit or taking an international assignment, there are many things you can do to improve your effectiveness as well as enhance your chances of having fun, including the following:

1. Read books, newspapers, magazines, and Web sites about the country.
2. Talk to people who already know the country and its culture.
3. Avoid literal translations of work materials, brochures, memos, and other important documents.
4. Watch locally produced television as well as monitor the local news through international news stations and Web sites.
5. After arriving in the new country, take time to tour local parks, monuments, museums, entertainment locations, and other cultural venues.
6. Share meals and breaks with local workers and discuss more than just work-related issues such as current local events and issues.
7. Learn several words and phrases in the local languages.

Regardless of what business profession you choose, globalization is a reality within the digital world. In addition to globalization, the proliferation of information systems is having specific ramifications for all business careers. This is discussed next.

For Accounting and Finance: In today's digital world, accounting and finance professionals rely heavily on information systems. Information systems are used to support various resource planning and control processes as well as to provide managers with up-to-date information. Accounting and finance professionals use a variety of information systems, networks, and databases to effectively perform their functions. In addition to changing the ways internal processes are managed and performed, information systems have also changed the ways organizations exchange financial information with suppliers, distributors, and customers. If you choose a career in accounting or finance, it is very likely that you will be working with various types of information systems every day.

For Operations Management: Information systems have also greatly changed the operations management profession. In the past, orders for supplies had to be placed over the phone, production processes had to be optimized using tedious calculations, and forecasts were sometimes only educated guesses. Today, enterprise resource planning and supply chain management systems have eliminated much of the "busywork" associated with making production forecasts and placing orders. Additionally, with the use of corporate extranets, companies are connecting to their suppliers' and distributors' networks, helping to reduce costs in procurement and distribution processes. If you choose operations management as your profession, the use of information systems will likely be a big part of your workday.

For Human Resources Management: The human resources management profession has experienced widespread use of information systems for recruiting employees via Internet job sites, distributing information through corporate intranets, or analyzing employee data stored in databases. In addition to using information systems within your daily work activities, you will also have to deal with other issues related to information systems use and misuse within your organization. For example, what are the best methods for motivating employees to use a system they do not want to use? What policies should you use regarding monitoring employee productivity or Internet misuse? If you choose human resource management as a profession, information systems have become an invaluable addition to the recruitment and management of personnel.

For Marketing: Information systems have changed the way organizations promote and sell their products. For example, business-to-consumer electronic commerce, enabled by the Internet, allows companies to directly interact with their customers without the need for intermediaries; likewise, customer relationship management systems facilitate the targeting of narrow market segments with highly personalized promotional campaigns. Marketing professionals must therefore be proficient in the use of various types of information systems in order to attract and retain loyal customers.

For Information Systems: Information systems have become a ubiquitous part of organizational life, where systems are used by all organizational levels and functions. Because of this, there is a growing need for professionals to develop and support these systems. To most effectively utilize the investment in information systems, professionals must be proficient in both business—management, marketing, finance, and accounting—and technology. In other words, information systems professionals must understand the business rationale for implementing a particular system as well as how organizations can use various systems to obtain a competitive advantage. Being able to bridge the business needs of the organization to information systems–based solutions will provide you with a competitive advantage in the job market.

Based on:

Treitel, R. (2000, October 9). Global Success. *Gantthead.com*. Retrieved May 17, 2008, from http://www.gantthead.com/articles/articlesPrint.cfm?ID=12706.

Key Points Review

1. *Explain what an information system is, contrasting its data, technology, people, and organizational components.* Information systems are combinations of hardware, software, and telecommunications networks that people build and use to collect, create, and distribute useful data, typically in organizational settings. When data are organized in a way that is useful to people, these data are defined as information. The term "information systems" is also used to represent the field in which people develop, use, manage, and study computer-based information systems in organizations. The field of IS is huge, diverse, and growing and encompasses many different people, purposes, systems, and technologies. The technology part of information systems is the hardware, software, and telecommunications networks. The people who build, manage, use, and study information systems make up the people component. They include systems analysts, systems programmers, information systems professors, and many others. Finally, information systems typically reside and are used within organizations, so they are said to have an organizational component. Together, these four aspects form an information system.

2. *Describe types of jobs and career opportunities in information systems and in related fields.* The people who help develop and manage systems in organizations include systems analysts, systems programmers, systems operators, network administrators, database administrators, systems designers, systems managers, and chief information officers. All of these types of people are in heavy demand; as a result, salaries are high and continue to rise. The field of IS has changed such that IS personnel are now thought of as valuable business professionals rather than as "nerds" or "techies." The need for technology-related knowledge and skills has spread to other careers as well in fields such as finance, accounting, operations management, human resource management, business law, and marketing.

3. *Describe the dual nature of information systems in the success and failure of modern organizations.* If information systems are conceived, designed, used, and managed effectively and strategically, then together with a sound business model they can enable organizations to be more effective, to be more productive, to expand their reach, and to gain or sustain competitive advantage over rivals. If information systems are not conceived, designed, used, or managed well, they can have negative effects on organizations such as loss of money, loss of time, loss of customers' goodwill, and, ultimately, loss of customers. Modern organizations that embrace and manage information systems effectively and strategically and combine that with sound business models tend to be the organizations that are successful and competitive.

Key Terms

chief information officer (CIO) 14
collaboration system 21
competitive advantage 27
computer-based information systems 11
data 8
downsizing 24
hardware 8
information 10

information systems (IS) 8
information technology (IT) 11
internetworking 20
knowledge 11
knowledge society 6
knowledge worker 5
new economy 6
office automation system 21

outsourcing 24
service mentality 23
software 8
strategic 27
systems integration 20
technology 11
telecommunications networks 8
wisdom 11

Review Questions

1. Define the term "knowledge worker." Who coined the term?
2. Describe and contrast the economic, cultural, and technological changes occurring in the digital world.
3. Define the term "information systems" (IS) and explain its data, technology, people, and organizational components.
4. Define and contrast data, information, knowledge, and wisdom.
5. Define and contrast technology, information technology, and information system.
6. Describe three or four types of jobs and career opportunities in information systems and in related fields.
7. What is a CIO, and why has the CIO grown in importance?
8. List and define three technical knowledge and/or skills core competencies.

9. List and define four business knowledge and/or skills core competencies.
10. List and define four of the systems knowledge and/or skills core competencies.
11. List and define five types of information systems used in organizations.
12. Describe the evolution of the information systems function within organizations.

Self-Study Questions

Visit the Interactive Study Guide on the Companion Web site for additional Self-Study Questions: www.pearsonhighered.com/valacich.

1. Information systems today are _____.
   A. slower than in the past
   B. continuing to evolve with improvements to the hardware and software
   C. utilized by only a few select individuals
   D. stable and should not change
2. Information systems are used in which of the following organizations:
   A. professional
   B. educational
   C. governmental
   D. all of the above
3. Whereas data are raw unformatted pieces or lists of words or numbers, information is _____.
   A. data that has been organized in a form that is useful
   B. accumulated knowledge
   C. what you put in your computer
   D. what your computer prints out for you
4. Computer-based information systems were described in this chapter as _____.
   A. any complicated technology that requires expert use
   B. a combination of hardware, software, and telecommunications networks that people build and use to collect, create, and distribute data
   C. any technology (mechanical or electronic) used to supplement, extend, or replace human, manual labor
   D. any technology used to leverage human capital
5. In the 1980s, which of the following became a popular new title given to executives who were responsible for the information systems function?
   A. CFO
   B. CIO

C. CEO
D. CMA

6. Other terms that can be used to represent the knowledge society include _____.
   A. the new economy
   B. the network society
   C. the digital world
   D. all of the above
7. Which of the following IS job titles is used for a person whose primary responsibility is directly doing maintenance on an information system?
   A. IS director
   B. maintenance manager
   C. systems analyst
   D. chief information officer
8. Which of the following is not classified as business knowledge and skills?
   A. management
   B. communication
   C. systems integration
   D. social
9. Which of the following was not discussed as a common type, or category, of information system used in organizations?
   A. transaction processing
   B. decision support
   C. enterprise resource planning
   D. Web graphics
10. Which of the following is not an example of an information system?
    A. an accounting system in a business
    B. a concession stand
    C. a combination of different software packages in a company
    D. a database of customers

Answers are on page 35.

Problems and Exercises

1. Match the following terms with the appropriate definitions:
   i. Wisdom
   ii. New economy
   iii. Information
   iv. Knowledge society
   v. Outsourcing
   vi. Systems integration
   vii. Downsizing
   viii. Chief information officer
   ix. Information systems
   x. Service mentality

   a. A society with a high proportion of knowledge workers who play an important leadership role
   b. An executive-level individual who has overall responsibilities for the information systems component within the organization and is concerned primarily with the effective integration of technology and business strategy
   c. Accumulated knowledge that represents broader, more generalized rules and schemas for understanding a specific domain or domains

d. The moving of routine jobs and/or tasks to people in another firm, in another part of the country, or in another country at less cost

e. Data that have been formatted in a way that is useful

f. The practice of slashing costs and streamlining operations by laying off employees

g. Connecting separate information systems and data to improve business processes and decision making

h. An economy in which information technology plays a significant role and enables producers of both the tangible (computers, shoes, etc.) and intangible (services, ideas, etc.) products to compete efficiently in global markets

i. The mind-set that your goal is to enable others to be successful and that the "customer is always right"

j. Combinations of hardware, software, and telecommunications networks that people build and use to collect, create, and distribute useful data, typically in organizational settings

2. Using the Web, research how FedEx has invested and updated its information systems and information technologies. List some of the most significant items and argue whether these investments have been good or bad. Discuss how you feel these investments affected FedEx's competitors.

3. Peter Drucker has defined the knowledge worker and knowledge society. What are his definitions? Do you agree with them? What examples can you give to support or disprove these concepts?

4. List three major IS professional core competencies or general areas from the textbook. Do you agree or disagree that all three are needed to become a professional? Why? What competencies do you currently possess, and what do you need to improve on or acquire? What is your strategy to acquire new skills? Where and when will you acquire them?

5. Of the several information systems listed in the chapter, how many do you have experience with? What systems would you like to work with? What types of systems do you encounter at the university you are attending? The Web is also a good source for additional information.

6. Consider an organization that you are familiar with, perhaps one that you have worked for or have done

business with in the past. Describe the types of information systems that organization uses and tell whether they are useful or up to date. List specific examples for updating or installing information systems that improve productivity or efficiency.

7. Identify someone who works within the field of information systems as an information systems instructor, professor, or practitioner (e.g., as a systems analyst or systems manager). Find out why this individual got into this field and what this person likes and dislikes about working within the field of IS. What advice can this person offer to someone entering the field?

8. Based on your previous work and/or professional experiences, describe your relationships with the personnel in the IS department. Was the IS department easy to work with? Why or why not? Were projects and requests completed on time and correctly? What was the organizational structure of this IS department? How do your answers compare with those of other classmates?

9. As a small group, conduct a search on the Web for job placement services. Pick at least four of these services and find as many IS job titles as you can. You may want to try monster.com or careerbuilder.com. How many did you find? Were any of them different from those presented in this chapter? Could you determine the responsibilities of these positions based on the information given to you?

10. What type of IT/IS investment should Starbucks Coffee have, and how would it be used in the corporate office and the individual stores? What would it need in order to track inventory and sales? Search the Web or visit a Starbucks Coffee store in your city to determine whether you can see what technology is available in your local store.

11. The IS support group within the School of Business at Indiana University changed its name from "Business Computing Facility" to "Technology Services." Along with the change in name came an appropriate change in services and offerings to their clientele. Research the evolution of the information systems support function within your university or within a company. Make sure you track name changes, reporting structures, service orientation, and so on.

12. Contrast, using specific examples in your own life, technology, information technology, and computer-based information systems.

13. Do information systems matter to modern organizations? Why or why not?

Application Exercises

 Note: The existing data files referenced in these exercises are available on the Student Companion Web site: www.prenhall.com/valacich.

 Spreadsheet Application: Ticket Sales at Campus Travel

The local travel center, Campus Travel, has been losing sales. The presence of online ticketing Web sites, such as

Travelocity.com and Expedia.com, has lured many students away. However, given the complexity of making international travel arrangements, Campus Travel could have a thriving and profitable business if it concentrated its efforts in this area. You have been asked by the director of sales and marketing to help with analyzing prior sales data in order to design better marketing strategies. Looking at these data, you realize that it is nearly impossible to perform a detailed analysis of ticket sales given that it is not summarized or organized in a useful way to inform business decision making. The spreadsheet TicketSales.csv contains the ticket sales data for spring 2009. Your director has asked you for the following information regarding ticket sales. Modify the TicketSales.csv spreadsheet to provide the following information for your director:

1. The total number of tickets sold for each month.
   a. Select the data from the "tickets sold" column.
   b. Then select the autosum function.
2. The largest amount of tickets sold by a certain salesperson to any one location.
   a. Select the appropriate cell.
   b. Use the "MAX" function to calculate each salesperson's highest ticket total in one transaction.
3. The least amount of tickets sold by a certain salesperson to any one location.
   a. Select the appropriate cells.
   b. Use the "MIN" function to calculate the "least tickets sold."
4. The average number of tickets sold.
   a. Select the cells.
   b. Use the "AVERAGE" function to calculate the "average number of tickets sold" using the same data you had selected in the previous steps.

Database Application: Tracking Frequent Flier Miles at the Campus Travel Agency

The director of sales and marketing of the travel agency would like to increase the efficiency of handling those who have frequent flier accounts. Often, frequent fliers have regular travel routes or want to change their preferred seating area or meal category. In the previous years, the data has been manually entered in a three-ring binder. In order to handle the frequent fliers' requests more efficiently, your director has asked you to build an Access database containing the following information:

- Name (first and last name)
- Address
- Phone number
- Frequent flier number
- Frequent flier airline
- Meal category
- Preferred seating area

To do this, you will need to do the following:

1. Create an empty database named "frequent flier."
2. Import the data contained in the file FrequentFliers.txt using the function "Get external Data >> Import . . .".
   Hint: Use tab delimiters when importing the data; note that the first row contains field names.

After importing the data, create a report displaying the names and addresses of all frequent fliers by doing the following:

1. Select "Create report by using Wizard."
2. Include the fields "first name," "last name," and "address" in the report.
3. Save the report as "frequent fliers."

Team Work Exercise: How to Find Out What Is Current in IS

Visit a Web site of an information systems–related content provider, such as *InformationWeek, Computerworld, CIO* magazine, or *NewsFactor,* and scan the current headlines. You can find these online resources at www.informationweek.com, www.computerworld.com, www.cio.com, and www.newsfactor.com. After having scanned the headlines, get together with your team and discuss your findings. What is the focus of the different sites? What are the hot technologies and related issues? Which seem to be most important to business managers? Prepare a brief presentation for your classmates.

Answers to the Self-Study Questions

1. B, p. 7	**2.** D. p. 20	**3.** A, p. 10	**4.** B, p. 8	**5.** B, p. 14
6. D, p. 7	**7.** B, p. 16	**8.** C, p. 17	**9.** D, p. 21	**10.** B, p. 13

Case ①

Click Clique—Facebook.com

Facebook.com calls itself "a social utility that helps people better understand the world around them . . . through social networks allowing people to share information online the same way they do in the real world." That it does. In late 2008, Facebook reported the following user statistics:

- More than 100 million active users—"active" means a user has visited the site in the last thirty days.

- Over 55,000 regional, work-related, collegiate, and high school networks
- Half of all users are outside of college
- Fastest-growing group of users is 25 and older
- Maintained an 85 percent market share of four-year American universities
- Number one photo sharing application on the Web

Founded by a group of Harvard University students and launched in February 2004, Facebook was set to provide everything a college student needs to know about other students. Users list their interests ("soccer," "buying shoes"), friends, classes, and any other "tasteful" information about themselves. Anyone can form a subgroup within Facebook, such as "Cancer Corner" for smokers, "Collars Up!" for members who like to wear their shirts with the collars turned up, and the self-described "Republican Princesses." Many active members post detailed profiles of themselves and admit to logging on to browse Facebook four or five times a day.

While Facebook can help people get acquainted, it can also be used as a "weapon," according to some users. "It's communication lean" and a little fake, says an undergraduate sociology major at George Washington University. But even so, she logs on to the site whenever she has some spare time.

Initially, Facebook provided students with a private online directory that could be accessed only by people having an e-mail address ending in ".edu" (an ending that is usually reserved for educational institutions). This constraint was the major difference between Facebook and other online friendship and dating Web sites. Students registered on Facebook apparently felt safe in divulging personal information, probably because the network is closed to campus outsiders. In some instances, however, sororities and fraternities ask students not to list their Greek affiliations on Facebook to prevent potential pledges from researching which students are members of which sororities and fraternities. This restriction protects sorority and fraternity members from being constantly approached, both online and in person, and it also reduces animosity and competition between students vying for certain sororities and fraternities.

Over time, Facebook realized that the restriction to just students alienated a large number of people. What was founded as a social networking site just for Harvard students was opened up to college students throughout the United States, to high school students, and, in 2006, to anyone who wanted to join. To give its members the feeling of protection, the privacy controls were expanded, allowing people to prevent being included in search results and being contacted by people outside their networks. Further, Facebook's college and work networks require authenticated e-mail addresses to join.

Due to such restrictions, Facebook is also a good place for announcements—or not. For example, one student advertised a party in an off-campus apartment complex. As expected, fellow students who were on Facebook learned about the time and location of the party, but, unfortunately (for the host), a pair of roommates living next door to the party site also read about the party on Facebook. The pair of roommates dreaded the impending commotion and advised the police to be on alert that night. The party started mildly at 8:00 P.M. but got rowdy by 9:00 P.M. The police cars that were parked just outside the apartment complex stopped the party promptly at 10:00 P.M. to comply with the city's noise ordinance. The moral is, don't advertise an event on Facebook unless you want a crowd to show up.

To summarize, Facebook provides a popular networking service for college students and others. Anyone belonging to the Facebook community can access other members' profiles and browse their interests and friends. The "wall" is another popular feature. Anyone can post messages to a member's wall, and members can delete posted messages. Other Facebook features include adding photo albums, listing coming activities, and "poking," a ritual equivalent to a handshake. Facebook also provides rating scales for music, books, movies, television series, and other interests and activities.

Facebook is not the first or the only Web site to deliver social networking activities. Other social networking sites include Friendster, MySpace, Tribe Networks, LinkedIn, NamesDataBase, and Google's Orkut, all of which have features similar to Facebook. Social networking sites use a variety of techniques to increase user base. Some allow direct registration from their Web sites; others do not. Those that do not allow direct registration follow the "viral marketing" premise, by which only those who receive an invitation from a registered friend may be allowed to join the network. This process not only reinforces the networking philosophy but also makes sure that an entire circle of friends is registered on one site.

Venture capitalists have expressed an interest in funding online social networking because of the advertising prospects. When friends recommend a product or service to friends, an ad has more impact. Therefore, when marketers use online social networks, sales can increase exponentially. Recently, Microsoft outbid Google in a bid for a 1.6 percent stake in Facebook, eventually paying $240 million.

Because often the only source of revenue is advertisements placed on every page, many online social networks have not yet paid off financially for founders, but the concept has definitely proven popular with users and will continue to attract those who simply enjoy being part of a cybercommunity.

Questions

1. Do you use a social networking site like Facebook.com? If so, why? If not, why not?
2. Besides advertising, how else could a social networking site generate revenue?
3. What are the pros and cons of using a social networking site?

Based on:

Anonymous (n.d.). Facebook statistics. Retrieved May 17, 2008, from http://www.facebook.com/press/info.php?statistics.

Arrington, M. (2006, March 28). Facebook is doing the Skype dance. *TechCrunch*. Retrieved May 17, 2008, from http://www.techcrunch.com/2006/03/28/facebook-is-doing-the-skype-dance/.

Barton, Z. (2005, October 17). Facebook's Greek drama. *CNET News.com*. Retrieved May 17, 2008, from http://news.com/Facebooks+Greek+drama/2100-1046_3-5895963.html.

Copeland, L. (2004, December 28). Click clique—Facebook's online college community. *WashingtonPost.com*. Retrieved May 17, 2008, from http://www.washingtonpost.com/wp-dyn/articles/A30002-2004Dec27.html.

Naraine, R. (2004, February 13). Social networks in search of business models. *Internetnews.com*. Retrieved May 17, 2008, from http://www.internetnews.com/bus-news/article.php/3312491.

Microsoft invests $240 million in Facebook (2007, October 24). Retrieved May 17, 2008, from http://www.msnbc.msn.com/id/21458486.

Case

Are We There Yet?—Online Map Services

Everyone who drives a car and/or uses a computer is familiar with online map services. Three of the best and most frequently used are Google maps (http://maps.google.com), MSN's MapBlast (http://www.mapblast.com), and Yahoo! Maps (http://maps.yahoo.com). The service is free for computer users who want to find the shortest route from point A to point B and now extends to laptop and mobile phones as well. Google has been especially popular for its satellite views and features such as real-time traffic information (in places like Southern California), or the display of user generated content (e.g., landmarks or restaurant reviews) (some of the overly inclusive satellite imagery of military bases has recently been taken down following a request by the U.S. military).

Maps have become so popular with consumers that they have also become a for-profit enterprise. For example, all three of the above services provide a for-fee option for businesses with Web sites for adding easy-to-use, interactive maps online. With these applications, organizations can show customers how to reach stores or service centers in their areas, and employees on the road can more easily reach customers in various locations, or find hotels and restaurants in their travel areas. Organizations can also track shipments or supply chains, manage employees and resources in the field, and insert relevant advertising into their customized maps when they are displayed on Web sites.

Beyond posting maps for viewing on Web sites and mobile phones, mapping is entering the consumer mainstream as a profitable enterprise. For example, in 2007 Google struck a deal with a company called Gilbarco Veeder-Root, which makes "smart" gas pumps that include an Internet connection and a kiosk. At the pump kiosk, customers could scroll through several categories to find landmarks, hotels, restaurants, and hospitals selected by the gas station's owner. In the beginning customers could not enter specific addresses, but that feature was said to be in the works.

Also in 2007, Google announced an extension of its earlier "Send to Car" maps partnership with BMW—first implemented only in Germany. The feature had been extended to Italy and the UK and would eventually reach the United States. Mercedes Benz also announced deals with both Google and Yahoo! called "Search and Send," where customers could send maps from either search engine to the Mercedes in-car telematics system. Maps and directions could be sent to Mercedes with the system via desktop PCs and mobile phones.

Personal in-car navigation systems that rely on global satellite positioning (GSP) technology are quickly turning into more comprehensive mobile search platforms that can be used in the car—stationary or on the go—or out of the car. This positions in-car search as a promising arena for search engine development and competition, for extending features offered in vehicles, and for potential advertising revenue.

Questions

1. Do you use Internet mapping sites like Google maps? Why or why not?
2. As outlined in the case, there are many innovative mapping products and services; describe a new service that you want that doesn't yet exist.
3. Do you think that mapping software can be an invasion of privacy? Why or why not?

Based on:

Bass, S. (2005, June 29). Maps for fun and business. *PCWorld*. Retrieved May 17, 2008, from http://www.pcworld.com:80/article/id,121387/article.html.

Claburn, T. (2008, March 7). U.S. military restricts Google maps. *InformationWeek*. Retrieved May 17, 2008, from http://www.informationweek.com/news/security/government/howArticle.jhtml?articleID=206902500.

Spring, T. (2008, January 16). Google maps the key locations of popular TV shows. *PCWorld*, Retrieved May 17, 2008, from http://blogs.pcworld.com/staffblog/archives/006311.html.

Sterling, G. (2007, August 29). Send to (German) car: The new local search front. *SearchEngineLand*. Retrieved May 17, 2008, from http://searchengineland.com/070829-183605.php.

Sterling, G. (2007, November 17). Search Google maps at the gas pump. *SearchEngineLand*. Retrieved May 17, 2008, from http://searchengineland.com/071107-101838.php.

Fueling Globalization Through Information Systems

After reading this chapter, you will be able to do the following:

1. Define globalization, describe how it evolved over time, and describe the key drivers of globalization.

2. Describe the emerging opportunities for companies operating in the digital world.

3. Explain the factors companies have to consider when operating in the digital world.

4. Describe international business and information systems strategies used by companies operating in the digital world.

Preview

In today's world, the effects of globalization can be seen everywhere. Whether you buy products or services, almost everything (except for maybe a haircut at your local barbershop) can be produced somewhere else in the world. For example, retailer Wal-Mart buys much of the products it sells from China—it is said that if Wal-Mart were a country, it would be China's eighth-largest trading partner, ahead of Russia, Australia, and Canada (Jingjing, 2004). Similarly, all kinds of services are now being outsourced to foreign countries, no matter whether the service is software development, the transcription of documents, or the design of components for large commercial aircraft. In this chapter, you will learn how globalization evolved and how information systems fuel this trend toward an ever-shrinking world.

The next section examines the evolution of globalization, followed by a discussion of challenges facing companies operating in a global digital world. Then different international business strategies and associated international information systems strategies are examined. Other aspects of the relationship between globalization and information systems, such as the *digital divide* (see Chapter 11—Managing Information Systems Ethics and Crime), will be examined throughout the remainder of the book. Finally, our discussion of globalization is intentionally limited to how information systems are fueling globalization; for more comprehensive discussions, see Friedman's *The World Is Flat* (2007) or Viotti and Kauppi's *International Relations and World Politics* (2009).

Managing in the Digital World: Infosys Technologies Ltd.

Those of us who thought the debate over whether the world is flat or round had been resolved centuries ago are wrong. Now we are told the world truly is flat. Thomas Friedman explains why the world is now flat in his book, *The World Is Flat: A Brief History of the Twenty-First Century*. Friedman concluded that the world is flat and started work on his book explaining when Nandan Nilekani, the Bangalore-based Infosys Technologies Ltd. CEO remarked "the global economic playing field is being leveled." "Level" to Friedman meant "flat," and this, he said, was his eureka moment. The concept of a flat world quickly became a phrase descriptive of globalization, with Friedman the guru.

Companies that help organizations compete and win in this flat, global world are called "flatteners." Infosys Technologies Ltd. is a flattener because the multinational information technology services company helps businesses think flat, which requires changing operational priorities and doing business in new ways. For example:

- Outsourcing: If an organization in a distant location can perform a portion of a business's services better and cheaper, hire that organization. In other words, it's no longer prudent or necessary for all of a business's services to be performed in one location, or under one roof.
- Supply Chains: Find the equipment and supplies needed to accomplish business goals efficiently and economically by using global, not just local, sources.
- Consulting: In order to compete in a flat world, it may make sense for businesses to consult information services that can advise them on how to become global. For example, Infosys Technologies consults with clients within eighteen industries, ranging from the aerospace industry, to health care, education, and utilities industries.
- Employment: To hire the best and the brightest, seek employees from countries around the world, or use the employment procurement services of a global employment service.

Infosys Technologies has been described as the brightest jewel in India's crown. It has maintained this reputation since seven individuals founded it in 1981, with $250 (U.S.) in borrowed capital. In 2008, the company reported consulting revenues of $4 billion and was valued at $30 billion.

After reading this chapter, you will be able to answer the following:

1. What events have led to the flat world?

2. What types of activities within an organization are better candidates for outsourcing?

3. How can you prepare yourself to compete in the flat world?

FIGURE 2.1

An employee walks in the Infosys Technologies campus in Electronics City in Bangalore, India.

Based on:

Anonymous (n.d.). What we do. Retrieved May 24, 2008, from http://www.infosys.com/about/what-we-do/default.asp.

Anonymous (n.d.). Flat world. Retrieved May 24, 2008, from http://www.infosys.com/flat-world/business/perspectives/default.asp.

Friedman, T. (2006, July). Think flat. Retrieved May 24, 2008, from http://www.infosys.com/flat-world/business/perspectives/FriedmanPerspective.pdf.

Friedman, T. (2007). The world is flat 3.0: A brief history of the twenty-first century. New York: Picador.

Infosys. (2008, May 21). In *Wikipedia, the free encyclopedia*. Retrieved May 24, 2008, from http://en.wikipedia.org/w/index.php?title=Infosys&oldid=213835069.

The world is flat. (2008, May 18). In *Wikipedia, the free encyclopedia*. Retrieved May 24, 2008, from http://en.wikipedia.org/w/index.php?title=The_World_Is_Flat&oldid=213282759.

Evolution of Globalization

Over the past centuries, **globalization**—the integration of economies throughout the world, enabled by innovation and technological progress (IMF, 2002)—has come a long way, from separate nation-states on different continents to what we see today, a world where people and companies can enjoy worldwide communication and collaboration, with fewer and fewer barriers. In his book *The World Is Flat, New York Times* foreign affairs columnist Thomas L. Friedman has characterized the evolution of globalization as having three distinct phases (see Figure 2.2), differing in the focal point and primary drivers of this evolution (see Table 2.1 for an overview of each phase). While it had taken humankind thousands of years to discover that the world is round, Friedman argues that forces of globalization are now creating a "flat," or connected, world, such that competitors in many areas of the world now have equal opportunities to access the global marketplace. As technologies have evolved and diffused broadly throughout the world, the pace and scope of globalization has accelerated. Next, we examine this evolution.

Globalization 1.0

The first stage, termed **Globalization 1.0** by Friedman, began in the late fifteenth century and ended about 1800. During those times, India was famous for its wealth of spices and other goods; however, getting there, for example, by traveling east was very cumbersome and dangerous, as no sea route had been discovered until the end of the fifteenth century. Even then, sailing to India going east included circumnavigating the entire continent of Africa, including a dangerous passage around the Cape of Good Hope (South Africa). When Christopher Columbus set sail in August 1492 to discover a westward route to India, he was convinced, contrary to popular belief at that time, that the earth was round. However, instead of discovering a new route to India, he discovered the Americas, opening up new areas for discovery and new sources for resources.

During Globalization 1.0, mainly European countries were globalizing, attempting to extend their territories into the New World. Power—from domesticated horses (for transportation and agriculture), wind (for grinding grain and sailing), and, in the late

FIGURE 2.2

Evolution of globalization.

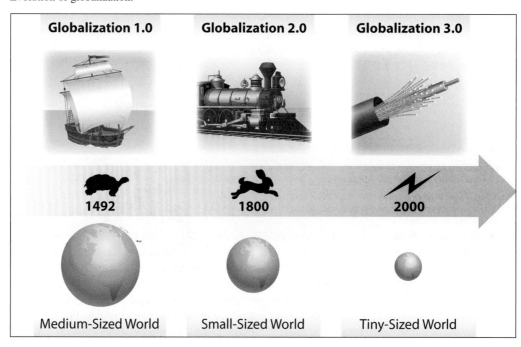

TABLE 2.1 **Phases of Globalization**

Globalization Phase	Time	Primary Entities Globalizing	Regions Globalizing
1.0	1492–1800	Countries	Europeans and Americans
2.0	1800–2000	Companies	Europeans and Americans
3.0	2000–now	Individuals and small groups	Worldwide

stages, steam (then used primarily for mining)—was the primary driver of this stage of globalization. Collectively, this evolution brought continents closer together, shrinking the world "from size large to size medium." During those times, industries changed slowly, and any change took generations. While many industries (such as the apparel industry) changed, most people didn't notice how it affected their lives because of the slow pace of change.

Globalization 2.0

In 1800, **Globalization 2.0** started, lasting up until the year 2000 (being interrupted only by the Great Depression and the two world wars). During Globalization 2.0, the world shrunk from "size medium to size small," as companies (rather than just countries) started to globalize. While people were constantly innovating, changes still took quite some time. For example, it took more than a generation before people felt the effects of the industrial revolution. In the early stages of Globalization 2.0, the steam engine led to falling costs for the transportation of goods, both on land using railroads and on sea using steamships. Technological innovations such as the telegraph and, later, telephones, personal computers, satellites, and early forms of the Internet, tremendously reduced telecommunication costs. The reduction of transportation and telecommunication costs spurred a growing market for products and labor. However, it was still mainly Americans and Europeans driving globalization.

Globalization 3.0

Around the year 2000, **Globalization 3.0** began, with individuals and small groups from virtually every nation joining the globalization movement, shrinking the world from "size small to size tiny." Not only did the world shrink, but this shrinking brought with it an even faster pace of change. People now feel the effects of industry changes within decades, and new industries have emerged that no one would have imagined only a few decades ago. For example, Google, the company that now dominates the search engine market and is one of the world's largest companies, was incorporated only in 1998. In the next sections, we will discuss the factors enabling Globalization 3.0 and how these factors have forever transformed the world.

Key Factors Enabling Globalization 3.0 In the last decade of the twentieth century, a number of technological and societal changes took place, ushering in Globalization 3.0. In his book, Friedman provides a list of ten forces enabling the transition from Globalization 2.0 to Globalization 3.0 (see Table 2.2). While the list of enablers could be extended almost endlessly (or be debated as to their ultimate significance), we will focus on those discussed by Friedman given their broad popularity.

ENABLER #1: NOVEMBER 9, 1989—THE FALL OF THE BERLIN WALL. The fall of the Berlin Wall and the downfall of communism is one of the key events flattening the world. Built in 1961 to keep East German citizens from emigrating (or escaping) to West Germany, the Berlin Wall quickly became the symbol of the division of Germany and the existence of an "iron curtain" between Western and communist countries. Following an autumn of mass demonstrations in 1989, the East German government announced on November 9, 1989, that its citizens were finally permitted to cross the border to West Germany; in the days and

TABLE 2.2 **Ten Enablers of Globalization 3.0**

Enabler	Event or Trend	Description
1	November 9, 1989	The fall of the Berlin Wall and the fall of communism opened up new markets for talent and products
2	August 9, 1995	Netscape went public; the company introduced the first mainstream Web browser
3	Work flow software	Standards and de facto standards enabling computers to "talk to each other" and facilitate collaboration
4	Uploading	The ability of individuals and companies to actively participate in content generation on the Web
5	Outsourcing	The moving of business processes or tasks (such as accounting or security) to another company
6	Offshoring	Companies moving business functions to different countries (often overseas) to reduce costs
7	Supply chaining	The use of information systems to tightly integrate retailers, their suppliers, and their customers
8	In-sourcing	The delegation of a company's logistics operations to a subcontractor that specializes in that operation
9	In-forming	Individuals' use of powerful search engines on the Internet, such as Google, Yahoo!, or MSN, to build their "own personal supply chain of information, knowledge, and entertainment" (Friedman, 2007, p.178)
10	The steroids	Technologies amplifying the other flatteners by making things digital, mobile, virtual, and personal

weeks after that date, people from all over the world participated in dismantling the wall (see Figure 2.3). The fall of the Berlin Wall and the opening of the border between East and West Germany marked the end of the Cold War between communist and capitalist countries and the breakup of the Eastern bloc, freeing millions of people. At once, people in many former communist countries could enjoy greater freedoms. For many companies, this meant a tremendous increase in potential customers as well as access to a huge, talented labor pool in the former Eastern bloc countries.

FIGURE 2.3

Enabler #1: People tearing down the Berlin Wall after November 9, 1989.

Around the same time, Microsoft released the first version of the Windows operating system, which over time became the de facto world standard in PC operating systems, enabling people from all over the world to use a common computing platform.

ENABLER #2: AUGUST 9, 1995—THE RELEASE OF THE NETSCAPE WEB BROWSER.   The second big flattener was the Internet browser—the "killer app" that enabled everyone who had a computer and a modem to view Web pages. While the first Web site went live in 1991, viewing and navigating early Web sites was very cumbersome, and the Internet, in its infancy, was not widely used by the general public (see Chapter 4—Managing the Information Systems Infrastructure). A company called Netscape released the first mainstream Web browser in 1994 and went public on August 9, 1995. Later in 1995, Netscape even integrated an e-mail component into its browser, allowing people not only to view Web pages but also to communicate using the Internet. Thus, the Netscape browser can be regarded as a cornerstone in giving individuals easy access to the Internet (see Figure 2.4). In addition to opening up the possibilities of the Internet for the general public, Netscape helped set a standard for the transport and display of data that other companies and individuals could build on, making the Internet even easier to use and more powerful than ever. Since then, Netscape has been acquired by AOL, which phased out the once popular browser in early 2008. Nevertheless, Netscape's legacy lives on, as both the open-source browser Mozilla Firefox and Netscape's successor Flock are based on Netscape's source code. Although many companies had some internal computer networks, it was the widespread adoption of the Internet that enabled companies to interconnect in new ways. Widespread adoption of the Internet also allowed organizations to benefit from the political and societal changes during that time.

In the final years of Globalization 2.0, the Internet really took off, and many young entrepreneurs envisioned a variety of new business models based on the possibilities the Internet offered. At the same time, companies supplying the network infrastructure saw the need to provide more and faster connections, leading to a tremendous *overinvestment* in telecommunications infrastructure, such as fiber-optic cable, which is used to transmit very large amounts of data at the speed of light (see Chapter 4). Only a few years later, many of the new ventures (most of which operated at a loss in order to gain initial market share) proved not to be viable, often because of inexperienced management and uncontrolled spending. With the bursting of the dot-com bubble, stock prices plummeted, causing many people to lose much of their retirement money that had been invested in the stock market. However, the burst of the dot-com bubble also helped make the transition from Globalization 2.0 to Globalization 3.0.

The burst of the dot-com bubble created less demand for and oversupply of the telecommunications infrastructure that had been installed just a few years before, which, in

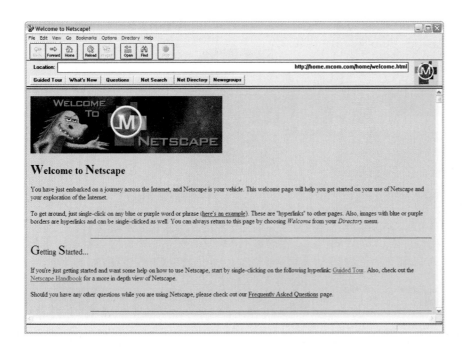

FIGURE 2.4

Enabler #2: The Netscape browser was a cornerstone in giving individuals easy access to the Internet.

Powerful Partnerships

Netscape's James H. Clark and Marc Andreessen

The WWW came into existence in 1993, and a year later James H. Clark and Marc Andreessen (see Figure 2.5) founded the first company to take advantage of the Web, called Mosaic Communications Corporation. The company's first product, released in October 1994, was a Web browser (an application used to view and navigate the World Wide Web and other Internet resources) called Mosaic Netscape 0.9. The browser was subsequently renamed "Netscape" in November 1994.

James Clark was born in Plainview, Texas, in 1944. He dropped out of high school after being suspended and spent four years in the navy. After Clark's discharge from the military, he earned bachelor's and master's degrees in physics from the University of New Orleans and then went on to earn a PhD in computer science from the University of Utah in 1974. Clark's computer science research concerned geometry pipelines, specialized software or hardware that accelerates the display of three-dimensional images.

Marc Andreessen was born in Cedar Rapids, Iowa, in 1971. He earned a bachelor's degree in computer science at the University of Illinois in Urbana-Champaign in 1993.

While still an undergraduate, he worked at the University's National Center for Supercomputing Applications (NCSA), where he and a salaried worker, Eric Bina, developed code for a user-friendly browser with integrated graphics that could work on a wide-range of computer platforms. They called the browser code Mosaic.

After college graduation, Andreessen took a job with Enterprise Integration Technologies in California, where he met James Clark, who had recently left Silicon Graphics, a successful company he founded with several others. Clark saw the potential in the browser code Andreessen had helped develop, and the two founded Mosaic Communications Corporation. However, the University of Illinois owned exclusively the Mosaic browser code Andreessen had helped develop at NCSA and claimed that Clark and Andreessen had stolen it from them, so Clark and Andreessen changed the name of their company to Netscape Communications Corporation. Nevertheless, they continued to distribute the software they marketed as Netscape Navigator, and in December 1994, Netscape Communications settled

FIGURE 2.5

Netscape's James H. Clark (left) and Marc Andreessen (below).

with the University of Illinois. The settlement cost Netscape Communications $3 million, including legal fees, but the University dropped all claims to Netscape.

At first Clark and Andreessen charged for the product, but there were a number of ways to receive the product free of charge, and most users did not pay. As the partners concentrated more on making their product ubiquitous, they worried less about making money from sales of the browser and hoped to make money in other ways, such as selling advertising. Superior features of Netscape, such as new HTML tags that allowed Web designers more control and creativity, soon made Netscape the browser of choice. Despite competition from Microsoft's Internet Explorer, by 1996, 75 percent of Web surfers used Netscape.

Fierce competition with Microsoft began almost immediately after Netscape was released when Microsoft released Internet Explorer 1.0 in 1995, as part of a Windows 95 Plus-Pack add-on. For the next few years, the two browser companies worked to outdo each other (often termed "browser wars"), adding features to their respective products so quickly that they often did not work correctly. Soon, Microsoft began bundling Internet Explorer with the Windows operating system, never charging extra for it, and by 1998, Netscape Communications was forced to offer its browser for free as well. Eventually Netscape Communications could no longer compete with Microsoft's superior financing assets and effectively dropped out of the race.

Critics of Netscape Communications have argued that racing to the market before browser versions were fully operational and bad company management contributed to the company's decline. The company rested on its laurels, some said, and soon Internet Explorer had superior features and better performance as a browser.

AOL acquired Netscape in 1999 for $10 billion in stock and hired Andreessen as chief technology officer. AOL has not promoted Netscape software, and decided to retire the browser in 2008 after its share of the browser market dropped to 1 percent. Both Clark and Andreessen have gone on to found several IT start-ups, and both are wealthy WWW pioneers.

Based on:

Anonymous (n.d.). Internet pioneers. Retrieved May 24, 2008 from http://www.ibiblio.org/pioneers/andreesen.html.

James H. Clark. (2008, May 22). In *Wikipedia, the free encyclopedia.* Retrieved May 24, 2008, from http://en.wikipedia.org/w/index.php?title=James_H._Clark&oldid=214262173.

Marc Andreessen. (2008, May 18). In *Wikipedia, the free encyclopedia.* Retrieved May 24, 2008, from http://en.wikipedia.org/w/index.php?title=Marc_Andreessen&oldid=213302804.

Netscape. (2008, May 23). In *Wikipedia, the free encyclopedia.* Retrieved May 24, 2008, from http://en.wikipedia.org/w/index.php?title=Netscape&oldid=214400768.

turn, caused infrastructure providers to fail, and much of the infrastructure had to be sold for a fraction of the cost. While the short-term consequences were devastating for many companies and individual investors, the most notable long-term consequence was falling telecommunications costs, enabling the collaboration of individuals and small groups we see today.

ENABLER #3: WORK FLOW SOFTWARE.   What Friedman broadly calls **work flow software** is a variety of software applications that allow for software-to-software interaction. Whereas the Netscape browser enabled people to access the Internet, other standards allowed different companies all over the world to communicate seamlessly. For example, eXtensible Markup Language (XML; see Chapter 9—Building Organizational Partnerships Using Enterprise Information Systems) enabled computer programs to "talk" to other programs so that, for example, a computer in an automobile manufacturing plant could automatically order a new shipment of windshield wipers from a supplier once the inventory reached a certain level. This and a variety of other transactions could be handled without human intervention, thanks to standards allowing different computers from different computer manufacturers, running different operating systems, to communicate. Today, XML is even used for saving document formatting information in open-source applications such as the OpenOffice.org Productivity Suite (see Chapter 4).

In addition to XML, various other de facto standards emerged, easing the ability for individuals and companies from all over the world to communicate and engage in commerce. Worldwide use of productivity software such as Microsoft Word or Adobe Acrobat enabled information sharing, while standard online payment systems such as PayPal (see Figure 2.6) provided a common global currency to fuel commerce (see Chapter 5—Enabling Commerce Using the Internet). Providing individuals anywhere in the world with the ability to communicate, share documents, or transfer money, regardless of the

FIGURE 2.6

Enabler #3: The online payment system PayPal provides a common global currency to fuel commerce.

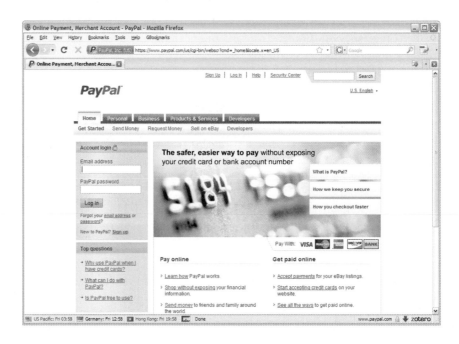

underlying computing platform or local currency, is fueling global collaboration of companies, small groups, and individuals.

ENABLER #4: UPLOADING.   The fourth enabler of Globalization 3.0 Friedman calls **uploading**, or the ability of individuals and companies to actively participate in content generation on the Web, enabling everyone to be a producer of information instead of merely a consumer. This enabler encompasses open-source software, wikis, and blogging/podcasting (see Chapter 6—Enhancing Collaboration Using Web 2.0 for a more detailed discussion of these Web 2.0 tools).

The ability to upload has been a catalyst for the growing popularity of open-source software products such as the Linux operating system, the Firefox Web browser, or the OpenOffice.org Productivity Suite. The open-source community has made different software, as well as the software's source code, freely available to everyone. With the power of uploading, software developers, geeks, and other techies all over the world use the communication and collaboration capabilities offered by the Internet to create and share new pieces of software. The software created in this way can be of very high quality, as people critique each other's work, improve the software, fix flaws, and so on. Despite the fact that open-source software development is often touted as a "hobbyist" movement, professional software developers are among the most active contributors to the creation and refinement of open-source software. In fact, more than one thousand developers working for more than one hundred different organizations participate in the development of the Linux operating system "kernel" (the core of the operating system that manages a computer's resources such as processor, memory, or input and output devices—see Chapter 4), and between 70 and 95 percent of these developers are being paid for their work. Whereas many companies use the Linux operating system but don't participate in further improvements, other companies, ranging from IBM to Intel, Google, Nokia, or Sony, actively participate in the development of future versions (http://www.linux-foundation.org/publications/linuxkerneldevelopment. php). The enormous success of open-source software, such as the Firefox Web browser or the Web server software Apache, has even forced established software companies to launch new and improved versions of their own proprietary software. The power of open-source software is further demonstrated by the fact that many established manufacturers (such as Dell, HP, Lenovo, or Asus) started offering laptop or desktop computers running different "flavors," or versions, of the open-source operating system Linux (see Chapter 4 and the Technology Briefing).

Another example of uploading is the successful online encyclopedia *Wikipedia* (see Figure 2.7), the content of which can be created and updated by anyone with an Internet

WIKIPEDIA

English
The Free Encyclopedia
2 683 000+ articles

日本語
フリー百科事典
550 000+ 記事

Deutsch
Die freie Enzyklopädie
847 000+ Artikel

Español
La enciclopedia libre
431 000+ artículos

Français
L'encyclopédie libre
746 000+ articles

Italiano
L'enciclopedia libera
527 000+ voci

Polski
Wolna encyklopedia
566 000+ hasel

Português
A enciclopédia livre
449 000+ artigos

Русский
Свободная энциклопедия
344 000+ статей

Nederlands
De vrije encyclopedie
508 000+ artikelen

FIGURE 2.7

Enabler #4: An example of uploading is Wikipedia, the content of which is created by its users.

connection. The term **wiki** refers to Web sites allowing users to add, remove, or edit content and is now often used synonymously with open-source dictionaries. Within a wiki community like Wikipedia, there is a huge number of people throughout the world reviewing all recent additions and edits; flaws in the content are usually quickly detected and fixed.

Finally, blogging allows individuals to upload content without editorial reviews, such that anyone can upload news or commentary comparable to an "open-source newsroom." Similarly, podcasting allows individuals to upload audio or video files that others can download and watch on their computers, MP3 players, or mobile devices. Uploading has made content, information, and software available to anyone with an Internet connection, enabling new and easier forms of collaboration for individuals, small groups, and organizations.

ENABLER #5: OUTSOURCING.   As defined in Chapter 1—Managing in the Digital World— outsourcing is the moving of business processes or tasks (such as accounting or security) to another company. The tremendous decrease in communication costs has added another dimension to outsourcing, as now companies can outsource business processes on a global scale (also referred to as **offshore outsourcing**). For example, companies commonly outsource customer service functions (such as call centers) or accounting to companies specializing in that service. Oftentimes companies located in countries such as India can provide these services much cheaper due to lower labor costs (see Figure 2.8).

FIGURE 2.8

Enabler #5: Many U.S.-based firms are outsourcing their call center operations to outsourcing providers such as Wipro.

TABLE 2.3 Outsourcing, Offshoring, and Offshore Outsourcing

Concept	Description	Example
Outsourcing	Business processes performed by another company	Payroll processing by a specialized provider, such as ADP
Offshoring	Business processes performed in-house, but in a different country	Boeing having aircraft design work performed at a Boeing design center in Moscow, Russia
Offshore outsourcing	Business processes performed by another company in a different country	A U.S. company having software developed by an Indian software firm, such as Wipro

ENABLER #6: OFFSHORING. As opposed to outsourcing, **offshoring** refers to having certain functions performed by the same company, but in a different country (see Table 2.3). For example, aircraft manufacturer Boeing offshored design work (such as computational fluid dynamics) for its new 787 Dreamliner aircraft to Russia, making use of the availability of highly skilled aeronautical engineers.

When China officially joined the World Trade Organization in 2001, it agreed to follow certain accepted standards of trade and fair business practices. Before, the slow opening of the Chinese market was seen as an opportunity to *sell products* to the huge Chinese market; afterward, companies saw the opportunity to *produce goods* in China (see Figure 2.9). Now, instead of just offshoring production to Mexico or Canada, companies set up entire factories in emerging countries, such as China, in order to mass-produce goods at a fraction of the price it would cost to produce these goods in the United States, Canada, or even in Mexico.

ENABLER #7: SUPPLY CHAINING. *Supply chaining* refers to the use of information systems to tightly integrate retailers, their suppliers, and their customers. One of the best-known examples is the supply chain of the giant retailer Wal-Mart (see Figure 2.10). Wal-Mart leverages the other enablers to create a seamless supply chain (see Chapter 9—Building

FIGURE 2.9

Enabler #6: Companies are offshoring production to overseas countries (such as China) to utilize talented workers or reduce costs.

FIGURE 2.10

Enabler #7: Wal-Mart is using supply chaining to tightly integrate the operations of its global suppliers and stores.

Organizational Partnerships Using Enterprise Information Systems) to get the goods from the manufacturers to the customers. Not only does Wal-Mart receive the information about their stores' sales, they also transmit this vital data to the manufacturers so that they can anticipate when the next shipment is needed, how their products sell, and what products may need improvement to increase sales. Wal-Mart has recently introduced *RFID (radio frequency identification)* tags into their supply chain, allowing them to track where the goods are in the supply chain as well as when their products are sold and to whom (see Chapter 9 for more on RFID).

ENABLER #8: IN-SOURCING.   The eighth major enabler is **in-sourcing**, which refers to the delegation of a company's logistics operations to a subcontractor that specializes in that operation. For example, United Parcel Service (UPS) is becoming a leading in-sourcing provider. In addition to providing their traditional service offering of delivering packages to worldwide destinations, UPS started offering complete supply chain solutions to companies (see Figure 2.11). Traditionally, online retailers, such as Nike.com, would handle all online customer orders themselves. However, through an in-sourcing arrangement, UPS manages Nike's warehouse and handles product packing and shipping as well as payment collection from customers so that Nike can concentrate on its core competencies, such as the design of new athletic shoes. Similarly, near their sort station in Lexington, Kentucky, UPS employees manage distribution facilities for a vast array of companies, even packaging bulk consumer electronics into retail packages or repairing Toshiba laptop computers. In some instances, it is not the manufacturer's repair team coming to a customer to perform on-site repair or maintenance but rather a team of certified UPS technicians. In these examples, UPS acts as a department within an organization. UPS employees come into an organization, analyze the organization's processes, and take over entire functions. Thus, such in-sourcing agreements require great amounts of trust, and for the outside observer, it is often hard to see that a different company (such as UPS) is performing the actual work. Given the scope of the in-sourcing arrangements and the nature of the tasks (i.e., complete logistics or supply chain solutions), such activities could usually not be performed from offshore locations.

ENABLER #9: IN-FORMING.   For the individual, **in-forming** allows individuals to utilize powerful search engines on the Internet, such as Google, Yahoo!, or MSN, to build their "own personal supply chain of information, knowledge, and entertainment" (Friedman,

Enabler #8: In-sourcing provider UPS manages entire warehouses for companies such as Nike.com.

2007, p. 178). With the Web and powerful search engines, such as Google, Yahoo!, or MSN, every person who has access to the Internet can now build his or her "own personal supply chain of information, knowledge, and entertainment" (Friedman, 2007, p. 178). Using the possibilities of the Internet, an incredible number of people all over the world now have access to all kinds of information; this access to information has enabled people to get a more complete picture of what's happening in the world, and people have to depend less on propaganda and censored media (see Figure 2.12). Now, people have an incredible amount of information at their fingertips, and in the near future, people will be able to access almost any book without even having to go to a physical library.

Enabler #9: Individuals can use powerful search engines such as Google for in-forming.

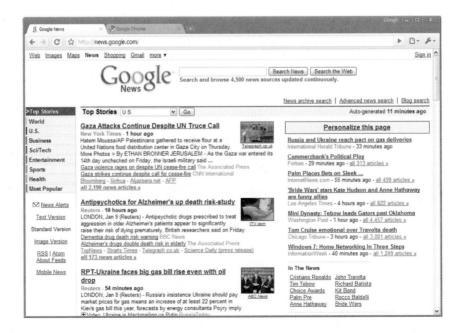

Net Stats

Online Searching

The Google search engine has become so popular with Internet users that the word "Google" is often used as a verb[1] (I "Googled" the restaurant to see its reviews.), but there are other well-known search engines, such as Yahoo! and Microsoft's MSN. Table 2.4 compares the percentage of Internet surfers that used each search engine (i.e., the search engines' market share) in 2008, as compared to 2006.

TABLE 2.4 **Top Three U.S. Search Engines by Market Share, October 2006 Compared with October 2008:**

Search Engine	October 2008 Market Share (%)	October 2006 Market Share (%)	Change (percentage points)
Google	71.9	60.9	11.0
Yahoo!	17.7	22.3	–4.6
MSN	4.2	10.7	–6.5

Based on: http://www.seoconsultants.com/search-engines

ENABLER #10: THE STEROIDS. The last group of enablers, which Friedman calls "the steroids," are technologies that make different forms of collaboration "digital, mobile, virtual, and personal" (p. 187). This group of technologies amplifies all the enablers discussed previously. By digitizing content—from books, to music, photographs, or virtually any business document—people can collaborate easier than ever before, benefiting from lightning-fast transmission of information. Similarly, the collaboration becomes virtual in that people using these technologies never have to think about the underlying standards or technologies enabling the collaboration; greater mobility enables collaboration from a wide variety of locations without being tied to one's office or desk (see Figure 2.13). Finally, certain enablers, such as in-forming, are available to everyone with an Internet connection, making the new forms of collaboration very personal.

What are some examples of these "steroids"? The tremendous increase in computing power and storage capacity is one of these steroids, enabling people to collaborate, manipulate pictures, or even record songs using their computers. Further, people can collaborate worldwide using technologies such as Skype, which allows free PC-to-PC video and voice calls to anywhere in the world. A final example is the growth in mobile infrastructures, to the point where people can access the vast resources enabled by the other nine enablers no matter where they are—be it on a train, in a coffee shop, or even aboard an aircraft.

Triple Convergence Although any one of these enablers may be powerful alone, it's their *convergence* that makes Globalization 3.0 possible; Friedman refers to this as a "triple convergence." First, between 2000 and 2003, the enablers started working together, making new forms of collaboration possible, such as the sharing of knowledge and work without regard to distance or geography, and soon even language. Second, this convergence enabled the move from vertical to horizontal collaboration, facilitating value creation and innovation. For example, employees of a global organization represent a vast global pool of specialists that can be assembled (and disassembled) as needed. Finally,

---

[1]Although "to google" is often used by people to refer to searching the Web, Google.com is becoming concerned that its use as a verb is a copyright infringement. See http://www.nzherald.co.nz/category/story.cfm?c_id=55&objectid=10396133.

FIGURE 2.13

Enabler #10: The "steroids" allow people to collaborate from almost anywhere.

people from countries such as China, India, or the former Soviet Union, could enter the playing field and connect and collaborate with others all over the world, enabling more people than ever to participate in new forms of collaboration. However, different countries and regions are at various stages of participation in the global village, so clearly we are only at the *beginning* of Globalization 3.0—the deep and pervasive impacts of this phase are in their infancy.

The Rise of Outsourcing

As discussed previously, one phenomenon that has seen a huge increase due to the decrease in telecommunication costs is *outsourcing,* both onshore (domestically) and offshore. Traditionally, organizations (domestically) outsourced business functions such as accounting to other companies. Early examples of offshore outsourcing included the manufacturing of goods in countries such as Mexico, based primarily on the cost of labor. For example, many U.S. companies produce their goods in so-called **maquiladoras**—assembly plants located on the Mexican side of the U.S.–Mexican border—to take advantage of lower wages and less stringent regulations. Then, in the years leading to Globalization 3.0, companies started to introduce offshore outsourcing of *services,* starting with the development of computer software and the staffing of customer support and telemarketing call centers. Today, a wide variety of services—ranging from telephone support to tax returns—are candidates for offshore outsourcing to different countries, be it Ireland, China, or India. Even highly specialized services, such as reading X-rays by skilled radiologists, are outsourced by U.S. hospitals to doctors around the globe, often while doctors in the United States are sleeping. However, companies operating in the digital world have to carefully choose offshore outsourcing locations, considering factors such as English proficiency, salaries, or geopolitical risk. While countries such as India remain popular for offshore outsourcing, other formerly popular countries (such as Singapore, Canada, or Ireland) are declining due to rising salaries. With these shifts, outsourcers are constantly looking at nascent and emerging countries such as Bulgaria, Egypt, Ghana, or Vietnam, each of which has some particular benefits to offer (see Table 2.5). Obviously, organizations have to weigh the potential benefits (e.g., cost savings) and drawbacks (e.g., higher geopolitical risk or less experience) of offshore outsourcing to a particular country.

In 2006, the global market for outsourcing was $930 billion. By the end of 2009, the global market is projected to be worth more than $1.43 trillion. The outsourcing market for IT services alone was $233 billion in 2006. Additionally, by 2006, nearly 90 percent of all

TABLE 2.5 Popular Offshore Outsourcing Destinations

Country	Ranking	English Proficiency	Yearly entry-level Programmer Salary (in US$1,000)	Relative Geopolitical Risk
Asia				
India	Leading	Very good	5–10	Moderate
China	Up and Coming	Poor	5–10	Moderate
Malaysia	Up and Coming	Fair	10–15	Moderate
Philippines	Up and Coming	Very good	5–10	High
Vietnam	Nascent	Fair	<5	Moderate
Thailand	Nascent	Poor	5–10	Moderate
Singapore	Declining	Fair	15–20	Low
Europe				
Czech Republic	Up and Coming	Good	10–15	Moderate
Poland	Up and Coming	Good	10–15	Moderate
Hungary	Up and Coming	Poor	10–15	Moderate
Russia	Up and Coming	Poor	10–15	Moderate
Romania	Emerging	Good	5–10	Moderate
Bulgaria	Emerging	Fair	5–10	Moderate
Ukraine	Emerging	Poor	5–10	Moderate
Ireland	Declining	Excellent	>20	Low
Middle East				
Egypt	Emerging	Very good	<5	High
Israel	Declining	Very good	15–20	Moderate
Africa				
South Africa	Challenging	Very good	10–15	Moderate
Ghana	Nascent	Very good	5–10	High
The Americas				
Mexico	Up and Coming	Poor	10–15	Moderate
Costa Rica	Emerging	Very good	10–15	Moderate
Brazil	Emerging	Poor	5–10	High
Argentina	Nascent	Fair	5–10	Moderate
Canada	Declining	Excellent	>20	Low

Based on: Overby, 2006.

large organizations used some type of offshore outsourcing of business functions. Companies are choosing to outsource business activities for a variety of reasons; the most important reasons include the following (King, 2003):

- To reduce or control costs
- To free up internal resources
- To gain access to world-class capabilities
- To increase revenue potential of the organization
- To reduce time to market
- To increase process efficiencies
- To be able to focus on core activities
- To compensate for a lack of specific capabilities or skills

Fueled by Globalization 2.0 and 3.0, outsourcing is now a fact of life, and no matter which industry you're in, you will likely feel the effects of (offshore) outsourcing (see Table 2.6). With Globalization 3.0, individuals will have to ask themselves how they can seize the global opportunities and how they will be able to compete with individuals from all over the world who might be able to do their job at the same quality but at a lower cost.

However, offshore outsourcing does not always prove to be the best approach for an organization. For example, only about a decade ago, German companies manufacturing highly specialized products such as large crankshafts, ship cranes, or road-paving equipment,

TABLE 2.6 Examples of Offshoring and Offshore Outsourcing

Industry	Examples	Offshoring/ Offshore Outsourcing
Airlines	British Airways moves customer relations and passenger revenue accounting to India.	Offshoring
	Delta outsources reservation functions to India.	Offshore outsourcing
Airplane design	Parts of Airbus and Boeing airplanes are designed and engineered in Moscow, Russia.	Offshoring
Consulting	McKinsey moves global research division to India.	Offshoring
	Ernst & Young moves part of its tax preparation to India.	Offshoring
Insurance	British firm Prudential PLC moves call center operations to India.	Offshoring
Investment banking	J.P. Morgan moves investment research to India.	Offshoring
Retail banking	Worldwide banking group HSBC moves back-office operations to India.	Offshoring
Credit card operations	American Express moves a variety of services to India.	Offshoring
Government	The Greater London Authority outsourced the development of a road toll system to India.	Offshore outsourcing
Telecommunications	T-mobile outsources part of its content development and portal configuration to India.	Offshore outsourcing

Based on: www.ebstrategy.com, 2006.

outsourced parts of their operations to Eastern European countries in order to cut costs. However, the cost savings have turned out to be negligible due to added overhead such as customs, shipping, or training, and quality problems ran rampant, leading to a reversal of this trend. Today, many companies are moving production back to Germany in order to better control production quality and costs. Similarly, *InformationWeek*, a leading publication targeting business IT users, found that 20 percent of the five hundred most innovative companies in terms of using IT took back previously offshored projects. Another recent trend is **nearshoring**—the use of locations closer to the home country in terms of geographical, political, linguistic, economic, or cultural distance. Nearshoring is thus the reversal of offshoring, such that, for example, U.S. companies move work from India to Mexico or British Columbia in order to address some of the challenges associated with overseas offshoring destinations.

The next sections will outline some opportunities made possible by increasing globalization.

Opportunities for Operating in the Digital World

Clearly, globalization has opened up many opportunities, brought about by falling transportation and telecommunication costs. Today, shipping a bottle of wine from Australia to Europe merely costs a few cents, and using the Internet, people can make PC-to-PC phone calls around the globe for free. To a large extent fueled by television and other forms of media, the increasing globalization has moved cultures closer together—to the point where people now talk about a "global village." Customers in all corners of the world can receive television programming from other countries or watch movies produced in Hollywood, Munich, or Mumbai (aka Bollywood), helping to create a shared understanding about

Brief Case ⊙

IT Globalization: Accenture in India

"**H**igh performers recognize shifts in the landscape before they happen." The Web site of the global management consulting and outsourcing company Accenture displays this axiom next to a photo of Tiger Woods in action. As one company competing with others in this unsettling age of globalization, Accenture has taken its own advice. The company that offers services in the general areas of consulting, technology, and outsourcing, has quickly risen to the top and become the benchmark for their competitors.

One reason for Accenture's success is that the company has always seen itself as a global organization. When most business consulting, technology, and outsourcing firms were just waking up to the fact that "globalization" was the key word, Accenture was already there. For example, 35,000 of the company's 160,000 employees are now located in India, where labor costs are less than half of those in the United States. Other companies in India saw Accenture as competition in the United States, but underestimated the company's ability to move quickly to other markets. "At one time I thought we'd be fortunate," says Pramod Bhasin, chief executive of Genpact, a top player among Indian companies handling business process outsourcing. "But [Accenture] really embraced [globalization]."

Accenture is quickly increasing its lead: in March 2008, the company announced plans to double its thirteen thousand business consultants over the next three years; one example of its hard-to-match services is the Life Sciences Center of Excellence in Bangalore, India. At the Center, dozens of physicians, pharmacists, mathematicians, statisticians, biologists, and PhDs work together to prepare clinical trial reports for the world's top drug companies. Robert Ruffalo, Jr., president of research and development at Wyeth Pharmaceuticals, Inc., an Accenture client, has said of the company: "We are launching drugs that otherwise would have been held up by our inability to handle the work . . . [Accenture] knew us and understood us. We don't have to educate them again and again."

Questions

1. What can you do to prepare yourself to work for an organization like Accenture?
2. Why do you think Accenture has been successful in the flat world?

Based on:

Anonymous (n.d.). Client successes. Retrieved May 24, 2008, from http://www.accenture.com/Global/Services/Client_Successes.

Hamm, E. (2007, April 23). How Accenture one-upped Bangalore. *Business Week*. Retrieved May 24, 2008, from http://www.businessweek.com/pdf/270499bwEprint.pdf.

---

forms of behavior or interaction, desirable goods or services, or even forms of government. Over the past decades, the world has seen a democratization of many nations, enabling millions of people to enjoy freedoms they had never experienced before. All of this makes operating in the digital world much easier than ever before.

Opportunities for Reaching New Markets

After the fall of communism, new markets opened up for countless companies. The fall of the Berlin Wall and the following reunification of Germany, for example, increased the size of the German market from sixty-four million to eighty million people. Similarly, the fall of communism in other Eastern Bloc countries, such as Poland, Romania, and the former Soviet Union, enabled the sales of products to literally millions of new customers (see Figure 2.14).

Opportunities of a Global Workforce

With the decrease in communication costs, companies can now draw on a large pool of skilled professionals from all over the globe. Some companies outsource to different regions because the availability of skilled labor is high. Many countries, such as Russia, China, and India, offer high-quality education, leading to an ample supply of well-trained people at low cost. While enrollment in the sciences or engineering is dropping in the United States, other countries are producing engineering graduates at an unprecedented pace (Mallaby, 2006). In 2005, for example, 200,000 young engineers graduated from

FIGURE 2.14

Former Eastern Bloc countries.

Indian universities, while the United States produced only about a third as many; like-wise, Europe produced only about half the number of India (see Figure 2.15). While the number of engineering students in the West is plummeting, enrollments in Asia and India in particular are rapidly expanding (e.g., India reported having over 450,000 students enrolled in engineering programs in 2005). Some countries are actively building entire industries around certain competencies, such as software development or tax preparation in India and call centers in Ireland. For companies operating in the digital world, this can be a huge opportunity, as they can "shop" for qualified, low-cost labor all over the world. On the other hand, the consulting company McKinsey believes that out of the 2.5 million Indian university graduates, only 10 to 25 percent (depending on the field of study) are considered employable by multinational companies, mainly because of differences in the quality of the education and the differences in language skills (Farrell, Kaka, and Stürze, 2005).

The factors discussed in this section translate into a number of direct opportunities for companies, including greater and larger markets to sell products and larger pools of quali-fied labor. Nevertheless, while globalization has brought tremendous opportunities to com-panies, they also face a number of daunting challenges when operating in the global mar-ketplace. Next, we highlight some of these challenges.

FIGURE 2.15

Engineering graduates in the United States, Europe, and India.

Based on: Mallaby, 2006

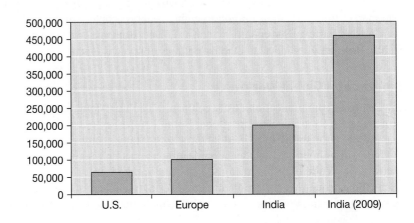

Challenges of Operating in the Digital World

Traditionally, companies acquired resources and produced and sold goods or services all within the same country. Such domestic businesses did not have to deal with any challenges posed by globalization but also could not leverage the host of opportunities. The challenges faced can be broadly classified into governmental, geoeconomic, and cultural challenges. See Table 2.7 for a summary of the challenges of operating in the digital world.

Governmental Challenges

Many challenges faced by companies operating in the digital world are of a governmental nature. These challenges are associated with factors such as the overall political system, regulations (including data sharing), or even Internet access. In the following sections, we will highlight some of these challenges.

Political System Challenges First and foremost, companies operating in the digital world have to consider the overall political climate of their host country. One factor to consider here is whether the host country is a market economy or whether it is a planned economy. When operating in a country that is less free than the home country, a company might face tight restrictions regarding what can be produced or sold, how much can be produced or sold, or to whom the products can be sold.

Further, although companies now have access to more countries than ever before, political stability is one issue to consider when operating outside one's home country. In many countries, the political systems are less stable than in the United States or in Western

TABLE 2.7 Challenges of Operating in the Digital World

Broad Challenges	Specific Challenges	Examples
Governmental	Political system	Market versus planned economy; political instability
	Regulatory	Taxes and tariffs; import and export regulations
	Data sharing	EU Data Protection Directive
	Internet access and individual freedom	Internet censorship in various countries
Geoeconomic	Time zone differences	Videoconferences across different time zones
	Infrastructure-related reliability	Differences in network infrastructures throughout the world
	Differences in welfare	Migration and political instability caused by welfare differences between rich and poor countries
	Demographic	Aging population in the United States and Western Europe; younger workforce in other countries
	Expertise	Availability of labor force and salary differences
Cultural	Working with different cultures	Differences in power distance, uncertainty avoidance, individualism/collectivism, masculinity/femininity, concept of time, and life focus
	Challenges of offering products or services in different cultures	Naming and advertising for products; intellectual property

Europe, and companies have to consider whether to invest huge sums into specific countries, as foreign companies operating in politically unstable countries risk losing their assets due to confiscation, military coups, upheavals, or civil wars.

Regulatory Challenges As most countries have their own sovereign governments, taxes, laws, and regulations differ from country to country, and companies have to follow the rules of their host countries. For example, many countries impose a variety of different taxes and **tariffs** in order to regulate the flow of goods and services into and out of the country. Such taxes and tariffs exist for almost all categories of products, from bananas to computer hardware, and differ widely depending on the product category. The nature and amount of such taxes and tariffs have to be considered when deciding whether to import or export goods and services, manufacture in a foreign country, and so on.

Other regulations concerning the flow of goods and services are embargoes and export regulations. **Embargoes** are typically limiting (or prohibiting) trade with one particular country. For example, the U.S. embargo of Cuba is intended to isolate the Cuban government economically; thus, it prohibits the export of goods into Cuba, the import of Cuban goods (such as rum or cigars) into the United States, and most forms of travel to Cuba. Other embargoes are targeted at countries accused of sponsoring terrorist activities; these countries include Syria, Iran, and North Korea, among others. Thus, embargoes limit many forms of trade with a specific country.

In contrast, **export regulations** are directed at limiting the export of certain goods to other countries. While the export of goods such as missile technology from the United States to almost any country is severely restricted, other products may be exported to some, but not other countries. The U.S. Department of Commerce maintains lists to cross-check which types of products cannot be exported to which countries. For some products, such regulations can be quite complicated. For example, while the desktop version of the computer program PGP (Pretty Good Privacy, a data encryption technology; see Chapter 7—Securing Information Systems) can be exported to almost any country (with the exception of embargoed countries), more sophisticated versions of the software can be freely sold to any user in European Union (EU) member countries and close trading partners, but only to nongovernmental users in other countries, and it cannot be sold at all to users in embargoed countries. As you can see, companies dealing with certain product categories have to be well aware of the laws and regulations governing the sale of their products.

Often companies have to produce in certain countries in order to win sales contracts. For example, Boeing produces some airplane parts in China for two important reasons. First, there are significant cost savings associated with manufacturing in China. Second and more important, the Chinese government requires the manufacturing of at least some aircraft components in China in exchange for large aircraft orders (Holmes, 2006). Similarly, the United States has various **quotas** permitting foreign businesses to bring only a certain number of products into the country; therefore, to overcome such quotas, many foreign car manufacturers (such as BMW, Toyota, or Mercedes-Benz) started producing automobiles in the United States.

Data-Sharing Challenges One area that has recently come to concern is the regulation of **transborder data flows**. Spurred by the decrease in telecommunications costs, companies started to use offshore outsourcing for many business functions; for example, companies today outsource integral functions such as accounting or human resources to India, where the same quality of service can be provided at a fraction of the cost of performing the same functions in the United States or the EU. However, to outsource such functions, much (sometimes sensitive) data has to be transferred to different countries, which is where the problems start. Recently, the EU passed a directive facilitating the transfer of data between member countries, while prohibiting the transfer of data to countries with less stringent data protection laws. Thus, while it is now easier to transfer data between countries within the EU, it is much harder to transfer data from an EU member country to a nonmember country. This poses not only challenges to companies from EU member countries (e.g., a German insurance company outsourcing its call center to India), but also introduces difficulties for international companies operating in the EU; for example, can a U.S.-based company transfer certain data from a European subsidiary back to the home office? In most cases no. As such, these limitations significantly restrict a company's ability to utilize common business processes (e.g., in the financial or health care sector), making it much more difficult and expensive to operate globally. However, currently, only a few countries have data protection laws as stringent as those of the EU, and a U.S. company outsourcing certain services to India, for example, does not face such challenges.

Standards Despite efforts to create globally accepted standards, there are many national or regional standards that differ across the world. Organizations operating on a global scale have to be aware of those issues and have to make sure to consciously think about those differences. For example, U.S. companies typically use the twelve-digit UPC (Universal Product Code) barcode to label their products, enabling the use of barcode scanners. However, when going global, companies may have to consider switching to EAN-13 (European Article Number), a standard that is widely used in Europe and Japan to mark goods (see Figure 2.16).

Other differences include the uses of measurement units. Whereas in the United States (and only two other countries, namely Liberia and Myanmar) distances are expressed in inches, feet, and miles, and weights are expressed in ounces and pounds, all other countries use the International System of Units (i.e., the metric system), using centimeters, meters, and kilometers for distances, and grams, kilograms, and tons for weights. This can create difficulties for companies operating internationally. For example, companies such as U.S. automaker Ford have to think about how to engineer their products. While U.S. auto repair garages typically have both metric and "standard" tools, garages (and mechanics) in Europe or Asia only have metric tools and will not be able to work on cars having "standard" fasteners. In addition to those differences, many other de facto standards emerged around the world. For example, Wal-Mart did not consider that the standard sizes of pillowcases differed between the United States and Germany, and as a result, Wal-Mart's German stores ended up sitting on huge piles of U.S.-sized pillowcases. These and other problems eventually caused the retail giant to withdraw from the highly competitive German retail market.

When operating international e-commerce sites, companies have to consider a variety of other standards across the world. For example, different countries have different formats for postal (ZIP) codes, with some consisting of letters and numbers (such as Canada), and other countries have no postal codes at all (e.g., Hong Kong). Similarly, phone numbers

FIGURE 2.16

Bar code standards differ throughout the world.

and addresses are standardized differently across countries. This has to be considered when designing data entry forms for international users.

Internet Access and Individual Freedom When operating in a global digital world, companies will also have to consider Internet access issues. People in many countries have access to almost all places on the Internet, but people in other places face many limitations in terms of the content they will be able to see or the applications they will be able to use. For example, in Germany and France, sites displaying fascist symbols and racist propaganda are banned by law; however, their citizens still have the possibility to visit prohibited content on sites hosted outside those countries. In other countries, certain content is completely blocked, and people have no way to access banned content. Likewise, China restricts the use of Voice over Internet Protocol (VoIP) technology (a technology enabling phone calls over the Internet; see Chapter 4) in order to be able to monitor phone conversations. Thus, Chinese Internet users typically are not able to use such technologies.

The French organization "Reporters without Borders" (www.rsf.fr) maintains a list of countries listed as "enemies of the Internet." Countries ranging from Belarus to Vietnam block all types of content that the governments deem inappropriate, with topics including primarily politics, religion, and sex. Whereas many countries regulate the Internet by maintaining blacklists of sites and providing Internet access only through state-owned Internet service providers, some countries (such as Cuba or North Korea) block Internet access altogether, allowing only a handful of people with special permission to access the Internet. Operating in such countries brings about all sorts of issues regarding mainly how to comply with such regulations and whether a company should comply with such rules on ethical grounds. For example, U.S. Internet search portals MSN and Yahoo! recently faced an ethical dilemma when they were requested to reveal the identity of Chinese citizens posting dissident messages on Web logs (i.e., blogs, see Chapter 6) hosted on those sites. Clearly, the Internet poses great challenges not only for companies operating globally but also for countries that are imposing control or limiting the freedom of their citizens.

Geoeconomic Challenges

These are just a few factors companies have to consider when operating in the digital world. Other factors to consider are of a **geoeconomic** nature, that is, the combination of economic and political factors that influence a region. Especially in the times before Globalization 3.0, the necessity to travel in order to conduct business in a foreign country was a big factor, considering the time needed to reach overseas destinations, the lost productivity due to time differences, and so on. For highly paid executives, a two-day trip to London can cost large sums of money, for airplane tickets, overnight stays, travel days, and lost productivity due to jet lag and other factors. The Internet in general and Globalization 3.0 in particular have reduced much of the need for business travel by enabling low-cost and high-quality videoconferencing. One such example is the partnership between computer company Hewlett-Packard and Dreamworks SKG (the makers of animated movies such as *Shrek* and *Kung Fu Panda*), which built a collaboration studio intended to simulate face-to-face meetings across the globe. Although only one such room costs about $400,000 and the monthly service fees can be as high as $18,000, the reduced need for business travel can still easily translate into significant savings in costs and time for companies conducting business globally.

Time Zone Challenges One factor that videoconferencing cannot resolve is the time difference between different countries. On the one hand, companies can use the time difference for their advantage; on the other hand, the time difference may actually hinder collaboration. For example, Symantec, a maker of antivirus software, has set up laboratories around the globe such that different teams can work on fighting viruses around the clock. When a team in California quits for the night, a team in Tokyo (where it's morning) can take over; when the team in Tokyo has finished their day's work, they hand off the project to a team in Europe, which then hands it back to the team in the United States (an approach called "following the sun"). However, the time differences can also

Ethical Dilemma

Underground Gaming Economy

In the United States in 2008, the real estate market was in dire straits, forcing many home owners (and speculators) into bankruptcy; gasoline prices rose to a phenomenal $4.00 per gallon and up; and health care costs again spiraled out of sight. It's the real world, and those of us who live and work in it develop skills to cope.

Things in Project Entropia, a virtual world with a real cash economy, aren't much better. Colonists on Calypso must still fight off dangerous enemies, the Ped is still worth only 10 cents against the U.S. dollar, and the price of ore-rich property is rising.

Project Entropia is one of many massively multiplayer online role-playing games (MMORPGs). Other online role-playing games include but are not limited to Sony's Everquest, George Lucas's Star Wars Galaxies, Second Life, and Ultima Online. Players pay monthly subscription fees and assume virtual identities called avatars. Estimates are that more than 100 million people play worldwide, and the gaming companies report that subscriptions total over $3.6 billion a year.

In most MMORPGs, gamers slay enemies, build houses and businesses, choose professions, pick up mystical attributes, and fill their virtual bank accounts with gold and cash. Each player's avatar "lives" in the game's virtual community. A recent trend, however, is for serious players to play to collect virtual tools, gold, or cash and then sell the booty for real cash. The dollar amounts involved are usually relatively small, say, $70 for 10 million gold sets in Ultima Online, but there have been notable exceptions. In November 2005, for example, Jon Jacobs, a film producer from Miami, Florida, paid $100,000 for a virtual resort in Project Entropia. "I have invested in a business that offers numerous opportunities for generating revenue," Jacobs said. He pointed out that the digital resort includes 1,000 hotel rooms that could be sold for $100 each, a stadium for hosting hunting or combat competitions, and a nightclub.

The practice of buying and selling assets from MMORPGs has become so prevalent that the virtual moguls have a name: "farmers." The popular auction site eBay.com daily lists thousands of items taken from MMORPGs under its Internet Games category. Items for sale range from characters that have advanced to higher levels of a game to weapons, gold, and other items captured in a game.

Farming has become especially popular in China, where companies employ rows of gamers who play for up to twelve hours at a time, collecting virtual assets and ascending to the highest levels of a game—all of which the companies will sell.

Critics of this new virtual economy say that it penalizes gamers who play strictly for fun but allows those with cash to spend to advance through levels of a game they have not mastered. Others say there is nothing wrong with players buying advantages that let them play at higher levels without putting in large amounts of time.

Some game companies have banned farmers from the playing field. For example, Blizzard Entertainment, the makers of World of Warcraft, a game that boasts more than six million subscribers, has permanently banned over five thousand users following its investigation into cheaters and farmers. By 2008, another 10,700 accounts were suspended for violations of the game's Terms of Use. Similarly, *PC Gamer,* America's largest gaming magazine, stopped taking advertisements from companies that trade in virtual goods and characters from MMORPGs, and in early 2007, eBay banned the sale of virtual goods such as currency or avatars.

The companies cite ethical reasons for penalizing farmers, but they also realize that farmers can eventually impact revenues, as gamers who don't buy and sell attributes refuse to play with those who do.

Based on:

Anonymous (n.d.). About Entropia universe. Retrieved May 24, 2008, from http://www.entropiauniverse.com/en/rich/5035.html.

Millard, E. (2006, January 4). Inside the underground economy of computer gaming. *Newsfactor.* Retrieved May 24, 2008, from http://www.newsfactor.com/story.xhtml?story_id=40592.

Spohn, D. (2006, April 12). Thousands banned from World of Warcraft. Retrieved May 24, 2008, from http://internetgames.about.com/b/2006/04/12/thousands-banned-from-world-of-warcraft.htm.

Wrolstad, J. (2005, November 11). Virtual resort sells for $100,000. *Newsfactor.* Retrieved May 24, 2008, from http://www.newsfactor.com/story.xhtml?story_id=39369.

cause friction, especially if real-time meetings (such as videoconferences) are needed. A good example is that of a U.S. telecommunications giant with subsidiaries in different European countries. Traditionally, the company's employees in Los Angeles prefer to hold weekly business meetings on a particular day of the week right after lunch. For employees of the European subsidiaries who have to "join" the conferences (via either phone or

FIGURE 2.17

International time zones.

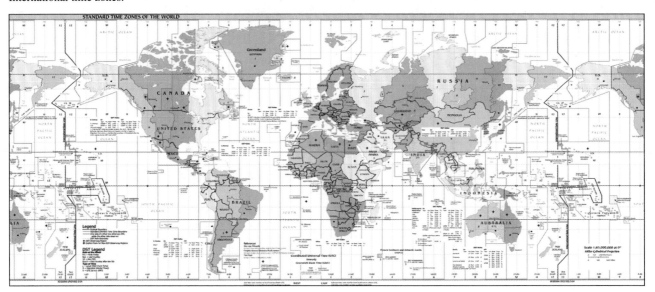

videoconferencing), this means coming in to work late in the evening once a week, as 1:00 P.M. in Los Angeles is 10:00 P.M. in Frankfurt (see Figure 2.17). Companies outsourcing call center operations to India face similar problems. To serve customers during North American daytime hours, call center workers in India have to work night shifts, leading to low worker morale, high attrition rates, and a general decline in customer service, which can be devastating for a company's reputation.

Infrastructure-Related Challenges Another challenge facing companies operating in the digital world is differences in infrastructure, both in terms of the classic infrastructure (such as roads, electricity, and sewage systems) and in terms of connectivity. While in most Western countries the telecommunications infrastructures are fast and reliable, in many other countries connectivity is not always a given. A network outage somewhere in Africa can effectively bring the communications infrastructure of an entire country to a screeching halt. Similarly, periodically, the undersea network cables linking different regions of the world are being accidentally cut, leading to massive problems in network access. Having backup plans for such incidents is imperative when operating in different regions that offer less reliable services. We will discuss infrastructure-related issues in more detail in Chapter 4.

Challenges Related to Economic Welfare Although the fall of communism and the other factors enabling Globalization 3.0 have helped to open up new markets and globalization has contributed to unprecedented growth in global per-capita gross domestic product (GDP), this growth has not been evenly distributed throughout the world. According to the International Monetary Fund, the gap between rich and poor countries has widened, as the per-capita GDP has increased sixfold in the richest 25 percent of all nations, whereas it only has increased threefold in the poorest 25 percent. For many companies, the poorest countries thus do not constitute viable markets, and attempting to expand their customer base by operating in such markets will not be worthwhile. Further, this inequality can have other (and potentially more serious) consequences, such as political instability or increased migration toward the richer countries.

For many established companies, there is also new competition coming from poorer countries. For example, companies like the Brazilian aircraft manufacturer Embraer, the Chinese appliances manufacturer Haier, or the Indian tractor and auto manufacturer Mahindra have gained extensive experience in operating in markets characterized by tough competition and low profit margins. Now these emerging giants have started entering the European and American markets, and established companies do not only face their competition in emerging markets but also in their traditional home markets, as the emerging giants can offer products at prices much below those established companies can offer (Engardio, Arndt, and Smith, 2006).

Demographic Challenges

Companies operating in the digital world will also have to consider different demographic trends occurring worldwide. Specifically, the populations of the United States, many European countries, and Japan are increasingly getting older. At the same time, the population of other countries is getting younger and younger. While this may be an opportunity for companies to try to replace their aging workforce with new talent, it can also pose a challenge, as much of this younger workforce is lacking the necessary work experience.

Many low-wage countries have an abundance of people; in addition, the populations of such countries are growing at much higher rates than those of most Western nations (see Figure 2.18). As these countries are very poor, however, it is unlikely that the population growth will directly translate into a larger qualified labor pool or a larger market for products and services.

Expertise-Related Challenges Relatedly, the nature of the workforce can also pose significant challenges for companies operating in the digital world. Different countries have different concentrations of skilled workers and differing costs for those workers (see Table 2.8). For example, most industrial nations have made significant investments in building a large base of skilled information systems personnel. However, these workers will typically also be much more costly to employ than those from less developed countries. The types of skills prevalent in different countries may also vary. Depending on the region, the lack of skilled labor can be a real problem for companies, as they might not always be able to hire people with the right set of skills. Further, cost advantages of offshore outsourcing can shrink as skill levels and wages are rising. As a case in point, the cost advantage of India has halved to about 1:3 (forbes.com), and attrition of qualified workers is a huge problem. The rising Indian rupee will soon further erode India's cost advantage, to a point that some have already forecast the coming death of offshore outsourcing to India. For these very reasons, Africa is seen as the next outsourcing destination, with low wages, cultural and language ties to many European countries, and closeness in terms of time zones (the same as Europe and closer than India for U.S. companies).

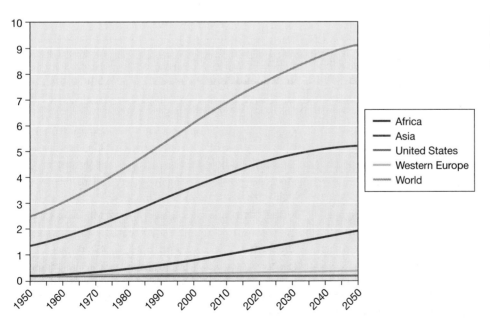

FIGURE 2.18

World population, 1950–2050 (in billions).

TABLE 2.8 Salary Differences Have Helped to Make Global Outsourcing Popular

2006 Average Salary for Experienced IT Managers in Various Countries		
Rank	Country	Pay (US$)
1	Switzerland	161,900
2	Germany	126,700
3	Denmark	116,000
4	Japan	112,300
5	Belgium	109,600
6	Ireland	108,800
7	United Kingdom	105,700
8	Hong Kong	97,600
9	Italy	93,900
10	Spain	93,200
14	**United States**	**89,100**
34	India	26,500

Based on: www.finfacts.com.

Cultural Challenges

The third broad class of challenges can be classified as cultural challenges. Although people speak of the emerging "global village," its existence is often very superficial, and companies operating in the digital world still have to consider a variety of cultural differences, some of which can pose quite complex challenges.

How National Cultures Differ Hofstede (2001) defines **culture** as the "collective programming of the mind that distinguishes the members of one group or category of people from another" (p. 9). Culture is manifested in how individuals view a variety of cultural dimensions, such as power distance, uncertainty avoidance, individualism/collectivism, masculinity/femininity, concept of time, and life focus (see Table 2.9). In essence, each nation has its own culture, which can often have important implications for companies operating in the digital world. One area where such challenges often surface is the interaction between a company's headquarters and a subsidiary in a different culture.

TABLE 2.9 Critical Cultural Dimensions for Various Countries

Critical Cultural Dimensions	Countries				
	Group 1: United States, Canada, Australia	Group 2: Germany, Austria, Switzerland	Group 3: Mexico, Venezuela, Peru	Group 4: Japan	Group 5: India, Hong Kong, Singapore
Power distance	Moderately low	Moderately low	Moderately high	Moderately high	High
Individualism/ collectivism	Highly individualistic	Moderately individualistic	Moderately to highly collectivistic	Moderately collectivistic	Moderately to highly collectivistic
Masculinity/ femininity	Moderately masculine	Moderately masculine	Moderately to highly masculine	Highly masculine	Masculine
Uncertainty avoidance	Moderately weak	Moderately strong	Moderately weak	Strong	Moderately weak
Concept of time	Long term	Long term	Short term	Long term	Short term
Life focus	Quantity	Quantity	Quality	More quality than quantity	Changing from quality to quantity

Based on: Verma (1997).

POWER DISTANCE.   **Power distance** refers to how different societies handle the issue of human inequality and sheds light on the inherent power structure within organizations and teams. Some cultures are higher in power distance, preferring strong authority or autocracy, while other cultures are lower in power distance, fostering more collaborative teamwork and less hierarchical structures. Consequently, differences in power distance can pose serious challenges.

UNCERTAINTY AVOIDANCE.   The degree of **uncertainty avoidance** helps in understanding the risk-taking nature of a culture. From an outsourcing perspective, this might result in workers from some cultures being more cautious; this can be particularly troublesome when some workers, because of high levels of uncertainty avoidance, are not eager to adopt new technologies or techniques.

INDIVIDUALISM/COLLECTIVISM.   A related dimension, **individualism/collectivism**, reflects the extent to which a society values the position of an individual versus the position of a group. In societies that are collectivist, peer pressure often plays an important role in shaping group interaction and decision making. Mixing both individually and collectively oriented individuals in an outsourcing project can often cause excessive conflict if not carefully managed.

MASCULINITY/FEMININITY.   Additionally, **masculinity/femininity** refers to the degree to which a society is characterized by masculine qualities, such as assertiveness, or by feminine characteristics, such as nurturance, which can have important implications in terms of user preferences for technology, how user requirements are collected, or how teams assign roles and collaborate.

CONCEPT OF TIME.   The **concept of time** can also differ across cultures, with some cultures having a relatively longer-term orientation, reflecting an appreciation for future rewards, perseverance, and long-term planning. On the other hand, cultures with shorter-term orientation focus on the past and the current situation.

LIFE FOCUS.   A last cultural dimension, **life focus**, contrasts the extent to which a culture focuses on the *quantity* versus the *quality* of life. A quantity-of-life orientation reflects a more competitive culture that values achievements and the acquisition of material goods. A quality-of-life orientation values relationships, interdependence, and concern for others. Life focus differences can influence group development, task and role assignments, and they can cause difficulties in the interaction between a company's headquarters and a subsidiary in a different culture.

Other Cultural Barriers In addition to the cultural barriers mentioned by Hofstede, there are many other barriers that can pose a challenge to companies operating in the digital world, including the following:

- *Language.* Communication language and norms
- *Work Culture.* Work skills, habits, and attitudes toward work
- *Aesthetics.* Art, music, and culture
- *Education.* Attitudes toward education and literacy
- *Religion, Beliefs, and Attitudes.* Spiritual institutions and values
- *Social Organizations.* Family and social cohesiveness

Each of these cultural elements can greatly influence interaction between employees in different countries, as outlined in Table 2.10. For example, the lack of a common language can often lead to disastrous results when communicating technical information, such as user requirements or design specifications. Likewise, differences in work culture can influence the employee's interaction. For instance, Europeans typically approach a project by focusing on its beginning and incrementally moving forward until the project is concluded. Americans, on the other hand, typically look at the end first and work backward to the start (Heichler, 2000). In sum, differences in language, work culture, and other cultural elements can have serious implications for managing in the digital world.

TABLE 2.10 How Various Cultural Elements Can Affect Communication, Interaction, and Performance

Cultural Element	How It Can Impact Globalization Success
Language	Communication problems can influence efficiency, understanding, and performance.
Work culture	Different skills, work habits, and attitudes can influence performance and manpower constraints.
Aesthetics	Art, music, and dance reflect nonwork interests that can be used to enrich team communication and cohesiveness.
Education	Lack of adequate education limits skill levels, technological sophistication, and infrastructure.
Religion, beliefs, and attitudes	Basic values and beliefs can influence attitudes toward work, promptness, punctuality, mutual trust, respect, and cooperation.
Social organization	Social norms of a society can influence formal and informal communication, including negotiations and job assignments.
Political life	Differing political systems can influence the delivery of supplies and equipment, human rights, legal system, and overall stability.

Based on: Verma (1997).

Environmental Challenges The manufacturing of goods in other countries can be a good way to reduce costs for a company. However, increasingly, organizations have to consider, defend, and try to minimize the environmental impact of their business practices. For example, companies producing goods in China or India cannot ignore issues such as energy consumption, air and water pollution, and workers' health, as, in addition to being unscrupulous, companies also risk damaging their reputation. Whereas just a few years

Coming Attractions

Learning Languages in Context

Have you struggled through years of classes in languages such as Spanish, French, or German (or English if it is not your first language), only to find that you cannot carry on a conversation in that language? As you might expect, the Internet can help.

For example, a start-up called Livemocha, based in Bellevue, Washington, uses social networking to motivate language students and help them learn. The site goes beyond the typical CD-ROM-based method of learning languages. Visitors can find structured lessons, help with grammar, and canned pronunciation guides, but one of the most valuable aspects of the site is the ability to practice conversing in a language with those who speak the native tongue. Presently, language learners can find instruction in English, Hindi, Mandarin Chinese, Spanish, French, and German, but CEO Shirish Nadkarni says plans for 2009 and beyond include adding instruction in twenty-five additional languages. Nadkarni hopes the online community will become involved: "We expect the community to come in

and use their native-language proficiencies to provide more explanation—grammar tips, alternate phrases, or colloquialisms—allowing people to build a much better understanding of the language and how it might be spoken in different parts of the world," Nadkarni says. "This is a lot more instructive and more dynamic than a static CD-ROM."

Gail Keech, who tested Livemocha early on, wanted to use the site to learn German, but when a flood of Chinese-speaking users asked her to help them with English, she saw the perfect opportunity to learn Chinese. Not only can site visitors learn new languages, they can hear firsthand opinions on everything from world affairs to the proper term for "ice cream" in German.

Based on:

Anonymous (n.d.). Learn languages and practice with native speakers. Retrieved May 24, 2008, from http://www.livemocha.com.

Naone, E. (2007, October 5). Learning languages in context. *Technology Review*. Retrieved May 24, 2008, from http://www.technologyreview.com/Biztech/19484/?a=f.

FIGURE 2.19

Electronic waste in China.

ago, companies moved their facilities offshore to avoid having to comply with stringent U.S. Environmental Protection Agency (EPA) regulations (which some companies still do), the enablers of Globalization 3.0 also help to uncover such unethical practices much more easily. In addition to the environmental impact of producing and disposing of goods (see Figure 2.19), a growing concern is the shipment of these goods to the final consumer, as the worldwide shipping traffic is a major player in terms of environmental impact, contributing between 5 and 6 percent to the world's emission of greenhouse gases (in addition to the emissions from airfreight and truck shipments). Clearly, organizations and society will have to consider these negative impacts of global trade.

Other Challenges of Offering Products or Services in Different Cultures
Companies selling their products in foreign markets also have to consider different local cultures when deciding what to sell and how to market their products. For example, different countries have different standards concerning what type of advertising is socially acceptable. Also, different cultures have different standards of dealing with intellectual property, such as computer software, digital music, or movies. In most Western nations intellectual property is considered very important and is even protected by law, but in other nations copying someone else's work is not seen as problematic. In fact, some cultures even regard it as flattery to copy the work of others. Thus, intellectual property infringements are common in many countries, reaching from counterfeiting Nivea Creme to mass-producing illegal copies of DVDs or computer software (see Figure 2.20). Finally, different norms and standards can cause problems for companies.

Network Readiness With the increased reliance on information and communication technologies, the development of economies and societies is heavily depending on access to the global networked economy (WEF, 2008). Enabling creative thinking and collaborative problem solving, the enablers of Globalization 3.0 provide vast opportunities for countries all over the globe. To assess how prepared the world's nations are for benefiting from these opportunities, the World Economic Forum and the French business school INSEAD annually collect data to calculate the countries' *Network Readiness Index*. This index assesses factors such as market conditions, political and regulatory environment, quality of education, government prioritization, and individual, business, or government usage of information and communication technologies. Not surprisingly, the top ten countries on the list comprise

e-Waste

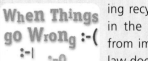

Americans bought an estimated $173 billion worth of consumer electronics in 2008—computers, monitors, cell phones, PDAs, DVD players, microwave ovens, and so on—and that number was projected to increase to $183 billion for 2009. When consumers replace old electronic products with newer versions, many of the discarded products could end up in landfills. This is an environmental concern because electronic products contain a mix of toxic components, such as lead, mercury, cadmium, or PVCs, which are released into the environment when incinerated or buried in a landfill. A conventional computer monitor alone, for example, contains four to eight pounds of lead, and newer LCD screens contain mercury.

So what happens to electronic gadgets when consumers no longer need or want them? Some owners hand them down to someone else or pack them away in the back of a closet or garage. Others donate the items—whether they still function or not—to a charitable organization, but when the products are hopelessly outdated, the donations probably aren't so welcome. Unfortunately, since local landfills generally won't take hazardous waste, some consumers bury discarded electronic products in ordinary household garbage, where they end up in landfills or incinerators despite the ban. In fact, an estimated 70 percent of discarded computers and monitors and over 80 percent of old TVs end up in landfills.

Currently, only 20 percent of e-waste is channeled through municipal drop-off sites or companies that offer disposal service, and even if such services are used, there's no guarantee that the waste will be disposed of properly.

In 2004 alone, Goodwill Industries International, Inc., was flooded with more than twenty-three million pounds of electronic goods, most of which were unusable. Since recycling electronics costs money, Goodwill spokesperson Christine Nyirjesy Bragale told a reporter in January 2006, "Electronic waste is becoming a costly problem for us."

Three U.S. states—California, Maine, and Maryland—have followed examples from Europe and Japan in handling electronic waste disposal in that they impose a mandatory recycling fee either on consumers or manufacturers, they require manufacturers to take back the equipment for recycling, or they place responsibility on local governments for providing recycling centers. Although federal law in the United States prevents businesses from improperly disposing of e-waste, this law does not extend to households.

Unfortunately, although the export of hazardous waste to developing countries was banned in 1992, between 50 and 80 percent of America's e-waste continues to be shipped to Third World countries, where environmental standards are less strict. So much e-waste has been deported that, in 2002, China banned its import. Now e-waste is smuggled into China, however, where resident scavengers know it is illegal but continue to earn payment for the precious metals and other materials extracted. The waste that doesn't reach China is diverted to other parts of Asia or is sent to West African countries like Ghana, Nigeria, and the Ivory Coast.

To reduce the environmental impact and to facilitate recycling efforts, as of mid-2006, the EU has banned toxic ingredients, such as lead, mercury, cadmium, and so on, from electronics, appliances, lighting equipment, medical equipment, and other consumer products. Prior to the EU mandate, few companies were concerned with the production of "green" hardware. Now, however, since Europe represents about 30 percent of the world market for electronic equipment, manufacturers are rushing to comply with the EU directive.

The need for stricter regulations concerning e-waste disposal has been recognized in the United States, and in March 2008, Congress appointed a working group to determine a course of action. In April 2008, the House Committee on Science and Technology held hearings on the e-waste problem, but legislation at the federal level has yet to be enacted. In the mean-time more states may decide to formulate their own legislation.

While Congress debates the problem, the U.S. Environmental Protection Agency estimates that thirty to forty million PCs will be ready for "end of life management" in each of the next few years. And computers are not the only electronic product heading for obsolescence. In 2009, American TVs that receive only analog signals no longer function without a set-top box as digital broadcasting becomes the norm, which means that about twenty-five million TVs will be taken out of service annually. Add to those numbers the ninety-eight million cell phones that have become unfashionable since 2005 and the garbage heap will grow exponentially. All told, the UN Environment Programme estimates that e-waste of all types could total fifty million tons a year worldwide.

Clearly, disposing properly of e-waste is a problem begging for a solution if the environment and human health are to be protected.

Based on:

Anonymous (2005, May 15). Waste electrical and electronic equipment. Retrieved May 24, 2008, from http://europa.eu.int/scadplus/leg/en/lvb/l21210.htm.

Anonymous (2006, January 6). Is America exporting a huge environmental problem? *ABC News*. Retrieved May 24, 2008, from http://www.abcnews.go.com/2020/Technology/story?id=1479506.

Anonymous (2008, January 7). 2008 consumer electronics sales seen up. *Reuters.com*. Retrieved May 24, 2008, from http://www.reuters.com/article/businessNews/idUSN0740878220080108.

Blouin, G. (n.d.). Is Canadian e-waste an environmental disaster in waiting? *Canada.com*. Retrieved May 24, 2008, from http://www.canada.com/topics/technology/story.html?id=e8def77a-3a8f-420b-ad29-a9e08d03fca0&k=4739&p=1.

Carroll, C. (2008, January). High tech trash. *National Geographic*. Retrieved May 24, 2008, from http://ngm.nationalgeographic.com/2008/01/high-tech-trash/carroll-text.

Mayfiel, K. (2003, January 10). E-waste: Dark side of digital age. *Wired*. Retrieved May 24, 2008, from http://www.wired.com/news/technology/0,57151-1.html?tw=wn_story_page_next1.

Watkins, S. (2006, January 2). E-waste epidemic. *Government Technology*. Retrieved May 24, 2008, from http://www.govtech.net/magazine/channel_story.php/97724.

several European nations, Singapore, and the United States; many countries in the developing world—e.g., Chad, Bangladesh, Bolivia, and so on—are still far behind, often due to political conditions, education, or lacking infrastructure (such as telephone lines or Internet servers).

Going Global: International Business Strategies in the Digital World

Before the era of globalization, most companies were solely operating in the domestic arena, conducting their activities exclusively in one country, starting from the acquisition of raw materials to the selling of final products. Although such businesses are likely to benefit from the enablers that also spurred Globalization 3.0, **domestic companies** do not have to deal with many of the challenges brought about by globalization.

In today's digital world, the number of domestic companies is continually shrinking, with most domestic companies being relatively small (often local) businesses, such as local

FIGURE 2.20

Illegally copied intellectual property is openly bought and sold in many countries.

International business strategies.

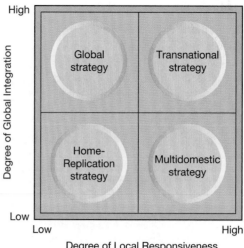

service providers, restaurants, farms, or independent grocery stores. Most of today's large companies, no matter if they are in car manufacturing (such as GM, Toyota, or Daimler), insurance (Allianz or Munich Re), or consumer goods (Nestlé or Procter & Gamble) have some **international business strategy** for competing in different global markets.

Such companies pursue either a home replication, multidomestic, global, or transnational strategy, depending on the degree of supply chain integration and necessary local customer responsiveness (Prahalad and Doz, 1987; Hitt, Ireland, and Hoskisson, 2009). On the one hand, businesses strive for global integration to realize economies of scale; on the other hand, a company's local subunits may benefit strongly from being able to quickly respond to changing conditions in local markets. Different international business strategies are suited better for different situations (see Figure 2.21 and Table 2.11).

Organizations use a variety of information systems strategies to manage international operations most effectively. For example, Nestlé, one of the world's largest food producers, with over five hundred factories and operations in more than seventy countries, is also considered to be one of the world's most globalized companies. In the following sections, we describe each of these various business strategies, along with the appropriate information systems strategies.

Home-Replication Strategy

The **home-replication strategy** (sometimes called export strategy or just international strategy) is the most basic form of going global. Companies using this strategy view international operations as secondary to their home operations. Thus, companies pursuing a

TABLE 2.11 When to Use International Business Strategies

Strategy	Description	Strengths	Weaknesses	When to Use
Home-Replication	International business seen as extension of home business	Focus on core competencies in home market	Inability to react to local market conditions	Homogeneous markets
Global	Centralized organization with standardized offerings across markets	Standardized product offerings allow achieving economies of scale	Inability to react to local market conditions	Homogeneous markets
Multidomestic	Federation of associated business units; decentralized	Ability to quickly react to local conditions	Differing product offerings limit economies of scale, and limited interunit communication limits knowledge sharing	Very heterogeneous markets
Transnational	Some aspects centralized, others decentralized; integrated network	Can achieve benefits of multidomestic and global strategies	Difficult to manage; very complex	Integrated global markets

home-replication strategy focus on their domestic customers' needs and wants, and merely export their products to generate additional sales. This allows companies to focus on their core competencies in their respective domestic markets. In some cases, selling products internationally is used as a way to extend the life of products nearing the end of their life cycles domestically (e.g., last year's tennis shoe may still be considered "hip" in some countries). As the company only places secondary emphasis on international operations, there is no expectation of obtaining additional knowledge from foreign operations. For example, it can be argued that German automaker Porsche pursues a home-replication strategy. Specifically, Porsche designs very high performance automobiles geared toward driving on German Autobahns (many of which have no speed limits); although this style of driving is almost impossible in most countries, Porsche sells their cars with the promise of high performance, making only minor modifications for local markets. With a home-replication strategy, the organization provides a relatively low level of local responsiveness and requires a relatively low level of global integration. As such, information systems play a minor role in facilitating this strategy (see Table 2.12).

Global Business Strategy

Companies pursuing a **global business strategy** attempt to achieve economies of scale by producing identical products in large quantities for a variety of different markets. In contrast to the home-replication strategy, where a product is developed for the home country and then exported (with little or no modifications), companies pursuing a global strategy (such as Sony) develop products for the global market.

A global business strategy works much more in a centralized fashion. As the decisions are made at the headquarters, the organization can be characterized as a centralized hub (Bartlett and Goshal, 1998). The headquarters gives the overall strategic direction and thus has tight control of the entire company as well as the knowledge that is generated within the company. However, the need to achieve economies of scale prohibits implementation of local strategies, and thus a global company cannot quickly react to local challenges and opportunities. Here, data flows extensively from the subsidiaries to the home location, and the home location exerts strong control on the subsidiaries (see Figure 2.22). As the home office coordinates most of the strategic decisions of the local subsidiaries, companies pursuing a global business strategy utilize multiple networks between the home office and the subsidiaries to facilitate both communication and data sharing. The data does not stay at the local subsidiaries, which reduces the potential for duplication, but at the same time introduces issues related to transborder data flows (primarily in EU countries) (see Table 2.12).

The **multidomestic business strategy** is particularly suited for operations in markets differing widely. The multidomestic business strategy uses a loose federation of associated business units, each of which is rather independent in their strategic

TABLE 2.12 Global Information Systems Strategies

Business Strategy	Systems	Communications	Data Resources
Home-Replication	Domestic systems (if any)	Limited (if any)	Local databases (if any)
Multidomestic	Decentralized systems	Direct communication between home office and subsidiaries	Local databases
Global	Centralized systems	Multiple networks between home office and subsidiaries	Data sharing between central home office and subsidiaries
Transnational	Distributed/shared systems; Internet-enabled applications	Enterprise-wide linkages	Common global data resources

Based on: Alavi and Young (1992), Karimi and Konsynski (1991), Ramarapu and Lado (1995).

FIGURE 2.22

Global business strategy.

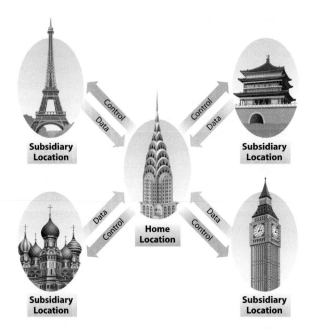

decisions. In other words, the degree of integration is very low, and the individual sub-units can respond quickly to their respective market demands (Ghoshal, 1987). Multidomestic companies can thus be extremely flexible and responsive to the needs and demands of local markets, and any opportunities arising in local markets can be quickly seized. An example of a multidomestic company is the international arm of General Motors, the national subsidiaries of which produce cars that are customized to the specific local markets (e.g., Opel in Germany and Vauxhall in Great Britain). However, working in a decentralized fashion, much of the knowledge generated is retained at the local subsidiaries, and knowledge transfer between the individual sub-sidiaries is often limited, leading to inefficiencies and mistakes that potentially can be repeated across subsidiaries (Bartlett and Ghoshal, 1998). In sum, for companies fol-lowing a multidomestic business strategy, very little data and control information flows between the home and subsidiary locations (see Figure 2.23).

FIGURE 2.23

Multidomestic business strategy.

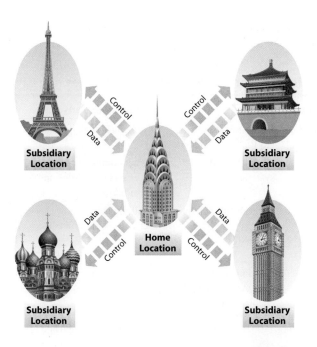

In order to support the loose confederacy of various different local subsidiaries and the decentralized nature of the decision making within companies utilizing a multidomestic business strategy, each organizational subsidiary has its own decentralized information systems. Although the systems within the different business units may be integrated, there is no centralized IS infrastructure. The communications take place primarily between the different subsidiaries and the home office; thus, there is no focus on the communication between the different subsidiaries (this is why there is only limited knowledge transfer among the subsidiaries). As the different subsidiaries are very independent, they retain the decentralized local data processing centers that are responsive to local needs and regulations and at the same time use information technology to integrate them loosely into the framework of the parent organization (see Table 2.12).

Transnational Business Strategy

An emerging strategy is the **transnational business strategy**. Having realized the benefits and drawbacks of multidomestic and global business strategies, companies using a transnational business strategy selectively decide which aspects of the organization should be under central control and which should be decentralized. This business strategy allows companies to leverage the flexibility offered by a decentralized organization (to be more responsive to local conditions), while at the same time reaping economies of scale enjoyed by centralization. An example of a transnational company is Unilever, which decides when to centralize and when to decentralize, depending on the products and the local markets. However, this business strategy is also the most difficult, as the company has to strike a balance between centralization and decentralization. In contrast to global organizations, where most of the resources are centralized in each company's home country, different resources in a transnational company can be centralized in different countries, depending on where the company can achieve the greatest returns or cost savings. Further, different decentralized resources are interdependent; this is in contrast to the other organizational forms, where there is usually one direction of the flow of resources. In a transnational company, for example, semiconductors for computer chips might be produced in a state-of-the-art factory in Dresden, Germany; shipped to a Southeast Asian country to be assembled into a final product; and then shipped back to Western Europe to be sold to an individual customer. Bartlett and Ghoshal (1998) characterize transnational companies as integrated networks requiring a great deal of effort in terms of managing the different interdependencies, tasks, and communication among the different units. In sum, both data and control can flow in any direction, depending on the specific business process (see Figure 2.24).

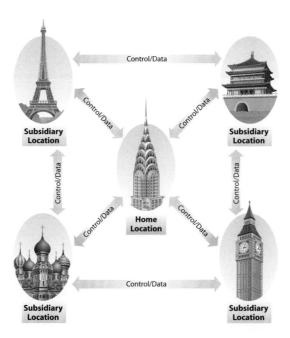

FIGURE 2.24

Transnational business strategy.

Companies utilizing a transnational business strategy need to create an integrated network between the home office and the multiple local subsidiaries. Because of this requirement, there is much communication among the different subunits as well as between the home office and the subunits. Many systems are distributed and/or shared; in this way, a subsidiary can access the systems and resources of other subsidiaries. Similarly, key data is shared throughout the company to enable a seamless integration of processes. Much of the communication, data, and application sharing is enabled by intranet, extranet, and Web-based applications (see Table 2.12).

Industry Analysis

The Automobile Industry

Could Ford Motor Company end up as the last of Detroit's "big three" car companies to be based in the United States? By late 2008, the big three were battling for survival, asking the U.S. Congress for loans to help deal with a major global recession. Although most Americans think of the big three as "U.S. firms," all major automobile companies (both foreign and domestic) have global operations.

Auto industry experts have claimed for years that globalization—the flattening of the world—would result in a widespread consolidation of automakers.

What is happening within the auto industry is indicative of globalization in general. A "flattened" world implies that the world is becoming more homogeneous. As the process continues, distinctions between national markets are fading and, for some products, may disappear entirely.

For instance, for decades manufacturers within the automobile industry have worked toward developing a "world car"—a basic car that with a few modifications can be sold all over the world. In the 1990s, three attempts were made to produce and market a world car: Honda's Accord, Ford's Mondeo/Contour, and GM's Cadillac Catera/Opel Omega. None of the models sold as well as hoped in North America, Europe, and Asia for several reasons:

- Consumers in different areas of the world have different tastes in automobiles. For example, small cab size has long been accepted in Europe, but American consumers prefer larger cabs.
- Europeans prefer steel construction over plastic, as in door panels, which are largely used in car manufacturing in the United States.
- Differences in infrastructure among countries lead to varying preferences in cars. Asians, for example, prefer smaller-sized cars that can maneuver well

through narrow, crowded streets, while Americans are fond of SUVs and pickups.
- The price of gasoline varies throughout the world. Europeans think first of fuel economy when buying a car, while this line of thinking is only slowly being adopted in the United States.
- Variations in regulations governing cars, such as emission standards, also vary with countries and affect car buyers' choices.

The development of a "world car" may yet be accomplished but probably not until cultural and economic conditions undergo even more globalization.

In the meantime, the automobile industry continues to move beyond geographic boundaries. Auto companies traditionally based in the United States are moving plants overseas, and foreign manufacturers are moving production facilities to the United States. The Japanese auto manufacturer Toyota operates production plants in many U.S. states, including Alabama, Texas, and West Virginia. The Ford Motor Company is based in the United States but operates satellite companies in Asia and Europe. A Chinese car manufacturer recently planned to buy a Brazilian auto engine manufacturing plant and transport it to China (the plant was eventually purchased by Italian multinational Fiat).

Another significant change in the auto industry involves sales channels. Traditionally, U.S. automakers maintain localized franchises that handle auto sales in a specific region. Now there are Internet franchises that have also created worldwide sales centers that did not previously exist.

Clearly, the global marketplace has changed the automobile industry profoundly, by allowing the automakers to build global networks of suppliers (such as Bosch and Continental from Germany, Magna and Lear from the U.S., or Yazaki from Japan) and selling to customers from all over the world. Although this has created new opportunities, the auto crisis in late 2008 has shown that in the age of Globalization 3.0, the success or failure of any major global firm has ripple effects far beyond its home country.

Questions

1. How is Globalization 3.0 fueling change in the auto industry?
2. Examine how cultural differences make it difficult to create a world car.

Based on:

Chandler, C. (2000, May 22). Globalization: The automobile industry's quest for a 'world car' strategy. Retrieved May 24, 2008, from http://globaledge.msu.edu/NewsAndViews/views/papers/0018.pdf.

Emmons, G. (2006, May 10). American auto's troubled road. *Working Knowledge*. Retrieved May 24, 2008, from http://hbswk.hbs.edu/item.jhtml?id=5290&t=innovation.

Webster, S. (2006, July 2). Future of autos is global. *Detroit Free Press*. Retrieved May 24, 2008, from http://www.freep.com/apps/pbcs.dll/article?AID=/20060702/BUSINESS01/607020577/1014/BUSINESS.

Key Points Review

1. **Define globalization, describe how it evolved over time, and describe the key drivers of globalization.** Globalization is the integration of economies throughout the world, fueled by technological progress and innovation. Over the past centuries, globalization has come a long way; starting with Columbus's discovery of America, Globalization 1.0 was fueled by power. Then, in 1800, Globalization 2.0 started, fueled mainly by a fall in transportation and telecommunications costs. Globalization 3.0 started in 2000 and was enabled by the convergence of a number of enablers, namely, the fall of the Berlin Wall, Netscape going public, work flow software, uploading, outsourcing, offshoring, supply chaining, in-sourcing, in-forming, and "the steroids." This has led to a rise in outsourcing and has helped to shape the world as we know it today.

2. **Describe the emerging opportunities for companies operating in the digital world.** Companies operating in the digital world see a number of opportunities, many of which are enabled by Globalization 3.0. For companies, the primary opportunities are the access to new markets for their products and services as well as the access to a talented labor pool in countries with lower wages.

3. **Explain the factors companies have to consider when operating in the digital world.** In addition to the opportunities, operating in the digital world also poses a number of challenges to companies. The first broad set of challenges is of governmental nature and includes challenges related to the political system (such as market versus planned economy or political instability), regulatory challenges, data-sharing challenges, and challenges related to Internet access and individual freedom.

The next class of challenges is of geoeconomic nature. Such challenges arise due to differences in world time zones, communication reliability, and workforce quality. Further, differences in economic welfare potentially lead to challenges, both for companies and for countries. Another set of challenges relates to national cultural differences, including differences in power distance, uncertainty avoidance, individualism/collectivism, masculinity/femininity, concept of time, and life focus as well as differences in language, education, and religion. Finally, companies face various challenges when offering products or services in many countries, depending on what is considered a socially acceptable product or advertisement, or environmental concerns related to operating in the digital world.

4. **Describe international business and information systems strategies used by companies operating in the digital world.** Companies operating in the digital world can use different business strategies. Some companies pursue a home-replication strategy, which entails selling products developed for the home market internationally. In contrast, other companies develop products for the global market. This strategy, known as global business strategy, includes having a centralized organization to offer standardized products in different markets. This helps to achieve economies of scale and is best suited for homogeneous markets. Information systems used by organizations pursuing this strategy are very centralized, and much data flows from the subsidiaries to the headquarters. The multidomestic business strategy is best suited for heterogeneous markets, as it allows to quickly respond to changing local conditions; this strategy includes having a decentralized federation of loosely associated business units in different

countries. Companies pursuing this strategy employ decentralized systems, and data sharing is very limited. The transnational business strategy is very well suited for operating in the digital world, as it combines the benefits of the multidomestic and the global business strategies by enabling economies of scale while being responsive to local market conditions. In a transnational business strategy, some aspects of the company are centralized, while others are decentralized. The information systems used are distributed, allowing for increased communication between the headquarters and the subsidiaries as well as between the subsidiaries, and common access to critical data. Transnational information systems are primarily enabled by intranets, extranets, and the Internet.

Key Terms

concept of time 65
culture 64
domestic company 69
embargoes 58
export regulations 58
geoeconomic 60
global business strategy 71
globalization 40
Globalization 1.0 40
Globalization 2.0 41
Globalization 3.0 41

home replication strategy 70
individualism/collectivism 65
in-forming 49
in-sourcing 49
international business strategy 70
life focus 65
maquiladoras 52
masculinity/femininity 65
multidomestic business strategy 72
nearshoring 54
offshoring 47

offshore outsourcing 47
power distance 65
quotas 58
tariffs 58
transborder data flows 58
transnational business strategy 72
uncertainty avoidance 65
uploading 46
wiki 47
work flow software 45

Review Questions

1. List the ten factors that led to Globalization 3.0.
2. How did the fall of the Berlin Wall flatten the world according to Friedman?
3. Describe work flow software. How did this technology drive the flattening of the world?
4. Compare outsourcing, offshoring, and offshore outsourcing.
5. Describe in-sourcing and provide examples of how organizations use in-sourcing.
6. List and describe several reasons why companies are choosing to outsource business activities.
7. List and contrast several challenges of operating in the digital world.
8. Explain the concept of geoeconomic challenges and how organizations can overcome these challenges.
9. What is meant by transborder data flows, and why is this a concern?
10. Define culture and describe how it affects globalization.
11. List and describe several ways in which cultures differ.
12. Describe the multidomestic business strategy and how it affects the flow of control information.

Self-Study Questions

Visit the Interactive Study Guide on the Companion Web site for additional Self-Study Questions: www.pearsonhighered.com/valacich.

1. What stage of globalization started with expansion of trade to India, where the horse and wind and in later stages steam were the primary drivers?
   A. Globalization 0.5
   B. Globalization 1.0
   C. Globalization 2.0
   D. Globalization 3.0

2. The release of the Netscape Web browser had the following effects on the flattening of the world *except*:
   A. setting the standard for Web browsing
   B. providing easy access to the Internet
   C. providing integrated e-mail
   D. launching the World Wide Web

3. Which of the following is *not* considered an enabler of a flat world by Friedman?
- A. uploading
- B. supply chaining
- C. in-forming
- D. customer service software

4. Which of the following is *not* considered open-source software:
- A. Microsoft Office
- B. OpenOffice.org
- C. Firefox
- D. Linux

5. The assembly plants on the Mexican side of the U.S.–Mexican border that mass-produce goods for the U.S. market are called _____.
- A. Mexicanizations
- B. maquiladoras
- C. Mexcaias
- D. gringoias

6. Embargoes are considered which part of the following challenges operating in the digital world?
- A. regulatory
- B. data sharing
- C. political system
- D. governmental

7. One of the geoeconomic challenges that videoconferencing *cannot* resolve is _____.
- A. time zone challenges
- B. regulatory challenges
- C. data-sharing challenges
- D. cultural challenges

8. Which of the cultural dimensions is described as "the extent to which a culture focuses on the quantity versus the quality of life"?
- A. concept of time
- B. uncertainty avoidance
- C. life focus
- D. work culture

9. _____ reflects the extent to which a society values the position of an individual versus the position of a group.
- A. masculinity/femininity
- B. uncertainty avoidance
- C. individualism/collectivism
- D. life focus

10. What emerging strategy do companies use when deciding which aspect should be under central control and which should be decentralized?
- A. global business strategy
- B. transnational business strategy
- C. multidomestic business strategy
- D. operational business strategy

Answers are on page 79.

Problems and Exercises

1. Match the following terms to the appropriate definitions:
- i. transnational business strategy
- ii. multidomestic business strategy
- iii. in-forming
- iv. Globalization 3.0
- v. quotas
- vi. offshore outsourcing
- vii. geoeconomic
- viii. uncertainty avoidance
- ix. nearshoring
- x. embargoes
  - a. The reversal of overseas offshoring to address challenges related to geographical, political, linguistic, or economic distance.
  - b. The outsourcing of business processes on a global scale.
  - c. Stage of globalization encompassing virtually every nation and shrinking the world from "size small to size tiny."
  - d. An international business strategy employed to be flexible and responsive to the needs and demands of heterogeneous local markets.
  - e. The combination of economic and political factors that influence a region.
  - f. Using the Internet to access information, enabling people to get a more complete picture of what is happening in the world.
  - g. Regulations typically limiting (or prohibiting) trade with one particular country.
  - h. The cultural characteristic that helps in understanding the risk-taking nature of a culture.
  - i. The act of foreign governments to limit the importing of certain products.
  - j. An international business strategy that allows companies to leverage the flexibility offered by a decentralized organization (to be more responsive to local conditions), while at the same time reaping economies of scale enjoyed by centralization.

2. Visit the Go4Customer Web site (www.go4customer.com). What does this company do? Where are they located? Who are Go4Customer customers? Give an example of how a U.S. company would use Go4Customer.

3. Visit Wal-Mart China (www.wal-martchina.com/english/index.htm). Compare and contrast your local Wal-Mart with Wal-Mart China. Are the items sold in China the same as your local Wal-Mart? How does Wal-Mart China differ from your Wal-Mart? Explain your answer.

4. Interview an IS professional and document his or her views on offshore outsourcing. Specifically, find out if his or her company is using offshore outsourcing; if so, what does the company outsource and why? If not, why not? If it utilizes offshore outsourcing, have the IS professional critique its quality, cost, and so on.

5. What search engine do you use? Compare and contrast your search engine preference with one of the other big search engines available (google.com, msn.com, yahoo.com). How would these search engines be used to create your "own personal supply chain"?

6. What digital news media do you use to get your news? According to this textbook's definitions, are you in-forming? If you are in-forming, describe how. What other ways could you in-form?

7. What are some examples of key technologies that utilize "steroids"? Using the technology definition provided by this textbook, how do you use technological steroids in your everyday life?

8. Should the U.S. government allow companies to use offshore outsourcing if qualified U.S. citizens are willing and able to do a job? Should the government regulate the amount that can be outsourced by any company? Why or why not?

9. Work flow software allows an organization to move documents and/or tasks through a work process. Using your own experiences and observations, either professionally or personally, describe how the work flow software worked.

10. As outlined in the chapter, UPS provides in-sourcing services for many businesses. Visit www.ups.com and identify some examples of UPS providing in-sourcing services and include a listing of some of UPS's in-sourcing customers.

11. Interview an IS professional regarding some possible uses for open-source software. Is open-source software being used in the IS professional's organization? If so, document what software it uses and how it is working; if not, document why it is not using open-source software.

12. List ten reasons why you would (or would not) be a good global manager.

13. Global outsourcing appears to be here to stay. Use the Web to identify a company that is providing low-cost labor from some less developed part of the world. Provide a short report that explains who the company is, where it is located, who its customers are, what services and capabilities it provides, how long it has been in business, and any other interesting information you can find in your research.

14. Examine Table 2.9 and rate yourself for each of the critical cultural dimensions. Do your ratings match those of your country in every instance? If so, why do you think this occurred? If not, why?

15. Download and use the open source Firefox Web browser (www.mozilla.com/firefox/) and compare and rank its features against those of Microsoft Internet Explorer or Flock. Which do you prefer and why?

Application Exercises

 Note: The existing data files referenced in these exercises are available on the Student Companion Web site: www.pearsonhighered. com/ valacich.

 Spreadsheet Application: Building a Business Case for Online Ticketing

On graduation, you were hired by Campus Travel to assist in creating an infrastructure to sell travel services over the Internet. One aspect of this online system is a module to handle travel-related requests so that the customers can see whether a particular product or service is available. In order to do this, you will have to be able to manipulate data to allow for management to see what is really going on. To do so, your manager has asked for the following:

1. Sort the data by date, then by sales.
   a. Open the file sortdata.csv.
   b. Highlight all data.
   c. Select sort from the "Data" menu.
   d. Sort by "Date Sold," then by "Salesperson." Print out a copy of each for your instructor.

2. Count the number of tickets sold in the provided table.
   a. In cell H3, enter the countif formula to count the number of tickets each salesperson has sold. Hint: Use "=countif(b2:b36,g3)."
   b. Copy cell H3 down to the other salespeople.
   c. Sum the total number of tickets sold in the appropriate field.

 Database Application: Locating Campus Travel Agencies

Campus Travel is now trying to market to specific customers in its frequent flier database. This includes targeting customers from certain airlines that reside in certain areas. You have been asked to import the frequent flier database and then to filter records accordingly. To do so, you must complete the following:

1. Open the file frequentflier.mdb.
2. Use "filter by selection" to filter records from customers in Pullman.
3. Filter customers by "Delta Airlines."

Team Work Exercise: Becoming a Global Leader

Many universities believe, rightfully so, that they have a duty to help internationalize students through a variety of events, courses, and experiences in order to help prepare students for managing in the digital world. Work in teams of four or five students and compile a list of all the different things you feel your school is doing to help students develop into better global leaders.

Answers to the Self-Study Questions

1. B, p. 40   2. D, p. 43   3. D, p. 42   4. A, p. 46   5. B, p. 52
6. A, p. 58   7. A, p. 60   8. C, p. 65   9. C, p. 65   10. B, p. 72

Case ❶

Global Picture Sharing: Flickr

Has there been a wedding, birth, confirmation, graduation, one-hundredth birthday celebration, or other commemorative event in your family lately? Would you like to see the photos your sister, Uncle Walt, and Grandma Mary took at the event? Invite everyone who attended to post their photos on Flickr.com—one of the easiest and most popular means of sharing photos online.

Flickr.com was developed by Ludicorp, a Vancouver, Canada–based company founded in 2002 and launched online in 2004. Yahoo! purchased Flickr in 2005. In just over a year after Flickr's launch, the site had over 350,000 members, who had collectively uploaded 31 million images.

Flickr didn't invent online photo sharing, but the tools members can use to navigate the photos on the site are unique. "Tags" let photo owners and viewers label photos to prescribe a category that makes them easier to find. For example, popular tags include summer, winter, cute, Europe, dog, cat, and so on. Flickr takes the tag concept further with clustering, a better way to explore photos through tags. Key in "summer beach vacations," for instance, and you can view a page of clustered photos with just those tags. Clustering has resulted in such far-out photo categories as confusing street signs, dogs' noses, Halloween costumes, margaritas, and mannequins.

Flickr sees photo sharing and the use of tags as a social process users call "folksonomy." That is, since viewers can add comments to photos, there is a level of involvement similar to a social gathering. For a person who is browsing through a set of photos, the notes on the photos tell little stories, as if that person were sitting by the photographer, who is explaining the photo.

Flickr photo viewers can also rate a photo according to "interestingness." Each calendar day, a few highly ranked photos are posted to a common page for easier viewer exploration.

Flickr also allows for basic photo manipulation, such as rotation, ordering prints, sending to a group of people, adding to a blog or even a map, and so on. Photos can be open for everyone everywhere to view, or viewing can be restricted to one's friends and family.

User space on Flickr is unlimited; however, there is a restriction based on the bandwidth used per month. (For only a few dollars per month, there are no bandwidth restrictions.)

Since Flickr's basic photo-sharing service is free, revenue for the company is based on Yahoo!-placed ads on Flickr Web pages. Photographers who post images on the Flickr site, however, are free to sell their photos. The legal aspects of copyright are handled by a license called the "creative commons." This license has many different levels of copyright protection but is primarily for not-for-profit use of a user's photographs. Flickr offers a simple interface that allows photographers to choose a license for protecting copyright.

For programming enthusiasts, Flickr has released all application program interfaces (APIs) for public use. For example, programmers have used the APIs to develop uploading applications for the Mac, Windows, camera phones, and other devices.

Flickr is also one of the first Web sites to join the OpenID project. With OpenID, Internet users don't need multiple IDs and passwords; after registering once with the free service, the same login ID and password can be used to enter any site that participates in OpenID. The worldwide popularity of Flickr is another way in which information systems are fueling a flatter world.

Questions

1. Why do you think Flickr has been so popular throughout the world?
2. What lessons could a Web site for a local business learn from Flickr?
3. How do Web sites like Flickr act to increase globalization?

Based on:

Anonymous (2005, August 1). The new new things. *Flickr Blog.* Retrieved May 24, 2008, from http://blog.flickr.com/flickrblog/2005/08/the_new_new_thi.html.

Anonymous (2005, December 16). Shedding light on Flickr. *News.com.* Retrieved May 24, 2008, from http://news.com.com/Shedding+light+on+Flickr/2100-1025_3-5997943.html.

Anonymous (n.d.). OpenID. Retrieved May 24, 2008, from http://openid.net.

Stone, B. (2004, March 11). Photos for the masses. *MSNBC-Newsweek.* Retrieved May 24, 2008, from http://www.newsweek.com/id/48941.

Terdiman, D. (2005, November 16). Tagging gives web a human meaning. *News.com.* Retrieved May 24, 2008, from http://news.com.com/Tagging+gives+Web+a+human+meaning/2009-1025_3-5944502.html.

Case ❷

Enabling Global Payments at PayPal

If you have used eBay (and who hasn't?) you know how easy it is to pay for items you buy and to receive payment for items you have sold. Checks, credit card charges, and money orders are unnecessary. Instead of these traditional methods of payment, digital money is easily and effortlessly zapped to and from accounts at PayPal, the most frequently used digital money transfer service online.

Peter Thiel, a hedge fund manager, and Max Levchin, an online security specialist, founded what was to become PayPal—it was first named Field Link and then Confinity and finally, in 2001, PayPal. The company went online rather naively in 1999. The founders' vision was to create a digital currency exchange service free of government controls, but the site quickly became a target for hackers, con artists, and organized crime groups, who used the site for scams and money laundering. Tighter security measures halted criminal activity and helped assuage customer complaints, but government regulators moved in. Attorneys General in several states investigated PayPal's business practices, and New York and California levied fines for violations. Louisiana banned the company from operating in that state. (The ban has since been lifted.)

When PayPal began, payment for Web products was made through credit card charges at the purchase site and via checks and money orders sent through the postal service. Other companies, such as Beenz.com and Flooz.com, had tried to establish electronic payment systems based on a special digital currency, but merchants, banks, and customers were hesitant to accept "money" that wasn't based on real dollars. Thiel and Levchin saw the need for an electronic payment system that relied on real currency, especially when eBay became popular, and PayPal filled that niche.

After PayPal solved its security and customer support problems, customers liked the convenience and ease of using the service, and its client base grew. Buyers like not having to reveal their credit card numbers to every online merchant, and merchants appreciate having PayPal handle payment collection. New PayPal clients establish an account with a user name and password and fund the account by giving PayPal a credit card number or bank account transaction information. Although PayPal prefers the latter (because bank account transactions are cheaper than credit card transactions), half of PayPal's accounts are funded via credit cards.

EBay bought PayPal in 2002 for $1.5 billion and since then has also been a major source of income for the money transfer site. At the same time, PayPal has expanded its client base both in the United States and abroad, and is generating much revenue by charging fees for payment processing for a wide variety of online vendors, auction sites, and corporations. Services to buyers are free, but sellers are charged a fee, which is generally lower than fees charged by major credit card companies. PayPal now offers special merchant accounts for transferring larger amounts of money and also offers a donation box feature for blogs and other Web sites where visitors can make donations.

PayPal spawned many rivals after its initial launch, but most have since died, including Citigroup's C2it and Bank One's Email Money. Currently, PayPal operates in 190 markets in thirteen countries, and manages over 164 million accounts. PayPal allows customers to send, receive, and hold funds in seventeen currencies worldwide. While the company has had its share of problems with fraud and phishers (scamsters who send fradulent e-mail messages and duplicate legitimate Web sites), PayPal continues to be the number one method of payment for the world's buyers and sellers.

Questions

1. Why do you think PayPal has been so successful throughout the world?
2. How has PayPal acted to increase globalization?
3. Do you use PayPal? Why or why not?

Based on:

Anonymous (n.d.). PayPal company history. Retrieved May 24, 2008, from http://www.fundinguniverse.com/company-histories/PayPal-Inc-Company-History.html.

Grabianowski, E. (n.d.). How PayPal works. Retrieved May 24, 2008, from http: /computer.howstuffworks.com/paypal3.htm.

PayPal. (2008, May 24). In *Wikipedia, the free encyclopedia*. Retrieved May 24, 2008, from http://en.wikipedia.org/w/index.php?title=PayPal&oldid=214626566.

Walker, L. (2005, May 19). PayPal looks to evolve beyond its auction roots. *Washingtonpost.com*. Retrieved May 24, 2008, from http://www.washingtonpost.com/wp-dyn/content/article/2005/05/18/AR2005051802187.html?nav=rss_opinion/columns.

Valuing Information Systems Investments

After reading this chapter, you will be able to do the following:

1. Discuss how organizations can use information systems for automation, organizational learning, and strategic advantage.

2. Describe how to formulate and present the business case for an information system.

3. Explain why and how companies are continually looking for innovative ways to use information systems for competitive advantage.

4. Describe freeconomics and how organizations can leverage digital technologies to provide free goods and services to customers as a business strategy for gaining a competitive advantage.

Preview

This chapter will examine how organizations evaluate information systems investments and how these investments can be used strategically, enabling firms to gain or sustain competitive advantage over their rivals. As described in Chapter 1—Managing in the Digital World, a firm has competitive advantage over rival firms when it can do something better, faster, more economically, or uniquely. We will show why it is vital but sometimes difficult for people to determine the value of an information systems investment. Presenting the "case" for an information system is necessary for making good investment decisions; these decisions are particularly difficult given the pace of technological innovations.

In this chapter, we begin by examining how organizations can gain the greatest value from their information systems investments. We then describe what it means to make the business case and examine several factors that must be identified and considered when building a successful business case. Finally, we talk about the continual need to find innovative ways to succeed with and through information systems.

Managing in the Digital World: TiVo

"You've got a life. TiVo gets it." With that catchy motto, in 1999 TiVo® Incorporated introduced a service that gave users unprecedented control over television viewing. Hate to miss that football game for your sister's wedding? TiVo will record it for you, and you can watch it at your convenience. Are there certain shows you always have to miss because you work late hours? TiVo solves the problem again. On the TiVo Web site, the service describes itself: "Your TiVo® box, powered by the amazing TiVo® service, automatically finds and digitally records all of your favorite shows, every time they're on. Every episode of your favorite series. Every Coppola movie. Every home improvement program. Even Dora cartoons! Whatever you choose. All while you're out living life. Plus, only TiVo lets you watch your favorite shows any time, anywhere."

Mike Ramsay and Jim Barton developed their TiVo business plan in 1997. The first TiVo "boxes" were shipped to customers in 1999. A 2008 subscriber to TiVo's service got the box, ranging from the basic model priced at $150 that records up to eighty hours of TV up to the high end $600 model with 1 terabyte of storage space that allowed recording of up to 150 hours of high-definition programming and supported Dolby THX audio. Monthly subscription fees were $12.95 and prepay options were also available. Customers could even chose a $399 lifetime plan that included subscription for the life of the TiVo device purchased. The subscription service allows users to select shows to record without knowing scheduled times.

TiVo is basically a simple computer with a hard drive recorder that incorporates the following capabilities:

- Automatic recording of your favorite shows whenever they are on; works with cable, satellite dish, or antenna
- A search engine to find and automatically record the shows that match your interests (by title, actor, director, category, and even key word)
- Easy home networking features that enable the use of online services like Podcasts, Yahoo! Weather and Traffic, and the ability to purchase movie tickets from Fandango
- Easy-to-use to-go features that let you transfer shows to your laptop or portable device or easily burn them to DVD
- Scheduling last-minute shows from the Web

TiVo makes TV watching an interactive experience in that you can pause the action if the phone rings, you can answer the phone and then either return to the show exactly where you left off or fast-forward to the story where it is when you return. You can also do instant replay without missing a moment of the action.

The internal architecture of a TiVo box consists of a microprocessor, a video encoder/decoder chip, and an internal hard drive. The hard drive's capacity initially was 13 to 60 GB, which has steadily increased over the years to 1 TB. The new TiVo models have the capability to record high-definition TV, record from two channels simultaneously, and connect to Ethernet and wireless networks. Licensed manufacturers produce all the hardware, and TiVo provides the software that runs the hardware. The software is a Linux-based operating system and has frequent updates.

FIGURE 3.1

TiVo allows consumers to watch television programming on their time schedule.

The variety of selections available to users include the following:

- You can select a genre of movies, such as comedy, mystery, or romance, and request that your TiVo record them.
- You can select only those shows for recording that have your favorite actor.
- You can select specific types of shows that have your favorite actor.
- You can drill down selections to include one person or item, such as recipes for asparagus.
- In addition, if you connect the TiVo box to your home computer network, you can play music from your computer on your TiVo system.
- You can access your entire MP3 library without moving from the living room couch.
- You can view photos stored on your computer using TiVo. They are displayed on the TV screen, so everyone does not have to crowd around the computer to see photos.
- You can watch a variety of content available on the Web via Real Simple Syndication (RSS) feeds, including everything from nightly newscasts and The Sesame Street podcast to daily headlines from MTV News and College Humor from CHTV.
- You can watch YouTube videos directly on your TV.

TiVo has recently launched an online service called TiVo Central, which allows users to schedule the recording of any program by accessing the Internet from any location, regardless of the location of the TiVo box.

As with any successful new technology, other companies have imitated TiVo. Several cable TV companies offer digital video recorders (DVRs) to customers that can record programs for later viewing. To date, however, the competition does not offer the wide variety of services TiVo offers.

Rivalry affected TiVo's customer base, however, forcing the company to change its marketing plan accordingly. For example, TiVo has joined with Comcast Cable Company to provide service to their customers. In March 2006, TiVo struck a deal with Verizon Wireless that allowed Verizon cell phone users to program their TiVo recorders from their cell phones. In another venture called TiVoToGo, TiVo is providing software to users that will let them move recorded programming from the TiVo recorder to laptop computers. Furthermore, in the future TiVo may add an advertisement display feature since marketers have complained that TiVo users can fast-forward to skip ads. (This feature will undoubtedly raise the ire of some TiVo customers.)

TiVo announced a new service in March 2006 called KidZone, where parents could look for shows appropriate for their children and then separate that content from recorded adult shows.

Time marches on and so does TiVo. By mid-2008 TiVo had formed an alliance with RealNetworks' Rhapsody music service and was offering a service that made TiVo Series 2, 3, and HD set top boxes conduits for content from Amazon's Video on Demand service. Thus, TiVo offered the first single box solution that intermingles downloadable broadband video and traditional TV in one place.

Clearly, TiVo will continue innovating and changing its services to meet customer needs and preferences.

After reading this chapter, you will be able to answer the following:

1. What would your "business case" be to convince your family or roommates to purchase TiVo?

2. In what way was TiVo a disruptive innovation?

3. How would you forecast the future of TiVo in regard to the advent of on-demand video where any type of video content is available at any time on any device?

Based on:

Lam, B. (2007, February 7). Breaking: Tivo boxes to download Amazon Unboxed videos. *Gizmodo.com*. Retrieved May 11, 2008, from http://gizmodo.com/gadgets/home-entertainment/breaking-tivo-boxes-to-download-amazon-unboxed-videos-234557.php.

McCarthy, C. (2007, October 10). No fast-forwarding at TiVo, Rhapsody party. *CNET News.com*. Retrieved May 11, 2008, from http://www.news.com/8301-13577_3-9794674-36.html.

Olsen, S. (2006, February 14). Love in the time of TiVo. *CNET News.com*. Retrieved May 11, 2008, from http://news.com.com/Love+in+the+time+of+TiVo/2100-1041_3-6039433.html.

Reardon, M. (2006, March 7). TiVo looks to Verizon phones for TV recording. *CNET News.com*. Retrieved May 11, 2008, from http://news.com.com/TiVo+looks+to+Verizon+phones+for+TV+recording/2100-1039_3-6046759.html.

Spring, T. (2008, January 9). TiVo boosts service, supports video podcasts. *PCWorld.com*. Retrieved May 11, 2008, from http://blogs.pcworld.com/staffblog/archives/006244.html.

TiVo DVR: Your ultimate source for entertainment. (n.d.). Retrieved May 11, 2008, from http://www.tivo.com.

Valuing Information Systems

In Chapter 1, we introduced the notion that information systems can have strategic value to an organization. Here, we describe three ways to use an information system: for automating, for organizational learning, and for achieving strategy (see Figure 3.2). These three activities are not necessarily mutually exclusive, but we believe that each is progressively more useful to the firm and thus adds more value to the business. In the final category,

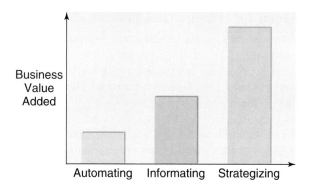

FIGURE 3.2

The business value added from automating, informating (learning), and strategizing with IS.

information systems are used to support a firm's strategy and to enable a firm to gain or sustain competitive advantage over rivals.

Information Systems for Automating: Doing Things Faster

Someone with an **automating** perspective thinks of technology as a way to help complete a task within an organization faster, more cheaply, and perhaps with greater accuracy and/or consistency. Let us look at a typical example. A person with an automating mentality would take a loan application screening process and automate it by inputting the loan applications into a computer database so that those involved in decision making for the loans could process the applications faster, more easily, and with fewer errors. Such a system might also enable customers to complete the loan application online. A transition from a manual to an automated loan application process might enable the organization to deploy employees more efficiently, leading to even more cost savings (see Table 3.1).

TABLE 3.1   Activities Involved Under Three Different Loan Application Processes and the Average Time for Each Activity

Primary Activities of Loan Processing	Manual Loan Process (Time)	Technology-Supported Process (Time)	Fully Automated Process (Time)
1. Complete and submit loan application	Customer takes the application home, completes it, returns it (1.5 days)	Customer takes the application home, completes it, returns it (1.5 days)	Customer fills out application from home via the Web (1 hour)
2. Check application for errors	Employee does this in batches (2.5 days)	Employee does this in batches (2.5 days)	Computer does this as it is being completed (3.5 seconds)
3. Input data from application into the information system	Applications are kept in paper form, although there is handling time involved (1 hour)	Employee does this in batches (2.5 days)	Done as part of the online application process (no extra time needed)
4. Assess loan applications under $250,000 to determine whether to fund them	Employee does this completely by hand (15 days)	Employee does this with the help of the computer (1 hour)	Computer does this automatically (1 second)
5. Committee decides on any loan over $250,000	(15 days)	(15 days)	(15 days)
6. Applicant notified	Employee generates letters manually in batches (1 week)	Employee generates letters with the help of a computer (1 day)	System notifies applicant via e-mail (3.5 seconds)
Total Time:	Anywhere from **25 to 40 days**, depending on size of loan	Anywhere from **5 to 20 days**, depending on size of loan	Anywhere from **1 hour to 15 days**, depending on size of loan

Many online loan application services can now give you instant "tentative" approval pending verification of data you report in your online application. Also, only some of the activities within the manual and technology-supported processes can occur in parallel.

Information Systems for Organizational Learning: Doing Things Better

We can also use information systems to learn and improve. Shoshana Zuboff (1988) described this as **informating**. Zuboff explained that a technology informates when it provides information about its operation and the underlying work process that it supports. The system helps us not only to automate a business process but also to learn to improve the day-to-day activities within that process. **Business processes** are the activities organizations perform in order to reach their business goals, including core activities that transform inputs and produce outputs, and supporting activities that enable the core activities to take place.

The learning mentality builds on the automating mentality because it recognizes that information systems can be used as a vehicle for **organizational learning**—the ability of an organization to use past behavior and information to improve its business processes—and change as well as for automation. In a 1993 *Harvard Business Review* article, David Garvin described a **learning organization** as one that is "skilled at creating, acquiring, and transferring knowledge, and at modifying its behavior to reflect new knowledge and insights."

To illustrate a learning mentality, let us think again about our loan processing example. Figure 3.3 shows how a computer-based loan processing system tracks types of loan applications by date, month, and season. The manager easily sees the trends and can plan for the timely ordering of blank application forms and the staffing and training of personnel in the loan department. The manager can also more efficiently manage the funds used to fulfill loans.

A learning approach allows people to track and learn about the types of applications filed by certain types of people at certain times of the year (e.g., more auto loan applications in the fall, mostly from men in their twenties and thirties), the patterns of the loan decisions made, or the subsequent performance of those loans. This new system creates data about the underlying business process that can be used to better monitor, control, and change that process. In other words, you *learn* from this information system about loan applications and approvals; as a result, you can do a better job at evaluating loan applications.

A combined automating and learning approach, in the long run, is more effective than an automating approach alone. If the underlying business process supported by technology is inherently flawed, a learning use of the technology might help you detect the problems with the process and change it. For instance, in our loan processing example, a learning use of technology may help us uncover a pattern among the accepted loans that enables us to distinguish between low- and high-performing loans over their lives and subsequently to change the criteria for loan acceptance.

If, however, the underlying business process is bad and you are using technology only for automating (i.e., you would not uncover the data that would tell you this process is bad), you are more likely to continue with a flawed or less-than-optimal business process. In fact, such an automating use of technology may mask the process problems.

With a bad underlying set of loan acceptance criteria (e.g., rules that would allow you to approve a loan for someone who had a high level of debt as long as they had not been late on any payments recently), a person might manually review four applications in a day and, because of the problematic criteria used, inadvertently accept on average two "bad" applications per week. If you automated the same faulty process, with no learning aspects built in, the system might help a person review twelve applications per day, with six "bad"

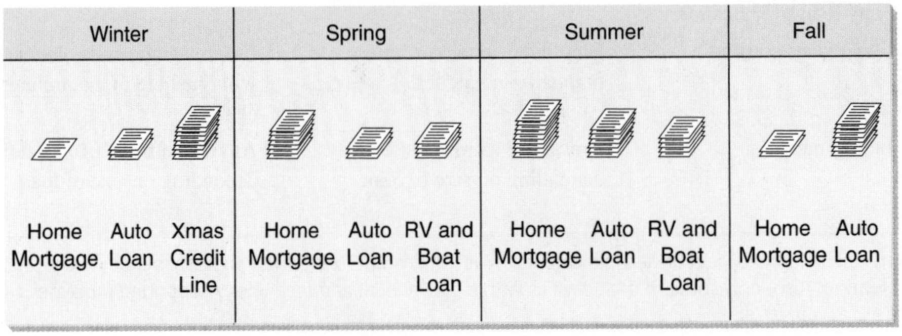

FIGURE 3.3

A computer-based loan processing system enables the bank manager to identify trends in loan applications.

Winter			Spring			Summer			Fall	
Home Mortgage	Auto Loan	Xmas Credit Line	Home Mortgage	Auto Loan	RV and Boat Loan	Home Mortgage	Auto Loan	RV and Boat Loan	Home Mortgage	Auto Loan

applications accepted per week on average. The technology would serve only to magnify the existing business problems (see Figure 3.4). Without learning, it is more difficult to uncover bad business processes underlying the information system.

Information Systems for Supporting Strategy: Doing Things Smarter

Using information systems to automate or improve processes has advantages, as described previously. In most cases, however, the best way to use an information system is to support the organization's strategy in a way that enables the firm to gain or sustain competitive advantage over rivals. To understand why, think about **organizational strategy**—a firm's plan to accomplish its mission and goals as well as to gain or sustain competitive advantage over rivals—and how it relates to information systems. When senior managers conduct **strategic planning**, they form a vision of where the organization needs to head, convert that vision into measurable objectives and performance targets, and craft a strategy to achieve the desired results. In Figure 3.5, we show some common organizational strategies. An organization might decide to pursue a **low-cost leadership strategy**, as do Wal-Mart and Dell, by which it offers the best prices in its industry on its goods and/or services. Alternatively, an organization might decide to pursue a **differentiation strategy**, as do Porsche, Nordstrom, and IBM, by which it tries to provide better products or services than its competitors. A company might aim that differentiation broadly at many different types of consumers, or it might focus on a particular segment of consumers, as Apple did for many years with its focus on high-quality computers for home and educational markets. Still other organizations might pursue a middle-of-the-road strategy, following a **best-cost provider strategy**, offering products or services of reasonably good quality at competitive prices, as does Target.

A person with a strategic mentality toward information systems goes beyond mere automating and learning and instead tries to find ways to use information systems to achieve the organization's chosen strategy. This individual wants the benefits of automating and learning but also looks for some strategic, competitive advantage from the system.

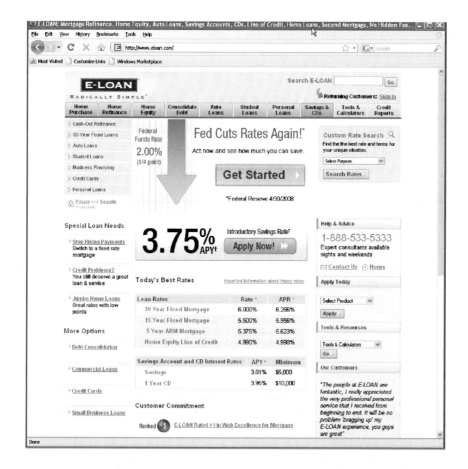

FIGURE 3.4

Automating a loan processing system requires sound underlying business processes.

FIGURE 3.5

Five general types of organizational strategy: broad differentiation, focused differentiation, focused low-cost, overall low-cost leadership, and best-cost provider.

Source: Courtesy A. A. Thompson and A. J. Strickland III, *Strategic Management: Concepts and Cases,* 8th ed. (Homewood, Ill.: Richard D. Irwin, 1995).

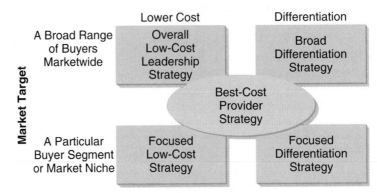

In fact, in today's business environment, if a proposed information system isn't going to clearly deliver some strategic value (i.e., help to improve the business so that it can compete better) while also helping people to work smarter and save money in the process, then it isn't likely to be funded.

Sources of Competitive Advantage

How do business firms typically get a competitive advantage? An organization has competitive advantage whenever it has an edge over rivals in attracting customers and defending against competitive forces (Porter, 1985, 2001). In order to be successful, a business must have a clear vision, one that focuses investments in resources such as information systems and technologies to help achieve a competitive advantage. Some sources of competitive advantage include the following (see Figure 3.6):

- Having the best-made product on the market
- Delivering superior customer service
- Achieving lower costs than rivals
- Having a proprietary manufacturing technology
- Having shorter lead times in developing and testing new products
- Having a well-known brand name and reputation
- Giving customers more value for their money

Companies can gain or sustain each of these sources of competitive advantage by effectively using information systems. Returning to our loan example, a person with a strategic view of information systems would choose a computer-based loan application process because it can help achieve the organization's strategic plan to process loan appli-

FIGURE 3.6

Sources of competitive advantage.

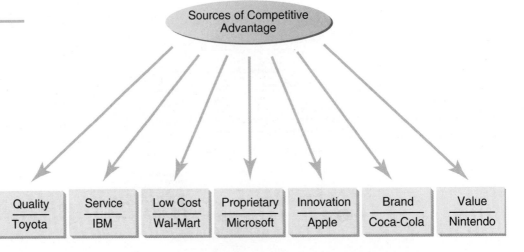

The IT Department Often *Knows*

Picture this scenario: You are a member of the IT department, working for a large international company. As part of your regular duties, consistent with the company's Internet usage policy that you helped develop, you are monitoring employees' Web surfing habits using a product developed for that purpose when you discover that a well-liked senior executive has visited several pornographic sites. He has also downloaded pornographic photos of women and children to his company computer's hard drive. What do you do? Do you follow the policy, risking the wrath of the executive in question who has hiring and firing authority? Or do you say nothing, rationalizing that alienating this executive, whom you have liked and trusted, could make your life miserable?

Such ethical dilemmas are becoming increasingly common, as technology for monitoring Internet use has improved and as IT departments are more often charged with this duty. Furthermore, IT team members within an organization have privileged access to large amounts of digital information—both work-related and private—and the technical savvy to manipulate that information. IT workers can uncover information they would rather not know, as in the above scenario, or they can uncover evidence of crimes such as embezzlement or industrial espionage. They can peek at private salary information and private e-mails or invade their coworkers' private cyberspace and cover their tracks so no one knows.

As in any profession, there are laws, codes of ethics, company policies, and standards of professional and personal behavior to guide IT employees, but the line between ethical and unethical behavior often blurs. If the behavior in question, such as peeking at salary figures, is not against the law, is it unethical? IT professionals often grapple with such decisions. According to the experts, the following strategies can help:

The company should have an easily understood policy for the use of IT equipment and company data, including guidelines for using the Internet, and should make sure that employees understand the policy. Employees should also be told what to do if they discover improper or illegal use of company equipment and/or data, and how to report violations up the chain of command. A clearly understood company policy, with whistle-blower provisions that protect employees who report infractions, can remove fear of reprisal or reluctance to report a friend.

If you, as an IT employee, discover data or behavior that violates company policy, report the infraction and then let the company handle it. In a perfect world, the company's management will make the appropriate decision. In the real-life scenario detailed above, however, the IT employee followed this procedure but the senior executive manufactured an excuse that the company accepted. The executive who stored pornography on his company-owned computer was not fired but was transferred to another country. The IT employee who reported the violation followed protocol but has since wished he had notified the FBI. He feared for his job, however, so he did not. Not the best of outcomes, but one the employee has had to accept.

Just as medical professionals, attorneys, and engineers have professional codes of ethics, IT professionals also need such a document so that both IT personnel and their employers are clear on the standards of the profession. For instance, should an employer ask his IT team to install unlicensed software on company PCs? Should an IT employee use his technical skills to steal information from the company that might be personally beneficial to him or her? Should a systems manager use nonprofessional methods to solve a company's networking problems, knowing that the network will crash when his or her replacement, who goes strictly by the book, tries to modify the system? A professional code of IT ethics would make clear, both to IT personnel and their employers, that the answer to all three questions is "no."

When people think of ethics they often think of personal values, says Stephen Northcutt, director of training and certification for the SANS Institute, and coauthor with Cynthia Madden of *IT Ethics Handbook: Right and Wrong for IT Professionals*. While the authors state that personal values are undoubtedly an important part of ethics, because of rapid advances in information technology, businesses must not rely entirely on employees' personal standards. Furthermore, businesses must also be aware of the ethical standards necessary for the entire organization as a whole. If ethical standards are not emphasized for IT departments, chances are the entire business cuts ethical corners in other areas as well, and the result is often disastrous. Think Enron.

Based on:

Harbert, T. (2007, October 29). Ethics in IT: Dark secrets, ugly truths—and little guidance. *Computerworld*. Retrieved May 11, 2008, from http://www.computerworld.com/action/article.do?command=viewArticleBasic&articleId=304308.

Monaghan, J. (2005, August 15). Ethics in system management. *Computerworld*. Retrieved May 11, 2008, from http://blogs.computerworld.com/node/777.

Norcutt, S., and Madden, C. 2004. *IT ethics handbook: Right and wrong for IT professionals*. Rockland, MA: Syngress.

SANS Institute (n.d.). Retrieved May 11, 2008, from http://www.sans.org/training/description.php?tid=2072.

cations faster and better than rivals and to improve the selection criteria for loans. This process and the supporting information system add value to the organization and match the organization's strategy. It is, therefore, essential to the long-term survival of the organization. If, on the other hand, managers determine that the organization's strategy is to grow and generate new products and services, the computer-based loan application process and the underlying system might not be an efficient, effective use of resources, even though the system could provide automating and learning benefits.

Information Systems and Value Chain Analysis

Managers use value chain analysis to identify opportunities to use information systems for competitive advantage (Porter, 1985, 2001; Shank and Govindarajan, 1993). Think of an organization as a big input/output process. At one end, supplies are purchased and brought into the organization (see Figure 3.7). The organization integrates those supplies to create products and services that it markets, sells, and then distributes to customers. The organization provides customer service after the sale of these products and services. Throughout this process, opportunities arise for employees to add value to the organization by acquiring supplies in a more effective manner, improving products, and selling more products. This set of activities that add value throughout the organization is known as the **value chain** within an organization.

Value chain analysis is the process of analyzing an organization's activities to determine where value is added to products and/or services and what costs are incurred for doing so. Because IS can automate many activities along the value chain, value chain analysis has become a popular tool for applying IS for competitive advantage. In value chain analysis, you first draw the value chain for your organization by fleshing out each of the activities, functions, and processes where value is or should be added. Next, you determine the costs—and the factors that drive costs or cause them to fluctuate—within each of the areas in your value chain diagram. You then benchmark (compare) your value chain and associated costs with those of your competitors. You can then make changes and improvements in your value chain to either gain or sustain competitive advantage.

The Role of Information Systems in Value Chain Analysis

The use of information systems has become one of the primary ways that organizations improve their value chains. In Figure 3.8 we show a sample value chain and some ways that use of information systems can improve productivity within it. For example, many organizations use the Internet to connect businesses with one another electronically so they can exchange orders, invoices, and receipts online in real time. Using the Internet has become a popular method for improving the front end of the organizational value chain. In fact, many firms now use the Internet for such business-to-business interactions; these systems are called *extranets* (described in greater detail in Chapter 5—Enabling Commerce Using the Internet).

FIGURE 3.7

A sample generic organizational value chain.

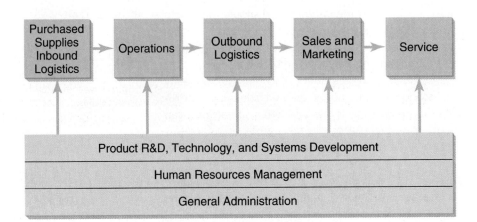

FIGURE 3.8

Sample value chain and corresponding sample uses of information systems to add value.

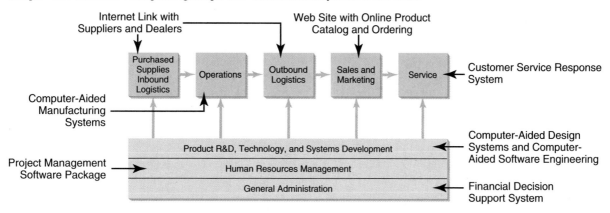

The Technology/Strategy Fit

You might be asking: If any information system helps do things faster and better and helps save money, who cares whether it matches the company's strategy? Good question. If money grew on trees, you probably would build and use just about every information system you could imagine. Organizations could build many different valuable systems, but they are constrained by time and money to build only those that add the most value: those that help automate and learn as well as have strategic value. In most cases, you do not want systems that do not match the strategy, even if they offer automating and learning benefits. Further, while spending on information systems is rising, most companies are willing to spend money on projects only when they can see clear, significant value.

Given this focus on the value that the system will add, you probably do not want a system that helps differentiate your products based on high quality when the organizational strategy is to be the overall industry low-cost leader. In other words, if a firm were pursuing a strategy for low-cost leadership, investments to help drive costs down would be valued over those that didn't.

We should also caution that merely choosing and implementing an emerging information system is not sufficient to gain or sustain competitive advantage. In any significant information systems implementation, there must be commensurate, significant organizational change. This typically comes in the form of *business process management (BPM)* and other similar methods of improving the functioning of the organization as opposed to merely dropping in an information system with no attempts at changing and improving the organization. We will talk more in Chapter 9—Building Organizational Partnerships Using Enterprise Information Systems—about the role of BPM for transforming organizational business processes.

Making the Business Case for an Information System

Given that money does not grow on trees, people in organizations are constantly asking for justification before spending money on anything, especially information systems. Before people are willing to spend money to build a new information system or spend more money on an existing system, they want to be convinced that this will be a good investment. Will the system provide automating, learning, and/or strategic benefits? The phrase that is used to describe the process of identifying, quantifying, and presenting the value provided by an information system is **making the business case**.

Business Case Objectives

What does making the business case for an information system mean? Think for a moment about what defense lawyers do in court trials. They carefully build a strong, integrated set of arguments and evidence to prove that their clients are innocent: They build and present

Rootkits: Sony's Secret

In November 2005, Mark Russinovich was testing computer security software he had cowritten when he discovered something new and uninvited hiding deep inside his PC. Russinovich is an experienced programmer who has written a book about the Windows operating system, and even he could not immediately identify the interloper. Russinovich finally traced the foreign object to code left behind when he purchased and played a Van Zant album from Amazon.com.

The album was produced by Sony BMG Music Entertainment and had been advertised as "copyright protected" when Russinovich bought it. He later found that the "protection" consisted of code called a "rootkit," a cloaking mechanism that was installed on his hard drive without his permission. Each time the CD was played, the program behind the rootkit notified Sony BMG.

Russinovich posted his discovery on his blog, immediately igniting a discussion about Sony BMG's methods. Copyright protection was one thing, the debaters said, but Sony BMG had gone too far.

The rootkit itself was not harmful to computers, experts explained, but it could serve as a hidden portal for viruses and Trojan horses. Shortly after the Sony rootkit news was publicized, virus makers did, indeed, exploit the rootkit access to spread infection via a Trojan horse. Thereafter, Sony announced it would quit distributing CDs that contained the rootkit, and the company has since issued uninstall instructions to customers.

Sony BMG argued that it sought only to protect the copyright of songs it produced. The British company that authored the software Sony used said it had tested the program and had not found it a problem. CD customers, however, begged to differ. It was sneaky, they countered, and not only took away control of their own computers but also left them vulnerable to malicious intruders. Attorneys General in Texas and California filed lawsuits that Sony settled in December 2006, paying $1.5 million in penalties. Consumers were offered refunds in a class action lawsuit settled in May 2006, and the Texas and California litigation also compensated consumers for damage the rootkit code caused.

In 2007, Sony was again under fire when a rootkit was discovered in the company's biometric Micro Vault USM-F thumb drive, which could allow hackers access to users' PCs. Sony denied any knowledge of the rootkit, claiming the Taiwanese authors of the software were apparently unaware of the potential for compromised computer security.

Which side of the debate could you argue?

Based on:

Borland, J. (2005, November 11). FAQ: Sony's 'rootkit' CDs. *CNET News.com.* Retrieved May 11, 2008, from http://www.news.com/FAQ-Sonys-rootkit-CDs/2100-1029_3-5946760.html.

Kirk, J. (2008, March 28). Analyst: Money will lead to more mobile spying programs. *Computerworld.* Retrieved May 11, 2008, from http://www.computerworld.com/action/article.do?command=viewArticleBasic&articleId=9072798.

Marson, I. (2006, January 17). "Sony rootkit victims in every state, researcher says," *CNET News.com.* Retrieved May 11, 2008, from http://www.news.com/Sony-rootkit-victims-in-every-state,-researcher-says/2100-1029_3-6027857.html.

Reimer, J. (2007, September 2). Another Sony rootkit worms its way to the surface. *ars technica.* Retrieved May 11, 2008, from http://arstechnica.com/news.ars/post/20070902-another-sony-rootkit-worms-its-way-to-the-surface.html.

---

their case to those who will pass judgment on their clients. In much the same way, people in business often have to build a strong, integrated set of arguments and evidence to prove that an information system is adding value to the organization or its constituents. This is, in business lingo, "making the business case" for a system.

As a business professional, you will be called on to make the business case for systems and other capital investments. As a finance, accounting, marketing, or management professional, you are likely to be involved in this process and will therefore need to know how to effectively make the business case for a system and to understand the relevant organizational issues involved. It will be in the organization's best interest—and in your own—to ferret out systems that are not adding value. In these cases, you will need to either improve the systems or replace them.

Making the business case is as important for proposed systems as it is for existing systems. For a proposed system, the case will be used to determine whether the new system is a "go" or a "no go." For an existing system, the case will be used to determine whether the company will continue to fund the system. Whether a new system or an existing one is being considered, your goal is to make sure that the system adds value, that it helps the firm to achieve its strategy and competitive advantage over its rivals, and that money is being spent wisely.

The Productivity Paradox

Unfortunately, while it is easy to quantify the costs associated with developing an information system, it is often difficult to quantify tangible productivity gains from its use. Over the past several years, the press has given a lot of attention to the impact of information systems investments on worker productivity. In many cases, IS expenditures, salaries, and the number of people on the IS staff have all been rising, but results from these investments have been disappointing. For instance, the information and technology research firm Gartner reports that worldwide spending on IS surpassed $3.4 trillion in 2008 and is forecast to increase to $3.6 trillion in 2009. American and Canadian companies are spending, on average, 3.9 percent of company revenues on IS investments. As a result, justifying the costs for IS investments has been a hot topic among senior managers at many firms. In particular, "white-collar" productivity, especially in the service sector, has not increased at the rate one might expect, given the trillions of dollars spent.

Why has it been difficult to show that these vast expenditures on information systems have led to productivity gains? Have information systems somehow failed us, promising increases in performance and productivity and then failing to deliver on that promise? Determining the answer is not easy. Information systems may have increased productivity, but other forces may have simultaneously worked to reduce it, the end results being difficult to identify. Factors such as government regulation, more complex tax codes and stricter financial reporting requirements (such as the Sarbanes-Oxley Act; see Chapter 7—Securing Information Systems), and more complex products can all have major impacts on a firm's productivity.

It is also true that information systems built with the best intentions may have had unintended consequences—employees spending excessive amounts of time surfing the Web to check sports scores on the ESPN Web site, volumes of electronic junk mail being sent by Internet marketing companies or from personal friends, and company PCs being used to download and play software games (see Figure 3.9). In these situations, information systems can result in less efficient and less effective communication among employees and less productive uses of employee time than before the IS was implemented. Does this kind of employee behavior affect productivity figures? You bet it does. Still, in general, sound IS investments should increase organizational productivity. If this is so, why have organizations not been able to show larger productivity gains? A number of reasons have been given for the apparent **productivity paradox** of IS investments (Figure 3.10). This is examined next.

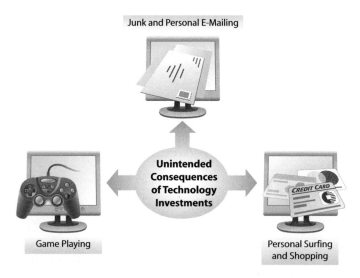

FIGURE 3.9

Unintended consequences can limit the productivity gains from information systems investments.

Measurement Problems In many cases, the benefits of information systems are difficult to pinpoint because firms may be measuring the wrong things. Often, the biggest increases in productivity result from increased **system effectiveness** (i.e., the extent to which a system enables people and/or the firm to accomplish goals or tasks well). Unfortunately, many business metrics focus on **system efficiency** (i.e., the extent to which a system enables people and/or the firm to do things faster, at lower cost, or with relatively little time and effort). Although information systems may have real benefits, those benefits may not be detected. Effectiveness improvements are sometimes difficult to measure. Also, expected benefits from IS are not always defined in advance, so they are never seen: In order to see something, you usually have to know what to look for. Measurement problems are not limited to traditional office information systems either. All types of systems have potential measurement problems.

A good example of measurement problems associated with IS investment is the use of automatic teller machines (ATMs). How much have ATMs contributed to banking productivity? Traditional statistics might look at the number of transactions or output as some multiple of the labor input needed to produce that output (e.g., a transaction). However, such statistics do not work well for the ATM example. The number of checks written may actually decrease with ATMs, making productivity statistics appear lower. On the other hand, can you imagine a bank staying competitive without offering ATM services? The value added for the customer in terms of improved delivery of services almost dictates that banks offer a wide range of ATM services in today's competitive market. Deploying these information systems has become a **strategic necessity**—something an organization must do in order to survive.

Time Lags A second explanation for why productivity is difficult to demonstrate for IS investments is that a significant time lag may occur from when a company makes the investment until that investment is translated into improvement in the bottom line. Brynjolfsson (1993) reports that lags of two to three years are typical before strong organizational impacts of IS investments are felt.

The explanation for lags is fairly simple. At one level, it takes time for people to become proficient at using new technologies. Remember the first time you ever used a computer? It probably seemed difficult and cryptic to use. It may have taken you more time to figure out how to use the computer than it would have to complete a task manually. Nonetheless, the computer probably became easier to use as you became more proficient

FIGURE 3.10

Factors leading to the information systems productivity paradox.

Measurement

Time Lags

Productivity Paradox

Redistribution

Mismanagement

with it. If you multiply this learning curve over everyone in an organization who may be using a given technology, you can see that until a firm has some experience in using a technology, the benefits associated with using it may be deferred. Everyone must become proficient with that technology in order to gain the benefits from its use.

It may also take some time before the tangible benefits of a new information system can be felt. Let us return to our ATM example. It may take years from the first implementation of this new system before the benefits may be felt. The system must first be implemented, which could take years in a large, widely distributed financial institution. Then the system must be fine-tuned to operate optimally and must be tied into all of the necessary subsystems. Employees and customers must be trained in how to use the system properly, and it may take years before they become truly proficient and comfortable with using it.

When the system is working well and people are using it efficiently, productivity gains may be measured. It takes time for the system to produce any labor savings within the organization and for customers' satisfaction levels to rise. Given that the ATMs have become a strategic necessity, perhaps one of their benefits is that they enable banks to gain—or simply keep—customers. It can take years for a financial institution to feel the effects of its deployment of ATM machines.

If time lags are the reason IS investments do not show up in productivity figures, then eventually IS managers should be able to report some very good news about organizational return on IS investment. Still, for managers faced with the day-to-day pressures of coming up with a demonstrable impact on firm performance, the explanation of time lags may not be very helpful or comforting.

Redistribution   A third possible explanation for why IS productivity figures are not easy to find is that IS may be beneficial for individual firms but not for a particular industry or the economy as a whole. Particularly in competitive situations, IS may be used to redistribute the pieces of the pie rather than making the whole pie bigger. In other words, strategic information systems may help one firm to increase its market share; however, this may come at the expense of another firm, which loses its market share as consumers transfer to the first firm. The result for the industry or economy as a whole is a wash—that is, the same number of products is being sold and the same number of dollars is being spent across all the firms. The only difference is that now one firm is getting a larger share of the business, while another firm is getting a smaller share.

While such an explanation may be feasible for some markets and industries, it does not fully explain why productivity figures would be stagnant at the level of one individual firm. Shouldn't each organization be more productive than before? Part of the problem is that our expectations of performance are somewhat biased. We tend to take for granted that technology fundamentally enables people to do things that would otherwise be nearly impossible. In effect, we continue to "raise the bar" with our expectations of what people can accomplish when supported by technology. For example, you might wonder whether the electronic spreadsheet on the PC on your desk is really helping you do your job better. To best answer this, you should think back to what it was like to create a spreadsheet by hand. It was a much slower process, was far more likely to produce errors, and left people significantly less time to work on other, more important tasks.

Mismanagement   A fourth explanation is that the IS has not been implemented and managed well. Some believe that people often simply build bad systems, implement them poorly, and rely on technology fixes when the organization has problems that require a joint technology/process solution. Rather than increasing outputs or profits, IS investments might merely be a temporary bandage and may serve to mask or even increase organizational slack and inefficiency. Also, as we mentioned in Chapter 1, an information system can be only as effective as the business model that it serves. Bad business models can't be overcome by good information systems. Similarly, the rapid decrease in processing time enabled by IS can result in unanticipated bottlenecks. For example, if automation has increased the potential output of a system but part of that system relies on human input, then the system can operate only as fast as the human can feed input into or through that system.

Powerful Partnerships

Microsoft's Bill Gates and Paul Allen

Think of who's who in IT and the first names that come to mind are probably William (Bill) Henry Gates III and Paul Gardner Allen. The two are almost cliché in the annals of technology: nerds as high school students at Lakeside School in Seattle, who begged, borrowed, and stole computer usage time; college students with a brilliant idea; entrants on the ground floor of computer technology when their programming skills paid off.

Both Gates and Allen were born in Seattle to upper-middle-class, educated parents, and both attended Lakeside High School in Seattle, where they formed a friendship based on their mutual interest and skills in computer technology. Gates went to Harvard after graduating from high school in 1973, but he dropped out in 1975 to run the business he and Allen cofounded called "Micro-Soft." The two worked out of company headquarters in Albuquerque, New Mexico, selling a language interpreter for BASIC, the programming language Gates wrote while a student at Harvard.

Allen, born in 1953, is two years older than Gates, so was halfway through Washington State University in Pullman when Gates enrolled in Harvard. Both men dropped out of college in 1975 to devote all their time to their new project, now called Microsoft.

A partnership formed with IBM to install Microsoft's MS-DOS operating system on all IBM PCs was profitable early on and set the stage for Microsoft to become a major player in the PC operating system business. Windows. Enough said.

Allen stepped down from his position at Microsoft in 1983 after a bout with Hodgkin's Disease. His cancer was successfully treated with radiation treatments and a bone marrow transplant, and Allen went on to found new profitable ventures on his own.

In 1998, Microsoft was prosecuted for violations of the Sherman Anti-Trust Law. In *United States v. Microsoft*, prosecutors alleged that Microsoft had committed monopoly violations in operating system and Web browser sales. In his trial testimony, Gates was described as arrogant, evasive, and uncooperative. Other Microsoft executives who testified were also labeled uncooperative, and the company was found guilty of monopolization under the Sherman Anti-Trust Law. Through a series of appeals, penalties against Microsoft have been modified, but the original verdict was allowed to stand. Microsoft agreed to settle the case in 2001. As of 2008, Microsoft continued to comply with the settlement terms.

FIGURE 3.11

Microsoft's Bill Gates and Paul Allen.

Both Gates and Allen have withdrawn from active involvement with Microsoft's management. Gates announced in 2006 that he was retiring from Microsoft and would instead focus his attention on the charitable foundation he and his wife, Melinda, formed in 2000. The Bill & Melinda Gates Foundation is the largest charitable organization in the world, with assets that have allowed the foundation to give away approximately $29 billion to various charities since 2001. Warren Buffet, Gates' friend, who is rated number one on the *Forbes* list of wealthiest people in the world, matches Gates' foundation grants with his own.

Today Bill Gates is number three on the list of the world's richest people, with a net worth of approximately $58 billion. Paul Allen, worth about $16.8 billion, is not within the top twenty on the world's billionaires list, but he has found satisfaction as owner of the Seattle Seahawks and chairman of Vulcan Inc., his private asset management company. Allen also donates to favorite causes, and he continues to serve as a consultant to Microsoft.

Regardless of Microsoft's future direction, Bill Gates and Paul Allen will always be at the top of the list of powerful partners in information technology.

Based on:

Bill Gates. (2008, May 10). In *Wikipedia, the free encyclopedia*. Retrieved May 12, 2008, from http://en.wikipedia.org/w/index.php?title=Bill_Gates&oldid=211389102.

Paul Allen. (2008, May 8). In *Wikipedia, the free encyclopedia*. Retrieved May 12, 2008, from http://en.wikipedia.org/w/index.php?title=Paul_Allen&oldid= 210974855.

U.S. vs. Microsoft: Current case. (n.d.). Retrieved May 11, 2008, from http://www.usdoj.gov/atr/cases/ms_index.htm.

United States Microsoft antitrust case. (2008, May 5). In *Wikipedia, the free encyclopedia*. Retrieved May 12, 2008, from http://en.wikipedia.org/w/index.php?title=United_States_Microsoft_antitrust_case&oldid=210317436.

Eli Goldratt very aptly showed how this happens in his best-selling book *The Goal*, in which he uses the format of a novel to show how people can think logically and consistently about organizational problems in order to determine true cause-and-effect relationships between their actions and the results. In the novel, the characters do this so well that they save their manufacturing plant and make it successful. Spending money on IS does not help increase the firm's productivity until all of the bottlenecks are addressed. From a management standpoint, this means that managers must be sure that they evaluate the entire process being automated, making changes to old processes as necessary, in order to truly benefit from IS investment. If managers simply overlay new technology on old processes, sometimes known as "paving the cow path," then they will likely be disappointed in the meager productivity gains reaped from their investment.

If it is so difficult to quantify the benefits of information systems for individual firms and for entire industries, why do managers continue to invest in information systems? The answer is that competitive pressures force managers to invest in information systems whether they like it or not. You might ask, then, so why waste time making the business case for a system? Why not just build them? The answer: Money doesn't grow on trees. These are typically expensive projects for companies, and a strong case must be made for investing in them.

Making a Successful Business Case

People make a variety of arguments in their business cases for information systems. When managers make the business case for an information system, they typically base their arguments on faith, fear, and/or facts (Wheeler, 2002a). (Wheeler also adds a fourth "F," that being for "fiction," and notes that, unfortunately, managers sometimes base their arguments on pure fiction, which is not only bad for their careers but also not at all healthy for their firms.) Table 3.2 shows examples of these three types of arguments.

Do not assume that you must base your business case on facts only. It is entirely appropriate to base the business case on faith, fear, or facts (see Figure 3.12). Indeed, the strongest and most comprehensive business case will include a little of each type of argument. In the following sections, we talk about each of these types of arguments for the business case.

TABLE 3.2 Three Types of Arguments Commonly Made in the Business Case for an Information System

Type of Argument	Description	Example
Faith	Arguments based on beliefs about organizational strategy, competitive advantage, industry forces, customer perceptions, market share, and so on.	"I know I don't have good data to back this up, but I'm convinced that having this customer relationship management system will enable us to serve our customers significantly better than our competitors do and, as a result, we'll beat the competition. . . . You just have to take it on faith."
Fear	Arguments based on the notion that if the system is not implemented, the firm will lose out to the competition or, worse, go out of business.	"If we don't implement this enterprise resource planning system, we'll get killed by our competitors because they're all implementing these kinds of systems. . . . We either do this or we die."
Fact	Arguments based on data, quantitative analysis, and/or indisputable factors.	"This analysis shows that implementing the inventory control system will help us reduce errors by 50 percent, reduce operating costs by 15 percent a year, increase production by 5 percent a year, and will pay for itself within eighteen months."

Business Case Arguments Based on Faith In some situations, arguments based on faith (or fear) can be the most compelling and can drive the decision to invest in an information system despite the lack of any hard data on system costs or even in the face of some data that say that the dollar costs for the system will be high. Arguments based on faith often hold that an information system must be implemented in order to achieve the organization's strategy effectively and to gain or sustain a competitive advantage over rivals, despite the dollar costs associated with that system. Given the power of modern information systems, their rapid evolution, and their pervasiveness in business today, information systems have become a common tool for enabling business strategy. Consequently, the business cases for systems are frequently grounded in strategic arguments.

For example, a firm has set as its strategy that it will be the dominant, global force in its industry. As a result, this firm must adopt a global telecommunications network and a variety of collaboration technologies, such as e-mail, desktop videoconferencing, and groupware tools, in order to enable employees from different parts of the globe to work together effectively and efficiently. Similarly, a firm that has set as its strategy that it will have a broad scope—producing products and services across a wide range of consumer needs—must adopt some form of an enterprise resource planning system to coordinate business activities across its diverse product lines. For example, Procter & Gamble produces dozens of household products that are consumed under various brand names

FIGURE 3.12

A successful business case will be based on faith, fear, and fact.

throughout the world—Noxzema, Folgers coffee, Tide laundry detergent, Cover Girl cosmetics, Crest toothpaste, and Pringles potato chips, to name a few. Integration across various product lines and divisions is a key goal for IS investments. Such integration allows Procter & Gamble to streamline inventory, thus improving efficiency.

In short, successful business case arguments based on faith should clearly describe the firm's mission and objectives, the strategy for achieving them, and the types of information systems that are needed in order to enact the strategy. A word of caution is warranted here. In today's business environment, cases based solely on strategic arguments, with no hard numbers demonstrating the value of the information system under consideration, are not likely to be funded.

Business Case Arguments Based on Fear There are several different factors to take into account when making a business case in which you will provide arguments based on fear. These include a number of factors involving competition and other elements of the industry in which the firm operates, which are shown in Figure 3.13 (Harris and Katz, 1991). For example, a mature and stable industry, such as the automotive industry, may need IS simply to maintain the current pace of operations. While having the newest IS available may be nice, it may not be needed to stay in business. However, a company in a newer, more volatile industry, such as the cellular phone industry, may find it more important to be on the leading edge of technology in order to compete effectively in the marketplace. Likewise, some industries are more highly regulated than others. In these cases, companies can use IS to control processes and ensure compliance with appropriate regulations. The argument for the business case here would be something like "If we do not implement this information system, we run the risk of being sued or, worse, being thrown in jail" (see Chapter 7 and the discussion related to IS controls).

Probably the most important industry factor that can affect IS investment is the nature of competition or rivalry in the industry. For example, when competition in an industry is high and use of information systems is rampant, as it is in the personal computer industry, strategic necessity, more than anything else, forces firms to adopt information systems. Given how tight profit margins are in the PC industry, Dell and other manufacturers must use inventory control systems, Web-based purchasing and customer service, and a host of other systems that help them to be more effective and efficient. If they do not adopt these information systems, they will likely go out of business. One framework often used to analyze the competition within an industry is Porter's notion of the five primary competitive forces (Porter, 1979): (1) the rivalry among competing sellers in your industry, (2) the threat of potential new entrants into your industry, (3) the bargaining power that customers have within your industry, (4) the bargaining power that suppliers have within your industry, and (5) the potential for substitute products from other industries (see Figure 3.14).

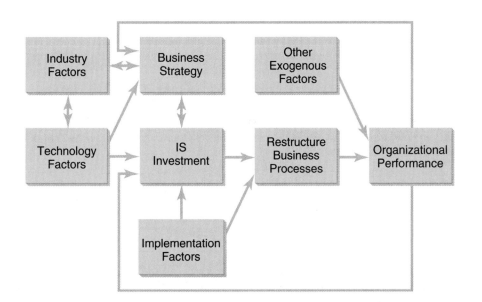

FIGURE 3.13

Factors in IS investment decisions.

FIGURE 3.14

Five forces influence the level of
competitiveness in an industry.

Table 3.3 provides examples of how IS can have an impact on the various competitive
forces in an industry.

Porter's five-forces model of competition can help you determine which specific technologies will be more or less useful, depending on the nature of your industry. You can
then use these as the basis for your arguments as to whether to invest in new or existing
information systems. This kind of industry-based business case might not enable you to
attach specific monetary benefits to particular information systems, but it can show you
and others that specific uses of particular systems are necessary to compete in your markets. Business case arguments formulated this way sound something like "If we do not
implement this information system, our competitors are going to beat us on price, we will
lose market share, and we will go out of business."

Business Case Arguments Based on Fact   Many people, including most chief financial officers, want to see the business case for an information system based on some convincing, quantitative analysis that proves beyond the shadow of a doubt that the benefits of
the system will outweigh the costs. The most common way to prove this is to provide a

TABLE 3.3 IS Impact on Competitive Forces

Competitive Force	Implication for Firm	Potential Use of IS to Combat Competitive Force
Traditional rivals within your industry	Competition in price, product distribution, and service	Implement enterprise resource planning system to reduce costs and be able to act and react more quickly, implement Web site to offer better service to customers
Threat of new entrants into your market	Increased capacity in the industry, reduced prices, and decreased market share	Better Web site to reach customers and differentiate product; inventory control system to lower costs and better manage excess capacity
Customers' bargaining power	Reduced prices, need for increased quality, demand for more services	Implement customer relationship management system to serve customers better, implement computer-aided design and/or computer-aided manufacturing system to improve product quality
Suppliers' bargaining power	Increased costs, reduced quality	Use Internet to establish closer electronic ties with suppliers and to create relationships with new suppliers located far away
Threat of substitute products from other industries	Potential returns on products, decreased market share, losing customers for life	Use decision support system and customer purchase database to better assess trends and customer needs, use computer-aided design systems to redesign products

Based on: Applegate, Austin, and McFarlan (2007).

detailed cost-benefit analysis of the information system. Although this step is critical, the manager must remember that there are inherent difficulties in and limits to cost-benefit analyses for information systems. To illustrate how a cost-benefit analysis could be used to build a fact-based business case, let us consider the development of a Web-based order entry system for a relatively small firm.

Identifying Costs.   One goal of a cost-benefit analysis is to accurately determine the **total cost of ownership (TCO)** for the IS investment. TCO is focused on understanding not only the total cost of *acquisition* but also all costs associated with ongoing *use and maintenance* of a system. Consequently, costs can usually be divided into two categories: **nonrecurring costs** and **recurring costs**. Nonrecurring costs are one-time costs that are not expected to continue after the system is implemented. These include costs for things such as the Web server, telecommunications equipment, Web server software, HTML editors, Java, Flash, and other tools. These one-time costs also include the costs of attracting and training a Webmaster, renovating some office space to serve as the location of the Web server, and paying analysts and programmers to develop the system.

Recurring costs are ongoing costs that occur throughout the life cycle of systems development, implementation, and maintenance. Recurring costs include the salary and benefits of the Webmaster and any other personnel assigned to maintain the system, upgrades and maintenance for the system components, monthly fees paid to a local Internet service provider, and the continuing costs for the space in which the Webmaster works or the *collocation facility* where the server resides. Personnel costs are usually the largest recurring costs, and the Web-based system is no exception in this regard. These recurring expenses can go well beyond the Webmaster to include expenses for help desk personnel, maintenance programmers, IS management, and data entry personnel.

The sample costs described thus far have been fairly **tangible costs** that are easy to quantify. Some **intangible costs** ought to be accounted for as well, even though they will not fit neatly into the quantitative analysis. These might include the costs of reducing traditional sales, losing some customers that are not "Web ready," or losing customers if the Web application is poorly designed or not on par with competitors' sites. You can choose either to quantify these in some way (i.e., determine the cost of losing a customer) or simply to reserve these as important costs to consider outside of—but along with—the quantitative cost-benefit analysis.

Identifying Benefits.   Next, you determine both **tangible benefits** and **intangible benefits**. Some tangible benefits are relatively easy to determine. For example, you can estimate that the increased customer reach of the new Web-based system will result in at least a modest increase in sales. Based on evidence from similar projects, you might estimate, say, a 5 percent increase in sales the first year, a 10 percent increase the second year, and a 15 percent increase the third year. In addition, you might also include as tangible benefits the reduction of order entry errors because orders will now be tracked electronically and shipped automatically. You could calculate the money previously lost on faulty and lost orders, along with the salaries and wages of personnel assigned to find and fix these orders, and then consider the reduction of these costs as a quantifiable benefit of the new system. Cost avoidance is a legitimate, quantifiable benefit of an information system. Similarly, the new system may enable the company to use fewer order entry clerks or redeploy these personnel to other, more important functions within the company. You could consider these cost reductions as benefits of the new system.

A Web-based system has intangible benefits as well. Some intangible benefits of this new system might include faster turnaround on fulfilling orders and resulting improvements in customer service. These are real benefits, but they might be hard to quantify with confidence. Perhaps an even more intangible benefit would be the overall improved perception of the firm. Customers might consider it more progressive and customer-service-oriented than its rivals; in addition to attracting new customers, this might increase the value of the firm's stock if it were a publicly traded firm. Another intangible benefit might be simply that it was a strategic necessity to offer customers Web-based ordering to keep pace with rivals. While these intangibles are difficult to quantify, they must be considered along with the more quantitative analysis of benefits. In fact, the intangible benefits of this

Web-based system might be so important that they could carry the day despite an inconclusive or even negative cost-benefit analysis.

Performing Cost-Benefit Analyses.   An example of a simplified **cost-benefit analysis** that contrasts the total expected tangible costs versus the tangible benefits is presented in Figure 3.15. Notice the fairly large investment up front, with another significant outlay in the fifth year for a system upgrade. You could now use the net costs/benefits for each year as the basis of your conclusion about this system. Alternatively, you could perform a **break-even analysis**—a type of cost-benefit analysis to identify at what point (if ever) tangible benefits equal tangible costs (note that breakeven occurs early in the second year of the system's life in this example)—or a more formal **net-present-value analysis** of the relevant cash flow streams associated with the system at the organization's **discount rate** (i.e., the rate of return used by an organization to compute the present value of future cash flows). In any event, this cost-benefit analysis helps you make the business case for this proposed Web-based order fulfillment system. It clearly shows that the investment for this system is relatively small, and the company can fairly quickly recapture the investment. In addition, there appear to be intangible strategic benefits to deploying this system. This analysis—and the accompanying arguments and evidence—goes a long way toward convincing senior managers in the firm that this new system makes sense.

FIGURE 3.15

Worksheet showing a simplified cost-benefit analysis for the Web-based order fulfillment system.

		2010	2011	2012	2013	2014
Costs						
Nonrecurring						
Hardware		$ 20,000				
Software		$ 7,500				
Networking		$ 4,500				
Infrastructure		$ 7,500				
Personnel		$100,000				
Recurring						
Hardware			$ 500	$ 1,000	$ 2,500	$ 15,000
Software			$ 500	$ 500	$ 1,000	$ 2,500
Networking			$ 250	$ 250	$ 500	$ 1,000
Service fees			$ 250	$ 250	$ 250	$ 500
Infrastructure				$ 250	$ 500	$ 1,500
Personnel			$ 60,000	$ 62,500	$ 70,000	$ 90,000
Total costs		$139,500	$ 61,500	$ 64,750	$ 74,750	$110,500
Benefits						
Increased sales		$ 20,000	$ 50,000	$ 80,000	$115,000	$175,000
Error reduction		$ 15,000	$ 15,000	$ 15,000	$ 15,000	$ 15,000
Cost reduction		$100,000	$100,000	$100,000	$100,000	$100,000
Total benefits		$135,000	$165,000	$195,000	$230,000	$290,000
Net costs/benefits		$ (4,500)	$103,500	$130,250	$155,250	$179,500

Comparing Competing Investments.   One method for deciding among different information systems investments or when considering alternative designs for a given system is **weighted multicriteria analysis**, as illustrated in Figure 3.16. For example, suppose that for a given system being considered, there are three alternative designs that could be pursued—A, B, or C. Let's also suppose that early planning meetings identified three key system requirements and four key constraints that could be used to help make a decision on which alternative to pursue. In the left column of Figure 3.16, three system requirements and four constraints are listed. Because not all requirements and constraints are of equal importance, they are weighted on the basis of their relative importance. In other words, you do not have to weight requirements and constraints equally; it is certainly possible to make requirements more or less important than constraints. Weights are arrived at in discussions among the analysis team, users, and sometimes managers. Weights tend to be fairly subjective and, for that reason, should be determined through a process of open discussion to reveal underlying assumptions, followed by an attempt to reach consensus among stakeholders. Notice that the total of the weights for both the requirements and constraints is 100 (percent).

Next, each requirement and constraint is rated on a scale of 1 to 5. A rating of 1 indicates that the alternative does not meet the requirement very well or that the alternative violates the constraint. A rating of 5 indicates that the alternative meets or exceeds the requirement or clearly abides by the constraint. Ratings are even more subjective than weights and should also be determined through open discussion among users, analysts, and managers. For each requirement and constraint, a score is calculated by multiplying the rating for each requirement and each constraint by its weight. The final step is to add up the weighted scores for each alternative. Notice that we have included three sets of totals: for requirements, for constraints, and for overall totals. If you look at the totals for requirements, alternative B or C is the best choice because each meets or exceeds all requirements. However, if you look only at constraints, alternative A is the best choice because it does not violate any constraints. When we combine the totals for requirements and constraints, we see that the best choice is alternative C. Whether alternative C is actually chosen for development, however, is another issue. The decision makers may choose alternative A, knowing that it does not meet two key requirements because, it has the lowest cost. In short, what may appear to be the best choice for a systems development project may not always be the one that ends up being developed. By conducting a thorough analysis, organizations can greatly improve their decision-making performance.

Presenting the Business Case

Up to this point, we have discussed the key issues to consider as you prepare to make the business case for a system. We have also shown you some tools for determining the value that a system adds to an organization. Now you are actually ready to make the case—to

FIGURE 3.16

Criteria	Weight	Alternative A		Alternative B		Alternative C	
		Rating	Score	Rating	Score	Rating	Score
Requirements							
Real-time data entry	18	5	90	5	90	5	90
Automatic reorder	18	1	18	5	90	5	90
Real-time data query	14	1	14	5	70	5	70
	50		122		250		250
Constraints							
Developer costs	15	4	60	5	75	3	45
Hardware costs	15	4	60	4	60	3	45
Operating costs	15	5	75	1	15	5	75
Ease of training	5	5	25	3	15	3	15
	50		220		165		180
Total	100		342		415		430

Alternative projects and system design decisions can be assisted using weighted multicriteria analysis.

Net Stats

Who Is Sharing Files?

Since the recording and entertainment industries have gone after P2P program developers, users, and customers, the term "P2P" has been mostly associated with illegally sharing music and/or video files. The fact is, however, as bandwidth has increased and has become financially and geographically available to more people, the P2P landscape has evolved. Consequently, marketers would do well to target the increasing numbers of computer users who use file sharing to download digital content.

In 2008, Michael Miraflor, a columnist for Clickz, conducted his own online survey, scouring chat rooms, bulletin boards, and online forums where file sharers hang out, to determine who the individuals are that make up the large P2P market. He found that:

- Personalities varied, but all were active consumers who had become accustomed to an on-demand lifestyle.
- All were well informed about current events (including the 2008 U.S. presidential election) and used the Internet as their primary source of information.
- Favorite topics of conversation were the latest technical gadgets, car accessories, and home theater setups; online deals and discounts were also hot topics.

- PC users did not dominate among P2P aficionados—many were Mac addicts.
- Gaming was a part of daily life, and Xbox LIVE accounts were rampant.
- There was much discussion about marketing campaigns for alternate reality games (ARG).
- They wanted to share files when and where it pleased them, and they expressed frustration with digital rights management (DRM) attached to files downloaded from such legitimate sites as iTunes.
- Many were frustrated with the music and entertainment industries for punishing consumers for wanting to download their content.
- Quality in video and audio downloads was important.

While Miraflor's informal survey was not an organized, scientific study, it did reveal the type of computer users to whom P2P marketers might aim their advertising.

Based on:

Miraflor, M. (2008, April 8). Pirates vs. ninjas: Marketing in P2P environments. *The Clickz Network*. Retrieved May 11, 2008, from http://www.clickz.com/showPage.html?page=3629000.

Miraflor, M. (2008, May 2). P2P: Understanding the file-sharing audience. *The Clickz Network*. Retrieved May 11, 2008, from http://www.clickz.com/showPage.html?page=3629334.

present your arguments and evidence to the decision makers in the firm. This task is much like that of a lawyer presenting a persuasive written and oral argument to win a judgment in her client's favor. Making a business case for IS really is not much different. You are simply trying to clearly articulate the value of the investment to your organization.

Know the Audience Depending on the firm, a number of people from various areas of the firm might be involved in the decision-making process for a new IS investment. People from different areas of the firm typically hold very different perspectives about what investments should be made and how those investments should be managed (see Table 3.4). Consequently, presenting the business case for a new IS investment can be quite challenging. Ultimately, a number of factors come into play in making investment decisions, and numerous outcomes can occur (see Figure 3.17). Understanding the audience and the issues important to them is a first step in making an effective presentation. Various ways to improve the development of a business case are examined next.

Convert Benefits to Monetary Terms When making the case for an information systems investment, it is desirable to translate all potential benefits into monetary terms. For example, if a new system saves department managers an hour per day, try to quantify that savings in terms of dollars. Figure 3.18 shows how you might convert time savings into

TABLE 3.4 Characteristics of Different Stakeholders Involved in Making Information Systems Investment Decisions

Stakeholder	Perspective	Focus/Project Characteristics
Management	Representatives or managers from each of the functional areas within the firm	Greater strategic focus; largest project sizes; longest project durations
Steering committee	Representatives from various interest groups within the organization (they may have their own agendas at stake when making investment decisions)	Cross-functional focus; greater organizational change; formal cost-benefit analysis; larger and riskier projects
User department	Representatives of the intended users of the system	Narrow, nonstrategic focus; faster development
IS executive	Has overall responsibility for managing IS development, implementation, and maintenance of selected systems	Integration with existing systems focus; fewer development delays; less concern with cost-benefit analysis

Based on: McKeen, Guimaraes, and Wetherbe (1994).

dollar figures. While merely explaining this benefit as "saving managers' time" makes it sound useful, managers may not consider it a significant enough inducement to warrant spending a significant amount of money. Justifying a $50,000 system because it will "save time" may not be persuasive enough. However, an annual savings of $90,000 is more likely to capture the attention of decision makers and is more likely to result in project approval. Senior managers can easily rationalize a $50,000 expense for a $90,000 savings and can easily see why they should approve such a request. They can also more easily rationalize their decision later on if something goes wrong with the system.

Devise Proxy Variables The situation presented in Figure 3.18 is fairly straightforward. Anyone can see that a $50,000 investment is a good idea because the return on that investment is $90,000 the first year. Unfortunately, not all cases are this clear-cut. In cases in which it is not as easy to quantify the impact of an investment, you can come up with **proxy variables** (i.e., alternative measures of outcomes) to help clarify what the impact on the firm will be. Proxy variables can be used to measure changes in terms of their perceived value to the organization. For example, if mundane administrative tasks are seen as a low value (perhaps a 1 on a 5-point scale), but direct contact with customers is seen as a high value (a rating of 5), you can use these perceptions to indicate how new systems will add value to the organization. In this example, you can show that a new system will allow personnel to have more contact with customers while at the same time reducing the

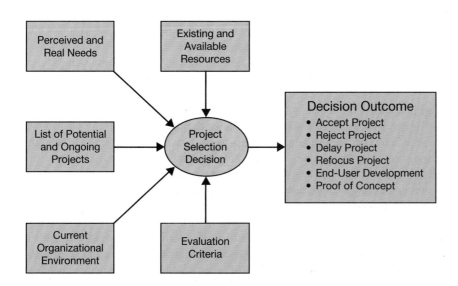

FIGURE 3.17

Investment selection decisions must consider numerous factors and can have numerous outcomes.

FIGURE 3.18

Converting time savings into
dollar figures.

Benefit:	
New system saves at least one hour per day for 12 mid-level managers.	
Quantified as:	
Manager's salary (per hour)	$30.00
Number of managers affected	12
Daily savings (one hour saved × 12 managers)	$360.00
Weekly savings (daily savings × 5)	$1,800.00
Annual savings (weekly savings × 50)	$90,000.00

administrative workload. Senior managers can quickly see that individual workload is being shifted from low-value to high-value activities.

Alternatively, you can create a customer contact scale from 1 to 5, with 1 representing very low customer contact and 5 representing very high customer contact. You can argue that currently your firm rates a 2 on the customer contact scale and that with the new information system your firm will rate a significantly higher number on the scale.

You can communicate these differences using percentages, increases or decreases, and so on—whatever best conveys the idea that the new system is creating changes in work, in performance, and in the way people think about their work. This gives decision makers some relatively solid data on which to base their decision.

Measure What Is Important to Management One of the most important things you can do to show the benefits of a system is one of the simplest: measure what senior managers think is important. You may think this is trivial advice, but you would be surprised how often people calculate impressive-looking statistics in terms of downtime, reliability, and so on, only to find that senior managers disregard or only briefly skim over those figures. You should concentrate on the issues senior business managers care about. The "hot button" issues with senior managers should be easy to discover, and they are not always financial reports. Hot issues with senior managers could include cycle time (how long it takes to process an order), customer feedback, and employee morale. By focusing on what senior business managers believe to be important, you can make the business case for systems in a way that is more meaningful for those managers, which makes selling systems to decision makers much easier. Managers are more likely to buy in to the importance of systems if they can see the impact on areas that are important to them.

Assessing Value for the Information Systems Infrastructure

Howard Rubin, executive vice president of Meta Group, argued that we should take a more holistic view when assessing IS value (*CIO,* June 2004), particularly in areas such as IS infrastructure, where assessing tangible value may be difficult (see Chapter 4). IS infrastructure includes an organization's hardware, software, personnel, and so on. While these things are important and expensive to acquire and maintain, they are often difficult to place a value on. Rubin suggested four categories for assessing investments in regard to their value to the overall infrastructure.

Economic Value First, economic value is the contribution an investment makes toward improving the infrastructure's ability to enhance the profitability of the business. Rubin recommended that we use important business metrics in order to gauge the economic value of a given investment. An airline, for example, might use a metric such as revenue per passenger per mile per year to determine effectiveness. To assess an investment, the airline could then calculate the IS infrastructure cost per passenger mile and observe how investments in the infrastructure over time has an impact on profitability.

Architectural Value Second, architectural value is derived from an investment's ability to extend the infrastructure's capabilities to meet business needs today and in the future. To measure architectural value, "before and after" assessments of infrastructure characteristics such as interoperability, portability, scalability, recoverability, and compatibility can be taken. Rubin recommended that for each area of the business, infrastructure characteristics be rated on a scale of 1 to 10 as to how well various investments influence the infrastructure's ability to meet those needs.

Operational Value Third, operational value is derived from assessing an investment's impact on enabling the infrastructure to better meet business processing requirements. To assess this, Rubin recommended that we measure the impact of not investing in a particular project. For example, what would be the cost of not investing in a new customer relationship management system in terms of lost staff productivity, lost business revenue, or even lost customers?

Regulatory and Compliance Value Fourth, regulatory and compliance value is derived from assessing the extent to which an investment helps to meet requirements for control, security, and integrity as required by a governing body or a key customer. For example, what is the impact of, say, noncompliance with government reporting requirements necessitated by the Sarbanes-Oxley Act of 2002?

Rubin also argues that, where possible, all evaluation measures should be compared with external benchmarks. In any event, these provide a useful framework for more broadly evaluating a particular investment.

Changing Mind-sets About Information Systems

Perhaps the most significant change in the information systems field has been in mind-sets about technology rather than in technology itself. The old way for managers to think about information systems was that information systems are a necessary service, a necessary evil, and a necessary, distasteful expense that is to be minimized. Managers cannot afford to think this way anymore. Successful managers now think of information systems as a competitive asset to be nurtured and invested in. This does not mean that managers should not require a sound business case for every information systems investment. Nor does this mean that managers should not also need to have facts as part of a business case for a system. It does mean, however, that managers must stop thinking about systems as an expense and start thinking about systems as an asset to invest in wisely. Managers have to become strategic about information systems and think of them as an enabler of opportunities.

Valuing Innovations

To differentiate itself, an organization often must deploy new, state-of-the-art technologies to do things even better, faster, and more cheaply than rivals that are using older technologies. Although firms can choose to continually upgrade older systems rather than investing in new systems, these improvements can at best give only a short-lived competitive edge. To gain and sustain significant competitive advantage, firms must often deploy the latest technologies or redeploy and reinvest in existing technologies in clever, new ways.

But with the plethora of new information technologies and systems available, how can you possibly choose winners? Indeed, how can you even keep track of all the new breakthroughs, new products, new versions, and new ways of using technologies? For example, in Figure 3.19 we present a small subset of some new information technologies and systems, ranging from some that are here now and currently being used to some that are easily a decade away from being a reality. Which one is important for you? Which one will make or break your business? Does this list even include the one that you need to be concerned about?

The Need for Constant IS Innovation

Sir John Maddox, a physicist and the editor of the influential scientific journal *Nature* for twenty-two years, was quoted in *Scientific American* in 1999 as saying, "The most important discoveries of the next 50 years are likely to be ones of which we cannot now even conceive." Think about that for a moment. Most of the important discoveries of the next

Brief Case ⊙

For Sale by Owner: Your Company's Name.com

They don't sell houses or land, but they do deal in Internet real estate, and most turn a handsome profit. "They" are called domainers, and the real estate they buy and sell consists of domain names. Although they keep a low profile and usually don't flaunt their success, domainers participated in a virtual land grab worth $9 billion in 2006, and those figures were projected to soar to $23 billion by 2009.

As you know, every Web site on the Internet has a domain name, also called a uniform resource locator (URL) or Web address. Domain names may or may not identify the business or person who owns the Web site. For example, msn.com, yahoo.com, and google.com are domain names that do, in fact, identify the Web site owner by name. Domain names such as xa2z7.com, however, do not.

Domainers trade on the fact that many businesses, organizations, and celebrities want domain names for their Web sites that clearly identify the site's owner and are, therefore, easy for Internet surfers to find. A domainer might buy the domain name "fordmotorcompany.com," for instance, and then try to sell it to the Ford Motor Company; that is exactly how the domain-buying business operated in the 1990s. Buy a name, hold it, and wait for a buyer who wanted it to make an offer. But when pay-per-click advertising was developed, the game changed. Currently, domainers can profit most by renting advertising space on the domain names they hold to marketers. Here is how the domainer makes his or her profit from renting ad space:

1. Buy and hold a general domain name, such as "candy.com" or "cellphones.com." (The financial wisdom in buying such domain names became apparent to domainers when they realized that many Internet surfers conduct searches simply by entering a search word or term followed by .com in the URL address box of their browsers.) Alternatively, domainers buy domain names that represent common misspellings of popular domains (such as amazon.com), hoping to benefit from Web surfers' typos.
2. Direct Web traffic to a middleman, called an aggregator, who designs a Web site and then taps into Yahoo!, Google, or Microsoft's advertising networks and lists the best-paying clients. When a searcher enters the domain name, such as "cellphone.com," the "cellphone.com" Web page comes up with a list of cell phone Web site URLs.
3. Each time a searcher clicks on one of the URLs listed on the domain name's page, the search engine owner (Yahoo!, Google, or Microsoft) or advertiser pays the domainer a fee.

Renting domain names is a secondary market for domainers that can bring in hundreds of dollars per day. The key to this market is not necessarily search engine traffic—rather it is type-in traffic or user-directed navigation because millions of Internet users type what they are looking for directly in the address bar of their browser, such as "candy.com." (Candy.com was recently sold for over $100,000 and makes a profit of $1,000 a week for its owner.)

Figures are not available for this type of URL type-in traffic since the larger search engines, such as Yahoo! and Google, do not disclose how much of their revenue comes from domain name rental. Experts report, however, that as much as 15 percent of Google's and Yahoo!'s revenue may come from per-click advertising.

Domainers could face a loss of revenue if, as has been suggested, Google, Yahoo!, and Microsoft cut out the domainer in the middle and served Internet browser type-in traffic directly. But until that happens, domainers are raking in the cash.

In March 2008, *Domainer's Magazine* editor Mike St. John, expressed concern over the Anti-Phishing Consumer Protection Act of 2008, introduced in Congress but not yet passed. If the bill were to become law, St. John warned, domainers found to have purloined trademarked or government names, such as FordsRUs.com or IRS.com, would face prosecution by the Federal Trade Commission and the U.S. Attorney General and fines of up to $6 million for each violation, plus attorneys' fees. St. John thought the punishment outlined in the bill was excessive. Others may disagree.

Questions
1. How do you feel about domainers? Is it an ethical business?
2. Discuss the pros and cons of having Google, Yahoo!, MSN, and others "cut out" domainers as middle men in the Web search process.

Based on:

Domainers magazine (n.d.). Retrieved May 11, 2008, from http://www.domainersmagazine.com.

Sloan, P. (2005, December 1). Masters of their domains. *CNN Money.com*. Retrieved May 11, 2008, from http://money.cnn.com/magazines/business2/business2_archive/2005/12/01/8364591/index.htm.

What's on the Horizon?

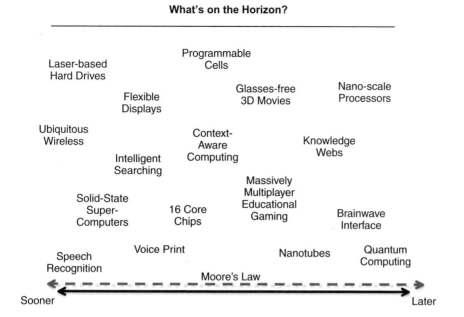

FIGURE 3.19

Some enabling technologies on the horizon.

fifty years are likely to be things that, at present, we have no clue about. To illustrate that point, think back to just a short decade ago about what the state of the Internet was. Then, the Internet was not on the radar screens of many business organizations. Those that had Web sites were mostly providing an electronic brochure to customers and weren't exploiting the technology to streamline business processes as is the norm today. Look now at how the Internet has transformed modern business. How could something so transformational not have been easier for businesses to imagine or predict a decade earlier? Well, it is difficult to see these things coming. Next, we examine how you can improve your ability to spot and exploit new innovations.

Successful Innovation Is Difficult

As we hinted at previously, there are limits to using emerging information systems to gain or sustain a competitive advantage. Information systems are often bought from or built by someone else. They are often either purchased from a vendor or developed by a consultant or outsourcing partner. In these situations, the information systems are usually not proprietary technologies owned by the organization. For example, although a soft-drink company can patent the formula of a cola or a pharmaceutical company can patent a new drug, an organization typically cannot patent its use of an information system, particularly if someone else developed it. The data in the system may be proprietary, but the information system typically is not. One classic counterexample, however, is Amazon.com's patented "one-click" ordering process that has been successfully defended in the courts.

Innovation Is Often Fleeting Given the pace of change in the digital world, advantages gained by innovations often have a limited life span. For example, even in situations where an organization has developed an innovative information system in-house, they usually do so with hardware, software, and networking components others can purchase. In short, rivals can copy emerging information systems, so this form of competitive advantage can be short lived. Indeed, if use of the new system causes one organization to gain a significant advantage over others, smart rivals are quick to duplicate or improve on that use of the system.

Innovation Is Often Risky Developing innovative information systems always entails risk. The classic example from consumer electronics is the choice of a VCR in the early days of that technology and the competing Betamax (developed by Sony) and VHS (developed by JVC) designs. Most experts agreed that the Betamax had superior recording and playback quality, but VHS ultimately won the battle in the marketplace.

FIGURE 3.20

Sony integrated a Blu-ray disc drive into its PlayStation 3 gaming console.

People who made the "smart" choice at the time probably would have chosen a VCR with the Betamax design. Ultimately, however, that turned out to be an unfortunate choice. Recently, consumers again had to choose between two competing formats, namely for high-definition DVD players, where the Blu-ray and HD DVD format competed to become the industry standard. In this battle, Microsoft, Toshiba, and many others backed the HD DVD format while Sony led the fight for Blu-ray (and even incorporated it into its PlayStation 3 gaming console, see Figure 3.20). This time around, Sony (and the Blu-ray format) won the "format war," with the dissolution of the HD DVD Promotion Group in early 2008, effectively making Blu-ray the dominant format for high-definition video discs.

Innovation Choices Are Often Difficult Choosing among innovative information systems–related investments is just as difficult as choosing consumer electronics. In fact, for organizations, choosing among the plethora of available innovative technologies is far more difficult, given the size and often mission-critical nature of the investment. Choosing a suboptimal DVD player, although disappointing, is usually not devastating.

Choosing new technologies in the information systems area is like trying to hit one of several equally attractive fast-moving targets. You can find examples of the difficulty of forecasting emerging technologies in the experiences that many organizations have had in forecasting the growth, use, and importance of the Internet. The 1994 Technology Forecast prepared by the major consulting firm Price Waterhouse (now PriceWaterhouseCoopers) mentioned the word "Internet" on only five pages of the 750-page document. The next year, more than seventy-five pages addressed the Internet. Only three years later, in the 1997 briefing, the Internet was a pervasive topic throughout. Back in 1994, it would have been difficult, perhaps even foolish, to forecast such pervasive, rapidly growing business use of the Internet today. Table 3.5 illustrates how many people and organizations have had difficulty making technology-related predictions.

Given the pace of research and development in the information systems and components area, staying current has been nearly impossible. Probably one of the most famous metrics of computer evolution has been "Moore's Law." Intel founder Gordon Moore predicted that the number of transistors that could be squeezed onto a silicon chip would double every eighteen months, and this prediction has proven itself over the past forty years (see Chapter 4). In fact, some computer hardware and software firms roll out new versions of their products every three months. Keeping up with this pace of change can be difficult for any organization.

TABLE 3.5 Some Predictions About Technology That Were Not Quite Correct

Year	Source	Quote
1876	Western Union, internal memo	"This 'telephone' has too many shortcomings to be seriously considered as a means of communication. The device is inherently of no value to us."
1895	Lord Kelvin, president, British Royal Society	"Radio has no future. Heavier-than-air flying machines are impossible. X-rays will prove to be a hoax."
1899	C. H. Duell, commissioner, U.S. Office of Patents	"Everything that can be invented has been invented."
1927	H. M. Warner, Warner Brothers	"Who the hell wants to hear actors talk?"
1943	Thomas Watson, chairman, IBM	"I think there is a world market for maybe five computers."
1949	*Popular Mechanics*	"Where a calculator on the ENIAC is equipped with 18,000 vacuum tubes and weighs 30 tons, computers in the future may have only 1,000 vacuum tubes and weigh only 1.5 tons."
1957	Editor, business books, Prentice Hall	"I have traveled the length and breadth of this country and talked with the best people, and I can assure you that data processing is a fad that won't last out the year."
1968	*Business Week*	"With over 50 foreign cars already on sale here, the Japanese auto industry isn't likely to carve out a big slice of the U.S. market."
1977	Ken Olsen, president, Digital Equipment Corporation	"There is no reason anyone would want a computer in their home."

Organizational Requirements for Innovation

Certain types of competitive environments require that organizations remain at the cutting edge in their use of information systems. For example, consider an organization that operates within an environment with strong competitive forces (Porter, 1979). The organization has competitive pressures coming from existing rival firms or from the threat of entry of new rivals. It is critical for these organizations to do things better, faster, and more cheaply than rivals. These organizations are driven to deploy innovative information systems.

These environmental characteristics alone, however, are not enough to determine whether an organization should deploy a particular information system. Before an organization can deploy any new system well, its processes, resources, and risk tolerance must be capable of adapting to and sustaining the development and implementation processes.

Process Requirements To deploy innovative information systems well, people in the organization must be willing to do whatever they can to bypass and eliminate internal bureaucracy, set aside political squabbles, and pull together for the common good. Can you imagine, for example, a firm trying to deploy a Web-based order entry system that enables customers to access inventory information directly when people in that firm do not even share such information with each other?

Resource Requirements Organizations deploying innovative information systems must also have the human capital necessary to deploy the new systems. The organization must have enough employees available with the proper systems knowledge, skills, time, and other resources to deploy these systems. Alternatively, the organization must have resources and able systems partners available to outsource the development of such systems if necessary.

Risk Tolerance Requirements The last characteristic of an organization ready for the deployment of innovative information systems is that its members must have the appropriate tolerance for risk and uncertainty as well as the willingness to deploy and use new systems that may not be as proven and pervasive as more traditional technologies. If people within the organization desire low risk in their use of information systems, then gambling on cutting-edge systems will probably not be desirable or tolerable for them.

Predicting the Next New Thing

As you can see, using innovative information systems toward a strategic end will be difficult to identify, implement, and sustain. As Bakos and Treacy (1986) and others have argued, if you are using information systems to gain a competitive advantage in the area of operating efficiencies, it is likely that your rivals can just as easily adopt the same types of information systems and achieve the same gains. For example, you might set up a Web site that enables customers to check on the status of their order without requiring help from a customer service representative, and this might enable you to cut costs. Rivals could, however, easily copy this approach and match your cost reductions. The competitive advantage thus turns into strategic necessity for anyone in this industry.

On the other hand, there are ways to use information systems to gain a competitive advantage in a way that is easier to sustain. For example, Bakos and Treacy argued that if you

Coming Attractions

What Were You Thinking? Brain Sensor for Market Research

Remember the 2007 Super Bowl ad that depicted a man and a woman in a horse-drawn carriage traveling down a wooded lane on a frosty evening? The man has worked hard to create a romantic setting for his beautiful blond date, and she is smiling as he hands her a candle and opens a basket that contains several chilled bottles of Budweiser beer. Then the horse has, ummm, a moment of flatulence, the candle explodes into flame, and the beautiful blond's hairdo is charred. Did you think the ad was funny, as Anheuser-Busch undoubtedly intended, or were you outraged and offended by the ad's coarse content? Budweiser pulled the ad shortly after its initial airing, but spokespersons for the company insisted they had not wanted to offend viewers.

If only there was a product that could tell, before commercials are aired, how potential viewers would react. Ad designers could then adjust advertising content to appeal to the audience they are trying to reach and could avoid marketing faux pas such as the one detailed above. It happens that research in this area is in progress.

For example, Emsense, a San Francisco–based company founded in 2004, has developed a sensor-laden headset for tracking brain activity that occurs while wearers watch various commercials and other video material. The headset is wired with one electroencephalography (EEG) sensor at the forehead and also has sensors for monitoring breathing and heart rate, head motion, blink rate, and skin temperature—all of which are intended to detect when the wearer is concentrating or excited. According to Hans Lee, chief technology officer at Emsense, the company has also devised algorithms that translate physiological data from the sensors into information about emotions that a marketer can use. "Our technology allows us to col-

lect moment-by-moment metrics while avoiding the cognitive bias that can interfere with self-reporting and focus groups," Lee told a writer for *Technology Review* in 2007.

Using the device, game makers can tell those points in a game when players are involved or bored. Ad designers can tell which content is offensive and which is humorous. Marketers can also use data from the device to tell how males differ from females or younger people from older people in their reactions to content.

Scientists among critics for most devices that use EEG data to postulate brain activity maintain that placing sensors on the scalp, rather than using MRI data, is not reliable because information is lost or diluted as it travels from the brain to the skin of the scalp. Despite those who say the research to date has not produced viable marketing projection products, Emsense spokespersons say their technology is superior—because the company was founded by five MIT graduates and because their proprietary algorithms provide the most reliable feedback about how physiological changes relate to reactions.

The science and technology appear promising, but time will tell. In the meantime, letters to publication editors and television networks are still one reliable, if nontechnical, way for consumers to respond to marketing campaigns that excite their emotions.

Based on:

EmSense Corporation. (n.d.). Retrieved May 11, 2008, from http://www.emsense.com.

Greene, K. (2007, December 7). Brain sensor for market research. *Technology Review.* Retrieved May 11, 2008, from http://www.technologyreview.com/Biztech/19833/?a=f.

SAM technology (n.d.). Retrieved May 11, 2008, from http://www.eeg.com.

can use information systems to make your products or services unique or to cause your customers to invest heavily in you so that their switching costs are high (i.e., switching to a competitor's product involves significant investment in terms of time and/or money for the customer), then you are better able to develop a competitive advantage that is sustainable over the long haul. For example, you might combine heavy investments in computer-aided design systems with very bright engineers in order to perfect your product and make it unique, something relatively difficult to copy. Alternatively, you might use a customer relationship management system to build an extensive database containing the entire history of your interaction with each of your customers and then use that system to provide very high-quality, intimate, rapid, customized service that would convince customers that if they switched to a rival, it would take them years to build up that kind of relationship with the other firm.

The Innovator's Dilemma

Deciding which innovations to adopt and pursue has never been easy. In fact, there are many classic examples where so-called industry leaders failed to see the changing opportunities introduced by new innovations (see Table 3.5). In his influential book *Diffusion of Innovations*, Everett Rogers (2003) theorized that the adoption of innovations usually follows an S-shaped curve (see Figure 3.21). When an innovation is brought to market, initially, only a small group of "innovators" will adopt that innovation. After some time, sales pick up as the innovators are followed by the "early adopters" and the "early majority," and the increase in sales is strongest. Then, sales slowly level off when the "late majority" starts adopting the innovation. Finally, sales stay level as only the "laggards" are left to adopt the innovation.

However, some innovations are more disruptive, turning entire industries upside down. Clayton Christensen's *The Innovator's Dilemma* outlines how *disruptive innovations* undermine effective management practices, often leading to the demise of an organization or an industry. **Disruptive innovations** are new technologies, products, or services that eventually surpass the existing dominant technology or product in a market (see Table 3.6). For example, retail giant Sears nearly failed in the early 1990s when it did not recognize the transformational power of the disruptive innovation discount retailing; today, discounters like Wal-Mart and segment-specific stores like Home Depot dominate retailing.

Within every market, there are customers who have relatively high, moderate, or low performance requirements from the existing product offerings. For example, within the mobile phone industry today, some low-performance customers demand very basic phones and services (e.g., no text messaging, camera, or data services), while high-performance customers use devices and services that rival the capabilities of some personal computers with high-speed Internet connections. Over time, as disruptive innovations and incremental improvements are introduced into an industry, the capabilities of the products in all segments (i.e., low to high performance) improve; as product capabilities improve at the

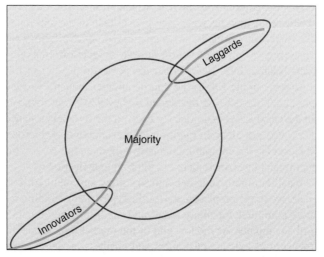

Cumulative Adoptions

Over Time

FIGURE 3.21

Diffusion of innovations.

Based on: Rogers (1962).

TABLE 3.6 **Examples of Disruptive Innovations and Their Associated Displaced or Marginalized Technology**

Disruptive Innovation	Displaced or Marginalized Technology
Digital photography	Chemical photography
Mobile telephony	Wire-line telephony
Handheld digital appliances	Notebook computers
Xbox, PlayStation	Desktop computers
Online stock brokerage	Full-service stock brokerages
Online retailing	Bricks-and-mortar retailing
Free, downloadable greeting cards	Printed greeting cards
Distance education	Classroom education
Unmanned aircraft	Manned aircraft
Nurse practitioners	Medical doctors
Semiconductors	Vacuum tubes
Desktop publishing	Traditional publishing
Automobiles	Horses
Airplanes	Trains
Compact discs	Cassettes and records
MP3 players and music downloading	Compact discs and music stores

high-performance end of the market, the number of potential customers for these products gets relatively smaller. At the same time, as the low-end products also improve, they are increasingly able to capture more and more of the mainstream marketplace.

To illustrate this progression, Christensen provides compelling examples within several industries. In particular, the collapse of 1970s mid-range (minicomputer) giant Digital Equipment Company (DEC) (and the entire mid-range industry for that matter) clearly illustrates the innovator's dilemma. DEC was ultimately surpassed in the marketplace by microprocessor-based computers, with the microprocessor being the disruptive innovation.

In the 1970s, when microcomputers were first introduced, DEC (and its customers) deemed them to be toys and ignored their potential. It is important to note that DEC was a well-run company and was touted as having one of the finest executive teams in the world. Additionally, DEC used leading management techniques, such as conducting extensive market research with its existing customers and industry (i.e., they put "marketing" ahead of technology; for a divergent view, see the discussion of the E-Business Innovation Cycle later in this chapter). When surveyed, none of DEC's customers indicated a need for microcomputers, and thus DEC concluded that developing improved capabilities within its *existing* mid-range computer product line is where they should focus. At this time, DEC's goal was to serve the needs of "high" and "mid" performance users, which made up the largest part of the total market for computers (see Figure 3.22). The increasing performance of DEC's products started meeting the needs of customers who would traditionally purchase mainframe computers, and so DEC could try to "up sell" to mainframe customers of IBM, Burroughs, and Honeywell, where the margins were even greater than in the mid-range computer industry.

Initially, there were virtually no competitive product offerings serving the needs of the low-performance users; in other words, current product offerings by established computer manufacturers, such as DEC, were either too powerful or too expensive (or both) for these low-end customers. In the 1980s, the microcomputer industry was launched by Apple, and the (disruptive) microprocessor, developed in the 1970s, was now being turned into a product that had the capabilities and price for users in the low-performance category of the marketplace. DEC was not alone in ignoring the introduction of microcomputers; virtually all established players in the computing industry continued to focus on their existing customers and existing product lines, incrementally improving their products over time. Meanwhile, in just a few years, the microcomputer industry grew and matured, going from toy to office automation device (e.g., a replacement for the typewriter or adding machine) to a multipurpose business computer for many small and medium-sized businesses that could never before afford a computer. As the low end of the market took shape in the 1980s, DEC continued to focus on its existing customers and business model (e.g., direct selling, personal service, and so on). Rapidly, the capabilities of the "disruptive" microcomputers improved,

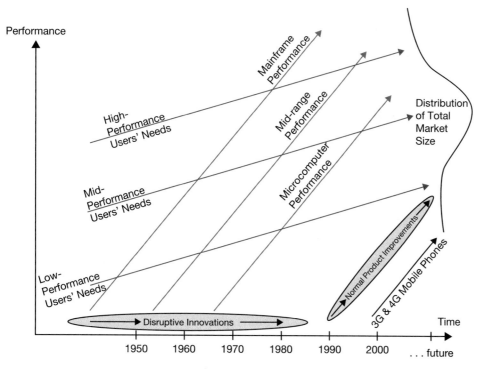

FIGURE 3.22

Innovator's dilemma view of the evolution of the computing industry.

meeting the needs of not only the low end but also the mid-performance range of the marketplace, which was traditionally served by DEC's mid-range computers. Being far more inexpensive than DEC's products, the microcomputers took over the bulk of the market. Sadly, DEC continued to ignore the microcomputer industry until it was too late, and DEC could do nothing but watch the loss of its biggest traditional market segment. By January 26, 1998, what was left of DEC was sold to Compaq Computers; Compaq was later acquired by Hewlett-Packard in 2002.

Today, microprocessor-based computers from Dell, Sony, Apple, and others meet or exceed the needs of much of the *entire* marketplace; additionally, only a handful of high-end computer manufacturers remain. So what is next for this industry? Many believe that the next disruptive innovations are 3G and 4G mobile phones from companies like Apple, Motorola, and HTC (see the Information Technology Briefing). Another example of an industry that has been transformed by disruptive technologies is the photo industry (see the Industry Analysis at the end of the chapter). What DEC experienced, so too have countless other companies in numerous industries. Table 3.7 summarizes the typical progression and effects of a disruptive innovation on an industry.

Organizing to Make Innovation Choices Given the evolution of industries outlined in the innovator's dilemma, how do organizations make decisions on which innovations to embrace and which to ignore? In his follow-up book, *The Innovator's Solution,* Christensen outlines a process called the *disruptive growth engine,* which all organizations can follow to more effectively respond to disruptive innovations in their industry. This process has the following steps:

1. *Start Early.* To gain the greatest opportunities, become a leader in identifying, tracking, and adopting disruptive innovations by making these processes a formal part of the organization (i.e., budgets, personnel, and so on).
2. *Executive Leadership.* To gain credibility as well as to bridge sustaining and disruptive product development, visible and credible leadership is required.
3. *Build a Team of Expert Innovators.* To most effectively identify and evaluate potential disruptive innovations, build a competent team of expert innovators.
4. *Educate the Organization.* To see opportunities, those closest to customers and competitors (e.g., marketing, customer support, and engineering) need to understand how to identify disruptive innovations.

TABLE 3.7 Typical Progression and Effects of Disruptive Innovations on an Industry

1. First mover introduces a new technology. It is expensive, focusing on a small number of high-performance, high-margin customers.
2. Over time, the first mover focuses on improving product capabilities to meet the needs of higher-performance customers in order to continue to reap the highest margins.
3. Later entrants, using a disruptive innovation, have an inferior market position, focusing on lower-performance, lower-margin customers.
4. Over time, later entrants focus on incremental product improvements to serve the needs of more lower-performance customers, also focusing on cost efficiencies to offset lack of margins with economies of scale.
5. As the market matures, all products improve, competition increases, and margins diminish; the first mover rarely learns the efficiencies of the later entrants and is entrenched in high-margin business practices; the first mover's market share rapidly erodes as that of the later entrants rapidly grows.
6. Ultimately, the later entrants' products meet or exceed the requirements for the vast majority of the marketplace, they "win" with efficient, low-cost business processes demanded by the majority of the marketplace.

In addition to formalizing the identification of innovations with the organization, shifts in business processes and the fundamental thinking about disruptive innovations are needed. Next, we examine how to implement the innovation identification process.

Implementing the Innovation Process Executives today who are serious about using information technology in innovative ways have made it a point to have their people be continually on the lookout for new disruptive innovations that will have a significant impact on their business. Wheeler (2002b) has summarized this process nicely as the **E-Business Innovation Cycle** (see Figure 3.23). Like the term "e-commerce," "e-business" refers to the use of information technologies and systems to support the business. Whereas "e-commerce" generally means the use of the Internet and related technologies to support commerce, **e-business** has a broader meaning: the use of nearly any information technologies or systems to support every part of the business. The model essentially holds that the key

FIGURE 3.23

The E-Business Innovation Cycle.

Based on: Wheeler (2002).

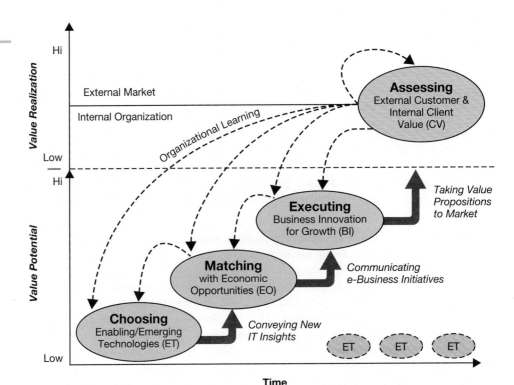

to success for modern organizations is the extent to which they use information technologies and systems in timely, innovative ways. The vertical dimension of the E-Business Innovation Cycle shows the extent to which an organization derives value from a particular information technology, and the horizontal dimension shows time. Next, we examine the cycle.

Choosing Enabling/Emerging Technologies.   The first bubble left of the graph shows that successful organizations first create jobs, groups, and processes that are all devoted to scanning the environment for new emerging and **enabling technologies** (i.e., information technologies that enable a firm to accomplish a task or goal or to gain or sustain competitive advantage in some way; also called disruptive innovations) that appear to be relevant for the organization. For example, an organization might designate a small group within the Information Systems department as the "Emerging Technologies" unit and charge them with looking for new technologies that will have an impact on the business. As part of their job, this group will pore over current technology magazines, participate in Internet discussion forums on technology topics, go to technology conferences and conventions, and have strong, active relationships with technology researchers at universities and technology companies.

Matching Technologies to Opportunities.   Next, in the second bubble, the organization matches the most promising new technologies with current **economic opportunities**. For example, the Emerging Technologies group might have identified advances in database management systems (and a dramatic drop in data storage costs) as a key emerging technology that now enables a massive data warehouse to be feasible. In addition, managers within the marketing function of the firm have recognized that competitors have really dropped the ball in terms of customer service and that there is an opportunity to gain customers and market share by serving customers better.

Executing Business Innovation for Growth.   The third bubble represents the process of selecting among myriad opportunities to take advantage of the database and data storage advances and addressing the current opportunity to grab customers and market share. The organization decides to implement an enterprise-wide data warehouse that enables them to have at their fingertips integrated corporate-wide data and an unparalleled capability to understand, react to, and better serve customers.

Assessing Value.   The fourth bubble represents the process of assessing the value of that use of technology, not only to customers but to internal clients (i.e., sales representatives, marketing managers, the chief operating officer, and so on) as well.

The E-Business Innovation Cycle suggests three new ways to think about investments in disruptive innovations:

1. ***Put Technology Ahead of Strategy.*** This approach says that technology is so important to strategy and to success that you have to begin with technology. Notice that the first bubble involves understanding, identifying, and choosing technologies that are important. The first bubble does not begin with strategy, as a traditional approach to running a business organization would suggest. In fact, many would argue that given how important technology is today and how fast it changes, if you start with a strategy and then try to retrofit technology into your aging strategy, you are doomed. This approach argues that you begin by understanding technology and develop a strategy from there. This approach is admittedly very uncomfortable for people who think in traditional ways and/or who are not comfortable with technology. We believe, however, that for many modern organizations, thinking about technology in this way is key.

2. ***Put Technology Ahead of Marketing.*** The second way that this approach turns conventional wisdom on its head is that, like strategy, marketing also takes a backseat to the technology. Think about it carefully, and you will see that marketing does not come into play until later in this model. A very traditional marketing-oriented approach would be to go first to your customers and find out from them what their needs are and what you ought to be doing with technology (as did DEC). The trouble with this approach is that, given the rapid evolution of technology, your customers are not likely to know about new technologies and their capabilities. In some sense, they are the last place you ought to be looking for ideas about new technologies and their impact on your business.

Indeed, if they know about the new technology, then chances are your competitors already do too, and that technology is not one to rest your competitive advantage on. As Steve Jobs of Apple put it, "You can't just ask people what they want and then try to give that to them. By the time you get it built, they'll want something new."

3. ***Innovation Is Continuous.*** The third way that this approach is interesting—and potentially troubling—is that the process has to be ongoing. As shown along the time dimension along the bottom of the graph, the first bubble repeats over and over again as the Emerging Technologies group is constantly on the lookout for the "next new thing" that will revolutionize the business. The rate of information technology evolution is not likely to slow down, and innovative organizations truly cannot—and do not—ever rest.

Today, dealing with rapid change caused by disruptive innovations is a reality for most industries. If you are a leader in an industry, you must continually learn to embrace and exploit disruptive innovations, potentially *destroying* your existing core business while at the same time building a new business around the disruptive innovation. If you fail to do this, your competition may do it for you.

Freeconomics: Why Free Products Are the Future of the Digital World

Chris Anderson, editor in chief of *Wired Magazine,* has put forth a provocative idea that charging customers nothing for products and services may be the future of business in the digital world. In fact, he argues that this strategy is a viable approach for making a fortune in virtually any industry. Of course, obvious examples not likely to be easily replicated include Google making billions from its free search engine or Yahoo! making millions from its free Web e-mail service. Anderson convincingly argues, however, that such money-making principles are not limited to Google and Yahoo!, but can be applied to countless industries. Here we examine how **freeconomics**—the leveraging of digital technologies to provide *free* goods and services to customers as a business strategy for gaining a competitive advantage—can be utilized by organizations from virtually any industry in the highly competitive digital world.

How Freeconomics Works

According to basic economics within a competitive marketplace, the price of something is set by its marginal cost—the cost of producing an additional unit of output. Given the push toward globalization, the world has never been more competitive (see Chapter 2). Likewise, given the exponential increases in processing power (see Moore's Law in Chapter 4), along with even greater increases in storage and networking capacity, the price of computer processing, storage, and bandwidth are on a free fall. For example, after Yahoo! has built its Web e-mail environment, the cost to provide this service for each additional person is nearly zero. Consequently, the marginal cost for Web e-mail services is essentially zero. At the same time, huge profits are made giving away this service to more and more customers. For every additional customer, Yahoo! receives payments from companies placing banner advertisements on pages within the Web e-mail service (see Figure 3.24).

It is important to note that *any* industry that utilizes digital technologies (not just those like Google or Yahoo!) is on a path toward increasingly lower costs, ultimately toward a price of free—or at least "free" for consumers. As digital technologies increase in capabilities and at the same time decreases in cost, the industry as a whole will see rapid cost reductions. As costs are reduced, prices for consumers will drop. Moreover, as that industry relies more and more on digital technologies to further reduce costs and to further increase efficiencies, the competitiveness of the industry will further increase, pushing the price closer and closer toward its marginal cost. In other words, as an industry relies more and more on digital technologies, free becomes the inevitable price.

The Freeconomics Value Proposition

Within freeconomics, just because products are free to consumers doesn't mean that someone, somewhere, isn't paying for it; and, most importantly, that someone else isn't also making a lot of money. For example, Google gets paid ad revenue from companies when

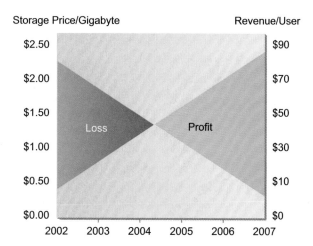

Storage Price/Gigabyte

Revenue/User

FIGURE 3.24

How Yahoo! makes millions of dollars from its *free* Web-based e-mail service—as the cost of storage has dropped, revenue per user has increased.

someone using a Google search clicks on a sponsored link. Here the **value proposition**—what a business provides to a customer and what that customer is willing to pay for that product or service—is larger than simply buyers and sellers. For Google, the value proposition includes a broad ecosystem of many participants, only some of which exchange payments (see Figure 3.25). This value proposition is very similar to that of the radio and television broadcast industries, where consumers receive free content, while advertisers make payments to stations to broadcast commercials. Freeconomics is therefore an extension of this basic advertising model and can be applied to virtually any industry. Additionally, this basic model can be applied in a variety of creative ways beyond advertising.

Appling Freeconomics in the Digital World

To demonstrate how freeconomics can be applied to a variety of industries beyond Web e-mail or online searches, Anderson explains how cable TV giant Comcast gave a free DVR (Digital Video Recorder) to millions of its customers, leading to huge profits for the company. The DVR cost Comcast around $250 each, so giving them away needed to stimulate some other type of revenue. Specifically, once consumers had the DVR, they were charged a monthly subscription fee to utilize its capabilities. Comcast was also able to create a stronger relationship with its customers, leading to other revenue streams including high-speed Internet access, digital telephony services, and pay-per-view movies. In the end, this free DVR is generating tremendous revenue and profits for Comcast.

In another example, the music icon Prince gave away 2.8 million copies of his latest CD, *Planet Earth,* retail value $19, inside the Sunday edition of London's *Daily Mail.* Although Prince lost money on the giveaway—he received 36 cents per disc from the newspaper while the cost to produce each disc was around $2—he more than made up for this loss through the sale of concert tickets. After the giveaway, he sold out a record breaking twenty-one shows in The O$_2$ Arena in London, netting the entertainer nearly $19 million in revenue after expenses (see Figure 3.26). Indeed, there are many approaches for making money by giving things away.

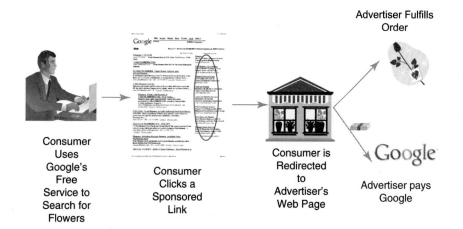

Consumer Uses Google's Free Service to Search for Flowers

Consumer Clicks a Sponsored Link

Consumer is Redirected to Advertiser's Web Page

Advertiser Fulfills Order

Advertiser pays Google

FIGURE 3.25

Google uses a value proposition similar to that of television and radio broadcasting advertising.

FIGURE 3.26

Music icon Prince used concepts of freeconomics to thrive in the digital world.

Table 3.8 outlines six general approaches for applying the concepts of freeconomics to a broad range of industries. For example, the online photo sharing application Flickr (owned by Yahoo!) allows users to store, share, organize, and tag a limited number of pictures for free; applying the *freemium* approach, users can upgrade to a paid "pro account," providing additional features such as unlimited storage and advertisement-free browsing, or can use other paid services such as printing through HP's print services, creating photo gifts, or creating books using Blurb.com. Understanding how to leverage the value of information systems investments is fundamental to thriving in the digital world.

TABLE 3.8 General Approaches for Applying Freeconomics to Various Industries

Approach	What It means	Examples
Advertising	Free services are provided to customers and paid for by 3rd party	• Yahoo!'s banner ads • Google's pay-per-click • Amazon's pay-per-transaction "affiliate ads"
Freemium	Basic services are offered for free, but a premium is charged for special features	• Flickr • Skype • FreeDrive.com • Trillian
Cross-Subsidies	Sale of one item is reduced in order to sell something else of value	• Comcast DVR • Free theatre ticket for those willing to buy a large popcorn and beverage • Free Wii to those willing to buy five new games • Free cell phone with two-year contract
Zero Marginal Cost	Products are distributed to customers without an appreciable cost to anyone	• Online music downloading at iTunes • Software distribution • Video content on YouTube
Labor Exchange	Services are provided to customers; the act of using the services creates value for the company	• Yahoo! Answers • Google's 411 service • Digg rating services
Gift Economy	Environments are created that allow people to participate and collaborate to create something of value for everyone	• Open-source software development • Wikipedia • Freecycle—free secondhand goods to anyone willing to haul them away

Based on: Anderson (2008).

Industry Analysis

Photo Industry

Have you tried lately to purchase a roll of Kodak 35-mm color film with 12 exposures? It's hard to find because the 12-exposure option is no longer manufactured—24 or 36 exposures are still for sale, but for how long?

Soon new cameras that use film will also be hard to find. For instance, Canon, number one in digital camera sales in the United States in 2006 (Sony was second and Kodak third), announced in June 2006 that the company would no longer develop new film cameras. Canon will concentrate instead on improving its digital cameras and developing new digital models. Other camera/film companies are following Canon's lead:

- Earlier in 2006, Konica Minolta Holdings said it would stop making film cameras, lenses, and even film, then announced it was selling its assets to rival Sony.
- Nikon, a world leader in high-quality camera products, said in January 2006 that it would stop making most models of film cameras to focus solely on digital. Nikon now makes only two film cameras, the F6 for professionals and the FM10 for beginners.

In just over four years (2002–2006), photography moved from film to digital dominance. "The shift from film to digital was way faster than we expected," said Kakushi Kiuchi, an executive in charge of professional photography for Fuji Film at the Photo Imaging Expo in Tokyo in 2006. Digital technology was clearly a disruptive innovation in the photo industry.

Just as PC technology has progressed at a dizzying rate over the past ten years, so too has digital photography. Film photography has dominated the industry for over one hundred years, but once digital cameras came online, the digital photography market exploded.

Apple manufactured the first digital cameras sold to the general public in 1994. One year later, Kodak introduced its first digital camera, the Kodak DC40. The DC40 was extremely successful, and soon several competing camera companies, including Canon, Sony, and Fuji, introduced digital cameras to the consumer market. (Experts predict that Kodak's mainstay—35-mm movie film products—will inevitably also go completely digital, as digitized movies become the rule, both for theater and for home viewing.)

Polaroid, the first camera company to manufacture a camera that could also instantly develop photos captured on film, has also had to change significantly as digital became the rule. The company has battled back from bankruptcy twice in 1993 and 2004 with a line of nonphotography business products, including commercial ID printing and DVD players. Given consumer demand for digital pictures and increasing options such as high-quality desktop printing, focusing exclusively on instant photos was no longer profitable for Polaroid.

Without the changes in their business models that moved the companies away from film photography and into the digital market, Kodak and Polaroid would probably not have survived. With Kodak, Polaroid, Canon, and other camera and film companies leading the way, the photography industry now focuses on the digital electronics consumers prefer. The result is that new electronic products, from cell phones to laptops, now have photographic capabilities.

Clearly, as the world continues to flatten, the motto for the photography industry, and other industries as well, is that digital dominates.

Questions

1. What competitive dynamics are affecting the digital camera marketplace?
2. Contrast the evolution of the digital camera industry with the cellular phone industry. What is similar? What is unique?

Based on:

Doi, E. (2006, June 26). As film fades, Japan's camera industry changes focus. *CNET News.com.* Retrieved May 11, 2008, from http://www.cnet.com.au/digitalcameras/cameras/0,239036184, 240063968,00.htm.

Lidor, D. (2006, May 9). Perez' Kodak loses no. 1 U.S. digital camera spot. *Forbes.com.* Retrieved May 11, 2008, from http://www.forbes.com/2006/05/09/kodak-digital-cameras-cx_gl_.0509autofacescan15.html.

Polaroid Commercial ID launches fully integrated product suite offering improved quality, functionality, and features. (2006, April 4). Retrieved May 11, 2008, from http://www.polaroid.com/global/printer_friendly.jsp?PRODUCT%3C%3Eprd_id=845524441764406&FOLDER%3C%3Efolder_id=282574488338473&bmUID=1210567208438&bmLocale=en_US.

Polaroid dips into DVD recorder market (2006, May 9). Retrieved May 11, 2008, from http://www.dvdrecorderworld.com/news/359.

Key Points Review

1. *Discuss how information systems can be used for automation, organizational learning, and strategic advantage.*   Automating business activities occurs when information systems are used to do a business activity faster or more cheaply. IS can be used to help automate. It can also be used to improve aspects of an operation in order to gain dramatic improvements in the operation as a whole. When this occurs, technology is said to help us learn because it provides information about its operation and the underlying work process that it supports. Using information systems to automate and learn about business processes is a good start. However, information systems can add even more value to an organization if they are conceived, designed, used, and managed with a strategic approach. To apply information systems strategically, you must understand the organization's value chain and be able to identify opportunities in which you can use information systems to make changes or improvements in the value chain to gain or sustain a competitive advantage. This requires a change in mind-set from thinking about information systems as an expense to be minimized to thinking of information systems as an asset to be invested in.

2. *Describe how to formulate and present the business case for a system.*   Making the business case is the process of building and presenting the set of arguments that show that an information system is adding value to the organization and/or its constituents. It is often difficult to quantify the value that an information system provides because of measurement problems, time lags before benefits are realized, industry redistribution, and mismanagement. You must also understand your organization's particular business strategy in order to make an effective business case for systems. In short, technology investments should be closely linked to the organization's business strategy because these investments are becoming one of the major vehicles by which organizations can achieve their strategy. After you gain an understanding of your organization's position in the marketplace, its strategy for investing in systems that add value, and firm-level implementation factors, you can quantify the relative costs and benefits of the system. Considering all of these factors simultaneously will help you formulate an effective business case. In order to make a convincing presentation, you should be specific about the benefits this investment will provide for the organization. To do this, you must convert the benefits into monetary terms, such as the amount of money saved or revenue generated. If you have difficulty identifying specific monetary measures, you should devise some proxy measures to demonstrate the benefits of the system. Finally, make sure that you measure things that are important to the decision makers of the organizations. Choosing the wrong measures can yield a negative decision about a beneficial system.

3. *Explain why and how companies are continually looking for innovative ways to use information systems for competitive advantage.*   Organizations are finding innovative ways to use new technologies to help them do things faster, better, and more efficiently than rivals. Being at the technological cutting edge has its disadvantages and is typically quite difficult to execute. Given that new technologies are not as stable as traditional ones, relying on innovative information systems and technologies can be problematic. Because constantly upgrading to newer and better systems is expensive, relying on emerging systems can hurt a firm financially. In addition, using innovative information systems for competitive advantage can provide short-lived advantages; competitors can quickly jump on the technological bandwagon and easily mimic the same system. Not every organization should deploy innovative information systems. Those organizations that find themselves in highly competitive environments probably most need to deploy new technologies to stay ahead of rivals. To best deploy these new technologies, organizations must be ready for the business process changes that will ensue, have the resources necessary to deploy new technologies successfully, and be tolerant of the risk and problems involved in being at the cutting edge. Deploying emerging information systems is essentially a risk/return gamble: the risks are relatively high, but the potential rewards are great. Organizations successfully utilizing innovative systems and technologies today have people (and in some cases, special units) who scan the environment, looking out for emerging and enabling (and potentially disruptive) technologies that can help their firm. They then narrow down the list to technologies that match with the challenges a firm faces or create economic opportunities. Next, they choose a particular technology or a set of technologies and implement them in a way that enables them to gain or sustain a competitive advantage. Finally, they assess these technology projects in terms of their value, not only to internal people and groups but also to external clients and partners. This process is ongoing, as information technologies and systems continually evolve.

4. *Describe freeconomics and how organizations can leverage digital technologies to provide free goods and services to customers as a business strategy for gaining a competitive advantage.* Freeconomics refers to the leveraging of digital technologies to provide *free* goods and services to customers as a business strategy for gaining a competitive advantage. Virtually *any* industry that utilizes digital technologies (not just those like Google or Yahoo!) is on a path toward increasingly lower costs, ultimately toward a price of free—or at least "free" for consumers. Industries can apply freeconomics in a variety of ways to gain a competitive advantage, including using advertising (e.g., Yahoo! banner ads), providing a freemium (e.g., Flickr providing limited storage for free to gain customers and then charging a fee to those customers who need additional storage and features), having one product cross-subsidize another (e.g., Comcast giving away DVRs to charge for programming), having zero marginal costs for additional product offerings (e.g., constant expansion of content on iTunes), gaining labor exchanges for services (e.g., Yahoo!'s answer service), or facilitating a gift economy where people freely collaborate to create something of value to everyone (e.g., open-source software development).

Key Terms

automating 85
best-cost provider strategy 87
break-even analysis 102
business processes 86
cost-benefit analysis 102
differentiation strategy 87
discount rate 102
disruptive innovations 114
e-business 116
E-Business Innovation Cycle 116
economic opportunities 117
enabling technology 117
freeconomics 118

informating 86
innovator's dilemma 113
intangible benefit 101
intangible cost 101
learning organization 86
low-cost leadership strategy 87
making the business case 91
net-present-value analysis 102
nonrecurring costs 101
organizational learning 86
organizational strategy 87
productivity paradox 93
proxy variables 105

recurring costs 101
strategic necessity 94
strategic planning 87
system effectiveness 94
system efficiency 94
tangible benefit 101
tangible cost 101
total cost of ownership (TCO) 101
value chain 90
value chain analysis 90
value proposition 119
weighted multicriteria analysis 103

Review Questions

1. Compare and contrast automating and learning.
2. Describe the attributes of a learning organization.
3. List five general types of organizational strategy.
4. Describe competitive advantage and list six sources.
5. Describe the productivity paradox.
6. Describe how to make a successful business case, contrasting faith-, fear-, and fact-based arguments.
7. Compare and contrast tangible and intangible benefits and costs.
8. Contrast the perspectives of different stakeholders involved in making information systems investment decisions.
9. Define a proxy variable and give an example.
10. Why is successful application of innovative technologies and systems often difficult?
11. What is the "innovator's dilemma"?
12. Using past examples, explain what is meant by a disruptive innovation.
13. Describe the E-business Innovation Cycle.
14. What is freeconomics, and what are several approaches for applying its concepts to various industries?

Self-Study Questions

Note: Visit the Interactive Study Guide on the Companion Web site for additional Self-Study Questions: www.pearsonhighered.com/valacich.

1. _____ is using technology as a way to help complete a task within an organization faster and, perhaps, more cheaply.
   A. automating
   B. learning
   C. strategizing
   D. processing

2. What are new technologies, products, or services that eventually surpass the existing dominant technology or product in a market called?
   A. surpassing event
   B. disruptive innovation
   C. innovative technology
   D. technology change

3. Which of the following is an intangible benefit?
   A. reduction of data entry errors
   B. improved company reputation
   C. increase in sales
   D. reduction of personnel costs

4. Which of the following is *not* improving the value chain?
   A. improving procurement processes
   B. increasing operating costs
   C. minimizing marketing expenditures
   D. selling more products

5. Which of the following is not one of the three types of arguments commonly made in the business case for an information system?
   A. fear
   B. fact
   C. faith
   D. fun

6. A company is said to have _____ when it has gained an edge over its rivals.
   A. monopoly
   B. profitability
   C. competitive advantage
   D. computer advantage

7. Each of the following was described in this chapter as a source of competitive advantage except for _____.
   A. delivering superior customer service
   B. achieving lower cost than rivals
   C. being the subject of a hostile takeover
   D. having shorter lead times in developing and testing new products

8. Making the _____ is the process of building and presenting the set of arguments that show that an information system is adding value to the organization.
   A. organizational chart
   B. organizational case
   C. law case
   D. business case

9. _____ refers to the emergence of disruptive innovations that undermine effective management practices, often leading to the demise of an organization or an industry.
   A. bad luck
   B. technological obsolescence
   C. life cycle analysis
   D. innovator's dilemma

10. What is a process of choosing, matching, executing, and assessing innovative technologies called?
    A. environmental scanning
    B. E-Business Innovation Cycle
    C. strategic planning
    D. none of the above

Answers are on page 126.

Problems and Exercises

1. Match the following terms with the appropriate definitions:

   i. Value chain analysis
   ii. Tangible costs
   iii. Total cost of ownership (TCO)
   iv. Productivity paradox
   v. Learning organization
   vi. Value chain
   vii. E-Business Innovation Cycle
   viii. Proxy variable
   ix. Disruptive innovation
   x. Innovator's dilemma

   a. The notion that disruptive innovations can cause established firms or industries to lose market dominance, often leading to failure
   b. Costs that are quantifiable or have physical substance
   c. The process of analyzing an organization's activities to determine where value is added to products and/or services and the costs that are incurred for doing so
   d. New technologies, products, or services that eventually surpass the existing dominant technology or product in a market

   e. Alternative measurement of outcomes, used when it is difficult to determine and measure direct effects

   f. The cost of owning and operating a system, including the total cost of acquisition, as well as all costs associated with its ongoing use and maintenance

   g. An organization that is able to learn, grow, and manage its knowledge well

   h. The extent to which an organization uses information technologies in innovative ways and derives value from these technologies over time

   i. The observation that productivity increases at a rate that is lower than expected when new technologies are introduced

   j. The set of primary and support activities in an organization where value is added to a product or service

2. After reading this chapter, it should be fairly obvious why an IS professional should be able to make a business case for a given system. Why, however, is it just as important for non-IS professionals? How are they involved in this process? What is their role in making information systems investment decisions?

3. Why is it important to look at industry factors when making a business case? What effect might strong competition have on IS investment and use? What effect might weak competition have on IS investment and use? Why?

4. Argue for or against the following statement: "When making the business case, you should concentrate on the decision makers' 'hot buttons' and gloss over some of the other details."

5. What role does the organizational culture play in IS investments? Is this something that can be easily adjusted when necessary? Why or why not? Who is in control of a firm's organizational culture? Do you have personal experiences with this issue?

6. Why can it be difficult to develop an accurate cost-benefit analysis? What factors may be difficult to quantify? How can this be handled? Is this something that should just be avoided altogether? What are the consequences of that approach?

7. Within a small group of classmates, describe any involvement you have had with making the business case for buying something for yourself or within an organization. To whom were you making the case? Was it a difficult sell? Why? To what extent did you follow the guidelines set forth in this chapter? Were your arguments based on faith, fear, fact, or fiction? How did your business case differ from those of others in your group? Were you successful? Why or why not? Were they successful? Why or why not?

8. Of the five industry forces presented in the chapter (Porter's model), which is the most significant for an organization in terms of making IS investment decisions? Why? Which is the least significant? Why?

9. Discuss the following in a small group of classmates or with a friend. Describe a situation from your own experience in which something was purchased where a cost-benefit analysis showed it to have a negative return when based on tangible factors. Was the purchase decision based on intangible factors? Have these intangible factors proven themselves to be worth the investment? Was it harder to convince others of the purchase because of these intangible factors?

10. Contrast the total cost of acquisition versus the total cost of ownership for the purchase of a new car. Demonstrate how the type of car, year, make, model, and so on change the values of various types of costs and benefits.

11. Identify and describe three different situations where fear, faith, or fact arguments would be most compelling when making an information systems investment decision.

12. Talk to an information systems manager and have him or her describe a system that took some length of time to improve organizational productivity in some significant way. Specifically, find out how long and why it took this much time. Was the time frame longer than expected? Why or why not? Was this a typical situation or a unique one?

13. Contrast the differing perspectives of different stakeholders involved in making information systems investment decisions.

14. Why shouldn't every organization deploy innovative information systems? What are some of the recommended characteristics of an organization that are necessary in order for that organization to successfully deploy innovative technologies?

15. Identify examples not discussed in the chapter of disruptive innovations that successfully displaced or marginalized an industry or technology.

16. Apply the progression and effects of disruptive innovation on an industry (see Table 3.7), describing the evolution of a disruptive technology to a product or industry.

17. Find an example not discussed in the book that demonstrated the freeconomics concept of freemium.

18. Find an example not discussed in the book that demonstrated the freeconomics concept of cross-subsidy.

19. Find an example not discussed in the book that demonstrated the freeconomics concept of zero marginal cost.

20. Find an example not discussed in the book that demonstrated the freeconomics concept of labor exchange.

Application Exercises

 Note: The existing data files referenced in these exercises are available on the Student Companion Web site: www.pearsonhighered.com/valacich.

 Spreadsheet Application: Valuing Information Systems

The cost of maintaining information systems is high for Campus Travel. You have been assigned to evaluate the total cost of ownership (TCO) of a few systems that are currently in use by Campus Travel employees. Take a look at the TCO.csv file to obtain the list of systems that are in use and the costs associated with maintaining the software, hardware, and the associated personnel for each type of system. Calculate the following for your operations manager:

1. The costs for server hardware by adding a new column to include Web servers. This includes $4,500 for the main campus and $2,200 for the other campuses.
2. The TCO for the entire IS in Campus Travel
   Hint: Sum all the values for all the systems together.
3. The TCO for servers and network components of the IS.

4. Make sure that you format the table, including using the currency format, in a professional manner.

 Database Application: Building a System Usage Database

To understand the assets in Campus Travel, the IS manager has asked you to design a database that would be able to store all the assets. Your manager asks you to do the following:

1. Create a new blank database called asset.mdb.
2. Create a new table called "assets" in the asset database with the following fields:
   a. Item ID (Text field)
   b. Item Name (Text field)
   c. Description (Memo field)
   d. Category (hardware, software, other)
   e. Condition (new, good, fair, poor)
   f. Acquisition Date (Date field)
   g. Purchase Price (Currency field)
   h. Current Value (Currency field)

Team Work Exercise: Pizza, Anyone?

Compare with your classmates your experiences with ordering pizza over the phone for delivery to your home. When you call to order the pizza, do you have to give them your full name, address, and phone number every time you call them, or do they merely ask your phone number and then automatically know who you are and where you live? If it is the latter, then they are using an information system to keep track of you so that they do not continually have to

annoy you by asking you for your name, address, and phone number every time you call. How important is this to you? Is this giving the pizza company a competitive advantage? Is it as important to you as the price of the pizza or how fast it is delivered? Are there conditions under which superior use of information systems can compensate for inferior products (think about products other than pizza, too)?

Answers to the Self-Study Questions

1. A, p. 85
2. B, p. 114
3. B, p. 101
4. B, p. 90
5. D, p. 97
6. C, p. 85
7. C, p. 88
8. D, p. 91
9. D, p. 114
10. B, p. 116

Case ❶

Netflix

Remember the old brick-and-mortar movie rental services? You drove to the physical location, scanned shelves for your movie of choice (too frequently, it wasn't in), paid the clerk, and left. The flick was due back in twenty-four hours (or, at most, three to five days later), or you were billed a hefty late fee. In some cases, forgetful customers answered the door to find a police officer asking why they hadn't returned a rental movie.

Movie rental stores still exist, of course—Blockbuster may come to mind first, although many of its stores have closed—but now there are alternatives. Pay-per-view is an option for cable and satellite dish TV subscribers, but choices are limited to the services' picks and are available only after movies have been offered as rental DVDs and videos for thirty days. Since customers are not always satisfied with limits inherent in these options—late fees, unavailability of newer films, short turnaround times, and so on—it had to follow that someone would come up with the idea to offer a click-based online movie rental service.

Enter Netflix in 2002, the first and now the largest online movie rental service. As of 2008, Netflix offered 8.4 million subscribers 100,000 movie choices. The term "subscriber" is the key to Netflix's unique idea. Movie aficionados subscribe to the Netflix service by paying a monthly fee based on the number of movies they want to rent each month. For $4.99 per month (the lowest-priced plan), customers can rent two movies per month. Fees continue upward as the number of movie rentals per month increase, with the top fee set at $16.99 per month—three DVDs out at a time and unlimited rentals per month. For all plans, postage is paid each way, the U.S. Postal Service handles mailed DVDs both ways, and there are no late fees. When one movie is returned, a second is mailed from a list of preferences the customer sets.

Soon after Netflix's inception in 2002, Blockbuster, the nation's largest movie rental chain, and Wal-Mart, the largest business in the United States,

began to offer in-store subscription services similar to Netflix's model. By 2006, however, Wal-Mart had dropped its movie rental subscription service, and Blockbuster's subscription service was losing money.

Netflix's extraordinary and, therefore, popular service has outpaced competitive movie rental services, including pay-per-view, because it personalizes a customer's movie rental experience to a degree not possible before. This personalized service asks the customer to rate up to forty movies. From this information, software called Cinematch creates a profile of each customer and a list of recommended movies. If, for example, a customer liked *Troy*, he or she may also like *Alexander*, and that movie will be included in a list the customer accesses by clicking on "recommendations." The customer can then opt to place any of the recommended movies in his or her queue. Customers manipulate the movies listed in the queue by adding new titles to the list, removing titles, and moving titles to the top or to other locations on the list. Netflix's Cinematch system allows customers to tap a wide database of movies, many of which they may not have been aware of at all since it will move to the next movie in a customer's queue if a more recent and popular listing is not immediately available.

Another strategy employed by Netflix is the "friends" feature, which allows subscribers to share and recommend movies to one another. Although not a unique idea to the Internet, this creates online communities of Netflix customers that further drive the business. A service added in 2007 lets customers view movies immediately on their PCs or Macs. In 2008 Netflix introduced a service that allowed subscribers to instantly watch streamed content on their TVs through Netflix-ready devices such as internet enabled Blu-ray players or Microsoft's Xbox 360.

Netflix is not without critics. It turns out that the service "rewards" customers with the fewest monthly rentals and "punishes" those with the most rentals in

terms of popular movie availability and promptness of shipping. This policy is spelled out in the company's Terms of Service, published on the Netflix Web site:

In determining priority for shipping and inventory allocation, we may utilize many different factors, including without limitation, the number and type of DVDs you rent through our service, the subscription plan you select, as well as other uses of our service by you. For example, if all other factors are the same, we give priority to those members who receive the fewest DVDs through our service.

According to the Netflix site, when you add a popular movie that is currently unavailable, you are added to the internal list that rates customers according to profitability. There is an assumption by the customers that the service is linear, meaning that the first customer to request the movie would be the first customer to get the movie—or first in, first out. In reality, the priority service equation selects customers on the basis of their profitability. With shipping being the major cost for the online movie distributor, customers who cost the most in terms of shipping may not receive popular movies first.

What does this mean for the customers? If you are a customer who uses the service infrequently, then you are highly profitable for Netflix since your shipping costs are low. Therefore, your selections are prioritized. The customers who use the service frequently or what Netflix would deem "overfrequently" are seen as not as profitable and therefore do not receive priority.

In 2004, this policy caused a "frequent" Netflix customer to sue the company in a class action lawsuit titled *Chavez v. Netflix, Inc.* The plaintiff in the case, Frank Chavez, claimed Netflix's claims that a subscriber could rent "unlimited" DVDs each month and receive them in "a day's time" were false. (Chavez had attempted to rent hundreds of DVDs a month but sued when he found he could not.) Although Netflix denied any wrong-doing, they settled the suit in 2005. Chavez received $2,000, and his lawyers got over $2.5 million. Certain Netflix cus-tomers who joined the class action suit were upgraded to a higher plan for a short period, and Netflix instituted a limited try-the-plan-for-three-months-free offer.

Although some customers have expressed dissatisfaction, Netflix cus-tomer numbers have increased rather than decreased.

Questions

1. Can local video stores survive in the digital world? Contrast their evolution with that of local bookstores. What is similar? What is unique?
2. Forecast the future of Netflix in regard to the advent of on-demand video where any type of video content is available at any time on any device.
3. Discuss whether you believe Netflix's Terms of Service are fair.

Based on:

Elgan, M. (2006, January 30). How to hack Netflix. *Information Week*. Retrieved May 12, 2008, from http://www.informationweek.com/news/showArticle.jhtml?articleID=177105341.

Frauenfelder, M. (2005, November 2). Netflix settlement details. *Boing Boing*. Retrieved May 12, 2008, from http://www.boingboing.net/2005/11/02/netflix_lawsuit_sett.html.

Mullaney, T. J., and R. Hof (2005, November 10). Netflix starring in merger story? *Business Week Online*. Retrieved May 12, 2008, from http://www.businessweek.com/technology/content/nov2005/tc20051110_143721.htm.

Netflix terms of use (n.d.). Retrieved May 12, 2008, from http://www.netflix.com/TermsOfUse.

O'Brien, J. M. (2002, December). The Netflix effect. *Wired*. Retrieved May 12, 2008, from http://www.wired.com/wired/archive/10.12/netflix.html.

Case ❷

LinkedIn

Netflix is for video entertainment; iTunes services music lovers; YouTube, Facebook, and MySpace are primarily for socializing; Flickr is for photo exchange; Second Life and World of Warcraft are for participating in virtual communities; Gamezone and Shockwave are for gamesters; and so on and on. It would seem that the WWW has anticipated all of our needs and responded. But wait, what's out there for those of us who want to fur-ther our professional lives—to visit with others in our field of expertise, to look at jobs that are available in other parts of the world, to find out what's happening in the business world outside our own familiar circle and to garner introductions to those who might help us succeed? LinkedIn is an online service that fills this niche. LinkedIn advertises itself as: "an online network of over 22 million experienced professionals from around the world, rep-resenting over 150 industries."

Reid Hoffman, a former executive vice president of PayPal, founded LinkedIn in 2002; the service was launched in May 2003. Hoffman remains chairman of the board at LinkedIn, which is based in Mountain View, California, but also has offices in Omaha, New York, and London. His LinkedIn profile is available at: http://www.linkedin.com/in/reidhoffman.

Joining LinkedIn is free; upgrading to a paid account with additional "tools" is optional. Newcomers to LinkedIn create a profile, listing professional accomplish-ments. Each newcomer then links trusted colleagues, contacts, and clients—called *connections*—by inviting them to join and linking to him or her. In this way, LinkedIn participants create their own professional networks, where contacts may number in the thousands. Connec-tions can be used in many ways:

- Users list trusted contacts, who then list their contacts, called second degree connections. Second degree connections list their trusted contacts, called third degree connections. In this way, the original LinkedIn user brings together thousands of professionals, gaining many valuable contacts.
- Users can then find jobs, people, and business opportunities recommended by someone in the network.

- Employers using the network can list jobs and search for available candidates to fill job openings.
- Job seekers can search the connections of potential employers and find mutual connections who might introduce them.

A free feature called "LinkedIn Answers" lets users ask business-related questions for the community to answer. LinkedIn Groups is another free feature that allows users to make additional con-tacts by joining alumni, professional, or other job-related groups.

A mobile version of LinkedIn, avail-able in six languages, was launched in February 2008.

There are ways to enhance one's use of professional profile sites such as LinkedIn, writes Kevin Donlin for the *Minneapolis-St. Paul Star Tribune*. First, enhance your profile. One way to do this is to jazz up your profile with a few perti-nent details and statements from col-leagues. For example, staff members at LinkedIn advised Guy Kawasaki, manag-ing director of Garage Technology Ventures in San Francisco, California, to add the following statement from a former colleague at Apple Computers, where Guy said he was "Chief Evangelist." "Spirited and exceptionally bright with a highly developed sense of humor, Guy continues to be one of the most gifted marketing executives I know."

Enhance your profile, Donlin advises, but "keep your dirt to yourself."

According to NBC News, 77 percent of employers will search the Internet to check your background, and 35 percent of employers have eliminated a candidate for consideration after finding 'digital dirt' about them online." So don't post that video of yourself imbibing too much at a party on Facebook, and remember that potential employers may not appre-

ciate the video of the tasteless practical joke you played on a friend, so keep it off YouTube.

Clearly, professional networking sites such as LinkedIn are yet another valuable technological tool for Internet users and entrepreneurs alike.

Questions

1. Do you think it is ethical for employers to search the Internet for information on potential employees?
2. Describe several ways to enhance/hurt a person's profile on a site like LinkedIn.
3. Have you joined, or do you plan to join, LinkedIn (or a similar type of site)? Why or why not?

Based on:

Donlin, K. (2008, April 9). Three ways to get found and hired. *Star Tribune.* Retrieved May 12, 2008, from http://www.startribune.com/jobs/career/15116626.html.

Kawasaki, G. (2007, January 16). LinkedIn profile extreme makeover. Retrieved May 12, 2008, from http://blog.guykawasaki.com/2007/01/linkedin_profil.html.

LinkedIn. (2008, May 6). In *Wikipedia, the free encyclopedia.* Retrieved May 12, 2008, from http://en.wikipedia.org/w/index.php?title=LinkedIn&oldid=210484559.

What is LinkedIn? (n.d.). Retrieved May 12, 2008, from http://www.linkedin.com/static?key=what_is_linkedin&trk=hb_what.

Managing the Information Systems Infrastructure

After reading this chapter, you will be able to do the following:

1. List the essential information systems infrastructure components and describe why they are necessary for satisfying an organization's informational needs.

2. Describe the components of an organization's hardware infrastructure and highlight current trends.

3. Describe the components of an organization's software infrastructure and highlight current trends.

4. Describe the components of an organization's communications and collaboration infrastructure and highlight current trends.

5. Describe the components of an organization's data and knowledge infrastructure.

Preview

As any city depends on a functioning infrastructure, companies operating in a digital world are relying on a comprehensive information systems infrastructure to support their business processes and competitive strategy. With ever-increasing speed, transactions are conducted; likewise, with ever-increasing amounts of data to be captured, analyzed, and stored, companies have to thoroughly plan and manage their infrastructure needs in order to gain the greatest returns on their information systems investments. When planning and managing their information systems architectures, organizations must answer many important and difficult questions. For example, how will we utilize information systems to enable our competitive strategy? What technologies and systems best support our core business processes? Which vendors should we partner with, which technologies do we adopt, and which do we avoid? What hardware, software, or services do we buy, build, or have managed by an outside service provider? How can the organization get the most out of the data captured from internal and external sources? Clearly, effectively managing an organization's information systems infrastructure is a complex but necessary activity in today's digital world.

This chapter focuses on helping managers understand the key components of a comprehensive information systems infrastructure and why its careful management is necessary. With an increasing complexity of an organization's information needs and an increasing complexity of the systems needed to satisfy these requirements, the topic of infrastructure management is fundamental for managing in the digital world.

Managing in the Digital World: "I Googled You!"

You're researching a paper for a physics class, and you need information on quarks. Google it (see Figure 4.1). You'd like to locate a high school classmate, but no one in your graduating class knows where she is. Google her. You're watching a movie, and a character says she "googled" a blind date. The term "google" has become so familiar to Internet users that it's often used as a verb. In fact, the term has become so common that Google is becoming concerned that its use as a verb is a copyright infringement, asking dictionaries such as *Merriam-Webster* to change their definition of Google to "to use the Google search engine to obtain information . . . on the World Wide Web."

When Larry Page and Sergey Brin started work on a search engine called BackRub in January 1996, they probably had no idea they were creating an Internet Age phenomenon. When they saw the infinite possibilities for their brainchild, however, the two changed the name of their project to "Google." According to the Google.com Web site, "Google is a play on the word googol, which was coined by Milton Sirotta, nephew of American mathematician Edward Kasner, and was popularized in the book *Mathematics and the Imagination* by Kasner and James Newman. It refers to the number represented by the numeral 1 followed by 100 zeros. Google's use of the term reflects the company's mission to organize the immense, seemingly infinite amount of information available on the Web."

Google has continued to innovate far beyond its 1996 beginning and to move beyond the search engine market, following its mission "to organize the world's information and make it universally accessible and useful." The company offers e-mail, instant messaging, and mobile text messaging services. Other Google services include an automated news site, a Web blogging site, free imaging software, and a site for programmers interested in creating new applications. In mid-2006, Google was poised to challenge PayPal in the Internet account business and to give eBay a run for its money in the online auction business.

Google's e-mail service, like the company itself, is unique. Launched in 2004 as "Gmail," it was initially available to newcomers only by invitation from someone who already had the service. Gmail incorporates e-mail and instant messaging so that users can e-mail in the traditional manner and/or "meet" in real time.

The highest revenue generator for Google is its AdSense program. This program allows any Web site to publish advertisements on each of its pages. The Web site publisher is paid every time someone clicks on an ad originating from that page. The AdSense program also lets Web site publishers analyze how many people look at the site, the cost per click, click-through rates, and so on. The AdSense program can tailor the type of ads that are placed on a Web site—that is, publishers can block ads they don't want to appear, such as competitor ads, ads concerning death or war, and ads for "adult" material.

Another Google service popular with users is Froogle, which uses Google search technology to let consumers search for and compare products by product type, price, and so on. Other features include the following:

- The Google News service, which automatically combines news clippings from various online newspapers and provides them on one page for users' convenience.
- Google Scholar, which helps researchers search through publications.

FIGURE 4.1

Google search page.

- Google Finance, which searches for finance-related news and stock information.
- Other specialized search capabilities, including video search, image search, mail-order catalog search, book search, blog search, and university search.

In addition, these services can also be accessed through mobile phones using the Google mobile products. Google continues to add to its list of features:

- 2007: A free 411 service (GOOG-411) allows users to name a city and state, then ask for the telephone number of a specific business; calls are directly routed to the business or results are sent via text message or Google Maps to the user's phone.
- 2007: Knol—a service that combines aspects of Wikipedia and Squidoo to create a user-generated knowledge base of everything. Critics called Knol a shift in Google's operating focus—instead of organizing existing Web content for search access, Google was moving into creating content. Since Knol content could be listed first in Google search results, critics also saw this feature as unfair competition for other knowledge-based sites.
- 2007: Google launches OpenSocial, a set of three common application programming interfaces (APIs) that would allow developers to access core functions and information at social networks, including (1) profile information; (2) friends information; and (3) activities. OpenSocial allows developers to create applications that work on all social networks that support OpenSocial and thus eliminates the necessity for social network developers to learn and maintain yet another markup language for each additional social network. Relatedly, Google Friend Connect lets site owners add social networking content to their sites.
- 2008: Google launches Android, an open-source operating system for mobile phones, directly competing against Apple's iPhone, Research in Motion's BlackBerry, and Window's Mobile operating system.
- 2008: Google launches Chrome, a browser lauded for its speed and unique features, starting yet another "browser war."

Google has clearly become a significant player on the Internet and in users' daily lives. Look for new Google products and services at **http://labs.google.com/**.

After reading this chapter, you will be able to answer the following:

1. What are the infrastructure needs for Google if it were to continue expanding at its current pace?
2. How does Google benefit from a well-functioning infrastructure?
3. How would you rank order the various infrastructure components described in this chapter in their importance to Google's success? Explain your rationale.

Based on:

Anonymous (n.d.). Company overview. Retrieved September 19, 2008, from http://www.google.com/intl/en/corporate/.

Anonymous (n.d.). Google milestones. Retrieved May 16, 2008, from http://www.google.com/corporate/history.html.

Arrington, M. (2007, April 6). Google launches free 411 service. *TechCrunch.* Retrieved May 16, 2008, from http://www.techcrunch.com/2007/04/06/google-launches-free-411-business.

Arrington, M. (2007, October 30). Details revealed: Google OpenSocial to launch Thursday. *TechCrunch.* Retrieved May 16, 2008, from http://www.techcrunch.com/2007/10/30/details-revealed-google-opensocial-to-be-common-apis-for-building-social-apps.

Claburn, T. (2006, January 19). Feds seek Google search records in child porn investigation. *InformationWeek.* Retrieved May 16, 2008, from http://www.informationweek.com/internet/showArticle.jhtml?articleID=177101999.

Gonsalves, A. (2005, October 25). Google testing possible eBay competition. *InformationWeek.* Retrieved May 16, 2008, from http://www.informationweek.com/story/showArticle.jhtml?articleID=172900366.

Riley, D. (2007, December 14). Google Knol: A step too far? *TechCrunch.* Retrieved May 16, 2008, from http://www.techcrunch.com/2007/12/14/google-knol-a-step-too-far.

Sinrod, E. J. (2006, January 19). Google in a patent pickle. *CNetNews.com.* Retrieved May 16, 2008, from http://news.com/Google+in+a+patent+pickle/2010-1071_3-6027546.html.

Snyder, J. (2008, January 13). First Google Android phone suite completed. *Infoworld.* Retrieved May 16, 2008, from http://weblog.infoworld.com/techwatch/archives/015486.html.

The Information Systems Infrastructure

Any area where people live or work needs a supporting **infrastructure**, which entails the interconnection of all basic facilities and services enabling the area to function properly. The infrastructure of a city, for example, includes components such as streets, power, telephone, water, and sewage lines but also schools, retail stores, and law enforcement. Both the area's inhabitants and the businesses depend on that infrastructure; cities with a good infrastructure, for example, are considered more livable than cities with poorer infrastructure and are much more likely to attract businesses and residents. Likewise, valuable employees often choose firms with better facilities, management, and business processes.

For organizations, many decisions are based on the provision of such infrastructure, for example when choosing a site for a new manufacturing plant or company headquarters.

Indeed, many municipalities attempt to attract new businesses and industries by setting up new commercial zones with a well-planned infrastructure. In some cases, specific infrastructure components are of special importance. One such example is search engine giant Google, which has data centers located all over the world to offer the best performance to its users. Google's newest data center was built in the small town of The Dalles, Oregon, located on the banks of the Columbia River (see Figure 4.2). Why would a company such as Google choose such a rural location? First, the location offered connectivity, using a state-of-the-art fiber-optic network to provide high-speed data transfer to the Internet backbone. Second—and maybe more important—the location on the river would give the data center access to water for its cooling needs (as a large number of computers generates a tremendous amount of heat) and uninterrupted power from a nearby hydroelectric dam; in addition to being relatively inexpensive, this renewable source of energy contributes to Google's efforts to be carbon neutral from 2007 onward. As you can see from this example, companies such as Google must consider far more than just the need for increased data storage space and processing power.

For organizations operating globally, managing a comprehensive, worldwide infrastructure poses additional challenges. This is particularly acute when operating in developing nations. For example, in many parts of the world, organizations cannot count on an uninterrupted supply of water or electricity. Consequently, many of the large call centers in India that support customers around the world for companies like Dell Computers or Citibank have, for example, installed massive power generators to minimize the effects of frequent power outages or have set up their own satellite links to be independent from the local, unreliable communications networks.

As people and companies rely on basic infrastructures to function, businesses also rely on an **information systems infrastructure** (consisting of hardware, software, communication and collaboration networks, data, facilities, and human resources) to support their decision making, business processes, and competitive strategy. Almost all of an organization's business processes depend on the underlying information systems infrastructure, albeit to different degrees. For example, an organization's management needs an infrastructure to support a variety of activities, including reliable communication networks to support collaboration between suppliers and customers, accurate and timely data and knowledge to gain business intelligence, and information systems to aid decision making and support business processes. In sum, organizations rely on a complex, interrelated information systems infrastructure to effectively thrive in the ever-increasing, competitive

FIGURE 4.2

Google data center in The Dalles, Oregon.

FIGURE 4.3

The information systems
infrastructure.

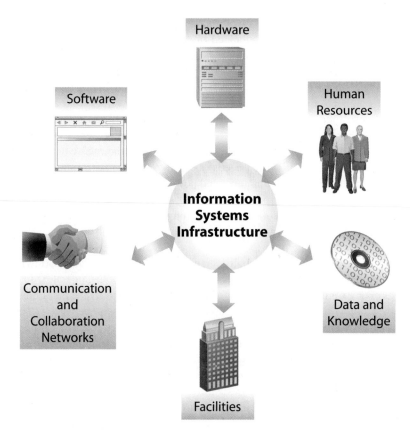

digital world. A modern organization's information systems infrastructure includes the following components (see Figure 4.3):

- Hardware
- Software
- Communications and collaboration networks
- Data and knowledge
- Human resources
- Facilities

In the rest of this chapter, we will discuss each of these components, highlight their role in an organization's information systems infrastructure, and present current approaches to addressing infrastructure-related challenges[1]. To dig deeper into the technical aspects of the various infrastructure components, refer to the Technology Briefing.

Information Systems Hardware Infrastructure

Information systems hardware is an integral part of the IS infrastructure and is broadly classified into three types: input, processing, and output technologies (see Figure 4.4). **Input technologies** are used to enter information into a computer. **Processing technologies** transform inputs into outputs. Finally, **output technologies**, such as a computer monitor and printer, deliver information to you in a usable format. This section describes each of these three key elements of information systems hardware (for more, see the Technology Briefing or Evans et al., 2009.)

Input Technologies

For information systems hardware to perform a task, data must be input into the system. Certain types of data can be entered more easily using one type of input device than another. There are four general categories of input devices: entering text and numbers,

[1] Human resources were discussed in Chapter 1; Facilities are discussed in Chapter 7.

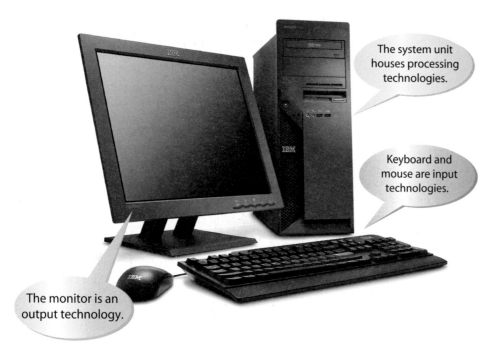

FIGURE 4.4

Input, processing, and output technologies.

pointing and selecting information, entering **batch data** (i.e., large amounts of routine information, such as checks at a bank), and entering audio and video (see Table 4.1). For example, **keyboards** are currently the primary means to enter text and numbers. Alternatively, architects and engineers can use **scanners** to enter their designs and drawings into computers. When interacting with your computer, the most common **pointing device** you use is the **mouse** to select menu items or drag and drop items. A great deal of research and development are conducted to identify optimal ways to input various types of information and to build and sell new input devices (Te'eni, Carey, and Zhang, 2007).

Processing Technologies

In this section we provide a brief overview of computer processing. To begin, we describe how data and information are represented within a computer. Next, we briefly describe the internal processing components of a desktop computer, focusing primarily on the central processing unit and data storage technologies.

TABLE 4.1 Methods for Input into an Information System

Category	Typical Devices	Emerging Technology
Entering original text/numbers	QWERTY keyboard	Laser keyboard
	Ergonomic keyboard	Voice-to-text
Selecting and pointing	Mouse	Eye tracking
	Trackball	
	Joystick	
	Touch screen	
	Light pen	
	Touch pad	
Entering batch data	Scanner	Biometric reader
	Bar-code/optical character reader	RFID scanner
Entering audio and video	Microphone	Digital video
	Digital camera	

Binary Code Your brain can readily process written words, photographs, music, an instructor's lecture (at least some of the time), videos, and much more. If you grew up speaking English, your brain will process incoming information in that language. Similarly, computers can process incoming data, but only after the words, photos, music, and other information have been translated into a language they can understand. The language that computers understand is called **machine language**. In machine language, the instructions the computer has to perform are represented using **binary code**, which means that all incoming data is translated into the 1s and 0s of binary math. Binary, or base-2 math (2, 4, 8, 16, 32, and so on), is used by computers instead of the more familiar base 10 because it matches the way a computer's hardware works. The basic instruction units for all the work the computer does represent on/off commands for tiny electric switches inside the computer's processor, with a 1 representing the flow of an electric current and a 0 representing no electrical flow. The individual 1s and 0s that make up the code are called **bits**—short for "binary digits." Eight bits equal a **byte**, or about one typed character, such as the letter "A" or the number "6" on the keyboard. You will often see computer storage and memory sizes expressed in multiples of bytes (see Table 4.2). Companies such as Google already have databases far larger than a petabyte (1 quadrillion bytes), but memory and storage capacities will soon be measured in exabytes (1 quintillion bytes) and zettabytes (1 sextillion bytes).

One of the biggest challenges for the computer industry has been to determine how to translate all the different types of information into digital data that a computer can understand. Early computers could not translate incoming data at all. They used paper cards on which strings of 1s and 0s were represented by punched holes. Later, computers received information from a keyboard, which was the first time a translation was made from text that the users could understand to bits that the computer can understand. Today's computers can translate many types of data, including words, photos, sound, and video, to binary code, then they manipulate it and store it. One of the main reasons computers become so quickly outdated is that newer models keep coming out that can process larger amounts and more types of information.

Programs (applications) you run on your computer contain instructions, such as telling the computer to open a specific file, move data from one location to another, open a new window on the monitor screen, add a column of figures, and so on. Before the computer can follow program instructions, however, those instructions must be converted to machine language. The central processing unit (described later) translates incoming data and instructions into binary code. Then, the bits are organized into groups—for instance, 64-bit instructions—that represent specific operations and storage locations.

Once the computer receives instructions from a program, it processes the information and presents it in a form that you, the computer user, can understand. In a word processing program, for example, the letters and numbers you type are displayed on the monitor just as they would appear on a sheet of paper if you were using an old-fashioned typewriter. But, unlike on the typewriter, when you press, for example, the "L" key on the computer keyboard, the computer is actually receiving the information as a series of 1s and 0s, specifically "01001100." As you type a letter or a term paper, the data is processed, and

TABLE 4.2 Elements of Computer Storage

Measurement	No. of Bits	No. of Bytes	No. of Kilobytes	No. of Megabytes	No. of Gigabytes
Byte	8	1			
Kilobyte* (K)	8,192	1,024	1		
Megabyte (MB)	8,388,608	1,048,576	1,024	1	
Gigabyte (GB)	8,589,934,592	1,073,741,824	1,048,576	1,024	1
Terabyte (TB)	8,796,093,022,208	1,099,511,627,776	1,073,741,824	1,048,576	1,024

*A kilobyte equals a little more than 1,000 bytes, but the number is usually rounded to 1,000. The same is true for the number of kilobytes in a megabyte, and so on.

Ethical Dilemma

Cookies: Harmless Identifiers or Privacy Violations?

Most online businesses use "cookies" to collect data about visitors to their Web sites. Cookies are bits of code that a Web server can store on a computer user's hard disk. Contrary to many media definitions, they are not programs and don't function like programs. They can't gather all kinds of information about you from your computer, like your bank account balance, eBay account number, or your credit card number. In fact, each Web site that places a cookie on your machine can retrieve only the information in that cookie, such as a user ID and/or password for the Web site, or what you bought on a shopping site.

Web sites use cookies in many different ways:

- Recognizing the user ID and password for a particular visitor, so that each visit does not require reentering passwords and IDs. These cookies let sites "recognize" you and greet you by name.
- Counting site visitors: Sites can determine how many users have visited, how many times a single user has visited, and can distinguish between first-time visitors and returning visitors.
- Customizing sites: Sites can store user preferences, so that the site can be customized for each visitor.
- Shopping carts and quick checkout options: The only way sites can offer these options is to use cookies that keep track of items selected for purchase.

Cookies, in reality, are benign entities that let certain Web site features function correctly. So why so many articles about cookies and privacy concerns? Because:

- Cookies are downloaded to hard drives without computer users' knowledge or consent.
- Cookies can be used to track preferences, and marketers like to target those consumers most likely to buy their products. Therefore, if you look at an item of clothing online, chances are you will be presented online ads from several retailers offering similar products when you visit other sites. You may find this annoying, but marketers tried to target you before the Internet, and probably aren't soon going to stop.
- Since cookies save certain information about your purchases and shopping habits, when this information is sold to others, marketers can precisely target advertising, which makes consumers

uncomfortable, because it feels too much like spying.
- Unique to the Internet are companies that place ads on multiple Web sites. DoubleClick is a famous example. Many Web sites used DoubleClick to place banner ads on multiple sites. This capability allowed DoubleClick to place small cookies on the hard drives of computers whose users visited the sites with DoubleClick banner ads. DoubleClick could then aggregate information from the cookies to create rich profiles of the visitors to these sites. When DoubleClick threatened to link the profiles back to user names and addresses and sell the information, the public was outraged.

Some sites have strict privacy policies that forbid selling cookie-collected information, and an increasing number of informed Web users are demanding such policies.

Users of most browsers can opt not to accept cookies, to be warned before accepting cookies, and to delete cookies presently on the hard drive, but there are downsides to each option. If you ask to be warned, the warning will constantly pop up as you surf the Web. If you refuse to accept cookies, or if you opt to delete cookies already stored on your computer's hard drive, many of the Web sites you visit will not function correctly. For example, if you have asked for stock market reports or otherwise customized home pages and other data you receive, this information will no longer be available unless you again accept cookies at those sites. If you have entered passwords and IDs to use sites such as your bank, Amazon.com, or a book club, you will not be able to access those sites if cookies on your hard drive have been deleted. In addition, most shopping sites will not function correctly, since online shopping carts usually work with cookies.

Perhaps the best policy concerning privacy and cookies is for Internet users to be aware of a Web site's privacy policy or lack thereof, and, since cookies are the one electronic tracking device users can control, to periodically delete those cookies that are no longer in use.

Based on:

Anonymous (n.d.). CookieCentral—ActiveFAQ. Retrieved May 16, 2008, from http://www.cookiecentral.com/faq.htm.

Brain, M. (n.d.). How Internet cookies work. Retrieved May 16, 2008, from http://computer.howstuffworks.com/cookie1.htm.

FIGURE 4.5

Information is translated into binary code so that the computer can store and manipulate the information.

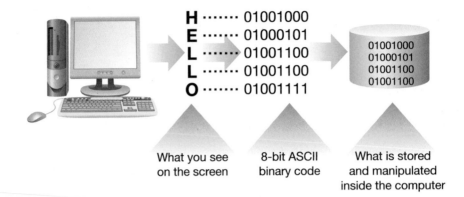

What you see on the screen	8-bit ASCII binary code	What is stored and manipulated inside the computer

then displayed on the monitor in a form that makes sense to you. The binary code the computer actually uses is hidden from your view (see Figure 4.5). You see words, lines, and paragraphs that you can print out on paper, store on the computer's hard disk, or even post to an Internet Web site.

System Unit A computer's **system unit** is the physical box that houses all of the electronic components that do the work of the computer and allows for accessing CD-ROM or DVD drives or connecting peripheral hardware, such as a keyboard, a mouse, speakers, printers, scanners, audio or video equipment, USB devices, or memory cards.

Central Processing Unit The **central processing unit (CPU)** is often called the computer's brain. It is also called a **microprocessor**, processor, or chip, and is responsible for performing all of the operations of the computer. Its job includes loading the operating system (e.g., Windows Vista, MAC OS X, Linux) when the machine is first turned on and performing, coordinating, and managing all the calculations and instructions relayed to it while the computer is running.

The CPU consists of two main sections: the **arithmetic logic unit (ALU)** and the **control unit**. The ALU performs mathematics, including all forms of addition, subtraction, multiplication, and division. It also performs logical operations, which involve comparing packets of data, then executing appropriate instructions. Combined in various ways, these functions allow the computer to perform complicated operations rapidly. The control unit works closely with the ALU, fetching and decoding instructions as well as retrieving and storing data.

The CPU, a small device made of silicon, is composed of millions of tiny transistors arranged in complex patterns that allow it to interpret and manipulate data. For example, Intel's latest generation CPUs pack more than 1.9 billion transistors into an area about the size of a dime. These transistors are so small that you could fit a hundred inside a single human cell. These CPUs are packaged in containers that are bigger than a dime because additional wiring is used to connect all of these transistors of the CPU to the motherboard (see Figure 4.6). The inner workings of a CPU are very complex, and, for

FIGURE 4.6

Using 45 nm transistor technology, 30 million transistors fit on the head of a pin.

most of us, it is easiest to think of a CPU as being a "black box" where all the processing occurs.

MOORE'S LAW. The general trend in computing is toward smaller, faster, and cheaper devices. But for how long can this trend continue? In the 1970s, Dr. Gordon Moore, then a researcher at Intel, hypothesized that computer processing performance would double every eighteen months. When Moore made this bold prediction, he did not limit it to any specified period of time. This prediction became known as **Moore's Law**. Interestingly, the first CPU had 2,200 transistors, so Dr. Moore has been basically correct so far. Feature size—the size of lines on the chip through which signals pass—has been reduced from about the width of a human hair in the 1960s (20 microns—a micron is equal to 1 millionth of a meter), to the size of a bacterium in the 1970s (5 microns), to smaller than a virus today (.032 micron, or 32 nm). As feature size is reduced, a greater number and variety of circuits can be packed increasingly closer together. Both feature density and complexity have facilitated the continued performance increases that microprocessors have realized. Figure 4.7 shows this trend. For more on Moore's Law, visit Intel's Web site (http://www.intel.com/technology/mooreslaw/index.htm); if you search on the Web using the phrase "Moore's Law," you will get many interesting pages to review.

The number of transistors that can be packed into a modern CPU and the speed at which processing and other activities occur are remarkable. For example, the Intel Core 2 Extreme CPU can complete hundreds of millions of operations every second. To achieve these incredible speeds, the CPU must execute instructions very rapidly. In addition to the number of transistors on the CPU, three other factors greatly influence its speed—its system clock speed (the number of instructions a CPU can execute in a fixed amount of time), registers, and cache memory; please refer to the Technology Briefing for more details on these factors.

Primary Storage Computers need temporary storage space, called **primary storage,** for current information. Typically, primary storage consists of **registers** and **cache** (used to store data for immediate use by the CPU), **random-access memory** (RAM, used to store the programs and data currently in use) and **read-only memory** (ROM, used to store programs and instructions that are automatically loaded when the computer is turned on, such as the **basic input/output system [BIOS]**). RAM provides temporary storage of data for the CPU. Because instructions and work stored in RAM are lost when the power to the computer is turned off or when new data is placed there, it is referred to as **volatile memory**. In contrast, ROM is **nonvolatile memory**, which means that it does not lose its instructions when the power to the computer is shut off.

Secondary Storage **Secondary storage** is for permanently storing data to a large-capacity storage component, such as a **hard disk** (or **hard drive**), **diskette**, CD-ROM disk, **magnetic tape**, or, of course, a flash drive (see Table 4.3). Hard disks and diskettes are magnetic media.

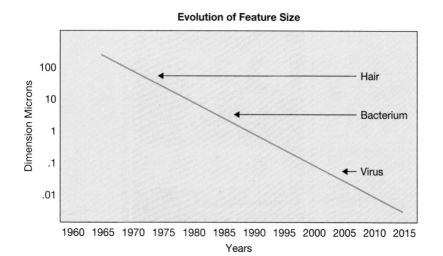

Evolution of Feature Size

FIGURE 4.7

Moore's law predicted that computer processing performance would double every eighteen months. To increase performance, feature size has to shrink.

TABLE 4.3 Comparing Methods of Secondary Storage.

Type	Speed	Method of Data Access	Relative Cost/MB
Magnetic tape	Slow	Sequential	Low
Floppy disk	Slow	Direct	Low
Hard drive	Fast	Direct	High
Compact discs	Medium	Direct	Low
Optical disks	Fast	Direct	Medium
Flash drive	Fast	Direct	High

That is, diskettes and the disks inside a hard disk drive are coated with a magnetic material. Reading data from the disks involves converting magnetized spots representing data to electrical impulses that can be understood by the processor. Writing to the disks is the reverse—converting electrical impulses to magnetized spots representing data.

Optical disks, such as **CD-ROMs** or **DVDs** (which have higher capacity than CD-ROMs), are coated with a metallic substance, and are written to when a laser beam passing over the surface of the disk burns small spots into the disk surface, each one representing a data packet. The data can be read when a laser scans the surface of the disk and a lens picks up various light reflections from the data spots. Some optical disks are read-only. That is, information is entered on them by a manufacturer. The information cannot be changed nor can new information be written to the disk by the computer user. Other optical disks can be written to by the user.

A variation of ROM used as secondary storage is erasable ROM, referred to as **electrically erasable programmable read-only memory (EEPROM)**. You may have heard EEPROM referred to by a more user-friendly term, **flash memory**. This type of memory can be repeatedly written to and erased like RAM, but, unlike RAM, it retains its information after power is turned off. Flash memory is the storage technology behind many popular consumer devices such as digital cameras, MP3 players, cellular phones, and portable storage devices called **flash drives** (see Figure 4.8).

FIGURE 4.8

Flash memory is used as a storage technology in a variety of devices.

BlackBerry

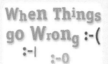

What would physicians, emergency medical technicians, trial attorneys, government decision makers, military officers, and countless other professionals do without their pagers, cell phones—and BlackBerries?

In 1999, Research in Motion (RIM), based in Waterloo, Ontario, introduced a wireless device it named BlackBerry, after the berry-like buttons on the product. A BlackBerry fits in a user's palm and is operated using a trackwheel and buttons. When first introduced, BlackBerries concentrated on e-mail, but they now support push e-mail (received in real time), mobile telephoning, Internet faxing, text messaging, Web browsing, and other wireless information services.

In the early 2000s, NTP, Incorporated, a Virginia-based patent-holding company, sent notice of their wireless telecommunications patents to several fledgling wireless companies, offering to license their patents to them. None of the companies bought patent licenses from NTP. NTP then sued one of the companies, RIM, claiming patent infringement. RIM claimed in court that a functional wireless e-mail system was already in the public domain before NTP's inventions. The jury, however, found for NTP, and RIM was fined several million dollars. The case continued through several appeals but was finally settled in 2006. RIM agreed to pay NTP $612.5 million "in full and final settlement of all claims." RIM also announced the use of newly developed technology that would remove all question of whether the BlackBerry used NTP-patented technology. BlackBerry users, who totaled more than 3 million in March 2006, were relieved when the case was settled since many had feared that the beloved devices would be shut down by court order. In fact, the U.S. Department of Defense had testified during the patent infringement lawsuit that loss of the BlackBerry network would be a threat to national security since so many government employees used the device.

Although NTP's patent infringement case was settled, the situation raised several questions. When similar innovations are developed independently but simultaneously, who actually "owns" the invention? If a company pays to license a patent, how long should the company pay royalties on the product using the patent? And, perhaps most important, how secure is intellectual property in a flat world, where technological advances emerge virtually overnight?

Despite patent problems, the BlackBerry product remained secure in its market share through 2007, because BlackBerries had long been noted for their reliability, offering connectivity when other telecommunication devices fail. Then on February 11, 2008, the unthinkable occurred: the BlackBerry network went down. ABC News senior political reporter, Rick Klein, told Cecilia Kang, a *Washington Post* staff writer, that the outage was his "worst nightmare." Checking e-mail messages vital to content for his political blog, "The Note," during his train ride home, Klein's e-mail service went down without warning and the outage lasted three hours. "It was like being underwater without an oxygen tank," Klein recalled. "It felt like every minute was an hour."

The failure apparently affected all North American users from 3:30 to 6:50 P.M., Eastern Time, but affected e-mail only—phone service was not interrupted. Research in Motion, the company that makes BlackBerries, said a system upgrade caused the outage. They were attempting to increase capacity when the unexpected down time occurred.

The temporary BlackBerry outage was noteworthy because it illustrates how dependent wireless devices are on network infrastructure, and how dependent some users have become on the wireless services devices like BlackBerry provide.

Based on:

BlackBerry. (2008, May 17). In *Wikipedia, the free encyclopedia.* Retrieved May 17, 2008, from http://en.wikipedia.org/w/index.php?title=BlackBerry&oldid=212965497.

Heinzl, M., & A. Sharma. (2006, March 4). RIM to pay NTP $612.5 million to settle BlackBerry patent suit. *Wall Street Journal.* Retrieved May 16, 2008, from http://online.wsj.com/article_email/SB114142276287788965-lMyQjAxMDE2NDAxMzQwMjMyWj.html.

Kang, C. (2008, February 12). BlackBerry outage strands users. *Washingtonpost.com.* Retrieved May 16, 2008, from http://www.washingtonpost.com/wp-dyn/content/article/2008/02/11/AR2008021101947.html?wpisrc=newsletter&wpisrc=newsletter.

Reed, B. (2008, February 12.). RIM blames BlackBerry outage on service infrastructure upgrade. *Networkworld.com.* Retrieved May 16, 2008, from http://www.networkworld.com/news/2008/021208-blackberry-outage-blame.html.

Output Technologies

After information is input and processed, it must be presented to the user. Computers can display information on a screen, print it, or emit sound. The sections that follow discuss details about how each of these output technologies operates.

Video Output **Monitors** and **projectors** are used to display information from a computer. No matter what type of display is used, it needs to be connected to a computer's video card. A **video card** (or **graphics card**) tells the monitor which dots to activate to produce the text or image. For many applications video cards that are integrated into the computer's motherboard are sufficient, but other applications (such as 3-D games or animation software) require the use of high-end video cards having a dedicated processor (called graphics processing unit, or GPU) and 1 GB or more of RAM. An emerging output technology is *electronic paper*, used for applications such as cellular phones or e-book readers (see the Technology Briefing for more on e-paper).

Printers and Plotters Information can be printed in several different ways. For example, **plotters** are used for transferring engineering designs from the computer to drafting paper using various types and colors of pens. **Dot matrix printers** are older, electric typewriter–based devices now mostly used for printing voluminous batch information, such as periodic reports and forms. For printing your term papers, you will most likely use either **ink-jet printers**, which use a small cartridge to spray ink onto paper, or **laser printers,** which are the most commonly used printers today; they use an electrostatic process to force ink onto the paper, literally "burning" the image onto the paper. The resulting high quality is considered necessary for almost all business letters and documents.

Audio Output In addition to transmitting text as output, most computers can also transmit audio as output. With the use of a **sound card** and speakers, a computer can produce stereo-quality sound. The computer's sound card translates the bits into tones that are then sent to the speakers for output. A sound card is also used to capture and convert audio for storage or processing.

Types of Computers

Depending on their computing needs, individuals and organizations can choose between a variety of different types of computers. The four general classes of computers are super-computer, mainframe, midrange, and microcomputer. A **supercomputer** is the most expensive and most powerful kind of computer; it is used primarily to assist in solving massive scientific problems. In contrast, a **mainframe**, while being very large, is primarily used as the main, central computing system for governmental agencies such as the Internal Revenue Service, or major corporations, such as Alamo Rent a Car, or Bank of America. **Midrange computers** (sometimes called **workstations**) offer lower performance than mainframes but higher performance than microcomputers and are typically used for engineering and midsized business applications. A **microcomputer** is used for personal computing, for small business computing, and as a workstation attached to large computers or to other small computers on a network. Portable computers—notebook computers, tablet PCs, and handheld computers—are a special type of microcomputer designed to support mobility (see Table 4.4).

Now that you understand how computer hardware works, we will discuss several trends to address organizations' information systems hardware infrastructure needs.

Hardware Infrastructure Trends

Both businesses and research facilities face an ever-increasing need for computing performance. For example, auto manufacturers, such as the GM German subsidiary Opel or Japanese Toyota, use large supercomputers to simulate automobile crashes as well as evaluate design changes for vibrations and wind noise. Research facilities such as the U.S. Department of Energy's Lawrence Livermore National Laboratory use supercomputers for

TABLE 4.4 **Characteristics of Computers Currently Being Used in Organizations**

Type of Computer	Number of Simultaneous Users	Physical Size	Typical Use	Memory	Typical Cost Range
Supercomputer	1 to many	Like an automobile to as large as multiple rooms	Scientific research	5,000+ GB	Low: $1 million High: more than $20 million
Mainframe	1,000+	Like a refrigerator	Large general purpose business and government	Up to 1500+ GB	Low: $1 million High: $10 million
Midrange	5 to 500	Like a file cabinet	Midsized general purpose business	Up to 64 GB	Low: $10,000 High: $100,000
Microcomputer	1	Handheld to fitting on a desktop	Personal productivity	512 MB to 4 GB	Low: $200 High: $5,000

simulating nuclear explosions, while others simulate earthquakes using supercomputers (see Figure 4.9); such research sites have a tremendously complex hardware infrastructure.

While not every organization faces such large-scale computing problems, the demands for computing resources are often fluctuating, leading to either having too few resources for some problems or having too many idle resources most of the time. Additionally, constant innovations within the information technology sector lead to rapid obsolescence of information systems hardware. Consequently, organizations often face many difficult and complex decisions. To address this problem, many organizations now turn to *on-demand computing* for fluctuating computation needs, *grid computing* for solving large-scale problems, and *edge computing* for increasing Web application performance. Further, organizations increasingly turn to *green computing* to reduce energy consumption and lower costs.

On-Demand Computing In almost every organization, demand for individual IS resources is highly fluctuating. For example, some high-bandwidth applications, such as videoconferencing, may be needed only during certain times of the day, or some resource-intensive data-mining applications may only be used in irregular intervals. Rather than maintaining the resources needed for peak demand, organizations can allocate resources

FIGURE 4.9

The earth simulator supercomputer creates a "virtual twin" of the earth.

based on users' needs, a concept called **on-demand computing**. For example, more bandwidth will be allocated to a videoconference, while other users who do not need the bandwidth at that time receive less. Similarly, a user running complex data-mining algorithms would receive more processing power than a user merely doing some word processing. A variation of on-demand computing is **utility computing**; in this case, organizations "rent" resources such as processing, data storage (from a **storage service provider (SSP)** such as Amazon S3), or networking from an external provider on an as-needed basis; the organization receives a bill for the services used from the provider at the end of each month (see Figure 4.10). Utility computing is an effective way for managing fluctuating demand as well as controlling costs; in essence, all tasks associated with managing, maintaining, and upgrading the infrastructure are left to the external provider and are typically bundled into the "utility" bill—if you don't use, you don't pay. This offers tremendous benefits in terms of **scalability** (i.e., the ability to adapt to increases or decreases in demand for processing or data storage), which is especially important for companies just starting to operate in the digital world.

Grid Computing Although today's supercomputers have tremendous computing power, some tasks are even beyond the capacity of a supercomputer. Indeed, some complex simulations can take a year or longer to calculate even on a supercomputer. Sometimes, an organization or a research facility would have the need for a supercomputer but may not be able to afford one because of the extremely high cost. For example, the fastest supercomputers can cost more than $200 million, and this does not represent the "total cost of ownership," which also includes all the other related costs for making the system operational (e.g., personnel, facilities, storage, software, and so on; see Chapter 3—Valuing Information System Investments). Additionally, the organization may not be able to justify the costs because the supercomputer may be needed only occasionally to solve a few complex problems. In these situations, organizations have had to either rent time on a supercomputer or decided simply not to solve the problem.

However, a relatively recent infrastructure trend for overcoming cost or use limitations is to utilize **grid computing**. Grid computing refers to combining the computing power of a large number of smaller, independent, networked computers (often regular desktop PCs) into a cohesive system in order to solve problems that only supercomputers were previously capable of solving. While supercomputers are very specialized, grid computing allows organizations to solve both very large-scale problems as well as mul-

FIGURE 4.10

Utility computing allows companies to pay for computing resources on an as-needed basis.

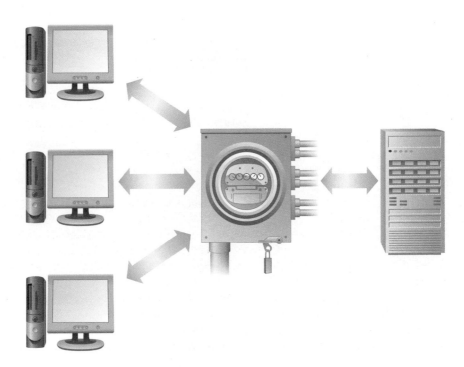

FIGURE 4.11

Grid computing uses resources from various different computers located around the world.

tiple (concurrent) smaller problems. To make grid computing work, large computing tasks are broken into small chunks, each of which can then be completed by individual computers (see Figure 4.11). However, as the individual computers are also in regular use, the individual calculations are performed during the computers' idle time so as to maximize the use of existing resources. For example, when writing this book, we used only minimal resources on our computers (i.e., we typically used only a word processor, the Internet, and e-mail); if our computers were part of a grid, the unused resources could be utilized to solve large-scale computing problems. This is especially useful for companies operating on a global scale. In each country, many of the resources are idle during the night hours, often more than twelve hours per day. Because of time zone differences, grid computing helps utilize those resources constructively. One way to put these resources into use would be to join the Berkeley Open Infrastructure for Network Computing (BOINC), which lets individuals "donate" computing time for various research projects, such as searching for extraterrestrial intelligence (SETI@home) or running climate change simulations.

However, as you can imagine, grid computing poses a number of demands in terms of the underlying network infrastructure or the software managing the distribution of the tasks. Further, the slowest computer often creates a bottleneck, thus slowing down the entire grid. A **dedicated grid**, consisting of a large number of homogeneous computers (and not relying on underutilized resources) can help overcome these problems. A dedicated grid is easier to set up and manage, and for many companies, much more cost-effective than purchasing a supercomputer.

Edge Computing Another recent trend in IS hardware infrastructure management is **edge computing**. With the decrease in cost for processing and data storage, computing tasks are now often solved at the edge of a company's network. In other words, rather than having massive, centralized computers and databases, multiple smaller servers are located closer to the individual users. This way, network bandwidth is saved and access time decreases. If a computer needs several hours to compute a certain problem, it might be a good choice to send the task over a network to a more powerful computer that might be able to solve that problem faster. However, as computing power has increased tremendously over the past years, many problems can now be computed locally within a matter of seconds, so it is not economical to send such problems over a network to a remote computer (Gray, 2004). Many businesses use edge computing to improve performance of their online commerce sites. In such cases, customers interact with the servers of an edge-computing service provider (such as Akamai). These edge servers, in turn, communicate with the business's computers (see Figure 4.12). This form of edge computing helps to reduce wait times for the consumers, as the sites (or media content, such as images or videos) are replicated on the provider's servers, while at the same time

FIGURE 4.12

Edge computing brings computing resources closer to the end user.

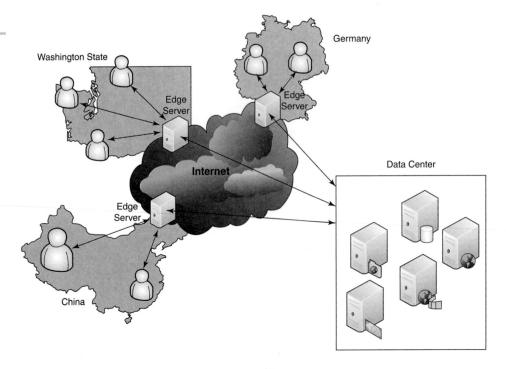

reducing the number of requests to the company's own infrastructure. This process not only saves valuable resources such as bandwidth but also offers superior performance that would otherwise be too expensive for organizations to offer. Akamai's services are utilized by organizations such as NBC, Fox Sports, BMW, and Victoria's Secret.

Green Computing Fueled by the rapid advances of developing nations, the world has seen a tremendous increase in demand for, and cost of, energy. Although you may not feel the impact of your personal computer usage on your home energy bill, for organizations having hundreds or thousands of computers, rising energy costs are becoming a major issue. **Green computing** is a recent trend to use computers more efficiently, doing the same (or more) with less. For example, organizations can save large amounts of money for power and cooling by using *virtualization* to replace hundreds of individual servers with just one powerful mainframe computer. Using **virtualization**, multiple **virtual machines**, each with its own applications, can be configured to run on one single computer. Other—fairly simple—approaches to green computing include installing sophisticated power management software on individual desktops to save energy that is wasted by leaving computers idling or on standby overnight; General Electric saved $6.5 million in electricity annually by changing the power saving settings for its computers (Wheeland, 2007).

Information Systems Software Infrastructure

Various types of software enable companies to utilize their information systems hardware and networks and assist organizations in executing their business processes and competitive strategy. Software consists of programs, or sets of instructions, that tell the computer to perform certain processing functions. Software's job is to provide instructions that allow all the hardware components in your computer system to speak to each other. The two basic types of information systems software are systems software and application software. In the next section, we discuss systems software and how it supports the overall operation of the computer hardware.

Systems Software/Operating System

Systems software is the collection of programs that control the basic operations of computer hardware. The most prominent type of systems software, the **operating system**, coordinates the interaction between hardware devices (e.g., the central processing unit

Powerful Partnerships

Google's Larry Page and Sergey Brin

According to Google lore, company founders Larry Page and Sergey Brin argued about everything when they first met as Stanford University graduate students in computer science in 1995 (see Figure 4.13). Larry was a twenty-four-year-old University of Michigan alumnus on a weekend visit; Sergey, twenty-three at that time, was among a group of students assigned to show him around. Both had strong opinions and divergent viewpoints, but they eventually found common ground in a unique approach to solving one of computing's biggest challenges: retrieving relevant information from a massive set of data.

By January 1996, Page and Brin had begun collaboration on a search engine called BackRub, named for its unique ability to analyze the "back links" pointing to a given Web site. Page, who had always enjoyed tinkering with machinery and had gained some notoriety for building a working printer out of LEGO™ bricks, took on the task of creating a new kind of server environment that used low-end PCs instead of big expensive machines. Afflicted by the perennial shortage of cash common to graduate students everywhere, the pair took to haunting the department's loading docks in hopes of tracking down newly arrived computers that they could borrow for their network.

In 1998, Page and Brin were still operating out of a dorm room. They maxed out credit cards buying a ter-abyte of memory to hold their data and went looking for investors to help them further develop their search engine technology. David Filo, a friend and one of the developers of Yahoo!, told the two their technology was solid and convinced them to start up their own company.

Page and Brin put out feelers for investors and found Andy Bechtolsheim, a friend of a faculty member, who wrote them a check for $100,000 after one brief meeting. Since the check was made out to "Google Inc.," Page and Brin scrambled to establish a corporation so they could deposit the check. Other investors joined, and Google Inc. began operations in September 1998 in Menlo Park, California—in a friend's garage that included a washer and dryer and a hot tub. The first employee hired was Craig Silverstein, director of technology.

From the start, Google, still in beta in 1998, handled 10,000 search queries a day. The company soon captured the attention of the press and was extolled in *USA Today*, *Le Monde*, and *PC Magazine*, which named Google the best search engine of 1998.

Google quickly outgrew its garage location, and by February 1999 the company had moved into an office in Palo Alto, California, and now had eight employees and was handling more than 500,000 search queries a day.

The company continued to expand, removed the "beta" label from the search engine in 1999, and that same year they moved into the Googleplex, its current headquarters in Mountain View, California.

In May 2000, Google was already the world's largest search engine answering 18 million queries a day and was awarded a Webby Award and a People's Voice Award for technical achievement. (Already, by the end of 2000, Google was answering 100 million search queries a day.)

On April 29, 2004, Google filed with the Securities and Exchange Commission for its initial public offering (IPO). In an unprecedented move, the IPO was sold at auction in order to make the shares more widely available. Shares were priced at $85, and Google hoped to raise $3 billion from the initial offering. Expert opinions on the success of the auction were mixed. Some said the stock price was inflated; others said the stock would eventually tank. Experts who warned of doomsday, however, were eventually proved wrong. In September 2008,

FIGURE 4.13

Google's Larry Page and Sergey Brin.

Google's stock was selling for $430 a share and was expected to rise even further.

Since that IPO, Google's revenue-earning ventures have expanded to include online and mobile advertising related to its Internet search, e-mail, online mapping, office productivity, social networking, and video sharing enterprises. The company also sells advertising-free versions of the same technology. As of March 2008, Google employed 19,156 full-time employees, and its revenue was listed as just over $16.5 billion, up 56 percent over 2007.

Google's unique corporate culture has revolved around the personal and business philosophy of the founding partners, and the company has worked hard to maintain a "flat" organization with no hierarchy and a collaborative environment that encourages innovation. At Google headquarters, for instance, there are no cubicles, and employees often sit on exercise balls in front of computers. Dogs roam the halls at will and seem as congenial as the company's human employees. In 2006, fearful that the company's growth was hindering its "anti-corporate" environment, Google hired a Chief Culture Officer who also serves as Human Relations Director.

As have many corporations in the United States, Google has gone green. In 2007, the company announced the Climate Savers Computing Initiative, a joint effort with more than thirty organizations to save energy and reduce greenhouse gas emissions by using more energy-efficient computers and computer equipment. The same year, Google.org announced the RechargeIT Plug-In Hybrid Car Initiative and installed 1.6 megawatts of solar panels at

company headquarters in Mountain View. Google also announced plans to make the company completely carbon neutral by 2008.

What do Larry and Sergey have planned for 2009 and beyond? Google stays pretty secretive: "What's next from Google? It's hard to say. We don't talk much about what lies ahead, because we believe one of our chief competitive advantages is surprise. And then there's innovation and an almost fanatical devotion to our users. These are the things that fuel us, and, we hope, fuel your own dreams."

"You can always take a peek at some of the ideas our engineers are currently kicking around by visiting them at play in Google Labs. Have fun, but be sure to wear your safety goggles."

Based on:

Anonymous (n.d.). Google milestones. Retrieved May 16, 2008, from http://www.google.com/corporate/history.html.

Anonymous (n.d.). Google solar panel project. Retrieved May 16, 2008, from http://www.google.com/corporate/solarpanels/home?gsessionid=Om9EfuNB7k4.

Anonymous (n.d.). The Google culture. Retrieved May 16, 2008, from http://www.google.com/corporate/culture.html.

Reicher, D. (2007, June 18). A clean energy update. Retrieved May 17, 2008, from http://googleblog.blogspot.com/2007/06/climate-savers-computing-initiative.html.

Weihl, B. (2007, June 12). Climate savers computing initiative. Retrieved May 16, 2008, from http://googleblog.blogspot.com/2007/06/climate-savers-computing-initiative.html.

[CPU] and the monitor), peripherals (e.g., printers), application software (e.g., office programs), and users, as shown in Figure 4.14. Additionally, given that microprocessors are embedded in countless devices including cell phones, digital video recorders like TiVo, and automobiles, you are likely interacting with operating systems more than you realize. For example, the I-Drive system utilized within luxury BMW automobiles is enabled by a Microsoft operating system. Likewise, the onboard passenger entertainment systems within many aircraft are powered by the Linux operating system.

Operating systems are often written in assembly language, a very low-level computer programming language that allows the computer to operate quickly and efficiently. The operating system is designed to insulate you from this low-level language and make computer operations unobtrusive. The operating system performs all of the day-to-day operations that we often take for granted when using a computer, such as updating the system clock, printing documents, or saving information to a disk. Just as our brain and nervous system control our body's breathing, heartbeat, and senses without our conscious realization, the systems software transparently controls the computer's basic operations.

Common Systems Software Functions Many tasks are common to almost all computers. These include getting input from a keyboard or mouse, reading from and/or writing to a storage device (such as a hard disk drive), and presenting information to you via a monitor. Each of these tasks is performed by the operating system, just as a manager of a firm oversees people and processes (as depicted in Figure 4.15). For example, if you

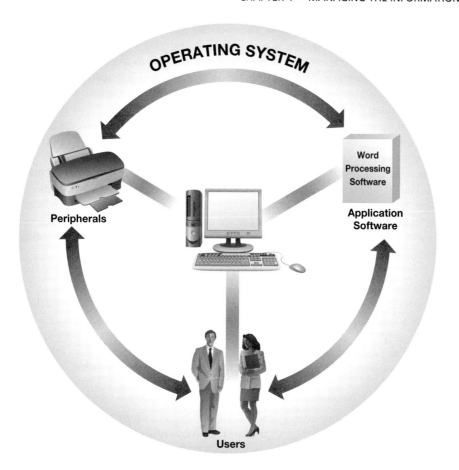

FIGURE 4.14

Operating systems coordinate the interaction between users, application software, hardware, and peripherals.

want to copy a word processing file from a flash drive onto your computer, the operating systems make this very easy for you, as all it takes is simply using the mouse to point at a graphic icon of the word processing file on the flash drive, then click and drag it onto an icon of your hard disk. The operating system makes this process appear easy. However, underlying the icons and simple dragging operations is a complex set of coded instructions that tell the electronic components of the computer that you are transferring a set of bits and bytes located on the flash drive to a location on your internal hard disk. Imagine if you had to program those sets of instructions every time you wanted to copy a file from one place to another. The operating system manages and executes these types of system operations so that you can spend your time on more important tasks.

FIGURE 4.15

A manager oversees organizational resources, whereas an operating system oversees computer resources.

Interfaces: Command Versus GUI The operating system is stored on the hard disk, and a portion of the operating system is transferred into primary storage when the computer boots up. After the operating system is in memory, it begins to manage the computer and provide a **user interface**. Different operating systems and application programs use different types of user interfaces, with the most typical being command and GUI. It is through this interface that you interact with the computer. The **command line interface** requires that you type text commands into the computer to perform basic operations. You could type the command "DELETE File1" to erase the file with the name "File1." Unix is an example of an operating system that uses a command line user interface.

The most common type of interface for the PC is called a **graphical user interface** (**GUI**). The GUI uses pictures, icons, and menus to send instructions from the user to the computer system. GUIs eliminate the need for users to input arcane commands into the computer and are, therefore, a popular interface. Examples of systems software using a GUI are Windows Vista, Mac OS X, or various versions of the open-source operating system Linux (using desktop environments such as KDE or GNOME).

Application Software

Unlike systems software, which manages the operation of the computer, **application software** lets a user perform specific tasks, such as writing a business letter, processing payroll, managing a stock portfolio, or manipulating a series of forecasts to come up with the most efficient allocation of resources for a project. The application program interacts with the systems software, which, in turn, interacts with the computer hardware.

Software Infrastructure Trends

With growing use of information systems to support organizations' business processes and the need for business intelligence, organizations have to rely on a variety of different software. Consequently, effectively utilizing software resources is becoming increasingly critical and complex. For example, companies have to manage the software installed on each and every computer used including managing updates, fixing bugs, and managing issues related to software licenses. In addition, companies have to decide whether to upgrade their software or switch to new products and when to do so.

Continuously upgrading operating systems and applications software can be a huge cost factor for organizations, both in terms of labor and in terms of costs for the actual products needed. To reduce such costs, many companies are now increasingly turning to using open-source software, application service providers, or implementing service-oriented architectures for their software needs. These various trends are discussed next.

Open-Source Software Open source is a philosophy that promotes developers' and users' access to the source of a product or idea (see Chapter 2—Fueling Globalization Using Information Systems). Particularly in the area of software development, the open-source movement has taken off with the advent of the Internet, and people around the world are contributing their time and expertise to develop or improve software, ranging from operating systems to applications software. As the programs' source code is freely available for use and/or modification, this software is referred to as **open-source software**.

OPEN-SOURCE OPERATING SYSTEMS. One of the most prevalent examples of open-source software is the operating system Linux, which was developed as a hobby by the Finnish university student Linus Torvalds in 1991. Having developed the first version himself, he made the source code of his operating system available to everyone who wanted to use it and improve on it. Because of its unrivaled stability, Linux has become the operating system of choice for Web servers, **embedded systems** (such as TiVo boxes, handheld computers, and network routers; see Figure 4.16), and supercomputers alike (as of 2008, over 80 percent of the world's 500 fastest supercomputers ran Linux operating systems; Top 500, 2008).

OPEN-SOURCE APPLICATION SOFTWARE. In addition to the Linux operating system, other open-source software has been gaining increasing popularity because of its stability and low cost. For example, in 2008, one-half of all Web sites were powered by the Apache Web

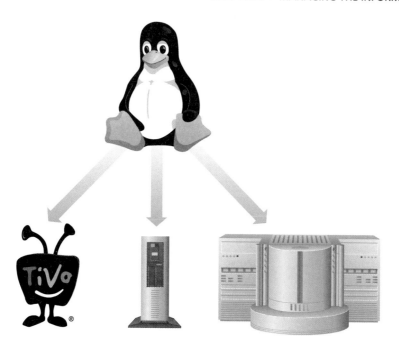

FIGURE 4.16

Linux is the operating system of choice for embedded systems, Web servers, and supercomputers (the penguin "Tux" is the official mascot of Linux).

server, another open-source project (Netcraft, 2008). Other popular examples of open-source application software include the Firefox Web browser (see Figure 4.17) and the office productivity suite OpenOffice. While there are many benefits to open-source software, vendors of proprietary software are still highlighting "hidden" costs of running open-source software, such as obtaining reliable customer support.

Application Service Providers As discussed in Chapter 3—Valuing Information Systems Investments—the total cost of ownership for software consists not only of the purchase price, but also of costs related to installing, maintaining, and updating the software. One popular way to address these issues is using **software as a service (SaaS)**. Rather than owning and supporting its own software, a company uses the Web to access

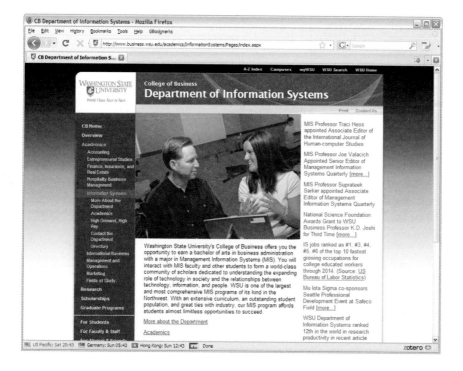

FIGURE 4.17

The Firefox Web browser.

software that is hosted by another company (or, **application service provider**). These concepts are further discussed in Chapter 10—Developing and Acquiring Information Systems.

Service Oriented Architecture Increased domestic and international competition, rapidly changing customer demand, and the emergence of electronic commerce has forced organizations to integrate their information systems across business functions. In the 1990's *Enterprise Resource Planning (ERP)* systems emerged, helping to integrate various business activities, to streamline and better manage interactions with customers, and to coordinate better with suppliers in order to meet changing customer demands more efficiently and effectively. However, although such systems can offer tremendous benefits for an organization, the implementation is typically time consuming, and some organizations feared losing the ability to quickly respond to changing business conditions due to the monolithic nature of ERP systems. Recently, organizations have turned to *Service Oriented Architectures (SOA)*, which allow breaking down business processes into distinct services that can be linked to provide the desired functionality. Using SOA, organizations can rapidly react to changing business conditions, and the reusable nature of services tremendously reduces the cost of developing new applications. Both ERP and SOA are further discussed in Chapter 9—Building Organizational Partnerships Using Enterprise Information Systems.

Communications and Collaboration Infrastructure

As you have read in the previous chapters, one of the reasons why information systems in organizations have become so powerful and important is the ability to interconnect, allowing internal and external constituents to communicate and collaborate with each other. The infrastructure supporting this consists of a variety of components, such as the networking hardware and software that facilitate the interconnection of different computers, enabling collaboration literally around the world.

Human Communication and Computer Networking

Human communication involves the sharing of information and messages between senders and receivers. The sender of a message formulates the message in her brain and codes the message into a form that can be communicated to the receiver—through voice,

---

 Net Stats

Broadband Access Increases

Recent reports show that broadband penetration in the United States is growing steadily, with 57 percent of all households having access to broadband connections in 2008. Among all *active* Internet users, broadband penetration reached 89 percent in 2008. Broadband penetration trends are shown in Figure 4.18.

FIGURE 4.18

U.S. Broadband penetration.

Source: http://www.websiteoptimization.com/bw/0804.

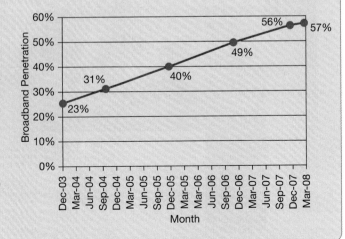

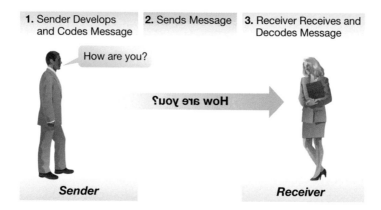

FIGURE 4.19

Communication requires senders, a message to share, and receivers.

for example. The message is then transmitted along a communication pathway to the receiver. The receiver, using his ears and brain, then attempts to decode the message, as shown in Figure 4.19. This basic model of human communication helps us to understand telecommunications or computer networking. **Computer networking** is the sharing of information or services. As with human communication, all computer networks require three things:

- Senders and receivers that have something to share
- A pathway or transmission medium, such as a cable, to send the message
- Rules or protocols dictating communication between senders and receivers

The easiest way to understand computer networking is through the human communication model. Suppose you are applying for a job in France after graduation. You need information about different employers. The first requirement for a network—information to share—has now been met. After contacting a few potential employers, a company sends you information about their hiring process (the encoded message) via e-mail. This is the second requirement: a means of transmitting the coded message. The Internet is the pathway or transmission medium used to contact the receiver. **Transmission media** refers to the physical pathway—cable(s) and wireless—used to carry network information. At this point, you may run into some difficulties. If the potential employer has sent you information in French, you may not understand what they have written—decode their message—because you don't speak French. Although you have contacted the receiver, you and the receiver of your message must meet the third requirement for a successful network: you must establish a language of communication—the rules or protocols governing your communication. **Protocols** define the procedures that different computers follow when they transmit and receive data. You both might decide that one communication protocol will be that you communicate in English. This communication session is illustrated in Figure 4.20.

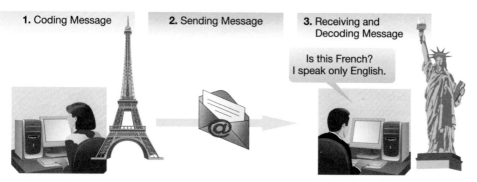

FIGURE 4.20

Coding, sending, and decoding a message.

FIGURE 4.21

In human communication, words are spoken and transmitted in the air. In computer communication, digital data are transmitted over some type of communication medium.

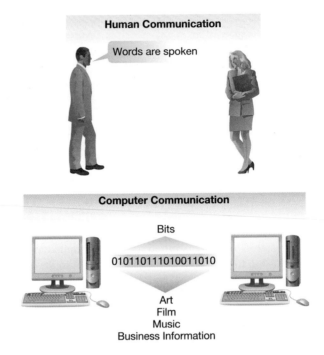

Computer Networks

A fundamental difference between human and computer communication is that human communication consists of words, whereas computer communication consists of bits, the fundamental information units of computers, as depicted in Figure 4.21. Virtually all types of information can be transmitted on a computer network—documents, art, music, or film—although each type of information has vastly different requirements for effective transmission. For example, a single screen of text is approximately 14 KB of data, whereas a publication-quality photograph could be larger than 200 MB of data (see Table 4.5). The process of converting a photograph or a song into digital information, or bits, is called

TABLE 4.5 Communication and Storage/Bandwidth Requirements for Different Types of Information.

Type of Information	Raw Size	Compressed Size
Voice		
Telephone	64 Kbps	16–32 Kbps
Teleconference	96 Kbps	32–64 Kbps
Compact disc	1.41 Mbps	63–128 Kbps
Data		
Single screen of text	14.4 KB	4.8–7 KB
Typed page, single-spaced	28.8 KB	9.6–14.4 KB
Faxed page (low to high resolution)	1.68–3.36 MB	130–336 KB
Super VGA screen image	6.3 MB	315–630 KB
Digital X-ray	50.3 MB	16.8–25.1 MB
Publication-quality photograph	230.4 MB	23–46 MB
Video		
Video telephony	9.3 Mbps	64–384 Kbps
Video teleconferencing	37.3 Mbps	384 Kbps–1.92 Mbps
Studio-quality digital TV	166 Mbps	1.7 Mbps
High-definition television	1.33 Gbps	20–50 Mbps

Note: KB = kilobytes, MB = megabytes; Kbps = kilobits per second; Mbps = megabits per second; Gbps = gigabits per second.

Based on *Business Data Communications*, 2nd ed., by Stallings/VanSlyke © 1997. Reprinted by permission of Prentice Hall, Inc., Upper Saddle River, NJ.

digitizing. After information is converted into bits, it can travel across a network. To transmit either the screen of text or the picture in a timely manner from one location to another, adequate bandwidth is needed. **Bandwidth** is the transmission capacity of a computer or communications channel, measured in bits per second (bps) or multiples thereof, and represents how much binary data can be reliably transmitted over the medium in one second. To appreciate the importance of bandwidth for speed, consider how long it would take to transmit a document the length of this book (about 2 million characters, or 16 million bits). It would take about 1.6 seconds at 10 megabits per second (Mbps) and .16 seconds at 100 Mbps. In contrast, using an old-fashioned PC modem that transmits data at a rate of 56 kilobits per second (Kbps), it would take nearly five minutes to transmit the same document. Hence, different types of information have different communication bandwidth requirements (see http://www.numion.com/Calculators/Time.html for a tool that helps you calculate download times). Typical local area networks have a bandwidth of 10 Mbps to 100 Mbps, and some have 1 Gbps, or even more.

Networking Fundamentals

Telecommunications advances have enabled individual computer networks—constructed with different hardware and software—to connect together in what appears to be a single network. Networks are increasingly being used to dynamically exchange relevant, value-adding knowledge and information throughout global organizations and institutions. The following sections take a closer look at the fundamental building blocks of these complex networks and the services they provide.

Servers, Clients, and Peers A **network** consists of three separate components—servers, clients, and peers—as depicted in Figure 4.22. A **server** is any computer on the network that makes access to files, printing, communications, and other services available to users of the network. Servers only provide services. A server typically has a more advanced microprocessor, more memory, a larger cache, and more disk storage than a single-user workstation. A **client** is any computer, such as a user's workstation or PC on the network, or any software application, such as a word processing application, that uses the services provided by the server. Clients only request services. A client usually has only one user, whereas many different users share the server. A **peer** is any computer that may both request and provide services. The trend in business is to use **server-centric networks** in which servers and clients have defined roles. However, **peer-to-peer networks** (often abbreviated as P2P) that enable any computer or device on the network to provide and request services can be found in small offices and homes. In P2P networks, all peers have equivalent capabilities and responsibilities; this is the network architecture behind popular

FIGURE 4.22

A server is a computer on the network that enables multiple computers (or "clients") to access data. A peer is a computer that may both request and provide services.

file sharing applications such as BitTorrent and KaZaa, where peers are able to connect directly to the hard drives of other peers on the Internet that are utilizing the software.

Types of Networks Computing networks are commonly classified by size, distance covered, and structure. The most commonly used classifications are a **private branch exchange**, **personal area network, local area network, campus area network, metropolitan area network,** and **wide area network** (see Table 4.6). For more on the different types of networks, see the Technology Briefing.

Transmission Media Every network uses one or more types of transmission media—the physical pathways to send data and information between two or more entities on a network. To send messages, computers send energy-based signals—electric currents using electromagnetic waves—to contact each other. These electromagnetic waves can be altered by semiconductor materials to represented bits, which are transmitted over physical pathways, or media, as computers communicate with each other.

When deciding which type of medium to use in a network, an organization should consider bandwidth, **attenuation** (the weakening of a signal as it travels), immunity from **electromagnetic interference** (**EMI**, disturbance due to electromagnetic radiation), and **eavesdropping**. Two forms of media are used in networks: cable and wireless media.

CABLE MEDIA. **Cable media** physically link computers and other devices in a network. Cable media are used when mobility is of no (or less) concern, and factors such as bandwidth are the deciding criteria. For example, LANs, CANs, MANs, and WANs typically use cable media to transfer large amounts of information. The most common forms of cable media are **twisted pair**, **coaxial**, and **fiber-optic**. The trade-offs of cable media are summarized in Table 4.7. For more on the different cable media, consult the Technology Briefing.

WIRELESS MEDIA. **Wireless media** transmit and receive electromagnetic signals using methods such as infrared line of sight, high-frequency radio, and microwave systems. **Infrared line of sight** uses high-frequency light waves to transmit data on an unobstructed path between nodes—computers or some other devices such as printers—on a network at a distance of up to 24.4 meters. The remote controls for most audiovisual equipment, such as your TV, stereo, and other consumer electronics equipment, use infrared light. **High-frequency radio** signals can transmit data at rates of up to several hundred Mbps to network nodes up to approximately 40 kilometers apart, depending on the nature of any obstructions between them. The flexibility of the signal path makes high-frequency radio ideal for mobile trans-

TABLE 4.6 **Types of Networks.**

Type	Usage	Size
Private Branch Exchange (PBX)	Telephone system serving a particular location	Within a business
Personal Area Network (PAN)	Wireless communication between devices, using technologies such as Bluetooth	Under 10 meters
Local Area Network (LAN)	Sharing of data, software applications, or other resources between several users	Typically within a building
Campus Area Network (CAN)	Connect multiple LANs, used by single organization	Spanning multiple buildings, e.g., a university or business campus
Metropolitan Area Network (MAN)	Connect multiple LANs, used by single organization	Larger than LAN or CAN, e.g., covering the area of a city
Wide Area Network (WAN)	Connect multiple LANs, distributed ownership and management	Large physical distance, up to world wide (Internet)

TABLE 4.7 **Key Benefits and Drawbacks of Different Cable Media**

Medium	Key Benefit(s)	Drawback(s)
Twisted pair cable	Inexpensive; easy to install and reconfigure	Highly susceptible to EMI, eavesdropping, and attenuation; unsuitable for high speeds
Coaxial cable	Higher bandwidth than twisted pair; lower susceptibility to EMI, eavesdropping, and attenuation than twisted pair	More expensive than twisted pair; more difficult to install, reconfigure, and manage than twisted pair; bulky
Fiber optic cable	Very high bandwidth; low attenuation; immune to EMI and eavesdropping	Expensive cable and hardware; complex installation and maintenance

missions. For example, most police departments use high-frequency radio signals that enable police vehicles to communicate with each other as well as with a dispatch office.

Two common applications of high-frequency radio communication are cellular phones and wireless networks. **Wireless local area networks (WLANs)**, also referred to as **wireless fidelity (Wi-Fi)**, are based on a family of standards called **802.11**. The ease of installation has made WLANs popular for business and home use to share Internet access, files, and peripheral devices. One example where high-frequency radio is being used is in the operation of PANs, which use low-powered **Bluetooth** radio-wave technology to connect cell phones to headsets, MP3 players to music servers, automobiles to cell phones, and countless other applications. Recently, Nokia released a new standard for PANs, called **Ultra Low Power (ULP) Bluetooth**; with low cost, small size, and ultra-low power consumption, ULP Bluetooth can bring wireless connectivity into even more devices, such as heart rate monitors, MP3 players, remote controls, or even golf clubs.

Microwave transmission is a high-frequency radio signal that is sent through the air using either terrestrial (earth-based) systems or satellite systems. Both terrestrial and satellite microwave transmissions require line-of-sight communications between the signal sender and the signal receiver. **Terrestrial microwave** systems are used to cross inaccessible terrain or to connect buildings where cable installation would be expensive. **Satellite microwave** uses a relay station that transfers signals between antennae located on earth and a **satellite** (i.e., a microwave station located in outer space) orbiting the earth. This technology has become very viable for media such as radio. A strength of satellite communication is that it can be used to access very remote and undeveloped locations on the earth. Such systems are extremely costly because their use and installation depends on space technology. As with cable media, there are key differences between the types of wireless media (see Table 4.8).

TABLE 4.8 **Key Benefits and Drawbacks of Different Wireless Media**

Medium	Key Benefit(s)	Drawback(s)
Infrared line of sight	Easy to install and configure; inexpensive	Very limited bandwidth; line of sight required; environmental factors influence signal quality
High-frequency radio	Mobile stations; low attenuation	Frequency licensing; complex installation
Terrestrial microwave	Can access remote locations or congested areas; high bandwidth; low attenuation	Frequency licensing; complex installation; environmental factors influence signal quality
Satellite microwave	Can access remote locations; high bandwidth; earth stations can be fixed or mobile	Frequency licensing; complex installation; environmental factors influence signal quality; propagation delays

A popular application of satellite communication is the **Global Positioning System (GPS)**. The GPS uses twenty-four active satellites to allow users to triangulate their position anywhere on the planet. At any point in time, at any place on earth, signals from at least four GPS satellites can be picked up by a GPS receiver; each of the satellites sends a signal containing a time stamp. Using this time stamp, the GPS receiver can determine the distance from each satellite and can thus triangulate its own position on earth with very high accuracy. GPS technology includes the first generation systems having location resolution down to 10 square meters (about 107 square feet) and the newer second generation technology having location resolution down to 10 square centimeters (about 1.5 square inches). Originally developed by the military, GPS technology is being used for a variety of civilian devices, including navigation systems, cell phones, or digital cameras.

Having a number of interconnected computers is necessary but not sufficient for enabling communication and collaboration; companies also need various other hardware and software. For example, e-mail servers, along with communication software, such as Microsoft Outlook, are needed to enable a broad range of internal and external communication. Similarly, companies have to decide on whether to utilize other communication tools, such as instant messaging, and which system to use for such applications (see Figure 4.23). Further, it has become increasingly important for companies to be able to utilize videoconferencing to bridge the distances between a company's offices or between a company and its business partners, saving valuable travel time and enhancing collaboration. However, as there are vast differences in terms of quality, costs, and functionality of these systems, companies have to assess their communication needs and carefully decide which combination of technologies best support the goals of the organization.

One global network that has enabled organizations and individuals to interconnect in a variety of ways is the **Internet**, which is a large worldwide collection of networks that use a common protocol to communicate with each other. The name Internet is derived from the concept of *internetworking,* which means connecting host computers and their networks together to form even larger networks.

How Did the Internet Get Started?

You can trace the roots of the Internet back to the late 1960s, when the U.S. **Defense Advanced Research Projects Agency (DARPA)** began to study ways to interconnect networks of various kinds. This research effort produced the **Advanced Research Projects Agency Network (ARPANET)**, a large wide area network (WAN) that linked many universities and research centers. The first two nodes on the ARPANET were the University of California, Los Angeles, and the Stanford Research Institute, followed by the University of Utah.

FIGURE 4.23

Companies have to decide how to best address their communication needs.

Brief Case ⊘

Autonomic Computing

Have you ever wondered why you constantly have to upgrade your computer or download software patches for your application software or operating systems? As no system is without flaws, and users and developers periodically find programming errors or security holes, the need arises to fix these, especially if they compromise the security of the system. At other times, a system just breaks down. With increasing complexity of information systems, the time and money needed to manage these increase tremendously; however, the time and money needed doesn't add value to an organization. In fact, some people believe that for large organizations, the costs of managing their systems undermine the benefits these systems provide.

Why can't systems be designed that are easier and less resource-intensive to manage? This question becomes increasingly important due to organizations' growing needs for complex information systems, paired with a shortage of skilled systems administrators. Recently, academic and industry researchers (e.g., at IBM) have begun working on autonomic computing systems designed to overcome these issues. **Autonomic computing** systems are self-managing and thus need only minimal human intervention to operate. In other words, in a traditional computing environment, system operators often have to fine-tune the computer's configuration in order to most efficiently solve a particular type of complex problem. In an autonomic computing environment, the ultimate goal is to allow the system to do everything else on its own, completely transparent to the user. In order to achieve this, an autonomic computing system must know itself and be self-configuring, self-optimizing, self-healing, and self-protecting.

How can a system be built to be autonomic, resembling a self-managing biological system? In organizational environments, conditions frequently change and are often unpredictable. In order to optimally perform under such conditions and swiftly react to any changes to the environment, an auto-nomic system must know itself; that is, it must know its configuration, capacity, and current status, but it must also know which resources it can draw on. Second, in order to be able to use different resources based on different needs, the system should be self-configuring so that the user does not have to take care of any configuration issues. Further, as any parts of a system can malfunction, an autonomic system should be self-healing so that any potential problems are detected, and the system is reconfigured so as to allow the user to continue performing the tasks, even if parts of the system are not operational. Finally, as almost any computer system can be the target of an attack (see Chapter 7—Securing Information Systems), autonomic computing systems must be aware of any potential dangers and must be able to protect themselves from any malicious attacks (e.g., by automatically quarantining infected parts of the system). In sum, an autonomic computing system should be flexible in regard to changing conditions, always accessible to the user, and transparent, freeing the users from tasks associated with managing the system.

Clearly, these are some formidable tasks researchers have to address, but considering the time and money that is currently spent on managing and maintaining IT infrastructures, autonomic computing systems are promising for the future.

Questions

1. How can an autonomic computing system foresee changing conditions and react as required by the situation?
2. How do you feel about autonomic computing systems? Would you be comfortable interacting with such a machine?

Based on:

Anonymous (n.d.). Autonomic computing. Retrieved May 27, 2008, from http://www.research.ibm.com/autonomic/index.html.

ARPANET quickly evolved and was combined with other networks. For example, in 1986, the U.S. **National Science Foundation (NSF)** initiated the development of the **National Science Foundation Network (NSFNET)**, which became a major component of the Internet. Other networks throughout the United States and the rest of the world were interconnected and/or morphed into the growing "Internet." Throughout the world, support for the Internet has come from a combination of federal and state governments, universities, national and international research organizations, and industry.

The Internet Uses Packet-Switching Technology

The Internet relies on packet-switching technology to deliver data and information across networks. **Packet switching** is based on the concept of turn taking and enables millions of users to send large and small chunks of data across the Internet concurrently. To minimize delays, network technologies limit the amount of data that a computer can transfer on each turn. Consider a conveyor belt as a comparison. Suppose that the conveyor belt connects a warehouse and a retail store. When a customer places an order, it is sent from the store to the warehouse, where a clerk assembles the items in the order. The items are placed on the conveyor belt and delivered to the customer in the store. In most situations, clerks finish sending items from one order before proceeding to send items from another order. This process works well when orders are small, but when a large order with many items comes in, sharing a conveyor belt can introduce delays for others. Consider waiting in the store for your one item while another order with fifty items is being filled.

Local area networks (LANs), WANs, and the Internet all use packet-switching technologies so that users can share the communication channel and minimize delivery delays. Figure 4.24 illustrates how computers use packet switching. Computer A wants to send a message to computer C; similarly, computer B wants to send a message to computer D. For example, computer A is trying to send an e-mail message to computer C, while computer B is trying to send a word processing file to computer D. The outgoing messages are divided into smaller packets of data, and then each sending computer (A and B) takes turns sending the packets over the transmission media. The incoming packets are reassembled at their respective destinations, using previously assigned packet sequence numbers.

For packet switching to work, each packet being sent across a network must be labeled with a header. This header contains the network address of the source (sending computer) and the network address of the destination (receiving computer). Each computer attached to a network has a unique network address. As packets are transmitted, network hardware detects whether a particular packet is destined for a local machine. Packet-switching systems adapt instantly to changes in network traffic. If only one computer needs to use the network, it can send data continuously. As soon as another computer needs to send data, packet switching, or turn taking, begins. Now let us see how the Internet handles this packet switching.

Transmission Control Protocol/Internet Protocol

Organizations use diverse network technologies that may or may not be compatible with the technologies of other organizations. Because so many different networks are interconnected today, they must have a common language, or protocol, to communicate. The protocol used by the Internet is called **Transmission Control Protocol/Internet Protocol (TCP/IP)**. The first part, TCP, breaks information into small chunks called data packets and manages the transfer of those packets from computer to computer (via packet switching, as described previously). For example, a single document may be broken into several packets, each containing several hundred characters, as well as a destination address (the IP part of the protocol). The IP defines how a data packet must be formed and to where a **router** (an intelligent device used to connect two or more individual networks) must forward each packet. Packets travel independently to their destination, sometimes following different paths and arriving out of order. The destination computer reassembles all the

FIGURE 4.24

Computers A and B use packet switching to send messages or files to computers C and D.

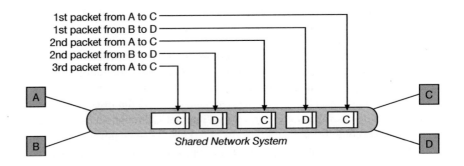

packets on the basis of their identification and sequencing information. Together, TCP and IP provide a reliable and efficient way to send data across the Internet.

A data packet that conforms to the IP specification is called an **IP datagram**. Datagram routing and delivery are possible because, as previously mentioned, every computer and router connected to the Internet is assigned a unique address, called its **IP address**. When an organization connects to the Internet, it obtains a set of IP addresses that it can assign to its computers. TCP helps IP guarantee delivery of datagrams by performing three main tasks. First, it automatically checks for datagrams that may have been lost en route from their source to their destination. Second, TCP collects the incoming datagrams and puts them in the correct order to re-create the original message. Finally, TCP discards any duplicate copies of datagrams that may have been created by network hardware.

World Wide Web

One of the most powerful uses of the Internet is something that you probably use almost every day—the World Wide Web. More than likely, you have probably browsed the Web using Microsoft's Internet Explorer, Mozilla Firefox, Flock, or some other popular Web browser. A **Web browser** is a software application that can be used to locate and display Web pages, including text, graphics, and multimedia content. Browsers have become a standard Internet tool. As previously mentioned, the **World Wide Web (WWW)** is a graphical user interface to the Internet that provides users with a simple, consistent interface to access a wide variety of information.

History of the World Wide Web Prior to the invention of the Web by Tim Berners-Lee in 1991, content posted on the Internet could be accessed through the Internet tool **Gopher**. Gopher provided a menu-driven, hierarchical interface to organize files stored on servers, allowing to tie together related files from different Internet servers across the world. The Web took Gopher one step further by introducing **hypertext**. A hypertext document, otherwise known as a **Web page**, contains not only information, but also **hyperlinks**, which are references or links to other documents. The standard method of specifying the format of Web pages is called **Hypertext Markup Language (HTML)**. Specific content within each Web page is enclosed within codes, or markup tags, that stipulate how the content should appear to the user. These Web pages are stored on **Web servers**, which process user requests for pages using the **Hypertext Transfer Protocol (HTTP)**. Web servers typically host a collection of interlinked Web pages (called a **Web site**) that are owned by the same organization or by an individual. Web sites and specific Web pages within those sites have a unique Internet address. A user who wants to access a Web site enters the address, and the Web server hosting the Web site retrieves the desired page from its hard drive and delivers it to the user.

The introduction of the Web was the first of three events that led to its proliferation. The second event was the Information Infrastructure Act (Berghel, 1996) passed by the U.S. government in 1992, which opened the Web for commercial purposes. Prior to this legislation, universities and government agencies were the Web's main users. The third event was the arrival of a graphical Web browser, Mosaic, which quickly transcended Gopher by adding a graphical front end to the Web. Mosaic's graphical interface allowed Web pages to be constructed to deliver an extended range of content, including images, audio, video, and other multimedia, all of which could be included and displayed within the same Web page. Mosaic was the basis for popular browsers such as Internet Explorer and Mozilla Firefox.

Web Domain Names and Addresses A **Uniform Resource Locator (URL)** is used to identify and locate a particular Web page. For example, www.google.com is the URL used to find the main Google Web server. The URL has three distinct parts: the domain, the top-level domain, and the host name (see Figure 4.25).

The **domain name** is a term that helps people recognize the company or person that the domain name represents. For example, Google's domain name is google.com. The prefix *google* lets you know that it is very likely that this domain name will lead you to the

FIGURE 4.25

Dissecting a URL.

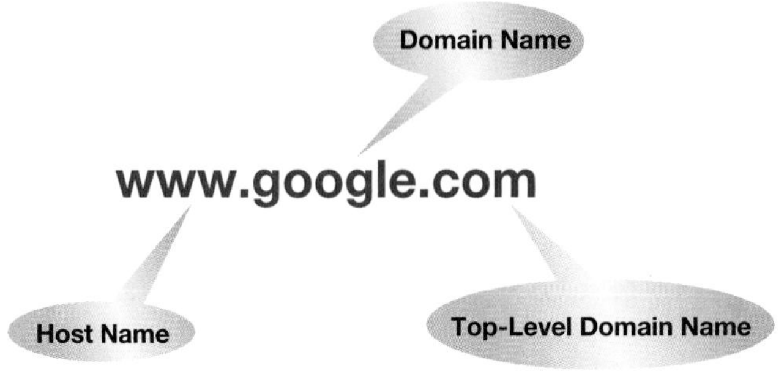

Web site of Google. Domain names also have a suffix that indicates which **top-level domain** they belong to. For example the "com" suffix is reserved for commercial organizations. Some other popular suffixes are listed here:

- edu—educational institutions
- org—organizations (nonprofit)
- gov—United States governmental entity
- net—network organizations
- de—Germany (there are over 240 two-letter "country code top-level domains")

Domain names ending with .com, .net, or .org can be registered through many different companies (known as registrars) that compete with one another. Given the proliferation of domain names, more of these top-level domain categories are being added, such as .aero for the air transport industry, .name for individuals, .coop for business industry cooperatives, and .museum for museums.

The host name is the particular Web server or group of Web servers (if it is a larger Web site) that will respond to the Web request. In most cases, the "www" host name refers to the default Web site or the home page of the particular domain. Other host names can be used. For example, spreadsheets.google.com will take you to the group of Web servers that are responsible for serving up Google's spreadsheet application. Larger companies have several host names for their different functions. Some examples used in Google are the following:

- mail.google.com (Google's free e-mail service)
- labs.google.com (Google's test applications)
- trends.google.com (see what other people are searching)
- maps.google.com (Google's mapping application)

All of the domain names and the host names are associated with one or more IP addresses. For example, the domain name google.com represents about a dozen underlying IP addresses. IP addresses serve to identify all the computers or devices on the Internet (or on any TCP/IP network). The IP address serves as the destination address of that computer or device and enables the network to route messages to the proper destination. The format of an IP address is a 32-bit numeric address written as four numbers separated by periods. Each of the four numbers can be any number between 0 and 255. For example, 134.121.0.99 is the underlying IP address of www.wsu.edu, Washington State University's main Web page. You could set up a private network using the TCP/IP protocol and assign your own domain names and IP addresses for computers and other devices on that network. On the other hand, if you wish to connect to the Internet, you must use registered IP addresses.

IP addresses can also be used as a URL to navigate to particular Web addresses. This practice is not done regularly, as IP addresses are far more difficult to remember than domain names.

World Wide Web Architecture The Web uses Web browsers, Web servers, and the TCP/IP networking protocol to facilitate the transmission of Web pages over the Internet. Figure 4.26 depicts the architecture of the Web. To access information on the Web, a Web browser, as well as the TCP/IP protocol, must be installed on a user's computer. Users can access Web pages by entering into their Web browser the URL of the Web page. Once the user enters the URL in the Web browser, TCP/IP breaks the request into packets and routes

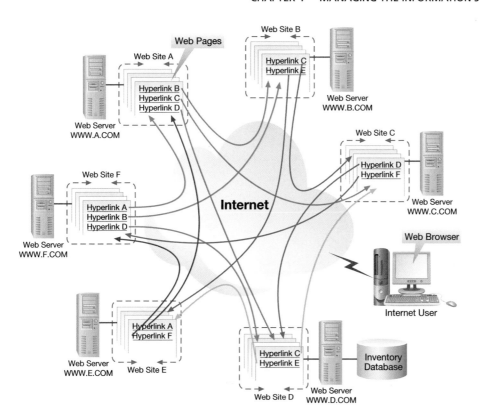

FIGURE 4.26

World Wide Web architecture.

them over the Internet to the Web server, where the requested Web page is stored. When the packets reach their destination, TCP/IP reassembles them and passes the request to the Web server. The Web server understands that the user is requesting a Web page (indicated by the http:// prefix in the URL) and retrieves the Web page, which is packetized by TCP/IP and transmitted over the Internet back to the Web browser. TCP/IP reassembles the packets at the destination and delivers the Web page to the Web browser. In turn, the Web browser translates the HTML code contained in the Web page, formats its physical appearance, and displays the results. If the Web page contains a hyperlink, the user can click on it and the process repeats.

Managing the Communication and Collaboration Infrastructure

Today, much of an organization's communication and collaboration needs are supported by Internet technologies; for example, e-mail has become the communications medium of choice for many people. However, for some topics, other forms of communication are more suited, so managers turn to the telephone, instant messaging, meetings, or videoconferences. One recent trend to satisfy such diverse communication and collaboration needs is the growing convergence of computing and telecommunications.

Convergence of Computing and Telecommunications The computing industry is experiencing an ever-increasing convergence of functionality of various devices. Whereas just a few years ago a cell phone was just a cell phone and a PDA was just a personal digital assistant (see the Technology Briefing), such devices are now converging such that the boundaries between devices are becoming increasingly blurred. Today, an increasing number of devices offer a variety of different functionalities—formerly often available only on separate dedicated devices—to address differing needs of knowledge workers and consumers alike (e.g., phones, PDAs, cameras, music players, and so on).

In addition to a convergence of capabilities of devices, there is also increasing convergence within the underlying infrastructures. For example, in the past, the backbone networks for the telephone and Internet were distinct. Today, increasingly, most voice and data traffic shares a common network infrastructure. To facilitate this convergence, also termed **IP convergence**, the use of IP for transporting voice, video, fax, and data traffic has

FIGURE 4.27

IP convergence allows various
devices to communicate using IP
technologies.

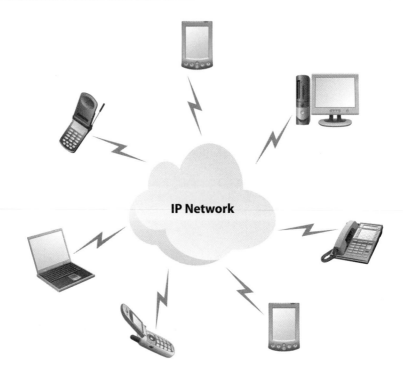

allowed enterprises to make use of new forms of communication and collaboration (e.g., instant messaging and online whiteboard collaboration) as well as traditional forms of communication (such as phone and fax) at much lower costs (see Figure 4.27). In the following sections, we will discuss two uses of IP for communication: voice over IP and videoconferencing over IP.

VOICE OVER IP. Voice over IP (VoIP) (or IP telephony) refers to the use of Internet technologies for placing telephone calls. Whereas just a few years ago the quality of VoIP calls was substandard, recent technological advances now allow the quality of calls to equal or even surpass the quality of traditional calls over (wired) telephone lines. In addition to the quality, VoIP offers a number of other benefits; for example, users can receive calls from almost anywhere they connect to the Internet. In other words, knowledge workers are not bound to their desk to receive VoIP calls; instead, using IP routing, their telephone number "follows" them to wherever they connect to the Internet. For example, Christoph, who lives in Hong Kong, has VoIP telephone numbers in the United States and Germany, so that friends and family members living in these countries can call him at local rates. Organizations can also benefit from tremendous cost savings, as often there is little cost incurred over and above the costs for a broadband Internet connection (e.g., VoIP software such as Skype or Gizmo allows home users to make free PC-to-PC calls; see Figure 4.28).

VIDEOCONFERENCING OVER IP. In addition to voice communications, IP can also be used to transmit video data. Traditionally, videoconferences were held either via traditional phone lines, which were not made to handle the transfer of data needed for high-quality videoconferencing, or via dedicated digital lines, which was a very costly option. Similar to VoIP, the Internet also helped to significantly reduce costs and enhance the versatility of videoconferences by enabling **videoconferencing over IP**.

For some videoconferences, desktop videoconferencing equipment (consisting of a webcam, a microphone, speakers, and software such as Microsoft Office Live Meeting or Skype) may be sufficient; for others higher-end equipment may be needed. Such infrastructure can include specific videoconferencing hardware, or it can even be a $400,000 HP HALO meeting room featuring life-sized images allowing people from across the globe to meet as if they were sitting in the same room (see Figure 4.29). In contrast to other applications, with the HALO room, HP provides a videoconferencing service to its customers, offering features such as access to a dedicated network infrastructure and support services for a fixed monthly fee. We will discuss videoconferencing in more detail in Chapter 8.

FIGURE 4.28

VoIP technology enables organizations and individuals to reduce their telecommunications costs.

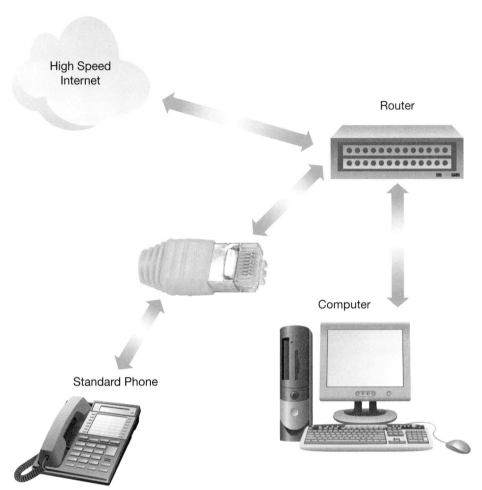

High Speed Internet

Router

Computer

Standard Phone

Increasing Mobility Changes in communication media—such as the growth of e-mail or instant messaging—has led to changes in the way we communicate. In today's digital world, knowledge workers want to be connected, whenever and wherever they are, so that they are able to quickly respond to any communication or use any spare minute to clean up their e-mail in-box. One infrastructure component supporting this need for connectivity is the provision of a wireless infrastructure.

WIRELESS INFRASTRUCTURES. Today's knowledge workers use two primary categories of wireless devices for their communication needs: (1) communication devices that use the public telephone infrastructure (such as cell phones) and (2) wireless devices capable of connecting to an organization's internal network. The convergence of devices and infrastructures allows the sending and receiving of e-mails using a cell phone. Thus,

FIGURE 4.29

The HP Halo meeting room features life-sized images.

Coming Attractions

TV for the Visually Impaired

According to the American Macular Degeneration Foundation (AMDF), approximately 10 million Americans over age fifty-five have macular degeneration; it is the leading cause of severe vision loss. Since the disease most often affects older individuals, that number will increase as the number of aging citizens continues to increase.

Patients who suffer from macular degeneration find that gray or blank spots mask the center of their vision, but peripheral vision is usually not affected. They may need more light to read newspapers and magazine print that is now harder to see, road signs are fuzzy, and television images are blurred and distorted. What has happened is that with age the tissue in the macula—the part of the retina responsible for central vision—deteriorates. The damage can't be reversed, but early diagnosis and treatment often helps reduce the degree of vision loss.

High-frequency waves in the visible spectrum are most difficult for people with macular degeneration to see—a major reason that they see distorted television images. Now researchers at the Schepens Eye Research Institute, an affiliate of Harvard Medical School, have developed software that lets users manipulate the contrast to create specially enhanced images that are easier

for viewers with macular degeneration to see. The researchers designed an algorithm that specifically increases contrast over the middle- and low-frequency ranges that macular degeneration patients can still detect. Once installed in a television set, the system can be adjusted much like one adjusts a volume knob.

In mid-2008, at least one company, Analog Devices, was building a prototype utilizing the algorithm. Researchers who have developed the system hope that one day it will be installed as an option in all television sets. Ideally, visually impaired viewers with macular degeneration will have an option to enhance images much like hearing impaired viewers can opt for closed captioning.

Based on:

Anonymous (n.d.). American macular degeneration foundation. Retrieved May 16, 2008, from http://www.macular.org.

Anonymous (n.d.). Schepens eye research institute. Retrieved May 16, 2008, from http://www.schepens.harvard.edu.

Sauser, B. (2008, January 28). TV for the visually impaired. *Technologyreview.com*. Retrieved May 16, 2008, from http://www.technologyreview.com/Infotech/20117/?a=f.

knowledge workers no longer need a laptop computer nor do they need to be connected to an organization's network to get useful tasks completed. Similarly, using Web-enabled cell phones or PDAs, knowledge workers can access their company's networks and informational resources (see Chapter 5—Enabling Commerce Using the Internet—for a discussion of corporate intranets). However, for many applications, having access to an organization's network can offer many advantages in terms of speed, ease of use, and so on. Thus, organizations are increasingly using wireless (Wi-Fi) infrastructures. However, having an (unsecured) wireless network is equal to having a live network cable lying in the company's parking lot, and securing wireless infrastructures still poses challenges for organizations, which have to strike a balance between providing relatively easy access for authorized individuals and limiting access for outsiders (see Chapter 7).

Data and Knowledge Infrastructure

Data and knowledge are probably among the most important assets an organization has, as data and knowledge are essential for both executing business processes and gaining business intelligence. **Databases**, which are collections of related data organized in a way that facilitates data searches, are vital to an organization's success. Information once taken for granted or never collected at all is now used to make organizations more productive and competitive. Stock prices in the market, potential customers who meet a company's criteria for its products' target audiences and the credit rating of wholesalers and customers are all types of information that organizations collect and analyze.

For example, Adidas uses databases to design and produce its clothing catalog and to market and sell products. Companies such as Adidas also use databases to gather and store information about customers and their purchasing behavior. Companies such as Nordstrom and Victoria's Secret even produce tailor-made catalogs and other mailings for specific individuals, based on the purchasing information stored in corporate databases. Additionally, database technology fuels electronic commerce on the Web, from tracking available products for sale to providing customer service.

As these examples make clear, database management systems have become an integral part of the total information systems infrastructure for most organizations. Database management systems allow organizations to retrieve, store, and analyze information easily. Next we examine some basic concepts, advantages of the database approach, and database management.

The Database Approach: Foundation Concepts

The database approach now dominates nearly all of the computer-based information systems used today. To understand databases, we must familiarize ourselves with some terminology. In Figure 4.30 we compare database terminology (middle column) with equivalents in a library (left column) and a business office (right column). We use **database management systems (DBMSs)** to interact with the data in databases. A DBMS is a software application with which you create, store, organize, and retrieve data from a single database or several databases. Microsoft Access is an example of a popular DBMS for personal computers. In the DBMS, the individual database is a collection of related attributes about entities. An **entity** is something you collect data about, such as people or classes (see Figure 4.31). We often think of entities as **tables**, where each row is a **record** and each column is an **attribute** (also referred to as field). A record is a collection of related attributes about a single entity. Each record typically consists of many attributes, which are individual pieces of information. For example, a name and a Social Security number are attributes of a person.

Advantages of the Database Approach

Before there were DBMSs, organizations used the file processing approach to store and manipulate data electronically. Data were usually kept in a long, sequential computer file, which was often stored on tape. Information about entities often appeared in several different

Library	DBMS Equivalent	Office
Card Catalog	DBMS	File Cabinet
Card Drawer	Database	File Drawer
Catalog Card	Record	File Folder
Card Data	Attributes	Report

FIGURE 4.30

Computers make the process of storing and managing data much easier.

FIGURE 4.31

This sample data table for the entity Student includes eight attributes and eleven records.

ID Number	Last Name	First Name	Street Address	City	State	Zip code	Major
209345	Judson	Jackie	216 Main	Pullman	WA	99164	Information Systems
213009	Schirmer	Birgit	233 Webb	Pullman	WA	99163	History
345987	Valacich	Jordan	1212 Valley View	Pullman	WA	99163	Computer Science
457838	Wright	Eliabeth	426 Main	Pullman	WA	99163	Nursing
459987	Schmidt	Lisa-Marie	1824 Lamont	Pullman	WA	99164	Pre-Medicine
466711	Ferrell	Lauren	412 C Street	Pullman	WA	99164	Business Management
512678	Gatewood	Lael	200 Hill	Pullman	WA	99163	Psychology
691112	Fuller	Grace	312 Mountain Drive	Pullman	WA	99164	Veterinary Medicine
910234	Hardin	Ethan	200 Sunset	Pullman	WA	99164	Sociology
979776	Valacich	James	1212 Valley View	Pullman	WA	99163	Computer Science
983445	Kabbe	Joshua	825 Skylark	Pullman	WA	99164	Human Resources

places throughout the information system, and the data was often stored along with, and sometimes embedded within, the programming code that used the data. People had not yet envisioned the concept of separately storing information about entities in non-redundant databases, so files often had repetitive data about a customer, a supplier, or another entity. When someone's address changed, it had to be changed in every file where that information occurred, an often tedious process. Similarly, if programmers changed the code, they typically had to change the corresponding data along with it. Further, the programmer would have to know *how* the data are stored in order to make any changes. This was often no better than the pen-and-paper approach to storing data.

It is possible for a database to consist of only a single file or table. However, most databases managed under a DBMS consist of several files, tables, or entities. A DBMS can manage hundreds or even thousands of tables simultaneously by linking the tables as part of a single system. The DBMS helps us manage the tremendous volume and complexity of interrelated data so that we can be sure that a change is automatically made for every instance of that data. For example, if a student or customer address is changed, that change is made through all the parts of the system where that data might occur. Using the DBMS prevents unnecessary and problematic redundancies of the data, and the data are kept separate from the programming code in applications. This means that the database does not need to be changed if a change is made to an application. Consequently, there are numerous advantages to using a database approach to managing organizational data; these are summarized in Table 4.9. Of course, moving to the database approach comes with some costs and risks that must be recognized and managed (see Table 4.10). Nonetheless, most organizations have embraced the database approach because most feel that the advantages far exceed the risks or costs.

Effective Management of Databases

Now that we have outlined why databases are important to organizations, we can talk about how organizational databases can be managed effectively. The best database in the world is no better than the data it holds. Conversely, all the data in the world will do you no good if they are not organized in a manner in which there are few or no redundancies and in which you can retrieve, analyze, and understand them. The two key elements of an organizational database are the data and the structure of that data. The structure of the data is typically captured in a **data model**, i.e., a map or diagram that represents entities and their relationships. A common way to represent a data model is

TABLE 4.9 **Advantages of the Database Approach.**

Advantages	Description
Program–data independence	Much easier to evolve and alter software to changing business needs when data and programs are independent.
Minimal data redundancy	Single copy of data ensures that storage requirements are minimized.
Improved data consistency	Eliminating redundancy greatly reduces the possibilities of inconsistency.
Improved data sharing	Easier to deploy and control data access using a centralized system.
Increased productivity of application development	Data standards make it easier to build and modify applications.
Enforcement of standards	A centralized system makes it much easier to enforce standards and rules for data creation, modification, naming, and deletion.
Increased security	A centralized system makes it easier to enforce access restrictions.
Improved data quality	Centralized control, minimized redundancy, and improved data consistency help to enhance the quality of data.
Improved data accessibility	Centralized system makes it easier to provide access for new personnel within or outside organizational boundaries.
Reduced program maintenance	Information changed in the central database is replicated seamlessly throughout all applications.

an **entity-relationship diagram (ERD)**. Further, the structure of the data is documented to facilitate management of the database.

Data Dictionary Each attribute in the database needs to be of a certain type. For example, an attribute may contain text, numbers, or dates. This **data type** helps the DBMS organize and sort the data, complete calculations, and allocate storage space.

Once the data model is created, a format is needed to enter the data in the database. A **data dictionary** is a document that database designers prepare to help individuals enter data. The data dictionary explains several pieces of information for each attribute, such as its name, whether it is a key or part of a key, the type of data expected (dates, alphanumeric, numbers, and so on), and valid values. Data dictionaries can include information such as why the data item is needed, how often it should be updated, and on which forms and reports the data appears.

TABLE 4.10 **Costs and Risks of the Database Approach.**

Cost or Risk	Description
New, specialized personnel	Conversion to the database approach may require hiring additional personnel.
Installation and management cost and complexity	Database approach has higher up-front costs and complexity in order to gain long-term benefits.
Conversion costs	Extensive costs are common when converting existing systems, often referred to as *legacy systems*, to the database approach.
Need for explicit backup and recovery	A shared corporate data resource must be accurate and available at all times.
Organizational conflict	Ownership—creation, naming, modification, and deletion— of data can cause organizational conflict.

Data dictionaries can be used to enforce **business rules**. Business rules, such as who has authority to update a piece of data, are captured by the designers of the database and included in the data dictionary to prevent illegal or illogical entries from entering the database. For example, designers of a warehouse database could capture a rule in the data dictionary to prevent invalid ship dates from being entered into the database.

The **database administrator (DBA)** is responsible for the development and management of the organization's databases. The DBA works with the systems analysts (described in Chapter 10) and programmers to design and implement the database. The DBA must also work with users and managers of the firm to establish policies for managing an organization's databases. The DBA implements security features for the database, such as designating who can look at the database and who is authorized to make changes. The DBA should not make these decisions unilaterally; rather, the DBA merely implements the business decisions made by organizational managers. A good DBA is fundamental to adequately leveraging the investment in database technology. For further discussion of modeling data, such as database *keys*, *associations*, or *normalization*, please see the Technology Briefing.

FIGURE 4.32a

A preprinted form used for gathering information that could be stored in a database.

Application for Employment	Pine Valley Furniture

Personal Information

Name: Date:

Social Security Number:

Home Address:

City, State, Zip

Home Phone: Business Phone:

U.S. Citizen?   If Not, Give Visa No. & Expiration:

Position Applying For

Title: Salary Desired:

Referred By: Date Available:

Education

High School (Name, City, State):

Graduation Date:

Business or Technical School:

Dates Attended: Degree, Major:

Undergraduate College:

Dates Attended: Degree, Major:

Graduate School:

Dates Attended: Degree, Major:

References

Form #2019
Last Revised:3/22/09

Key Database Activities

In this section, we describe the key activities involved in the design, creation, use, and management of databases (for more information, see Hoffer, Prescott, and Topi, 2009). We start by describing how people use databases, beginning with the entry of data.

Entering and Querying Data DBMS software enables end users to create and manage their own database applications. At some point, data must be entered into the database. A clerk or other data entry professional creates records in the database by entering data. These data may come from telephone conversations, preprinted forms that must be filled out, historical records, or electronic files (see Figure 4.32a). Most applications use a graphical user interface (GUI) to present the user with a **form** (see Figure 4.32b), which typically has blanks where the user can enter the information or make choices, each of which represents an attribute within a database record. This form presents the information to the user in an intuitive way so that the user can easily see and enter the data. The form might be online or printed, and the data could even be entered directly by the customer rather than by a data entry clerk. Forms can be used to add, modify, and delete data from the database.

To retrieve information from a database, we use a **query**. **Structured Query Language (SQL)** is the most common language used to interface with databases. Figure 4.33 is an example of an SQL statement used to find students who earned an "A" in a particular course, sorted by student ID number. Writing SQL statements requires time and practice, especially when you are dealing with complex databases with many entities or when you are writing complex queries with multiple integrated criteria—such as adding numbers while sorting on two different attributes. Many DBMS packages have a simpler way of interfacing with the databases—using a concept called **query by example (QBE)**. QBE capabilities in a database enable us to fill out a grid, or template, in order to construct a sample or description of the data we would like to see. Modern DBMS packages, such as Microsoft Access, let us take advantage of the drag-and-drop features of a GUI to create a query quickly and easily. Conducting queries in this manner is much easier than typing the corresponding SQL commands. In Figure 4.34, we provide an example of the QBE grid from Microsoft Access's desktop DBMS package.

Creating Database Reports DBMS packages include a report generation feature. A **report** is a compilation of data from the database that is organized and produced in printed format. Reports are traditionally produced on paper, but today, many reports are presented to users on-screen, reducing the amount of paper used. **Report generators** are software tools that help users to quickly build reports and describe the data in a useful format.

FIGURE 4.32b

A computer-based form used for gathering information that could be stored in a database.

Reproduced with permission of 2008 by Yahoo!

```
SELECT DISTINCTROW STUDENT_ID, GRADE
FROM GRADES
WHERE GRADE="A"
ORDER BY STUDENT_ID;
```

An example of a report is a quarterly sales report for a restaurant. Adding the daily sales totals, grouping them into quarterly totals, and displaying the results in a table of totals creates a quarterly sales report. Reports are not limited to text and numbers. Report generators enable us to create reports using any data in the databases at whatever level we choose. For example, we could add to the restaurant report breakdowns of the data that show the average daily sales totals by days of the week. We could also show the quarterly sales totals in a bar chart, as shown in Figure 4.35. Each of these reports could be presented to the user either on paper or online. We could create automatic links between the underlying sales data located in the database and the attributes on the report in which the underlying data is used so that the reports could be updated automatically.

How Organizations Get the Most from Their Data

Modern organizations are said to be drowning in data but starving for information. Despite being a mixed metaphor, this statement seems to portray quite accurately the situation in many organizations. The advent of Internet-based electronic commerce has resulted in the collection of an enormous amount of customer and transactional data. How this data is collected, stored, and manipulated is a significant factor influencing the success of a commercial Internet Web site. In this section we discuss how organizations are getting the most from their data.

Online Transaction Processing Fast customer response is fundamental to having a successful Internet-based business. **Online transaction processing (OLTP)** refers to immediate automated responses to the requests of users. OLTP systems are designed to

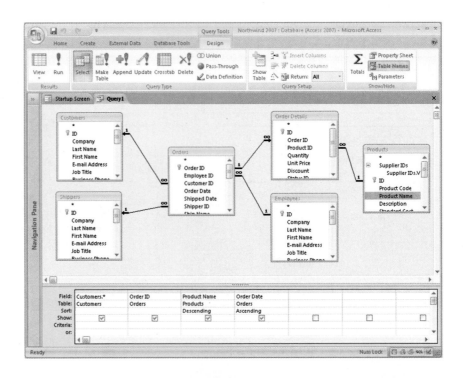

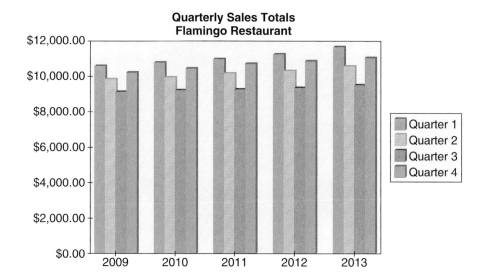

FIGURE 4.35

The quarterly sales report could show either text and numbers or a bar chart and could include the level of detail captured by the database data.

handle multiple concurrent transactions from customers. Typically, these transactions have a fixed number of inputs, such as order items, payment data, and customer name and address, and a specified output, such as total order price or order tracking number. In other words, the primary use of OLTP systems is gathering new information, transforming that information, and updating information in the system. Common transactions include receiving user information, processing orders, and generating sales receipts. Consequently, OLTP is a big part of interactive electronic commerce applications on the Internet. Since customers can be located virtually anywhere in the world, it is critical that transactions be processed efficiently (see Figure 4.36). The speed with which database management systems can process transactions is, therefore, an important design decision when building Internet systems. In addition to which technology is chosen to process the transactions, how the data is organized is also a major factor in determining system performance.

LINKING WEB SITE APPLICATIONS TO ORGANIZATIONAL DATABASES. A recent database development is linking Web sites and organizational databases to provide dynamic and customized, rather than static, information. For example, many companies are enabling users of their Web site to view product catalogs, check inventory, and place orders—all actions that ultimately read and write to organizations' databases. Similarly, information about products (name, description, dimensions, shipping weight, and so on) is stored in a database and dynamically inserted into a Web page, freeing the company from having to develop a separate Web site for each individual product. Traditionally, databases would have to be located together or have complex software connecting them in order to utilize each other's data. Using Internet technology, data can now easily be integrated into many applications from many sources regardless of where the database physically resides.

Some Internet electronic commerce applications can receive and process millions of transactions per day. To gain the greatest understanding of customer behavior and to ensure adequate system performance for customers, you must manage online data effectively. For example, Amazon.com is the world's largest bookstore, with more than 2.5 million titles, and is open 24 hours a day, 365 days a year, with customers from all over the world order-ing books and a broad range of other products. Amazon's servers log millions of transac-tions per day. Amazon is a vast departure from a traditional physical bookstore. In fact, the largest physical bookstore carries "only" about 170,000 titles, and it would not be econom-ically feasible to build a physical bookstore the size of Amazon; a physical bookstore that carried Amazon's 2.5 million titles would need to be the size of nearly twenty-five football fields. The key to effectively designing an online electronic commerce business is clearly the effective management of online data.

Although the database operations behind most transactions are relatively simple, designers often spend considerable time making adjustments to the database design in

FIGURE 4.36

Global customers require that online transactions be processed efficiently.

order to "tune" processing for optimal system performance. Once an organization has all this data, it must design ways to gain the greatest value from its collection; each individual OLTP system could be queried individually, but the real power for an organization comes from analyzing the aggregation of data from different systems, or *data mining*, using methods such as *online analytical processing* (quickly conducting complex analysis of data stored in a database, typically using graphical software tools; see Chapter 8—Enhancing Business Intelligence Using Information Systems).

Merging Transaction and Analytical Processing The requirements for designing and supporting transactional and analytical systems are quite different. In a distributed online environment, performing real-time analytical processing diminishes the performance of transaction processing. For example, complex analytical queries require the locking of data resources for extended periods of execution time, whereas transactional events—data insertions and simple queries from customers—are fast and can often occur simultaneously. Thus, a well-tuned and responsive transaction system may have uneven performance for customers while analytical processing occurs. As a result, many organizations replicate all transactions on a second database server so that analytical processing does not slow customer transaction processing performance. This replication typically occurs in batches during off-peak hours, when site traffic volumes are at a minimum.

The systems that are used to interact with customers and run a business in real time are called **operational systems**. Examples of operational systems are sales order processing and reservation systems. The systems designed to support decision making based on stable

TABLE 4.11 **Comparison of Operational and Informational Systems.**

Characteristic	Operational System	Informational System
Primary purpose	Run the business on a current basis	Support managerial decision making
Type of data	Current representation of state of the business	Historical or point-in-time (snapshot)
Primary users	Online customers, clerks, salespersons, administrators	Managers, business analysts, customers (checking status, history)
Scope of usage	Narrow and simple updates and queries	Broad and complex queries and analyses
Design goal	Performance	Ease of access and use

point-in-time or historical data are called **informational systems**. The key differences between operational and informational systems are shown in Table 4.11. Using a process called **Extraction, Transformation, and Loading (ETL)**, data from informational systems are being consolidated with other organizational data into a comprehensive *data warehouse* to facilitate the use of data mining techniques to gain the greatest and broadest understanding from the data. First, the data need to be extracted from various different systems. In the transformation stage, data are being cleansed and manipulated to fit the needs of the analysis (such as by creating new calculated fields or summary values). **Data cleansing** refers to the process of standardizing the format of data retrieved from different systems (such as differences in the way dates or ZIP codes are stored) and removing inaccurate records. Finally, the transformed data is loaded into the data warehouse and is ready for being used for complex analyses (see Figure 4.37).

Data Warehousing Large organizations, such as Walmart, UPS, and Alaska Airlines, have built **data warehouses** that integrate multiple large databases and other information sources into a single repository. This repository is suitable for direct querying, analysis, or processing. Much like a physical warehouse for products and components, a data warehouse stores and distributes data on computer-based information systems. A data warehouse is a company's virtual storehouse of valuable data from the organization's disparate information systems and external sources. It supports the online analysis of sales, inventory, and other vital business data that have been culled from operational systems. The purpose of a data warehouse is to put key business information into the hands of more decision makers. Table 4.12 lists sample industry uses of data warehouses. Data warehouses can take up hundreds of gigabytes (even terabytes) of data. They usually run on fairly powerful mainframe computers and can cost millions of dollars.

Data warehouses represent more than just big databases. An organization that successfully deploys a data warehouse has committed to pulling together, integrating, and sharing critical corporate data throughout the firm.

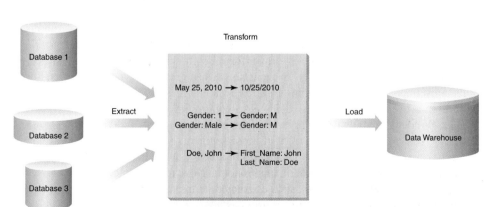

FIGURE 4.37

Extraction, transformation, and loading are used to consolidate data from operational systems into a data warehouse.

TABLE 4.12 **Sample Industry Uses of Data Warehousing.**

Use of Data Warehousing	Representative Companies
Retail	
Analysis of scanner checkout data	Safeway
Tracking, analysis, and tuning of sales promotions and coupons	Costco
	CVS Corporation
Inventory analysis and redeployment	Home Depot
Price reduction modeling to "move" the product	Office Depot
Negotiating leverage with suppliers	Sears
Frequent buyer program management	Target
Profitability analysis	Walgreen
Product selections of granular market segmentation	Walmart
	Williams-Sonoma
Telecommunications	
Analysis of call volume, equipment sales, customer profitability, costs, inventory	AT&T
	Comcast Cable
Inventory analysis and redeployment	Hong Kong CSL
Purchasing leverage with suppliers	Telefonica SA
Frequent buyer program management	T-Mobile
Resource and network utilization	Verizon
Problem tracking and customer service	
Banking and Financing	
Relationship banking	Bank of America
Cross-segment marketing	Citigroup
Risk and credit analysis	HSBC
Merger and acquisition analysis	Goldman Sachs
Customer profiling	Morgan Stanley
Branch performance	UBS
Portfolio management	Wells Fargo
Automotive	
Inventory and supply chain management	Daimler AG
Resource utilization	Ford
Negotiating leverage with suppliers	General Motors
Warranty tracking and analysis	Honda
Profitability analysis and market segmentation	Toyota

Data Marts Rather than storing all enterprise data in one data warehouse, many organizations have created multiple data marts, each containing a subset of the data for a single aspect of a company's business—for example, finance, inventory, or personnel. A **data mart** is a data warehouse that is limited in scope. It contains selected information from the data warehouse such that each separate data mart is customized for the decision support applications of a particular end-user group. Data marts have been popular among small and medium-sized businesses and among departments within larger organizations, all of which were previously prohibited from developing their own data warehouses because of the high costs involved.

Williams-Sonoma, for example, known for its high-class home furnishing stores, is constantly looking to find new ways to increase sales and reach new target markets. Some of the most important data are coming from their catalog mailings, a database that contains 33 million active U.S. households. Using SAS data-mining tools and different statistical models, Williams-Sonoma can segment customers into groups of 30,000 to 50,000 households and can predict the profitability of those segments based on the prior year's purchases. These models resulted in the creation of a new catalog for a market segment that had up to then not been served by Williams-Sonoma. Now, for example, Williams-Sonoma markets a variety of new products, such as fringed lamps, chic furniture, and cool accessories, to an identified market segment using its Pottery Barn Teen catalog.

Data marts typically contain tens of gigabytes of data as opposed to the hundreds of gigabytes in data warehouses. Therefore, data marts can be deployed on less powerful hardware. The differences in costs between different types of data marts and data warehouses can be significant. The cost to develop a data mart is typically less than $1 million, while the cost for a data warehouse can exceed $10 million. Clearly, organizations committed to getting the most out of their data must make a large investment in database technology.

Industry Analysis

Movie Industry

Do you remember the original *Star Wars* movies or movies such as *King Kong* (1976) or *Godzilla*? Compare these to recent box office hits such as the *Lord of the Rings Trilogy* (2001–2003), *Star Wars Episode III: Revenge of the Sith* (2005), *King Kong* (2005), or animated movies such as *Bee Movie* (2007) or *Madagascar: Escape 2 Africa* (2008). The tremendous increase in computing power has enabled film studios such as Dreamworks or Universal Studios or special effects studios such as Weta Digital or Pixar to create animations and special effects of hitherto unimaginable quality using specialized powerful software- and hardware for computer-generated imagery (CGI, also known as computer graphics, CG).

As for major studios, rapidly evolving digital technology (specifically, recording hardware and sophisticated, yet easy-to-use digital editing software) has opened vast opportunities for independent filmmakers who are producing studio-quality films without having to rely on expensive lighting, film development, and postproduction facilities. Thus, people who could never afford all the necessary equipment can now produce movies digitally. Further, digital cameras and projectors and advances in software have made the transition from celluloid to digital more attainable for filmmakers who until recently used traditional technology. In fact, over 30 percent of the submissions to the Sundance Film Festival (the primary film festival for independent movies, comparable to festivals in Cannes or Berlin for mainstream movies) are now in digital format.

However, the impact of technology on the movie industry does not stop with movie production. Many movie theaters across the world have shifted to digital projection technologies, reducing the need for duplicating and shipping large reels of film, reducing distribution costs by up to 90 percent, while speeding up the time from the studio to the theater. Rather than shipping reels of film (that are susceptible to out-of-focus projection, scratches, or pops), the movies are stored on central servers, from which they are accessed and downloaded via the Internet by individual theaters. Theater owners can much more swiftly react to fluctuating demand and easily show movies in more than one screen in case of high demand. In addition, digital technology is a requirement for new 3-D techniques such as "3ality," the technology used for U2's 2007 3-D concert film, which premiered at the 2008 Sundance Film Festival.

Clearly, the use of information systems has tremendously changed the movie industry.

Questions

1. Can digital technologies help movie theaters compete with the increasing trend toward more sophisticated home theaters? How?
2. What are the ethical issues associated with special effects becoming more and more realistic with the help of digital technologies?
3. From the perspective of movie studios and theaters, list the pros and cons of using digital distribution technologies.

Based on:

Anonymous (n.d.). U2 3D: The first live-action 3D concert movie, featuring U2. Retrieved May 16, 2008, from http://www.u23dmovie.com.

Jardin, X. (2005, July 28). Hollywood plots end of film reels. *Wired.* Retrieved May 16, 2008, from http://www.wired.com/entertainment/music/news/2005/07/68332.

Meyers, M. (2006, January 18). Tech plays supporting role at Sundance festival. *CNET News.com.* Retrieved May 16, 2008, from http://news.com.com/Tech+plays+supporting+role+at+Sundance+festival/2100-1025_3-6028354.html.

Key Points Review

1. *List the essential information systems infrastructure components and describe why they are necessary for satisfying an organization's informational needs.* Modern organizations heavily rely on information systems infrastructure; its components include hardware, software, communications and collaboration, data and knowledge, and human resources. While the computing hardware is integral to an organization's IS infrastructure, as it is also needed to store and process organizational data, networking hardware is needed to connect the different systems to allow for collaboration and information sharing. Software assists organizations in executing their business processes and competitive strategy. Consequently, with increased reliance on information systems for managing organizations, effectively utilizing software resources is becoming increasingly critical and complex. Communication and collaboration is one of the reasons why information systems have become so powerful and important to modern organizations. The ability to interconnect computers, information systems, and networks ultimately allows the interconnection of both internal and external business processes, facilitating improved communication and collaboration. Data and knowledge are probably among the most important assets an organization has, as data and knowledge are essential for both gaining business intelligence and executing business processes.

2. *Describe the components of an organization's hardware infrastructure, and highlight current trends.* Information systems hardware is classified into three types: input, processing, and output technologies. Input hardware consists of devices used to enter information into a computer. Processing hardware transforms inputs into outputs. The central processing unit is the device that performs this transformation, with the help of several other closely related devices that store and recall information. Finally, output-related hardware focuses on delivering information in a usable format to users. Many organizations now turn to on-demand computing for fluctuating computation needs, utility computing for "renting" of resources, grid computing for solving large-scale problems, edge computing for providing a more decentralized use of resources, and green computing for reducing energy costs.

3. *Describe the components of an organization's software infrastructure, and highlight current trends.* Systems software is the collection of programs that form the foundation for the basic operations of the computer hardware. Systems software, or the operating system, performs tasks such as booting your computer, reading programs into memory, managing where programs and files are located in secondary storage, formatting disks, controlling the computer monitor, and sending documents to the printer. The systems software manages the dialogue you can have with a computer using either a command-based or graphical interface. A command-based interface requires that text commands be typed into the computer, whereas a graphical user interface uses pictures and icons as well as menus to send instructions back and forth between the user and the computer system. Application software allows the user to perform specific tasks, such as writing business letters, analyzing data, or processing payroll. To manage the ever-increasing complexity of software needs, organizations turn to open-source software to increase their independence, use software as a service to free themselves from having to manage the software infrastructure, or use service-oriented architectures to integrate various systems and processes.

4. *Describe the components of an organization's communications and collaboration infrastructure, and highlight current trends.* As with human communication, a computer network needs senders, receivers, transmission media, and protocols. There are several types of computer networks, which are classified by use and geographic area. Commonly used networks include private branch exchanges (PBX), personal area networks (PANs), local area networks (LANs), campus area networks (CANs), wireless LANs (WLANs), metropolitan area networks (MANs), and wide area networks (WANs). Transmission media can be classified as cable or wireless media. The most widely used network is the Internet, which is composed of networks that are developed and maintained by many different entities. The Internet relies on packet-switching technology to deliver data and information across networks. Routers are used to interconnect independent networks. Because so many different networks are connected to the Internet, they use a common communication protocol (TCP/IP). TCP/IP is divided into two parts. TCP breaks information into datagrams that are transferred from computer to computer. IP defines how a data packet must be formed and how a router must forward each packet. All computers, including routers, are assigned unique IP addresses, enabling data routing and delivery. Together, TCP and IP provide a reliable

and efficient way to send data across the Internet. The World Wide Web provides a graphical user interface to the Internet by using HTML documents called Web pages containing hyperlinks to other pages. The convergence of computing and telecommunications has helped organizations address their diverse communication needs, such as by enabling Voice over IP or videoconferencing over IP. Often, companies implement wireless infrastructures to increase their employees' mobility.

5. *Describe the components of an organization's data and knowledge infrastructure.* A database is a collection of related data organized in a way that facilitates data searches. A database contains entities, attributes, records, and tables. Entities are things about which we collect data, such as people, courses, customers, or products. Attributes are the individual pieces of information about an entity, such as a person's last name or Social Security number, that are stored in a database record. A record is the collection of related attributes about an entity; usually, a record is displayed as a database row. A table is a collection of related records about an entity type; each row in the table is a record, and each column is an attribute. A database management system is a software application with which you create, store, organize, and retrieve data from a single database or several databases. The data within a database must be adequately organized so that it is possible to store and retrieve information effectively. To support more effective business processes and to gather business intelligence, organizations have to find ways to manage vast amounts of data, usually using online transaction processing and online analytical processing. Data warehouses and data marts support the integration and analysis of large data sets.

Key Terms

802.11 157
Advanced Research Projects Agency
  Network (ARPANET) 158
application service provider 152
application software 150
arithmetic logic unit (ALU) 138
attenuation 156
attribute 167
autonomic computing 159
bandwidth 155
basic input/output system
  (BIOS) 139
batch data 135
binary code 136
bit 136
Bluetooth 157
business rule 170
byte 136
cable media 156
cache 139
campus area network (CAN) 156
CD-ROM 140
central processing unit 138
client 155
coaxial cable 156
command line interface 150
computer networking 153
control unit 138
data cleansing 175
data dictionary 169
data mart 176
data model 168
data type 169

data warehouse 175
database 166
database administrator (DBA) 170
database management system
  (DBMS) 167
dedicated grid 145
Defense Advanced Research Projects
  Agency (DARPA) 158
digitizing 155
diskette 139
domain name 161
dot matrix printer 142
DVD 140
eavesdropping 156
edge computing 145
electrically erasable programmable
  read-only memory
  (EEPROM) 140
electromagnetic interference
  (EMI) 156
embedded system 150
entity 167
entity-relationship diagram
  (ERD) 168
extraction, transformation, and
  loading (ETL) 175
fiber-optic cable 156
flash drive 140
flash memory 140
form 171
global positioning system
  (GPS) 158
gopher 161

graphical user interface (GUI) 150
graphics card 142
green computing 146
grid computing 144
hard disk 139
hard drive 139
high-frequency radio 156
hyperlink 161
hypertext 161
hypertext markup language
  (HTML) 161
hypertext transfer protocol
  (HTTP) 161
information systems
  infrastructure 133
informational system 175
infrared line of sight 156
infrastructure 132
ink-jet printer 142
input technologies 134
Internet 158
IP address 161
IP convergence 163
IP datagram 161
keyboard 135
laser printer 142
local area network (LAN) 156
machine language 136
magnetic tape 139
mainframe 142
metropolitan area network
  (MAN) 156
microcomputer 142

microprocessor 138
microwave transmission 157
midrange computer 142
monitor 142
Moore's Law 139
mouse 135
National Science Foundation
     (NSF) 159
National Science Foundation
     Network (NSFNET) 159
network 155
nonvolatile memory 139
on-demand computing 144
online transaction processing
     (OLTP) 172
open-source software 150
operating system 146
operational system 174
optical disk 140
output technologies 134
packet switching 160
peer 155
peer-to-peer networks 155
personal area network (PAN) 156
plotter 142
pointing device 135
primary storage 139
private branch exchange (PBX) 156
processing technologies 134

projector 142
protocol 153
query 171
query by example (QBE) 171
random-access memory (RAM) 139
read-only memory (ROM) 139
record 167
registers 139
report 171
report generator 171
router 160
satellite 157
satellite microwave 157
scalability 144
scanner 135
secondary storage 139
server 155
server-centric networks 155
software as a service (SaaS) 151
sound card 142
storage service provider (SSP) 144
structured query language
     (SQL) 171
supercomputer 142
system unit 138
systems software 146
table 167
terrestrial microwave 157
top-level domain 162

Transmission Control
     Protocol/Internet Protocol
     (TCP/IP) 160
transmission media 153
twisted pair cable 156
ultra low power (ULP)
     Bluetooth 157
uniform resource locator (URL) 161
user interface 150
utility computing 144
video card 142
videoconferencing over IP 164
virtual machine 146
virtualization 146
voice over IP (VoIP) 164
volatile memory 139
Web browser 161
Web page 161
Web server 161
Web site 161
wide area network (WAN) 156
wireless fidelity (Wi-Fi) 157
wireless local area network
     (WLAN) 157
wireless media 156
workstation 142
World Wide Web (WWW) 161

Review Questions

1. Information systems hardware is classified into what three major types?
2. How do a computer's primary storage, secondary storage, ROM, and RAM interact?
3. Describe the different types of computers and their key distinguishing characteristics.
4. Define grid computing and describe its advantages and disadvantages.
5. What is the difference between a command-based interface and a graphical user interface?
6. Describe why companies would choose to implement open-source software over fully licensed software.
7. What are the major types of networks?

8. What is TCP/IP, and what roles does it play in the use of the Internet?
9. What is the World Wide Web, and what is its relationship to the Internet?
10. What are URLs, and why are they important to the World Wide Web?
11. Describe what is meant by the term IP convergence.
12. Describe why databases have become so important to modern organizations.
13. Describe how the following terms are related: entity, attribute, record, and table.
14. Compare and contrast data warehouses and data marts.

Self-Study Questions

Visit the Interactive Study Guide on the Companion Web site for additional Self-Study Questions: www.pearsonhighered.com/valacich.

1. A system unit contains all of the following except
   _____.
   A. CD-ROM
   B. central processing unit
   C. power supply
   D. monitor

2. _____ is a special form of on-demand computing which is typically used to solve large-scale computing problems.
   A. grid
   B. utility
   C. access
   D. edge

3. An operating system performs which of the following tasks?
   A. booting the computer
   B. managing where programs and files are stored
   C. sending documents to the printer
   D. all of the above

4. Which of the following is *not* an example of open-source software?
   A. Linux
   B. OpenOffice
   C. Apache
   D. Windows Vista

5. Which of the following is a type of wireless medium?
   A. fiber-optic
   B. TCP/IP
   C. infrared
   D. microterminal

6. Which of the following is the protocol of the Internet?
   A. URL
   B. TCP/IP
   C. PAN
   D. HMTL

7. All of the following are correct domain suffixes except
   A. edu—educational institutions
   B. gov—U.S. government
   C. neo—network organizations
   D. com—commercial businesses

8. Web sites and specific Web pages within those sites have a unique Internet address called a URL, or
   _____.
   A. Universal Resource Login
   B. Universal Router Locator
   C. Uniform Resource Locator
   D. Uniform Resource Language

9. A database comprises _____.
   A. attributes
   B. records
   C. organized data for querying
   D. all of the above

10. What method is used to effectively process customer transactions?
    A. OLTP
    B. Web services
    C. OLAP
    D. data mining

Answers are on page 183.

Problems and Exercises

1. Match the following terms with the appropriate definitions:
   i. Utility computing
   ii. Output technologies
   iii. System Unit
   iv. Systems software
   v. Voice over IP
   vi. OLTP
   vii. Bandwidth
   viii. Transmission media
   ix. Data warehouse
   x. Graphical user interface
      a. The integration of multiple large databases into a single repository
      b. The use of Internet technology for placing telephone calls
      c. The physical box that houses the electronic components of a computer

   d. Technology used for immediate automated response to requests of the users
   e. The physical pathways to send data and information between two or more entities on a network
   f. The transmission capacity of a computer or communications channel
   g. A form of on-demand computing where resources are rented on an as-needed basis
   h. Technology used to deliver information to the user in a usable format
   i. The collection of programs that control the basic operations of computer hardware
   j. A computer interface that enables the user to select pictures or icons to send instructions to the computer.

2. Go visit a computer shop or look on the Web for mice or touch pads. What is new about how these input

devices look, or how they are used? What are some of the advantages and disadvantages of each device?

3. What types of printers are most common today? What is the cost of a color printer versus a black-and-white one? Compare and contrast laser and ink-jet printers in terms of speed, cost, and output quality. What kind of printer would you buy or have you bought?

4. What happens when a computer runs out of RAM? Can more RAM be added? Is there a limit? How does cache memory relate to RAM? Why is RAM so important in today's modern information systems world? Search the Web for RAM retailers. Compare their prices and options.

5. How do software programs affect your life? Give examples of software from areas other than desktop computers. Are the uses for software increasing over time?

6. Interview an IS professional, and ask him or her about open-source software. Does he or she see all types of information systems to be candidates for open-source software? Additionally, find out what systems are most likely and least likely to be open source.

7. Discuss the difference between LANs and WLANs. What are the advantages of each? What are possible disadvantages of each? When would you recommend one over the other?

8. Personal area networks using Bluetooth are becoming increasingly popular. Visit www.bluetooth.com and investigate the types of products that this wireless technology is being used to enhance. Find three products that you find interesting and prepare a ten-minute presentation on what these products are and how Bluetooth is enhancing their operation and usage.

9. Scan the popular press and/or the Web for clues concerning emerging technologies for computer networking. This may include new uses for current technologies or new technologies altogether. Discuss as a group the "hot" issues. Do you feel they will become a reality in the near future? Why or why not? Prepare a ten-minute presentation of your findings to be given to the class.

10. Do you have your own Web site with a specific domain name? How did you decide on the domain name? If you don't have your own domain, research possibilities of obtaining one. Would your preferred name be available? Why might your preferred name not be available?

11. Search through recent articles in your favorite technology publication—whether print or online. What are some of the issues being discussed that relate to the Internet and/or the Web in particular? Have you experienced any of these technologies, applications, and/or issues? What is your opinion about them? How will they affect your life and career? Prepare a ten-minute presentation to the class of your findings.

12. How and why are organizations without extensive databases falling behind in competitiveness and growth? Is this simply a database problem that can be fixed easily with some software purchases? Search the Web for stories or news articles that deal with the issue of staying competitive by successfully managing data. How are these stories similar to each other? How are they different? Prepare a ten-minute presentation to the class on your findings.

13. Based on your experience with online transaction processing systems (in everyday life or in the workplace), which ones seem to work best? What characteristics did you judge the success of these systems by? Would you make any adjustments to the system?

14. Choose an organization with which you are familiar that uses databases. Then brainstorm how this organization could use data mining to gain an understanding of their customers, products, or marketplace. What are some key pieces of information that should be data mined for this organization?

15. Using a search engine, enter the key phrase "data warehousing." Who are the large vendors in this industry? What type of solutions do they offer to their clients? Do you see any common trends in the data warehousing business?

Application Exercises

Note: The existing data files referenced in these exercises are available on the Student Companion Web site: www. pearsonhighered.com/valacich.

Spreadsheet Application: Tracking Frequent Flier Mileage

You have recently landed a part-time job as a business analyst for Campus Travel. In your first meeting, the operations manager learned that you are taking an introductory MIS class. As the manager is not very proficient in using office software tools, he is doing all frequent flier mileage in two separate Excel worksheets. One is the customer's contact information and the second is the miles flown. Being familiar with the possibilities of spreadsheet applications, you suggest setting up one worksheet to handle both functions. To complete this, you must do the following:

1. Open the spreadsheet frequentflier2.csv. You will see a tab for customers and a tab labeled "miles flown."

2. Use the vlookup function to enter the miles flown column by looking up the frequent flier number (Hint:

If done correctly with absolute references, you should be able to enter the vlookup formula in the first cell in the "miles flown" column and copy it down for all the cells).

3. Use conditional formatting to highlight all frequent fliers who have less than 4,000 total miles.

4. Finally, sort the frequent fliers by total miles in descending order and print out the spreadsheet.

A Database Application: Building a Knowledge Database

Campus Travel seems to be growing quite rapidly. Now they have franchises in three different states, totaling sixteen locations. As the company has grown tremendously over the past few years, it has become increasingly difficult to keep track of the areas of expertise of each travel consultant; often, consultants waste valuable time trying to find out who in the company possesses the knowledge about a particular region. Impressed with your skills, the general manager of Campus Travel has asked you to add, modify, and delete the following records from its employee database:

1. Open employeedata.mdb.

2. Select the "employee" tab.

3. Add the following records:
   a. Eric Tang, Spokane Office, Expert in Southwest, Phone (509)555-2311
   b. Janna Connell, Spokane Office, Expert in Delta, Phone (509)555-1144

4. Delete the following record:
   a. Carl Looney from the Pullman office

5. Modify the following:
   a. Change Frank Herman from the Pullman office to the Spokane office
   b. Switch Ramon Sanchez's home number to (208)549-2544

Team Work Exercise: Your Personal Communication Infrastructure Assessment

Work in a team of four or five students and have each person list the number of wired telephone calls, cellular telephone calls, instant messages, e-mail messages, and so on. For each instance, also inventory the total time spent, who the call was to, and the purpose of the call. Have each person also document his or her demographic and relevant personal information (e.g., age, gender, relationship status, children, and so on). Combine the results of all team members and discuss patterns and anomalies.

Answers to the Self-Study Questions

1. D, p. 135	**2.** A, p. 144	**3.** D, p. 146	**4.** D, p. 150	**5.** C, p. 156
6. B, p. 160	**7.** C, p. 162	**8.** C, p. 161	**9.** D, p. 166	**10.** A, p. 172

Case ❶

DATABASE AS A SERVICE: Amazon's SimpleDB

As you know by now, databases are not simple to construct or maintain, but nothing beats a computer-based database for managing large amounts of information. Corporations can ask IT personnel to construct custom database software from scratch, which generally proves time-consuming and expensive, or the IT department can purchase off-the-shelf DBMS software. Whether created in-house or purchased from a software vendor, DBMS software lets users set up a database, create tables, forms, and reports. DBMS users can then insert, sort, update, analyze, and report on the data stored in the database, thus converting the data within the database into useful information.

But why expend the time and expense necessary to create a database when, as is currently true in so many areas, the Internet offers a much easier and less costly solution? Duplicating Google's game plan of becoming a provider of online hosted services, in 2007, Amazon launched its SimpleDB—a service for enterprises that can't afford to construct in-house databases or simply want the convenience of letting a hosted service do most of the work. Database developers sign up for the service, which operates in conjunction with Amazon's Storage Service (S3) and Elastic Compute Cloud (EC2), and pay only for time and storage space used, at beginning rates of 14¢ per machine hour and 10¢ per GB in and 18¢ per GB out. For start-up companies, scalability is an important feature, as the database can grow with the business's needs.

Amazon points out that, traditionally, database construction and use requires a clustered relational database, with considerable investment, complexity, and management requirements. "Many developers," the company says, "simply want to store, process, and query their data without worrying about managing schemas, maintaining indexes, tuning performance, or scaling access to their data."

Therefore, there is no need for data modeling or for fine-tuning the database for performance. Amazon's SimpleDB is automatically indexed for "fast real-time look-up and querying capabilities." The company compares a SimpleDB domain to a spreadsheet, with items as rows of data, attributes as column headers, and values as the data in each cell. In contrast to a spreadsheet, however, cells can have multiple values, such as "small," "medium,"or "large" for the attribute "size" of a clothing item. If an organization needs a full relational database, it can host its own within Amazon's EC2 service.

With the hosting services it now makes available, Amazon has been compared to Google as a host of online services. The prediction is that 90 percent of the world's software will someday be online and available through hosting services such as Google and Amazon for a fee. Both companies are poised to take full advantage of the hosting trend.

Questions

1. Would you trust an external provider with your organization's data? Why or why not? What would be needed to raise your trust in the reliability, security, and privacy of the data?
2. What are the potential drawbacks of using a relatively simple database with limited capabilities? Do the benefits outweigh these limitations? Why or why not?
3. In what types of business environments would Amazon's SimpleDB be a good match? Where would it not?

Based on:

Anonymous (n.d.). Amazon SimpleDB—Limited Beta. Retrieved May 16, 2008, from http://www.amazon.com/gp/browse.html?node=342335011.

Levine, B. (2007, December 17). Amazon launching database-as-a-service. *Newsfator.com*. Retrieved May 31, 2008, from http://www.newsfactor.com/story.xhtml?story_id=110003L9MFM8.

Case ❷

Broadband Service on Airplanes: WiFi in the Sky

Broadband connectivity is fast becoming a competitive area in the airline industry. Since many passengers on long flights don't want to be deprived of their WiFi-enabled digital devices, the industry is rushing to comply.

Between 2004 and 2006, Boeing tried offering broadband service to passengers through its service called Connexion by Boeing. The infrastructure for the system included phased array antennae or mechanically steered Ku-band antennae on the aircraft, leased satellite transponders, and ground stations located in Vancouver, B.C.; Russia; Switzerland; the United States; and Japan. However, following the terrorist attacks of September 11, 2001, many U.S. domestic carriers faced severe financial difficulties and could not justify the costs associated with installing Connexion's systems. Thus, Connexion was launched internationally, and the first airline to use the service in 2004 was Lufthansa German Airlines. Signing up later in 2004 were ANA, Japan Airlines, and SAS. In 2005, airlines contracting for the service included China Airlines, Singapore Airlines, Asiana Airlines, Korean Air, El-Al Israel Airlines, and Etihad Airlines. In 2005, Connexion by Boeing added the first live streaming TV service on Singapore Airlines.

Costs to passengers using Connexion were $9.95 for one hour of access, $14.95 for less than three hours of access, $19.95 for three to six hours of access, and $29.95 for unlimited access. Despite indications supported by Boeing's market research, Boeing's broadband service was not as popular with passengers as anticipated, and Connexion was discontinued in 2006.

In 2008, broadband service was again positioned to take off, and Alaska, American, Southwest and Virgin America all announced that they would launch broadband access to flight passengers within a few months. Alaska and Southwest Airlines would use satellite-based services via California-based Row 44. American and Virgin America Airlines would use a cell phone tower system from Aircell, a company based in Illinois. It has been determined that cell phone signals don't interfere with a plane's instrumentation, but their use is prohibited in the United States while planes are in flight because they annoy other passengers.

The two types of broadband service to be offered include:

- Aircell cell phone towers: Ninety-two existing cell towers covering the entire continental United States relay data from tower to tower. Coverage is good, but the system will initially work only in the lower forty-eight states. The cost to passengers is $12.95 per flight.

- Row 44 satellite service: Geosynchronous satellites generate signals and the system can work across international borders and over oceans, but will be offered at first only over North America. Passengers can expect to log on via lower end DSL speeds and will pay about $6.00 per flight.

In the mean time, the European Commission has lifted the cell phone ban

aboard aircraft in European airspace. Under the new rules, airlines would have to install small mobile base stations aboard their aircraft, and passengers could use their cell phones once the aircraft has reached 10,000 feet. The onboard base station would limit the transmission power and possible interference with the aircrafts' navigation systems and could be turned off or set to only allowing text messaging during night flights. As of summer 2008, Air France, Ryanair, and BMI were planning to make the service available. Other airlines, such as Qatar, installed the necessary equipment, but will only allow text messaging during the flight. Whether or not the latest broadband and mobile services for airline passengers will succeed remains to be seen, but WiFi in the sky is definitely a concept that airlines will continue to pursue.

Questions

1. How much would you be willing to pay for Wi-Fi access in the sky? Under which circumstances would you be willing to pay a higher price?
2. How do you feel about cell phone use during the flight? Would you switch to or abandon carriers if cell phone use was allowed on one but not the other? Why?
3. Do you think that using the Internet or cell phones creates any security problems on a flight? Why or why not?

Based on:

Anonymous (2008, April 7). Europe clears mobiles on aircraft. Retrieved May 31, 2008, from http://news.bbc.co.uk/2/hi/technology/7334372.stm.

Anonymous (2008, January 29). JetBlue providing WIFI/TV for other airlines? *Techdirt*. Retrieved May 16, 2008, from http://www.techdirt.com/articles/2008129/141951112.shtml.

Anonymous (n.d.). Lessons from the failure of Connexion-by-Boeing. Retrieved May 16, 2008, from http://www.tmfassociates.com/LessonsfromConnexion.pdf.

Gammon, K. (2008, April 21). Coming this summer: Fly the Wi-Fi skies. *Wired*. Retrieved May 16, 2008, from http://www.wired.com/techbiz/it/magazine/16-05/st_wifi.

Hamblen, M. (2008, January 23). Southwest, American test inflight Wi-Fi. *Macworld*. Retrieved May 16, 2008, from http://www.macworld.com/article/131781/2008/01/wifi.html.

Keenan, S. (2008, May 7). Qatar bans inflight mobile calls. Retrieved May 31, 2008, from http://travel.timesonline.co.uk/tol/life_and_style/travel/news/article3887510.ece.

Enabling Commerce Using the Internet

After reading this chapter, you will be able to do the following:

1. Describe electronic commerce, how it has evolved, and the strategies that companies are adopting to compete in cyberspace.

2. Explain the differences between extranets and intranets and show how organizations utilize these environments.

3. Describe the stages of business-to-consumer electronic commerce and understand the keys to successful electronic commerce applications.

4. Describe emerging trends in consumer-to-consumer e-commerce and the key drivers for the emergence of mobile commerce.

5. Explain different forms of e-government as well as regulatory threats to e-commerce.

Preview

This chapter focuses on electronic commerce (e-commerce, or EC), explaining how companies conduct business with customers, business partners, and suppliers over the Internet. The Internet and World Wide Web are extremely well suited for conducting business electronically on a global basis. Web-based EC has introduced unprecedented opportunities for the marketing of products and services, accompanied by features, functionality, and innovative methods to serve and support consumers.

With EC representing a growing proportion of overall retail sales, an understanding of EC can be a powerful tool in your arsenal. People with EC skills are in high demand in the marketplace; therefore, the more you know about EC, the more valuable you will become.

Doing Virtual Business: Second Life

The rise and fall of the Arbitrage Wise financial empire was a business saga worth following. Wise bought empire-builder Xavier Mohr's holdings when Mohr tired of business and wanted out. At the height of his success, Wise ran a variety of companies under the Wise Metaverse title. His holdings included the SL Capital Exchange, JT Financial, SL Reports, a financial newspaper, and Wise Metaverse Ad Network, which sold advertising space on all ATMs. Then the financial world suffered setbacks—high interest rates, a prohibition on local gambling, and a stock exchange theft were primarily to blame—and Wise's empire crumbled. At that time, JT Financial was one of the largest banks in Wise's holdings, with over L$82 million on deposit. At the current exchange rate of L$265 to US$1 that amount equates to approximately US$309,443.00. A disillusioned Wise cashed out and got out of the business.

Does the above account sound as though it tracks the rise and fall of a Wall Street mogul? Almost, but not quite. If you have ever played the MMOG (massively multiplayer online game) "Second Life (SL)," you probably recognized some of the terms as those used in the virtual world: "L$" refers to Lindens, the currency SL avatars use in financial dealings. "US$" is "U.S. Dollars," indicating how much Lindens are actually worth when converted to real-world dollars. Yes, Lindens do convert to real dollars. After business fees are paid (Linden Lab collects fees for doing business), SL residents can opt to cash out.

Is there a real opportunity within the MMOG virtual world for participants to earn money? Second Life's Web site boasts, "Thousands of residents are making part or all of their real life income from their Second Life businesses." With an estimated 8.5 million "residents," SL would seem an entrepreneur's paradise. Avatars can buy property, build businesses and homes, shop for clothing and other items, invest money, and otherwise function much as real residents in real communities function. The reality, however, according to some sources, may not be so optimistic. Frank Rose's 2007 article in *Wired* magazine, "How Madison Avenue Is Wasting Millions on a Deserted Second Life," points out that often, individuals create multiple avatars or their owners had not logged in within the last thirty days. (An August 2007 article in *Technology Review* estimates SL's population at about 1.6 million *active* users.) "Then there's the question of what people do when they get there," Rose's article continues. "Once you put in several hours flailing around learning how to function in Second Life, there isn't much *to* do." The biggest draw for avatars, Rose claims, is free Linden giveaway events at Money Island and kinky sex.

And yet, corporate marketers are eager to establish an SL presence; American Apparel, Reebok, Scion, Coca Cola, IBM, NBA, Coldwell-Banker, Adidas, H&R Block, Sears, CNET, Reuters, and so on and on—about fifty real-world companies have invested money and established presences in SL, and a small industry has sprung up to help them. The Electric Sheep Company, for instance, was paid to establish SL locations for such clients as AOL, Major League Baseball, the NBA, Nissan, Pontiac, and Sony BMG Music. ". . . [W]e can hardly keep up with the Fortune 500 companies who are contacting us," Sibley Verbeck, CEO and founder of the Electric Sheep Company, is quoted in Rose's *Wired* article.

Market and advertising experts claim that traditional advertising methods, such as thirty-second television commercials, are less effective than they used to be, therefore, some businesses see virtual world environments as a chance to reach a different audience. Some are proceeding

FIGURE 5.1

Avatars within Second Life interacting.

slowly and cautiously, while others are jumping in just to avoid missing what might be the next big Web innovation.

After the 2007 demise of Arbitrage Wise's financial empire and other Second Life banking meltdowns, in January 2008, Linden Lab evicted SL's banks, causing avatar owners to lose real-life money. To protect avatars that fall for deals that are too good to be true, Linden Lab abruptly banned virtual banks that could not furnish "proof of an applicable government registration statement or financial institution charter." What? In a virtual world, real-world financial regulations apply? Apparently so, if real money is on the line.

Virtual worlds continue to capture Web developers' imaginations, and predictions are that environments like Second Life will in the future be posted in 3-D, more closely resembling real communities. Will entrepreneurs have the same opportunities that exist in the real world? Time will tell.

After reading this chapter, you will be able to answer the following:

1. What are the pros and cons of establishing a business within Second Life?

2. What business opportunities would you invest in within Second Life?

3. How would you forecast the future of Second Life as an opportunity for business?

Based on:

Gardenvale, P. (2008, February). Fool's gold: The rise and demise of Second Life finance. *The Seventh Sun.* Retrieved May 22, 2008, from http://www.theseventhsun.com/0208_foolsGold004.htm.

Naone, E. (2007, August 8). Money trouble in Second Life. *Technology Review.* Retrieved May 22, 2008, from http://www. technologyreview.com/Biztech/19193.

Naone, E. (2007, August 14). Making money in Second Life. *Technology Review.* Retrieved May 22, 2008, from http://www. technologyreview. com/Biztech/ 19242.

Rose, F. (2007, July 24). How Madison Avenue is wasting millions on a deserted Second Life. *Wired.* Retrieved May 22, 2008, from http://www.wired.com/techbiz/media/magazine/15-08/ff_sheep.

Talbot, D. (2008, January 10). Second Life closes banks. *Technology Review.* Retrieved May 22, 2008, from http://www. technologyreview.com/Biztech/20037.

Electronic Commerce Defined

The Internet provides a set of interconnected networks for individuals and businesses to complete transactions electronically. We define **electronic commerce** very broadly as the online exchange of goods, services, and money[1] among firms, between firms and their customers, and between customers. The Census Bureau of the Department of Commerce reported that annual online retail sales were up by 19 percent and that e-commerce accounted for 3.4 percent of total retail sales in 2007, resulting in sales of more than $136.4 billion for that year (see Figure 5.2). Surprisingly, these figures only include traditional online store sales and do not account for auction sales (e.g., eBay), movie and music content rentals (e.g., iTunes or Netflix), or sales through online classifieds (e.g., Craigslist). Forrester Research estimated all online retail revenues at $175 billion in 2007, up 21 percent from 2006, and predicted a growth to $335 billion by 2012. Considering all online markets, it is clear that online transactions have become a major segment of the global economy. With this much money at stake, it is little wonder that no other information systems issue has captured as much attention as has EC. Although EC was being used as far back as 1948 during the Berlin Airlift (Zwass, 1996), the emergence of the Internet and Web has fueled a revolution in the manner in which products and services are marketed and sold. Their far-reaching effects have led to the creation of an electronic marketplace where a virtually limitless array of new services, features, and functionality can be offered. As a result, a presence on the Web has become a strategic necessity for companies.

Contrary to popular belief, EC goes beyond merely buying and selling products online. EC can involve the events leading up to the purchase of a product as well as customer service after the sale. Furthermore, EC is not limited to transactions between businesses and consumers, which is known as **business-to-consumer (B2C)** EC. EC is also used to conduct business with business partners such as suppliers and intermediaries. This form of EC is commonly referred to as **business-to-business (B2B)** EC. Some companies use both forms for conducting business, such as the clothing and home furnishing retailer Eddie Bauer, while other firms concentrate solely in B2C or B2B. Some forms of EC happen between businesses and their employees; these are referred to as **business-to-employee (B2E)**. Some forms of EC do not even involve business firms, as would be the

[1]EC can also include the distribution of digital products such as software, music, movies, and digital images.

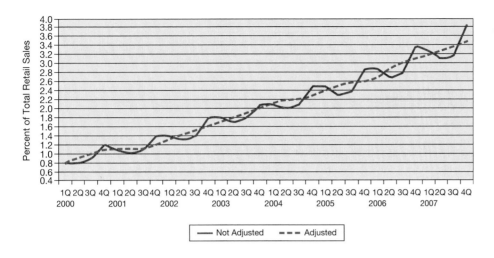

FIGURE 5.2

Electronic commerce continues to grow rapidly.

Source: http://www.census.gov/mrts/www/data/html/07Q4.html.

case with an online auction site such as eBay; these forms of EC are referred to as **consumer-to-consumer (C2C)**. Finally, there are forms of electronic commerce that involve a country's government and its citizens (*government-to-citizen [G2C]*), businesses (*government-to-business [G2B]*), and other governments (*government-to-government [G2G]*). These basic types of EC are summarized in Table 5.1.

Furthermore, there is a wide variety of ways to conduct business in each arena. In the following section, we examine the reasons that Web-based EC is revolutionizing the way business is being done. This is followed by an in-depth analysis of how companies are utilizing EC in their daily operations.

Internet and World Wide Web Capabilities

Technological forces are driving business, and the Internet and Web emerged as a strong new agent of change. The resulting technological revolution has essentially broken down the barriers to entry, leveled the playing field, and propelled commerce into the electronic domain (Looney and Chatterjee, 2002). Companies are exploiting the capabilities of the Web to reach

TABLE 5.1 Types of Electronic Commerce

Type of EC	Description	Example
Business-to-consumer (B2C)	Transactions between businesses and their customers	A person buys a book from Amazon.com
Business-to-business (B2B)	Transactions among businesses	A manufacturer conducts business over the Web with its suppliers
Business-to-employee (B2E)	Transactions between businesses and their employees	An employee uses the Web to make a change to his or her health benefits
Consumer-to-consumer (C2C)	Transactions between people not necessarily working together	A person purchases some memorabilia from another person via eBay.com
Government-to-citizen (G2C)	Transactions between a government and its citizens	A person files his or her income taxes online
Government-to-business (G2B)	Transactions between a government and businesses	A government purchases supplies using an Internet-enabled procurement system
Government-to-government (G2G)	Transactions among governments	A foreign government uses the Internet to access information about U.S. federal regulations

TABLE 5.2 **Capabilities of the Web**

Web Capability	Description	Example
Global information dissemination	The ability to market products and services over vast distances.	Almost anyone can access Amazon.com
Integration	Web sites can be linked to corporate databases to provide real-time access to personalized information.	Customers can check account balances at www.alaskaair.com
Mass customization	Firms can tailor their products and services to meet a customer's particular needs.	Customers can build their own messenger bag on www.timbuk2.com
Interactive communication	Companies can communicate with customers, improving the image of responsiveness.	Customers can receive real-time computer support from www.geeksquad.com
Collaboration	Different departments of a company can use the Web to collaborate.	Virgin Megastores uses a collaboration site to improve managers' efficiency
Transactional support	Clients and businesses can conduct business online without human support	Customers can build and purchase their own PC online without human interaction on www.dell.com

a wider customer base, offer a broader range of products, and develop closer relationships with customers by striving to meet their unique needs (Valacich, Parboteeah, & Wells, 2007). These wide-ranging capabilities include global information dissemination, integration, mass customization, interactive communication, collaboration, and transactional support (Chatterjee and Sambamurthy, 1999; Looney and Chatterjee, 2002; see Table 5.2).

Information Dissemination The powerful combination of Internet and Web technologies has given rise to a global platform where firms from across the world can effectively compete for customers and gain access to new markets. EC has wide geographical potential, given that many countries have at least some type of Internet access. The worldwide connectivity of the Internet enables **global information dissemination**, a relatively economical medium for firms to market their products and services over vast distances. This increased geographical reach has been facilitated by virtual storefronts that can be accessed from every Web-enabled computer in the world.

Integration Web technologies also allow for **integration** of information via Web sites that can be linked to corporate databases to provide real-time access to personalized information. No longer must customers rely on old information from printed catalogs or account statements that arrive in the mail once a month. For example, when Alaska Airlines (www.alaskaair.com) updates fare information in their corporate database, customers can access the revisions as they occur simply by browsing the company's Web site. As with nearly every other major airline, the Web allows Alaska Airlines to disseminate real-time fare pricing. This is particularly important for companies operating in highly competitive environments such as the air transport industry. Furthermore, Alaska Airlines offers their valued customers the ability to check the balances of their frequent flier accounts, linking customers to information stored on the firm's corporate database (see Figure 5.3). Customers do not have to wait for monthly statements to see if they are eligible for travel benefits and awards.

Mass Customization Web technologies are also helping firms realize their goal of mass customization. **Mass customization** helps firms tailor their products and services to meet a customer's particular needs on a large scale. For instance, bag manufacturer Timbuk2 (www.Timbuk2.com) has developed an application called Custom Messenger Bag Builder, which allows customers to create a virtual bag that is modeled just for them (see Figure 5.4).

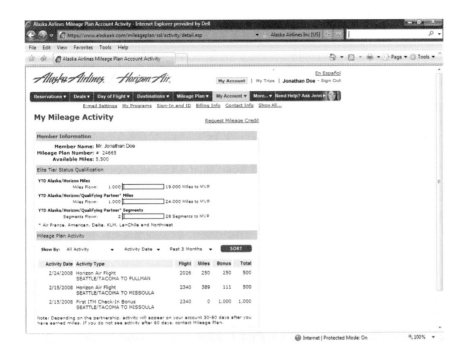

FIGURE 5.3

Alaska Airlines' mileage plan
Web site. Used with permission
of Alaska Airlines.

FIGURE 5.4

Timbuk2 bags can be customized
in a variety of ways.

Customers can configure the virtual bag based on a number of criteria such as size, fabrics, colors, accessories, and even use (e.g., for carrying a laptop). The virtual model application also assists Timbuk2 in tracking customers' preferred styles and colors, allowing them to target marketing efforts to individual customers.

Interactive Communication **Interactive communication** via the Web enables firms to build customer loyalty by providing immediate communication and feedback to/from customers, which can dramatically improve the firm's image through demonstrated responsiveness. Many firms are augmenting telephone-based ordering and customer support with Web-based applications and electronic mail. In some cases, online chat applications are provided to allow customers to communicate with a customer service representative in real time through the corporate Web site.

Best Buy, for example, has entered into the computer repair and support business with their brand Geek Squad (see Figure 5.5). Traditionally, customers having computer problems would have to take their computer to a Best Buy store for repair. Geek Squad online (www.geeksquad.com) has implemented a feature whereby customers can contact customer support representatives at any time of the day to receive real-time online support. Support options include operation system diagnostics, software installation issues, and computer optimization. Interactive communication agents aid the customers online in real time. This feature allows the customer service agent to walk the customer through the troubleshooting process step-by-step while the customer is at home. This customer-driven approach far outdistances traditional, nonelectronic means in terms of tailoring and timeliness.

Transaction Support By providing ways for clients and firms to conduct business online without human assistance, the Internet and Web have greatly reduced transaction costs while enhancing operational efficiency. Many companies, such as Dell Computer Corporation, are utilizing the Web to provide automated **transaction support** (see Figure 5.6). Dell began selling computers on the Web in mid-1996. By early 1998, Dell was experiencing around $2 million in online sales per day. Dell derives about 90 percent of its overall revenues from sales to medium-sized and large businesses, yet more than half of its Web-based sales have been from individuals and small businesses that typically buy one computer at a time. As a result, Dell is experiencing significant cost savings per sale by reducing the demand for phone representatives on the smaller purchases. Individual customers can access product

FIGURE 5.5

Geek Squad offers 24-hour computer support.

FIGURE 5.6

Customers can build their own computers at www.dell.com.

information anytime from anywhere, benefiting not only the end consumer but also Dell. Customer service representatives can focus on lucrative corporate customers, reducing labor costs involved in servicing small-ticket items.

By streamlining operations and greatly increasing sales through both online and traditional channels, Dell has grown into one of the world's largest personal computer manufacturers, with revenue of nearly $61 billion annually for the fiscal year 2007. This phenomenon of cutting out the "middleman" and reaching customers more directly and efficiently is known as **disintermediation**. Disintermediation creates both opportunities and challenges. While disintermediation allows producers or service providers to offer products at lower prices (or reap greater profits), they also have to take on those activities previously performed by the middleman. For example, when airlines started selling tickets online and dealing directly with customers, they disintermediated travel agents. To make up for this lost revenue, travel agents now charge booking fees when arranging a person's travel. In contrast, **reintermediation** refers to the design of business models that reintroduce middlemen in order to reduce the chaos brought on by disintermediation. For example, without middlemen like Travelocity.com, Orbitz.com, and other travel Web sites, a consumer would have to check all airline Web sites in order to find the flight with the best connection or lowest price.

Electronic Commerce Business Strategies

Given the vast capabilities of the Internet, the Web has transformed traditional business operations into a hypercompetitive electronic marketplace. Companies must strategically position themselves to compete in the new EC environment. At one extreme, companies following a **brick-and-mortar business strategy** choose to operate solely in the traditional physical markets. These companies approach business activities in a traditional manner by operating physical locations such as department stores, business offices, or manufacturing plants. In other words, the brick-and-mortar business strategy does not include EC. In contrast, companies following a **click-only business strategy** (i.e., **virtual companies**) conduct business electronically in cyberspace. These firms have no physical store locations, allowing them to focus purely on EC. An example of a click-only company might be the popular eBay.com trading and exchange Web site, which does not have a physical storefront in the classic sense. In e-business terminology, click-only companies are sometimes called "pure play companies," focusing on one very distinct way of doing business; other firms choose to straddle the two environments, operating in both physical

Virtual Crime

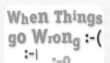

In one weekend in November 2007, ATM thieves stole $11,500. It seems the banks involved did not check first to be sure ATM customers had enough cash in their accounts to cover withdrawals. An egregious banking error, for sure, but not too likely to occur in the real world. The banks were located in Second Life (SL), a virtual world created and owned by Linden Lab. Since the banks all used the same software, the thieves were able to skim money from several ATMs.

How can virtual money be stolen by thieves and the loss measured in real money? SL is one of the virtual worlds that has allowed a financial system to develop where virtual dollars (Lindens) can actually be converted to U.S. dollars. As detailed in this chapter's opening case, SL's banking industry was evicted in January 2008, and fraud and theft were largely responsible.

Virtual crime, or crime occurring within MMOGs, is possible because players invest large amounts of time and energy, and dollars if allowed, to create avatars that succeed, and maybe even become wealthy, in the game environment. Because virtual communities and real communities have many aspects in common—objects and property collected within MMOGs have value—criminal activity sometimes spills over from virtual worlds to the real world and vice-versa.

To prevent criminal activity related to theft and fraud, many MMOGs, such as World of Warcraft (WOW) and other Blizzard Entertainment games, do not allow in-game objects to have monetary value. Since in-game objects have been stolen and auctioned on eBay, the popular auction site now prohibits the buying and selling of any in-game objects.

Virtual crimes are an international problem:

- In South Korea, virtual world gamers have organized into crime gangs, whose members terrorize other in-world residents and extort protection money.
- In China, an MMOG player "loaned" a sword from the game to another player and that player auctioned the sword off on eBay (before eBay prohibited the practice) for real money. The person who loaned the sword then actually killed the player who sold it.
- In Japan, a twelve-year-old player was actually arrested for stealing from other players' in-world accounts.

Some game developers have given up on prohibiting in-world crime and have simply made crime inherent in the game's design. For example, All Points Bulletin (APB) and CrimeCraft entice players with opportunities to blow up objects, join criminal gangs, and complete story-driven gangster missions.

With crime becoming yet another element within MMOG games, can laws, police forces, courts, trials, and prisons be far behind?

Based on:

Kagotani, C. (2005, September 7). Japan: MMOG crime rising. *Next Generation*. Retrieved May 22, 2008, from http://www.nextgen.biz/index.php?option=com_content&task=view&id=974&Itemid=2.

Knight, W. (2005, August 18). Computer characters mugged in virtual crime spree. *New Scientist*. Retrieved May 22, 2008, from http://www.newscientist.com/article.ns?id=dn7865.

Reuters, E. (2007, November 20). Second Life banks hacked in virtual crime wave. *Reuters/Second Life*. Retrieved May 22, 2008, from http://secondlife.reuters.com/stories/2007/11/20/second-life-banks-hacked-in-virtual-crime-wave.

Virtual crime. (2008, May 9). In *Wikipedia, the free encyclopedia*. May 21, 2008, from http://en.wikipedia.org/w/index.php?title=Virtual_crime&oldid=211236917.

and virtual arenas. These firms employ a **click-and-mortar business strategy** approach (also referred to as the **bricks-and-clicks business strategy**). The three general approaches are depicted in Figure 5.7 (Looney and Chatterjee, 2002).

The Click-and-Mortar Strategy The greatest impact of the Web-based EC revolution has occurred in companies adopting the click-and-mortar approach. Click-and-mortars continue to operate their physical locations and have added the EC component to their business activities. With transactions occurring in both physical and virtual environments, it is imperative that click-and-mortars learn how to fully maximize commercial opportunities in both domains. Conducting physical and virtual operations presents special chal-

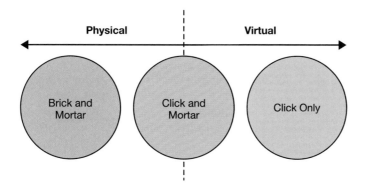

FIGURE 5.7

General approaches to electronic commerce.

lenges for these firms, as business activities must be tailored to each of these different environments in order for the firms to compete effectively.

Another challenge for click-and-mortars involves increasing information system complexity. Design and development of complex computing systems are required to support each aspect of the click-and-mortar approach. Furthermore, different skills are necessary to support Web-based computing, requiring substantial resource investments. Companies must design, develop, and deploy systems and applications to accommodate an open computing architecture that must be globally and persistently available. For instance, with total client assets of over $1 trillion, hundreds of thousands of daily trades by customers, a variety of ways that global customers use their Web site, and a dynamic, fast-changing set of online products and services, the click-and-mortar brokerage firm Charles Schwab has a large, complex information systems staff and a set of interrelated information systems (see Figure 5.8).

The Click-Only Strategy Click-only companies can often compete more effectively on price since they do not need to support the physical aspects of the click-and-mortar approach. Thus, these companies can reduce prices to rock-bottom levels (although a relatively small click-only firm may not sell enough products and/or may not order enough from suppliers to be able to realize economies of scale and thus reduce prices). Click-only firms, such as Amazon.com or eBay.com, also tend to be highly adept with technology and can innovate very rapidly as new technologies become available. This can enable

FIGURE 5.8

Brokerage firm Charles Schwab offers a variety of services online to meet the needs of its global customers.

TABLE 5.3 **Components of a Business Model**

Components	Description	Questions to ask?
Revenue model	The way a firm generates income. For more detail, see Table 5.4.	What are you selling? How much are you selling it for?
Value proposition	The utility that the product/service has to offer.	Why do customers need your product/service?
Competitive environment	The existing players in the market and the nature of the competition.	Who are your competitors? How fierce is the competition?
Marketing strategy	The promotion plan of your product/service.	How do you plan to let your potential customers know about your product/service?
Management team	The background and experience of the company leadership.	Can your leaders get the job done? How do they add value to the company?

them to stay one step ahead of their competition. However, conducting business in cyberspace has some problematic aspects. For example, it is more difficult for a customer to return a product to a purely online company than simply to return it to a local department store. In addition, some consumers may not be comfortable making purchases online. Individuals may be leery about the security of giving credit card numbers to a virtual company.

You must also develop a sound business model to be successful with EC. A **business model** is a summary of how a company will generate revenue, identifying its product offering, value-added services, revenue sources, and target customers. In other words, a business model reflects the following:

1. What does a company do?
2. How does a company uniquely do it?
3. In what way (or ways) does the company get paid for doing it?
4. How much gross margin does the company earn per average unit sale?

There are several components of a proper business model (see Table 5.3). Perhaps the most important ingredient for EC is a firm's revenue model. A **revenue model** describes how the firm will earn revenue, generate profits, and produce a superior return on invested capital. Table 5.4 describes the most common revenue models for EC, including advertising, subscription, transaction fee, sales, and affiliate marketing.

As you can see, firms can conduct EC in a variety of ways. In the next section, we describe in greater detail how firms have evolved toward using the Internet and Web to support internal operations and to interact with each other.

Business-to-Business Electronic Commerce: Extranets

In order to communicate proprietary information with authorized users outside organizational boundaries, a company can implement an **extranet**. An extranet enables two or more firms to use the Internet to do business together. Using the Internet to support business-to-business (B2B) activities has become one of the best ways for organizations to gain a positive return on their technology-based investments. For example, The Boeing Company, the U.S. aerospace giant, launched an extranet that can be accessed by over 1,000 authorized business partners. One of Boeing's business partners, aluminum supplier Alcoa, accesses the extranet to coordinate its shipments to Boeing as well as to check Boeing's raw materials supply to ensure appropriate inventory levels. Customers, such as the U.S. Department of Defense, log in to Boeing's extranet to receive status updates on the projects Boeing is working on for them. Overall, countless organizations are gaining benefits from

TABLE 5.4 **Typical Revenue Models for Electronic Commerce Businesses**

Revenue Type	Description	Who is doing this?
Affiliate marketing	Paying businesses that bring or refer customers to another business. Revenue sharing is typically used.	Amazon.com's Associates program
Subscription based	Users pay a monthly or yearly recurring fee for the use of the product/service.	Netflix.com, World of Warcraft
Transaction fees	Commission paid to the business for aiding in the transaction.	Paypal.com, eBay.com
Traditional sales	A consumer buying a product/service from the Web site.	Nordstrom.com, iTunes.com
Web advertising	A free service/product is supported by advertising displayed on the Web site.	Facebook.com, Digg.com

 Net Stats

E-Business Is BIG Business

Statistics show that increasing numbers of consumers are shopping online. According to a report by Forrester Research, online retail revenues totaled $175 billion in 2007, a 21 percent increase over 2006. (Note that revenues for traditional online stores—e.g., not including auction sites, entertainment downloads, and so on—were estimated by the Census Bureau to be nearly $137 billion in 2007.) Total online retail revenues are forecast to reach a whopping $335 billion by 2012. Table 5.5 shows where e-business revenues were generated in 2007.

Based on:

Burns, E. (2006, June 5). Online revenues to reach $200 billion. *Clickz*. Retrieved May 22, 2008, from http://www.clickz.com/stats/sectors/retailing/article.php/3611181.

Mulpuru, S. Johnson, C., McGowan, B., and Wright, S. (2008, January 18). US eCommerce Forecast: 2008 To 2012. *Forrester Research*. Retrieved October 13, 2008, from http://www.forrester.com/Research/Document/Excerpt/0,7211,41592,00.html.

TABLE 5.5 **E-Business Revenues by Product Category, 2007**

Product Category	Actual Revenues 2007	Projected Revenues 2012
Apparel, accessories, and footwear	$22.7 billion	$41.8 billion
Computer hardware and software	$20.7 billion	$37.1 billion
Autos and auto parts	$16.8 billion	$30.9 billion
Consumer electronics	$13.5 billion	$29.5 billion
Home furnishings	$12.3 billion	$26.7 billion
Office supplies	$7.7 billion	$17.1 billion
Food, beverages, and groceries	$6.2 billion	$13.7 billion
Pet supplies	$1.1 billion	$3.4 billion
Cosmetics and fragrances	$1 billion	$2 billion

B2B electronic commerce with nearly all *Fortune* 1000 companies deploying some type of B2B application.

Interestingly, there is a long history of organizations using proprietary networks to share business information. In this section, we will examine the evolution to the present-day extranets and review how organizations are utilizing extranets to improve organizational performance and gain a competitive advantage.

The Need for Organizations to Exchange Data

Prior to the introduction of the Internet and Web, business-to-business EC was facilitated using **Electronic Data Interchange (EDI)**. The use of EDI was generally limited to large corporations that could afford the associated expenses of having dedicated telecommunication networks between suppliers and customers in order to exchange business documents and other information. Today, the Internet and Web have become an economical medium over which this business-related information can be transmitted, enabling even small to midsized enterprises to participate in electronic B2B markets. Companies have devised a number of innovative ways to facilitate B2B transactions using these technologies. Web-based B2B systems range from simple extranet applications to complex trading exchanges where multiple buyers and sellers come together to conduct business. In the following sections, we examine the stages under which modern B2B EC is done, shedding light on the different approaches and their suitability for different business requirements.

Exchanging Organizational Data Using Extranets

Today's trend in business is to use the Web as the vehicle for business-to-business EC. With the entrance of buyers and suppliers of all shapes and sizes, the mass adoption of these technologies has propelled B2B into the forefront of modern commerce. To use the Web for business-to-business EC, companies are creating extranets, which can be regarded as a private part of the Internet that is cordoned off from ordinary users. In other words, although the content is "on the Web," only authorized users can access it after logging on to the company's extranet Web site.

Benefits of Extranets

Extranets, as well as *intranets* (discussion to follow), benefit corporations in a number of ways, so it is no surprise that firms have readily and rapidly adopted these technologies.

Information Timeliness and Accuracy First and foremost, extranets can dramatically improve the timeliness and accuracy of communications, reducing the number of misunderstandings within the organization as well as with business partners and customers. In the business world, very little information is static; therefore, information must be continually updated and disseminated as it changes. Extranets facilitate this process by providing a cost-effective, global medium over which proprietary information can be distributed. Furthermore, they allow central management of documents, thus reducing the number of versions and the amount of out-of-date information that may be stored throughout the organization. While security is still considered to be better on proprietary networks, the Internet can be made to be a relatively secure medium for business.

Technology Integration Web-based technologies are cross-platform, meaning that disparate computing systems can communicate with each other provided that standard Web protocols have been implemented. For example, an Apple MacBook Air can request Web pages from a Linux Apache Web server. Even though the computers are running under different operating systems, they can communicate with each other over the Internet. The cross-platform nature of the Web makes implementing extranets extremely attractive as a way to connect disparate computing environments.

Low Cost–High Value In addition, extranets do not require large expenditures to train users on the technologies. Since many employees, customers, and business partners are familiar with the tools associated with the Web, they do not require special training to familiarize them with extranet interfaces. In other words, extranets look and act just like public Web sites. As long as users are familiar with a Web browser, they can utilize extranets with little difficulty.

Above all, extranets impact a company's bottom line. A company can use them to automate business transactions, reducing processing costs and achieving shortened cycle times. Extranets can also reduce errors by providing a single point of data entry from which the information can be updated on disparate corporate computing platforms without having to reenter the data. Management can then obtain real-time information to track and analyze business activities. Extranets are incredibly powerful and intensely popular. We describe in the following sections how they work and how they are being effectively utilized.

Extranet System Architecture

An extranet looks and acts just like a typical Internet-based application, using the same software, hardware, and networking technologies to communicate information (see Figure 5.9). However, an extranet uses the Internet infrastructure to connect two or more business partners and, thus, requires an additional component. Specifically, companies use *firewalls* to secure proprietary information stored within the corporate LAN and/or WAN so that the information can be viewed only by authorized users. Firewalls with specialized software are placed between the organization's LAN or WAN and the Internet, preventing unauthorized access to the companies' proprietary information. Organizations can connect their internal intranet infrastructures (see discussion of intranets to follow) together using a *virtual private network,* or *VPN,* to facilitate the secured transmission of proprietary information between business partners. You will learn more about VPNs in Chapter 7—Securing Information Systems. To access information on an extranet, authorized business partners access their business partner's main extranet Web page using their Web browsers.

Extranet Applications

As the use of extranets has increased, a common set of applications has been found to be particularly beneficial to organizations. The primary use of extranets in organizations is for managing their supply chains; in other words, organizations exchange data and handle transactions with their suppliers or organizational customers. One way to handle transactions with suppliers and buyers is the use of enterprise portals, through which a business partner accesses secured, proprietary information from an organization. We will discuss different portals as well as emerging technologies enabling B2B EC in detail in Chapter 9—Building Organizational Partnerships Using Enterprise Information Systems.

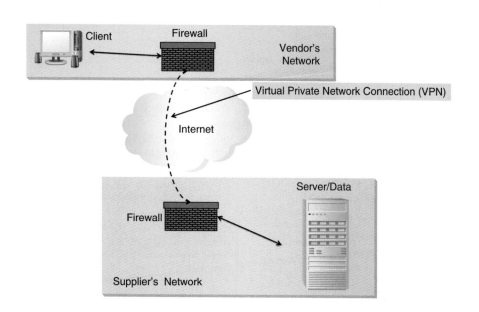

FIGURE 5.9

Typical extranet system architecture.

Ethical Dilemma

Monitoring Productive Employees

"You have zero privacy; get over it," Scott McNeely, cofounder and long-time chief executive officer of Sun Microsystems, once said. He was speaking about privacy expectations of Internet users in general, but the quote can also apply to privacy expectations of employees in the workplace.

If you work for a company where Internet connectivity is provided, it is legal for that company to track your computer use, including e-mails sent and received, Web sites visited, and downloads to your workstation computer. The question of whether such surveillance is ethical, however, is still under debate. The essence of the debate is this: Employers want employees to do a good job without abusing computer resources. Employees don't want their every keystroke and Web site visit tracked.

New technologies make it possible for employers to monitor employees' activities on the job, especially telephone use, electronic and voice mail, computer terminals, and Internet use. To date, such monitoring is unregulated; thus, your employer can listen to, watch, and read most of your on-the-job communications.

An American Management Association (AMA) survey in 2005 found that 75 percent of the employers surveyed monitor their employees' Internet use in order to prevent inappropriate surfing. Sixty-five percent use software to block employees' access to inappropriate Web sites. Approximately 30 percent track keyboard strokes and amount of time spent at the keyboard. Over 50 percent review and retain employee e-mail messages. Eighty percent of the companies surveyed disclose their monitoring practices to employees. In most cases, new employees are asked to sign the privacy practice disclosure and agree to abide by its provisions.

Increasingly, companies are vigorously enforcing technology policies. The AMA survey reported that 26 percent of survey respondents had fired employees for misusing the Internet. Another 25 percent had fired employees for e-mail abuses.

While employee monitoring practices may be legal, are they ethical? On the employee side of the monitoring debate is the argument that when employers spy on employees, they are violating the individuals' privacy rights. Employers say they monitor to increase productivity but also to prevent liability. For instance, since employ-

ers are expected to maintain a workplace environment free of sexual harassment, shouldn't they be allowed to monitor e-mail messages that could implicate them in a sexual harassment suit?

Some legal experts argue that ethical questions about employee monitoring come down to the issue of contract. David D. Friedman, an economist and law professor at the University of Southern California, has said, "There isn't an agreement that is morally right for everybody. The important thing is what the parties agree to. If the employer gives a promise of privacy, then that should be respected." If, on the other hand, Friedman continues, the employer reserves the right to read e-mail or monitor Web browsing, the worker can either accept those terms or look elsewhere for employment. Friedman's comments do not address the issue of low-income employees who have no choice but to accept any job offered, regardless of employers' privacy policies.

In 2008, a federal government employee's right to e-mail privacy became an issue when members of Congress discovered that managers at the Small Business Administration had tracked a staff whistle-blower's e-mail. The worker had served as a confidential source for the Senate Committee on Small Business and Entrepreneurship, submitting anonymous testimony for a committee hearing. After Congress learned of the e-mail monitoring activities within the SBA, the agency took steps to limit the policy.

In any case, business law and ethics experts agree that employers who monitor should do so only if the surveillance serves a legitimate purpose, should follow clear procedures to protect a worker's personal life, and should inform workers about monitoring practices.

Based on:

Anonymous (2006, February). Employee monitoring: Is there privacy in the workplace? *Privacy Rights Clearinghouse*. Retrieved May 22, 2008, from http://www.privacyrights.org/fs/fs7-work.htm.

AMA ePolicy Institute Research (n.d.). 2005 Electronic monitoring and surveillance survey. *American Management Association*. Retrieved May 22, 2008, from http://www.amanet.org/research/pdfs/EMS_summary05.pdf.

Loten, A. (2008, January 11). SBA whistleblower's email tracked. *New York Times*. Retrieved May 22, 2008, from http://www.nytimes.com/inc_com/inc1199710983718. html?ref=smallbusiness.

Schulman, M. (1998, Spring). Little brother is watching you. *Issues in Ethics 9, no. 2*. Retrieved May 22, 2008, from http://www.scu.edu/ethics/ publications/iie/v9n2/brother.html.

Business-to-Employee Electronic Commerce: Intranets

Once organizations realize the advantage of using the Internet and Web to communicate public information outside corporate boundaries, Web-based technologies can also be leveraged to support proprietary, internal communications within an organization through the implementation of an **intranet**[2] to support business-to-employee (B2E) electronic commerce. Like an extranet, an intranet consists of a private network using Web technologies, but it is used to facilitate the secured transmission of proprietary information *within* an organization. Intranets take advantage of standard Internet and Web protocols to communicate information to and from authorized employees. As was the case with extranets, intranets provide many benefits to the organization, including improved information timeliness and accuracy, global reach, cross-platform integration, low-cost deployment, and a positive return on investment.

As with the use of the Internet to support business-to-business activities, using the Internet to support internal organizational communication and processes—business-to-employee—is also rapidly expanding. For example, like their use of the Internet to support B2B activities, The Boeing Company also operates an intranet with more than 1 million pages registered with its internal search engine, serving nearly 200,000 employees. The intranet has become pervasive, impacting every department within the organization. Employees rely on the intranet to assist them in their daily business activities, ranging from tracking vacation benefits to monitoring aircraft production. In the remainder of this section, we examine the characteristics of an organizational intranet as well as the types of applications being deployed.

Intranet System Architecture

An intranet looks and acts just like a publicly accessible Web site and uses the same software, hardware, and networking technologies to communicate information. As with an extranet, users access their company's intranet using their Web browser. All intranet pages are behind the company's firewall, and in the simplest form of an intranet, communications only take place within the confines of organizational boundaries and do not travel across the Internet. However, increases in employees' mobility necessitate that an intranet be accessible from anywhere. Thus, most companies allow their employees to use VPNs to connect to the company's intranet while on the road or working from home (i.e., telecommuting). Figure 5.10 depicts a typical intranet system architecture (see Chapter 7 for more on firewalls and VPNs).

Intranet Applications

Organizations are deploying a variety of common intranet applications to leverage their EC investments. In this section, we briefly review a few of the most significant: training, application integration, online entry of information, real-time access to information, and collaboration.

Training Using its intranet, The Boeing Company offers training for nearly 200,000 of its employees. In addition to intranet-based training about quality standards and procedures using a system called "Quality eTraining," employees can choose from a wide range of course offerings, including educational programs or supervisor training. Boeing's intranet contains an online catalog summarizing course offerings and provides a feature that allows employees to register for courses using their Web browsers. Once registered for a course, users can access multimedia content, including video lectures, presentation slides, and other course materials, directly from their desktops. Boeing's intranet-based training initiative has led to dramatic business improvements and cost reductions. The intranet helped eliminate redundant courses and standardized course material. It virtually eliminated travel costs associated with sending employees to training sites. In addition, employees can take

---

[2]It can be argued that, on a technological level, intranets and extranets are variants of the same thing in that both employ firewalls to cordon off ordinary users. However, given that intranets and extranets have very different purposes from a business point of view, we chose to distinguish between the two.

FIGURE 5.10

Typical intranet system
architecture.

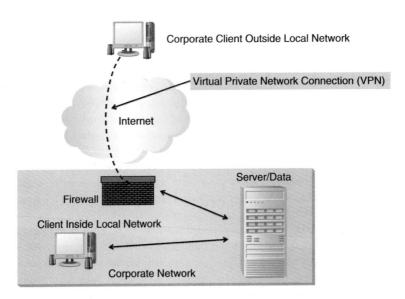

courses on a time-permitting basis, meaning that they can learn at a pace that accommodates their work schedule. At Boeing, employee training is no longer subject to the physical and time constraints associated with traditional forms of education.

Personalized Intranet Pages Many companies such as Boeing provide customized intranet pages for each employee depending on job functions or even geographical location. Whereas each employee's pages has the same look and feel and draws on the same underlying data, each employee can only access the information he or she needs to perform his or her job function. For example, if an employee from human resources logs onto the intranet Web site they would only see content that pertains to their job, such as payroll information or hiring statistics; if someone from the accounting department logged into the intranet Web site, they would see information such as profit/loss statements or balance sheets; if employees from Hong Kong logged into their company's intranet, they would see the information in Chinese or English, depending on their preferences.

Application Integration Many organizations have invested substantial sums of money and resources in a variety of software applications such as *enterprise resource planning, customer relationship management, sales force automation,* and various other packages to support internal operations (see Chapter 9). Often these disparate applications are installed on different computing platforms where each may be running under a different operating system, using a different database management system, and/or providing a different user interface. Because of these disparate environments, it may be difficult for, say, a salesperson to consolidate information from different systems in order to answer a customer request. Intranets can be used to alleviate this problem by providing application integration.

For example, by installing a product such as Netegrity's SiteMinder on the intranet Web server, information from separate applications can be consolidated and presented to the user through a single Web browser interface. Now, when the salesperson needs information related to sales calls and customer support activities, the request is routed to the intranet Web server running SiteMinder, which accesses the relevant data from various applications. The intranet server consolidates the information and delivers it to the salesperson, displaying all the information necessary to make business decisions in a single Web page.

Online Entry of Information Companies can use intranets to streamline routine business processes because an intranet provides a Web browser interface to facilitate online entry of information. Microsoft has implemented an intranet-based expense reporting application called MSExpense that allows employees from across the world to submit expense reports online, dramatically reducing the inefficiencies and expenses associated with paper-based expense report processing.

Prior to MSExpense, 136 different expense report templates existed within the corporation, and information such as mileage rates was often outdated. These issues cost Microsoft employees precious time and effort in locating the appropriate template and ensuring that the expenses they were submitting were accurate. With MSExpense, expense report templates and expense rates are centrally managed on the intranet Web server, where modifications can be made instantaneously as conditions change. Now, Microsoft employees submit the appropriate template electronically with the assurance that they have used the correct version and up-to-date expense rates.

The implementation of the MSExpense intranet application reduced the cost of processing employee expense reports by over $4.3 million per year (or from $21 to $8 per expense report), shortened the time to receive reimbursements from three weeks to three days, and dramatically reduced error rates by providing a single point of entry (Microsoft, 2002). Furthermore, applications such as MSExpense provide management with accurate, up-to-date information to track and analyze the costs associated with key business activities as well as a way to enforce business policies to take advantage of reduced corporate rates offered by airlines, rental car companies, and hotels.

Real-Time Access to Information Unlike paper-based documents, which need to be continually updated and distributed to employees when changes occur, intranets make it less complicated to manage, update, distribute, and access corporate information.

Boeing disseminates corporate news using multimedia files distributed over the company's intranet. Formerly, news releases were produced on videotape, duplicated, and distributed via surface mail to each corporate office around the world. With the intranet-based solution, the company has eliminated the videotape reproduction process by allowing employees to view digital copies of company news releases as they occur, from the convenience of their desktops. Boeing can now disseminate news in a more timely fashion while, in the process, saving millions annually in distribution costs.

With intranet-based solutions such as those deployed at Boeing, up-to-date, accurate information can be easily accessed on a company-wide basis from a single source that is both efficient and user-friendly. Companies can become more flexible with resources required to create, maintain, and distribute corporate documents, while in the process employees become more knowledgeable and current about the information that is important to them. Employees develop a sense of confidence and become self-reliant, reducing time spent dealing with employment-related issues and allowing them to focus on their work responsibilities.

Collaboration One of the most common problems occurring in large corporations relates to the communication of business activities in a timely fashion across divisional areas of the organizations. For instance, Boeing uses its intranet to facilitate collaborative efforts, such as in the process of designing new aircraft components. In this process, three-dimensional digital models of aircraft designs frequently need to be shared between aerospace engineers. Using Boeing's intranet, an engineer can share a drawing with another engineer at a remote location; the second engineer revises the drawing as necessary and uploads the updated drawing to a shared folder on the intranet. The Boeing intranet provides the company with the capability of reducing product development cycles as well as the ability to stay abreast of current project, corporate, and market conditions.

Further, intranets are now being used to facilitate communication within organizations outside of traditional workflow. For example, Atomic Energy of Canada Labs (AECL), the manufacturer of the CANDU, one of the world's most popular nuclear reactors, has been using an intranet for employee blogs, to poll staff about current issues, to communicate new executive initiatives, and more. AECL's, intranet collaboration tools empower employees to communicate with each other and executives in a secure nonpublic forum.

Brief Case ◑

Human-Powered Search Engines: ChaCha

It's finally here: a free search service for mobile phones. Imagine you are in Chicago and you would like directions to the super new pizza restaurant you have seen advertised. Simply text your question to ChaCha, and within minutes the answer is texted back to you. It's handier than unwieldy maps, more accurate than asking directions from passers by, and it's free.

Scott Jones, inventor and entrepreneur, and Brad Bostic, chairman of Bostech Corporation, came up with the idea, and the service was launched first in alpha then in beta versions in 2006. Indiana-based ChaCha is handier for people on the go to use than most computer search engines because it is human-powered. Humans, called "guides" actually read the question you ask, find the answer, and get back to you. Since ChaCha's introduction, other services have followed, including Mahala.com, iRazoo.com, and Findinfo.com.

ChaCha selects guides from applicants who pass a series of tests. These applicants then are trained via ChaCha's Search University and a simulation program to become certified live ChaCha guides. ChaCha's technology also "learns" from the answers guides provide, thus becoming more accurate over time.

To test the ChaCha service for yourself, simply use your mobile phone to text your question to "242242" (spells "ChaCha"), or call 1-800-2chacha to verbally ask a question. The answer to your question will be sent back to you via a text message. If your phone has a Web browser, you can access the short link provided with the answer to see more information. The service itself is free, but standard mobile phone text messaging and voice rates apply.

Questions

1. Describe a situation where you could have used ChaCha.
2. When do you think "old fashioned" search engines would be more effective than ChaCha? When would ChaCha be preferred?

Based on:

Anonymous (n.d.). About us. Retrieved May 22, 2008, from http://info.chacha.com/AboutUs/tabid/54/Default.aspx#.

ChaCha (search engine). (2008, May 2). In *Wikipedia, the free encyclopedia*. May 21, 2008, from http://en.wikipedia.org/w/index.php?title=ChaCha_%28search_engine%29&oldid=209595864.

Iskold, A. (2006, December 14). ChaCha: A human-powered search engine. *ReadWriteWeb*. Retrieved May 22, 2008, from http://www.readwriteweb.com/archives/chacha_human-powered_search.php.

Mills, E. (2008, January 3). ChaCha gives you answers via text message. *CNET News.com*. Retrieved May 22, 2008, from http://www.news.com/8301-10784_3-9838019-7.html.

Business-to-Consumer Electronic Commerce

The Internet and Web have evolved with mind-boggling speed, achieving mass acceptance faster than any other technology in modern history. The widespread availability and adoption of the Internet and Web, which are based on an economical, open, ubiquitous computing platform, have made Internet access affordable and practical, allowing consumers to participate in Web-based commerce. In addition, a great number of businesses have similarly benefited from the revolution and have implemented Web-based systems in their daily operations. This heightened level of participation by both consumers and producers has made the emergence of business-to-consumer (B2C) EC economically feasible. Unlike B2B, which concentrates on business-to-business relationships at the wholesale level, or B2E, which focuses on internal organizational communication and processes, B2C focuses on retail transactions between a company and end consumers. Table 5.6 provides a high-level comparison between these three approaches to utilizing Internet technologies.

Stages of Business-to-Consumer Electronic Commerce

With millions of B2C-oriented Web sites in existence, Web sites range from passive to active. At one extreme are the relatively simple, passive Web sites that provide only product information and the company address and phone number, much like a traditional brochure would do. At the other extreme are the relatively sophisticated, active Web sites that enable customers to see products, services, and related real-time information and actually make purchases online. As shown in some early, pioneering research on EC (Quelch

TABLE 5.6 Characteristics of the Internet, Intranet, and Extranet

	Focus	Type of Information	Users	Access
The Internet	External communications	General, public, and "advertorial" information	Any user with an Internet connection	Public and not restricted
Intranet	Internal communications	Specific, corporate, and proprietary information	Authorized employees	Private and restricted
Extranet	External communications	Communications between business partners	Authorized business partners	Private and restricted

Based on Szuprowicz, 1998; Turban et al., 2008.

and Klein, 1996; Kalakota, Olivia, and Donath, 1999), companies usually start out with an electronic brochure and pass through a series of stages as depicted in Figure 5.11, adding additional capabilities as they become more comfortable with EC. These stages can be classified as **e-information** (i.e., providing electronic brochures and other types of information for customers), **e-integration** (i.e., providing customers with the ability to gain personalized information by querying corporate databases and other information sources), and **e-transaction** (i.e., allowing customers to place orders and make payments).

Just a few years ago, integrating transactional capabilities into a company's Web site was very difficult, especially for smaller companies on a tight budget. Now, search engines such as Google and online stores such as Amazon.com offer small businesses the possibility to sell their goods and services online without having to invest large sums in an e-transaction infrastructure. Two major categories of e-transactions are the online sales of goods and services (or *e-tailing*) and financial transactions (such as *online banking*). These two categories will be discussed next.

E-Tailing: Selling Goods and Services in the Digital World

The online sales of goods and services, or **e-tailing**, can take many forms. For example, using the Internet, bricks-and-clicks retailers such as Walmart.com or click-only companies such as Amazon.com sell products or services in ways similar to traditional retail channels. In contrast, virtual companies such as Priceline.com have developed innovative ways of generating revenue, such as offering consumers discounts on airline tickets, hotel rooms, rental cars, new cars, home financing, and long-distance telephone service. The revolutionary aspect of the Priceline.com Web site lies in its **reverse pricing system** called *Name Your Own Price* (see Figure 5.12). Customers specify the product they are looking for and how much they are willing to pay for it. This pricing scheme transcends traditional **menu-driven pricing**, in which companies set the prices that consumers pay for products. After a user enters the product and price, the system routes the information to appropriate brand-name companies, such as United Airlines and Avis Rent-a-Car, which either accept or reject the consumer's offer. In a recent business quarter, Priceline.com sold 6.0 million hotel room nights, 639,000 airline tickets, and 2.0 million rental car days for a gross booking of a little

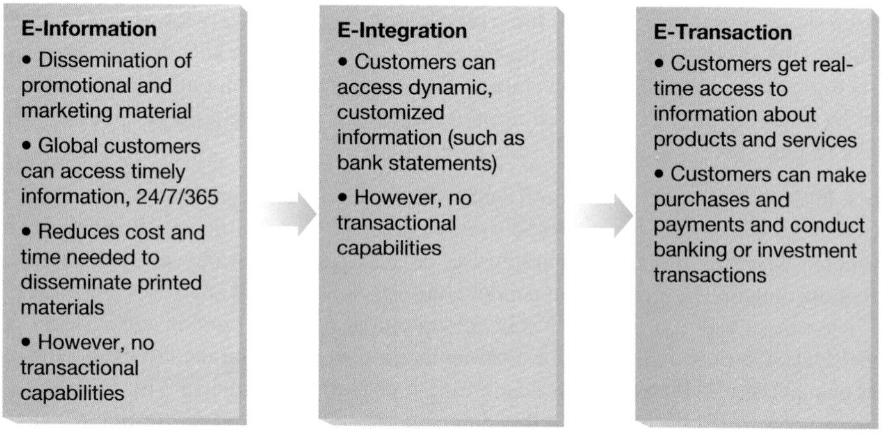

E-Information
- Dissemination of promotional and marketing material
- Global customers can access timely information, 24/7/365
- Reduces cost and time needed to disseminate printed materials
- However, no transactional capabilities

E-Integration
- Customers can access dynamic, customized information (such as bank statements)
- However, no transactional capabilities

E-Transaction
- Customers get real-time access to information about products and services
- Customers can make purchases and payments and conduct banking or investment transactions

FIGURE 5.11

Stages of business-to-consumer electronic commerce.

FIGURE 5.12

Priceline.com lets consumers name their own price for travel related services.

under $1 billion (Priceline.com, 2007). E-tailing has both benefits and drawbacks, which are examined next.

Benefits of E-Tailing Using the marketing concepts of product, place, and price, e-tailing can provide many benefits over traditional brick-and-mortar retailing.

PRODUCT BENEFITS. Web sites can offer a virtually unlimited number and variety of products because e-tailing is not limited by physical store and shelf space restrictions. For instance, e-tailer Amazon.com offers millions of book titles on the Web, compared to a local brick-and-mortar–only book retailer, which can offer "only" a few thousand titles in a store because of the restricted physical space.

For online customers, comparison shopping is much easier on the Web. In particular, a number of comparison shopping services that focus on aggregating content are available to consumers. Some companies fulfilling this niche are AllBookstores (www.allbookstores. com), BizRate (www.bizrate.com), or Google's Froogle (www.froogle.com). These comparison shopping sites can literally force sellers to focus on relatively low prices in order to be successful. If sellers do not have the lowest price, they must be able to offer better quality, better service, or some other advantage. These comparison shopping sites generate revenue by charging a small commission on transactions, by charging usage fees to sellers and/or through advertising on their site.

PLACE BENEFITS. As company storefronts (virtually) exist on every computer that is connected to the Web, e-tailers can compete more effectively for customers, giving e-tailers an advantage. Whereas traditional retailing can be accessed only at physical store locations during opening hours, e-tailers can conduct business anywhere at any time.

The ubiquity of the Internet has enabled companies to sell goods and services on a global scale. Consumers looking for a particular product are not limited to merchants from their own country; rather, they can search for the product where they are most likely to get it or where they may get the best quality. For example, if you're looking for fine wines from

France, you can order directly from the French site Chateau Online (www.chateauonline.fr). This truly shows how the Internet has fueled globalization.

PRICE BENEFITS. E-tailers can also compete on price effectively since they can turn their inventory more often because of the sheer volume of products and customers who purchase them. Companies can sell more products, reducing prices for consumers while at the same time enhancing profits for the company. Further, virtual companies have no need to rent expensive retail space, allowing them to further reduce prices.

The Long Tail Together, these benefits of e-tailing have enabled a form of business model centered on "The Long Tails." Coined by Chris Anderson (2004, 2006), the concept of the **Long Tail** refers to a focus on niche markets, rather than purely on mainstream products. The distribution of consumers' needs and wants can be compared to a statistical normal distribution, where there are people with very diverse needs and wants on the tails (and very few people want the same products or services) and many people with "mainstream" needs and wants in the center of the distribution (see Figure 5.13). Due to high storage and distribution costs, most traditional brick-and-mortar retailers and service providers are forced to limit their product offerings to serving the needs and wants of the mainstream customers in the center of the distribution. For example, most independent movie productions are not shown at local cinemas, as they are unlikely to draw a large enough audience to cover the movie theater's costs to show the movie. Similarly, record stores only carry CDs of which a certain number of copies will be sold each year to cover the costs for shelf space, sales personnel, and so on. Given the limited local reach of brick-and-mortar stores, this ultimately limits the stores' product selection.

In contrast, made possible by their extended reach, many e-tailers can focus on the "Long Tails," that is, on products outside the mainstream tastes. Whereas a local Blockbuster store is unlikely to have a large selection of documentaries (due to a lack of local demand), Netflix can afford to have a very large selection of rather unpopular movies and still make a profit with it. Rather than renting a few "blockbusters" to many people, many (often outside the mainstream) titles are rented to a large number of people spread out on the "Long Tails." Similarly, online bookseller Amazon.com can carry a tremendous selection of (often obscure) titles, as the costs for storage are far less than those of their offline competitors. In fact, more than half of Amazon's book sales are titles that are *not* carried by the average physical bookstores, not even by megastores such as Barnes & Noble. In other words, focusing on those titles that are on the "Long Tails" of the distribution of consumers' wants can lead to a very successful business model in the digital world. A similar strategy is the mass-customization strategy pursued by Dell, which offers customized computers based on people's diverse needs and wants.

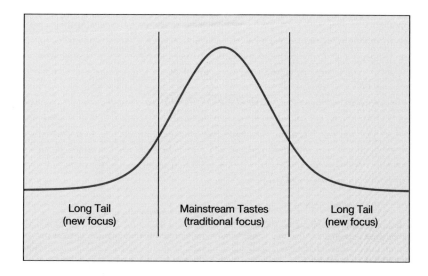

FIGURE 5.13

The Long Tails.

Drawbacks to E-Tailing Despite all the recent hype associated with e-tailing, there are some downsides to this approach, in particular, issues associated with product delivery and the inability to adequately experience the capabilities and characteristics of a product prior to purchase.

PRODUCT DELIVERY DRAWBACKS. Excepting products that you can download directly, such as music or an electronic magazine, e-tailing requires additional time for products to be delivered. If you have run out of ink for your printer and your research paper is due this afternoon, chances are that you will drive to your local office supply store to purchase a new ink cartridge rather than ordering it online. The ink cartridge purchased electronically needs to be packaged and shipped, delaying use of the product until it is delivered. Other issues can also arise. The credit card information that you provided online may not be approved, or the shipper may try to deliver the package when you are not home.

DIRECT PRODUCT EXPERIENCE DRAWBACKS. Another problem associated with e-tailing relates to a lack of sensory information, such as taste, smell, and feel. When trying on clothes with your virtual model at Lands' End, how can you be sure that you will like the feel of the material? Or what if you discover that the pair of size 9 EE hockey skates you just purchased online fits you like an 8 D? Products such as fragrances and foods can also be difficult for consumers to assess via the Web. Does the strawberry cheesecake offered online actually taste as good as it looks? How do you know if you will really like the smell of a perfume without actually sampling it? Finally, e-tailing eliminates the social aspects of the purchase. Although growing in popularity, e-tailers won't soon replace the local shopping mall because going to the mall with some friends is still an important social experience that cannot be replicated online.

E-Commerce Web Sites: Attracting and Retaining Online Customers

The basic rules of commerce are to offer valuable products and services at fair prices. These rules apply to EC as well as to any other business endeavor. However, having a good product at a fair price may not be enough to compete in the EC arena. Companies that were traditionally successful in the old markets will not necessarily dominate the new electronic markets. Successful companies are found to follow a basic set of principles, or rules, related to Web-based EC.[3] These rules are the following:

Rule 1—The Web site should offer something unique.
Rule 2—The Web site must be aesthetically pleasing.
Rule 3—The Web site must be easy to use and *fast*.
Rule 4—The Web site must motivate people to visit, to stay, and to return.
Rule 5—You must advertise your presence on the Web.
Rule 6—You should learn from your Web site.

RULE 1—THE WEB SITE SHOULD OFFER SOMETHING UNIQUE. Providing visitors with information or products that they can find nowhere else leads to EC profitability. Many small firms have found success on the Web by offering hard-to-find goods to a global audience at reasonable prices. Such niche markets can be in almost any category, be it diapers for birds (http://www.flightquarters.com), elk meat, art supplies, or hard-to-find auto parts.

RULE 2—THE WEB SITE MUST BE AESTHETICALLY PLEASING. Successful firms on the Web have sites that are nice to look at. People are more likely to visit, stay at, and return to a Web site that looks good. Creating a unique look and feel can separate a Web site from its competition. Aesthetics can include the use of color schemes, backgrounds, and high-quality images. Furthermore, Web sites should have a clear, concise, and consistent layout, taking care to avoid unnecessary clutter.

---

[3]Note that these rules apply mainly to how to make a Web site more successful. Realize that the underlying business model must be sound and that there are a host of similar rules that information systems personnel must follow to ensure that (1) the Web site works well, (2) it interacts properly with back-end business information systems, and (3) the site is secure.

RULE 3—THE WEB SITE MUST BE EASY TO USE AND *FAST*. As with nearly all software, Web sites that are easy to use are more popular. If Web surfers have trouble finding things at the site or navigating through the site's links or have to wait for screens to download, they are not apt to stay at the site long or to return. In fact, studies suggest that the average length of time that a Web surfer will wait for a Web page to download on his screen is only a couple of seconds. Rather than presenting a lot of information on a single page, successful Web sites present a brief summary of the information with hyperlinks, allowing users to "drill down" to locate the details they are interested in.

RULE 4—THE WEB SITE MUST MOTIVATE PEOPLE TO VISIT, TO STAY, AND TO RETURN. Given the pervasiveness of e-tailing, online consumers can choose from a vast variety of vendors for any (mainstream) product they are looking for and are thus less likely to be loyal to a particular e-tailer. Rather, people go to the Web sites that offer the lowest prices, or they visit Web sites with which they have built a relationship such as one that provides useful information, product ratings and customer reviews, or offers free goods and services that they value. For instance, one of the reasons that Microsoft's Web site is popular is that users can download free software. Other firms and organizations motivate visitors to visit their Web sites by enabling them to interact with other users who share common interests. These sites help to establish an online community where members can build relationships, help each other, and feel at home. For example, at the BMW Car Club of America Web site (www.BMWcca.org), visitors can share suggestions and ideas with other BMW fanatics, post requests for maintenance, repair, and other items, and follow electronic links to other BMW resources. At this Web site, visitors carry out transactions with one another as well as share advice and enthusiasm for BMW products. Likewise, e-tailers such as Amazon.com try to "learn" about their customers' interests in order to provide customized recommendations and strengthen virtual relationships.

RULE 5—YOU MUST ADVERTISE YOUR PRESENCE ON THE WEB. Like any other business, a Web site cannot be successful without customers. Companies must attract visitors to their site and away from the thousands of other sites they could be visiting. One method of attracting visitors involves advertising the Web site. The first way to advertise your firm's presence on the Web is to include the Web site address on all company materials, from business cards and letterheads to advertising copy. It is now common to see a company's URL listed at the end of its television commercials.

In addition to advertising its URL on company materials, a firm can advertise its Web site on other commerce sites or Web sites containing related information. Advertising your presence on other popular Web sites, such as that of *USA Today* (www.usatoday.com), can cost as much as $20,000 to $30,000 per month, but they can promise that more than a million users a day will visit their sites. Given the high cost of advertising on these sites and the fact that many of those Web surfers do not even look at the online ads, the trend in Web advertising is moving away from high, fixed monthly charges to a **pay-per-click** scheme. Under this type of pricing scheme, the firm running the advertisement pays only when a Web surfer actually clicks on the advertisement (usually between $0.01 and $0.50 per click). The performance of this form of advertising can be assessed by metrics such as **click-through-rate,** reflecting the ratio of surfers who click on an ad (i.e., clicks) divided by the number of times it was displayed (i.e., impressions), or **conversion rate**, reflecting the percentage of visitors who actually perform the marketer's desired action (such as making a purchase). Another option, **affiliate marketing,** allows individual Web site owners to post companies' ads on their pages; the Web site owner can earn money from referrals or ensuing sales. However, such pay-per-click models can also be abused by repeatedly clicking on a link to inflate revenue to the host or increase the costs for the advertiser; this is known as **click fraud**. The first form of click fraud is called **network click fraud**, where a site hosting an advertisement creates fake clicks in order to get money from the advertiser. In other cases, a person—competitor, disgruntled employee, and so on— inflates an organization's online advertising costs by repeatedly clicking on an advertiser's link; this is called **competitive click fraud**. In addition to using advertising or affiliate marketing, companies use *search engine marketing* (discussed later) to increase traffic to their Web sites.

RULE 6—YOU SHOULD LEARN FROM YOUR WEB SITE. Smart companies learn from their Web sites. A firm can track the path that visitors take through the many pages of its Web site and record the length of the visits, page views, common entry and exit pages, and even the user's region or Internet service provider (ISP), among other statistics. The company can then use this information to improve its Web site. If 75 percent of the visitors leave the company's site after visiting a certain page, the company can then try to find out why the surfers leave and redesign the page to entice the users to stay. Similarly, pages that go unused can be eliminated from the site, reducing maintenance and upkeep. This process of analyzing Web surfers' behavior in order to improve Web site performance (and, ultimately, maximize sales) is known as **Web analytics** (for more on this topic, see Chapter 8—Enhancing Business Intelligence Using Information Systems).

E-Business Strategy

All businesses, large and small, eventually have to make decisions on how and if they should bring their business to the Internet. In Chapter 3—Valuing Information Systems Investments, the value chain was presented to inform about the production and distribution of goods/services that provide customer value. Here we are extending the value chain thinking to include dimensions of e-Business Strategy (Wells and Gobeli, 2003, and Evan and Wurster, 1999).

There are two fundamental mistakes companies can make when taking a current business online or creating an online business. The first is assuming that if you build it they will come. As with an offline business, marketing is a critical activity in any online endeavor. For many online businesses, search marketing (discussed next) is the first step to success. The second mistake is providing an online means for an old product. For example, many new Web businesses are selling CDs online. Why sell an old format (the CD) via a new technology (the Internet)? Apple started iTunes, which moved away from the old format (CD) and offered digital downloads of music via the Internet. Apple's approach has been very successful, and many others have since followed. In fact, in early 2006 Apple announced it had sold its one billionth song. Now, Apple is the number two music retailer in the United States, behind only Wal-Mart. Next, we examine various aspects of an e-business strategy.

Search Marketing

To be successful, companies must advertise their presence on the Web. In the United States, it has been predicted that by 2012 search marketing will account for 7.5 percent of the total $340 billion spent on all advertising (see Table 5.7). Traditionally, companies would advertise their products and services in regional or national newspapers or place listings in the yellow pages. With the advent of the Internet and the growth of search engines, Web surfers are using other ways to find information. A common way to find a company is to just enter the name of a product into a search engine and then visit the resulting pages. However, given the incredible numbers of results that are returned for common searches such as "apparel," "sportswear," or "digital camera," most surfers visit

TABLE 5.7 Search Marketing Spend 2009–2012 (U.S. dollars in millions)

	2009	2010	2011	2012
Paid search	$7,054	$8,220	$9,237	$10,129
Paid inclusion	1,198	1,342	1,469	1,773
Contextual ads	1,464	2,013	3,359	4,558
SEO	3,594	5,200	6,928	8,863
TOTAL	13,310	16,775	20,993	25,323

Based on VanBoskirk, S. (2007, Oct. 10). U.S. interactive marketing forecast, 2007 to 2012. *Impaqt.com.* Retrieved September 16, 2008, from http://www.impaqt.com/downloads/US_Interactive_Marketing_Forecast.pdf.

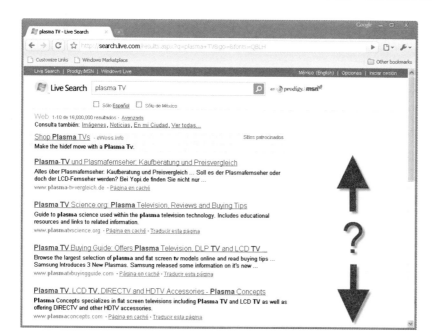

FIGURE 5.14

It is hard to influence the ranking of your company's page.

only the first few links that are presented and rarely go beyond the first results page. Thus, companies are trying to increase their visibility in search engine results, a practice known as **search marketing** (see Figure 5.14). However, when a Web site is first launched, it may take a while until it is included in a search engine's results. With most search engines, companies can speed up that process by paying a fee for being *listed* in the search engine's results (**paid inclusion**); however, a company cannot influence the *ranking* of its site on the results page. Therefore, companies turn to other forms of search engine marketing, such as *search engine advertising* and *search engine optimization.* Search marketing is now big business. Research firm Forrester reports that by 2012, interactive marketing in general (i.e., including e-mail marketing, online video marketing, and so on) could reach 18 percent on all marketing spending in the United States (see Table 5.7). Included in search marketing is paid search, paid inclusion, contextual ads, and search engine optimization (SEO). Search advertising and search engine optimization are discussed next.

Search Advertising A way to ensure that your company's site is the first result users see when searching for a specific term is using **search advertising** (or **sponsored search**). For example, using Google's "AdWords," a company can bid for being listed in the sponsored search results for the word "televisions" (see Figure 5.15). In order to present the most relevant ads to its users, Google then determines the relevance of the ad's content to the search term, and, depending on the amount of the bid, the company's Web site is listed in the sponsored results; the search engine receives revenue on a pay-per-click basis. As you can imagine, this can quickly become very expensive for advertisers, especially when the sponsored link is associated with a popular search term. On the other hand, a system such as Google's AdWords ensures high-quality leads, as the ads are only presented to users actually searching for a specific key word. Nevertheless, companies are looking for less expensive ways to improve their site's position in the search results.

Search Engine Optimization Internet search engines such as Google, Yahoo!, and MSN order the results of a user's search according to complex, proprietary formulas, and the position of the link to a company's Web site on a search results page is outside the control of the company. However, although the exact formulas for a Web site's location on a search engine's results page are kept as trade secrets, the major search engines give tips on how to optimize a site's ranking. The methods to improve a site's ranking are referred to as

FIGURE 5.15

Companies pay per click for being included in the sponsored listings.

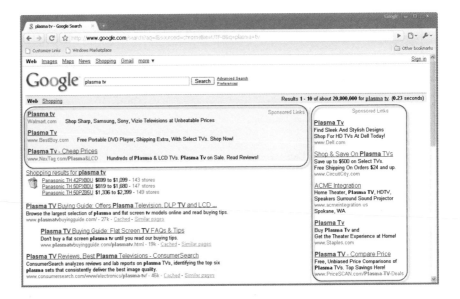

search engine optimization (SEO) and include having other pages link to one's site, keeping the content updated, and including key words a user may query for. In other words, if a Web site is frequently updated, has content relevant to the search term, and is popular (as indicated by other pages linking to it), chances are that it will be positioned higher in the search results.

There are a multitude of companies promising to improve a page's ranking, but because search engines' algorithms are usually proprietary, are changed frequently, and there can be literally hundreds of factors influencing a site's rank, the success of using such services is often limited. Further, search engines such as Google try to figure out whether a site is using unethical "tricks" (such as "hidden" key words) to improve its ranking and ban such sites from the listing altogether.

Securing Payments in the Digital World

In addition to increasing the visibility of their Web sites, companies have to ensure that consumers can make transactions on the Web site. However, one factor that still keeps people from engaging in online shopping, online banking, or online investing is the transfer of money. Recent polls revealed that 90 percent of all adult Internet users have changed their online behavior because of fears of threats like *identity theft* (see Chapter 11—Managing Information Systems Ethics and Crime), and about a third of those who do purchase goods or services online have decided to cut back on their online purchasing (Princeton Survey, 2005). These and other factors (such as impatience, lengthy checkout procedures, or comparison shopping) lead shoppers to frequently abandon their shopping carts and to not follow through with a purchase—reports show that more than half of the online shopping carts are abandoned. Traditionally, paying for goods and services was limited to using credit and debit cards, but now different companies offer payment services for buying and selling goods or services online. These different forms of online payment will be discussed next.

Credit and Debit Cards Credit and debit cards are still among the most accepted forms of payment in B2C e-commerce. For customers, paying online using a credit card is easy; all the customer needs to do is to enter his or her name, billing address, credit card number, and expiration date to authorize a transaction. In many cases, the customer is also asked to provide the so-called **Customer Verification Value (CVV2)**, a three-digit code located on the back of the card (see Figure 5.16). This is one way to combat fraud in online purchases, as the code is used for authorization by the card-issuing bank. As the CVV2 is not included in the magnetic strip information, a person using a credit card for online transactions has to physically possess the actual credit card (see Table 5.8 for other guidelines on how to conduct safe transactions on the Internet).

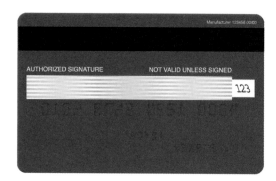

FIGURE 5.16

The three-digit Customer Verification Value (CVV2) is printed on the back of a credit card.

As for each transaction, an online customer has to transmit much personal information to a (sometimes unknown) merchant, many Internet users (sometimes rightfully) fear being defrauded by an untrustworthy seller or falling victim to some other form of computer crime (see Chapter 11). Further, ordinary people can only make payments using credit cards—to receive payments, one has to open up a merchant account to accept credit card payments. For people who are only once in a while selling things online (such as on the online auction site eBay, see the discussion later in this chapter), this is not a good option. To combat these problems, online shoppers (and sellers) are increasingly using third-party payment services. These are discussed next.

Payment Services Concerns for security have led to the inception of independent payment services such as PayPal (owned by eBay) or Google Checkout. These services allow online customers to purchase goods online without having to give much private information to the actual sellers. Rather than paying a seller by providing credit card information, an online shopper can simply pay by using his or her account with the payment service. Thus, the customer only has to provide the (sensitive) payment information to the payment service, which keeps this information secure (along with other information such as e-mail address or purchase history) and does not share it with the online merchant. Google linked its payment service to the search results so that Internet users looking for a

TABLE 5.8 Ways to Protect Yourself When Shopping Online

Tip	Example
Use a secure browser	Make sure that your browser has the latest encryption capabilities; also, always look for the padlock icon in your browser's status bar before transmitting sensitive information
Check the site's privacy policy	Make sure that the company you're about to do business with does not share any information you would prefer not to be shared
Read and understand the refund and shipping policies	Make sure that you can return unwanted/defective products for a refund
Keep your personal information private	Make sure that you don't give out information, such as your Social Security number, unless you know what the other entity is going to do with it
Give payment information only to businesses you know and trust	Make sure that you don't provide your payment information to fly-by-night operations
Keep records of your online transactions and check your e-mail	Make sure that you don't miss important information about your purchases
Review your monthly credit card and bank statements	Make sure to check for any erroneous or unauthorized transactions

Based on Federal Trade Commission (2008). A consumer's guide to e-payments. *Federal Trade Commission.* Retrieved October 31, 2008, from http://www.ftc.gov/bcp/edu/pubs/consumer/tech/tec01.shtm.

Powerful Partnerships

YouTube's Steve Chen and Chad Hurley

Steve Chen (born in 1978) and Chad Hurley (born in 1977) met and became friends while both were PayPal employees. After taking video clips of a dinner party with friends, they found it difficult and time consuming to share these clips. For instance, when they tried to send the videos in e-mail messages, services refused them because the files were too large; uploading the videos to Web sites that would accept them also proved difficult. Proving once again the adage, "Necessity is the mother of invention," Chen and Hurley then began work on a service that would allow anyone to upload a video and others to view the video at will.

YouTube went online in 2005, and within eleven months became one of the most popular sites on the Web, showing 30 million videos a day from 9.1 million people. Why was the site so quickly successful? Hurley and Chen designed the site exclusively for videos and for ease of use. When YouTube was posted, no one else had yet come up with an easy, fast method to electronically share videos that by-passed the usual process of attaching videos to e-mail messages. "From Day One we concentrated on building a service and community around video," Chen told *Business Week* in April 2006. "That made us a lot different from the iTunes and the Googles out there."

Google Inc. bought YouTube in October 2006 for a reported $1.76 billion in stock. Consequently, Hurley, Chen, and Jawed Karim, a third PayPal employee who worked on the venture but left the YouTube company early on, joined the ranks of dot.com multimillionaires.

Hurley, YouTube's chief executive officer, grew up in the Philadelphia suburbs and had a feel for business early on—at five he sold his own paintings from his front yard. He studied design at Indiana University of Pennsylvania, and applied for a job at PayPal after reading about it in *Wired* magazine. Hurley designed a logo for the company that is still in use today.

Chen, YouTube's chief technology officer, attended the Illinois Math and Science Academy and majored in computer science at the University of Illinois in Urbana-Champaign. PayPal recruited Chen during his last semester of college.

Despite legal problems over the posting of copyrighted videos on YouTube, the company has survived and continues to be high on the list of favorites for users. YouTube has consistently catered to the wishes of users, but spokespersons insist the site has also attempted to work with the entertainment and music industries to discourage copyright violations. Now special software compares YouTube's content to video clips submitted for protection, and when copyrighted material that was not approved for submission is detected, it is removed.

Like many dot.com success stories, YouTube has provided a service that illustrates the recipe for success for future Web 2.0 entrepreneurs—design sites that are easy to use then let *users* create the content.

FIGURE 5.17

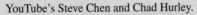

YouTube's Steve Chen and Chad Hurley.

Based on:

Anonymous (n.d.). Agenda setter 2006. *Silicon.com.* Retrieved May 22, 2008, from http://www.silicon.com/research/specialreports/as2006/0,3800012300,39162381,00.htm.

Anonymous (2006, April 10). YouTube: Way beyond home videos. *BusinessWeek.com.* Retrieved May 22, 2008, from http://www.businessweek.com/magazine/content/06_15/b3979093.htm?chan=tc&chan=technology_technology+index+page_more+of+today's+top+stories.

Chad Hurley. (2008, May 10). In *Wikipedia, the free encyclopedia.* Retrieved May 21, 2008, from http://en.wikipedia.org/w/index.php?title=Chad_Hurley&oldid=211521444.

Steve Chen (YouTube). (2008, May 10). *In Wikipedia, the free encyclopedia.* Retrieved May 21, 2008, from http://en.wikipedia.org/w/index.php?title=Steve_Chen_%28YouTube%29&oldid=211521405.

YouTube. (2008, May 21). In *Wikipedia, the free encyclopedia.* Retrieved May 21, 2008, from http://en.wikipedia.org/w/index.php?title=YouTube&oldid=213855846.

specific product can immediately see whether a merchant offers this payment option; this is intended to ease the online shopping experience for consumers, thus reducing the number of people abandoning their shopping carts.

Another payment service, PayPal, goes a step further by allowing anyone with an e-mail address to send and receive money. In other words, using this service, you can send money to your friends or family members, or you can receive money for anything you're selling. This easy way to transfer money has been instrumental in the success of the online auction eBay, where anyone can sell or buy goods from other eBay users (see the discussion of consumer-to-consumer e-commerce later).

Managing Financial Transactions in the Digital World

One special form of services frequently offered online is managing financial transactions. Whereas traditionally consumers had to visit their bank to conduct financial transactions, they can now manage credit card, checking, or savings accounts online using **online banking** or pay their bills using **electronic bill pay** services. However, concerns about security of online transactions have worried many online users.

In addition to online banking, **online investing** has seen steady growth over the past several years. The Internet has changed the investment landscape considerably; now, people use the Internet to get information about stock quotes or to manage their portfolios. For example, many consumers turn to sites such as MSN Money, Yahoo! Finance, or CNN Money to get the latest information about stock prices, firm performance, or mortgage rates. Then they can use online brokerage firms to buy or sell stocks.

Consumer-to-Consumer E-Commerce

Consumer-to-consumer (C2C) commerce has been with us since the start of commerce itself. Whether it was bartering, auctions, or tendering, commerce has always included consumer-to-consumer economics. According to the American Life Project, 17 percent of online American adults, or 25 million people, have used the Internet to sell things. C2C relationships can be categorized based on the number of sellers (one or many) and the number of buyers (one or many) involved, giving four distinct categories of C2C e-commerce (see Figure 5.18). This electronically facilitated interaction creates unique opportunities (such as a large pool of potential buyers) and unique problems (such as the potential of being defrauded; see Table 5.9). This section will discuss *e-auctions,* one of the most popular mechanisms consumers use to buy, sell, and trade with other consumers.

E-Auctions

As seen throughout this text, the Internet has provided the possibility to disseminate information and services that were previously unavailable in many locations. This dissemination can be seen clearly in the emergence of electronic auctions, or **e-auctions**. E-auctions

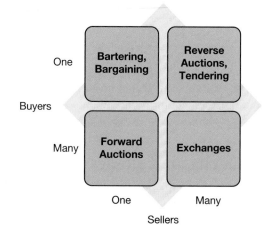

FIGURE 5.18

Types of consumer-to-consumer e-commerce.

Adapted from Turban, E., Lee, J., King, D., McKay, J., and Marshall, P. 2008. *Electronic Commerce 2008: A Managerial Perspective.* Upper Saddle River, NJ: Prentice Hall.

TABLE 5.9 Opportunities and Threats of Consumer-to-Consumer E-Commerce

Opportunities	Threats
Consumers can buy and sell to broader markets	No quality control
Eliminates the middleman that increases the final price of products and services	Higher possibility of fraud
Always available for consumers, 24/7/365	Harder to use traditional methods to pay (checks, cash, ATM cards)
Market demand is an efficient mechanism for setting prices in the electronic environment	
Increases the numbers of buyers and sellers who can find each other	

provide a place where sellers can post goods and services for sale and buyers can bid on these items. This method of transaction is called **forward auction**, where the highest bid wins. A **reverse auction** is where buyers post a *request for quote (RFQ)*, which is similar to a request for proposal (RFP) (for more on RFPs, see Chapter 10—Developing and Acquiring Information Systems) in that the sellers respond with bids (and the seller with the lowest bid wins), rather than posting items or services for auction. Auctions are typically characterized as dynamic and competitive environments where market forces set the prices.

The largest e-auction site you probably know is eBay (www.ebay.com). eBay has evolved from only offering forward auctions to now offering every type of auction from forward auctions to reverse auctions to exchanges. Its revenue model is based on small fees that are associated with posting items, but these small fees quickly add up so that in 2007 eBay's gross revenue exceeded $7 billion. Next the threats in online auctions will be discussed.

According to the National Fraud Information Center & Internet Fraud Watch (NFIC/IFW), e-auctions are marred with more fraud than any commerce activity conducted over the Internet (Fraud.org, 2007). E-auction fraud accounted for 45 percent of all Internet fraud-related complaints filed with the NFIC/IFW, with an average loss of $724 in 2007. There are several different types of e-auction fraud:

- ▪ *Bid Luring.* Luring bidders to leave a legitimate auction to buy the same item at a lower price outside the auction space; return policies and buyer protection do not apply
- ▪ *Reproductions.* Selling something that is said to be an original, but it turns out to be a reproduction
- ▪ *Bid Shielding.* Sometimes called "shill bidding." Using two different accounts to place a low followed by a very high bid on a desired item, leading other bidders to drop out of the auction. The high bid is then retracted, and the item is won at the low bid
- ▪ *Shipping Fraud.* Charging excessive shipping and handling fees, far above actual cost
- ▪ *Payment Failure.* Buyers not paying for item after auction conclusion
- ▪ *Nonshipment.* Sellers failing to ship item after payment has been received

E-auction providers such as eBay use sophisticated business intelligence applications (see Chapter 8) to detect and minimize e-auction fraud, attempting to make consumer-to-consumer electronic commerce a safer shopping experience.

Emerging Topics in Electronic Commerce

Although electronic commerce is only a little over a decade old, radical developments in technology and systems have brought e-commerce from a fringe economic activity to one of the most prevalent in today's global economy. This innovation has not slowed down and has opened some promising new areas within electronic commerce. This section will outline some emerging topics within electronic commerce. This will include innovations in *mobile commerce* (or *m-commerce*) and *location-based m-commerce*. Also included in this section are descriptions of two exploding trends, *mobile entertainment* and *e-government*. Both have grown from concepts to implementation in a short period of time.

The Rise in M-Commerce

One exciting new form of e-commerce is mobile electronic commerce, or **m-commerce**. M-commerce is defined as any electronic transaction or information interaction conducted using a wireless, mobile device and mobile networks (wireless or switched public network) that leads to the transfer of real or perceived value in exchange for information, services, or goods (MobileInfo, 2008).

The most common platform for m-commerce is the use of powerful "smart phones" like Apple's iPhone or RIM's BlackBerry, supporting high-speed data transfer and "always-on" connectivity over high-speed cellular networks (see the accompanying Technology Briefing for a detailed description of these and other handheld devices). These powerful devices provide a wide variety of services and capabilities in addition to voice communication, such as multimedia data transfer, video streaming, video telephony, and full Internet access. In Table 5.10, we list some sample m-commerce applications.

Location-Based M-Commerce One form of m-commerce is **location-based services**, which are highly personalized mobile services based on a user's location. Location-based services are implemented via the cellular network and global positioning system (GPS) functionality—now built into most modern cell phones—or by using personal area network technologies such as Bluetooth. When using Bluetooth, consumers must be within range of a transmitter sending content to all available devices. Using Bluetooth, a city can provide directions to popular locations (e.g., restaurants), provide current movie listings, or any other information that might be valued. Also, businesses can use this technology to provide information about current products or sales as consumers pass by a shop. Whereas some of these applications are pull-based (e.g., the consumer trying to find information about restaurants, ATMs, or movie listings), others are push-based, providing the consumer with (sometimes unwanted) information based on his or her current location (such

TABLE 5.10 Some M-Commerce Applications

Purchasing and Other Financially Related Transactions

• Online purchasing of goods or services

• In-store purchases

• Directory/store-finder services

• M-wallets

• Vending machine purchases

• Stock trading and other investments

• Paying bills

Reserving and/or Booking

• Reserving and/or purchasing tickets for airlines, movies, concerts, or sporting events

• Reservations for restaurants or hotels

Entertainment and Information

• Downloading and playing games

• Streaming media for movies or music

• General information such as news and weather

• Accessing corporate extranets/intranets

as information about a sales event). However, current anti-spam legislation has put a damper on push-based marketing using location-based services in some countries.

These and other location-based capabilities can be provided via one or more networking technologies. One example of a very useful GPS-enabled location-based service is **e911**, or *enhanced* 911 (which is part of a federal mandate to improve the effectiveness and reliability of the 911 emergency service). When someone in distress would dial 911 from an older cell phone, the call would most likely be routed to the wrong 911 dispatch center, and the dispatcher would have no way to find out the location of the caller. GPS-enabled location-based services enable correct routing of 911 calls and also provide dispatchers with location information on the wireless 911 calls. This includes information on the phone number used to call and GPS information that would indicate where the cell phone is located within fifty meters. Another popular GPS-enabled location-based service is the phone locator, which uses GPS phone tracking capabilities. This service, offered by major U.S. and European wireless providers, allows for users to log on to Web sites and view the location of family members' cell phones. Marketed as tracking capability built for family safety, phone locator applications can include everything from maps of a person's current location to messaging systems that alert parents when their child leaves a certain area (see Figure 5.19).

In addition to these location-based services, there is now a variety of consumer-oriented phone software that uses GPS and Bluetooth functionalities in cell phones. Table 5.11 lists a sample of GPS-enabled applications.

Social activities are another area that is supported by GPS technology in cell phones. With the success of social networking sites, such as Facebook.com and MySpace.com, many innovators are looking to social networks and cell phone technology to be the next big thing. Already several Web sites are providing social networking cell service. This includes Dodgeball.com, which is a social networking cell phone pioneer offering a service that allows users to view location information regarding friends and social gatherings. If you have a buddy who is having a burger at the local burger joint, an SMS text message will be sent automatically letting the user know the location of the restaurant and who is all in attendance. Many

FIGURE 5.19

Parents can track their children's movements using cell phones.

TABLE 5.11 **GPS-Enabled Location-Based Services**

Service	Example
Location	Determining the basic geographic position of the cell phone
Mapping	Capturing specific locations to be viewed on the phone
Navigation	The ability to give route directions from one point to another
Tracking	The ability to see another person's location

predict that within two years, 5 percent of all text messages will be cell phone social networking related. Not bad considering that the current SMS market is annually close to $3 billion.

Key Drivers for M-Commerce Several factors have led to the rapid rise of m-commerce. First, there is exponential growth of consumer interest in and adoption of the Internet and e-commerce in general. Second, there is now development and deployment of real-time transfer of data over 3G and soon 4G cellular networks that have enabled faster data transmission and "always-on" connectivity, resulting in tremendous growth in mobile telephony and availability of powerful wireless, handheld devices. We describe these types of cellular networks in detail in the accompanying Technology Briefing.

Through a convergence of Internet and wireless technologies, m-commerce promises to propel business by enabling the electronic exchange of capital, goods, and commercial information via mobile, un-tethered computing devices (Looney, Jessup, and Valacich, 2004). Indeed, the m-commerce market is predicted to grow to over $88 billion by 2009, up from only $19 billion in 2007.[4]

Mobile Entertainment

Another e-commerce innovation in the entertainment industry involves media dissemination. With the advent of products such as **Slingbox** and TiVo, the entertainment industry, including the major U.S. network television stations and the major Hollywood studios, has no choice but to adopt the Internet as a viable dissemination medium. These industry players are now making their TV shows and movies available via Apple's iTunes and YouTube.com, responding to innovations such as Slingbox. A Slingbox, connected to a user's set-top box, acts as a personal media server and "placeshifts" television content to any Internet-enabled device. In other words, the television signal is received in the user's house and then relayed via the Internet so that the users can access TV shows or movies while traveling, being in the office, or sitting in the backyard.

E-Government

E-government is the use of information systems to provide citizens, organizations, and other governmental agencies with information about public services and to allow for interaction with the government. E-government has become more widespread since the 1998 Government Paperwork Elimination Act. Similar to the e-commerce business models, electronic government involves three distinct relationships (see Figure 5.20).

Government-to-Citizens The first form of e-government is known as **government-to-citizen (G2C)** e-commerce. This category allows for interactions between federal, state, and local governments and their constituents. The Internal Revenue Service's

[4]Burger, K. (2007, March 4) M-Commerce Hot Spots, Part 1: Beyond Ringtones and Wallpaper. E-Commerce Time. Retrieved May 13, 2008, from http://www.ecommercetimes.com/story/ 57109.html?welcome= 1210701360

Coming Attractions

Transforming Communication: Ribbit

On the one hand you have your landline telephone and on the other hand your computer, and never the two shall meet. Right? As of 2008, and a start-up Silicon Valley telephony company called Ribbit—wrong. "Ribbit is an open platform for telephony innovation," the company's Web site explains. "Unlike any other phone company, we are giving our developers unprecedented access to our technology, through the Ribbit API and allowing them to innovate at will."

Sounds promising for developers, but what can Ribbit do for consumers? Imagine one phone number for your landline telephones, mobile phones, and voice over Internet phones, no matter which service you use for each. When using Ribbit's service "amphibian," all the phones will ring, but answer one and the others get the message that the phone has been answered. In addition, imagine answering a telephone call or checking voice mail on a Web page. Amphibian even offers speech-to-text conversion, so that you can receive your voice mail via text messages on your cell phone. Integrating social networking technology, you can learn about what your callers are doing, what they are blogging about, or watch the latest video your caller uploaded on YouTube.

Ribbit's SmartSwitch software was built to communicate with traditional phones, mobile phones, and a variety of Voice over Internet protocols (VoIPs). Like the switches after which it is modeled, Ribbit's software has the capability for 911 calls, is robust enough to survive damage to some individual elements, and can be enabled with common features such as call forwarding and call waiting. Adobe Flash has also been added to the system's technology, so that Ribbit-enabled phones can operate within browsers, like other Flash media.

What do you get when you cross a telephone with a computer? A Ribbit.

Based on:

Anonymous (n.d.). If you have a mobile phone and use the Internet, you need Amphibian. Retrieved May 22, 2008, from http://www.ribbit.com/ everyday/index.php.

Anonymous (n.d.). Ribbit. An open platform for telephony innovation. Retrieved May 22, 2008, from. http://www.ribbit.com/about

Naone, E. (2008, January 4). Transforming communication. *Technology Review*. Retrieved May 22, 2008, from http://www.technologyreview.com/Infotech/19999.

FIGURE 5.20

E-government initiatives include interaction with citizens, corporations, and other governments.

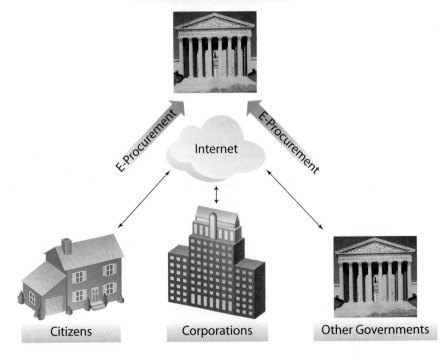

Internet tax filing, or *e-filing,* is one of the more recognizable government-to-citizen tools. Another e-government tool in wide use today is grants.gov. Of the over 2,200 funding opportunities for federal discretion, 54 percent were available for online submission (www.whitehouse.gov). Some states have begun working on e-voting initiatives, allowing citizens to vote online. However, concerns over security and protection from manipulation have thus far slowed the adoption of e-voting.

Government-to-Business **Government-to-business (G2B)** is similar to G2C, but this form of EC involves businesses' relationships with all levels of government. This includes e-procurement, in which the government streamlines its supply chain by purchasing materials directly from suppliers using its proprietary Internet-enabled procurement system. Also included in G2B initiatives are forward auctions that allow businesses to buy seized and surplus government equipment. Similar to eBay.com, the government launched AuctionRP.com to provide a marketplace for real-time auctions for surplus and seized goods. Other G2B services include online application for export licenses, verification of employees' Social Security numbers, and online tax filing.

Government-to-Government Finally, **government-to-government (G2G)** EC is used for electronic interactions that take place between countries or between different levels of government within a country. Since 2002, the U.S. government has provided comprehensive e-government tools that allow foreign entities to find government-wide information related to business topics. This includes Regulations.gov and Export.gov; both allow information to be accessed regarding laws and regulations relevant to federal requirements. In addition, e-government has aligned its electronic capabilities with world issues. For example, the Consolidated Health Informatics Initiative has adopted electronic standards to allow worldwide health organizations to share information securely with government agencies. Other G2G transactions relate to the intergovernmental collaboration at the local, state, federal, and tribal levels.

Issues in E-Commerce

Although electronic commerce is now a viable and well-established business practice, there are issues that have changed the landscape for businesses and consumers and continue to do so. These threats to the current electronic business models typically take the form of policy changes. This section outlines the major factors influencing these legal developments. This includes such subjects as the USA PATRIOT Act, Internet taxation, Net neutrality, and censorship, all of which are outlined next.

The USA PATRIOT Act The **USA PATRIOT Act** (officially known as *Uniting and Strengthening America by Providing Appropriate Tools to Intercept and Obstruct Terrorism*) was introduced shortly after the 9/11 terrorist attacks in 2001. The intent of this law is to give law enforcement agencies at the local, state, and federal levels broader ranges of power to aid in the protection of Americans. There have been several critics of this law, including the American Civil Liberties Union, who have expressed grave concerns, including (1) reduced checks and balances on surveillance, (2) lack of focus on terrorism, and (3) surveillance on Americans by U.S. intelligence agencies. For some examples of elements included in the USA PATRIOT Act, see Table 5.12.

Taxation Although this issue is a relatively old one, it remains controversial within the American legal system. With e-commerce global transactions increasing at an exponential rate, many governments are concerned that sales made via electronic sales channels have to be taxed in order to make up for the lost revenue in traditional sales methods. As people shop less in local retail stores, cities, states, and even countries are now seeing a decrease in their sales tax income because of electronic commerce. Table 5.13 highlights issues associated with Internet taxation.

TABLE 5.12 **Examples of the Provisions Allowed by the USA PATRIOT Act**

Provision	Description
View electronic messages	Permits authorities to intercept communications to and from a trespasser within a computer system
Permits "roving" surveillance	Permits court orders omitting the identification of the particular instrument, facilities, or place where the surveillance is to occur
Pen register	Authorizes pen register and trap and trace device orders for e-mail as well as telephone conversations
Tangible items inclusion	Sanctions court ordered access to *any* tangible item rather than only business records held by lodging, car rental, and locker rental businesses
Banking regulations	Establishes minimum new customer identification standards and record keeping and recommending an effective means to verify the identity of foreign customers
Counterfeiting	Increases the penalties for counterfeiting
Finding terrorists	Increases the rewards for information in terrorism cases

Based on Congressional Research Service, *Intelligence and Related Issues*, 2008.

THE INTERNET TAX FREEDOM ACT. Starting in 1998, the **Internet Tax Freedom Act**, passed by the U.S. Senate, created a moratorium on EC taxation in the hopes of creating incentives for electronic commerce. The most recent version called the Internet Tax Nondiscrimination Act was signed into law in late 2004 by President George Bush. According to these tax laws (in addition to other provisions, such as a ban on Internet access or e-mail taxes), sales on the Internet were to be treated the same way as mail-order sales. As with mail-order sales, a company was required to collect sales tax only from customers residing in a state where the business had substantial presence. In other words, if an EC business had office facilities or a shipping warehouse in a certain state (say, California), it would have to collect sales tax only on sales to customers from that state (in that case, California). Many EC businesses thus strategically selected their home bases to offer "tax-free shopping" to most customers. For example, Jeff Bezos, the founder of Amazon.com, closely examined several states before choosing the state of Washington for Amazon.com's head office. This way, initially only the 6 million Washington State residents had to pay tax on Amazon.com purchases. As Amazon.com expands, it continues to be very selective in where it locates shipping facilities and warehouses. For example, Amazon.com selected Reno, Nevada to serve the Californian market in order to allow its 36 million potential customers to avoid paying sales tax on purchases. Currently, Amazon.com collects sales tax only on purchases from customers located in Kansas, Kentucky, North Dakota, and Washington State. Walmart.com, on the

TABLE 5.13 **Arguments For and Against Internet Taxation**

For	Against
Loss in tax income of local, state, and federal governments	Slows e-commerce growth and opportunity
	Creates an opportunity for consumer fraud
Unfair advantage for e-tailers over brick-and-mortar stores	Creates a nongeographic economy where poorer states could grow
Creates accountability for e-tailers	Drives e-commerce businesses to other countries

other hand, charges taxes on all of their U.S. EC transactions, as they are physically present in every U.S. state.

USE TAX. However, the situation is not as easy as it seems. Even if the EC business does not *collect* sales tax on goods or services purchased outside your home state, you are still liable for *paying* "use tax" (usually equal to your state's sales tax) on those goods and services. For example, if an out-of-state e-tailer does not collect sales tax from its California customers, these customers are asked to report that purchase and mail a check for the tax amount to the state. Other states have started adding a line for the use tax on their state income tax returns, and people have to report the taxes they owe on out-of-state purchases or else face stiff penalties for misrepresenting their tax liabilities.

The State of New York attempted to close this tax loophole by arguing that any Web site that would earn referral fees for directing customers to an e-tailer such as Amazon.com would constitute active solicitation through an in-state entity. Thus, if one or more of the countless "Amazon Associates" has an address in the State of New York, Amazon would have to collect sales and use tax from its New York state customers. In early 2008, Amazon sued the State of New York, claiming that the associates are not its agents, but are only Web sites that display Amazon's ads; no ruling has been issued at the time of publication of this book, but any ruling will certainly have an effect on other states' treatment of sales and use tax for e-tailers.

THE STREAMLINED SALES TAX PROJECT. With the tremendous growth in e-commerce, many states have proposed that EC businesses should be forced to collect the appropriate use tax from their customers. However, this poses tremendous problems because of local differences in taxation. For example, in Washington, fruit juice made from 100 percent juice is tax free, whereas in New York, the threshold is 70 percent juice. In some states, taxation even differs from county to county. If an EC business were to collect use tax from all its customers, it would have to know these differences in taxation to charge the correct amount to the customers' bills. Thus, over forty-four states are participating as of March 2008 in an effort to propose new laws (such as the **Streamlined Sales Tax Project**) to simplify the tax codes and make it mandatory for out-of-state sellers to collect taxes. It may not be too long until you will have to pay taxes on every purchase you make on the Internet.

Net Neutrality Columbia University professor Tim Wu originally coined the term **Net neutrality**. The underlying concept is that data that is sent over the Internet should be routed and handled in a neutral matter, regardless of the content of the data. In other words, all traffic over the Internet must be treated the same way, and your e-mail is sent, routed, and received no differently than an Amazon.com Web page or even a streaming video from Comedy Central.

Proponents of Net neutrality have asked for the Internet to be a service similar to a utility, such as power. When you are using power, it does not matter what you use your power for; the usage is metered, and you are charged accordingly. Many ISPs and telephone companies, however, have asked the U.S. government to change the nature of the Internet to allow for a prioritizing of particular applications. They believe that several large Internet companies are abusing the Internet (e.g., for bandwidth-hungry applications such as video over IP) and that this abuse causes problems for traditional Internet traffic. Their solution involves a two-tiered Internet where data is either sped up or slowed down, depending on what the data is being used for. For example, YouTube.com, the wildly popular Web site that streams millions of videos a day to users around the world, would be targeted. Telephone companies and ISPs would argue that YouTube.com causes problems for other traffic and therefore should either pay more or be "deprioritized."

Censorship **Censorship** is another hot-button issue that has gained importance. Censorship refers to governmental attempts to control Internet traffic, thus preventing some material from being viewed by a country's citizens. Several countries, including

China and North Korea, have strict guidelines on what can be viewed by their citizens. Certain key words and topics are not permitted for one reason or another.

Within the United States, there is also a concerted effort to censor content, specifically the content children can view. The **Child Online Protection Act (COPA)** exemplifies this approach. This law requires Internet users to verify their age before being able to view content that is deemed inappropriate for minors. In addition to concerns about explicit material that children view, there is concern with hate sites. Although difficult to do, the advocates of censorship argue that it is the ISP's responsibility to control the user's content. Many ISPs have embraced this point of view, including AOL, which strictly censors any hate sites or serial killer enthusiasts' sites.

Industry Analysis

Retailing

You may make most of your large purchases online in order to benefit from greater convenience or lower prices, but most likely, you will be setting your feet into a brick-and-mortar retail store at least once in a while, and you may have noticed some changes brought by technology. A few decades ago, large retail chains started introducing computerized point-of-sale (POS) inventory systems consisting of checkout computers and an inventory control system. A simple bar code scan captures a sale, and the item is automatically deducted from the store's inventory, allowing real-time tracking of purchases so that the retailer knows when to reorder merchandise or restock shelves. In addition to a speedier check-out process, such systems help to reduce stock outs, increasing customer satisfaction. In many grocery stores, this system has been taken a step further, allowing the customers to conduct the check-out process themselves, saving time and labor costs.

In the near future, many items will be equipped with radio frequency identification (RFID) tags (see Chapter 9), eliminating the need to scan every individual item so that the total price for a cart full of merchandise can be calculated within a second, saving even more time and adding convenience for the customer. Imagine the time you'll save when all you have to do is pass with your cart through an RFID reader and swipe your credit card. Similarly, a store's shelves will be equipped with RFID technology, tracking when an item is removed from the shelf or enabling the use of electronic shelf labels that can present much more than a product's price. "Smart" dressing rooms, equipped with RFID technology, can help the customer find more information about a product, such as the availability of an item in additional sizes or different colors or it can even suggest other matching items. Thus, the customer does not have to wait for a sales associate to go and look for items. A similar technology currently in use is handheld computers with bar code scanners. Linked to the store's inventory control system using wireless technologies, these handheld computers allow the sales associates to inquire about stock levels at the same store or even inquire about the availability at other stores of the same chain.

As you can see, information systems had a huge impact on retailing, and many more changes are yet to hit the shelves.

Questions

1. How can technology help brick-and-mortar retailers compete against e-tailers?
2. Privacy advocates criticize the use of RFID, as it allows better tracking of purchasing habits. How can brick-and-mortar retailers alleviate these concerns?
3. As you read, some of the "human element" in retailing is replaced by technology. How can brick-and-mortar stores avoid becoming too "sterile" when using information systems to compete against e-tailers?

Based on:

Anonymous (n.d.). Metro Group future store initiative–Supermarket. Retrieved May 17, 2008, from http://www.future-store.org/servlet/PB/menu/1007144_l2_yno/index.html.

Anonymous (n.d.). Metro Group future store initiative–Department Store. Retrieved May 17, 2008, from http://www.future-store.org/servlet/ PB/menu/1007142_l2_yno/index.html.

Key Points Review

1. *Describe electronic commerce, how it has evolved, and the strategies that companies are adopting to compete in cyberspace.* Electronic commerce is the online exchange of goods, services, and money between firms and between firms and their customers. Although EC was being used as far back as 1948 during the Berlin Airlift, the emergence of the Internet and World Wide Web has fueled a revolution in the manner in which products and services are marketed and sold. Their far-reaching effects have led to the creation of a global electronic marketplace that offers a virtually limitless array of new services, features, and functionality. Unlike the situation with traditional storefronts, time limitations are not a factor, allowing firms to sell and service products seven days a week, twenty-four hours a day, 365 days a year to anyone, anywhere. Companies are exploiting one or more of the capabilities of the Web to reach a wider customer base, offer a broader range of product offerings, and develop closer relationships with customers by striving to meet their unique needs. These wide-ranging capabilities include global information dissemination, integration, mass customization, interactive communication, collaboration, and transactional support. The Web has transformed the traditional business operation into a hypercompetitive electronic marketplace. Companies must strategically position themselves to compete in the new EC environment. At one extreme, companies known as brick-and-mortars choose to operate solely in the traditional, physical markets. In contrast, click-only (or virtual) companies conduct business electronically in cyberspace. These firms have no physical locations, allowing them to focus purely on EC. Click-and-mortar (or bricks-and-clicks) companies straddle the two environments, operating in both physical and virtual arenas. Companies must also select a specific business model that defines how they will earn money, which markets they intend to serve, whom they will compete with, what competitive advantage they will have, how they will market themselves, and so on. Firms in cyberspace must also define a revenue model that can be based on advertising revenue, subscription revenue, transaction fee revenue, sales revenue, or some combination.

2. *Explain the differences between extranets and intranets and show how organizations utilize these environments.* Extranets enable two or more firms to use the Internet to engage in business-to-business (B2B) electronic commerce. Extranets provide timely and accurate information, allow for technology integration, and provide high value at low cost. Also referred to as business-to-employee (B2E) electronic commerce, an intranet refers to the use of the Internet within an organization to support internal business processes and activities. Examples of the types of processes or activities that might be supported include things such as training, application integration, online entry of information, real-time access to information, and employee collaboration. Both extranets and intranets provide significant benefits to organizations and are being very widely adopted by firms both big and small.

3. *Describe the stages of business-to-consumer electronic commerce and understand the keys to successful electronic commerce applications.* Business-to-consumer (B2C) electronic commerce focuses on retail transactions between a company and end consumers. Business Web sites can be relatively simple or very sophisticated and can be classified as e-information, e-integration, or e-transaction sites. E-information sites simply provide electronic brochures and other types of information for customers. E-integration sites provide customers with the ability to gain personalized information by querying corporate databases and other information sources. E-transaction sites allow customers to place orders and make payments. For successful e-commerce applications, companies should follow several rules. The basic rules of commerce are to offer valuable products and services at fair prices. These rules apply to EC as well as to any business endeavor. In addition to having a sound business model and plan for generating revenue, successful companies are found to follow a basic set of principles, or rules, related to Web-based EC. These rules include having a Web site that offers something unique, is aesthetically pleasing, is easy to use, and is fast and that motivates people to visit, to stay, and to return. A company should also advertise its presence on the Web (e.g., using search engine marketing) and should try to learn from its Web site (using Web analytics).

4. *Describe emerging trends in consumer-to-consumer e-commerce and the key drivers for the emergence of mobile commerce.* The Internet has fueled the development of a variety of ways people can trade goods, socialize, or voice their thoughts and opinions. Specifically, e-auctions allow private people to sell goods to large markets. Mobile electronic commerce, or m-commerce, enables people to take full advantage of the Internet

on portable, wireless devices, such as smart phones. M-commerce is rapidly expanding with the continuing expansion of worldwide Internet adoption as well as the continued evolution of faster cellular networks, more powerful handheld devices, and more sophisticated applications. Location-based services, based on GPS technology, are a key driver enabling even more creative m-commerce applications.

5. *Explain different forms of e-government as well as regulatory threats to e-commerce.* E-government is a government's use of information systems to provide a variety of services to citizens, businesses, and other governmental agencies. Depending on the services, e-government initiatives can be targeted at citizens (government-to-citizens),

businesses (government-to-business), or other governmental agencies (either within a country or between countries; government-to-government). Governments' attempts to regulate electronic commerce have created some threats to EC. Most notably, the USA PATRIOT Act limits civil liberties by loosening restrictions on electronic surveillance, the Streamlined Sales Tax Project attempts to make tax collection mandatory for all out-of-state sellers (both online and offline), opponents of Net neutrality attempt to prioritize the delivery of online data depending on its use, and censorship (both outside and within the United States) attempts to limit the nature of content Internet users can view.

Key Terms

affiliate marketing 209
bid luring 216
bid shielding 216
brick-and-mortar business
strategy 193
bricks-and-clicks business
strategy 194
business model 196
business-to-business (B2B) 188
business-to-consumer (B2C) 188
business-to-employee (B2E) 188
censorship 223
Child Online Protection Act
(COPA) 224
click-and-mortar business
strategy 194
click fraud 209
click-only business strategy 193
click-through rate 209
competitive click fraud 209
consumer-to-consumer (C2C) 189
conversion rate 209
Customer Verification Value
(CVV2) 212
disintermediation 193
e911 218

e-auctions 215
e-government 219
e-information 205
e-integration 205
electronic bill pay 215
electronic commerce (EC) 188
Electronic Data Interchange
(EDI) 198
e-tailing 205
e-transaction 205
extranet 196
forward auction 216
global information
dissemination 191
government-to-business (G2B) 220
government-to-citizen (G2C) 219
government-to-government
(G2G) 220
integration 191
interactive communication 192
Internet Tax Freedom Act 222
intranet 201
location-based services 217
Long Tail 207
mass customization 191
m-commerce 217

menu-driven pricing 205
Net neutrality 223
network click fraud 209
nonshipment 216
online banking 215
online investing 215
paid inclusion 211
payment failure 216
pay-per-click 209
reintermediation 193
reproductions 216
revenue model 196
reverse auction 216
reverse pricing system 205
search advertising 211
Search Engine Optimization
(SEO) 211
search marketing 211
shipping fraud 216
Slingbox 219
sponsored search 211
Streamlined Sales Tax Project 223
transaction support 192
USA PATRIOT Act 221
virtual company 193
Web analytics 210

Review Questions

1. What is electronic commerce (EC), and how has it evolved?
2. How have the Web and other technologies given rise to a global platform?
3. Compare and contrast two electronic commerce business strategies.

4. Explain the differences between the Internet, an intranet, and an extranet. What is the common bond among all three?
5. List and explain three benefits of using extranets.
6. What are the three stages of business-to-consumer electronic commerce?

7. Describe the differences between SEO, search marketing, and sponsored search.
8. List and describe six elements of or rules for a good Web site.
9. List and describe three emerging trends in consumer-to-consumer e-commerce.
10. Explain the different forms of online auctions.
11. Describe m-commerce and explain how it is different from regular e-commerce.
12. What are the primary forms of e-government? Provide examples for each.
13. What type of regulations can be considered threats to e-commerce?

Self-Study Questions

Visit the Interactive Study Guide on the Companion Web site for additional Self-Study Questions: www.pearsonhighered.com/valacich.

1. Electronic commerce is the online exchange of _____ between firms and between firms and their customers.
   A. goods
   B. services
   C. money
   D. all of the above
2. _____ are those companies that operate in the traditional, physical markets and do not conduct business electronically in cyberspace.
   A. brick-and-mortars
   B. click-onlys
   C. both A and B
   D. dot-coms
3. A _____ is a summary of how a company will generate revenue, identifying its product offering, value-added services, revenue sources, and target customers.
   A. profit-and-loss statement
   B. revenue model
   C. business model
   D. annual report
4. According to the text, the three stages of Web sites include all of the following except _____.
   A. e-tailing
   B. e-integration
   C. e-transaction
   D. e-information
5. The revolutionary aspect of the Priceline.com Web site lies in its _____ system called Name Your Own Price. Customers specify the product they are looking for and how much they are willing to pay for it.
   A. immediate pricing
   B. menu-driven pricing
   C. forward pricing
   D. reverse pricing
6. A type of e-auction fraud where bidders are lured to leave a legitimate auction in order to buy the same item at a lower price.
   A. bid luring
   B. product luring
   C. customer luring
   D. low-price luring
7. A Web site should _____.
   A. be easy to use and fast
   B. offer something unique and be aesthetically pleasing
   C. motivate people to visit, to stay, and to return
   D. all of the above
8. Trying to "outsmart" a search engine to improve a page's ranking is known as _____.
   A. rank enhancement
   B. SEO
   C. search engine hacking
   D. Google fooling
9. C2C e-commerce can be categorized according to _____.
   A. the number of goods sold
   B. the number of buyers and sellers
   C. the payment methods accepted
   D. all of the above
10. Net neutrality implies _____.
    A. that all people on the Internet have equal rights
    B. that all companies and organizations on the Internet have equal rights
    C. both A and B are true
    D. that all data sent over the Internet is routed and treated the same

Answers are on page 229.

Problems and Exercises

1. Match the following terms with the appropriate definitions:
   i. Search marketing
   ii. Electronic commerce
   iii. Web analytics
   iv. Paid inclusion
   v. E-transaction
   vi. Long Tails
   vii. Web analytics
   viii. Search engine optimization
   ix. E-government
   x. E-integration

    a. The practice of trying to increase a company's visibility in search engine results

    b. The online sale of goods and services between firms using proprietary networks that the firms have developed and paid for entirely themselves

    c. A business model focusing on niche markets, rather than purely on mainstream products

    d. A stage that takes the e-integration stage one step further by adding the ability for customers to enter orders and payments online

    e. A stage in which Web pages are created on the fly to produce tailored information that addresses the particular needs of a consumer

    f. The use of information systems to provide citizens and organizations with handy information about public services

    g. Methods used to improve a site's ranking

    h. The analysis of Web surfers' behavior in order to improve a site's performance

    i. The practice of paying a fee to be included in a search engine's listing

    j. The process of analyzing Web surfers' behavior to improve Web site performance

2. Visit Alaska Airlines' Web site (www.alaskaair.com) for real-time pricing and test the custom messenger bag builder at www.timbuk2.com. How have Internet technologies improved over the years?

3. Search the Web for a company that is purely Web based. Next, find the Web site of a company that is a hybrid (i.e., they have a traditional brick-and-mortar business plus a presence on the Web). What are the pros and cons of dealing with each type of company?

4. Do you feel that e-commerce will help or hurt shipping companies such as FedEx, UPS, and USPS? Have you purchased anything over the Internet? If so, how was it delivered?

5. Do you receive advertisements through e-mail? Are they directed toward any specific audience or product category? Do you pay much attention or just delete them? How much work is it to get off an advertising list?

6. What is it about a company's Web site that draws you to it, keeps you there on the site longer, and keeps you coming back for more? If you could summarize these answers into a set of criteria for Web sites, what would those criteria be?

7. Visit the following services for comparison shopping: BestBookBuys (www.bestwebbuys.com/books/), Bizrate (www.bizrate.com), and mySimon (www.mysimon.com). These companies focus on aggregating content for consumers. What are the advantages of these Web sites?

8. Compare three different search engines. What tips do they provide to improve a page's rankings? How much does it cost to advertise a page on their results pages? If you were a company, could you think of any situation where you would pay almost any amount to have the first listing on the first results page?

9. Describe your experiences in online shopping. How did you pay for your purchases? What information did you have to reveal to the merchant? Did you feel comfortable giving out that information?

10. Go to Amazon.com's affiliate site. How does affiliate marketing at Amazon.com work? How do Amazon.com business partners get paid? Who can sign up for this service?

11. Have you ever used a mobile, wireless device such as a smart phone? If so, what do you like or dislike about it? In what ways could your use of that device be made better? If you are not using one, what is preventing you from using one? What would have to happen before you would begin using such a device?

12. Visit www.firstgov.gov. What kind of services do you see that would help you? What services would you use? What areas are missing?

13. When you shop online, is sales tax a criterion for you? Do you try to purchase goods where you do not have to pay sales tax? If you would have to pay sales tax for everything you buy online, would that change your online shopping behavior?

Application Exercises

 Note: The existing data files referenced in these exercises are available on the Student Companion Web site: www.pearsonhighered.com/valacich.

Spreadsheet Application: Analyzing Server Traffic

Campus Travel has recently found that its Internet connections between offices are becoming slow, especially during certain periods of the day. Since all the online traffic is maintained by another company, an increase in capacity requires a formal approval from the general manager. The IS manager has proposed to increase the capacity of the company's network; in a few days, he has to present the business case for this proposal at the weekly meeting of the depart-ment heads. You are asked to prepare graphs for the presentation to support the IS manager's business case. In the file ServerLogs.csv, you will find information about the network traffic for a one-week period. Prepare the following graphs:

1. Total bandwidth used for each day (line graph)

2. Bandwidth used per day, by time period (line graph)

3. Average bandwidth used in each two-hour period (line graph)

Format the graphs in a professional manner and print out each graph on a separate page (Hint: If you are using Microsoft Excel's Chart Wizard, select "Place chart: As New Sheet" in step 4).

Database Application: Tracking Network Hardware

As Campus Travel is new to e-commerce, the management suggests following a stepwise approach for using the Internet to conduct business. Before using the Internet for conducting transactions, the managers recommend setting up a site that provides information to customers. Part of this informational site is an agency locator that shows the services each agency has. You have been asked to create a new database. This includes creating relationships in the current database. To create this new database, do the following:

1. Create a database called "agency."

2. Create a table called "agencies" and include agency ID, street address, city, state, ZIP code, phone number, number of service agents, and working hours for fields.

3. Create a table called "services" that includes service ID, name (i.e., type of service) and description.

4. Create a third table called "agencyservices" that includes the agency ID field from the agencies table and the service ID field from the services table.

5. Once these tables are created, go to the relationship view and connect the agencies (one side) and agencyservices (many side) tables, and the services (one side) and agencyservices (many side) tables using two one-to-many relationships (i.e., each agency can offer many services; each service can be offered by many agencies).

Team Work Exercise: So Many Books, So Little Time

Have you ever bought books online? Compare and contrast your experiences with your classmates. What types of books have you purchased? Which Web sites did you use? How did you like your online purchase experience? Do you tend to stick with the same online bookstore, or do you shop around for the best bargains? Discuss strategies the different stores use to keep you from switching to another bookstore. If you have not yet bought books online, visit the Web sites of Amazon.com and Barnes & Noble as well as comparison sites, such as www.allbookstores.com, and evaluate their offerings. Summarize the benefits and drawbacks of purchasing books online.

Answers to the Self-Study Questions

1. D, p. 188	**2.** A, p. 193	**3.** C, p. 196	**4.** A, p. 205	**5.** D, p. 205
6. A, p. 216	**7.** D, p. 208	**8.** B, p. 211	**9.** B, p. 215	**10.** D, p. 223

Case ❶

Crowdsourcing

Outsourcing certain business functions, such as customer service, accounting, or IT to an external service provider, has helped many businesses lower costs and thus increase profits. But outsourcing is so 1980s. In today's e-commerce world, think crowdsourcing.

For example, a T-shirt company in Chicago sponsors an online contest periodically that calls for the general public to submit designs. The designs are posted on the company's Web site, and visitors to the site are asked to vote for their favorite design. Visitors can also opt to pre-order a T-shirt displaying their favorite design. The company's employees count votes for the various designs and also determine which ones have the largest number of pre-orders. A winner is easily determined, and that design typically also has the largest number of pre-orders. The T-shirt company awards the contest winner a $2,000 prize—a worthy sum, but less than the company would pay a full-time designer. The T-shirt company wins twice, in that it gains a top-quality design at a discounted price, and it already has pre-orders for shirts with the winning design.

iStockphoto is another example of crowdsourcing at its best. A Web site that grew from a sharing site for graphic designers, iStockphoto lets amateur photographers offer their work for sale. Due to the site's access to top-quality material—from members of the general public as well as professional photographers—iStockphoto can offer images for licensing for as little as $1 each, whereas a professional photographer might price his or her work at $300 and up per image.

Texas Governor Rick Perry has also found a way to implement crowdsourcing in preventing illegal immigration across the Texas-Mexico border. In November 2007, Perry's administration funded the installation of two hundred video cameras to record live in strategic high-traffic areas along the border and invited all Internet users to become border patrol persons, reporting illegal

crossings and border crime. The effectiveness of the Texas crowdsourcing experiment had already been demonstrated. A month-long test run of nine cameras in 2006, before full funding was obtained, led authorities to ten undocumented aliens, a drug deal, and one human smuggling route.

Similarly, in 2008, researchers at Purdue University were working on developing a system of networked cell phones that would detect and track radiation to help prevent terrorist attacks with "dirty bombs" and other nuclear weapons. Cell phones already have GPS capability, and Purdue's project would also give them

radiation detection capability, in order to blanket the nation with millions of cell phones comprising a citizen radiation-tracking system.

Crowdsourcing is yet another example of Web 2.0's aims to enhance creativity and Internet user collaboration. It blurs the line between professionals and amateurs and lets hobbyists, talented computer geeks, and virtually anyone anywhere contribute their own unique talents to online endeavors. Crowdsourcing also offers another Web-based platform for new businesses and resources for older, established businesses—both brick-and-mortar and online.

Questions

1. Have you participated in crowdsourcing? If so, describe. If not, describe something you know or can do that would be of value to someone running a crowdsourcing activity.
2. Does crowdsourcing take advantage of people? Why or why not?
3. Describe a business or activity not described in the case that would benefit from crowdsourcing.

Based on:

Anonymous (2007, November 19). Border Web cams go online again. Perry says he's found the funds to have virtual watch up and running as early as January. *TMCNet.com*. Retrieved May 22, 2008, from http://www.tmcnet.com/usubmit/2007/11/19/3105892.htm.

Carr, N. (2006, November 5). Crowdsourcing surveillance. Retrieved May 22, 2008, from http://www. roughtype.com/archives/2006/11/crowdsourcing_l.php.

Crowdsourcing (2008, May 19). In *Wikipedia, the free encyclopedia*. Retrieved May 22, 2008, from http://en.wikipedia.org/w/index.php?title=crowdsourcing&oldid=213560796.

Howe, J. (2006, June). The rise of crowdsourcing. *Wired*. Retrieved May 22, 2008, from http://www.wired.com/wired/archive/14.06/crowds.html.

Venere, E., & E. K. Gardner (2008, January 22). Cell phone sensors detect radiation to thwart nuclear terrorism. Retrieved May 22, 2008, from http://www.purdue.edu/UNS/ x/2008a/080122Fischbachnuclear.html.

Case ❷

YouTube

It's the Web site everyone visits at least once, and most surfers come back again and again. It's the ubiquitous YouTube. Where else can you watch a video of a cat swimming contentedly in a bathtub, a twelve-year-old rendering a professional performance of the "The Star Spangled Banner" at a small town basketball game, or a public political debate where candidates answer questions visitors to the site have submitted?

YouTube, a video-sharing Web site, went online in 2005. Two former PayPal employees, Steve Chen and Chad Hurley, created the site, and it was practically an overnight success. The San Bruno,

California–based service uses Adobe Flash technology to display a wide variety of user-generated video content, including movie and TV clips, music videos, videoblogging, and short original videos. In July 2006, YouTube reported that visitors to the site were viewing more than 100 million video clips a day—a fact that compelled Google Inc. to buy the site that year for $1.76 billion in stock.

YouTube is free and registration is not necessary for visitors to view videos. To upload videos, however, registration is required. Videos with pornographic content and those showing nudity or that

defame or harass are prohibited, as well as advertising and anything encouraging criminal conduct.

After several lawsuits were filed alleging copyright violations over copyrighted material posted on YouTube, the company agreed to remove copyrighted material upon request. In addition, in October 2007, YouTube installed software intended to automatically detect and remove copyrighted clips. In order to function correctly, however, the software needed to compare clips of copyrighted material to YouTube content, which meant that music, movie, and television companies would have to send decades of clips of copyrighted material to YouTube so that comparisons could be made.

YouTube's critics, including some competitors, argue that spotting copyrighted material on the site isn't that difficult. For instance, Rob Gould, vice president of marketing for Broadcaster.com, a rival video site, told FoxNews.com in 2007: "If there has been a clip from 'American Idol' posted to the site by Joe Schmoe in Oklahoma instead of Fox, you can be pretty sure it's not supposed to be there."

As YouTube has gained in popularity, police forces around the country have used the service to help catch criminals. In February 2008, for example, the Arlington County Police in Virginia posted a video of a bank robbery. The two-minute video was viewed 1,000 times in two days, and the police claimed posting the video produced a credible lead that they were investigating. Some police departments, however, such as St. George County, Virginia, said they would not use YouTube for catching criminals, because posting police videos next to those with "crazy" content would be "bad publicity" for the police.

Regardless of the propensity for catching criminals or lack thereof, YouTube remains popular with Web users. In 2008, about 83.5 million videos were posted on YouTube, via 3.8 million registered users. Bandwidth expenses for the service were estimated at $1 million per day in 2007, and that same year YouTube consumed an amount of bandwidth comparable to the entire Internet in the year 2000. In fact, a September 2008 edition of the British publication, the *Telegraph*, expressed fears that the Internet could "grind to a halt within two years," without massive upgrades to the Internet infrastructure. Bill Thompson, visiting lecturer at City University, London, told the *Telegraph*: "I think we're in trouble. If you've got kids on YouTube and parents on iPlayer and other things going on, it all starts to go very slow."

Whatever YouTube's future, it's not likely that Internet users will soon lose interest in video sharing.

Questions

1. Do you use YouTube? If so, what is your favorite type of content? If not, why not?
2. Some view the content on YouTube as being objectionable or of bad taste (e.g., videos of terrorists killing prisoners). Should some content on YouTube be banned? Explain your answer.
3. Should YouTube content have less priority for Internet bandwidth than other types of content (e.g., e-mail)? Why or why not?

Based on:

Anonymous (2007, March 14). Viacom sues Google's YouTube for alleged copyright infringement, seeks $1B in damages. *International Herald Tribune*. Retrieved May 22, 2008, from http://www.iht.com/articles/ap/2007/03/14/business/NA-FIN-US-Viacom-YouTube-Lawsuit.php.

Anonymous (2007, October 17). YouTube installs copyright-protection filters. *Fox News*. Retrieved May 22, 2008, from http://www.foxnews.com/story/0,2933,302376,00.html?sPage=fnc.scitech/personaltechnology.

Carroll, J. (2008, January 16). The shrinking planet and YouTube. Retrieved May 22, 2008, from http://blogs.zdnet.com/carroll/?p=1789.

Carter, L. (2008, April 9). Web could collapse as video demand soars. *Telegraph.co.uk*. Retrieved May 22, 2008, from http://www.telegraph.co.uk/news/uknews/1584230/Web-could-collapse-as-video-demand-soars.html.

Delaney, K. (2006, June 27). With NBC pact, YouTube site tries to build a lasting business. *Wall Street Journal*. Retrieved May 22, 2008, from http://online.wsj.com/article/SB115137083424491406.html?mod= googlenews_wsj.

Delaney, K., & E. Smith. (2006, September 19). YouTube model is compromise over copyrights. *Wall Street Journal*. Retrieved May 22, 2008, from http://online.wsj.com/public/article/SB115862128600366836-HfXOBEjVMilRqWxOu6LMMFpVMKo_20061018.html?mod= tff_main_tff_top.

Sachoff, M. (2008, February 4). YouTube used by police for leads. *WebProNews*. Retrieved May 22, 2008, from http://www.webpronews.com/topnews/2008/02/04/youtube-used-by-police-for-leads.

YouTube. (2008, May 21). In *Wikipedia, the free encyclopedia*. Retrieved 23:10, May 21, 2008, from http://en.wikipedia.org/w/index.php?title=YouTube&oldid=213855846.

Enhancing Collaboration Using Web 2.0

After reading this chapter, you will be able to do the following:

1. Describe Web 2.0, its components, the strategies that companies are adopting to embrace these emerging capabilities, and its future.

2. Understand the importance of empowering users to generate content using wikis, tags, blogs, netcasts, and self-publishing.

3. Explain different collaboration tools and techniques, including social networking, virtual teams, viral marketing, and crowdsourcing.

Preview

This chapter focuses on the revolution that is changing the World Wide Web, electronic commerce (EC), and business in general. Web 2.0 is the term used to describe the wave of change in business models and in Web site functionality that has transformed the online landscape. Web 2.0 introduces unprecedented ways to connect to friends, share knowledge with your colleagues, or collaborate with a team of engineers five thousand miles away.

With Web 2.0 providing a new set of capabilities for individuals and businesses, an understanding of how these techniques are applied can be very helpful. Being able to understand and apply these emerging capabilities and strategies that are associated with Web 2.0 is a highly marketable skill.

Managing in the Digital World: Digg.com: Changing How News Is Delivered

Submit a news story or link to Digg.com, and if site users like it (that is, "dig" it), the story moves to the front page. If the story proves unpopular, site users vote to "bury" it and it disappears.

In October 2004, Kevin Rose, a former regular on the TechTV show *The Screen Savers* and his friends Owen Byrne, Ron Gorodetzky, and Jay Adelson began playing around with the idea of a user-controlled, community-based news Web site. They launched the site on December 5, 2004, and it immediately began drawing visitors. The original design was advertisement free, but that has changed since Google AdSense was added to the site.

Digg has so many users that "digging" a news story or Web link posting can sometimes cause a phenomenon called the "Digg effect," whereby increased traffic to a linked Web site can cause it to either slow considerably or to even crash. According to a Compete.com survey, by 2008, Digg.com was attracting 236 million visitors annually.

While Digg remains popular, critics argue that:

- The site gives users too much control over content, resulting in misinformation and sensationalism.
- Companies paying for submissions have skewed the site's original purpose.
- The site's operators, which are its founders, exert too much control over front page and forum content.
- The "bury" option is undemocratic because those who vote to bury an item are allowed to remain anonymous.
- The site is too susceptible to "gaming"—to groups or Web site operators who deliberately try to dictate content.

In May 2007, when the Advanced Access Content System (AACS) Consortium objected to Digg posts containing encryption-breaking code for HD-DVD and Blu-ray disks, management heeded advice from attorneys and took the offending articles and posts down. A user-revolt followed that prompted Digg's Kevin Rose to post a comment that reversed direction: "We hear you, and effective immediately we won't delete stories or comments containing the code and will deal with whatever the consequences might be. If we lose, then what the hell, at least we died trying."

As of late 2008, Digg.com was far from dead and continues to exemplify the spirit of user-provided-content and community-based Web 2.0 start-ups.

After reading this chapter, you will be able to answer the following:

1. What effect does the "Digg effect" have on Web sites that are featured on Digg.com?

2. What are the positives and negatives to a news site that organizes its stories using user input?

3. How do you think Digg.com generates revenue? How do you think Digg.com will do in the future? What are main threats to its current business?

FIGURE 6.1

Digg.com (as displayed in Internet Explorer 8) is a popular social content Web site.

Based on:

Arrington, M. (2006, March 18). The power of Digg. *Techcrunch.com.* Retrieved June 4, 2008, from http://www. techcrunch.com/2006/03/18/the-power-of-digg.

Digg. (2008, June 2). In *Wikipedia, the free encyclopedia.* Retrieved June 4, 2008, from http://en.wikipedia.org/w/index.php? title=Digg&oldid=216676222.

Railsback, K. (2007, May 1). Digg losing control of their site. *Infoworld.com.* Retrieved June 4, 2008, from http://weblog. infoworld.com/railsback/archives/2007/05/digg_losing_con.html.

Rose, K. (2007, May 1). Digg This: 09-f9-11-02-9d-74-e3-5b-d8-41-56-c5-63-56-88-c0. Retrieved June 4, 2008, from http://blog.digg. com/?p=74.

Defining Web 2.0

Over the past few years, **Web 2.0** has received much attention from the popular press. Typically, the term has been used to express: (1) how technology has enabled integrating more interactive features into Web sites, and (2) the change in strategies of EC-based businesses. In the mid-1990s, fueled by the growth of the Internet and the availability of venture capital, thousands of new e-business models emerged, and entrepreneurs started "dot-com" businesses selling everything from fashions to pet food. However, many of these start-ups didn't have sustainable business models, and, in 2001, a variety of external (e.g., rising interest rates) and internal (e.g., the focus on fast growth rather than on the bottom line) factors led to the collapse of this "dot-com bubble." A consequence of this collapse was the bankruptcy of many of these start-up companies and the evaporation of more than $5 trillion in market value over a two-year period. Many online businesses, however, survived. Also, in the aftermath of the burst of the dot-com bubble, many new online businesses started and became very successful, indicating that e-commerce was far from dead.

One of the key questions asked by business leaders during this period related to identifying what differentiated the businesses that failed (such as online pet supplier Pets.com) from those that survived (such as online retailer Amazon.com). Relatedly, in 2001 when brainstorming for new conference ideas, O'Reilly Media and MediaLive International contrasted early Web business characteristics (called "Web 1.0" capabilities) with current and potentially future capabilities of successful Web-based organizations (called "Web 2.0" capabilities). Table 6.1 contrasts the capabilities and characteristics of the Web 1.0 versus the Web 2.0 eras. In 2006, Tim O'Reilly refined the definition of Web 2.0 as "the business revolution in the computer industry caused by the move to the Internet as a platform and an attempt to understand the rules for success on that new platform." Thus, Web 2.0 is not just about an upgrade in Internet technology, but rather, it is about how the Internet is being used to execute successful business models. Although the term was coined after the dot-com bubble burst, Web 2.0 uses

TABLE 6.1 **Contrasting Web 1.0 to Web 2.0**

Web 1.0	Web 2.0
Banner ads	Keyword ads
Uploading media to a Web site	Uploading and tagging media
Downloading music	Renting movies
Artist producing promo songs	Artist giving away albums
Print encyclopedias	Wikipedia
Personal Web sites	Personal blogs
Domain name squatting	Search engine optimization (SEO)
Buying books online	Writing and publishing online
Bookmarks	Really simple syndication (RSS)
Outsourcing	Crowdsourcing

many older technologies to offer interactive business environments, such as Web Services (from 1998), AJAX (from 1998), and Web content syndication (from 1997), which are underlying many current Web technologies, such as wikis, podcasts, RSS feeds, blogs, and social networking sites. All of these topics will be discussed in detail later in this chapter.

Pillars of Web 2.0

When the dot-com bubble burst in 2001, many believed the Web's usefulness as a business vehicle was over. Time would quickly show, however, that in most cases dot-com failures simply eliminated concepts not well suited to the online environment (remember sites for buying groceries[1]) and made room for those that were. Those dot-com businesses that survived the shake-up had certain characteristics in common (O'Reilly, 2006). This is explained next.

Utilizing the Web as a Platform In Web 2.0, the Internet is not just an add-on to the PC, but it is the platform for a business. Using the Internet, software can be provided as a continually updated service, and businesses can focus on the Long Tails of customer demand (see Chapter 5—Enabling Commerce Using the Internet). Further, successful Web 2.0 sites make use of users' resources. Whereas some Web business sites must add their *own* resources (such as servers) to satisfy increased demand, others take advantage of *users'* resources; thus, as the number of users grows, so does the capacity to satisfy the user base. For example, users are encouraged to download the openSUSE operating system (sponsored by Novell) from other users (and make it available to yet other users) using **peer-to-peer** technology. Peer-to-peer software uses the network bandwidth of all users of the software to improve download performance. As such, Novell reduces the load on its servers while at the same time improving download speeds for users by utilizing a peer-to-peer platform.

Harnessing Collective Intelligence Successful Web 2.0 sites not only provide content; they also allow users to contribute, thus improving the content. For example, Amazon.com engages users by allowing them to post book or product reviews. Likewise, the online encyclopedia Wikipedia is entirely based on its users' contributions. Open-source software is another example of the power of collective intelligence. High-quality software such as the Firefox Web browser, the Linux operating systems, or the OpenOffice office suite are created by thousands of volunteers located all over the world.

Leveraging the Data Many of the most successful online businesses base their success on powerful databases containing tremendous amounts of useful information. For example, Amazon would not be successful without its database of products and customers, and eBay bases its success on gaining valuable business intelligence from its online auction database. Similarly, Google's success is based on its data about Web pages, and increasingly, the data about customers using its search technology and applications. Clearly, for many companies operating in the digital world, data is arguably their most valuable asset.

Implementing Innovative Web Capabilities For successful Web 2.0 companies, technology is key to a competitive advantage. For Google, constantly monitoring and upgrading their systems is crucial. Web 2.0 companies also treat users as codevelopers, learning from their users' behavior to improve products or services (e.g., as more people call Goog411, Google can use the voice data to improve its speech recognition technology). Similarly, *scripting languages* (see the accompanying Technology Briefing) allow simple and dynamic composition of Web 2.0 applications, which eases application development and reduces costs. Because these scripting languages are quick and easy to learn, users can create new applications by combining (or "mashing up") existing Web applications. Together, these technologies can tremendously help in creating a rich user experience; for example, Microsoft uses AJAX technology for its Windows Live suite of

---

[1]Amazon.com recently launched "Amazon Fresh," delivering groceries (including produce, frozen foods, and even alcoholic beverages) to customers in the Seattle area.

services to provide the type of functionality usually reserved for desktop applications (such as right clicking objects in an e-mail message, dragging and dropping elements to create customized home pages, or formatting text using keyboard shortcuts).

Although this list of key Web 2.0 characteristics is not exhaustive, it can help to assess the potential for success of a new online venture. Needless to say, an organization that is successfully deploying all of these characteristics will be very likely to succeed. Nevertheless, many successful Web 2.0 ventures succeed by excelling at only one or two of these characteristics. Failure would be likely to occur if a venture was unable to excel in any, or were simply mediocre at many.

Key Web 2.0 Capabilities

One of the most important pillars of Web 2.0 is the Web as a platform. Although Web 2.0 is more than aesthetics and functionality, both have played an important role in the identity of Web 2.0. The ability for Web 2.0 sites to offer a rich Internet experience stems from technologies such as AJAX, Adobe Flash, Microsoft's Silverlight, Java, and others. The key capability of these technologies is that they allow parts of the Web page to be refreshed without needing to refresh the entire page. For example, Washington State University's athletics team, the Cougars, uses a combination of technologies including Adobe Flash and Java to create a rich multimedia Web site, allowing visitors to follow football games on the Internet in real-time, or review the entire game at a later time (see Figure 6.2). NBC's site dedicated to the 2008 Olympic Games in Beijing, China, offered a similar rich media experience. In this case, users could simultaneously watch live video, archived video, and real-time statistics for any given event in a single Web page.

Web Services For companies operating in the digital world, online collaboration with suppliers, business partners, and customers is crucial to being successful. To enable seamless collaboration, organizations need to allow outsiders access to their data, typically using the Internet. However, the Internet was originally designed to enable human to computer interaction, with Web pages being a collection of text that hyperlinked to other Web pages. A computer could not use data from other computers without explicit knowledge of the physical location and the security configuration of the remote computer network. Today, **Web services** are one of the critical components of sharing data. Web

FIGURE 6.2

The Washington State Cougars use Web 2.0 technologies to provide a rich user experience (as displayed in the Firefox browser).

services allow data to be accessed without intimate knowledge of other organizations' systems, enabling machine-to-machine interaction over the Internet. The central idea behind Web services is that *any device* can use *any network* to access *any service* (see Figure 6.3). A Web service can offer several benefits for organizations, including:

1. Utilizing the existing Internet infrastructure (i.e., no new technologies are needed).
2. Accessing remote or local data without having to know the complexities of this access.
3. Creating unique and dynamic applications quickly and easily.

Many organizations have recognized the power and benefits from offering free Web services to the public, with an increasing number of organizations offering free access to parts of their databases. Why are companies doing this? By providing access to useful Web services, organizations build and strengthen customer relationships, providing a base for revenue-generating services. For example, Facebook.com has been using this idea to gain market share in the competitive social networking market space. Also, Google has perfected this strategy by offering a host of Web services to the public, including:

- Android: A Web service used for building mobile phone applications
- Search: A Web service allowing users to create customized search features in Google
- Calendar: A Web service for managing personal calendars
- Maps: A Web service used to integrate Google's mapping system into Web sites
- OpenSocial: A Web service designed to allow users to build applications that work with multiple social communities such as Friendster.com and MySpace.com.

Widgets Widgets provide a clear example of how Web 2.0 technology has changed the look and feel of the Web pages. Specifically, **widgets** are small interactive tools used for a single purpose such as taking notes, viewing pictures, or simply displaying a clock. Widgets can either be placed on a desktop or be integrated into a Web page (see Figure 6.4). Apple pioneered the concept of widgets in its early version of the Mac operating system, and Microsoft followed by developing its active desktop environment. Widgets have now moved to the Web platform where they can access data from Web sites to do more complicated things such as translate languages, provide weather forecasts, display stock prices, and stream music. Often, widgets use Web services to pull their information from a remote source, such as Weather.com for weather information or Marketwatch.com for stock market information. Widgets currently have no standard format. For example, a Google developed

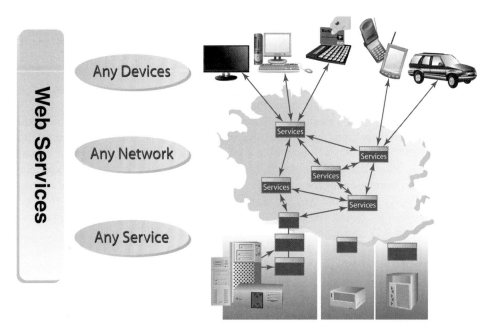

FIGURE 6.3

Web services allow any device to use any network to access any service.

FIGURE 6.4

Users can choose between a variety of widgets to create a personalized "iGoogle" home page.

widget can only run on a Google Web page or a Google desktop widget engine; a Yahoo!-developed widget can only run on Yahoo!'s platforms. The World Wide Web Consortium (W3C) is currently working toward a standard so that all widgets will run on any platform or Web page.

Mashups Together, Web services and widgets enable the creation of **mashups.** The idea of mashups came from popular music where many songs are produced by mixing two or more existing songs together; in Web 2.0 terminology, a mashup is a new application (or Web site) that integrates one or more Web services. One Web service frequently used to display geospatial information in mashups is Google Maps. For instance, Craigslist developed a dynamic map of all available apartments in the United States (www.housingmaps.com). Similarly, during the 2007 wildfires in Southern California, KPBS, San Diego's local public television station, created a mashup displaying the locations of the fires, evacuation zones, and emergency shelters, such that residents and friends and family members could easily get the latest information on the situation. Everyblock.com is a mashup of Web services aggregating content from newspapers, blogs, and government databases to enable citizens of cities such as Chicago, New York, and Seattle to find out what's happening in their neighborhoods (see Figure 6.5), including crime information, restaurant inspections, or local photos posted on Flickr. For a list of useful mashups, visit www.programmableweb.com.

There are several large organizations that see value in end users creating unique applications using other's data. Yahoo! and Microsoft have specialized Web editors that allow users to create mashups from several data sources. Yahoo! was one of the first to offer this service (called "Yahoo! Pipes"), providing a graphical user interface that can aggregate RSS feeds (described later), Web services, or Web pages. The software works by connecting "pipes" of information together to create a single Web page that fits the user's needs. Microsoft's Popfly (see Figure 6.6) is a similar project, offering pre-configured "blocks" that allow the user to connect feeds. The goal of both projects is to allow a typical nonprogrammer Web user to create unique Web sites from existing Web content.

Tools for Collaboration

If you have ever worked on a team project for your class (and you probably have), you have noticed that there are many different communication needs such as talking, sharing documents, or making decisions. Just as there are many things to discuss within your team project,

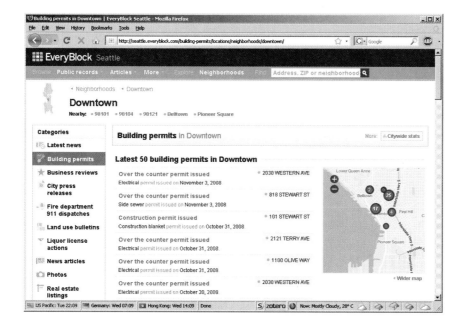

FIGURE 6.5

Everyblock.com is a mashup
of Web services aggregating
content from newspapers, blogs,
and government databases,
enabling citizens of cities
such as Chicago, New York,
and Seattle to find out
what's happening in their
neighborhoods.

there are also many ways that you can communicate and collaborate. In fact, the Internet and various Web 2.0 technologies provide many capabilities that have forever transformed the way teams can work together. Here, we present the major categories of collaboration tools (see Table 6.2), followed by an examination of two popular collaboration environments.

Web-Based Collaboration Tools For organizations and individuals, **Web-based collaboration tools** can offer a number of benefits. For example, Web-based collaboration tools allow for easy access and easy transferability from one person to another, as the tools can run on any computer with a Web browser and Internet connectivity. Further, users don't have to e-mail documents back and forth or worry about having the latest version of the software installed. On the other hand, using Web-based collaboration tools requires a live Internet connection to work on shared documents, and thus users may not be able to

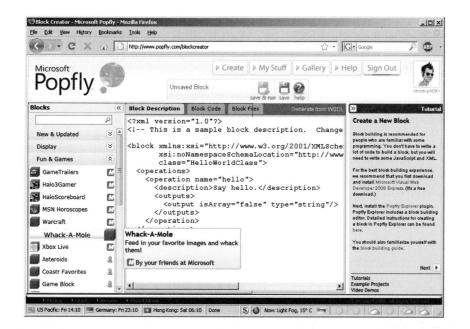

FIGURE 6.6

Microsoft's Popfly allows end
users to create their own
mashups.

TABLE 6.2 **Categories of Collaborative Tools**

Title	Description	Instances	Examples
Electronic Communication Tools	Tools allowing users to send files, documents, and pictures to each other and share information.	Fax, e-mail, voice mail, blogs, wikis, static Web sites.	MS Outlook, Blogger.com, Wikipedia.com
Electronic Conferencing Tools	Tools allowing information sharing and rich interactions between users.	Internet forums, instant messaging, application sharing, video conferencing.	Apple Discussion Forum, Skype, AOL IM, WebEx
Collaboration Management Tools	Tools used to facilitate virtual or co-located meetings and manage group activities.	Electronic calendars, knowledge management systems, intranets, online document systems.	Google Docs, MS Office Live, MS SharePoint

work when traveling or when having Internet connectivity problems. Also, the applications are limited in what they can do. For example, an online spreadsheet can only do basic formulas. Table 6.3 outlines various benefits and risks of Web-based collaboration tools.

Organizations and individuals can choose from different options for using Web 2.0 collaboration tools. In the following sections, we will discuss collaboration tools offered by Google and Microsoft, the major applications in use today.

GOOGLE APPS. Google Apps is a family of Web-based collaboration tools designed to function similar to an offline office software suite, while also allowing for easy collaboration (see Figure 6.7). The following outlines various Google Apps tools:

1. Gmail: a Web-based e-mail client allowing users to send large attachments and offering large storage space and superior filing and search capabilities; users can select a custom domain name for an additional fee (i.e., joe@outfitter.com).
2. Google Calendar: a Web-based collaborative calendar that allows users to share events, send invitations to events, subscribe to public calendars for new events (e.g., Netflix's calendar for new DVD releases), and so on.

TABLE 6.3 **Benefits and Risks of Web-Based Collaboration Tools**

Domain	Benefit	Risk
IT	Reduced costs and risks when using preexisting, easily deployed, and low cost Web-based tools (versus in-house developed tools).	Loss of control regarding data and service quality (data and tools will likely reside on the provider's server).
Organization	Tools are easy to use, facilitating widespread adoption throughout an organization.	Little or no documentation, training, or support for system complexities or problems.
Competition	More efficient and effective than e-mail, FTP, or legacy collaboration tools; potentially speeding up product development cycles and enabling quick responses to competitors' actions.	Security and compliance policies are nearly impossible to enforce, which may increase the possibility of exposing sensitive corporate data; increased threat of industrial espionage.
Upgrade Cycles	No need to purchase software upgrades.	Tools and features in the collaboration environment can change without notice, potentially causing problems with users and corporate IT strategy.

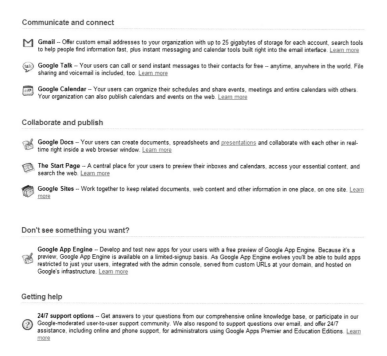

FIGURE 6.7

Google offers a variety of collaboration tools.

3. Google Talk: an instant messaging client.
4. Google Docs: an online office suite comprised of a spreadsheet application, a word processor, and a presentation application. The documents, spreadsheet, and presentations can be created in the Web application or imported from other tools (e.g., Microsoft Office).
5. Google Sites: An enterprise-level collaboration tool that allows users to create group Web sites and share team information.

A variety of other providers offer similar Web-based collaboration tools (see Table 6.4).

Although there are several Web-based office suites available, Google Apps has been adopted by many users. Backed by Google, one of the world's most recognized companies, Google Apps are free for individual users and educational institutions and are provided on a per-user fee for commercial organizations. In fact, in October of 2006, Lakehead University in Thunder Bay, Canada, adopted Google Apps for all of its 38,000 users. Similarly, in 2008, Boise State University in Boise, Idaho, migrated from the Novell Groupwise e-mail system to GMail for all faculty, staff, and students, and rolled out Google Apps for document sharing and collaboration.

MICROSOFT SHAREPOINT AND GROOVE. Microsoft has also integrated collaboration capabilities into several of its current business tools, including Microsoft SharePoint and Microsoft Groove. In contrast to stand-alone Web collaboration tools such as Google

TABLE 6.4 Web-Based Collaboration Tools

Type	Name
Spreadsheets	Bad Blue, EditGrid, Simple Sheets, Google Docs, Zoho Sheets
Word processors	ajaxWrite, Adobe's Buzzword, Think Free, Zoho Writer, Google Docs, ZCubes
Presentation	PresenterNet, Slide, vMix, Acrobat Connect, Google Docs, Zoho Show
Office suites	eDesk Online, Zoho, Share Office, Google Docs
Project	Trac, eGroupWare, Open-Xchange, dotProject

Docs, Microsoft SharePoint is a document management platform that can be used to host Web sites that enable shared workspaces and integrate other collaborative applications such as wikis and blogs. SharePoint also includes workflow functionality such as to-do lists, discussion boards, and messaging alerts. Because SharePoint has been designed to be easily customizable, it has been installed in a variety of businesses, which can personalize the collaborative SharePoint Web sites to meet their needs. For example, Mary Kay Cosmetics uses SharePoint to distribute product and company information to its over 30,000 Canadian consultants. Whereas SharePoint's strength is content management in organizations, Microsoft Groove is designed specifically for working in small teams. Groove is an application that allows secure access to workspaces, where users can share calendars, discussions, files, pictures, and so on (see Figure 6.8). In fact, the team that wrote and developed this book used Groove as a shared workspace.

Content Management Systems

A **content management system** allows users to publish, edit, version track, and retrieve digital information (or *content*, such as documents, images, audio files, videos, or anything that can be digitized). A content management system allows the assignment of different roles for different users; some users can create and edit content, others can edit but not create, and yet others can only view content contained in the system. Typical roles in a content management system include:

- Creator—responsible for publishing new information.
- Editor—responsible for editing the content into a final form.
- Administrator—responsible for managing account access levels to the digital information.
- Guest—a person who can only view the digital information.

Content management systems are also known by several other names, including digital asset management system, document management system, and enterprise content system. In addition to Microsoft SharePoint, which offers extensive content management capabilities (see Figure 6.9), IBM and Adobe are major players in this market space. For example, the All England Lawn Tennis and Croquet Club, the host of the annual Wimbledon tennis tournament, selected IBM's content management system to help distribute interactive digital content (such as videos) to fans worldwide. Similarly, as more and more content in the health care industry is stored in digital format, content management systems are becoming very valuable. CIGNA Healthcare, one of the first health

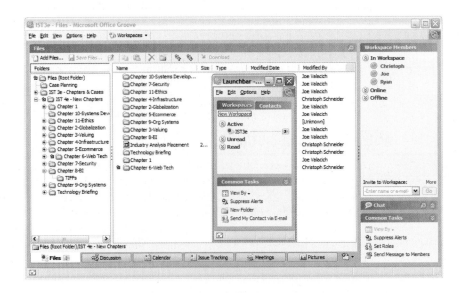

FIGURE 6.9

Washington State University uses the Microsoft SharePoint content management system to provide students and faculty with access to important information.

management organizations (HMO) to use Adobe's content management system to publish, edit, share, and secure health information, estimates that changing to a content management system saves millions, which can ultimately help improve the patients' quality of care.

The Web of the Future

Web technologies and collaboration are ever evolving topics, and many developments have yet to be fully realized. This section briefly forecasts future capabilities of the Web, in particular, focusing on efforts to create the semantic Web and characteristics of Web 3.0.

Semantic Web   Since the Web opened up for public use, the number of Web pages and sites has grown exponentially. Although this increase in Web pages should mean that we have ever more information at our fingertips, it also means that the information is increasingly harder to find. What if the information on the Web was organized in a way that users could more easily find information or related media? At present, search engines cannot help to solve this formidable task, as Web pages can be understood by people, but not by computers. For example, when you now go to Google.com and search for "what eats penguins," it returns Web sites that may have this information but it is more likely to have the words or key terms, "what" and "eats" and "penguins." For Larry Page, cofounder of Google, the perfect search engine would return only *one* result, namely, the one page that provides the best answer to the user's query. Currently, however, search engines are not sophisticated enough to be able to find and integrate information presented on Web pages. The **semantic Web**, originally envisioned by one of the founders of the Internet, Tim Berners-Lee, is a set of design principles that will allow computers to be able to better index Web sites, topics, and subjects. When Web pages are designed using semantic principles, computers will be able to read the pages, and search engines will be able to give richer and more accurate answers. Google Sets (labs.google.com/sets) provides an example of an attempt at using a search engine to categorize data using semantic Web principles. For example, when entering key words such as Ford, Audi, GMC, and Volvo into the Google Sets engine, Google Sets predicts other items belonging to the set (in this case, this would be other car brands such as Mercedes, Fiat, Saturn, and so on). Although

Ethical Dilemma

Virtual Reality People

Virtual reality (VR) is not limited just to a computer-generated environment where participants wear special headsets and other gear that allows them to interact with virtual situations. We experience virtual reality when we watch television or play computer games. Nature shows on television are enjoyed from the comfort of our living rooms, and there are no biting mosquitoes and gnats, and we don't get hot and sweaty hiking for miles, nor dunked in icy streams.

We all know by now that too much time spent watching television or using computers and game consoles is bad for our health, since the sedentary lifestyle leads to obesity, diabetes, deteriorating muscles and social lives, and other unhealthy conditions. But what happens when virtual reality becomes more desirable than experiencing nature in the wild?

Researchers Oliver Pergams and Patricia Zaradic reported in a February 2008 edition of the *Proceedings of the National Academy of Sciences* that camping, fishing, and visitors to national parks were all declining.

"Declining nature participation has crucial implications for current conservation efforts," Pergams and Zaradic wrote. "We think it probable that any major decline in the value placed on natural areas and experiences will greatly reduce the value people place on biodiversity conservation."

Pergams and Zaradic called the observed shift away from outdoor activities particularly damaging to children, and they refer to the preference for indoor, VR activities as "videophilia."

By studying visits to national and state parks and the issuance of hunting and fishing licenses, the researchers documented declines of between 18 percent and 25 percent in various types of outdoor recreation:

- The decline, found in both the United States and Japan, apparently began in the 1980s and 1990s, the period of rapid growth of video games.
- The number of people fishing peaked in 1981 and had declined 25 percent by 2005. The number of hunters stayed relatively stable, possibly because deer populations across the United States exploded.
- Visits to U.S. national parks peaked in 1987, but had dropped 23 percent by 2006. Similarly, visits to Japan's national parks dropped by 18 percent between 1991 and 2005.
- Hiking on the Appalachian Trail peaked in 2000 and was down 18 percent by 2005.

Ethical implications of videophilia concern the fact that if people do, indeed, prefer virtual nature to reality, will nature conservation and concern for our natural environment deteriorate to the point that we no longer have an enjoyable and productive natural environment? It seems unlikely, with all the hullabaloo about going "green" in the twenty-first century, but it may be worth studying as Web 2.0 assumes a more prominent place in our lives.

Based on:

Pergams, O. R. W., & Zaradic, P. A. (2008). Evidence for a fundamental and pervasive shift away from nature-based recreation. *Proceedings of the National Academy of Sciences, 105,* 7, pp. 2295–2300.

---

the semantic Web is largely unrealized, Google's efforts show that the semantic Web experience is getting closer.

Web 3.0 In many ways, Web 2.0 has already replaced Web 1.0, and the question is, What will replace Web 2.0? For some, Web 2.0 is just a short transitionary period before the next wave of Internet technologies, which is predicted to last from 2010 to 2020. There are several ideas on what this next wave, Web 3.0, will entail. Eric Schmidt, CEO of Google views **Web 3.0** as technologies providing for ubiquitous data access where the data is viewed as being in a "cloud," and applications that access this data can be run on any device, PC, or mobile phone. Although there are different points of view on what will

Powerful Partnerships

Digg's Kevin Rose and Jay Adelson

Kevin Rose, born February 21, 1977, studied computers and animation in high school in Las Vegas, Nevada, and attended the University of Nevada Las Vegas, studying computer science until he dropped out in 1999 to take part in the dot-com boom.

Rose was working in Los Angeles in 2003, hosting and contributing content to the TechTV show *The Screen Saver,* when he set up an interview with Jay Adelson, the founder and chief technology officer of data center company Equinix Inc. The two became friends, and in 2004, Rose came up with the idea of Digg, a social content

FIGURE 6.10

Digg's Kevin Rose and Jay Adelson.

Web site where users would post the content—news stories and links. Rose offered Adelson the position of CEO of Digg, and Adelson accepted. (Adelson corrects interviewers who write that he helped found Digg. Rose founded Digg.com, but Adelson serves as its CEO.) Rose was also involved in founding the Internet start-ups Revision3 and Pownce. Today, Rose spends much of his time podcasting, climbing, and inventing Digg's next generation features.

Jay Adelson, born September 7, 1970, was suckered out of the world of film and broadcasting and into the Internet industry to found Equinix Inc. in 1998. When he accepted the job as Digg's CEO, it meant leaving his wife and three children in New York while he commuted to Digg's San Francisco headquarters. Adelson, seven years older than Rose, has commented that he is the "adult" of the pair, reminding Rose to pull up his jeans to cover his boxers on a number of occasions. (Advice that he claims Rose usually ignores.) Information about Adelson at the Digg Web site states: "Jay has testified before Congress and advised the government and other groups with his knowledge of the Internet's workings, and he habitually speaks at industry events and conferences."

Since the advent of Equinix and Digg, both Adelson and Rose continue to be involved in other successful Web 2.0 start-ups.

Based on:

Anonymous (n.d.). Jay Adelson—chief executive officer. Retrieved June 5, 2008, from http://digg.com/about/jay.

Anonymous (n.d.). Kevin Rose—founder and chief architect. Retrieved June 5, 2008, from http://digg.com/about/Kevin.

Grossman, L. (2008, May 5). Jay Adelson—The 2008 *Time* 100. *Time.com.* Retrieved June 5, 2008, from http://www.time.com/time/specials/2007/article/0,28804,1733748_1733758_1736343,00.html.

Jay Adelson. (2008, April 12). In *Wikipedia, the free encyclopedia.* Retrieved June 5, 2008, from http://en.wikipedia.org/w/index.php?title=Jay_Adelson&oldid=205169257.

Kevin Rose. (2008, June 2). In *Wikipedia, the free encyclopedia.* Retrieved June 5, 2008, from http://en.wikipedia.org/w/index.php?title=Kevin_Rose&oldid=216727691.

Lacy, S., & J. Hempel (2006, August 14). Valley boys. *BusinessWeek.* Retrieved June 5, 2008, from http://www.businessweek.com/magazine/content/06_33/b3997001.htm.

dominate Web 3.0, there are certain topics that are universally accepted as coming trends. These topics include:

1. ***The World Wide Database***—The ability for databases to be distributed and accessed from anywhere
2. ***Open Technologies***—The design of Web sites and other software so that they can be easily integrated
3. ***Open ID***—The provision of an online identity that can easily be ported to mobile devices, PCs, and more, allowing for easy authentication across different Web sites
4. ***Integration of Legacy Devices***—The ability to use current mobile devices such as iPhones, laptops, and so on, as credit cards, tickets, and reservations
5. ***Intelligent applications***—The use of agents (discussed in Chapter 8—Enhancing Business Intelligence Using Information Systems), machine learning, and semantic Web concepts to complete intelligent tasks for users

Although you may have already seen some of these emerging technologies in practice, the coming trends involve true integration of the devices and connectivity to create powerful socially aware Internet appliances. Stay tuned to see what the future holds.

False Stories Receive Attention: Madness of the Crowds

With Digg.com's popularity has come admonishments for users to be more responsible. So many visitors are now posting stories, URL links, and comments that their opinions and statements can actually move others to action. For example:

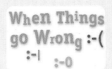

1. In 2007, a Digg user posted a story stating that Nancy Pelosi, the U.S. Speaker of the House of Representatives, wanted to hear the opinions of Americans regarding the possible impeachment of President George W. Bush and Vice President Dick Cheney. Her House of Representatives telephone number was listed, and readers were encouraged to call and express their support for impeachment.
2. A Digg user accused Steve Mallett, a writer for the Fox News O'Reilly show, of stealing code from Digg.
3. A Digg user posted encryption-busting code for HD-DVD and Blu-ray disks. When Digg's management took the posts containing the code down, users revolted, flooding the site with messages and comments containing the code.

In each of the above cases, the stories became popular on Digg, and the influence of the crowd is evident:

- Nancy Pelosi was flooded with telephone messages, but the message posted on Digg was false. No impeachment plan was in the works, and no plea for public opinion.
- Steve Mallett did not steal code from Digg; rather, he used material in his blog that he thought was reliable, but did contain code that had been stolen from Digg. Although Mallett was unjustly accused, he was flooded with angry e-mails from those who believed the tale.
- Digg's users so influenced the site's management that they took a risk in leaving up the legally protected DVD encryption code.

The above Digg incidents illustrate what blog writer Nat Torkington calls a "classic Web 2.0 problem: It's hard to aggregate the wisdom of the crowd without aggregating their madness as well."

If "aggregating the wisdom of the crowd" is to be used to full advantage, Digg users and others who post observations and stories on the Web will need to learn what journalists have known for years—without reputable sources for the information you post, it becomes fodder for the rumor mill and nothing more.

Based on:

Chen, D. (2007, May 7). The power of Digg: With great power comes great responsibility. Retrieved June 5, 2008, from http://nomorequo.blogspot.com/2007/05/power-of-digg-with-great-power-comes.html.

Marshall, M. (2006, January 10). Digg suffers madness of crowds . . . and of open source movement. *Siliconbeat.com.* Retrieved June 5, 2008, from http://www.siliconbeat.com/entries/2006/01/10/digg_suffers_madness_of_crowdsand_of_open_source_movement.html.

Torkington, N. (2006, January 9). Digging the madness of the crowds. *O'Reilly Radar.* Retrieved June 5, 2008, from http://radar.oreilly.com/archives/2006/01/digging-the-madness-of-crowds.html.

Empowering Individuals with Web 2.0

In the new Web environment, the users are central and no longer just passive viewers of information. Web sites are embracing their users to help create content, to review products, and even edit stories. Users are adding value to Web sites by contributing to *wikis*, or *tagging* sites or images. Web 2.0 allows everyone to publish original content using *blogs*, *netcasts*, or *printing-on-demand* (see Figure 6.11). Publishing has gone from a strictly business-to-consumer domain to a viable consumer-to-consumer practice, allowing people to voice their thoughts or opinions with little or no editorial review (a practice known as **self-publishing**). Because of the global flattening discussed in Chapter 2—Fueling Globalization Using Information Systems—people can now write, edit, and even publish without ever leaving their home. This is another example of a business model focusing on the "Long Tails." Rather than focusing on the mass market, people can publish work that may or may not appeal to the mainstream. In the remainder of this section, we examine several ways that Web 2.0 capabilities are empowering individuals.

Wikis

Ever since the inception of the online encyclopedia Wikipedia, wikis have become mainstream and are used for a variety of collaboration tasks. As discussed in Chapter 2, a wiki is a Web site allowing people to post, add, edit, comment, and access information. In contrast to a regular Web site, a wiki is linked to a database keeping a history of all prior versions and changes, and thus, a wiki allows viewing prior versions of the site, as well as reversing any changes made to the content. The idea behind wikis is that they allow anyone to contribute information or edit others' contributions. Whereas some wikis can be public and open to anyone who wished to contribute, others are private so only certain registered users can contribute. The most popular wiki is the online encyclopedia **Wikipedia**, which has over 10 million articles in 253 languages.[2] These articles have been created by registered users of Wikipedia, and almost any of these articles can be edited by either anonymous or registered users. By allowing easy access, Wikipedia has grown exponentially in a short amount of time. However, Wikipedia is not without its critics. Some argue that by allowing anyone to edit and create an article, a systematic bias in the content can occur. This includes the ability for users to add misinformation that is hard to verify. For example, in January of 2006, it was revealed that staffers for several congressmen deleted negative information about their particular bosses while adding negative comments to members of the other party. Sometimes, so-called "wiki wars" arise, where contributors continuously edit each others' posts. Also, Wikipedia has been found to have a significant cultural bias, as most contributors are males from either North America or Europe. Since the information is often not backed by verifiable sources, Wikipedia is not considered a credible source, and many universities discourage users from citing Wikipedia. In fact, in some instances professors have been failing students for using Wikipedia as their primary (or only) source. Wikipedia openly acknowledges this situation and encourages users to check the facts against multiple sources,

Wikis have been used for many more things than just an online encyclopedia. The ability for users to contribute and edit content has a wide variety of applications such as designing software, helping people find media, and even helping people play video games.

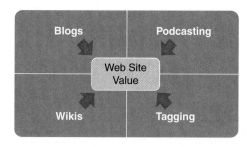

[2]Wikipedia. (2008, May 11). In *Wikipedia, the free encyclopedia*. Retrieved May 12, 2008, from http://en.wikipedia.org/w/index.php?title=Wikipedia&oldid=211701674.

FIGURE 6.11

In Web 2.0, users can add value in various ways.

TABLE 6.6 **Examples of Wikis**

Title	Description
Welker's Wikinomics (http://welkerswikinomics.wetpaint.com)	A learning wiki for understanding concepts in Advanced Placement Economics.
Second Life Wiki (http://wiki.secondlife.com/wiki/Main_Page)	A wiki dedicated to the Massive Multiplayer game Second Life.
Visual FoxPro Wiki (http://fox.wikis.com)	A wiki designed to help with questions on creating database applications using Microsoft's Visual FoxPro programming language.
WikiDot (http://www.wikidot.com)	A site providing free wiki hosting to everyone (also known as wiki farm).
Lostpedia (http://www.lostpedia.com)	A wiki for the fans of the NBC TV show *Lost*.
Muppet Wiki (http://muppet.wikia.com)	A wiki for Jim Henson's Muppets.

In fact, many organizations are using wiki technology to create internal knowledge repositories. Table 6.6 lists examples of several different uses of wikis.

Tagging

Another way that users can contribute and add value to Web sites is known as **tagging**, or adding descriptive information to Web site content. In other words, tagging is the practice of describing a piece of information such as a map, a picture, or a Web page by adding key words or relevant terms, thus making it searchable. Figure 6.12 shows some popular key words and terms that have been used to tag the concept "Web 2.0." Tags are commonly added to pictures and videos in Web sites such as Flickr, a picture and video hosting Web site that allows users to upload their content. As of May 2008, Flickr, owned by Yahoo!, boasted millions of active users and over 2 billion pieces of media, making it all but impossible to find images related to a certain topic. However, because many of the images have been tagged by users, they can be easily searched by various descriptive tags (see Figure 6.13). Another popular Web site that relies on users to tag content is the cleverly named site Del.icio.us. Del.icio.us is a bookmarking site that allows users to tag, share, and save bookmarks to Web sites. Del.icio.us, also owned by Yahoo!, combines the key words added to the bookmarks by the users to recommend Web sites based on common interests.

Geo-tagging Tagging information to maps, also known as **geo-tagging**, has also become a common practice on the Web. Google Maps, for example, allows users to add pictures or information such as restaurant reviews to its maps. By allowing geo-tagging, Google can offer a map experience with pictures of attractions, reviews, and things to do without having to take a single picture or write a single review themselves.

FIGURE 6.12

Key words commonly associated with Web 2.0.

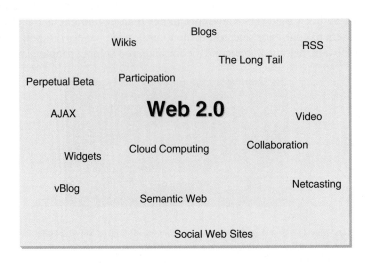

FIGURE 6.13

Users can search images by tags on Flickr.com

Reproduced with permission of 2008 by Yahoo! Inc. YAHOO! and the YAHOO! logo are trademarks of Yahoo! Inc.

Metadata **Metadata** can be simply thought of as data about data (see Table 6.8). For example. if you were to search Google for "42," what are the possible Web sites that it would return? Could it be someone's height in inches, someone's apartment number, or even the answer to the ultimate question of life, the universe, and everything? By specifying the metadata we can understand the context and meaning of the data. Tagging is one form of manually adding metadata to pieces of information. For example, by adding the key words "Washington State Basketball" to a picture on Flickr, we are adding metadata about the context of the picture. This metadata will help return this picture as one of the results whenever a user searches Flickr for basketball pictures. Another example of metadata is the date a picture was taken, allowing a user to search pictures taken within a certain time period.

Blogging

In addition to contributing to wikis or tagging images on sites such as Flickr, users can express their views, opinions, or experiences through blogs. Blogging originally started out as a novice's way of expressing themselves using very simple Web pages. **Blogging** (or **Weblogging**) is the process of creating an online text diary (i.e., a **blog**, or **Web log**) made up of chronological entries that comment on everything from one's everyday life, to wine and food, or even computer problems (see Figure 6.14). Rather than trying to produce physical books to sell or use as gifts, bloggers (i.e., the people maintaining blogs) merely want to share stories about their lives or voice their opinions. Blogging has exploded into its own industry, and many companies and even the mainstream media embrace blogging (see Table 6.5). Engadget.com is one instance of a blogging business. Started in 2004 and later bought by AOL in 2005, Engadget.com focuses on news and rumors from the customer electronics and gadgets areas. Engadget.com now employs several story editors

TABLE 6.8 **Metadata Examples**

Data	Metadata
42	Inches
Leopard	Operating system
Capri	Model of car
Louis Louis	Song title
Gibson	Guitar
Latitude	Laptop

FIGURE 6.14

A young woman updates her blog.

and a multitude of reporters to cover the electronics industry. The influence in blogging has also hit the mainstream media. Many traditional media giants, such as CNN, now use blogs to paint a richer picture of the stories they produce. Anderson Cooper, one of CNN's anchors, currently edits and writes for CNN's flagship blog called Anderson Cooper 360. There are now blogs for corporations, such as Google's Corporate Blog, used by company executives to give their views on the industry and their organization.

TABLE 6.5 **Examples of Prominent Blogs**

Type of Blog	Example	Description
Technology	www.engadget.com	Consumer electronics blog
	www.cnet.com/macalop	Apple news and rumor site
	www.roughtype.com	Blog of Nicholas Carr, author of the book *IT Doesn't Matter* and former executive editor of the *Harvard Business Review*
Financial	www.marketbeat.com	*Wall Street Journal's* David Gaffen reports on stock market happenings
	www.dvorak.org/blog	John Dvorak from *Market Watch* reports on technology stocks
Entertainment	www.perezhilton.com	A gossip and news blog run by TV personality Mario Armando Lavandeira Jr.
	www.tmz.com	A celebrity gossip site started by Warner Brothers and AOL that now has its own VH1 television show
Political	www.nationalreview.com/thecorner	A blog run by *The National Review*, a magazine started in 1955 by William F. Buckley
	www.huffingtonpost.com	One of the most powerful political blogs. The Huffington Post, founded by Arianna Huffington, won the "Webby Award" as best political blog in 2006 and 2008.

Blogs have infiltrated small, medium, and large organizations and have become important voices that can sway public opinion. One such example of the power of blogging is the 2004 election scandal known as "Rathergate." Dan Rather, appearing on *60 Minutes,* reported on some suspect findings concerning President George W. Bush's record of military service. Bloggers soon after (correctly) reported that the documents used in this news story were falsified. Without the bloggers' visibility, this misrepresentation could have gone unnoticed. Because of the bloggers' reports, Dan Rather resigned from *60 Minutes,* and some say that this eventually caused his dismissal from CBS News.

Blogs are not without controversy. Nicholas Carr, noted technology journalist (and active blogger himself), classifies blogging as the **"amateurization" of journalism**. Often the value of blogging is the ability to bring breaking news to the public in the fastest possible way. By doing so, some bloggers cut journalistic corners, rendering some of the posts on the blogs less than accurate. For example, in May of 2007, Engadget.com reported that Apple's iPhone and OSX operating system were going to be delayed. This news spurred a 4 percent downturn in Apple's stock price in less than twenty minutes. Soon after the story was released, users questioned the validity of the story, and Engadget.com retracted the story. Further, blogs have been criticized for frequently providing the biased opinions of the writers, particularly because many of the authors' sources cannot or have not been verified.

Nevertheless, Blogs have massively influenced the way in which people gather and consume information. In fact, turning to free information from blogs and other online sources, many readers have cancelled newspaper subscriptions. In turn, diminishing readership in traditional newspapers has enticed advertisers to begin to withdraw from this traditional medium, leading to budget cuts and layoffs at reputable newspapers such as the *San Francisco Chronicle, New York Times, Washington Times,* and many others; in December 2008, newspaper giant Tribune Co., owner of the *Los Angeles Times,* the *Chicago Tribune,* and other newspapers, was forced to file for Chapter 11 bankruptcy protection, facing dwindling advertising revenues and a huge debt burden. Unfortunately, and ironically, this may erode the very sources that many bloggers base their information on. To show just how severe this problem is today, a Google Maps Web service has been created to visually show where layoffs are occurring at newspapers across the United States (http://graphicdesignr.net/papercuts). These examples show both the power of the blogs and some of the problems associated with them. The influence of blogs has also been called the power of the **blogosphere** (i.e., the community of all blogs).

Netcasts

Despite widespread availability of the Internet, access to blogs (consisting of written text) and other Web resources is often difficult or impossible when physically traveling. Just as Apple's iPods, Microsoft's Zune, and other digital music players have transformed the way people listen to music while on the go, they are also transforming how people can consume information that was previously only available when accessing the Internet. **Netcasting** (or **podcasting**) is the distribution of digital media, such as audio or video files via *syndication feeds* for playback on digital media players. The term podcasting, derived from combining the terms "broadcasting" and "iPod," is a misnomer, as **netcasts** (or **podcasts**) can be played on a variety of devices in addition to Apple's iPods. As with blogging, netcasting has grown substantially, with traditional media organizations now podcasting everything from NPR radio shows, to Fox's *Family Guy,* to the *Oprah Winfrey Show* (see Figure 6.15). All of this is made possible using syndication feeds that allow netcast publishers (called **netcasters**) to publish and push current shows to the watchers/listeners. In addition to media organizations and independent netcasters, the educational sector uses netcasts for providing students access to lectures, lab demonstrations, or sports events; this allows students to review lectures or prepare for class during their morning and evening commutes. In 2007, Apple launched iTunes U, which offers free content provided by major U.S. universities such as Stanford, Berkeley, and MIT.

Real Simple Syndication **Real Simple Syndication (RSS)** is a family of syndication feeds used to publish the most current blogs, podcasts, videos, and news stories. RSS feeds are offered by organizations so that the users can view the most current information, and users can subscribe to RSS feeds from different sources. Rather than users actively having

FIGURE 6.15

Students watch a video netcast on their iPod.

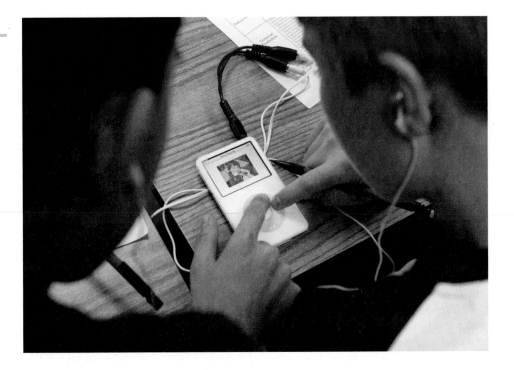

to check multiple sources for the latest news, RSS readers automatically check the feeds for updated content. RSS feeds typically contain a synopsis of a document or the full text. For example, CNN.com publishes RSS feeds for each of its areas, such as world news, sports news, and entertainment news, and NBC uses RSS feeds to allow viewers to download the most current version of shows such as *Meet the Press* and *NBC's Nightly News*.

RSS feeds can be read by most Web browsers (see Figure 6.16) and even e-mail clients such as Microsoft's Outlook, allowing users to browse different feeds as they would browse different bookmarks. Similarly, iGoogle, Google's personalized home page, allows users to add multiple RSS feeds to a single page. Finally, there are several stand-alone applications that can aggregate RSS feeds such as NewsBreak for Windows Mobile users, Liferea for Linux users, and Attensa for Mac users.

Printing-On-Demand

In addition to offering online distribution of content through blogs and netcasts, Web 2.0 facilitates self-publishing for everyday people. Traditionally, self-publishing refers to the publishing of original material (such as books) by an author, which tended to be a risky

FIGURE 6.16

RSS feeds can be displayed by most Web browsers.

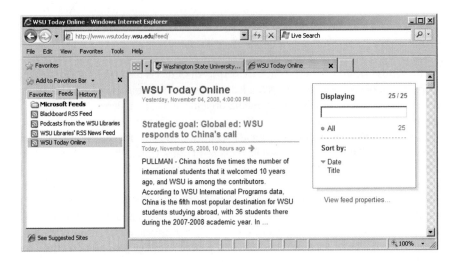

Netstats

Top Web 2.0 Sites

As Web 2.0 has become increasingly important, various publications and news sites publish rankings of the top Web 2.0 sites (and Web sites in general). These rankings are based on a variety of metrics, developed by different companies, including:

- **Yahoo!:** Yahoo! Site Explorer provides statistics about inbound links. The number of links pointing toward a particular Web site is used as a proxy for "popularity"; the more links point to a Web site, the more popular it is (this approach is also used within Google's PageRank algorithm).
- **Compete:** Compete.com uses statistics to estimate traffic to a variety of Web sites based on the usage data of a panel consisting of over 2 million Web users. This usage data is then extrapolated to the usage behavior of all U.S. Internet users.
- **Quantcast:** Quantcast.com estimates Web site traffic by combining panel data (similar to Compete) and data from traffic counters that are incorporated into participating Web sites' code. Thus, Quantcast is able to provide audience profiles and also hopes to provide more accurate traffic statistics.
- **Alexa:** Alexa.com ranks Web sites based on statistics provided by users who have the Alexa toolbar installed within their browser, as well as on other, third party statistics. This allows Alexa to incorporate both reach (i.e., the number of users) and the number of page views into the rankings.

As there are many ways to determine the "top" Web sites, which site is considered "top" varies. Further, as there are many ways to arrive at a certain metric, rankings are bound to differ. For instance, for September 2008, Quantcast estimated 68.3 monthly U.S. visitors to MySpace.com, whereas Compete estimated 56.5 million visitors. Alexa.com estimated 335,770 inbound links for

TABLE 6.7 Top Web 2.0 Sites

Web Site	
MySpace.com	IMDb.com
Wikipedia.org	Digg.com
YouTube.com	WordPress.com
Facebook.com	Hi5.com
Photobucket.com	Friendster.com
Craigslist.org	Orkut.com
Flickr.com	

MySpace.com, whereas Yahoo! reported 873,470 inbound links. Further, due to changes in popularity, the ordering of the top sites changes slightly from month to month. Nevertheless, several sites (as listed in Table 6.7) are consistently highly rated in these various rankings.

Based on:

Anonymous (2008). How does Compete estimate site traffic and Internet rank? *Compete.com.* Retrieved November 4, 2008, from http://www.compete.com/help/q18.

Anonymous (2008). What kind of information can I see using Site Explorer? *Yahoo.com.* Retrieved November 4, 2008, from http://help.yahoo.com/l/us/yahoo/search/siteexplorer/about/siteexplorer-15.html.

Anonymous (n.d.). Frequently asked questions. *Alexa.com.* Retrieved November 4, 2008, from http://www.alexa.com/site/help/?index=12.

Anonymous (n.d.). How Quantcast works. *Quantcast.com.* Retrieved November 4, 2008, from http://www.quantcast.com/docs/how-quantcast-works.

Top 25 Web 2.0 sites October 2008 (n.d.). *eBizMBA.* Retrieved November 3, 2008, from http://www.ebizmba.com/articles/user-generated-content.

Top Web 2.0 Sites (2008). *Movers 2.0.* Retrieved November 3, 2008, from http://movers20.esnips.com/TableStatAction.ns?reportId=100.

option as the author would have to bear high costs for typesetting and printing and had to sell enough books to recover his costs before making any profits. With increasingly sophisticated text editing and typesetting software targeted at the consumer market, **printing-on-demand** (i.e., customized printing that is done in small batches), is becoming increasingly popular. Open-source versions of the software needed are available for free on the Internet, and small-batch book printing machines minimize set-up and per print run costs. Thus, the cost of print-on-demand is fixed per unit produced, and almost anyone can publish his or her own books. This makes printing-on-demand particularly attractive to first-time authors

FIGURE 6.17

Everyone can publish and sell books using Blurb.com.

who want to sell books, but also for people who want to produce a professional looking book of recipes, wedding pictures, or travel diaries to place on their own coffee table or give away as a present. The leading print-on-demand companies include BookSurge, Lulu, and Blurb (see Figure 6.17), and many print-on-demand services also offer distribution services. BookSurge (owned by Amazon.com) provides this end-to-end service where authors can submit their manuscript, and the online publisher will edit, format, print, and sell the work. These services are provided for a small sales commission, and the rest of the revenue is returned to the author.

Enhancing Collaboration with Web 2.0

Web technologies, such as those outlined above, also enable **collaboration** (i.e., two or more people working together). Web 2.0 exemplifies how people from different places can work together for a common goal using Web technologies. People frequently collaborate on many different tasks, whether it be writing software, preparing a business plan, or even writing a textbook. When collaborating on projects, communication can be either **synchronous** (i.e., at the same time) or **asynchronous** (i.e., not coordinated in time). For example, chatting online is an example of synchronous communication, whereas e-mail is an example of asynchronous communication; a student might send his professor an e-mail message at 7 A.M. and the professor might reply at 1 P.M. With increasing globalization and increasing use of the Internet, collaborators on projects do not have to be co-located, and meetings typically take the form of **virtual meetings** using an online environment. Virtual meetings can be done synchronously, like a teleconference, or asynchronously, using technologies like online discussion boards.

Collaboration is often thought of as peers working together on a specific task. In addition, collaboration can also be a way for management and employees to interact. For example, the coffee giant Starbucks was dealing with problems stemming from its rapid growth and huge success (see Figure 6.18). Prior to implementing a Web portal to provide a centralized location for third-party vendor ordering, manifests and other resources were needed for managing inventory, training employees, and other communication and collaboration activities, and most correspondence between stores and corporate offices was very slow and inefficient using traditional paper-based mail and faxes. With over 100,000 employees, it was critical that Starbucks find a solution to improve its communication and collaboration between headquarters and stores. To achieve this, a corporate Web portal was implemented in 2003. Today, this portal is the primary communication channel between the corporate office and stores, allowing managers to focus more time on increasing sales and providing superior customer service (Microsoft, 2007).

FIGURE 6.18

Starbucks utilizes information systems to improve collaboration.

Virtual Teams

In today's business environment, project teams comprise highly specialized members, many of whom may not be co-located. Thus, rather than forming traditional teams, **virtual teams**, comprised of members from different geographic areas, are assembled to collaborate on a project (Sarker and Sahay, 2002). Virtual teams are commonly used for tasks such as developing systems and software; for example, the programmers are located in India, the project managers are in the United States, and the testers are in Europe. However, systems development is not the only place you will find virtual teams. For instance, the health care industry has embraced the idea of using technology to create superior care for patients. At the Rush University Medical Center in Chicago, team members may include dieticians, physicians, surgeons, pharmacists, and social workers from different cities, all of whom can coordinate care of the patient using various Web technologies to collaborate. This allows the patients to get the best health care professionals regardless of where they reside. Rush University Hospital is finding that patients under "virtual team care" report fewer trips to the emergency room and gain a better understanding of the health care system.

Social Online Communities

In addition to direct collaboration, **social networking** has become one of the most popular uses of the Internet over the past few years. Social networking sites are referred to as **social online communities**, where individuals with a broad and diverse set of interests meet and collaborate. MySpace.com and Facebook.com exemplify this trend, being the Web sites with the greatest number of users, accounting together for more than 6 percent of all Internet site visits in the United States in mid-2008 (Hitwise, 2008) (see Table 6.9). Reportedly, in 2008, MySpace had over 100 million users, growing at more than 230,000 users per day. MySpace.com originally was designed to provide users with information regarding their favorite bands and a place where users were allowed to view other users' favorite bands and link to these users, thus creating a social network based on musical interests. Soon after its release, however, the actual use of MySpace changed significantly from its original purpose. Typical users are teens and young adults who utilize MySpace to link to friends having little or nothing to do with musical interest. MySpace.com and

Coming Attractions

Virtual Extras

In the past, computer-generated crowd scenes in video games and animated movies have portrayed the group as an amorphous, blurry entity, with all individuals acting in approximately the same way. That portrayal could be changing, thanks to software that gives computer-generated crowd members traits of their own.

Demitri Terzopoulous, a computer science professor at the University of California, Los Angeles, has designed crowd-generating software that he says can handle as many as 1,400 autonomous "people" at once. In late 2007, the software was used to create a simulation of Pennsylvania Station in New York City. The 1,000 crowd members portrayed in the simulation act and react the same as real people in the station would act at any given time. They:

- Avoided oncoming traffic as they lined up to enter and exit narrow entrances
- Gathered in small groups of two or three to visit in different locations around the station
- Formed lines at ticket booths and drinking fountains to buy tickets or get a drink
- Sat down on benches to rest
- Aggregated to watch a performer in the station and clustered together when traffic disembarking from trains became heavy
- Navigated narrow stairways in a predictable manner—by staying to the right side on the stairway

This sort of animation is important in games and movies, because it allows abnormal behavior to stand out in the crowd, as relevant to the story.

Terzopoulous' program portrays subjects' behavior at three different layers:

1. A motion layer shows movement such as walking, running, sitting, or standing still.
2. A reactive layer allows subjects to react to obstacles, such as walking around a bench before sitting on it.
3. A cognitive layer shows behavior when people can think about what they are going to do ahead of time, such as getting in line for a drink of water.

With software like Terzopoulous has created, moviemakers will no longer have to rely on computerized crowd scenes based on flocking behavior, where all the subjects behave alike, as in the stampede scenes in *The Lion King*. Instead, games and animated movies can show people in crowds as they would normally appear, adding yet another factor in making the "virtual" appear real.

Based on:

Graham-Rowe, D. (2007, December 19). Virtual extras: Giving each member of a digital crowd its own personality could make animated mob scenes more realistic. *TechnologyReview.com*. Retrieved June 5, 2008, from http://www.technologyreview.com/Infotech/19964/?a=f

See also http://www.technologyreview.com/player/07/12/19Rowe Video/2.aspx.

---

other similar social online communities, such as Facebook and LinkedIn, have created unique and prolific electronic business opportunities. In fact, MySpace has been so successful that in 2005, it was purchased by Rupert Murdoch's NewsCorp for $580 million (see Figure 6.19). Cyworld is another successful social online community that is vastly popular, especially in Asia; in South Korea, for example, Cyworld's per capita penetration is greater than that of MySpace in the United States (Schonfeld, 2006).

Although largely popular among preteens, teens, and young adults, social networking is not only used for entertainment purposes. Several social online communities are targeted at professional audiences allowing users to meet business contacts, post career profiles, present themselves in professional context, ask for expert advice, or be contacted regarding job opportunities. For example, LinkedIn has more than 20 million users, and Xing (which is widely popular in Europe) has more than 5.5 million users.

The Social Network Economies These social online communities have created a large underground economy based on social networking. T-shirts, jeans, and various items are being sold because of MySpace associations. Although the likes of MySpace or Cyworld

TABLE 6.9 Top 10 Social Networking Sites

Name of Community	Description	Monthly Visitors
MySpace.com	Started as a site allowing bands to post their profiles, MySpace.com has grown to the largest social networking Web site in the world.	~66 Million
Facebook.com	Started by a Harvard student to network with other Harvard students online, Facebook is now open to everyone.	~29 million
Classmates.com	This site focuses on keeping in touch with past classmates from high school and college.	~22 million
Myyearbook.com	Social networking site similar to Classmates.com, focusing on the high school market.	~19 million
Bebo.com	Acquired by AOL in 2005, Bebo has a large international presence. Bebo stands for Blog early and blog often.	~16 million
Livejournal.com	A social networking site geared toward users creating and sharing daily entries about their activities.	~13 million
Blackplanet.com	A niche social networking site targeted at African American users.	~11 million
Hi5.com	A social networking site popular among users located in Central America.	~11 million
LinkedIn.com	A business-oriented Web site where people can post jobs, résumés, and profiles for professional networking.	~10 million
Tagged.com	An early adopter of the use of slideshows and YouTube videos.	~10 million

Based on Freiert, M. (2008, March 7). February top social networks—Make way for the new guys. *Compete.com*. Retrieved May 5, 2008 from http://blog.compete.com/2008/03/07/top-social-networks-traffic-feb-2008.

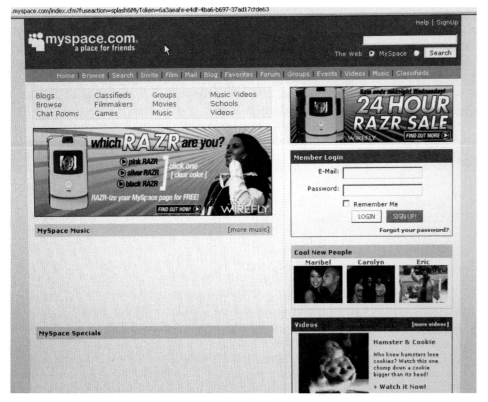

FIGURE 6.19

MySpace.com is one of the most popular social networking sites.

do not make money from this trade, they do make significant profits. In the case of MySpace, targeted ads generate about $2.17 per user per year (Schonfeld, 2006). Cyworld's revenue comes from the sale of virtual items that can be used within the site to improve its look and feel. Sales are estimated at nearly $300,000 a day, or more than $7 per user per year. Facebook.com also allows targeted ads, but does so by allowing advertisers to create applications specifically for Facebook.com such as Diet Pepsi's 80s trivia application or Microsoft's Zune application that allows users to see the music their friends are listening to.

Network Effects in Web Sites Although there are a multitude of highly successful social networking sites, there have been many others that have failed. Large companies such as Walmart, Yahoo!, and Google all have tried and failed to start successful social networks. The **network effect** describes why certain social Web sites succeed and why others fail. The network effect refers to the belief that the value of a network is dependent on the number of other users. In other words, if a network has few users, it has little or no value (e.g., how useful would e-mail be if none of your friends or family members had access to it?). For example, eBay would not be an effective auction Web site if only a few bidders were present. In order for eBay auctions to be valued, there must be a large number of users that are involved in the auctions. As more users hear about eBay and then become active buyers and sellers, the value of eBay continues to grow. These network effects also occur in social networks, where the network's utility is related to the number of registered users on the network. If your friends are already on Facebook.com, why would you change to another network?

Viral Marketing

In the offline world, marketing one's products or services is one of the most important aspects of successfully running a business. In an online context, marketing Web sites, products, and services is equally important, and business organizations use techniques such as search marketing, paid inclusion, and banner advertisements to promote their Web sites (see Chapter 5). With the growth of social networking, advertisers have turned to **viral marketing** to promote their Web sites, products, or services. Viral marketing is using the network effect to increase brand awareness. The term *viral marketing* was coined by Harvard business professor Jeffery Rayport to describe how good marketing techniques can be driven by word-of-mouth or person-to-person communication, similar to how real viruses are transmitted through offline social networks. Rather than creating traditional banner ads or sending out massive amounts of spam, businesses create advertisements in a way that entices the viewers to share the message with their friends through e-mail or social networks, so that the message will spread like a virus. Viral marketing can take many forms such as video clips, ebooks, flash games, and even text messages.

The power of viral marketing can be a great tool, and there are several techniques that are critical to making a successful viral marketing campaign. Writer and Interaction Designer Thomas Baekdal has outlined some critical factors in viral marketing, including (Baekdal, n.d.):

1. Do something unexpected
2. Make people feel something
3. Make sequels
4. Allow sharing and easy distribution
5. Never restrict access to the viral content

Following these principles entices users to view an ad, share it with their friends, and revisit the site to look for new ads. For example, BMW created a series of short films directed by popular directors. Rather than being traditional car ads, these films told stories, presenting the vehicles in a certain context. Viewers would watch the films because of the content, would share the films, and come back to the BMW films Web site to watch the next film.

Another successful viral marketing campaign was used by Hotmail's founders during the launch of the free Hotmail e-mail service. One of the techniques involved adding a

Brief Case ⊘

The Internet Movie Database (IMDb)

If you love movies, there have probably been times when a film-related question drove you crazy. A friend bet you that the blond bombshell who played Irina Spalko in *Indiana Jones and the Kingdom of the Crystal Skull* was Nicole Kidman, and you knew he was wrong, but how to prove it? Which Native American actor played sidekick Tonto in Clayton Moore's *Lone Ranger*? Which television show made Robert Blake famous, and what animal was his costar on the show?

Of course, you could conduct a general Web search and find the answers to all of the above questions, but it might take you a while. Instead, you can visit one Web site—The Internet Movie Database (IMDb)—and find all of the above answers and more in minutes.

What began as a Usenet list posted on the Internet in 1990 (the World Wide Web did not yet exist) has become the largest online accumulation of data about films, actors, film production and distribution crews and companies, television programs, direct-to-video productions, video games, movie trivia, plots, and quotes, and more to be found at one Web site. Amazon.com bought IMDb in 1998, allowing devoted IMDb volunteers to finally quit their day jobs and earn a living maintaining and expanding the site.

Any computer user with a Web browser and an e-mail account can set up a free account that lets him or her submit information, leave comments for actors, and otherwise interact with the site, but setting up an account is not necessary to simply look up information about movies, television shows, and actors. In 2002, IMDb created a for-profit subscription service,

IMDbPro, to provide additional information for business professionals. A résumé subscription service begun in 2006 lets actors and production crew members post photos and additional information about themselves for an annual fee.

IMDb founder and current managing director Col Needham says that "the IMDb didn't start as a dream to build a business or a Web site. It started as a dream to make a tool that we, as movie fans, would find really useful and fun. Over the years, millions of other movie fans have found it useful and fun too." (IMDb serves on average 65 million requests per month, and, as of October 2007, had 17 million registered users.)

So who was the blond in the Indiana Jones movie mentioned above? Who was the Native American actor who played Tonto? What show made Robert Blake famous, and what animal was his costar? Visit IMDb and find out.

Questions

1. How can IMDb be used to promote movies for the studios? How can it be used to promote actors?
2. What is the future for IMDb? What service or products could be added to the Web site to enhance user experience?

Based on:

IMDb history (n.d.). Retrieved June 5, 2008, from http://www.imdb.com/help/show_leaf?history.

Internet Movie Database. (2008, June 4). In *Wikipedia, the free encyclopedia*. Retrieved June 5, 2008, from http://en.wikipedia.org/w/index.php?title=Internet_Movie_Database&oldid=217164249.

footer to every outbound message. This footer gave a short message about Hotmail.com's free e-mail service, and the message about the service was spread with every e-mail sent through the service (see Figure 6.20). This campaign proved very effective (Hotmail spent only $500,000 to get 12 million subscribers), and Microsoft later bought Hotmail.

In July of 2006, a series of simple videos was posted to YouTube.com by a user called lonelygirl15. The supposed user was a teenage girl named Bree, who in short video blogs regularly talked about her friends and family. Lonelygirl15 gained worldwide attention, and her videos were watched by over 70 million viewers. A *New York Times* story eventually outed loneygirl15 as a paid actress who was hired by a small production company. This entertainment company, LG15, now produces several mock video blogs that remain popular.

Facebook.com, a social networking Web site, has taken viral marketing to the next level. Viral marketing is the cornerstone of its business where applications are distributed via the social network. For example, one popular application in use by the Facebook.com community is called "Launch a Package." Users can send a virtual package to any other user in their network for occasions such as a birthday or anniversary. This application is sponsored by FedEx, which pays Facebook.com a fee for every viral package sent by its users.

FIGURE 6.20

Hotmail uses viral marketing by adding a footer containing information about the e-mail service to each e-mail.

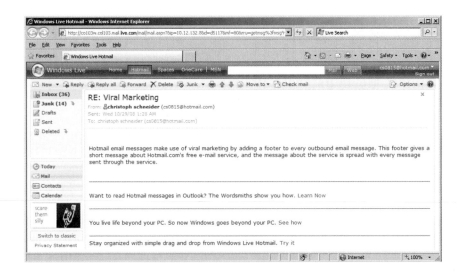

Crowdsourcing

Another way individuals can collaborate with organizations is through crowdsourcing. When companies look for cheap labor, many immediately think about outsourcing work to *companies* in different countries, such as India, China, or Russia (see Chapter 2). However, companies have now found a way to use *everyday people* as a cheap labor force, a phenomenon called **crowdsourcing**, which ingeniously uses the pillars of Web 2.0.

For example, up until a few years ago, book publishers such as Pearson Prentice Hall had to rely on so-called stock photography for many of a book's images; in other words, publishers had to pay large sums for pictures taken by professional photographers. Clearinghouses for stock photography had to charge high fees just to cover their expenses, as they had to purchase pictures from professional photographers. Today, high-quality digital cameras can be had for far less than $1,000, and, with the right editing software, amateur photographers can create images that almost match those of professional photographers. Amateur photographers can upload their pictures to image sharing sites such as iStockphoto.com, where interested parties can license and download the images for $1 to $5 per image, which is a fraction of the price of a regular stock photo. Given overhead costs that are almost negligible, iStockphoto can make a profit while still sharing part of the revenue with the pictures' creators.

Similarly, pharmaceutical giant Eli Lilly created a site called InnoCentive, where companies can post scientific problems, and everybody can take a shot at solving the problem. Usually, a reward is paid to a successful solver. This way, an ad-hoc R&D network is created, and companies have to rely less on a dedicated R&D department or on hiring specialists to solve a certain problem. At the same time, people can use their spare time and expertise to solve problems and earn rewards for their contributions.

Amazon.com took crowdsourcing mainstream with its mturk (mechanical turk) application. Using the mechanical turk, requesters can crowdsource so-called human intelligence tasks (HITs), which are small, self-contained tasks that humans can solve easily, but would be difficult for a computer to solve. Examples of HITs include tagging images, generating potential search key words for a product, fixing product titles on e-commerce sites, and so on. Users can find HITs that are of interest to them, solve the tasks, and earn money that is credited to their Amazon.com account.

As you can see, for companies, crowdsourcing is an innovative way to reduce costs by using the expertise of the crowds. Similar to grid computing (see Chapter 4), a person's "idle time" is used for a certain business task, and many people are willing to provide their resources in exchange for a relatively small amount of money. Just imagine that you could pay for your textbooks using the money you earned from the collection of digital pictures you've taken, all for almost no extra effort. Another emerging trend is **e-lancing**. Traditionally, companies have used self-employed freelancers to work on individual projects or provide content. E-lancing takes this concept a step further by enabling people to work in more flexible ways on a variety of Internet-related projects.

Industry Analysis

Online Travel

Spring break is coming, and you've decided to go to Puerto Vallarta this year. Chances are your first step will be to check the Expedia, Travelocity, and Orbitz Web sites for flights to and hotels in your chosen destination. (Expedia's 2008 first-quarter report showed that it accounted for 32 percent of worldwide bookings.)

We all know the big three online travel agencies (OTAs). In today's digital world, they dominate the travel industry. They took the old brick-and-mortar travel industry and turned it into an online service where you can click to book flights and hotel reservations, change or cancel flights, reserve rental cars—even plan a vacation. In Internet terms, you can think of the big three as still being in Online Travel 1.0. But technology marches relentlessly on, and Online Travel 2.0 is in the works.

Travel service providers and travel customers—airlines, hotels, and car rental companies—pay fees to online travel agencies. And travel service providers selling through OTAs do not have the opportunity to build customer relationships. Therefore, some providers, including JetBlue and InterContinental Hotels, would rather have customers book directly from them. That way, they (and their customers) avoid OTA fees, and they are better able to satisfy customers since they can provide up-to-the-minute information.

Enter Online Travel 2.0—the travel search engines. They don't book travel services for you, but they locate and list URLs for hundreds of suppliers, and when you choose one, you can then click the link to the supplier's Web site. Travel search engines becoming increasingly popular with online consumers include Kayak, Vayama, Mobissimo, and Yahoo!'s FareChase.

If you want to book a travel package, especially to an international destination, OTAs may be the best choice. But if you can navigate travel services yourself, are in a hurry, or want to deal directly with travel service providers, travel search engines can fill the bill.

Questions

1. Do you use online travel agencies for assisting you with travel plans? If so, which service provider do you use, and why did you make this choice? If not, why not?
2. Forecast the future of traditional travel agencies. What electronic commerce business strategy would you recommend? Why?

Based on:

Smith, B. (2006, April 27). Yahoo's FareChase: The stealth disruptor? *SearchEngineWatch*. Retrieved June 8, 2008, from http://searchenginewatch.com/searchday/article.php/3601971.

Key Points Review

1. **Describe Web 2.0, its components, the strategies that companies are adopting to embrace these emerging capabilities, and its future.** The term Web 2.0 has been heavily used in the popular press to express: (1) how the Web site interface has changed to allow more interactive features and (2) the change in strategies for EC-based businesses. Using Web 2.0 concepts and technologies has helped many companies survive the burst of the "dot-com bubble." These concepts include utilizing the Web as a platform, harnessing collective intelligence, leveraging data, and implementing innovative Web capabilities. Web 2.0 technologies enabling a rich user experience include Web services, widgets, and mashups. These and other technologies have enabled Web-

based collaboration tools such as Google Apps or Microsoft Sharepoint, as well as content management systems. However, many see Web 2.0 only as a transitional period and regard the semantic Web and Web 3.0 trends such as the World Wide Database, open technologies, open ID, integration of legacy devices, and intelligent applications as the future of the Web.

2. **Understand the importance of empowering users to generate content using wikis, tags, blogs, netcasts, and self-publishing.** The users are central to the new Web environment and are no longer passive viewers of information. As the Web has evolved, individuals can now generate content using several methods, such as wikis, which are Web sites in which people can post, edit, comment,

and access information. The idea behind wikis is that they allow anyone to contribute information or edit prior contributions. A second method, tagging, refers to the adding of key words or relevant terms to a piece of information such as a map, picture, or Web page, thus describing the piece of information for others and making it searchable. A third method, blogging (or Weblogging) is the process of creating an online text diary (i.e., a blog, or Web log) made up of chronological entries that comment on virtually any topic of interest to the author. A fourth, netcasting, also known as podcasting, is the distribution of digital media, such as audio or video files via syndication feeds for playback on digital media players such as iPods, Zunes, or other portable music devices. Finally, self-publishing refers to the publishing of original material (such as books) by the author through the use of customized printing services available on the Web, referred to as printing-on-demand, that is done in small, relatively inexpensive batches.

3. *Explain the different collaboration tools and techniques, including social networking, virtual teams, viral marketing, and crowdsourcing.*

Web 2.0 technologies have enabled new forms of collaboration for organizations and individuals. With increasing globalization, virtual teams and virtual meetings have become more important for organizations. For individuals, social networking has become an important way to meet new friends, connect with family members, or meet new colleagues and business partners. MySpace.com and Facebook.com exemplify this trend, being the Web sites with the highest market share and having created a large underground economy based on social networking. Although there are many highly successful social networking sites, there have been many others that have failed. The network effect describes why certain social Web sites succeed and why others fail. The reach of social networks is also used by business organizations to market their products or services through viral marketing. Viral marketing resembles offline word-of-mouth communication, in which advertising messages are spread like viruses through social networks. Another emerging topic in the Web 2.0 environment is crowdsourcing, or the use of everyday people as a cheap labor force.

Key Terms

amateurization of journalism 251
asynchronous 254
blog 249
blogging 249
blogosphere 251
collaboration 254
content management system 242
crowdsourcing 260
e-lancing 261
geo-tagging 248
mashup 238
metadata 249
netcast 251

netcaster 251
netcasting 251
network effect 257
peer-to-peer 235
podcast 251
podcasting 251
printing-on-demand 253
Real Simple Syndication (RSS) 251
self-publishing 247
semantic web 244
social networking 255
social online community 255
synchronous 254

tagging 248
viral marketing 257
virtual meeting 254
virtual team 255
Web 2.0 234
Web 3.0 244
Web log 249
Web service 237
Web-based collaboration tool 239
Weblogging 249
widget 237
Wikipedia 247
World Wide Database 246

Review Questions

1. What is Web 2.0? Give some examples of Web 2.0 capabilities.
2. What are the four pillars of Web 2.0?
3. Describe and contrast Web services, widgets, and mashups.
4. What are the advantages and disadvantages of Web-based collaboration tools?
5. Compare and contrast Google Apps and Microsoft SharePoint.
6. What are the four roles users can have in a content management system? Why does a content management system need specific roles?
7. What capabilities will define the Web of the future?

8. What is a wiki? Why would an organization want to implement a wiki?
9. Explain the concept of metadata. Give three examples of metadata.
10. What is tagging, and how are organizations using it in their Web sites?
11. What is blogging, and why are blogs sometimes controversial?
12. Describe what RSS does and why it is an important technology for today's Web environment.
13. There are several ways to self-publish in today's world. Compare and contrast two ways of self-publishing.

14. What is the difference between synchronous and asynchronous collaboration? Give two examples for both synchronous and asynchronous collaboration.
15. What are virtual teams and how do they help to improve an organization's capabilities?
16. Social online communities are in wide use. Explain why some social communities are adopted and others fail.

17. What is viral marketing? What capabilities of the Web help to spread the virus?
18. Explain what is meant by crowdsourcing and how the Web is enabling this form of collaboration.

Self-Study Questions

Visit the Interactive Study Guide on the Companion Web site for additional Self-Study Questions: www.pearsonhighered.com/valacich.

1. Which of the following is NOT a pillar of Web 2.0?
   A. Innovative Web technologies
   B. Leveraging the data of all customers
   C. Use the most current technologies available
   D. Using the Web as the business platform
2. Which of the following can NOT be considered content?
   A. Videos
   B. Blogs
   C. Shopping carts
   D. Pictures
3. Tagging is adding _____ to a piece of information such as a map, picture, or Web page.
   A. Key words
   B. Comments
   C. Blogs
   D. RSS
4. The process of adding information to online maps such as Google Maps or Microsoft's Virtual Earth is called
   _____.
   A. Flagging
   B. Posting
   C. Geotagging
   D. Podcasting
5. Which of the following could be considered metadata?
   A. Inches
   B. Printers
   C. Song title
   D. All of the above

6. _____ is the process of creating an online diary made up of chronological entries.
   A. Wiki-ing
   B. Tagging
   C. Blogging
   D. None of the above
7. Netcasts are also known as _____.
   A. Podcasts
   B. Blogcasts
   C. Radiocasts
   D. Blogging
8. RSS allows you to do all of the following except what?
   A. Publish a video blog
   B. Publish current news stories
   C. Download a Netcast
   D. Edit a Netcast
9. Wikis are a type of Web site where people can _____.
   A. Post information
   B. Comment on information
   C. Access information
   D. All of the above
10. _____ communication is when people are all meeting at the same time or in real time.
   A. Synchronous
   B. Asynchronous
   C. Collaboration
   D. None of the above

Answers are on page 265.

Problems and Exercises

1. Match the following terms with the appropriate definitions:
   i. Printing-on-demand
   ii. Asynchronous
   iii. Metadata
   iv. Social networking
   v. RSS
   vi. Web services
   vii. Netcasts
   viii. Mashups
   ix. Content management system
   x. Blogging

   a. Technologies allowing organizations to access data without intimate knowledge of each other's systems behind the firewall.
   b. The distribution of digital media, such as audio or video files via syndication feeds for playback on digital media players such as iPods, Zunes, or other portable music devices.
   c. A family of syndication feeds used to publish the most current blogs, podcasts, videos, and news stories.
   d. Software allowing users to publish, edit, version track, and retrieve digital information.

e. Web applications that integrate one or more Web services.

f. The process of creating an online text diary made up of chronological entries.

g. Data about data.

h. Customized printing that is done in small batches.

i. Using Web-based services to link friends or colleagues.

j. Not coordinated in time.

2. Visit popular social online communities (such as www.myspace.com or www.facebook.com). What features would entice you to visit such sites over and over again? Do you have a page in an online community? If yes, why? If no, what is keeping you from having such a site? Is there any content you definitely would or would not post on such page?

3. Go to the Web site Programmable Web (www.programmableweb.com). List some interesting mashups you find. What factors do you think make a good mashup Web site?

4. Go to Amazon's Mechanical Turk Web site (www.mturk.com). Which of the HITs do you think could be completed using a computer, and which could not? Why?

5. Search the Web for a social networking site that you have not heard about before. Describe the users of this social online community. Are the features of this site different from those you are familiar with? If so, describe those features. If not, describe common features.

6. Visit: Google Page Creator (pages.google.com) and Microsoft Live Office (Officelive.com). Compare and contrast the features for each Web site. Which Web site would you choose to use and why?

7. Have you ever blogged or read someone's blog? If so, what did you like or dislike about the experience? What do you see for the future in blogs? Are they going to be around for a while? Are they a temporary fad?

8. Do you use a Web site that uses Web 2.0 principles? What do you like or dislike about this Web site? If you were a company, would you choose to use the current Web technologies? Why?

9. Envision and describe general features of Web 3.0 applications. Describe a feature you would like to see in the next version of the Web.

10. Describe an application or service you would like to be able to use on the Web today that is not yet available. Describe the potential market for this application or service. Forecast how long you believe it will take before this will occur.

11. Search the Web for definitions of metadata. Give examples of how people are using metadata.

12. Have you listened to or watched a netcast (or podcast)? If so, describe your experience. If not, why?

13. Describe the pros and cons of collaborating with colleagues over the Web. What is useful about this form of collaboration? What is difficult?

14. Describe an example of viral marketing that you have experienced.

Application Exercises

Note: The existing data files referenced in these exercises are available on the Student Companion Web site: www.pearsonhighered.com/valacich.

Spreadsheet Application: Online vs. Traditional Spreadsheets

Campus Travel is currently evaluating the possibility of using an online spreadsheet as opposed to the traditional locally installed spreadsheet. There are a variety of issues involved in this decision. The company wants you to investigate the possibilities that are currently available while also paying special attention to the company requirements. Campus Travel has the following requirements: (1) The ability to share spreadsheets easily, (2) the ability to secure this information, (3) the ability to save the spreadsheets into other forms (i.e., CSV files), and (4) the ability to do work from anywhere in the world. Prepare the following information:

1. Look through the different options for spreadsheets and list the available options.

2. Using the company requirements, list the pros and cons for each spreadsheet option.

3. Summarize the findings and provide a recommendation to the company.

Database Application: Tracking Web Site Visits

As Campus Travel expands its Web presence, the importance of tracking what the competitors are doing has become very important. This includes making sure Campus Travel tracks the prices of packages and services that its closest competitor offers. To do so, a database must be created to track this information. Follow these steps to create the database:

1. Create a database called "tracking."

2. Create a table called "company_info." In this table, create fields for company_name and company_URL.

3. Create a table called "products." In this table create fields for the company_name, product_name, product_description, product_price, and date_retrieved.

4. Create a table called "services." In this table create fields for company_name, service_name, service description, service_price, and date_retrieved.

5. Once these tables are created, go to the relationship view and connect the company_info (one side) and products (many side) tables, and the company_info (one side) and service (many side) tables.

6. Make sure that when you create the relationships that referential integrity option is selected. (This will make sure that when you delete a company that the products associated with the company are also deleted.)

7. Test the referential integrity by adding data to the tables and make sure when a company is deleted in the company table that the products table is updated too.

Team Work Exercise: Online Social Communities

Do you use online social communities to communicate with your friends and family? Are you a member of multiple social communities? Compare and contrast your experiences in social networking with your classmates. Which Web sites do you use, and why do you use these Web sites? Can you see yourself changing to another social network Web site? What would make you change? Discuss strategies that these social community Web sites are using to keep you active in the Web site. Visit LinkedIn (www.linkedin.com), Classmates (www.classmates.com), and Facebook (www.facebook.com). What are the similarities in these Web sites? What are the main differences in these three social community Web sites?

Answers to the Self-Study Questions

1. C, p. 235   2. C, p. 242   3. A, p. 248   4. C, p. 248   5. D, p. 249
6. C, p. 249   7. A, p. 251   8. D, p. 251   9. D, p. 247   10. A, p. 254

Case ❶
Google's OpenSocial API

Key to Web 2.0 is that the Web is a social place, and the exploding popularity of social networking Web sites like Facebook, YouTube, MySpace, and Digg have confirmed that fact.

When Web site developers want to create a social networking site, (and many do given the concept's popularity) open-source application programming interfaces (APIs) make the task easier. Easier, that is, to some extent. If each social networking site uses a different API, developers must learn new programming languages for each API. Facebook, for example, has opened its API to developers, but the programs created are operational only on Facebook's Web site.

In October 2007, Google announced it would soon release to developers its new social networking API, called OpenSocial. MySpace, still holding first place in the social networking popularity race, reported soon after Google's announcement that it would join forces with Google to support OpenSocial. "Our partnership with Google allows developers to gain massive distribution without unnecessary specialized development for every platform," said MySpace CEO and cofounder Chris DeWolfe in a statement for the press. "This is about helping the start-up spend more time building a great product rather than rebuilding it for every social network. We're pleased to collaborate with Google to establish a landmark standard for social applications."

Unlike Facebook's API, OpenSocial offers a common set of APIs that its partners or "hosts" can use on their networks. MySpace is an OpenSocial partner, as stated above, as are Orkut (Google's social network that took off in Brazil, but is not as popular in the United States), Salesforce, LinkedIn, Xing, Plaxo, Friendster, and more. But not Facebook—at least not yet in mid-2008.

Developers using OpenSocial have access to three JavaScript and Gdata APIs to access social functions. OpenSocial apps can also use Flash and can interact with other Web sites. Google stated that the "ultimate goal" of OpenSocial "is for any social Web site to be able to implement the API and host third-party applications . . .

"Google's gadget caching technology can ease your bandwidth demands," Google's OpenSocial information Web page continues, "should your app suddenly become a worldwide success."

Questions:

1. Do you see Google's OpenSocial affecting your social networking experience? If so, how will users be affected by this technology?
2. If you were running a social networking Web site such as Facebook or MySpace, would you implement Google OpenSocial? What are the pros and cons of implementing Google's system?
3. What other Web sites would benefit from Google's OpenSocial API other than those previously mentioned? How would they benefit from this technology?

Based on:

Anonymous (n.d.). OpenSocial. Retrieved June 5, 2008, from http://code.google.com/apis/opensocial.

Arrington, M. (2007, October 30). Details revealed: Google OpenSocial to launch Thursday. *TechCrunch*. Retrieved June 5, 2008, from http://www.techcrunch.com/2007/10/30/details-revealed-google-opensocial-to-be-common-apis-for-building-social-apps.

Cheng, J. (2007, November 1). Google goes after Facebook with new OpenSocial social networking API (Updated: Now with more MySpace). *ArsTechnica*. Retrieved June 5, 2008, from http://arstechnica.com/news.ars/post/20071031-google-goes-after-facebook-with-new-opensocial-social-networking-api.html.

Helft, M., & B. Stone (2007, October 31). Google and friends to gang up on Facebook. *New York Times*. Retrieved June 5, 2008, from http://www.nytimes.com/2007/10/31/technology/31google.html.

Lenssen, P. (2007, October 31). Google's OpenSocial API? *Google Blogoscoped*. Retrieved June 5, 2008, from http://blogoscoped.com/archive/2007-10-31-n58.html.

Case ❷

Wikipedia: Who Is Editing?

Research almost any topic on the Web and a URL for a Wikipedia entry will likely appear on the list of resources. Wikipedia is a free, online encyclopedia that gets its millions of entries, called "Wikies," from users—be they amateurs, professionals, or pranksters with nothing better to do. ("Wiki wiki" is the Hawaiian term for "quick.") Users who are logged in are also able to edit entries, but the Wikipedia site keeps detailed logs of the sources (IP addresses) of all changes. User/editors are anonymous in that only their user names are known, but IP addresses can be traced back to the source.

Cal Tech computation and neural-systems graduate student Virgil Griffith got curious about Wikipedia's anonymous editors in 2007, when he read that congressional aides had been editing entries about their employers—the senators and representatives of the U.S. Congress. Griffith wondered if other companies and organizations were doing the same thing, so he created a program to find out. Griffith created a database of all Wikipedia entries and changes, including the information logged each time an anonymous editor made a change. Griffith isolated the XML-based records of changes and IP addresses, then identified the owners of the IP addresses using public net-address look-up services, such as ARIN, as well as private domain name data obtained through IP2location.com.

Griffith's system revealed such information about editors as:

- Someone on a computer at voting-machine maker Diebold Election Systems deleted fifteen paragraphs from a Wikipedia article about electronic voting that were critical of Diebold's machines.
- Walmart made changes to improve its image.
- Politicians are frequent editors. For instance, a former U.S. senator from Montana made changes to indicate he was a voice for farmers in his state.

- Dave Winer, a famous blogger and developer of RSS, notes that his Wikipedia entry has been edited several times, removing all mention of his contributions to RSS, blogging, and podcasting.
- ExxonMobil deleted information about its nonpayment of damages to 32,000 Alaska fishermen after the *Exxon Valdez* oil spill.
- A computer registered to Disney deleted information critical of the company's digital rights management software.

Griffith emphasizes that his system, WikiScanner, cannot identify Wikipedia editors as agents of certain companies or organizations. It can only identify IP addresses that come from networks registered to a company or organization.

Since Wikipedia entries can be written and edited by any user registered at the site, its accuracy should obviously not be completely trusted. If one uses other reputable sources in addition to

Wikipedia, however, it can often be a starting point for further research on a topic. Dave Winer, for instance, writes in March 2008 that he finds Wikipedia "a useful personal resource." He was "working his way" through all episodes of *Battlestar Galactica* and found it helpful to read a synopsis of each episode on Wikipedia after he had watched the episode.

When used in conjunction with other sources, Wikipedia can have value. Just don't depend on it exclusively when researching a topic, and verify facts read there before quoting them as fact.

Questions:

1. Do you use Wikipedia for your research? Why or why not?
2. Have you ever made a change to a Wikipedia entry? If you were to see an obvious mistake (in your opinion), would you take the time to change it? Why or why not?
3. Anyone can edit entries on Wikipedia. Do you see this as a curse or as a blessing? Explain.

Based on:

Blakely, R. (2007, August 16). Wal-Mart, CIA, and ExxonMobil changed Wikipedia entries. *Foxnews.com*. Retrieved June 8, 2008, from http://www.foxnews.com/story/0,2933,293389,00.html.

Borland, J. (2007, August 14). See who's editing Wikipedia—Diebold, the CIA, a campaign. *Wired.com*. Retrieved June 8, 2008, from http://www.wired.com/politics/onlinerights/news/2007/08/wiki_tracker?currentPage=all.

Risley, D. (2008, March 21). Wikipedia accuracy: Dave Winer's criticism. *PCMech.com*. Retrieved June 8, 2008, from http://www.pcmech.com/article/wikipedia-accuracy-dave-winers-criticism.

Winer, D. (2008, March 10). What's wrong with Wikipedia. *Scripting News*. Retrieved June 8, 2008, from http://www.scripting.com/stories/2008/03/20/whatsWrongWithWikipedia.html.

Securing Information Systems

After reading this chapter, you will be able to do the following:

1. Explain what is meant by the term "information systems security" and describe the primary threats to information systems security and how systems are compromised.

2. Describe both technology- and human-based safeguards for information systems.

3. Discuss how to better manage information systems security and explain the process of developing an information systems security plan.

4. Describe how organizations can establish IS controls to better ensure security.

Preview

As organizations become more dependent on information systems for enabling organizational strategy, they also become more vulnerable to catastrophic security disasters. Because of this, organizations are focusing more of their attention on information systems security. In this chapter, we explain how you can manage the security of information systems and the critical information they hold.

Managing in the digital world requires careful attention to information systems security. Having thorough plans for dealing with information systems security attacks and natural disasters is critical for effectively managing information systems resources within organizations.

Managing in the Digital World: Drive-by Hacking

How did businesses and individuals do without wireless networks before they became widely available? We can check e-mail messages while waiting in airports, access the Web using laptops in classrooms, keep a business running while attending conventions and meetings worldwide, and perform any number of additional tasks via wireless networks. A downside to the ease of communicating wirelessly, however, is that hackers have also migrated to wireless networks. Lax security on wireless networks has allowed hackers to join networks and launch malicious attacks. Recent surveys show that between 60 and 80 percent of wireless corporate networks do not use security. (A shocking statistic, considering the prevalence of destructive hacker attacks.)

Until recently, hackers were focused on discovering new ways to bypass firewalls and other security measures used to protect wired networks. Now, however, with the increasing availability of insecure wireless networks (Wi-Fi), hackers have found a new playground. Thus, hackers have instituted a new type of pursuit called "war driving," whereby they drive around densely populated areas looking for unsecured networks and usually find literately hundreds of unsuspecting victims.

One common attack that war drivers perpetrate is called "war spamming," where hackers link into an e-mail server of an unsecured Wi-Fi network and send out millions of junk e-mails without the network administrators' knowledge. War spamming costs companies millions in bandwidth fees but is difficult to trace, so spammers are seldom caught. Some businesses are fighting back by using a technology that generates thousands of bogus wireless network access points, thus stymieing hackers trying to access personal or corporate Wi-Fi networks. Software tools called wireless camouflage, such as FakeAP, offer such protection by confusing war drivers so that they are not able to locate the "real" access point among the thousands of bogus ones. However, using network scanners such as Netstumbler or Kismet and even some of Windows' built-in tools, one can distinguish between genuine access points and the thousands of bogus access points. Most war drivers use these tools to find open networks, but organizations can also use network scanners to find holes in their protection (see Figure 7.1).

All wireless access points have built-in security in the form of Wired Equivalent Privacy (WEP). WEP uses a 64-bit key to encrypt the wireless signals, which, theoretically, allows only those network users with the 64-bit code to use the Wi-Fi signal. WEP, however, has documented security flaws. These flaws allow hackers to circumvent the security and easily access the Wi-Fi network. Recently, the engineering security community within the IEEE (Institute of Electrical and Electronics Engineers) has worked to fix WEP security flaws by adopting "Fast Packet Keying," which is designed to repair security flaws and to finally create a truly secure wireless network.

As with all new technologies, however, there are problems with Fast Packet Keying. For instance, it is difficult to administer and deploy. Network administrators must choose between allowing users easy access and thus compromising security or installing Fast Packet Keying, which tightens security but makes day-to-day network operations more difficult.

Since war driving, war spamming, and other forms of hacker theft cost companies millions in damages, some businesses are looking to cyber-insurance policies to help recoup losses. According to an article in *Economic Times*, in 2007 approximately twenty-five stand-alone cyber-insurance polices were sold, but the

FIGURE 7.1

Accessories for "war driving" are easily obtainable, causing security concerns for organizations.

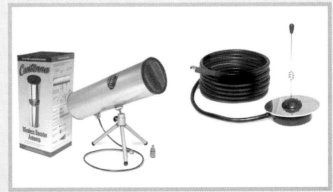

Source: http://shop.netstumbler.com/SearchResult.aspx?CategoryID=26.

number was expected to greatly increase in 2008 and beyond, as cyber-crime escalates. The policies are expensive, but may provide one more hedge for businesses suffering from the rising tide of cybercrime.

After reading this chapter, you will be able to answer the following:

1. How can organizations better secure their wireless networks to reduce security vulnerabilities?

2. Is using a wireless network without the owner's permission wrong? If so, why? If not, why not? Are there any ethical issues associated with "piggybacking" on your neighbor's unsecured wireless network?

3. Some believe that all wireless networks should be "open" to anyone. What are the pros and cons of this perspective?

Based on:

Sengupta, D. (2008, January 31). IT cos seek insurance cover against virtual fraud. *Economic Times.* Retrieved May 12, 2008, from http://economictimes.indiatimes.com/infotech/it_cos_seek_insurance_cover_against_virtual_fraud/articleshow/2744918.cms.

Wearden, G. (2002, September 5). Heard of drive-by hacking? Meet drive-by spamming. *ZDNET,* Retrieved May 12, 2008, from http://news.zdnet.co.uk/internet/0,39020369,2121857,00.htm.

Welcome to the world of drive-by hacking. (2001, November 6). *BBC News.* Retrieved May 12, 2008, from http://news.bbc.co.uk/1/hi/sci/tech/1639661.stm.

Information Systems Security

How do you secure information systems from viruses and other threats? The rule of thumb for deciding whether an information system is at risk is simple: All systems connected to networks are vulnerable to security violations from outsiders as well as insiders and to virus infections and other forms of computer crime. Threats to information systems can come from a variety of places inside and external to an organization. **Information systems security** refers to precautions taken to keep all aspects of information systems (e.g., all hardware, software, network equipment, data, and facilities) safe from unauthorized use or access. That means that you have to secure not only the personal computers on people's desks but also the notebook computers, the handhelds, the servers: all levels of the network and any gateway between the network and the outside world.

As use of the Internet and related telecommunications technologies and systems has become more pervasive, use of these networks now creates a new vulnerability for organizations. These networks can be infiltrated and/or subverted in a number of ways. As a result, the need for tight computer and network security has increased dramatically. Fortunately, there are a variety of managerial methods and security technologies that can be used to manage information systems security effectively. In the remaining sections of this chapter, we address this new reality.

Primary Threats to Information Systems Security

Everyone who uses an information system knows that disasters can happen to stored information or to entire systems. Some disasters are accidents caused by power outages, inexperienced computer users, or mistakes, while others are caused on purpose by malicious crackers (see Chapter 11—Information Systems Ethics and Crime). The primary threats to the security of information systems include the following (see Figure 7.2):

- *Accidents and Natural Disasters.* Inexperienced or careless computer operators, cats walking across keyboards, power outages, hurricanes, and so on;
- *Employees and Consultants.* People within an organization who have access to electronic files;
- *Links to Outside Business Contacts.* Electronic information can be at risk when it travels between or among business affiliates as part of doing business; and
- *Outsiders.* Hackers and crackers who penetrate networks and computer systems to snoop or to cause damage (viruses, currently rampant on the Internet, are included in this category).

FIGURE 7.2

Threats to information systems
security.

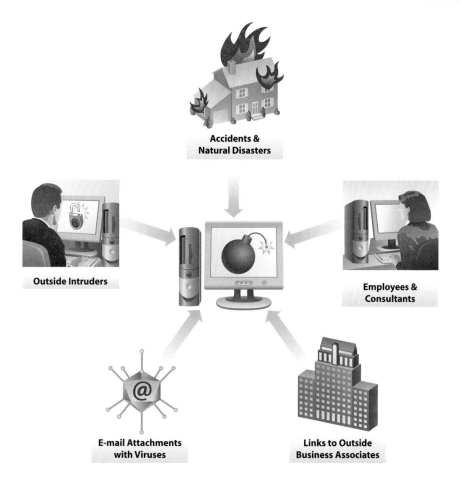

**Accidents &
Natural Disasters**

Outside Intruders

**Employees &
Consultants**

**E-mail Attachments
with Viruses**

**Links to Outside
Business Associates**

Information systems are most often compromised through one or more of the follow-ing: unauthorized access, information modification, denial of service, and viruses, as well as spam, spyware, and cookies. Next, each of these is examined.

Unauthorized Access **Unauthorized access** occurs whenever people who are not authorized to see, manipulate, or otherwise handle information look through electronically stored information files for interesting or useful data, peek at monitors displaying proprietary or confidential information, or intercept electronic information on the way to its destination.

Unauthorized access can be gained by physically stealing computers, stealing stor-age media (e.g., removable flash drives, CD-ROMs, or backup tapes), using someone else's password, or simply opening files on a computer that has not been set up to limit access. When computer information is shared by several users, as in an organization, in-house system administrators can prevent casual snooping or theft of information by requiring correct permissions. Further, administrators can log attempts of unautho-rized individuals trying to obtain access. Determined attackers, however, will try to gain access by giving themselves system administrator status or otherwise elevating their permission level—sometimes by stealing passwords and logging on to a system as authorized users (see Figure 7.3).

Information Modification **Information modification** occurs when someone accesses electronic information and then changes the information in some way, such as when employees give themselves electronic raises and bonuses or when crackers hack into government Web sites and change information (see Figure 7.4).

Backhoe Cyberthreat

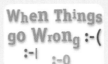

When you hear the word "cyberthreat," what comes to mind? Worms, viruses, and Trojan horses? These maladies are, indeed, serious cyberthreats. Take, for example, the notorious Storm Worm, which was not really a worm at all, but a new type of botnet using peer-to-peer control, with hundreds of thousands of infected computers (note that worms and viruses will be discussed below). Storm infections started spreading in 2007, with an e-mail message that said, "230 dead as storm battles Europe." Several variants of the message (including Valentine's and April Fools' Day themes) kept the infection on the rampage into 2008, causing annoyance as well as costs for organizations.

A less obvious type of cyberthreat, however—a threat usually considered only by security experts—is the threat to the "hard" infrastructure of the Internet. For instance, in early 2006, workers burying a TV cable in Arizona mistakenly dug up an unmarked fiber-optic cable. The workers had dutifully called the "call before you dig" number provided at the site and were given the go-ahead to bury the TV cable. This mishap had widespread consequences since the cable was part of the huge Internet backbone. Even though the cable was part of a self-healing ring, many Internet and cell phone users were immediately disconnected. Adding to the problem was the fact that other parts of the ring had been damaged earlier during a mudslide in California.

The fact that over 675,000 incidents have been reported in only one year, in which telephone lines, fiber-optic cables, water lines, or gas pipelines were accidentally damaged, illustrates how vulnerable the telecommunications infrastructure is. Even more worrisome, since information about the location of the infrastructure is publicly available, is the possibility for terrorists to exploit this vulnerability using nothing more than a backhoe.

In 2008, for example, underwater Internet cables serving certain sections of the Middle East were cut, disrupting service connecting Europe with the Middle East, North Africa, and the Indian subcontinent. Some suspicious Net users were sure Al Qaeda was to blame, but telecommunications expert Stephan Beckert of TeleGeography Research said, "Cable cuts happen on average once every three days." In fact, twenty-five large ships do nothing but fix cable cuts and bends. Early reports blamed an errant ship's anchor for cutting the cable, but the cause was not confirmed.

While some cable cuts happen naturally or due to human error, the ease with which one could deliberately attack the telecommunications infrastructure was demonstrated by a graduate student who, for his dissertation, mapped the major fiber-optic cables across the United States. Interestingly, he found that most of the cables are buried along major interstate highways and railroads and that there are only two routes through which most of the Internet traffic flows. His dissertation soon got attention from the Department of Homeland Security, which realized that it would be disastrous if it fell into the wrong hands. (On the other hand, publicizing this type of information might have helped to sensitize the public as well as the authorities about how vulnerable the telecommunications infrastructure really is and what can be done to protect it.)

Based on:

Blumenfeld, L. (2003, July 8). Dissertation could be security threat. *Washington Post*. Retrieved May 12, 2008, from http://www.washingtonpost.com/ac2/wp-dyn/A23689-2003Jul7.

Poulsen, K. (2006, January 19). The backhoe: A real cyberthreat. *Wired*. Retrieved May 12, 2008, from http://www.wired.com/news/technology/1,70040-0.html.

Singel, R. (2008, January 31). Fiber optic cable cuts insulate millions from Internet, future cuts likely. *Wired*. Retrieved May 12, 2008, from http://blog.wired.com/27bstroke6/2008/01/fiber-optic-cab.html.

Singel, R. (2008, February 6). Cable cut fever grips the web. *Wired*. Retrieved May 12, 2008, from http://blog.wired.com/27bstroke6/2008/02/who-cut-the-cab.html.

Top ten cyber security menaces for 2008 (n.d.). Retrieved May 12, 2008, from http://www.sans.org/2008menaces.

Computer Viruses **Viruses** are extensively discussed in Chapter 11, but they are mentioned here because they pose one of the greatest risks to computer security (see Figure 7.5). Viruses consist of destructive code that can erase a hard drive, seize control of a computer, or otherwise do damage. When viruses corrupt and destroy data, large amounts of company and individual time, money, and resources are spent to repair the damage they do. **Worms**, a variation of a virus that is targeted at networks, take advantage

FIGURE 7.3

Unauthorized access can occur in many ways.

of security holes in operating systems and other software to replicate endlessly across the Internet, thus causing servers to crash, which denies service to Internet users.

Denial of Service **Denial of service** attacks occur when electronic intruders deliberately attempt to prevent legitimate users of a service from using that service, often by using up all of a system's resources. To execute such attacks, intruders often create armies of **zombie computers** by infecting computers that are located in homes, schools, and businesses, with

FIGURE 7.4

Information modification attack.

FIGURE 7.5

Anatomy of a virus attack.

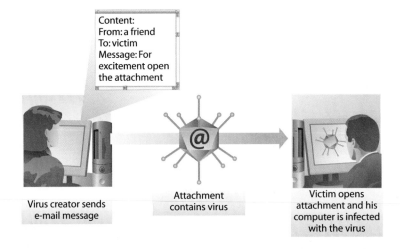

Content:
From: a friend
To: victim
Message: For
excitement open
the attachment

Virus creator sends
e-mail message

Attachment
contains virus

Victim opens
attachment and his
computer is infected
with the virus

viruses or worms. Computers can be infected if they are not protected by firewalls and antivirus software and are, therefore, open to attacks and to being used as zombies (in fact, some security experts believe that more than 10 percent of all computers connected to the Internet are used as zombies, unbeknown to the owner). The zombie computers, without users' knowledge or consent, are used to spread the virus to other computers and to launch attacks on popular Web sites. The Web site servers under attack crash under the barrage of bogus computer-generated visitors, causing a *denial of service* to those Internet users who are legitimately trying to visit the sites (see Figure 7.6). For example, MyDoom was able to recruit an army of zombies that bombarded Microsoft's Web site with traffic and literally locked out legitimate customers. (Microsoft is a popular target for virus writers, and the company must constantly provide downloadable patches to those using its software in order to prevent unauthorized intrusion.)

FIGURE 7.6

Denial of service attack.

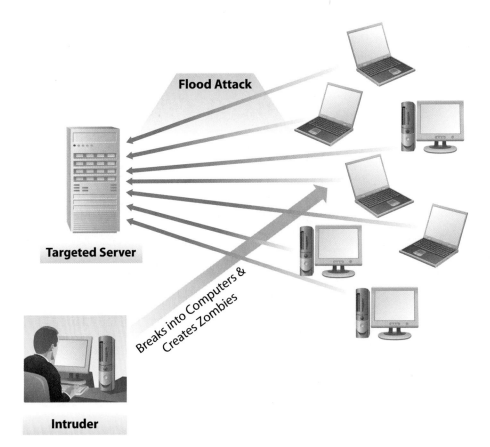

Flood Attack

Targeted Server

Breaks into Computers &
Creates Zombies

Intruder

Spyware, Spam, and Cookies Three additional ways in which information systems can be threatened is by spyware, spam, and cookies.

SPYWARE. **Spyware** is any software that covertly gathers information about a user through an Internet connection without the user's knowledge. Spyware is sometimes hidden within freeware or shareware programs. In other instances, it is embedded within a Web site and is downloaded to the user's computer, without the user's knowledge, in order to track data about the user for marketing and advertisement purposes. Spyware can monitor your activity and secretly transmit that information to someone else. E-mail addresses, passwords, credit card numbers, and Web sites you have visited are among the various types of information that spyware can gather. Spyware presents problems because it uses your computer's memory resources, eats network bandwidth as it sends information back to the spyware's home base via your Internet connection, causes system instability or, worse, system crashes, and exposes users to identity theft, credit card fraud, and other types of crime. **Adware** (free software paid for by advertisements appearing during the use of the software) sometimes contains spyware that collects information about a person's Web surfing behavior in order to customize Web browser banner advertisements. It is important to note that spyware is not currently illegal, although there is ongoing legislative hype about regulating it in some way. Fortunately, firewalls and spyware protection software can be used to scan for and block spyware.

SPAM. Another prevalent form of network traffic that invades our e-mail is spam. **Spam** is electronic junk mail or junk newsgroup postings, usually for the purpose of advertising for some product and/or service (see Figure 7.7). In addition to being a nuisance and wasting our time, spam also eats up huge amounts of storage space and network bandwidth. Spammers commonly use zombie computers to send out millions of e-mail messages, unbeknown to the computer users. Some spam consists of hoaxes, asking you to donate money to nonexistent causes or warning you of viruses and other Internet dangers that do not exist (see Figure 7.8). Other times, spam includes attachments that carry destructive computer viruses. As a result, Internet service providers and those who manage e-mail within organizations often use **spam filters** to fight spam. For example, Washington State University utilizes a spam filter to fight spam and other e-mail threats

Net Stats

Adware/Spyware Lurks on Most PCs

According to Webroot, a company that produces software to scan for and eliminate adware/spyware, 66 percent of all Webroot-scanned personal computers are infected with at least twenty-five adware/spyware programs. While statistics show that incidents of spyware found on personal computers are declining slightly, it is still a disturbing presence. "Even if it is a totally opt-in ad with consent, it adds to resource demand," explains Richard Steinnon, Webroot's vice president of threat research. "If you have five to seven [adware programs], the average we are finding, your system is not going to work."

McAfee research found in 2006 that the most prolific distributors of adware/spyware were celebrity Web sites—not adult and pornographic sites as previously believed. The research also found that the numbers of PCs infected with unwanted adware/spyware were increasing at exponential rates. By August 2006, there were approximately 450 adware families with 4,000 variants.

Based on:

Burns, E. (2005, May 6). Spyware lurks on most PCs. *Clickz.* Retrieved May 12, 2008, from http://www.clickz.com/stats/sectors/security/article.php/3503156.

McAfee, Inc. reports on adware and spyware growth (2006, September 11). Retrieved May 12, 2008, from http://www.mcafee.com/us/about/press/corporate/2006/20060911_182130_g.html.

McAfee Threat Center (n.d.). Retrieved May 12, 2008, from http://www.mcafee.com/us/threat_center/default.asp.

FIGURE 7.7

Spam is rampant and consumes an enormous amount of human and technology resources.

such as directory harvest attacks (i.e., attempts to determine valid e-mail addresses for spam databases), phishing attacks, viruses, and more. Typical spam filters use multiple defense layers to help reduce the amount of spam processed by the central e-mail servers and delivered to users' in-boxes. The IT administrator sets the parameters for spam filtering and can determine how aggressively e-mail will be filtered. Usually, e-mail that is suspected to be spam can be blocked outright or sent to a quarantine folder that is managed by the e-mail owner through a Web interface. The user can visit their quarantine folder and quickly mark and delete spam messages. The IT administrator has a log of all messages that are received, even those that are blocked outright, and can release messages if any are blocked unintentionally. Such instances are known as *false positives*, when a legitimate e-mail is inadvertently identified as spam and blocked. Most spam filters learn

FIGURE 7.8

Spam classifications.

Source: Websense Security Labs Quarterly Research Highlights, Q3–Q4 2007.

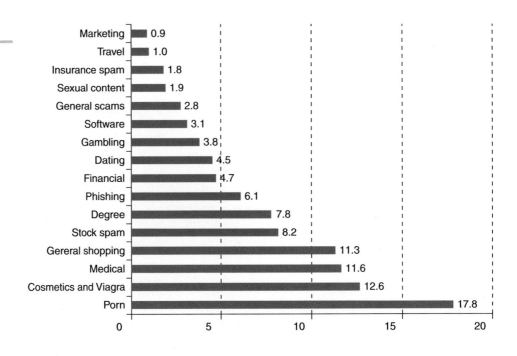

over time—through a process known as Bayesian analysis—so that any future messages from known sources of spam are automatically blocked by the firewall.

Some spam e-mail is used for **phishing** (or spoofing), which are attempts to trick financial account and credit card holders into giving away their authorization information, usually by sending spam messages to literally millions of e-mail accounts (i.e., attackers are "phishing" [fishing] for victims). These phony messages contain links to Web sites that duplicate legitimate sites to capture account information. For example, most e-mail users regularly receive phishing attempts from various spoofed banks, eBay, or PayPal (see Figure 7.9). In Chapter 11, we extensively discuss phishing and other computer crimes.

It is important to stress that it is never advisable to reply to a spam message—although if it might feel good to do so at the moment—even if the message contains instructions for removing your e-mail address from the recipients list. Replying to the message can actually be counterproductive because the spammer (i.e., the person who sent the spam) may simply note that someone actually responded and mark your address for future mailings. In addition to e-mail–based spam, spam over text messaging and spam over instant messaging—called **spim**—are becoming increasingly used. Spim is particularly tricky because messages—typically a Web site link and some text saying how great the site is—are formatted to mimic communication chat sessions.

Often, spammers post their spam messages in online forums, blogs, or wikis, or create thousands of e-mail accounts at free providers such as Yahoo! or Hotmail to send out their messages. Rather than manually going through such tedious tasks to set up these accounts or post thousands of messages, spammers use bots (i.e., software robots that work in the background to provide services to their owners, see Chapter 8—Enhancing Business Intelligence Using Information Systems and Chapter 11) to do this. Faced with this problem, e-mail providers and managers of online forums are attempting to prevent spammers from using bots to automatically submit online forms. One commonly used approach for preventing bots from submitting forms is the use of CAPTCHAs. A **CAPTCHA** (Completely Automated Public Turing Test to Tell Computers and Humans Apart) typically consists of a distorted image displaying a combination of letters and/or numbers that a user has to input into a form (in addition to other required information) before submitting it. As the image is distorted, (currently) only humans can interpret the letters/numbers, preventing the use of automated bots for creating accounts or posting

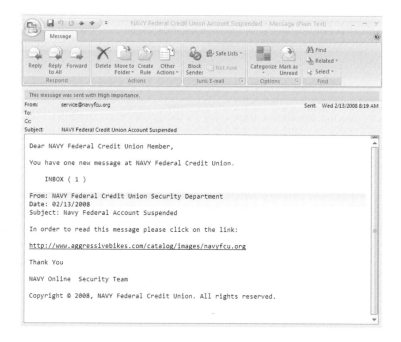

FIGURE 7.9

A phishing e-mail message.

FIGURE 7.10

A CAPTCHA is used to prevent bots from submitting an online form.

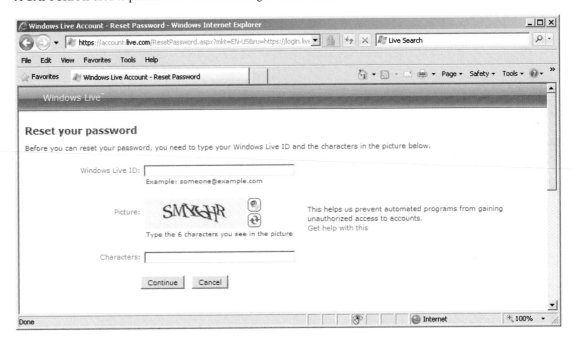

spam to forums, blogs, or wikis. CAPTCHAs are also used to prevent bots from trying to break passwords using a brute force approach (see Figure 7.10).

Unfortunately, in addition to posing challenges for the disabled, CAPTCHAs are becoming increasingly ineffective. Whereas some spammers try to break CAPTCHAs using sophisticated character recognition technology, others use cheap human labor; recently, inventive spammers created a strip-tease game, where the "players" had to solve CAPTCHAs for "Melissa" to expose herself. Unbeknown to the users, the program would send the results to a remote server, which would use the information for malicious purposes. Increasingly, Web masters are using a combination of multiple techniques to stop spammers, such as detecting mouse movements (as automated agents do not use a mouse), or the rate at which text is entered into forms, or incorporate invisible fields (which would be "seen" and filled out by an automated agent, but not a human user), together with CAPTCHAs in order to distinguish between malicious bots and legitimate users.

COOKIES. Another nuisance in Internet usage are cookies. A **cookie** is a message passed to a Web browser on a user's computer by a Web server. The browser then stores the message in a text file, and the message is sent back to the server each time the user's browser requests a page from that server.

Cookies are normally used for legitimate purposes, such as identifying a user in order to present a customized Web page or for authentication purposes. For example, some Web sites ask you to provide your name and interests or to simply provide your ZIP code. This information is packaged into a cookie, which is sent to your Web browser to be stored on your computer for later use. The next time you go to the same Web site, your browser will send the cookie back to the Web server so that it can then present you with a custom-made Web page based on your name and interests, or perhaps the Web server provides you with local news and weather forecasts based on your ZIP code. Often, cookies store information provided by users on a Web form (e.g., when ordering products). In such cases, cookies may contain sensitive information (such as credit card numbers) and thus pose a security risk in case unauthorized persons gain access to the computer.

Specific cookie management or cookie killer software can be used to manage cookies, but an even simpler way to manage cookies is through the settings in your Web browser. In the set-

FIGURE 7.11

Managing cookies within the Firefox Web browser.

tings for the Firefox Web browser, for example, you can set levels of restrictions on the use of cookies, you can stop the use of them altogether, and if you do allow them, you can go in periodically and delete them from your computer (see Figure 7.11). (In Chapter 11 we talk about the ethical concerns over spyware, spam, and cookies, particularly as an invasion of privacy.)

Other Threats to Information Systems Security   Many times, computer security is breached simply because organizations and individuals do not exercise proper care in safeguarding information. Some examples follow:

- Employees keep passwords or access codes on slips of paper in plain sight.
- Individuals have never bothered to install antivirus software, or they install the software but fail to keep it up to date.
- Computer users within an organization continue to use default network passwords after a network is set up instead of passwords that are more difficult to break.
- Employees are careless about letting outsiders view computer monitors, or they carelessly give out information over the telephone.
- Organizations fail to limit access to company files and system resources.
- Organizations fail to install effective firewalls or intrusion detection systems, or they install an intrusion detection system but fail to monitor it regularly.
- Proper background checks are not done on new hires.
- Employees are not properly monitored, and they steal company data or computer resources.
- Fired employees are resentful and install harmful code, such as viruses, worms, or Trojan horses, when they leave the company.

While there are many threats to computer security, there are also ways to combat those threats. Next, we discuss safeguards organizations and individuals can use to improve information systems security.

Safeguarding Information Systems Resources

Any good approach to securing information systems begins first with a thorough audit of all aspects of those systems, including hardware, software, data, networks, and any business processes that involve them. By doing this, you can then decide which aspects of the various systems within the organization are most vulnerable to break-ins by unauthorized users and/or misuse by authorized users. After such an audit, you can then design and implement a security plan that makes the best use of the available resources in order to protect the systems and guard against (or at least minimize) any problems. People within the information

Brief Case ⊘

Hacking an Airplane

The fact that the latest generation of aircraft uses information technology as never before is undoubtedly beneficial for the pilots, ground control centers, and passengers, but, once again, hackers can become a problem.

For example, according to the U.S. Federal Aviation Administration (FAA), Boeing's 787 Dreamliner passenger jet, due to enter service in 2010, could have a serious security vulnerability in its onboard computer networks that would allow passengers to access the plane's control systems. The FAA report reveals that the computer network in the Dreamliner's passenger compartment, designed to give passengers in-flight Internet access, is connected to the plane's control, navigation, and communication systems. This physical connection of the networks makes the plane's control system vulnerable to hackers. IT security experts said that a more secure system would physically separate the two systems, a solution that Boeing executives said would soon be tested.

"This is serious," said Mark Loveless, a network security analyst with Autonomic Networks, a company that presented a conference talk in 2007, "Hacking the Friendly Skies." "This isn't a desktop computer. It's controlling the systems that are keeping people from plunging to their deaths. So I hope they are really thinking about how to get this right."

Questions

1. If a passenger hacked into a plane's control system, even if they did no damage, how seriously do you think they should be punished?
2. Given that air travel can never be perfectly safe, how safe should the networks be on modern aircraft?

Based on:

Zetter, K. (2008, January 4). FAA: Boeing's new 787 may be vulnerable to hacker attack. *Wired.* Retrieved May 12, 2008, from http://www.wired.com/politics/security/news/2008/01/dreamliner_security.

---

systems department are usually responsible for implementing the security measures chosen, though people from throughout the organization should participate in the systems security audit. Some organizations even go so far as to pay an external consulting firm to attempt to break in and breach their systems so that vulnerabilities will be uncovered and fixed.

It would not make sense to spend literally millions of dollars a year to protect an asset, the loss of which would cost the organization only a few thousand dollars. As a result, organizations frequently conduct information systems audits (discussed later in this chapter). One critical component of a good information systems audit is a thorough risk analysis. **Risk analysis** is a process in which you assess the value of the assets being protected, determine their likelihood of being compromised, and compare the probable costs of their being compromised with the estimated costs of whatever protections you might have to take. People in organizations often perform risk analyses for their systems to ensure that information systems security programs make sense economically (Stallings & Brown, 2008).

Risk analysis then enables us to determine what steps, if any, to take to secure systems. There are three general ways to react:

1. *Risk Reduction.* Taking active countermeasures to protect your systems, such as installing firewalls like those described later in this chapter
2. *Risk Acceptance.* Implementing no countermeasures and simply absorbing any damages that occur
3. *Risk Transference.* Having someone else absorb the risk, such as by investing in insurance or by outsourcing certain functions to another organization with specific expertise

Large organizations typically use a balance of all three approaches, taking steps in **risk reduction** for some systems, accepting risk and living with it in other cases (i.e., **risk acceptance**), and also insuring all or most of their systems activities as well (i.e.,

risk transference). There are two broad categories of safeguards for reducing risk—technological- and human-based approaches—and any comprehensive security plan will include both.

Technological Safeguards

There are six commonly used methods in which technology is employed to safeguard information systems:

- Physical access restrictions
- Firewalls
- Encryption
- Virus monitoring and prevention
- Audit-control software
- Dedicated facilities

Within any type of safeguard, there are a variety of ways in which it can be deployed. Next, we briefly review each of these methods.

Physical Access Restrictions Organizations can prevent unauthorized access to information systems by keeping stored information safe and allowing access only to those employees who need it to do their jobs. Of course, organizations can protect computers and data resources by physically securing computers to desks or requiring users to lock hard drives with keys when leaving a computer unattended. However, most organizations don't go to such lengths and only control access by requiring some form of **authentication**. The most common form of authentication is the use of passwords, which are effective only if chosen carefully and changed frequently (see Figure 7.12). Besides passwords, employees may be asked to provide an ID combination, a security code sequence, or personal data, such as a mother's maiden name. Employees authorized to use computer systems may also be issued keys to physically unlock a computer, photo ID cards, smart cards with digital

FIGURE 7.12

The most common form of authentication is through passwords.

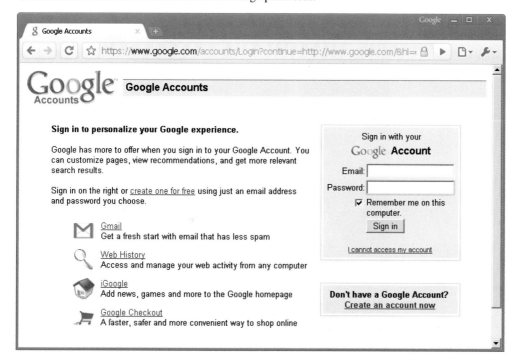

ID, and other physical devices allowing computer access. In sum, access is usually limited by making it dependent on one of the following:

- *Something You Have.* Keys, picture identification cards, smart cards, or smart badges that contain memory chips with authorization data on them (see Figure 7.13)
- *Something You Know.* Passwords, code numbers, PIN numbers, lock combinations, or answers to secret questions (your pet's name, your mother's maiden name, and so on)
- *Something You Are.* Unique attributes, such as fingerprints, voice patterns, facial characteristics, or retinal patterns (collectively called *biometrics*)

Some measures that limit access to information are more secure than others. For example, smart cards and smart badges, passwords, lock combinations, and code numbers can be stolen. Biometric devices are difficult to fool, but determined intruders may sometimes devise ways to bypass them. Any of the previously mentioned single items can be used, but it is safer to use combinations of safeguards, such as a password *and* a smart card. Next, we examine various methods for implementing physical access control.

BIOMETRICS. Biometrics is one of the most sophisticated forms of restricting computer user access. Biometrics is a form of authentication used to govern access to systems, data, and/or facilities. With biometrics, employees may be identified by fingerprints, retinal patterns in the eye, body weight, or other bodily characteristics before being granted access to use a computer or to enter a facility (see Figure 7.14). Once users have been authenticated, they are allowed to access certain systems, computers, data, and/or facilities with specified privileges. After the hijackings and attacks on September 11, 2001, the use of better security methods became a high priority for airports, large corporate buildings, and computers. Biometrics has the promise of providing very high security while at the same time authenticating people extremely efficiently, so many governments and companies are investigating how best to use this technology. For example, residents of Hong Kong can quickly pass through immigration checkpoints by using a smart card and their thumbprints.

A smart card.

FIGURE 7.14

Biometric devices are used to verify a person's identity.

Source: ©AP/Wide World Photos.

ACCESS-CONTROL SOFTWARE. Special software can also be used to help keep stored information secure. **Access-control software**, for example, may allow computer users access only to those files related to their work. The user might even be restricted to these resources only at certain times or for specified periods of time, and, depending on the access level, the user can be restricted to being able to only read a file, to read and edit the file, to add to the file, and/or to delete the file. Many common business systems applications now build in these kinds of security features so that you do not have to have additional, separate access-control software running on top of your applications software. Whether you are restricting user access within the application software or with the help of additional access-control software, the common approach is to authenticate that the user is indeed who he or she claims to be by requiring something that the user knows (e.g., a password) together with something that the user physically carries or has access to (e.g., an identification card).

WIRELESS LAN CONTROL. Given how easy and inexpensive wireless local area networks (LANs) are to install and use, their use has skyrocketed, leaving many systems open to attack. Whereas traditional LANs use physical transmission media such as copper wire and optical fiber, wireless LANs use radio waves for transmission. As a result, while traditional LANs operate by sending signals through wires or fibers in cables, wireless LANs spread their signals widely over the airwaves, allowing attackers to access the network and intercept messages relatively easily. Unauthorized people can thus easily "steal" company resources (e.g., by surfing the Web for free, which is illegal in many countries) or do considerable damage to the network. A new form of attack known as **drive-by hacking** has arisen (see the chapter-opening case), where an attacker accesses the network, intercepts data from it, and even uses network services and/or sends attack instructions to it without entering the home, office, or organization that owns the network (see Figure 7.15).

As described in more detail in the Information Technology Briefing, the main standard for wireless LANs is the IEEE 802.11 family of standards. The 802.11 signals can travel up to several hundred feet away from the wireless access point that generates the signals. These wireless LANs can be extended to cover entire buildings by placing multiple access points around the premises. Unfortunately, covering great distances in this way can also give easy access to attackers both within and external to the organization. When using wireless LANs, whether in the home or in the office, it is important to configure the wireless access points such that they do not allow open access. Many of these access points can be configured, for example, to allow access only to computers using preauthorized wireless network interface cards.

FIGURE 7.15

Drive-by hacking is on the rise given the proliferation of unsecured wireless LANs.

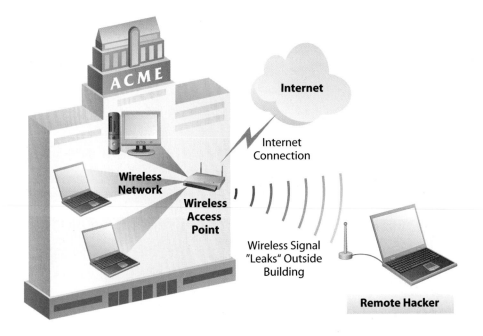

VIRTUAL PRIVATE NETWORKS. A **virtual private network (VPN)** is a network connection that is constructed dynamically within an existing network—often called a secure tunnel—in order to connect users or nodes (see Figure 7.16). For example, a number of companies and software solutions enable you to create virtual private networks within the Internet as the medium for transporting data. These systems use authentication and encryption (discussed later) and other security mechanisms to ensure that only authorized users can access the VPN and that the data cannot be intercepted and compromised; the practice of creating an encrypted "tunnel" to send secure (private) data over the (public) Internet is known as **tunneling**. For example, Washington State University requires VPN software to be used when connecting remotely to the campus network or e-mail system, or when using the on-campus wireless LAN.

FIGURE 7.16

A virtual private network (VPN) allows remote sites and users to connect to organizational network resources using a secure tunnel.

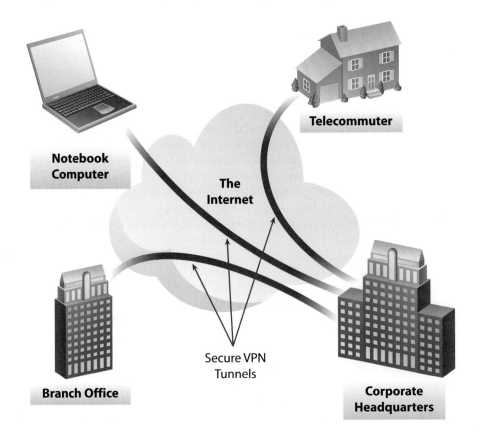

Ethical Dilemma

Stealing WiFi

If your neighbor is watering his lawn and accidentally waters some of your grass, have you "stolen" your neighbor's water? When you tune a station on your car radio, are you illegally using the "free" radio? Similarly, here is a question for the millions of laptop computer users: If you are sitting in your car in front of a business with in-house WiFi service and you are surfing the Net by "piggy-backing" on the businesses' Internet access, are you stealing Internet service? (Piggy-backing refers to using someone else's WiFi service without their knowledge or consent.) Most Internet service providers would probably answer that question with a resounding "Yes." Why? Because piggy-backing allows you to use, for free, a service that costs the business.

According to a 2007 survey by security firm Sophos, piggy-backing is a popular activity. Fifty-four percent of the 560 Sophos survey respondents reported using someone else's bandwidth via piggy-backing. But is it really theft? Great Britain says it is and arrests bandwidth thieves when they can catch them. The WiFi "theft" issue is loosely defined under the United States Computer Fraud and Abuse Act—paragraph (a)(2) covers anyone who "intentionally accesses a computer without authorization or exceeds authorized access"—but when the 1986 law was passed, no one had anticipated 802.11x wireless links. WiFi mooching, however, has lead to arrests in some states, where laws may differ somewhat from federal law. For example, in Alaska, a twenty-one-year-old man was arrested while accessing a public library's WiFi service from his car, a Wisconsin man was arrested for accessing a café's free WiFi service, as was a Florida man driving around a neighborhood looking for WiFi access.

Some people see the ethics of piggy-backing differently. For example, one person posted a comment in response to an online article about piggy-backing by Michael Santo: "My home router is intentionally left open, with some antispam restrictions. There are 2–5 connections weekly. I've no problem with people in need using it from time to time."

Just as hacking led to the 1986 Computer Fraud and Abuse Act, unauthorized WiFi use will eventually be conclusively addressed in federal legislation. Until then, the practice is largely an ethical issue that should be addressed by individual computer users. If an airport, Internet café, or public library advertises "take advantage of our free WiFi service," computer users can conclude that WiFi use in those facilities is legal and, therefore, worry-free. If, on the other hand, a neighbor has not invited you to use his WiFi service, perhaps your conscience should tell you that using his broadband service uninvited and without his knowledge is not a good idea.

Based on:

Bangemen, E. (2008, January 3). The ethics of "stealing" a WiFi connection. *ars technica*. Retrieved May 12, 2008, from http://arstechnica.com/news.ars/post/20080103-the-ethics-of-stealing-a-wifi-connection.html.

Cheng, J. (2007, May 22). Michigan man arrested for using cafe's free WiFi from his car. *ars technica*. Retrieved May 12, 2008, from http://arstechnica.com/news.ars/post/20070522-michigan-man-arrested-for-using-cafes-free-wifi-from-his-car.html.

Man arrested over wi-fi 'theft' (2007, August 22). *BBC News*. Retrieved May 12, 2008, from http://news.bbc.co.uk/2/hi/uk_news/england/london/6958429.stm.

McCullagh, D. (2005, July 8). FAQ: Wi-Fi mooching and the law. *CNET News*. Retrieved May 12, 2008, from http://www.news.com/FAQ-Wi-Fi-mooching-and-the-law/2100-7351_3-5778822.html?tag=news.1.

Santo, M. (2007, November 17). Wi-Fi piggybacking widespread: Study. *Realtechnews*. Retrieved May 12, 2008, from http://www.realtechnews.com/posts/5070.

Firewalls A **firewall** is a system designed to detect intrusion and prevent unauthorized access to or from a private network. Think of a firewall essentially as a security force around the perimeter of an organization that spots any intruders that penetrate the organization's outer defenses.

Firewalls can be implemented in hardware, in software, or in a combination of both. Firewalls are frequently used to prevent unauthorized Internet users from accessing private networks connected to the Internet, especially private corporate intranets, described in Chapter 5—Enabling Commerce Using the Internet. All messages entering or leaving the intranet pass through the firewall, which examines each message and blocks those that do not meet the specified security criteria. Firewalls employ several different approaches:

■ *Packet Filtering.* A firewall may examine each data packet entering or leaving the network and then accept or reject each packet based on predefined rules. **Packet filtering** is fairly effective and is transparent to users, but it takes more time to set up and may slow the network.

■ *Application-Level Control.* A firewall might perform certain security measures only on specific applications, such as file transferring. **Application-level control** is also fairly effective but may degrade performance for those applications that are monitored by the firewall.

■ *Circuit-Level Control.* A firewall may be used to detect when a certain type of connection (or "circuit") has been made between specified users or systems on either side of the firewall. Once the connection has been made, packets can flow between the two entities without further checking. **Circuit-level control** is effective for targeted types of connections that need fast, unrestricted network performance once they are connected.

■ *Proxy Server.* A firewall can serve as or create the appearance of an alternative (or "proxy") server that intercepts all messages entering and leaving the network. The use of the **proxy server** thus effectively hides the true network addresses, and potential attackers "see" only the network address of the firewall (this is also known as **network address translation [NAT]**). Proxy servers are also commonly used to locally store (cache) frequently viewed Web sites to provide for faster access.

FIREWALL ARCHITECTURE. In Figure 7.17, we show a variety of different **firewall architectures** that depict how firewalls can be used within a network. Figure 7.17a depicts a basic firewall for a home network, where the firewall is implemented as software on the single computer being used. Figure 7.17b depicts a firewall router being used for either a small office or a home office. Here the firewall is implemented as hardware, and is integrated into the router (this is typically the case if you connect to the Internet via cable or DSL). Figure 7.17c depicts a firewall architecture comprising several layers for a larger organization (Stallings & Brown, 2008). The point here is not that you can decipher the details in these network architecture diagrams; rather, the point is to show you how the complexity and power of the firewall solution changes as the situation gets more complex.

Encryption In any discussion of systems security, the problem of unauthorized eavesdroppers arises. Organizations can use secure channels not available to computer users outside their networks, but the Internet, public telephone lines, and airwaves are not subject to the same restricted use. Most of us send e-mail around the globe; call friends, family, and colleagues on wireless telephones; and trust our desktop, notebook, and server computers with all manner of personal, financial, and corporate secrets. Until recent years, we may have felt secure in our activities. Now, however, news stories about corporate spies, malicious hackers, curious neighbors and coworkers and suspicious government agencies have us wondering if every transfer of information is somehow subject to unseen eavesdroppers.

When you do not have access to a secure channel for sending information, encryption is the best bet for keeping snoopers out. **Encryption** is the process of encoding messages before they enter the network or airwaves, then decoding them at the receiving end of the transfer so that the intended recipients can read or hear them (see Figure 7.18). The process works because if you scramble messages before you send them, eavesdroppers who might intercept them cannot decipher them without the decoding key. (The science of encryption is called *cryptography*.)

Encryption software allows users to ensure the following:

■ *Authentication.* The ability to prove one's identity in a more secure form than just name-based or address-based authentication, both of which are subject to falsification.

■ *Privacy/Confidentiality.* Ensuring that no one can read the message except the intended recipient.

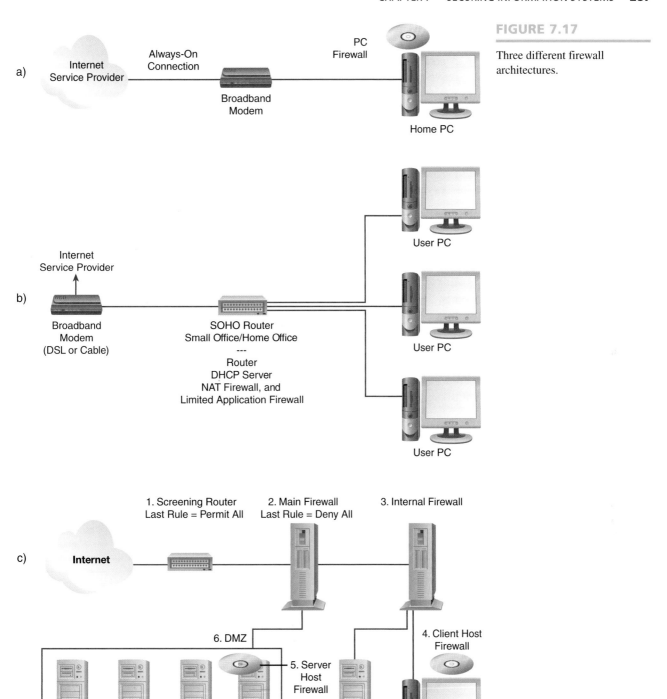

FIGURE 7.17

Three different firewall architectures.

FIGURE 7.18

Encryption is used to encode information so that unauthorized people cannot understand it.

```
Ciphertext letters:
JOGPSNBUJPO TZTUFNT UPEBZ
Equivalent plaintext letters:
INFORMATION SYSTEMS TODAY
```

■ *Integrity.* Assuring the recipient that the received message has not been altered in any way from the original that was sent.

■ *Nonrepudiation.* The use of a **digital signature**, available through most browsers, to prove that a message did, in fact, originate from the claimed sender.

We now have access to encryption software that scrambles text and voice messages and also allows us to send digital signatures that guarantee we are who we say we are when we send a message.

HOW ENCRYPTION WORKS. All encryption systems use a key—the code that scrambles and then decodes messages. When both sender and recipient use the same key, this is called a **symmetric secret key system**. This method of encrypting messages was used for centuries. One problem with symmetric secret key encryption is that, since both sender and recipient must keep their key secret from others, key management can be a problem. If too many people use the same key, the system can soon become ineffective. If different keys are used for sending messages to different people, the number of keys can become unmanageable.

Key management problems of secret key encryption systems were eliminated with the development of **public key technology**. Public key encryption is asymmetric since it uses two keys—a private key and a public key (see Figure 7.19). An eccentric former hacker and researcher from the Massachusetts Institute of Technology (MIT) named Whit Diffie is credited with first envisioning the possibility of using two keys—public and private—to encrypt and decode messages. He and two coworkers published their concept in 1976. Each person has his own key pair: a public key that is freely distributed and a private key that is kept secret. Say you want to send a message to Jane using this encryption system. First, you get Jane's public key, which is widely available, and you use it to scramble your message. Now even you cannot decode the encrypted message. When Jane receives the message, she uses her private key, known only to her, to unscramble it. Public key systems also allow you to authenticate messages. If you encrypt a message using your private key, you have "signed" it. A recipient can verify that the message came from you if your public key can be used to decode it.

Implementing public key encryption on a large scale, such as on a busy Web site, requires a more sophisticated solution. Here, a third party, called a **certificate authority**,

FIGURE 7.19

How asymmetrical keys are used to encrypt and decrypt information.

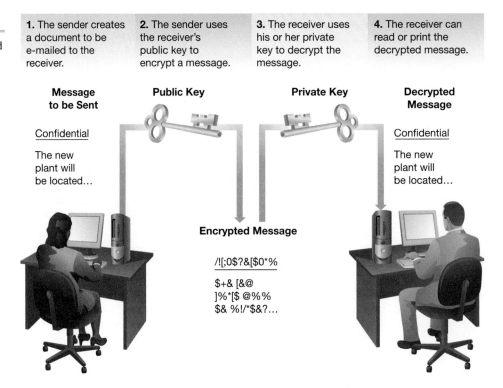

1. The sender creates a document to be e-mailed to the receiver.

2. The sender uses the receiver's public key to encrypt a message.

3. The receiver uses his or her private key to decrypt the message.

4. The receiver can read or print the decrypted message.

| Message to be Sent | Public Key | Private Key | Decrypted Message |

Confidential

The new plant will be located...

Encrypted Message

/![;0$?&[$0*%

$+& [&@]%*[$ @%% $& %!/*$&?...

Confidential

The new plant will be located...

is used. The certificate authority acts as a trusted middleman between computers and verifies that a Web site is a trusted site. The certificate authority knows that each computer is who it says it is and provides the public keys to each computer. **Secure Sockets Layer (SSL),** developed by Netscape, is a popular public key encryption method used on the Internet.

OTHER ENCRYPTION APPROACHES. Other encryption breakthroughs followed Diffie's public–private key revelation. In 1977, three MIT professors, Ron Rivest, Adi Shamir, and Len Adleman, created RSA (named for the surname initials of the inventors), a system based on the public–private key idea. They licensed the technology to several companies, including Lotus and Microsoft, but federal laws against exporting encryption technology kept the companies from incorporating RSA into their software. In 1991, Phil Zimmermann devised Pretty Good Privacy (PGP), a versatile encryption program that he gave away free to anyone who wanted to try it. It soon became the global favorite for encrypting messages.

While innovative encryption aficionados were mainstreaming the encryption concept, the government fought to keep control over keys that would allow its agents to decode communications deemed suspicious. There is great fear by legitimate governments that encryption technology will fall into the wrong hands, making it very difficult to monitor illegal activity or rogue governments. Consequently, in 1993, President Bill Clinton endorsed the Clipper Chip, a chip that could generate uncrackable codes. The catch was that the U.S. government would have the key to decode any messages scrambled via the Clipper Chip. Opponents criticized the idea as a threat to personal liberty. But when a flaw was found in the chip, which under certain conditions would allow users to take advantage of the chip's strong encryption capabilities without giving the government the key, the Clipper Chip idea was scrapped before it could become reality.

The government finally loosened its control over encryption technology when, in 1999, federal regulations were written allowing the export of strong encryption programs. This paved the way for software developers to build encryption options into their products and made it easier for any computer user to take advantage of encryption technology. Nevertheless, the U.S. government has maintained Department of Commerce regulations against the export of strong encryption programs, but in 2003 President George W. Bush's administration promised not to enforce some of the encryption regulations that might stifle encryption research. This has solved problems some encryption researchers have had when they wanted to distribute codes for widespread use on the Internet, but future presidents' administrations may decide to strictly enforce encryption export regulations, at which time cryptography researchers may again find themselves wrangling with the federal government.

THE FUTURE OF ENCRYPTION. Private security and encryption researchers are working to develop products that can serve military as well as civilian needs without violating the privacy rights of individuals. Future encryption programs will provide the following:

- *Strong Security.* Generally, the larger the key used for encryption, the more secure it is. But larger keys also work at slower speeds; therefore, the trend has been toward shorter keys, which are easier to break.
- *High Speed.* Encryption is not effective if it works so slowly that it is noticeable.
- *Usable on Any Platform.* Encryption programs designed for computers have not been transferable to cellular telephones and other electronic devices. New encryption must work on a variety of platforms, such as PCs, workstations, high-end mainframes, cellular telephones, and personal digital assistants (PDAs).

While encryption cannot solve all privacy issues, such as the trading of consumer information collected on the Web or deliberate leakage of e-mail messages the sender intended to be kept private, it is definitely effective in keeping snoopers out when both senders and receivers desire privacy. Perhaps eventually encryption will protect medical records, credit histories, credit card databases, and other information that should be marked "keep out" to unauthorized viewers.

Powerful Partnerships

The Disruptive Duo, Niklas Zennström and Janus Friis.

Niklas Zennström was born in Sweden in 1966 and was educated at Uppsala University in Sweden and the University of Michigan in Ann Arbor. Zennström met Janus Friis, ten years his junior, in 1996, when both men were working in Denmark, Friis' native country.

Zennström and Friis developed a peer-to-peer file sharing service called KaZaA, which could be used to exchange many file types, such as video, music, applications, and documents (peer-to-peer software uses the combined network bandwidth of the users of the software to improve performance). KaZaA soon became the application of choice for illegally downloading and sharing music files, and Zennström and Friis' company was sued in the Netherlands by the music recording industry for copyright infringement. Further, KaZaA has been accused of being bundled with various programs considered adware and spyware, drawing much criticism from computer security experts. In 2001, the duo sold KaZaA and KaZaA's user base has dwindled since tight restrictions were implemented into the software to prevent illegal file sharing.

In 2003, Zennström and Friis created Skype, a program that lets users make voice calls over the Internet using peer-to-peer technology. Calls are free to other Skype users, but there are charges for calls to land lines and mobile phones, based on location. Voice mail, call

FIGURE 7.20

The disruptive duo, Niklas Zennström and Janus Friis.

forwarding, instant messaging, file transfer, and video-conferencing services are also available to users. In 2005, eBay bought Skype for $3.1 billion. In 2008, Skype released "Skype for your mobile"—a downloadable mini version of Skype that works on approximately fifty of the most popular java-based mobile phones.

As of 2008, Skype reported 370 million registered users globally. Customer service and security have reportedly been issues of concern for users, but user testimonials posted at Skype.com are, of course, enthusiastic about the service.

The duo's latest creation is Joost, a system for broadcasting television programs over the Internet, again using peer-to-peer technology. In 2007, CNNMoney.com rated the two entrepreneurs twenty-seventh on the publication's list of "The 50 Who Matter Now." "Call them the disruptive duo," the article began. "First they undermined the music industry by unleashing the KaZaA file-sharing network. Then they rattled the telephone industry by creating Skype, a free Internet phone network." The partners' disruptive genius rolls on, the article continues, as their joint ventures move into the television industry with Joost, "a full-screen, peer-to-peer TV network that you can watch on your laptop." Joost provided 353 channels in 2008, and 17,000 programs. Having made their fortune with disruptive innovations, in 2007, Zennström and Friis founded Atomico, a venture capital group to invest in disruptive entrepreneurs working in the consumer Internet technology sector.

Which industry will the "disruptive duo" transform next? Who knows.

Based on:

Ilett, D. (2004, November 26). CA slaps spyware label on Kazaa. *CNET News.* Retrieved November 7, 2008, from http://news.cnet.com/CA-slaps-spyware-label-on-Kazaa/2100-1025_3/5467539.html.

Interview: Janus Friis (2008, January 15). *Netmag.co.uk.* Retrieved May 12, 2008, from http://www.netmag.co.uk/zine/discover-interview/janus-friis.

Janus Friis. (2008, March 22). In *Wikipedia, the free encyclopedia.* Retrieved May 12, 2008, from http://en.wikipedia.org/w/index.php?title=Janus_Friis&oldid=200061453.

Kazaa. (2006, March 22). *Stopbadware.org.* Retrieved November 7, 2008, from http://www.stopbadware.org/reports/reportdisplay?reportname=kazaa.

Naraine, R. (2006, March 32). Spyware trail leads to Kazaa, big advertisers. *eWeek.com*. Retrieved November 7, 2008, from http://www.eweek.com/c/a/Security/Spyware-Trail-Leads-to-Kazaa-Big-Advertisers.

Niklas Zennström. (2008, April 12). In *Wikipedia, the free encyclopedia*. Retrieved May 12, 2008, from http://en.wikipedia.org/w/index.php?title=Niklas_Zennstr%C3%B6m&oldid=205080241.

Niklas Zennström (n.d.). Retrieved May 12, 2008, from http://www.web2summit.com/cs/web2006/view/e_spkr/2976.

Skype. (2008, May 12). In *Wikipedia, the free encyclopedia*. Retrieved May 12, 2008, from http://en.wikipedia.org/w/index.php?title=Skype&oldid=211923420.

Skype. (n.d.). Retrieved May 12, 2008, from http://www.skype.com/.

The 50 who matter now: Janus Friis and Niklas Zennstrom. (n.d.). *CNNMoney.com*. Retrieved May 12, 2008 from http://money.cnn.com/galleries/2007/biz2/0706/gallery.50whomatter.biz2/24.html.

Virus Monitoring and Prevention **Virus prevention**, which is a set of activities for detecting and preventing computer viruses, has become a full-time, important task for information systems departments within organizations and for all of us with our personal computers. While viruses often have colorful names—Melissa, I Love You, Naked Wife—they can be catastrophic from a computing perspective. Here we describe some precautions you can take to ensure that your computer is protected:

- Purchase and install antivirus software, then update frequently to be sure you are protected against new viruses. These programs can actively scan your computer, locate viruses, inform you of the presence of viruses, destroy and/or neutralize viruses, and keep your computer updated with the most up-to-date antivirus protection. This software is available relatively inexpensively from several software vendors and can be downloaded over the Internet from their Web sites; updates are typically available over the Internet as well.

- Do not use flash drives, disks, or shareware from unknown or suspect sources and be equally careful when downloading material from the Internet, making sure that the source is reputable.

- Delete without opening any e-mail message received from an unknown source. Be especially wary of opening attachments. It is better to delete a legitimate message than to infect your computer system with a destructive germ.

- Do not blindly open e-mail attachments, even if they come from a known source (such as a friend or coworker). Many viruses are spread without the sender's knowledge, so it is better to check with the sender before opening a potentially unsafe attachment.

- If your computer system contracts a virus, report the infection to your school or company's IT department so that appropriate measures can be taken.

Information systems security—especially issues of unauthorized computer access, sending spam e-mail, deploying spyware, or spreading computer viruses—is at a minimum an ethical issue and at most a computer crime. (In Chapter 11, we will continue this discussion by exploring the ethical and legal implications of information systems security and use.)

Audit-Control Software **Audit-control software** is used to keep track of computer activity so that auditors can spot suspicious activity and take action. The software is designed so that any user—authorized or unauthorized—leaves electronic footprints that auditors can trace. The record showing who has used a computer system and how it was used is called an *audit trail*. For the software to effectively protect security, of course, auditors within an organization—most often someone in the IT department or information security department—must monitor and interpret results.

Facilities Specialized facilities are an important component of creating a reliable and secure information systems infrastructure. In addition to technical requirements (such as power and cooling), organizations face the need to protect important equipment from both outside intruders and the elements, such as water or fire. The most prominent threats to an organization's IS facilities come from floods, seismic activity, rolling blackouts,

FIGURE 7.21

Potential threats to IS facilities include floods, hurricanes, terrorism, power outages, and seismic activity.

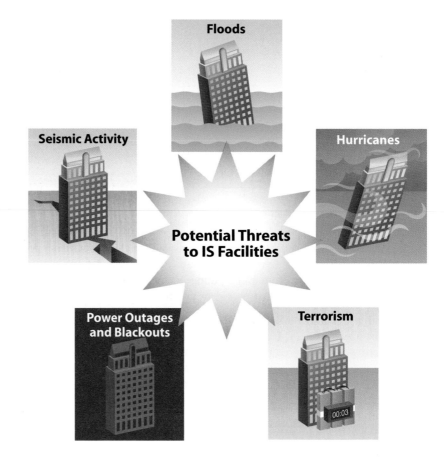

hurricanes, and the potential of criminal activities (see Figure 7.21). How can an organization reliably protect its facilities from such threats?

ENSURING AVAILABILITY. As many potential causes of disasters cannot be avoided (there's no way to stop a hurricane), organizations should attempt to plan for the worst and protect their infrastructure accordingly. For companies operating in the digital world, the information systems infrastructure is often critical for most business processes, so special care has to be taken to secure it. Whereas some applications can tolerate some downtime in case something malfunctions or disaster strikes, other applications (such as UPS's package tracking databases) can't tolerate any downtime—these companies need 24/7/365 reliability (see Figure 7.22).

In order to provide for uninterrupted service, the infrastructure is usually housed in high-availability facilities; such facilities are equipped with different features to assure availability and reliability. The facilities for UPS in Atlanta, Georgia, and Mahwah, New Jersey, are prime examples for such high-availability facilities. To ensure uninterrupted service, the data centers are self-sufficient, and each can operate for up to two days on self-generated power. The power is needed not only for the computers but also for air conditioning, as each facility needs air-conditioning capacity equaling that of or more than 2,000 homes. In case power fails, the cooling is provided using more than 600,000 gallons of chilled water, and the UPS facilities even have backup wells in case the municipal water supply should fail. Other protective measures include raised floors (to protect from floods) and buildings designed to withstand winds of 200 miles per hour. As you can imagine, such facilities are highly complex, and monitoring the operations can be a difficult task, as there are more than 10,000 data points to observe (such as temperature readings, power surges, and so on). To help manage this infrastructure component, these facilities have been designed so that they can be monitored from a single laptop computer.

Many (especially smaller) organizations do not need facilities the size of one of the UPS data centers; instead, they may just need space for a few servers. For such needs,

FIGURE 7.22

UPS's servers handle up to 20 million requests per day.

companies can turn to **collocation facilities**. Organizations can rent space (usually in the form of cabinets or shares of a cabinet; see Figure 7.23) for their servers in such collocation facilities, and the organizations managing collocation facilities provide the necessary infrastructure in terms of power, backups, connectivity, and security.

SECURING THE FACILITIES INFRASTRUCTURE. An organization's information systems infrastructure always needs to be secured to prevent it from outside intruders. Thus, no matter whether your server is located in a cabinet within your organization or you have rented space in a collocation facility, you should have physical safeguards in place to secure the

FIGURE 7.23

Collocation facilities allow organizations to rent secure space for their infrastructure.

Source: http://www.sungard.com/corporate/general_pictures.htm.

equipment. Absolute protection against security breaches remains out of reach, but here are a few additional safeguards organizations can employ:

- ■ *Backups.* Organizations and individual computer users should perform **backups** of important files to external hard drives, CDs, tapes, or online backup service providers at regular intervals. Some systems can be set to perform automatic backups at specified intervals, such as at the end of a working day. Information maintained in current databases and transferred to backup tapes should be encrypted so that if crackers enter databases or thieves steal tapes, the information is useless to them.

- ■ *Backup Sites.* **Backup sites** are critical for business continuity in the event a disaster strikes; in other words, backup sites can be thought of as a company's office in a temporary location. Commonly, a distinction is made between cold and hot backup sites. A **cold backup site** is nothing more than an empty warehouse with all necessary connections for power and communication but nothing else. In the case of a disaster, a company has to first set up all necessary equipment, ranging from office furniture to Web servers. While this is the least expensive option, it also takes a relatively longer time before a company can resume working after a disaster. A **hot backup site**, in contrast, is a fully equipped backup facility, having everything from office chairs to a one-to-one replication of the most current data. In the event of a disaster, all that has to be done is to relocate the employees to the backup site to continue working. Obviously, this is a very expensive option, as the backup site has to be kept fully equipped and all the information systems infrastructure duplicated. Further, hot backup sites also have a redundant backup of the data so that the business processes are interrupted as little as possible. To achieve this redundancy, all data are **mirrored** on separate servers (i.e., everything is stored synchronously on two independent systems). This might seem expensive, but for a critical business application involving customers, it may be less expensive to run a redundant backup system in parallel than it would be to disrupt business or lose customers in the event of catastrophic system failure.

- ■ *Redundant Data Centers.* Often, companies choose to replicate their data centers in multiple locations. Thinking about the location of redundant systems is an important aspect of disaster planning. If a company relies on redundant systems, all of which are located within the same building, a single event can incapacitate all of the systems. Similarly, events such as a hurricane can damage systems that are located across town from each other. Thus, even if the primary infrastructure is located in-house, it pays to have a backup located in a different geographic area to minimize the risk of a disaster happening to both systems. For example, given that data is the lifeblood for UPS, they have replicated their infrastructure in two locations—New Jersey and Georgia—to ensure speed and reliability.

- ■ *Closed-Circuit Television (CCTV).* While installation and monitoring a CCTV system is costly, the systems can monitor for physical intruders in data centers, server rooms, or collocation facilities. Video cameras display the physical interior and/or exterior of a facility and record all activity on tape. In-house security personnel or an outside security service can watch computer monitors and immediately report suspicious activity to the police. Digital video recording can be used to store this information digitally, even from remote cameras connected to the system via a company's intranet, wireless LANs, or the Internet.

- ■ *Uninterruptible Power Supply (UPS).* A UPS does not protect against intruders, but it protects against power surges and temporary power failures that can cause information loss.

Clearly, there are a broad range of technology-based approaches for securing information systems. A comprehensive security plan will include numerous technological methods. Next, we examine human-based methods.

Human Safeguards

In addition to the technological safeguards, there are various human safeguards that can help to safeguard information systems, specifically ethics, laws, and effective management (see Figure 7.24). Information systems *ethics,* discussed thoroughly in Chapter 11, relates

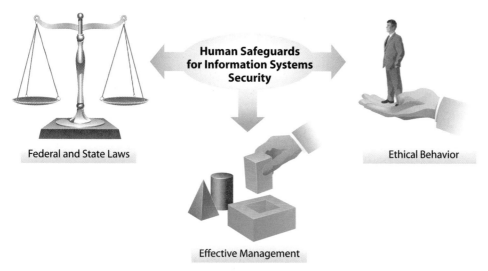

FIGURE 7.24

Human safeguards for information systems security.

to a broad range of standards of appropriate conduct by users. Educating potential users at an early age as to what constitutes appropriate behavior can help, but unethical users will undoubtedly always remain a problem for those wanting to maintain information systems security. Additionally, there are numerous federal and state laws against unauthorized use of networks and computer systems. Unfortunately, individuals who want unauthorized access to networks and computer systems usually find a way to exploit them; often, after the fact, laws are enacted to prohibit that activity in the future.

Additionally, beyond ethics and laws, the quality of information security in any organization depends on *effective management.* Managers must continuously check for security problems, recognize that holes in security exist, and take appropriate action. We discuss methods for effectively managing information systems security next.

Managing Information Systems Security

Very often some of the best things that people can do to secure their information systems are not necessarily technical in nature. Instead, they may involve changes within the organization and/or better management of people's use of information systems. For example, one of the outcomes of the systems security risk analysis described here may well be a set of computer and/or Internet use policies (sometimes referred to as **acceptable use policies**) for people within the organization, with clearly spelled out penalties for noncompliance (see Figure 7.25). More fundamental to security than management techniques such as these is that you make every effort to hire trustworthy employees and treat them well. Trustworthy employees who are treated well are less likely to commit offenses affecting the organization's information systems.

Developing an Information Systems Security Plan

All organizations should develop an information systems security plan. An **information systems security plan** involves assessing risks, planning ways to reduce risk, implementing the plan, and ongoing monitoring. This planning process should be ongoing and include these five steps:

1. *Risk Analysis.* Organizations should do the following:
   a. Determine the value of electronic information.
   b. Assess threats to confidentiality, integrity, and availability of information.
   c. Determine which computer operations are most vulnerable to security breaches.
   d. Assess current security policies.
   e. Recommend changes to existing practices and/or policies that will improve computer security.

FIGURE 7.25

Most organizations provide
employees or customers with an
acceptable use policy.

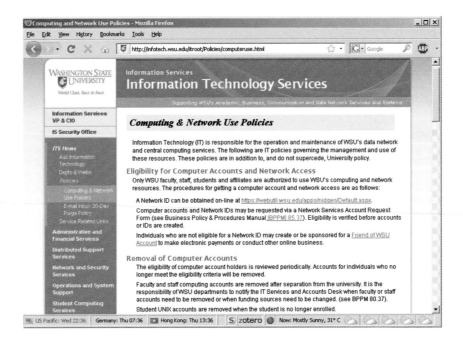

2. ***Policies and Procedures.*** Once risks are assessed, a plan should be formulated that
   details what action will be taken if security is breached. Policies and procedures
   related to computer security generally include the following:
   a. *Information Policy.* Outlines how sensitive information will be handled, stored,
      transmitted, and destroyed.
   b. *Security Policy.* Explains technical controls on all organizational computer
      systems, such as access limitations, audit-control software, firewalls, and so on.
   c. *Use Policy.* Outlines the organization's policy regarding appropriate use of in-
      house computer systems. May mandate no Internet surfing, use of company
      computer systems only for employment-related purposes, restricted use of e-mail,
      and so on.
   d. *Backup Policy.* Explains requirements for backing up information.
   e. *Account Management Policy.* Lists procedures for adding new users to systems
      and removing users who have left the organization.
   f. *Incident Handling Procedures.* Lists procedures to follow when handling a
      security breach.
   g. *Disaster Recovery Plan.* Lists all the steps an organization will take to restore
      computer operations in case of a natural or deliberate disaster. Each department
      within the organization generally has its own disaster recovery plan (see
      discussion below).
3. ***Implementation.*** Once policies and plans are established, organizations can decide
   which security mechanisms to use and train personnel regarding security policies
   and measures. During this phase, network security mechanisms, such as firewalls,
   are put in place, as are intrusion detection systems, such as antivirus software,
   manual and automated log examination software, and host- and network-based
   intrusion detection software. Encryption information, passwords, and smart cards
   and smart badges are also disseminated and explained during this phase. The
   information technology department is usually responsible for instituting security
   measures.
4. ***Training.*** Personnel within an organization should know the security policy and the
   plan for disaster recovery and be prepared to perform assigned tasks in that regard—
   both routinely on a daily basis and disaster related.
5. ***Auditing.*** Auditing is an ongoing process that assesses policy adherence, the
   security of new projects, and whether the organization's computer security can be

penetrated. Penetration tests are conducted in-house and/or by an outside contractor to see how well the organization's computer security measures are working. Can the intrusion detection system detect attacks? Are incident response procedures effective? Can the network be penetrated? Is physical security adequate? Do employees know security policies and procedures?

Disaster Planning In some cases, all attempts to provide a reliable and secure information systems infrastructure are in vain, and disasters cannot be avoided. Thus, organizations need to be prepared for when something catastrophic occurs. The most important aspect of preparing for disaster is creating a **business continuity plan**, which describes how a business resumes operation after a disaster. A subset of the business continuity plan is the **disaster recovery plan**, which spells out detailed procedures for recovering from systems-related disasters, such as virus infections and other disasters that might cripple the information systems infrastructure. This way, even under the worst-case scenario, people will be able to replace or reconstruct critical files or data, or they will at least have a plan readily available to begin the recovery process. A typical disaster recovery plan includes information that answers the following questions:

- What events are considered a disaster?
- What should be done to prepare the backup site?
- What is the chain of command, and who can declare a disaster?
- What hardware and software are needed to recover from a disaster?
- Which personnel are needed for staffing the backup sites?
- What is the sequence for moving back to the original location after recovery?
- Which provider can be drawn upon to aid in the disaster recovery process?

Designing the Recovery Plan When planning for disaster, two objectives should be considered by an organization: recovery time and recovery point objectives. **Recovery time objectives** specify the maximum time allowed to recover from a catastrophic event. For example, should the organization be able to resume operations in minutes, hours, or days after the disaster? Having completely redundant systems helps to minimize the recovery time and might be best suited for mission-critical applications, such as e-commerce transaction servers. For other applications, such as data mining, while important, the recovery time can be longer without disrupting primary business processes.

Additionally, **recovery point objectives** specify how current the backup data should be. Imagine that your computer's hard drive crashes while you are working on a term paper. Luckily, you recently backed up your data. Would you prefer the last backup to be a few days old, or would you rather have the last backup include your most recent changes to the term paper? Having completely redundant systems that mirror the data helps to minimize (or even avoid) data loss in the event of a catastrophic failure.

Responding to a Security Breach Organizations that have developed a comprehensive information systems security plan, as outlined previously, will have the ability to rapidly respond to any type of security breach to their information systems resources or to a natural disaster. In addition to restoring lost data using backups, common responses to a security breach include performing a new risk audit and implementing a combination of additional (more secure) safeguards (as described previously). Additionally, when intruders are discovered, organizations can contact local law enforcement agencies and the FBI for assistance in locating and prosecuting them. Several online organizations issue bulletins to alert organizations and individuals to possible software vulnerabilities or attacks based on reports from organizations when security breaches occur. Additionally, the Computer Emergency Response Team Coordination Center (CERT/CC), established by the federal government in 1988 as a major center of Internet security expertise, provides additional resources for organizations by publishing security alerts, conducting and publishing research, and providing training to incident response professionals. Its Web site is at www.cert.org.

The State of Systems Security Management

We continue to hear and read about cases where a breach of computer security was catastrophic and/or had potentially dire consequences. For example, a stolen laptop computer in May 2006 reportedly put 26.5 million U.S. military personnel at risk for *identity theft* because it contained a large database that included Social Security numbers, birth dates, and other personal information. Nevertheless, even with these highly publicized incidents, systems security measures are paying off for most organizations. According to the annual Computer Security Institute (CSI) Computer Crime and Security Survey (2007), the total financial losses resulting from cybercrime are decreasing. Key findings from their survey include the following:

- Financial fraud attacks result in the greatest financial losses for organizations; other significant costs were due to viruses, data theft, unauthorized access, and denial of service attacks.
- Relatively few organizations (about 29 percent) utilize cyberinsurance (to cover losses incurred from attacks), even though it is widely available.
- Relatively few organizations (about 29 percent) report computer intrusions to law enforcement due to various fears such as how negative publicity would hurt stock values or how competitors might gain an advantage over news of a security incident.
- Most organizations do not outsource security activities.
- Nearly all organizations conduct routine and ongoing security audits.
- The majority of organizations believed security training of employees is important, but most respondents said their organization did not spend enough on security training.

In addition to these findings, organizations use a broad variety of security technologies (see Figure 7.26). Clearly, because malicious crackers won't become complacent anytime soon, it is encouraging that organizations appear to be gaining ground to guard against attacks. The lesson learned here is that we need to continue to implement vigilant approaches to better manage systems security in the digital world.

FIGURE 7.26

Security technologies used by respondents of the 2007 CSI Computer Crime and Security Survey.

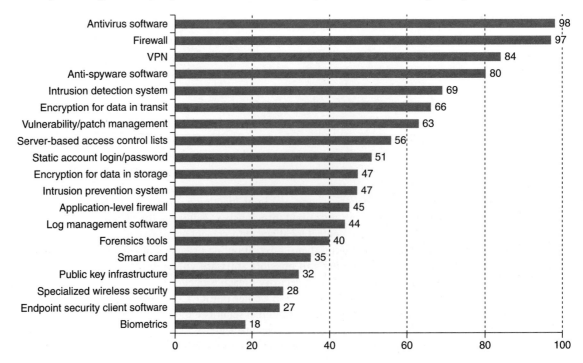

Coming Attractions

Recharging Gadgets Wirelessly

Cell phones, MP3 players, digital cameras, and laptop computers are indispensable tools in today's world. They also have at least one downside—especially for travelers. Batteries run down and have to be recharged, which means carrying a charger for each device, since one charger does *not* fit all. At least not yet.

A Delaware-based company, WildCharge, has developed a flat, metal charger, about the size of a piece of copy paper, that can recharge several digital devices at once, simply by placing a device equipped with an adapter on the charger. The company has come out with

an adapter for one product—Motorola's Razr phones—and others are in development, including an adapter for charging an iPhone. According to the company, *Time* chose WildCharge as one of 2007's best inventions.

Based on:

Greene, K. (2007, December 13). Recharging gadgets wirelessly: A metal pad that can recharge devices placed on top of it has come to market. *Technologyreview.com.* Retrieved May 12, 2008, from http://www.technologyreview.com/Infotech/19894/?a=f.

WildCharge (n.d.). Retrieved May 12, 2008, from http://www.wildcharge.com.

Information Systems Controls, Auditing, and the Sarbanes-Oxley Act

As you have seen, there are a variety of issues to consider when managing information systems security. To ensure security, control costs, gain and protect trust, remain competitive, or comply with internal or external governance (e.g., the Sarbanes-Oxley Act, discussed later in this section), **information systems controls** have to be put into place. Such controls, which help ensure the reliability of information, can consist of a variety of different measures, such as policies and their physical implementation, access restrictions, or record keeping, to be able to trace actions and transactions and who is responsible for these. IS controls thus need to be applied throughout the entire IS

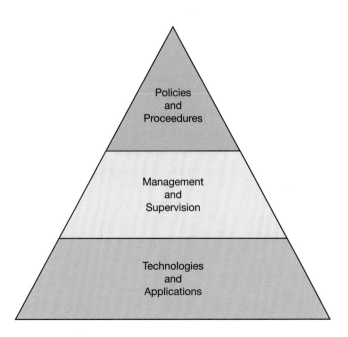

FIGURE 7.27

Hierarchy of IS controls.

Based on http://infotech.aicpa.org.

infrastructure. To be most effective, controls should be a combination of three types of controls:

■ Preventive controls (to prevent any potentially negative event from occurring, such as by preventing outside intruders from accessing a facility)
■ Detective controls (to assess whether anything went wrong, such as unauthorized access attempts)
■ Corrective controls (to mitigate the impact of any problem after it has arisen, such as restoring compromised data)

One way to conceptualize the different forms of controls is by a hierarchy ranging from high-level policies to the implementation at the application level (see Figure 7.27 for the hierarchy of controls); Table 7.1 gives a brief explanation of the different types of controls and presents examples for each. You have learned about a variety of IS controls in prior sections, and, while reading this book, you will continue to come across the different elements of control. In the following sections, we will describe how companies use IS

TABLE 7.1 Different Types of Information Systems Controls

Type of Control	What Is It For?	Examples
Policies	Define aims and objectives of the organization	General policies about: Security and privacy Rights of access Data and systems ownership End-user development Access to sensitive areas (e.g., high-availability facilities) Disaster planning
Standards	Support the requirements of policies	Standards about: Systems development process Systems software configuration Application controls Data structures Documentation
Organization and management	Define lines of reporting to implement effective control and policy development	Policies about: Security and use Account authorization Backup and recovery Incident reporting
Physical and environmental controls	Protect the organization's IS assets	High-availability facilities Collocation facilities
Systems software controls	Enable applications and users to utilize the systems	Control access to applications Generate activity logs Prevent outside intrusion (e.g., by hackers)
Systems development and acquisition controls	Ensure that systems meet the organization's needs	Document user requirements Use formal processes for systems design, development, testing, and maintenance
Application-based controls	Ensure correct input, processing, storage, and output of data; maintain record of data as it moves through the system	Input controls (such as automated checking of the inputs into a Web form) Processing controls Output controls (comparing the outputs against intended results) Integrity controls (ensure that data remains correct) Management trail (keep record of transactions to be able to locate sources of potential errors)

auditing to assess the IS controls in place and whether further IS controls need to be implemented or changed.

Information Systems Auditing

Analyzing the IS controls should be an ongoing process for organizations. However, often it can be beneficial for organizations to periodically have an external entity review the controls so as to uncover any potential problems. An **information systems audit**, often performed by external auditors, can help organizations assess the state of their information systems controls to determine necessary changes and to help ensure the information systems' availability, confidentiality, and integrity. The response to the strengths and weaknesses identified in the IS audit is often determined by the potential risks an organization faces. In other words, the IS audit has to assess whether the IS controls in place are sufficient to address the potential risks. Thus, a major component of the IS audit is a risk assessment (discussed in prior sections), which aims at determining what type of risks the organization's IS infrastructure faces, the criticality of those risks to the infrastructure, and the level of risks the organization is willing to tolerate.

Once the risk has been assessed, auditors have to evaluate the organization's internal controls. During such audits, the auditor tries to gather evidence regarding the effectiveness of the controls. However, testing all controls under all possible conditions is very inefficient and often infeasible. Thus, auditors frequently rely on **computer-assisted auditing tools (CAAT)**, which is specific software to test applications and data, using test data or simulations. In addition to using specific auditing tools, auditors use audit sampling procedures to assess the controls, enabling the audit to be conducted in the most cost-effective manner. Once the audit has been performed and sufficient evidence has been gathered, reports are issued to the organization. Usually, such reports are followed up with a discussion of the results and potential courses of action.

The Sarbanes-Oxley Act

Performing an IS audit can help an organization reduce costs or remain competitive by identifying areas where IS controls are lacking and need improvement. Another major factor that has contributed to a high demand for IS auditors is the need to comply with government regulations, most notably the **Sarbanes-Oxley Act** of 2002 (hereafter S-OX). Formed as a reaction to large-scale accounting scandals that led to the downfall of corporations such as WorldCom and Enron; S-OX primarily addresses the accounting side of organizations. However, given the importance of an IS infrastructure and IS controls for an organization's financial applications, it is of major importance to include IS controls in compliance reviews.

According to S-OX, companies have to demonstrate that there are controls in place to prevent misuse or fraud, controls to detect any potential problems, and effective measures in place to correct any problems; S-OX goes so far that corporate executives face jail time and heavy fines if the appropriate controls are not in place or are ineffective. The information systems architecture plays a key role in S-OX compliance, given that many controls are information-systems based, providing capabilities to detect information exceptions and to provide a management trail for tracing exceptions. However, S-OX itself barely addresses IS controls specifically; rather, it addresses general processes and practices, leaving companies wondering how to comply with the guidelines put forth in the act. Further, it is often cumbersome and time-consuming for organizations to identify the relevant systems to be audited for S-OX compliance. Thus, many organizations find it easier to review their entire IS infrastructure, following objectives set forth in guidelines such as the **control objectives for information and related technology (COBIT)**—a set of best practices that helps organizations both maximize the benefits from their IS infrastructure and establish appropriate controls.

Another issue faced by organizations because of S-OX is the requirement to preserve evidence to document compliance and for potential lawsuits. Since the inception of S-OX, e-mails and even instant messages have achieved the same status as regular business documents and thus need to be preserved for a period of time, typically up to seven years.

Failure to present such documents in the case of litigious activity can lead to severe fines being imposed on companies and their executives, and courts usually will not accept the argument that a message could not be located. For example, the investment bank Morgan Stanley faced fines up to $15 million for failing to retain e-mail messages. On the surface, it seems easiest for an organization to simply archive all the e-mail messages sent and received. However, such a "digital landfill," where everything is stored, can quickly grow to an unmanageable size, and companies cannot comply with the mandate to present evidence in a timely manner. Thus, many organizations turn to e-mail management software that archives and categorizes all incoming and outgoing e-mails based on key words. Even using such specialized software, finding e-mails related to a certain topic within the archive, can pose a tremendous task: Some analysts estimate that a business with 25,000 employees generates over 4 billion e-mail messages over the course of seven years (not counting any increase in e-mail activity), which will be hard to handle for even the most sophisticated programs.

Industry Analysis

Banking Industry

Like many other industries moving into the Internet age, the banking business is changing. Since the nineteenth century, banks in the United States have been heavily regulated. Federal and state laws passed in the 1800s and the 1930s have limited banks to certain geographic locations and have determined the services they could offer. For example, in many states each bank could maintain locations for accepting deposits in only that one state, and in some states they were allowed to maintain offices in just one county. Banks could offer traditional banking services, including deposits and loans, but little more. Insurance services were banned, and securities underwriting was limited. The many banking laws and regulations were intended to limit the number of bank failures after the Great Depression and to make banks safer, but they also limited services that banks could provide to customers, which prevented them from competing with stockbrokers and insurance companies.

Nearly all these banking restrictions were eased or eliminated from the 1970s to the present, when banking deregulation took place. Deregulation resulted in increased acquisitions and consolidations, integration across state lines, and a larger market share for better-run banks as they gained ground over their less-efficient rivals. As a result, banks could offer more customer services at lower prices, benefiting the country's overall economy.

Today, the Internet provides banks with another way to serve customers and another venue for competition. Banks can now offer customers the convenience and security of online banking services—from account management to loan applications and certificate of deposit

purchases. No longer do customers judge banks simply according to hours open, ATM locations, fees charged, or travel distance to a brick-and-mortar site. Now banks offering online services can also expect potential customers to judge them according to the following:

1. The degree to which the online banking experience can be personalized
2. Ease of use
3. Responsiveness of the site

Technological and global changes will undoubtedly change the banking industry further as the twenty-first century progresses.

Questions

1. What are your biggest security concerns related to online banking? How does/should your bank address these concerns?
2. Deregulation of the banking industry allowed banks to more freely operate across state lines; should international banks be allowed to operate in domestic markets? Why or why not?

Based on:

Delivering on the promise to change the banking experience (2005, November 15). Retrieved May 12, 2008, from http://www.microsoft.com/presspass/features/2005/nov05/11-15Banking.mspx.

Poole, W. (1999, January 12). The structure of our changing banking industry: Let the market decide. *St. Louis Fed.* Retrieved May 12, 2008, from http://stlouisfed.org/news/speeches/1999/01_12_99.html.

Strahan, P. E. (2003, July). The real effects of banking deregulation. Retrieved May 12, 2008, from http://research.stlouisfed.org/publications/review/03/07/Strahan.pdf.

Key Points Review

1. *Explain what is meant by the term "information systems security" and describe the primary threats to information systems security and how systems are compromised.* Information systems security refers to precautions taken to keep all aspects of information systems (e.g., all hardware, software, network equipment, and data) safe from unauthorized use or access. The primary threats to information systems include accidents and natural disasters, employees and consultants, links to outside business contacts, and outsiders. Information systems are most often compromised through one or more of the following: unauthorized access, information modification, denial of service, and viruses, as well as spam, spyware, and cookies.

2. *Describe both technology- and human-based safeguards for information systems.* There are five general categories of technological safeguards: physical access restrictions, firewalls, encryption, virus monitoring and protection, and audit-control software. Physical access restrictions prevent unauthorized access using authentication through something a person has (e.g., identification card), something a person knows (e.g., password), or something a person is (e.g., unique human attribute). Many organizations use some combination of methods to best control information systems assets. A variety of technologies can be deployed to enhance system security, including firewalls, biometrics, virtual private networks, encryption, and virus protection tools. Firewalls are hardware or software used to detect intrusion and prevent unauthorized access to or from a private network. Biometrics is the use of technology to better authenticate users by matching fingerprints, retinal patterns in the eye, body weight, or other bodily characteristic before granting access to a computer. Virtual private networks use authentication and encryption to provide a secure tunnel within a public network such as the Internet so that information can pass securely between two computers. Encryption— the process of encoding messages before they enter the network or airwaves—is very useful for securing information when you do not have access to a secure telecommunications channel. Virus monitoring and protection utilizes a set of hardware and software to detect and prevent computer viruses. Audit-control software is used to keep track of computer activity so that auditors can spot suspicious activity and take action if necessary. Other technological safeguards include backups, closed-circuit television, and uninterruptible power supplies. Human safeguards include ethical standards, federal and state laws, and effective management. Organizations typically utilize a combination of both technological and human safeguards when protecting their information systems resources.

3. *Discuss how to better manage information systems security and explain the process of developing an information systems security plan.* Because no system is 100 percent secure, organizations must utilize all available resources for implementing an effective information systems security plan. The planning process includes a risk analysis, the development of policies and procedures, implementation, training, and ongoing auditing. Relatedly, organizations should develop a business continuity plan and a disaster recovery plan that specifies how to react to a disaster. After a security breach, organizations should perform new audits, implement new countermeasures, and possibly inform law enforcement agencies of the breach.

4. *Describe how organizations can establish IS controls to better ensure security.* IS controls can help ensure a secure and reliable infrastructure; such controls should be a mix of preventive, detective, and corrective controls. To assess the efficacy of these controls, organizations frequently conduct information systems audits to determine the risks an organization faces and how far the IS controls can limit any potentially negative effects. Further, organizations perform IS audits to comply with government regulations, most notably the Sarbanes-Oxley Act of 2002. According to S-OX, companies have to demonstrate that there are controls in place to prevent misuse or fraud, controls to detect any potential problems, and effective measures to correct any problems; S-OX goes so far that a business executive could face heavy fines or substantial jail time if appropriate controls are not in place or are ineffective. Performing thorough IS audits on a regular basis can help assess compliance to these regulations.

Key Terms

acceptable use policies 295
access-control software 282
adware 275

application-level control 285
audit-control software 291
authentication 281

backup site 293
backup 293
biometrics 282

business continuity plan 297
CAPTCHA 277
certificate authority 288
circuit-level control 286
cold backup site 293
collocation facility 293
computer-assisted auditing tools
  (CAAT) 301
confidentiality 287
control objectives for information
  and related technology
  (COBIT) 301
cookie 278
denial of service 273
digital signature 287
disaster recovery plan 297
drive-by hacking 283
encryption 287
firewall 285

firewall architecture 287
hot backup site 293
information modification 271
information systems audit 300
information systems controls 299
information systems security 270
information systems security
  plan 296
integrity 287
mirrored 294
network address translation
  (NAT) 286
nonrepudiation 287
packet filtering 285
phishing 277
privacy 287
proxy server 286
public key technology 288
recovery point objectives 297

recovery time objectives 297
risk acceptance 281
risk analysis 280
risk reduction 281
risk transference 281
Sarbanes-Oxley Act (S-OX) 301
Secure Sockets Layer (SSL) 288
spam 275
spam filter 275
spim 277
spyware 275
symmetric secret key system 287
tunneling 285
unauthorized access 271
virtual private network (VPN) 284
virus 272
virus prevention 290
worm 272
zombie computer 273

Review Questions

1. List and describe the primary threats to information systems security.
2. List and describe how information systems are most often compromised.
3. Describe risk analysis as it relates to information systems security and explain three ways to approach systems security risk.
4. What are physical access restrictions, and how do they make an information system more secure?
5. What is a firewall?
6. Describe encryption and how it helps to secure information.
7. Describe several methods for preventing and/or managing the spread of computer viruses.
8. What is audit-control software?
9. Describe three human-based approaches for safeguarding information systems.
10. What is an information systems security plan, and what are the five steps for developing such a plan?
11. Contrast cold and hot backup sites.
12. Describe how the Sarbanes-Oxley Act impacts the information systems security of an organization.

Self-Study Questions

Visit the Interactive Study Guide on the Companion Web site for additional Self-Study Questions: www.pearsonhighered.com/valacich.

1. What is the common rule for deciding if an information system faces a security risk?
   A. Only desktop computers are at risk.
   B. Only network servers are at risk.
   C. All systems connected to networks are vulnerable to security violations.
   D. Networks have nothing to do with computer security.
2. Primary threats to the security of electronic information include which of the following?
   A. small children and household pets
   B. defective power connections
   C. accidents and natural disasters
   D. none of the above
3. Which of the following does *not* pose a threat to electronic information?
   A. unauthorized access

B. denial of service
   C. unauthorized information modification
   D. all of the above can compromise information
4. Information modification attacks occur when _____.
   A. an authorized user changes a Web site address
   B. a Web site crashes
   C. the power is cut off
   D. someone who is not authorized to do so changes electronic information
5. Technical safeguards used to protect information include _____.
   A. laws
   B. effective management
   C. firewalls and physical access restrictions
   D. ethics
6. Limiting access to electronic information usually involves _____.
   A. something you have

B. something you know

C. something you are

D. all of the above

7. Which of the following is the process of determining the true, accurate identity of a user of an information system?

A. audit

B. authentication

C. firewall

D. virtual private network

8. Which of the following approaches to information systems security is aimed at assessing the value of the assets being protected, determining their likelihood of being compromised, and comparing the probable costs of their being compromised?

A. keeping stored information safe with passwords and allowing access only to those employees who need it to do their jobs

B. using biometrics that may include fingerprints, retinal scans, or other bodily characteristics

C. making every effort to hire good employees and treat them well

D. conducting a risk analysis

9. A(n) _____ is a system composed of hardware, software, or both that is designed to detect intrusion and prevent unauthorized access to or from a private network.

A. encryption

B. firewall

C. alarm

D. logic bomb

10. _____ is the process of encoding messages before they enter the network or airwaves, then decoding them at the receiving end of the transfer so that recipients can read or hear them.

A. encryption

B. biometrics

C. authentication

D. disaster recovery

Answers are on page 307.

Problems and Exercises

1. Match the following terms to the appropriate definitions:

   i. Acceptable use policy

   ii. Authentication

   iii. Biometrics

   iv. Encryption

   v. Firewall

   vi. Phishing

   vii. Risk analysis

   viii. Spyware

   ix. Unauthorized access

   x. Zombie computer

   a. A type of security that grants or denies access to a computer system through the analysis of fingerprints, retinal patterns in the eye, or other bodily characteristics

   b. Specialized hardware and software that are used to keep unwanted users out of a system or to let users in with restricted access and privileges

   c. The process of encoding messages before they enter the network or airwaves, then decoding them at the receiving end of the transfer so that recipients can read or hear them

   d. The process of identifying that the user is indeed who he or she claims to be, typically by requiring something that the user knows (e.g., a password) together with something that the user carries with him or her or has access to (e.g., an identification card or file)

   e. Computer and/or Internet use policy for people within an organization, with clearly spelled-out penalties for noncompliance

   f. A process in which the value of the assets being protected is assessed, the likelihood of their being compromised is determined, and the costs of their being compromised are compared with the costs of the protections to be taken

   g. An e-mail that attempts to trick financial account and credit card holders into giving away their private information

   h. A computer that has been infected with a virus allowing an attacker to control it without the knowledge of the owner

   i. Software that covertly gathers information about a user through an Internet connection without the knowledge of the owner

   j. An information systems security breach where an unauthorized individual sees, manipulates, or otherwise handles electronically stored information

2. There are many brands of software firewalls, with ZoneAlarm, Norton's Internet Security, and McAfee's Personal Firewall being three popular choices. Search for these products on the Web and learn more about how a firewall works and what it costs to give you this needed protection; prepare a one-page report that outlines what you have learned.

3. Search for further information on encryption. What is the difference between 128-bit and 40-bit encryption? What level of encryption is used in your Web browser? Why has the U.S. government been reluctant to release software with higher levels of encryption to other countries?

4. What levels of user authentication are used at your school and/or place of work? Do they seem to be

effective? What if a higher level of authentication were necessary? Would it be worth it, or would the added steps cause you to be less productive?

5. Search for more information on the Computer Emergency Response Team Coordination Center and the Computer Security Division of the U.S. National Institute of Standards and Technology's Information Technology Laboratory. What role do you envision they will continue to play in the development of better information systems security? Do either of these seem to be organizations you might want to work for? Are they hiring?

6. Should the encryption issue be subject to ethical judgments? For instance, if an absolutely unbreakable code becomes feasible, should we use it with the knowledge that it may help terrorists and other criminals evade the law? Should governments regulate which encryption technology can be used so that government law enforcement agents can always read material generated by terrorists and other criminals? Explain your answer. Should the government continue to regulate the exportation of encryption technology to foreign countries, excluding those that support terrorism as it does now? Why or why not?

7. Assess and compare the security of the computers you use regularly at home, work, and/or school. What measures do you use at home to protect security? What measures are taken at work or school to protect security? (If possible, interview IT/IS personnel at work and/or at school to determine how security is protected in the workplace and in classrooms.) Describe any security vulnerabilities you find and explain how they might be corrected.

8. Take a poll of classmates to determine who has had personal experience with computer virus infections, identity theft, or other computer/information intrusions. How did victims handle the situation? What are classmates who have not been victimized doing to secure computers and personal information?

9. Research the statistics for the number of unauthorized intrusions into computer systems last year. Which type was most prevalent? Which groups committed the highest number of intrusions—hackers, employees, and so on?

10. What is the outlook for computer security in the future? Are there new techniques/laws and so on that will improve security?

11. Visit the Web site for the Computer Emergency Response Team at www.cert.org/tech_tips/denial_of_service.html and answer the following:
   a. What are the three basic types of denial of service attacks?
   b. What impact can denial of service attacks have on an organization?
   c. What other devices or activities within an organization might be impacted by denial of service attacks?
   d. Name three steps organizations might take to prevent denial of service attacks.

   If the previously given URL is no longer active, conduct a Web search for "denial of service attacks." Other active links can provide answers to the questions.

Application Exercises

 Note: The existing data files referenced in these exercises are available on the Student Companion Web site: www.pearsonhighered.com/valacich.

Spreadsheet Application: Tracking Web Site Visits at Campus Travel

Campus Travel has recently started selling products on the Internet; the managers are eager to know how the company's Web site is accepted by the customers. The file CampusTravel.csv contains transaction information for the past three days, generated from the company's Web server, including IP addresses of the visitors, whether or not a transaction was completed, and the transaction amount. You are asked to present the current status of the e-commerce initiative. Use your spreadsheet program to prepare the following graphs:

1. A graph highlighting the total number of site visits and the total number of transactions per day

2. A graph highlighting the total sales per day

Make sure to format the graphs in a professional manner, including headers, footers, and the appropriate labels, and print each graph on a separate page (Hint: To calculate the total number of site visits and the total number of transactions, use the "countif" function to count the number of Yes answers).

Database Application: Creating Forms at Campus Travel

After helping Campus Travel to a good start with its databases, you have decided that it should enter in data using forms rather than doing it from tables. From your experience, you know that employees have an easier time being able to browse, modify, and add records from a form view. As this can be implemented using your existing database, you decide to set up a form. You can accomplish this by doing the following:

1. Open the employees' database (employeeData.mdb).

2. Select the employee table in the database window.

3. Create a form using the table (Hint: This can be done by selecting the Autoform Wizard in the Forms view).

4. Save the form as "employees."

Team Work Exercise: Should Security Upgrades Be Made Available for Pirated Software?

Microsoft and other software producers make free upgrades available to legitimate buyers of applications when security risks are exposed. You probably have firsthand experience with updating Microsoft's products as new security risks are identified; only those who purchased and registered the software are eligible to receive these free downloads. Unfortunately, some people use pirated copies of Microsoft software and are, of course, not eligible to receive security downloads. An argument has been made that these security upgrades should be free to everyone because individuals using software with security vulnerabilities are a threat to everyone using the Internet since their computers are more easily converted to zombies that can spew spam in ever-increasing numbers, and they are more likely to contract

and spread viruses. Those who argue that security patches should be available to everyone say that there will always be pirated software in use—especially in those countries that have no laws against it or weak laws against it—so if we are ever to tighten security on the Internet, software manufacturers must provide security patches as a public service. Do you agree that security patches for popular software should be available free to everyone, no questions asked? Explain your answer. Do you agree that software vulnerable to security breaches threatens all computer users? Why or why not? In your opinion, is it possible for the Internet community to solve this problem without asking software developers to give away their product? Explain your answer.

Answers to the Self-Study Questions

1. C, p. 270   2. C, p. 270   3. D, p. 271   4. D, p. 271   5. C, p. 281
6. D, p. 282   7. B, p. 287   8. D, p. 280   9. B, p. 285   10. A, p. 287

Case ①

Under Attack

By now you know the scam. You receive an e-mail from eBay or maybe from PayPal, American Express, or your bank or credit card company that says they are "updating" your account information. The e-mail letterhead looks legitimate, so you read on. If you will just use the Web site address provided, the e-mail promises, the problem can be remedied, and your account won't be canceled. If you visit the URL provided, the site looks legitimate—that is, it's been "spoofed" to fool you—but the scam artists have posted it to steal your account information. By now you probably also know better than to respond to such a request. The scam is called "phishing"—meaning to "fish" for user

information—and it's akin to identity theft. If you are conned into revealing account numbers, the scam artists will use that information to steal from you.

Phony e-mail is just one version of the phishing scam. Others include the following:

- Phishing via instant message, whereby users are sent a link to click on. Similar to the e-mail phishing, the user is directed to a fraudulent Web site that asks for sensitive information.
- Phishing via malware. Malware (short for "malicious software") is a malicious program that is installed on an unsuspecting user's

computer via a virus or Trojan horse. This *malware* then runs in the background waiting for the user to go to, for example, a financial site. As soon as the *malware* detects the user going to a prime site, a pop-up window appears asking for sensitive information. This pop-up cannot be blocked since it is generated from the infected PC, not the Web server.

Phishing con artists also like to take advantage of special times of the year, such as April 15, when tax returns are due. Taxpayers must now beware of bogus e-mails from the Internal Revenue Service that say something like this: "You are eligible to receive a tax refund of $285.67. To access the form for your tax refund, please click here." Clicking on the URL provided, of course, takes you to a counterfeit form, asking for personal information that the phishing thieves can use to steal from you. Fake IRS sites have also bilked taxpayers of personal information.

All types of phishing are a significant problem for Internet businesses and consumers. Over 57 million Americans were reportedly exposed to e-mail phishing in 2005, and 5 percent of those e-mail recipients were victimized. The Anti-Phishing Working Group (APWG) reported in 2007 that the number of e-mail phishing attacks spiked by 73 percent in 2007. In one year—2005 to 2006—the scam grew from a nuisance to a $2.8-billion-a-year problem in the United States. In 2007, losses from phishing attacks had reached $3 billion.

What is even more troublesome is the fact that 101 brands have been highjacked or spoofed with over 92 percent of these occurring in the financial sector. (PayPal is the country's number one financial victim, and American Express is number two.) Clearly, phishing thieves are not only persistent but often successful at gaining access to users' sensitive information.

In an effort to defeat phishers, PayPal has stopped using e-mail to contact account holders. Instead, PayPal has its own proprietary messaging system that handles all transactions. If PayPal needs to contact you regarding your account, they will send a single e-mail message saying that there is a message waiting on the Web site messaging system. This procedure may further complicate access for an account holder, but it also adds a necessary layer of security.

Questions

1. What types of companies are most susceptible to phishing attacks?
2. Assume you have replied to a phishing e-mail; research on the Web what steps you should follow to limit any possible consequences.
3. Research on the Web for the telltale signs of a phishing message.

Based on:

About e-mail fraud (n.d.). Retrieved May 12, 2008, from http://www10.americanexpress.com/sif/cda/page/0,1641,21372,00.asp.

Chickowski, E. (2007, December 19). Email phishing attacks still on the rise. *Baselinemag.* Retrieved May 12, 2008, from http://www.baselinemag.com/c/a/Projects-Security/Email-Phishing-Attacks-Still-on-the-Rise.

Crimeware double threat menaces Internet (n.d.). Retrieved May 12, 2008, from http://www.antiphishing.org.

Dignan, L. (2008, January 14). Phishing for your tax return. *ZDNet.* Retrieved May 12, 2008, from http://blogs.zdnet.com/security/?p=805.

Gartner survey shows phishing attacks escalated in 2007; more than $3 billion lost to these attacks. (2007, December 17). Retrieved May 12, 2008, from http://www.gartner.com/it/page.jsp?id=565125.

Case ❷

China's Great (Fire)Wall

When you were younger did your parents forbid you to socialize with certain kids? Was off-color reading material declared off-limits? Was your computer use monitored and restricted? If so, you probably remember your absolute determination to circumvent the parental restrictions and censorship.

Similarly, as an adult, you would probably be insulted and outraged if the government attempted to assume the parental role and told you when and where you could travel, what types of literature you could purchase, which Web sites were off-limits, and which e-mail and snail mail content was acceptable.

Welcome to modern-day China. Researchers at Harvard Law School's Berkman Center for Internet and Society have found that the Chinese government blocks Web site access to the country's 210 million Internet users on such subjects as democracy, Tibet, Taiwan, health, education, news, entertainment, religion, or revolution. Chat rooms, blogs, photo and video sharing sites, gaming and podcasting sites, and bulletin boards are also forbidden stops on the Web. And, of course, if surfing from China, don't even think about googling "Tiananmen Square massacre" or anything remotely considered pornographic.

Building censorship into China's Internet infrastructure is step one for the country's government in controlling access to politically sensitive material. To accomplish this, the Chinese government has prevented ISPs—many of them privately held businesses, some with foreign investments—from hosting any material the government calls politically objectionable. The government does this by holding the ISPs liable for content and imposing severe penalties for violations, including imprisonment.

The second step the Chinese government follows for censoring the Internet is to target Internet content providers (ICPs—organizations and individuals who post Web sites, both nonprofit and for profit). ICPs are required to register for and post a license to operate legally, and like ISPs are held liable for politically incorrect content. To keep a license,

ICPs must police sites for objectionable content and must take down those sites that violate regulations governing content. Yahoo!, Microsoft's MSN, and Google all act as ICPs in China, and all have been criticized for complying with China's strict Internet censorship policy. Yahoo!, the only non-Chinese company providing e-mail service to the People's Republic of China (PRC), has also turned over e-mail content to the authorities, resulting in the prosecution and conviction of at least four persons for criticizing the government. Relatedly, in late 2008, a team of Canadian researchers discovered that hundreds of thousands of chat messages sent via the Chinese version of Skype were archived using a huge surveillance system, potentially enabling the government to prosecute senders of offensive messages.

As is true of most attempts to censor the Internet (you *will* continue to receive spam), tech-savvy users in China find ways to circumvent the government's firewall. Proxy servers have helped poke holes in the wall at Internet gateways and ISP levels. Users with the right knowledge can configure browsers to access the Internet through proxy servers located in other countries. The use of proxies slows the service, but does allow surfers in China to visit "forbidden" Web sites. Estimates are, however, that only about 14 percent of the millions of Chinese Internet users are willing or able to use proxy servers.

Wired reported in October 2007 that even a much-heralded addition to Beijing's surveillance arsenal, a program called the Golden Shield, was showing signs of cracking. The Golden Shield, which took eight years to produce at a cost of $700 million, was supposed to automatically monitor, filter, and block undesirable online content. But it wasn't the perfect solution the Chinese government thought it would be.

While it's true that government surveillance is an ongoing activity for Internet users in China and dissidents are severely punished, those who want the freedom to peruse content at will are chipping away at the wall, through circumvention methods, unstoppable blogs, and other Web content, and through the objections of cyberprotestors around the world.

Questions

1. U.S. companies like Yahoo!, Google, and Microsoft point out that European, Japanese, or other firms would quickly fill any gap left if American companies withheld their expertise. Nevertheless, should these companies provide their technologies to China, even if they are used to limit the individual freedom of Chinese citizens? Why or why not?
2. Given that it is estimated that China will have the largest number of Internet users by 2010, do you think they can ultimately succeed in controlling information? Why or why not?
3. Should the rest of the world care if China limits information access within China? Why or why not?

Based on:

August, O. (2007, October 23). The great firewall: China's misguided—and futile—attempt to control what happens online. *Wired.* Retrieved May 12, 2008, from http://www.wired.com/politics/security/magazine/15-11/ff_chinafirewall.

China's Internet censorship (2002, December 3). *CBS News.* Retrieved May 12, 2008, from http://www.cbsnews.com/stories/2002/12/03/tech/main531567.shtml.

Markoff, J. (2008, October 1). Surveillance of Skype messages found in China. *New York Times.* Retrieved January 15, 2009, from http://www.nytimes.com/2008/10/02/technology/internet/02skype.htm.

Race to the bottom: Corporate complicity in Chinese Internet censorship. (2006, August). *Human Rights Watch.* Retrieved May 12, 2008, from http://www.hrw.org/reports/2006/china0806.

Enhancing Business Intelligence Using Information Systems

After reading this chapter, you will be able to do the following:

1. Describe the concept of business intelligence and how it is used at the operational, managerial, and executive levels of an organization.

2. Explain the three components of business intelligence: information and knowledge discovery, business analytics, and information visualization.

Preview

Today, organizations operate in a global, highly competitive, and rapidly changing environment. A key to effective management is high-quality and timely information to support decision making. This high-quality and timely information, or business intelligence, can be provided from a variety of information systems. In this chapter, we first describe business intelligence, followed by the primary information systems components utilized by organizations to gain business intelligence. Every day, the capabilities of these various information systems are expanding, making it difficult to provide clear-cut distinctions between the capabilities of one type of system versus another. Nevertheless, it is important to understand that organizations are comprised of different decision-making levels and business functions, which execute various business processes in order to realize the strategic goals of the organization. Likewise, it is also important to distinguish among the various technologies utilized by modern organizations to gain business intelligence. To this end, this chapter has two primary objectives.

This chapter focuses on why organizations need business intelligence and how they are utilizing various information systems to best support *internal* business processes. In Chapter 9—Building Organizational Partnerships Using Enterprise Information Systems, we focus on systems that support business processes spanning multiple organizational functions and potentially multiple organizations, critical in today's competitive global environment.

Managing in the Digital World: Providing Business Intelligence to eBay Customers

You are probably very familiar with the online auction Web site eBay (see Figure 8.1). Founded in 1995, it is the global online marketplace where practically anyone can trade practically anything, from baseball cards, to rare vinyl records, to even a private jet. Today, around 84 million people from thirty-nine countries have active eBay accounts, trading over $2,000 worth of goods, every second of every day. In 2007, total auction sales were around $30 billion, a large portion of the overall U.S. Internet retail sales of $116 billion in 2007.

With this amount of transactions, tremendous data is being processed on a daily basis, including seller and buyer data, current auction listings, and final sales. For eBay as well as its sellers, this massive amount of data can be a virtual gold mine. When is the best time to list a new item? What are the best strategies to respond to seasonal changes in demand? How can you learn from past auctions to adjust your strategies for future auctions? Which items are selling well, and which aren't worth listing? What is the best strategy for setting starting bids or reserve prices? These are questions that both private and commercial sellers are facing on a daily basis, hoping to improve the return on their auctions.

How can sellers gain this insight and benefit from the tremendous amounts of historical data? eBay offers a variety of tools and reports that help sellers analyze their past auctions; similarly, third-party providers offer different tools that help sellers get most of the data. However, it is not just the sellers that can benefit from the data that is being collected from everyday transactions; eBay itself is crunching the numbers on a daily basis. With growing auction volumes, eBay has to fine-tune its systems to offer maximum performance and minimize delays or system failures, as any technical problem will lead to customer dissatisfaction and lost revenues. Thus, it is critical for eBay to analyze bidding behavior over the life of an auction and how this behavior influences demand on its systems. In eBay's early days, performing such complex analyses had taken days or weeks. However, in 2000, a large data warehouse was implemented that allowed eBay to quickly perform complex analyses on its data. With the help of this data warehouse and sophisticated business intelligence software, eBay has managed to be the online auction site of choice for buyers and sellers alike.

Despite (or due to) its popularity and success, there are downsides to doing business on eBay, namely, account hijacking; counterfeit, doctored, or misrepresented merchandise; and payment fraud.

FIGURE 8.1

eBay is the largest Internet auction site in the world.

Account hijacking, the biggest and most dangerous problem on eBay, refers to criminals taking over a legitimate eBay account with good feedback in order to buy merchandise with stolen credit cards or to sell expensive items that are never delivered to customers.

Given the need to maintain customer and seller confidence, eBay is exerting a lot of effort and spending a lot of resources to maintain and improve the integrity of the site through the development of sophisticated business intelligence tools. Unfortunately, as with all forms of Internet crime, eBay cannot offer absolute protection for its customers.

For instance, in 2003, the Salt Lake City police arrested a thirty-one-year-old man who was accused of perpetrating one of the biggest scams in eBay history. Hundreds of customers complained that they sent $1,000 to a company called Liquidation Universe for laptop computers they never received. Early in the investigation, police determined that the suspect scammed over 1,000 eBay customers to the tune of $1 million in just a few weeks. eBay worked with the victims of the scam to help them get their money back, but the company does not reimburse customers for items not received. In other cases, crooks were offering counterfeited products—anything from collectables to software—on eBay. By the time a buyer finds out, the seller's account is often closed. In fact, in 2005, over 16,000 entries offering pirated products were closed by the Business Software Alliance. In 2007, eBay said data on 1,200 eBay members had probably been stolen via a phishing scam. The members' data was posted to the company's Trust & Safety discussion forum. Likewise, in 2008, several members of a family who sold counterfeit designer handbags were sentenced to several years in prison. Needless to say, these examples represent only a small fraction of the criminal activities on eBay. It is clearly a big problem.

Likewise, eBay is dealing with other types of auction fraud, such as shill bidding, where sellers use multiple accounts to bid on their own items, thus driving up the highest bid. Although such behavior only occurs at a small percentage of all auctions, buyers are losing large amounts of money due to the high number of transactions. For eBay, determining patterns of fraudulent behavior is in its own best interest, as such behavior ultimately drives away both buyers and legitimate sellers. Again, mining its massive data warehouse can help to find such patterns, helping to detect fraudsters and close accounts that are engaging in these behaviors.

It should be clear that, owing to eBay's success, criminals who prowl the Internet will continue to make it one of their biggest targets. The best hope for honest users is that technology designed to thwart scam artists can keep up and provide both buyers and sellers with needed intelligence to make good decisions.

After reading this chapter, you will be able to answer the following:

1. How can eBay utilize its transactional data to help both buyers and sellers?

2. Given the speed and volume of transactions on eBay, what business analytics and visualization tools could be used to better track and reduce fraudulent transactions?

3. How could legitimate buyers and sellers help eBay improve its tools for fighting fraud?

Based on:

Anonymous (2006, December 5). Online auction fraud: Data mining software fingers both perpetrators and accomplices. *Science Daily.* Retrieved May 24, 2008, from http://www.sciencedaily.com/releases/2006/12/061205143326.htm.

Anonymous (n.d.). Analyzing your eBay data. *Allbusiness.com.* http://www.allbusiness.com/sales/internet-ebay/3236-1.html.

Colet, E. (n.d.). Using data mining to detect fraud in auctions. *DSStar.* Retrieved May 24, 2008, from http://www.allbusiness.com/sales/internet-ebay/3236-1.html.

Shah, H., N. Joshi, and P. Wurman (2002, May 24). Mining for bidding strategies on eBay. Retrieved May 24, 2008, from http://www4.ncsu.edu/~wurman/Papers/Shah-WebKDD.pdf.

Sullivan, B. (2003, June 12). Man arrested in huge eBay fraud. *MSNBC.* Retrieved May 24, 2008, from http://msnbc.msn.com/id/3078461.

Business Intelligence

In Chapter 3—Valuing Information Systems Investments, you learned about the importance of business planning for gaining and sustaining competitive advantage. To stay ahead of the competition, organizations have turned to **business intelligence** (BI), or the use of information systems to gather and analyze information from internal and external sources in order to make better business decisions. Business intelligence also refers to the information gained from the use of such systems. Next, the need for business intelligence is examined.

Why Organizations Need Business Intelligence

Although a company's overall direction is decided upon at the strategic level, business processes span all organizational levels and are highly interconnected. Recall from Chapter 3 that business processes refer to the activities that organizations perform in order to reach their business goals. Unfortunately, the business processes outlined within strategic plans are often not implemented as envisioned at the managerial and operational levels of the organization because the information needed to effectively monitor and control these processes is simply not available. This "missing" information, in fact, exists, but often resides in disconnected spreadsheets, reports, or databases. Consequently, to realize the goals of their strategic plans, organizations must have up-to-date, accurate, and *integrated* information to monitor and fine-tune a broad range of business processes. To make this possible, information systems that provide business intelligence—by collecting, analyzing, and delivering needed information to the right decision maker and at the right time—facilitate the effective management of modern organizations. Additionally, business intelligence allows organizations to better respond to ongoing threats and opportunities as well as to better plan for the future.

Responding to Threats and Opportunities External factors such as globalization, competitive pressures, consumer demands, and governmental regulations can create opportunities as well as threats for modern organizations. For example, increasing globalization provides opportunities to compete in new markets, but it also creates the challenge of gaining new types of information in order to effectively manage these opportunities. Globalization can also lead to the threat of increased competition from developing countries, forcing organizations to rethink strategies or to further improve business processes. Thus, as the world becomes increasingly flatter, market opportunities will expand, but, at the same time, markets will also become increasingly more competitive. This means that today's business environment is characterized by factors such as unstable market conditions, fierce competition, shorter product life cycles, and wider choices for customers than ever before. Business intelligence can help organizations make better decisions in this increasingly complex, fast-changing, and competitive environment, by more effectively collecting and analyzing both internal and external data (see Figure 8.2).

Effective Planning Is Continuous In the past, organizations lacked the necessary information and tools to continuously plan for their future. Typically, organizations would first develop a strategic plan for some planning cycle (say, a year); then, once a strategic plan was agreed upon, managers of various business units would prepare

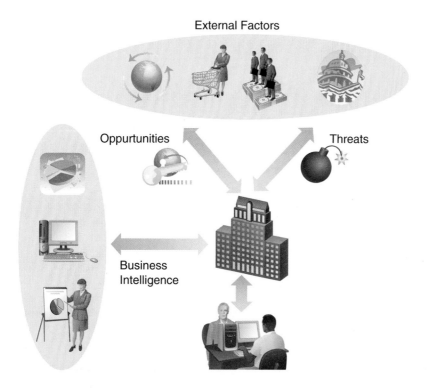

External Factors

Oppurtunities

Threats

Business
Intelligence

FIGURE 8.2

Business intelligence helps organizations swiftly respond to external threats and opportunities.

budgets for executing their portion of the plan. These budgets were often "backward looking" because they were typically based on historical data, rather than being based on a clear understanding of current conditions and forecasts of future trends. Over time, managers would then execute their portion of the plan. For many organizations, this method of planning and managing was adequate given the relatively slow pace of change.

Today, however, given the need to swiftly respond to a highly competitive and rapidly changing environment, organizations must implement new ways of planning. In fact, successful organizations are utilizing a **continuous planning process** (see Figure 8.3). In a continuous planning process, organizations *continuously* monitor and analyze business processes; the results lead to ongoing adjustments to not only how the organization is managed, but these results are also reflected in ongoing updates to the organizational plans. It is only through timely and accurate business intelligence that continuous planning can be executed.

Continuous planning involves decision makers from all levels of an organization. In the next section, we will describe these levels.

Business Intelligence and Organizational Decision-Making Levels

Every organization is composed of decision-making levels, as illustrated in Figure 8.4. Each level of an organization has different responsibilities and, therefore, different informational needs. In this section, we describe each of these levels.

Operational Level   At the **operational level** of a firm, the routine, day-to-day business processes and interactions with customers occur. Information systems at this level are designed to automate repetitive activities, such as sales transaction processing, and to improve the efficiency of business processes and the customer interface. Operational planning typically has a time frame of a few hours or days, and the managers at the operational level, such as foremen or supervisors, make day-to-day decisions that are highly structured and recurring. **Structured decisions** are those in which the procedures to follow for a given situation can be specified in advance. For example, a supervisor may decide when to reorder supplies or how best to allocate personnel for the completion of a

FIGURE 8.3

Effective business planning is continuous.

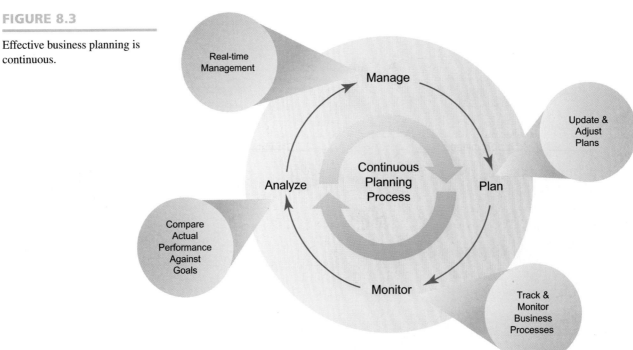

FIGURE 8.4

Organizations are composed of different levels, each using business intelligence to assist in decision making.

project. Because structured decisions are relatively straightforward, they can be programmed directly into operational information systems so that they can be made with little or no human intervention. For example, an inventory management system for a shoe store in the mall could keep track of inventory and issue an order for additional inventory when levels drop below a specified level. Operational managers within the store would simply need to confirm with the inventory management system that the order for additional shoes was needed. At the operational level, business intelligence applications are typically used to optimize processes and to better understand the underlying causes of any performance problems. Using business intelligence to optimize processes at the operational level can offer quick returns on the information systems investment, as activities at this level are clearly delineated and well focused. Figure 8.5 summarizes the general characteristics of the operational level.

Managerial/Tactical Level At the **managerial level** of the organization, functional managers (e.g., marketing managers, finance managers, manufacturing managers, and human resource managers) focus on monitoring and controlling operational-level activities and providing information to higher levels of the organization (see Figure 8.6). Managers at this level, referred to as midlevel managers, focus on effectively utilizing and deploying

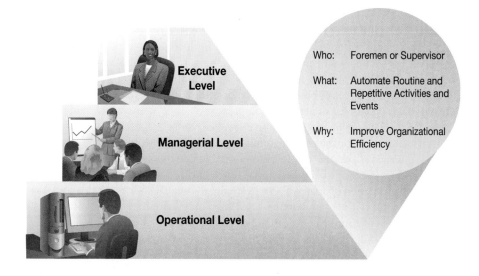

Who: Foremen or Supervisor

What: Automate Routine and Repetitive Activities and Events

Why: Improve Organizational Efficiency

FIGURE 8.5

The operational level of an organization uses business intelligence to improve efficiency by automating routine and repetitive activities.

FIGURE 8.6

The managerial level of an organization uses business intelligence to improve effectiveness by automating the monitoring and controlling of operational activities.

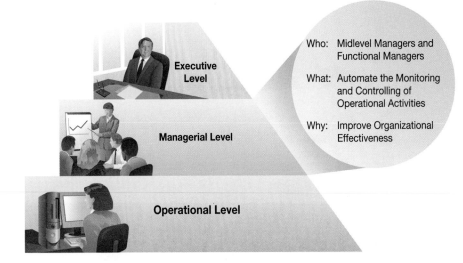

organizational resources to achieve the strategic objectives of the organization. Midlevel managers typically focus on problems within a specific business function, such as marketing or finance. Here, the scope of the decision usually is contained within the business function, is moderately complex, and has a time horizon of a few days to a few months (also referred to as tactical planning). For example, a marketing manager at Nike may decide how to allocate the advertising budget for the next business quarter or some other fixed time period.

Managerial-level decision making is not nearly as structured or routine as operational-level decision making. Managerial-level decision making is referred to as semistructured decision making because solutions and problems are not clear-cut and often require judgment and expertise. For **semistructured decisions**, some procedures to follow for a given situation can be specified in advance but not to the extent where a specific recommendation can be made. For example, a business intelligence application could provide a production manager at Nike with performance analytics and forecasts about sales for multiple product lines, inventory levels, and overall production capacity. The metrics deemed most critical to assessing progress toward a certain goal (referred to as **key performance indicators [KPIs]**) are displayed on performance *dashboards* (described later). The manager could use this information to create multiple production schedules. With these schedules, the manager could then perform predictive analyses to examine inventory levels and potential sales profitability, depending on the order in which manufacturing resources were used to produce each type of product.

Executive/Strategic Level At the **executive level** of the organization, managers focus on long-term strategic issues facing the organization, such as which products to produce, which countries to compete in, and what organizational strategy to follow (see Figure 8.7). Managers at this level include the president and chief executive officer (CEO), vice presidents, and possibly the board of directors; they are referred to as "executives." Executive-level decisions deal with complex problems with broad and long-term ramifications for the organization. Executive-level decisions are referred to as unstructured decisions because the problems are relatively complex and nonroutine. In addition, executives must consider the ramifications of their decisions in terms of the overall organization. For **unstructured decisions**, few or no procedures to follow for a given situation can be specified in advance. For example, top managers may decide to develop a new product or discontinue an existing one. Such a decision may have vast, long-term effects on the organization's levels of employment and profitability. To assist executive-level decision making, business intelligence applications are used to obtain aggregate summaries of trends and projections of the future. At the executive level, business

FIGURE 8.7

The executive level of an organization uses business intelligence to improve strategy and planning by providing summaries of past data and projections of the future.

intelligence applications provide KPIs that are focused on balancing performance across the organization, such that, for example, product launches are staggered to smooth out the effects of spikes in demand on the supply chain. Other KPIs are used to benchmark the organization's performance against its competitors.

In summary, most organizations have three general levels: operational, managerial, and executive. Each level has unique activities and business processes, each requiring different types of information. The next section examines transaction processing systems and how they provide important input into business intelligence applications.

Providing Inputs into Business Intelligence Applications

To make sound operational, tactical, and strategic business decisions, it is imperative that decisions made in different departments are based on the same underlying data, definitions, and assumptions, that is, there is a "single version of the truth." For example, do the marketing and accounting departments have the same definitions of a customer or a sale? Does a "customer" entail anyone who may be interested in the company's product or service (marketing view), or only those who actually made a purchase (accounting view)? Especially for large organizations, arriving at a single version of the truth can be a challenge, as data often has to be integrated from multiple systems. Business intelligence applications achieve this by enabling access to multiple databases or by using a data warehouse that integrates data from various operational systems. One fundamental type of operational system used for both day-to-day business processes and as input for business intelligence applications is a transaction processing system.

Transaction Processing Systems

Many organizations deal with repetitive activities. Grocery stores scan groceries at the checkout counter. Banks process checks drawn on customer accounts. Fast-food restaurants process customer orders. All of these repetitive activities are examples of **transactions** that occur as a regular part of a business's day-to-day operations. A **transaction processing system (TPS)** is a special class of an information system designed to process business events and transactions. Consequently, TPSs often reside close to customers, at the operational level of the organization (see Figure 8.5). The goal of transaction processing systems is to automate repetitive business processes within organizations to increase speed and accuracy and to lower the cost of processing each transaction—that is, to make the organization more efficient. Because TPSs are used to process large volumes of information, organizations spend considerable resources designing and fine-tuning these systems. A TPS can reduce or eliminate people from the process, thereby reducing

Bad Intelligence—Anonymous Hackers Punish the Wrong Person

In 1953, science fiction author L. Ron Hubbard founded a religion called the Church of Scientology. The religion's guiding principle is a concept called "dianetics," based on the Greek words for "through" and "mind." In short, Scientologists believe that by clearing one's mind of certain harmful impulses and thoughts one can achieve a higher level of function. Several American movie stars follow Scientology, including such famous actors as John Travolta, Kelly Preston, Kirstie Alley, Katie Holmes, and Tom Cruise.

In January 2008, an interview with Tom Cruise was placed on several Web sites, including YouTube, Google Video, Radar, Defamer, and Gawker, where Cruise expressed his views concerning Scientology. "When you're a Scientologist, and you drive by an accident, you know you have to do something about it," Cruise states in the videotaped interview, "because you know you're the only one who can really help . . . We are the way to happiness. We can bring peace and unite cultures."

The Church of Scientology has long been known for taking legal action when it perceives an attack, and it forced many of the sites to take down the Tom Cruise interview shortly after it was posted, citing copyright violations.

After the Cruise interview was removed from most of the Web sites that had posted it, a group of hackers called Anonymous declared war on the Church of Scientology. They flooded the church's servers with fake data requests, reportedly saying the attacks were retribution for Scientology's influence in the removal of the Cruise video from the Internet and for brainwashing its members. Anonymous dubbed the attack Project Chanology and encouraged its members to launch denial of service attacks, make prank telephone calls, post

online proprietary Scientology documents, and fax blank pages to the church's fax machines.

As Anonymous members responded to the call, other hacker groups who opposed Anonymous entered the fray, and a Stockton, California, couple was caught in the crosshairs. Fifty-nine-year-old John Lawson and his wife received anonymous calls threatening their lives, and the couple's names, address, telephone number, and Mrs. Lawson's Social Security number were posted online. Lawson, who said he doesn't "even really know how to use a computer," and his wife were somehow mistakenly targeted as pro-Scientology hackers. Lawson notified local police and news outlets and placed fraud protection alerts on his and his wife's credit reports, but the couple was resigned to simply waiting anxiously for the harassment to end.

As the hacker war waged, other mistaken targets included a school in The Netherlands. This attack was brief, but the Anonymous–Scientology war illustrates a principle often violated on the Internet: When hackers see their views as righteous and use illegal methods to make a point, innocent citizens can get caught in the cross fire.

Based on:

Anonymous (n.d.). The Cruise indoctrination video Scientology tried to suppress. Retrieved May 24, 2008, from http://gawker.com/5002269/the-cruise-indoctrination-video-scientology-tried-to-suppress.

Singel, R. (2008, January 23). War breaks out between hackers and Scientology—There can be only one. *Wired.* Retrieved May 24, 2008, from http://blog.wired.com/27bstroke6/2008/01/anonymous-attac.html.

Singel, R. (2008, January 29). Anonymous hackers track saboteur, find and punish the wrong guy. *Wired.* Retrieved May 24, 2008, from http://blog.wired.com/27bstroke6/2008/01/anonymous-hac-1.html.

transaction costs and reducing the likelihood of data entry errors. Examples of business processes supported by TPSs include the following:

- Payroll processing
- Sales and order processing
- Inventory management
- Product purchasing, receiving, and shipping
- Accounts payable and receivable

Architecture of a TPS The basic architecture of a TPS is shown in Figure 8.8, using an input, process, and output model—the basic systems model (for a thorough discussion, see Checkland, 1981), which can be used to describe virtually all types of systems.

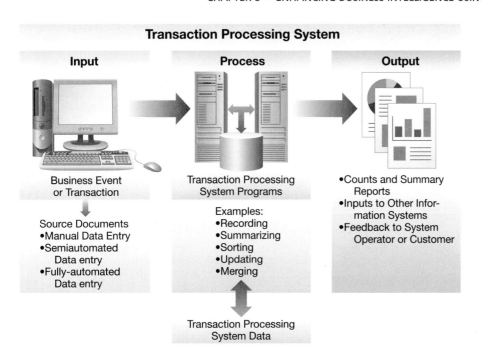

FIGURE 8.8

Architecture of a transaction processing system using the basic systems model.

Source documents, paper or electronic, describe a specific business transaction and serve as a stimulus to a TPS from some external source. For example, when you fill out a driver's license application, the form serves as a source document for a TPS that processes the applications to check against search warrants and that records and stores all licensed drivers in a state. Source documents can be processed as they are created—referred to as online processing—or they can be processed in batches—referred to as batch processing. **Online processing** of transactions provides immediate results to the system operator or customer. For example, an interactive class registration system that immediately notifies you of your success or failure to register for a class is an example of an online TPS. **Batch processing** of transactions occurs when source documents are collected and then processed together as a "batch" at some later time. Banks often use batch processing when reconciling checks drawn on customer accounts. Likewise, your university uses batch processing to process end-of-term grade reports; all inputs must be periodically processed in batches to calculate your grade-point average. Online processing is used when customers need immediate notification of the success or failure of a transaction. Batch processing is used when immediate notification is not needed or is not practical. Table 8.1 lists several examples of online and batch transaction processing systems. Additionally, as summarized in Table 8.2, information can be entered into a TPS in one of three ways: **manual data entry** (i.e., information is entered by hand), **semiautomated data entry** (i.e., information is entered using some type of data capture device), or **fully automated data entry** (i.e., information is entered without human intervention).

TABLE 8.1 **Examples of Online and Batch Transaction Processing Systems**

Online TPS	Batch TPS
University class registration processing	Students' final grades processing
Airline reservation processing	Payroll processing
Concert/sporting event ticket reservation processing	Insurance forms processing
Grocery store checkout processing	Bank check processing

TABLE 8.2 Ways Information Can Be Entered into a Transaction Processing System

Data Entry Method	Description	Example
Manual	Having a person enter the source document information by hand.	When applying for a new driver's license, a clerk manually enters information about you into a driver's license recording system, often copying the information from a form that you filled out by hand.
Semiautomated	Capturing data using a device such as a scanner to speed the entry and processing of a transaction.	When purchasing groceries in a store, the cashier uses a bar code scanner to record each item, allowing for a speedy checkout and better inventory management.
Fully-automated	Computer-to-computer communication without any human intervention.	When the inventory of a car manufacturer falls below a certain level, the manufacturer's inventory system automatically notifies the supplier's system that more materials are needed.

The characteristics of a TPS are summarized in Table 8.3. Inputs to a TPS are business events or transactions. The processing activities of a TPS include recording, summarizing, sorting, updating, and merging transaction information with organizational databases. Outputs from a TPS include summary reports, inputs to other systems, and operator notification of processing completion. People who are very close to day-to-day operations most often use TPSs. For example, a checkout clerk at the grocery store uses a TPS to record your purchases. Supervisors may review transaction summary reports to control inventory, to manage operations personnel, or to provide customer service. Additionally, inventory management systems may monitor transaction activity and use this information to manage inventory reordering. This is an example of the output from a TPS being the input to another system.

TPS and Business Intelligence Depending on the nature of the system, transaction processing systems can generate a wealth of data that can serve as useful inputs into business intelligence applications. For example, a grocery checkout system processes a specific transaction (the purchase) that can be linked to an inventory system (for reordering purposes), but can also capture valuable data such as time of the purchase, items purchased together, form of payment, or preferred customer program details. Coupled with external data (such as store location, weather data, or competitor information), this data can be analyzed for spending patterns, effectiveness of sales promotions, or customer profiling. As you can see, TPS can provide valuable input into business intelligence applications, clearly helping organizations improve their business decision making.

TABLE 8.3 Characteristics of a Transaction Processing System

Inputs	Business events and transactions
Processing	Recording, summarizing, sorting, updating, merging
Outputs	Counts and summary reports of activity; inputs to other information systems; feedback to system operators or customers
Typical users	Operational personnel, supervisors, and customers

The Demise of Broadcast TV

Recent studies of the TV-viewing habits of various age groups indicate that the TV industry is in trouble. Fifty-six percent of viewers 18–34 aren't watching TV on TV. Instead, they tune in online or record shows for viewing on DVD—minus the commercials. Since advertisers are the financial life's blood for the TV industry, and viewers who don't watch commercials are on the rise, the industry will need to rethink its business plan if it wants to survive. As streaming video, DVD recording, online movie rental, and downloading sites compete with TV, the future of the industry seems in doubt, unless the medium can embrace the Web and come to terms with viewers' changing habits.

Based on:

Anonymous (2007, December 5). Nielsen: Young people don't watch TV on TV. *MarketingVox.* Retrieved May 24, 2008, from http://www.marketingvox.com/nielsen-young-people-dont-watch-tv-on-tv-035031.

Carton, S. (2007, December 10). TV's last gasp. *Clickz.com.* Retrieved May 24, 2008, from http://www.clickz.com/showPage.html?page=3627808.

Business Intelligence Components

Business intelligence applications comprise a wide variety of tools. In general, however, there are three categories of business intelligence tools: tools for aiding information and knowledge discovery, tools for analyzing data to improve decision making, and tools for visualizing complex data relationships. Although each category can be very valuable to an organization by itself, it is their convergence that enables organizations to gain and sustain competitive advantage through improved business intelligence. In the following sections, we will discuss each of these categories as well as the various systems and technologies that each encompasses.

Information and Knowledge Discovery

Information and knowledge discovery tools are primarily used to extract information from existing data. Sometimes, information and knowledge discovery is completely atheoretical, and a system is used to search for hidden relationships between data, akin to searching for the "needle in the haystack." In other cases, business users formulate hypotheses (such as "customers with a household income of $150,000 are twice as likely to respond to our marketing campaigns as customers with an income of $60,000 or less"), and these hypotheses are tested against existing data. In the following sections, we will describe some of the applications used for discovering new and unexpected relationships and for testing hypotheses.

Ad Hoc Queries and Reports Business users across an organization need the right information at the right time. Such information is typically presented as reports based on data stored in organizational databases and can take the form of **scheduled reports, drill-down reports**, **exception reports**, and **key-indicator reports** (see Table 8.4). These reports are either produced at pre-specified intervals or created whenever a pre-specified event happens. However, decision makers frequently have information needs that are unforeseen and may never arise again. In such instances, the users need to run **ad hoc queries** (i.e., queries created due to unplanned information needs that are typically not saved for later use). Ad hoc query tools provide an easy-to-use interface, allowing managers to run queries and reports themselves, without having to know query languages, or the structure of the underlying data. Installed on a person's desktop or notebook computer, the tools can be used to run queries and reports whenever an unplanned information need arises, without having to resort to calling the IT department for help in creating a complex query or a special report.

TABLE 8.4 **Common Reports and Queries**

Report/Query	Description
Scheduled reports	Reports produced at predefined intervals—daily, weekly, or monthly—to support routine decisions
Key indicator reports	Reports that provide a summary of critical information on a recurring schedule
Exception reports	Reports that highlight situations that are out of the normal range
Drill-down reports	Reports providing greater detail as to why a key indicator is not at an appropriate level or an exception occurred
Ad hoc queries	Queries answering unplanned information requests to support a nonroutine decision; typically not saved to be run again

Online Analytical Processing **Online analytical processing (OLAP)** refers to the process of quickly conducting complex, multidimensional analyses of data stored in a database that is optimized for retrieval, typically using graphical software tools. OLAP tools enable users to analyze different dimensions of data beyond simple data summaries and data aggregations of normal database queries. Typical questions asked would be "What were the profits for each week in 2008 by sales region and customer type?" In contrast to relatively simple ad hoc queries, running such multidimensional queries requires a deeper understanding of the underlying data. Given the high volume of transactions within Internet-based systems, and the potential business value in the data, analysts must provide extensive OLAP capabilities to managers. The chief component of an OLAP system is the **OLAP server** that understands how data is organized in the database and has special functions for analyzing the data. The use of dedicated databases allows for tremendous increases in retrieval speed. In the past, multidimensional queries against large transactional databases could take hours to run; in contrast, OLAP systems pre-aggregate data, so that only the subset of the data necessary for the queries is extracted, greatly improving performance.

MEASURES AND DIMENSIONS. Whenever a business transaction occurs, associated data can be stored and then analyzed from a variety of perspectives. To facilitate efficient processing of transactions, databases supporting online transaction processing systems treat all data in similar ways. In contrast, OLAP systems are designed for efficient retrieval of data, and categorize data as measures and dimensions. **Measures** (or sometimes called **facts**) are the values or numbers the user wants to analyze, such as the sum of sales or the number of orders placed. **Dimensions** provide a way to summarize the data, such as region, time, or product line. Thus, sales (a measure) could be analyzed by product, time (year, quarter, week), geographical region, or distributor (the dimensions). To enable the analysis of data at more or less detailed levels, the dimensions are organized as hierarchies (such as in day, month, quarter, year). For example, when analyzing sales by geographical regions, a user can **drill down** from state, to county, to city, and to the individual store location or **roll up** from state, to sales region (northwest, south, southeast, and so on), to country, or to continent.

CUBES, SLICING, AND DICING. To enable such multidimensional analyses, OLAP arranges the data as so-called cubes. An **OLAP cube** is a data structure allowing for multiple dimensions to be added to a traditional two-dimensional table (see Figure 8.9). Although the figure only shows three dimensions, data can be analyzed in more than three dimensions. Analyzing the data on subsets of the dimensions is referred to as **slicing and dicing**. For example, a slice may show sales by product type and region only for the second quarter of 2009. Another slice may only show sales for desktops in the western region (see Figure 8.10).

Data Mining **Data mining** complements OLAP in that it provides capabilities for discovering "hidden" predictive relationships in the data. Using powerful multiprocessor computers and complicated algorithms, data-mining applications can analyze massive amounts of data to identify characteristics of profitable customers, purchasing patterns, or even fraudulent credit card transactions. Typically, data-mining algorithms search for

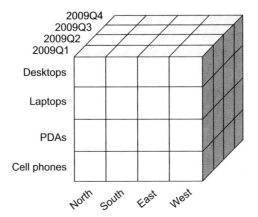

FIGURE 8.9

An OLAP cube allows for analyzing data by multiple dimensions.

hidden patterns, trends, or rules that are hidden in the data. Results from a data-mining exercise (such as the characteristics of customers most likely to respond to a marketing campaign for a specific new product) can then be used in an ad hoc query (e.g., to identify customers sharing the characteristics so as to target them in the next campaign). It is important to note that any interesting predictive model derived from data mining should be tested against "fresh" data to determine if the model actually holds what it promises.

In order to increase predictive power, data-mining algorithms are run against large data warehouses. In Chapter 4, we discussed the importance of extraction, transformation, and loading transactional data into a data warehouse, so as to enable analysis. Still, depending on the size of the data warehouse (large data warehouses often contain many terabytes of data), data-mining algorithms can take a long time to run. Thus, an important preparatory step to running data-mining algorithms is **data reduction**, i.e., to reduce the complexity of the data to be analyzed. This can be achieved by rolling up a data cube to the smallest level of aggregation needed, reducing the dimensionality, or dividing continuous measures into discrete intervals.

ASSOCIATION DISCOVERY. One frequently used application of data mining is **association discovery**. Association discovery is a technique used to find associations or correlations among sets of items. For example, a supermarket chain wants to find out which items are typically purchased together to redesign the store's layout and optimize the customer's "navigational path" through the store or to launch a new promotion. Mining sales transactions over the past five years may reveal that 80 percent of the time, people who purchase coffee also purchase sugar (see Figure 8.11). Association rules typically contain two numbers: a percentage indicating support (e.g., how often does the combination of coffee and sugar occur in all transactions analyzed) and a confidence level indicating the reliability (e.g., 80 percent of the transactions that contain coffee also contain sugar). These numbers help managers decide if the association rule is meaningful, and if any changes based on the findings are worthwhile. Similar to association discovery, **sequence discovery** is used to

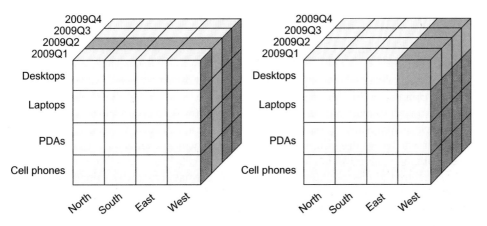

FIGURE 8.10

Slicing and dicing allows for analyzing subsets of the dimensions.

FIGURE 8.11

Association rules symbolize
associations among sets of items.

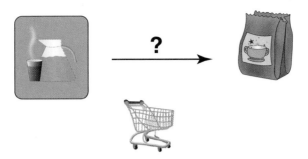

Coffee → Sugar [Support 20%, Confidence 80%]

discover associations over time. For example, it may be discovered that 55 percent of all customers who purchase a new high-definition TV set also purchase a high-definition video player within the next two months.

CLUSTERING AND CLASSIFICATION. Another useful application of data mining is clustering and classification. **Clustering** is the process of grouping related records together on the basis of having similar values for attributes. For example, an airline may cluster its frequent fliers based on miles flown or the number of flight segments. These results can then be used for targeting certain groups of customers in marketing campaigns. In contrast, **classification** is used when the groups ("classes") are known beforehand, and records are segmented into these classes. For example, a bank may have found that there are different classes of customers, who differ in their likelihood of defaulting on a loan. As such, all customers can be classified into different (known) risk categories in order to assure that the bank does not exceed a desired level of risk within its loan portfolio. Typically, classification would use a decision tree to classify the records.

Text Mining As networking and processing speeds continue to increase, creative analytical approaches are being developed to gain business intelligence from sources that could previously not be analyzed. An example of this is **text mining**, which refers to analytical techniques for extracting information from textual documents. Text mining can be applied to a variety of documents, from Web sites to transcripts, customer calls, and student college applications. For example, Verizon could use text mining to analyze customer service transcripts to determine the most important issues customers have and how they can be solved most effectively.

Web Mining Relatedly, **Web mining** is an approach to analyze the usage or content of Web pages. **Web usage mining** is used by organizations such as Amazon.com to determine patterns in customers' usage data, such as how users navigate through the site or how much time they spend on different pages. By analyzing users' **clickstream data** (i.e., a recording of the users' path through a Web site), a business such as Amazon can find its pages' "**stickiness**" (i.e., the ability to attract and keep visitors), and how customers navigate through different item categories, ultimately helping Amazon to optimize the structure of its Web site.

Web content mining refers to extracting textual information from Web documents. For example, eBay.com could use Web content mining to analyze distinct groups of vendors according to their textual profiles rather than just product offerings, volume, and other analytics common within data-mining applications.

To extract information from the overall Internet (or from some subset of Web sites), for example, a Web crawler would gather sites and documents that matched some prespecified criteria and place this information in a massive document warehouse. Once collected, the text mining system would apply a variety of analytical techniques to produce reports that can be used to gain additional insights beyond what is typically gained using data-mining analytics alone (see Figure 8.12).

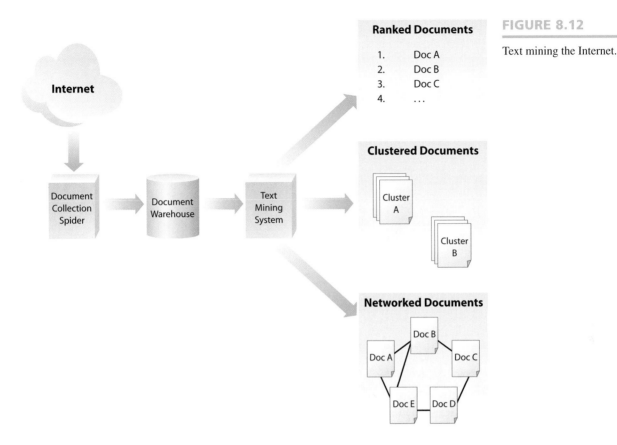

FIGURE 8.12

Text mining the Internet.

The tools used for information and knowledge discovery can be embedded into a broad range of managerial, executive, and functional area information systems (see the following discussion) as well as into decision support and intelligent systems. Results from these analyses can be provided on digital dashboards, paper reports, Web portals, e-mail alerts (using monitoring or data-mining agents), and mobile devices as well as a variety of information systems (see Figure 8.13).

Business Analytics to Support Decision Making

The second class of business intelligence applications comprises systems to support human and automated decision making. We will first discuss applications designed to support human decision makers in making unstructured decisions. Then, we will provide an overview of intelligent systems, which are designed to take some of these decisions out of the hands of the human decision makers, thus freeing up valuable resources. Finally, we examine various tools for enhancing organizational collaboration.

Management Information Systems **Management information system (MIS)** is a term with two meanings. It describes the field of study that encompasses the development, use, management, and study of computer-based information systems in organizations. It also refers to a specific type of information system that is used to produce reports to support the ongoing, recurring business processes associated with managing an entire business or a functional area within a business. An MIS is designed to get the right information to the right people in the right format at the right time to help midlevel managers make more effective decisions and consequently, often resides at the managerial level of the organization, as shown in Figure 8.6.

MISs can be found throughout the organization. For example, a marketing manager for Nike may have an MIS that contrasts sales revenue and marketing expenses by geographic region so that he or she can better understand how regional marketing for the

FIGURE 8.13

Data-mining results can be delivered to users in a variety of ways.

"Tiger Woods" golf promotions are performing. Examples of the types of business processes supported by MISs include the following:

- Sales forecasting
- Financial management and forecasting
- Manufacturing planning and scheduling
- Inventory management and planning
- Advertising and product pricing

ARCHITECTURE OF AN MIS. The basic architecture of an MIS is shown in Figure 8.14. At regular intervals, managers need to review summary information of some organizational activity. For example, a sales manager at a Ford dealership may review the weekly performance of all his sales staff. To aid his review, an MIS summarizes the total sales volume of

FIGURE 8.14

Architecture of a management information system using the basic systems model.

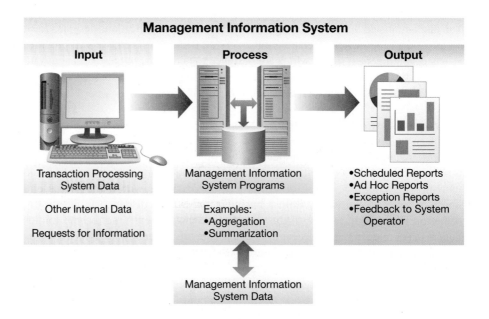

TABLE 8.5 Characteristics of a Management Information System

Inputs	Transaction processing data and other internal data; scheduled and ad hoc requests for information
Processing	Aggregation and summary of data
Outputs	Scheduled, exception, and ad hoc reports; feedback to system operator
Typical users	Midlevel managers

each salesperson in a report. This report may provide a plethora of information about each person, including the following:

- What are this salesperson's year-to-date sales totals?
- How do this year's sales figures compare with last year's?
- What is the average amount per sale?
- How do sales change by the day of the week?

The characteristics of an MIS are summarized in Table 8.5. In general, inputs to an MIS are transaction processing data produced by a TPS, other internal data (such as sales promotion expenses), and ad hoc requests for special reports or summaries. The processing aspect of an MIS focuses on data aggregation and summary. Outputs are formatted reports that provide scheduled and nonrecurring information to midlevel managers. For example, a store manager can use an MIS to review sales information to identify products that are not selling and are in need of special promotion.

Executive Information Systems In addition to operational personnel and midlevel managers, top-level managers or executives can use business intelligence applications to support business processes such as cash and investment management, resource allocation, and contract negotiation (see Figure 8.7). An information system designed to support the highest organizational manager is called an **executive information system (EIS)**. An EIS (sometimes referred to as an *executive support system*) consists of technology (hardware and software), data, procedures, and the people needed to consolidate information from internal and external sources to assist executive-level decision making. An EIS provides information to executives in a highly aggregated form so that they can scan information quickly for trends and anomalies. For example, executives may track various market conditions—such as the Dow Jones Industrial Average—to assist in making investment decisions. Although EISs are not as widely used as other types of information systems, this trend is rapidly changing because more and more executives are becoming comfortable with information technology and because an EIS can provide substantial benefits to the executive. Business processes supported by an EIS include the following:

- Executive-level decision making
- Long-range and strategic planning
- Monitoring of internal and external events and resources
- Crisis management
- Staffing and labor relations

An EIS can deliver both "soft" and "hard" data to the executive decision maker. **Soft data** include textual news stories or other nonanalytical information. **Hard data** include facts and numbers. While lower-level TPSs and MISs generate much of the hard data provided by an EIS, providing timely soft information to executive decision makers has been much more of a challenge. For example, deciding how to get the late-breaking news stories and information to the system in a format consistent with the EIS philosophy was a significant challenge to organizations. Many investment organizations, for example, subscribe to online services such as Dow Jones as a source for their stock market data. However, executives typically want to view only data that are aggregated and summarized

Ethical Dilemma

Too Much Intelligence? RFID and Privacy

Radio frequency identification (RFID) tags are the latest in technological tracking devices. Each tag generates a signature signal that an RFID reader can identify. The identification is then sent to the information system that can identify the product that was tagged. For example, the pharmaceutical industry has recently begun tagging certain drugs in large quantities, such as 100-pill bottles of Viagra and Oxycontin, in order to track them as they move through the supply chain and thus prevent counterfeits from reaching the public.

As is true with all electronic tracking devices, privacy advocates are concerned about misuse. Since, theoretically, RFID tags can be read by anyone who has an RFID reader, the tags have the potential of revealing private consumer information. For example, if you buy a product that has an RFID tag, someone with an RFID reader can possibly identify where you bought the product and how much you paid for it. The amount of information imprinted on an RFID tag is limited, however, and since few retail businesses have purchased RFID writers, readers, or the erasers that can clear information from the tags before they leave the store, the likelihood of privacy abuse is currently slim. Although pharmaceutical companies use RFID tags to track certain products, drug company spokespersons say it is highly unlikely that consumers will take home tracking devices with their heart medications or birth control pills.

Two states—California and Washington—have initiated legislation that partially addresses RFID tags and privacy, but both state laws are limited in scope. Washington's law applies primarily to identity theft and other criminal acts, and California's law prohibits the forced RFID tagging of humans. As of 2008, there were no federal laws covering RFID and privacy. A twenty-year-old federal law mandates that drugs be tracked every time they change hands from the factory to the pharmacy, but the U.S. Food and Drug Administration (FDA) has put off enforcing the requirement until RFID technology becomes more widely used. As the technology becomes more widely used, consumer protection laws and policies will undoubtedly need to be in place.

Based on:

Chartier, D. (2008, March 28). Washington State passes RFID privacy law: Where's Uncle Sam? *ArsTechnica*. Retrieved May 24, 2008, from http://arstechnica.com/news.ars/post/20080328-washington-state-passes-rfid-privacy-law-wheres-uncle-sam.html.

Jones, K. (2007, September 4). California passes bill to ban forced RFID tagging. *RFIDWorld*. Retrieved May 24, 2008, from http://www.rfid-world.com/news/201804991?queryText=RFID+California+law.

Long, M. (2005, December 29). Mind being tracked by a tiny chip? *Newsfactor*. Retrieved May 24, 2008, from http://www.newsfactor.com/story.xhtml?story_id=40435.

in a user-friendly format. To get the right information into the hands of the executives, personnel or specially designed systems select appropriate information and translate the information into a user-friendly format.

The Internet has made it much easier to gather soft data to support executive decision making. The use of numerous Web-based news portals such as FOXNews.com, CNN.com, ABCNews.com, and MSNBC.com allow users to easily customize news content so that assistants can quickly summarize and evaluate information for viewing by executives. In addition, online streaming media—video and audio—is radically changing how many executives gain soft information. Various subscription-based services from Yahoo!, CNN, and others provide customized content on almost any subject or industry, virtually as it hits the newswires. Figure 8.15 shows an example of the range of content available from Yahoo! Finance. Two very powerful features of these services make them particularly attractive for gathering soft data. First, these services can be customized to filter information so that they deliver only the information deemed relevant to the executive. For example, if an executive is interested in the software, Internet/online, and telecommunications industries, these industries can be specifically tracked. Second, these services will deliver this information to virtually any device, literally tracking you until

FIGURE 8.15

Yahoo! Finance provides a broad range of soft information that can be integrated into applications or sent to a variety of devices.

you receive the message. For example, they can be customized so that important information is sent to a computer (using e-mail, instant messaging, or a Web link), a cell phone (via voice or text message), or a BlackBerry PDA. The goal is to get the right information to a customer, using the most convenient medium.

ARCHITECTURE OF AN EIS. The architecture of an EIS is shown in Figure 8.16. Inputs to an EIS are all internal data sources and systems, external data sources such as Dow Jones and CNN that contain information on competitors, financial markets, news (local, national, and international), and any other information the executive deems important in making day-to-day decisions. However, an EIS could "overload" the executive with too much information from too many sources, so systems designers use filtering software to customize the EIS so that only key information is provided, in its most effective form, to executives. Also, system designers provide output information to executives in a highly aggregated form, often using graphical icons to make selections and bar and line charts to summarize data, trends,

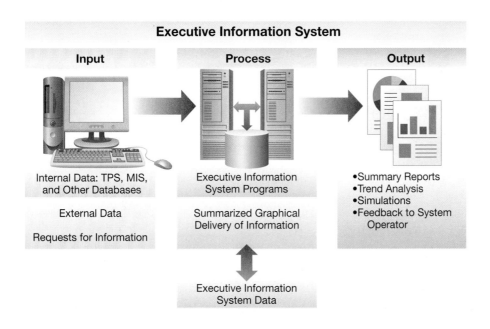

FIGURE 8.16

Architecture of an executive information system using the basic systems model.

TABLE 8.6 Characteristics of an Executive Information System

Inputs	Aggregate internal and external data
Processing	Summarizing, graphical interpreting
Outputs	Summary reports, trends, and simulations; feedback to system operator
Typical users	Executive-level managers

and simulations. Multiple monitors are often used to display the information so that it is easier to view. The characteristics of an EIS are summarized in Table 8.6.

Decision Support Systems A **decision support system (DSS)** is a special-purpose information system designed to support organizational decision making related to a particular recurring problem. DSSs are typically used by managerial-level employees to help them solve semistructured problems such as sales and resource forecasting, yet a DSS can be used to support decisions at virtually all levels of the organization. A DSS augments human decision-making performance and problem solving by enabling managers to examine alternative solutions to a problem via "what-if" analyses. A **what-if analysis** allows you to make hypothetical changes to the data associated with a problem (e.g., loan duration or interest rate) and observe how these changes influence the results. For example, a cash manager for a bank could examine what-if scenarios of the effect of various interest rates on cash availability. With a DSS, the manager uses decision analysis tools such as Microsoft Excel—a widely used DSS environment—to either analyze or create meaningful information to support the decision making related to nonroutine problems. In contrast to the systems described previously—MIS and EIS—that primarily present the outputs in a passive way, a DSS is designed to be an "interactive" decision aid. The results from any analysis are displayed in both textual and graphical formats.

ARCHITECTURE OF A DSS. Like the architecture of all systems, a DSS consists of input, process, and output components as illustrated in Figure 8.17 (Sprague, 1980). Within the process component, models and data are utilized. The DSS uses **models** to manipulate data. For example, if you have some historic sales data, you can use many different types of mod-

FIGURE 8.17

Architecture of a decision support system using the basic systems model.

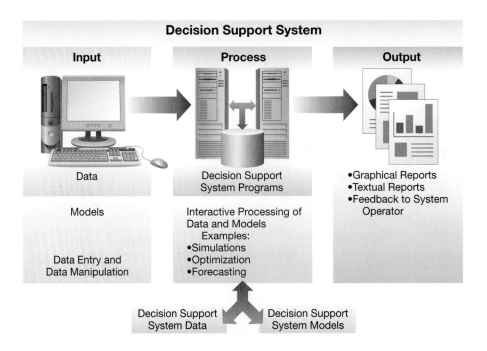

TABLE 8.7 Common DSS Models for Specific Organizational Areas

Area	Common DSS Models
Corporate level	Corporate planning, venture analysis, mergers and acquisitions
Accounting	Cost analysis, discriminant analysis, break-even analysis, auditing, tax computation and analysis, depreciation methods, budgeting
Finance	Discounted cash flow analysis, return on investment, buy or lease, capital budgeting, bond refinancing, stock portfolio management, compound interest, after-tax yield, foreign exchange values
Marketing	Product demand forecast, advertising strategy analysis, pricing strategies, market share analysis, sales growth evaluation, sales performance
Human resources	Labor negotiations, labor market analysis, personnel skills assessment, employee business expenses, fringe benefit computations, payroll and deductions
Production	Product design, production scheduling, transportation analysis, product-mix, inventory levels, quality control, plant location, material allocation, maintenance analysis, machine replacement, job assignment, material requirements planning
Management science	Linear programming, decision trees, simulation, project evaluation and planning, queuing, dynamic programming, network analysis
Statistics	Regression and correlation analysis, exponential smoothing, sampling, time-series analysis, hypothesis testing

els to create a forecast of future sales. One technique is to take an average of the past sales. The formula you would use to calculate the average is the model. A more complicated forecasting model might use time-series analysis or linear regression. See Table 8.7 for a summary of the models used to support decision making in organizations. Data for the DSS can come from many sources, including a TPS or an MIS. The user interface is the way in which the DSS interacts with the user by collecting inputs and displaying output and results.

Table 8.8 summarizes the characteristics of a DSS. Inputs are data and models. Processing supports the merging of data with models so that decision makers can examine alternative solution scenarios. Outputs are graphs and textual reports.

Functional Area Information Systems A **functional area information system** is a cross-organizational-level information system designed to support the business processes of a specific functional area (see Figure 8.18). A functional area represents a discrete area of an organization that focuses on a specific set of activities. For example, people in the marketing function focus on the activities that promote the organization and its products in a way that attracts and retains customers. People in accounting and finance focus on managing and controlling capital assets and financial resources of the organization. Table 8.9 lists various organizational functions, describes the focus of each one, and lists examples of the types of information systems used in each functional area.

TABLE 8.8 Characteristics of a Decision Support System

Inputs	Data and models; data entry and data manipulation commands (via user interface)
Processing	Interactive processing of data and models; simulations, optimization, forecasts
Outputs	Graphs and textual reports; feedback to system operator (via user interface)
Typical users	Midlevel managers (although a DSS could be used at any level of the organization)

FIGURE 8.18

Business processes supported by various functional area information systems.

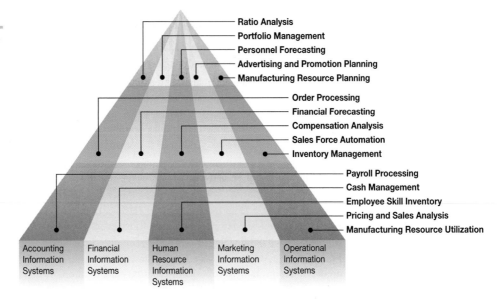

Collaboration Systems To be competitive, organizations constantly need to bring together the right combinations of people who have the appropriate set of knowledge, skills, information, and authority to solve problems quickly and easily. Traditionally, organizations have used task forces, which are temporary work groups with a finite task and life cycle, to solve problems that cannot be solved well by existing work groups. Unfortunately, traditional task forces, like traditional organizational structures, cannot always solve problems quickly. Structure and logistical problems often get in the way of people trying to get things done quickly.

Organizations need flexible teams that can be assembled quickly and can solve problems effectively and efficiently. Time is of the essence. Membership on these virtual teams

TABLE 8.9 Organizational Functions and Representative Information Systems

Functional Area	Information System	Examples of Typical Systems
Accounting and finance	Systems used for managing, controlling, and auditing the financial resources of the organization	• Inventory management • Accounts payable • Expense accounts • Cash management • Payroll processing
Human resources	Systems used for managing, controlling, and auditing the human resources of the organization	• Recruiting and hiring • Education and training • Benefits management • Employee termination • Workforce planning
Marketing	Systems used for managing new product development, distribution, pricing, promotional effectiveness, and sales forecasting of the products and services offered by the organization	• Market research and analysis • New product development • Promotion and advertising • Pricing and sales analysis • Product location analysis
Production and operations	Systems used for managing, controlling, and auditing the production and operations resources of the organization	• Inventory management • Cost and quality tracking • Materials and resource planning • Customer service tracking • Customer problem tracking • Job costing • Resource utilization

Brief Case ⊙

Instant Messaging at Work

You know the drill. You download the software necessary for instant messaging (IM) from a popular public instant messaging service such as Microsoft's Windows Live Messenger, iChat, Jabber, Google Talk, Yahoo! Messenger, Skype, ICQ, or AOL Instant Messenger, and you're off. You can then invite your contacts to participate, and if they have downloaded IM software from a compatible service and they accept your invitation, they can contact you and vice versa—all in real time. It's a convenient and fast way to communicate directly with friends and family.

Companies have also found IM a great way to hold interactive conversations and share information with their customers and colleagues. In fact, the real-time communication environment created by IM has proven especially adaptable to organizations. The predominant business advantage to IM is that it saves time—an organizational IM user knows immediately if a contact is available as opposed to playing "telephone or e-mail tag" or, worse, waiting for snail mail deliveries. Furthermore, text and graphic files can be instantly transported for perusal during an IM conversation—a process that is more unwieldy and inconvenient via fax or e-mail.

Since the secure transport of information is vital to corporations, businesses prefer more secure alternatives over using public instant messaging services. Organizations can establish their own IM network, using software designed specifically for that purpose. Organizations can choose among a variety of IM protocols for establishing an IM network, but any protocol selected should fit business-use requirements, which include the following:

1. The secure transfer of messages.
2. The ability to handle hundreds or even thousands of employee accounts.
3. Compatibility with operating systems used within the organization (e.g., Windows, Linux, and so on).
4. Access from outside the company's network.
5. The ability to load existing user data to facilitate setup and ensure proper access rights.

Alternatives to establishing one's own IM system within a corporation include (1) use of the public instant messaging services and (2) using an IM hosting service targeted at business needs. Disadvantages to using the public providers for business IM communication are clear:

1. Security cannot be enforced based on the corporation's needs.
2. Data resides on the provider's servers and in some cases becomes its property.
3. The corporation cannot block access to the network based on its own needs.
4. The corporation has no control over the stability and availability of the network. (Major public IM providers such as ICQ have blocked access to entire countries at times.)
5. The corporation cannot automate processes such as adding new employees to existing rosters.

The second alternative of the two listed here—using an IM-hosting service—is better from security and availability standpoints than using the public Internet, but such services can be costly, and there are additional disadvantages:

- Data still resides on the provider's servers and is only as secure as the provider decides to make it.
- Privacy concerns may arise when the provider has access to all conversations.
- Although automation is possible, it will not be as flexible.

A face-to-face visit may still be the preferred method of doing business, but business IM is running a close second. In fact, increasingly, workers are exchanging instant messaging IDs with business contacts instead of or in addition to exchanging e-mail addresses and telephone numbers.

Questions

1. How can IM be used to better manage a distributed workforce?
2. If you were the owner of a small company, would you allow your employees to use IM while working? If so, what rules would you impose? If not, why?

Based on:

Altunergil, O. (2005, October 6). Company-wide instant messaging with Jabberd. *Onlamp*. Retrieved May 24, 2008, from http://www.onlamp.com/pub/a/onlamp/2005/10/06/jabberd.html.

Instant messaging & messengers. (2008, May 22). In *Wikipedia, the free encyclopedia*. Retrieved May 25, 2008, from http://en.wikipedia.org/w/index.php?title=Instant_messaging_%26_messengers&oldid=214130757.

is fluid, with teams forming and disbanding as needed, with team size fluctuating as necessary, and with team members coming and going as they are needed. Employees may, at times, find themselves on multiple teams, and the life of a team may be very short. In addition, team members must have easy, flexible access to other team members, meeting contexts, and information. Think of these virtual teams as highly dynamic task forces.

Traditional office technologies, such as telephones or e-mail, are of some use to members of virtual teams but are not well suited to support the types of collaboration described previously. Telephones and pagers are not useful for rich, rapid, multiple-person team collaboration. This technology is best suited for person-to-person communication. E-mail is a useful technology for teams, but it does not provide the structure needed for effective multiperson, interactive problem solving. Companies need technologies that enable team members to interact through a set of media either at the same place and time or at different times and in different locations, with structure to aid in interactive problem solving and access to software tools and information. A number of technologies, described next, fit the bill.

GROUPWARE. The term **groupware** refers to a class of software that enables people to work together more effectively. As mentioned previously, groupware and other collaboration technologies are often distinguished along two dimensions:

1. Whether the system supports groups working together at the same time (synchronous groupware) or at different times (asynchronous groupware)
2. Whether the system supports groups working together face-to-face or distributed

Using these two dimensions, groupware systems can be categorized as being able to support four types of group interaction methods as shown in Figure 8.19. With the increased use of group-based problem solving and virtual teams, there are many potential benefits of utilizing groupware systems. These benefits are summarized in Table 8.10.

FIGURE 8.19

Groupware supports various modes of group interaction.

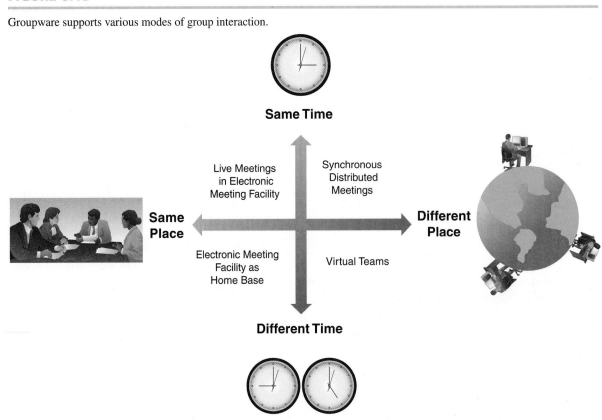

TABLE 8.10 Benefits of Groupware

Benefits	Examples
Process structuring	Keeps the group on track and helps it avoid costly diversions (i.e., doesn't allow people to get off topic or the agenda)
Parallelism	Enables many people to speak and listen at the same time (i.e., everyone has an equal opportunity to participate)
Group size	Enables larger groups to participate (i.e., brings together broader perspectives, expertise, and participation)
Group memory	Automatically records member ideas, comments, votes (i.e., allows members to focus on content of discussions, rather than on recording comments)
Access to external information	Can easily incorporate external electronic data and files (i.e., plans and proposal documents can be collected and easily distributed to all members)
Spanning time and space	Enables members to collaborate from different places at different times (i.e., reduces travel costs or allows people from remote locations to participate)
Anonymity	Member ideas, comments, and votes are not identified to others, if desired (i.e., can make it easier to discuss controversial or sensitive topics without fear of identification or retribution)

A large number of asynchronous groupware tools are becoming commonplace in organizations, including e-mail, newsgroups and mailing lists, work flow automation systems, intranets, group calendars, and collaborative writing tools. One of the most popular groupware systems—and arguably the system that put groupware into the mainstream—appeared in 1989 when Lotus Development released its Notes software product (today, Lotus is owned by IBM). In recent years, many new groupware products have emerged, most of which work through or with the Internet. Even with all of these alternative asynchronous groupware systems available, Notes continues to be an industry leader and is widely deployed throughout the world (see Figure 8.20).

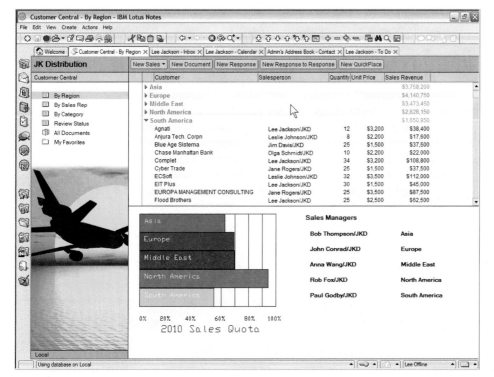

FIGURE 8.20

Lotus Notes is an award-winning groupware application with an installed base of millions of users worldwide.

Like asynchronous groupware, there are also many forms of synchronous groupware available to support a wide variety of activities, including shared whiteboards, online chat, electronic meeting support systems, and, of course, video communication systems (discussed in the following section). Although many forms of groupware can be used to help groups work more effectively, one category of groupware focuses on helping groups have better meetings. These systems are commonly referred to as **electronic meeting systems (EMS)**. An EMS is essentially a collection of personal computers networked together with sophisticated software tools to help group members solve problems and make decisions through interactive electronic idea generation, evaluation, and voting. Some typical uses for an EMS include strategic planning sessions, marketing focus groups, brainstorming sessions for system requirements definition, business process management, and quality improvement. EMSs have traditionally been housed within a dedicated meeting facility, as shown in Figure 8.21. However, EMSs are also being implemented with notebook computers so that the system can be taken on the road. Additionally, Web-based implementations are supporting distributed meetings where group members access the EMS software from their computers in their offices or from home. While EMS and related software have been around for quite some time, organizations are now beginning to discover how useful these tools can be to support e-meetings and other forms of teamwork. Evidence that groupware has become mainstream is the recent media blitz for Microsoft Live Meeting and Cisco's WebEx online meeting software.

VIDEOCONFERENCING. In the 1960s, at Disneyland and other theme parks and special events, the picturephone was first being demonstrated to large audiences. The phone companies estimated that we would be able to see a live picture with our phone calls in the near future. It took another thirty years, but that prediction has come true within many organizations. Many organizations are conducting **videoconferencing** to replace traditional meetings, using either desktop videoconferencing or dedicated videoconferencing systems that can cost from a few thousand dollars up to $500,000 (see Figure 4.29 on page 165).

(see Figure 4.29 on page 165)

FIGURE 8.21

A computer-supported meeting facility, complete with networked PCs and electronic meeting system software.

Courtesy of Groupsystems.com.

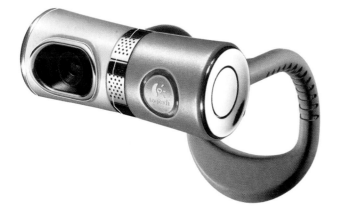

FIGURE 8.22

Logitech's popular QuickCam.

Desktop videoconferencing has been enabled by the growing power of processors powering personal computers and faster Internet connections. A desktop videoconferencing system usually comprises a fast personal computer, a **Web cam** (i.e., a small camera, often with a fixed focus, although zooming and panning features are available) (see Figure 8.22), a speaker telephone or separate microphone, videoconferencing software (e.g., Skype, Gizmo, Yahoo! Messenger, or Windows Live Messenger), and a high-speed Internet connection.

Dedicated videoconferencing systems are typically located within organizational conference rooms, facilitating meetings with customers or project team members across town or around the world. These systems can be highly realistic—as if you are almost co-located with your colleagues—but high-end systems can be extremely expensive. No matter what type of dedicated videoconferencing system utilized by an organization, this collaboration technology has come a long way from the demonstration at Disneyland in the 1960s, becoming mainstream in most modern organizations.

Intelligent systems **Artificial intelligence (AI)** is the science of enabling information technologies—software, hardware, networks, and so on—to simulate human intelligence, such as reasoning and learning, as well as gaining sensing capabilities, such as seeing, hearing, walking, talking, and feeling. AI has had a strong connection to science fiction writers where AI-enabled technologies aid humans (e.g., Mr. Data in *Star Trek: The Next Generation*) (Figure 8.23) or attempt world domination (e.g., *The Matrix*). The current reality of AI is that it is lagging far behind the imagination of most science fiction writers, but, nevertheless, great

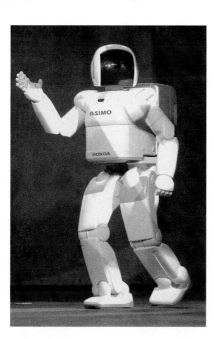

FIGURE 8.23

Artificial intelligence in the real world lags behind the imagination of science fiction writers.

Source: http://world.honda.com/ ASIMO.

strides have been made. Most notably, the development of several types of intelligent systems is having great successes for a variety of applications. An **intelligent system**—comprised of sensors, software, and computers embedded in machines and devices—emulates and enhances human capabilities. Intelligent systems are having a tremendous impact in a variety of areas, including banking and financial management, medicine, engineering, and the military. Three types of intelligent systems—expert systems, neural networks, and intelligent agents—are particularly relevant in business contexts and are discussed next.

EXPERT SYSTEMS. An **expert system (ES)** is a type of intelligent system that uses reasoning methods based on knowledge about a specific problem domain in order to provide advice, much like a human expert. ESs are used to mimic human expertise by manipulating knowledge (understanding acquired through experience and extensive learning) rather than simply manipulating information (for more information, see Turban, Aronson, Liang, and Sharda, 2007). Human knowledge can be represented in an ES by facts and rules about a problem coded in a form that can be manipulated by a computer. When you use an ES, the system asks you a series of questions, much as a human expert would. It continues to ask questions, and each new question is determined by your response to the preceding question. The ES matches the responses with the defined facts and rules until the responses point the system to a solution. A **rule** is a way of encoding knowledge, such as a recommendation, after collecting information from a user. Rules are typically expressed using an "if–then" format. For example, a rule in an expert system for assisting with decisions related to the approval of automobile loans for individuals could be represented as follows: *If* personal income is $50,000 or more, *then* approve the loan.

Given that most experts make decisions with limited information as well as use general categories of information when making judgments, researchers have developed **fuzzy logic** to broaden the capabilities of ESs and other intelligent systems. Specifically, fuzzy logic allows ES rules to be represented using approximations or subjective values in order to handle situations where information about a problem is incomplete. For example, a loan officer, when assessing a customer's loan application, may generally categorize some of the customer's financial information such as income and debt level, as high, moderate, or low rather than using precise amounts. In addition to numerous business applications, fuzzy logic is used to better control antilock braking systems and household appliances as well as when making medical diagnoses or filtering offensive language in chat rooms.

The most difficult part of building an ES is acquiring the knowledge from the expert and gathering and compiling it into a consistent and complete form capable of making recommendations. ESs are used when expertise for a particular problem is rare or expensive, such as in the case of a complex machine repair or medical diagnosis (see Figure 8.24). Using fuzzy logic, ESs are also utilized when knowledge about a problem is incomplete.

As with other information systems, the architecture of an ES (and other intelligent systems) can be described using the basic systems model (see Figure 8.25). Inputs to the system are questions and answers from the user. Processing is the matching of user questions and answers to information in the knowledge base. The processing in an expert system is called **inferencing**, which consists of matching facts and rules, determining the sequence of questions presented to the user, and drawing a conclusion. The output from an ES is a recommendation. The general characteristics of an ES are summarized in Table 8.11.

NEURAL NETWORKS. A **neural network** attempts to approximate the functioning of the human brain. Typically, a neural network is *trained* by having it categorize a large database of past information for common patterns. Once these patterns are established, new data can be compared to these learned patterns and conclusions drawn. For example, many financial institutions use neural network systems to analyze loan applications. These systems compare a person's loan application data with the neural network containing the *intelligence* of

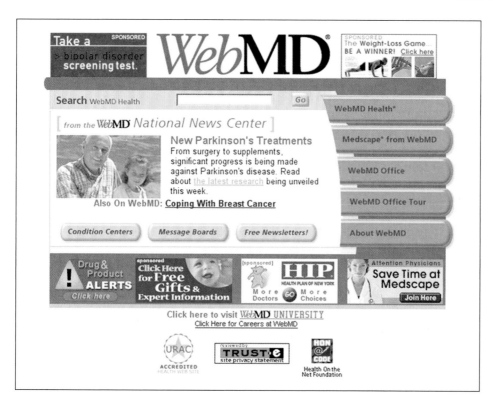

FIGURE 8.24

WebMD uses expert systems to make medical recommendations.

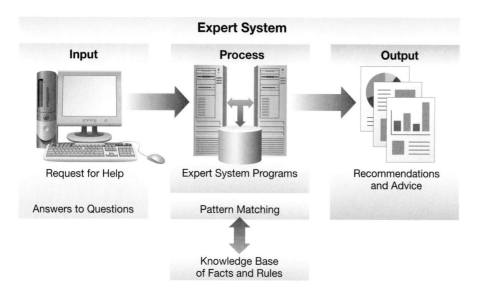

FIGURE 8.25

Architecture of an expert system using the basic systems model.

TABLE 8.11 Characteristics of an Expert System

Inputs	Request for help, answers to questions
Processing	Pattern matching and inferencing
Outputs	Recommendation or advice
Typical users	Midlevel managers (although an expert system could be used at any level of the organization)

the success and failure of countless prior loans, ultimately making a loan acceptance (or rejection) recommendation (see Figure 8.26).

INTELLIGENT AGENT SYSTEMS. An **intelligent agent**, or simply an *agent* (also called a **bot**—short for "software robot"), is a program that works in the background to provide some service when a specific event occurs. There are several types of agents for use in a broad range of contexts, including the following:

1. *User Agents.* Agents that automatically perform a task for a user, such as automatically sending a report at the first of the month, assembling customized news, or filling out a Web form with routine information
2. *Buyer Agents (Shopping Bots).* A type of user agent that searches to find the best price for a particular product you wish to purchase
3. *Monitoring and Sensing Agents.* Agents that keep track of key information such as inventory levels or competitors' prices, notifying the user when conditions change
4. *Data-Mining Agents.* Agents that continuously analyze large data warehouses to detect changes deemed important by a user, sending a notification when such changes occur
5. *Web crawlers.* Agents that continuously browse the Web for specific information (e.g., used by search engines)—also known as **Web spiders**
6. *Destructive Agents.* Malicious agents designed by spammers and other Internet attackers to farm e-mail addresses off Web sites or deposit spyware on machines

FIGURE 8.26

Neural networks approximate the functioning of the brain by creating common patterns in data and then compare new data to learned patterns to make a recommendation.

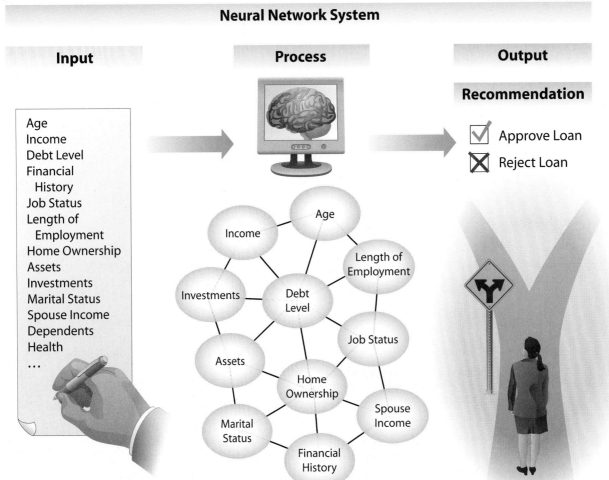

In sum, there are ongoing developments to make information systems *smarter* so that organizational decision makers gain business intelligence. Although systems such as ESs, neural networks, and intelligent agents have yet to realize the imagination of science fiction writers, they have taken great strides in helping information systems support business intelligence.

Knowledge Management Systems There is no universal agreement on what exactly is meant by the term "knowledge management." In general, however, **knowledge management** refers to the processes an organization uses to gain the greatest value from its knowledge assets. In Chapter 1, we contrasted data and information as well as knowledge and wisdom. Recall that data are raw material—recorded, unformatted information, such as words or numbers. Information is data that have been formatted and organized in some way so that the result is useful to people. We need knowledge to understand relationships between different pieces of information; wisdom is accumulated knowledge. Consequently, what constitutes **knowledge assets** are all the underlying skills, routines, practices, principles, formulas, methods, heuristics, and intuitions, whether explicit or tacit. All databases, manuals, reference works, textbooks, diagrams, displays, computer files, proposals, plans, and any other artifacts in which both facts and procedures are recorded and stored are considered knowledge assets (Winter, 2001). From an organizational point of view, properly used knowledge assets enable an organization to improve its efficiency, effectiveness, and, of course, profitability. Additionally, as many companies are beginning to lose a large number of baby boomers to retirement, companies are using knowledge management systems to capture these crucial knowledge assets

Coming Attractions

Very Smart Phones

Mobile phones have quickly evolved from voice transmission devices to handheld computers. Now researchers at MIT, Intel, and Palo Alto Research Center (PARC) are working on software that turns a mobile phone into a personal assistant, keeping track of users' activities and recommending activities that fit users' lifestyles. PARC, for example, created Magitti, an application that uses a combination of user cues, such as time of day, location, past behaviors, and text messages, to suggest activities. For example, if it's morning Magitti might suggest IHOP for breakfast; if it's 3 P.M. the location of the nearest shopping mall; 9 P.M. a conveniently located pub.

Similarly, researchers at MIT's Media Laboratory have developed data-analysis software for mobile phones that, like Magitti, collects information from mobile phones' GPS locators, call logs, and other behavior indicators, then processes the data to predict behavior. Making sense of the data assembled through mobile phone use will mean that the devices can schedule meetings, suggest activities, and otherwise predict behavior.

In fact, Apple's popular iPhone already has many sensors "under the hood," such as tiny accelerometers,

light sensors, and infrared sensors that are just waiting for software to take advantage of the many possibilities. Accelerometers, for example, as presently used in the Nokia 5500, allow joggers to keep track of distances and speeds and let users play accelerometer-based games.

Mobile phones of the future will definitely provide more than just person-to-person communication. They are poised to become artificial intelligence wonders that remind us of all the daily activities necessary to keep us living a healthy, goal-focused, stimulating lifestyle.

Based on:

Greene, K. (2006, November 1). From the labs: Information technology. *Technology Review.* Retrieved May 24, 2008, from http://www.technologyreview.com/Infotech/17729/page2.

Green, K. (2007, November 13). Smart phone suggests things to do. *Technology Review.* Retrieved May 24, 2008, from http://www.technologyreview.com/Biztech/19698/?a=f.

Greene, K. (2007, June 29). The iPhone's untapped potential. *Technology Review.* Retrieved May 24, 2008, from http://www.technologyreview.com/Infotech/18990/?a=f.

(Leonard, 2005). Clearly, effectively managing knowledge assets will enhance business intelligence.

Knowledge assets can be distinguished as being either explicit or tacit. **Explicit knowledge assets** reflect knowledge that can be documented, archived, and codified, often with the help of information systems. Explicit knowledge assets reflect much of what is typically stored in a database management system. In contrast, **tacit knowledge assets** reflect the processes and procedures that are located in a person's mind on how to effectively perform a particular task (see Figure 8.27). Identifying key tacit knowledge assets and managing these assets so that they are accurate and available to people throughout the organization remains a significant challenge.

Tacit knowledge assets often reflect an organization's **best practices**—procedures and processes that are widely accepted as being among the most effective and/or efficient. Identifying how to recognize, generate, store, share, and manage this tacit knowledge is the primary objective for deploying a knowledge management system. Consequently, a **knowledge management system** is typically not a single technology but rather a collection of technology-based tools that include communication technologies—such as e-mail, groupware, instant messaging, and the like—as well as information storage and retrieval systems, such as a database management system, to enable the generation, storage, sharing, and management of tacit and explicit knowledge assets (Malhotra, 2005).

BENEFITS OF KNOWLEDGE MANAGEMENT SYSTEMS. Many potential benefits can come from organizations' effectively capturing and utilizing their tacit knowledge assets (Santosus and Surmacz, 2001) (see Table 8.12). For example, innovation and creativity may be enhanced by the free flow of ideas throughout the organization. Also, by widely sharing best practices, organizations should realize improved customer service, shorter product development, and streamlined operations. Enhanced business operations not only will improve the overall organizational performance but also will enhance employee retention rates by recognizing the value of employees' knowledge and rewarding them for sharing it. Thus, organizations can realize many benefits from the successful deployment of a knowledge management system.

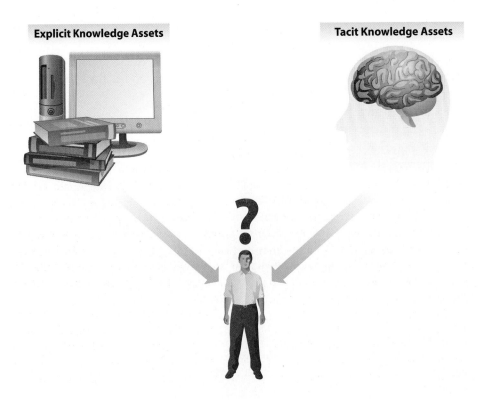

FIGURE 8.27

Explicit knowledge assets can easily be documented, archived, and codified, whereas tacit knowledge assets are located in a person's mind.

TABLE 8.12 Benefits and Challenges of Knowledge Management Systems

Benefits	Challenges
• Enhanced innovation and creativity	• Getting employee buy-in
• Improved customer service, shorter product development, and streamlined operations	• Focusing too much on technology
	• Forgetting the goal
• Enhanced employee retention	• Dealing with knowledge overload and obsolescence
• Improved organizational performance	

Although there are many potential benefits for organizations that effectively deploy knowledge management systems, to do so requires that several substantial challenges be overcome (Table 8.12). First, effective deployment requires employees to agree to share their personal tacit knowledge assets and to take extra steps to utilize the system for identifying best practices. Therefore, to encourage employee buy-in and also to enable the sharing of knowledge, organizations must create a culture that values and rewards widespread participation. Second, experience has shown that a successful deployment must first identify what knowledge is needed, why it is needed, and who is likely to have this knowledge. Once an organization understands "why, what, and who," identifying the best technologies for facilitating knowledge exchange is a much easier task. In other words, the best practices for deploying knowledge management systems suggest that organizations save the "how"—that is, what collaboration and storage technologies to use—for last.

Third, the successful deployment of a knowledge management system must be linked to a specific business objective. By linking the system to a specific business objective and coupling that with the use of an assessment technique, such as return on investment, an organization can then identify costs and benefits and can also be sure that the system is providing value in an area that is indeed important to the organization. Fourth, the knowledge management system must be easy to use, not only for putting knowledge in but also for getting knowledge out. Similarly, the system cannot overload users with too much information or with information that is obsolete. Just as physical assets can erode over time, knowledge, too, can become stale and irrelevant. Therefore, an ongoing process of updating, amending, and removing obsolete or irrelevant knowledge must occur or the system will fall into disarray and will not be used. In sum, to gain the greatest benefits from an investment in a knowledge management system, the organization must take care to overcome various challenges.

HOW ORGANIZATIONS UTILIZE KNOWLEDGE MANAGEMENT SYSTEMS. The people using a knowledge management system will be working in different departments within the organization, doing different functions, and will likely be located in different locations around the building, city, or even the world. Each person—or group of people—can be thought of as a separate island that is set apart from others by geography, job focus, expertise, age, and gender. Often, a person on one island is trying to solve a problem that has already been solved by another person located on some other island. Finding this "other" person is often a significant challenge (see Figure 8.28). The goal of a successful knowledge management system is to facilitate the exchange of needed knowledge between these separate islands. To find and connect such separate islands, organizations use **social network analysis**. Social network analysis is a technique that attempts to find groups of people who work together, to find people who don't collaborate but should, or to find experts in particular subject areas. To do this, people's contacts are mapped, so that connections or missing links within the organization can easily be discovered.

Once organizations have collected their knowledge into a repository, they must find an easy way to share it with employees (often using an intranet), customers, suppliers (often with an extranet), or the general public (often using the Internet). These **knowledge portals** can be customized to meet the unique needs of their intended users. For example, the FDA is responsible for keeping the public (e.g., citizens, researchers, and industry)

FIGURE 8.28

In a large or global organization, finding the person with the right knowledge can be a significant challenge.

"I wonder who knows?"

informed on the most up-to-date information related to food (e.g., information on mad cow disease or product recalls) and drugs (e.g., the status of a drug trial). The FDA Web site uses a Google *search appliance*—a special type of computer that analyzes and indexes information within a Web site—so that visitors can quickly search and find needed information within the FDA's more than 1 million documents (see Figure 8.29).

In addition to the FDA, countless other organizations, such as Ford Motor Company, Eli Lilly, Wal-Mart, and Dell Computers, are also rapidly deploying knowledge management

FIGURE 8.29

Countless organizations are using Web-based knowledge portals to provide information to employees, customers, and partners.

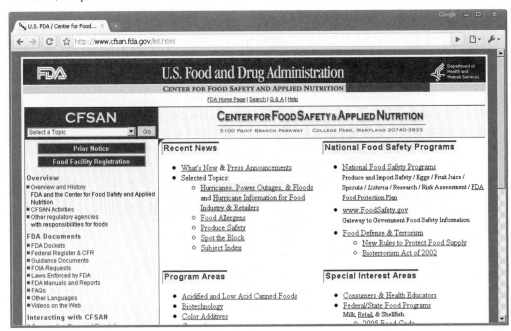

Powerful Partnerships

Adobe's John Warnock and Chuck Geschke

John Warnock was born October 6, 1940, in Salt Lake City, Utah. He earned undergraduate and master's degrees in mathematics and a PhD in electrical engineering, all from the University of Utah. Chuck Geschke was born in Cleveland, Ohio, on September 11, 1939. He holds a PhD in computer science from Carnegie Mellon University in Pittsburgh. Warnock worked for Charles Geschke at Xerox Corporation's Palo Alto Research Center (PARC) from 1978 to 1982, where they developed the foundation for PostScript, a technology aimed at simplifying the process of printing documents directly from a computer. Warnock and Geschke left Xerox in 1982 to start Adobe Systems Inc. to bring their technology to the market (see Figure 8.30).

Being perceived as a wealthy Internet entrepreneur, Geschke was kidnapped from the Adobe parking lot in Mountain View, California, in 1992, ten years after the company was founded. The abductors claimed to be members of a Middle Eastern organization and told Geschke they would kill him after they collected the ransom they were asking. The kidnappers also claimed to have planted explosives that would destroy Geschke's house and his neighbors' houses. Five days after his ordeal began, the FBI recovered Geschke unharmed. The kidnappers were arrested and sentenced to life in prison.

Today, Adobe is one of the biggest software companies, and its portfolio includes several industry-leading software products, including Acrobat (the PDF file format is the de facto standard for sharing documents on the Web), ColdFusion, Dreamweaver, Flash, Photoshop, and many others. Geschke retired as Adobe's president in 2000; Warnock retired in 2000 as the company's CEO and in 2001 as CTO. Warnock and Geschke continue to be cochairmen of Adobe's board, helping to guide the future for the $3 billion company they cofounded.

Based on:

Anonymous (n.d.). Executive profiles. Retrieved May 24, 2008, from http://www.adobe.com/aboutadobe/pressroom/executivebios/charlesgeschke.html.

Belden, A. (1997, October 13). A dramatic kidnapping revisited. *Los Altos Town Crier.* Retrieved May 25, 2008, from http://www.latc.com/1997/10/13/special_sect/exclusive1.html.

Charles Geschke. (2008, May 21). In *Wikipedia, the free encyclopedia.* Retrieved May 25, 2008, from http://en.wikipedia.org/w/index.php?title=Charles_Geschke&oldid=214062509.

John Warnock. (2008, May 21). In *Wikipedia, the free encyclopedia.* Retrieved May 25, 2008, from http://en.wikipedia.org/w/index.php?title=John_Warnock&oldid=214062599.

FIGURE 8.30

Adobe's John Warnock and Chuck Geschke.

systems. We are learning from these deployments that all organizations, whether for-profit or nonprofit, struggle to get the right information to the right person at the right time. Through the use of a comprehensive strategy for managing knowledge assets, organizations are much more likely to gain a competitive advantage and a positive return on their information systems investments.

Information Visualization

The third pillar of business intelligence applications is information visualization. **Visualization** refers to the display of complex data relationships using a variety of graphical methods, enabling managers to quickly grasp the results of the analysis. For example, Figure 8.31 shows the visualization of Hurricane Katrina in 2005 as the storm was gaining strength. The image shows towering thunderclouds (in red), called hot towers, which were spotted just before Katrina intensified to a Category 5 hurricane. Once represented visually, analysts can view changes over time and perform what-if analyses to better understand the behavior of hurricanes. In similar ways, organizations around the world are utilizing visualization technologies to enhance business intelligence.

Visual Analytics As discussed in previous sections, business intelligence systems can provide business decision makers with a wide variety of analyses to support decision making. However, in the end, it is still the humans who have to interpret the output from these systems. With growing complexity of the underlying data (such as multiple dimensions, including spatial dimensions), interpreting the outputs becomes extremely challenging. **Visual analytics** is the combination of various analysis techniques and interactive visualization to solve complex problems. By combining human intelligence and reasoning capabilities with technology's retrieval and analysis capabilities, visual analytics can help in decision making, as the strengths of both the human and the machine are merged. With the humans' ability to make sense of "noisy" data, unexpected patterns or relationships in the data can be discovered, and results of complex queries can be quickly interpreted. Visual analytics is used in a variety of settings, ranging from homeland security to disaster relief.

FIGURE 8.31

Visualization is the display of complex data relationships using a variety of graphical methods.

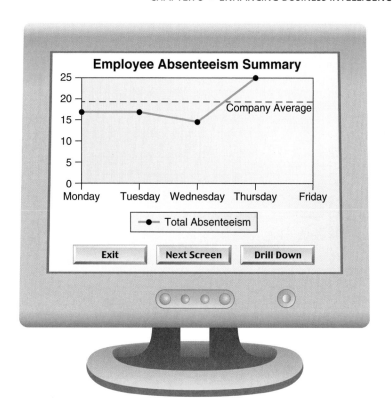

FIGURE 8.32

A digital dashboard showing a total employee absenteeism line chart.

Dashboards **Digital dashboards** are commonly used to present KPIs and other summary information used by managers and executives to make decisions. Within systems like an EIS, digital dashboards deliver information, possibly from multiple sources, to provide warnings, action notices, and summaries of business conditions. Although data are typically provided in a very highly aggregated form, the executive also has the capability to drill down and see the details if necessary. For example, suppose a digital dashboard within an EIS summarizes employee absenteeism, and the system shows that today's numbers are significantly higher than normal. The executive can see this information in a running line chart, as illustrated in Figure 8.32. If the executive wants to understand why absenteeism is so high, a selection on the screen can provide the details behind the aggregate numbers, as shown in Figure 8.33. By drilling down into the data, the executive can see that the spike in absenteeism was centered in the manufacturing area. Also, the digital dashboard can connect the data in the system to the organization's internal communication systems (e.g., electronic or voice mail) so that the executive can quickly send a message to the appropriate managers to discuss solutions to the problem discovered in the drill-down.

Dashboards make use of a variety of design elements to present the data in the most user-friendly way. To highlight deviations that need to be addressed or to symbolize changes over time, dashboards use maps, charts, sparklines, or graphics symbolizing traffic lights, thermometers, or speedometers (see Figure 8.34).

Geographic Information Systems One type of visualization system that is growing in popularity is called a **geographic information system (GIS)**. A GIS is a system for creating, storing, analyzing, and managing geographically referenced information. For example, a GIS can be used by a retail company to identify the optimal location for a new store or help a farmer identify areas too wet to fertilize. Using GIS, analysts can combine geographic, demographic, and other data for locating target customers, finding optimal site locations, or determining the right product mix at different locations; additionally, GIS can perform a variety of analyses, such as market share analysis and competitor analysis. Cities, counties, and states also use GIS for

FIGURE 8.33

Drill-down numbers for
employee absenteeism.

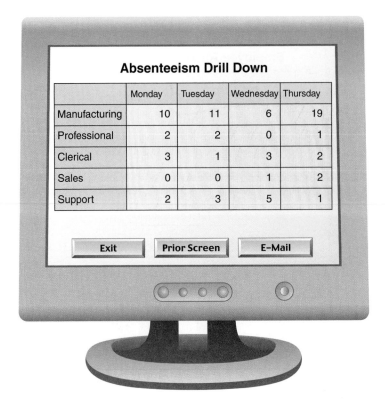

	Monday	Tuesday	Wednesday	Thursday
Manufacturing	10	11	6	19
Professional	2	2	0	1
Clerical	3	1	3	2
Sales	0	0	1	2
Support	2	3	5	1

aiding in infrastructure design and zoning issues (e.g., where should the new elementary school be located?).

Businesses typically face many decisions with a spatial dimension, such as Where are my customers located? Where is the best location to open a new store? Which areas should be included in the next mailing? or How far are my customers willing to drive? **Customer dot mapping** is used to map current customers. Comparing customers' locations with the location of one's business can help in deciding whether the store has the optimal location, or whether opening a new store would be warranted. Relatedly, **trade area analysis** helps to assess where customers are coming from by combining location information with, for example, drive time information, to determine if certain areas are underserved, or if two stores' trade areas overlap. **Thematic mapping** is another widely

FIGURE 8.34

Dashboards use various
graphical elements to highlight
important information.

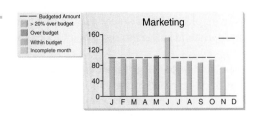

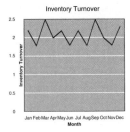

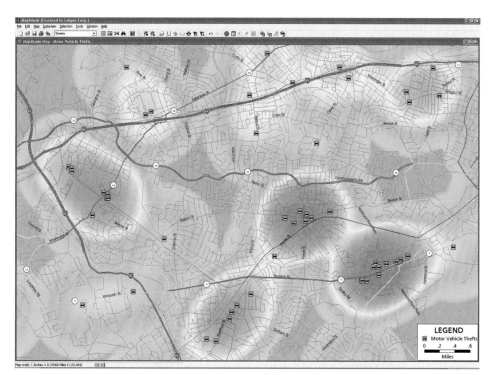

FIGURE 8.35

A thematic map showing car thefts in a town.

used GIS technique. Thematic maps color code data that is aggregated for specific geographic regions. For example, a thematic map could display the median household income in different blocks, or it could display average household sizes, helping a business to identify areas with the most promising target population; similarly, an insurance company could use GIS to determine where certain crimes (such as car theft) most frequently occur (see Figure 8.35).

Clearly, GIS, like all the systems described in this chapter, are providing organizations with business intelligence to better compete in the digital world.

Industry Analysis

Healthcare

Do you remember the times when your doctor wrote a prescription, and the handwriting was worse than your professor's, making you wonder how the pharmacist could ever decipher it and dispense the correct drugs? If you recently went to a doctor, you may have noticed that information systems have had a huge impact on the health care field. Now, many doctors carry laptops or PDAs, allowing them to digitally store any diagnosis, facilitating the sharing of information between the physician, nurses, and even your medical insurance. In addition to providing access to electronic patient records, the laptop or PDA provides your physician access to medical and drug information, as offered by the "physician's desk ref-

erence" Web site (www.pdr.net). At pdr.net, your physician can obtain the latest information about drugs and clinical guidelines, or check interactions between different drugs. Electronic patient records are now even moving toward the Web. Pioneered by Microsoft's HealthVault and Google, Web-based electronic patient records free the patient from having to carry medical records from doctor to doctor.

Information systems have also tremendously changed diagnosis and monitoring of patients. For example, modern EEG and EKG devices heavily depend on computer technology, and, as the name implies, computer tomography (used to produce images of internal organs) could not be performed without computer technology. Even diagnostic tests such as x-rays now use digital technology, allowing the doctor to digitally enhance the image for improved diagnosis or to electronically transmit the image to a remote specialist. Following the diagnosis of a serious condition, technology can even help in the operating room. For example, many modern clinics use surgical robots and endoscopes for delicate procedures such as neurosurgery or gastrointestinal surgery. Taken a step further, such systems can be used for what is referred to as telemedicine, including remote diagnosis and remote surgery. Whereas traditionally, a patient had to travel thousands of miles to visit a specialized surgeon, many surgeries can now be performed remotely, reducing the strain on the patient and potentially saving precious time. Further, telemedicine applications can be used for remote locations, battlefields, or even prisons, reducing costs for transporting patients and improving care.

No matter if you're visiting your doctor regarding a condition or just for a routine checkup, you'll be likely to encounter various information systems that change the doctors' and nurses' lives.

Questions:

1. Discuss the benefits and drawbacks of online medical records.
2. Computer-aided diagnosis can replace years of experience, providing opportunities for young, inexperienced physicians. Contrast the benefits and drawbacks for the patients and the physicians.
3. Will there be a place for physicians without computer skills in the future? Why or why not?

Based on:

Anonymous (2007, April 29). World's first image-guided surgical robot to enhance accuracy and safety of brain surgery. *Science Daily.* Retrieved May 24, 2008, from http://www.sciencedaily.com/releases/2007/04/070417114732.htm.

Anonymous (n.d.). Welcome to HealthVault. Retrieved May 24, 2008, from http://www.healthvault.com.

Anonymous (n.d.). Welcome to PDR.net. Retrieved May 24, 2008, from http://www.pdr.net.

Key Points Review

1. *Describe the concept of business intelligence and how it is used at the operational, managerial, and executive levels of an organization.* Businesses need business intelligence to quickly respond to external threats and opportunities arising from unstable market conditions, fierce competition, short product life cycles, and fickle customers. Business intelligence supports this by enabling a closed-loop approach to planning at all levels of the organization. At the operational level of the firm, the routine day-to-day business processes and interaction with customers occur, and information systems are designed to automate repetitive activities. Business intelligence is used to optimize processes and to understand the underlying causes of performance problems. At the managerial level of the organization, functional managers focus on monitoring and controlling operational-level activities and providing information to higher levels of the organization. Midlevel or functional managers use business intelligence to achieve the organization's strategic objectives. At the executive level of the organization, decisions are often very complex problems with broad and long-term ramifications for the organization. Executive-level decisions are often referred to as being messy or unstructured because executives must consider the ramifications for the overall organization. Business intelligence applications provide the necessary input, focusing on balancing performance across the organization. Transaction processing systems are designed to process business events and transactions and reside close to customers at the operational level of the organization. Primarily used to automate repetitive information-processing activities to increase speed and accuracy and to lower the cost of processing each transaction, these systems provide valuable input into business intelligence applications.

2. *Explain the three components of business intelligence: information and knowledge discovery, business analytics, and information visualization.* Information and knowledge discovery tools are used to discover "hidden" relationships in data. Ad hoc query tools allow decision makers to run queries whenever needed. OLAP tools extend this capability by offering the ability to perform complex multidimensional queries. Data mining is used for association discovery and clustering and classification. Text and Web mining are used to

extract information from textual documents. Decision support and intelligent systems are used to support human and automated decision making. Management information systems reside at the managerial level and are designed to aid midlevel managers in their decision making. Executive information systems are used to provide information to executives in a very highly aggregate form so that information can be scanned quickly for trends and anomalies. Decision support systems (DSS) support organizational decision making and are typically designed to solve a particular recurring problem in the organization. DSSs are most commonly used to support semistructured problems that are addressed by managerial-level employees. A DSS is designed to be an interactive decision aid. Collaboration technologies such as videoconferencing, groupware, and electronic meeting systems are used to support the communication and teamwork of virtual teams. Intelligent systems such as expert systems, neural networks, and intelligent agents work to emulate and enhance human capabilities. Expert systems (ESs) apply knowledge within some topic area to provide

advice by mimicking human expertise (understanding acquired through experience and extensive learning). ESs are used when expertise for a particular problem is rare or expensive. Neural networks attempt to approximate the functioning and decision making of the human brain by comparing patterns in new data versus complex patterns learned from prior data. Intelligent agents are programs that can be applied to a broad variety of situations, typically operating in the background to provide some service when a special event occurs or when a request is made. Knowledge management systems are a collection of technology-based tools that enable the generation, storage, sharing, and management of knowledge assets. Visualization combines the human visual system and analysis techniques to aid in the analysis of complex relationships. Dashboards are often used to provide decision makers with the right information in an easy-to-understand way. Geographic information systems aid in storing, analyzing, and managing geographically referenced information, such as for locating target customers or finding optimal store locations.

Key Terms

ad hoc query 321
artificial intelligence (AI) 337
association discovery 323
batch processing 319
best practices 342
bot 340
business intelligence 312
buyer agent 340
classification 324
clickstream data 324
clustering 324
continuous planning process 314
customer dot mapping 348
data mining 322
data-mining agent 340
data reduction 323
decision support system (DSS) 330
desktop videoconferencing 337
destructive agent 340
digital dashboard 347
dimension 322
drill down 322
drill-down report 321
electronic meeting system (EMS) 336
exception report 321
executive information system (EIS) 327
executive level 316

expert system 338
explicit knowledge asset 342
fact 322
fully automated data entry 319
functional area information system 331
fuzzy logic 338
geographic information system (GIS) 347
groupware 334
hard data 327
inferencing 338
intelligent agent 340
intelligent system 338
key performance indicator (KPI) 316
key-indicator report 321
knowledge asset 341
knowledge management 341
knowledge management system 342
knowledge portal 343
management information system (MIS) 325
managerial level 315
manual data entry 319
measure 322
model 330
monitoring and sensing agent 340

neural network 338
OLAP cube 322
OLAP server 322
online analytical processing (OLAP) 322
online processing 319
operational level 314
roll up 322
rule 338
scheduled report 321
semiautomated data entry 319
semistructured decision 316
sequence discovery 323
shopping bot 340
slicing and dicing 322
social network analysis 343
soft data 327
source document 319
stickiness 324
structured decision 314
tacit knowledge asset 342
text mining 324
thematic mapping 348
trade area analysis 348
transaction 317
transaction processing system (TPS) 317
unstructured decision 316
user agent 340
videoconferencing 336

visual analytics 346

visualization 346

Web cam 337

Web content mining 324

Web crawler 340

Web mining 324

Web spider 340

Web usage mining 324

what-if analysis 330

Review Questions

1. Compare and contrast the characteristics of the operational, managerial, and executive levels of an organization.
2. Describe the differences between online processing and batch processing. Give examples of each.
3. What are the three methods used for inputting data into a transaction processing system? Provide examples of each.
4. Describe how OLAP enables a user to conduct multidimensional queries.
5. What is the meaning of support and confidence in the context of data mining?
6. Explain the difference between clustering and classification.
7. Describe and give examples of two types of Web mining.
8. How does a management information system differ from a transaction processing system in terms of purpose, target users, capabilities, and so forth?
9. How does an executive information system "drill down" into the data?
10. Explain the purpose of a model within a decision support system.
11. Provide some examples of functionally specific information systems and needs within an organization.
12. What is groupware, and what are the different types?
13. Compare and contrast stand-alone videoconferencing and desktop videoconferencing.
14. Describe four types of intelligent agents. How can they be used to benefit organizations?
15. What is a knowledge management system, and what types of technologies make up a comprehensive system?
16. How can visualization be used to gain business intelligence and improve decision making?
17. What are the different types of GIS applications?

Self-Study Questions

Visit the Interactive Study Guide on the Companion Web site for additional Self-Study Questions: www.pearsonhighered.com/valacich.

1. At the _____ level of the organization, functional managers (e.g., marketing managers, finance managers, manufacturing managers, and human resource managers) focus on monitoring and controlling operational-level activities and providing information to higher levels of the organization.
   A. operational
   B. managerial
   C. organizational
   D. executive
2. A(n) _____ report provides a summary of critical information on a recurring schedule.
   A. scheduled
   B. exception
   C. key indicator
   D. drill-down
3. A supervisor's having to decide when to reorder supplies or how best to allocate personnel for the completion of a project is an example of a _____ decision.
   A. structured
   B. unstructured
   C. automated
   D. delegated
4. _____ is used to determine the likelihood of new customers to default on a loan.
   A. Association discovery
   B. Sequence discovery
   C. Classification
   D. Clustering
5. Market share analysis is a type of model typically used by the _____ function of an organization.
   A. marketing
   B. accounting
   C. production
   D. management science
6. E-mail is an example of a(n) _____ groupware system.
   A. synchronous
   B. anonymous
   C. asynchronous
   D. parallel
7. Examples of the types of activities that can be supported by expert systems include all of the following except _____.
   A. payroll calculations
   B. financial planning
   C. machine configuration
   D. medical diagnosis

8. _____ agents keep track of key information such as inventory levels, notifying the users when conditions change.
   - A. User
   - B. Buyer
   - C. Monitoring and sensing
   - D. Data-mining
9. What is true about knowledge management?
   - A. As baby boomers retire at an increasing rate, knowledge management is helping organizations capture their knowledge.
   - B. A knowledge management system is not a single technology but a collection of technology-based tools.
   - C. Finding the right technology to manage knowledge assets is much easier than identifying what knowledge is needed, why it is needed, and who has this knowledge.
   - D. All of the above are true.
10. Which of the following is not a commonly used GIS application?
   - A. customer dot mapping
   - B. thematic mapping
   - C. trade area analysis
   - D. regional sales analysis

Answers are on page 355.

Problems and Exercises

1. Match the following terms with the appropriate definitions:
   - i. Operational level
   - ii. Transactions
   - iii. Virtual teams
   - iv. Source document
   - v. Online processing
   - vi. Data mining
   - vii. Expert system
   - viii. Digital dashboard
   - ix. Geographic information system
   - x. Decision support system
     - a. An information system designed to analyze and store spatially referenced data
     - b. A special-purpose information system designed to mimic human expertise by manipulating knowledge (understanding acquired through experience and extensive learning) rather than simply information
     - c. The bottom level of an organization, where the routine day-to-day interaction with customers occurs
     - d. A set of applications used to find hidden predictive relationships in a data set.
     - e. Processing of information immediately as it occurs
     - f. Repetitive events in organizations that occur as a regular part of conducting day-to-day operations
     - g. A special-purpose information system designed to support organizational decision making primarily at the managerial level of an organization
     - h. A document created when a business event or transaction occurs
     - i. A user interface visually representing summary information about a business's health, often from multiple sources
     - j. Teams forming and disbanding as needed, with team size fluctuating as necessary and with team members coming and going as they are needed

2. Visit guide.real.com on the Web. RealNetworks provides information on almost any subject or industry, virtually as it hits the newswires. What types of "hard" and "soft" data can you find?

3. Do you feel that, as much as possible, transaction processing systems should replace human roles and activities within organizations? Why or why not? How much cost savings will there be if these humans are still needed to run the systems? What if you were the person being replaced? Will all errors necessarily be eliminated? Why or why not?

4. Imagine that your boss has asked you to build an inventory transaction system that would enable the receiving and shipping clerks to enter inventory amounts for purchases and sales, respectively. Discuss the pros and cons of building this system as an online processing system versus a batch processing system. Which would you recommend to your boss?

5. The national sales manager for ABC Corp. is interested in purchasing a software package that will be capable of providing "accurate" sales forecasts for the short term and the long term. She has asked you to recommend the best type of system for this purpose. What would you recommend? Do you have any reservations about such a system? Why or why not?

6. Visit MSN Money (www.moneycentral.msn.com/ investor/calcs/n_expect/main.asp) on the Web to determine your life expectancy using a decision support system. What did you learn? Is there a difference between life expectancies for different genders? If you browse through MSN Money, what other interesting stuff do you find? Also check out www.bigcharts.com.

7. Interview a top-level executive within an organization with which you are familiar and determine the extent to

which the organization utilizes executive information systems (or information aggregation technologies like digital dashboards). Does this individual utilize an executive information system in any way? Why or why not? Which executives do utilize an executive information system?

8. Think about the junk mail you receive every day in your postal mail. Which mailings do you believe to be a result of data mining? How have the companies chosen you for their targeted mailings?

9. Using any program you choose or using the Web site www.moneycentral.com, find or create a template that you could use in the future to determine monthly payments on car or home loans. Compare your template with the one at www.bankrate.com/brm/auto-loan-calculator.asp. Would you have categorized the program you used to create this template as a decision support system before doing this exercise?

10. Describe your experiences with expert systems, or go to www.exsys.com or www.easydiagnosis.com on the Web and spend some time interacting with their demonstration systems. Now choose a problem that you know a lot about and would like to build your own expert system for. Describe the problem and list the questions you would need to ask someone in order to make a recommendation.

11. Go out onto the Web and compare three shopping bots for a product you are interested in (e.g., www.bottom-dollar.com, www.mysimon.com, www.shopzilla.com, www.shopping.com, or www.pricegrabber.com). Did the different agents find the same information, or were there any differences? Did you prefer one over the others? Why?

12. Have you seen or used ad hoc, exception, key-indicator, and/or drill-down reports? What is the purpose of each report? Who produces and who uses the reports? Do any of these reports look or sound familiar from your work experience?

13. Interview an information systems manager within an organization. What types of information and knowledge discovery tools does the organization use? Was there an increase or decrease in the last few years? What predictions does this manager have regarding the future of these systems? Do you agree? Prepare a ten-minute presentation to the class on your findings.

14. For your university, identify several examples of various knowledge assets and rate these assets on their value to the university on a 10-point scale (1 = low value to 10 = high value).

15. Examine your university Web site to identify examples where a knowledge management system could be used, or is being used, to help provide improved services to students.

16. How do you prefer your desired information to be presented? Do you use any type of visualization tools? If so, which ones?

Application Exercises

Note: The existing data files referenced in these exercises are available on the Student Companion Web site: www.pearsonhighered.com/valacich.

Spreadsheet Application: Travel Loan Facility

A new aspect of the business has been added to Campus Travel. Students can apply for a loan to help pay for their travels. However, loans for travel are available only to students who are traveling outside the country for at least two weeks. Since the costs for this type of international travel differ depending on how you travel, where you stay, and what you do at the destination, different loan packages are available. For a month in Europe, you have decided to take out a loan. You have already taken a look at several offers but are unsure whether you can afford it. Set up a spreadsheet to calculate the payments per month for the following situations:

1. Two weeks in Eastern Europe; Price: $2,000; Percentage Rate: 5.5%; Time: one year

2. Two weeks in Western Europe; Price: $3,000; Percentage Rate: 6.0%; Time: one year

3. Three weeks in Eastern Europe; Price: $3,000; Percentage Rate: 6.5%; Time: two years

4. Three weeks in Western Europe; Price: $3,500; Percentage Rate: 5.5%; Time: two years

5. Four weeks in Eastern Europe; Price: $4,000; Percentage Rate: 6.0%; Time: two years

6. Four weeks in Western Europe; Price: $5,000; Percentage Rate: 6.5%; Time: three years

Once you have calculated the payments, calculate the total amount to be paid for each option as well as the total interest you would pay over the course of the loan. Make sure to use formulas for all calculations and print out a professionally formatted page displaying the results and a page displaying the formulas (Hint: In Microsoft Excel, use the "PMT" function in the category "Financial" to calculate the payments. Use Ctrl + ` [grave accent] to switch between formula and data views).

Database Application: Tracking Regional Office Performance at Campus Travel

The general manager wants to know which offices were most profitable during the previous year and asks you to prepare several reports. In the file FY2006.mdb, you find information about the offices, sales agents, and destinations. Use the report wizard to generate the following reports:

1. List of all sales agents grouped by office (including total number of agents per office)

2. List of sales agents for each destination (grouped by destination, including total number of agents)

3. Destinations sold by each sales agent (including total number of destinations)

Team Work Exercise: What's the Hot Topic?

Visit a Web site of an information systems–related content provider, such as *InformationWeek, Computerworld, CIO*, or *NewsFactor*, and scan the current headlines. You can find these online resources at www.informationweek.com, www.computerworld.com, www.cio.com, and www.newsfactor.com. After having scanned the headlines, get together with your team and discuss your findings. What is the focus of the different sites? What are the hot technologies and related issues? Which seem to be most important to business managers? Prepare a brief presentation for your classmates.

Answers to the Self-Study Questions

1. B, p. 315
2. C, p. 322
3. A, p. 314
4. C, p. 324
5. A, p. 331
6. C, p. 335
7. A, p. 338
8. D, p. 340
9. D, p. 341
10. D, p. 348

Case ❶

The Netflix Prize

Netflix is the world's largest online movie provider. For a flat monthly fee, subscribers can opt to receive from one to an unlimited number of movies per month, all mailed from the Netflix distribution center (there are over 100) nearest the customer. On the Netflix Web site, the subscriber maintains a queue of movies he or she wants to watch, listed in order of viewing preference. Netflix chooses which movies to mail next from the queue, and when one movie is returned another is mailed. Customers are never charged late fees, and after viewing a movie or DVD, simply drop it in a mailbox using the prepaid envelope Netflix provides.

Netflix has consistently ranked high in customer satisfaction surveys. In fact, the service has proved so successful that in February 2007, the company reported that a billion DVDs had been mailed.

Besides the DVD rental service, Netflix also sells used DVDs, and in 2007 rolled out its "Watch Instantly" feature, which allows subscribers above the basic enrollment to stream certain movies and TV shows for instant viewing. In January 2008, Netflix announced plans to sell an HDTV set-top box that would allow subscribers to stream "Watch Instantly" movies and TV shows directly to a TV.

A key feature of the Netflix service is customers' ability to rate the movies they have seen on a five-point scale from "hated it" to "loved it." Based on customers' ratings, Netflix's movie recommendation system, Cinematch[SM], then displays other movie titles customers might enjoy. While the system works well for Netflix's purpose, it admits that improvements are possible. With that in mind, since 2006 Netflix has sponsored a contest to improve their movie rating/recommendation system. The grand prize is $1 million, but to win the prize, contestants must improve Cinematch's results by 10 percent—a difficult task. According to the contest rules published at the Netflix Prize Web site:

"It's 'easy' really. We provide you with a lot of anonymous rating data and a prediction accuracy bar that is 10 percent better than what Cinematch can do on the same training data set. (Accuracy is a measurement of how closely predicted ratings of movies match subsequent actual ratings.) If you develop a system that we judge most beats that bar on the qualifying test set we provide, you get serious money and the bragging rights. But (and you knew there would be a catch, right?) only if you share your method with us and describe to the world how you did it and why it works."

Contestants register for the contest as teams, and entries are limited to one per day. Any team whose members come up with an algorithm that improves Cinematch performance by 1 percent wins $50,000. The $50,000 prize is awarded once annually. It was awarded in 2007, but as of mid-2008, had not yet been won for that year.

Entries will continue to be accepted in the Netflix Prize contest until the $1 million prize is awarded or until 2011, whichever comes first. Netflix has also reserved the right to cancel the contest at any time.

Questions

1. Do you use Netflix? If so, how do you like it? If not, why not?
2. What are the pros and cons of having the winner of the Netflix Prize share the improved Cinematch method?
3. Describe another problem in business or society that could utilize an approach similar to that for winning the Netflix Prize (i.e., a contest that anyone can try to solve).

Based on:

Anonymous (n.d.). The Netflix prize. Retrieved May 24, 2008, from http://www.netflixprize.com.

Netflix prize. (2008, May 18). In *Wikipedia, the free encyclopedia.* Retrieved May 25, 2008, from http://en.wikipedia.org/w/index.php?title=Netflix_Prize&oldid=213245872.

Case ❷

Applications to Make You Smarter

In 2008, Jill Price, a forty-two-year-old California resident, published her memoir, *The Woman Who Can't Forget*. Price's phenomenal memory allowed her to remember every day of her childhood since the age of eight. Give her a date, interviewers discovered, and she could tell you the day of the week, what the weather was like on that day, and what she did that day. "On Friday afternoon, October 19, 1979," she writes, "I came home from school and had some soup because it was unusually cold that day." She isn't a genius by I.Q. test standards and was an average student in school, but she remembers remarkably well the things that *happened* to her.

What would it be like to remember almost every day of your childhood? Most of us will never know, but what would really be useful is if we could just remember such things as advanced math formulas, how to conjugate verbs in a foreign language, or even the position of all the states on a map of the United States and all of their capital cities.

As you might suspect, memory researchers—particularly Petro Wozniak in Poland—have formulated techniques to improve memory, which are incorporated in software designed for that purpose. For example, SuperMemo, which embodies

Wozniak's techniques, has enthusiastic users around the world, most of whom are self-improvement aficionados.

Wozniak's research found that there are optimum times for remembering data, and SuperMemo maximizes the concept. Practice a new concept too soon, and it won't stick in your memory bank. Practice too late and you've forgotten the material and have to start relearning it from the beginning. The right time to practice, so that the material can later be recalled at will, is just when you are about to forget. That optimum moment for learning is different for each person and for each type of data.

SuperMemo, frequently used to help people learn foreign languages, helps users determine the right time to practice for memorization to occur. (Whether or not memorization equals learning is a debate better left to psychologists.) Because human remembering and forgetting follows a pattern, computers are well suited for mapping such patterns. Wozniak realized twenty years ago that computers could easily calculate the moment of forgetting if he could just create the right algorithm. He also deduced that if we input the right personal data, computers can help us achieve top performance in all areas of our lives. In fact,

Wozniak's life is an ongoing experiment based on this premise.

SuperMemo is an application designed to keep track of bits of information that you have learned and want to remember. Learning a foreign language is a good example of the program's function. For example, you are studying German and you have been practicing one particular phrase. Your chances of remembering the phrase decline as time passes, on a predictable curve. SuperMemo keeps track of the learning curve and reminds you to practice recalling the phrase at the optimum time for remembering it to occur. When you learn a new German word or phrase, your chance for recalling it will drop quickly. But with SuperMemo working for you, reminding you of the word or phrase, forgetting time levels out. The program tracks the next forgetting time and waits longer to remind you of the word or phrase the next time.

As of 2008, Wozniak had never visited an English-speaking country. Yet, using the spacing principles incorporated into SuperMemo, he taught himself to speak fluent English. (In April 2008, he told Gary Wolf, in an interview for *Wired* how he "entered a mnemonic in SuperMemo: clear/

clever" to help him remember the difference in meaning between "perspicuous and perspicacious.")

Using SuperMemo may not increase your memory of daily childhood events, but its Web site informs that you may find it helpful for other memory tasks, such as learning foreign languages, speed-learning software programs, or improving creativity. Proving once again that a computer may not make us inherently smarter, but it can help with certain study skills and memorization, and possibly, as Wozniak illustrates, to structure a personal way of life that optimizes our abilities.

Questions

1. How could you use SuperMemo?
2. What are the pros and cons of using a tool like SuperMemo?
3. In addition to improving memory, what other type of software could be developed to extend human capabilities?

Based on:

Adler, J. (2008, May 19). Unable to forget. *Newsweek*. Retrieved May 24, 2008, from http://www.newsweek.com/id/136334.

Anonymous (n.d.). Super memory. Retrieved May 24, 2008, from http://www.supermemo.com.

Wolf, G. (2008, April 21). Want to remember everything you'll ever learn? Surrender to this algorithm. *Wired*. Retrieved May 24, 2008, from http://www.wired.com/medtech/health/magazine/16-05/ff_wozniak?currentPage=all.

Building Organizational Partnerships Using Enterprise Information Systems

After reading this chapter, you will be able to do the following:

1. Describe what enterprise systems are and how they have evolved.

2. Describe enterprise resource planning systems and how they help to improve internal business processes.

3. Describe customer relationship management systems and how they help to improve downstream business processes.

4. Describe supply chain management systems and how they help to improve upstream business processes.

5. Understand and utilize the keys to successfully implementing enterprise systems.

Preview

This chapter describes how companies are deploying enterprise-wide information systems to build and strengthen organizational partnerships. Enterprise systems help to integrate various business activities, to streamline and better manage interactions with customers, and to coordinate better with suppliers in order to meet changing customer demands more efficiently and effectively.

Large companies continue to find that they need systems that span their entire organization to tie everything together. As a result, an understanding of enterprise systems is critical to succeed in today's competitive and ever-changing digital world.

Managing in the Digital World: Amazon.com

In the years since the company's inception in 1994, Amazon.com, founded and headed by Jeff Bezos, has grown from a garage-based online book reseller to one of the world's largest retailers for music, DVDs, videos, computer and video games, photography equipment, toys, software, tools and hardware, wireless products, electronics, and kitchen and housewares. In fact, Amazon is a world of online commerce, boasting nearly 615 million visitors to the site annually—more than twice the number that visited Walmart.com during the same time period.

Amazon's commitment to be "customer-centric" has resulted in a satisfied, returning customer base unequaled in the dot-com marketplace. Among the innovations that make customers smile and return are:

- The Amazon.com Web site greets you by name each time you visit.
- The site remembers your recent purchases and recommends similar products you might like.
- At the top of Amazon.com's home page, a "gold box," custom-tailored for each returning customer, contains books, music, video, and DVDs he or she might want to buy—all at deep discounts.
- Amazon.com offers free shipping on most orders over $25.00 and offers "Amazon Prime," where customers pay a small monthly fee and receive complimentary upgrades on shipping.

To offer these features, Amazon not only needs a sophisticated information systems infrastructure, it also needs to be able to excel at managing its supply chain. Included in this is not only efficiently shipping the physical goods from its warehouses to the customers, but acquiring and receiving the right goods at the right time. On the "upstream" side of the supply chain, seasonality of products, short product cycles, or changes in consumer tastes make it very difficult to accurately forecast demand, and thus control inventory levels. These problems are exacerbated by the broad selection and by product lines such as consumer electronics that tend to change frequently. On the "downstream" side, Amazon has to optimize the operation of their fulfillment centers to most efficiently ship the products to the customers. For example, insufficient inventory levels increase Amazon's shipping costs, as partial shipments or long-zone deliveries are needed. Further, Amazon's reliance on a few select shipping companies can have a negative impact on customer experience if any of these companies experience problems.

Over the years, Amazon has spent tremendous efforts to address these issues and has built a network of twelve North American and seven international fulfillment centers, along with a sophisticated information systems infrastructure. Recently, Amazon realized that it could gain additional revenue by utilizing this infrastructure in novel ways. "We have this beautiful, elegant, high-I.Q. part of our business that we have been working hard on for many years," Jeff Bezos told the *New York Times* in 2007. "We've gotten good at it. Why not make money off it another way?"

FIGURE 9.1

Companies can rent Amazon's warehouse infrastructure on an as-needed basis.

One step was managing the online store and fulfillment for large companies such as Target.com. For small Internet start-up companies, a solid and highly scalable infrastructure is also a prime need; however, such infrastructure can require huge investments and diverts the company's resources away from its primary tasks of attracting new customers and growing the business. Amazon Web Services allows companies to do just that. Based on Amazon's solid and reliable infrastructure, start-up companies can rent computing resources or storage space from Amazon on an as-needed basis. In addition to providing reliability and ease of use, it saves the start-up money, as they only pay for the resources used, which are scalable upward and downward, depending on demand. Fulfillment by Amazon extends Amazon Web Services from the computing infrastructure to the physical warehouse and fulfillment infrastructure. Fulfillment by Amazon lets independent retailers who list their goods on Amazon.com, or even elsewhere on the Web, use its network of distribution centers to store products and ship orders. This frees smaller companies from the need to have a warehouse of their own and to deal with the myriad processes involved in getting a product to the customer, nearly creating a virtual business. As with Amazon Web Services, a seller only pays fulfillment fees for picking, packing, and shipping whenever an item is sold. Thus, the fixed cost of renting a warehouse is turned into a variable cost that depends on sales volume. As you can see,

optimizing its supply chain has helped Amazon even beyond its own business.

After reading this chapter, you'll be able to answer the following questions:

1. How has an effective and efficient supply chain helped Amazon's success?

2. How can Amazon balance the goals of supply chain effectiveness and supply chain efficiency?

3. What other core competencies could Amazon rent out on an as-needed basis?

Based on:

Anonymous (2008, April 18). 2007 Annual Report. Retrieved May 20, 2008, from http://media.corporate-ir.net/media_files/irol/97/97664/2007AR.pdf.

Anonymous (n.d.). Amazon fulfillment Web service. Retrieved May 20, 2008, from http://www.amazon.com/b?ie=UTF8&node=402340011.

Anonymous (n.d.). Fulfillment by Amazon. Retrieved May 20, 2008, from http://www.amazon.com/gp/seller/fba/fulfillment-by-amazon.html.

Anonymous (n.d.). History of e-commerce. Retrieved May 20, 2008, from http://www.ecommerce-land.com/history_ecommerce.html.

Stone, B. (2007, April 27). Sold on eBay, shipped by Amazon.com. *New York Times.* Retrieved May 20, 2008, from http://www.nytimes.com/2007/04/27/technology/27amazon.html?_r=2.

Enterprise Systems

Traditionally, companies are organized around four distinct functional areas, namely, Marketing and Sales, Supply Chain Management, Accounting and Finance, and Human Resources. Each of these functional areas is responsible for several well-defined business functions, such as marketing a product, sales forecasting, manufacturing goods, planning and budgeting, or recruiting, hiring, and training. Although this model suggests that a company can be regarded, as being comprised of distinct silos, the different functional areas are highly interrelated (see Figure 9.2). In fact, most business processes cross the boundaries of business functions, so it is helpful for managers to think in terms of business processes from a customer's (both internal and external) view. In most cases, the customers do not care about how things are being done, they only care that things are being done to their satisfaction. When you buy a book at Amazon.com, you typically do not care which functional areas are involved in the transaction, you only care about getting the right book for the right price in the right time.

In order to efficiently conduct business processes, the different functional areas within a company need to share data. For example, data about your book needs to be shared between Accounting and Finance (for billing purposes), Marketing and Sales (e.g., to feed into product recommendations for other customers), and Supply Chain Management (e.g., to fulfill the order and replenish the inventory). Businesses have leveraged information systems to support business processes for decades, beginning with the installation of applications to assist companies with specific business tasks such as issuing paychecks. Often different systems were built on different computing platforms, such as mainframes and midrange computers, each operating in unique hardware and software environments. Applications running on different computing platforms are more difficult to integrate, as custom interfaces are required in order for one system to communicate with another.

FIGURE 9.2

A company's functional areas should be interrelated.

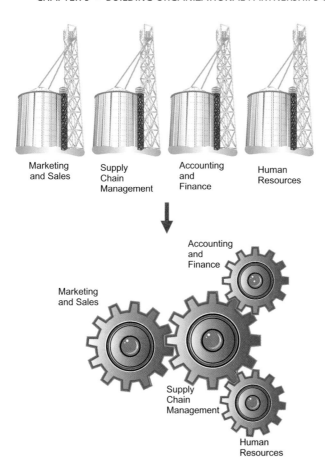

Marketing and Sales

Supply Chain Management

Accounting and Finance

Human Resources

Accounting and Finance

Marketing and Sales

Supply Chain Management

Human Resources

Utilizing different applications on separate computing platforms can create tremendous inefficiencies within organizations because data cannot readily be shared between the systems. To utilize this data to facilitate business processes and decision making, information must be reentered from one system to the next or be consolidated by a third system. Further, the same pieces of data may also be stored in several (sometimes conflicting) versions throughout the organization, making the information harder to consolidate. **Enterprise-wide information systems** (or **enterprise systems**) are information systems that allow companies to integrate information across operations on a company-wide basis. Rather than storing information in separate places throughout the organization, enterprise systems provide a central repository common to all corporate users. This, along with a common user interface, allows personnel to share information seamlessly no matter where the data is located or who is using the application (see Figure 9.3).

The emergence of the Internet and the Web has resulted in the globalization of customer and supplier networks, opening up new opportunities and methods to conduct business. Customers have an increasing number of options available to them, so they are demanding more sophisticated products that are customized to their unique needs. They also expect higher levels of customer service. If companies cannot keep their customers satisfied, the customers will not hesitate to do business with a competitor. Companies need to provide quality customer service and develop products faster and more efficiently to compete in global markets. Enterprise systems can be extended to streamline communications with customers and suppliers. Rather than focusing only on internal operations, these systems can also focus on business activities that occur outside organizational boundaries. Enterprise systems can help companies find innovative ways to increase accurate on-time shipments, avoid (or at least anticipate) surprises, minimize costs, and ultimately increase customer satisfaction and the overall profitability of the company.

Enterprise systems come in a variety of shapes and sizes, each providing a unique set of features and functionality. When deciding to implement enterprise solutions, managers need to be aware of a number of issues. One of the most important involves selecting and

FIGURE 9.3

Enterprise systems allow companies to integrate information across operations on a company-wide basis.

Legacy system approach:
Separate information storage files for different business activities.

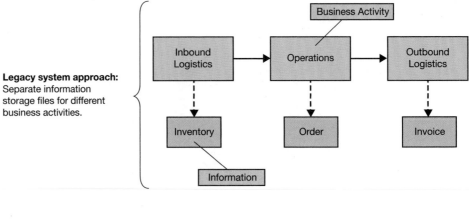

Enterprise systems approach:
Consolidated information storage for different business activities.

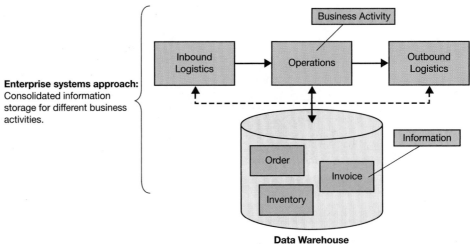

implementing applications that meet the requirements of the business as well as of its customers and suppliers. In the following sections, we examine the ways in which information systems can be leveraged to support business processes. This is followed by an in-depth analysis of how enterprise systems have evolved and how companies are using these systems to support their internal and external operations.

Supporting Business Processes

As we talked about in Chapter 3—Valuing Information Systems Investments—information systems can be used to increase competitive advantage by supporting and/or streamlining business processes (Porter and Millar, 1985). For example, an information system could be used to support a billing process in such a way that it reduces the use of paper and, more important, the handling of paper, thus reducing material and labor costs. This system can help managers keep track of that same billing process more effectively because they will have more accurate, up-to-date information about the billing process, enabling them to make smart, timely business decisions.

Information systems can be used to support either internally or externally focused business processes. **Internally focused systems** support functional areas, business processes, and decision making *within* an organization. These activities can be viewed as a series of links in a chain along which information flows within the organization. At each stage (or link) in the process, value is added in the form of the work performed by people associated with that process, and new, useful information is generated. Information begins to accumulate at the point of entry and flows through the various links, or business processes, within the organization, progressing through the organization with new, useful information being added every step of the way (see Figure 9.4).

In contrast, **externally focused systems** coordinate business processes with customers, suppliers, business partners, and others who operate *outside* an organization's

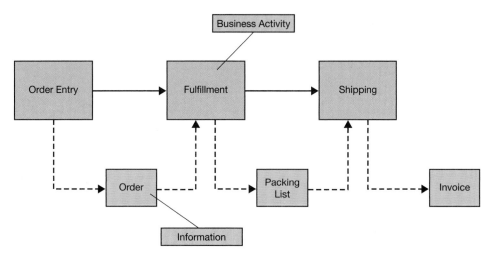

FIGURE 9.4

Information flow for a typical order.

boundaries. A system that communicates across organizational boundaries is sometimes referred to as an **interorganizational system (IOS)** (Kumar and Crook, 1999). The key purpose of an IOS is to streamline the flow of information from one company's operations to another's (e.g., from a company to its potential or existing customers).

Competitive advantage can be accomplished here by integrating multiple business processes in ways that enable a firm to meet a wide range of unique customer needs. Sharing information between organizations helps companies to adapt more quickly to changing market conditions. For instance, should consumers demand an additional component to be added to a product, a company can gain this information from its information systems that support sales and pass it along to its component suppliers in real time. Information systems allow the company and its suppliers to satisfy the needs of customers efficiently, since changes can be identified and managed immediately, creating a competitive advantage for companies that can respond quickly. We can view processes and information flows across organizations just as we previously viewed the processes and information flows within an organization. At each stage (or link) in the process, value is added by the work performed, and new, useful information is generated and exchanged between organizations (see Figure 9.5). Using IOS, one company can create information and transmit it electronically to another company.

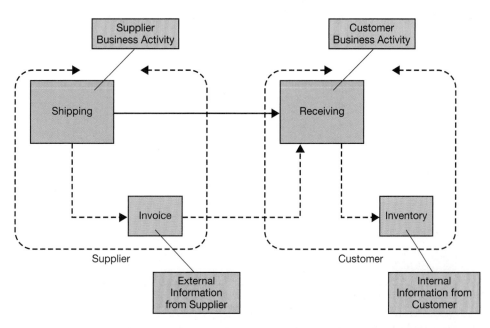

FIGURE 9.5

Information flow for a typical shipment across organizational boundaries.

Coming Attractions

Three-Dimensional Fabrication

Traditionally, manufacturing prototypes—cars, specialized machinery, prostheses, and the like—has been a slow and arduous process. No more. Prototyping for many products is now fast and precise because of a process called "fabbing," also known as three-dimensional (3-D) printing or desktop manufacturing.

Although 3-D printing has been in use since 1988, it was not commercially viable until recently. New technology in printing allows for creating 3-D, usable, moving parts instead of simply block models as in the past.

Three-dimensional printing is accomplished by using two printer heads. The first printer head lays down a fine powder, and the second head is a gluing agent. With each pass of the printer heads, another thin layer of glued powder is laid down. As each layer is added, a 3-D model emerges.

Not only is fabbing now more applicable, it has also increased in speed. The process has gone from taking days to create a prototype to finishing a model in hours, allowing engineers to produce several models in a short period of time.

Hewlett-Packard (HP) has been a leader in developing 3-D printers. Once priced at $100,000, a 3-D HP printer now sells for $1,000. Engineers, IS personnel, hardware vendors, and consumers have benefited from the development, refinement, and availability of 3-D printers since designs can now be more quickly transformed into finished products.

Based on:

Gardiner, B. (2007, November 21). 3-D printers redefine industrial design. *Wired*. Retrieved May 27, 2008, from http://www.wired.com/gadgets/miscellaneous/news/2007/11/3d_printers.

Hanluain, D. (2003, August 11). 3-D printing's great leap forward. *Wired*. Retrieved March 27, 2008, from http://www.wired.com/news/technology/0,1282,59648,00.html.

Leberecht, T. (2007, December 17). Trends 2008: Will 3-D printing finally go mainstream? *CNET News*. Retrieved May 27, 2008, from http://news.cnet.com/8301-13641_3-9835160-44.html.

Internally Focused Applications

Because different companies within certain industries operate their businesses differently, one of the first challenges an organization must face is to understand how it can use information systems to support its unique internal business activities. Generally, the flow of information through a set of business activities is referred to as a *value chain* (Porter and Millar, 1985), in which information flows through functional areas that facilitate the internal activities of the business. Figure 9.6 depicts the value chain framework. In Chapter 3, we spoke of the strategic value of analyzing a value chain; now, we will show you how to use value chain analysis to implement enterprise systems.

Functional areas can be broken down into core and support activities. *Core activities* are functional areas within an organization that process inputs and produce outputs. *Support activities* are those activities that enable core activities to take place. In the fol-

FIGURE 9.6

Value chain framework.

Adapted from Porter and Millar (1985).

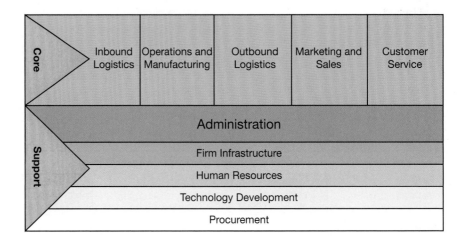

lowing sections, we focus on core activities and then turn our attention to the support activities that make them possible.

Core Activities **Core activities** include inbound logistics, operations and manufacturing, outbound logistics, marketing and sales, and customer service. These activities may differ widely, depending on the unique requirements of the industry in which a company operates, although the basic concepts hold in most organizations.

INBOUND LOGISTICS ACTIVITIES. Inbound logistics involves the business activities associated with receiving and stocking raw materials, parts, and products. For example, inbound logistics at Cisco Systems involves the receipt of electronic components that go into making their end products, such as routers. Shippers deliver electronic components to Cisco, where employees unwrap the packages and stock the components in the company's inventory. Cisco can automatically update inventory levels at the point of delivery, allowing purchasing managers to access real-time information related to inventory levels and reorder points.

OPERATIONS AND MANUFACTURING ACTIVITIES. Once the components have been stocked in inventory, the functional area of operations and manufacturing takes over. Operations and manufacturing can involve such activities as order processing and/or manufacturing processes that transform raw materials and/or component parts into end products. Companies such as Dell utilize Web-based information systems to allow customers to enter orders online. This information is used to coordinate the manufacturing of a customized personal computer in which the component parts are gathered and assembled to create the end product. During this process, inventory levels from inbound logistics are verified; if the appropriate inventory exists, workers pick the components from existing supplies and build the product to the customer's specifications. When components are picked, items are deducted from inventory; once the product is assembled, inventory levels for the final product are updated.

OUTBOUND LOGISTICS ACTIVITIES. The functional area of outbound logistics mirrors that of inbound logistics. Instead of involving the receipt of raw materials, parts, and products, outbound logistics focuses on the distribution of end products. For example, outbound logistics at Amazon.com involves the delivery of books that customers have ordered. Orders that have been processed by the operations area are forwarded to outbound logistics, which picks the products from inventory and coordinates delivery to the customer. At that point, items are packaged and deducted from the company's inventory, and an invoice is created that will be sent to the customer. Amazon.com can automatically update sales information at the point of distribution, allowing managers to view inventory and revenue information in real time.

MARKETING AND SALES ACTIVITIES. The marketing and sales functional area facilitates the presales (i.e., before the sale) activities of the company. These include such things as creation of marketing literature, communication with potential and existing customers, and pricing of goods and services. As discussed in Chapter 5—Enabling Commerce Using the Internet—many companies support the business activity of marketing and sales by creating an e-brochure. Other companies, such as Amtrak, a U.S. passenger train service, use information systems to update pricing information and schedules. This information is entered directly into the pricing and scheduling systems, allowing the information to become immediately accessible throughout the organization and to end consumers through the organization's Web site.

CUSTOMER SERVICE ACTIVITIES. Whereas marketing and sales focus on presales activities, customer service focuses on the post-sales (i.e., after the sale) activities. Customers may have questions and need help from a customer service representative. Many companies, such as Hewlett-Packard (HP), are utilizing information systems to provide customer service. These applications allow customers to search for and download information related to the products that they have purchased. For example, HP customers may need to install drivers for the printers they have just purchased. Rather than calling a customer service representative, customers can easily find the needed information through a self-service customer support application.

Companies can use information systems to track service requests. When a customer calls in for repairs to a product, customer service representatives can access a bevy of information related to the customer. For instance, an agent can access technical information concerning the specific product as well as review any problems the customer has encountered in the past. This enables customer service representatives to react quickly to customer concerns, improving the customer service experience.

Support Activities Support activities are business activities that enable the primary activities to take place. Support activities include administrative activities, infrastructure, human resources, technology development, and procurement.

ADMINISTRATIVE ACTIVITIES. Administrative activities focus on the processes and decision making to orchestrate the day-to-day operations of an organization, particularly those processes that span organizational functions and levels. Administration includes systems and processes from virtually all functional areas—accounting, finance, marketing, operations, and so on—as well as both the executive and the managerial level.

INFRASTRUCTURE ACTIVITIES. Infrastructure refers to the hardware and software that must be implemented to support the applications that the primary activities use. An order entry application requires that employees who enter orders have a computer and the necessary software to accomplish their business objectives. In turn, the computer must be connected via the network to a database containing the order information so that the order can be saved and recalled later for processing. Infrastructure provides the necessary components to facilitate the order entry process (see Chapter 4—Managing the Information Systems Infrastructure).

HUMAN RESOURCE ACTIVITIES. Human resources involves the business activities associated with employee management, such as hiring, interview scheduling, payroll, and benefits management. Human resources is classified as a support activity since the primary activities cannot be accomplished without the employees to perform them. In other words, all the primary activities use the human resource business activity. For example, if a company needs a new customer service representative to serve the growing volume of customers, the request is processed through the human resource function, which creates the job description and locates the appropriate person to fill the job.

TECHNOLOGY DEVELOPMENT ACTIVITIES. Technology development includes the design and development of applications that support the primary business activities. If you are planning on pursuing a career in the management information systems field, the technology business activity is likely where you will find a job. Technology can involve a wide array of responsibilities, such as the selection of packaged software or the design and development of a custom application to meet a particular business need. Many companies are leveraging the technology business activity to build Internet, intranet, and extranet applications for these purposes. As seen in previous chapters, companies use these systems to support a wide variety of primary business activities.

PROCUREMENT ACTIVITIES. Procurement refers to the purchasing of goods and services that are required as inputs to the primary activities. Allowing each functional area to send out purchase orders can create problems for companies, such as maintaining relationships with more suppliers than necessary and not taking advantage of volume discounts. The procurement business activity can leverage information systems by accumulating purchase orders from the different functional areas within the corporation. By having this information at their disposal, procurement personnel can combine multiple purchase orders containing the same item into a single purchase order. Ordering larger volumes from its suppliers means that the company can achieve dramatic cost savings through volume discounts. Procurement receives, approves, and processes requests for goods and services from the primary activities and coordinates the purchase of those items. This allows the primary activities to concentrate on running the business rather than adding to their workload.

Externally Focused Applications

The flow of information can be streamlined not only within a company but outside organizational boundaries as well. A company can create additional value by integrating internal applications with suppliers, business partners, and customers. Companies accomplish this by connecting their internal value chains to form a **value system** (Porter and Millar, 1985), in which information flows from one company's value chain to another company's value chain. Figure 9.7 depicts the value system framework. In this diagram, three companies are aligning their value chains to form a value system. First, company A processes information through its value chain and forwards the information along to its customer, company B, which processes the information through its value chain and sends the information along to its customer, company C, which processes the information through its value chain. Adding additional suppliers, business partners, and customers can create complex value systems. However, for our purposes, we simply view an organization's information systems as a value chain that interacts with the value chains of other organizations.

Externally focused systems can be used to coordinate a company's value chain with another company's value chain or with consumers (such as in business-to-consumer electronic commerce). Any information that feeds into a company's value chain, whether its source is another company's value chain or an end consumer, is considered part of the value system.

The value system can be viewed as a river of information that flows from a source to an ultimate destination. Like a river, at any particular point there is a flow coming from upstream and progressing downstream. Value systems comprise upstream and downstream information flows. An **upstream information flow** consists of information that is received from another organization, whereas a **downstream information flow** relates to the information that is produced by a company and sent along to another organization. For instance, using the value system depicted in Figure 9.7 as an example, the upstream and downstream information flows for company B become quite evident. In this case, company B receives information from its upstream supplier, processes the information through its internal value chain, and subsequently passes information downstream to its distributors and/or customers. These flows of external information into and from a company can be leveraged to create additional value and competitive advantage.

The Rise of Enterprise Systems

Software programs come in two forms—packaged and custom. **Packaged applications** are software programs written by third-party vendors for the needs of many different users and organizations, whereas **custom applications** are software programs that are designed and developed exclusively for a specific organization (see Chapter 10—Developing and Acquiring Information Systems). Packaged applications that you are likely familiar with

FIGURE 9.7

Three companies combine their value chains, forming a value system. Based on Porter and Millar (1985), Christensen (1997).

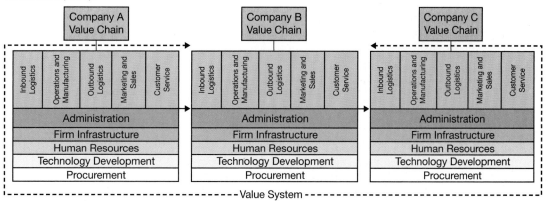

Brief Case ⊘

Outsourcing Your McDonald's Order

Dial the customer service telephone number for countless companies, and chances are you will speak to a representative based in India, the Dominican Republic, Thailand, or another offshore location. The practice of outsourcing is becoming increasingly prominent in our lives: Customer service and catalog sales representatives are often located offshore. More than 50 percent of U.S. income tax returns are prepared outside the United States. And the largest major industry to outsource? Surprisingly, it's fast food. Since outsourcing lends itself to services and products not used or consumed where they are purchased, fast-food drive-through kiosks have proved the perfect opportunity for outsourcing.

McDonald's, one of America's largest success stories, is synonymous with fast food. Founded in 1948 in San Bernardino, California, the company has parlayed its original 15-cent hamburgers and 1-cent French fries into a worldwide, multibillion-dollar business. The company strives for uniformity in its thousands of locations around the globe (see Figure 9.8). That is, if a customer orders a quarter-pounder with fries in Tokyo, the meal should be of the same quality as the quarter-pounder with fries ordered in Moscow, Shanghai, or Chicago.

FIGURE 9.8

McDonald's can be found in most places in the world.

As McDonald's became increasingly globalized, it made financial sense for the company to search for outsourcing possibilities. The drive-through service seemed especially well suited because of the repetitive nature of the service and the fact that it is difficult to retain staff in the low-paying drive-through positions.

McDonald's was not interested in investing millions of dollars in a new drive-through ordering system to facilitate outsourcing. Any changes made in technology had to be easy and cheap, and outsourcing fit the bill. McDonald's restaurants everywhere were already connected to the Internet, since corporate offices downloaded daily sales from the restaurants and uploaded price changes to the outlets. Therefore, the software was updated to allow for orders to be processed overseas and be entered into McDonald's food management queue. It didn't matter if the order was taken 20 feet or 20,000 miles away; the process was the same—only the network was different.

Like most organizations, the Internet and information technology are vital in allowing McDonald's to improve its business processes. Now your McDonald's order might be going from router to router at light speed and arriving at a foreign destination, to be relayed back to the local McDonald's where your order will actually be served. For McDonald's, the end goal is the same as it was sixty years ago—customers will receive the same quality product at any McDonald's restaurant, but their orders may be routed to the Dominican Republic, India, or Thailand before they are filled and the food is served.

Questions

1. From the perspective of both McDonald's and its customers, what are the pros and cons of outsourcing drive-through ordering?
2. What risks does a local McDonald's restaurant assume when utilizing outsourced drive-through service? How can these risks be minimized?

Based on:

Richtel, M. (2006, April 11). The long-distance journey of a fast-food order. *New York Times*. Retrieved May 27, 2008, from http://www.nytimes.com/2006/04/11/technology/11fast.html.

are Microsoft Money and Quicken, which are software packages users can purchase off the shelf to help them with their financial matters. Packaged systems are highly useful for standardized, repetitive tasks such as making entries in a check register. They can be quite cost effective since the vendor that builds the software application can spread out development costs through selling to a large number of users.

Yet packaged applications may not be well suited for tasks that are unique to a particular business. In these cases, companies may prefer to develop (or have developed for them) custom applications that can accommodate their particular business needs. The development costs of custom systems are much higher than for packaged applications because of the time, money, and resources that are required to design and develop them. Furthermore, applications need to be maintained internally when changes are required. With packaged applications, the vendor makes the changes and distributes new versions to its customers. In all, there are trade-offs when choosing between the packaged and custom application routes. Managers must consider whether packaged applications can meet the business requirements and, if not, conduct a cost-benefit analysis to ensure that taking the custom application approach will prove worthwhile to the company.

Figure 9.9 provides a high-level overview of how enterprise systems typically evolve. As companies begin to leverage information systems applications, they typically start out by fulfilling the needs of particular business activities in a particular department within the organization. Systems that focus on the specific needs of individual departments are not designed to communicate with other systems in the organization and are, therefore, referred to as **stand-alone applications**. Stand-alone applications usually run on a variety of computing hardware platforms, such as mainframes and midrange computers. Together, stand-alone applications and the computers they run on are often referred to as **legacy systems**, given that they are typically older systems that are either fast approaching or beyond the end of their useful life within the organization. Legacy systems tend to require substantial resources to maintain them in order to accommodate emerging business needs.

Legacy Systems When companies first use information systems to support business activities, they usually begin by implementing systems in various departments rather than starting with a single application that can accommodate all aspects of the business. Each

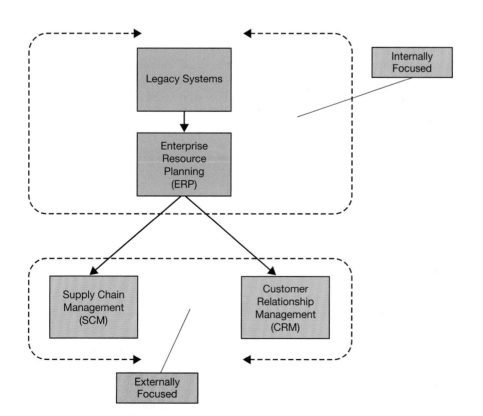

FIGURE 9.9

Stages of enterprise systems evolution.

department implements applications to assist it with its daily business activities, which are optimized for its unique needs and the manner in which personnel in a particular unit accomplish job tasks. These applications tend to be infrastructure specific, meaning they run on particular hardware and software platforms. As a result, each department normally has its own computing system that runs its necessary applications. Although departmental systems enable departments to conduct their daily business activities efficiently, these systems often are not very helpful when people from one part of the firm need information from another part of the firm (e.g., people in manufacturing need forecasts from sales).

Given that these older systems were not necessarily designed to communicate with other applications beyond departmental boundaries, they are classified as "legacy" systems, or systems that operate within the confines of a particular business need. Legacy systems and their associated stand-alone applications can prove problematic when information from multiple departmental systems is required to support business processes and decision making (as is often the case). For example, if the applications for inbound logistics and operations are not integrated, companies will lose valuable time in accessing information related to inventory levels. When an order is placed through operations, personnel need to verify that the components are available in inventory before the order can be processed.

If the inventory and order-entry systems are not integrated, personnel may have to access two separate applications or use a custom interface that pulls information from both systems. Figure 9.10 provides an example of how information flows through legacy systems within an organization. As the diagram depicts, information is generated by the inbound logistics business activity, but it does not flow through to the next business activity, in this case operations. Since the inbound logistics and operations departments use different legacy systems, information cannot readily flow from one business activity to another. Understandably, this creates a highly inefficient process for operations personnel, who must have access to two systems or a common interface that pulls information together in order to get both the order entry and the inventory information. In some cases, inventory information may be stored on both systems, creating the potential for inaccuracies. Should data be updated in one system but not the other, the data becomes outdated and inaccurate. In addition, there are further, unnecessary costs associated with entering, storing, and updating data redundantly.

The Need for Integrated Enterprise Systems Companies can gain several advantages by integrating and converting legacy systems so that information stored on separate computing platforms can be consolidated to provide a centralized point of access. The process of **conversion** transfers information stored on legacy systems to a new, integrated computing platform, which typically comes in the form of *enterprise resource planning (ERP)* applications (discussed later in this chapter). Although such applications do an

FIGURE 9.10

Information flows using legacy systems.

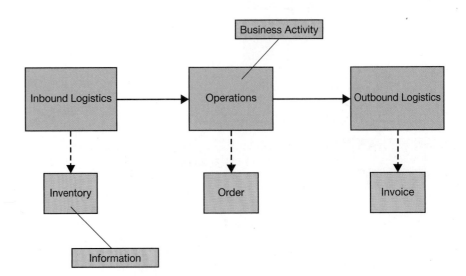

TABLE 9.1 **Key Components of SAP's mySAP Business Suite**

mySAP Customer Relationship Management	mySAP Supplier Relationship Management
mySAP ERP	mySAP Supply Chain Management
mySAP Product Life-Cycle Management	

excellent job of serving the needs of internal business operations on an organization-wide basis, they are not necessarily designed to completely accommodate the communication of information outside the organization's boundaries.

Systems that facilitate interorganizational communications focus on either the upstream or the downstream information flows. Since these systems coordinate business activities across organizational boundaries, they are classified as externally focused applications. *Customer relationship management* applications concentrate on the downstream information flows, integrating the value chains of a company and its distributors or customers (discussed later). In contrast, *supply chain management* applications operate on the upstream information flows, integrating the value chains of a company and its suppliers (also discussed later).

Improving Business Processes through Enterprise Systems Because all companies are different, no packaged software application will exactly fit the unique requirements of a particular business. Likewise, enterprise systems come in a variety of shapes and sizes, each designed to accommodate certain transaction volumes, industries, and business processes. Thus, enterprise systems providers such as SAP offer different **modules**, which are components that can be selected and implemented as needed. The modules provided by different vendors may vary in the specific business processes they support as well as what they are called (see Tables 9.1 and 9.2 for examples of modules and key capabilities of SAP's mySAP business suite).

TABLE 9.2 **Key Capabilities of SAP's mySAP Enterprise System**

Capability	Explanation
Business analysis	Enables organizations to evaluate business performance by providing functionality for analyzing workforce, operations, and supply chain.
Financial and management accounting	Allows organizations to manage corporate finance functions by automating financial supply chain management, financial accounting, and management accounting.
Human capital management	Gives organizations the tools needed to maximize the profitability potential of the workforce, with functionality for employee transaction management and employee life-cycle management.
Operations management	Empowers organizations to streamline operations with integrated functionality for managing end-to-end logistics processes, while expanding collaborative capabilities in supply chain management, product life-cycle management, and supplier relationship management.
Corporate services management	Allows organizations to optimize centralized and decentralized services for managing real estate, corporate travel, and incentives and commissions.
Self-services	Provides an employee-centric portal that enables both employees and managers to create, view, and modify key information. Uses a broad range of interaction technologies, including Web browser, voice, and mobile devices, for easy access to internal and external business content, applications, and services.

VANILLA VERSUS CUSTOMIZED SOFTWARE. As the naming and capabilities differ between the software vendors, it is critical for managers to understand the vendors' naming conventions and software modules to gain an understanding of how these features can be implemented to support the company's business processes. The features and modules that an enterprise system comes with out of the box are referred to as the **vanilla version**. If the vanilla version does not support a certain business process, the company may require a customized version. **Customization** either provides additional software that is integrated with the enterprise system or direct changes to the vanilla application itself. SAP, for example, includes literally thousands of elements in its various enterprise systems that can be customized, and it also offers many industry-specific versions that have already been customized for a particular industry based on SAP's perceptions of the best way to do things (i.e., best practices). Companies must take special care when dealing with customization issues. Customizations can be extremely costly, and maintaining and upgrading customizations can be troublesome. For example, a customization made to the vanilla version will need to be reprogrammed when a new release of the system is implemented because subsequent releases of the software will not include the previous customizations. In other words, new vanilla versions must be continually upgraded to accommodate the company-specific customizations. This process can involve a substantial investment of time and resources.

BEST PRACTICES–BASED SOFTWARE. One of the major hurdles posed to companies that implement enterprise systems involves changing business processes to accommodate the manner in which the software works. Enterprise system implementations are often used as a catalyst for overall improvement of underlying business processes. As with SAP, most enterprise systems are designed to operate according to industry-standard business processes, or best practices. In fact, most enterprise system vendors build best practices into their applications to provide guidelines for management to identify business activities within their organizations that need to be streamlined. Implementations and future upgrades to the system will go more smoothly when companies change their business processes to fit the way the enterprise system operates.

Many organizations have spent many years developing business processes that provide them with a competitive advantage in the marketplace. Adopting their industry's best practices may force these companies to abandon their unique ways of doing business, putting them on par with their industry competitors. In other words, companies can potentially lose their competitive advantages by adopting the best practices within their industry. Best practices is an area that managers must carefully consider before selecting any type of enterprise system because some enterprise system vendors build their entire systems around best practices, and companies that reject best practices are in for a long and time-consuming implementation (although the vendors and external consultants typically offer help in the process). Other vendors provide a series of options that companies select before implementing the software, allowing them some (but not complete) flexibility in changing their business processes to accommodate the enterprise system modules. Given the importance and difficulty of changing business processes with enterprise and other systems implementations, we now briefly describe business process management.

BUSINESS PROCESS MANAGEMENT. Since the first publishing of *The Principles of Scientific Management* by Fredrick Taylor in 1911 (and probably even before that), organizations have focused on improving business processes. Over the years, various approaches for improving business processes have been developed (see Table 9.3). Given the magnitude of change that an enterprise system can impose on an organization's business processes, understanding the role of business process management in the implementation of an enterprise system is necessary. **Business process management (BPM)** is a systematic, structured improvement approach by all or part of an organization whereby people critically examine, rethink, and redesign business processes in order to achieve dramatic improvements in one or more performance measures, such as quality, cycle time, or cost.

TABLE 9.3 **Some Other Terms Closely Related to Business Process Management**

Business activity modeling	Business process redesign
Business activity monitoring	Business process reengineering (BPR)
Business architecture modernization (BAM)	Functional process improvement
Business process improvement (BPI)	Workflow management

BPM became very popular in the 1990s (and was then called **business process reengineering [BPR]**) when Michael Hammer and James Champy published their best-selling book *Reengineering the Corporation.*

Hammer and Champy and their proponents argued that radical redesign of an organization was sometimes necessary in order to lower costs and increase quality, and that information systems were the key enabler for that radical change. The basic steps in BPM can be summarized as follows:

1. Develop a vision for the organization that specifies business objectives, such as reducing costs, shortening the time it takes to get products to market, improving quality of products and/or services, and so on
2. Identify the critical processes that are to be redesigned
3. Understand and measure the existing processes as a baseline for future improvements
4. Identify ways that information systems can be used to improve processes
5. Design and implement a prototype of the new processes

BPM is similar to quality improvement approaches such as *total quality management* and *continuous process improvement* in that they are intended to be cross-functional approaches to improve an organization. BPM differs from these quality improvement approaches, however, in one fundamental way. These quality improvement approaches tend to focus on incremental change and gradual improvement of processes, while the intention behind BPM is radical redesign and drastic improvement of processes.

When BPR was introduced in the 1990s, many efforts were reported to have failed. These failures occurred for a variety of reasons, including the lack of sustained management commitment and leadership, unrealistic scope and expectations, and resistance to change. In fact, BPR gained the reputation of being a nice way of saying "downsizing."

Nevertheless, BPR (and its successors such as BPM) lives on today and is still a popular approach to improving organizations. No matter what it is called, the conditions that appear to lead to a successful business process improvement effort include the following:

- Support by senior management
- Shared vision by all organizational members
- Realistic expectations
- Participants empowered to make changes
- The right people participating
- Sound management practices
- Appropriate funding

In any event, it is clear that successful business process change, especially involving enterprise systems, requires a broad range of organizational factors to occur that are far beyond the technical implementation issues. Next, we examine the three most popular forms of enterprise systems.

Powerful Partnerships

SAP—Dietmar Hopp, Hans-Werner Hector, Hasso Plattner, Klaus Tschira, and Claus Wellenreuther

In what seems like the Dark Ages to today's computer users, five former IBM employees had a vision. The year was 1972, and Dietmar Hopp, Hans-Werner Hector, Hasso Plattner, Klaus Tschira, and Claus Wellenreuther founded a small company in Mannheim, Germany, to develop and sell business software for real-time processing (see Figure 9.11). They called the fledgling company **S**ystems, **A**pplications, and **P**roducts in Data Processing. After the first year, "R/1" was added to the product's name, "R" standing for "real-time" data processing.

The company continued to grow and in the 1980s R/2 was born. During this decade, SAP expanded internationally with the opening of subsidiaries in Denmark, Sweden, Italy, and the United States. Client-server architecture had become the standard in business software and SAP was poised to meet the need.

Today SAP is the world's largest business software company, employing 39,300 people. It is third interna-

tionally in terms of revenue. Areas of concentration for SAP software developers include:

1. Enterprise Resource Planning (ERP)—SAP's latest version, R/3 (the number 3 representing a three-tier architecture comprising client, server, and database), helps integrate the various data sources and processes of an organization into a unified system
2. Customer Relationship Management (CRM)—helps companies win and retain customers, gain marketing and customer insight, and focus on customers
3. Product Life-Cycle Management (PLM)—helps manufacturers set up a single source for all product-related information necessary for communicating closely with business partners and supporting product lines
4. Supply Chain Management (SCM)—helps companies enhance operational flexibility across global enterprises and provide real-time visibility for customers and suppliers
5. Supplier Relationship Management (SRM)—allows customers to collaborate closely with suppliers and organize sourcing processes that enhance transparency and lower costs

SAP's original founders have remained with the company and are often found in publications naming the world's wealthiest individuals. Plattner pledged large amounts of his personal fortune to fund higher education, such as the Hasso Plattner Institute at the University of Potsdam (Germany), the library at the University of Mannheim (Germany), and the Hasso Plattner Institute of Design (aka d.school) at Stanford University. Klaus Tschira launched a foundation supporting research in informatics, mathematics, and the natural sciences.

Based on:

Anonymous (n.d.). SAP history. Retrieved May 27, 2008, from http://www.sap.com/company/history.epx.

SAP AG. (2008, May 26). In *Wikipedia, the free encyclopedia.* Retrieved May 27, 2008, from http://en.wikipedia.org/w/index. php?title=SAP_AG&oldid=215048864.

FIGURE 9.11

SAP, like many great technology companies, was built with a powerful partnership.

Enterprise Resource Planning

When companies realize that legacy systems can create dramatic inefficiencies within their organizations, the next step is to integrate legacy information on a company-wide basis. As previously described, applications that integrate business activities across departmental boundaries are often referred to as **enterprise resource planning (ERP)** systems. In the 1990s, we witnessed companies' initial push to implement integrated applications, as exhibited by skyrocketing ERP sales at that time. Be aware that the terms "resource" and "planning" are somewhat misnomers, meaning that they do not accurately describe the purpose of ERP since these applications do very little in the way of planning or managing resources. The reason for the term "enterprise resource planning" is that these systems evolved in part during the 1990s from material requirements planning (MRP) and manufacturing resource planning (MRP II) packages. Do not get hung up on the words "resource" and "planning." The key word to remember from the acronym ERP is "enterprise."

Integrating Data to Integrate Applications

ERP takes stand-alone applications a step further by providing a common data warehouse and similar application interfaces that service the entire enterprise rather than portions of it. Information stored on legacy systems is converted into large, centralized data repositories known as data warehouses (see Chapter 4 for more information on data warehouses). Data warehouses are databases that store information related to the various business activities of an organization. Data warehouses alleviate the problems associated with multiple computing platforms by providing a single place where all information relevant to the company and particular departments can be stored and accessed, as depicted in Figure 9.12.

In contrast to legacy systems where it is difficult to share information between business activities, ERP applications make accessing information easier by providing a central information repository. For example, where an ERP solution is used, both inbound logistics and operations have access to inventory data because both business activities have access to the same pieces of information. Rather than information flowing from one department to the next, data can be accessed and updated at will, meaning that the next business activity can access information in the data warehouse whenever it needs to. This gives personnel access to accurate, real-time information. The beauty of ERP lies in the fact that information can be shared throughout the organization. For example, inventory information is accessible not only to inbound logistics and operations but also to accounting and customer service personnel. If a customer calls in wondering about the status of an order, customer service representatives can find out by accessing the data warehouse through the ERP application. Prior to the emergence of ERP, customer service representatives may have had to retrieve information from two or more separate computing systems, making their job extremely difficult while

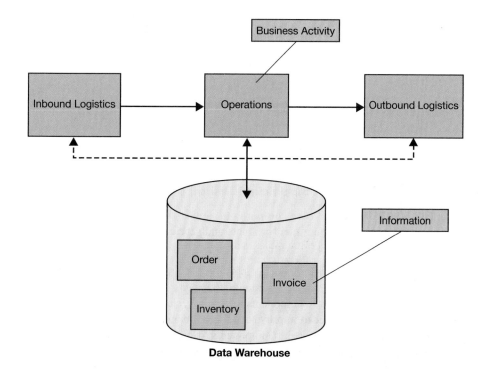

Data Warehouse

FIGURE 9.12

Information storage using an ERP solution.

potentially resulting in dissatisfied customers. Storing data in a single place and making it available to everyone within the organization empowers everyone in the organization to be aware of the current state of business and to perform their jobs better.

ERP applications that access the data warehouse are designed to have the same look and feel, regardless of the unique needs of a particular department. Inbound logistics and operations personnel will use a common user interface to access the same pieces of information from the data warehouse. Although the inbound logistics screens and the operations screens will have different features tailored to the unique needs of the business activity, the screens will look comparable, with similar designs, screen layouts, menu options, and so on. The Microsoft Office products provide a useful analogy. Microsoft Word and Microsoft Excel are designed to serve separate functions (word processing and spreadsheets, respectively), but overall the products look and feel very similar to one another. Word and Excel have similar user interfaces, but differ vastly in the purpose, features, and functionality that each application offers.

Choosing an ERP System

When selecting an appropriate ERP application for an organization, management needs to take many factors into careful consideration. ERP applications come as packaged software, which means a one-size-fits-all strategy. However, businesses have unique needs even within their own industries. In other words, like snowflakes, no two companies are exactly alike. Management must carefully select an ERP application that will meet the unique requirements of the particular company. Companies must consider a number of factors in the ERP selection. Among the most prevalent issues facing management are ERP control and ERP business requirements.

ERP Control ERP control refers to the locus of control over the computing systems and decision making regarding these systems. Companies typically either opt for centralized control or allow particular business units to govern themselves. In the context of ERP, these decisions are based on the level of detail in the information that must be provided to management. Some corporations want to have as much detail as possible made available at the executive level, whereas other companies do not require such access. For instance, an accountant in one company may want the ability to view costs down to the level of individual transactions, while an accountant in another company may want only summary information. Another area related to control involves the consistency of policies and procedures. Some companies prefer that policies and procedures remain consistent throughout an organization. Other companies want to allow each business unit to develop its own policies and procedures to accommodate the unique ways that they do business. ERP applications vary widely in their allowance for control, typically assuming either a corporate or a business-unit locus of control. Some ERP applications allow users to select or customize the locus of control. In either case, management must consider the ERP's stance on control to ensure it will meet the business requirements of the company.

ERP Business Requirements When selecting an ERP system, organizations must choose which modules to implement from a large menu of options—most organizations only adopt a subset of the available ERP components. There are two major categories of ERP components—ERP *core* components and ERP *extended* components (see Figure 9.13). Most ERP vendors provide components that are tailored to specific industry best practices and, of course, allow customization if desired by the customer.

ERP CORE COMPONENTS. **ERP core components** support the important *internal* activities of the organization for producing their products and services. These components support internal operations, such as the following:

1. *Financial Management.* Components to support accounting, financial reporting, performance management, and corporate governance.
2. *Operations Management.* Components to simplify, standardize, and automate business processes in order to improve collaboration and decision making.
3. *Human Resource Management.* Components to support employee recruitment, assignment tracking, performance reviews, payroll, and regulatory requirements.

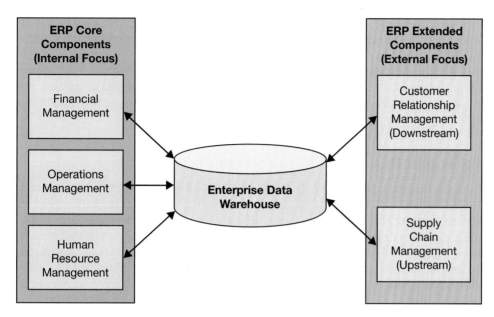

FIGURE 9.13

An ERP system consists of core and extended components.

ERP EXTENDED COMPONENTS. **ERP extended components** support the primary *external* activities of the organization for dealing with suppliers and customers. Specifically, ERP extended components primarily focus on customer relationship management and supply chain management. Both are discussed in detail later in this chapter.

ERP Limitations

While ERP helps companies to integrate systems across the organization, it falls short in communicating across organizational boundaries (Larson and Rogers, 1998). Since ERP

Census Computers

In April 2006, the U.S. Department of Commerce announced that it had awarded $600 million to Harris Corporation to supply wireless personal digital assistants (PDAs) to the 600,000 census takers in 2010. For the first time since census counts began in 1790, technology was to take precedence over paper and pencil. The use of the PDAs, the government insisted, would actually save the taxpayers money in the long run.

In the short run, however, a test run of the PDAs was unsatisfactory. When workers representative of the volunteer census workers tried to use the devices, they proved too complex. Plus, the PDAs were not programmed to transmit the large amounts of data they would be collecting. Then there were the contract overruns. What started as a $597 million contract ballooned to $647 million and kept growing, with government officials worrying the total cost for the handhelds could reach $2 billion.

Finally, in the face of mounting costs and other difficulties, Commerce Secretary Carlos Gutierrez announced in April 2008 that plans to use the PDAs for the 2010

census were scrapped. Harris would still receive its $600 million, of course, but the Department of Commerce would collect data in 2010 the usual way—with pencil and paper. Some of the scaled-back devices might still be used, but only to verify addresses.

What began as a giant step for the government into technological advancement ended as a retreat to simpler times. Costs for the census are still projected at a hefty $14 billion, but census workers who don't already have computer skills can rest easy in the knowledge that they won't be required to learn the tech skills necessary to operate the PDAs.

Based on:

Bosavage, J. (2008, April 4). U.S. census: PDA promise slips away. *CRN.com*. Retrieved May 27, 2008, from http://www.crn.com/government/207001895.

Melanson, D. (2008, March 26). Problems with census PDAs could prompt a return to pencil and paper. *Endgadget.com*. Retrieved May 27, 2008, from http://www.engadget.com/2008/03/26/problems-with-census-pdas-could-prompt-a-return-to-pencil-and-pa.

core components are designed to service internal business activities, they tend not to be well suited for managing value system activities. Companies wanting to integrate their value chains with the business activities of their suppliers, business partners, and customers typically choose to implement systems other than (or in addition to) ERP to manage the upstream and/or downstream flows of information. These types of applications, designed to coordinate activities outside organizational boundaries, are discussed in the following sections.

Customer Relationship Management

With the changes introduced by the Web, in most industries a company's competition is simply a mouse click away. It is increasingly important for companies not only to generate new business but also to attract repeat business from existing customers (see Figure 9.14). This means that to remain competitive, companies must keep their customers satisfied. In today's highly competitive markets, customers hold the balance of power because if they become dissatisfied with the levels of customer service they are receiving, they have many alternatives readily available. The global nature of the Web has affected companies worldwide in virtually all industries. An economic transformation is taking place, shifting the emphasis from conducting business transactions to managing relationships. Marketing researchers have found that the cost of trying to get back customers that have gone elsewhere can be up to fifty to one hundred times as much as keeping a current one satisfied. Thus, companies are finding it imperative to develop and maintain customer satisfaction and widen (by attracting new customers), lengthen (by keeping existing profitable customers satisfied), and deepen (by transforming minor customers into profitable customers) the relationships with their customers in order to compete effectively in their markets (see Figure 9.15).

Customer relationship management (CRM) is a corporate-level strategy to create and maintain, through the introduction of reliable systems, processes, and procedures, lasting relationships with customers by concentrating on the downstream information flows.

FIGURE 9.14

Organizations must work harder than ever to attract and retain customers where comparison shopping is the norm and competitors are just a click away.

FIGURE 9.15

Companies search for ways to widen, lengthen, and deepen customer relationships.

| **Widen** | **Lengthen** | **Deepen** |
| Attract New Customers | Keep Current Customers Satisfied | Transform Minor Customers into Profitable Customers |

Applications focusing on downstream information flows have two main objectives: to attract potential customers and create customer loyalty. The appropriate CRM technology combined with business process management of sales-related business processes can have tremendous benefits to an organization (see Table 9.4). To pursue customer satisfaction as a basis for achieving competitive advantage, organizations must be able to access information and track customer interactions throughout the organization, regardless of where, when, or how the interaction occurs. This means that companies need to have an integrated system that captures information from retail stores, Web sites, call centers, and various other ways that organizations communicate downstream within their value chain. More important, managers need the capability to monitor and analyze factors that drive customer satisfaction as changes occur according to prevailing market conditions.

CRM applications come in the form of packaged software that is purchased from software vendors. CRM applications are commonly integrated with a comprehensive ERP implementation to leverage internal and external information to better serve customers. Like ERP, CRM applications come with various features and modules. Management must

TABLE 9.4 Benefits of a Customer Relationship Management System

Benefit	Examples
Enables 24/7/365 operation	Web-based interfaces provide product information, sales status, support information, issue tracking, and so on.
Individualized service	Learn how each customer defines product and service quality so that customized product, pricing, and services can be designed or developed collaboratively.
Improved information	Integrate all information for all points of contact with the customers—marketing, sales, and service—so that all who interact with customers have the same view and understand current issues.
Speeds problem identification/resolution	Improved record keeping and efficient methods of capturing customer complaints help to identify and solve problems faster.
Speeds processes	Integrated information removes information handoffs, speeding both sales and support processes.
Improved integration	Information from the CRM can be integrated with other systems to streamline business processes and gain business intelligence as well as making other cross-functional systems more efficient and effective.
Improved product development	Tracking customer behavior over time helps to identify future opportunities for product and service offerings.
Improved planning	Provides mechanisms for managing and scheduling sales follow-ups to assess satisfaction, repurchase probabilities, time frames, and frequencies.

carefully select a CRM application that will meet the unique requirements of their business processes.

Companies that have successfully implemented CRM can experience greater customer satisfaction and increased productivity of their sales and service personnel, which can translate into dramatic enhancements to the company's profitability. CRM allows organizations to focus on driving revenue as well as reducing costs as opposed to emphasizing only cost cutting. Cost cutting tends to have a lower limit because there are only so many costs that companies can reduce, whereas revenue generation strategies are bound only by the size of the market itself. The importance of focusing on customer satisfaction is emphasized by findings from the National Quality Research Center, which estimates that a 1 percent increase in customer satisfaction can lead to a threefold increase in a company's market capitalization.

Developing a CRM Strategy

To develop a successful CRM strategy, organizations must do more than simply purchase and install CRM software. A successful CRM strategy must include enterprise-wide changes, including the following:

- *Policy and Business Process Changes.* Organizational policies and procedures need to reflect a customer-focused culture.
- *Customer Service Changes.* Key metrics for managing the business need to reflect customer-focused measures for quality and satisfaction as well as process changes to enhance the customer experience.
- *Employee Training Changes.* Employees from all areas—marketing, sales, and support—must have a consistent focus that values customer service and satisfaction.
- *Data Collection, Analysis, and Sharing Changes.* All aspects of the customer experience—prospecting, sales, support, and so on—must be tracked, analyzed, and shared to optimize the benefits of the CRM.

In sum, the organization must focus and organize its activities to provide the best customer service possible (see Figure 9.16). Additionally, successful CRM strategy must carefully consider ethical and privacy concerns of customers' data (discussed later in this chapter).

FIGURE 9.16

A successful CRM strategy requires enterprise-wide changes.

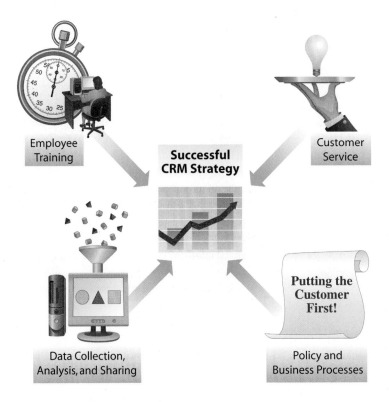

Employee Training

Customer Service

Successful CRM Strategy

Data Collection, Analysis, and Sharing

Putting the Customer First!

Policy and Business Processes

Architecture of a CRM

A comprehensive CRM system provides three primary components:

1. *Operational CRM.* Systems for automating the fundamental business processes—marketing, sales, and support—for interacting with the customer
2. *Analytical CRM.* Systems for analyzing customer behavior and perceptions (e.g., quality, price, and overall satisfaction) in order to provide business intelligence
3. *Collaborative CRM.* Systems for providing effective and efficient communication with the customer from the entire organization

Operational CRM is commonly referred to as a **front-office system** because it enables direct interaction with customers. In contrast, analytical CRM is commonly referred to as a **back-office system** because it provides the analysis necessary to more effectively manage the sales, service, and marketing activities. Additionally, all systems that are not accessible or visible to the customer, including inventory management, producing goods and services, and other supply chain activities, are referred to as back-office systems. Whereas analytical CRM aids in the development of a company's CRM strategy, operational CRM helps in the execution of CRM strategy; thus, either component alone provides no real benefit for a business. Finally, collaborative CRM provides the communication capabilities of the CRM environment (see Figure 9.17). Next, we examine each of these architecture components.

Operational CRM **Operational CRM** includes the systems used to enable customer interaction and service. With an effective operational CRM environment, organizations are able to provide personalized and highly efficient customer service. Customer-focused personnel are provided complete customer information—history, pending sales, and service requests—in order to optimize interaction and service. It is important to stress that the operational CRM environment provides *all* customer information regardless of the touch point. This means that marketing, sales, and support personnel see *all* prior and current interactions with the customer regardless of where it occurred within the organization. To facilitate the sharing of information and customer interaction, three separate systems are utilized (see Figure 9.18).

FIGURE 9.17

A comprehensive CRM environment provides operational, analytical, and collaborative components.

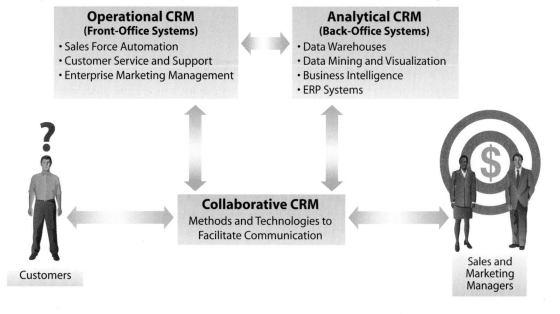

FIGURE 9.18

An operational CRM is used to enable customer interaction and service.

SALES FORCE AUTOMATION. The first component of an operational CRM is **sales force automation (SFA)**. SFA refers to systems to support the day-to-day sales activities of an organization. SFA supports a broad range of sales-related business processes, including the following:

- Order processing and tracking
- Account and contact management
- Opportunity management
- Sales management
- Territory management
- Customer history, preferences (product and communication), and management
- Sales forecasting and performance analyses

SFA systems provide advantages for sales personnel, sales managers, and marketing managers. For sales personnel, SFA helps them use their time more efficiently and ultimately focus more on selling than on paperwork and other nonselling tasks (see Table 9.5). Likewise, for sales managers, the SFA system provides improved information, allowing for better day-to-day management of the sales function and improved forecasting of future events (see Table 9.6). For example, SFA allows sales managers to track a plethora of sales performance measures, including the following:

- Revenue per salesperson, per territory, or as a percentage of sales quota
- Margins by product category, customer segment, or customer
- Number of calls per day, time spent per contact, revenue per call, cost per call, or ratio of orders to calls
- Number of lost customers per period or cost of customer acquisition
- Percentage of goods returned, number of customer complaints, or number of overdue accounts

TABLE 9.5 Advantages of Sales Force Management Systems for *Sales Personnel*

Advantages	Examples
Less paperwork	Customer contact information is recorded using e-forms that automatically provide known customer data; fill-in-the-blank forms are used to capture new information.
Fewer handoffs	Information is automatically routed to other team members and managers.
Fewer errors	E-forms ensure that customer data is automatically entered; forms can require necessary updates to be entered before saving and sharing.
Better information	Sales personnel have accurate, up-to-date, complete information on all interactions with customers as well as higher-quality sales leads.
Better training	Common systems ensure that sales personnel follow common processes and procedures.
Improved teamwork	Sharing of all sales-related information facilitates successful team selling and the sharing of best practices.
Improved morale	Improved training and less "busywork" allows a greater focus on selling and revenue generation.
Higher sales	Streamlined selling processes and improved communications allow sales personnel to focus more on selling than on nonselling activities.

Finally, SFA improves the effectiveness of the marketing function by providing an improved understanding of market conditions, competitors, and products. This enhanced information will provide numerous advantages for the management and execution of the marketing function. Specific advantages include the following:

- Improved understanding of markets, segments, and customers
- Improved understanding of competitors
- Enhanced understanding of the organization's strengths and weaknesses
- Better understanding of the economic structure of the industry
- Enhanced product development
- Improved strategy development and coordination with the sales function

In sum, the primary goals of SFA are to better identify potential customers, streamline selling processes, and improve managerial information. Next, we examine systems for improving customer service and support.

CUSTOMER SERVICE AND SUPPORT. The second component of an operational CRM system is **customer service and support (CSS)**. CSS refers to systems that automate service requests, complaints, product returns, and information requests. In the past, organizations had *help desks* and *call centers* to provide customer service and support. Today, organizations are deploying a **customer interaction center (CIC)**, using multiple communication channels to support the communication preferences of customers, such as the Web, face-to-face contact, telephone, fax, and so on (see the section "Collaborative

TABLE 9.6 Advantages of Sales Force Management Systems for *Sales Managers*

Advantages	Examples
Improved information	Sales performance data is automatically tabulated and presented in easy-to-understand tables, charts, and graphs.
Improved time usage	Less time summarizing and tracking information allows greater time for advising and coaching sales personnel.
Better planning and forecasts	Improved accuracy and timeliness of information leads to better forecasts and plans.
Improved scheduling	Accurate and real-time data allow managers to more effectively deploy sales personnel.
Improved coordination	Accessible information allows better coordination with marketing, production, and finance.
Better sales force tracking	Systems allow managers to track a greater number of up-to-date measures, leading to improved management and faster response when problems arise.

CRM" later in this chapter). The CIC utilizes a variety of communication technologies for optimizing customers' communications with the organization. For example, automatic call distribution systems forward calls to the next available person; while waiting to connect, customers can be given the option to use key or voice response technologies to check account status information. In essence, the goal of the CSS is to provide great customer service—anytime, anywhere, and through any channel—while at the same time keeping service and support costs low. Customers can log service requests or gain updates to pending support requests using a variety of self-service or assisted technologies (see Figure 9.19). Successful CSS systems enable faster response times, increased first-contact resolution rates, and improved productivity of service and support personnel. Managers can utilize digital dashboards to monitor key metrics such as first-contact resolution and service personnel utilization, which allows for improved management of the service and support functions (see Chapter 8—Enhancing Business Intelligence Using Information Systems).

ENTERPRISE MARKETING MANAGEMENT. The third component of an operational CRM system is **enterprise marketing management (EMM)**. EMM tools help a company in the execution of the CRM strategy by improving the management of marketing campaigns. Today, many companies use a variety of channels (such as e-mail, telephone, and so on) to reach potential customers. Using EMM tools can help integrate those campaigns such that

FIGURE 9.19

A customer interaction center allows customers to use a variety of self-service and assisted technologies to interact with the organization.

the right messages are sent to the right people through the right channel. This necessitates that customer lists are managed carefully to avoid targeting people who have opted out of receiving marketing communication and to be able to personalize messages that can deliver individualized attention to each potential customer. At the same time, EMM tools provide extensive analytical capabilities that can help to analyze the effectiveness of marketing campaigns and can help to efficiently route sales leads to the right salespeople, leading to better conversion rates.

Analytical CRM **Analytical CRM** focuses on analyzing customer behavior and perceptions in order to provide the business intelligence necessary to identify new opportunities and to provide superior customer service. Organizations that effectively utilize analytical CRM can more easily customize marketing campaigns from the segment level to even the individual customer. Such customized campaigns help to increase cross- or up-selling (i.e., selling more or more profitable products) as well as retaining customers by having accurate, timely, and personalized information.

Key technologies within analytical CRM systems include data mining, decision support, and other business intelligence technologies that attempt to create predictive models of various customer attributes (see Chapter 8). These analyses can focus on enhancing a broad range of customer-focused business processes, including the following:

- Marketing campaign management and analysis
- Customer campaign customization
- Customer communication optimization
- Customer segmentation and sales coverage optimization
- Pricing optimization and risk assessment and management
- Price, quality, and satisfaction analysis of competitors
- Customer acquisition and retention analysis
- Customer satisfaction and complaint management
- Product usage, life-cycle analysis, and product development
- Product and service quality tracking and management

Once these predictive models are created, they can be delivered to marketing and sales managers using a variety of visualization methods, including digital dashboards and other reporting methods. To gain the greatest value from the analytical CRM process, data collection and analysis must be continuous so that all decision making reflects the most accurate, comprehensive, and up-to-date information.

Collaborative CRM **Collaborative CRM** refers to systems for providing effective and efficient communication with the customer from the entire organization. Collaborative CRM systems facilitate the sharing of information across the various departments of an organization in order to increase customer satisfaction and loyalty. Sharing useful customer information on a company-wide basis helps improve information quality and can be used to identify products or services a customer may be interested in. A collaborative CRM system supports customer communication and collaboration with the entire organization, thus providing more streamlined customer service with fewer handoffs. The CIC (as described previously) enables customers to utilize the communication method they prefer when interacting with the organization. In other words, collaborative CRM integrates the communication related to all aspects of the marketing, sales, and support processes in order to better serve and retain customers. Collaborative CRM enhances communication in the following ways:

- ***Greater Customer Focus.*** Understanding customer history and current needs helps to focus the communication on issues important to the customer.
- ***Lower Communication Barriers.*** Customers are more likely to communicate with the organization when personnel have complete information and when they utilize the communication methods and preferences of the customer.
- ***Increased Information Integration.*** All information about the customer as well as all prior and ongoing communication is given to all organizational personnel interacting with the customer; customers can get status updates from any organizational touch point.

In addition to these benefits, collaborative CRM environments are flexible such that they can support both routine and nonroutine events.

Ethical Concerns with CRM

Although CRM has become a strategic enabler for developing and maintaining customer relationships, it is not viewed positively by those who feel it invades customer privacy and facilitates coercive sales practices. Proponents of CRM warn that relying too much on the "systems" profile of a customer, based on statistical analysis of past behavior, may categorize customers in a way that they will take exception to. Additionally, given that a goal of CRM is to better meet the needs of customers by providing highly *personalized* communication and service, at what point does the communication get *too* personal? It is intuitive to conclude that when customers feel the system knows too much about them, personalization could backfire on a company. Clearly, CRM raises several ethical concerns in the digital world (see Chapter 10—Information Systems Ethics and Crime for a comprehensive discussion of information privacy). Nevertheless, as competition continues to increase in the digital world, CRM will be a key technology for attracting and retaining customers.

Ethical Dilemma

Customer Relationship Management (CRM)—Targeting or Discriminating?

Customer relationship management (CRM) systems could be called a marketer's dream, because they promise companies the capability of getting to know their customers and at the same time maximizing the benefit gained from every customer. Through the use of sophisticated features, CRM software can let companies take a close look at customer behavior, drilling down to smaller and smaller market segments. Once so segmented, customers can be targeted with specific "special offers" or promotions. For the company, this process reaps the greatest returns from marketing efforts since only those customers are targeted who are likely to respond to the marketing campaign.

From a consumer's perspective, CRM systems seem like a great idea. Finally, you stop receiving advertisements for reams of stuff that doesn't interest you. But what if a company uses its CRM software in a more discriminating way? Where do companies draw the line between using CRM data to offer certain clients customized deals and unethically discriminating against other customers? For example, banks, which have the ability to segment their customers according to their creditworthiness, might use this credit risk data to target customers having a low credit rating. Although these customers are more risky for the banks, the higher fees and interest for credit make these customers especially lucrative.

A fine line exists between using CRM data for targeted marketing purposes and using such data to take advantage of certain groups. Some companies sell the customer data they have collected through CRM programs—without customer knowledge or consent. For example, a customer buys a Kenmore stove and completes the registration card for the appliance. She thinks she is sending the card to Kenmore, but instead it goes to a large database company, which puts the stove buyer's information on a list with data collected from other customers and sells the list. Such data-sharing alliances benefit from the use of CRM programs and they are legal; but are they ethical?

"Among my client base, these issues are very sensitive," Emma Warrillow, a customer intelligence and data use consultant based in Toronto, is quoted in a 2006 article published in *CRM News*. Warrillow recommends that companies collecting customer data through the use of CRM software and by other means test their ethics by asking themselves, "How would the customer feel? It may be legal, but is it ethical?"

Based on:

Jourdier, A. (2002, May 1). Privacy & ethics: Is CRM too close for comfort? *CIO.com*. Retrieved May 27, 2008, from http://www.cio.com/article/31062/Privacy_Ethics_Is_CRM_Too_Close_for_Comfort_.

Shermach, K. (2006, August 25). Data mining: Where legality and ethics rarely meet. *CRMBuyer.com*. Retrieved May 27, 2008, from http://www.crmbuyer.com/story/52616.html?welcome=1211140308.

Supply Chain Management

In the previous section, we looked downstream at CRM applications. Now we turn our attention upstream. Getting the raw materials and components that a company uses in its daily operations is an important key to business success. When deliveries from suppliers are accurate and timely, companies can convert them to finished products more efficiently. Coordinating this effort with suppliers has become a central part of companies' overall business strategies, as it can help them reduce costs associated with inventory levels and get new products to market more quickly. Ultimately, this helps companies drive profitability and improve their customer service since they can react to changing market conditions swiftly. Collaborating, or sharing information, with suppliers has become a strategic necessity for business success. In other words, by developing and maintaining stronger, more integrated relationships with suppliers, companies can more effectively compete in their markets through cost reductions and responsiveness to market demands.

What Is Supply Chain Management?

The term **supply chain** is commonly used to refer to the producers of supplies that a company uses. Companies often procure specific raw materials and components from many different suppliers. These suppliers, in turn, work with their suppliers to obtain goods; their suppliers work with additional suppliers and so forth. The further out in the supply chain one looks, the more suppliers are involved. As a result, the term "chain" becomes somewhat of a misnomer since it implies one-to-one relationships facilitating a chain of events flowing from the first supplier to the second to the third and so on. A more descriptive term to describe the flow of materials from suppliers to a company is **supply network** because multiple suppliers are involved in the process of servicing a single organization (see Figure 9.20).

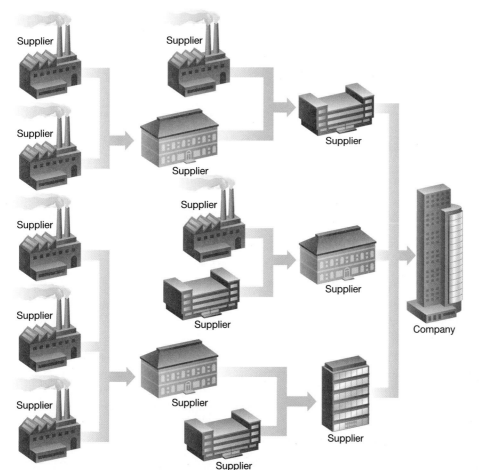

FIGURE 9.20

A typical supply network.

Several problems can arise when firms within a supply network do not collaborate effectively. Information can easily become distorted as it moves from one company down through the supply network, causing a great deal of inefficiency. Problems such as excessive inventories, inaccurate manufacturing capacity plans, and missed production schedules can run rampant, causing huge ripple effects that lead to degradations in profitability and poor customer service by everyone within the supply network. Such ripple effects are referred to as the "**bullwhip effect**." Each business forecasting demand typically includes a safety buffer in order to prevent possible stockouts. However, forecast errors and safety stocks multiply when moving up the supply chain, such that a small fluctuation in demand for an end product can lead to tremendous fluctuation in demand for the raw materials. Implementing integrated business processes allows a company to better coordinate the entire supply network and reduce the impact of the bullwhip.

Information systems focusing on improving upstream information flows have two main objectives: to accelerate product development and to reduce costs associated with procuring raw materials, components, and services from suppliers. These systems, called **supply chain management (SCM)**, improve the coordination of suppliers, product or service production, and distribution. When executed successfully, SCM helps in not only reducing inventory costs but also enhancing revenue through improved customer service. SCM is often integrated with ERP to leverage internal and external information in order to better collaborate with suppliers. Like ERP and CRM applications, SCM packages are delivered in the form of modules (see Table 9.7) that companies select and implement according to their differing business requirements.

TABLE 9.7 Functions That Optimize the Supply Network

Module	Key Uses
Supply chain collaboration	Share information and integrate processes up and down the supply chain
	Provide Internet-enabled processes such as collaborative planning, forecasting, and replenishment (CPFR) and vendor managed inventory
Collaborative design	Streamline product design processes across supply chain partners to reduce time to market
	React quickly to changing market conditions
Collaborative fulfillment	Commit to delivery dates in real time
	Fulfill orders from channels on time with order management, transportation planning, and vehicle scheduling
	Support the entire logistics process, including picking, packing, shipping, and international activities
Collaborative demand and supply planning	Develop a one-number forecast of customer demand by sharing demand and supply forecasts instantaneously across multiple tiers
	Enable suppliers and vendors to use shared forecasts and real-time demand signals to replenish stock automatically
Collaborative procurement	Provide global visibility into direct material spending
	Allow partners to leverage buying clout and reduce ad hoc buying
Production planning	Support both discrete and process manufacturing
	Optimize plans and schedules while considering resource, material, and dependency constraints
Supply chain event management	Monitor every stage of the supply chain process, from price quotation to the moment the customer receives the product, issuing alerts when problems arise
	Capture data from carriers, vehicle on-board computers, GPS systems, and other sources
Supply chain exchange	Create an online supply chain community that enables partners to collaborate on design, procurement, demand and supply management, and other supply chain activities
Supply chain performance management	Report key measurements in the supply chain, such as order cycle times and percent of capacity utilized
	Integrate planning and execution functions with competitive information and market trends

Based on http://www.sap.com.

As discussed previously, ERP and CRM are primarily used to optimize (reengineer) business processes *within* the organization, whereas SCM is used to improve business processes that *span* organizational boundaries. Given its scope, SCM is adopted primarily by large organizations with a large and/or complex supplier network. To reap the greatest benefits from the SCM processes and systems, organizations need to extend the system to include all trading partners regardless of size, providing a central location for information integration and common processes so that all partners benefit.

SCM Architecture

An SCM system includes more than simply hardware and software; it also integrates business processes and supply chain partners. As shown in Table 9.7, an SCM system consists of many modules or applications. Each of these applications supports either supply chain planning or supply chain execution. Both are described next.

Supply Chain Planning **Supply chain planning (SCP)** involves the development of various resource plans to support the efficient and effective production of goods and services (see Figure 9.21). Four general types of plans are developed within the SCP process:

1. **Demand Planning and Forecasting.** SCP begins with product demand planning and forecasting. To develop these plans, SCM modules examine historical data to develop the most accurate forecasts possible. The accuracy of these plans will be influenced greatly by the stability of the data. When historic data is stable, plans can be longer in duration, whereas if historic data shows unpredictable fluctuations in demand, the forecasting time frame must be narrowed. Demand planning and forecasting leads to the development of the overall *demand forecast.*
2. **Distribution Planning.** Once final product planning forecasts are complete, plans for moving products to distributors can be developed. Specifically, distribution planning focuses on delivering products or services to consumers as well as the warehousing, delivering, invoicing, and payment collection. Distribution planning leads to the development of the overall *transportation schedule.*
3. **Production Scheduling.** Production scheduling focuses on the coordination of all activities needed to create the product or service. When developing this plan, analytical tools are used to optimally utilize materials, equipment, and labor. Production also involves product testing, packaging, and delivery preparation. Production scheduling leads to the development of the *production plan.*
4. **Procurement Planning.** Procurement planning focuses on the development of inventory estimates using inventory simulations and other analytical techniques. Once inventory levels are estimated, suppliers are chosen who contractually agree to preestablished delivery and pricing terms. *Inventory simulation* is a key element of the procurement planning process.

As suggested, various types of analytical tools—such as statistical analysis, simulation, and optimization—are used to forecast and visualize demand levels, distribution and warehouse locations, resource sequencing, and so on. Once these plans are developed, they are used to guide supply chain execution. Additionally, it is important to note that SCM planning is an ongoing process—as new data are obtained, plans are updated.

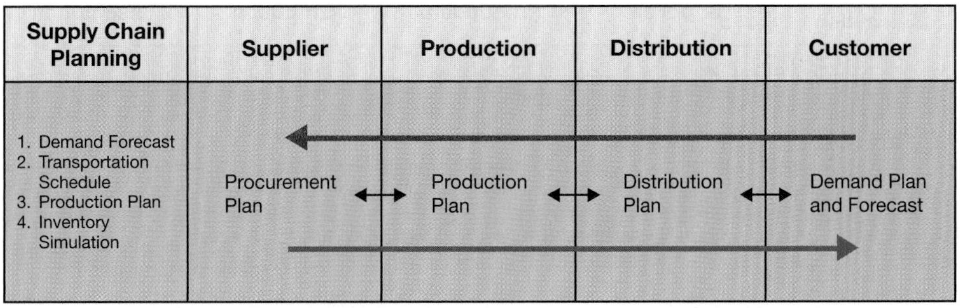

Supply Chain Planning	Supplier	Production	Distribution	Customer
1. Demand Forecast 2. Transportation Schedule 3. Production Plan 4. Inventory Simulation	Procurement Plan	Production Plan	Distribution Plan	Demand Plan and Forecast

FIGURE 9.21

Supply chain planning is used to create demand forecasts, transportation schedules, production plans, and inventory simulations.

Supply Chain Execution Supply chain execution (SCE) is the execution of supply chain planning. Essentially, SCE puts the SCM planning into motion and reflects the processes involved in improving the collaboration of all members of the supply chain—suppliers, producers, distributors, and customers. SCE involves the management of three key elements of the supply chain: product flow, information flow, and financial flow (see Figure 9.22). Each of these flows is discussed next.

THE PRODUCT FLOW. Product flow refers to the movement of goods from the supplier to production, from production to distribution, and from distribution to the consumer. Although products primarily "flow" in one direction, an effective SCM system will also automate product returns. Effectively processing returns and customer refunds is a critical part of supply chain execution. Thus, an SCM system should support not only the physical product production process but also the necessary processes in place to efficiently receive excessive or defective products from customers (e.g., ship replacements or credit accounts).

THE INFORMATION FLOW. Information flow refers to the movement of information along the supply chain, such as order processing and delivery status. Like the product flow, information can also flow up or down the supply chain as needed. The key element to the information flow is the complete removal of paper documents. Specifically, all orders, fulfillment, billing, and consolidation information is shared electronically. These paperless information flows save not only paperwork but also time and money. Additionally, because the SCM system uses a central database to store information, all supply chain partners have access to all the current information at all times.

THE FINANCIAL FLOW. Financial flow refers primarily to the movement of financial assets throughout the supply chain. Financial flows also include information related to payment schedules, consignment and ownership of products and materials, and other relevant information. Linkages to electronic banking and financial institutions allow payments to automatically flow into the accounts of all members within the supply chain.

Developing an SCM Strategy

When developing a supply chain management strategy, an organization must consider a variety of factors that will affect the efficiency and effectiveness of the supply chain. **Supply chain efficiency** is the extent to which a company's supply chain is focusing on minimizing procurement, production, and transportation costs, sometimes by reducing customer service. In contrast, **supply chain effectiveness** is the extent to which a company's supply chain is focusing on maximizing customer service, regardless of procurement, production, and transportation costs. In other words, the design of the supply chain must consider natural trade-offs between a variety of factors and should reflect the organization's competitive strategy. For example, an organization utilizing a low-cost provider competitive strategy would likely focus on supply chain efficiency. In contrast, an organization pursuing a superior customer service differentiation strategy would focus on supply chain effectiveness. Of course, it is also likely that, because of the availability and locations of major suppliers and customers, hybrid strategies would be implemented. Nevertheless, organizations must match their overall supply chain strategy to their overall competitive strategy to reap the greatest benefits (see Figure 9.23).

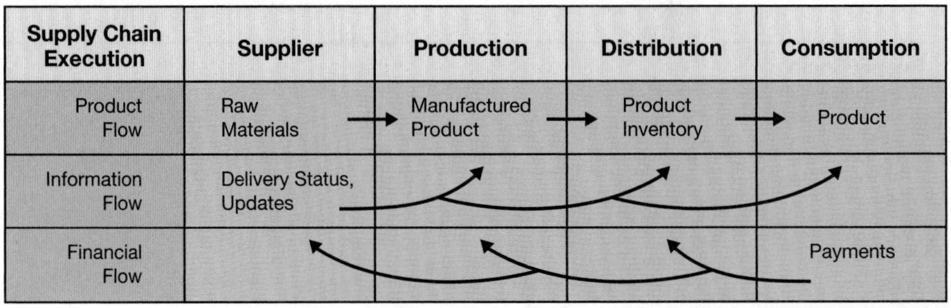

FIGURE 9.22

Supply chain execution focuses on the efficient and effective flow of products, information, and finances along the supply chain.

Supply Chain Execution	Supplier	Production	Distribution	Consumption
Product Flow	Raw Materials	Manufactured Product	Product Inventory	Product
Information Flow	Delivery Status, Updates			
Financial Flow				Payments

Supply Chain Strategy	Procurement	Production	Transportation
Effectiveness ⬍ **Efficiency**	More Inventory Multiple Inventory Sources ... ⬍ ... Single Inventory Source Less Inventory	General Purpose Facilities More Facilities Higher Excess Capacity ... ⬍ ... Less Excess Capacity Fewer Facilities Special Purpose Facilities	Fast Delivery Times More Warehouses ... ⬍ ... Fewer Warehouses Longer Delivery Times

FIGURE 9.23

A supply chain strategy requires balancing supply chain efficiency and effectiveness.

Emerging SCM Trends

As is the case with all technologies, SCM is evolving. One key trend is the development of enterprise portals, which provide an alternative to proprietary supply linkages. In addition, new technologies are helping to add greater value to SCM. These topics are briefly examined next.

Enterprise Portals Most SCM systems are tightly integrated with a relatively small number of suppliers or customers. The goal of SCM is to optimize the flow rather than minimize costs or maximize revenue. For example, it may make sense for an organization to have a close, proprietary relationship with suppliers of rare, unique, or critical components to a product. However, for other more standard components, it may be more advantageous to utilize some form of Web-based business-to-business (B2B) marketplace, bringing together companies and their business partners. These B2B marketplaces are referred to as **enterprise portals**. Portals, in the context of B2B supply chain management, can be defined as access points (or front doors) through which a business partner accesses secured, proprietary information from an organization (typically using extranets). Enterprise portals provide a single point of access to this type of information that may be dispersed throughout an organization. Thus, enterprise portals can provide substantial productivity gains and cost savings by creating a single point of access where the company can conduct business with any number of business partners.

Enterprise portals come in two basic forms: distribution portals and procurement portals. Distribution portals automate the business processes involved in selling or distributing products from a single supplier to multiple buyers. On the other end of the spectrum, procurement portals automate the business processes involved in purchasing or procuring products between a single buyer and multiple suppliers (see Figure 9.24). Distribution and procurement portals can vary depending on the number of buyers and suppliers that utilize

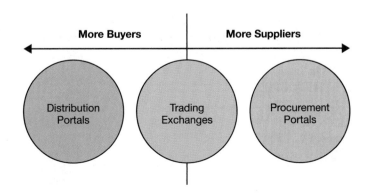

FIGURE 9.24

Distribution portals, trading exchanges, and procurement portals.

the portal. Further, a few companies can share distribution portals to purchase products from many suppliers. When the balance between buyers and sellers nears a point of equilibrium, these systems are classified as **trading exchanges**.

Distribution portals, procurement portals, and trading exchanges commonly service specific industries or groups of firms that rely on similar products or services. Tailoring products and services to particular companies creates a **vertical market**, or a market that services the needs of a specific sector. Vertical markets can create tremendous efficiencies for companies since they bring together numerous participants along the supply network.

DISTRIBUTION PORTALS. Distribution portals are designed to automate the business processes that occur before, during, and after sales have been transacted between a supplier and multiple customers. In other words, distribution portals provide efficient tools for customers to manage all phases of the purchasing cycle, including product information, order entry, and customer service. Dell services business customers through its distribution portal Premier.Dell.com (see Figure 9.25).

PROCUREMENT PORTALS. Procurement portals are designed to automate the business processes that occur before, during, and after sales have been transacted between a buyer and multiple suppliers. Procurement portals provide efficient tools for suppliers to manage all phases of the distribution cycle, including dissemination of product information, purchase order processing, and customer service. The Boeing Company has implemented a procurement portal called Boeing Supplier Portal, where suppliers come to share information and conduct business with Boeing.

Trading Exchanges

Enterprise portals tend to be beyond the reach of small to midsized businesses because of the costs involved in designing, developing, and maintaining this type of system. Many of these firms do not have the necessary monetary resources or skilled personnel to develop large-scale SCM applications on their own. To service this market niche, a number of trading exchanges, or electronic marketplaces, have sprung up. Trading exchanges are operated by third-party vendors, meaning they are built and maintained by a particular company. These companies generate revenue by taking a small commission for each transaction that occurs, by charging usage fees, by charging association fees, and/or by

FIGURE 9.25

Distribution portal
Premier.Dell.com.

Source: http://www.dell.com.

generating advertising revenues. Unlike distribution and procurement portals, trading exchanges allow many buyers and many sellers to come together, offering firms access to real-time trading with other companies in their vertical markets. Some popular trading exchanges include www.e-steel.com and www.scrapsite.com (steel), www.paperspace.com (paper), and www.biosupplynet.com and www.sciquest.com (medical equipment).

Key Technologies for Enhancing SCM Several new technologies are helping organizations gain even more from their investments in SCM systems. In this section, we briefly review two that are providing significant benefits to managing supply chains.

EXTENSIBLE MARKUP LANGUAGE (XML). **Extensible Markup Language (XML)** is a data presentation standard first specified by the World Wide Web Consortium, an international consortium of companies whose purpose is to develop open standards for the Web. XML allows designers of Web documents to create their own customized tags, enabling the definition, transmission, validation, and interpretation of data between applications and between organizations (see the Technology Briefing for more on XML).

XML does not specify any particular formatting; rather, it specifies the rules for tagging elements. A **tag** is a command that is inserted in a document in order to specify how the document or a portion of the document should be formatted and/or used. As described in the Technology Briefing, hypertext markup language (HTML) uses tags to instruct a Web browser how data on a Web page should be laid out cosmetically on a user's screen. Much like HTML, XML also uses tags in Web documents, but they go well beyond HTML. XML instructs systems as to how information should be interpreted and used. For example, the tags <UPC>. . .</UPC> would instruct the application reading the XML file that the numbers enclosed in the tags should be interpreted as a product's universal product code. The application could use this information when displaying a product on a Web page, or when updating inventory records. As a result, XML is a powerful information tagging system that can be tailored to share similar data across applications over the Web. With these advanced data definition characteristics built into Web applications, organizations can then use the Web as the worldwide network for business-to-consumer electronic commerce and business-to-business supply chain management.

Many people think that XML is on its way to becoming the standard for automating data exchange between business information systems and may well replace all other formats for electronic data interchange (EDI). Companies can, for example, use XML to create an application for doing Web-based ordering, for checking on and managing inventory, for signaling to a supplier that more parts are needed, for alerting a third-party logistics company that a delivery is needed, and so on. All of these various applications can work together using the common language of XML.

XML is customizable, and a number of variations of XML have been developed. For example, **Extensible Business Reporting Language (XBRL)** is an XML-based specification for publishing financial information. XBRL makes it easier for public and private companies to share information with each other, with industry analysts, and with shareholders. XBRL includes tags for data such as annual and quarterly reports, Securities and Exchange Commission filings, general ledger information, and net revenue and accounting schedules.

XML is not, however, a panacea for SCM. Support for and use of XML is growing rapidly, but all the necessary standards and agreements are not yet in place to enable XML-based applications to work seamlessly with all other applications and systems. Further, while nearly anyone can learn to use a text editor to create a basic HTML document, XML is far more complex and requires not only knowledge of XML but also expertise in distributed database design and management. Nevertheless, XML holds great promise for managing supply chains by its ability to inject more information into the process.

RADIO FREQUENCY IDENTIFICATION. Another exciting technology now being used within SCM systems is **radio frequency identification (RFID)**, which is starting to replace standard bar codes you find on almost every product. RFID is the use of the electromagnetic energy to transmit information between a reader (transceiver) and a processing device, or **RFID tag**.

RFID tags can be used just about anywhere that a unique identification system might be needed, such as on clothing, pets, cars, keys, missiles, or manufactured parts. RFID tags can range in size from being a fraction of an inch, which can be inserted beneath an animal's skin, up to several inches across and fixed on a product or shipping container (see Figure 9.26). The tag can carry information as simple as the name of the owner of a pet or as complex as how a product is to be manufactured on the shop floor.

RFID systems offer advantages over standard bar-code technologies in that RFID eliminates the need for line-of-sight reading. RFID also does not require time-consuming hand scanning, and RFID information is readable regardless of the entity's position or whether the tag is plainly visible (see Figure 9.27). RFID tags can also contain more information than bar codes. It is possible to retrieve information about an entity's version, origin, location, maintenance history, and other important information and to manipulate that information on the tag. RFID scanning can also be done at greater distances than can barcode scanning. *Passive tags* are small and relatively inexpensive (less than $1) and typically have a range up to a few feet. *Active tags,* on the other hand, cost upward of $5, include a battery, and can transmit hundreds of feet.

RFID systems offer great opportunities for managing supply chains. For example, airlines are strapped for cash and think a lot about those metal, rolling serving carts that are used on airplanes and that can cost as much as $1,000 each. "We've heard horrific stories of airlines losing up to 1,500 of these things in three months," says Tony Naylor, vice pres-

FIGURE 9.26

An RFID tag is small but contains a lot of information.

Source: METRO AG.

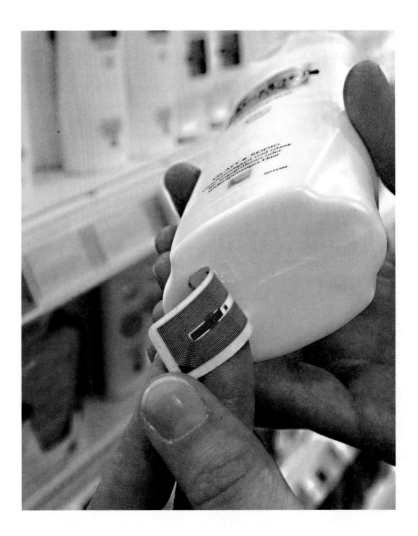

FIGURE 9.27

A pallet of inventory being processed as it passes through an RFID gate.

Source: METRO AG.

ident of in-flight solutions for eLSG.SkyChefs, a technology provider for the airline catering industry, based in Irving, Texas (Edwards, 2003). To keep tabs on their vanishing carts, eLSG.SkyChefs now uses an RFID system with an RFID tag on each cart.

Additionally, virtually all major retailers are adopting RFID to better manage their supply chains, as are governments for tracking military supplies and weapons, drug shipments and ingredients (i.e., for eliminating counterfeit drugs), and citizens with RFID chips on passports. While RFID's deployment is growing rapidly, the systems are still relatively expensive, there isn't yet a clear set of data standards, and global radio frequencies

Net Stats

RFID on the Rise

The market for radio frequency identification (RFID) tags, those high-tech devices that let businesses keep track of certain products via radio frequency transmitters and receivers, is exploding. According to industry estimates, the total RFID market (including related services) is expected to grow from $5.29 billion in 2008 to $12.3 billion in 2010, making RFID tags the hottest wireless item since cell phones first came out. Experts predict that supply chain elements, such as shipping cartons and labels, will account for most of the growth. The second-largest segment of growth will be consumer items—everything from drug containers to clothing. In terms of total revenues, the largest RFID market sector is security and access control applications (62.6 percent), followed by animals (28.8 percent), and supply chain

applications (4.9 percent). Consumer products, large freight, and RFID implants for human bodies are trailing far behind, with less than 1 percent of total revenues (each).

Based on:

Das, R., and Harrop, P. (2008). RFID forecasts, players & opportunities 2008–2018. Retrieved May 27, 2008, from http://www.idtechex.com/products/en/view.asp?productcategoryid=151.

McGann, R. (2005, January 18). RFID tag market to swell tenfold by 2009. *Clickz.com*. Retrieved May 27, 2008, from http://www.clickz.com/showPage.html?page=3460851.

McGrath, D. (2006, January 26). RFID market to grow 10 fold by 2016, firm says. *EE Times*. Retrieved May 27, 2008, from http://www.eetimes.com/news/latest/showArticle.jhtml?articleID=177104240.

differ between countries. Fortunately, these hurdles are being overcome by cooperation between vendors. In any event, RFID is clearly a valuable new technology for managing supply chains.

The Formula for Enterprise System Success

To summarize, the main objective of enterprise systems is to create competitive advantage by streamlining business activities within and outside a company. However, many implementations turn out to be more costly and time consuming than originally envisioned. It is not uncommon to have projects that run over budget, meaning that identifying common problems and devising methods for dealing with these issues can prove invaluable to management. Surveys suggest that 40 to 60 percent of companies that undertake enterprise system implementations do not fully realize the results that they had hoped for (Langenwalter, 2000). Companies that have successfully installed enterprise systems are found to follow a basic set of recommendations related to enterprise system implementations (Koch, Slater, and Baatz, 2000). Although the following list is not meant to be comprehensive, these recommendations will provide an understanding of some of the challenges involved in implementing enterprise systems:

> *Recommendation 1.* Secure executive sponsorship
> *Recommendation 2.* Get help from outside experts
> *Recommendation 3.* Thoroughly train users
> *Recommendation 4.* Take a multidisciplinary approach to implementations
> *Recommendation 5.* Look beyond ERP

Secure Executive Sponsorship

The primary reason that enterprise system implementations fail is believed to be a direct result of lack of top-level management support. Although executives do not necessarily need to make decisions concerning the enterprise system, it is critical that they buy into the decisions made by project managers. Many problems can arise if projects fail to grab the attention of top-level management. In most companies, executives have the ultimate authority regarding the availability and distribution of resources within the organization. If executives do not understand the importance of the enterprise system, this will likely result in delays or stoppages because the necessary resources may not be available when they are needed.

A second problem that may arise deals with top-level management's ability to authorize changes in the way the company does business. When business processes need to be changed to incorporate best practices, these modifications need to be completed. Otherwise the company will have a piece of software on its hands that does not fit the way people accomplish their business tasks. Lack of executive sponsorship can also have a trickle-down effect within the organization. If users and midlevel management perceive the enterprise system to be unimportant, they are not likely to view it as a priority. Enterprise systems require a concentrated effort, and executive sponsorship can propel or stifle the implementation. Executive management can obliterate any obstacles that arise.

Get Help from Outside Experts

Enterprise systems are complex. Even the most talented information systems departments can struggle in coming to grips with ERP, CRM, and SCM applications. Most vendors have trained project managers and consultants to assist companies with installing enterprise systems. Using consultants tends to move companies through the implementation more quickly and tends to help companies train their personnel on the applications more effectively. However, companies should not rely too heavily on consultants and should plan for the consultants leaving once the implementation is complete. When consultants are physically present, company personnel tend to rely on them for assistance. Once the application goes live and the consultants are no longer there, users have to do the job themselves. A key focus should therefore be facilitating user learning.

Thoroughly Train Users

Training is often the most overlooked, underestimated, and poorly budgeted expense involved in planning enterprise system implementations. Enterprise systems are much more complicated to learn than stand-alone systems. Learning a single application requires users to become accustomed to a new software interface, but enterprise system users regularly need to learn a new set of business processes as well. Once enterprise systems go live, many companies experience a dramatic drop-off in productivity. This issue can potentially lead to heightened levels of dissatisfaction among users, as they prefer to accomplish their business activities in a familiar manner rather than doing things the new way. By training users before the system goes live and giving them sufficient opportunities to learn the new system, a company can allay fears and mitigate potential productivity issues.

Take a Multidisciplinary Approach to Implementations

Enterprise systems affect the entire organization; thus, companies should include personnel from different levels and departments in the implementation project (Kumar and Crook, 1999). In CRM and SCM environments in which other organizations are participating in the implementation, it is critical to enlist the support of personnel in their organizations as well. Project managers need to include in the implementation personnel from midlevel management, the information systems department, external consultants, and, most important, end users.

Failing to include the appropriate people in the day-to-day activities of the project can prove problematic in many areas. From a needs analysis standpoint, it is critical that all the business requirements be sufficiently captured before selection of an enterprise solution. Since end users are involved in every aspect of daily business activities, their insights can be invaluable. For instance, an end user might make salient a feature that no one on the project team had thought of. Having an application that does not meet all of the business's requirements can result in poorly fitting software or customizations. Another peril in leaving out key personnel is the threat of alienation. Departments and/or personnel that do not feel included may develop a sense of animosity toward the new system and view it in a negative light. In extreme cases, users will refuse to use the new application, resulting in conflicts and inefficiencies within the organization.

Look Beyond ERP

As you can see, implementing ERP systems is a highly complex undertaking; although a successful implementation can have huge payoffs for an organization, some organizations fear losing the ability to quickly respond to changing business requirements, particularly since large ERP systems are difficult to install, maintain, and upgrade. A recent trend is to move away from such large, comprehensive systems to a **service-oriented architecture (SOA)**. Using SOA, business processes are broken down into individual components (or **services**) that are designed to achieve the desired results for the service consumer (which can be either an application, another service, or a person). To illustrate this concept, think about the next oil change for your car. As you can't be expert in everything, it is probably more effective to have someone change the oil for you. You may take your car to the dealership, you may go to an independent garage or oil change service, or you may ask your friend to do it for you. In all cases, the desired service will be performed, but at different levels of quality and cost.

By breaking down business processes into individual services, organizations can more swiftly react to changing business needs. For example, using an ERP approach, one application would handle all aspects of the customer order process; in contrast, using an SOA approach, multiple services (such as check inventory, or order supplies) would be orchestrated to handle the individual tasks associated with the order process, and could be changed relatively easily, if the business process changes. Web services, discussed in Chapter 6—Enhancing Collaboration Using Web 2.0—are services that are invoked via a network, and typically use standards such as XML. By using and reusing individual services as "building blocks" systems can be easily built and reconfigured as requirements change. To achieve these benefits, services have to follow three main principles:

1. Reusability—A service should be usable in many different applications.
2. Interoperability—A service should work with any other service.
3. Componentization—A service should be simple and modular.

Following these principles, multiple applications can invoke the same services. For example, both an organization's point-of-sale system and e-commerce Web site could invoke the service "process credit card," and the executive dashboard could invoke the services "display products," "display inventory," and "display sales" (see Figure 9.28). Using SOA can be very beneficial for an organization. For example, the Virgin Entertainment Group, which has twenty-three mega-record stores in North America and several more in Europe, implemented SOA to prevent employee theft and shrinkage in its stores. SOA was used to develop a real-time loss-prevention system that could monitor point-of-sale activity, along with receiving systems. By breaking this complex business process into several small services, the theft prevention system could easily be integrated into the company's current enterprise system. The SOA approach was successful for Virgin as losses and employee theft decreased 50 percent.

Recently, large ERP vendors such as Oracle or SAP introduced platforms enabling the transition to SOA. Such solutions allow incremental migration from an ERP system to SOA, without having to immediately retire the ERP system. Further, these solutions allow the use of services from other systems or vendors, increasing an organization's flexibility.

Although expansive enterprise system implementations, as well as SOA approaches, are often cumbersome and difficult, the potential payoff is huge. As a result, organizations are compelled to implement these systems. Further, given the popularity and necessity of integrating systems and processes on an organization-wide basis, you are likely to find yourself involved in the implementation and/or use of such a system. We are confident that after reading this chapter, you will be better able to understand and help with the development and use of such systems.

FIGURE 9.28

Using SOA, multiple applications can invoke multiple services.

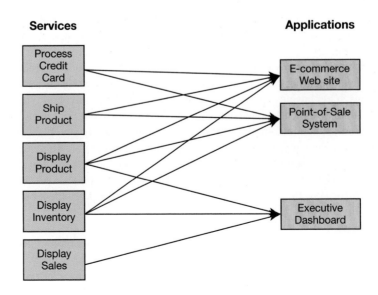

Industry Analysis

Manufacturing

Regardless of whether you're thinking about a new computer, a TV, an automobile, or a toy for your baby brother, most of today's consumer products have undergone an elaborate design and manufacturing process, and few companies fail to make heavy use of information systems in the process. Traditionally, designers and engineers used large drawing boards to sketch detailed drawings of each component of a product. Today, designers use **computer-aided design (CAD)** software for this task, allowing them to create drawings faster and more accurately, thus cutting down cycle time (i.e., the time from inception to the shipment of the first product) tremendously. At the same time, CAD allows easier sharing of designs, and can be used to produce three-dimensional drawings of a new product. However, although you can create realistic 3-D drawings of a new product, people often still need to hold a physical model in their hands to evaluate it. 3-D printing, sometimes known as "fabbing," can greatly speed up the creation of models. In essence, 3-D printers add successive layers of material onto a surface, thus building a three-dimensional model out of myriads of individual slices. In fact, some 3-D printers even use materials such as titanium, allowing battleships to produce spare parts on an as-needed basis, rather than carrying warehouses full of parts.

Engineers use **computer-aided engineering (CAE)** tools to test these designs. Whereas traditionally, many features of a new product could only be tested after building prototypes, CAE allows for the testing and modification of features before the first prototypes are ever built, resulting in substantial savings of both time and money. For example, almost all automobile manufacturers now use CAE tools to perform tests for wind resistance, noise, vibrations, or simulating wear and tear. Rather than having to build prototype after prototype to test different design changes, these are tested on the computer, and the first working prototype is closer to the final model than ever.

Finally, **computer-aided manufacturing (CAM)** is the use of information systems to control the production of the final product. CAM systems take design input from a CAD system and then automatically control the manufacturing of a product's components, ranging from sheet metal presses to the spray painting of a car's exterior by "painting robots." This integration of design, engineering, and manufacturing has reduced manufacturing costs and at the same time improved product quality.

The use of technology doesn't stop there. Inventory planning, job scheduling, or warehouse management are all supported by information systems, often in the form of enterprise resource planning systems. Once a product leaves the manufacturer, information systems are being used throughout the distribution of the product, from transportation scheduling to route optimization to improvement of the trucking company fleet's fuel efficiency. Clearly, information systems have changed and will continue to change the process of designing, manufacturing, and shipping products to you.

Based on:

Gardiner, B. (2007, November 21). 3-D printers redefine industrial design. *Wired*. Retrieved May 27, 2008, from http://www.wired.com/gadgets/miscellaneous/news/2007/11/3d_printers.

Leberecht, T. (2007, December 17). Trends 2008: Will 3-D printing finally go mainstream? *CNET News*. Retrieved May 27, 2008, from http://news.cnet.com/8301-13641_3-9835160-44.html.

Key Points Review

1. *Describe what enterprise systems are and how they have evolved.* Enterprise systems are information systems that span the entire organization and can be used to integrate business processes, activities, and information across all the functional areas of a firm. Enterprise systems can be either prepackaged software or custom-made applications. The implementation of enterprise systems often involves business process management, a systematic, structured improvement approach by all or part of an organization that critically examines, rethinks, and redesigns processes in order to achieve dramatic improvements in one or more performance measures, such as quality, cycle time, or cost. Enterprise systems evolved from legacy systems that supported distinct organizational activities by combining data and applications into a single comprehensive system.

2. *Describe enterprise resource planning (ERP) systems and how they help to improve internal business processes.* ERP systems evolved from "material requirements planning" systems during the 1990s and are, for the most part, used to support internal business processes. ERP systems allow information to be shared throughout the organization through the use of a large data warehouse, helping to streamline business processes and improve customer service. When selecting an ERP system, organizations must choose which modules to implement from a large menu of options—most organizations adopt only a subset of the available ERP components. ERP core components support the major internal activities of the organization for producing their products and services, while ERP extended components support the primary external activities of the organization for dealing with suppliers and customers.

3. *Describe customer relationship management (CRM) systems and how they help to improve downstream business processes.* CRM is a corporate-level strategy to create and maintain lasting relationships with customers by concentrating on the downstream information flows through the introduction of reliable systems, processes, and procedures. Applications focusing on downstream information flows have two main objectives—to attract potential customers and create customer loyalty. To develop a successful CRM strategy, organizations must do more than simply purchase and install CRM software; they must also make changes to policy and business processes, customer service, employee training, and data utilization. A CRM consists of three primary components: operational CRM, analytical CRM, and collaborative CRM. Operational CRM focuses on front-office activities that deal directly with customers. Analytical CRM focuses on back-office activities that aid managers in analyzing the sales and marketing functions. Finally, collaborative CRM provides effective communication capabilities within the organization and externally with customers.

4. *Describe supply chain management (SCM) systems and how they help to improve upstream business processes.* SCM systems focus on improving upstream information flows and have two main objectives—to accelerate product development and to reduce costs associated with procuring raw materials, components, and services from suppliers. SCM consists of supply chain planning (SCP) and supply chain execution (SCE) components. SCP involves the development of various resource plans to support the efficient and effective production of goods and services. SCE puts the SCP into motion and reflects the processes involved in improving the collaboration of all members of the supply chain—suppliers, producers, distributors, and customers. SCE involves the management of three key elements of the supply chain: product flow, information flow, and financial flow. When developing a supply chain management strategy, an organization must consider a variety of factors that will affect the efficiency and effectiveness of the supply chain. Specifically, organizations must match their overall supply chain strategy to their overall competitive strategy to reap the greatest benefits.

5. *Understand and utilize the keys to successfully implementing enterprise systems.* Experience with enterprise system implementations suggests that there are some common problems that can be avoided and/or should be managed carefully. Organizations can avoid common implementation problems by (1) securing executive sponsorship, (2) getting necessary help from outside experts, (3) thoroughly training users, (4) taking a multidisciplinary approach to implementations, and (5) looking beyond ERP.

Key Terms

analytical CRM 385
back-office system 380
bullwhip effect 388
business process management
(BPM) 372
business process reengineering
(BPR) 373
collaborative CRM 385
computer-aided design (CAD) 399
computer-aided engineering
(CAE) 399
computer-aided manufacturing
(CAM) 399
conversion 370
core activities 365
custom application 367
customer interaction center (CIC) 384
customer relationship management
(CRM) 379
customer service and support
(CSS) 384
customization 372
distribution portal 392
downstream information flow 367

enterprise marketing management
(EMM) 385
enterprise portal 391
enterprise resource planning
(ERP) 375
enterprise system 361
enterprise-wide information
system 361
ERP core components 376
ERP extended components 378
Extensible Business Reporting
Language (XBRL) 393
Extensible Markup Language
(XML) 393
externally focused system 362
financial flow 390
front-office system 380
information flow 390
internally focused system 362
interorganizational system (IOS) 363
legacy system 369
module 371
operational CRM 381
packaged application 367

procurement portal 392
product flow 390
radio frequency identification
(RFID) 393
RFID tag 394
sales force automation (SFA) 382
service 397
service-oriented architecture 397
stand-alone application 369
supply chain 387
supply chain effectiveness 390
supply chain efficiency 390
supply chain execution (SCE) 390
supply chain management (SCM) 388
supply chain planning (SCP) 389
supply network 387
support activities 366
tag 393
trading exchange 392
upstream information flow 367
value system 367
vanilla version 372
vertical market 392

Review Questions

1. Describe what enterprise systems are and how they have evolved.
2. Contrast internally and externally focused systems.
3. What are the core and support activities of a value chain?
4. Give an example of upstream and downstream information flows in a value system.
5. Compare and contrast customized and packaged applications as well as vanilla versions versus best practices–based software.
6. What are the core components of an enterprise resource planning system?
7. What is a customer relationship management system, and what are its primary components?

8. What is supply chain management, and how does supply chain planning differ from supply chain execution?
9. How does customer relationship management differ from supply chain management?
10. Contrast distribution portals, procurement portals, and trading exchanges.
11. What is XML, and how will it impact supply chain management?
12. What is RFID, and how will it impact supply chain management?
13. What are the keys to successfully implementing an enterprise system?

Self-Study Questions

Visit the Interactive Study Guide on the Companion Web site for additional Self-Study Questions: www.pearsonhighered.com/valacich.

1. _____ are information systems that allow companies to integrate information and support operations on a company-wide basis.
   A. customer relationship management systems
   B. enterprise systems
   C. WANs
   D. interorganizational systems

2. Which of the following is a core activity according to the value chain model?
   A. firm infrastructure
   B. customer service
   C. human resources
   D. procurement

3. According to the value chain model, which of the following is a support activity?
   A. technology development

B. marketing and sales

C. inbound logistics

D. operations and manufacturing

4. All of the following are true about legacy systems except _____.

A. they are stand-alone systems

B. they are older software systems

C. they are enterprise resource planning systems

D. they may be difficult to integrate into other systems

5. A comprehensive customer relationship management system includes all but which of the following components?

A. operational CRM

B. analytical CRM

C. diagnostic CRM

D. collaborative CRM

6. Sales force automation is most closely associated with what?

A. enterprise resource planning

B. customer relationship management

C. supply chain management

D. legacy systems

7. Which of the following is commonly used to refer to the producers of supplies that a company uses?

A. procurement

B. sales force

C. supply network

D. customers

8. Which type of flow does supply chain execution not focus on?

A. procurement flow

B. product flow

C. information flow

D. financial flow

9. RFID tags can be used for _____.

A. tracking military weapons

B. eliminating counterfeit drugs

C. tracking passports

D. all of the above

10. _____ is a systematic, structured improvement approach by all or part of an organization that critically examines, rethinks, and redesigns processes in order to achieve dramatic improvements in one or more performance measures such as quality, cycle time, or cost.

A. Systems analysis

B. Business process management

C. Customer relationship management

D. Total quality management

Answers are on page 404.

Problems and Exercises

1. Match the following terms with the appropriate definitions:

   i. Enterprise systems

   ii. Legacy systems

   iii. Supply chain

   iv. ERP extended components

   v. Customer relationship management

   vi. Customer interaction center

   vii. Supply chain management

   viii. Business process management

   ix. Enterprise portal

   x. RFID

   a. Components that support the primary *external* activities of the organization for dealing with suppliers and customers

   b. Information systems that provide a single point of access to secured, proprietary information that may be dispersed throughout an organization

   c. The use of electromagnetic energy to transmit information between a reader (transceiver) and a processing device, used to replace bar codes and bar code readers

   d. Older systems that are not designed to communicate with other applications beyond departmental boundaries

   e. Information systems that allow companies to integrate information on a company-wide basis

   f. Applications that concentrate on downstream information flows, integrating the value chains of a company and its distributors or customers

   g. Commonly used to refer to the network of producers of supplies that a company uses

   h. A systematic, structured improvement approach by all or part of an organization whereby people critically examine, rethink, and redesign business processes in order to achieve dramatic improvements in one or more performance measures such as quality, cycle time, or cost

   i. The use of multiple communication channels to support the communication preferences of customers

   j. Applications that operate on upstream information flows, integrating the value chains of a company and its suppliers

2. Find an organization that you are familiar with and determine how many software applications it is utilizing concurrently. Is the company's information system cohesive, or does it need updating and streamlining?

3. What part does training users in an ERP system play, and how important is it in job satisfaction? What productivity problems can result in an ERP implementation?

4. What are the payoffs from taking a multidisciplinary approach to an ERP implementation? What departments are affected, and what is the typical time frame?

Research an organization that has recently implemented an ERP system. What could the company have done better, and what did it do right?

5. What companies are using data warehouses? Research this question and determine the cost and size of a data warehouse. What are the advantages and disadvantages of data warehouses, especially for implementing enterprise systems? What is the typical time frame for implementation?

6. Based on your own experiences with applications, have you used customized or off-the-shelf applications? What is the difference, and how good was the system documentation?

7. Search the Web for the phrase "best practices," and you will find numerous sites that summarize the best practices for a variety of industries and professions. Choose one and summarize these best practices into a one-page report.

8. Choose a company you are familiar with and examine how efficiently or effectively it has designed the procurement, production, and transportation aspects of its business.

9. Assume you are a sales manager. What sales performance measures would you want the customer relationship management system to provide you in order to better manage your sales force? For each measure, describe how you would use it and at what interval you would need to update this information.

10. Find an organization that is utilizing customer relationship management (visit vendor Web sites for case studies or industry journals such as *CIO Magazine* or *Computerworld*). Who within the organization is most involved in this process, and who benefits?

11. Discuss the ethical trade-offs involved when using large databases that profile and categorize customers so that companies can more effectively market their products. Think about products that are "good" for the consumer versus those that are not.

12. Search the Web for recent articles on business process management and related approaches (e.g., business process reengineering) for improving organizations. What is the current state of the art for these approaches? To what extent are these "headlines" about information systems implementations, especially regarding enterprise systems?

13. Use the Web to visit a distribution portal, procurement portal, and trading exchange. What do they have in common? What do they have that is unique?

14. Search the Web for recent stories about the use of SOA. To what extent does it appear that SOA will be replacing ERP systems?

15. What applications other than those mentioned in the chapter are there for RFID tags? What must happen in order for the use of RFID to become more widespread?

Application Exercises

 Note: The existing data files referenced in these exercises are available on the Student Companion Web site: www.pearsonhighered.com/valacich.

Spreadsheet Application: Choosing an ERP System at Campus Travel

Campus Travel is interested in integrating its business processes to streamline processes such as purchasing, sales, human resource management, and customer relationship management. Because of your success in implementing the e-commerce infrastructure, the general manager asks you for advice on what to do to streamline operations at Campus Travel. Use the data provided in the file ERPSystems.csv to make a recommendation about which ERP system to purchase. The file includes ratings of the different modules of the systems and the weights assigned to these ratings. You are asked to do the following:

1. Determine the product with the highest overall rating (Hint: Use the SUMPRODUCT formula to multiply each vendor's scores with the respective weights and add the weighted scores.)

2. Prepare the necessary graphs to compare the products on the different dimensions and the overall score.

3. Be sure to professionally format the graphs before printing them out.

Database Application: Managing Customer Relations at Campus Travel

Not all frequent fliers accumulate large amounts of miles. There are many who never travel for years but have frequent flier accounts. As manager of sales and marketing, you want to find out how to target these individuals with promotions and special offers. To accomplish this task, you will need to create the following reports:

1. A report displaying all frequent fliers, sorted by distance traveled

2. A report displaying all frequent fliers, sorted by the total amount spent on air travel.

In the file InfrequentFliers.mdb, you find travel data of the members of a frequent flier program for the year 2008. Prepare professionally formatted printouts of all reports, including headers, footers, dates, and so on. (Hint: Use the report wizard to create the reports; use queries to sum up the fares and distances for each traveler before creating the respective reports.)

Team Work Exercise: ERP, CRM, and SCM

Work in a small group with classmates and use a search engine such as Google to search the Web for sites with information on ERP, CRM, and SCM. What types of Web sites are you finding? Choose a particular software package related to ERP, CRM, or SCM and split up your group to research the company's site as well as related articles on the system at an online magazine such as *InformationWeek* or *Computerworld*. Get back together with your group and discuss your findings. How is the system portrayed by the company/vendors and by the magazines? Does the product seem to deliver what the company promises? Prepare a brief presentation of your findings.

Answers to the Self-Study Questions

1. B, p. 361	**2.** B, p. 365	**3.** A, p. 366	**4.** C, p. 369	**5.** C, p. 380
6. B, p. 381	**7.** C, p. 387	**8.** A, p. 390	**9.** D, p. 395	**10.** B, p. 372

Case ❶

The Battle for the Dashboard

Competition is stiff among electronics manufacturers as they battle for dominance of consumers' living rooms, desktops, and mobile devices. Now the battle extends to the automobile industry.

For the first time in the event's history, when the International Consumer Electronics Show (CES) opened in Las Vegas on January 8, 2008, an executive from the automobile manufacturing industry delivered the keynote address. General Motors Corporation CEO Rick Wagoner arrived on stage in GM's electric-powered Chevy Volt and told the audience that if the automobile were invented in 2008, he was "pretty sure" it would debut at the CES. GM views electronics as a new frontier for automobile manufacturers. Just as the electronics industry "stays young" by constantly coming up with new gadgets, Wagoner commented, GM intended to stay young by "reinventing the automobile . . . with a lot of that based on electronics."

Cars already incorporate many of the electronics consumers have grown to love, such as GPS, TV screens, voice-activated radios, touch-screen monitors, BlackBerry enabled ports, and mobile phone dialing. Coming soon are headrests with computers in them (with monitors in the back of the headrest), WiFi in dashboards, cars that talk to each other, and, according to GM's Wagoner, cars that drive themselves.

Yes, drive themselves. Cars of the near future will contain electronic sensors to alert drivers to objects in the road ahead or behind if the vehicle is in reverse, and vehicle-to-vehicle (V2V) transponder systems will let other cars know when conditions are changing, as when one car in a row of cars is braking. Electronics will also eventually keep cars spaced appropriately during highway driving, make cars obey all traffic signals, and allow cars to communicate with highway information centers along main routes.

As the highlight of his 2008 CES address, Wagoner introduced GM's Cadillac Provoq, powered by the company's fifth-generation fuel cell system and a lithium-ion battery pack. The Provoq relies on three electric motors and can drive up to 300 miles on a single fill of hydrogen or 20 miles using electricity alone.

As the electronics and auto industries merge, the technology-dominated home and workplace environments will no longer be separate from the automobile environment. According to GM's head of research and development, Larry Burns, "Consumers don't want to have a different experience when they're in their car versus when they're outside their car, so I think that tying in with consumer electronics is going to be really important for the future of our industry. Connectivity will be mainstream with the auto industry."

Questions

1. How can enterprise systems help companies like GM better manage supplier and customer relationships, especially as the automobile industry is transformed?
2. Which capabilities of enterprise systems will be most critical for manufacturing or selling the cars of the future?
3. What capabilities would you like to see in the car of the future?

Based on:

Abuelsamid, S. (2008, January 8). CES 2008: Live blogging the Rick Wagoner keynote on Electric Avenue. *Autoblog.com*. Retrieved May 27, 2008, from http://www.autoblog.com/2008/01/08/ces-2008-live-blogging-the-rick-wagoner-keynote.

Hartley, M. (2008, January 9). The battle for the dashboard. *Reportonbusiness.com.* Retrieved May 27, 2008, from http://www.theglobeandmail.com/servlet/story/LAC.20080109.RCES09/TPStory/Business.

Massy, K. (2008, January 8). GM's Wagoner addresses CES, unveils Cadillac Provoq. *CNET.com.* Retrieved May 27, 2008, from http://ces.cnet.com/8301-1_1-9846322-67.html.

Case ❷

Real or Fake? Tech May Tell

Fake currency, credit cards, passports, and identification. Knock-off designer bags and clothing, and forged masterpiece paintings. Piracy of software, movies, and music CDs. Scams selling fake vintage wines, adulterated or completely fake brand-name drugs, and . . . counterfeit seeds. Counterfeiting is all pervasive. Customers who buy knock-off designer bags or not-so-vintage wines are gypped and inconvenienced; piracy fleeces the music and entertainment industries of profits. Horror stories abound about people who purchase drugs over the Internet only to receive a harmful version of the medicine they thought they were buying.

Can technology come to the rescue? With counterfeiting at an all-time high, there is a growing need, internationally, for a quick and easy way to detect fraudulent products, and authentication technologies and products may be the answer. The role of authentication technology is to allow inspection agencies—customs agents, food and drug inspectors, police—to detect which products are genuine and which are fake in ways that are not obvious.

Counterfeit detection often depends on layered systems that, on first glance, make the product look genuine, but in underlying layers betray the product as fake. For example, hologram images embedded within a wine label or other product tags that are not readily visible to the naked eye, but can be read using a simple laser pointer. The use of technology to detect counterfeit products includes the following specific examples:

- Xerox Corporation's Anti-Counterfeit Detection (ACD) technology was developed in response to U.S. government regulations requiring photocopier suppliers to use technology that deters people from using copy machines to counterfeit currency, stock warrants, and bonds. The ACD system can recognize certain currency and other documents and prevent their reproduction, display, or transmission on machines that have installed the system.
- ProTag from Germain's Technology Group protects seeds, seed treatments, and packaging with a polymer security coating. The system consists of a tagged, chemically inert but stable polymer and a dedicated reader that uses nuclear magnetic resonance (NMR) technology to quickly detect counterfeits.
- The Rapid Assessment of Infringement and Diversioning (RAID) program runs a sweep of a company's product line to reveal certain counterfeit activities and other forms of fraud. The program is intended for use in detecting intellectual property theft, copyright infringement, supply chain diversion, licensed plant over-production, and product cloning.

In recent legislation—the FDA Revitalization Act—the U.S. government mandated that counterfeiting detection technology be employed to verify the authenticity of drugs sold to the American public. The bill also had implications for radio frequency identification (RFID), since it mandates RFID technology for the unique numerical identifiers used for drug packaging.

Indeed, technology seems a practical and reliable solution for distinguishing between fake products and the real thing.

Questions

1. What are the pros and cons of knowingly buying a fake/knock-off product?
2. Should it be illegal to knowingly own a fake/knock-off product?
3. Beyond what was described in the case, what other ways might technology assist in identifying or limiting the distribution of fake/knock-off products?

Based on:

Anonymous (2006, April). The role of authentication technologies in combating counterfeiting. *WIPO Magazine.* Retrieved May 27, 2008, from http://www.wipo.int/wipo_magazine/en/2006/02/article_0004.html.

Anonymous (2008, April 21). Grand ISS continues to innovate counterfeiting solutions with the release of its R.A.I.D. program. *Newswire Today.* Retrieved May 27, 2008, from http://www.newswiretoday.com/news/33011.

Anonymous (n.d.). Anti-counterfeit detection. Retrieved May 27, 2008, from http://www.xeroxtechnology.com/acd.

Anonymous (n.d.). Brand protection—counterfeit seed technology. *BPCouncil.* Retrieved May 27, 2008, from http://www.bpcouncil.com/apage/569.php.

Anonymous (n.d.). New U.S. legislation mandates "counterfeit-resistant technologies." *BPCouncil.* Retrieved May 27, 2008, from http://www.bpcouncil.com/apage/394.php.

Developing and Acquiring Information Systems

After reading this chapter, you will be able to do the following:

1. Understand the process used by organizations to manage the development of information systems.

2. Describe each major phase of the systems development life cycle: systems planning and selection; systems analysis; systems design; systems implementation and operation.

3. Describe prototyping, rapid application development, and object-oriented analysis and design, along with each approach's strengths and weaknesses.

4. Understand the factors involved in building a system in-house, along with situations in which it is not feasible.

5. Explain three alternative systems development options: external acquisition, outsourcing, and end-user development.

Preview

As you have read throughout this book and have experienced in your own life, information systems are of many different types, including electronic commerce (EC) systems to efficiently process online transactions, decision support systems (DSS) to aid managerial decision making, or customer relationship management (CRM) systems to provide improved customer service. Just as there are different types of systems, different approaches have been found to be more appropriate for developing some types of systems and less appropriate for others. Learning all the possible ways to develop or acquire information systems and, more important, how to identify the optimal approach takes years of study and experience.

If you are a business student majoring in areas such as marketing, finance, accounting, human resources, operations, and so on, you might be wondering why we have a chapter on building and acquiring information systems. The answer is simple: No matter what area of an organization you are in, you will be involved in the systems development or acquisition process. In fact, research indicates that the IS spending in most organizations is controlled by specific business functions, rather than by the information systems (IS) department. What this means is that even if your career interests are in something other than IS, it is very likely that you will be involved in the IS development or acquisition process. Understanding all available options is important to your future success.

Managing in the Digital World: Casual Gaming: You, Me, and Wii

Think of "gamers" and chances are you visualize a portly, unkempt couch potato hunched over a game controller, fingers flying, for hours or maybe days at a time. Or maybe you see a hard-core nerd whose brain functions well only in virtual mode. In the past, the term "gamers" referred mostly to participants in role-playing or war games, but today it refers also to casual gamers who indulge occasionally for fun, but also maintain a functioning life in the "real" world.

For gamers—both hard-core and casual—the big three in gaming consoles have been Sony PlayStation, Microsoft's Xbox, and in third place, Nintendo's GameCube. Then in 2006 Nintendo differentiated itself from its competitors by introducing the Wii that offered a level of *physical* gamer participation hitherto unknown (see Figure 10.1). Instead of exercising just the fingers to move around a game, the Wii's wireless, motion-sensing controllers let players get entire bodies involved. Wii Sports, for example, gets players of all ages off the couch and swinging a baseball bat (with the help of a special interactivity-enabling device called the Wiimote), lobbing tennis balls, or driving golf balls.

The Wii also introduced a different way for players to interact with each other. Instead of going online to compete with players in distant locations, Wii gamers can participate with family members and friends in their own living rooms. Dance together (on a special dance pad), form bowling teams, or call friends together for a complete group workout using special mat-like controllers that detect distribution of weight.

Nintendo's gamble that consumers would enjoy playing games that require less time, less skill, and more closely parallel real-life activities paid off. Seven months after the Wii's introduction, production had not kept up with demand and would-be buyers were lining up in front of stores such as Toys "R" Us and Best Buy, only to find that the latest shipment of the product was already sold out.

One important reason for the Wii's success was that the product targeted casual gamers—those who did not play games at all or played them only occasionally because of the time required to master most games and the dexterity required. The multibillion-dollar gaming industry had long been concerned that devoted gamers would eventually move on to other types of entertainment, but the casual gaming market has given the industry new life. Games that take minutes to master on platforms such as Wii and Nintendo's DS are currently popular, as are inexpensive, downloadable games such as *MapleStory* and *KartRider,* and free, non-timed games such as *Bejeweled* that computer users can play online without downloading or using any special software or equipment.

The key to any successful product is volume, and the time has come for casual gaming. Game developers are working hard to provide shorter, less complicated, more interactive games for those who want to play occasionally, but don't want games to be their one consuming passion.

FIGURE 10.1

The Nintendo Wii puts the gamer into the game.

After reading this chapter, you will be able to answer the following:

1. What process would you use if you were designing a new computer game?

2. How would the process of determining system requirements differ if you were designing a new payroll system versus a new game?

3. How important is system testing for an online game versus a traditional type of software, such as a payroll system?

Based on:

Bishop, T. (2007, July 12). New Wii controller turns your video game into workout. *SeattleP.,com.* Retrieved May 12, 2008, from http://seattlepi.nwsource.com/business/323343_nintendosony12.html.

Gaudiosi, J. (2007, April 24). Games continue record pace. *Home Media Magazine.* Retrieved May 12, 2008, from http://www.homememediamagazine.com/news/html/breaking_article.cfm?article_id=10568.

Kim, R. (2007, May 18). Wii needs more games: Developers push to meet demand on popular box. *SFGate.com.* Retrieved May 12, 2008, from http://www.sfgate.com/cgi-bin/article.cgi?f=/c/a/2007/05/18/BUG0FPT1J31.DTL.

Kohler, C. (2007, June 11). Triumph of the Wii: How fun won out in the console wars. *Wired.* Retrieved May 12, 2008, from http://www.wired.com:80/gaming/hardware/news/2007/06/wii?currentPage=2.

Kohler, C. (2008, February 6). Game biz guns for mainstream by going casual. *Wired.* Retrieved May 12, 2008, from http://www.wired.com/gaming/gamingreviews/news/2008/02/dice_walkup.

Rosmarin, R. (2007, November 16). Wii rules! *Forbes.com.* Retrieved May 12, 2008, from http://www.forbes.com/2007/11/15/wii-games-xbox-technology-personaltech-cx_rr_1116wii.html.

Seven months later, Wii demand still outpaces supply. (2007, July 2). Retrieved May 12, 2008, from http://www.foxnews.com/story/0,2933,287678,00.html?sPage=fnc.scitech/videogaming.

Customized Versus Off-the-Shelf Software

When deciding to implement new systems to support their operations in order to gain or sustain a competitive advantage, organizations can typically choose between customized and off-the-shelf software. Many types of application software (such as word processors, spreadsheet, or accounting software) can be used by a variety of businesses within and across industries. These types of general purpose systems are typically purchased off-the-shelf. Oftentimes, however, organizations have very specific needs that cannot be met by generic software. This is especially true for companies trying to capitalize on a first-mover advantage and therefore may not be able to purchase an existing system to meet their specific needs. For example, pioneers in online retailing (such as Amazon.com) or budget air travel (such as Southwest Airlines) needed entirely new systems to support their revolutionary business models and had to develop (or have someone else develop) customized solutions. The approaches to developing or acquiring customized and off-the-shelf systems are quite different, but also have many similarities. Before going into the details of developing or acquiring such systems, we'll first contrast these two types of software.

Customized Software

Customized software is developed to meet the specifications of an organization. This software may be developed in-house by the company's own information systems staff, or it may be contracted, or outsourced, to a specialized vendor charged with developing the software to the company's contractual specifications. Customized application software has two primary advantages over general purpose commercial software:

1. *Customizability.* It can be tailored to meet unique organizational requirements. Such requirements, for example, can reflect a desire to achieve a competitive advantage through a specific type of system (e.g., Amazon's one-click ordering) or to better fit business operations, characteristics of the organizational culture, proprietary security requirements, or to better interface with existing systems.

2. *Problem Specificity.* The company pays only for the features specifically required for its users. For example, company- or industry-specific terms or acronyms can be included in the program, as can unique types of required reports. Such specificity is not typically possible in off-the-shelf programs that are targeted to a general audience.

TABLE 10.1 Examples of Off-the-Shelf Application Software

Category	Application	Description	Examples
Business information systems	Payroll	Automation of payroll services, from the optical reading of time sheets to generating pay checks	www.zpay.com www.payroll.com
	Inventory	Automation of inventory tracking, order processing, billing, and shipping	www.QuickBooksRetailers.com www.inventorysoft.com
Office automation	Personal productivity	Support for a wide range of tasks from word processing to graphics to e-mail	www.openoffice.org www.corel.com www.microsoft.com/office

Today, building a complete system from scratch is quite rare; most information systems that are developed within an organization for its internal use typically include a large number of preprogrammed, reusable modules that are purchased from development organizations or consultants.

Off-the-Shelf Software

Although customized software has advantages, it is not automatically the best choice for an organization. **Off-the-shelf software** (or packaged software) is typically used to support common business processes that do not require any specific tailoring. In general, off-the-shelf software is less costly, faster to procure, of higher quality, and less risky than customized software. Table 10.1 summarizes examples of off-the-shelf application software.

Combining Customized and Off-the-Shelf Software

It is possible to combine the advantages of customized and off-the-shelf software. Companies can purchase off-the-shelf software and then modify it for their own use. For example, a retailer may want to purchase an off-the-shelf inventory management program and then modify it to account for the specific products, outlets, and reports it needs to conduct its day-to-day business. In some cases, the company selling the software makes these customized changes for a fee. Other vendors, however, do not allow their software to be modified.

Commercial, off-the-shelf software is always acquired from an external vendor (unless you *are* the vendor, such as personnel within Microsoft using Word for their word processing tasks), whereas customized software can be either developed in-house or developed by an outside vendor (see Figure 10.2).

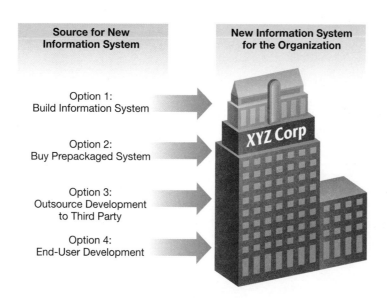

FIGURE 10.2

There are a variety of sources for information systems.

Coming Attraction

Microsoft's Surface

If you have ever watched the television show *CSI Miami*, you have seen Surface in action (not the actual machine, but a demonstration of the technology). A technician uses her fingers to manipulate images—photos, microscope slides, documents—on a flat horizontal surface in front of her, and she can "throw" the images to a larger screen that displays them vertically. If you thought the concept was still science fiction, you were wrong.

The technology exists, and Microsoft introduced it to the public commercially in April 2008. At that time, select hotels, restaurants, retail outlets, and public entertainment venues were to begin using the technology. The computer, which one only needs fingers to operate, is called Surface (see Figure 10.3).

With Surface, Microsoft reveals, "We can actually grab data with our hands and move information between objects with natural gestures and touch." No keyboards, no mice, just a thirty-inch tabletop display where fingers do the walking . . . and drawing . . . and writing . . . and tapping. And more than one user at once can manipulate data. Users can also place physical objects, like cell phones and even drinks, on the surface to see additional information revealed, such as the features present in the cell phone or the ingredients in a drink. Surface uses cameras to sense objects, hand gestures, and touch. User input is processed and the results are projected on the tabletop surface.

Microsoft chose AT&T to present Surface to the public. In select cities—New York, Atlanta, San Francisco, and San Antonio—shoppers can interact with Surface to see how certain AT&T cell phones compare or to examine a map of an area in the city. Later, users purchasing cell phones will be able to drag and drop ringtones, graphics, and videos into the phones. Also in the future: Tabletops in restaurants can use Surface to display menus and to analyze drinks, as in the above example. Users can place an MP3 player on Surface, quickly see a menu of tunes, and tap on titles to play them.

Microsoft's Surface looks fun and looks like an interesting way to involve more than one user at a time in game playing or other digital activities, but its commercial success is yet to be determined. If it flies in the retail world, it could become as familiar as the past's mall kiosks, library, and restaurant touch-screens or even last year's monitor.

FIGURE 10.3

The Microsoft Surface.

Based on:

Chen, J. (2008, May 8). Microsoft Surface + Xbox 360 = What? *Gizmodo*. Retrieved May 12, 2008, from http://gizmodo.com/388749/microsoft-surface-%252B-xbox-360–what.

Costa, D. (2007, May 30). Hands on with "Microsoft Surface": The coffee-table PC. *PC Mag*. Retrieved May 12, 2008, from http://www.pcmag.com/article2/0,1759,2138251,00.asp.

Derene, G. (2007, July). Microsoft Surface: Behind-the-scenes first look. *Popular Mechanics*. Retrieved May 12, 2008, from http://www.popularmechanics.com/technology/industry/4217348.html.

Microsoft Surface (n.d.). Retrieved May 12, 2008, from http://www.microsoft.com/surface/index.html.

Riley, D. (2008, April 1). Microsoft Surface coming to AT&T stores. *Techcrunch*. Retrieved May 12, 2008, from http://www.techcrunch.com/2008/04/01/microsoft-surface-coming-to-att-stores.

Regardless of the source of the new information system, the primary role of managers and users in the organization is to make sure that any new system will meet the organization's business needs. This means that managers and users must understand the systems development process to ensure that the system will meet their needs. In the following section, we will first describe the general structured process of developing an information system, followed by a discussion of the options organizations have when implementing new systems.

The Need for Structured Systems Development

No matter if a software company such as Microsoft is planning to build a new version of its popular Office software suite or a company such as Netflix is trying to build a system to improve its movie recommendations, companies have to follow a standardized approach. This process of designing, building, and maintaining information systems is often referred to as **systems analysis and design**. Likewise, the individual who performs this task is referred to as a **systems analyst**. Because few organizations can survive without effectively utilizing information and computing technology, the demand for skilled systems analysts is very strong. In fact, *US News and World Report* named being a systems analyst one of the thirty-one best jobs for 2009. Likewise, the U.S. Bureau of Labor Statistics ranks systems analysts near the top of all professions for job stability, income, and employment growth through 2016, with average growth exceeding 29 percent. Organizations want to hire systems analysts because they possess a unique blend of managerial and technical expertise—systems analysts are not just "techies." In fact, systems analysts remain in demand precisely because of this unique blend of abilities, but it was not always this way.

The Evolution of Information Systems Development

In the early days of computing, systems development was considered an art that only a few technical "gurus" could master. Unfortunately, the techniques used to construct systems varied greatly from individual to individual. This variation made it difficult to integrate large organizational information systems. Furthermore, many systems were not easily maintainable after the original developer left the organization. As a result, organizations were often left with systems that were very difficult and expensive to maintain. Many organizations, therefore, underutilized these technology investments and failed to realize all possible benefits from their systems.

To address this problem, information systems professionals concluded that system development needed to become an engineering-like discipline (Nunamaker, 1992). Common methods, techniques, and tools had to be developed to create a disciplined approach for constructing information systems. This evolution from an "art" to a "discipline" led to the use of the term **software engineering** to help define what systems analysts and programmers do. Transforming information systems development into a formal discipline would provide numerous benefits. First, it would be much easier to train programmers and analysts if common techniques were widely used. In essence, if all systems analysts had similar training, it would make them more interchangeable and more skilled at working on the systems developed by other analysts. Second, systems built with commonly used techniques would be more maintainable. Both industry and academic researchers have pursued the quest for new and better approaches for building information systems.

Information Systems Development in Action

The tools and techniques used to develop information systems are continually evolving with the rapid changes in information systems hardware and software. As you will see, the information systems development approach is a very structured process that moves from step to step. Systems analysts become adept at decomposing large, complex problems into many small, simple problems. They can then easily solve each simple

FIGURE 10.4

Problem decomposition makes solving large, complex problems easier.

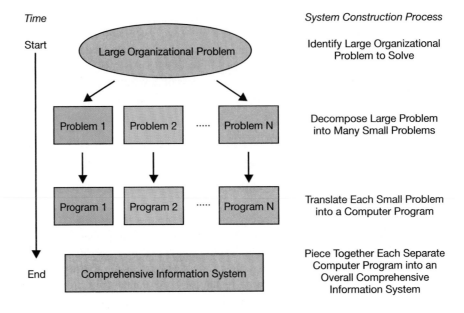

problem by writing a relatively short computer program (or by purchasing prepackaged modules that meet their needs). The goal of the systems analyst is to build the final system by piecing together the many small programs and modules into one comprehensive system. This process of decomposing a problem is outlined in Figure 10.4. An easy way to think about this is to think about using LEGO blocks for building a model of a medieval castle. Each individual block is a small, simple piece that is nothing without the others. When put together, the blocks can create a large and very complex design. When systems are built in this manner, they are much easier to design, program, and, most important, maintain.

The Role of Users in the Systems Development Process

Most organizations have a huge investment in transaction processing and management information systems. These systems are most often designed, constructed, and maintained by systems analysts within the organization, using a variety of methods. When building and maintaining information systems, systems analysts rely on information provided by system users, who are involved in all phases of the system's development process. To effectively participate in the process, it is important for all members of the organization to understand what is meant by systems development and what activities occur. A close, mutually respectful working relationship between analysts and users is a key to project success. Now that you understand the history and need for systems development, it is time to consider some of the relevant techniques that are used in systems development.

Steps in the Systems Development Process

Just as the products that a firm produces and sells follow a life cycle, so does an organizational information system. For example, a new type of tennis shoe follows a life cycle of being designed, introduced to the market, being accepted into the market, maturing, declining in popularity, and ultimately being retired. The term **systems development life cycle (SDLC)** describes the life of an information system from conception to retirement (Valacich, George, and Hoffer, 2009). The SDLC has four primary phases:

1. Systems planning and selection
2. Systems analysis
3. Systems design
4. Systems implementation and operation

Figure 10.5 is a graphical representation of the SDLC containing four boxes connected by arrows. Within the SDLC, arrows flow from systems planning and selection, to

Conquering Computer Contagion

Blue Security, an Israel-based Internet security company start-up, thought it had the answer to spammers. For every unwanted spam message that the half million clients of the company's service, Blue Frog, received, a message was returned to the advertiser. As a result, six of the top ten spammers were inundated by the opt-out messages and were forced to eliminate Blue Frog's clients from their mailing list. One spamming company, however, decided to fight back. According to Blue Security, PharmaMaster responded by sending so many spam messages to Blue Frog's clients that several Internet service provider servers crashed. Under PharmaMaster's threat of continuing and expanded attacks, on May 2, 2006, Blue Security folded. "We cannot take the responsibility for an ever-escalating cyberwar through our continued operations," said Eran Reshef, chief executive officer (CEO) and founder of Blue Security.

Like PharmaMaster, all authors of malware (destructive computer code such as viruses, Trojan horses and worms, and intrusive pop-up and spam ads) have continued to flout efforts to cleanse the Internet of their disruptive and exasperating wares, as evidenced by statistics gathered for just two months in 2008. The top 10 malware reported to Sophos, an Internet security firm, in June 2008 are shown in Table 10.2.

Unfortunately, the battle against malware will probably rage as long as the Internet exists. On the plus side, however, the battle has given rise to new enterprises dedicated solely to protecting Internet users—the "white knights" who will continue to come to the rescue as long as the malware threat exists.

Based on:

Lemos, R. (2006, May 17). Blue Security folds under spammer's wrath. *SecurityFocus*. Retrieved May 12, 2008, from http://www.securityfocus.com/news/11392.

Top 10 malware reported to Sophos in June 2008 (n.d.). Retrieved July 12, 2008, from http://www.sophos.com/security/top-10.

TABLE 10.2 Top 10 Malware Reported to Sophos in June 2008

Rank	Virus	Percent of Reports
1	Troj/Agent	19.9
2	Troj/Pushdo	18.6
3	W32/Netsky	17.6
4	Troj/Dropr	8.3
5	Mal/Iframe	7.4
6	W32/Traxg	5.6
7	Troj/Clagger	5.6
8	W32/MYtob	4.5
9	W32/MYDoom	3.3
10	W32/Bagle	1.3
	Others	7.9

Source: http://www.sophos.com/security/top-10.

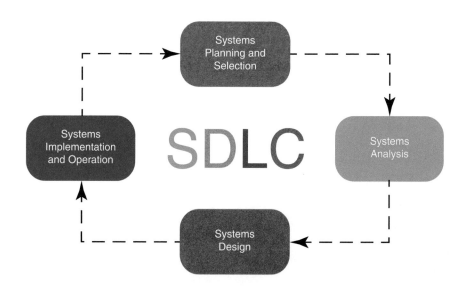

FIGURE 10.5

The systems development life cycle defines the typical process for building systems.

systems analysis, to systems design, and, finally, to systems implementation and operation. Once a system is in operation, it moves into an ongoing maintenance phase that parallels the initial development process. For example, when new features are added to an existing system, analysts must first plan and select which new features to add, then analyze the possible impact of adding these features to the existing system, then design how the new features will work, and, finally, implement these new features into the existing system. In this way, the SDLC becomes an ongoing *cycle*.

Phase 1: Systems Planning and Selection

The first phase of the SDLC is **systems planning and selection**, as shown in Figure 10.6. Understanding that it can work on only a limited number of projects at a given time because of limited resources, an organization must take care that only those projects that are critical to enabling the organization's mission, goals, and objectives are undertaken. Consequently, the goal of systems planning and selection is simply to identify, plan, and select a development project from all possible projects that could be performed. Organizations differ in how they identify, plan, and select projects. Some organizations have a formal **information systems planning** process whereby a senior manager, a business group, an IS manager, or a steering committee identifies and assesses all possible systems development projects that an organization could undertake. Others follow a more ad hoc process for identifying potential projects. Nonetheless, after all possible projects are identified, those deemed most likely to yield significant organizational benefits, given available resources, are selected for subsequent development activities.

It is important to note that different approaches for identifying and selecting projects are likely to yield different organizational outcomes (see Table 10.3). For example, projects identified by top management more often have a strategic organizational focus, and projects identified by steering committees more often reflect the diversity of the committee and therefore have a cross-functional focus. Projects identified by individual

FIGURE 10.6

Phase 1 of the SDLC focuses on project identification, planning, and selection.

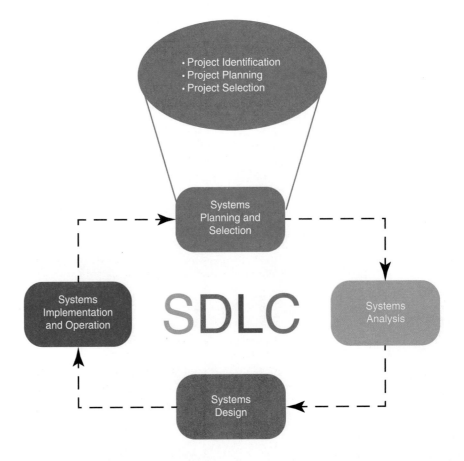

TABLE 10.3 **Sources of Systems Development Projects and Their Likely Focus**

Project Source	Primary Focus
Top management	Broad, strategic
Steering committee	Cross-functional
Individual departments and business units	Narrow, tactical
Systems development group	Integration with existing information systems

Adapted from McKeen, Guimaraes, and Wetherbe (1994).

departments or business units most often have a narrow, tactical focus. Finally, the typical focus of projects identified by the development group is the ease with which existing hardware and systems can be integrated with the proposed project. Other factors—such as project cost, duration, complexity, and risk—are also influenced by the source of a given project. The source of projects has been found to be a key indicator of project focus and success.

Just as there are often differences in the source of systems projects within organizations, there are often different evaluation criteria used within organizations when classifying and ranking potential projects. During project planning, the analyst works with the customers—the potential users of the system and their managers—to collect a broad range of information to gain an understanding of the project size, potential benefits and costs, and other relevant factors. After collecting and analyzing this information, the analyst can bring it together into a summary planning document that can be reviewed and compared with other possible projects. Table 10.4 provides a sample of the criteria often used by organizations. When reviewing a potential development project, organizations may focus on a single criterion but most often examine multiple criteria to make a decision to accept or reject a project. If the organization accepts the project, systems analysis begins.

Phase 2: Systems Analysis

The second phase of the SDLC is called **systems analysis**, as highlighted in Figure 10.7. One purpose of the systems analysis phase is for designers to gain a thorough understanding of an organization's current way of doing things in the area for which the new information system will be constructed. The process of conducting an analysis requires that many tasks, or subphases, be performed. The first subphase focuses on determining system requirements. To determine the requirements, an analyst works closely with users to determine

TABLE 10.4 **Possible Evaluation Criteria for Classifying and Ranking Projects**

Evaluation Criteria	Description
Strategic alignment	The extent to which the project is viewed as helping the organization achieve its strategic objectives and long-term goals.
Potential benefits	The extent to which the project is viewed as improving profits, customer service, and so forth, and the duration of these benefits.
Potential costs and resource availability	The number and types of resources the project requires and their availability.
Project size and duration	The number of individuals and the length of time needed to complete the project.
Technical difficulty and risks	The level of technical difficulty involved in successfully completing the project within a given time and resource constraint.

Source: Valacich, George, and Hoffer (2009).

FIGURE 10.7

Phase 2 of the SDLC focuses on collecting requirements and modeling data, processes, and logic.

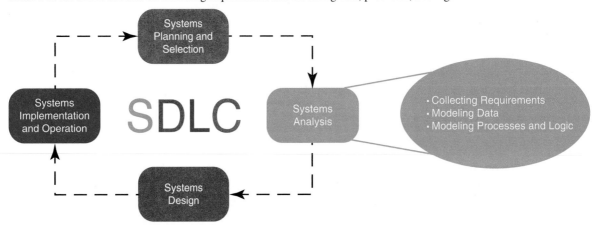

what is needed from the proposed system. After collecting the requirements, analysts organize this information using data, process, and logic modeling tools. These elements will be illustrated and discussed later in the chapter.

Collecting Requirements The collection and structuring of requirements is arguably the most important activity in the systems development process because how well the information system requirements are defined influences all subsequent activities. The old saying "garbage in, garbage out" very much applies to the systems development process. **Requirements collection** is the process of gathering and organizing information from users, managers, business processes, and documents to understand how a proposed information system should function. Systems analysts use a variety of techniques for collecting system requirements, including the following (Valacich et al., 2009):

▪ *Interviews.* Analysts interview people informed about the operation and issues of the current or proposed system.
▪ *Questionnaires.* Analysts design and administer surveys to gather opinions from people informed about the operation and issues of the current or proposed system.
▪ *Observations.* Analysts observe workers at selected times to see how data are handled and what information people need to do their jobs.
▪ *Document Analysis.* Analysts study business documents to discover issues, policies, and rules as well as concrete examples of the use of data and information in the organization.

In addition to these techniques, there are other contemporary approaches for collecting system requirements, including the following:

▪ *Critical Success Factors Methodology.* A **critical success factor (CSF)** is something that must go well to ensure success for a manager, department, division, or organization. To understand an organization's CSFs, a systems analyst interviews people throughout the organization and asks each person to define his or her own personal CSFs. After the analyst collects these individual CSFs, he or she can merge, consolidate, and refine them to identify a broad set of organization-wide CSFs, as shown in Figure 10.8. Table 10.5 summarizes the strengths and weaknesses of the CSF approach.
▪ *Joint Application Design.* **Joint application design (JAD)** is a process used for requirements collection. Using JAD, all (or most) users meet with the analyst at the same time in a special type of a group meeting. During this meeting, the users *jointly* define and agree on system requirements or designs. This process can result in dramatic reductions in the length of time needed to collect requirements or specify designs. The JAD meeting can be held in a normal conference room or special-purpose JAD room (see Figure 10.9). Table 10.6 summarizes the strengths and weaknesses of the JAD approach.

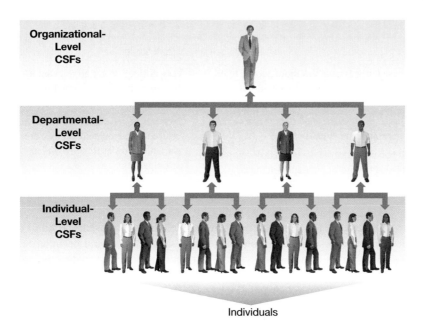

FIGURE 10.8

Merging individual CSFs to represent organization-wide CSFs.

TABLE 10.5 Strengths and Weaknesses of the CSF Approach

Strengths	Weaknesses
Senior managers intuitively understand the approach and support its usage.	High-level focus can lead to an oversimplification of a complex situation.
Provides a method for understanding the information needs of the organization in order to make effective decisions.	Difficulty in finding analysts trained to perform the CSF process, which requires both understanding of information systems and being able to communicate effectively with senior executives.
	Method is analyst focused, rather than being user centered.

Based on Boynton and Zmud (1984).

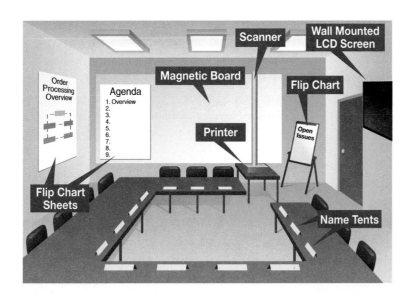

FIGURE 10.9

A JAD room.

Based on: J. Wood and D. Silver, *Joint Application Design* (New York: John Wiley & Sons, 1989).

TABLE 10.6 **Strengths and Weaknesses of the JAD Approach**

Strengths	Weaknesses
Group-based process enables more people to be involved in the development effort without adversely slowing the process.	Very difficult to get all relevant users to the same place at the same time to hold a JAD meeting.
Group-based process can lead to higher levels of system acceptance and quality.	Requires high-level executive sponsor to ensure that adequate resources are available in order to allow widespread participation.
Group involvement in the design and development process helps to ease implementation, user training, and ongoing support.	

Modeling Data Data are facts that describe people, objects, or events. A lot of different facts can be used to describe a person: name, age, gender, race, and occupation, among others. To construct an information system, systems analysts must understand what data the information system needs in order to accomplish the intended tasks. To do this, they use data modeling tools to collect and describe the data to users to confirm that all needed data are known and presented to users as useful information. Figure 10.10 shows an *entity-relationship diagram (ERD)*, a type of data model describing students, classes, majors, and classrooms at a university. Each box in the diagram is referred to as a data entity. Each data entity may have one or more attributes that describe it. For example, a "student" entity may have attributes such as ID, Name, and Local Address. Additionally, each data entity may be "related" to other data entities. For example, because students take classes, there is a relationship between students and classes: "Student Takes Class(es)" and "Class Has Student(s)." Relationships are represented in the diagram by lines drawn between related entities. Data modeling tools enable the systems analyst to represent data in a form that is easy for users to understand and critique. For more information on databases and data modeling, see the Technology Briefing.

Modeling Processes and Logic As the name implies, **data flows** represent the movement of data through an organization or within an information system. For example, your registration for a class may be captured in a registration form on paper or on a computer terminal. After it is filled out, this form probably flows through several processes to validate and record the class registration, as shown as "Data Flows" in

FIGURE 10.10

A sample ERD for students.

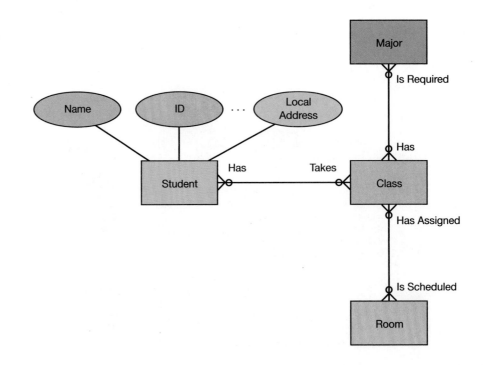

Figure 10.11. After all students have been registered, a repository of all registration information can be processed for developing class rosters or for generating student billing information, which is shown as "Data" in Figure 10.11. **Processing logic** represents the way in which data are transformed. Processing logic is often expressed in **pseudocode**, which is independent of the actual programming language being used. As there are no standards for pseudocode, the level of detail can vary. For example, the

Requirements

FIGURE 10.11

Four key elements to the development of a system: Requirements, Data, Data Flows, and Processing Logic.

Data

Name	Class	GPA
Patty Nicholls	Senior	3.7
Brett Williams	Grad	2.9
Mary Shide	Fresh	3.2

Data Flows

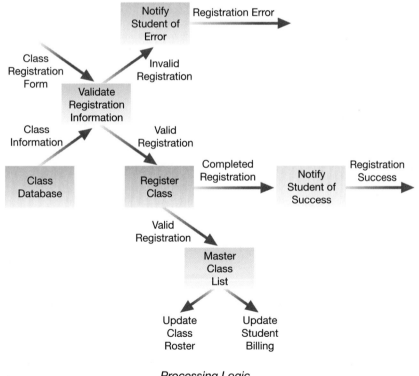

Processing Logic

```
i = read (number_of_classes)
total_hours = 0
total_grade = 0
total_gpa = 0
for j = 1 to i do
        begin
                read (course [ j ], hours [ j ], grade [ j ])
                total_hours = total_hours + hours [ j ]
                total_grade = total_grade + (hours [ j ] * grade [ j ])
        end
current_gpa = total_grade/total hours
```

Powerful Partnerships

MySpace: Tom Anderson and Chris DeWolfe

Anyone under thirty is familiar with the MySpace universe. That's right, MySpace isn't a Web page; it's a universe. And the creators of that universe are Tom Anderson (born in 1970) and Chris DeWolfe (born in 1966) (see Figure 10.12). The two had earlier created an Internet marketing firm that they sold to Intermix, but the big bang came in 2003, when Anderson and DeWolfe decided the world was ready for an online bulletin board on steroids—a place where users could put up personal pages to broadcast their personality traits, interests, goals, and anything else they had to say about themselves. The site was almost instantly successful—by December 2006, beating out eBay, Amazon.com, and Google in page views.

FIGURE 10.12

MySpace founders Chris DeWolfe and Tom Anderson.

DeWolfe and Anderson met during the dot-com boom, when DeWolfe was vice president of sales and marketing at Xdrive, an online storage company, and Anderson was a film student who volunteered to try the company's products. DeWolfe was so impressed with Anderson's comments that he hired him as a copy editor at Xdrive. By 2001, the team had created their first business together—an Internet advertising firm called RB Marketing. When they began thinking about MySpace, Friendster, also a social interaction site, was already up and running, but Anderson and DeWolfe were not concerned. Somewhat revolutionary in their approach to business, the two didn't create a detailed business plan. Instead, they let the site evolve as users commented on their preferences and dislikes. "I tend to see people trying to do stuff that is an uphill struggle," Anderson told *USA Today* in 2006. "Pay attention to what works, and do that."

And they did. MySpace took off from the beginning. So much so, in fact, that the founders did not need to advertise for new users, since word of mouth brought them in by the tens of thousands. One reason the site was successful so quickly was that artists and music groups that wanted to promote themselves were prohibited on other similar sites, but welcomed on MySpace (popular artists like Madonna and U2 and unknown garage bands alike have pages on the site). Unknown bands, for example, were encouraged to post performance schedules and clips of songs for visitors to sample.

Rupert Murdoch bought MySpace in 2005, but the original team still runs the site. DeWolfe, Anderson, and their employees check content constantly, weeding out pornography and other inappropriate content, but they admit that occasionally some of it gets through. As of October 2008, Anderson had more than 245 million "friends" in his profile on MySpace (DeWolfe did not make his profile public).

Based on:

Horning, F. (2007, January 15). "We have replaced MTV." *Spiegel Online.* Retrieved May 12, 2008, from http://www.spiegel.de/international/spiegel/0,1518,459685,00.html.

Pace, N. (2004, January 4). Q&A: MySpace founders Chris DeWolfe and Tom Anderson. *Forbes.com.* Retrieved May 12, 2008, from http://www.forbes.com/2006/01/04/myspace-dewolfe-anderson-cx_np_0104myspace.html.

pseudocode used to calculate students' grade-point averages at the conclusion of a term is shown in the "Processing Logic" section in Figure 10.11.

After the data, data flow, and processing logic requirements for the proposed system have been identified, analysts develop one or many possible overall approaches—sometimes called designs—for the information system. For example, one approach for the system may possess only basic functionality but has the advantage of being relatively easy and inexpensive to build. An analyst might also propose a more elaborate approach for the system, but it may be more difficult and more costly to build. Analysts evaluate alternative system approaches with the knowledge that different solutions yield different benefits and different costs. After a system approach is selected, details of that particular system approach can be defined.

Phase 3: Systems Design

The third phase of the SDLC is **systems design**, as shown in Figure 10.13. As its name implies, it is during this phase that the proposed system is designed; that is, the details of the chosen approach are developed. As with analysis, many different activities must occur during systems design. The elements that must be designed when building an information system include the following:

- Human–computer interface
- Databases and files
- Processing and logic

Designing the Human–Computer Interface Just as people have different ways of interacting with other people, information systems can have different ways of interacting with people. A **human–computer interface (HCI)** might be text-based—communicating with you through text and forcing you to communicate with it the same way. Alternatively, an HCI

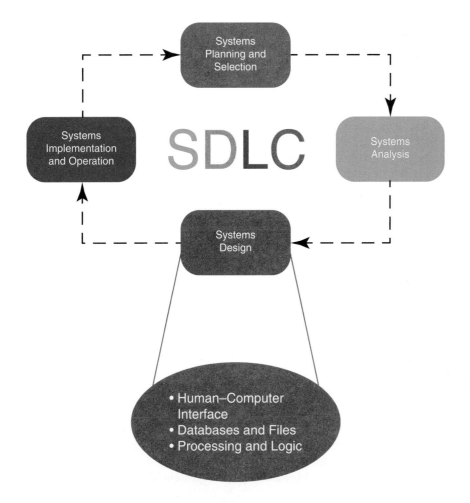

FIGURE 10.13

Phase 3 of the SDLC focuses on developing the details of the chosen approach.

FIGURE 10.14

Yahoo! account registration form.

could use graphics and color as a way to interact with you, providing you with color-coded windows and special icons. For example, both the Mac and the Windows operating systems use an HCI that enables the user to select pictures, icons, and menus to send instructions to the computer; such an interface is referred to as a graphical user interface (GUI) (see Chapter 4—Managing the Information Systems Infrastructure). Over the past several years, standards for user interfaces have emerged, making things easier for both designers and users.

In addition to the HCI, analysts take great care in designing data entry forms and management reports. A form is a business document containing some predefined data, often including some areas where additional data can be filled in (see Figure 10.14). Similarly, a report is a business document containing only predefined data for online viewing or printing (see Figure 10.15).

Designing Databases and Files To design databases and files, a systems analyst must have a thorough understanding of an organization's data and informational needs. As described previously, a systems analyst often uses data modeling tools to first gain a comprehensive understanding of all the data used by a proposed system. After the conceptual data model has been completed, typically using an entity-relationship diagram, it can be easily translated into a *physical* data model in a database management system. For example, Figure 10.16 shows a physical data model to keep track of student information in a Microsoft Access database. The physical data model is more complete (shows each attribute of the student) and more detailed (shows how the information is formatted) than a conceptual data model. For example, contrast Figure 10.16 with the student information contained in the conceptual data model in Figure 10.11.

Designing Processing and Logic The processing and logic operations of an information system are the steps and procedures that transform raw data inputs into new or modified information. For example, when calculating your grade-point average, your school needs to perform the following steps:

1. Obtain the prior grade-point average, credit hours earned, and list of prior courses
2. Obtain the list of each current course, final grade, and course credit hours
3. Combine the prior and current credit hours into aggregate sums
4. Calculate the new grade-point average

The logic and steps needed to make this calculation can be represented in many ways, including structure charts, decision trees, pseudocode, programming code, and so on (see Figure 10.11). Regardless of how the logic is represented, the process of converting

FIGURE 10.15

Sales summary report.

Ascend Systems Incorporated
SALESPERSON ANNUAL SUMMARY REPORT 2010

REGION	SALESPERSON	SSN	QUARTERLY ACTUAL SALES			
			FIRST	SECOND	THIRD	FOURTH
Northwest and Mountain						
	Wachter	999-99-0001	16,500	18,600	24,300	18,000
	Mennecke	999-99-0002	22,000	15,500	17,300	19,800
	Wheeler	999-99-0003	19,000	12,500	22,000	28,000
Midwest and Mid-Atlantic						
	Spurrier	999-99-0004	14,000	16,000	19,000	21,000
	Powell	999-99-0005	7,500	16,600	10,000	8,000
	Topi	999-99-0006	12,000	19,800	17,000	19,000
New England						
	Speier	999-99-0007	18,000	18,000	20,000	27,000
	Morris	999-99-0008	28,000	29,000	19,000	31,000

pseudocode, structure charts, or decision trees into actual program code during system implementation is a relatively straightforward process.

Phase 4: Systems Implementation and Operation

Many separate activities occur during **systems implementation**, the fourth phase of the SDLC, as highlighted in Figure 10.17. One group of activities focuses on transforming the system design into a working information system that can be used by the organization. These activities include software programming and testing. A second group of activities focuses on preparing the organization for using the new information system. These activities include system conversion, documentation, user training, and support. This section briefly describes what occurs during systems implementation.

C:\MSOFFICE\ACCESS\STUDENT.MDB   Saturday, June 23, 2010
Table: Students   Page: 1

Properties
Date Created: 6/23/10 10:35:41 PM   Def. Updatable: Yes
Last Updated: 6/23/10 10:35:43 PM   Record Count: 0

Columns

Name	Type	Size
StudentID	Number (Long)	4
FirstName	Text	50
MiddleName	Text	30
LastName	Text	50
Address	Text	255
City	Text	50
State	Text	50
Region	Text	50
PostalCode	Text	20
PhoneNumber	Text	30
EmailName	Text	50
Major	Text	50
Note	Memo	-

FIGURE 10.16

The physical data model for student information from an Access database.

FIGURE 10.17

Phase 4 of the SDLC focuses on programming, testing, conversion, documentation, training, and support.

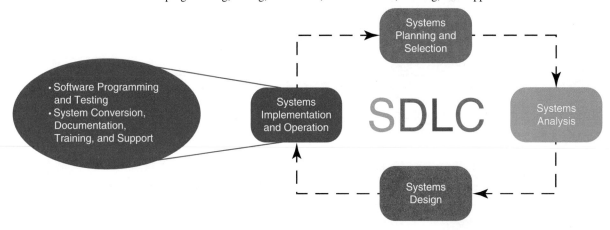

Software Programming and Testing Programming is the process of transforming the system design into a working computer system. During this transformation, both processing and testing should occur in parallel. As you might expect, a broad range of tests are conducted before a system is complete, including **developmental testing**, **alpha testing**, and **beta testing** (see Table 10.7).

System Conversion, Documentation, Training, and Support **System conversion** is the process of decommissioning the current system (automated or manual) and installing the new system in the organization. Effective conversion of a system requires not only that the new software be installed but also that users be effectively trained and supported. System conversion can be performed in at least four ways, as shown in Figure 10.18.

Many types of documentation must be produced for an information system. Programmers develop system documentation that details the inner workings of the system to ease future maintenance. A second type of documentation is user-related documentation, which is typically written not by programmers or analysts but by users or professional technical writers. The range of documents can include the following:

- User and reference guides
- User training manuals and tutorials
- Installation procedures and troubleshooting suggestions

In addition to documentation, users may also need training and ongoing support to use a new system effectively. Different types of training and support require different levels of investment by the organization. Self-paced training and tutorials are the least expensive options, and one-on-one training is the most expensive. Table 10.8 summarizes various user training options.

Besides training, providing ongoing education and problem-solving assistance for users may also be necessary. This is commonly referred to as system support, which is

TABLE 10.7 **General Testing Types, Their Focus, and Who Performs Them**

Testing Type	Focus	Performed by
Developmental	Testing the correctness of individual modules and the integration of multiple modules	Programmer
Alpha	Testing of overall system to see whether it meets design requirements	Software tester
Beta	Testing of the capabilities of the system in the user environment with actual data	Actual system users

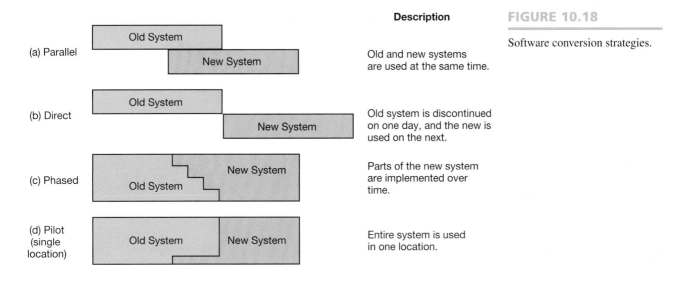

Description

FIGURE 10.18

Software conversion strategies.

(a) Parallel — Old and new systems are used at the same time.

(b) Direct — Old system is discontinued on one day, and the new is used on the next.

(c) Phased — Parts of the new system are implemented over time.

(d) Pilot (single location) — Entire system is used in one location.

often provided by a special group of people in the organization who make up an information center or help desk. Support personnel must have strong communication skills and be good problem solvers in addition to being expert users of the system. An alternative option for a system not developed internally is to outsource support activities to a vendor specializing in technical system support and training. Regardless of how support is provided, it is an ongoing issue that must be managed effectively for the company to realize the maximum benefits of a system.

Ongoing Systems Maintenance

After an information system is installed, it is essentially in the maintenance phase of the SDLC, in which an information system is systematically repaired and/or improved. During maintenance, one person within the systems development group is responsible for collecting maintenance requests from system users. These requests are then analyzed so that the developer can better understand how the proposed change might alter the system and what business benefits and necessities might result from such a change. If the change request is approved, a system change is designed and then implemented. As with the initial development of the system, implemented changes are formally reviewed and tested before installation into operational systems. The **systems maintenance** process parallels the process used for the initial development of the information system, as shown in Figure 10.19. Interestingly, it is during system maintenance that the largest part of the system development effort occurs.

The question must be, then, why does all this maintenance occur? It is not as if software wears out in the physical manner that cars, buildings, or other physical objects do.

TABLE 10.8 User Training Options

Training Option	Description
Tutorial	One person taught at a time by a human or by paper-based exercises
Course	Several people taught at a time
Computer-aided instruction	One person taught at a time by the computer system
Interactive training manuals	Combination of tutorials and computer-aided instruction
Resident expert	Expert on call to assist users as needed
Software help components	Built-in system components designed to train users and troubleshoot problems
External sources	Vendors and training providers to provide tutorials, courses, and other training activities

FIGURE 10.19

Mapping of systems
maintenance activities to the
SDLC.

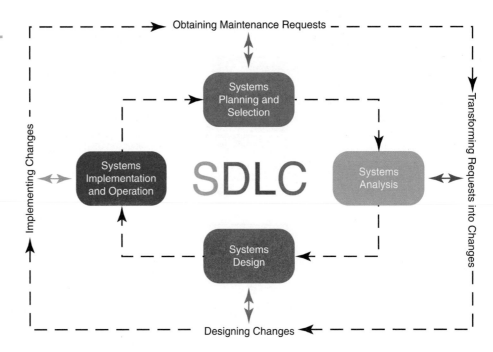

Correct? Yes, but software must still be maintained. The types of maintenance are summarized in Table 10.9.

As with **adaptive maintenance**, both **perfective maintenance** and **preventive maintenance** are typically a much lower priority than **corrective maintenance**, which deals with repairing flaws in the system. Corrective maintenance is most likely to occur after initial system installation, as well as over the life of a system after major system changes. This means that adaptive, perfective, and preventive maintenance activities can lead to corrective maintenance activities if they are not carefully designed and implemented.

Today, vendors of commercial off-the-shelf software packages incorporate **patch management systems** to facilitate the different forms of software maintenance for the user; patch management systems use the Internet to check the software vendor's Web site for available patches and/or updates. If the software vendor offers a new patch, the application will download and install the patch in order to fix the software bug. An example of a patch management system in wide use is the Windows Update Service. The user's operating system automatically connects to a Microsoft Web service to download critical operating system patches for corrective (e.g., to fix bugs in the Windows operating system) or preventive maintenance (e.g., to fix security holes that could be exploited by malicious hackers).

TABLE 10.9   Types of Software Maintenance

Maintenance Type	Description
Corrective maintenance	Making changes to an information system to repair flaws in the design, coding, or implementation
Adaptive maintenance	Making changes to an information system to evolve its functionality, to accommodate changing business needs, or to migrate it to a different operating environment
Perfective maintenance	Making enhancements to improve processing performance or interface usability, or adding desired but not necessarily required system features (in other words, "bells and whistles")
Preventive maintenance	Making changes to a system to reduce the chance of future system failure

As you can see, there is more to system maintenance than you might think. Lots of time, effort, and money are spent in this final phase of a system's development, and it is important to follow prescribed, structured steps. In fact, the approach to systems development described in this chapter—from the initial phase of identifying, selecting, and planning for systems to the final phase of system maintenance—is a very structured and systematic process. Each phase is fairly well prescribed and requires active involvement by systems people, users, and managers. It is likely that you will have numerous opportunities to participate in the acquisition or development of a new system for an organization for which you currently work or will work in the future. Now that you have an understanding of the process, you should be better equipped to make a positive contribution to the success of any systems development project.

Brief Case ⊘

Hackers, Patches, and Reverse Engineering

Microsoft dominates the market for operating systems, which is good news and bad news for the company. It's good news for Microsoft's bottom line but bad news in that its prominence has made its software a popular target for hackers (those who break into computer systems for the purpose of stealing or manipulating data) and other computer criminals. When security experts discover a breach, Microsoft releases a code "patch" to plug security holes. Downloading and installing these patches has become a regularly performed ritual for Windows users (this is often performed in the background).

You might reasonably expect that after an operating system, browser, or other application has been on the market for several years, all security holes will have been detected and closed. Not so. Unfortunately, there are invariably hackers who find new holes that have not yet been detected.

How do hackers find security holes? Smart hackers may study an application until they recognize an entrance hole, while not-so-smart hackers simply "free ride" on the efforts of others by following "recipes" posted on hacker Web sites.

Lately, the frequent release of patches has provided hackers another means of discovering security holes that require less time and effort than studying a program's code. When Microsoft, Mozilla, or other software producers release a security patch, hackers use special software tools to backtrack or reverse engineer the patch. Once they determine the location of the security hole for which the patch was issued, they work on ways to circumvent the patch and exploit the security hole in a new, unpatched way. (**Reverse engineering** is not always destructive and may be legally used to improve a program, but use of the term here implies using the process for unauthorized entry into a computer system.)

Thus, the dilemma for software manufacturers and security companies is this: if they do not release patches, hackers can exploit security holes; if they do release patches, more people will know about the security holes and will attempt to exploit them. Yet consumers using software with security holes expect patches to be issued. The solution? Microsoft tries to deter hackers from reverse engineering by withholding detailed information about patches for security holes for three months after discovery of the hole, but that strategy does not usually deter hackers. There will always be hackers looking for security holes in software, but, fortunately, there will also always be software engineers, programmers, and security experts who can foil hackers' attempts to breach security. Solutions may come after the fact, but they do arrive.

Questions

1. Explain what type(s) of maintenance Microsoft is performing when fixing security holes and releasing patches to its customers.
2. Are there situations where it is justified for hackers to find and exploit security holes in software? If so or if not, explain.

Based on:

Espiner, T. (2008, May 6). Defend against patch-based exploits, warns Sans. *ZDNet*. Retrieved May 12, 2008, from http://news.zdnet.co.uk/security/0,1000000189,39411112,00.htm.

Lemos, R. (2008, April 23). Patches pose significant risk, say researchers. *SecurityFocus*. Retrieved May 12, 2008, from http://www.securityfocus.com/news/11514.

Other Approaches to Designing and Building Systems

The SDLC is one approach to managing the development process, and it is a very good approach to follow when the requirements for the information system are highly structured and straightforward—for example, for a payroll or inventory system. Today, in addition to "standard" systems such as payroll and inventory systems, organizations need a broad variety of company-specific information systems, for which requirements either are very hard to specify in advance or are constantly changing. For example, an organization's Web site is likely to evolve over time to keep pace with changing business requirements. How many Web sites have you visited in which the content or layout seemed to change almost every day? For this type of system, the SDLC might work as a development approach, but it would not be optimal. In this section, we describe three more flexible approaches for developing information systems: prototyping, rapid application development, and object-oriented analysis and design.

Prototyping

Prototyping is a systems development methodology that uses a trial-and-error approach for discovering how a system should operate. You may think that this does not sound like a process at all; however, you probably use prototyping all the time in many of your day-to-day activities, but you just do not know it. For example, when you buy new clothes, you likely use prototyping—that is, trial and error—by trying on several shirts before making a selection.

Figure 10.20 diagrams the prototyping process when applied to identifying/determining system requirements. To begin the process, the system designer interviews one or several users of the system, either individually or as a group using a JAD session.

FIGURE 10.20

The prototyping process uses a trial-and-error approach to discovering how a system should operate.

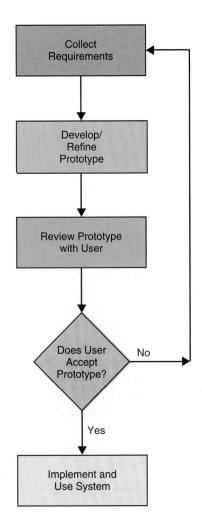

After the designer gains a general understanding of what the users want, he or she develops a prototype of the new system as quickly as possible to share with the users. The users may like what they see or ask for changes. If the users request changes, the designer modifies the prototype and again shares it with them. This process of sharing and refinement continues until the users approve the functionality of the system.

Rapid Application Development

Rapid application development (RAD) is a four-phase systems development methodology that combines prototyping, computer-based development tools, special management practices, and close user involvement (Martin, 1991; McConnell, 1996; Valacich et al., 2009). RAD has four phases: (1) requirements planning, (2) user design, (3) construction, and (4) the move to the new system. Phase 1, requirements planning, is similar to the first two phases of the SDLC, in which the system is planned and requirements are analyzed. To gain intensive user involvement, the RAD methodology encourages the use of JAD sessions to collect requirements. Where RAD becomes *radical* is during phase 2, in which users of the information system become intensively involved in the design process. Computer-aided software engineering (CASE) and other development tools (see the Technology Briefing) are used to structure requirements and develop prototypes quickly. As prototypes are developed and refined, they are continually reviewed with users in additional JAD sessions. Like prototyping, RAD is a process in which requirements, designs, and the system itself are developed via iterative refinement, as shown in Figure 10.21. In a sense, with the RAD approach the people building the system and the users of that system keep cycling back and forth between phase 2 (user design) and phase 3 (construction) until the system is finished. As a result, RAD requires close cooperation between users and designers to be successful.

Object-Oriented Analysis and Design

Object-oriented analysis and design (OOA&D) is another alternative approach for developing a system (see George, Batra, Valacich, and Hoffer, 2007). In the conventional SDLC approach, analysts model data and processes separately; the outputs of these modeling processes are handed over to a programmer who writes the program code and implements the database. In contrast, rather than artificially separating data and processes, the analyst

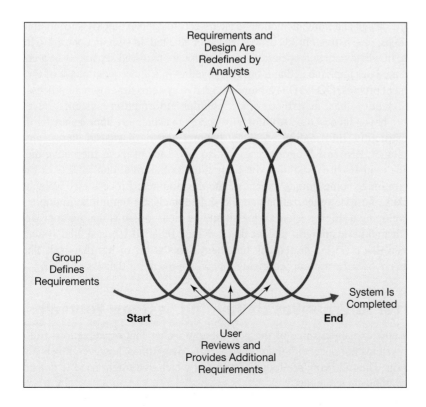

FIGURE 10.21

Iterative refinement is a key to the success of RAD.

FIGURE 10.22

When performing object-oriented analysis and design, analysts use diagramming methods that integrate all aspects of the system.

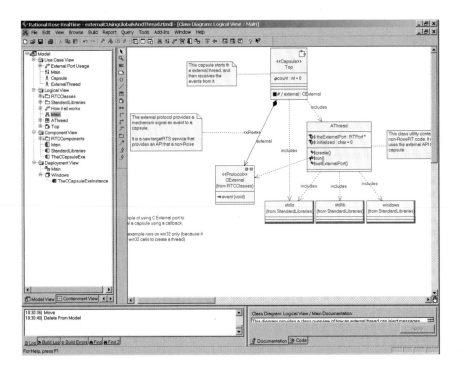

using an OOA&D approach thinks in terms of common modules (called objects), which combine the "what" (the data) and the "how" (the operations to be performed), as he or she defines the relevant system components. An example of an object would be a specific student who has a name, an address, date of birth (i.e., the "what"), but can also perform certain operations, such as register for a class (the "how"). Thus, with the tight coupling between the methods and data, objects are a closer representation of our view of the world, and OOA&D can turn every programmer into an analyst and every analyst into a programmer. Additionally, analysts typically use somewhat different diagramming methods when performing OOA&D to better integrate various aspects of the system, and to be able to develop a conceptual model that is tightly coupled with its actual implementation (see Figure 10.22). Furthermore, if an object-oriented programming language is being used, it enables the design and implementation of the objects to happen quickly and simultaneously, as oftentimes, preexisting objects can be reused or adapted. In sum, in contrast to the SDLC approach, in which data and operations on the data are modeled separately at a conceptual level and are later implemented and brought together in a subsequent phase of the systems development process, OOA&D is a more integrative systems development process.

This section has described other popular information systems development approaches beyond the SDLC. Additionally, there are even more approaches for designing and constructing information systems beyond those discussed here (e.g., Agile Methodologies, EXtreme Programming, and so on). Each of these alternative methodologies focuses either on overcoming the limitations to the traditional SDLC or on finding ways to optimize some unique aspect of the development process (see Valacich et al., 2009). Thus, the wise organization and the skilled analyst often utilize multiple methods when developing a single system. What should be clear to you is that no approach is perfect and that all have strengths and weaknesses (see Table 10.10); a skilled systems developer, much like a skilled craftsman, has many tools at his or her disposal. The skilled craftsman chooses the most appropriate tool and approach for the task at hand.

Need for Alternatives to Building Systems Yourself

We have now explained some of the general approaches that organizations follow when building systems in-house with their own IS staff. Many times, however, this is not a feasible solution. The following are four situations in which you might need to consider alternative development strategies.

TABLE 10.10 Strengths and Weaknesses of Prototyping, RAD, and Object-Oriented Analysis and Design Approaches

Approach	Strengths	Weaknesses
Prototyping	Develops close working relationship between designer and users; works well for messy and hard-to-define problems	Not practical with a large number of users; system may be built too quickly, which could result in lower quality
Rapid application development	Active user involvement in design process; easier implementation due to user involvement	Systems are often narrowly focused, which limits future evolution; system may be built too quickly, which could result in lower quality
Object-oriented analysis and design	Integration of data and processing during design should lead to higher-quality systems; reuse of common modules makes development and maintenance easier	More difficult to train analysts and programmers on the object-oriented approach; unnecessary re-creation of common objects across different systems

Situation 1: Limited IS Staff

Often, an organization does not have the capability to build a system itself. Perhaps its IS staff is small or deployed on other activities, such as maintaining a small network and helping users with problems on a day-to-day basis. This limited staff may simply not have the capability to take on an in-house development project without hiring several analysts or programmers, which is very expensive in today's labor market.

Situation 2: IS Staff Has Limited Skill Set

In other situations, the IS staff may not have the skills needed to develop a particular kind of system. This has been especially true with the explosion of the Web; many organizations are having outside groups manage their sites. For example, the Seattle Seahawks of the National Football League (NFL) have their fan Web site developed and maintained by an outside organization; internal Seahawk personnel dictate Web site content and policies, while the outside organization implements these into the Web site. A similar "division of labor" is utilized by countless organizations where specialized skills that are not present within the existing IS staff are readily available on the open market.

Situation 3: IS Staff Is Overworked

In some organizations, the IS staff may simply not have the time to work on all the systems that the organization requires or wants. Obviously, the number of people dedicated to new development is not infinite. Therefore, you must have ways to prioritize development projects. In most cases, systems that are of strategic importance or that affect the whole organization are likely to receive a higher priority than those that offer only minor benefits or affect only one department or a couple of people in a department. Nonetheless, the IS manager must find a way to support all users, even when the IS staff may be tied up with other "higher-priority" projects.

Situation 4: Problems with Performance of IS Staff

Earlier in this book we discussed how and why systems development projects could sometimes be risky. Often the efforts of IS departments are derailed because of staff turnover, changing requirements, shifts in technology, or budget constraints. Regardless of the reason, the result is the same: another failed (or flawed) system. Given the large expenditures in staff time and training as well as the high risk associated with systems development efforts, the prudent manager tries to limit the risk of any project as much as possible. What if it were possible to see the completed system to know what it looked like before development began? Being able to see into the future would certainly help you learn more about the system and whether it would meet your needs, and it would help to lower the risk of a project. When building a system in-house, it is obviously not possible to see into the future. However, using some of the alternative methods described in this chapter, you can, in fact, see what a completed system might look like. These methods will enable you to know what you are buying, which greatly lowers the risk of a project.

Common Alternatives to In-House Systems Development

Any project has at least four different systems development options. The first option is building the system in-house with your IS staff following the methodologies discussed previously. However, as discussed, this option is not always feasible. The other options include:

- External Acquisition of a Prepackaged System
- Outsourcing Systems Development
- End-User Development

The following sections examine each of these options in closer detail to see how one or more of them might fit the four situations described in the preceding section.

External Acquisition

Purchasing an existing system from an outside vendor such as IBM, EDS, or Accenture is referred to as **external acquisition**. How does external acquisition of an information system work? Think about the process that you might use when buying a car. Do you simply walk into the first dealership you see, tell them you need a car, and see what they try to sell

---

Net Stats

Adopting New Technology

The technology industry, laboring under Moore's Law, depends on users to regularly adopt new hardware and software. Millions of users, however, used to the tried-and-true, would rather stick with those products they know—at least as long as possible. Sometimes the reason for not rushing to replace the old with the new is familiarity with and an acquired expertise in using the older version of a product or service. Or the reason may be prohibitive costs or that the new product or service has yet to prove itself to users as superior to the old. Microsoft's Vista operating system is a case in point. According to W3Counter, an Internet traffic monitoring site, by 2008, Vista had picked up only 3 percent of the operating system market and continued to lag far behind Microsoft's earlier XP.

Other examples of technology users being slow to adopt new technology include, as reported in the *New York Times*:

- In early 2008, more than nine million people still used AOL's dial-up Internet access service, even when broadband was available at comparable prices.
- Yahoo! updated its e-mail service in 2007, but millions of subscribers opted to stick with the older version.
- More than a million Internet users continue to use Netscape, even though AOL has discontinued support for this once popular browser.

Individual computer users are free to opt to be tortoises or hares regarding the adoption of new technology. IT directors, however, must usually follow company culture and management preferences when opting whether or not to adopt new technology. If management is comfortable with risk and likes to be on the cutting edge, for example, IT directors can probably feel safe in adopting new technology early on. A staid, risk-averse management attitude, however, would probably not appreciate an IT director who rushes to adopt new technology.

In any event, whether or not to adopt new technology immediately as it becomes available is a decision that will always be with us.

Based on:

Helft, M. (2008, March 12). Tech's late adopters prefer the tried and true. *New York Times*. Retrieved May 12, 2008, from http://www.nytimes.com/2008/03/12/technology/12inertia.html?th&emc=th.

Internet statistics reveal Vista's lack of acceptance (n.d.). Retrieved May 12, 2008, from http://vistasucks.wordpress.com/2007/09/03/internet-statistics-reveal-vistas-lack-of-acceptance.

Warren, S. (2005, November 17). Adopting new tech: Conservative or aggressive? *Earthweb*. Retrieved May 12, 2008, from http://itmanagement.earthweb.com/erp/article.php/3565056.

you? You had better not. Probably you have done some up-front analysis and know how much money you can afford to spend and what your needs are. If you have done your homework, you probably have an idea of what you want and which dealership can provide the type of car you desire.

This up-front analysis of your needs can be extremely helpful in narrowing your options and can save you a lot of time. Understanding your needs can also help you sift through the salespeople's hype that you are likely to encounter from one dealer to the next as each tries to sell you on why his or her model is perfect for you (see Figure 10.23). After getting some information, you may want to take a couple of promising models for a test drive, actually getting behind the wheel to see how well the car fits you and your driving habits. You might even talk to other people who have owned this type of car to see how they feel about it. Ultimately, you are the one who has to evaluate all the different cars to see which one is best for you. They may all be good cars; however, one may fit your needs just a little better than the others.

The external acquisition of an information system is very similar to the purchase of a car. When you acquire an IS, you should do some analysis of your specific needs. For example, how much can you afford to spend, what basic functionality is required, and approximately how many people will use the system? Next, you can begin to "shop" for the new system by asking potential vendors to provide information about the systems that they have to offer. After you evaluate this information, it may become clear that several vendors have systems that are worth considering. You may ask those vendors to come to your organization and set up their systems so that you and your colleagues are able to "test-drive" them. Seeing how people react to the systems and seeing how each system performs in the organizational environment can help you "see" exactly what you are buying. By seeing the actual system and how it performs with real users, with real or simulated data, you can get a much clearer idea of whether that system fits your needs. When you take a car for a test-drive, you learn how the car meets your needs. By seeing how the system meets your needs before you buy, you can greatly reduce the risk associated with acquiring that system.

Steps in External Acquisition In many cases, your organization will use a competitive bid process for making an external acquisition. In the competitive bid process, vendors are given an opportunity to propose systems that meet the organization's needs. The goal of the competitive process is to help the organization ensure that it gets the best system at the

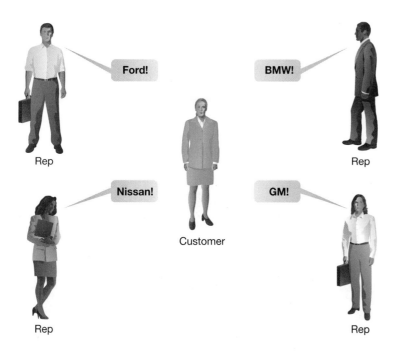

FIGURE 10.23

Multiple car dealers canvass a prospective car buyer.

lowest possible price. Most competitive external acquisition processes have at least five general steps:

1. Systems planning and selection
2. Systems analysis
3. Development of a request for proposal
4. Proposal evaluation
5. Vendor selection

You have already learned about the first two steps because they apply when you build a system yourself as well as when you purchase a system through an external vendor. Step 3, development of a request for proposal, is where the external acquisition process differs significantly from in-house development.

Development of a Request for Proposal A **request for proposal (RFP)** is simply a document that is used to tell vendors what your requirements are and to invite them to provide information about how they might be able to meet those requirements (see Figure 10.24). An RFP is sent to vendors who might potentially be interested in providing hardware and/or software for the system.

Among the areas that may be covered in an RFP are the following:

- A summary of existing systems and applications
- Requirements for system performance and features
- Reliability, backup, and service requirements
- The criteria that will be used to evaluate proposals
- Timetable and budget constraints (how much you can spend)

The RFP is then sent to prospective vendors along with an invitation to present their bids for the project. Eventually, you will likely receive a number of proposals to evaluate. If, on the other hand, you do not receive many proposals, it may be necessary to rethink the requirements—perhaps the requirements are greater than the budget limitations or the timetable is too short. In some situations, you may first need to send out a preliminary request for information simply to gather information from prospective vendors. This will help you determine whether, indeed, the desired system is feasible or even possible. If you determine that it is, you can then send out an RFP. Often, rather than trying to identify all potential vendors and sending out RFPs, companies set up a project Web site, allowing potential bidders to find out more about the organization and its current and planned information systems.

FIGURE 10.24

Sample RFP document for an information systems project.

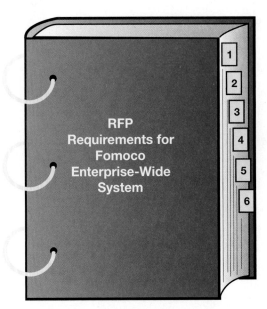

RFP Requirements for Fomoco Enterprise-Wide System

1. Summary of existing systems and applications
2. System performance and features
3. Reliability, backup, and service requirements
4. Evaluation criteria
5. Timetable
6. Budget

Proposal Evaluation The fourth step in external acquisition is to evaluate proposals received from vendors. This evaluation may include viewing system demonstrations, evaluating the performance of those systems, and examining criteria important to the organization and judging how the proposed systems "stack up" to those criteria. Demonstrations are a good way to get a feel for the different systems' capabilities. Just as you can go to the showroom to look over a new car and get a feel for whether it meets your needs, it is also possible to screen various systems through a demonstration from the vendor. During a demonstration, a sales team from the vendor gives an oral presentation about their system, its features and cost, followed by a demonstration of the actual system. In some cases, this may take place at your location; other times, it may take place at the vendor's facility or at one of the vendor's clients, particularly when the system is not easily transportable. Although such demonstrations are often useful in helping you understand the features of different systems being proposed, they are rarely enough in and of themselves to warrant purchasing the system without further evaluation.

One of the ways you can use to evaluate a proposed system is **systems benchmarking**, which is the use of standardized performance tests to facilitate comparison between systems. Benchmark programs are sample programs or jobs that simulate your computer workload. You can have benchmarks designed to test portions of the system that are most critical to your needs, based on your systems analysis. A benchmark might test how long it takes to calculate a set of numbers, how long it takes to access a set of records in a database, or how long it would take to access certain information given a certain number of concurrent users. Some common system benchmarks include the following:

- Response time given a specified number of users
- Time to sort records
- Time to retrieve a set of records
- Time to produce a given report
- Time to read in a set of data

In addition, vendors may also supply benchmarks that you can use, although you should not rely solely on vendor information. For popular systems, you may be able to rely on system benchmarks published in computer trade journals such as *PC Magazine* or on industry Web sites such as CNet.com. However, in most cases, demos and benchmarks alone do not provide all the information you need to make a purchase. The systems analysis phase should have revealed some specific requirements for the new system. These requirements may be listed as criteria that the organization can use to further evaluate vendor proposals. Depending on what you are purchasing—hardware, software, or both—the criteria you use will change. Table 10.11 provides examples of commonly used evaluation criteria.

Vendor Selection In most cases, more than one system will meet your needs, just as more than one car will usually meet your needs. However, some probably "fit" better than others. In these cases, you should have a way of prioritizing or ranking competing proposals. One way of doing this is by devising a scoring system for each of the criteria and benchmarking results. For example, an organization might create a scoring system in

TABLE 10.11 Commonly Used Evaluation Criteria

Hardware Criteria	Software Criteria	Other Criteria
Clock speed of CPU	Memory requirements	Installation
Memory availability	Help features	Testing
Secondary storage (including capacity, access time, and so on)	Usability	Price
	Learnability	
Video display size	Number of features supported	
Printer speed	Training and documentation	
	Maintenance and repair	

which benchmarking results are worth 100 total points, while online help features are worth only 50 points. All the points for each criterion are then summed to give an overall score for each system. Then the system with the highest score (or one of the systems among several with the highest scores) is selected. Figure 10.25 shows an example of a form that could be used to evaluate systems and choose a vendor using this method.

In the example shown in Figure 10.25, system A looks like the best solution because it scored highest. Using such an evaluation method, it is possible that scoring low on a given criterion might exclude otherwise outstanding systems from being purchased. You can see that systems B and C fared very poorly on the vendor support criterion. It is possible that those systems do not have very good vendor support. However, it is also possible that the vendor did not adequately communicate its commitment to support, perhaps because it did not realize it was such an important issue. Therefore, it is very important for you to communicate with vendors about the evaluation process and which criteria you value most highly.

Companies may use other, less formalized approaches to evaluate vendors. Sometimes they use simple checklists; other times they use a more subjective process. Regardless of the mechanism, eventually a company completes the evaluation stage and selects a vendor, ending the external acquisition process.

Managing Software Licensing When purchasing commercial, off-the-shelf software, companies usually have to agree to some license agreement. In general, software licenses can be classified based on the restrictiveness, or the freedom they offer to use or modify the software. Software licensing has been a hot button topic for software companies as they lose billions in piracy and mislicensed customers (see Chapter 11—Managing Information Systems Ethics and Crime). Traditionally, software licensing is defined as the permission and rights that are imposed on applications; the use of software without a proper license is illegal in most countries.

Most software licenses differ in terms of restrictiveness, ranging from no restrictions at all to completely restricted. Note that although freeware or shareware is freely available, the copyright owners often retain their rights and do not provide access to the program's source code. For organizations using proprietary software, two types of licenses are of special importance. The first type includes **shrink-wrap licenses** and **click-wrap licenses** that accompany the software and are used primarily for generic off-the-shelf application and systems software. The shrink-wrapped contract has been named as such because the contract is activated when the shrink wrap on the packaging has been removed; similarly, a click-wrap license refers to a license primarily used for downloaded software that requires computer users to click on "I accept" before installing the software. The second type of license is an **enterprise license** (also known as a **volume license**). Enterprise licenses can vary greatly and are usually negotiated. In addition to rights and permissions, enterprise licenses usually contain limitations of liability and warranty disclaimers that protect the software vendor from being sued if their software does not operate as expected.

As shown in Table 10.12, there are a variety of software licenses. For different business needs, organizations are often depending on a variety of software, each having different licenses, which can cause headaches for many organizations. Not knowing about the software an organization has can have a variety of consequences. For example, companies

FIGURE 10.25

Sample system evaluation form with subset of criteria.

Criterion	Max Points (or weight)	Systems Being Evaluated (Score)		
		A	B	C
Disk capacity	20	10	17	12
Compatibility	50	45	30	25
Usability	30	12	30	20
Vendor support	35	27	16	5
Benchmark results	50	40	28	30
(add as needed...)				
Total	185	134	121	92

TABLE 10.12 **Different Types of Software Licenses**

Restrictiveness	Software Type	Rights	Restrictions	Examples
Full rights	Public domain software	Full rights	No restrictions; owner forsakes copyright	Different programs for outdated IBM mainframes
	Nonprotective open source (e.g., Berkeley software development [BSD] license)	Freedom to copy, modify, and redistribute the software; can be incorporated into a commercial product	Creator retains copyright	FreeBSD operating system; BSD components in (proprietary) Mac OS X operating system
	Protective open source (e.g., general public license [GPL])	Freedom to copy, modify, and redistribute the software	Modified or redistributed software must be made available under the same license; cannot be incorporated into commercial product	Linux operating system
	Proprietary software	Right to run the software (for licensed users)	Access to source code severely restricted; no rights to copy or modify software	Windows operating system
No rights	Trade secret	Software typically only used internally	Access to source code severely restricted; software is not distributed outside the organization	Google PageRank™ algorithm

are not able to negotiate volume licensing options, unused licenses strain the organization's budget, or license violations can lead to fines or public embarrassment. **Software asset management** helps organizations to avoid such negative consequences. Usually, software asset management consists of a set of activities, such as performing a software inventory (either manually or using automated tools), matching the installed software with the licenses, reviewing software-related policies and procedures, and creating a software asset management plan. The results of these processes help organizations to better manage their software infrastructure by being able to consolidate and standardize their software titles, decide to retire unused software, or decide when to upgrade or replace software.

External Acquisition Through Application Service Providers As introduced in Chapter 4, another way to acquire software externally is by the use of *application service providers (ASP)*. Undoubtedly, managing the software infrastructure is a complex task, often resulting in high operating costs for organizations; further, many systems are not scalable in response to large increases in demand. To deal with these issues, business organizations increasingly use the services of ASPs that provide Software as a Service (SaaS)—i.e., clients access applications on an as-needed basis over the Web using standard Web-enabled interfaces. For organizations, using SaaS provides a variety of benefits, such as a reduced need to maintain or upgrade software, a variable fee based on the actual use of the services (rather than fixed IT costs), and the ability to rely on a provider that has gained considerable expertise because of a large number of clients.

One example of a simple, free application service is Google calendar that allows users to organize their schedules, share calendars, and coordinate meetings with other users. To address different business needs, there are a variety of application service providers (see Table 10.13 for examples of different ASPs).

Outsourcing Systems Development

Outsourcing systems development is a way to acquire new information systems that closely resembles the process of in-house development. However, in the case of outsourcing, the responsibility for some or all of an organization's information systems development (and potentially the day-to-day management of its operation) is turned over to an outside firm. Information systems outsourcing includes a variety of working relationships.

TABLE 10.13 **Examples of Different Types of Application Service Providers (ASPs)**

Type	Service Offered	Example
Specialist or functional ASP	Single application	ASP providing payroll processing software for companies to use
Vertical market ASP	Solution package for a specific industry	ASP providing property management systems and reservation systems for hotels
Enterprise ASP	Broad solutions for the needs of different organizations	ASP offering complete enterprise resource planning solutions to different industries
Local ASP	Services for small businesses within a limited geographic area	ASP providing software to small-business owners in a community

The outside firm, or service provider, may develop your information systems applications and house them within their organization; they may run your applications on their computers; or they may develop systems to run on existing computers within your organization. Anything is fair game in an outsourcing arrangement. Today, outsourcing has become a big business and is a very popular option for many organizations (see Chapter 1 for more information on outsourcing).

Why Outsourcing? A firm might outsource some (or all) of its information systems services for many reasons. Some of these are old reasons, but some are new to today's environment (Applegate, Austin, and McFarlan, 2007):

- *Cost and Quality Concerns.* In many cases it is possible to achieve higher-quality systems at a lower price through economies of scale, better management of hardware, lower labor costs, and better software licenses on the part of a service provider.
- *Problems in IS Performance.* IS departments may have problems meeting acceptable service standards because of cost overruns, delayed systems, underutilized systems, or poorly performing systems. In such cases, organizational management may attempt to increase reliability through outsourcing.
- *Supplier Pressures.* Perhaps not surprisingly, some of the largest service providers are also the largest suppliers of computer equipment (e.g., IBM or Hewlett-Packard). In some cases, the aggressive sales forces of these suppliers are able to convince senior managers at other organizations to outsource their IS functions.
- *Simplifying, Downsizing, and Reengineering.* Organizations under competitive pressure often attempt to focus on only their "core competencies." In many cases, organizations simply decide that running information systems is not one of their core competencies and decide to outsource this function to companies such as IBM and EDS, whose primary competency is developing and maintaining information systems.
- *Financial Factors.* When firms turn over their information systems to a service provider, they can sometimes strengthen their balance sheets by liquidating their IT assets. Also, if users perceive that they are actually paying for their IT services rather than simply having them provided by an in-house staff, they may use those services more wisely and perceive them to be of greater value.
- *Organizational Culture.* Political or organizational problems are often difficult for an IS group to overcome. However, an external service provider often brings enough clout, devoid of any organizational or functional ties, to streamline IS operations as needed.
- *Internal Irritants.* Tension between end users and the IS staff is sometimes difficult to eliminate. At times this tension can intrude on the daily operations of the organization, and the idea of a remote, external, relatively neutral IS group can be appealing. Whether the tension between users and the IS staff (or service provider) is really eliminated is open to question; however, simply having the IS group external to the organization can remove a lingering thorn in management's side.

Genetic Testing

The Human Genome Project has been big news since its beginning in 1990. U.S. government funded, the project allowed scientists around the world to map the 20,000 to 25,000 genes within the twenty-three pairs of human chromosomes. Groundbreaking science, for sure, but also a source of ethical dilemmas in a number of industries because of the personal information genetic testing can reveal. Do you carry genes for chronic diseases that may make you a bad risk for health insurance companies or for potential employers who provide health insurance for their employees? Would you want to know if you carry the gene or genes for a fatal disease for which there is currently no treatment or cure, such as Alzheimer's disease? How ethical are mail-order genetic testing laboratories that offer genetic analyses without counseling to help clients interpret results? Is genetic testing another example of technology outpacing legal and ethical issues?

As early as 1990, Lisa N. Geller and her Harvard Medical School colleagues were conducting a study of genetic discrimination in the United States. Out of 917 questionnaires sent out, 455 respondents in Geller's study said they had experienced genetic discrimination. The often-quoted study revealed that a number of institutions were reported to have engaged in genetic discrimination, including health and life insurance companies, health care providers, blood banks, adoption agencies, the military, and schools. For instance:

- A health maintenance organization refused to pay for occupational therapy for a child born with a disabling hereditary disease, on grounds that the condition was "preexisting."
- Medical professionals reportedly pressured patients at risk for passing on defective genes to undergo prenatal diagnostic testing or to avoid having children.
- In one case, a twenty-four-year-old respondent reported that she was denied life insurance due to her family history of Huntington's chorea (a hereditary, disabling, inevitably fatal disease). She had not been genetically tested for the gene causing Huntington's, and the insurance company did not want to risk issuing a policy to her, in case she later developed the disease.

In May 2008, Congress passed the Genetic Information Nondiscrimination Act to bar discrimination based on genes. "People know we all have bad genes, and we are all potential victims of genetic discrimination," said Representative Louise M. Slaughter, New York, who proposed the legislation. The bill prohibited health insurance companies from using genetic information to deny benefits or raise premiums for individual policies. Furthermore, employers who use genetic information to make decisions about hiring, firing, or salaries could face hefty fines.

Technology has opened the door to the possibility of genetic discrimination. In 2008, a plethora of genetic testing laboratories could be found online. "Paternity tests for $99," one lab advertised. A more extensive genetic profile could be obtained for $1,000 from a number of testing facilities. Companies will take a sample of your DNA from cheek cells (you spit into a vial), scan it, and send you information about your genetic future, as well as your family tree. You and members of your family can track inherited traits such as athletic endurance, heart disease, breast cancer, colorectal cancer, and lactose intolerance. Other companies focus on matching the genes you have discovered you have to current medical research, calculating your genetic risk for developing a wide range of diseases.

The new genomics age comes with great promise and opportunity, but it also raises ethical questions that will be difficult to answer. How will knowing your genetic profile affect your life and your future? And how can we protect such information from those who would abuse it? Linda Avey and Anne Wojcicki, cofounders of a genetic testing company called "23andMe," emphasize that one's genome is simply information. Information about our health or potential health to add to the information we're already collecting, such as blood pressure, cholesterol level, and height/weight comparisons. Using such information wisely and without prejudice is the challenge for the twenty-first century.

Based on:

Goertz, T. (2007, November 17). 23AndMe will decode your DNA for $1,000. Welcome to the age of genomics. *Wired*. Retrieved May 12, 2008, from http://www.wired.com:80/medtech/genetics/magazine/15-12/ff_genomics.

Harmon, A. (2008, May 2). Congress passes bill to bar bias based on genes. *New York Times*. Retrieved May 12, 2008, from http://www.nytimes.com:80/2008/05/02/health/policy/02gene.html?th&emc=th.

Human genome project information (n.d.). Retrieved May 12, 2008, from http://www.ornl.gov/sci/techresources/Human_Genome/home.shtml.

Judson K., C. Harrison, and S. Hicks (2006). *Law & ethics for medical careers*. Boston: McGraw-Hill.

Landau, M. (n.d.). Genetics testing leads to discrimination. Retrieved May 12, 2008, from http://focus.hms.harvard.edu/1996/Apr12_1996/Genetics.html.

Managing the IS Outsourcing Relationship McFarlan and Nolan (1995) argue that the ongoing management of an outsourcing alliance is the single most important aspect of the outsourcing project's success. Their recommendations for the best management are as follows:

1. A strong, active chief information officer (CIO) and staff should continually manage the legal and professional relationship with the outsourcing firm.
2. Clear, realistic performance measurements of the systems and of the outsourcing arrangement, such as tangible and intangible costs and benefits, should be developed.
3. The interface between the customer and the outsourcer should have multiple levels (e.g., links to deal with policy and relationship issues and links to deal with operational and tactical issues).

Managing outsourcing alliances in this way has important implications for the success of the relationship. For example, in addition to making sure a firm has a strong CIO and staff, McFarlan and Nolan (1995) recommend that firms assign full-time relationship managers and coordinating groups lower in the organization to "manage" the IS outsourcing project. This means that as people within the IS function are pulled away from traditional IS tasks, such as systems development, they are moved toward new roles and organized into new groups. The structure and nature of the internal IS activities change from exclusively building and managing systems to including managing relationships with outside firms that build and manage systems under legal contract.

Not All Outsourcing Relationships Are the Same Most organizations no longer enter into a strictly legal contract with an outsourcing vendor but rather into a mutually beneficial relationship with a strategic partner. In such a relationship, both the firm and the vendor are concerned with—and perhaps have a direct stake in—the success of the other. Yet other types of relationships exist, meaning that not all outsourcing agreements need to be structured the same way (Fryer, 1994). In fact, at least three different types of outsourcing relationships can be identified:

- Basic relationship
- Preferred relationship
- Strategic relationship

A basic relationship can best be thought of as a "cash-and-carry" relationship in which you buy products and services on the basis of price and convenience. Organizations should try to have a few preferred relationships in which the buyer and supplier set preferences and prices to the benefit of each other. For example, a supplier can provide preferred pricing to customers that do a specified volume of business. Most organizations have just a few strategic relationships in which both sides share risks and rewards.

We have now discussed two systems development alternatives that rely on external organizations to alleviate, either completely or partially, the burden of managing IS development projects in-house. In some cases, however, it may not be possible or convenient to rely on agencies outside the organization for development. In these cases, organizations may rely on another option for systems development projects.

End-User Development

In many organizations, the growing sophistication of users offers IS managers another alternative for systems development. This alternative is **end-user development**—having users develop their own applications. This means that the people who are actually going to use the systems are also those who will develop those systems. End-user development, then, is one way IS departments can speed up application development without relying on external entities such as vendors or service providers. In the following sections, we will discuss the benefits and drawbacks of end-user development.

Benefits of End-User Development To help you better understand the benefits of end-user development, you should quickly review some of the problems with conventional development that are suggested by the four situations presented earlier in this chapter:

- *Cost of Labor.* Conventional systems development is labor intensive. With the increasing complexity of information systems, the costs of purchasing or developing software have increased while hardware costs have declined, as shown in Figure 10.26. Thus, providing end users with the right equipment to develop their own systems has become a viable option, and an IS manager can significantly reduce the cost of application development simply by giving end users the tools they need and enabling them to develop their own applications. Better yet, the various departments within the organization can purchase their own equipment, and the IS staff can simply provide guidance and other services.
- *Long Development Time.* New systems can take months or even years to develop, depending on the scale and scope of the new system and the backlog of systems waiting to be developed. As a result, users' needs may significantly change between when a system is initially proposed and when it is actually implemented. In these cases, the system may be virtually obsolete before it has even been implemented. End-user–developed systems can "skip" the queue of systems waiting to be developed by the IS organization, resulting in more rapidly developed systems.
- *Slow Modification or Updates of Existing Systems.* Related to the time it takes to develop new systems is the problem of maintaining existing systems. Often, updates to existing systems are given a lower priority than developing new systems. Unfortunately, this can result in systems that are unable to keep pace with changing business needs, becoming antiquated and underused. When end users develop their own systems, the users have the responsibility for maintaining and updating applications as needed. Also, when systems are implemented, they often cause changes to the underlying business process. These changes may necessitate further change or modification to the application, as highlighted in Figure 10.27. Rather than rely on IS staff to make these changes, users are able to modify the application in a timely manner to reflect the changed business process.
- *Work Overload.* One reason for long development times and slow modifications is that IS departments are often overloaded with work. When you leverage the talents of end-user developers, you can, in effect, increase the size of the development staff by shifting some of the workload normally handled by IS professionals to end users, as depicted in Figure 10.28.

End-user development can radically decrease the development workload in the IS department. However, such a shift may cause other areas within IS, such as a help desk, to become flooded with requests for assistance. Nonetheless, end-user development can be an excellent option for organizations faced with some of the problems previously described.

Encouraging End-User Development End-user development sounds great, but how can organizations encourage and enable users to develop their own systems? Fortunately, the availability of easy-to-use, fourth-generation development tools (see the Technology

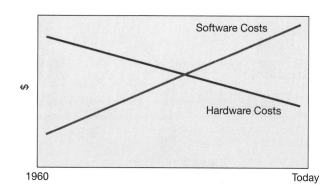

FIGURE 10.26

Rising software costs versus declining hardware costs.

FIGURE 10.27

Continuous cycle of development. A system is developed and implemented. However, it eventually becomes inadequate, and new development takes place.

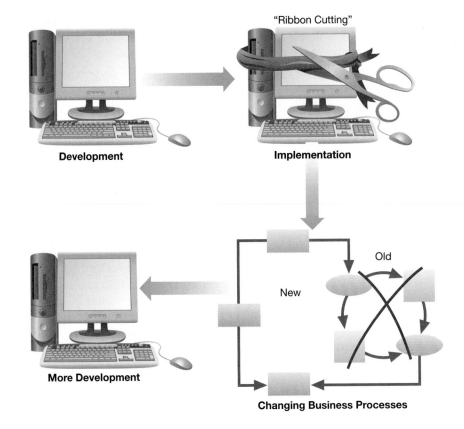

Briefing) has enabled end-user development to become more practical today than in the early to mid-1980s. There are five categories of fourth-generation tools that are summarized in Table 10.14.

End-User Development Pitfalls This chapter has painted a pretty rosy picture of end-user development so far. However, it is important to understand that along with the benefits come some problems. The information systems and computer science professions have established software development standards and generally accepted practices that are used throughout different organizations and across different types of systems. Unfortunately, users may not be aware of these standards, such as the need for adequate documentation,

FIGURE 10.28

Shifting systems development workload as end-user development has become more prevalent.

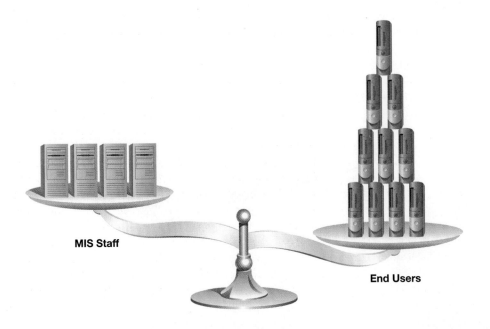

TABLE 10.14 Categories of Fourth-Generation Programming Tools

Fourth-Generation Programming Tools	Description
Personal computing tools	Tools such as spreadsheets, database management systems, and graphics programs, enabling users to build their own applications using macro languages or embedded tools within the software
Query languages/report generators	Capabilities within database systems and other applications enabling users to search a database by entering various search criteria or to produce various types of textual and graphical reports
Graphics generators	Tools allowing users to extract relevant information from databases to generate pie charts, line graphs, area plots, or other types of graphics
Decision support or modeling tools	Spreadsheets and other dedicated decision support tools enabling the analysis of routine and more complex, multidimensional problems
Application generators	Tools for developing small customized systems where the user specifies what analysis is to be done in a relatively user-friendly language rather than in the more tedious commands of a lower-level programming language

built-in error checking, and testing procedures. In small, personal applications, not adhering to the standards may not present a problem. However, if the system manages or interconnects with important business data, then lack of adherence to sound principles can quickly become a big problem if data becomes corrupted or is not secure.

Another problem for end-user–developed systems is a potential lack of continuity. Suppose James develops a new system that meets his needs perfectly. James understands the system and uses it every day. However, one day James is transferred and is replaced by Jordan, a new hire to the company. The system that was intuitive for James to use may not be so intuitive for Jordan. Jordan may quickly abandon James' system or may be forced to develop her own system. This example shows how end-user development can easily result in a lack of continuity among applications, leading to redundant development efforts and a lot of wasted productivity in the organization. In organizations where turnover is frequent, a lot of time can be lost "reinventing the wheel" simply because systems that are in place are undocumented and cannot easily be used by new employees. Likewise, end users in different parts of an organization might create systems for handling similar tasks, unbeknown to each other, leading to redundant efforts.

Related to the continuity problem is the question of whether users and managers should be spending their time on IS development. That is, the organization has hired individuals to be financial managers, production managers, marketers, or salespeople. The organization expects these employees to add value to the organization based on the skills that they have to offer. If their time and energy are diverted to developing new systems, then the organization loses out on the potential productivity these individuals have to offer in other ways. Also, individual motivation, morale, and performance might suffer if the employee is unable to concentrate on his or her area of expertise and instead spends too much time worrying about developing new systems.

Fortunately, organizations that have been successful in moving to end-user development are aware of many of these problems and have established some controls to avoid them. One control mechanism is an information center (IC), which is charged with encouraging end users to develop their own applications while at the same time providing some management oversight. The IC staff can assist or train end users in proper development techniques or standards, prevent redundancy in application development, and ensure that systems are documented properly. IC staff are often not functional-area experts but are typically experts in using the fourth-generation tools. Working together, end users and the IC staff can develop useful systems for an organization.

Industry Analysis

Broadcasting

Only a few years ago, radio and television were among the primary sources for satisfying the desire for both entertainment and up-to-date news and information. Over the past few years, this situation has changed dramatically, with many people turning to the Internet for both information and entertainment. For traditional broadcasting media, this change in technology and their consumers' habits has caused both tremendous opportunities and tremendous headaches.

For many television news companies, the Internet has opened opportunities, as news features can be easily transmitted over the Internet, allowing easier connection between the newsrooms and the "action" on the field. At the same time, viewing habits have changed, and many viewers prefer to obtain their latest news via the Internet. As a reaction, television stations (both focusing on news and entertainment) have started using the Internet as a distribution medium for their content. Internet TV uses the Internet's TCP/IP protocol to transmit content, and viewers can watch parts of a provider's content at their home computers. This shift has also prompted television stations to change the format of their broadcasts—typically to include shorter segments to cater to ever-shortening attention spans. Some stations even started to produce limited-budget episodes of popular TV shows specifically for the Internet.

These changes force TV stations to adjust their revenue models. Whereas traditionally, large revenues were derived from TV advertising, advertisers are now less willing to pay high advertising fees in light of dwindling viewership. On the other hand, TV stations can potentially charge more for advertising tied to online shows, as the Internet offers benefits such as advertising targeted at the individual viewer, and provides detailed tracking metrics such as click-through rates, allowing the advertiser to directly evaluate the success of a campaign.

For radio stations, the situation is similar. With more and more people listening to various Internet radio stations, or (legally or illegally) downloading music, the number of listeners to traditional radio has dwindled and along with it advertising revenues. In 2007, for instance, online advertising for the first time surpassed radio advertising spending. Facing competition from Internet radio, satellite radio, or even podcasting, many radio stations will have to find new ways in order to survive the next decade.

Questions

1. What is the effect of the Internet on television and radio content? With revenues from advertising in traditional channels diminishing, how can television and radio stations continue to produce high-quality content?
2. Today there are thousands of AM/FM stations competing with Internet radio stations and music downloading. Forecast their future and provide a strategy for retaining and gaining market share.

Based on:

Macklin, B. (2007, August). Radio trends: On air and online. *eMarketer*. Retrieved May 12, 2008, from http://www.emarketer.com/Report.aspx?code=emarketer_2000409.

TV networks looking for new eyeballs online. (2008, April 20). Retrieved May 12, 2008, from http://www.msnbc.msn.com/id/24096815.

Key Points Review

1. *Understand the process used by organizations to manage the development of information systems.* The development of information systems follows a process called the systems development life cycle (SDLC). The SDLC is a process that first identifies the need for a system and then defines the processes for designing, developing, and maintaining an information system. The process is very structured and formal and requires the active involvement of managers and users.

2. *Describe each major phase of the SDLC: systems identification, selection, and planning; systems analysis; systems design; systems implementation and operation.* The SDLC has four phases: systems planning and selection; systems analysis; systems design; systems implementation and operation. Systems identification, selection, and planning is the first phase of the SDLC, in which potential projects are identified, selected, and planned. Systems analysis is the second phase of the SDLC, in which the current ways of doing business are studied and alternative replacement systems are proposed. Systems design is the third phase of the SDLC, in which all features of the proposed system are described. Systems implementation and operation is the fourth phase of the SDLC, in which the information system is programmed, tested, installed, and supported. Systems maintenance is an ongoing process focused on repairing and improving the system.

3. *Describe prototyping, rapid application development, and object-oriented analysis and design methods of systems development, along with each approach's strengths and weaknesses.* Prototyping is an iterative systems development process in which requirements are converted into a working system that is continually revised through a close working relationship between analysts and users. The strengths of prototyping are that it helps develop a close working relationship between designers and users and that it is a good approach for hard-to-define problems. Its weaknesses are that it is not a practical approach for a large number of users and that it can at times lead to a lower-quality system if the system is built too quickly. Rapid application development (RAD) is a systems development methodology that combines prototyping, computer-based development tools, special management practices, and close user involvement. The strength of RAD is that users are actively involved in the design process, making system implementation much easier. The weaknesses of RAD are that systems are sometimes narrowly focused—which might limit future evolution—and that quality problems might result if a system is designed and built too quickly (as is the case with prototyping). Object-oriented analysis and design (OOA&D) is a systems development approach that focuses on bundling data and operations together as objects, rather than on modeling these separately. The strengths of OOA&D are the integration of data and processing during the design phase, which should lead to higher-quality systems, and the reuse of common objects, which should make

development and maintenance easier. The weaknesses of OOA&D are that it is more difficult to train analysts and programmers in the object-oriented approach and that analysts often re-create common objects.

4. *Understand the factors involved in building a system in-house, along with situations in which it is not feasible.* It is not feasible for an organization to build a system in-house in at least four situations. First, some organizations have limited IS staffing and, therefore, do not have the capability to build a system themselves. Second, an organization may have IS staff with a limited skill set. Existing IS staff may be highly skilled at producing traditional applications, but they may not have the skills to build new types of systems or systems that require emerging development tools. Third, in many organizations, the IS staff does not have the time to work on all the systems that the organization desires. Fourth, some organizations have performance problems with their IS staff whereby staff turnover, changing requirements, shifts in technology, or budget constraints have resulted in poor results. In any of these situations, it may be advantageous to an organization to consider an alternative to in-house systems development.

5. *Explain three alternative systems development options: external acquisition, outsourcing, and end-user development.* External acquisition is the process of purchasing an existing information system from an external organization or vendor. External acquisition is a five-step process. Steps 1 and 2 mirror the first two steps of the SDLC. Step 3 is the development of a request for proposal (RFP). An RFP is a communication tool indicating an organization's requirements for a given system and requesting information from potential vendors on their ability to deliver such a system. Step 4 is proposal evaluation, which focuses on evaluating proposals received from vendors. This evaluation may include viewing system demonstrations, evaluating the performance of those systems, and examining criteria important to the organization and the ways the proposed systems meet those criteria. Step 5 is vendor selection, which focuses on choosing the vendor to provide the system. Outsourcing refers to the turning over of partial or entire responsibility for information systems development and management to an outside organization. End-user development is a systems development method whereby users in the organization develop, test, and maintain their own applications.

Key Terms

adaptive maintenance 426
alpha testing 424
beta testing 424
click-wrap license 436
corrective maintenance 426
critical success factor (CSF) 416
customized software 408
data flows 418
developmental testing 424
end-user development 440
enterprise license 436
external acquisition 432
human-computer interface
   (HCI) 421
information systems planning 413

joint application design (JAD) 416
object-oriented analysis and design
   (OOA&D) 429
off-the-shelf software 409
patch management system 426
perfective maintenance 426
preventive maintenance 426
processing logic 419
prototyping 428
pseudocode 419
rapid application development
   (RAD) 429
request for proposal (RFP) 434
requirements collection 416
reverse engineering 427

shrink-wrap license 436
software asset management 437
software engineering 411
system conversion 424
systems analysis 415
systems analysis and design 411
systems analyst 411
systems benchmarking 435
systems design 421
systems development life cycle
   (SDLC) 412
systems implementation 423
systems maintenance 425
systems planning and selection 413
volume license 436

Review Questions

1. What are the four phases of the systems development life cycle (SDLC)?
2. List and describe six techniques used in requirements collection.
3. What are the four major components/tasks of the system design phase of the SDLC?
4. What are the four options for system conversion? How do they differ from each other?
5. Compare and contrast the four types of system maintenance.
6. What are three alternative approaches to the SDLC for designing and building systems?
7. What are the advantages and disadvantages of prototyping?
8. List and define the four phases of rapid application development.
9. What is object-oriented analysis and design, and what are its strengths and weaknesses?
10. Define outsourcing and list three major types.
11. List and describe two main types of software licenses.
12. What is software asset management and why is it important for organizations?
13. What is system benchmarking, and what are some common benchmarks?
14. What are some of the reasons outsourcing is more popular than ever?
15. What are the three recommendations made in this chapter for managing an outsourcing IS relationship?
16. Describe five categories of fourth-generation tools.
17. End-user developers have what advantages and disadvantages?

Self-Study Questions

Visit the Interactive Study Guide on the Companion Web site for additional Self-Study Questions: www.pearsonhighered.com/valacich.

1. Which of the following is not one of the four phases of the systems development life cycle?
   A. systems analysis
   B. systems implementation
   C. systems design
   D. systems resource acquisition
2. _____ is the process of gathering and organizing information from users, managers, business processes, and documents to understand how a proposed information system should function.
   A. Requirements collection
   B. Systems collection
   C. Systems analysis
   D. Records archiving
3. Which of the following is the correct order of phases in the systems development life cycle?
   A. analysis, planning, design, implementation
   B. analysis, design, planning, implementation
   C. planning, analysis, design, implementation
   D. design, analysis, planning, implementation
4. In the systems design phase, the elements that must be designed when building an information system include all of the following except _____.
   A. reports and forms

B. questionnaires

C. databases and files

D. interfaces and dialogues

5. _____ maintenance involves making enhancements to improve processing performance or interface usability or adding desired (but not necessarily required) system features (in other words, "bells and whistles").

A. Preventive

B. Perfective

C. Corrective

D. Adaptive

6. Which of the following is an alternative to building a system in-house?

A. external acquisition

B. end-user development

C. outsourcing

D. all of the above

7. A _____ is a report that an organization uses to tell vendors what its requirements are and to invite them to provide information about how they might be able to meet those requirements.

A. request letter

B. vendor request

C. request for proposal

D. requirements specification

8. Which of the following is not a type of outsourcing?

A. basic

B. elite

C. strategic

D. preferred

9. Which of the following factors is a good reason to outsource?

A. problems in IS performance

B. supplier pressures

C. financial factors

D. all of the above

10. Most competitive external acquisition processes have at least five general steps. Which of the following is not one of those steps?

A. vendor selection

B. proposal evaluation

C. development of a request for proposal

D. implementation

Answers are on page 449.

Problems and Exercises

1. Match the following terms with the appropriate definitions:

    i. Request for proposal
    ii. Systems benchmarking
    iii. Alpha testing
    iv. Systems development life cycle
    v. End-user development
    vi. Prototyping
    vii. Pilot conversion
    viii. Systems analysis
    ix. Outsourcing
    x. External acquisition
    xi. Data flows
    xii. Requirements collection

    a. The movement of data through an organization or within an information system

    b. Term that describes the life of an information system from conception to retirement

    c. The second phase of the systems development life cycle

    d. The process of gathering and organizing information from users, managers, business processes, and documents to understand how a proposed information system should function

    e. Testing performed by the development organization to assess whether the entire system meets the design requirements of the users

    f. Using a new system in one location before rolling it out to the entire organization

    g. A systems development methodology that uses a trial-and-error approach for discovering how a system should operate

    h. The practice of turning over responsibility for some or all of an organization's information systems development and operations to an outside firm

    i. The development, testing, and maintenance of applications by users in an organization

    j. The process of purchasing an existing system from an outside vendor

    k. A way to evaluate a proposed system by testing a portion of it with the system workload

    l. A report that is used to tell vendors what the requirements are and to invite them to provide information about how they might be able to meet those requirements

2. Explain the differences between data and data flows. How might systems analysts obtain the information they need to generate the data flows of a system? How are these data flows and the accompanying processing logic used in the system design phase of the life cycle? What happens when the data and data flows are modeled incorrectly?

3. When Microsoft posts a new version of Internet Explorer on its Web site and states that this is a beta version, what does it mean? Is this a final working version of the software, or is it still being tested? Who is doing the testing? Search the Web to find other companies that

have beta versions of their products available to the public. You might try Corel (www.corel.com) or Adobe (www.adobe.com). What other companies did you find?

4. Why is the system documentation of a new information system so important? What information does it contain? For whom is this information intended? When will the system documentation most likely be used?

5. Conduct a search on the Web for "systems development life cycle," using any search engine. Check out some of the hits. Compare them with the SDLC outlined in this chapter. Do all these life cycles follow the same general path? How many phases do the ones you found on the Web contain? Is the terminology the same or different? Prepare a ten-minute presentation to the class on your findings.

6. Choose an organization with which you are familiar that develops its own information systems. Does this organization follow an SDLC? If not, why not? If so, how many phases does it have? Who developed this life cycle? Was it someone within the company, or was the life cycle adopted from somewhere else?

7. Describe your experiences with information systems that were undergoing changes or updates. What kind of conversion procedure was being used? How did this affect your interaction with the system as a user? Who else was affected? If the system was down altogether, for how long was it down? Do you or any of your classmates have horror stories or were the situations not that bad?

8. Compare and contrast RAD and object-oriented methodologies. What are the strengths and weaknesses of each? Visit Object FAQ at www.objectfaq.com/oofaq2.

9. Conduct a search on the Web for "object-oriented analysis and design" using any search engine you wish. Check out some of the hits. You should have found numerous articles regarding OOA&D's use by IS departments. Are these articles positive or negative regarding OOA&D? Do you agree with the articles? Prepare a ten-minute presentation to the class on your findings.

10. Interview an IS manager within an organization with which you are familiar. Determine whether the organization uses methodologies such as prototyping, RAD, and/or OOA&D for system projects. Who chooses the methodology? If the organization has not used a methodology, is it because of choice or because of a lack of need, understanding, or capability of using the methodology?

11. Choose an organization with which you are familiar and determine whether it builds its applications in-house. How many IS staff members does the organization have, and how large is the organization they support?

12. Think about the requirements of a career in IS. Do IS positions generally require people to work 40 hours a week or more if a project has a deadline? Do positions in the IS department require people skills? To find these answers, visit the IS department at your university, a local business, or an online clearinghouse of jobs, such as hotjobs.yahoo.com or www.job-hunt.org.

13. Find an organization on the Internet (e.g., at www.computerworld.com or www.infoworld.com) or a company you may want to work for in the future that outsources work. What are the managerial challenges of outsourcing, and why is this a popular alternative to hiring additional staff?

14. Interview an IS professional about his or her company's use of software asset management processes. How does the company keep track of the different software installed? If anyone asked you about the software installed on your computer, would you know what you have installed? Would you be able to produce the licenses for all software installed?

Application Exercises

Note: The existing data files referenced in these exercises are available on the Student Companion Web site: www.pearsonhighered.com/valacich.

Spreadsheet Application: Outsourcing Information Systems at Campus Travel

Campus Travel wants to increase its customer focus and wants to be able to better serve its most valued customers. Many members of the frequent flier program have requested the ability to check on the status of their membership online; furthermore, the frequent fliers would welcome the opportunity to book reward flights online. As you know that there are a number of companies specializing in building such transactional systems, you have decided to outsource the development of such a system. The following weights are assigned to evaluate the different vendors' systems:

- Online booking capability: 20 percent
- User friendliness: 25 percent

- Maximum number of concurrent users: 20 percent
- Integration with current systems: 10 percent
- Vendor support: 10 percent
- Price: 15 percent

To evaluate the different offers, you need to calculate a weighted score for each vendor using the data provided in the Outsourcing.csv spreadsheet. To calculate the total points for each vendor, do the following:

1. Open the file Outsourcing.csv.

2. Use the SUMPRODUCT formula to multiply each vendor's scores with the respective weights and add the weighted scores.

3. Use conditional formatting to highlight all vendors falling below a total of 60 percent and above a total of 85 percent to facilitate the vendor selection.

A Database Application: Building a Special Needs Database for Campus Travel

In addition to international travel, travel reservations for people with special needs is an area of specialty of Campus Travel. However, to be able to recommend travel destinations and travel activities you should know what facilities are available at each destination. Therefore, you have been asked to create a database of the destinations and the type of facilities that are available for people with special needs. In order to make the system as useful as possible for all, you need to design reports for the users to retrieve information about each destination. Your manager would like to have a system that contains the following information about the destinations:

- Location
- Availability of facilities for the physically handicapped
- Distance to medical facilities
- Pet friendliness

Each location may have one or more handicap facility (e.g., hearing, walking, sight, and so on). A type of handicap facility can be present at multiple locations. Also, each location has to have one pet friendly accommodation/activity and may also have accommodation for different types of pets (dogs, cats, and so on). After designing the database, please design three professionally formatted reports that (1) list the locations in alphabetical order, (2) list all locations that have the handicap facilities for those that find it difficult to walk, and (3) list all locations that have a cat-friendly policy.

Hint: In Microsoft Access, you can create queries before preparing the reports. Enter a few sample data sets and print out the reports.

Team Work Exercise: Determining a Development Approach

You have just been hired by an organization, and you have been charged with purchasing ten new standard desktop computers. Compile a list of criteria you will use to evaluate the vendor to choose. Having determined the different criteria, discuss the importance of these factors and rank them accordingly. Prepare a report explaining the criteria and rankings.

Answers to the Self-Study Questions

1. D, p. 412   **2.** A, p. 416   **3.** C, p. 412   **4.** B, p. 421   **5.** B, p. 426
6. D, p. 432   **7.** C, p. 434   **8.** B, p. 440   **9.** D, p. 438   **10.** D, p. 434

Case ❶

The Emergence of Open-Source Software

You're probably well aware, by now, that some software, such as the Linux operating system and the Firefox browser, is *open source*. That is, creators of the programs made the source code available so that anyone could program changes to improve the application's performance.

Bruce Perens and Eric S. Raymond, two prominent proponents of open-source software, formed the Open Source Initiative (OSI) in 1998, a nonprofit organization dedicated to promoting open-source software. The OSI formulated an *open-source definition* to determine whether software can be considered for an open-source license. An open-source license is a copyright license for software that specifies that the source code is available for redistribution and modification without programmers having to pay the original author. OSI conditions for meeting the open-source definition include the following:

1. The software can be redistributed for free.
2. Source code is freely available.
3. Redistribution of modifications must be allowed.
4. Licenses may require that modifications be available only as patches.
5. Rights attached to the program must apply to all to whom the program is redistributed.
6. No one who wants to modify the code can be locked out.
7. Commercial software users cannot be excluded.
8. License may not be restricted to a specific product.

9. Licenses cannot specify that any other software distributed with the licensed software must also be open code.
10. No click-wrap acceptance of the license shall be required.

One category of open-source software that meets these criteria and that has gained widespread acceptance is operating systems, including the following:

- Linux (www.linux.org). The most used Unix-like operating system on the planet. Versions have been run on anything from handheld computers and regular PCs to the world's most powerful supercomputers. For a list of popular Linux distributions, see www.linuxiso.org.
- FreeBSD (www.freebsd.org), OpenBSD (www.openbsd.org/), and NetBSD (www.netbsd.org). The BSDs are all based on the Berkeley Software Distribution of the Unix

operating system, developed at the University of California, Berkeley. Another BSD-based open-source project is *Darwin* (developer. apple.com/opensource/index.html), which is the base of Apple's Mac OS X.

In addition, many of the router boxes and root DNS servers that keep the Internet working are based on one of the BSDs or on Linux. Microsoft also uses BSD to keep their Hotmail and MSN services working. Other open-source software that keeps the Internet working includes the following:

- Apache (www.apache.org), which runs over 70 percent of the world's Web servers (see www. securityspace.com/s_survey/data/ 200804/index.html).
- BIND (www.isc.org/index.pl?/sw/ bind), the software that provides the DNS (domain name service) for the entire Internet.

- Sendmail (www.sendmail.org), the most important and widely used e-mail transport software on the Internet.
- Firefox (www.firefox.com), the open-source redesign of the Netscape Browser, is recovering ground lost by Netscape in the "browser wars." (Netscape's fight with Microsoft over the dominance of Internet Explorer). With each new release, Firefox has added functionality, stability, cross-platform consistency, and features that are not available from any other browser; many of the popular features (such as tabbed browsing) have since been copied by its competitors.
- OpenSSL (www.openssl.org) is the standard for secure communication (strong encryption) over the Internet.

The Internet has clearly taken advantage of the open-source concept and will undoubtedly continue to do so.

Questions:

1. What are the pros and cons of having so much open-source software enabling the Internet?
2. For what types of applications do you think open-source is better than non–open-source software? When is it worse?
3. Find a for-profit company that is distributing open-source software. What is the software? How does the company make money? Is its revenue model sustainable?
4. Do you use any open-source software on your personal computer, such as the Linux operating system or the Firefox browser? Why or why not?

Based on:

Coar, K. (2006, July 7). The open source definition. *Open Source Initiative*. Retrieved May 12, 2008, from http://www.opensource.org/docs/osd.

Kunkel, R. G. (2002, September). Recent developments in Shrinkwrap, Clickwrap and Browsewrap licenses in the United States. *E Law*. Retrieved May 12, 2008, from http://www.murdoch.edu.au/elaw/issues/v9n3/kunkel93_text.html#Shrinkwrap%20License%20Cases_T.

Tiemann, M. (2006, September 19). History of the OSI. *Open Source Initiative*. Retrieved May 12, 2008, from http://opensource.org/history.

Case ❷

FBI Database to Expand

As crime-solving aides, first there was fingerprinting; decades later came DNA analysis. Next, according to recent information from the FBI, is a $1 billion, ten-year plan to compile palm prints, iris eye patterns, photos of scars and tattoos, and distinctive facial characteristics for a far-reaching criminal identification database. In the past, fingerprints have been the most widely used means of uniquely

identifying people, with the FBI keeping fifty-five million sets of fingerprints on file. The next step would be additional biometric characteristics. Unfortunately, taken alone, many of those have been proven to be rather unreliable (facial recognition accuracy in public places can be as low as 10 to 20 percent, depending on lighting conditions), such that a real increase in identification accuracy can

only come from combining the results of multiple biometrics.

In defense of the FBI's extensive program, Kimberly Del Greco, the FBI's Biometric Services section chief, said adding to the database is "important to protect the borders to keep the terrorists out, protect our citizens, our neighbors, our children so they can have good jobs and have a safe country to live in."

Some privacy experts disagreed. The American Civil Liberties Union (ACLU) saw the program as the beginning of super surveillance tactics that would allow the government to track individuals anywhere, anytime. In addition, privacy advocates fear the potential of widespread mistakes (as frequently happens with no-fly lists at airports). As more than half of all background checks involve people applying for certain jobs, any error in the system could prevent you from getting that job, or even being fired from a job, in case your record mistakenly changes. Others said the program may actually provide more personal privacy, in that it could prevent identity theft and similar misuse of personal information.

While the FBI maintains the program will be strictly limited to criminals, privacy advocates are nervous and worried that it represents yet another case of Big Brother too closely watching private lives.

Questions

1. Should the FBI expand its database to include palm prints, iris eye patterns, photos of scars and tattoos, and so on, of suspected criminals and terrorists? Why or why not?
2. Who should verify that information in this database is true and accurate?
3. Some privacy advocates argue that biometric systems can become unreliable and single out innocent people, especially over time as these databases become less accurate due to a person's natural aging process, weight loss, weight gain, injury, or permanent disability. Discuss the problems associated with having these systems single out innocent people.

Based on:

Arena, K. and C. Cratty (2008, February 4). FBI wants palm prints, eye scans, tattoo mapping. *CNN.com*. Retrieved May 12, 2008, from http://www.cnn.com/2008/TECH/02/04/fbi.biometrics/index.html.

Managing Information Systems Ethics and Crime

After reading this chapter you will be able to do the following:

1 Describe the advent of the Information Age and how computer ethics impact the use of information systems.

2 Discuss the ethical concerns associated with information privacy, accuracy, property, and accessibility.

3 Define computer crime and list several types of computer crime.

4 Describe and explain the differences between cyberwar and cyberterrorism.

Preview

Given that computers and information systems are now a fundamental part of life, opportunities for misusing and abusing information, computers, and systems now abound. This digital world we live in causes us to ask some important new ethical questions. Who owns information, particularly information about us? Who is responsible for the accuracy of information? Should guidelines be set for how business organizations and business professionals use information, computers, and information systems, and, if so, what should these guidelines be? What penalties should be assessed for computer crime and abuses?

This chapter focuses on the last major topic related to managing in the digital world, specifically, various issues associated with information systems ethics and computer crime. Both of these topics are becoming increasingly important to successfully manage information systems.

Managing in the Digital World: BitTorrent

In 1999, Shawn Fanning, a student at Northeastern University in Boston, thought he had a groundbreaking idea for a Web site. Tired of searching IRC or Lycos to find music, Fanning devised a *peer-to-peer* file-sharing system that allowed users to exchange music files directly. Under Fanning's unique system, files were not stored on a central server but were uploaded and downloaded from the hard drives of users' computers. For example, if a user wanted to download a Linkin Park song, he or she could search among other users to locate that song and then download the tune from another user's computer.

Fanning called his service Napster, and it was phenomenally successful since users could download hit tunes as MP3 files without buying CDs loaded with "filler" songs and could locate and download hard-to-find songs not available anywhere else. The trouble was, the Motion Picture Association of America (MPAA) and the Recording Industry Association of America (RIAA) soon discovered the site and filed copyright infringement suits against Fanning. Heavy metal band Metallica and rapper Dr. Dre also brought copyright violation suits against Fanning. The courts sided with the music industry and shut Napster down in 2001. As part of the court's decision, Fanning paid music creators and copyright holders $26 million in damages.

Napster filed for bankruptcy in 2001 and was sold. The site continues to exist as a free service for users to listen to music selections, but users who want to download tunes must pay (see www.napster.com). Over the past decade, the music and movie industries have won a series of legal victories against file-sharing sites that followed Napster, including Grokster, Morpheus, and KaZaA. Like Napster, some of these sites continue to operate as legitimate businesses.

The hugely successful peer-to-peer file-sharing system Fanning originated did not disappear with the demise of Napster. The latest star in the file-sharing constellation is BitTorrent. The difference between Napster and BitTorrent is that BitTorrent is not a program or a file server. BitTorrent is a protocol designed for transferring files. This protocol lets users connect to ad hoc peer-to-peer networks, allowing users to communicate directly with each other to send and receive files. Although there is a central server called a tracker, it simply manages the connection and does not have any knowledge of the files being transported between users.

BitTorrent's key concept is that users can upload at the same time they are downloading by breaking data down into smaller, more easily transferred chunks. This feature lets users connect to several other users and either helps others download or uses the combined bandwidth of a group of users to download large files at lightning-fast speeds, thus optimizing available bandwidth. The protocol is designed to work better with more users on the network. Supportive sharing has built-in growth since each new user brings supply as well as demand.

BitTorrent technology has contributed new catchwords to the computer lexicon. For example, "leechers" are users who download content without sharing that content with anyone else. "Seeders" are users who not only download content but also provide content to be downloaded using their hard drives and bandwidth. Many users will not allow their content to be

Napster is synonymous with music downloading.

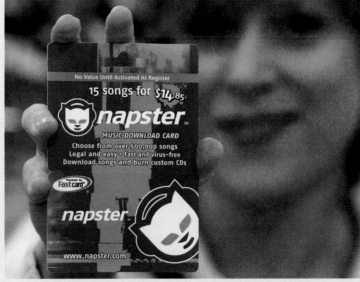

downloaded by leechers and will block leechers when they see them.

Why hasn't this service been stopped via lawsuits? Primarily because BitTorrent servers only manage the BitTorrent protocol connection and do not store files for downloading. The software that allows for users to download and upload files is not associated with BitTorrent. In other words, anyone can create a BitTorrent program, and many developers have.

Surprisingly, the MPAA has embraced BitTorrent's strategy instead of fighting it. In 2006, Warner Brothers Home Entertainment Group launched a legal peer-to-peer service in Germany called In2Movies. Subscribers used Warner Brothers' client-based software that, in turn, used the BitTorrent network protocol to manage connections among Warner Brothers' clients. Subscribers could download films on the same day the product was released. The business model was simple: Users paid a certain fee for each movie they downloaded. In turn, as an incentive, users received bonus points for sharing movies they downloaded using In2Movies and could use these bonus points to "pay" for downloading additional content. The consumers "downloaded to own" (or "ownloaded") the movies (i.e., they could watch the movies as often as they desired), but could not play burnt copies using a stand-alone DVD player.

Warner Brothers' strategy was considered revolutionary since the entertainment industry considers the file-sharing battle a lost cause. Warner Brothers' strategy not only shows how to reduce distribution costs by maximizing network effectiveness but also provided a speedy download experience for the consumer. Warner Brothers' move gave the company positive press and exposure to the music-sharing communities and allowed them to save millions in their digital distribution. However, as any peer-to-peer application, this system depended heavily on the number of users. Faced with a low subscriber base (possibly due to the relatively high prices for purchasing movies), the service was shut down in mid-2008.

Another company using BitTorrent technology to its advantage is Blizzard Entertainment. Blizzard's hit game title *World of Warcraft* uses the BitTorrent protocol for patches and update information. When gamers update or patch their current *World of Warcraft* installation, they do not download the necessary files from Blizzard's servers. Instead, they connect to other users worldwide using the BitTorrent protocol to download the files. Thus, they use the users' combined bandwidth to accomplish digital distribution. With over three million users, *World of Warcraft* is a widely profitable title for Blizzard, and since Blizzard uses the BitTorrent distributed file-sharing technology, scalability costs are marginal.

Despite the entertainment industry's efforts to shut down sites illegally sharing movie and music files, the trend has increased as more and more computer users have access to broadband connections, which allow file sharers to accomplish uploading and downloading at ever-increasing speeds. And file-sharing services based on the BitTorrent protocol continue to increase at the fastest rate.

After reading this chapter, you will be able to answer the following:

1. What ethical issues do technologies like BitTorrent raise?

2. What are the ethical issues associated with seeders and leechers?

3. If you were a popular performer in the music industry, how would you feel about file sharing?

Based on:

BitTorrent (protocol). (2008, October 12). In *Wikipedia, the free encyclopedia*. Retrieved October 12, 2008, from http://en.wikipedia.org/w/index.php?title=BitTorrent_(protocol)&oldid=244680255.

Napster. (2009, January 1). In *Wikipedia, the free encyclopedia*. Retrieved January 4, 2009, from http://en.wikipedia.org/w/index.php?title=Napster&oldid=261207872.

McBride, S. (2006, January 30). Warner Bros. to try file sharing of films, TV shows in Germany. *Wall Street Journal*. Retrieved October 12, 2008, from http://online.wsj.com/article/SB113858875415059685.html.

Pfanner, E. (2008, February 3). Pirate Bay defiant despite criminal charges. *International Herald Tribune*. Retrieved October 12, 2008, from http://www.iht.com/articles/2008/02/01/business/PIRATES04.php.

What is BitTorrent? (n.d.). Retrieved October 12, 2008, from http://www.bittorrent.com/introduction.html.

Information Systems Ethics

In his book *The Third Wave*, futurist Alvin Toffler describes three distinct phases, or "waves of change," that have taken place in the past or are presently taking place within the world's civilizations (see Figure 11.2). The first wave—a civilization based on agriculture and handwork—was a comparatively primitive stage that began as civilizations formed and lasted for thousands of years. The second wave of change—the Industrial Revolution—overlapped with the first wave. The Industrial Revolution began in Great Britain toward the end of the eighteenth century and continued over the next 150 years, moving society from a predominantly agrarian culture to the urbanized machine age. Where once families supported themselves by working the land or handcrafting items for

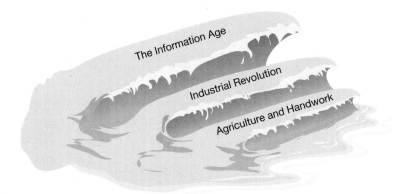

FIGURE 11.2

The Information Age is the biggest wave of change.

sale or trade, now mothers, fathers, and children left home to work in factories. Steel mills, textile factories, and eventually automobile assembly lines replaced farming and handwork as the principal source of family income.

As the Industrial Revolution progressed, not only did occupations change to accommodate the mechanized society, but so did educational, business, social, and religious institutions. On an individual level, now punctuality, obedience, and the ability to perform repetitive tasks were qualities to be instilled and valued in children in public schools and, ultimately, in workers. Although industrialization has brought about many positive changes, technology introduced challenges for individuals, societies, and the environment. Many felt threatened by these changes, and some—called **Luddites** (see later in this chapter for more)—resorted to protesting against the technology; some others even resorted to destroying the technology that they felt threatened their livelihoods.

The Information Age Arrives

In a much shorter period of time than it took for civilization to progress past the first wave, societies worldwide moved from the machine age into the **Information Age**—a period of change Toffler has dubbed the "third wave." As the third wave gained speed, information became the currency of the realm. For thousands of years, from primitive times through the Middle Ages, information, or the body of knowledge known to that point, was limited. It was transmitted verbally within families, clans, and villages, from person to person and generation to generation. Then came Johann Gutenberg's invention of the printing press with movable type in the middle of the fifteenth century, and a tremendous acceleration occurred in the amount and kind of information available to populations (see Figure 11.3). Now knowledge could be imparted in written form and sometimes came from distant locations. Information could be saved, absorbed, debated, and written about in publications, thus adding to the exploding data pool.

Computer Literacy and the Digital Divide

Most modern-day high school and university students have grown up in a computerized world. If by some chance they do not know how to operate a computer by the time they graduate from high school, they soon acquire computer skills because in today's work world knowing how to use a computer—called **computer literacy** (or information literacy)—can mean the difference between being employed and being unemployed. Knowing how to use a computer can also open up myriad sources of information to those who have learned how to use the computer as a device to gather, store, organize, and otherwise process information. In fact, some fear that the Information Age will not provide the same advantages to "information haves"—those computer-literate individuals who have unlimited access to information—and "information have-nots"—those with limited or no access or skills.

The first computer-related occupations have evolved as computers have become more sophisticated and more widely used. Where once we thought of computer workers primarily as programmers, data entry clerks, systems analysts, or computer repairpersons, today many more job categories in virtually all industries, from accounting to the medical field (see

FIGURE 11.3

The printing press gave birth to the Information Age.

Figure 11.4) involve the use of computers. In fact, today there are few occupations where computers are not somehow in use. Computers manage air traffic, perform medical tests, monitor investment portfolios, enable online shopping, and more. Since they are especially adept at processing large amounts of data, they are used extensively by universities and public schools, in businesses of all sizes, and in all levels and departments of government. Engineers, architects, interior designers, and artists use special purpose computer-aided design programs. Musicians play computerized instruments, and they write and record songs with the help of computers. Not only do we use computers at work, we also use them in our personal lives. We teach our children on them, manage our finances, do our taxes, compose letters and term papers, create greeting cards, send and receive electronic mail, surf the

FIGURE 11.4

Computers are used in countless types of jobs and industries, including the medical field.

Source: © Getty Images/Eye Wire, Inc.

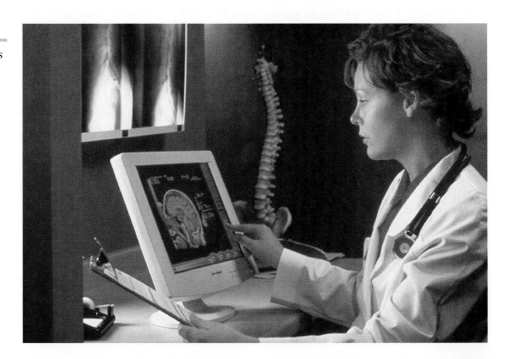

Internet, purchase products, and play games on them. With the increasing use of computers in all areas of society, many argue that being computer literate—knowing how to use a computer and use certain applications—is not sufficient in today's world; rather, **computer fluency**—the ability to independently learn new technologies as they emerge and assess their impact on your work and life—is what will set you apart in the future.

Unfortunately, there are still many people in our society who are being left behind in the Information Age. The gap between those individuals in our society who are computer literate and have access to information resources like the Internet and those who do not is referred to as the **digital divide**. The digital divide is one of the major ethical challenges facing society today when you consider the strong linkage between computer literacy and a person's ability to compete in the Information Age. For example, access to raw materials and money fueled the Industrial Revolution, "but in the informational society, the fuel, the power, is knowledge," emphasized John Kenneth Galbraith, an American economist who specialized in emerging trends in the U.S. economy. "One has now come to see a new class structure divided by those who have information and those who must function out of ignorance. This new class has its power not from money, not from land, but from knowledge."

The good news is that the digital divide in America is rapidly shrinking, but there are still major challenges to overcome. In particular, people in rural communities, the elderly, people with disabilities, and minorities lag behind national averages for Internet access and computer literacy (see Figure 11.5). Outside the United States, the gap gets even wider and the obstacles much more difficult to overcome, particularly in the developing countries, where infrastructure and financial resources are lacking. For example, most developing countries are lacking modern informational resources such as affordable Internet access or efficient electronic payment methods like credit cards. In an attempt to shrink the digital divide, a global project called **One Laptop per Child (OLPC)** is attempting to distribute very low-cost laptop computers to children in developing countries around the world (see Figure 11.6). The goal is to price these computers at $100 each for governments and charitable organizations to purchase and distribute. The project is making progress, but there are numerous obstacles to providing a low-cost computer to children throughout the developing world (for more on OLPC and other efforts to develop computers for children in the developing world, see Case 1—Bridging the Digital Divide—at the end of this chapter). Clearly, the digital divide is a major ethical concern facing the Information Age.

A broad range of ethical issues have emerged through the use and proliferation of computers. Just as the Luddites opposed technological progress during industrialization, **neo-Luddites** oppose information systems, fearing negative impacts such as social decay,

FIGURE 11.5

The digital divide even exists in the developed world.

FIGURE 11.6

One Laptop per Child (OLPC) laptop.

increased consumerism, or loss of privacy. **Computer ethics** is used to describe the issues and standards of conduct as they pertain to the use of information systems. In 1986, Richard O. Mason wrote a classic article on the issues central to this debate—information privacy, accuracy, property, and accessibility. These issues are still at the forefront of most ethical debates related to how information systems store and process information (see Figure 11.7). Next, we examine each of these issues.

FIGURE 11.7

Information privacy, accuracy, property, and accessibility are central to most ethical concerns about information technology.

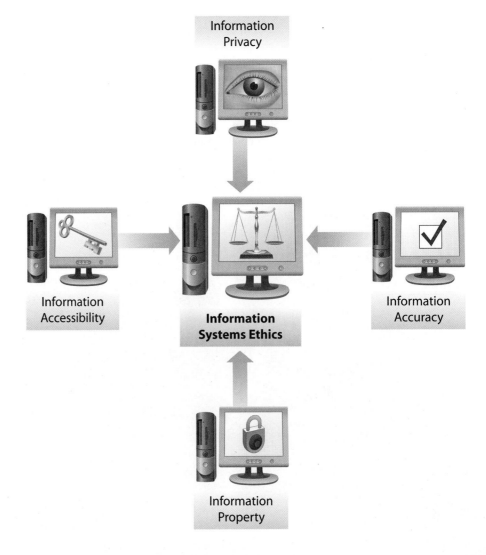

Information Privacy

If you use the Internet regularly, sending e-mail messages and visiting Web sites, you may have felt that your personal privacy is at risk. Several Web sites where you like to shop greet you by name and seem to know which products you are most likely to buy (see Figure 11.8). Every day, the inbox in your browser's mail program is full to overflowing with messages urging you to buy something. As a result, you may feel as though eyes are on you every time you go online. **Information privacy** is concerned with what information an individual should have to reveal to others in the workplace or through other transactions, such as online shopping.

While the Information Age has brought widespread access to information, the downside is that others may now have access to personal information that you would prefer to keep private. Personal information, such as Social Security numbers, credit card numbers, medical histories, and even family histories, is now available on the Internet. Using search engines, your friends, coworkers, current or future employers, or even your spouse can find out almost anything that has been posted by or about you on the Internet. For example, it is very easy to locate your personal blog, your most recent party pictures posted on MySpace or Facebook, or even sensitive questions you asked in a public discussion forum about drug use or mental health. Moreover, many of these pages are stored in the search engines' long-term cache, so they remain accessible for a long time even after they have been taken off the Web.

One of the fastest-growing "information" crimes in recent years has been **identity theft** (see Figure 11.9). Identity theft is the stealing of another person's Social Security number, credit card number, and other personal information for the purpose of using the victim's credit rating to borrow money, buy merchandise, and otherwise run up debts that are never repaid. In some cases, thieves even withdraw money directly from victims' bank accounts. Since many government and private organizations keep information about individuals in accessible databases, opportunities abound for thieves to retrieve it. Reclaiming one's identity and restoring a good credit rating can be frustrating and time-consuming for victims.

The solution to identity theft lies in the government and private sector working together to change practices used to verify a person's identity. For example, a mother's maiden name and an individual's Social Security number are too easily obtained. Other methods of personal identification, such as biometrics and encryption, may need to be used

FIGURE 11.8

Amazon.com is famous for personalizing its Web site to individual customers.

FIGURE 11.9

Identity theft is one of the fastest growing information crimes.

if the problem is to be solved. Methods of information security, including biometrics and encryption, were discussed in Chapter 7—Securing Information Systems.

Before moving on, it is important to distinguish between unethical behavior and a crime. Identity theft is clearly a crime. However, many "misuses" of computers and information may not be crimes but would be considered unethical by most people. As technology moves forward and allows humans to do things not possible before, existing laws often do not apply to these emerging situations. One of the ongoing debates regarding technological innovations revolves around the question, "Just because it is not a crime, does that make it okay to do it?"

How to Maintain Your Privacy Online When you make Web purchases, vendors are not required by law to respect your privacy. In other words, a vendor can track what pages you look at, what products you examine in detail, which products you choose to buy, what method of payment you choose to use, and where you have the product delivered. After collecting all that information, unscrupulous vendors can sell it to others, resulting in more direct-mail advertising, electronic spam in your e-mail inbox, or calls from telemarketers.

When surveyed about concerns related to online shopping, most consumers list issues of information privacy as a top concern. As a result, governments have pressured vendors to post their privacy policies on their Web sites. Unfortunately, these policies do not often protect the privacy of consumers. To protect yourself, you should always review the privacy policy of all companies you do business with and refuse to do business with those that do not have a clear policy or do not respect your privacy. According to the Consumer Protection Working Group of the American Bar Association at safeshopping.org, a seller's privacy policy should indicate at least the following:

- What information the seller is gathering from you
- How the seller will use this information
- Whether and how you can "opt out" of these practices

To make sure your shopping experience is a good one, you can take a few additional steps to maintain your privacy:

- ***Choose Web Sites That Are Monitored by Independent Organizations.*** Several independent organizations monitor the privacy and business practices of Web sites (see, for example, www.epubliceye.com).

▓ *Avoid Having "Cookies" Left on Your Machine.* Many commercial Web sites leave cookies on your machine so that the owner of the site can monitor where you go and what you do on the site (see Chapter 7). To enhance your privacy, you should carefully manage your browser's cookie settings or get special "cookie management" software (see www.cookiecentral.com).

▓ *Visit Sites Anonymously.* There are ways to visit Web sites anonymously. Using services provided by companies such as Anonymizer (www.anonymizer.com), you have a high degree of privacy from marketers, identity thieves, or even coworkers when surfing the Web.

▓ *Use Caution When Requesting Confirmation E-Mail.* When you buy products online, many companies will send you a confirming e-mail message to let you know that the order was received correctly. A good strategy is to have a separate e-mail account, such as one that is available for viewing via a Web browser, that you use when making online purchases.

Of course, there are no guarantees that all your online experiences will be problem free, but if you follow the advice provided here, you are much more likely to maintain your privacy.

Avoid Getting Conned in Cyberspace The Internet has fundamentally changed the way consumers gather information, shop, and do business. Unfortunately, con artists and other lawbreakers have gone high tech and are using the Internet to cheat consumers in a number of clever ways. The U.S. Federal Trade Commission has compiled advice on how not to get taken by crafty con artists on the Internet (www.ftc.gov/bcp/edu/pubs/consumer/tech/tec09.shtm). Among the listed "dot-cons" were offers to let you see adult images in exchange for revealing your credit card number, auction cheats, charges for a "free" Web site appearing on telephone bills, and various investment, travel and vacation, business, and health care products scams (see Table 11.1).

Information Accuracy

The issue of **information accuracy** has become highly charged in today's wired world. Information accuracy is concerned with ensuring the authenticity and fidelity of information as well as with identifying who is responsible for informational errors that harm people. With all the computerization that has taken place, people have come to expect to receive and retrieve information more easily and quickly than ever before. In addition, because computers "never make mistakes," we have come to expect this information to be accurate. A case in point is at the bank. The combination of automated teller machines, computerized record systems, and large, electronic client and transaction databases should provide customers with quick and accurate access to their account information. However, we continue to hear about and experience record-keeping errors at banks.

An error of a few dollars in your banking records does not seem significant. However, what if it were an error of hundreds or thousands of dollars in the bank's favor? What if the error caused one of your important payments (such as a home mortgage payment) to bounce? Bank errors can have quite significant consequences.

Now, imagine how significant a data accuracy error might be in other settings. Hospitals use similar automation and computer-intensive record keeping. What would happen if prescription information appeared incorrectly on a patient's chart, and the patient became fatally ill as a result of the medicine that was mistakenly dispensed to him? The significance of such a data accuracy error could be tremendous. Furthermore, it would not be clear who was to blame. Would this be the fault of the doctor, the pharmacist, the programmer, the data entry clerk, or maybe some combination of errors by the system designer, the system analyst, the system programmer, the database administrator, and the vendor? It would be too easy simply to blame the computer; some one person would need to be found at fault. As a case in point, in late 2000, a software flaw in a radiation therapy device in a cancer treatment center in Panama City, Panama, increased exposure levels by up to 100%, causing multiple deaths and countless injured patients. Blame was placed on

TABLE 11.1 **Top Ten List of Dot-Cons from the Federal Trade Commission and Advice on How Not to Get Conned**

The Con	The Bait	The Switch	Advice
Internet auctions	Great deals on great products.	After sending money, consumers receive inferior item or nothing at all.	Investigate the seller carefully. Use a credit card or escrow service to pay.
Internet access service	Free money, simply for cashing a check.	After cashing "free" check, consumers are locked into long-term Web service with steep penalties for early cancellation.	Read both sides of the check, the fine print, or any documentation that comes with the check.
Credit card fraud	View online adult images for free, just for sharing your credit card number to "prove" you are over eighteen.	Fraudulent promoters run up unauthorized charges on consumers' cards.	Share your credit card numbers only when you are buying from a company you trust. Dispute unauthorized charges (federal law limits your liability to $50).
International modem dialing	Free access to adult material by downloading "viewer" or "dialer."	Exorbitant long-distance phone bills as the viewer or dialer reconnects to an international carrier.	Do not download programs providing "free" access without carefully reading all the fine print. Dispute unauthorized charges to your account.
Web cramming	Free custom-designed Web site for thirty-day trial.	Telephone is billed even when consumers do not accept the offer or agree to continue service.	Review phone bill carefully, and challenge all charges you do not recognize.
Multilevel marketing plans/pyramids	Make money from selling products as well as from products sold by people you recruit to sell.	Consumers are required to recruit other distributors, but products sold to distributors do not qualify for commissions.	Avoid programs that require you to recruit distributors, buy expensive inventory, or commit to a minimum sales volume.
Travel/vacations	Great trips for bargain prices.	Low-quality accommodations and services, often with hidden charges.	Get references and the details of the trip in writing.
Business opportunities	Be your own boss, and earn a high salary.	Consumers invest in unproven or insecure ventures.	Talk with others who have made the same investment, get all promises in writing and study the contract carefully. Consult with a lawyer or accountant.
Investments	Realize huge investment returns.	Big profits always mean big risks.	Check with state and federal securities and commodities regulators; insist on talking with other investors.
Health care products/services	Cure serious illness or fatal health problems.	Consumers put faith in unproven solutions and put off pursuing needed health care.	Consult with health professionals to evaluate cure-alls or promises to provide fast or easy cure.

Based on http://www.ftc.gov/bcp/edu/pubs/consumer/tech/tec09.shtm.

the software and also on the doctors who didn't manually double check the device's settings. As the device and the software were manufactured in the United States, the U.S. FDA filed an injunction to force the manufacturer to stop manufacturing and distributing software for radiation therapy devices; the physicians involved were indicted for murder under Panama law.

Computer-based information systems and the data within those systems are only as accurate and as useful as they have been made to be. This suggests the need for better precautions and greater scrutiny when modern information systems are designed, built, and used. This means that everyone must be concerned with data integrity, from the design of the system, to the building of the system, to the person who actually enters data into the system, to the people who use and manage the system. Perhaps more important, when data errors are found, people should not blame the computer. After all, people designed it, built it, and entered data into it in the first place.

Information Property

It happens to all of us. Nearly every day in the mail, we receive unwanted solicitations from credit card companies, department stores, magazines, or charitable organizations (see Figure 11.10). Many of these envelopes are never opened. We ask the same question over and over again: "How did I get on another mailing list?" Your name, address, and other personal information were most likely sold from one company to another for use in mass mailings. You probably did not give anyone permission to buy or sell information about you, but that is not a legal issue or a matter of concern for some firms. **Information property** focuses on who owns information about individuals and how information can be sold and exchanged.

Data Privacy Statements Who owns the computerized information about people—the information that is stored in thousands of databases by retailers, credit card companies, and marketing research companies? The answer is that the company that maintains the database of customers or subscribers legally owns the information and is free to sell it. Your name, address, and other information are all legally kept in a company database to be used for the company's future mailings and solicitations. However, the company can sell its customer list or parts of it to other companies who want to send similar mailings. This is where the problems begin. For instance, the apparel retailer The Gap could sell names and addresses from its customer database to companies looking for a similar customer base or buying pattern. Of course, The Gap would not likely sell parts of its list to competitors (see www.gap.com/customerService/info.do?cid=2331). Still, many people are concerned that these companies have full ownership of their purchasing habits and demographic data.

There are limits, however, to what a company can do with such data. For example, if a company stated at one time that its collection of marketing data was to be used strictly internally as a gauge of its own customer base and then sold that data to a second company years later, it would be unethically and illegally breaking its original promise. Companies collect data from credit card purchases (by using a credit card, you indirectly allow this) or from surveys and questionnaires you fill out when applying for a card. They also collect data when you fill in a survey at a bar, restaurant, supermarket, or the mall about the quality of the service or product preferences. By providing this information, you implicitly agree that this data can be used as the company wishes (within legal limits, of course).

FIGURE 11.10

Selling personal information has become big business.

What is even more problematic is the combination of this survey data with transaction data from your credit card purchases. Using the demographic data (Who am I, and where do I live?) and the psychographic data (What are my tastes and preferences?), companies can create a highly accurate profile of customers. How do you know who is accessing these databases? This is an issue that each company must address at both a strategic/ethical level (Is this something that we should be doing?) and a tactical level (If we do this, what can we do to ensure the security and integrity of the data?). The company needs to ensure proper hiring, training, and supervision of employees who have access to the data and implement the necessary software and hardware security safeguards.

Spam, Cookies, and Spyware In addition to the information you knowingly share with a Web site when purchasing a product, spam, cookies, and spyware are three additional ways that information property about individuals and organizations is being collected and (ab)used on the Internet. *Spam,* discussed in Chapter 7, refers to unsolicited e-mail that promotes a product or service or makes some other type of solicitation. If you have ever signed up for a contest online, filled out a registration form for an Internet service, or even bought a book from a little-known bookseller on the Internet, chances are your e-mail address was sold to e-marketers. Although there are federal, state, and international laws related to spam, most notably the CAN-SPAM Act of 2003, very little can be done to stop a motivated spammer (see www.spamlaws.com for more information).

Also described in Chapter 7, a *cookie* is a small text file on your computer that stores information about your Web-browsing activity at a particular site. Although you can choose to not accept the storage of cookies, you may not be able to visit the site, or it may not function properly. For example, to read the *New York Times* online, you must register by entering your name and other information. When you go through the registration process, cookies are stored on your machine. If you don't accept cookies or you delete the stored cookies, you are not allowed to access the online newspaper without reregistering. Similarly, you will have to accept cookies when purchasing from many e-tailers, as most online shopping carts require cookies to function properly. Although the use of cookies is a relatively well-known mechanism for "enhancing" your surfing experience, many privacy advocates believe that it is a form of spyware. If you like the personalized touch cookies can provide, or you want to be able to shop online, you will have to decide if the subsequent loss of your information property is a fair trade-off.

Spyware is any technology that is used to collect information about a person or organization without their knowledge (again, see Chapter 7). In other words, spyware is software that runs on a person's computer to collect information about the user and to transmit this information to some other party. This collected information is typically used for advertising purposes, although it can also be used for committing various types of computer crimes. Unfortunately, most privacy advocates feel that it is unlikely that spyware will become illegal or heavily regulated anytime soon. Fortunately, there are many effective tools available to monitor and remove unwanted spyware (see Figure 11.11).

Cybersquatting Another information property issue relates to **cybersquatting**, the dubious practice of registering a domain name, then trying to sell the name for big bucks to the person, company, or organization most likely to want it. Domain names are one of the few scarce resources on the Internet, and victims of cybersquatting include Panasonic, Hertz, Avon, and numerous other companies and individuals. Fortunately, the U.S. government passed the Anti-Cybersquatting Consumer Protection Act in 1999, which made it a crime to register, traffic in, or use a domain name to profit from the goodwill of a trademark belonging to someone else. Fines for cybersquatting can reach as high as $100,000 in addition to the forfeiture of the disputed domain name. As a result, recent court cases have not been kind to squatters. Many feel, however, that it is often much easier simply to pay the cybersquatter because that will likely be much faster and cheaper than to hire a lawyer and go through the lengthy legal process. Others, such as rapper Eminem, who won a case against a company that had registered the domain name eminemmobile.com, use a fast-track procedure of the World Intellectual Property Organization of the United Nations to stop others from using their names without

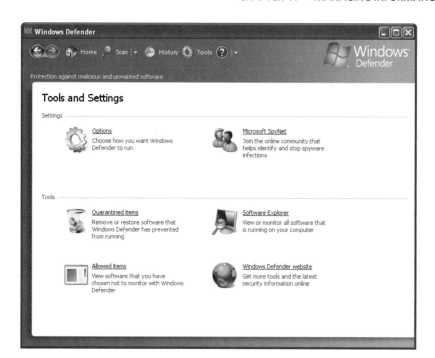

FIGURE 11.11

Windows Defender is a widely used spyware monitoring and removal tool.

permission (see Figure 11.12). No matter how companies or individuals deal with this problem, valuable resources of time and money are wasted resolving these disputes.

Digital Rights Management With consumers increasingly using e-commerce as viable alternatives for traditional commerce, the entertainment industry has no choice but to embrace the Internet as a distribution medium. This transformation of the entertainment industry has undergone a very public and very controversial scrutiny. This controversy centers on **digital rights management (DRM)**, which is a technological solution that allows publishers to control their digital media (music, movies, and so on) to discourage, limit, or prevent illegal copying and distribution. DRM restrictions include which devices

FIGURE 11.12

Rap artist Eminem was a victim of cybersquatting.

will play the media, how many devices the media will play on, and even how many times the media can be played. If you ever downloaded a song or video from Apple's iTunes, then you have experienced DRM, which includes prohibiting users from copying the media or even playing the media on other (non-Apple) devices.

The entertainment industry argues that DRM allows copyright holders to minimize sales losses by preventing unauthorized duplication. Critics refer to DRM as "digital restriction management," stating that publishers are arbitrary on how they enforce DRM. Further, critics argue that DRM enables publishers to infringe on existing consumer rights and to stifle innovation.

Apple and other online music retailers, such as Amazon, are now offering DRM-free downloads. Many users want the ability to freely move their media, typically music or videos, from one device to another with ease. For instance, to remove DRM limitations, iTunes charges a 30¢ per song premium when downloading a song. Without DRM the song can be easily moved and transferred to any device. To prevent illegal sharing of DRM-free content, it is often watermarked so that any illegal copy can be traced to the original purchaser. A digital **watermark** is an electronic version of physical watermarks placed on paper currency to prevent counterfeiting (see Figure 11.13).

Information Accessibility

With the rapid increase in online databases containing personal information and the surge in the use of computer-based communication between individuals, ethical concerns have been raised concerning who has the right to access and monitor this information. **Information accessibility** focuses on defining what information a person or organization has the right to obtain about others and how this information can be accessed and used.

For example, almost everyone sends and receives electronic mail, whether or not they have a PC. All that is needed to participate is access to the Internet, whether through a home PC, a school's computer lab, a wireless phone, a handheld computer, or any of several other devices that provide Internet access. E-mail is one of the most popular software applications of all time, and projections are that its use will only continue to increase. That is why e-mail aficionados and privacy groups were chilled when the Federal Bureau of Investigation (FBI) under the Clinton administration demonstrated a software application named Carnivore to telecommunications industry representatives. Carnivore was designed to be connected to the computers of ISPs, where it would lurk undetected by ISP subscribers and eavesdrop on *all* communications delivered by the ISP, including e-mail, instant messaging, and visits to chat rooms and Internet sites. If the FBI detected communications that it decided were threatening, as in, for example, activities of terrorists, members of organized crime groups, and hackers, they could unleash Carnivore (see Figure 11.14).

FIGURE 11.13

Watermarking is used to prevent counterfeiting currency and digital content.

FIGURE 11.14

How Carnivore works.

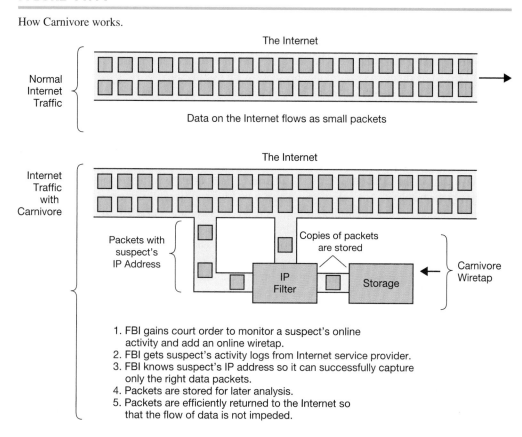

1. FBI gains court order to monitor a suspect's online activity and add an online wiretap.
2. FBI gets suspect's activity logs from Internet service provider.
3. FBI knows suspect's IP address so it can successfully capture only the right data packets.
4. Packets are stored for later analysis.
5. Packets are efficiently returned to the Internet so that the flow of data is not impeded.

In 2005, the FBI abandoned Carnivore in favor of commercially available eavesdropping software. Nevertheless, Carnivore and its successors are extremely controversial. The FBI claims that its cyberwiretaps will provide a "surgical ability" to intercept and collect only those communications that are the subject of lawful wiretaps. However, privacy advocates, such as Marc Totenberg, director of the Electronic Privacy Information Center, counter that unlike police searches of cars and houses for drugs, these cyberwiretaps will allow "dragnet fishing" while sifting through all the traffic on an ISP. Clearly, Carnivore and other eavesdropping technologies will be central to numerous ethical discussions.

Beyond the government's accessing information, recent court cases have not supported computer privacy for employee e-mail transmissions and Internet usage. For example, although most companies provide employees with access to the Internet and other outside e-mail systems, many periodically monitor the e-mail messages that employees send and receive. Monitoring employee behavior is nothing new, and it was to many businesses a natural extension to monitor e-mail messages.

Surprisingly, there is little legal recourse for those who support e-mail privacy. In 1986, Congress passed the Electronic Communications Privacy Act (ECPA), but it offered far stronger support for voice mail than it did for e-mail communications. This act made it much more difficult for anyone (including the government) to eavesdrop on phone conversations. E-mail privacy is, thus, much harder to protect. In addition, no other laws at the federal or state levels protect e-mail privacy. However, some states, most notably California, have passed laws that define how companies should inform their employees of this situation and in which situations monitoring is legal. Even so, this law is more of a guideline for ethical practice than a protection of privacy (Sipior and Ward, 1995).

Fortunately, the ECPA and the court case judgments thus far on e-mail monitoring suggest that companies must be prudent and open about their monitoring of e-mail messages and Internet usage. Companies should use good judgment in monitoring e-mail and should make public their policy about monitoring messages. One primary reason that employees perceive their e-mail to be private is the fact that they are never told otherwise

(Weisband and Reinig, 1995). In addition, employees should use e-mail only as appropriate, based on their company's policy and their own ethical standards. Given recent actions and rulings on the capture and usage of e-mail messages over the Internet, it appears that online privacy is in jeopardy, in and out of business organizations. As a general rule, we all need to realize that what we type and send via e-mail in and out of the workplace is likely to be read by others for whom the messages were not intended. It is wise to generate only those e-mail messages that would not embarrass us if they were made public.

The Need for a Code of Ethical Conduct

Not only has the Internet age found government playing catch-up to pass legislation pertaining to computer crime, privacy, and security, it has also created an ethical conundrum. For instance, the technology exists to rearrange and otherwise change photographs, but is the practice ethical? After all, if photographs no longer reflect absolute reality, how can we trust published images? In the fashion industry, it is common practice to "enhance" photographs of supermodels, and sophisticated software has made this process much easier than ever before. On the other hand, on several occasions, journalists and photographers have been fired from reputable sources such as Reuters or the *Los Angeles Times* for digitally altering pictures to "improve the composition" (an *LA Times* photographer altering an Iraq war scene in 2003) or make certain situations more dramatic (a Reuters freelancer altering pictures of an Israeli air raid on Beirut in 2006). It may not be illegal for you to "steal" computer time from your school or place of employment to do personal business, but many people would consider this unethical. Is it ethical for companies to compile information about your shopping habits, credit history, and other aspects of your life for the purpose of selling such data to others? Should guidelines be in place to dictate how businesses and others use information and computers? If so, what should the guidelines include, and who should write them? Should there be penalties imposed for those who violate established guidelines? If so, who should enforce such penalties?

Many businesses have devised guidelines for the ethical use of information technology and computer systems, and many computer-related professional groups have also published guidelines for their members. Such organizations include the Assistive Devices Industry Association of Canada, the Association for Computing Machinery, the Australian Computer Society, the Canadian Information Processing Society, the Association of Information Technology Professionals, the Hong Kong Computer Society, the Institute of Electrical and Electronics Engineers, the International Federation for Information Processing, the International Programmers Guild, and the National Society of Professional Engineers.

Most universities and many public school systems have written guidelines for students, faculty, and employees about the ethical use of computers. EduCom, a nonprofit organization of colleges and universities, has developed a policy for ethics in information technology that many universities endorse. In part, the EduCom statement concerning software and intellectual rights says,

> Because electronic information is volatile and easily reproduced, respect for the work and personal expression of others is especially critical in computer environments. Violations of authorial integrity, including plagiarism, invasion of privacy, unauthorized access, and trade secret and copyright violations, may be grounds for sanctions against members of the academic community.

Most organization and school guidelines encourage all system users to act responsibly, ethically, and legally when using computers and to follow accepted rules of online etiquette as well as federal and state laws.

Responsible Computer Use The Computer Ethics Institute is a research, education, and policy study organization with members from the IT-related professions and from academic, corporate, and public policy communities. The group studies how advances in information technology have impacted ethics and corporate and public policy and has issued widely quoted guidelines for the ethical use of computers. The guidelines prohibit the following:

- Using a computer to harm others
- Interfering with other people's computer work
- Snooping in other people's files
- Using a computer to steal
- Using a computer to bear false witness
- Copying or using proprietary software without paying for it
- Using other people's computer resources without authorization or compensation
- Appropriating other people's intellectual output

The guidelines recommend the following:

- Thinking about social consequences of programs you write and systems you design
- Using a computer in ways that show consideration and respect for others

Responsible computer use in the Information Age includes following the guidelines mentioned here. As a computer user, when in doubt, you should review the ethical guidelines

Powerful Partnerships

Flickr's Caterina Fake and Stewart Butterfield

What's the tagline for a Web 2.0 company? Let them come and *they* will build it. Caterina Fake, 37, marketing expert and art director, and her husband, Web designer Stewart Butterfield, 33, represent the next generation of successful Web business gurus. Already operating a fledgling gaming company, Ludicorp, the pair was impressed when a coworker devised a photo-sharing program for Web users. They added tools for users to add captions and keywords to locate photos and Flickr was born. The service went online in February 2004, and about three million users have since posted over 130 million photos.

According to Fake, "Will you start a business with me?" came before "Will you marry me?" Two weeks after returning from their honeymoon, the couple started GameNeverending, a Vancouver, British Columbia–based business that designed a site for visitors to interact as they made virtual products, traded, bought, and sold. GameNeverending morphed into Flickr, replacing objects of the game with photos, and now Ludicorp, based in Silicon Valley.

In the beginning, Fake said she and a colleague greeted every single person who visited Flickr. "We introduced them to people, we chatted with them. This is a social product. People are putting things they love—photographs of their whole lives—into it. All of these people are your potential evangelists. You need to show those people love." The personal attention paid off.

Since Web 2.0 businesses have proved cheaper to build, thanks to lower broadband and software costs, Fake and Butterfield started Flickr with no venture capital. They borrowed money from relatives, friends, and angel investors to start Flickr, and investors must have been pleased when Yahoo! bought the business for $30 million in 2005.

FIGURE 11.15

Flickr's Stewart Butterfield and Caterina Fake.

Based on:

Butterfield, S., and C. Fake (2006, December 1). How we did it: Stewart Butterfield and Caterina Fake, co-founders, Flickr. *Inc.com*. Retrieved October 12, 2008, from http://www.inc.com/magazine/20061201/hidi-butterfield-fake.html.

Quittner, J. (2006, April 30). The Flickr founders. *Times*. Retrieved October 12, 2008, from http://www.time.com/time/magazine/article/0,9171,1186931,00.html.

published by your school, place of employment, and/or professional organization. Some users bent on illegal or unethical behavior are attracted by the anonymity they believe the Internet affords. But the fact is that we leave electronic tracks as we wander through the Web, and some perpetrators have been traced and successfully prosecuted when they thought they had hidden their trails. For example, a college student cracking the e-mail account of 2008 U.S. vice presidential candidate Sarah Palin was quickly identified and indicted, even though he used an anonymous proxy server in an attempt to cover his tracks. The fact is, too, that if you post objectionable material on the Internet and people complain about it, your ISP can ask you to remove the material or remove yourself from the service.

Computer Crime

Computer crime is defined as the act of using a computer to commit an illegal act. This broad definition of computer crime can include the following:

- Targeting a computer while committing an offense. For example, someone gains unauthorized entry to a computer system in order to cause damage to the computer system or to the data it contains.
- Using a computer to commit an offense. In such cases, computer users may steal credit card numbers from Web sites or a company's database, skim money from bank accounts, or make unauthorized electronic fund transfers from financial institutions.
- Using computers to support a criminal activity, despite the fact that computers are not actually targeted. For example, drug dealers and other professional criminals may use computers to store records of their illegal transactions.

According to the Computer Security Institute (CSI), the overall trend for computer crime has been declining over the past several years, although there was an uptick in 2006 due to the proliferation of financial fraud attacks (CSI, 2007). The reported losses for organizations due to computer crime have been tremendous. For example, a recent CSI survey of 494 organizations estimated that the various computer crimes cost the organizations over $66 million (see Figure 11.16). Note that this survey represents only a fraction of actual losses to the world economy, where worldwide losses for computer viruses alone were estimated to exceed $13.3 billion in 2006 (see Figure 11.17). Many organizations do not report incidents of computer crime because of fear that negative publicity could hurt stock value or provide advantages to competitors. Thus, experts believe that many incidents are never reported. It is clear that computer crime is a fact of life. In this section, we briefly introduce this topic of growing importance.

The Computer Access Debate

Traditionally, there have been two sides to the issue of computer access. On one side are liberal civil rights champions, the information industry, communications service providers, and hackers who want to prosecute computer criminals under the law but at the same time not severely limit or prevent the free exchange of information. On the opposing side are privacy advocates, government agencies, law enforcement officials, and businesses that depend on the data stored in computers who take a much stricter position, advocating the free exchange of information *only* among those with authorization for access. Anyone who breaks into a computer is trespassing, they say, and all intruders should be subject to penalties under the law.

In today's Information Age, however, the debate has expanded, and lines between the two sides may not be as clearly drawn. The global reach of computer networks has raised concern over copyrights, privacy, and security among all user groups. Most computer users now agree that ownership rights of those who create software and other copyrighted materials disseminated over networks must be protected. And when financial or health-related data is collected about individuals and stored on computers, that information should not be freely available to anyone who can retrieve it. Both sides of the information access argument agree that one of the major challenges of the Information Age will be to protect privacy and security while at the same time allowing authorized access to digitized information.

FIGURE 11.16

Types of computer crime and estimated financial losses for 194 respondents from a variety of organizations.

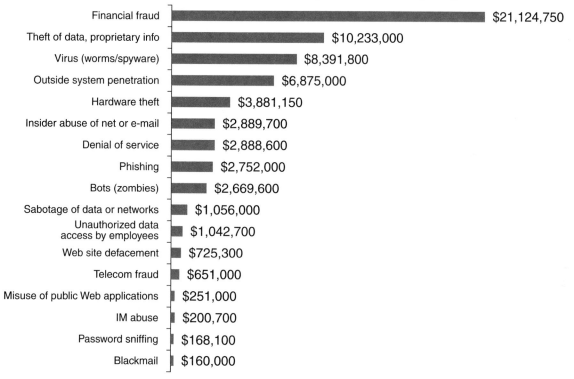

Source: 2007 CSI Computer Crime and Security Survey, Computer Security Institute.

Unauthorized Computer Access

A person who gains unauthorized access to a computer system has committed a computer crime. Unauthorized access means that the person who has gained entry to a computer system has no authority to use such access. Here are a few additional examples from recent media reports:

- Employees steal time on company computers to do personal business.
- Intruders break into government Web sites and change the information displayed.
- Thieves steal credit card numbers and Social Security numbers from electronic databases, then use the stolen information to charge thousands of dollars in merchandise to victims.

Financial Impact of Virus Attacks 1995–2006
Worldwide Impact (US $)

2006	$13.3 billion
2005	14.2 billion
2004	17.5 billion
2003	13.0 billion
2002	11.1 billion
2001	13.2 billion
2000	17.1 billion
1999	13.0 billion
1998	6.1 billion
1997	3.3 billion
1996	1.8 billion
1995	500 million

FIGURE 11.17

Financial impact of virus attacks, 1995–2006.

Source: http://www. computereconomics.com.

However, research conducted by the CSI has found that the frequency of (successful) attacks on computer systems has been declining (see Figure 11.18). Of 436 respondents, representing organizations large and small from a variety of industries, "only" 25 percent reported unauthorized computer use in 2007—this is down from a high of 70 percent in 2000. Although computer crime has decreased somewhat, there is an increasing demand for more and broader federal and state laws to expressly prohibit various crimes, given the widespread and increasing dependence on computer and networking technologies.

Federal and State Laws

In the United States, there are two main federal laws against computer crime: the Computer Fraud and Abuse Act of 1986 and the Electronic Communications Privacy Act of 1986. The Computer Fraud and Abuse Act of 1986 prohibits the following:

- Stealing or compromising data about national defense, foreign relations, atomic energy, or other restricted information
- Gaining unauthorized access to computers owned by any agency or department of the U.S. government
- Violating data belonging to banks or other financial institutions
- Intercepting or otherwise intruding on communications between states or foreign countries
- Threatening to damage computer systems in order to extort money or other valuables from persons, businesses, or institutions

In 1996, the Computer Abuse Amendments Act expanded the Computer Fraud and Abuse Act of 1986 to prohibit the dissemination of computer viruses and other harmful code.

The Electronic Communications Privacy Act of 1986 makes it a crime to break into any electronic communications service, including telephone services. It prohibits the interception of any type of electronic communications. Interception, as defined by the law, includes listening in on communications without authorization and recording or otherwise taking the contents of communications. In 2002, however, the U.S. Congress passed the USA PATRIOT Act (Patriot Act) to extend the Computer Fraud and Abuse Act (see also Chapter 5—Enabling Commerce Using the Internet). Under the prior law, investigators could not monitor voice communication—or stored voice communication—when investigating someone suspected of violating the Computer Fraud and Abuse Act. Under the Patriot Act, investigators can gain access to voice-related communications much more easily, and this makes it a very controversial law. What also raises scrutiny is that it was passed only 45 days after the September 11, 2001, terrorist attacks, under the fear of further attacks, and with very little debate or public awareness. Civil libertarians feel that the Patriot Act greatly erodes many existing constitutional protections. Although the Patriot Act was scheduled to expire on December 31, 2005, it was initially extended and then reauthorized in March 2006. In this reauthorization, fourteen of its sixteen provisions were made into permanent law; two are slated to expire in 2010. Given the polarized views regarding the war on terror and the uneasy trade-offs between civil liberty and homeland security, it is likely that the Patriot Act will continue to be hotly debated long into the future.

FIGURE 11.18

Percentage of organizations reporting incidents of unauthorized computer access has been declining.

Source: 2007 CSI Computer Crime and Security Survey, Computer Security Institute.

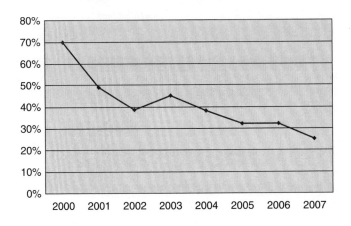

In addition to the primary laws discussed here, other federal laws may apply to computer crime. Patent laws protect some software and computer hardware, and contract laws may protect trade secrets that are stored on computers. In 1980, the U.S. Copyright Act was amended to include computer software, making it a violation of this act to post online written compositions, photos, sound files, and software without the permission of the copyright holder.

The FBI and the U.S. Secret Service jointly enforce federal computer crime laws. The FBI is in charge when crimes involve espionage, terrorism, banking, organized crime, and threats to national security. The Secret Service investigates crimes against U.S. Treasury Department computers and against computers that contain information protected by the Right to Financial Privacy Act. Information protected by the Financial Privacy Act includes credit card information, credit reporting information, and data on bank loan applications. In some federal computer crime cases, the U.S. Customs Department, the Commerce Department, or the military may have jurisdiction. In addition to federal laws against computer crime, all fifty states have passed laws prohibiting computer crime. Many foreign countries also have similar laws.

Some violations of state and federal computer crime laws are charged as misdemeanors. These violations are punishable by fines and by not more than one year in prison. Other violations are classified as felonies and are punishable by fines and by more than one year in prison. The Patriot Act converted many misdemeanors into felony-level offenses. Nevertheless, intent can often determine whether crimes are prosecuted as misdemeanors or felonies. If intruders breach computer systems with intent to do harm, they may be charged with a felony. If a break-in is classified as reckless disregard but causes no damage, the offense may be classified as a misdemeanor.

Some critics argue that laws do not go far enough to prosecute computer crimes, while others believe they should not be invoked when systems are breached but no damage is done. Even the definition of "damage" is debatable. For instance, has damage occurred if someone gains unauthorized access to a computer system but does not steal or change information?

There are additional difficulties in legislating and enforcing laws that affect global networks. Since many countries can be involved when break-ins and other crimes occur, who has jurisdiction? Should e-mail messages be monitored for libelous or other illegal content, and, if so, who should have monitoring responsibility? Is e-mail subject to the same laws as mail delivered by the U.S. Postal Service, or is it more akin to telephone conversations and the laws that apply to them?

Computer Forensics

As computer crime has gone mainstream, law enforcement has had to become much more sophisticated in their computer crime investigations. **Computer forensics** is the use of formal investigative techniques to evaluate digital information for judicial review. Most often, computer forensics experts evaluate various types of storage devices to find traces of illegal activity or to gain evidence in related but noncomputer crimes. In fact, in most missing person or murder cases today, investigators immediately want to examine the victim's computer for clues or evidence.

Organizations and governments are increasingly utilizing *honeypots* to proactively gather intelligence to improve their defenses or to catch cybercriminals. A **honeypot** is a computer, data, or network site that is designed to be enticing to crackers, so as to detect, deflect, or counteract illegal activity. For instance, the FBI operated a cybercrime clearinghouse called "DarkMarket" where unsuspecting hackers, credit card swindlers, and identity thieves bought and sold products and information (Poulsen, 2008). Products for sale included electronic banking logins, stolen personal data, and even specialized hardware for producing counterfeit credit cards. The FBI operated DarkMarket for more than two years to collect information on the global marketplace for cybercriminals. In late 2008, DarkMarket was shut down because it had become known to the criminals. It is without question that countless other honeypots are being operated by governments and computer forensics experts to track criminals and gather information.

Net Stats

Top Cyber Threats

Robert Morris's worm, a bug that crashed a record six thousand computers (a statistic compiled from an estimate that there were sixty thousand computers connected to the Internet at the time and the worm affected 10 percent of them), now seems as antiquated as the 1911 Stutz Bearcat automobile. Morris was a student at Cornell University in 1988 when he devised a program that he later insisted was intended simply to gauge how many computers were connected to the Internet. Errors in Morris's program turned it into a self-replicating monster that overloaded computers and threatened frightened Internet users. Dubbed simply the Internet Worm, Morris's program was the precursor for today's multitude of malevolent codes. For example, in 2008, these five cyber threats made the top of the list for most prevalent:

1. Bots and botnets: networked computers that perform automated spamming activities. The Storm worm botnet will continue to hassle harried IT security experts, since it has managed to evade most antivirus detection programs.
2. Phishing sites will continue to swindle Internet users out of personal information in order to steal from them.
3. Vishing: A new trend in cybercrime, "vishing" is the term for stealing personal and financial

information using voice over Internet protocol (VoIP) telephony.

4. Rootkits: Malware that avoids antivirus detection to take control of a computer's system.
5. Mobile malware: Viruses and spyware previously confined to computers have wormed their way into mobile phones. Programs designed to detect and clean viruses from mobile phones are in use and will continue to develop as new mobile malware threats arise.

One small bit of good news on the malware scene is that adware is continuing to decline, thanks to successful legal prosecutions of some of the largest players.

Based on:

Markoff, J. (1990, May 5). Computer intruder is put on Probation and fined $10,000. *New York Times.* Retrieved October 12, 2008, from http://query.nytimes.com/gst/fullpage.html?res= 9C0CE1D71038F936A35756C0A966958260.

Top 10 Threat Predictions for 2008 (2007, December 3). *CXO Today.* Retrieved October 12, 2008, from http://www.cxotoday.com/India/ Market_Scan/Top_10_Threat%20Predictions_for_2008/551-84917- 1009.html.

Top five cyber threats in 2008 (2008, February 4). *India Times.* Retrieved October 12, 2008, from http://economictimes.indiatimes. com/infotech/internet/Top_five_cyber_threats_in_2008/articleshow/ 2754391.cms.

Although computer forensics experts are extremely skilled in investigating prior and ongoing computer crime, many computer criminals are also experts, making the forensics process extremely difficult in some cases. Some criminals, for example, have special "booby-trap" programs running on computers to destroy evidence if someone other than the criminal uses the machine. Using special software tools, computer forensics experts can often restore data that has been deleted from a computer's hard drive. Clearly, computer forensics will continue to evolve as criminals utilize more sophisticated computer-based methods for committing and aiding criminal activities.

Hacking and Cracking

Those individuals who are knowledgeable enough to gain access to computer systems without authorization have long been referred to as **hackers**. The name was first used in the 1960s to describe expert computer users and programmers who were students at the Massachusetts Institute of Technology. They wrote programs for the mainframes they used and freely exchanged information, but they followed unwritten rules against damaging or stealing information belonging to others. They claimed that their motives for roaming freely through computer systems were based entirely on curiosity and the desire to learn as much as possible about computers.

As computer crime became more prevalent and damaging, true hackers—those motivated by curiosity and not by a desire to do harm—objected to use of the term to describe computer criminals. Today, those who break into computer systems with the intention of doing damage or committing a crime are usually called **crackers**. Some computer criminals attempt to break into systems or deface Web sites to promote political, or ideological goals (such as free speech, human rights, and antiwar campaigns); these Web vandals are referred to as **hacktivists**.

 # Ethical Dilemma

Ethical Hacking

Some hackers who are skilled in "unauthorized computer access" have found that it makes more economic sense to be paid for their computer skills than to continue to operate outside the law. Marc Maiffret, cofounder of a computer security firm, is a case in point.

Maiffret has always been interested in figuring out how things work. When he was small, he took apart various household items to see how they worked, then "tried" to put them back together. He came relatively late to computers, however, but when he got his first machine at the age of fifteen, he immediately tried to figure out how the machine worked.

Maiffret soon discovered the online hacker culture and was intrigued by how they were thinking and approaching problems. To Maiffret, it seemed that hackers were among the greatest thinkers of society, particularly in regard to pushing the limits and understanding things. The progression for him was to go from just trying to understand how software and hardware worked to getting the hard- and software to do what he wanted it to do—beyond what the original manufacturer intended.

By the ripe old age of seventeen, Maiffret knew, through experience, that there were few, if any, computer systems that could keep him out. He had dropped out of high school and was looking for work when he was introduced to Jordanian businessman Firas Bushnaq, then the chief executive officer of eCompany, a software firm. Maiffret offered Bushnaq a deal—if he could break into Bushnaq's corporate network, Bushnaq would hire him as a security expert. Bushnaq agreed, and Maiffret cracked (broke into) eCompany's network in less than an hour. Bushnaq hired Maiffret and taught him how to write commercial software and, perhaps most important, how to run a business.

In 1997, Maiffret and Bushnaq started their own company, eEye Digital Security. The company finds holes in different types of software for its software-vendor clients. It then devises and sells software to prevent unauthorized visitors from breaching a client's system. In other words, eEye sells software that can find the ways a hacker could break into a computer system or network; then, eEye offers information on how those security holes can be fixed. When asked to reveal some of the techniques he uses to discover software vulnerabilities, Maiffret's standard reply is, "I could tell you, but I would have to kill you."

Maiffret's insights into the hacker culture have contributed to his business success. To Maiffret, the "computer underground" is appealing, as differences are accepted far more often than in the 'real' world. The hackers' way of thinking differs vastly from other people, and especially business people. This is partly because many of the best hackers don't have a formal education.

Maiffret's title at eEye was "Chief Hacking Officer." Check out the services offered on the company's Web site (www.eEye.com) to see how one "ethical hacker" has found success in the online business world. In 2007, Maiffret, now aged twenty-seven, left eEye to start his own non-security company.

While Maiffret has made a success of his security business, most hackers who dream of being recognized for their skills and hired by security firms will be disappointed. For example, the president of Rent-A-Hacker, a security troubleshooting firm headquartered in Boulder, Colorado, has said he rejects job-seeking crackers every day. The company employs hackers, but not for illegal activities, and the chief executive officer of Rent-A-Hacker won't hire anyone with a criminal record. The hackers who haven't been arrested are the true experts, the man maintains, and he has employed nearly one hundred of them.

Based on:

Higgins, K. J. (2007, December 12). Maiffret says bye to eEye. *DarkReading*. Retrieved October 12, 2008, from http://www.darkreading.com/document.asp?doc_id=141256.

Rent-a-Hacker (n.d.). Retrieved October 12, 2008, from http://www.rent-a-hacker.com.

Types of Computer Criminals and Crimes

Computer crimes are almost as varied as the users who commit them. Some involve the use of a computer to steal money or other assets or to perpetrate a deception for money, such as advertising merchandise for sale on a Web auction site, collecting orders and payment, and then sending either inferior merchandise or no merchandise at all. Other computer crimes involve stealing or altering information. Some of those thieves who steal information or disrupt a computer system have demanded a ransom from victims in exchange for returning the information or repairing the damage. Cyberterrorists have planted destructive programs in computer systems, then threatened to activate them if a ransom is not paid (see more on cyberterrorism later in this chapter). Crimes in the form of electronic vandalism cause damage when offenders plant viruses, cause computer systems to crash, or deny service on a Web site.

Use of the Internet has fostered other types of criminal activity, such as the stalking of minors by sexual predators through newsgroups and chat rooms. Those who buy, sell, and distribute pornography have also found in the Internet a new medium for carrying out their activities.

Who Commits Computer Crimes? When you hear the term "cracker" or computer criminal, you might imagine a techno-geek, someone who sits in front of his or her computer all day and night, attempting to break the ultra-super-secret security code of one of the most sophisticated computer systems in the world, perhaps a computer for the U.S. military, a Swiss bank, or the Central Intelligence Agency. While this fits the traditional profile for a computer criminal, there is no clear profile today. More and more people have the skills, the tools, and the motives to hack into a computer system. A modern-day computer criminal could be a disgruntled, middle-aged, white-collar worker sitting at a nice desk on the fourteenth floor of the headquarters building of a billion-dollar software manufacturer. Computer criminals have been around for decades. For the most part, we associate hackers and crackers with their pranks and crimes involving security systems and viruses. Nevertheless, hackers and crackers have caused the loss of billions of dollars' worth of stolen goods, repair bills, and lost goodwill with customers.

Studies attempting to categorize computer criminals show that they generally fall into one of four groups. These groups are listed next, from those who commit most infractions to those who commit the fewest number of infractions:

1. Current or former employees who are in a position to steal or otherwise do damage to employers—World Security Corporation reported in 2004 that 85 percent to 95 percent of theft from businesses was perpetrated internally, while just 5 percent to 15 percent involved forced entry; most organizations report insider abuses as their most common crime (CSI, 2007).
2. People with technical knowledge who commit business or information sabotage for personal gain.
3. Career criminals who use computers to assist in crimes.
4. Outside crackers simply snooping or hoping to find information of value—crackers commit millions of intrusions per year, but most cause no harm. Estimates are that only around 12 percent of cracker attacks cause damage.

Some crackers probe others' computer systems, electronically stored data, or Web sites for fun, for curiosity, or just to prove they can. Others have malicious or financial motives and intend to steal for gain or do other harm. Whatever the motives, discovery, prosecution, fines, and jail terms can result.

Data Diddling, Salami Slicing, and Other Techno-Crimes As long as computers and the data they contain are an integral part of our daily lives, criminals will devise ways to take illegal advantage of the technology. Such crimes cost society billions of dollars annually. (The exact amount can only be estimated since many businesses do not report crimes for fear of losing customers or devaluing the company's stock if the offenses became public.) Over the years, colorful jargon has evolved to label the many types of computer crime, as summarized in Table 11.2. Additionally, technology facilitates many traditional types of crimes such as harassment (i.e., where individuals with grudges send threatening e-mail, post names and addresses of adversaries on Web sites, and so on) or the victimization of children and adults through stalking and other predatory practices.

Software Piracy

Software developers and marketers want you to buy as many copies of their products as you want, of course. But commercial software vendors do not want you or anyone else to buy one copy, then bootleg additional copies to sell or to give to others. Vendors also take a dim view of companies that buy one copy of a software application, then make many copies to distribute to employees. In fact, the practice is called **software piracy**, and it is illegal (see Figure 11.19).

TABLE 11.2 Types of Computer Crimes

Type of Crime	Description	Recent Examples
Carding	Stealing credit card information for one's own use or to sell	A carder code named Smak sells a CD with 100,000 credit card numbers to undercover law enforcement agents.
Cloning	Using scanners to steal wireless transmitter codes for cell phones, then duplicating the phone for illegal use	The practice was so prevalent in New York City in the mid-1990s that the mayor, police commissioner, and a city council member were victims.
Data diddling	Changing electronic data before or after it is entered on computers	A payroll clerk in a large company credits overtime hours to her own account, allowing her to steal hundreds of thousands of dollars from the company and her fellow employees.
Dumpster diving	Scouring wastebaskets and dumpsters for credit card receipts and other information, then using the information illegally or selling it	An identity thief searches garbage for store receipts, utility bills, bank statements, and so on, to defraud the unsuspecting victim.
Phishing or **spoofing**	Attempting to trick financial account and credit card holders into giving away their authorization information, usually by posting false Web sites that duplicate legitimate sites	Many account holders at eBay, the popular auction Web site, were duped by a false Web site into giving up account numbers.
Phreaking	Breaking into telephone systems to make free long-distance calls or for other purposes	John Draper (aka "Captain Crunch") used a whistle found in a box of breakfast cereal to imitate the phone system's connection tones, thus getting free access to long-distance calls.
Piggybacking or **shoulder-surfing**	Looking over a person's shoulder while he or she is using an automated teller machine, cell phone, or other device in order to steal access information	At the Port Authority Terminal in New York City, computer fraud officers have often arrested people using binoculars to filch codes from telephone calling cards.
Salami slicing	Stealing small amounts of money from a large number of financial accounts	A bank employee transfers one penny from the balance of thousands of accounts every day and puts the money in an account she has set up for herself. She accumulates hundreds of thousands of dollars before being discovered.
Social engineering or **masquerading**	Misrepresenting yourself in order to steal equipment or to trick others into revealing sensitive information	Famous cracker Kevin Mitnick, who served prison time in California under computer crime statutes, frequently used social engineering to get access to computer systems or facilities.
Vishing	Also known as voice phishing; instead of asking users to visit a Web site, asking users to call a fake telephone number and "confirm" their account information	An e-mail asks the recipient to call a phone number to confirm his credit card information. The fake phone number has been set up using VoIP technology, and the caller transfers his information to a scammer located somewhere around the globe, who is then able to run charges on the credit card.

FIGURE 11.19

In many parts of the world, using pirated software is a common practice.

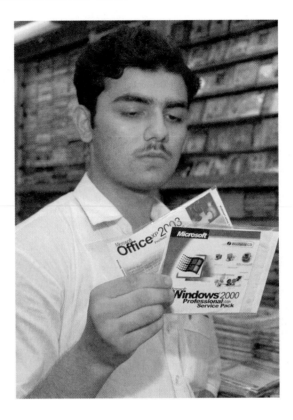

When you buy commercial software, it is legal for you to make one backup copy for your own use. It is also legal to offer shareware or public domain software for free through bulletin boards and other Web sites. But **warez** peddling—offering stolen proprietary software for free over the Internet—is a crime. ("Warez" is the slang term for such stolen software.)

Both patent and copyright laws can apply to software, which is a form of **intellectual property (IP)**—creations of the mind (e.g., music, software, etc.), inventions, names, images, designs, and other works used in commerce. Patents and copyrights are recognized and enforced by most countries, giving the creator exclusive rights to benefit from the creation for a limited period of time. **Patents** typically refer to process, machine, or material inventions. For example, Amazon.com's "one-click buying" process is protected by patent law and Apple is trying to patent its "pinch" for shrinking and expanding items on the iPhone. **Copyrights** generally refer to creations of the mind such as music, literature, or software. Copyright laws covering software include the 1980 Computer Software Copyright Act, a 1992 act that made software piracy a felony, and the 1997 No Electronic Theft (NET) Act, which made copyright infringement a criminal act even when no profit was involved.

Software piracy has become a problem because it is so widespread, costing the commercial software industry and the entire economy billions of dollars a year. A 2008 study conducted by the Business Software Alliance (BSA) suggested that reducing software piracy by only 10 percent over the next four years could generate 32,000 new jobs, $7 billion in tax revenues, and $41 billion in revenues for the software companies. The crime is difficult to trace, but many individuals and even companies have been successfully prosecuted for pirating software. Many software vendors are trying to limit software piracy by requiring the users to enter license keys, or verifying the key before allowing the customer to register or update the software. With its new operating system Windows Vista, Microsoft went even further. When a user first installs the software, and on every subsequent update to the operating system, the system attempts to validate itself in order to confirm that the software has been successfully registered. If the software has not been successfully registered, the user will have thirty days to enter a valid license key. After such time, Vista will switch into a *reduced functionality mode,* severely limiting what can be done on the computer. For example, a user will only be able to use the Web browser for one hour before being logged off, will not be allowed to use Microsoft Office tools to view or edit documents, and will only receive the most critical security updates. Some view Microsoft's new policy as being a bit Draconian, while others feel that such aggressive measures are long overdue.

Software Piracy Is a Global Business A major international issue businesses deal with is the willingness (or unwillingness) of governments and individuals to recognize and enforce the ownership of intellectual property—in particular, software copyright. Piracy of software and other technologies is widespread internationally. The Business Software Alliance points to countries such as Armenia (93 percent), Bangladesh (92 percent), Moldova (92 percent), Azerbaijan (92 percent), Zimbabwe (91 percent), and Sri Lanka (90 percent) as those with the highest percentages of illegal software (Business Software Alliance, 2008). In these countries, more than 90 percent of the software used consists of illegal copies. Worldwide losses due to piracy exceeded $48 billion in 2007. Countries with the lowest piracy rates include the United States (20 percent), Luxembourg (21 percent), New Zealand (22 percent), Japan (23 percent), and Austria (25 percent). Because technology usage varies significantly by region, average piracy levels and dollar losses greatly differ across regions (see Table 11.3). For instance, even though the United States has the lowest piracy rate, it also is where the greatest losses (more than $8 billion) occur due to its high level of computer usage.

In addition to being a crime, is software piracy also an ethical problem? Perhaps in part, but businesspeople must acknowledge and deal with other perspectives as well. In part, the problem stems from countries' differing concepts of ownership. Many of the ideas about intellectual property ownership stem from long-standing cultural traditions. For example, the concept of individual ownership of knowledge is traditionally a strange one in many Middle Eastern countries, where knowledge is meant to be shared. Plagiarism does not exist in a country where words belong to everyone. By the same token, piracy does not exist either. This view is gradually changing; the Saudi Arabia Patent Office granted its first patents several years ago, and their piracy rates have plummeted from 79 percent in 1996 to 51 percent in 2007.

In other cases, there are political, social, and economic reasons for piracy. In many countries, software publishers are not catering to the needs of consumers, who often simply do not have the funds to purchase software legitimately. This is true in many areas of South America and other regions with low per capita income. It is particularly true of students and other members of university communities whose needs are critical in some areas.

Other factors leading to piracy or infringement of intellectual property agreements throughout the world include lack of public awareness about the issue, lack of an industrial infrastructure that can produce legitimate software, and the increasingly high demand for computer and other technology products. The United States has repeatedly pressured and threatened other countries accused of pirating. It is interesting to note, however, that

TABLE 11.3 Software Piracy Levels and Dollar Losses by Region

Region	Piracy Level	Dollar Loss (million)
North America	21%	9,144
Western Europe	33%	11,655
Asia/Pacific	59%	14,090
Latin America	66%	4,123
Middle East/Africa	60%	2,446
Eastern Europe	68%	6,351
World Wide	35%	47,809

Source: Business Software Alliance (2008).

despite the fact that few of these cultural and economic explanations are valid in the United States, the U.S. leads the world in the sheer volume of illegal software in use. Businesses that operate in glass offices should surely not throw stones.

Computer Viruses and Other Destructive Code

Malware—short for "malicious software" such as viruses, worms, and Trojan horses—continues to have a tremendous economic impact on the world, costing organizations more than $13 billion in 2006 (computereconomics.com, 2008). Antivirus Web vendors report thousands of new forms of malware each month. *Viruses* are destructive programs that disrupt the normal functioning of computer systems. They differ from other types of malicious code in that they can reproduce themselves. Some viruses are intended to be harmless pranks, but more often they do damage to a computer system by erasing files on the hard drive or by slowing computer processing or otherwise compromising the system.

Viruses are planted in host computers in a number of ways (Figure 11.20). Boot sector viruses attach themselves to that section of a hard disk that lets the user boot up or start the computer. They are most often spread through malicious e-mail attachments or file downloads. File infector viruses attach themselves to files with certain extensions, such as .doc or .exe. Some viruses are a combination of boot sector and file infector viruses, and many of these can mutate in order to fool antivirus programs. Viruses transmitted through e-mail messages became popular in the late 1990s. When an unsuspecting recipient of an e-mail message opens the message or an attachment to the message, the virus is activated. Usually such e-mail viruses can then send copies of themselves to everyone in the victim's address book, thus spreading throughout networked computers at an alarming rate.

Worms, Trojan Horses, and Other Sinister Programs Viruses are among the most virulent forms of computer infections, but other destructive code can also be damaging. A *worm,* for example, usually does not destroy files, but, like a virus, it is designed to copy and send itself, spreading rapidly throughout networked computers. It eventually brings computers to a halt simply by clogging memory space with the outlaw code, thus preventing normal function.

Another destructive program is the **Trojan horse**. Unlike a virus, the Trojan horse does not copy itself, but, like viruses, it can do much damage. When a Trojan horse is

FIGURE 11.20

How a computer virus is spread.

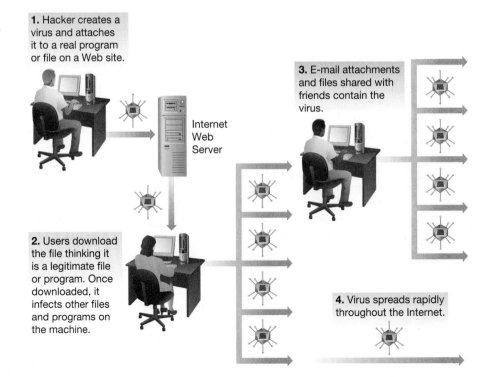

planted in a computer, its instructions remain hidden. The computer appears to function normally, but in fact it is performing underlying functions dictated by the intrusive code. For example, under the pretext of playing chess with an unsuspecting systems operator, a cracker group installed a Trojan horse in a Canadian mainframe. While the game appeared to be proceeding normally, the Trojan horse program was sneakily establishing a powerful unauthorized account for the future use of the intruders.

Logic bombs or **time bombs** are variations of Trojan horses. They also do not reproduce themselves and are designed to operate without disrupting normal computer function. Instead, they lie in wait for unsuspecting computer users to perform a triggering operation. Time bombs are set off by specific dates, such as the birthday of a famous person. Logic bombs are set off by certain types of operations, such as entering a specific password or adding or deleting names and other information to and from certain computer files. Disgruntled employees have planted logic and time bombs on being fired, intending for the program to activate after they have left the company. In at least one instance in recent history, a former employee in Minnesota demanded money to deactivate the time bomb he had planted in company computers before it destroyed employee payroll records.

The Rise of Botnets and the Cyberattack Supply Chain In Chapter 8, we briefly described bots—software robots, that work in the background to provide services to their owners. Destructive bots, working together on a collection of zombie computers via the Internet, called **botnets,** have become the standard method of operation for professional

Brief Case ⊘

The Vulnerabilities of Online Banking

Everyone who regularly uses online banking services agrees that it's convenient—you can make a deposit sitting at your desk in your pajamas, send in a car payment on your cell phone, and get up-to-the-minute statements via your computer so that you never have to worry about overdrawing your account. The bad news is, once again, that hackers have devised a malevolent program that can silently and without warning grab your banking information before it is encrypted and send it to the attacker's computer. This Trojan program, dubbed Silentbanker, is downloaded from infected Web sites and installed in unsuspecting computer users' Web browsers. It then silently captures screen images and steals passwords, account numbers, and other financial information from legitimate users' accounts.

While two-factor authentication systems that go beyond just a user name and password are in place on most electronic banking sites to protect customers, Silentbanker circumvents these systems. Users see what they expect to see, with no clue that a mute masked robber is stealing from their bank accounts. For many people, banking Trojans are worrying, but the scale and sophistication of the Silentbanker Trojan was troubling even for people who deal with these every day, such as Symantec security expert Liam O. Murchu.

In early 2008, Silentbanker had targeted over four hundred banks, both in the United States and abroad. The virus was relatively easy to remove, but wreaked havoc on untold bank accounts before it was detected. As of March 2008, security experts like Liam O. Murchu were working hard to eradicate Silentbanker, one of the latest—but unfortunately not the last—tools for cybercriminals.

Questions

1. What steps can you take to protect yourself when doing online banking?
2. Why do you think it is so hard to protect consumers from sinister programs like Silentbanker?

Based on:

Murchu, L. O. (2008, January 14). Banking in silence. Retrieved October 12, 2008, from https://forums.symantec.com/syment/blog/article?blog.id=malicious_code&thread.id=181.

Reed, B. (2008, January 14). New Trojan intercepts online banking information. *NetworkWorld.* Retrieved October 12, 2008 , from http://www.networkworld.com/news/2008/011408-silentbanker-trojan.html.

Weinberg, N. (2008, January 14). Two-factor authentication: Hot technology for 2008. *NetworkWorld.* Retrieved October 12, 2008, from http://www.networkworld.com/research/2008/011408-8-techs-authentication.html.

cybercriminals. For example, about 85 percent of all e-mail spam is sent out by only six major botnets. Attacks using botnets are emerging into a global supply chain of highly specialized criminals. For instance, a phishing attack can involve the following:

1. A *programmer* writes a phishing attack template and makes this available for purchase.
2. A *phisher* who wants to run an attack purchases the template and designs an attack (e.g., update your banking information at the Wells Fargo Bank).
3. The *phisher* contracts with a *cracker* to provide hosting space for the phishing Web sites.
4. The *phisher* contacts a **bot herder**—a criminal who has a botnet residing on a collection of zombie computers—to send out the spam e-mail that carries the attack to unsuspecting people.
5. After launching the attack and collecting information from those who responded to the phishing attack, the *phisher* provides the stolen personal information to a *collector* who specializes in removing funds from the affected financial institutions.
6. The *collector* works with a criminal called a *mule herder* who has a network of people who carry out the withdrawals from affected banks.

Each member of the supply chain has very specialized skills and can be located anywhere in the world. In fact, one of the difficulties in stopping this global crime syndicate is the difficulty of not only tracking the locations of these villains, but also prosecuting criminals across international borders. Today, a would-be cybercriminal does not need highly specialized computer skills to build a botnet; rather, the criminal can easily "rent" space on a botnet (including technical support from the bot herder, tremendous resources, and bandwidth) for around $1,000 per spam or denial of service attack.

Internet Hoaxes

An **Internet hoax** is a false message circulated online about new viruses; funds for alleged victims of crime or the September 11, 2001, terrorist attacks; kids in trouble; cancer causes; or any other topic of public interest. One especially effective virus hoax that was circulated in 2004 was an e-mail message that told recipients that someone they knew had inadvertently infected their computers with a virus. To rid themselves of the infection, message recipients were told to look for a certain file and delete it, then inform everyone in their address books of the virus. The message was a hoax. The file was a legitimate component of the Microsoft Windows operating system, and people who received the hoax message deleted it and told others to delete it also. Fortunately, the file was not crucial to the Windows operating system, and most computer operators who deleted it did not suffer any consequences. The message functioned as a virus in that unsuspecting recipients quickly passed it along, and recipients themselves destroyed files on hard drives.

In most cases, the consequences of passing on a hoax will be small, and your friends will just ridicule you; in other cases, spammers might "harvest" e-mail addresses from hoaxes, potentially causing your inbox to be flooded with junk mail. Several Web sites such as Hoaxbusters (hoaxbusters.ciac.org), Symantec, or McAfee publish lists of known hoaxes, and you should always check to see if a message is a hoax before you forward it to others.

Cyber Harassment, Stalking, and Bullying

The Internet has become a place where people utilize its anonymity to harass, bully, and stalk others. **Cyber harassment**, a crime in many states and countries, broadly refers to the use of a computer to communicate obscene, vulgar, or threatening content that causes a reasonable person to endure distress. A single offensive message can be considered cyber harassment.

Repeated contacts with a victim are referred to as **cyber stalking**. Cyber stalking can take many forms, including:

■ Making false accusations that damage the reputation of the victim on blogs, Web sites, chat rooms, or commerce sites (e.g., eBay).
■ Gaining information on a victim by monitoring online activities, accessing databases, and so on.

Coming Attraction

Invisibility on the Horizon?

Remember H. G. Wells' classic 1933 story, *The Invisible Man*, about a scientist who goes mad when he can't reverse the process that rendered him invisible? To be "seen" in public, the unfortunate scientist had to swathe himself in bandages, otherwise he remained completely invisible to human eyes—a prospect he couldn't abide.

Seventy-five years later, invisibility may, indeed, be an achievable concept—not exactly as Wells envisioned, but possible, nevertheless, from a scientific standpoint. The key word, scientists at Purdue University in West Lafayette, Indiana, have found, is *metamaterials* that bend light in extraordinary ways.

Metamaterials (Rodger M. Walser of the University of Texas at Austin coined the term in 1999) gain their properties from their structure, rather than from their composition. That is, according to Walser: "Macroscopic composites have a manmade, three-dimensional, periodic cellular architecture designed to produce an optimized combination, not available in nature, of *two or more responses* to specific excitation." In simpler terms, macromaterials have a negative index of refraction. They bend light in the opposite direction one would expect. Effectively, nanowires imbedded within the materials render objects invisible. Refraction-free lenses, powerful microscopes, and cloaking devices are possibilities for practical uses of macromaterials in the future. Invisible men? Probably not any time soon.

Based on:

Bullis, K. (2007, October 15). Invisibility made easier. *MIT Technology Review.* Retrieved October 12, 2008, from http://www.technologyreview.com/Nanotech/19576.

Graham-Rowe, D. (2007, April 11). How to make an object invisible. *MIT Technology Review.* Retrieved October 12, 2008, from http://www.technologyreview.com/Nanotech/18514.

Walser, R. M. (2003). Metamaterials: An introduction. In W. S. Weiglhofer and A. Lakhtakia (eds.), *Introduction to complex mediums for electromagnetics and optics* (pp. 295–316). Bellingham, WA: SPIE Press.

- Encouraging others to harass a victim by posting personal information about the victim on Web sites or in chat rooms.
- Attacking data and equipment of the victim by sending e-mail viruses and other destructive code.
- Using the Internet to place false orders for goods and services such as magazines, pornography, and other embarrassing items as well as having such items delivered to work addresses.

Many states, the U.S. government, and many countries have anti-cyber-stalking laws. Unfortunately, law enforcement has a difficult time catching most cyber stalkers. While cyber stalking can take many forms, and can go undetected by the victim, the intent of **cyber bullying** is to *deliberately* cause emotional distress in the victim. Cyber harassment, stalking, and bullying are typically targeted at a particular person or group as a means of revenge or hatred.

In contrast, **online predators** typically target vulnerable people, usually the young or old, for sexual or financial purposes. While online chat rooms and instant messaging systems have been the playground for online predators, these villains are also targeting many social networking sites like MySpace. To combat these online predators, parents must educate their children not to share personal information and possibly use monitoring software to track online activity. Fortunately, most social networking and online chat sites also provide ways to report abuse by these predators.

Cyberwar and Cyberterrorism

Over the past several years, individual computer criminals have caused billions of dollars in losses through the use of viruses, worms, and unauthorized access to computers. In the future, many believe that coordinated efforts by national governments or terrorist groups have the potential to do hundreds of billions of dollars in damage as well as put the lives of countless people at stake (Panko, 2007). Most experts believe that cyberwar and cyberterrorism are imminent threats to the United States and other technologically advanced countries. A major attack that cripples a country's information infrastructure or power grid or even the global Internet could have devastating implications for a country's (or the world's) economic system and make transportation systems, medical capabilities, and other key infrastructure extremely vulnerable to disaster.

Cyberwar

Cyberwar refers to an organized attempt by a country's military to disrupt or destroy the information and communication systems of another country. Cyberwar is often executed simultaneously with traditional methods to quickly dissipate the capabilities of an enemy. Given that the United States and the NATO alliance is the most technologically sophisticated war machine in the world—and also the most dependent on its networking and computing infrastructure—it is also the most vulnerable to a cyberwar (or cyberterrorism) attack.

Cyberwar Vulnerabilities The goal of cyberwar is to turn the balance of information and knowledge in one's favor in order to enhance one's capabilities while diminishing those of an opponent. Cyberwar will utilize a diverse range of technologies, including software, hardware, and networking technologies, to gain an information advantage over an opponent. These technologies will be used to electronically blind, jam, deceive, overload, and intrude into an enemy's computing and networking capabilities in order to diminish various capabilities, including the following:

- Command and control systems
- Intelligence collection and distribution systems
- Information processing and distribution systems
- Tactical communication systems and methods
- Troop and weapon positioning systems
- Friend-or-foe identification systems
- Smart weapons systems

Additionally, controlling the content and distribution of propaganda and information to an opponent's civilians, troops, and government is a key part of a cyberwar strategy. At the simplest level, **Web vandalism** can occur by simply defacing Web sites. Likewise, cyber propaganda can be quickly and easily distributed through chat rooms, Web sites, and e-mail. Espionage—stealing of secrets or modifying information—can occur if data and systems are not adequately protected and secure.

The New Cold War According to the 2007 annual report of the Internet security company McAfee, a *cyber cold war* is an imminent threat for the world's computers. They report that more than 120 nations are developing ways to use the Internet as a weapon to target financial markets, governmental computer systems, and key infrastructure. Reminiscent of the Cold War—a period of conflict, tension, and competition between the United States and the Soviet Union and their respective allies from the mid-1940s until the early 1990s (see Figure 11.21)—intelligence agencies from countries around the world are secretly testing networks and looking for weaknesses in their potential enemies' computer systems. There are several known attacks, although most governments deny involvement. Typically, governments accused of cyberwar activities blame uncontrolled **patriot hackers**—independent citizens or supporters of a country that perpetrate attacks on perceived or real enemies. Regardless of the source of these attacks, it is clear that one of the big challenges for governments moving forward will be to fully integrate a cyberwar strategy into their overall plans and capabilities. In 2006, for example, the U.S. launched the Air Force Cyber Command (see Figure 11.22), its newest major command with a mission to stand "alongside Air Force Space Command and Air Combat Command as the

FIGURE 11.21

The Cuban missile crisis was the height of the Cold War.

provider of forces that the president, combatant commanders, and the American people can rely on for preserving the freedom of access and commerce, in air, space, and now cyberspace" (Michael W. Wynne, Secretary, U.S. Air Force). By late 2008, some controversy had arisen regarding whether the Air Force alone or a multi-agency command would be best equipped to combat global cyberattacks for the United States. Regardless of how the Cyber Command is ultimately configured, it is clear that the United States, and most other nations, are making a major investment and commitment to cyberwar capabilities.

FIGURE 11.22

The U.S. Air Force Cyber Command was created for the cyber Cold War.

War and the Value of Networks

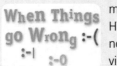

The Internet began as a Department of Defense (DoD) project—a network to connect scientists, mathematicians, technicians, military strategists, and others with an interest in networking information. The DoD, therefore, knows the value of networks. And technology has infiltrated every aspect of military operations, as few could foresee back when the Internet was in its infancy. Networks and technology have helped bring the sprawling, multifaceted DoD into the Information Age. Precision weapons that can take out a small group of enemy soldiers without harming civilians in the area, up-to-the-second battleground communications, GPS devices for troops to keep track of where their comrades are, lighter yet more accurate arms for infantry soldiers all add up to a technology-enabled, effective fighting force.

In Iraq, however, military commanders gradually learned that human networks operating within the country's population were as vital to military success as any technological network. To augment technical expertise, in 2007 the Army apportioned $41 million to build Human Terrain Teams (HTTs), consisting of 150 social scientists, computer software geeks, and experts on local culture. The HTTs were then embedded with twenty-six different military units in Iraq and Afghanistan, where their duties consist of advising local military commanders on cultural issues. The HTTs have been effective in areas where technology had faced a stalemate. For example, a village in Afghanistan was frequently bombed to rid the area of Taliban insurgents, but with little success. When an HTT visited the village, they learned from local residents that if the Americans would provide some security, members of the Taliban would stay away, thus removing the necessity for periodic bombings. (The villagers also requested a volleyball net.) The village got its security patrols and its volleyball net, and the Taliban lost another safe refuge.

Technology has definitely changed the way countries wage war, but superior technological ability doesn't always ensure success. American military commanders in Iraq and Afghanistan have learned that knowing the human residents in an occupied country is perhaps even more important than knowing how to enter coordinates to bomb a precise area in a crowded neighborhood.

Based on:

Shachtman, N. (2007, November 27). How technology almost lost the war: In Iraq, the critical networks are social—not electronic. *Wired*. Retrieved October 12, 2008, from http://www.wired.com/politics/security/magazine/15-12/ff_futurewar?currentPage=1.

Cyberterrorism

Unlike cyberwar, **cyberterrorism** is launched not by governments but by individuals and organized groups. Cyberterrorism is the use of computer and networking technologies against persons or property to intimidate or coerce governments, civilians, or any segment of society in order to attain political, religious, or ideological goals. One of the great fears about cyberterrorism is that an attack can be launched from a computer anywhere in the world—no borders have to be crossed, no bombs smuggled and placed, and no lives lost in carrying out the attack. Because computers and networking systems control power plants, telephone systems, and transportation systems, as well as water and oil pipelines, any disruption in these systems could cause loss of life or widespread chaos (Volonino and Robinson, 2004). Just as physical terrorist attacks have physical and psychological effects, so also do cyberattacks. Dealing with the unknown—where, when, and how—of an indiscriminant terrorist attack is what leads to "terror."

What Kinds of Attacks Are Considered Cyberterrorism? Cyberterrorism could involve physical destruction of computer systems or acts that destroy economic stability or infrastructure. Cyberterrorist acts could likely damage the machines that control traffic lights, power plants, dams, or airline traffic in order to create fear and panic. Attacks

TABLE 11.4 Categories of Potential Cyberterrorist Attacks

Category	Description
Coordinated bomb attacks	To distribute a number of devices—from small explosive devices to large weapons of mass destruction—that communicate with each other through the Internet or cellular phone network and are made to simultaneously detonate if one device stops communicating with the others
Manipulation of financial and banking information	To disrupt the flow of financial information with the objective of causing fear and lack of confidence in the world's or a country's financial system
Manipulation of the pharmaceutical industry	To make hard-to-detect changes in the formulas of medications in order to cause fear and lack of confidence in this important industry
Manipulation of transportation control systems	To disrupt airline and railroad transportation systems, possibly leading to disastrous collisions
Manipulation of the broader civilian infrastructures	To compromise the communication, broadcast media, gas lines, water systems, and electrical grids in order to cause panic and fear within the population
Manipulation of nuclear power plants	To disrupt cooling systems in order to cause a meltdown that would disperse radiation

launched in cyberspace could take many forms, such as viruses, denial of service, destruction of government computers, stealing classified files, altering Web page content, deleting or corrupting vital information, disrupting media broadcasts, and otherwise interrupting the flow of information. Table 11.4 summarizes several categories of attacks that experts believe cyberterrorists will try to deliver.

The goal of cyberterrorists is to cause fear, panic, and destruction. Through the power of computer technology and global networks, terrorists can gain access to critical parts of the world's infrastructure to produce both physical and virtual terror. Given the great potential for cyberterrorism, many experts believe that it will, unfortunately, become the weapon of choice for the world's most sophisticated terrorists.

How the Internet Is Changing the Business Processes of Terrorists Virtually all modern terrorist groups utilize the Internet (Weimann, 2006). Beyond using the Internet to wage cyberattacks, the Internet is a powerful tool for improving and streamlining the business processes of the modern terrorist (see Table 11.5). Just as the Internet has fueled globalization for organizations and societies, it too has fueled global terrorism. Clearly, the Internet is transforming the "business processes" of the modern terrorist.

Assessing the Cyberterrorism Threat Some experts claim that because of the general openness of access, the Internet infrastructure is vulnerable to cyberterrorism; such incidents are often cited by the media. For example, in a January 2000 article for *Blueprint Magazine,* "Get Ready for Cyberwar," author Sam Nunn reported the following:

■ In a 1997 operation called *Eligible Receiver,* the U.S. government hired thirty-five hackers to test the nation's vulnerability to cyberattacks. The attackers, dubbed "Red Team," quickly obtained access to thirty-six of the Department of Defense's forty thousand networks. They determined that they could have shut down large segments of the nation's power grid and disrupted communications of the Pacific Command in Honolulu.

TABLE 11.5 **How Terrorists Are Using the Internet**

Use	Description
Information dissemination	The use of Web sites to disseminate propaganda to current and potential supporters, to influence international public opinion, and to notify potential enemies of pending plans.
Data mining	The use of the vast amount of information available on the Internet regarding virtually any topic for planning, recruitment, and numerous other endeavors.
Fund-raising	The use of Web sites for bogus charities and nongovernmental organizations to raise funds and transfer currencies around the world.
Recruiting and mobilization	The use of Web sites to provide information for recruiting new members as well as utilizing more interactive Internet technologies, such as roaming online chat rooms and cybercafés for receptive individuals.
Networking	The use of the Internet to enable a less hierarchical, cell-based organizational structure that is much more difficult to combat; networking capabilities also allow different groups, with common enemies, to better share and coordinate information.
Information sharing	The use of the Internet as a powerful tool for announcing events as well as sharing best practices; for example, the official Hamas Web site details how to make homemade poisons and gases.
Planning and coordinating	The use of communication and information dissemination capabilities to facilitate designing and executing plans.
Information gathering	The use of mapping software such as Google Earth to locate potential targets for terrorist attacks.
Location monitoring	The use of public Web cams to monitor and study potential attack sites (e.g., Times Square or public resources such as tunnels or power generation facilities).

- In another systems vulnerability probe, the Defense Information Systems Agency followed the results of some 38,000 deliberate attacks. Only 5 percent of the systems administrators realized they were under attack, and only 4 percent of those reported the attacks to a higher authority.

The U.S. Department of Defense, a popular target for hackers and crackers, reported in late 2004 that it receives some sixty to ninety attacks by unauthorized intruders daily. However, many attacks are launched against other governmental institutions or countries. While the majority of such attacks have not done damage, a few were alarmingly successful:

- During the Gulf War in 1991, a group of Dutch crackers stole electronic information about U.S. troop movements and offered it for sale to Iraq. The Iraqis turned down the offer, thinking it was a hoax.
- In 1998, a twenty-year-old Israeli cracker, Ehud Tennebaum, also known as "The Analyzer," joined two crackers in California to disrupt U.S. troop movements by disabling computers at the Pentagon, the National Security Agency, and national labs.
- In 1999, crackers allegedly gained control of a British military communication satellite and held it for ransom. The British military denied that the satellite had ever been under the control of intruders.
- Also in 1999, during the Serbia/Kosovo war, Serb crackers allegedly gained access to NATO Web pages and flooded e-mail accounts with pro-Serb messages.

■ During the 2000 presidential election in the United States, Web attacks were reported that involved intruders with various political motives. Information was changed on targeted Web sites, snooping on political sites was rampant, and many denial of service attacks were launched.

■ In May 2003, Romanian crackers compromised systems that housed life support control for fifty-eight scientists and contractors in Antarctica. FBI agents assisted in the arrest of the crackers who attempted to extort money from the research station.

■ In May 2007, government networks and commerical banks within Estonia came under a very sophisticated cyberattack by cyberterrorists for the removal of a Soviet-era memorial to fallen soldiers.

While defense and security departments within the United States need to protect against cyberterrorism, the U.S. military has also researched methods of using information technology to its advantage in times of war. For example, the United States reportedly conducted its first cyberwar campaign during the seventy-eight-day Serbia/Kosovo war by establishing a team of information warriors to support its bombing campaign against Serbia. The U.S. information operation cell electronically attacked Serbia's critical networks and command and control systems.

While cyberterrorism obviously remains a threat to computer and network security, some experts point out that there are disadvantages to using acts of cyberterrorism as a weapon, including the following:

1. Computer systems and networks are complex, so cyberattacks are difficult to control and may not achieve the desired destruction as effectively as physical weapons.

2. Computer systems and networks change and security measures improve, so it requires an ever-increasing level of knowledge and expertise on the part of intruders for cyberattacks to be effective. This means that perpetrators will be required to continuously study and hone their skills as older methods of attack no longer work.

3. Cyberattacks rarely cause physical harm to victims; therefore, there is less drama and emotional appeal for perpetrators than using conventional weapons.

While cyberterrorism and cyberwar may be methods of choice for future generations with advanced computer knowledge, experts are hopeful that the increasing sophistication of computer security measures will help reduce the number of such incidents.

The Globalization of Terrorism With the proliferation and dependence on technology increasing at an astronomical rate, the threat of cyberterrorism will continue to increase. As has been true with virtually all governments and business organizations, fueled by the digitization of information and the Internet, terrorism has become a global business. To be adequately prepared, national governments along with industry partners must design coordinated responses to various attack scenarios. In addition to greater cooperation and preparedness, governments must improve their intelligence-gathering capabilities so that potential attacks are thwarted before they begin. Industry must also be given incentives to secure their information resources so that losses and disruptions in operations are minimized. International laws and treaties must rapidly evolve to reflect the realities of cyberterrorism, where attacks can be launched from anywhere in the world, to anywhere in the world. Fortunately, experts believe that the likelihood of a devastating attack that causes significant disruption in the major U.S. infrastructure systems is quite low because the attackers would need "$200 million, intelligence information, and years of preparation" to succeed (Volonino and Robinson, 2004). Nevertheless, small attacks have been occurring for years and are likely to increase in frequency and severity—even a "small" attack, like an individual suicide bomber, can cause tremendous chaos to a society. Clearly, there are great challenges ahead.

Industry Analysis

Cybercops Track Cybercriminals

The *CSI* (crime scene investigation) television shows have made "DNA testing" a household phrase. Virtually everyone knows that a criminal who leaves body cells or fluids—hair and skin cells, saliva, blood, semen, and so on—at the scene of a crime can be linked to the crime through DNA analysis. (DNA, or deoxyribonucleic acid, is present in all living tissue—plant or animal.) The *CSI* shows have helped to illustrate that just as crime laboratories have had to keep technologically current, so, too, have law enforcement officers at national, state, and local levels.

Because technological advancement has been rapid, law enforcement has lagged behind, but it is catching up. At the U.S. federal level, the Computer Crime and Intellectual Property Section within the Justice Department is devoted to combating cybercrime. In addition, the FBI has created computer crime squads in sixteen metropolitan areas around the country specifically to investigate cybercrime. In Washington, D.C., the FBI's National Infrastructure Protection Center acts as a clearinghouse for information and expertise relating to cybercrime. And each federal judicial district has at least one assistant U.S. attorney, called a computer and telecommunications crime coordinator, who has received special training in how to investigate and prosecute cybercrime.

Furthermore, every state now has a computer crime investigation unit available as a resource to local law enforcement agencies, and many municipal police departments have their own computer crime investigative units.

Software tools available to law enforcement agencies have also improved. Programs such as the Software Forensic Tool Kit provide police with the ability to search and re-create deleted files on computers. Also digitized for law enforcement use are criminal identification systems, such as the Statewide Network of Agency Photos (SNAP). Law enforcement officers can search SNAP's digital database for mug shots that show a criminal's distinguishing marks, such as scars and tattoos, making criminal identification simpler. SNAP is connected to the Automatic Fingerprint Identification Systems, which electronically transmits fingerprints at the time a person is arrested.

Similarly, the Classification System for Serial Criminal Patterns, developed by the Chicago Police Department, allows detectives to look for possible patterns connecting crimes.

Radio communication has also been updated to provide a secure means of voice communication for law enforcement officers. No longer can any interested civilian buy a receiver and monitor police calls since digital voice communication can now be encrypted, allowing for a higher level of security.

It's an unfortunate fact that criminals have discovered how to use the Internet to their advantage. Clearly, however, law enforcement is gaining on them as officers also use technological advancement to track, arrest, and prosecute online and offline criminals.

Questions

1. Today, is it harder or easier to be a criminal? Why?
2. Argue whether law enforcement can or cannot ever get ahead of criminals.

Based on:

Ashcroft, J. (2001, May 22). Remarks of Attorney General John Ashcroft. Retrieved October 12, 2008, from http://www.usdoj.gov/criminal/cybercrime/AGCPPSI.htm.

Justice Technology Information Network (n.d.). Retrieved October 12, 2008, from http://www.justnet.org/Pages/home.aspx.

Key Points Review

1. **Describe the advent of the Information Age and how computer ethics impacts the use of information systems.** The Information Age refers to a time in the history of civilization when information became the currency of the realm.

Being successful in many careers today requires that people be computer literate, since the ability to access and effectively operate computing technology is a key part of many careers. A digital divide is said to exist between people who are computer literate and those who are not. Because computer literacy is so critical in the Information Age, a major ethical concern for society centers on who is computer literate and who is not.

2. **Discuss the ethical concerns associated with information privacy, accuracy, property, and accessibility.** Information privacy is concerned with what information an individual should have to reveal to others through the course of employment or through other transactions, such as online shopping. Ensuring authenticity and fidelity of information, as well as identifying who is responsible for informational errors that harm people, is information accuracy. Information property focuses on who owns information about individuals and how information can be sold and exchanged. Information accessibility refers to what information a person or organization has the right to obtain about others and how this information can be accessed and used. While the Information Age has brought widespread access to information, the downside is that others may now have access to personal information that you would prefer to keep private. Because there are few safeguards for ensuring the accuracy of information, individuals and companies can be damaged by informational errors. Additionally, because information is so easy to exchange and modify, information ownership violations readily occur. Likewise, with the rapid increase in online databases containing personal information and the increase in the use of computer-based communication between individuals, who has the right to access and monitor this information has raised many ethical concerns.

3. **Define computer crime and list several types of computer crime.** Computer crime is defined as the act of using a computer to commit an illegal act, such as targeting a computer while committing an

offense, using a computer to commit an offense, or using computers in the course of a criminal activity. A person who gains unauthorized access to a computer system has also committed a computer crime. Those individuals who are knowledgeable enough to gain access to computer systems without authorization have long been referred to as hackers. Today, those who break into computer systems with the intention of doing damage or committing a crime are usually called crackers. Hackers and crackers can commit a wide variety of computer crimes, including data diddling, salami slicing, phreaking, cloning, carding, piggybacking or shoulder-surfing, social engineering and masquerading, dumpster diving, and spoofing. Crackers are also associated with the making and distributing of computer viruses and other destructive codes. Finally, making illegal copies of software, a worldwide computer crime, is called software piracy.

4. **Describe and explain the differences between cyberwar and cyberterrorism.** Cyberwar refers to an organized attempt by a country's military to disrupt or destroy the information and communication systems of another country. The goal of cyberwar is to turn the balance of information and knowledge in one's favor in order to diminish an opponent's capabilities and also to enhance those of the attacker. Cyberterrorism is the use of computer and networking technologies by individuals and organized groups against persons or property to intimidate or coerce governments, civilians, or any segment of society to attain political, religious, or ideological goals. Now that terrorist groups are increasingly using the Internet for their purposes, one of the great fears about cyberterrorism is that an attack can be launched from a computer anywhere in the world.

Key Terms

bot herder 482
botnet 481
carding 477
cloning 477
computer crime 470
computer ethics 458
computer fluency 457
computer forensics 473
computer literacy 455
copyright 478
cracker 475
cyber bullying 483
cyber harassment 482
cyber stalking 482

cybersquatting 464
cyberterrorism 485
cyberwar 484
data diddling 477
digital divide 457
digital rights management (DRM) 465
dumpster diving 477
hacker 474
hacktivist 475
honeypot 473
identity theft 459
information accessibility 466
information accuracy 461

Information Age 455
information privacy 459
information property 463
intellectual property (IP) 463
Internet hoax 482
logic bomb 481
Luddite 455
malware 480
masquerading 477
neo-Luddite 457
One Laptop per Child (OLPC) 457
online predator 483
patent 478
patriot hacker 484

phreaking 477
piggybacking 477
salami slicing 477
shoulder-surfing 477
social engineering 477

software piracy 477
spoofing 477
time bomb 481
Trojan horse 480
vishing 477

warez 478
watermark 466
Web vandalism 484

Review Questions

1. Describe the advent of the Information Age and how computer ethics impacts the use of information systems.
2. What is the difference between the digital divide and computer literacy?
3. Compare and contrast information accuracy, information privacy, and information property.
4. Compare and contrast a worm, a virus, a Trojan horse, and a logic or time bomb.
5. List five dot-cons that you find interesting and give the advice suggested for avoiding these traps.
6. What is identity theft, and what is the solution according to this chapter?
7. Define cybersquatting. What year did the U.S. government pass legislation to deter this action, and what is the name of the act?
8. Define computer crime and list several types of computer crime.
9. Explain the purpose of the Computer Fraud and Abuse Act of 1986 and the Electronic Communications Privacy Act of 1986.
10. Define unauthorized access and give several examples from recent media reports.
11. Viruses that are spread via e-mail transmitted over the Internet are also frequently in the news. What are five ways to prevent these viruses?
12. Define and contrast cyberwar and cyberterrorism.

Self-Study Questions

Visit the Interactive Study Guide on the Companion Web site for additional Self-Study Questions: www.pearsonhighered/valacich.

1. Being _____, or knowing how to use the computer as a device to gather, store, organize, and process information, can open up myriad sources of information.
   A. technology literate
   B. digitally divided
   C. computer literate
   D. computer illiterate
2. A broad definition of computer crime includes all of the following except _____.
   A. targeting a computer while committing an offense
   B. using computers in the course of a criminal activity, despite the fact that computers are not actually targeted
   C. using a computer to commit a legal act
   D. using a computer to commit an offense
3. _____ focuses on defining what information a person or organization has the right to obtain about others and how this information can be accessed and used.
   A. Information accessibility
   B. Information accuracy
   C. Information privacy
   D. Information property
4. The guidelines published by the Computer Ethics Institute prohibit all of the following except _____
   A. using a computer to harm others
   B. using a computer to bear false witness
   C. copying or using proprietary software without paying for it
   D. using computer resources with authorization
5. In the United States, two main federal laws have been passed against computer crime, including _____.
   A. the Computer Fraud and Abuse Act of 1986
   B. the Electronic Communications Privacy Act of 1986
   C. the E-Commerce Internet Act of 1996
   D. A and B
6. Those individuals who break into computer systems with the intention of doing damage or committing a crime are usually called _____.
   A. hackers
   B. crackers
   C. computer geniuses
   D. computer operatives
7. Which of the following copyright laws is applicable to illegal software piracy?
   A. the 1980 Computer Software Copyright Act
   B. a 1992 act that made software piracy a felony
   C. the 1997 No Electronic Theft (NET) Act that made copyright infringement a criminal act even when no profit was involved
   D. all of the above
8. The use of computer and networking technologies by individuals and organized groups against persons or property to intimidate or coerce governments, civilians, or any segment of society in order to attain

political, religious, or ideological goals is known as
_____.
A. cyberwar
B. cybercrime
C. cyberterrorism
D. none of the above

9. The use of formal investigative techniques to evaluate
digital information for judicial review is called _____.
A. data diddling
B. computer ethics
C. computer forensics
D. warez

10. Crimes committed against telephone company computers with the goal of making free long-distance calls,
impersonating directory assistance or other operator
services, diverting calls to numbers of the perpetrator's
choice, or otherwise disrupting telephone service for
subscribers is called _____.
A. phreaking
B. cloning
C. carding
D. data diddling

Answers are on page 495.

Problems and Exercises

1. Match the following terms with the appropriate
definitions:
   i. Digital divide
   ii. Information privacy
   iii. Cyberwar
   iv. Information accuracy
   v. Shoulder-surfing
   vi. Identity theft
   vii. Information accessibility
   viii. Worm
   ix. Computer ethics
   x. Social engineering
   a. The stealing of another person's Social
      Security number, credit card number, and other
      personal information for the purpose of using
      the victim's credit rating to borrow money, buy
      merchandise, and otherwise run up debts that
      are never repaid
   b. An area concerned with what information an
      individual should have to reveal to others
      through the course of employment or through
      other transactions, such as online shopping
   c. The gap between those individuals in our
      society who are computer literate and have
      access to information resources, such as the
      Internet, and those who do not
   d. Destructive computer code that is designed to
      copy and send itself throughout networked
      computers
   e. An area concerned with ensuring the
      authenticity and fidelity of information as
      well as identifying who is responsible for
      informational errors that harm people
   f. An ethical issue that focuses on defining what
      information a person or organization has the
      right to obtain about others and how this
      information can be accessed and used
   g. The issues and standards of conduct as they
      pertain to the use of information systems
   h. Gaining information needed to access
      computers by tricking company employees by
      means of posing as magazine journalists,
      telephone company employees, and forgetful
      coworkers in order to persuade honest
      employees to reveal passwords and other
      information
   i. The act of simply standing in line behind a card
      user at an automated teller machine, looking
      over that person's shoulder, and memorizing the
      card's personal identification number and then
      placing the stolen number on a counterfeit
      access card and using it to withdraw cash from
      the victim's account
   j. An organized attempt by a country's military to
      disrupt or destroy the information and
      communication systems of another country

2. The Electronic Frontier Foundation (www.eff.org) has
a mission of protecting rights and promoting freedom
in the "electronic frontier." The organization provides
additional advice on how to protect your online privacy. Review its suggestions and provide a summary of
what you can do to protect yourself.

3. In some cases, individuals engage in cybersquatting in
the hope of being able to sell the domain names to
companies at a high price; in other cases, companies
engage in cybersquatting by registering domain names
that are very similar to their competitors' product
names in order to generate traffic from people mis-
spelling Web addresses. Would you differentiate
between these practices? Why or why not? If so, where
would you draw the boundaries?

4. Do you consider yourself computer literate? Do you
know of any friends or relatives who are not computer
literate? What can you do to improve your computer
literacy? Is computer literacy necessary in today's job
market? Why or why not?

5. Look at the following Web sites for tips and articles on
identity theft: www.ftc.gov/bcp/edu/microsites/idtheft

and www.identitytheft.org. Did you find anything that you think might help you in the future? Did you bookmark any of these tips or e-mail them to your classmates or friends?

6. Complete the computer ethics quiz at web.cs.bgsu. edu/maner/xxicee/html/welcome.htm and visit www. onlineethics.diamax.com/CMS/computers/compcases/ killerrobot.aspx for more issues on computer ethics and social implications of computing. Should ethical codes apply to all professions?

7. Find your school's guidelines for ethical computer use on the Internet and answer the following questions: Are there limitations as to the type of Web sites and material that can be viewed (e.g., pornography)? Are students allowed to change the programs on the hard drives of the lab computers or download software for their own use? Are there rules governing personal use of computers and e-mail?

8. Do you believe that there is a need for a unified information systems code of ethics? Visit www.albion.com/ netiquette/corerules.html. What do you think of this code? Should it be expanded, or is it too general? Search the Internet for additional codes for programmers or Web developers. What did you find?

9. Visit the Consumer Sentinel (www.ftc.gov/sentinel) to learn about how law enforcement agencies around the world work together to fight consumer fraud. The site contains statistics on consumer complaints and sorts this data in many interesting ways. Prepare a report using the most current data on the top five complaint categories.

10. Choose an organization with which you are familiar. Determine what the company's computer ethics policy is by obtaining a written copy and reviewing it. In addition, asking questions and observing several employees may provide insight into the actual application. Does this organization adhere to a strict or casual ethics policy? Prepare a ten-minute presentation to the rest of the class on your findings.

11. Visit www.safeshopping.org and prepare a summary of its top ten safe online shopping tips. Did you find these tips useful enough to share with a friend or classmate? Did you bookmark the site or e-mail it to a friend?

12. To learn more about protecting your privacy, visit www.cookiecentral.com and www.epubliceye.com. Did you learn something that will help protect your privacy? Why is privacy more important than ever?

13. Should laws be passed to make spam a crime? If so, how should lawmakers deal with First Amendment rights? How would such laws be enforced?

14. Do you think that educational institutions should be allowed to monitor e-mail sent and received on school computers? Why or why not? Do you think that any e-mail messages sent or received over a computer at work should be considered company property? Why or why not?

15. Do you feel the media generate too much hype regarding hackers and crackers? Since prominent companies such as Microsoft are often hacked into, are you concerned about your bank account or other sensitive information?

16. Review Table 11.1's list of dot-cons from the Federal Trade Commission. Have any suspicious groups contacted you or any of your friends or classmates?

17. Identity theft is a new type of theft. Visit www.fraud. org to find ways to protect yourself. Search the Internet for additional sources that provide information on identity theft and make a list of other ways to safeguard against it. What are some of the losses in addition to stolen documents and additional bills to pay that may result from identity theft?

18. Search the Internet for information about the damaging effects of software piracy and/or look at the following Web sites: www.bsa.org and www.microsoft.com/ piracy. Is software piracy a global problem? What can you do to mitigate the problem? Prepare a short presentation to present to the class.

19. Check one or more of the following Web sites to see which hoaxes are currently circulating online: www. hoax-slayer.com, www.truthorfiction.com, or www. snopes.com/info/top25uls.asp. What are five popular hoaxes now circulating online?

20. What laws should be enacted to combat cyberterrorism? How could such laws be enforced?

21. Contrast cyber harassment, stalking, and bullying using real-world examples found from recent news stories.

Application Exercises

Note: The existing data files referenced in these exercises are available on the Student Companion Web site: www. pearsonhighered/valacich.

Spreadsheet Application: Analyzing Ethical Concerns at Campus Travel

Because of the employees' increased use of IT resources for private purposes at Campus Travel, you have announced that a new IT use policy will be implemented. You have set up a Web site for the employees to provide feedback to the proposed changes; the results of this survey are stored in the file EthicsSurvey.csv. Your boss wants to use the survey results to find out what the greatest concerns in terms of ethical implications are for the employees, so you are asked to do the following:

1. Complete the spreadsheet to include descriptive statistics (mean, standard deviation, mode, minimum,

maximum, and range) for each survey item. Use formulas to calculate all statistics for the responses to the individual questions

(Hint: In Microsoft Excel, you can look up the necessary formulas in the category "Statistical.")

2. Provide a graph highlighting the means of the different items.

Make sure to professionally format the pages before printing them out.

Database Application: Tracking Software Licenses at Campus Travel

Recently, you have taken on the position of an IS manager at Campus Travel. In your second week at work, you realize that many of the software licenses are about to expire or have already expired. As you know about the legal and eth-ical implications of unlicensed software, you have decided to set up a software asset management system that lets you keep track of the software licenses. You have already set up a database and stored some of the information, but you want to make the system more user-friendly. Using the SWLicenses.mdb database, design a form to input the fol-lowing information for new software products:

- Software title
- Installation location (office)
- License number
- Expiration date

Furthermore, design a report displaying all software licenses and expiration dates (sorted by expiration dates)

(Hint: In Microsoft Access, use the form and reports wizard to create the form.)

Team Work Exercise: Making Copies of Programs, Games, Music, and Videos

Have you ever gone to a friend's house with a blank CD or DVD and copied a program, a game, music, or a movie? Has anyone offered to give you a "free" copy of a program or game? Discuss the possible reasons for and against doing this with your team members. What would be the argu-ments of an open-source software proponent? Now that you have read this chapter, how do you feel about making an illegal copy of such items? Is it okay to let someone else copy your programs, games, music, or movies as long as your own copies are not pirated? If you had an illegal copy of your favorite musical group's latest CD, what would you say to them if they asked you why you made an illegal copy?

Answers to the Self-Study Questions

1. C, p. 455   **2.** C, p. 470   **3.** A, p. 466   **4.** D, p. 469   **5.** D, p. 472
6. B, p. 475   **7.** D, p. 478   **8.** C, p. 485   **9.** C, p. 473   **10.** A, p. 477

Case ❶

Bridging the Digital Divide

An important ethical issue related to computer use is the *digital divide*, which refers to the unequal access to computer technology within various populations. The divide occurs on several levels: socioeconomic (rich or poor); racial (majority/minority); and geographical (urban/rural and developed/undeveloped countries). Studies have shown that as the Information Age progresses, those individuals who have access to computer technology and to opportunities for learning computer skills generally have an educational edge.

To even the divide, Nicholas Negroponte, an architect and computer scientist who founded the Massachusetts Institute of Technology's (MIT's) Media Lab, announced the creation of One Laptop per Child (OLPC), a nonprofit organization, in 2005 at the World Economic Forum in Davos, Switzerland. As part of the project, the OX-1, a $100 computer, was designed expressly for child use. With $2 million start-up contri-butions, the OLPC began distributing the computers to children around the world, including locations within the United States. The computers were given to chil-dren at an early age, were designed for child ownership and use, had built-in Internet access, were intended to accompany children from school to homes, and were designed for free and open programming access.

The project's goal was to close the digital divide and transform education by providing access to computers to children who would otherwise not have the opportunity to fully participate in the Information Age.

Critics of the program, however, claimed that Negroponte's policy of dealing only with heads of state and of requiring countries to purchase machines in lots of one million seemed in direct opposition to stated goals. (These requirements have since been modified.) In 2007, when Intel mounted competitive campaigns to sell the Classmate PC, a low-cost computer also designed for individuals previously underserved in the

computer market, Negroponte complained about the competition, calling Intel's efforts "shameless."

The competition, however, is proving beneficial to those who would otherwise not have had access to low-cost, educationally focused, top-of-the-line computer technology.

Questions:

1. Why does the digital divide matter to children and their families?
2. Do you think the OLPC project will be successful? Why or why not?
3. Identify and discuss what you feel is the major challenge for making the OLPC a success. How can this challenge be overcome?

Based on:

Nicholas Negroponte (n.d.). Retrieved October 12, 2008, from http://web.media.mit.edu/~nicholas.

Vota, W. (2007, May 21). OLPC XO vs. Intel Classmate PC, a beneficial competition. *OLPC News*. Retrieved October 12, 2008, from http://www.olpcnews.com/sales_talk/countries/olpc_xo_intel_classmates.html.

Case ❷

Terrorists Invade Gaming

Second Life (SL) is a virtual world where you can do all the things you do in the real world and more. For instance, you can buy land, build a house or a skyscraper, go shopping, open a business, and deposit Lindens (SL currency) in your bank account. And you can participate in all these activities as the person of your dreams by creating an avatar that personifies the "you" you have always dreamed of becoming—no zits, freckles, weight problems, knobby knees, braces, or bad hair days. Sound ideal?

It was, for a while. Then the terrorists discovered Second Life is the perfect place to recruit cell members, practice various plans of attack, and even unleash biological weapons. Now, if you visit SL you risk stepping into the middle of a terrorist attack. Last year, for example, bombs destroyed ABC's headquarters in SL, and a group of jihadists flew a helicopter into the virtual Nissan building.

Then armed militants attacked a clothing store, killing two customers, and planted a bomb outside a Reebok outlet. Clearly out to overthrow SL's government, the militants terrorized Second Life's 13 million inhabitants, and even managed to transfer money into SL accounts and back to the real world, where Lindens could be exchanged for currency to fund terrorist activities. While the humans behind the avatars in SL were never in danger of injury or death, the terrorist activities rehearsed in SL gave real-life terrorists an idea of how the same methods of attack would play out in real cities like New York, Chicago, or Los Angeles.

Ramifications for the real world could also be seen when virtual terrorists recently invaded *World of Warcraft*, using suicide bombers to blow up themselves and others within explosion vicinities, and even deliberately spreading a disease called Corrupted Blood. The virtual

biowarfare actually gave scientists insight into how disease epidemics impact the real world, because since humans manipulate the 10 million avatars that inhabit *World of Warcraft*, they tend to behave in ways that are typical for the species.

Scientists could study how people reacted, how panic was or was not controlled, and which community services were most helpful to Warcraft's citizens.

The fact that behavior within Second Life and Warcraft environments so closely resembles actual human behavior is interesting, but sometimes alarming. Perhaps government security agencies, public health administrators, police departments, and others charged with public health and safety would do well to become familiar with virtual communities. A virtual world is never "real," of course, but it can be another technological tool for protecting citizens in actual communities.

Questions:

1. Should terrorists within virtual worlds be prosecuted? Why or why not?
2. Should governments be allowed to monitor and track citizens within virtual worlds? Why or why not?
3. Who should govern and police virtual worlds? How can laws be enforced?

Based on:

Kelm, B. (2007, August 22). Learning about disease from the World of Warcraft. *Wired*. Retrieved October 12, 2008, from http://blog.wired.com/wiredscience/2007/08/learning-about-.html.

O'Brien, N. (2007, July 31). Virtual terrorists. *The Australian*. Retrieved October 12, 2008, from http://www.theaustralian.news.com.au/story/0,25197,22161037-28737,00.html.

Their, D. (2008, March 20). World of Warcraft shines light on terror tactics. *Wired*. Retrieved October 12, 2008, from http://www.wired.com/gaming/virtualworlds/news/2008/03/wow_terror.

Advanced Topics and Trends in Managing the Information Systems Infrastructure

After reading this briefing, you will be able to do the following:

① Discuss advanced information systems hardware concepts.

② Describe advanced topics related to systems and application software, as well as the characteristics of various types of programming languages and application development environments.

③ Describe network software and hardware, including media access control, network topologies, and protocols, as well as advanced Internet concepts.

④ Explain advanced database management concepts.

Preview

In Chapter 4—Managing the Information Systems Infrastructure, you have learned about the basic hardware and software components of a computer, as well as foundational concepts that include networking, the Internet, and databases. This Technology Briefing will delve deeper into these infrastructure components, providing you with an advanced understanding of these topics.

Our approach in this technology briefing is not to bog you down with hardware facts and jargon but to supplement the managerial overview we have provided in Chapter 4.

Advanced Topics in Information Systems Hardware

In this section, we will delve deeper into topics related to information systems hardware. Specifically, we will discuss additional topics related to input, processing, and output technologies, giving you a deeper understanding of how a computer works.

Input Technologies

In Chapter 4, we discussed the typical input technologies used on today's computers, such as keyboards, scanners, or graphics tablets. In addition, there are several emerging trends in technology that have changed how we use computers by adding flexibility and utility. This is discussed next.

Entering Text and Numbers   Historically, entering text and numbers had to be done using a **QWERTY keyboard**. QWERTY stands for how the letters are arranged on the keyboard, with Q-W-E-R-T-Y being the first six letters going from left to right on the keyboard. Additionally, there are several different flavors of keyboards that can be used. For example, **ergonomic keyboards** resemble a widened V shape that is designed to reduce the stress placed on the wrists, hands, and arms when typing. Of course, both the standard and the ergonomic keyboards can be wireless, using either infrared or Bluetooth technologies. Another type of keyboard gaining popularity is the laser keyboard. The laser keyboard, also known as the virtual laser keyboard, uses both laser and infrared technology to project a full-sized QWERTY keyboard onto any surface (see Figure TB1).

Selecting and Pointing   In addition to the mouse, various other pointing devices are used to select items from menus, to point, and to sketch or draw. Several of the most popular types of pointing devices are listed in Table TB1. Other, more specialized pointing devices include a **graphics tablet,** used to simulate the process of drawing or sketching on a sheet of paper, or an **eye-tracking device,** an innovative pointing device primarily developed for the disabled for help with computer pointing. The eye tracker is used in cases where voice and finger manipulation is not possible. This device is built around a monitor and tracks the eye movements of the user, moving the pointer to where the user is focusing on; a "click" is signaled by blinking for a set amount of time.

FIGURE TB1

The virtual laser keyboard.

Source: http://www.sforh.com/ images/keyboards/virtual-keyboard-lg.jpg.

TABLE TB1 **Selecting and Pointing Devices**

Device	Description
Mouse	Pointing device that works by sliding a small box-like device on a flat surface; selections are made by pressing buttons on the mouse.
Trackball	Pointing device that works by rolling a ball that sits in a holder; selections are made by pressing buttons located near or on the holder.
Joystick	Pointing device that works by moving a small stick that sits in a holder; selections are made by pressing buttons located near or on the holder.
Touch screen	Pointing device using a touch sensitive computer display; selections are made by touching the display.
Light pen	Pointing device that works by placing a pen-like device near a computer screen; selections are made by pressing the pen to the screen.

Entering Batch Data Large amounts of routine information are often entered into the computer using scanners that convert printed text and images into digital data. Scanners range from small handheld devices that look like a mouse to large desktop boxes that resemble personal photocopiers (see Figure TB2). Rather than duplicating the image on another piece of paper, the computer translates the image into digital information that can be stored or manipulated by the computer. Insurance companies, universities, and other organizations that routinely process large batches of forms and documents are using scanner technology to increase employee productivity.

Once a document is converted into digital format, **text recognition software** uses optical character recognition (OCR) to convert typed, printed, or handwritten text into the computer-based characters that form the original letters and words.

Other special-purpose scanning technologies include optical mark recognition (OMR) devices, bar code readers, and magnetic ink character readers, as summarized in Table TB2. Also, RFID (radio frequency identification) scanners are a popular system input method for a variety of contexts (see Chapter 9—Building Organizational Partnerships Using Enterprise Information Systems).

FIGURE TB2

Handheld scanners are a type of batch input device.

TABLE TB2 **Specialized Scanners for Inputting Information**

Scanner	Description
Optical mark recognition (OMR)	Used to scan questionnaires and test answer forms ("bubble sheets") where answer choices are marked by filling in circles using pencil or pen
Optical character recognition (OCR)	Used to read and digitize typewritten, computer-printed, and even handwritten characters such as on sales tags on department store merchandise, patient information in hospitals, or address information on a piece of postal mail
Bar code reader	Used mostly in grocery stores and other retail businesses to read bar code data at the checkout counter; also used by libraries, banks, hospitals, utility companies, and so on
Magnetic ink character recognition (MICR)	Used by the banking industry to read data, account numbers, bank codes, and check numbers on preprinted checks
Biometric scanner	Used to scan human body characteristics of users to enable everything from secure access to payment procurement

OTHER SCANNING TECHNOLOGIES.   Used in many European and Asian countries, as well as at many colleges and universities, **smart cards** are special credit card-sized cards containing a microprocessor chip, memory circuits, and often a magnetic stripe. When issued by a school, smart cards are photo-identification cards that can also be used to unlock dormitory doors, make telephone calls, do laundry, make purchases from vending machines or student cafeterias, and more. Some smart cards allow for contactless transmission of data using RFID technology (e.g., the Exxon Speedpass for purchasing gasoline). Biometric devices, discussed in more detail in Chapter 7—Securing Information Systems, are being used primarily for identification and security purposes. These devices read certain features, including iris, fingerprints, and hand or face geometry, and compare them with stored profiles. Biometric devices are now also being included in consumer products, such as laptops, allowing users to log on to the laptop using a fingerprint scanner rather than the traditional keyboard entry of user name and password.

Entering Audio and Video   When entering **audio** (i.e., sound) and **video** (i.e., still and moving images) data into a computer, it has to be digitized before it can be manipulated, stored, and played or displayed. In addition to the manipulation of music, audio input is helpful for operating a computer when a user's hands need to be free to do other tasks. Video has become popular for assisting in security-related applications, such as room monitoring and employee verification. It has also gained popularity for videoconferencing and chatting on the Internet, using your PC and very inexpensive video cameras.

VOICE INPUT.   Perhaps one of the easiest ways to enter data into a computer is simply to speak into a microphone. With the increased interest in such applications as Internet-based telephone calls and videoconferencing, microphones have become an important component of computer systems. A process called **speech recognition** also makes it possible for your computer to understand speech. For many disabled people, the use of the keyboard is not an option for entering in text and numbers. For this reason, researchers have developed a variety of options for the disabled users, including voice-to-text translators. **Voice-to-text software** is an application that uses a microphone to monitor a person's speech and then converts the speech into text. There are consumer versions of voice-to-text software that are relatively cheap, but the professional software used by the disabled can be very expensive. Speech recognition technology can also be especially helpful for physicians and other medical professionals, airplane cockpit personnel, factory workers whose hands get too dirty to use keyboards, and computer users who cannot type and do not want to learn. Increasingly, **interactive voice response (IVR)**, based on speech recognition technology, is used for telephone surveys or to guide you through the various menu options when calling a company's customer service line.

OTHER FORMS OF AUDIO INPUT.   In addition to using a microphone, users can enter audio using electronic keyboards, or they can transfer audio from another device (such as an audio recorder). The users can then analyze and manipulate the sounds via sound editing software for output to MP3s, CDs, or other media.

VIDEO INPUT.   A final way in which information can be entered into a computer is through video input. Digital cameras record still images or short video clips in digital form, on small, removable memory cards rather than on film. Storage capacity is influenced by the resolution and size you select for pictures or the length of the recording for video. At any time you can connect the camera to a port on a PC for downloading to the computer's memory and then clear the memory card for later use. Digital camera technology has become so portable that it has been used in a variety of products, including cell phones and laptops. High-quality digital cameras are generally more expensive than film-based cameras, ranging in price from $150 to $10,000 or more. However, they offer three main advantages. You can record digital images without using a scanner, you can take photographs without having film developed, and you can record video. Presently, photos taken with high-end digital cameras are suitable for professional quality photos, but for video recordings, specialized digital video (DV) cameras are still the best choice. Since huge digital files are created when video clips are recorded, DV cameras use digital video tapes or DVDs rather than memory cards. Further, when the clips are downloaded to the computer, storage and processing requirements are demanding.

There are also lower-quality cameras that are priced from $30 to $200. These devices, often referred to as webcams, have become very popular with people wanting to use the Internet for chatting with friends and family, using programs like Skype, Google Talk, Windows Live Messenger or Yahoo! Messenger. Using the input of a webcam, a PC can create **streaming video**, which is a sequence of moving images in a compressed format that can be sent over the Internet; the images are displayed on the receiver's screen as they arrive. **Streaming media** encompasses both streaming video and streaming audio. With streaming media, a Web user does not have to wait for the entire file to be downloaded before seeing the video or hearing the sound. Instead, the media are sent in a continuous stream that is played as it arrives. This is why streaming has become popular for real-time chatting, and it is how live broadcasts, like the news on CNN (www.cnn.com) or even baseball games (www.mlb.com), can be viewed on a computer over the Internet.

We have described numerous options for providing input to a computer. After information is entered into a computer, it can be processed, stored, and manipulated. In the next section, we describe the processing aspects of information systems hardware.

Processing: Transforming Inputs into Outputs

In Chapter 4, we discussed how data and information are represented and processed within a computer. Next, we briefly describe different encoding standards and then highlight the different components of a desktop computer.

Binary Codes   Binary codes are used to relay data and instructions to and from the central processing unit. There are several different types of binary codes that have been developed. Some are in wide use, such as the **American Standard Code for Information Interchange (ASCII)**, and others are used for specialized equipment (see Table TB3).

System Unit   As discussed in Chapter 4, the system unit contains the motherboard, power supply and fan, central processing unit(s), RAM and ROM memory, hard drive, optical drives, ports for plugging in peripherals, and add-in slots for sound, video, internal LAN card, USB devices, and other cards. In all types and models of computers, the main circuit board or system board, most often called the motherboard, is the heart of the system unit.

MOTHERBOARD.   The **motherboard** is aptly named because it contains all of the components that do the actual processing work of the computer (see Figure TB3). It is a large printed plastic or fiberglass circuit board that holds or connects to all of the computer's electronic components. Plugged into or otherwise connected to the motherboard are the

TABLE TB3 **Types of Encoding for Information Systems**

Code	Name	Description	Variants
ASCII	American Standard Code for Information Interchange	Often pronounced "aski," a character encoding based on the English alphabet. ASCII codes represent symbols (letters and numbers) in binary form. Most character encodings have a historical basis in ASCII.	Extended US-ASCII IBM367
MIME	Multipurpose Internet Mail Extensions	This is the standard coding for the Internet. Virtually all e-mail is transmitted in MIME format.	RFC 2045 8BITMIM
MAC OS Roman		This encoding is used by Mac OS to represent text. It encodes 256 characters; this includes 128 characters that are identical to ASCII.	
Unicode		This encoding has become an industry standard that was designed to allow symbols from all languages, including Arabic, Chinese, and so on.	UTF-8 UTF-7 UCS-2

central processing unit (often referred to as the computer's brain) as well as the other components mentioned previously. These devices are described next.

The computer's **power supply** converts electricity from the wall socket to a lower voltage. Whereas typically power supplied by the utility companies can vary from 110 to 240 volts AC, depending on where you are in the world, a PC's components use lower voltages—3.3 to 12 volts DC. The power supply converts the power accordingly and also regulates the voltage to eliminate spikes and surges common in most electrical systems. For added protection against external power surges, many PC owners opt to connect their systems to a separately purchased voltage surge suppressor. The power supply includes one or several fans for air cooling the electronic components inside the system unit—that low humming noise you hear while the computer is running is the fan.

CLOCK SPEED. In Chapter 4, we discussed the influence of the number of transistors on the performance of the central processing unit (CPU). Other factors influencing performance are clock speed, registers, and cache memory. These are discussed next.

Within the computer, an electronic circuit generates pulses at a rapid rate, setting the pace for processing events to take place, rather like a metronome marks time for a musician. This circuit is called the **system clock**. A single pulse is a **clock tick**, and a fixed number of clock ticks is required to execute a single instruction. In microcomputers, the processor's **clock speed** is measured in hertz (Hz). One megahertz (MHz) is 1 million clock ticks, or instruction cycles, per second. Microprocessor speeds are measured in different units, depending on the type of computer. Personal computer speeds are most often measured in gigahertz (GHz, or 1 billion hertz). Microprocessor speeds improve so quickly that faster chips are on the market about every six months. Today, most new PCs operate at more than 3 GHz. To give you an idea of how things have changed, the original IBM PC had a clock speed of 4.77 MHz.

FIGURE TB3

A computer's motherboard holds or connects to all of the computer's electronic components.

See Table TB4 for a description of computer speeds. It takes a permanent storage device such as a hard disk (described later) about 10 milliseconds to access information. Within a CPU, however, a single transistor can be changed from a 0 to a 1 in about 10 picoseconds (10 trillionth of a second). Changes inside the CPU occur about 1 billion times faster than they do in a fixed disk because the CPU operates only on electronic impulses, whereas the fixed disks perform both electronic and mechanical activities, such as spinning the disk and moving the read/write head (described later). Mechanical activities are extremely slow relative to electronic activities.

PRIMARY STORAGE.   Random access memory (RAM), located on the motherboard, is used to store the data and programs currently in use. Within the CPU itself, registers provide temporary storage locations where data must reside while it is being processed or manipulated. For example, if two numbers are to be added together, both must reside in registers, with the result placed in a register. Consequently, one factor influencing the speed and power of a CPU is the number and size of the registers.

A cache (pronounced "cash") is a small block of memory used by processors to store those instructions most recently or most often used. Just as you might keep file folders you use most in a handy location on your desktop, cache memory is located within or close to the CPU. Thanks to cache memory, before performing an operation, the processor does not have to go directly to main memory, which is farther away from the microprocessor and takes longer to reach. Instead, it can check first to see if needed data is contained in the cache. Cache memory is another way computer engineers have increased processing speed.

Cache may be located inside the microprocessor—similar to registers—or outside of but close to the microprocessor. Special high-speed cache memory, called **internal cache** (also called Level 1, or L1, cache), is incorporated into the microprocessor's design. **External cache** (also called **secondary cache**, Level 2, or L2, cache) is usually not built into the CPU but is located within easy reach of the CPU on the motherboard. The more cache available to a CPU, the better the overall system performs because more information is readily available (although at a certain size, factors such as heat emission and power consumption become prohibitive to increasing the CPU cache).

SECONDARY STORAGE.   Hard disk drives, diskette drives, and tapes are secondary storage devices with **read/write heads** that inscribe data to or retrieve data from magnetic media. Hard disk, diskette, and tape drives are usually installed internally but may be externally located and attached via cables to ports on the system unit. Diskettes and tapes are removable secondary storage media. That is, they must be inserted into the appropriate drive (or tape reader) to be read from or written to and are removed when these tasks are accomplished, just as a flash drive has to be plugged into a USB port on your computer.

TABLE TB4   **Elements of Computer Time**

Name	Fraction of a Second	Description	Example
Millisecond	1/1000	One thousandth of a second	Fixed disks access information in about 10 to 20 milliseconds.
Microsecond	1/1,000,000	One millionth of a second	A 3.2-GHz CPU executes approximately 3.2 billion operations in a second (i.e., about 3,200 operations every microsecond).
Nanosecond	1/1,000,000,000	One billionth of a second	Most type of RAM used in PCs have access times (the time needed to read information from the RAM to the CPU) from 3 to 50 nanoseconds (lower is better). Most cache memory has access times less than 20 nanoseconds.
Picosecond	1/1,000,000,000,000	One trillionth of a second	Inside a CPU, the time that it takes to switch a circuit from one state to another is in the range of 5 to 20 picoseconds.
Femtosecond	$1/10^{15}$, or 10^{-15}	One quadrillionth of a second	Used in laser technology to measure the length of the laser pulse. Used for nanosurgery.
Attosecond	$1/10^{18}$, or 10^{-18}	One quintillionth of a second	A term used in photon research. Currently the shortest unit of time scientists are able to measure.

Most of the software run on a computer, including the operating system, is stored on the hard drive (or hard disk). The hard drive is a secondary storage device usually located inside the system unit of a computer. It writes data and programs to a fixed disk. The storage capacity of the hard drives for today's microcomputers is now measured in gigabytes (GB), or billions of bytes. It is not unusual for PCs currently on the market to come equipped with hard drives with 100-GB to 500-GB storage capacities. Modern supercomputers can have millions of gigabytes of storage. Most microcomputers have one hard drive, but additional drives can usually be added either internally or externally. To make sure critical data is not lost, some computers employ **redundant array of independent disks (RAID)** technology to store redundant copies of data on two or more hard drives. RAID is not typically used on an individual's computer but is very common for Web servers and many business applications. RAID is sometimes called a "redundant array of *inexpensive* disks" because it is typically less expensive to have multiple redundant disks than fewer highly reliable and expensive ones.

Hard drives consist of several disks, or platters, stacked on top of one another so that they do not touch (see Figure TB4). Each disk within a disk pack has an access arm with two read/write heads—one positioned close to the top surface of the disk and another positioned close to the bottom surface of the disk. (Both surfaces of each disk are used for data storage, usually with the exception of the top surface of the top disk and the bottom surface of the bottom disk.) When reading from or writing to the disks, the read/write heads are constantly repositioned to the desired storage location for the data while the disks are spinning at speeds of 5,400 to 15,000 RPM. The read/write heads do not actually touch either surface of the disks. In fact, a **head crash** occurs if the read/write head for some reason touches the disk, leading to a loss of data.

REMOVABLE STORAGE MEDIA. A diskette (or floppy disk) is a removable storage medium with a capacity of (typically) 1.44 megabytes, which can be read using a diskette drive. Because of the increase in use of relatively inexpensive flash memory having a capacity of up to 8 GB or more, most personal computers do not contain diskette drives any more. This technology will soon be phased out for more practical means of data transfer and storage.

As storage requirements have increased, optical disks (i.e., disks using laser beam technology) have become popular. One advantage to using optical disks for storage is that they can hold much more information than diskettes: A single optical disk can record the information from hundreds of diskettes. Optical disks have made possible the huge growth in multimedia software applications for PCs. For many years, CD-ROMs (compact disc— read-only memory) have been the standard for distributing data; because of their low cost and their storage capacity of 700 MB, CD-ROMs are often used to distribute software. As CD-ROMs cannot be written to, most computers support another type of optical disk that

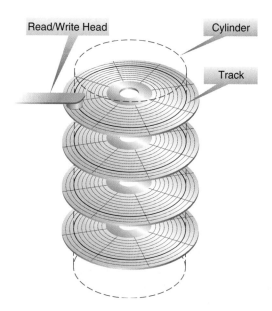

Read/Write Head   Cylinder

Track

FIGURE TB4

A hard drive consists of several disks that are stacked on top of one another and read/write heads to read and write information.

Source: Pfaffenberger/CIYF Brief 2003, Prentice Hall, 2003.

data can be written to, the **CD-R (compact disc—recordable)**. Whereas a CD-R can only be written onto once, a **CD-RW (compact disc—rewritable)** can be written onto multiple times using a CD-RW drive. However, many users desire higher storage capacity than CD-Rs or CD-RWs can offer for multimedia (such as video) or large data backups.

The **DVD-ROM (digital versatile disk—read-only memory)** has more storage space than a CD-ROM because DVD-ROM (or typically referred to as simply DVD) drives use a shorter-wavelength laser beam that allows more optical pits to be deposited on the disk. Like compact discs, there are recordable (DVD-R) and rewritable (DVD-RW) versions of this storage technology. DVDs used for the distribution of movies are also called **digital video disks**. The drive to offer high-definition (HD) video content led to the creation of Blu-Ray, a new DVD format that offers up to 50 GB of storage,

Magnetic tapes used for storage of computer information consist of narrow plastic tape coated with a magnetic substance. Storage tapes range from one-fourth inch wide, wound into a plastic cassette that looks much like a music cassette tape, to one-half inch wide, wound on a reel. As with other forms of magnetic storage, data are stored in tiny magnetic spots. The storage capacity of tapes is expressed as **density**, which equals the number of **characters per inch (CPI)** or **bytes per inch (BPI)** that can be stored on the tape. Mainframe computers use tape drives called stackers that wind tape from a supply reel to a take-up reel as data are read.

Magnetic tape is still used for storing large amounts of computer information, but it is gradually being replaced by high-capacity disk storage since disk storage is equally reliable. In fact, information stored on disks is easier and faster to locate because using disks, computers do not have to scan an entire tape to find a specific data file.

PORTS. To use the full functionality of a computer, you need to be able to connect various types of devices, such as mice, printers, and cameras, to the system unit. A **port** provides a hardware interface—plugs and sockets—for connecting devices to computers. The characteristics of various types of ports are summarized in Table TB5.

Now that you understand how information is input into a computer and how it is processed, we can turn our attention to the third category of hardware—output technologies.

Output Technologies

As you have learned in Chapter 4, computers can display information on a screen, print it, or emit sound. The following section provides further detail about various video output technologies.

Monitors are used to display information from a computer. Traditionally, monitors consist of a **cathode ray tube (CRT)**, which is similar to a television but with much higher resolution. Monitors can be color, black and white, or monochrome (meaning all one color, usually green or amber). Today, monochrome monitors are primarily used in cash registers and other point-of-sale applications. Notebooks and many desktop computers use lighter and thinner **liquid crystal displays (LCD)** to replace the bulky CRT monitor. Because display monitors are embedded into a broad range of products and devices, such as cell phones, digital cameras, or automobiles (e.g., to display route maps and other relevant information), they must be sturdy, reliable, lightweight, energy-efficient, and low in cost. Recent developments in monitor technologies have thus focused on other display technologies, such as **organic light-emitting diodes (OLED)**, which promise to require far less power and are much thinner than traditional LCD panels. Finally, projectors are used for presentation to an audience. Projectors have gone from large very expensive equipment ($5,000 or more) to very small, relatively inexpensive equipment ($200). This is due primarily to the development of LCD technology as previously discussed. In fact, projectors have become so affordable that they are now a consumer-grade product that competes with regular and flat-screen TVs.

Especially for mobile computing, monitor technology is still a challenge. In addition to screen size and power requirements of commonly used display technologies, glare is often an issue, and many laptop screens are hard to read in bright sunlight. For years, many futurists have envisioned a day when computer displays would be lightweight, thin, and flexible like paper, as well as be inexpensive and would require no external power to retain

TABLE TB5   Common Computer Ports, Their Applications, and Description

Port Name	Used to Connect	Description
Serial	Modem, mouse, keyboard, terminal display, MIDI	• Used to transfer one bit at a time • Slowest data transfer rates
Parallel	Printer	• Used to transfer several bits concurrently • Many times faster than serial
USB (Universal Serial Bus)	Printer, scanner, mouse, keyboard, digital camera and camcorders, external disk drives	• A very high speed data transfer method • Up to 480 million bytes per second • Up to 127 devices simultaneously connected
IEEE 1394 ("Fire Wire")	Digital cameras and camcorders, external disk drives	• Extremely high speed data transfer method • Up to 800 million bytes per second • Up to 63 devices simultaneously connected

an image. Recently, devices using **electronic paper** (or **e-paper**) have been introduced into the market. E-paper uses microscopic beads that change color (and retain this image indefinitely) in response to small electrical charges. These beads are encased between very thin sheets of flexible material. The primary benefits of e-paper are that it needs no backlight (as LCD displays do) and reflects like ordinary paper. Current applications of e-paper include electronic signs (that can be automatically updated by a wireless network), infinitely reusable newspapers and magazines, improved displays for mobile phones, and e-book readers such as the Amazon Kindle. The Kindle can hold up to 200 titles, which can be downloaded from Amazon.com via a wireless connection.

In the following sections, we provide a brief history of computers and further discuss the types of computers that people and organizations typically use.

Types of Computers

Over the past sixty years, information systems hardware has gone through many radical changes. When the Zuse Z1 Computer (a mechanical computer using program punch cards) was introduced in 1936, almost all business and government information systems consisted of file folders, filing cabinets, and document repositories. Huge rooms were dedicated to the storage of these records. Information was often difficult to find, and corporate knowledge and history were difficult to maintain. Only certain employees knew specific information. When these employees left the firm, so did all their knowledge about the organization. The computer provided the solution to the information storage and retrieval problems facing organizations up to the 1940s. Shifts in computing eras were facilitated by fundamental changes in the way computing technologies worked. Each of these fundamental changes is referred to as a distinct generation of computing. Table TB6 highlights the technology that defined the five generations of computing. We conclude this section of the Technology Briefing by briefly describing the four general types of computers currently being used in organizations.

Supercomputers   The most powerful and expensive computers that exist today are called supercomputers (see Figure TB5). Supercomputers are often used for scientific applications, solving massive computational problems that require processing large amounts of data. They can cost many millions of dollars. Rather than in clock speed (as your PC), supercomputers' processing speeds are measured in **flops (floating points operations per second)**. An example of one of the world's premier supercomputers is IBM's Roadrunner, which was the first to break the **petaflop** barrier (1 petaflop = 1,000 trillion flops). This supercomputer has been applied to several different problems, from forecasting

TABLE TB6 Five Generations of Computing

Generation	Time Line	Major Event	Characteristics
1	1946–1958	Vacuum tubes	• Mainframe era begins • ENIAC and UNIVAC were developed
2	1958–1964	Transistors	• Mainframe era expands • UNIVAC is updated with transistors
3	1964–1990s	Integrated circuits	• Mainframe era ends • Personal computer era begins • IBM 360 with general purpose operating system • Microprocessor revolution: Intel, Microsoft, Apple, IBM PC, MS-DOS
4	1990s–2000	Multimedia and low cost PCs	• Personal computer era ends • Interpersonal computing era begins • High-speed microprocessor and networks • High-capacity storage • Low-cost, high-performance integrated video, audio, and data
5	2000–present	Widespread Internet accessibility	• Interpersonal computing era ends • Internetworking era begins • Ubiquitous access to Internet with a broad variety of devices • Prices continue to drop; performance continues to expand

FIGURE TB5

Rows of IBM supercomputers at Lawrence Berkeley National Laboratory, California, USA.

climate change to tests of nuclear weapons systems. To achieve this incredible speed, supercomputers are equipped with numerous fast processors that work in parallel to execute several instructions simultaneously. An extensive staff is usually required to operate and maintain supercomputers and to support the researchers and scientists using them. Supercomputers often run only one application at a time in order to dedicate all processing capabilities to a single massive application.

Mainframes   The backbone of large corporate computing has historically been large, high-powered computers called mainframe computers (see Figure TB6). The general difference between a supercomputer and a mainframe is that supercomputers focus on calculation speed and are limited to one application at a time, whereas mainframes focus on input/output speed and reliability. Mainframes can be the size of a large refrigerator (and even larger), and they often cost several million dollars to purchase. Organizations normally use mainframe computers for processing large amounts of business data, and the machines are designed to support hundreds or even thousands of users simultaneously. In addition to businesses, many federal and state governments use mainframe computers to manage the massive amount of data generated by day-to-day governmental activities. Federal agencies, such as the Internal Revenue Service, have several mainframe computers to handle the massive databases related to individual and corporate payroll and tax information. Large corporations, such as Alamo Rent a Car, American Airlines, and Holiday Inn, use mainframes to perform repetitive tasks, such as processing reservations.

Midrange Computers   Midrange computers, often referred to as *minicomputers*, are scaled-down versions of mainframes that were created for companies that did not have the budgets for mainframes and did not need that amount of computing power. In the past few years, the distinction between large midrange computers and small mainframes has blurred in both performance and price. Nonetheless, midrange computers have become integral to many smaller and midsized organizations and typically cost tens to hundreds of thousands of dollars, supporting from five to five hundred users simultaneously. As with mainframes, IBM is a leader in the midrange computer market with its System i5 model (the successor of the AS/400), but other manufacturers, such as Hewlett-Packard, also service this market. The midrange market as a whole has been declining as microcomputers have become faster and have absorbed some of the functionality once required of midrange and mainframe computers.

Microcomputers   Microcomputers, also referred to as **personal computers (PCs)**, fit on desktops, generally cost between a few hundred dollars and $5,000 and are used in homes and offices (see Figure TB7). Microcomputers can be relatively stationary desktop models or portable, notebook-sized computers. High-end microcomputers can cost more

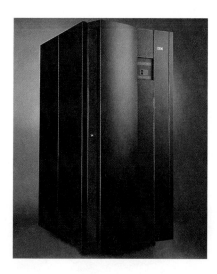

FIGURE TB6

IBM mainframe computer.

Source: Courtesy of IBM Corporate Archives.

FIGURE TB7

A personal computer.

Source: Courtesy of Apple Inc.

than $5,000 and can be used as design workstations for engineers or as servers that manage shared resources such as printers or large databases or that deliver content over the Internet. In the past few years, the popularity of microcomputers has exploded. Within organizations, microcomputers are the most commonly used computing technology for knowledge workers, and they have become as common as the telephone. In fact, more microcomputers than televisions are now sold in the United States each year. Next, we delve a bit deeper into the types of microcomputers.

NETWORK COMPUTERS. A **network computer** (sometimes called a **thin client**) is a microcomputer with minimal memory and storage that is designed to connect to networks, especially the Internet, to use the resources provided by servers. The concept of network computing is to reduce the obsolescence and maintenance of personal computers by allowing inexpensive machines to access servers that deploy resources—software programs, printers, and so on—to all machines on the network (see Figure TB8).

PORTABLE COMPUTERS. When computers appeared that could fit on a desktop, users considered them the ultimate in lighter, smaller, handier machines. Then came laptop computers you could carry, but the first models were heavy and bulky. Next on the portable computer scene were notebook computers that could fit in a backpack or briefcase. Today, battery-powered laptop and notebook computers are popular for both business and personal use (see Table TB7 for a summary of trade-offs between desktop and portable computers). These computers are equipped with a flat display panel; fold into a small, convenient carrying case; and can weigh as little as two pounds or less. With a portable computer, you can use a keyboard and a mouse as well as a trackball, touch pad, or other built-in pointing devices. Most portable computers come equipped with wireless networking capabilities and USB ports and can connect to printers, scanners, or other peripherals. Many students, employees, and others now use a portable computer as their only PC rather than buying both a desktop and a portable machine.

FIGURE TB8

A Sun Microsystems network computer.

Source: Chris LaGrand/Getty Images, Inc.

TABLE TB7 **Trade-Offs between Desktop and Portable Computers**

Desktop Computer	Portable Computer
One location for use	Mobile—any location for use
Lower price	Higher price
Expandable	Very limited expandability
Better ergonomics—full-size/high-resolution color screen, large keyboard, and so on	Cramped ergonomics—small screen, small keyboard, awkward pointing device, and so on
Relatively easy to service/repair	Hard to service/repair

Portable computers can also be easily converted into a desktop machine. This is done by using a **docking station** that allows the portable computer to be easily connected to desktop peripherals, including full-sized monitors, keyboards, and mice. Docking stations are common in many businesses and university settings, as they allow fully functional desktop usability while providing for the portable computer experience. The three most popular forms of portable computers—notebooks, tablets, and handhelds—are described next.

Mobile computers once weighed twenty pounds and were portable only in the sense that they could be moved—with difficulty—from one location to another. A few years ago, machines evolved to what was referred to as a laptop, weighed around ten pounds, and could be folded up and carried like a briefcase. The trend has been toward smaller, lighter, yet ever more powerful **notebook computers** some of which weigh only two pounds and can be easily carried in a briefcase or backpack (see Figure TB9). Modern **ultramobile PCs (UMPCs)**, sometimes referred to as **subnotebooks** or **netbooks**, such as the Asus Eee PC have the size of a hardcover book, making them even easier to take along.

A **tablet PC** is a type of notebook computer that uses a touch-sensitive display to accept input from an electronic pen (called a stylus) or a keyboard. So-called *slate* tablet PCs only provide a touch screen that requires a user to plug in a keyboard and other

FIGURE TB9

Notebook computers are very portable and often weigh less than five pounds.

Source: Courtesy of Apple Inc.

Tablet PCs are designed to
support mobile professionals.

input devices as needed. *Convertible* tablet PCs are quite similar to existing notebook computers but also have displays that swivel and fold flat to cover their keyboard (see Figure TB10).

Both slate and convertible models have a special type of screen that captures the movement of the stylus. Because tablet PCs have been designed to support mobile professionals in a work environment, all typically have built-in wireless Ethernet access for connecting to the Internet. Given these features, experts feel that tablet PCs will soon become a clear alternative to traditional notebook computers for many professionals such as doctors, architects, or even students.

First introduced around 1994, handheld computers failed to live up to expectations, perhaps because consumers had expected that they would replace PCs. Then in 1996, Palm introduced a handheld computer that was never intended to replace the PC but performed some essential computing tasks so well that users could often leave their laptop and notebook computers at home. Since then, referred to as **personal digital assistants (PDAs)**, handheld computers have filled a niche in the portable computer market. Today, the capabilities of many PDAs are beginning to rival the functionality of desktop PCs. For example, HP's iPAQ Pocket PC allows users to send and receive e-mail, work on documents and spreadsheets, surf the Web, and perform countless other activities. Handheld technologies are also being integrated into cell phones with many companies developing the PDA/cell phone. The most popular PDA/cell phones are made by RIM, which makes the BlackBerry (see Figure TB11), and Palm, which manufactures the Treo.

Now that you have learned in more detail about information systems hardware, we will focus on software, another important component of the information systems infrastructure.

Personal digital assistants allow
you to have a very powerful
computer in the palm of your
hand.

Advanced Topics in Information Systems Software

Software directs the functions of all computer hardware. Without software, the biggest, fastest, most powerful computer in the world is nothing more than a fancy paperweight. Software is intertwined with all types of products and services—toys, music, appliances, health care, and countless other products. As a result, the term *software* can be confusing because it is used in many different ways. We will unravel this confusion in the next section by describing the different types of software that are used in today's organizations.

Systems Software

In Chapter 4, you have learned about one type of systems software, the operating system, and its many different tasks. More specifically, common tasks of an operating system include the following:

- Booting (or starting) your computer
- Reading programs into memory and managing memory allocation
- Managing where programs and files are located in secondary storage
- Maintaining the structure of directories and subdirectories
- Formatting disks
- Controlling the computer monitor
- Sending documents to the printer

Just as there are many kinds of computers, there are many different kinds of operating systems (see Table TB8). In general, operating systems—whether for large mainframe computers or for small notebook computers—perform similar operations. Obviously, large multiuser supercomputers are more complex than small desktop systems; therefore, the operating system must account for and manage that complexity. However, the basic purpose of all operating systems is the same.

The second type of systems software, **utilities** (or **utility programs**), are designed to manage computer resources and files. Some are included in operating systems software. Others must be purchased separately and installed on your computer. Table TB9 provides a sample of a few utility programs that are considered essential.

TABLE TB8 Common Operating Systems

Operating System	Description
OS/390	A proprietary operating system developed specifically for large IBM mainframe systems.
Unix	A multiuser, multitasking operating system that is available for a wide variety of computer platforms. Commonly used because of its superior security.
Windows	Currently, by far the Windows desktop operating system is the most popular in the world. Variations are also used to operate large servers, small handhelds, and cell phones.
Mac OS	The first commercial graphical-based operating system making its debut in 1984.
Linux	A freely distributed operating system designed in 1991 by a Finnish student. Known for providing a secure, low-cost, multiplatform operating system. Also, Linux powers about one-third of all Web servers.
	Linux users can choose between different "flavors" (or distributions), depending on their needs (such as the novice-friendly Ubuntu)
Symbian OS	An operating system designed for mobile devices that was jointly developed by Ericsson, Nokia, and Psion.

TABLE TB9 Common Types of Computer Software Utilities

Utility	Description
Backup	Archives files from the hard disk to tapes, flash drive, or other storage devices
File defragmentation	Converts fragmented files (i.e., files not stored contiguously) on your hard disk into contiguous files that will load and be manipulated more rapidly
Disk and data recovery	Allows the recovery of damaged or erased information from hard and floppy disks
Data compression	Compresses data by substituting a short code for frequently repeated patterns of data, much like the machine shorthand used by court reporters, allowing more data to be stored on a disk
File conversion	Translates a file from one format to another, so it can be used by an application other than the one used to create it
Antivirus	Monitors and removes viruses
Device drivers	Allows adding new hardware to your computer system, such as a game controller, printer, scanner, and so on, to function with your operating system
Spam blockers	Monitors your incoming e-mail messages and filters or blocks unwanted messages from arriving
Spyware detection and removal	Monitors and removes spyware from your computer
Media players	Allows you to listen to music or watch video on a computer

As mentioned earlier, systems software (or the operating system) is the type of software that is needed to run a computer. However, with just the systems software alone, users can perform very few (if any) important business tasks. In the next section, we discuss a second type, application software that is used in today's information systems.

Application Software

Application software is categorized by its design and by the type of application or task it supports. The task-oriented categories for application software are (1) large business systems and office automation and (2) personal productivity tools. As discussed in Chapter 8—Enhancing Business Intelligence Using Information Systems—applications in the business category are purchased or developed by the organization to support the central, organization-wide operations of the company. Those in the office automation or personal productivity category are tools used to support the daily work activities of individuals and small groups (see Table TB10).

Open-Source Software   Open-source software refers to systems software, applications, and programming languages in which the source code (i.e., the actual program code) is freely available to the general public for use and/or modification. Many large mainstream software companies are actively involved in the open-source community. For example, IBM is playing a leading role in evolving the Linux operating system. Likewise, Sun Microsystems is active in developing and extending the OpenOffice Productivity Suite. This is reflected in a variety of popular open-source software, as presented in Table TB11.

Programming Languages and Development Environments

Each piece of application software is developed using some programming language. A programming language is the computer language the software vendor uses to write application programs. For application software, such as spreadsheets or database management systems, the underlying programming language is invisible to the user. However, pro-

TABLE TB10 **Examples of Productivity Software**

Tool	Examples
Word processor	Microsoft Word, Corel Word Perfect, OpenOffice Writer
Spreadsheet	Microsoft Excel, OpenOffice Calc, Google Spreadsheet, Simple Spreadsheets
Database management	OpenOffice Base, Microsoft Access, Borland Paradox, Microsoft SQL Server, IBM DB2, MySQL
Presentation software	Apple Keynote, OpenOffice Impress, Microsoft PowerPoint, Harvard Graphics
E-mail	Mozilla Thunderbird, Apple Mail, Opera M2, Microsoft Outlook and Outlook Express
Web browsers	Microsoft Internet Explorer, Mozilla Firefox, Opera Presto, Google Chrome
Chat	Microsoft Live Messenger, Yahoo! Messenger, Google GTalk, Trillian, Pidgin
Calendar and contact management	Lotus Notes, Microsoft Outlook and Outlook Express, ACT!

grammers in an organization's information systems group and, in some instances, end users can use programming languages to develop their own specialized applications. Many different types of programming languages exist, each with its own strengths and weaknesses. Popular languages used in businesses and industry today are summarized in Table TB12.

TABLE TB11 **Examples of Open-Source Software**

Type of Software	Description	Examples
Operating systems	This software operates the hardware on computers.	Ubuntu Linux (www.ubuntu.com)
		openSuSE Linux (www.opensuse.org)
		FreeBSD (freebsd.org)
Business information systems	A wide variety of applications used in everyday businesses.	Accounting: Turbo Cash (www.turbocashuk.com)
		GIS: NASA World Wind (worldwind.arc.nasa.gov)
		Office Suite: OpenOffice (www.openoffice.org)
		Antivirus: Open Antivirus (openantivirus.org)
		Firewall: FWBuilder (fwbuilder.org)
		Web browser: Firefox (www.mozilla.com/firefox)
		E-mail: Mozilla Thunderbird (www.mozilla.com/thunderbird)
Developer tools	Application development suites.	Languages: PERL (PERL.com)
		PHP (php.net)
		Version control: Microsoft Codeplex (codeplex.com)
Database management systems	Software for accessing and maintaining data in a database	MySQL (mysql.com)
Web servers	Software providing access to Web sites	Apache (www.apache.org)

TABLE TB12   **Popular Programming Languages**

Language	Application	Description
BASIC	General purpose	Beginner's All-Purpose Symbolic Interaction Code. An easy-to-learn language, BASIC works on almost all PCs.
C/C++	General purpose	C++ is a newer version of C. Developed at AT&T Bell Labs. Complex languages used for a wide range of applications.
COBOL	Business	COmmon Business-Oriented Language. Developed in the 1960s, it was the first language for developing business software. COBOL is used for most business transaction processing applications on mainframes.
FORTRAN	Scientific	FORmula TRANslator. The first commercial high-level language developed by IBM in the 1950s. Designed for scientific, mathematical, and engineering applications.
Pascal	Teaching structured programming	Named after the mathematician Blaise Pascal. Uses building block approach to programming. Useful in developing large programs.
HTML	World Wide Web	HyperText Markup Language. The most widely used language for developing Web pages. Markup languages simplify pages for transmission by using symbols that tell what document elements should look like when displayed.
Java	World Wide Web	An object-oriented programming language developed at Sun Microsystems in the early 1990s. It is a popular programming language for the Internet because it is highly transportable from one computer to another.
.NET Framework	World Wide Web	Microsoft offers a variety of programming languages (ASP.NET, C#, etc.) that can easily be integrated into Web applications.
LISP	Artificial intelligence	LISt Processor. Dates from the late 1950s. One of the main languages used to develop applications in artificial intelligence and high-speed arcade graphics.

Compilers and Interpreters   Programs created using programming languages must be translated into code—called assembly or machine language—that the hardware can understand. Most programming languages are translated into machine languages through a program called a **compiler**, as depicted in Figure TB12. The compiler takes an entire program written in a programming language, such as C#, and converts it into a completely new program in machine language that can be read and executed directly by the computer. Use of a compiler is a two-stage process. First, the compiler translates the computer program into machine language, and then the CPU executes the machine language program. Such programs are usually compiled before they are sold to the customers, speeding up the application.

Some programming environments do not compile the entire program into machine language. Instead, each statement of the program is converted into machine language and

FIGURE TB12

A compiler translates the entire computer program into machine language, then the CPU executes the machine language program.

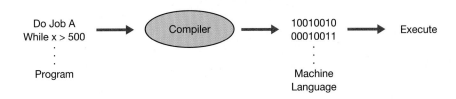

Do Job A
While x > 500
   .
   .
   .
Program

Compiler

10010010
00010011
   .
   .
   .
Machine
Language

Execute

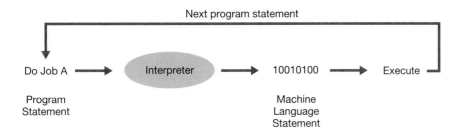

Interpreters read, translate, and execute one line of source code at a time.

executed "on the fly" (i.e., one statement at a time) as depicted in Figure TB13. The type of program that does the conversion and execution is called an **interpreter**. Programming languages can be either compiled or interpreted.

Programming Languages Over the past few decades, software has evolved. In the early days of computing, programming languages were quite crude by today's standards. Initially used in the 1940s, the first generation of programming languages was called machine languages. Programmers wrote in binary code to indicate to the computer which circuits to turn on and which to turn off. As you might guess, machine language is very unsophisticated and therefore very difficult to write. Because it is so difficult, very few programs are actually written in machine language. Instead, programmers rely on higher-level languages. In the early 1950s, a more sophisticated method for programming was developed in which the binary codes used in machine language were replaced by symbols. These symbolic languages were a lot easier for humans to understand. Programs written in symbolic language or any higher-level language still need to be converted into machine language in order to run.

In the mid-1950s, the first high-level programming language, called FORTRAN, was developed by IBM. The big innovation of high-level languages was that they used English-like words to instruct the computer. Consequently, high-level languages are much easier to program in than lower-level languages. Programmers must fully understand the tasks that are to be accomplished when writing a new application in order to choose the best programming language for those tasks.

In the 1970s, several user-oriented languages, called **fourth-generation languages (4GLs)**, were created. These languages are more like English than third-generation languages in that they focus on the desired output instead of the procedures required to get that output. Fourth-generation languages, also called outcome-oriented languages, are commonly used to write and execute queries of a database. For example, the widely used database query language called Structured Query Language (SQL) is a fourth-generation language. See Figure TB14 for several lines of SQL displayed in a sentence-like statement requesting that the last and first names of people in a database called "Customer" with credit limits equal to $100 be displayed.

> **SELECT LAST_NAME, FIRST_NAME**
> **FROM CUSTOMER**
> **WHERE CREDIT_LIMIT = 100**
>
> **DIEHR GEORGE**
> **JANKOWSKI DAVID**
> **FERRELL LAUREN**
> **HAGGARTY JOSEPH**
> **SCHNEIDER BIRGIT**
> **VALACICH JAMES**
> **VALACICH JORDAN**

A 4GL query using SQL that requests that the last and first names of those who have a credit limit equal to $100 be displayed from a database called "Customer."

More recently, **fifth-generation languages (5GLs)** have been developed for use within some expert system or artificial intelligence applications. 5GLs are called natural languages because they allow the user to communicate with the computer using true English sentences. For example, Hewlett-Packard and other software vendors have developed tools for document search and retrieval and database queries that let the user query the documents or databases using English-like sentences. These sentences are then automatically converted into the appropriate commands (in some cases SQL) needed to query the documents or databases and produce the result for the user. If the system does not understand exactly what the user wants, it can ask for clarification. The same code shown in Figure TB14 might appear as shown in Figure TB15 if a natural language were used. Although 5GL languages are not common and are still being further developed, they have been used to forecast the performance of financial portfolios, help diagnose medical problems, and estimate weather patterns.

Of course, programming languages continue to evolve, with object-oriented languages, visual programming languages, and Web development languages rapidly gaining popularity. We discuss these next.

OBJECT-ORIENTED LANGUAGES. **Object-oriented languages** are the most recent in the progression of high-level programming languages and are extremely popular with application developers. For important concepts related to object-oriented languages, see Table TB13. Object-oriented languages were further discussed in Chapter 10—Developing and Acquiring Information Systems.

VISUAL PROGRAMMING LANGUAGES. Just as you may have found it easier to use a computer operating system with a GUI, such as Windows Vista or Mac OS X, programmers using **visual programming languages** may also take advantage of the GUI. For instance, programmers can easily add a command button to a screen with a few clicks of a mouse (see Figure TB16) instead of programming the button pixel by pixel and using many lines of code. Visual Basic.NET and Visual C#.NET are two popular examples of visual programming languages.

WEB DEVELOPMENT LANGUAGES. If you have been surfing the Web for a while, you probably either already have a personal Web page or have thought of creating one. In that event, you have some experience with using a programming language. The language you used to create your Web page is called Hypertext Markup Language (HTML). HTML is a text-based file format that uses a series of codes (aka tags), to set up a document. Because HTML editing programs are visually oriented and easy to use, you do not need to memorize the language to set up a Web page. Programs for creating Web pages (such as Microsoft Expression Web and Macromedia Dreamweaver) are called **Web page builders** or **HTML editors**.

FIGURE TB15

A 5GL query using natural language to request the same information as the SQL query in Figure TB14.

> **BEGINNING WITH THE LAST NAME ON THE FOLLOWING LIST OF CUSTOMERS, FIND CUSTOMERS WHO HAVE A CREDIT LIMIT OF $100**
>
> **DIEHR GEORGE**
> **JANKOWSKI DAVID**
> **FERRELL LAUREN**
> **HAGGARTY JOSEPH**
> **SCHNEIDER BIRGIT**
> **VALACICH JAMES**
> **VALACICH JORDAN**

TABLE TB13 Concepts Related to Object-Oriented Languages

Concept	Description	Examples
Class	Modules that allow programmers to group properties and behavior together. Classes can be reused for different programs.	A "student" has an address and a GPA (properties) and can enroll in courses (behavior).
Encapsulation	Data and behavior of a class are hidden from other classes, and are thus protected from unexpected changes.	The registrar doesn't need to know how the GPA is calculated within the "student" class; the registrar only cares that it is updated.
Inheritance	More specific classes include the properties and behaviors of the more general class.	Both "distance degree student" and "on-campus student" inherit properties (such as address and GPA) and behaviors (such as enroll in a course) from the general class "student."
Event driven program execution	The programmer does not determine the sequence of execution for the program; the flow is determined by user input (e.g., mouse clicks) or messages from other applications.	A word processor reacts to your typing and clicking.

In HTML, the tags used to identify different elements on a page and to format the page are set apart from the text with angle brackets (< >). Specific tags are used to mark the beginning and the ending of an element or a formatting command. For example, if you want text to appear in bold type, the HTML tag to begin bolding is . The tag to turn off bolding, at the end of the selected text, is . The "a href" command sets up a hyperlink from a word or image on the page to another HTML document. Tags also denote document formatting commands, such as text to be used as a title, sizes of text in headings, the ends of paragraphs, underlining, italics, bolding, and places to insert pictures and sound (see Table TB14).

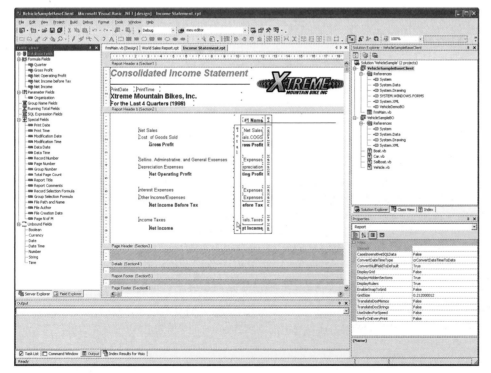

FIGURE TB16

Visual Basic.NET, a visual programming language, is used to create standard business forms.

Source: Hoffer, George, and Valacich, *Modern Systems Analysis and Design*, 5th ed. (Upper Saddle River, NJ: Prentice Hall, 2008)

TABLE TB14 **Common HTML Tags**

Tag	Description
<html> . . . </html>	Creates an HTML document
<head> . . . </head>	Sets off the title and other information that is not displayed on the Web page itself
<body> . . . </body>	Sets off the visible portion of the document
<b> . . . </b>	Creates bold text
<a href="URL"> . . . </a>	Creates a hyperlink
<a href=mailto:EMAIL> . . . </a>	Creates a link creating a new e-mail message
<p> . . . </p>	Creates a new paragraph
<table> . . . </table>	Creates a table

A good way to understand how HTML works is to find a Web page you like, then use the "View Source" command on your browser to see the hypertext that created the page (see Figure TB17). Once you have created your own Web page and saved it to a disk, you can upload it to an Internet account you have created through your Internet service provider.

Markup languages such as HTML are for laying out or formatting Web pages. If you want to add animated cartoons or other dynamic content or have users interact with your Web page other than by clicking on hypertext links, then you will need access to tools such as Java, Web services, a scripting language, and so on.

Java is a programming language that was developed by Sun Microsystems in the early 1990s. It lets you spice up your Web page by adding active content such as circles that whirl and change colors, hamsters marching to a tune, forms to help users calculate car payments at various interest rates, or any other such dynamic content. You can do this in one of two ways: by learning Java or a similar language and programming the content you want or by downloading free general purpose **applets** from the Web to provide the content you want on your Web page. Applets are small programs that are executed within another application, such as a Web page. When a user accesses your Web page, the applets you inserted are downloaded from the server along with your Web page to the user's browser, where they perform the desired action. Later, when the user leaves your Web page, the Web page and the applets disappear from his or her computer.

Microsoft.NET is a programming platform that is used to develop applications that are highly interoperable across a variety of platforms and devices. For example, .NET can create an application that runs on desktop computers, mobile computers, or Web-enabled phones. .NET applications can be constructed using a suite of visual programming lan-

FIGURE TB17

A Web page and the HTML commands used to create it.

Source: Courtesy Washington State University.

guages including Visual C# (pronounced as C-sharp), ASP.NET and Visual Basic. To gain its interoperability, .NET utilizes Web services.

Web services are Web-based software systems used to integrate information from different applications and databases over a network (see also Chapter 6—Enhancing Collaboration Using Web 2.0). To support the interoperability from machine to machine, Web services use XML. The *Extensible Markup Language (XML)* was designed (1) to be used as a Web page construction tool when users want to create their own markup tags and (2) to build database queries. One practical application of Web services is iGoogle, which lets users create personalized home pages by gathering information from several sources and aggregating the content (see Figure TB18).

The advantages of Web services include the following:

- Web services offer interoperability between a variety of software applications that are on different operating systems.
- Web services allow software and services from different companies and locations to be easily shared and combined to provide powerful integrated applications.
- Web services, similar to object-oriented languages, allow the reuse of components.
- Web services are easily distributed, thereby facilitating a distributed approach to application integration.

Scripting languages can also be used to supply interactive components to a Web page. These languages let you build programs or scripts directly into HTML page code. Web page designers frequently use them to check the accuracy of user-entered information, such as names, addresses, and credit card numbers. Two common scripting languages are Microsoft's VBScript and JavaScript.

JavaScript bears little resemblance to Java. The two are similar, however, in that both Java and JavaScript are useful component software tools for creating Web pages. That is, both allow users to add or create applets that lend dynamic content to Web pages. Both are also cross-platform programs, meaning they can typically be used by computers running Windows, Linux, Mac OS, and other operating systems.

The development of programming languages is an ongoing process of change and innovation. These changes often result in more capable and complex systems for the user. The popularity of the Internet has spurred the creation of innovative and evolving software. From the pace of change that is occurring, it is clear that many more innovations are on the horizon.

FIGURE TB18

Web services are enabling powerful applications.

Along with commercial products, there are several open-source tools in wide use today. The most common is PHP, originally designed as a high-level tool for producing dynamic Web content. Another open-source application used frequently is MySQL, a multiuser database management system with over six million customers. This robust database can be used instead of commercial products such as Oracle or Microsoft's SQL server.

Another common way to add dynamic content to Web sites is Flash. Using the application development suite Macromedia Flash, developers can create animation and video that can be compressed small enough for fast download speeds. When you browse the Web and see animation or complex data streams, this is usually done in Flash. Flash animation is displayed on your screen using the Adobe Flash player. Flash can also include Web services to allow data-driven animation. Some examples of data-driven flash animation on Web sites are the bag builder at Timbuk2 (www.timbuk2.com) and the live major league baseball game update at Yahoo!'s sports site (sports.yahoo.com/mlb/gamechannel).

Automated Development Environments Over the years, the tools for developing information systems have increased both in variety and in power. In the early days of systems development, a developer was left to use a pencil and paper to sketch out design ideas and program code. Computers were cumbersome to use and slow to program, and most designers worked out on paper as much of the system design as they could before moving to the computer. Today, system developers have a vast array of powerful computer-based tools at their disposal. These tools have changed forever the ways in which systems are developed. **Computer-aided software engineering (CASE)** refers to automated software tools used by systems developers to design and implement information systems. Developers can use these tools to automate or support activities throughout the systems development process with the objective of increasing productivity and improving the overall quality of systems. The capabilities of CASE tools are continually evolving and being integrated into a variety of development environments. Next we briefly review some of the interesting characteristics of CASE.

TYPES OF CASE TOOLS. Two of the primary activities in the development of large-scale information systems are the creation of design documents and the management of information. Over the life of a project, thousands of documents need to be created—from screen prototypes to database content and structure to layouts of sample forms and reports. At the heart of all CASE environments is a repository for managing information.

CASE also helps developers represent business processes and information flows by using graphical diagramming tools. By providing standard symbols to represent business processes, information flows between processes, data storage, and the organizational entities that interact with the business processes, CASE eases a very tedious and error-prone activity (see Figure TB19). The tools not only ease the drawing process but also ensure that the drawing conforms to development standards and is consistent with other design documents developed by other developers.

Another powerful capability of CASE is its ability to generate program source code automatically. CASE tools keep pace with contemporary programming languages and can automatically produce programming code directly from high-level designs in languages such as Java, Visual Basic.NET, and C#.NET. In addition to diagramming tools and code generators, a broad range of other tools assists in the systems development process. The general types of CASE tools used throughout the development process are summarized in Table TB15.

Advanced Topics in Networking

Telecommunications and networking technologies are taking on more and more importance as organizations rely more on computer-based information systems. Understanding how the underlying networking technologies work and where these technologies are heading will help you better understand the potential of information systems. The discussion begins with a description of the evolution of computer networking.

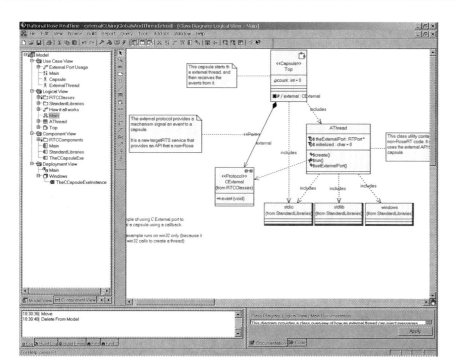

FIGURE TB19

High-level system design diagram from a CASE tool.

Source: Hoffer, George, and Valacich, *Modern Systems Analysis and Design*, 5th ed. (Upper Saddle River, NJ: Prentice Hall, 2008).

Evolution of Computer Networking

Over the past decades, computer networking underwent an evolution from centralized computing, to distributed computing, to collaborative computing. These eras of computer networking will be discussed next.

Centralized Computing   **Centralized computing**, depicted in Figure TB20, remained largely unchanged through the 1970s. In this model, large centralized computers, called mainframes, were used to process and store data. During the mainframe era (beginning in the 1940s), people entered data on mainframes through the use of local input devices called **terminals**. These devices were called "dumb" terminals because they did not conduct any processing, or "smart," activities. The centralized computing model is not a true network because there is no sharing of information and capabilities. The mainframe

TABLE TB15 General Types of CASE Tools

CASE Tool	Description
Diagramming tools	Tools that enable system process, data, and control structures to be represented graphically.
Screen and report generators	Tools that help model how systems look and feel to users. Screen and report generators also make it easier for the systems analyst to identify data requirements and relationships.
Analysis tools	Tools that automatically check for incomplete, inconsistent, or incorrect specifications in diagrams, screens, and reports.
Repositories	Tools that enable the integrated storage of specifications, diagrams, reports, and project management information.
Documentation generators	Tools that help produce both technical and user documentation in standard formats.
Code generators	Tools that enable the automatic generation of program and database definition code directly from the design documents, diagrams, screens, and reports.

Source: Hoffer, George, and Valacich, 2008. *Modern Systems Analysis and Design*, 5th ed., (Upper Saddle River, NJ: Prentice Hall).

FIGURE TB20

In the centralized computing model, all processing occurs in one central mainframe.

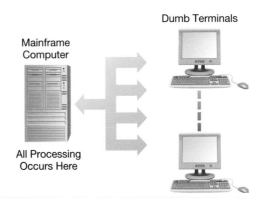

provides all the capabilities, and the terminals are only input/output devices. Computer networks evolved in the 1980s when organizations needed separate, independent computers to communicate with each other.

Distributed Computing The introduction of personal computers in the late 1970s and early 1980s gave individuals control over their own computing. Organizations also realized that they could use multiple small computers to achieve many of the same processing goals of a single large computer. People could work on subsets of tasks on separate computers rather than using one mainframe to perform all the processing. To achieve this goal, computer networks were needed so that information and services could be easily shared between these distributed computers. The 1980s were characterized by an evolution to a computing model called **distributed computing**, shown in Figure TB21, in which multiple types of computers are networked together to share information and services.

FIGURE TB21

In the distributed computing model, separate computers work on subsets of tasks and then pool their results by communicating over a network.

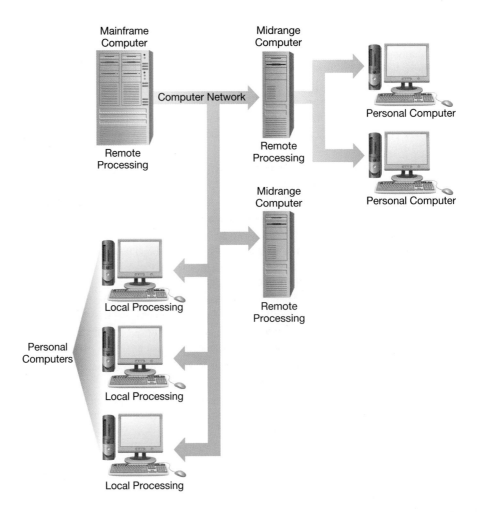

Collaborative Computing.   In the 1990s, a new computing model, called **collaborative computing**, emerged. Collaborative computing is a synergistic form of distributed computing in which two or more networked computers are used to accomplish a common processing task. That is, in this model of computing, computers are not simply communicating data but are also sharing processing capabilities. For example, one computer may be used to store a large employee database. A second computer may be used to process and update individual employee records selected from this database. The two computers collaborate to keep the company's employee records current, as depicted in Figure TB22.

Collaborative computing has also been introduced at the consumer level, such as with innovations in instant messaging (IM). All the major players have integrated collaborative functionality into their IM platforms, so that users can save files to particular folders that will then synchronize with other users' sharing folders.

Also in use are business-oriented Web collaborative tools. One example of this is Microsoft's SharePoint technology. SharePoint, like other Web-based collaborative tools, allows users to use office automation tools to create documents that are linked to Web sites that then can be distributed, checked out, modified, and even published to the public. With the rise in collaborative tools, most office automation applications now integrate some sort of collaborative components.

Types of Networks

Computing networks today include all three computing models: centralized, distributed, and collaborative. The emergence of new computing models did not mean that organizations completely discarded older technologies. Rather, a typical computer network includes mainframes, minicomputers, personal computers, and a variety of other devices. Computer networks are commonly classified by size, distance covered, and structure. The most commonly used classifications are a private branch exchange, local area network, campus area network, wide area network, and personal area network. Each is described in the following sections.

Private Branch Exchange   A private branch exchange (PBX) is a telephone system that serves a particular location, such as a business (see Figure TB23). It connects telephone extensions within the system and connects internal extensions to the outside telephone network. It can also connect computers within the system to other PBX systems, to an outside network, or to various office devices, such as fax machines or photocopiers. Since they use ordinary telephone lines, PBX systems have limited bandwidth, preventing them from transmitting such forms of information as interactive video, digital music, or high-resolution photos. Using PBX technology, a business requires few outside phone lines but has to purchase or lease the PBX equipment.

Local Area Network   A local area network (LAN), shown in Figure TB24, is a computer network that spans a relatively small area, allowing all computer users to connect with each other to share information and peripheral devices, such as printers. LAN-based communications may involve the sharing of data software applications, or other resources between several users. LANs typically do not exceed tens of kilometers in size and are typically contained within a single building or a limited geographical area. They typically use only one kind of transmission medium or cabling, such as twisted-pair wire or coaxial cable. There are also wireless local area network (WLAN) products available. These are

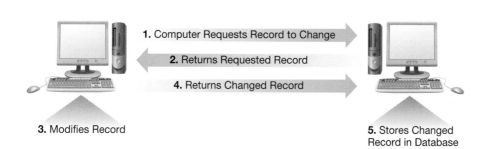

1. Computer Requests Record to Change
2. Returns Requested Record
4. Returns Changed Record

3. Modifies Record

5. Stores Changed Record in Database

FIGURE TB22

In the collaborative computing model, two or more networked computers are used to accomplish a common processing task.

A private branch exchange (PBX) supports local phone and data communications as well as links to outside phone and data networks.

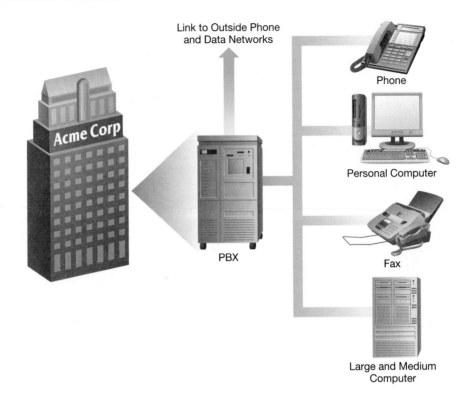

very popular because they are relatively easy to set up, and they enable you to have a network without any network cables strewn around your home or office. WLANs will be discussed more thoroughly later.

Campus Area Network   A campus area network (CAN) is a computer network that is used by a single organization to connect multiple LANs. A CAN typically spans multiple buildings, such as at a corporate or university campus.

Wide Area Network   A wide area network (WAN) is a computer network that spans a relatively large geographical area. WANs are typically used to connect two or more LANs. Different hardware and transmission media are often used in WANs because they must cover large distances efficiently. Used by multinational companies, WANs transmit and receive information across cities and countries. A discussion follows of four specific types of WANs—metropolitan area networks, enterprise networks, value-added networks, and global networks.

METROPOLITAN AREA NETWORKS.   A metropolitan area network (MAN) is a computer network of limited geographic scope, typically a citywide area, that combines both LAN and high-speed fiber-optic technologies. MANs are attractive to organizations that need high-speed data transmission within a limited geographic area.

A local area network (LAN) allows multiple computers located near each other to communicate directly with each other and to share peripheral devices, such as a printer.

ENTERPRISE NETWORKS.   An **enterprise network** is a WAN connecting disparate networks of a single organization into a single network (see Figure TB25).

VALUE-ADDED NETWORKS.   Medium-speed WANs, called **value-added networks (VANs)**, are private, third-party-managed networks that are shared by multiple organizations. VANs are economical because customers lease communication lines rather than investing in dedicated network equipment. The "added value" provided by VANs can include network management, e-mail, EDI, security, and other special capabilities. Consequently, VANs can be more expensive than generic communication lines leased from a common telecommunication company like AT&T or Sprint, but they provide valuable services for customers.

GLOBAL NETWORKS.   A **global network** spans multiple countries and may include the networks of several organizations. The Internet is an example of a global network. The Internet is the world's largest computer network, consisting of thousands of individual networks supporting millions of computers and users in almost every country of the world.

Personal Area Networks   A final type of computer network, called a personal area network (PAN), is an emerging technology that uses wireless communication to exchange data between computing devices using short-range radio communication, typically within an area of 10 meters (30 feet). The enabling technology for PAN is called Bluetooth, a specification for personal networking of desktop computers, peripheral devices, mobile phones, pagers, portable stereos, and other handheld devices. Bluetooth's founding members include Ericsson, IBM, Intel, Nokia, and Toshiba. Bluetooth is rapidly being integrated into a variety of personal devices to ease interoperability and information sharing (see Figure TB26).

Now that you have an understanding of the general types of networks, the next sections examine some of their fundamental components. This discussion is divided into two areas: networking fundamentals and network standards and technologies. Together, these sections provide a foundation for understanding various types of networks.

Networking Fundamentals

Telecommunications advances have enabled individual computer networks—constructed with a variety of hardware and software—to connect together in what appears to be a single network. Networks are increasingly being used to dynamically exchange relevant,

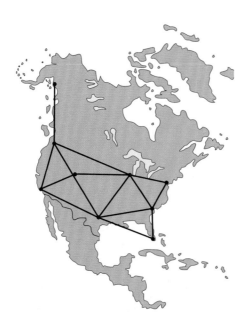

FIGURE TB25

An enterprise network allows an organization to connect distributed locations into a single network.

FIGURE TB26

BMW's new motorcycle helmet "System-Helmet 5" can be equipped with a Bluetooth network that allows riders to operate their Bluetooth-enabled cellular phones, using hands-free operation through the motorcycle's navigation system (note: BMW motorcycle helmets are not approved for use/sold in the USA).

value-added knowledge and information throughout global organizations and institutions. The following sections take a closer look at the fundamental building blocks of these complex networks and the services they provide.

Network Services   **Network services** are the capabilities that networked computers share through the multiple combinations of hardware and software. The most common network services are file services, print services, message services, and application services. **File services** are used to store, retrieve, and move data files in an efficient manner, as shown in Figure TB27a. An individual can use the file services of the network to move a certain file electronically to multiple recipients across the network. **Print services** are used to control and manage users' access to network printers and fax equipment, as shown in Figure TB27b. Sharing printers on a network reduces the number of printers an organization needs. **Message services** include the storing, accessing, and delivering of text, binary, graphic, and digitized video and audio data across a network. These services are similar to file services, but they also deal with communication interactions between users and applications. Message services include electronic mail or the transfer of messages between two or more networked computers, as shown in Figure TB27c. **Application services** run software for network clients and enable computers to share processing power, as shown in Figure TB27d. Application services highlight the concept of client/server computing, in which processing is distributed between the client and server. Clients request information or services from the servers. The servers store data and application programs. For example, the physical search of database records may take place on the server, while the user interacts with a much smaller database application that runs on the client.

When an organization decides to network its computers and devices, it must decide what services will be provided and whether these services will be centralized (a server-centric approach), distributed (a peer-to-peer approach), or some combination of both. These decisions ultimately affect the choice of the network operating system. The **network operating system (NOS)** is system software that controls the network and enables computers to communicate with each other. In other words, the NOS enables network services. In most LAN environments, the NOS consists of two parts. The first and most complex part is the system software that runs on the network server. The system software coordinates many functions, including user accounts, access information, security, and resource sharing. The second and much smaller part of the NOS runs on each workstation connected to the network. In peer-to-peer networks, usually a piece of the NOS is installed on each attached workstation and runs on top of the local operating system. Often, the second part of the NOS is integrated into the workstation operating system itself.

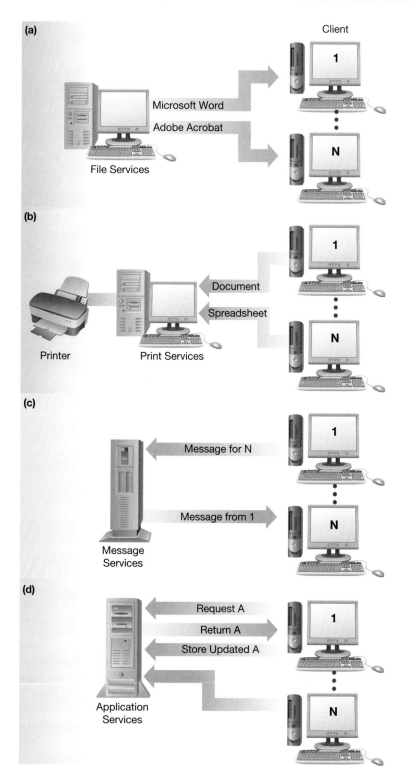

FIGURE TB27

Networks can provide (a) file, (b) print, (c) message, and (d) application services.

Cable Media   Cable media physically link computers and other devices in a network. The most common forms of cable media are twisted pair, coaxial, and fiber-optic.

TWISTED PAIR CABLE.   Twisted pair (TP) cable is made of two or more pairs of insulated copper wires twisted together (see Figure TB28). The cable may be unshielded (UTP) or shielded (STP). Telephone wire installations use UTP cabling. UTP is rated according to its quality; category 5 (Cat 5) and Cat 6 UTP are often used in network installations. Unshielded cable is cheap, easy to install, and has a capacity up to 1 Gbps at distances up to 100 meters (330 feet). However, like all copper wiring, it has rapid attenuation and is

(a) A cable spliced open showing several twisted pairs; (b) a sample network installation that utilizes many twisted pair cables at once.

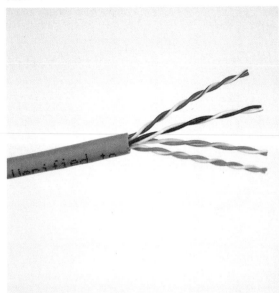

Sources: (a) ©Belkin Components; (b) ©Getty Images, Inc.

very sensitive to EMI and eavesdropping—the undetected capturing of network information. STP uses wires wrapped in an insulation, making it less prone to EMI and eavesdropping. STP cable is more expensive than unshielded twisted pair cable, and it is more difficult to install because it requires special grounding connectors to drain EMI. STP can support bandwidths up to 500 Mbps at distances up to 100 meters (330 feet). However, it is most commonly used to support networks running at 16 Mbps.

COAXIAL CABLE. Coaxial (or coax) cable contains a solid inner copper conductor surrounded by plastic insulation and an outer braided copper or foil shield (see Figure TB29). Coax cable comes in a variety of thicknesses—thinnet coax and thicknet coax—based on resistance to EMI. Though less costly than TP, thinnet coax is not commonly used in networks any more; thicknet coax is more expensive than TP. Coax cable is most commonly used for cable television installations and for networks operating at 10 to 100 Mbps. Its attenuation is lower than twisted pair cable's, and it is moderately susceptible to EMI and eavesdropping.

FIBER-OPTIC CABLE. Fiber-optic cable is made of a light-conducting glass or plastic core surrounded by more glass, called cladding, and a tough outer sheath (see Figure TB30). The sheath protects the fiber from changes in temperature as well as from bending or breaking. This technology uses pulses of light sent along the optical cable to transmit data. Fiber-optic cable transmits clear and secure data because it is immune to EMI and eaves-

These coaxial cables are ready to be connected to a computer or other device.

Source: ©Getty Images, Inc.

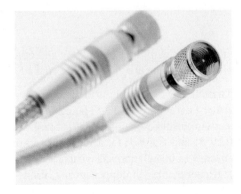

FIGURE TB30

Fiber-optic cable consists of a light-conducting glass or plastic core, surrounded by more glass, called cladding, and a tough outer sheath.

Source: ©Getty Images, Inc.

dropping. Transmission signals do not break up because fiber-optic cable has low attenuation. It can support bandwidths from 100 Mbps to greater than 2 Gbps (gigabits per second) and distances up to 25 kilometers (15 miles). It can transmit video and sound. Fiber-optic cable is more expensive than copper wire because the cost and difficulties of installation and repair are higher for fiber-optic. Fiber-optic cables are used for high-speed **backbones**—the high-speed central networks to which many smaller networks can be connected. A backbone may connect, for example, several different buildings in which other, smaller LANs reside.

Wireless Media   With the popularity of cellular phones, wireless media are rapidly gaining popularity. Wireless media transmit and receive electromagnetic signals using methods such as infrared line of sight, high-frequency radio, and microwave systems.

INFRARED LINE OF SIGHT.   Infrared line of sight uses high-frequency light waves to transmit data on an unobstructed path between nodes—computers or some other device such as a printer—on a network at a distance of up to 24.4 meters (80 feet). The remote controls for most audiovisual equipment, such as TVs, stereos, and other consumer electronics equipment, use infrared light. Infrared systems may be configured as either point-to-point or broadcast. For example, when you use your TV remote control, you have to be in front of the TV to have successful communication. This is an example of point-to-point infrared. Many printers and notebooks have the capability to transmit data using infrared communication, allowing these devices to be easily connected. With broadcast infrared communication, devices do not need to be positioned directly in front of each other but simply have to be located within some distance of each other. Infrared equipment is relatively inexpensive, but point-to-point systems require strict line-of-sight positioning. Installation and maintenance focus on ensuring proper optical alignment of nodes on the network. Point-to-point infrared systems can support up to 16 Mbps at 1 meter (3 feet), with transmission speeds reducing as distances increase; broadcast systems support less than 1 Mbps. Attenuation and susceptibility to EMI and eavesdropping are problematic, particularly when objects obstruct the light path or when environmental conditions such as smoke or high-intensity light are prevalent.

HIGH-FREQUENCY RADIO.   High-frequency radio signals can transmit data at rates of up to several hundred Mbps to network nodes from 12.2 up to approximately 40 kilometers (7.5 to 25 miles) apart, depending on the nature of any obstructions between them. The flexibility of the signal path makes high-frequency radio ideal for mobile transmissions. For example, most police departments use high-frequency radio signals that enable police vehicles to communicate with each other as well as with the dispatch office. This medium is expensive due to the cost of antenna towers and high-output transceivers. Installation is complex and often dangerous because of the high voltages. Although attenuation is fairly low, this medium is very susceptible to EMI and eavesdropping.

FIGURE TB31

A cellular network divides a geographic region into cells.

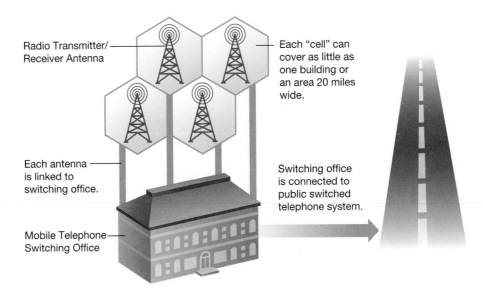

Radio Transmitter/Receiver Antenna

Each "cell" can cover as little as one building or an area 20 miles wide.

Each antenna is linked to switching office.

Switching office is connected to public switched telephone system.

Mobile Telephone Switching Office

Two common applications of high-frequency radio communication are cellular phones and wireless networks. A **cellular phone** gets its name from how the signal is distributed. In a cellular system a coverage area is divided into **cells** with a low-powered radio antenna/receiver in each cell; these cells are monitored and controlled by a central computer (see Figure TB31). Any given cellular network has a fixed number of radio frequencies. When a user initiates or receives a call, the mobile telephone switching office assigns the caller a unique frequency for the duration of the call. As a person travels within the network, the central computer at the switching office monitors the quality of the signal and automatically assigns the call to the closest cellular antenna. Cellular phones have gone through rapid changes since their first commercial use in the mid-1980s (see Table TB16). Cellular phones are now mostly digital in the United States except for a few rural areas. Digital transmission and reception offers many advantages over analog, some of which include wider reception range, less static, and the capability of data transmission.

TABLE TB16 Evolution of Cell Phone Technology

Generation	Description	Data Transfer	Advantages
0G	Preceded modern cellular mobile telephony and was usually mounted in cars or trucks; it was a closed circuit so you could call only other radio telephone users.	Analog	Communicate on the go.
1G	This technology, introduced in the 1980s, used circuit switching with poor voice quality, unreliable handoffs between towers, and non-existent security.	Analog	Can communicate with other cell phones and land lines.
2G	The first all-digital signal that was divided into TDMA and CDMA standards. Allowed for SMS (text) messaging and e-mails to be sent/received to the phones.	Digital (up to 9.6 Kbps transfer)	Lower-powered radio signals allow longer battery life. Digital format allows for clearer signal and reduced signal noise.
2.5G	Allows for faster data transmission via a packet-switched domain in addition to the circuit-switched domain.	Digital (up to 115 Kbps transfer)	Higher data speeds allow for more complex data to be transmitted (e.g., sports scores, news stories).
3G	Even faster. Requires a new cellular network, different from that already available in 2G systems.	Digital (up to 128 Kbps when moving and 2 Mbps when stationary)	Transfer full video and audio.
4G	Appears to be the future standard of wireless devices.	Digital (up to 100 Mbps when moving and 1 Gbps when stationary)	Data speeds similar to wired networks.

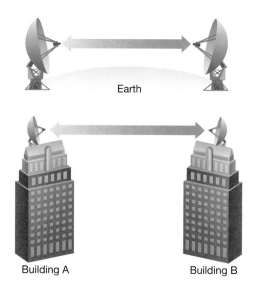

FIGURE TB32

Terrestrial microwave requires a line-of-sight path between a sender and a receiver.

High-frequency radio-wave technology is increasingly being used to support wireless local area networks (WLANs). WLANs based on a family of standards called 802.11 are also referred to as Wi-Fi (wireless fidelity). The 802.11 family of standards has been universally adopted and has transmission speeds up to 540 Mbps (using the 802.11n standard). The ease of installation has made WLANs popular for business and home use. For example, some homes and many buildings have (or want) multiple computers and need to share Internet access, files, and peripheral devices. Unfortunately, many older buildings and homes do not have a wired infrastructure to easily connect computers and devices, making wireless networking particularly attractive. Through the use of wireless technologies, many organizations are transforming their work environments into better team collaboration environments.

MICROWAVE. Microwave transmission is a high-frequency radio signal that is sent through the air using either terrestrial (earth-based) systems or satellite systems. Terrestrial microwave, shown in Figure TB32, uses antennae that require an unobstructed path or line of sight between nodes. The cost of a terrestrial microwave system depends on the distance to be covered. Typically, businesses lease access to these microwave systems from service providers rather than invest in antenna equipment. Data may be transmitted at up to 274 Mbps. Over short distances, attenuation is not a problem, but signals can be disrupted over longer distances by environmental conditions such as high winds and heavy rain. EMI and eavesdropping are significant problems with microwave communications.

Satellite microwave, shown in Figure TB33, uses satellites orbiting the earth as relay stations to transfer signals between ground stations located on earth. Satellites orbit from

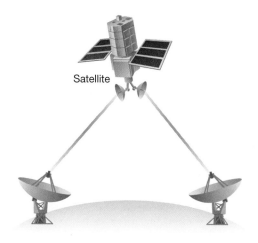

FIGURE TB33

Communications satellites are relay stations that receive signals from one earth station and rebroadcast them to another.

TABLE TB17 **Characteristics of Satellites with Different Orbits**

Name	Distance from Earth	Characteristics/Common Application
Low Earth Orbit (LEO) Satellite	400–1,000 miles	• Not fixed in space in relation to the rotation of the earth; circles the earth several times per day. • Photography for mapping and locating mineral deposits; monitoring ice caps, coastlines, volcanoes, and rain forests; researching plant and crop changes; monitoring wildlife and animal habitat and animal changes; search and rescue for downed aircraft or ships that are in trouble; researching projects in astronomy and physics.
Medium Earth Orbit (MEO)	1,000–22,300 miles	• Not fixed in space in relation to the rotation of the earth; circles the earth more than one time per day. • Primarily used in geographical positioning systems (GPS mapping) for navigation of ships at sea, spacecraft, airplanes, automobiles, and military weapons.
Geosynchronous Earth Orbit (GEO)	22,300 miles	• Fixed in space in relation to the rotation of the earth; circles the earth one time per day. • Because it is fixed in space, transmission is simplified. • Transmission of high-speed data for television, weather information, remote Internet connections, digital satellite radio, telecommunications (satellite phones).

400 to 22,300 miles above the earth and have different uses and characteristics (see Table TB17). Because of the distance signals must travel, satellite transmissions are delayed (also known as **propagation delay**). Satellite transmission has become very viable for media such as TV and radio, including the digital radio stations XM and Sirius, both of which have their own satellites that send out scrambled signals to proprietary receivers.

Another strength of satellite communication is that it can be used to access very remote and undeveloped locations on the earth. Such systems are extremely costly because their use and installation depends on space technology. Companies such as AT&T sell satellite services with typical transmission rates ranging from less than 1 to 10 Mbps, but the rates can be as high as 90 Mbps. Like terrestrial microwave, satellite systems are prone to attenuation and are susceptible to EMI and eavesdropping. Table TB18 compares wireless media across several criteria.

TABLE TB18 **Relative Comparison of Wireless Media**

Medium	Expense	Speed	Attenuation	EMI	Eavesdropping
Infrared line of sight	Low	Up to 16 Mbps	High	High	High
High-frequency radio	Moderate	Up to 54 Mbps	Low	High	High
Terrestrial microwave	Moderate	Up to 274 Mbps	Low	High	High
Satellite microwave	High	Up to 90 Mbps	Moderate	High	High

Note: Mbps = megabits per second.

TABLE TB19 Summary of Major LAN Standards

Network Standard	Access Control	Topology	Typical Media	Speed
Ethernet	CSMA/CD	Bus	Coax or twisted pair	10 Mbps–1 Gbps
Token ring	Token passing	Ring	Twisted pair	4–100 Mbps
ARCnet	Token passing	Star or bus	Coax or twisted pair	2.5–20 Mbps

Network Standards and Technologies

Standards play a key role in creating networks. The physical elements of networks—adapters, cables, and connectors—are defined by a set of standards that have evolved since the early 1970s. Standards ensure the interoperability and compatibility of network devices. The Institute of Electrical and Electronics Engineers (IEEE) has established a number of telecommunications standards. The three major standards for LAN cabling and media access control are Ethernet, token ring, and ARCnet. See Table TB19 for a summary of LAN standards. Each standard combines a media access control technique, network topology, and media in different ways. Software interacts with hardware to implement protocols that allow different types of computers and networks to communicate successfully. Protocols are often implemented within a computer's operating system or within the network operating system. Each of these topics is described more thoroughly next.

Media Access Control **Media access control** is the set of rules that governs how a given node or workstation gains access to the network to send or receive information. Without access control, collisions are likely to happen if two or more workstations simultaneously transmit messages onto the network. There are two general types of access control: distributed and random access. With distributed control, only a single workstation at a time has authorization to transmit its data. This authorization is transferred sequentially from workstation to workstation. Under random control, any workstation can transmit its data by checking whether the medium is available. No specific permission is required. The following sections describe each type in more detail.

DISTRIBUTED ACCESS CONTROL. The most commonly used method of distributed access control is called **token passing**. Token passing is an access method that uses a constantly circulating electronic token, a small packet of data, to grant workstations access to a ring-shaped network. A workstation must possess the token before it can transmit a message onto the network, which helps to prevent collisions and gives equal access to all workstations.

A workstation that receives the token and wants to send a message marks the token as busy, appends a message to it, and transmits both. The message and token are passed around the ring, as depicted in Figure TB34. Each workstation copies the message and retransmits the token/message combination. When it is received back at the originating workstation, the message is removed, the token is marked as free, and it is transmitted to the next workstation on the network.

RANDOM ACCESS CONTROL. The most commonly used method of random access control is called **carrier sense multiple access/collision detect (CSMA/CD)**. In CSMA/CD, each workstation "listens" to the network to determine whether a message is being transmitted. If the network is quiet, the workstation sends its message; otherwise, it waits. When a workstation gains access to the medium and sends information onto the network, messages are sent to all workstations on the network; however, only the destination with the proper address is able to "open" the message. If two or more workstations try to send a message simultaneously, all workstations detect that a collision has occurred, and all sending is ceased. After a short random period of time, the workstations again try to send their messages. When network traffic is light, there are few collisions, and data are quickly transmitted. However, the speed of transmission deteriorates rapidly under heavy traffic conditions.

Network Topologies **Network topology** refers to the shape of a network. The four common network topologies are star, ring, bus, and mesh.

FIGURE TB34

Station A receives the token and adds a message for station C; station C receives the message and token, then forwards both back to station A; station A removes the message and forwards the empty token on to the next station on the network.

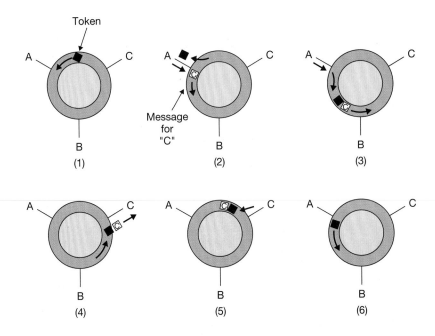

STAR NETWORK. A **star network** is configured, as you might expect, in the shape of a star, as shown in Figure TB35a. That is, all nodes or workstations are connected to a central hub, or concentrator, through which all messages pass. The workstations represent the points of the star. Star topologies are easy to lay out and modify. However, they are also the most costly because they require the largest amount of cabling. Although it is easy to diagnose problems at individual workstations, star networks are susceptible to a single point of failure at the hub that would result in all workstations losing network access.

RING NETWORK. A **ring network** is configured in the shape of a closed loop or circle with each node connecting to the next node, as shown in Figure TB35b. In ring networks, messages move in one direction around the circle. As a message moves around the circle, each workstation examines it to see whether the message is for that workstation. If not, the message is regenerated and passed on to the next node. This regeneration process enables ring networks to cover much larger distances than star or bus networks can. Relatively little cabling is required, but a failure of any node on the ring network can cause complete network failure. Self-healing ring networks avoid this by having two rings with data flowing in different directions; thus, the failure of a single node does not cause the network to fail. In either case, it is difficult to modify and reconfigure a ring network. Ring networks normally use some form of token-passing media access control method to regulate network traffic.

BUS NETWORK. A **bus network** is in the shape of an open-ended line, as shown in Figure TB35c; as a result, it is the easiest network to extend and has the simplest wiring layout. This topology enables all network nodes to receive the same message through the network cable at the same time. However, it is difficult to diagnose and isolate network faults. Bus networks use CSMA/CD for media access control.

MESH NETWORK. A **mesh network** consists of computers and other devices that are either fully or partially connected to each other. In a *full* mesh design, every computer and device is connected to every other computer and device. In a *partial* mesh design, many but not all computers and devices are connected (see Figure TB35d). Like a ring network, mesh networks provide relatively short routes from one node to another. Mesh networks also provide many possible routes through the network—a design that prevents one circuit or computer from becoming overloaded when traffic is heavy. Given these benefits, most WAN networks, including the Internet, use a partial mesh design.

Protocols In addition to media access control and network topologies, all networks employ protocols to make sure communication between computers is successful. Protocols are agreed-on formats for transmitting data between connected computers. They specify

FIGURE TB35

(a) The star network has several workstations connected to a central hub. (b) The ring network is configured in a closed loop, with each workstation connected to another workstation. (c) The bus network is configured in the shape of an open-ended line where each workstation receives the same message simultaneously. (d) The mesh network consists of computers and other devices that are either fully or partially connected to each other.

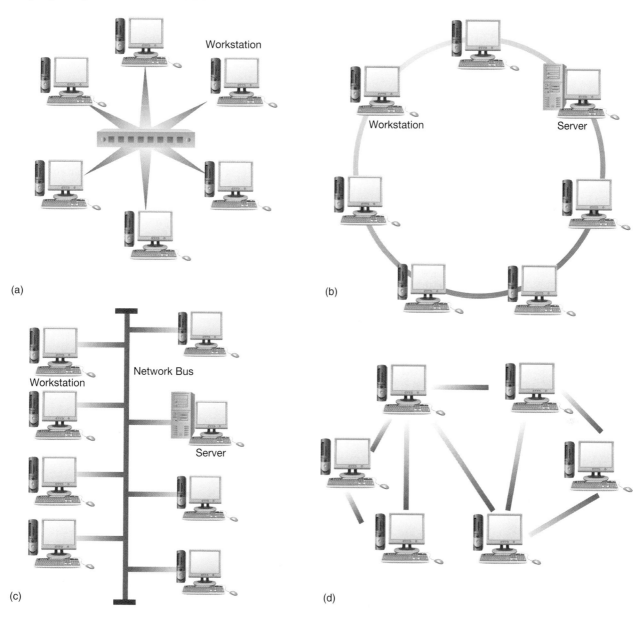

how computers should be connected to the network, how errors will be checked, what data compression method will be used, how a sending computer will signal that it has finished sending a message, and how a receiving computer will signal that it has received a message. Protocols allow packets to be correctly routed to and from their destinations. There are literally thousands of protocols for programmers to use, but a few are a lot more important than the others. In this section, we will first review the worldwide standard, called the OSI model, for implementing protocols. Next, we briefly review two of the more important network protocols: Ethernet and TCP/IP.

THE OSI MODEL. The need of organizations to interconnect computers and networks that use different protocols has driven the industry to an open system architecture in which different protocols can communicate with each other. The International Organization for

FIGURE TB36

The Open Systems Interconnection (OSI) model has seven layers and provides a framework for connecting different computers with different operating systems to a network.

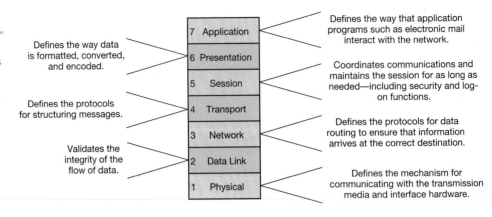

Standardization defined a networking model called Open Systems Interconnection (OSI), which divides computer-to-computer communications into seven connected layers. The **Open Systems Interconnection (OSI) model** is a protocol that represents a group of specific tasks, represented in Figure TB36 as successive layers that enable computers to communicate data. Each successively higher layer builds on the functions of the layers below. For example, suppose you are using a PC running Windows and are connected to the Internet and you want to send a message to a friend who is connected to the Internet through a large workstation computer running Unix—two different computers and two different operating systems. When you transmit your message, it is passed down from layer to layer in the Windows protocol environment of your system. At each layer, special bookkeeping information specific to the layer, called a header, is added to the data. Eventually, the data and headers are transferred from the Windows Layer 1 to Unix's Layer 1 over some physical pathway. On receipt, the message is passed up through the layers in the Unix application. At each layer, the corresponding header information is stripped away, the requested task is performed, and the remaining data package is passed on until your message arrives as you sent it, as shown in Figure TB37. In other words, protocols represent an agreement between different parts of the network about how data are to be transferred.

FIGURE TB37

Message passing between two different computers.

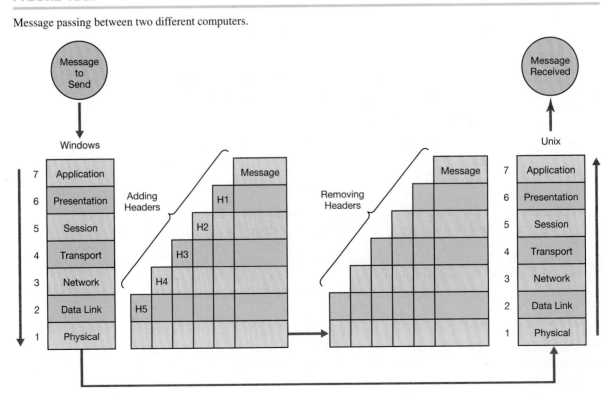

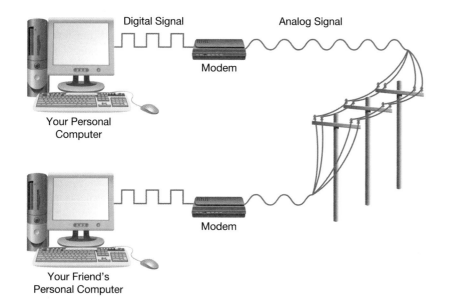

FIGURE TB38

Modems convert digital signals into analog and analog signals into digital.

ETHERNET. **Ethernet** is a LAN protocol developed by the Xerox Corporation in 1976. It uses a bus network topology and uses random access control to send data. The original Ethernet protocol supports data transfer rates of 10 Mbps. A later version, called 100Base-T or Fast Ethernet, supports transfer rates of 100 Mbps; the latest version, called Gigabit Ethernet, supports transfer rates of 1 gigabit, or 1,000 megabits, per second. Most new computers have an Ethernet card installed, allowing you to use this type of network connection.

TCP/IP. The Internet was based on the idea that individual networks could be separately designed and developed yet still connect their users to the Internet by using their own unique interfaces. Transmission Control Protocol/Internet Protocol (TCP/IP), the protocol of the Internet, allows different interconnected networks to communicate using the same language. For example, TCP/IP allows IBM, Macintosh, and Unix users to communicate despite any system differences. Computer scientist Vinton Cerf and engineer Robert Kahn defined the Internet Protocol (IP), by which packets are sent from one computer to another on their way to a destination, as part of the DARPA project (you learned about TCP/IP in Chapter 4).

Connectivity Hardware Stand-alone computers can be physically connected to create different types of networks. Most computers today are equipped with a **network interface card (NIC)**, which is a PC expansion board that plugs into a computer so that it can be connected to a network. Each NIC has a unique identifier (assigned by the manufacturer) that is used to identify the computer on the network. The PC is then connected to other network components via transmission media, such as Ethernet cables. Transmission media connectors, or simply **connectors**, are used to terminate the cables so that they can be plugged into a network interface card or into other network components. Connectors include T-connectors for coax cable and RJ-45 connectors (similar to a phone jack) for twisted pair cable. Some computers connect to networks using (slower) telephone lines. Because the dial-up telephone system was designed to pass the sound of voices in the form of analog signals, it cannot pass the electrical pulses—**digital signals**—that computers use. The only way to pass digital data over conventional voice telephone lines is to convert it to audio tones—**analog signals**—that the telephone lines can carry. A **modem** (MOdulator/DEModulator) converts digital signals from a computer into analog signals so that telephone lines may be used as a transmission medium to send and receive electronic information, as shown in Figure TB38. After individual devices are connected to the network, multiple segments of transmission media can be connected to form one large network. Repeaters, hubs, bridges, and multiplexers are used to extend the range and size of the network. These devices are described next.

Networking Hardware   Because of the complexity of current networks, there are several specialized pieces of equipment needed for computers to connect and transfer data. Not all pieces of equipment are necessary in order to connect computers together. The use of this equipment is dependent on the configuration of the network and the use of the network. As seen in Table TB20, each piece of network hardware is designed for a specific function at a specific OSI layer. Most Internet traffic will at some point have to cross both a gateway, which allows the packets to leave the LAN, and a router, which designates the addressing for the packets.

The Internet

The name Internet is derived from the concept of *internetworking,* which means connecting host computers and their networks to form even larger networks. The Internet is a large worldwide collection of networks that use a common protocol to communicate with each other. In Chapter 4, you learned that the Internet uses packet switching to transfer information from computer to computer. In the following sections, we will discuss in more detail how independent networks are connected to form the Internet, who manages the Internet, and how home and business users can connect to the Internet.

TABLE TB20 **Networking Hardware**

Networking Hardware	Description
Repeater	A **repeater** is used to regenerate or replicate a signal as it weakens when traveling on a network. A repeater also moves data from one media segment to another and effectively extends the size of the network.
Hub	A **hub** is used as a central point of connection between media segments. Like repeaters, hubs enable the network to be extended to accommodate additional workstations.
Bridge	A **bridge** is used to connect two different LANs or two segments of the same LAN by forwarding network traffic between network segments. Bridges determine the physical location of the source and destination computers, and are typically used to divide an overloaded network into separate segments, helping to minimize intersegment traffic. Bridges are also used to connect segments that use different wiring or network protocols.
Multiplexer	A **multiplexer (MUX)** is used to share a communications line or medium among a number of users. Sometimes the transmission medium provides more capacity than a single signal can occupy. To use the entire media bandwidth effectively, multiplexers are used to transmit several signals over a single channel.
Router	A router is an intelligent device used to connect two or more individual networks. When a router receives a signal, it looks at the network address and passes the signal or message on to the appropriate network.
Brouter	A **brouter**, short for bridge router, provides the capabilities of both a bridge and a router.
Channel service unit	A **channel service unit (CSU)** is a device that acts as a "buffer" between a LAN and a public carrier's WAN. CSUs ensure that all signals placed on the public lines from the LAN are appropriately timed and formed for the public network.
Gateway	A **gateway** performs protocol conversion so that different networks can communicate even though they "speak" different languages. For example, communications between a LAN and a large system, such as a mainframe, whose protocols are different, require a gateway.

Connecting Independent Networks   The Internet uses routers to interconnect independent networks. For example, Figure TB39 illustrates a router that connects networks 1, 2, and 3. A router, like a conventional computer, has a central processor, memory, and network interfaces. However, routers do not use conventional software, nor are they used to run applications. Their only job is to interconnect networks and forward data packets from one network to another. For example, in Figure TB46, computers A and F are connected to independent networks. If computer A generates a data packet destined for computer F, the packet is sent to the router that interconnects the two networks. The router forwards the packet onto network 2, where it is delivered to its destination at computer F.

Routers are the fundamental building blocks of the Internet because they connect thousands of LANs and WANs. LANs are connected to backbone WANs, as depicted in Figure TB40. A backbone network manages the bulk of network traffic and typically uses a higher-speed connection than the individual LAN segments. For example, a backbone network might use fiber-optic cabling, which can transfer data at a rate of 2 Gbps (gigabits per second), whereas a LAN connected to the backbone may use Ethernet with twisted pair cabling, transferring data at a rate of 10 Mbps to 1 Gbps. To gain access to the Internet, an organization installs a router between one of its own networks and the closest Internet site. Business organizations typically connect to the Internet not only with personal computers but with Web servers as well.

Who Manages the Internet?   As discussed in Chapter 4, individual computers on the Internet are identified by their IP addresses. So, who keeps track of these IP addresses on the Internet? A number of national and international standing committees and task forces have been used to manage the development and use of the Internet. Among these is the Coordinating Committee for Intercontinental Research Networks, which has helped to coordinate government-sponsored research in this area. The Internet Society is a professional membership society with over 150 organizational and 16,000 individual members around the world that helps to shape the future of the Internet and is home for the Internet Engineering Task Force and the Internet Architecture Board (IAB). These groups help manage Internet standards. For example, the IAB has guided the evolution of the TCP/IP Protocol Suite. The Internet Assigned Numbers Authority has provided the recording of system identifiers on the Internet and has helped to manage an **Internet Registry** that acts as a central repository for Internet-related information and that provides central allocation of network system identifiers. The Internet Registry also provides central maintenance of the **Domain Name System (DNS)** root database, which points to distributed DNS servers

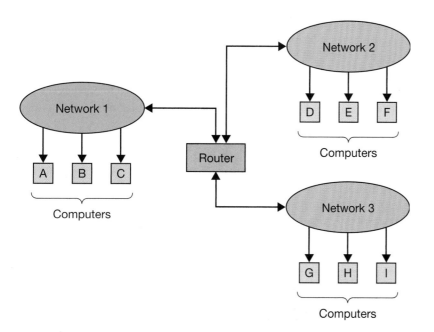

FIGURE TB39

Routers connect independent networks.

FIGURE TB40

LANs connect to wide area backbones.

Source: Douglas E. Comer, *The Internet Book*, 2nd ed. (Upper Saddle River, NJ: Prentice Hall, 1997).

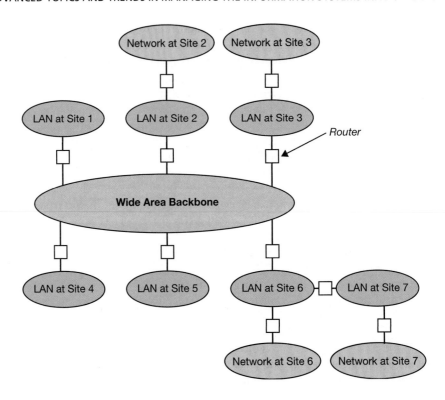

replicated throughout the Internet. This database is used to associate Internet host names with their Internet IP addresses. As mentioned previously, users can access Web sites using domain name or IP addresses. The functionality of the DNS is to provide users easy-to-remember domain names to access Web sites. In other words, it is far easier to remember www.apple.com than it is to remember 17.149.160.10 (the IP address of a server mirroring Apple's content as of mid-2008), but both will work as a URL in any Web browser, as the DNS servers will translate the domain names into the accompanying IP address.

In 1993, the NSF created **InterNIC**, a government–industry collaboration, to manage directory and database services, domain registration services, and other information services on the Internet. In the late 1990s, this Internet oversight was transitioned more fully out into industry when InterNIC morphed into the **Internet Corporation for Assigned Names and Numbers (ICANN)**, a nonprofit corporation that assumed responsibility for managing IP addresses, domain names, and root server system management. The number of unassigned Internet addresses is running out, so new classes of addresses are being added as we adopt **IPv6**, the latest version of the IP.

How to Connect to the Internet Now you can see how the Internet works and how it is managed. How do you connect to the Internet? For personal use (i.e., from home), we typically connect to the Internet through an **Internet service provider (ISP)**, also called Internet access provider. ISPs provide several different ways to access the Internet from home (see Table TB21).

ISPs connect to one another through **network access points (NAPs)**. Much like railway stations, these NAPs serve as access points for ISPs and are an exchange point for Internet traffic. They determine how traffic is routed and are often the points of most Internet congestion. NAPs are a key component of the **Internet backbone**, which is the collection of main network connections and telecommunications lines that make up the Internet (see Figure TB41).

The Internet follows a hierarchical structure, similar to the interstate highway system. High-speed central network lines are like interstate highways, enabling traffic from midlevel networks to get on and off. Think of midlevel networks as city streets that, in turn, accept traffic from their neighborhood streets or member networks. However, you cannot get on an interstate or city street whenever you want to. You have to share the highway and

TABLE TB21 **Methods for Connecting to the Internet**

Service	Current Status and Future Outlook	Typical Bandwidth
Dial-up	Although still used heavily in the United States, there are very few new dial-up customers. This market should dry up as broadband is moved to the rural areas of the United States.	52 Kbps
ISDN	This technology has limited market share because of its expense. Typically, ISDN connections are more expensive than broadband connections, although they offer less bandwidth.	128 Kbps
Cable	Coaxial cable used for cable TV provides much greater bandwidth than telephone lines and therefore is the market leader in broadband use for home users. Overselling of bandwidth that causes slower-than-average speeds tends to be a major problem for home users.	Upload: 768 Kbps Download: 30 Mbps
DSL	DSL technology has gained market share over cable. With many companies offering higher speeds at lower cost, DSL should continue to cut into cable's market share.	Upload: up to 3.5 Mbps Download: 1.5–30 Mbps
Satellite	Although satellite connectivity had a promising future, many users are moving away from this expensive technology in order to access faster and cheaper cable or DSL connections.	Upload: 50 Kbps Download: 5 Mbps
Wireless	Wireless offers the most promise of any of the current technologies, as the speeds are increasing while the coverage areas continue to grow.	Up to 54 Mbps
Fiber to the home	FTTH has been adopted by many major players in the ISP industry. Although the technology typically can be placed only in new developments, the demand for fast connections is helping make FTTH a significant technology for ISPs.	Up to 100 Mbps

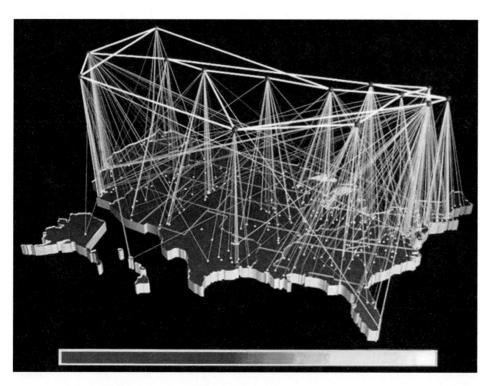

FIGURE TB41

The Internet backbone.

follow traffic control signs to arrive safely at your destination. The same holds true for traffic on the Internet. People can connect to the Internet in a number of ways. The following outline how typical home users connect to the Internet.

DIAL-UP. Traditionally, most people connected to the Internet through a telephone line at home or work. The term we use for standard telephone lines is **plain old telephone service (POTS)**. The speed, or bandwidth, of POTS is generally about 52 Kbps (52,000 bits per second). The POTS system is also called the **public switched telephone network (PSTN)**. Today, most people connect to the Internet using some form of digital, high-speed connection.

INTEGRATED SERVICES DIGITAL NETWORK. **Integrated services digital network (ISDN)** is a standard for worldwide digital communications. ISDN was designed in the 1980s to replace all analog systems, such as most telephone connections in the United States, with a completely digital transmission system. ISDN uses existing twisted pair telephone wires to provide high-speed data service. ISDN systems can transmit voice, video, and data. Because ISDN is a purely digital network, you can connect your PC to the Internet without the use of a traditional modem. Removing the analog-to-digital conversion for sending information and the digital-to-analog conversion for receiving information greatly increases the data transfer rate. However, a small electronic box called an "ISDN modem" is typically required so that computers and older, analog-based devices such as telephones and fax machines can utilize and share the ISDN-based service. While ISDN has had moderate success in various parts of the world, it has largely been surpassed by DSL and cable modems.

DIGITAL SUBSCRIBER LINE. **Digital subscriber line (DSL)** is one of the more popular ways of connecting to the Internet. DSL is referred to as a "last-mile" solution because it is used only for connections from a telephone switching station to a home or office and generally is not used between telephone switching stations.

The abbreviation DSL is used to refer collectively to **asymmetric digital subscriber line (ADSL)**, **symmetric digital subscriber line (SDSL)**, and other forms of DSL. DSL enables more data to be sent over existing copper telephone lines by sending digital pulses in the high-frequency area of telephone wires. Because these high frequencies are not used by normal voice communications, DSL enables your computer to operate simultaneously with voice connections over the same wires. ADSL speeds range from 1.5 to 30 Mbps downstream and from 16 Kbps to 3.5 Mbps upstream. SDSL is said to be symmetric because it supports the same data rates for upstream and downstream traffic (up to 3 Mbps). Like ISDN, ADSL and SDSL require a special modem-like device. ADSL is most popular in North America, whereas SDSL is being developed primarily in Europe.

CABLE MODEMS. In most areas, the company that provides cable television service also provides Internet service. With this type of service, a special **cable modem** is designed to transmit data over cable TV lines. Coaxial cable used for cable TV provides much greater bandwidth than telephone lines, and millions of homes in the United States are already wired for cable TV, so cable modems are a fast, popular method for accessing the Internet. Cable modems offer download speeds up to 30 Mbps.

SATELLITE CONNECTIONS. In many regions of the world, people can access the Internet via satellite, referred to as **Internet over satellite (IoS)**. IoS technologies allow users to access the Internet via satellites that are placed in a geostationary orbit above the earth's surface. With these services, your PC is connected to a satellite dish hanging out on the side of your home or placed out on a pole (much like satellite services for your television) and is able to maintain a reliable connection to the satellite in the sky because the satellite orbits the earth at the exact speed of the earth's rotation. Given the vast distance that signals must travel from the earth up to the satellite and back again, IoS is slower than high-speed terrestrial (i.e., land-based) connections to the Internet over copper or fiber-optic cables. In remote regions of the world, IoS is the only option available because installing the cables necessary for an Internet connection is not economically feasible or, in many cases, is just not physically possible.

BROADBAND WIRELESS. **Broadband wireless** is a technology that is becoming more prevalent with home users today. With speeds similar to DSL and cable, broadband wireless is usually found in rural areas where other connectivity options, such as DSL and cable, are not available. A common scenario is that the ISP will install an antenna at a high point, such as a large building or radio tower. The consumer will mount a small dish to the roof and point it at the antenna. Although broadband wireless can bridge a distance of up to 50 kilometers (30 miles), line of sight between the sender and receiver is necessary for wireless access to work.

MOBILE WIRELESS ACCESS. In addition to the fixed wireless approach, there are also many new **mobile wireless** approaches for connecting to the Internet. For example, there are Internet-enabled cellular phones that give you Internet access nearly anywhere. Also, special network adapter cards from a cellular service provider allow a notebook computer, tablet PC, or personal digital assistant (PDA) to connect to cellular networks. The advantage of these systems is that as long as you are in the coverage area of that cell phone provider you have access to the Internet (much like coverage with cellular phones). One other option for wireless access to the Internet is to use a wireless network adapter card (typically built into most mobile computers) when you are within the range of a wireless local area network (WLAN). Using a WLAN, you are free to roam around your office or building; with a cellular-based technology, you are able to connect anywhere within the cellular coverage area.

FIBER TO THE HOME. **Fiber to the home (FTTH)**, also known as **fiber to the premises (FTTP)**, refers to connectivity technology that provides a superspeed connection to people's homes. This is usually done by fiber-optic cabling running directly into new homes. With several players entering the FTTH marketplace, there will be wide use of this technology shortly. The growth in FTTH is dependent on new home building, as it is currently cost-prohibitive to distribute the technology to existing structures.

Until now, we have talked about ways that individuals rather than organizations typically access the Internet. In the following section, we talk more about ways that organizations typically access the Internet.

Business Internet Connectivity Although home users have enjoyed a consistent increase in bandwidth availability, the demand for corporate use has increased at a greater pace; therefore, the need for faster speeds has become of great importance. In addition to the home connectivity options, business customers also have several high-speed options, described next.

T1 LINES. To gain adequate access to the Internet, organizations are turning to long-distance carriers to lease dedicated **T1 lines** for digital transmissions. The T1 line was developed by AT&T as a dedicated digital transmission line that can carry 1.544 Mbps of information. In the United States, companies such as MCI that sell long-distance services are called **interexchange carriers (IXC)** because their circuits carry service between the major telephone exchanges. A T1 line usually traverses hundreds or thousands of miles over leased long-distance facilities.

AT&T and other carriers charge as little as $400 per month for a dedicated T1 circuit, and some providers will waive the installation fee if you sign up for some specified length of service. If you need an even faster link, you might choose a **T3 line**. T3 provides about 45 Mbps of service at about 10 times the cost of leasing a T1 line. Alternatively, organizations often choose to use two or more T1 lines simultaneously rather than jump to the more expensive T3 line. Higher speeds than the T3 are also available but are not typically used for normal business activity. For example, fiber-optic networks offer speeds considerably faster than T3 lines. See Table TB22 for a summary of telecommunication line capacities, including optical carrier (OC) lines that use the Synchronous Optical Network (SONET) standard.

ASYNCHRONOUS TRANSFER MODE. **Asynchronous transfer mode (ATM)** is a method of transmitting voice, video, and data over high-speed LANs at speeds of up to 2.2 Gbps. ATM has found wide acceptance in the LAN and WAN arenas as a solution to integrating

TABLE TB22 **Capacity of Telecommunication Lines**

Type of Line	Data Rate
T1	1.544 Mbps
T3	44.736 Mbps
OC-1	51.85 Mbps
OC-3	155.52 Mbps
OC-12	622.08 Mbps
OC-24	1.244 Gbps
OC-48	2.488 Gbps

disparate networks over large geographic distances. ATM uses a form of packet transmission in which data is sent over a packet-switched network in fixed-length, 53-byte cells. Although it is based on packet-switching technology, ATM has the potential to do away with routers, allocated bandwidth, and contention for communications media. Organizations in the movie and entertainment industries that need to deliver synchronized video and sound, for example, are particularly interested in ATM.

The Future of Connectivity   Although there are many options for both business and home user alike, there are still many innovations yet to gain widespread acceptance. One such innovation is broadband over power lines. **Power line communication**, or power line telecoms, is a system that uses the existing power distribution wires for data transmission. Currently, the data rates are 1 Mbps and increasing every year. This technology is promising, as the infrastructure is currently available to virtually all consumers. Consumers can also use their power lines to extend their home LANs without additional wiring.

WiMax is another promising innovation. WiMAX, or Worldwide Interoperability for Microwave Access, is a standards-based technology that enables the delivery of the "last mile" in wireless form. WiMax is similar to broadband wireless in that it offers high-speed stationary wireless, but is different in that it is not a line-of-sight technology. Further, WiMax can also be used for mobile applications. Currently, WiMax is being used primarily by corporate customers and ISPs because of the large investment needed in equipment. However, as equipment becomes less expensive, consumer versions of the technology will become available (see www.clearwire.com).

The Current State of Internet Usage   The Internet is now the most prominent global network. Internet World Stats (www.internetworldstats.com) reports that, as of late 2008, over 1.4 billion people worldwide use the Internet. This means that over 20 percent of the world's population has Internet access at home, an increase of 290 percent since 2000. Most Internet users are found in Asia, but North America has the largest percentage of users (73.1 percent of the North American population have access to the Internet). Africa, on the other hand, has the smallest percentage of its population using the Internet since 2000 (just 5.3 percent) but is experiencing rapid growth (1030 percent).

One other way to measure the rapid growth of the Internet, in addition to the number of users, is to examine the growth in the number of **Internet hosts**—that is, computers working as servers on the Internet—as shown in Figure TB42.

Advanced Topics in Database Management

In Chapter 4, you were introduced to foundational database concepts, such as attributes, entities, and relationships. In the following sections, we will delve deeper into the topic of database management to give you a better idea of the intricacies involved in designing a sound database.

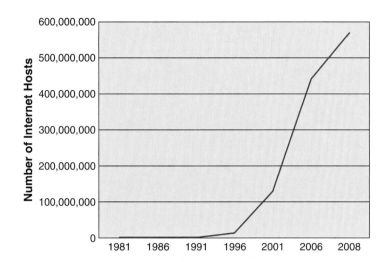

FIGURE TB42

Growth in Internet servers (hosts).

Source: Internet Systems Consortium. http://www.isc.org/index.pl?/ops/ds/host-count-history.php.

Database Design

Much of the work of creating an effective organizational database is in the creation of the data model. If the model is not accurate, the database will not be effective. A poor data model will result in data that are inaccurate, redundant, or difficult to search. If the database is relatively small, the effects of a poor design might not be too severe. A corporate database, however, contains many entities, perhaps hundreds or thousands. In this case, the implications of a poor data model can be catastrophic. A poorly organized database is difficult to maintain and process—thus defeating the purpose of having a database management system in the first place. Undoubtedly, your school maintains databases with a variety of entity types—for example, students and grades—with both of these entities having several attributes. Attributes of a Student entity might be Student ID, Name, Campus Address, Major, and Phone. Attributes of a Grades entity might include Student ID, Course ID, Section Number, Term, and Grade (see Figure TB43).

For the database management system (DBMS) to distinguish between records correctly, each instance of an entity must have one unique identifier. For example, each student has a unique Student ID. Note that using the student name (or most other attributes) would not be adequate because students may have the exact same name, live at the same address, or have the same phone number. Consequently, when designing a database, we

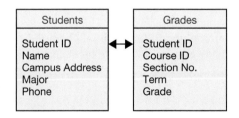

FIGURE TB43

The attributes for and links between two entities—students and grades.

Students

Student ID	Name	Campus Address	Major	Phone
555-39-3232	Joe Jones	123 Any Avenue	Finance	335-2211
289-42-8776	Sally Carter	1200 Wolf Street #12	Marketing	335-8702

Grades

Student ID	Course ID	Section No.	Term	Grade
555-39-3232	MIS 250	2	F'05	D+
555-39-3232	MIS 250	1	F'06	A–
289-42-8776	MIS 250	3	S'07	B+

TABLE TB24 **Rules for Expressing Relationships among Entities and Their Corresponding Data Structures**

Relationship	Examples	Instructions
One-to-one	Each team has only one home stadium, and each home stadium has only one team.	Place the primary key from one table (e.g., Stadium) into the other (e.g., Team) as a foreign key.
One-to-many	Each player is on only one team, but each team has many players.	Place the primary key from the table on the "one" side of the relationship (e.g., Team) as a foreign key in the table on the "many" side of the relationship (e.g., Player).
Many-to-many	Each player participates in many games and each game has many players.	Create a third table (e.g., Player Statistics) and place the primary keys from each of the original tables (e.g., Player and Team) together in the third as a combination primary key.

must always create and use a unique identifier, called a **primary key**, for each type of entity, in order to store and retrieve data accurately. In some instances, the primary key can also be a combination of two or more attributes, in which case it is called a **combination primary key**. An example of this is the Grades entity shown in Figure TB43, where the combination of Student ID, Course ID, Section Number, and Term uniquely refers to the grade of an individual student, in a particular class (section number), from a particular term. Attributes not used as the primary key can be referred to as **secondary keys** when they are used to identify one or more records within a table that share a common value. For example, a secondary key in the Student entity shown in Figure TB43 would be Major when used to find all students who share a particular major.

Associations   To retrieve information from a database, it is necessary to associate or relate information from separate tables. The three types of **relationships** (or **associations**) among entities are one-to-one, one-to-many, and many-to-many. Table TB24 summarizes each of these three associations and shows how they should be handled in database design for a basketball league.

   To understand how relationships work, consider Figure TB44, which shows four tables—Home Stadium, Team, Player, and Games—for keeping track of the information for a basketball league. The Home Stadium table lists the Stadium ID, Stadium Name, Capacity, and Location, with the primary key underlined. The Team table contains two attributes, Team ID and Team Name, but nothing about the stadium where the team plays. If we wanted to have such information, we could gain it only by creating a rela-

FIGURE TB44

Tables used for storing information about several basketball teams, with no foreign key attributes added; thus, associations cannot be made.

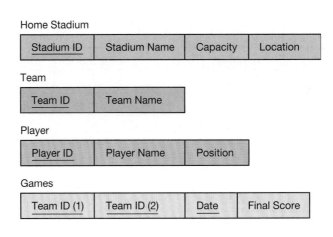

Home Stadium

| Stadium ID | Stadium Name | Capacity | Location |

Team

| Team ID | Team Name |

Player

| Player ID | Player Name | Position |

Games

| Team ID (1) | Team ID (2) | Date | Final Score |

tionship between the Home Stadium and Team tables. For example, if each team has only one home stadium and each home stadium has only one team, we have a one-to-one relationship between the team and the home stadium entities. In situations in which we have one-to-one relationships between entities, we place the primary key from one table in the table for the other entity and refer to this attribute as a **foreign key**. In other words, a foreign key refers to an attribute that appears as a nonprimary key attribute in one entity and as a primary key attribute (or part of a primary key) in another entity. By sharing this common—but unique—value, entities can be linked, or associated, together. We can choose in which of these tables to place the foreign key of the other. After adding the primary key of the Home Stadium entity to the Team entity, we can identify which stadium is the home for a particular team and find all the details about that stadium (see section A in Figure TB45).

When we find a one-to-many relationship—for example, each player plays for only one team, but each team has many players—we place the primary key from the entity on the "one" side of the relationship, the Team entity, as a foreign key in the table for the entity on the "many" side of the relationship, the Player entity (see section B in Figure TB45). In essence, we take from the one and give to the many, a Robin Hood strategy.

When we find a many-to-many relationship (e.g., each player plays in many games, and each game has many players), we create a third (new) entity—in this case, the Player Statistics entity and corresponding table. We then place the primary keys from each of the original entities together into the third (new) table as a combination primary key (see section C in Figure TB45).

You may have noticed that by placing the primary key from one entity in the table of another entity, we are creating a bit of redundancy. We are repeating the data in different places. We are willing to live with this bit of redundancy, however, because it enables us to keep track of the interrelationships among the many pieces of important organizational data that are stored in different tables. By keeping track of these relationships, we can quickly answer questions such as "Which players on the SuperSonics played in the game on February 16 and scored more than 10 points?" In a business setting, the question might be "Which customers purchased the 2009 forest-green Toyota Prius from Jeff at the James Toyota dealership in Moscow, Idaho, during the first quarter of 2009, and how much did each pay?" This kind of question would be useful in calculating the bonus money Jeff should receive for that quarter or in recalling those specific vehicles in the event of a recall by the manufacturer.

Entity-Relationship Diagramming   A diagramming technique that creates an entity-relationship diagram (ERD) is commonly used when designing databases, especially when showing associations between entities. To create an ERD, you draw entities as boxes and

A. One-to-one relationship: Each team has only one home stadium, and each home stadium has only one team.

Team

Team ID	Team Name	*Stadium ID*

B. One-to-many relationship: Each player is on only one team, but each team has many players.

Player

Player ID	Player Name	Position	*Team ID*

C. Many-to-many relationship: Each player participates in many games, and each game has many players.

Player Statistics

Team 1	*Team 2*	*Date*	*Player ID*	Points	Minutes	Fouls

FIGURE TB45

Tables used for storing information about several basketball teams, with foreign key attributes added in order to make associations.

FIGURE TB46

An entity-relationship diagram showing the relationships between entities in a basketball league database.

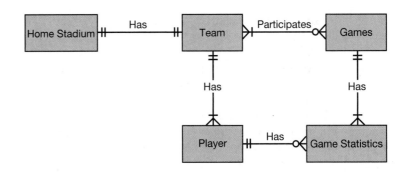

draw lines between entities to show relationships. Each relationship can be labeled on the diagram to give it additional meaning. For example, Figure TB46 shows an ERD for the basketball league data previously discussed. From this diagram, you can see the following associations:

- Each Home Stadium has a Team.
- Each Team has Players.
- Each Team participates in Games.
- For each Player and Game, there are Game Statistics.

When you are designing a complex database, with numerous entities and relationships, ERDs are very useful. They allow the designer to talk with people throughout the organization to make sure that all entities and relationships have been found.

The Relational Model   Now that we have discussed data, data models, and the storage of data, we need a mechanism for joining entities that have natural relationships with one another. For example, in the University database we described previously, there are several relationships among the four entities students, instructors, classes, and grades. Students are enrolled in multiple classes. Likewise, instructors teach multiple classes and have many students in their classes in a semester. At the end of the semester, instructors assign a grade to each student, and each student earns grades in multiple classes. It is important to keep track of these relationships. We might, for example, want to know which courses a student is enrolled in so that we can notify her instructors that she will miss courses because of an illness. The primary DBMS approach, or model, for keeping track of these relationships among data entities is the relational model. Other models—the hierarchical, network, and object-oriented models—are also used to join entities with commercial DBMSs, but this is beyond the scope of our discussion (see Hoffer, Prescott, and Topi, 2009).

The most common DBMS approach in use today is the **relational database model**. A DBMS package using this approach is referred to as a relational DBMS, or RDBMS. With this approach, the DBMS views and presents entities as two-dimensional tables, with records as rows and attributes as columns. Tables can be joined when there are common columns in the tables. The uniqueness of the primary key, as mentioned earlier, tells the DBMS which records should be joined with others in the corresponding tables. This structure supports very powerful data manipulation capabilities and linking of interrelated data. Database files in the relational model are three-dimensional: a table has rows (one dimension) and columns (a second dimension) and can contain rows of attributes in common with another table (a third dimension). This three-dimensional database is potentially much more powerful and useful than traditional, two-dimensional, "flat file" databases (see Figure TB47).

A good relational database design eliminates unnecessary data duplications and is easy to maintain. To design a database with clear, nonredundant relationships, you perform a process called normalization.

Department Records

Dept No	Dept Name	Location	Dean
Dept A			
Dept B			
Dept C			

FIGURE TB47

With the relational model, we represent these two entities, department and instructor, as two separate tables and capture the relationship between them with a common column in each table.

Instructor Records

Instructor No	Inst Name	Title	Salary	Dept No
Inst 1				
Inst 2				
Inst 3				
Inst 4				

Normalization   To be effective, databases must be efficient. Developed in the 1970s, **normalization** is a technique to make complex databases more efficient and more easily handled by the DBMS (Hoffer, George and Valacich, 2009). To understand the normalization process, let us return to the scenario in the beginning of this section. Think about your report card. It looks like nearly any other form or invoice. Your personal information is usually at the top, and each of your classes is listed, along with an instructor, a class day and time, the number of credit hours, and a location. Now think about how this data is stored in a database. Imagine that this database is organized so that in each row of the database, the student's identification number is listed on the far left. To the right of the student ID are the student's name, local address, major, phone number, course and instructor information, and a final course grade (see Figure TB48). Notice that there is redundant data for students, courses, and instructors in each row of this database. This redundancy means that this database is not well organized. If, for example, we want to change the phone number of an instructor who has hundreds of students, we have to change this number hundreds of times.

Elimination of data redundancy is a major goal and benefit of using data normalization techniques. After the normalization process, the student data is organized into five separate tables (see Figure TB49). This reorganization helps simplify the ongoing use and maintenance of the database and any associated analysis programs.

FIGURE TB48

Database of students, courses, instructors, and grades with redundant data.

ID	Student ID#	Student Name	Campus Address	Major	Phone	Course ID	Course Title	Instructor Name	Instructor Location	Instructor Phone	Term	Grade
1	A121	Lauren Ferrell	100 N. State Street	MIS	555-7771	MIS 350	Intro. MIS	Hess	T240C	555-2222	F'09	A
2	A121	Lauren Ferrell	100 N. State Street	MIS	555-7771	MIS 372	Database	Sarker	T240F	555-2224	F'09	B
3	A121	Lauren Ferrell	100 N. State Street	MIS	555-7771	MIS 375	Elec. Comm.	Wells	T240D	555-2228	F'09	B+
4	A121	Lauren Ferrell	100 N. State Street	MIS	555-7771	MIS 426	Strategic MIS	Fuller	T240E	555-2227	F'09	A-
5	A121	Lauren Ferrell	100 N. State Street	MIS	555-7771	MIS 374	Telecomm	Clay	T240A	555-2221	F'09	C+
6	A123	Ulrike Schirmer	123 S. State Street	MGT	555-1235	MIS 350	Intro. MIS	Hess	T240C	555-2222	F'09	A
7	A123	Ulrike Schirmer	123 S. State Street	MGT	555-1235	MIS 372	Database	Sarker	T240F	555-2224	F'09	B-
8	A123	Ulrike Schirmer	123 S. State Street	MGT	555-1235	MIS 375	Elec. Comm.	Wells	T240D	555-2228	F'09	A-
9	A123	Ulrike Schirmer	123 S. State Street	MGT	555-1235	MIS 426	Strategic MIS	Fuller	T240E	555-2227	F'09	C+
10	A124	Birgit Schneider	125 S. Elm	HIST	555-2214	MIS 350	Intro. MIS	Hess	T240C	555-2222	F'09	A-
11	A124	Birgit Schneider	125 S. Elm	HIST	555-2214	MIS 372	Database	Sarker	T240F	555-2224	F'09	A-
12	A124	Birgit Schneider	125 S. Elm	HIST	555-2214	MIS 375	Elec. Comm.	Wells	T240D	555-2228	F'09	B+
13	A124	Birgit Schneider	125 S. Elm	HIST	555-2214	MIS 374	Telecomm	Clay	T240A	555-2221	F'09	B
14	A126	Jackie Judson	224 S. Sixth Street	MKT	555-1245	MIS 350	Intro. MIS	Hess	T240C	555-2222	F'09	A
15	A126	Jackie Judson	224 S. Sixth Street	MKT	555-1245	MIS 372	Database	Sarker	T240F	555-2224	F'09	B+
16	A126	Jackie Judson	224 S. Sixth Street	MKT	555-1245	MIS 375	Elec. Comm.	Wells	T240D	555-2228	F'09	B+
17	A126	Jackie Judson	224 S. Sixth Street	MKT	555-1245	MIS 374	Telecomm	Clay	T240A	555-2221	F'09	A-

University: Student_Course_Grades
File Edit View Tools Window Help

Record 1 of 17

FIGURE TB49

Organization of information on students, courses, instructors, and grades after normalization.

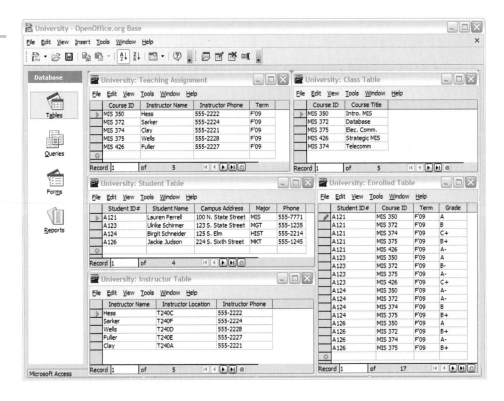

Key Points Review

1. **Discuss advanced information systems hardware concepts.** Information systems hardware is classified into three types: input, processing, and output technologies. Input hardware consists of devices used to enter information into a computer. Processing hardware transforms inputs into outputs. The central processing unit is the device that performs this transformation, with the help of several other closely related devices that store and recall information. Information is stored on primary and secondary storage devices. Finally, output-related hardware focuses on delivering information in a usable format to users. The four general classes of computers are supercomputer, mainframe, midrange, and microcomputer. A supercomputer is the most expensive and most powerful kind of computer; it is used primarily to assist in solving massive research and scientific problems. A mainframe is a very large computer that is the main, central computing system for major corporations and governmental agencies. Midrange computers offer lower performance than mainframes but higher performance than microcomputers and are typically used for engineering and midsized business applications. A microcomputer is used for personal computing, for small business computing, and as a workstation attached to large computers or to other small computers on a network. Portable computers—notebook computers, tablet PCs, and handheld computers—are a special type of microcomputer designed to support mobility.

2. **Describe advanced topics related to systems and application software, as well as the characteristics of various types of programming languages and application development environments.** Systems software, or the operating system, performs many different tasks. Some of these tasks include booting your computer, reading programs into memory, managing memory allocation to those programs, managing where programs and files are located in secondary storage, maintaining the structure of directories and subdirectories, and so on. Application software helps you to be productive with your computer. You can find a large number of computer software applications. For most personal productivity tools, you can find open-source alternatives. A programming language is the computer language programmers use to write application programs. In order to run on a computer, programs must be translated into binary machine language. Programming languages are translated into machine language through special

types of programs, called compilers and interpreters. Over the past several decades, programming languages have evolved. Early programmers used machine language to tell the computer exactly which circuits to turn on and which to turn off. Next, symbolic languages used symbols to represent a series of binary statements. This was followed by the development of high-level languages, such as FORTRAN, COBOL, C, and Java. The difference between these high-level languages and earlier languages is that the high-level languages use English-like words and commands, making it easier to write programs. Fourth-generation languages are called outcome-oriented languages because they contain even more English-like commands and tend to focus on what output is desired instead of the procedures required to get that output. Fifth-generation languages are called natural languages because they allow the user to communicate with the computer using true English sentences. In addition to this generational evolution, object-oriented programming, visual programming, and Web development languages are relatively new enhancements to programming languages. Object-oriented languages group together data and their corresponding instructions into manipulable objects. Visual programming languages use a graphical interface to build graphical interfaces for other programs. Web development languages are a rapidly evolving set of tools designed for constructing Internet applications and Web content. Finally, computer-aided software engineering environments help systems developers construct large-scale systems more rapidly and with higher quality.

3. *Describe network software and hardware, including media access control, network topologies, and protocols, as well as advanced Internet concepts.*   From the 1950s until the 1970s, the centralized computing model was dominant, where all processing occurs at a large central computer, and users interact with the system through the use of terminals. From the late 1970s until the late 1980s, a distributed computing model was dominant. In this model, separate computers work on subsets of tasks and then pool their results by communicating via a network. In the 1990s, the collaborative computing model emerged, where two or more networked computers work together to accomplish a common processing task. There are several types of computer networks, classified according to their use and distance covered. These include a personal area network (PAN), private branch exchange (PBX), local area network (LAN), wireless LAN, campus area network, and wide area network (WAN). WANs

can be further divided into: metropolitan area networks, enterprise networks, value-added networks, and global networks. In networking, a distinction is made between servers, clients, and peers. Networks provide file, print, message, and application services that extend the capabilities of stand-alone computers. The network operating system (NOS) is the major piece of software that controls the network. Networks exchange information by using cable or wireless transmission media. Cable media include twisted pair, coaxial, and fiber-optic. Wireless media include infrared line of sight, high-frequency radio, and microwave. Network access control refers to the rules that govern how a given workstation gains access to the network. There are two general types: distributed and random access. With distributed access, only a single workstation at a time has authorization to transmit its data. Under random access control, any workstation can transmit its data by checking whether the medium is available. The shape of a network can vary; the four most common topologies are star, ring, bus, and mesh configurations. Protocols are agreed-on formats for transmitting data between connected computers. The International Organization for Standardization defined a networking model called the Open Systems Interconnection (OSI) model that divides computer-to-computer communications into seven connected layers, allowing different networks to be more easily interconnected. Each successively higher layer builds on the functions of the layers below. Ethernet is an important protocol for LANs, whereas the Transmission Control Protocol/Internet Protocol is most widely used for the world's largest WAN, the Internet. In a network, each device or computer must be connected to the medium or cable segment using transmission media connectors, network interface cards, or modems. Multiple segments of transmission media can be connected to form one large network. A variety of different devices is used to extend the range and size of the network and to interconnect wide area networks. The Internet is composed of networks that are developed and maintained by many different entities; it follows a hierarchical structure, similar to the interstate highway system. High-speed central networks called backbones are like interstate highways, enabling traffic from midlevel networks to get on and off. Routers are used to interconnect independent networks. A collection of tools enables us to use the Internet in order to exchange messages, share information, or connect to remote computers. The most powerful application of the Internet is the World Wide Web, which binds together the various tools used on the Internet, providing users with a simple, consistent interface to a wide variety of information through the use of Web browsers.

4. *Explain advanced database management concepts.* In order to get the most of their data, organizations have to take care to create an accurate data model. A primary key is used to uniquely identify records in a database. A foreign key is used to link entities together. A useful diagramming technique is entity-relationship diagramming, displaying entities and the associations between them. Normalization is used to reduce redundancy in a database.

Key Terms

American Standard Code for Information Interchange (ASCII) 502
analog signal 540
applet 520
application service 528
association 548
asymmetric digital subscriber line (ADSL) 544
asynchronous transfer mode (ATM) 545
audio 501
backbone 531
bar code reader 501
biometric scanner 501
bridge 540
broadband wireless 545
brouter 540
bus network 536
bytes per inch (BPI) 506
cable modem 544
carrier sense multiple access/collision detect (CSMA/CD) 535
cathode ray tube (CRT) 506
CD-R (compact disc—recordable) 506
CD-RW (compact disc—rewritable) 506
cell 532
cellular phone 532
centralized computing 524
channel service unit (CSU) 540
characters per inch (CPI) 506
clock speed 503
clock tick 503
collaborative computing 525
combination primary key 548
compiler 516
computer-aided software engineering (CASE) 522
connector 539
density 506
digital signal 539
digital subscriber line (DSL) 544
digital video disk 506

distributed computing 524
docking station 511
domain name system (DNS) 541
DVD-ROM (digital versatile disk—read-only memory) 506
electronic paper 507
enterprise network 527
e-paper 507
ergonomic keyboard 499
ethernet 539
external cache 504
eye-tracking device 499
fiber to the home (FTTH) 545
fiber to the premises (FTTP) 545
fifth-generation language (5GL) 518
file services 528
flops (floating points operations per second) 507
foreign key 549
fourth-generation language (4GL) 517
gateway 540
global network 527
graphics tablet 499
head crash 505
HTML editor 518
hub 540
integrated services digital network (ISDN) 544
interactive voice response (IVR) 501
interexchange carrier (IXC) 545
internal cache 504
Internet backbone 542
Internet Corporation for Assigned Names and Numbers (ICANN) 542
Internet host 546
Internet over satellite (IoS) 544
Internet Registry 541
Internet service provider (ISP) 542
InterNIC 542
interpreter 517
IPv6 542
Java 520
JavaScript 521

joystick 500
light pen 500
liquid crystal display (LCD) 506
magnetic ink character recognition (MICR) 501
media access control 535
mesh network 536
message services 528
Microsoft.NET 520
mobile wireless 545
modem 540
motherboard 502
mouse 500
multiplexer (MUX) 540
netbook 511
network access point (NAP) 542
network computer 510
network interface card (NIC) 539
network operating system (NOS) 528
network service 528
network topology 535
normalization 551
notebook computer 511
object-oriented language 518
optical character recognition (OCR) 501
optical mark recognition (OMR) 501
organic light-emitting diode (OLED) 506
Open Systems Interconnection (OSI) model 538
personal computer (PC) 509
personal digital assistant (PDA) 512
petaflop 507
plain old telephone service (POTS) 544
port 506
power line communication 546
power supply 503
primary key 548
print services 528
propagation delay 534
public switched telephone network (PSTN) 544

QWERTY keyboard 499
read/write head 504
redundant array of independent disks
   (RAID) 505
relational database model 550
relationship 548
repeater 540
ring network 536
scripting language 521
secondary cache 504
secondary key 548
smart card 501
speech recognition 501

star network 536
streaming media 502
streaming video 502
subnotebook 511
symmetric digital subscriber line
   (SDSL) 544
system clock 503
T1 line 545
T3 line 545
tablet PC 511
terminal 524
text recognition software 500
thin client 510

token passing 535
touch screen 500
trackball 500
ultramobile PC (UMPC) 511
utilities 513
utility program 513
value-added networks (VANs) 527
video 501
visual programming language 518
voice-to-text software 501
Web page builder 518
WiMax 546

Review Questions

1. Describe the system unit and its key components.
2. What determines the speed of a CPU?
3. Compare and contrast the different types of secondary data storage.
4. Describe at least four different tasks performed by an operating system.
5. Describe the evolution of programming languages as well as various contemporary programming languages in use today.
6. What is CASE, and how can it help in the development of information systems?
7. Compare and contrast centralized, distributed, and collaborative computing.
8. What are the major types of network services available?
9. What is a network topology? Describe the four common topologies that are used today.
10. What is the purpose of the OSI model?
11. What are the alternatives available for corporations to connect to the Internet?
12. Compare and contrast the primary key, combination key, and foreign key within an entity.
13. What is the purpose of normalization?

Self-Study Questions

Visit the Interactive Study Guide on the Companion Web site for additional Self-Study Questions: www.pearsonhighered.com/valacich.

1. _____ can convert handwritten text into computer-based characters.
   A. Scanners
   B. Bar code/optical character readers
   C. Text recognition software
   D. Audio/video
2. Which of the following has the largest storage, along with video capacity?
   A. CD-ROM
   B. floppy disk
   C. DVD-ROM
   D. cache memory
3. Automated software tools used to develop information systems that can improve the overall system quality and increase programmer productivity are called _____.
   A. computerized programming
   B. automated development
   C. computer-aided programming
   D. none of the above
4. Fifth-generation languages are also referred to as _____ languages.
   A. assembly
   B. natural
   C. high-level
   D. low-level
5. What were first-generation programming languages called?
   A. natural language
   B. assembly language
   C. machine language
   D. none of the above
6. Which of the following is a type of computer on the network that makes access to files, printing, communications, and other services available to users of the network?
   A. server
   B. client

C. peer

D. pager

7. Which of the following are types of networks?

A. star, ring, bus

B. star, box, ring

C. star, ring, triangle

D. ring, bus, rectangle

8. After individual devices are connected to a network, multiple segments of transmission media can be connected to form one large network. All of the following except _____ are used to extend the range and size of the network.

A. bridges

B. repeaters

C. modems

D. hubs

9. Each team has only one home stadium, and each home stadium has only one team. This is an example of which of the following relationships?

A. one-to-one

B. one-to-many

C. many-to-many

D. many-to-one

10. _____ is a technique to make a complex database more efficient by eliminating redundancy.

A. Data repository

B. Associating

C. Normalization

D. Standardization

Answers are on page 557.

Problems and Exercises

1. Match the following terms with the appropriate definitions:

   i. Cache memory

   ii. Batch input

   iii. Applets

   iv. Interpreter

   v. Compiler

   vi. Token passing

   vii. Bus network

   viii. FTTH

   ix. Primary key

   x. Foreign key

   a. A network topology in which all stations are connected to a single open-ended line

   b. An attribute that appears as a nonprimary key attribute in one entity and as a primary key in another

   c. An access method that uses a constantly circulating electronic token (a small packet of data) to prevent collisions and give all workstations equal access to the network

   d. A software program that translates a program written in a programming language into machine language one statement at a time

   e. Software used to create and display dynamic content on Web sites

   f. A small block of memory used by the central processor to store those instructions most recently or most often used

   g. A field included in a database that assures that each instance of an entity is stored or retrieved accurately

   h. Connectivity technology that allows for superspeed connection to homes, usually done by fiber-optic cabling running directly into new homes

   i. A software program that translates an entire program written in a programming language into machine language that can be read and executed directly by the computer

   j. A type of input for large amounts of routine information

2. Imagine that you have just informed your supervisor that you will need to purchase new computers for yourself and three fellow employees. Your supervisor states that she has heard in the news that computer prices are dropping constantly, and she feels that you should wait a bit before making this purchase. She adds that you can still be 100 percent effective with your current computer and software. Develop a counterargument explaining why you should make the purchase now instead of waiting. Will this be a hard sell? Why or why not?

3. Based on your experiences with different input devices, which do you like the best and least? Why? Are your preferences due to the devices' design or usability, or are they based on the integration of the device with the entire information system?

4. Choose a few of the computer hardware vendors that sell computers to the general public. These include Dell, HP, Lenovo, Gateway, Apple, and many lesser-known brands. Using each company's home page on the Web, determine what options these vendors provide for input devices, processing devices, and output devices. Does it seem that this company has a broad range of choices for its customers? Is there something that you did not find available from this company? Present your findings in a ten-minute presentation to the rest of the class.

5. What are the implications for an organization of having more than one operating system? What might be the advantages? What are some of the disadvantages? Would

you recommend such a situation? Prepare a ten-minute presentation to the rest of the class on your findings.

6. Find an organization that does a lot of in-house programming and utilizes a variety of different programming languages. Determine the generation level of these languages. Are the same personnel programming in most (or all) of the languages, or are different personnel programming in each of the languages? Is this assignment of programmers intentional or unintentional?

7. Describe how you would handle resistance to implementing CASE tools by those who feel they will be replaced by technology. From whom is this resistance most likely to come? Is this fear legitimate? Why or why not?

8. Compare and contrast client-server and peer-to-peer networks. How do the computers and devices interact with each other in these networks? How does the term *client* relate to a peer-to-peer network? Under what circumstances is one type of network better than the other? Why?

9. Working in a group, have everyone describe what type of network would be most appropriate for a small office with about ten computers, one printer, and one scanner, all within one floor in one building and relatively close to one another. Be sure to talk about transmission media, network topology, hardware, and software. Did all group members come up with the same option? Why or why not? What else would you need to know to make a good recommendation?

10. Search the Web for background information on the origin and uses of the Ethernet protocol. How did it begin, and how popular is it today?

11. Search the Web for background information on the origin and uses of the TCP/IP protocol. Why has it become so popular and powerful?

12. Investigate the options for high-speed, broadband Internet access into your home. What options are available to you, and how much do they cost?

13. You have probably experienced several different types of connections—from the university T1 connections to a home DSL or even dial-up connection. If you had to balance between cost and speed, which connection would you choose?

14. You see an announcement for a job as a database administrator for a large corporation but are unclear about what this title means. Research this on the Web and obtain a specific job announcement.

15. Have several classmates interview database administrators within organizations with which they are familiar. To whom do these people report? How many employees report to these people? Is there a big variance in the responsibilities across organizations? Why or why not?

16. Based on your understanding of a primary key and the information in the following sample grades table, determine the best choice of attribute(s) for a primary key.

Student ID	Course	Grade
100013	Visual Programming	A
000117	Telecommunications	A
000117	Introduction to MIS	A

Answers to the Self-Study Questions

1. C, p. 500	**2.** C, p. 506	**3.** D, p. 522	**4.** B, p. 518	**5.** C, p. 516
6. A, p. 510	**7.** A, p. 535	**8.** C, p. 539	**9.** A, p. 548	**10.** C, p. 551

Acronyms

ADSL: Asymmetric Digital Subscriber Line

AI: Artificial Intelligence

ALU: Arithmetic Logic Unit

ARPANET: Advanced Research Projects Agency Network

ASCII: American Standard Code for Information Interchange

ASP: Application Service Provider

ATM: Asynchronous Transfer Mode

ATM: Automated Teller Machine

B2B: Business-to-Business

B2C: Business-to-Consumer

B2E: Business-to-Employee

BIOS: Basic Input-Output System

BPI: Bytes per Inch

BPM: Business Process Management

BPR: Business Process Reengineering

C2C: Consumer-to-Consumer

CAAT: Computer-Assisted Auditing Tools

CAD: Computer-Aided Design

CAE: Computer-Aided Engineering

CAN: Campus Area Network

CASE: Computer-Aided Software Engineering

CD-R: Compact Disk-Recordable

CD-RW: Compact Disk-Rewritable

CIC: Customer Interaction Center

CIO: Chief Information Officer

COBIT: Control Objectives for Information and Related Technology

COPA: Child Online Protection Act

CPI: Characters per Inch

CPU: Central Processing Unit

CRM: Customer Relationship Management

CRT: Cathode Ray Tube

CSF: Critical Success Factor

CSMA/CD: Carrier Sense Multiple Access/Collision Detect

CSS: Customer Service and Support

CSU: Channel Service Unit

CVV2: Customer Verification Value

DARPA: Defense Advanced Research Projects Agency

DBA: Database Administrator

DBMS: Database Management System

DNS: Domain Name System

DoS: Denial of Service

DRM: Digital Rights Management

DSL: Digital Subscriber Line

DSS: Decision Support System

DVD: Digital Versatile Disk

DVD: Digital Video Disk

EC: Electronic Commerce

EDI: Electronic Data Interchange

EEPROM: Electrically Erasable Programmable Read-Only Memory

EIS: Executive Information System

EMI: Electromagnetic Interference

EMM: Enterprise Marketing Management

EMS: Electronic Meeting System

ERD: Entity-Relationship Diagram

ERP: Enterprise Resource Planning

ES: Expert System

ETL: Extraction, Transformation, and Loading

5GL: Fifth-Generation Language

FLOPS: Floating Point Operations per Second

4GL: Fourth-Generation Language

FTTH: Fiber to the Home

FTTP: Fiber to the Premises

G2B: Government-to-Business

G2C: Government-to-Citizens

G2G: Government-to-Government

GEO: Geosynchronous Earth Orbit

GIS: Geographic Information System

GPS: Global Positioning System

GUI: Graphical User Interface

HCI: Human-Computer Interface

HTML: Hypertext Markup Language

HTTP: Hypertext Transfer Protocol

ICANN: Internet Corporation for Assigned Names and Numbers

IoS: Internet over Satellite

IOS: Interorganizational System

IP: Internet Protocol

IS: Information System

ISDN: Integrated Services Digital Network

ISP: Internet Service Provider

IT: Information Technology

IVR: Interactive Voice Response

IXC: Interexchange Carrier

JAD: Joint Application Design

KPI: Key Performance Indicator

LAN: Local Area Network

LCD: Liquid Crystal Display

LEO: Low Earth Orbit

MAN: Metropolitan Area Network

MEO: Middle Earth Orbit

MICR: Magnetic Ink Character Recognition

MIS: Management Information System

MUX: Multiplexer

NAP: Network Access Point

NAT: Network Address Translation

NIC: Network Interface Card

NOS: Network Operating System

NSF: National Science Foundation

NSFNET: National Science Foundation Network

OAS: Office Automation System

OCR: Optical Character Recognition

OLAP: Online Analytical Processing

OLED: Organic Light-Emitting Diode

OLTP: Online Transaction Processing

OMR: Optical Mark Recognition

OOA&D: Object-Oriented Analysis and Design

OSI: Open Systems Interconnection

PAN: Personal Area Network

PBX: Private Branch Exchange

PC: Personal Computer

PDA: Personal Digital Assistant

PIN: Personal Identification Number

PLC: Power Line Communication

POTS: Plain Old Telephone Service

PSTN: Public Switched Telephone Network

QBE: Query by Example

RAD: Rapid Application Development

RAID: Redundant Array of Independent Disks

RAM: Random Access Memory

RFID: Radio Frequency Identification

RFP: Request for Proposals

ROM: Read-Only Memory

RSS: Real Simple Syndication

SaaS: Software as a Service

SAM: Software Asset Management

SCE: Supply Chain Execution

SCM: Supply Chain Management

SCP: Supply Chain Planning

SDLC: Systems Development Life Cycle

SDSL: Symmetric Digital Subscriber Line

SEO: Search Engine Optimization

SFA: Sales Force Automation

SOA: Service-Oriented Architecture

SQL: Structured Query Language

SSP: Storage Service Provider

TCO: Total Cost of Ownership

TCP/IP: Transmission Control Protocol/Internet Protocol

TPS: Transaction Processing System

ULP: Ultra Low Power

UMPC: Ultra Mobile PC

URL: Uniform Resource Locator

VAN: Value Added Network

VoIP: Voice Over IP

VPN: Virtual Private Network

WiFi: Wireless Fidelity

WiMax: Worldwide Interoperability for Microwave Access

WLAN: Wireless Local Area Network

WWW: World Wide Web

XBRL: Extensible Business Reporting Language

XML: Extensible Markup Language

Glossary

802.11: Also known as Wi-Fi; family of universally adopted wireless transmission standards offering transmission speeds up to 54 Mbps.

Acceptable use policy: Computer and/or Internet usage policy for people within an organization, with clearly spelled-out penalties for noncompliance.

Access-control software: Software for securing information systems that only allows specific users access to specific computers, applications, or data.

Adaptive maintenance: Making changes to an information system to make its functionality meet changing business needs or to migrate it to a different operating environment.

Ad-hoc query: Request for information created due to unplanned information needs that is typically not saved for later use.

Advanced Research Projects Agency Network (ARPANET): A wide area network linking various universities and research centers; forerunner of the Internet.

Adware: Free software paid for by advertisements appearing during the use of the software; Adware sometimes contains spyware.

Affiliate marketing: A type of marketing that allows individual Web site owners to earn revenue by posting other companies' ads on their Web pages.

Alpha testing: Testing performed by the development organization to assess whether the entire system meets the design requirements of the users.

Amateurization of journalism: Replacement of professional journalism by amateur bloggers.

American Standard Code for Information Interchange (ASCII): Character encoding method based on the English alphabet that provides binary codes to represent symbols.

Analog signal: Audio tones used to transmit data over conventional voice telephone lines.

Analytical CRM: Systems for analyzing customer behavior and perceptions in order to provide business intelligence.

Applet: A program designed to be executed within another application (such as a Web page).

Application-level control: The prevention of unauthorized access to selected applications by some form of security.

Application service: Provision of software for network clients, enabling computers to share the server's processing power.

Application Service Provider (ASP): A company offering on-demand software on an as-needed basis to its clients over the Web.

Application software: Software used to perform a specific task that the user needs to accomplish.

Arithmetic logic unit (ALU): Part of the central processing unit (CPU) that performs mathematics and logical operations.

Artificial intelligence (AI): The science of enabling information technologies to simulate human intelligence as well as gaining sensing capabilities.

Association: *See* Relationship.

Association discovery: A data mining technique used to find associations or correlations among sets of items.

Asymmetric digital subscriber line (ADSL): A variant of DSL offering faster download speeds (1.5 Mbps to 30 Mbps) than upload speeds (16 Kbps to 3.5 Mbps).

Asynchronous: Not coordinated in time.

Asynchronous transfer mode (ATM): A method of transmitting voice, video, and data over high-speed LANs at speeds of up to 22 Gbps.

Attenuation: The weakening of an electric signal as it is sent over increasing distance.

Attribute: Individual piece of information about an entity in a database.

Audio: Analog or digital sound data.

Audit-control software: Software used to keep track of computer activity, enabling auditors to spot suspicious activity.

Authentication: The process of confirming the identity of a user who is attempting to access a restricted system or Web site.

Automating: Using information systems to do an activity faster, cheaper, and perhaps with more accuracy and/or consistency.

Autonomic computing: The use of self-managing computing systems needing only minimal human intervention to operate.

Backbone: High-speed central network to which many smaller networks can be connected.

Back-office system: A system designed to support business activities not involving direct customer contact.

Backup: Copy of critical data on a separate storage medium.

Backup site: A facility allowing businesses to continue functioning in the event a disaster strikes.

Bandwidth: The transmission capacity of a computer or communications channel.

Bar code reader: Specialized scanner used to read bar code data.

Basic Input-Output System (BIOS): Programs and instructions that are automatically loaded when the computer is turned on.

Batch data: Large amounts of routine data.

Batch processing: The processing of transactions after some quantity of transactions is collected and then processed together as a "batch" at some later time.

Best-cost provider strategy: Strategy to offer products or services of reasonably good quality at competitive prices.

Best practices: Procedures and processes used by business organizations that are widely accepted as being among the most effective and/or efficient.

Beta testing: Testing performed by actual system users with actual data in their work environment.

Bid luring: A type of e-auction fraud; bidders are lured to leave a legitimate auction in order to buy the same item at a lower price.

Bid shielding: Using two different accounts to place a low followed by a very high bid on a desired item, leading other bidders to drop out of the auction. The high bid is then retracted, and the item is won at the low bid. Sometimes called "shill bidding."

Binary code: Digital representation of data and information using sequences of zeros and ones.

Biometric scanner: Input technology used to scan a user's human body characteristics.

Biometrics: Body characteristics such as fingerprints, retinal patterns in the eye, or facial characteristics that allow the unique identification of a person.

Bit: Short for binary digit; the individual ones and zeros that make up a byte.

Blog: Short for Web log. Chronological online text diary.

Blogging: The creation of online text diaries, usually organized chronologically, that can focus on anything the user desires. Also called Weblogging.

Blogosphere: The community of all blogs.

Bluetooth: A wireless specification for personal area networking (PAN) of desktop computers, peripheral devices, mobile phones, pagers, portable stereos, and other handheld devices.

Bot: Short for "software robot"; a program that works in the background to provide some service when a specific event occurs.

Bot herder: Computer criminal "owning" a botnet.

Botnet: Collection of zombie computers used for destructive activities or spamming.

Break-even analysis: A type of cost-benefit analysis to identify at what point (if ever) tangible benefits equal tangible costs.

Brick-and-mortar business strategy: A business approach exclusively utilizing physical locations, such as department stores, business offices, and manufacturing plants, without an online presence.

Bricks-and-clicks business strategy: *See* Click-and-mortar business strategy.

Bridge: Device used to connect two different LANs or two segments of the same LAN by forwarding network traffic between network segments; unlike repeaters, bridges determine the physical location of the source and destination computers.

Broadband wireless: Wireless transmission technology with speeds similar to DSL and cable requiring line-of-sight between the sender and receiver.

Brouter: Short for bridge router (pronounced brow-ter); networking device providing the capabilities of both a bridge and a router for managing network traffic.

Bullwhip effect: Large fluctuations in suppliers' forecasts caused by small fluctuations in demand for the end product and the need to create safety buffers.

Business intelligence: The processes of gathering information from both external and internal sources to make better decisions and the data derived from these processes.

Business model: Summary of how a company will generate revenue, identifying the product offering, value-added services, revenue sources, and target customers.

Business processes: Activities organizations perform in order to reach their business goals, consisting of core processes and supporting processes.

Business process management (BPM): A systematic, structured improvement approach by all or part of an organization including a critical examination and redesign of business processes in order to achieve dramatic improvements in one or more performance measures such as quality, cycle time, or cost.

Business process reengineering (BPR): Legacy term for business process management (BPM).

Business rules: Policies by which a business runs.

Business-to-business (B2B): Electronic commerce between business partners, such as suppliers and intermediaries.

Business-to-consumer (B2C): Electronic commerce between businesses and consumers.

Business-to-employee (B2E): Electronic commerce between businesses and their employees.

Bus network: Network in the shape of an open-ended line.

Buyer agent: Intelligent agent used to find the best price for a particular product a consumer wishes to purchase. Also known as a shopping bot.

Byte: Typically 8 bits or about one typed character.

Bytes per inch (BPI): The numbers of bytes that can be stored on one inch of magnetic tape.

Cable media: Media physically linking computers and other devices in a network.

Cable modem: A specialized piece of equipment that enables a computer to access Internet service via cable TV lines.

Cache: A small block of special high-speed memory used by processors to store those instructions most recently or most often used (pronounced "cash").

Campus area network (CAN): Type of network spanning multiple buildings, such as a university campus.

CAPTCHA: Short for "Completely Automated Public Turing Test to tell Computers and Humans Apart." A system designed to prevent automated mechanisms from repeatedly attempting to submit forms or gain access to a system. A CAPTCHA requires the user to enter letters or numbers that are presented in the form of a distorted image before submitting an online form.

Carding: Stealing credit card information for one's own use, or to sell.

Carrier sense multiple access/collision detect (CSMA/CD): A random access control method in which each workstation "listens" to the network to determine whether a message is being transmitted. If the network is quiet, the workstation sends its message; otherwise, it waits. When a workstation gains access to the medium and sends information onto the network, messages are sent to all workstations on the network; however, only the destination with the proper address is able to "open" the message.

Cathode ray tube (CRT): Display technology similar to a television monitor.

CD-R (compact disc–recordable): A type of optical disk that data can be written to.

CD-ROM (compact disc–read-only memory): A type of optical disk that can only be read, but not written to.

CD-RW (compact disc–rewritable): A type of optical disk that be written onto multiple times.

Cell: A geographic area containing a low-powered radio antenna/receiver for transmitting telecommunications signals within that area; monitored and controlled by a central computer.

Cellular phone: Mobile phone technology using a communications system that divides a geographic region into sections called cells.

Censorship: Governmental attempts to control Internet traffic, thus preventing some material from being viewed by a country's citizens.

Central processing unit (CPU): Responsible for performing all the operations of the computer. Also called a microprocessor, processor, or chip.

Centralized computing: A computing model utilizing large centralized computers, called mainframes, to process and store data.

Certificate authority: A trusted middleman between computers that verifies that a Web site is a trusted site and that provides large-scale public-key encryption.

Channel service unit (CSU): A device that acts as a "buffer" between a LAN and a public carrier's WAN. CSUs ensure that all signals placed on the public lines from the LAN are appropriately timed and formed for the public network.

Characters per inch (CPI): The number of characters that can be stored on one inch of magnetic tape.

Chief information officer (CIO): Executive-level individual who is responsible for leading the overall information systems component within an organization and integrating new technologies into the organization's business strategy.

Child Online Protection Act (COPA): A law to protect minors from accessing inappropriate content on the Internet.

Circuit-level control: Firewall allowing unrestricted traffic for certain communication/circuits and blocking others.

Classification: A data mining technique grouping instances into predefined categories.

Click-and-mortar business strategy: A business approach utilizing both physical locations and virtual locations. Also referred to as bricks-and-clicks.

Click fraud: Abuse of pay-per-click advertising models by repeatedly clicking on a link to inflate revenue to the host or increase the costs for the advertiser.

Click-only business strategy: A business approach that exclusively utilizes an online presence. Companies using this strategy are also referred to as virtual companies.

Clickstream data: A recording of the users' path through a Web site.

Click-through rate: The ratio of surfers who click on an ad (i.e., clicks), divided by the number of times it was displayed (i.e., impressions).

Click-wrap license: A type of software license primarily used for downloaded software that requires computer users to click on "I accept" before installing the software.

Client: Any computer, such as a user's workstation or PC on a network, or any software application, such as a word processing application, that requests and uses the services provided by a server.

Clock speed: The speed of the system clock, typically measured in hertz (Hz).

Clock tick: A single pulse of the system clock.

Cloning: Using scanners to steal wireless transmitter codes for cell phones, then duplicating the codes for illegal use.

Clustering: Data mining technique grouping related records on the basis of having similar attributes.

Coaxial (coax) cable: Network cable containing a solid inner copper conductor, surrounded by plastic insulation and an outer braided copper or foil shield; most commonly used for cable television installations and for networks operating at 10 Mbps.

Cold backup site: A backup facility consisting of an empty warehouse with all the necessary connections for power and communication, but nothing else.

Collaboration: Cooperation between different individuals or entities.

Collaboration system: Software designed to enable people to communicate, collaborate, and coordinate with each other.

Collaborative computing: A synergistic form of distributed computing in which two or more networked computers are used to accomplish common processing tasks.

Collaborative CRM: Systems for providing effective and efficient communication with the customer from the entire organization.

Collocation facility: Facility in which businesses can rent space for servers or other information systems equipment.

Combination primary key: A unique identifier consisting of two or more attributes.

Command line interface: Computer interface that requires the user to enter text-based commands to instruct the computer to perform specific operations.

Competitive advantage: A firm's ability to do something better, faster, cheaper, or uniquely when compared with rival firms in the market.

Competitive click fraud: A competitor's attempt to inflate an organization's online advertising costs by repeatedly clicking on an advertiser's link.

Compiler: A software program that translates an entire program written in a programming language into machine language that can be read and executed directly by the computer.

Computer-aided design (CAD): Software used to create design drawings and three-dimensional models during the product design process.

Computer-aided engineering (CAE): Software used to complement or replace the process of building prototypes during product development.

Computer-aided manufacturing (CAM): The use of information systems to control the production process of a product.

Computer-aided software engineering (CASE): The use of software tools that provide automated support for some portion of the systems development process.

Computer-assisted auditing tools (CAAT): Software used to test information systems controls.

Computer-based information system: A combination of hardware, software, and telecommunication networks that people build and use to collect, create, and distribute data.

Computer crime: The use of a computer to commit an illegal act.

Computer ethics: A broad range of issues and standards of conduct that have emerged through the use and proliferation of information systems.

Computer fluency: The ability to independently learn new technologies as they emerge and assess their impact on one's work and life.

Computer forensics: The use of formal investigative techniques to evaluate digital information for judicial review.

Computer literacy: The knowledge of how to operate a computer.

Computer networking: The sharing of information or services between computers using wireless or cable transmission media.

Concept of time: A cultural characteristic that reflects the extent to which a culture has a longer- or shorter-term orientation.

Confidentiality: Ensuring that no one can read a message except the intended recipient.

Connector: Also called transmission media connector; used to terminate a cable in order to be plugged into a network interface card or into other network components.

Consumer-to-consumer (C2C): A form of electronic commerce that does not involve business firms, but enables transactions between consumers.

Content management system: Information system enabling users to publish, edit, version track, and retrieve digital information (or content).

Continuous planning: Strategic business planning process involving continuous monitoring and adjusting of business processes to enable rapid reactions to changing business conditions.

Control objectives for information and related technology (COBIT): A set of best practices that help organizations to both maximize the benefits from their information systems infrastructure and establish appropriate controls.

Control unit: Part of the central processing unit (CPU) that works closely with the ALU (arithmetic logic unit) by fetching and decoding instructions as well as retrieving and storing data.

Conversion: The process of transferring information from a legacy system to a new computing platform.

Conversion rate: The percentage of visitors to a Web site who perform the desired action.

Cookie: A message passed by a Web server to a Web browser to be stored on a user's computer; this message is then sent back to the server each time the user's browser requests a page from that server.

Copyright: A form of intellectual property, referring to creations of the mind such as music, literature, or software.

Core activities: The activities within a value chain that process inputs and produce outputs, including inbound logistics, operations and manufacturing, outbound logistics, marketing and sales, and customer service.

Corrective maintenance: Making changes to an information system to repair flaws in its design, coding, or implementation.

Cost–benefit analysis: Techniques that contrast the total expected tangible costs versus the tangible benefits for an investment.

Cracker: An individual who breaks into computer systems with the intention of doing damage or committing a crime.

Critical success factor (CSF): Something that must go well to ensure success for a manager, department, division, or organization.

Crowdsourcing: The use of everyday people as cheap labor force, enabled by information technology.

Culture: The collective programming of the mind that distinguishes the members of one group or category of people from another.

Custom applications: Software programs that are designed and developed for a company's specific needs, as opposed to being bought off-the-shelf.

Customer dot mapping: A type of geospatial analysis comparing the customers' locations with the location of a business.

Customer interaction center (CIC): A part of operational CRM that provides a central point of contact for an organization's customers, employing multiple communication channels to support the communication preferences of customers.

Customer relationship management (CRM): A corporate-level strategy designed to create and maintain lasting relationships with customers by concentrating on the downstream information flows through the introduction of reliable systems, processes, and procedures.

Customer service and support (CSS): A part of operational CRM that automates service and information requests, complaints, and product returns.

Customer verification value (CVV2): A three-digit code located on the back of a credit card; used in transactions when the physical card is not present.

Customization: Modifying software so that it better suits user needs.

Customized software: Software that is developed based on specifications provided by a particular organization.

Cyber bullying: The use of a computer to intentionally cause emotional distress to a person.

Cyber harassment: The use of a computer to communicate obscene, vulgar, or threatening content that causes a reasonable person to endure distress.

Cyber stalking: The use of a computer to repeatedly engage in threatening or harassing behavior.

Cybersquatting: The dubious practice of registering a domain name, then trying to sell the name to the person, company, or organization most likely to want it.

Cyberterrorism: The use of computer and networking technologies against persons or property to intimidate or coerce governments, individuals, or any segment of society to attain political, religious, or ideological goals.

Cyberwar: An organized attempt by a country's military to disrupt or destroy information and communications systems of another country.

Data: Recorded, unformatted information, such as words and numbers, that often has no meaning in and of itself.

Database: A collection of related data organized in a way to facilitate data searches.

Database administrator (DBA): A person responsible for the development and management of an organization's databases.

Database management system (DBMS): A software application used to create, store, organize, and retrieve data from a single database or several databases.

Data cleansing: The process of standardizing the form of data retrieved from different systems and removing inaccurate records.

Data dictionary: A document prepared by database designers to describe the characteristics of all items in a database.

Data diddling: A type of computer crime where the data going into or out of a computer is altered.

Data flows: Data moving through an organization or within an information system.

Data mart: A data warehouse that is limited in scope and customized for the decision support applications of a particular end-user group.

Data mining: A method used by companies to discover "hidden" predictive relationships in data to better understand their customers, products, markets, or any other phase of their business for which data has been captured.

Data-mining agent: An intelligent agent that continuously analyzes large data warehouses to detect changes deemed important by a user, sending a notification when such changes occur.

Data model: A map or diagram that represents the entities of a database and their relationships.

Data reduction: A preparatory step to running data mining algorithms, performed by rolling up a data cube to the smallest level of aggregation needed, reducing the dimensionality, or dividing continuous measures into discrete intervals.

Data type: The type (e.g., text, number, date) of an attribute in a database.

Data warehouse: An integration of multiple, large databases and other information sources into a single repository or access point that is suitable for direct querying, analysis, or processing.

Decision support system (DSS): A special-purpose information system designed to support organizational decision making.

Dedicated grid: A grid computing architecture consisting of homogeneous computers that are dedicated to performing the grid's computing tasks.

Defense Advanced Research Projects Agency (DARPA): The U.S. governmental agency that began to study ways to interconnect networks of various kinds, leading to the development of the ARPANET (Advanced Research Projects Agency Network).

Denial-of-service (DoS): Attack by crackers—often using zombie computers—that makes a network resource (e.g., Web site) unavailable to users or available with only a poor degree of service.

Density: The storage capacity of magnetic tape; typically expressed in characters per inch (CPI) or bytes per inch (BPI).

Desktop videoconferencing: The use of integrated computer, telephone, video recording, and playback technologies—typically by two people—to remotely interact with each other using their desktop computers.

Destructive agent: Malicious agent designed by spammers and other Internet attackers to farm e-mail addresses off Web sites or deposit spyware on machines.

Developmental testing: Testing performed by programmers to ensure that each module of a new program is error free.

Differentiation strategy: Strategy in which an organization differentiates itself by providing better products or services than its competitors.

Digital dashboard: A display delivering summary information to managers and executives to provide warnings, action notices, and summaries of business conditions.

Digital divide: The gap between those individuals in our society who are computer literate and have access to information resources like the Internet and those who do not.

Digital rights management (DRM): A technological solution that allows publishers to control their digital media (music, movies, and so on) to discourage, limit, or prevent illegal copying and distribution.

Digital signals: The electrical pulses that computers use to send bits of information.

Digital signature: A mechanism to prove that a message did, in fact, originate from the claimed sender.

Digital subscriber line (DSL): A high-speed data transmission method that uses special modulation schemes to fit more data onto traditional copper telephone wires.

Digital video disk: A DVD used for storing movies.

Digitizing: The process of converting analog into digital information, or bits, which can be used by computer-based information systems.

Dimension: A way to summarize data, such as region, time, or product line.

Disaster recovery plan: Organizational plan that spells out detailed procedures for recovering from systems-related disasters, such as virus infections and other disasters, that might strike critical information systems.

Discount rate: The rate of return used by an organization to compute the present value of future cash flows.

Disintermediation: The phenomenon of cutting out the "middleman" in transactions and reaching customers more directly and efficiently.

Diskette: A removable storage medium with a capacity of 1.44 MB; also called floppy disk.

Disruptive innovation: A new technology, product, or service that eventually surpasses the existing dominant technology, product, or service in a market.

Distributed computing: Using separate computers to work on subsets of tasks and then pooling the results by communicating over a network.

Distribution portal: Enterprise portal that automates the business processes involved in selling or distributing products from a single supplier to multiple buyers.

Docking station: Hardware that allows a portable computer to be easily connected to desktop peripherals including full-sized monitors, keyboards, and mice.

Domain name: Used in Uniform Resource Locators (URLs) to identify a source or host entity on the Internet.

Domain Name System (DNS): A database used to associate Internet host names with their IP addresses.

Domestic company: A company operating solely in its domestic market.

Dot matrix printer: A printing technology that forms characters and images using a series of small dots; most commonly used for printing voluminous batch information, such as periodic reports and forms.

Downsizing: The practice of slashing costs and streamlining operations by laying off employees.

Downstream information flow: Information flow that relates to the information that is produced by a company and sent along to another organization, such as a distributor.

Drill down: To analyze data at more detailed levels of a specific dimension.

Drill-down report: Report that provides details behind the summary values on a key-indicator or exception report.

Drive-by hacking: Computer attack in which an attacker accesses a wireless computer network, intercepts data, uses network services, and/or sends attack instructions without entering the office or organization that owns the network.

Dumpster diving: Going through dumpsters and garbage cans for company documents, credit card receipts, and other papers containing information that might be useful for committing computer crimes.

DVD: Digital versatile disk; high capacity optical storage medium available in read-only, recordable, and re-writable form.

DVD-ROM (digital versatile disk–read-only memory): A DVD that can only be read, but not written to.

E911: Enhanced 911; a part of a federal mandate to improve the effectiveness and reliability of 911 service.

E-auctions: Electronic auctions.

Eavesdropping: Intercepting communication intended for others.

E-business: Term used to refer to the use of a variety of types of information technologies and systems to support every part of the business.

E-Business Innovation Cycle: The extent to which an organization derives value from a particular information technology over time.

Economic opportunities: Opportunities that a firm finds for making more money and/or making money in new ways.

Edge computing: The location of relatively small servers close to the end users to save resources in terms of network bandwidth and provide improved access time.

E-government: The use of information systems to provide citizens, organizations, and other governmental agencies with information about and access to public services.

E-information: The use of the Internet to provide electronic brochures and other types of information for customers.

E-integration: The use of the Internet to provide customers with the ability to gain personalized information by querying corporate databases and other information sources.

E-lancing: Self-employed work, similar to freelancing, typically on Internet-related projects.

Electrically erasable programmable read-only memory (EEPROM): Storage medium similar to RAM, which can be repeatedly written to, but which also retains information after power is turned off; also known as Flash.

Electromagnetic interference (EMI): Disturbance due to electromagnetic radiation.

Electronic bill pay: The use of online banking for bill paying.

Electronic commerce (EC): Exchanges of goods and services via the Internet among and between customers, firms, employees, business partners, suppliers, etc.

Electronic Data Interchange (EDI): The digital, or electronic, transmission of business documents and related data between organizations via dedicated telecommunications networks.

Electronic meeting system (EMS): A collection of personal computers networked together with sophisticated software tools to help group members solve problems and make decisions through interactive, electronic idea generation, evaluation, and voting.

Electronic paper: Flexible output medium using microscopic beads that change color in response to small electrical charges.

Embargo: A type of export regulation concerning the flow of goods and services, typically limiting (or prohibiting) trade with one particular country.

Embedded system: Microprocessor-based system (such as a digital video recorder [TiVo] or a network router) designed to perform only a specific, predefined task.

Enabling technology: Information technology that enables a firm to accomplish a task or goal or to gain or sustain a competitive advantage in some way.

Encryption: The process of encoding messages or files so that only intended recipients can decipher and understand them.

End-user development: The development, testing, and maintenance of applications by users in an organization.

Enterprise license: *See* Volume license

Enterprise marketing management (EMM): CRM tools used to integrate and analyze marketing campaigns.

Enterprise network: A WAN connecting disparate networks of a single organization into a single network.

Enterprise portal: B2B marketplace that provides a single point of access to secured, proprietary information from an organization.

Enterprise Resource Planning (ERP): Information systems that integrate business activities across departmental boundaries, including planning, manufacturing, sales, marketing, and so on.

Enterprise systems: Information systems that span the entire organization and can be used to integrate business processes, activities, and information across all functional areas of a firm.

Enterprise-wide information systems: See enterprise systems.

Entity: Something data is collected about, such as people or classes.

Entity-relationship diagram (ERD): A diagram used to display the structure of data and show associations between entities.

E-paper: Electronic paper.

Ergonomic keyboard: Keyboard resembling a widened V shape that is designed to reduce the stress placed on the wrists, hands, and arms when typing.

ERP core components: The components of an ERP that support the internal activities of an organization for producing products and services.

ERP extended components: The components of an ERP that support the primary external activities of an organization for dealing with suppliers and customers.

E-tailing: Electronic retailing; the online sales of goods and services.

Ethernet: A local area network protocol that uses a bus network topology and random access control.

E-transaction: The use of the Internet to allow customers to place orders and make payments.

Exception report: Report providing users with information about situations that are out of the normal operating range.

Executive information system (EIS): An information system designed to provide information in a highly aggregated form so that managers at the executive level of the organization can quickly scan it for trends and anomalies.

Executive level: The top level of the organization, where executives focus on long-term strategic issues facing the organization.

Expert system (ES): A special-purpose information system designed to mimic human expertise by manipulating knowledge—understanding acquired through experience and extensive learning—rather than simply information.

Explicit knowledge assets: Knowledge assets that can be documented, archived, and codified.

Export regulations: Regulations directed at limiting the export of certain goods to other countries.

Extensible Business Reporting Language (XBRL): An XML-based specification for publishing financial information.

Extensible Markup Language (XML): A data presentation standard that allows designers to create customized features that enable data to be more easily shared between applications and organizations.

External acquisition: The process of purchasing an existing information system from an external organization or vendor.

External cache: Cache memory that is usually not built into the CPU, but is located within easy reach of the CPU on the motherboard.

Externally focused system: Information system that coordinates business activities with customers, suppliers, business partners, and others who operate outside an organization's boundaries.

Extraction, transformation, and loading (ETL): The process of consolidating, cleansing, and manipulating data before loading it into a data warehouse.

Extranet: A private Web site used by firms and companies for business-to-business interactions.

Eye-tracking device: A pointing device that uses the movement of someone's eyes to move the pointer.

Facts: *See* Measures.

Fiber-optic cable: Transmission medium made of light-conducting glass or plastic core, surrounded by more glass, called cladding, and a tough outer sheath; used for high-speed data transmission.

Fiber to the home (FTTH): *See* Fiber to the premises.

Fiber to the premises (FTTP): High-speed network connectivity to homes and offices that is implemented using fiber-optic cable. Also known as fiber to the home.

Fifth-generation language (5GL): Computer language using English sentences; developed for application within expert systems and artificial intelligence applications.

File services: Processes used to store, retrieve, and move data files in an efficient manner across a network.

Financial flow: The movement of financial assets throughout the supply chain.

Firewall: Hardware or software designed to keep unauthorized users out of network systems.

Firewall architecture: The manner in which a firewall is implemented, such as hardware only, software only, or a combination of hardware and software.

Flash drive: Portable, removable data storage device using flash memory.

Flash memory: *See* EEPROM.

Flops (floating point operations per second): Measure of processing speed, used for supercomputers.

Foreign key: An attribute that appears as a nonprimary key attribute in one entity and as a primary key attribute (or part of a primary key) in another entity.

Form: A business document that contains some predefined data and may include some areas where additional data is to be filled in, typically for a single record.

Forward auction: A form of e-auctions that allows sellers to post goods and services for sale and buyers to bid on these items.

Fourth-generation language (4GL): Outcome-oriented programming language using English-like sentences.

Freeconomics: The leveraging of digital technologies to provide *free* goods and services to customers as a business strategy for gaining a competitive advantage.

Front-office system: Systems designed for direct interaction between an organization and its customers.

Fully automated data entry: Data entry into an information system that does not require any human intervention.

Functional area information system: A cross-organizational-level information system designed to support a specific functional area.

Fuzzy logic: Type of logic used in intelligent systems that allows rules to be represented using approximations or subjective values in order to handle situations where information about a problem is incomplete.

Gateway: A networking hardware component used for protocol conversion so that different networks can communicate even though they "speak" different languages.

Geoeconomics: The combination of economic and political factors that influence a region.

Geographic information system (GIS): A system for creating, storing, analyzing, and managing geographically referenced information.

Geo-tagging: Adding geographically referenced information to maps.

Global business strategy: An international business strategy employed to achieve economies of scale by producing identical products in large quantities for a variety of different markets.

Global information dissemination: The use of the Internet as an inexpensive means for distributing an organization's information.

Global network: Network spanning multiple countries that may include the networks of several organizations. The Internet is an example of a global network.

Global positioning system (GPS): A worldwide navigation system that utilizes twenty-four middle earth orbiting (MEO) satellites to determine the exact position of a GPS receiver.

Globalization: The integration of economies throughout the world, enabled by innovation and technological progress.

Globalization 1.0: The first stage of globalization (fifteenth century through the 1800s), primarily driven by power from horses, wind, and steam. Countries (mainly European) were globalizing, shrinking the world from size large to size medium. Industries changed slowly and the effects of globalization on individuals was barely noticed.

Globalization 2.0: The second stage of globalization (1800 to 2000), driven by a reduction of transportation and telecommunication costs. Companies (mainly American and European) were globalizing, shrinking the world from size medium to size small. Changes were happening at a fairly slow pace.

Globalization 3.0: The third stage of globalization (starting around 2000), driven by the convergence of the ten "flatteners." Individuals and small groups from virtually every nation were globalizing, shrinking the world from size small to size tiny. Changes are happening at a faster pace, making people readily feel the effects of industry changes.

Gopher: A text-based, menu-driven interface that enables users to access a large number of varied Internet resources as if they were in folders and menus on their own computers.

Government-to-business (G2B): Electronic commerce that involves a country's government and businesses.

Government-to-citizens (G2C): Online interactions between federal, state, and local governments and their constituents.

Government-to-government (G2G): Electronic interactions that take place between countries, or between different levels of government within a country.

Graphical user interface (GUI): Computer interface that enables the user to select pictures, icons, and menus to send instructions to the computer.

Graphics card: *See* Video Card

Graphics tablet: An input device that simulates the process of drawing or sketching on a piece of paper.

Green computing: Attempts to use computing resources more efficiently, reducing energy needs.

Grid computing: A computing architecture that combines the computing power of a large number of smaller, independent, networked computers (often regular desktop PCs) into a cohesive system in order to solve large-scale computing problems.

Groupware: Software that enables people to work together more effectively.

Hacker: Individual who gains unauthorized access to computer systems.

Hacktivist: Cybercriminal pursuing political, religious, or ideological goals.

Hard data: Facts and numbers that are typically generated by transaction processing systems and management information systems.

Hard disk: *See* Hard drive.

Hard drive: A secondary storage device usually located inside the system unit of a computer for storing data. Also called hard disk.

Hardware: Physical computer equipment, such as the computer monitor, central processing unit, or keyboard.

Head crash: A hard disk failure occurring when the read/write head touches the disk, resulting in the loss of the data and/or the operation of the hard disk.

High-frequency radio: Wireless transmission medium that can transmit data at rates of up to 54 Mbps to network nodes up to 40 kilometers apart.

Home replication strategy: International business strategy that views the international business as extension of the home business.

Hot backup site: A fully equipped backup facility, having everything from hardware, software, current data, to office equipment.

HTML editor: *See* Web page builder.

Hub: Network device used as a central point of connection between media segments.

Human–computer interface (HCI): The point of contact between an information system and its users.

Hyperlink: A reference or link on a Web page to other documents that contain related information.

Hypertext: Text in a Web document that is linked to other text or files.

Hypertext Markup Language (HTML): The standard method of specifying the format of Web pages. Specific content within each Web page is enclosed within codes (called markup tags) that stipulate how the content should appear to the user.

Hypertext Transfer Protocol (HTTP): The standard regulating how servers process user requests for Web pages.

Identity theft: Stealing another person's Social Security number, credit card number, and other personal information for the purpose of using the victim's credit rating to borrow money, buy merchandise, and run up debts that are never repaid.

Individualism/collectivism: The extent to which a society values the position of an individual versus the position of a group.

Inferencing: The matching of user questions and answers to information in a knowledge base within an expert system in order to make a recommendation.

Informating: The ability of information technology to provide information about the operation within a firm and/or about the underlying work process that the system supports.

Information: Data that has been formatted and/or organized in some way as to be useful to people.

Information accessibility: An ethical issue that focuses on defining what information a person or organization has the right to obtain about others and how this information can be accessed and used.

Information accuracy: An ethical issue concerned with the authenticity and fidelity of information, as well as identifying who is responsible for informational errors that harm people.

Information Age: A period of time in society when information became a valuable or dominant currency.

Information flow: The movement of information along the supply chain.

Information modification: The intentional change of electronic information by unauthorized users.

Information privacy: An ethical issue that is concerned with what information an individual should have to reveal to others through the course of employment or through other transactions such as online shopping.

Information property: An ethical issue that focuses on who owns information about individuals and how information can be transferred, sold, and exchanged.

Information systems (IS): Assumed to mean computer-based information systems that are combinations of hardware, software, and telecommunications networks that people build and use to collect, create, and distribute useful data; this term is also used to represent the field in which people develop, use, manage, and study computer-based information systems in organizations.

Information systems audit: An assessment of the state of an organization's information systems controls to determine necessary changes and to help ensure the information systems' availability, confidentiality, and integrity.

Information systems controls: Controls helping to ensure the reliability of information, consisting of policies and their physical implementation, access restrictions, or recordkeeping of actions and transactions.

Information systems infrastructure: The hardware, software, networks, data, facilities, human resources, and services used by organizations to support their decision making, business processes, and competitive strategy.

Information systems planning: A formal organizational process for identifying and assessing all possible information systems development projects of an organization.

Information systems security: Precautions taken to keep all aspects of information systems safe from unauthorized use or access.

Information systems security plan: An ongoing planning process to secure information systems, involving risk assessment, risk-reduction planning, and plan implementation as well as ongoing monitoring.

Information technology (IT): Machine technology that is controlled by or uses information.

Informational system: System designed to support decision making based on stable point-in-time or historical data.

In-forming: Individuals' use of powerful search engines on the Internet to build their own personal supply chain of information, knowledge, and entertainment.

Infrared line of sight: The use of high-frequency light waves to transmit data on an unobstructed path between nodes—computers or some other device such as printers—on a network, at a distance of up to 24.4 meters.

Infrastructure: The interconnection of various structural elements to support an overall entity, such as an organization, city, or country.

Ink-jet printer: Type of printer that uses a small cartridge to spray ink onto paper.

Innovator's dilemma: The notion that disruptive innovations can cause established firms or industries to lose market dominance, often leading to failure.

Input technologies: Hardware that is used to enter information into a computer.

In-sourcing: The delegation of a company's logistics operations to a subcontractor that specializes in that operation.

Intangible benefit: A benefit of using a particular system or technology that is difficult to quantify.

Intangible cost: The cost of using a particular system or technology that is difficult to quantify.

Integrated services digital network (ISDN): A standard for worldwide digital telecommunications that uses existing twisted-pair telephone wires to provide high-speed data service.

Integration: The use of Web technologies to link Web sites to corporate databases to provide real-time access to personalized information.

Integrity: Assurance that a message has not been altered in any way from the original that was sent.

Intellectual property (IP): Creations of the mind that have commercial value.

Intelligent agent: A program that works in the background to provide some service when a specific event occurs.

Intelligent system: System comprised of sensors, software, and computers embedded in machines and devices that emulate and enhance human capabilities.

Interactive communication: Immediate communication and feedback between a company and its customers using Web technologies.

Interactive voice response (IVR): System using speech recognition technology to guide callers through online surveys or menu options.

Interexchange carriers (IXC): Companies that sell long-distance services with circuits carrying service between the major telephone exchanges.

Interface: The way in which the user interacts with the computer.

Internal cache: Special high-speed cache memory that is incorporated into the microprocessor's design.

Internally focused systems: Information systems that support functional areas, business processes, and decision making within an organization.

International business strategy: Set of strategies employed by organizations operating in different global markets.

Internet: A large worldwide collection of networks that use a common protocol to communicate with each other.

Internet backbone: The collection of primary network connections and telecommunications lines comprising the Internet.

Internet Corporation for Assigned Names and Numbers (ICANN): A nonprofit corporation that is responsible for managing IP addresses, domain names, and the root server system.

Internet hoax: A false message circulated online about any topic of public interest, typically asking the recipient to perform a certain action.

Internet host: Computer working as a server on the Internet.

Internet over Satellite (IoS): Technology that allows users to access the Internet via satellites that are placed in a geostationary orbit.

Internet Registry: A central repository for Internet-related information that provides a central allocation of network system identifiers.

Internet service provider (ISP): Individual or organization that enables other individuals and organizations to connect to the Internet.

Internet Tax Freedom Act: An act mandating a moratorium on electronic commerce taxation in order to stimulate electronic commerce.

Internetworking: Connecting host computers and their networks to form even larger networks.

InterNIC: A government–industry collaboration created by the NSF in 1993 to manage directory and database services, domain registration services, and other information services on the Internet.

Interorganizational system (IOS): An information system that communicates across organizational boundaries.

Interpreter: A software program that translates a programming language into machine language one statement at a time.

Intranet: An internal, private network using Web technologies to facilitate the secured transmission of proprietary information within an organization, thereby limiting the viewing access to authorized users within the organization.

IP address: A numerical address assigned to every computer and router connected to the Internet, serving as the destination address of that computer or device and enabling the network to route messages to the proper destination.

IP convergence: The use of the Internet protocol for transporting voice, video, fax, and data traffic.

IP datagram: A data packet that conforms to the Internet protocol specification.

IPv6: The latest version of the Internet protocol, also referred to as IPng (IP next generation).

Java: An object-oriented programming language developed by Sun Microsystems in the early 1990s that is used in developing applications on the Web and other environments.

JavaScript: A scripting language, created by Netscape, that allows developers to add dynamic content to Web sites.

Joint application design (JAD): A special type of a group meeting in which all (or most) users meet with the analyst to jointly define and agree on system requirements or designs.

Joystick: Pointing device that works by moving a small stick that sits in a holder.

Keyboard: Input device for entering text and numbers into a computer.

Key-indicator report: Report that provides a summary of critical information on a recurring schedule.

Key performance indicator (KPI): A metric deemed critical to assessing progress toward a certain organizational goal.

Knowledge: A body of governing procedures, such as guidelines or rules, that are used to organize or manipulate data to make it suitable for a given task.

Knowledge assets: The set of skills, routines, practices, principles, formulas, methods, heuristics, and intuitions (both explicit and tacit) used by organizations to improve efficiency, effectiveness, and profitability.

Knowledge management: The processes an organization uses to gain the greatest value from its knowledge assets.

Knowledge management system: A collection of technology-based tools that include communications technologies and information storage and retrieval systems to enable the generation, storage, sharing, and management of tacit knowledge assets.

Knowledge portals: Specific portals used to share knowledge collected into a repository with employees (often using an intranet), with customers and suppliers (often using an extranet), or the general public (often using the Internet).

Knowledge society: Term coined by Peter Drucker to refer to a society in which education is the cornerstone of society and there is an increase in importance of knowledge workers.

Knowledge worker: Term coined by Peter Drucker to refer to professionals who are relatively well educated and who create, modify, and/or synthesize knowledge as a fundamental part of their jobs.

Laser printer: An electrostatic printing process that forces toner onto the paper, literally "burning" text or images onto the paper.

Learning organization: An organization that is skilled at creating, acquiring, and transferring knowledge and at modifying its behavior to reflect new knowledge and insights.

Legacy systems: Older stand-alone computer systems within an organization with older versions of applications that are either fast approaching or beyond the end of their useful life within the organization.

Life focus: The extent to which a culture focuses on the quantity versus the quality of life.

Light pen: Pointing device that works by placing a pen-like device near a computer screen.

Liquid crystal display (LCD): A type of computer monitor that is most commonly used on notebook and desktop computers.

Local area network (LAN): A computer network that spans a relatively small area, allowing all computer users to connect with each other to share information and peripheral devices, such as printers.

Location-based services: Highly personalized mobile services based on a user's location.

Logic bomb: A type of computer virus that lies in wait for unsuspecting computer users to perform a triggering operation before executing its instructions.

Long tail: The parts of consumer demand that are outside the mainstream tastes (i.e., niche markets).

Low-cost leadership strategy: Strategy to offer the best prices in the industry on goods or services.

Luddite: People feeling threatened by and protesting against or destroying technology.

Machine language: A binary-level computer language that computer hardware understands.

Magnetic ink character recognition (MICR): Scanning technology used by the banking industry to read data, account numbers, bank codes, and check numbers on preprinted checks.

Magnetic tape: A secondary storage method that consists of narrow plastic tape coated with a magnetic substance.

Mainframe: A very large computer that is used as the main, central computing system by major corporations and governmental agencies.

Making the business case: The process of identifying, quantifying, and presenting the value provided by an information system.

Malware: Malicious software such as viruses, worms, or Trojan horses.

M-commerce: Any electronic transaction or information interaction conducted using a wireless, mobile device and mobile networks that leads to a transfer of real or perceived value in exchange for information, services, or goods.

Management information system (MIS): (1) A field of study that encompasses the development, use, management, and study of computer-based information systems in organizations. (2) An information system designed to support the management of organizational functions at the managerial level of the organization.

Managerial level: The middle level of the organization, where functional managers focus on monitoring and controlling operational-level activities and providing information to higher levels of the organization.

Manual data entry: The process of entering information by hand into an information system.

Maquiladoras: Assembly plants located on the Mexican side of the United States–Mexican border; utilized mainly to take advantage of lower wages and less stringent regulations.

Masculinity/Femininity: The degree to which a society is characterized by masculine qualities, such as assertiveness, or by feminine characteristics, such as nurturance.

Mashup: A new application or Web site created by integrating one or more Web services.

Masquerading: Misrepresenting oneself in order to steal equipment or to trick others into revealing sensitive information. Also called social engineering.

Mass customization: Tailoring products and services to meet particular needs of individual customers on a large scale.

Measures: The values and numbers a user wants to analyze.

Media access control: The rules that govern how a given node or workstation gains access to a network to send or receive information.

Menu-driven pricing: A pricing system in which companies set and present negotiable prices for products to consumers.

Mesh network: A network that consists of computers and other devices that are either fully or partially connected to each other.

Message services: The storing, accessing, and delivering of text, binary, graphic, digitized video, and audio data across a network.

Metadata: Data about data.

Metropolitan area network (MAN): A computer network of limited geographic scope, typically a city-wide area that combines both LAN and high-speed fiber-optic technologies.

Microcomputer: A category of computers that is generally used for personal computing, for small business computing, and as workstations attached to large computers or to other small computers on a network.

Microprocessor: see Central Processing Unit.

Microsoft.NET: A programming platform that is used to develop applications that are highly interoperable across a variety of platforms and devices.

Microwave transmission: Sending of messages through a high-frequency radio signal, using either terrestrial (earth-based) systems or satellite systems.

Midrange computer: Computers offering lower performance than mainframes but higher performance than microcomputers that are typically used for engineering and midsized business applications.

Mirrored: Data stored synchronously on independent systems to achieve redundancy for purposes of reliability and/or performance.

Mobile wireless: Transfer of data to a moving computer or handheld device.

Models: Conceptual, mathematical, logical, and analytical formulas used to represent or project business events or trends.

Modem: Short for modulator-demodulator; device or program that enables a computer to transmit data over telephone lines.

Modules: Components of a software application that can be selected and implemented as needed.

Monitor: A computer display screen.

Monitoring and sensing agent: Intelligent agent that keeps track of key information, notifying the user when conditions change.

Moore's Law: The prediction that computer processing performance would double every eighteen months.

Motherboard: A large printed plastic or fiberglass circuit board that holds or connects to all the computer's electronic components.

Mouse: Pointing device used to select menu items and drag and drop items.

Multidomestic business strategy: A decentralized international business strategy using a federation of associated business units, employed to be flexible and responsive to needs and demands of heterogeneous local markets.

Multiplexer (MUX): Networking hardware used to share a communications line or medium among a number of users.

National Science Foundation (NSF): The organization in the United States that initiated the development of the NSFNET (National Science Foundation Network), which became a major component of the Internet.

National Science Foundation Network (NSFNET): A network developed by the United States in 1986 that became a major component of the Internet.

Nearshoring: The reversal of offshoring; the use of locations closer to the home country in terms of geographical, political, linguistic, economic, or cultural distance.

Neo-Luddite: Person who opposes information systems, fearing negative impacts such as social decay, increased consumerism, or loss of privacy.

Netcast: A digital media stream that can be distributed to and played by digital audio players.

Netcaster: Person publishing a netcast.

Netcasting: The process of publishing netcasts.

Net neutrality: A concept that data sent over the Internet using Internet protocol should be routed and handled in a neutral matter, regardless of the content of the data.

Net-present-value analysis: A type of cost–benefit analysis of the cash flow streams associated with an investment.

Network: A group of computers and associated peripheral devices connected by a communication channel capable of sharing information and other resources (e.g., a printer) among users.

Network access point (NAP): Access points used by ISPs to connect to each other.

Network address translation (NAT): The process of hiding computers' true network addresses by replacing the computers' IP addresses with a firewall's address, allowing potential attackers to only "see" the network address of the firewall.

Network click fraud: A form of click fraud where a site hosting an advertisement creates fake clicks in order to get revenue from the advertiser.

Network computer: A microcomputer with minimal memory and storage designed to connect to networks, especially the Internet, to use the resources provided by servers.

Network effect: The notion that the value of a network is dependent on the number of its users, such that a network with more users becomes more useful for each user.

Network interface card (NIC): An expansion board that plugs into a computer so that it can be connected to a network.

Network operating system (NOS): System software that controls the network and enables computers to communicate with each other.

Network service: Capabilities of networked computers that enable them to share files, print, send and receive messages, as well as use shared software applications.

Network topology: The shape of a network; the three common network topologies are star, ring, bus, and mesh.

Neural network: An information system that attempts to approximate the functioning of a human brain.

New economy: An economy in which information technology plays a significant role and that enables producers of both tangible (computers, shoes, etc.) and intangible (services, ideas, etc.) goods to compete efficiently in global markets.

Nonrecurring costs: One-time costs that are not expected to continue after a system is implemented.

Nonrepudiation: A mechanism using a digital signature to prove that a message did, in fact, originate from the claimed sender.

Nonshipment: A type of e-auction fraud where a seller fails to ship an item after payment has been received.

Nonvolatile memory: Memory that does not lose its data after power is shut off.

Normalization: A technique for making complex databases more efficient and more easily handled by a database management system.

Notebook computer: A mobile microcomputer that can be easily carried in a briefcase or backpack.

Object-oriented analysis and design (OOA&D): Systems development methodologies and techniques based on objects rather than on data and processes.

Object-oriented language: Programming language that groups together data and its corresponding instructions into manipulatable objects.

Office automation system (OAS): A collection of software and hardware for developing documents, scheduling resources, and communicating.

Offshore outsourcing: Outsourcing of business processes on a global scale.

Offshoring: Having certain business functions performed by the same company, but in a different country.

Off-the-shelf software: Software designed and used to support general business processes that does not require any specific tailoring to meet an organization's needs.

OLAP cube: A data structure allowing for multiple dimensions to be added to a traditional two-dimensional table for detailed analysis.

OLAP server: The chief component of an OLAP system that understands how data is organized in the database and has special functions for analyzing the data.

On-demand computing: Allocation of computing resources on the basis of users' needs, often on a pay-per-use basis.

One Laptop per Child (OLPC): An initiative to distribute very low-cost laptop computers to children in developing countries around the world.

Online analytical processing (OLAP): The process of quickly conducting complex analyses of data stored in a database, typically using graphical software tools.

Online banking: The use of the Internet to conduct financial transactions.

Online investing: The use of the Internet to obtain information about stock quotes and manage financial portfolios.

Online predator: Cyber criminal using the Internet to target vulnerable people, usually the young or old, for sexual or financial purposes.

Online processing: Processing of source documents as they are created, providing immediate results to the system operator or customer.

Online transaction processing (OLTP): Immediate automated responses to the requests from multiple concurrent transactions from customers.

Open-source software: Software for which the source code is freely available for use and/or modification.

Open systems interconnection (OSI) model: A protocol that represents a group of specific communication tasks as successive layers.

Operating system: Software that coordinates the interaction between hardware devices, peripherals, application software, and users.

Operational CRM: Systems for automating the fundamental business processes—marketing, sales, and support—for interacting with the customer.

Operational level: The bottom level of an organization, where the routine, day-to-day business processes and interaction with customers occur.

Operational system: Any system that is used to interact with customers and run a business in real time.

Optical character recognition (OCR): Scanning technology used to read and digitize typewritten, computer-printed, or hand-printed characters.

Optical disk: A storage disk coated with a metallic substance that is written to (or read from) when a laser beam passes over the surface of the disk.

Optical mark recognition (OMR): Scanning technology used to scan questionnaires and test answer forms ("bubble sheets") where answer choices are marked by filling in circles using pencil or pen.

Organic light-emitting diode (OLED): Display technology using less power than LCD technology.

Organizational learning: The ability of an organization to learn from past behavior and information, improving as a result.

Organizational strategy: A firm's plan to accomplish its mission and goals as well as to gain or sustain competitive advantage over rivals.

Output technologies: Hardware devices that deliver information in a usable form.

Outsourcing: The moving of routine jobs and/or tasks to people in another firm, at less cost.

Packaged applications: Software programs written by third-party vendors for the needs of many different users and organizations.

Packet filtering: Prevention of unauthorized access to a computer network by a firewall at the data-packet level; data packets are accepted or rejected based on predefined rules.

Packet switching: The process of breaking information into small chunks called data packets and then managing the transfer of those packets from computer to computer via the Internet.

Paid inclusion: Inclusion of a Web site in a search engine's listing after payment of a fee.

Patch management system: An online system that utilizes Web services to automatically check for software updates, downloading and installing these "patches" as they are made available.

Patent: Type of intellectual property typically referring to process, machine, or material inventions.

Patriot hacker: Independent citizens or supporters of a country that perpetrate computer attacks on perceived or real enemies.

Pay-per-click: A payment model used in online advertising, where the advertiser pays the Web site owner a fee for visitors visiting a certain link.

Payment failure: A type of e-auction fraud where buyers fail to pay for an item after the conclusion of an auction.

Peer: Any computer that may both request and provide services.

Peer-to-peer: Technology using the network bandwidth of all users of the software to improve performance.

Peer-to-peer networks: Networks that enable any computer or device on the network to provide and request services.

Perfective maintenance: Making enhancements to improve processing performance, to improve interface usability, or to add desired, but not necessarily required, system features.

Personal area network (PAN): An emerging technology that uses wireless communication to exchange data between computing devices using short-range radio communication, typically within an area of 10 meters.

Personal computer (PC): A type of microcomputer that fits on desktops and is used in homes and offices.

Personal digital assistant (PDA): A handheld microcomputer.

Petaflop: 1,000 trillion flops.

Phishing: Attempts to trick financial account and credit card holders into giving away their authorization information, usually by sending spam messages to literally millions of e-mail accounts. Also known as spoofing.

Phreaking: Crimes committed against telephone company computers with the goal of making free long distance calls, impersonating directory assistance or other operator services, diverting calls to numbers of the perpetrator's choice, or otherwise disrupting telephone service for subscribers.

Piggybacking: *See* shoulder-surfing.

Plain old telephone service (POTS): Standard telephone lines with a speed, or bandwidth, that is generally about 52 Kbps (52,000 bits per second); also called public switched telephone network (PSTN).

Plotter: Device used for transferring engineering designs from the computer to drafting paper, which is often as big as 34 by 44 inches.

Podcast: *See* Netcast.

Podcasting: *See* Netcasting.

Pointing device: Input device for pointing at items and selecting menu items within a GUI.

Port: A hardware interface by which a computer communicates with another device or system.

Power distance: A cultural characteristic related to how different societies view authority and hierarchical structures.

Power line communication (PLC): A connectivity technology that uses existing power distribution wires for data transmission. Also referred to as power line telecoms (PLT).

Power line telecoms (PLT): *See* Power line communication.

Power supply: A device that converts electricity from the wall socket to a lower voltage appropriate for computer components and regulates the voltage to eliminate surges common in most electrical systems.

Preventive maintenance: Making changes to a system to reduce the chance of future system failure.

Primary key: A field included in a database that contains a unique value for each instance of an entity to assure that it is stored or retrieved accurately.

Primary storage: Temporary storage for current calculations.

Print services: Network applications used to control and manage users' access to network printers and fax equipment.

Printing-on-Demand: Publishing original works using customized printing that is done in small batches.

Privacy: Ensuring that no one can read the message except the intended recipient.

Private branch exchange (PBX): A telephone system that serves a particular location, such as a business, connecting one telephone extension to another within the system and connecting the internal extensions to the outside telephone network.

Processing logic: The steps by which data is transformed or moved, as well as a description of the events that trigger these steps.

Processing technologies: Computer hardware that transforms inputs into outputs.

Procurement portals: Enterprise portals that automate the business processes involved in purchasing, or procuring, products between a single buyer and multiple suppliers.

Product flow: The movement of goods from the supplier to production, from production to distribution, and from distribution to the consumer.

Productivity paradox: The observation that productivity increases at a rate that is lower than expected when new technologies are introduced.

Projector: Video output device used to project an image onto a large screen.

Propagation delay: The delay in the transmission of a satellite signal because of the distance the signal must travel.

Protocols: Procedures that different computers follow when they transmit and receive data.

Prototyping: An iterative systems development process in which requirements are converted into a working system that is continually revised through close work between analysts and users.

Proxy server: A firewall that serves as, or creates the appearance of, an alternative server that intercepts all messages entering and leaving the network, effectively hiding the true network addresses. Proxy servers are also commonly used to locally store (cache) Web sites to provide faster access of popular sites.

Proxy variables: Alternative measurements of outcomes, used when it is difficult to determine and measure direct effects.

Public key technology: A data encryption technique that uses two keys—a private key and a public key—to encrypt and decode messages.

Public switched telephone network (PSTN): *See* Plain old telephone service (POTS).

Query: Method used to retrieve information from a database.

Query by example (QBE): A capability of a DBMS that enables data to be requested by providing a sample or a description of the types of data the user would like to see.

Quota: Regulation permitting foreign businesses to export only a certain number of products into a specific country.

QWERTY keyboard: The default keyboard layout for entering numbers and letters (QWERTY stands for how the letters are arranged on the keyboard, with Q-W-E-R-T-Y being the first six letters going from left to right on the keyboard).

Radio frequency identification (RFID): The use of the electromagnetic energy to transmit information between a reader (transceiver) and a processing device, used to replace bar codes and bar code readers.

Random-access memory (RAM): A type of primary storage that is volatile and can be accessed randomly by the CPU.

Rapid application development (RAD): A four-phase systems development methodology that combines prototyping, computer-based development tools, special management practices, and close user involvement.

Read-only memory (ROM): A type of primary storage on which data has been prerecorded and is nonvolatile.

Read/write head: Components that inscribe data to or retrieve data from hard disks, diskettes, and tapes.

Real Simple Syndication (RSS): A set of standards for sharing updated Web content, such as news and sports scores, across sites.

Record: A collection of related attributes about a single entity.

Recovery point objectives: Objectives specifying how timely backup data should be preserved.

Recovery time objectives: Objectives specifying the maximum time allowed to recover from a catastrophic event.

Recurring costs: Ongoing costs that occur throughout the life cycle of systems development, implementation, and maintenance.

Redundant array of independent (inexpensive) disks (RAID): A secondary storage technology that makes redundant copies of data on two or more hard drives.

Registers: Temporary storage locations inside the CPU where data must reside while being processed or manipulated.

Reintermediation: The design of business models that reintroduce middlemen in order to reduce the chaos brought on by disintermediation.

Relational database model: The most common DBMS approach in which entities are presented as two-dimensional tables, with records as rows and attributes as columns.

Relationship: An association between entities in a database to enable data retrieval.

Repeater: A network device used to regenerate or replicate a signal as it weakens when traveling on a network and to move data from one media segment to another, thereby effectively extending the size of the network.

Report: A compilation of data from a database that is organized and produced in printed format.

Report generator: Software tool that helps users build reports quickly and describe the data in a useful format.

Reproductions: A type of e-auction fraud where something is sold as an original but is actually a reproduction.

Request for proposal (RFP): A communication tool indicating buyer requirements for a given system and requesting information or soliciting bids from potential vendors.

Requirements collection: The process of gathering and organizing information from users, managers, business processes, and documents to understand how a proposed information system should function.

Revenue model: Organization model that describes how the organization will earn revenue, generate profits, and produce a return on invested capital.

Reverse auction: A type of auction in which buyers post a request for proposal (RFP) and sellers respond with bids.

Reverse pricing system: A pricing system in which customers specify the product they are looking for and how much they are willing to pay; this information is routed to appropriate companies who either accept or reject this offer.

RFID tag: The processing device used in an RFID system that uniquely identifies an object.

Ring network: A network that is configured in the shape of a closed loop or circle, with each node connecting to the next node.

Risk acceptance: A computer system security policy in which no countermeasures are adopted, and any damages that occur are simply absorbed.

Risk analysis: The process in which the value of the assets being protected are assessed, the likelihood of their being compromised is determined, and the costs of their being compromised are compared with the costs of the protections to be taken.

Risk reduction: The process of taking active countermeasures to protect information systems.

Risk transference: A computer system security policy in which someone else absorbs the risk, as with insurance.

Roll up: To analyze data at less detailed levels of a certain dimension.

Router: An intelligent device used to connect and route data traffic across two or more individual networks.

Rule: A way of encoding knowledge, typically expressed using an "if-then" format, within an expert system.

Salami slicing: A form of data diddling that occurs when a person shaves small amounts from financial accounts and deposits them in a personal account.

Sales force automation (SFA): CRM systems to support the day-to-day sales activities of an organization.

Sarbanes-Oxley Act: Government regulation formed as a reaction to large-scale accounting scandals that led to the downfall of large corporations that includes the use of information systems controls in compliance reviews.

Satellite: A device launched to orbit earth and enable network communication.

Satellite microwave: Microwave transmission using satellites as relay stations to transfer high-frequency radio signals between antennas located on earth.

Scalability: The ability to adapt to increases or decreases in demand for processing or data storage.

Scanner: Input device that converts printed text and images into digital data.

Scheduled reports: Reports produced at predefined intervals—daily, weekly, or monthly—to support the routine informational needs of managerial-level decision making.

Scripting language: A programming technique for integrating interactive components into a Web page.

Search advertising: Attempting to ensure that a company's Web site is the first site a user sees when searching for a specific term.

Search engine optimization (SEO): Methods for improving a site's ranking in search engine results.

Search marketing: Any attempts to increase a Web site's visibility in search engine results.

Secondary cache: *See* external cache.

Secondary key: Attribute that can be used to identify one or more records within a table that share a common value.

Secondary storage: Methods for permanently storing data to a large-capacity storage component, such as a hard disk, diskette, CD-ROM disk, or tape.

Secure Sockets Layer (SSL): A popular public-key encryption method used on the Internet.

Self-publishing: Publishing written documents with little or no editorial review.

Semantic web: A set of design principles that will allow computers to be able to index Web sites, topics, and subjects, enabling computers to read Web pages, and search engines to give richer and more accurate answers.

Semiautomated data entry: Data entry into an information system using some type of data capture device, such as a grocery store checkout scanner.

Semistructured decision: Decisions where problems and solutions are not clear-cut and often require judgment and expertise.

Sequence discovery: Data mining technique used to discover associations over time.

Server: Any computer on the network that enables access to files, printing, communications, and other services available to users of the network; it typically has a more advanced microprocessor, more memory, a larger cache, and more disk storage than a single-user workstation.

Server-centric networks: Networks in which servers and clients have defined roles.

Service: Individual software component designed to perform a specific task.

Service mentality: The belief among information systems personnel that their chief goal is satisfying their systems customers within the firm while fundamentally believing that the customers, not the systems personnel, own the technology and the information.

Service-oriented architecture (SOA): A software architecture in which business processes are broken down into individual components (or services) that are designed to achieve the desired results for the service consumer (which can be either an application, another service, or a person).

Shipping fraud: Charging irregular shipping and handling fees far above actual cost in e-auctions.

Shopping bot: *See* Buyer agent.

Shoulder-surfing: Looking over a person's shoulder while he or she is using an automated teller machine, cell phone, or other device in order to steal access information.

Shrink-wrap license: A type of software license that is used primarily for consumer products; the contract is activated when the shrink wrap on the packaging has been removed.

Slicing and dicing: Analyzing data on subsets of certain dimensions.

Slingbox: A device acting as a personal media server that can "placeshift" television content to any Internet-enabled device.

Smart card: Special credit card-sized card containing a microprocessor chip, memory circuits, and often a magnetic stripe.

Social engineering: *See* Masquerading.

Social network analysis: A technique that attempts to find groups of people who work together, to find people who don't collaborate but should, or to find experts in particular subject areas.

Social networking: Connecting to colleagues, family members, or friends for business or entertainment purposes.

Social online community: Web site enabling social networking.

Soft data: Textual news stories or other nonanalytical information.

Software: A program or set of programs that tell the computer to perform certain processing functions.

Software as a Service (SaaS): Software that is accessed via the Web and is hosted by an application service provider.

Software asset management (SAM): A set of activities performed to better manage an organization's software infrastructure by being able to consolidate and standardize their software titles, decide to retire unused software, or decide when to upgrade or replace software.

Software engineering: A disciplined approach for constructing information systems through the use of common methods, techniques, or tools.

Software piracy: A type of computer crime where individuals make illegal copies of software protected by copyright laws.

Sound card: A specialized circuit board that supports the ability to convert digital information into sounds that can be listened to on speakers or headphones plugged into the card; a microphone can also be plugged into the card for capturing audio for storage or processing.

Source document: Document that serves as a stimulus to a transaction processing system from some external source.

Spam: Electronic junk mail.

Spam filter: Hardware or software device used to fight spam and other e-mail threats such as directory harvest attacks, phishing attacks, viruses, and more.

Speech recognition: The process of converting spoken words into commands and data.

Spim: Spam sent via instant messaging.

Sponsored search: *See* Search advertising.

Spoofing: *See* phishing.

Spyware: Software that covertly gathers information about a user through an Internet connection without the user's knowledge.

Stand-alone applications: Systems that focus on the specific needs of individual departments and are not designed to communicate with other systems in the organization.

Star network: A network with several workstations connected to a central hub.

Stickiness: A Web site's ability to attract and keep visitors.

Storage service provider (SSP): Online provider offering hosted storage solutions.

Strategic: A way of thinking in which plans are made to accomplish specific goals.

Strategic necessity: Something an organization must do in order to survive.

Strategic planning: The process of forming a vision of where the organization needs to head, converting that vision into measurable objectives and performance targets, and crafting a plan to achieve the desired results.

Streaming media: Audio or video that can be sent over the Internet and is played/displayed as it arrives on the receiver's computer; developed so that Web users do not have to wait for an entire file to be downloaded before seeing a video or hearing a sound.

Streaming video: A sequence of compressed moving images that can be sent over the Internet.

Streamlined Sales Tax Project: A project to simplify tax codes and make it mandatory for out-of-state sellers to collect sales tax.

Structured decisions: Decisions where the procedures to follow for a given situation can be specified in advance.

Structured Query Language (SQL): The most common language used to interface with databases.

Supercomputer: The most expensive and most powerful category of computers. It is primarily used to assist in solving massive research and scientific problems.

Supply chain: The producers of supplies that a company uses.

Supply chain effectiveness: The extent to which a company's supply chain is focusing on maximizing customer service, regardless of procurement, production, and transportation costs.

Supply chain efficiency: The extent to which a company's supply chain is focusing on minimizing procurement, production, and transportation costs, sometimes by reducing customer service.

Supply Chain Execution (SCE): The execution of supply chain planning involving the management of product flows, information flows, and financial flows.

Supply Chain Management (SCM): Information systems focusing on improving upstream information flows with two main objectives—to accelerate product development and to reduce costs associated with procuring raw materials, components, and services from suppliers.

Supply Chain Planning (SCP): The process of developing various resource plans to support the efficient and effective production of goods and services.

Supply network: The network of multiple (sometimes interrelated) producers of supplies that a company uses.

Support activities: Business activities that enable the primary activities to take place. Support activities include administrative activities, infrastructure, human resources, technology development, and procurement.

Symmetric digital subscriber line (SDSL): A variant of DSL that supports the same data rates (up to 3 Mbps) for upstream and downstream traffic.

Symmetric secret key system: An encryption system where both the sender and recipient use the same key for encoding (scrambling) and decoding the message.

Synchronous: Coordinated in time.

System clock: An electronic circuit inside a computer that generates pulses at a rapid rate for setting the pace of processing events.

System conversion: The process of decommissioning the current system and installing a new system into the organization.

System effectiveness: The extent to which a system enables people and/or the firm to accomplish goals or tasks well.

System efficiency: The extent to which a system enables people and/or a firm to do things faster, at lower cost, or with relatively little time and effort.

System unit: The physical box that houses all the electronic components that do the work of the computer.

Systems analysis: The second phase of the systems development life cycle in which the current ways of doing business are studied and alternative replacement systems are proposed.

Systems analysis and design: The process of designing, building, and maintaining information systems.

Systems analyst: The primary person responsible for performing systems analysis and design activities.

Systems benchmarking: A standardized set of performance tests designed to facilitate comparison between systems.

Systems design: The third phase of the systems development life cycle in which details of the chosen approach are developed.

Systems development life cycle (SDLC): A model describing the life of an information system from conception to retirement.

Systems implementation: The fourth phase of the systems development life cycle in which the information system is programmed, tested, installed, and supported.

Systems integration: Connecting separate information systems and data to improve business processes and decision making

Systems maintenance: The process of systematically repairing and/or improving an information system.

Systems planning and selection: The first phase of the systems development life cycle in which potential projects are identified, selected, and planned.

Systems software: The collection of programs that controls the basic operations of computer hardware.

T1 line: A dedicated digital transmission line that can carry 1.544 Mbps of information.

T3 line: A digital transmission line that provides about 45 Mbps of information at about 10 times the cost of leasing a T1 line.

Table: A collection of related records in a database where each row is a record and each column is an attribute.

Tablet PC: Notebook computer accepting input from a stylus or a keyboard.

Tacit knowledge assets: Knowledge assets that reflect the processes and procedures located in employees' minds.

Tag: A command that is inserted into a document to specify how the document is to be formatted or used.

Tagging: The adding of keywords or relevant terms to a piece of information such as a map, picture, or Web page, thus describing the piece of information for others and making it searchable.

Tangible benefit: A benefit of using a particular system or technology that is quantifiable.

Tangible cost: A cost of using a particular system of technology that is quantifiable

Tariff: Government-imposed fees to regulate the flow of goods and services in and out of a country.

Technology: Any mechanical and/or electrical means to supplement, extend, or replace manual operations or devices.

Telecommunications network: A group of two or more computer systems linked together with communications equipment.

Terminal: Local input device used to enter data onto mainframes in centralized computing systems.

Terrestrial microwave: Microwave transmission using earth-based antennas that require an unobstructed path or line-of-sight between nodes; often used to cross inaccessible terrain or to connect buildings where cable installation would be infeasible or expensive.

Text mining: Analytical techniques for extracting information from textual documents.

Text recognition software: Software designed to convert handwritten text into computer-based characters.

Thematic mapping: A GIS technique using color coding to display aggregated data (such as median household income) for specific geographic regions.

Thin client: *See* Network computer.

Time bomb: A type of computer virus that lies in wait for a specific date before executing its instructions.

Token passing: An access method that uses a constantly circulating electronic token (a small packet of data) to prevent collisions and give all workstations equal access to the network.

Top-level domains: The highest level of Internet domain names in the domain name system, as indicated by their suffix (i.e., .com, .edu, or .org).

Total cost of ownership (TCO): The cost of owning and operating a system, including the total cost of acquisition, as well as all costs associated with its ongoing use and maintenance.

Touch screen: Pointing device using a touch sensitive computer display.

Trackball: Pointing device that works by rolling a ball that sits in a holder.

Trade area analysis: GIS technique used to assess where customers are coming from by combining location information with, for example, drive time information, to determine if certain areas are underserved or if two stores' trade areas overlap

Trading exchange: A Web site where multiple buyers and sellers come together to conduct business; also called an electronic marketplace.

Transaction processing system (TPS): An information system designed to process day-to-day business-event data at the operational level of the organization.

Transactions: Repetitive events in organizations that occur as a regular part of conducting day-to-day operations.

Transaction support: Utilizing the Web to provide automatic support to clients and firms for conducting business online without human assistance.

Transborder data flows: Data flowing across national boundaries.

Transmission control protocol/Internet protocol (TCP/IP): The protocol of the Internet, which allows different interconnected networks to communicate using the same language.

Transmission media: The physical pathways to send data and information between two or more entities on a network.

Transnational business strategy: An international business strategy that allows companies to leverage the flexibility offered by a decentralized organization (to be more responsive to local conditions), while at the same time reaping economies of scale enjoyed by centralization; characterized by a balance between centralization and decentralization and interdependent resources.

Trojan horse: Destructive computer code whose instructions remain hidden to the user because the computer appears to function normally but, in fact, is performing underlying functions dictated by the intrusive code.

Tunneling: A technology used by VPNs to encapsulate, encrypt, and securely transmit data over the public Internet infrastructure, enabling business partners to exchange information in a secured, private manner between organizational networks.

Twisted pair cable: Cable made of two or more pairs of insulated copper wires twisted together.

Ultra low power (ULP) bluetooth: New standard for PANs, characterized by low cost, small size, and low power consumption.

Ultramobile PC (UMPC): Laptop approximately the size of a hardcover book.

Unauthorized access: An information systems security breach where an unauthorized individual sees, manipulates, or otherwise handles electronically stored information.

Uncertainty avoidance: A cultural characteristic related to the risk-taking nature of a culture.

Uniform Resource Locator (URL): The unique Internet address for a Web site and specific Web pages within sites.

Unstructured decision: Decision where few or no procedures to follow for a given situation can be specified in advance.

Uploading: The ability of individuals and companies to actively participate in content generation on the Web.

Upstream information flow: An information flow consisting of information received from another organization, such as from a supplier.

USA PATRIOT Act: Officially known as Uniting and Strengthening America by Providing Appropriate Tools to Intercept and Obstruct Terrorism, a law giving law enforcement agencies, at both the local and federal levels, broader ranges of power to aid in the protection of U.S. citizens.

User agent: Intelligent agent that automatically performs specific tasks for a user, such as automatically sending a report at the first of the month, assembling customized news, or filling out a Web form with routine information.

Utilities: *See* Utility programs

Utility computing: A form of on-demand computing where resources in terms of processing, data storage, or networking are rented on an as-needed basis. The organization receives a bill for the services used from the provider at the end of each month.

Utility programs: Software designed to manage computer resources and files.

Value-added networks (VANs): Private, third-party-managed WANs that are shared by multiple organizations, and include leased communication lines, e-mail services, EDI, security, and other special capabilities.

Value chain: The set of primary and support activities in an organization where value is added to a product or service.

Value chain analysis: The process of analyzing an organization's activities to determine where value is added to products and/or services and the costs that are incurred for doing so.

Value proposition: What a business provides to a customer and what that customer is willing to pay for that product or service.

Value system: A collection of interlocking company value chains.

Vanilla version: The features and modules that a packaged software system comes with out of the box.

Vertical market: A market comprised of firms within a specific industry sector.

Video: Still and moving images that can be recorded, manipulated, and displayed on a computer.

Video card: A computer interface card that tells the monitor which dots to activate to produce text or images.

Videoconferencing: The use of integrated telephone, video recording, and playback technologies by two or more people to interact with each other from remote sites.

Videoconferencing over IP: The use of Internet technologies for videoconferences.

Viral marketing: Type of marketing that resembles offline word-of-mouth communication, in which advertising messages are spread similar to how real viruses are transmitted through social networks.

Virtual company: *See* Click-only business strategy.

Virtualization: The use of multiple virtual machines (run on large servers) to reduce energy needs.

Virtual machine: A computer that does not exist as a physical machine, but is implemented in software, allowing multiple computers to be run on a single server.

Virtual meeting: A meeting taking place using an online environment.

Virtual private network (VPN): A network connection that is constructed dynamically within an existing network—often called a secure tunnel—in order to securely connect remote users or nodes to an organization's network.

Virtual team: Work team that is composed of members that may be from different organizations and different locations that form and disband as needed.

Viruses: Destructive programs that disrupt the normal functioning of computer systems.

Virus prevention: Set of activities designed to detect and prevent computer viruses.

Vishing: Phone scams that attempt to defraud people by asking them to call a bogus telephone number to "confirm" their account information. Also known as voice phishing.

Visual analytics: The combination of various analysis techniques and interactive visualizations to solve complex problems.

Visual programming language: Programming language that has a graphical user interface (GUI) for the programmer and is designed for programming applications that will have a GUI.

Visualization: The display of complex data relationships using a variety of graphical methods.

Voice over IP (VoIP): The use of Internet technologies for placing telephone calls.

Voice-to-text software: An application that uses a microphone to monitor a person's speech and then converts the speech into text.

Volatile memory: Memory that loses its contents when the power is turned off.

Volume license: A type of software license that is usually negotiated and covers all users within an organization. Also known as enterprise license.

Warez: Slang term for stolen proprietary software that is sold or shared for free over the Internet.

Watermark: A digital or physical mark that is difficult to reproduce, used to prevent counterfeiting.

Web 2.0: Term used to express: (1) how technology has enabled integrating more interactive features into Web sites, and (2) the change in strategies for EC-based businesses.

Web 3.0: The next wave of the Internet using technologies providing for ubiquitous data access where the data is viewed as being in a "cloud," and applications that access this data can be run on any device, PC, or mobile phone.

Web analytics: The analysis of Web surfers' behavior in order to improve a site's performance

Web-based collaboration tool: Tool enabling teams to collaborate on projects using the Internet.

Web browser: A software application that can be used to locate and display Web pages including text, graphics, and multimedia content.

Web cam: A small camera that is used to transmit real-time video images within desktop videoconferencing systems.

Web content mining: Extracting textual information from Web documents.

Web crawler: Intelligent agent that continuously browses the Web for specific information (e.g., used by search engines). Also known as Web spider.

Web log: *See* Blog.

Weblogging: *See* Blogging.

Web mining: Analyzing the content or usage of Web pages.

Web page: A hypertext document stored on a Web server that contains not only information, but also references or links to other documents that contain related information.

Web page builder: Program for assisting in the creation and maintenance of Web pages.

Web server: A computer used to host Web sites.

Web service: Component that allows data to be accessed without intimate knowledge of other organizations' systems, enabling machine-to-machine interaction over the Internet.

Web site: A collection of interlinked Web pages typically belonging to the same person or business organization.

Web spider: *See* Web crawler.

Web usage mining: Analysis of a Web site's usage patterns, such as navigational paths or time spent.

Web vandalism: The act of defacing Web sites.

Weighted multicriteria analysis: Method for deciding among different information systems investments or alternative designs for a given system, in which requirements and constraints are weighted based on their importance.

What-if analysis: An analysis of the effects hypothetical changes to data have on the results.

Wide area network (WAN): A computer network that spans a relatively large geographic area; typically used to connect two or more LANs.

Widget: Small interactive tool used for a single purpose such as taking notes, viewing pictures, or simply displaying a clock.

Wiki: Web site allowing people to post, edit, comment, and access information. In contrast to a regular Web site, a wiki is linked to a database keeping a history of all prior versions and changes; therefore, a wiki allows viewing prior versions of the site, as well as reversing any changes made to the content.

Wikipedia: Online encyclopedia using wiki technology.

WiMax: Short for Worldwide Interoperability for Microwave Access (IEEE 802.16). High-speed wireless transmission technology that can be used for stationary and mobile applications and does not require a line of sight.

Wireless fidelity (Wi-Fi): Wireless LAN, based on the 802.11 family of standards.

Wireless local area network (WLAN): Local area network using a wireless transmission protocol.

Wireless media: The pathways used to transmit and receive electromagnetic signals using methods such as infrared line-of-sight, high-frequency radio, and microwave systems.

Wisdom: Accumulated knowledge, gained through a combination of academic study and personal experience, that goes beyond knowledge by representing broader, more generalized rules and schemas for understanding a specific domain or domains; wisdom allows you to understand how to apply concepts from one domain to new situations or problems.

Work flow software: Software applications that allow people worldwide to communicate.

Workstation: *See* Midrange computer.

World wide database: The ability of databases to be distributed and accessed from anywhere.

World Wide Web (WWW): A system of Internet servers that support documents formatted in HTML, which supports links to other documents, as well as graphics, audio, and video files.

Worm: Destructive computer code that is designed to copy and send itself throughout networked computers.

Zombie computers: Virus-infected computers that launch attacks on Web sites.

References

CHAPTER 1

Browning, R., and S. Reiss (1998). *Encyclopedia of the New Economy*. San Francisco, CA: Wired Magazine Group, Inc.

Carr, N. (2004). *Does IT matter? Information technology and the corrosion of competitive advantage*. Boston: Harvard Business School Press.

Carr, N. (2003). IT doesn't matter. *Harvard Business Review* 81(5): 41–49.

CIO.com. (2004). Metrics: Offshore spending swells. Retrieved February 3, 2007, from www2.cio.com/metrics/2004/metric667.html.

Collett, S. (2006). Hot skills, cold skills: The IT worker of 2010 won't be a technology guru but rather a "versatilist." *Computerworld*. Retrieved July 15, 2008, from www.computerworld.com/action/article.do?command=viewArticleTOC&articleId=112360.

Drucker, P. (1959). *Landmarks of tomorrow*. New York: Harper.

Evans, A., M. A. Poatsy, and K. Martin (2010). *Technology in action, complete*, 6th ed. Upper Saddle River, NJ: Prentice Hall.

Ferguson, T. (2008). Heathrow terminal 5 suffers first day baggage chaos. *Silicon.com*. Retrieved July 9, 2008, from www.silicon.com/retailandleisure/0,3800011842,39177659,00.htm.

Lundberg, A. (2004, May 1). Interview with N. Carr. *CIO.com*. Retrieved July 15, 2008, from www.cio.com/article/32264/Interview_Nicholas_Carr_The_Argument_Over_IT.

Mandel, M. (2007, June 18). The real cost of offshoring. *BusinessWeek*. Retrieved July 9, 2008, from www.businessweek.com/magazine/content/07_25/b4039001.htm?chan=top+news_top+news+index_businessweek+exclusives.

Michaeli, R. (2009). *Competitive intelligence: Competitive advantage through analysis of competition, markets and technologies*. New York: Springer.

Porter, M. E. (1985). *Competitive advantage: Creating and sustaining superior performance*. New York: Free Press.

Porter, M. E., and V. Millar (1985). How information gives you competitive advantage. *Harvard Business Review* 63(4): 149–161.

Rifkin, J. (1987). *Time wars: The primary conflict in human history*. New York: Henry Holt.

Rothfeder, J., and L. Driscoll (1990). CIO is starting to stand for "career is over": Once deemed indispensable, the chief information officer has become an endangered species. *BusinessWeek* February 26: 78–80.

Sims-Taylor, K. (1998). The brief reign of the knowledge worker: Information technology and technological unemployment. Paper presented at the International Conference on the Social Impact of Information Technologies, St. Louis, Missouri, October 12–14, 1998.

Stevens, D. (1994). Reinvent IS or Jane will. *Datamation* 40(24): 84.

Tapscott, D. (2004, May 1). The engine that drives success: The best companies have the best business models because they have the best IT strategies. *CIO.com*. Retrieved October 22, 2008, from www.cio.com/article/32265/IT_The_Engine_That_Drives_Success.

Todd, P., J. McKeen, and R. Gallupe (1995). The evolution of IS job skills: A content analysis of IS jobs. *MIS Quarterly* 19(1): 1–27.

Yeo, V. (2008, June 27). Offshoring: India still no. 1. *ZDNet*. Retrieved July 9, 2008, from news.zdnet.com/2424-9595_22-208741.html.

CHAPTER 2

Bartlett, C., and S. Ghoshal (1998). *Managing across borders: The transnational solution*. Boston: Harvard Business School Press.

Cavusgil, T., G. Knight, and J. Riesenberger (2008). *International business: Strategy, management, and the new realities*. Upper Saddle River, NJ: Prentice Hall.

Deresky, H. (2008). *International management: Managing across borders and cultures*, 6th ed. Upper Saddle River, NJ: Prentice Hall.

Engardio, P., M. Arndt, and G. Smith (2006, July 31). Emerging giants. *BusinessWeek*. Retrieved July 9, 2008, from www.businessweek.com/magazine/content/06_31/b3995001.htm.

Farrell, D., N. Kaka, and S. Stürze (2005). Ensuring India's offshoring future. *McKinsey Quarterly*, September. Retrieved July 9, 2008, from www.mckinsey.com/mgi/publications/India_offshoring.asp.

Friedman, T. L. (2007). *The world is flat 3.0: A brief history of the twenty-first century*. New York: Farrar, Straus and Giroux.

Ghoshal, S. (1987). Global strategy: An organizing framework. *Strategic Management Journal* 8(5): 425–440.

Griffin, R. W., and M. W. Pustay (2007). *International business*, 5th ed. Upper Saddle River, NJ: Prentice Hall.

Heichler, F. (2000, June 15). A head for the business. *CIO.com*. Retrieved February 3, 2007, from www.cio.com/archive/061500_head.html.

Hitt, M. A., R. D. Ireland, and R. E. Hoskisson (2009). *Strategic management. Competitiveness and globalization*, 8th ed. Boston, MA: South-Western.

Hofstede, G. (2001). *Culture's consequences: Comparing values, behaviors, institutions, and organizations across nations*. Thousand Oaks, CA: Sage Publications.

Holmes, S. (2006, January 30). Boeing's global strategy takes off. *BusinessWeek*. Retrieved July 9, 2008, from yahoo.businessweek.com/magazine/content/06_05/b3969417.htm.

International Monetary Fund (2002). Globalization: Threat or opportunity? Retrieved July 9, 2008, from www.imf.org/external/np/exr/ib/2000/041200to.htm.

Jinging, J. (2004, November 11). Wal-Mart's China inventory to hit US$18b this year. *China Daily*. Retrieved July 9, 2008, from www.chinadaily.com.cn/english/doc/2004-11/29/content_395728.htm.

King, J. (2003, September 15). IT's global itinerary: Offshore outsourcing is inevitable. *Computerworld*. Retrieved July 9, 2008, from www.computerworld.com/managementtopics/outsourcing/story/0,10801,84861,00.html.

Mallaby, S. (2006, January 2). In India, engineering success. *Washington Post*, January 2. Retrieved July 9, 2008, from www.washingtonpost.com/wp-dyn/content/article/2006/01/02/AR2006010200566.html.

Netcraft (2008). June 2008 Web server survey. *Netcraft.* Retrieved July 9, 2008, from news.netcraft.com/archives/2008/06/22/june_2008_web_server_survey.html.

Prahalad, C. K., and Y. L. Doz (1987). *The multinational mission: Balancing local demands and global vision.* New York: Free Press.

Ramarapu, N. K., and A. A. Lado (1995). Linking information technology to global business strategy to gain competitive advantage: An integrative model. *Journal of Information Technology* 10: 115–124.

Viotti, P. R., and M. V. Kauppi (2009). *International relations and world politics: Security, economy, identity,* 4th ed. Upper Saddle River, NJ: Prentice Hall.

World Economic Forum (WEF) (2008). Global information technology report 2007–2008. Retrieved July 9, 2008, from www.insead.edu/v1/gitr/wef/main/home.cfm.

CHAPTER 3

Anderson, C. (2008, February 25). Free! Why $0.00 is the future of business. *Wired.* Retrieved July 15, 2008, from www.wired.com/techbiz/it/magazine/16-03/ff_free.

Applegate, L. M., R. D. Austin, and F. W. McFarlan (2007). *Corporate information strategy and management,* 7th ed. Burr Ridge, IL: Richard D. Irwin.

Bakos, J. Y., and M. E. Treacy (1986). Information technology and corporate strategy: A research perspective. *MIS Quarterly* 10(2): 107–120.

Brynjolfsson, E. (1993). The productivity paradox of information technology. *Communications of the ACM* 36(12): 66–76.

Christensen, C. M. (1997). *The innovator's dilemma.* Boston: Harvard Business School Press.

Christensen, C. M., and M. E. Raynor (2003). *The innovator's solution: Creating and sustaining successful growth.* Boston: Harvard Business School Press.

Christensen, C. M., E. A. Roth, and S. D. Anthony (2004). *Seeing what's next: Using theories of innovation to predict industry change.* Boston: Harvard Business School Press.

Garvin, D. A. (1993). Building a learning organization. *Harvard Business Review* 71(4): 78–91.

Goldratt, E. M., and J. Cox (1992). *The goal: A process of ongoing improvement.* Great Barrington, MA: North River Press.

Harris, S. E., and J. L. Katz (1991). Organizational performance and information technology investment intensity in the insurance industry. *Organization Science* 2(3): 263–295.

Maddox, J. (1999). The unexpected science to come. *Scientific American* 281(December): 62–67.

McKeen, J. D., T. Guimaraes, and J. C. Wetherbe (1994). A comparative analysis of MIS project selection mechanisms. *Database* 25(2): 43–59.

Porter, M. E. (2001). Strategy and the internet. *Harvard Business Review* 79(3): 62–78.

Porter, M. E. (1985). *Competitive advantage: Creating and sustaining superior performance.* New York: Free Press.

Porter, M. E. (1979). How competitive forces shape strategy. *Harvard Business Review* 57 (March–April): 137–145.

Rogers, E. (2003). *Diffusion of innovations.* 5th ed. New York: Free Press.

Rubin, H. (2004, June 1). Practical counsel for capturing IT value: The elusive value of infrastructure. *CIO.com.* June 1. Retrieved July 15, 2008, from www.cio.com/article/32321/Real_Value_The_Elusive_Value_of_Infrastructure.

Shank, J., and V. Govindarajan (1993). *Strategic cost management: Three key themes for managing costs effectively.* New York: Free Press.

Valacich, J. S., J. F. George, and J. A. Hoffer (2009). *Essentials of systems analysis and design.* Upper Saddle River, NJ: Prentice Hall.

Wheeler, B. C. (2002a). Making the business case for IT investments through facts, faith, and fear. Online teaching case and teaching note. Retrieved July 15, 2008, from www.aisworld.org/onlineteachingcases/cases/ConsumerProductsIntl.doc.

Wheeler, B. C. (2002b). NeBIC: A dynamic capabilities theory for assessing net-enablement. *Information Systems Research* 13(2), 125–146.

Zuboff, S. (1988). *In the age of the smart machine: The future of work and power.* New York: Basic Books.

CHAPTER 4

Aksoy, P., and L. Denardis (2008). *Information technology in theory.* Boston: Course Technology.

Amer, B. (2007). *Computers in our world,* 2nd ed. Boston: Course Technology.

Berghel, H. (1996). U.S. technology policy in the information age. *Communications of the ACM* 39(6): 15–18.

Evans, A. D., K. E. Martin, and M. A. Poatsy (2009). *Technology in action, complete,* 5th ed. Upper Saddle River, NJ: Prentice Hall.

FitzGerald, J., and A. Dennis (2007). *Business data communications and networking,* 9th ed. New York: Wiley.

Gray, J. (2004). Distributed computing economics, in A. Herbert and K. Sparck Jones, eds. *Computer systems theory, technology, and applications, a tribute to Roger Needham.* New York: Springer, pp. 93–101.

Hoffer, J., M. Prescott, and H. Topi (2009). *Modern database management,* 9th ed. Upper Saddle River, NJ: Prentice Hall.

Netcraft (2008). June 2008 Web server survey. *Netcraft.* Retrieved July 9, 2008, from news.netcraft.com/archives/2008/06/22/june_2008_web_server_survey.html.

Te'eni, D., J. M. Carey, and P. Zhang (2007). *Human-computer interaction: Developing effective organizational information systems.* New York: Wiley.

Top 500 (2008). Retrieved July 9, 2008, from www.top500.org/lists/2008/06.

Wheeland, M. (2007). Green computing at Google. Retrieved July 9, 2008, from www.climatebiz.com/feature/2007/05/03/green-computing-google.

CHAPTER 5

Advertising Age (2007, November 5). Search marketing fact pack 2007, a supplement to *Advertising Age.* Retrieved October 22, 2008, from adage.com/images/random/datacenter/2007/searchfactpack2007.pdf.

American Life Project (2005). Reports: Online activities and pursuits. About 25 million people have used the internet to sell something. Retrieved July 14, 2008, from www.pewinternet.org/PPF/r/169/report_display.asp.

Anderson, C. (2006). *The long tail: Why the future of business is selling less of more*. New York: Hyperion.

Anderson, C. (2004). The long tail. *Wired*. Retrieved July 14, 2008, from www.wired.com/wired/archive/12.10/tail.html.

Chatterjee, D., and V. Sambamurthy (1999). Business implications of web technology: An insight into usage of the world wide web by U.S. companies. *Electronic markets* 9(2): 126–131.

Evan, P., and T. Wurster (1999). *Blown to bits: How the new economics of information transforms strategy*. Boston: Harvard Business School Press.

Fraud (2005). 2005 Internet fraud report. Retrieved July 14, 2008, from www.fraud.org/2005_Internet_Fraud_Report.pdf.

Google (2007). Marketing and advertising using Google. Retrieved October 22, 2008, from books.google.com/intl/en/googlebooks/pdf/MarketingAndAdvertisingUsingGoogle.pdf.

Kalakota, R., R. A. Oliva, and E. Donath (1999). Move over, e-commerce. *Marketing Management* 8(3): 23–32.

Laudon, K., and C. Guercio Traver (2007). *E-commerce: Business, technology, society*. New York: Pearson Addison Wesley.

Looney, C., and D. Chatterjee (2002). Web enabled transformation of the brokerage industry: An analysis of emerging business models. *Communications of the ACM* 45(8): 75–81.

Looney, C., L. Jessup, and J. Valacich (2004). Emerging business models for mobile brokerage services. *Communications of the ACM* 47(6): 71–77.

Microsoft Corporation (2005). Virgin entertainment group uses Microsoft SharePoint products and technologies to boost sales and reduce operational costs. Retrieved July 14, 2008, from members.microsoft.com/customerevidence/search/EvidenceDetails.aspx?EvidenceID=2959&LanguageID=1&PFT=developers&TaxID=25396.

Microsoft Corporation (2002). Microsoft IT: MS expense: U.S.-based employees. Retrieved July 14, 2008, from www.microsoft.com/resources/casestudies/CaseStudy.asp?CaseStudyID=13724.

MobileInfo (2008). M-commerce. *MobileInfo.com*. Retrieved July 14, 2008, from www.mobileinfo.com/Mcommerce/index.htm.

Priceline (2007). Annual report. Retrieved July 14, 2008, from sec.edgar-online.com/2007/03/01/0001104659-07-015407/Section27.asp.

Princeton Survey Research Associates (2005). Leap of faith: Using the Internet despite the dangers. Retrieved July 14, 2008, from www.consumerwebwatch.org/pdfs/princeton.pdf.

Quelch, J. A., and L. R. Klein (1996). The Internet and internal marketing. *Sloan Management Review* 63 (Spring): 60–75.

Schonfeld, E. (2006, July 27). Cyworld ready to attack MySpace. *Business 2.0*. Retrieved July 14, 2008, from money.cnn.com/2006/07/27/technology/cyworld0727.biz2/index.htm.

Szuprowicz, B. (1998). *Extranet and Intranet: E-commerce business strategies for the future*. Charleston, SC: Computer Technology Research Corporation.

Turban, E., J. K. Lee, D. King, J. McKay, and P. Marshall (2008). *Electronic commerce 2008. A managerial perspective*, 5th ed. Upper Saddle River, NJ: Pearson Education.

U.S. Census Bureau News (2006). Report No. CB06-19. Washington, DC: U.S. Department of Commerce.

Valacich, J. S., D. V. Parboteeah, and J. D. Wells (2007). The online consumer's hierarchy of needs. *Communications of the ACM, 50*(9), 84–90

Vollmer, K. (2003). IT trends 2003: Electronic data interchange. Retrieved July 14, 2008, from www.forrester.com/findresearch/results?SortType=Date&geo=0&dAg=10000&N=50645+10849.

Wells, J., and D. Gobeli (2003). The three R framework: Improving e-strategy across reach, richness and range. *Business Horizons* 46(2): 5–14.

Zwass, V. (1996). Electronic commerce: Structures and issues. *International Journal of Electronic Commerce* 1(1): 3–23.

CHAPTER 6

Adobe Corporation (2008). Cigna Healthcare. Retrieved July 14, 2008, from www.adobe.com/products/contribute/customers/.

Amazon.com (2008). Amazon fresh. Retrieved October 22, 2008, from fresh.amazon.com.

Anderson, C. (2006). *The long tail: Why the future of business is selling less of more*. New York: Hyperion.

Anderson, C. (2004). The long tail. *Wired*. Retrieved July 14, 2008, from www.wired.com/wired/archive/12.10/tail.html.

Arrington, M. (2007). Engadget knocks $4 billion off Apple market cap on bogus iphone email. Retrieved July 14, 2008, from www.techcrunch.com/2007/05/16/engadget-knocks-4-billion-of-apple-market-cap-on-bogus-iphone-email/.

Carr, N. (2005). The amorality of Web 2.0. Retrieved July 14, 2008, from www.roughtype.com/archives/2005/10/the_amorality_o.php.

CBS (2005). CBA ousts 4 for Bush guard story. Retrieved July 14, 2008, from www.cbsnews.com/stories/2005/01/10/national/main665727.shtml.

Gambino, M. (2008). Patricia Zaradic, conservation ecologist, Pennsylvania. Retrieved July 14, 2008, from www.smithsonianmag.com/science-nature/interview-patricia-zaradic.html.

Google (2008). Lakehead University success story. Retrieved July 14, 2008, from www.google.com/a/help/intl/en/admins/case_studies/lakehead.html.

Hitwise (2007). iMeem and Bebo are the fastest movers. Retrieved July 14, 2008, from www.hitwise.com/press-center/hitwiseHS2004/socialnetworkingmarch07.php.

Ho, V. (2008). Silverlight to shine in NBC's Olympics coverage. *CNET.com*. Retrieved July 14, 2008, from news.cnet.com/Silverlight-to-shine-in-NBCs-Olympics-coverage/2100-1026_3-6238260.html?hhTest=1.

IBM Corporation (2008). Wimbledon delivers a previously unimagined tennis experience. Retrieved July 14, 2008, from www-935.ibm.com/services/au/igs/pdf/wimbledon-case-study.pdf.

Keen, W. (2007). *The cult of the amateur: How today's Internet is killing our culture*. New York: Doubleday.

LaMonica, M. (2007). Microsoft's popfly: Mashup creation for the masses. *CNET.com*. Retrieved July 14, 2008, from news.cnet.com/8301-17939_109-9720583-2.html?hhTest=1.

MacManus, R. (2007). Eric Schmidt defines Web 3.0. Retrieved July 14, 2008, from www.readwriteweb.com/archives/eric_schmidt_defines_web_30.php.

MedicineNet (2008). "Virtual" health teams boost patient care. Retrieved July 14, 2008, from www.medicinenet.com/script/main/art.asp?articlekey=89224.

Microsoft Corporation (2007, February 20). Leading global coffee retailer improves business processes and enhances store

Web portal with Microsoft Office SharePoint Server. Retrieved October 22, 2008, from http://www.microsoft.com/casestudies/casestudy.aspx?casestudyid=201085.

Microsoft Corporation (2007, February 15). Major cosmetics producer deploys Microsoft search technology to increase efficiency. Retrieved October 22, 2008, from www.microsoft.com/casestudies/casestudy.aspx?casestudyid=201075.

O'Reilly, T. (2005, September 30). What is Web 2.0? Retrieved July 14, 2008, from www.oreillynet.com/pub/a/oreilly/tim/news/2005/09/30/what-is-web-20.html.

Rayport, J. (1996, December). The virus of marketing. *Fast Company.com.* Retrieved October 22, 2008, from www.fastcompany.com/magazine/06/virus.html.

Sarker, S., and S. Sahay (2002). Understanding virtual team development: An interpretive study. *Journal of the AIS* 3: 247–285.

Schonfeld, E. (2006, August 1). Cyworld attacks. *Business 2.0 Magazine.* Retrieved October 22, 2008, from http://money.cnn.com/magazines/business2/business2_archive/2006/08/01/8382263/index.htm.

Shankland, S. (2008). Google wants businesses to have faith in the cloud. *ZDNET.* Retrieved July 14, 2008, from news.zdnet.co.uk/internet/0,1000000097,39446767,00.htm.

Wikipedia. (2008, October 22). In *Wikipedia, The Free Encyclopedia.* Retrieved October 22, 2008, from http://en.wikipedia.org/w/index.php?title=Wikipedia&oldid=246862400.

World Wide Web Consortium (2008). Widgets 1.0: Requirements. Retrieved July 14, 2008, from www.w3.org/TR/2008/WD-widgets-reqs-20080625.

CHAPTER 7

Addison-Hewitt Associates (2005). The Sarbanes-Oxley Act. Retrieved July 15, 2008, from www.soxlaw.com/index.htm.

CAPTCHA (2008). Telling humans and computers apart automatically. Retrieved July 15, 2008, from www.captcha.net/.

CERT (2008). CERT Coordination Center (CERT/CC). Retrieved July 15, 2008, from www.cert.org/certcc.html.

Champlain, J. (2003). *Auditing information systems.* Hoboken, NJ: John Wiley & Sons.

Computer Security Institute (2007). *CSI Survey 2007: The 12th annual computer crime and security survey.* Retrieved July 15, 2008, from i.cmpnet.com/v2.gocsi.com/pdf/CSISurvey2007.pdf.

Electronic Privacy Information Center (2008). The clipper chip. Retrieved July 15, 2008, from epic.org/crypto/clipper/.

Fitzgerald, T. (2008). The ocean is full of phish. *Information Systems Security.* Retrieved July 15, 2008, from www.infosectoday.com/Articles/Phishing.htm.

Leyden, J. (2002, March 27). Drive-by hacking linked to cyberterror. *The Register.* Retrieved July 15, 2008, from www.theregister.co.uk/2002/03/27/driveby_hacking_linked_to_cyberterror/.

Mann, C. (2008). A primer on public key encryption. *MyCrypto.com.* Retrieved July 15, 2008, from www.mycrypto.net/encryption/public_key_encryption.html.

Martin, L. (2008). Protecting your data: It's not your father's encryption. *Information Systems Security.* Retrieved July 15, 2008, from www.infosectoday.com/Articles/Protecting_Your_Data.htm.

Panko, R. (2007). *Corporate computer and network security.* Upper Saddle River, NJ: Pearson Prentice Hall.

Reuters (2006). Morgan Stanley offers $15M fine for e-mail violations. *ComputerWorld.* Retrieved July 15, 2008, from www.computerworld.com/hardwaretopics/storage/story/0,10801,108687,00.html.

SearchCIO (2007). Disaster recovery planning for CIOs. *SearchCIO.com.* Retrieved July 15, 2008, from searchcio.techtarget.com/generic/0,295582,sid182_gci1206807,00.html#planning.

Stallings, W., (2008). *Network security essentials: Applications and standards.* Upper Saddle River, NJ: Prentice Hall.

Stallings, W., and L. Brown (2008). *Computer security: Principles and practices.* Upper Saddle River, NJ: Prentice Hall.

Sullivan, B. (2004). New MyDoom virus spreads quickly. *MSNBC.* Retrieved July 15, 2008, from www.msnbc.msn.com/id/5518331/.

CHAPTER 8

Awad, E. M., and H. M. Ghaziri (2004). *Knowledge management.* Upper Saddle River, NJ: Pearson Prentice Hall.

Checkland, P. B. (1981). *Systems thinking, systems practice.* Chichester, UK: John Wiley.

Larose, D. T. (2006). *Data mining methods and models.* New York: Wiley.

Lo, C. P., and A. K. W. Yeung (2007). *Concepts and techniques of geographic information systems,* 2nd ed. Upper Saddle River, NJ: Prentice Hall.

Leonard, D. (2005, May 1). How to salvage your company's deep smarts. *CIO.com.* Retrieved February 3, 2007, from www.cio.com/archive/050105/keynote.html.

Levinson, M. (2008). ABC: An introduction to knowledge management. *CIO.* Retrieved July 9, 2008, from www.cio.com/article/40343/ABC_An_Introduction_to_Knowledge_Management_KM_/1.

Malhotra, Y. (2005). Integrating knowledge management technologies in organizational business processes: Getting real time enterprises to deliver real business performance. *Journal of Knowledge Management* 9(1): 7–28.

Myatt, G. J. (2007). *Making sense of data: A practical guide to exploratory data analysis and data mining.* New York: Wiley.

Saarenvirta, G. (2004). The untapped value of geographic information. *Business Intelligence Journal* 9(1): 58–63.

Santosus, M., and J. Surmacz (2001, May 23). The ABCs of knowledge management. *CIO.com.* Retrieved February 3, 2007, from www.cio.com/research/knowledge.edit/kmabcs.html.

Sprague, R. H., Jr. (1980). A framework for the development of decision support systems. *MIS Quarterly* 4(4): 1–26.

Turban, E., J. E. Aronson, T. P. Liang, and R. Sharda (2007). *Decision support systems and business intelligence systems,* 7th ed. Upper Saddle River, NJ: Prentice Hall.

Turban, E., R. Sharda, J. E. Aronson, and D. King (2008). *Business intelligence.* Upper Saddle River, NJ: Prentice Hall.

White, C. (2005). Bridging the planning and business performance gap. SAP BI Research. Retrieved July 9, 2008, from www.sap.com/platform/netweaver/pdf/BWP_AR_BI_Research.pdf.

Winter, S. G. (2001). Framing the issues: Knowledge asset strategies. Wharton Impact Conference on Managing Knowledge Assets: Changing Rules and Emerging Strategies. Retrieved July 9, 2008, from emertech.wharton.upenn.edu/ConfRpts_Folder/WhartonKnowledgeAssets_Report.pdf.

CHAPTER 9

Brown, P. C. (2007). *Succeeding with SOA: Realizing business value through total architecture.* New York: Addison Wesley.

Edwards, J. (2003, February 15). RFID creates fast asset identification and management. *CIO.* Retrieved July 9, 2008, from www.cio.com/archive/021503/et_article.html.

Erl, T. (2008). *SOA principles of service design.* Upper Saddle River, NJ: Prentice Hall.

Hammer, M., and J. Champy (1993). *Reengineering the corporation: A manifesto for business revolution.* New York: Harper Business Essentials.

Harrison, A., and R. Van Hoek (2008). *Logistics management and strategy: Competing through the supply chain,* 3rd ed. Upper Saddle River, NJ: Prentice Hall.

Koch, C., D. Slater, and E. Baatz (1999, December 22). The ABCs of ERP. *CIO.com.* Retrieved August 6, 2001, from www.cio.com/research/erp/edit/122299_erp.html.

Kumar, R. L., and C. W. Crook (1999). A multi-disciplinary framework for the management of interorganizational systems. *The DATABASE for Advances in Information Systems* 30(1): 22–36.

Langenwalter, G. A. (2000). *Enterprise resource planning and beyond.* Boca Raton, FL: St. Lucie Press.

Larson, P. D., and D. S. Rogers (1998). Supply chain management: Definition, growth, and approaches. *Journal of Marketing Theory and Practice* 6(4): 1–5.

Monk, E., and B. Wagner (2006). *Concepts in enterprise resource planning,* 2nd ed. Boston: Course Technology.

Porter, M. E., and V. E. Millar (1985). How information gives you competitive advantage. *Harvard Business Review* (July–August): 149–160.

Wagner, W., and M. Zubey (2006). *Customer relationship management.* Boston: Course Technology.

CHAPTER 10

Applegate, L. M., R. D. Austin, and F. W. McFarlan (2007). *Corporate information strategy and management,* 6th ed. Chicago: Irwin.

Boynton, A. C., and R. W. Zmud (1984). An assessment of critical success factors. *Sloan Management Review* 25(4): 17–27.

Fryer, B. (1994). Outsourcing support: Kudos and caveats. *Computerworld.* Retrieved February 3, 2007, from www.computerworld.com.

Fuller, M. A., J. S. Valacich and J. F. George (2008). *Information systems project management: A process and team approach.* Upper Saddle River, NJ: Prentice Hall.

George, J. F., D. Batra, J. S. Valacich, and J. A. Hoffer (2007). *Object-oriented systems analysis and design,* 2nd ed. Upper Saddle River, NJ: Prentice Hall.

Hoffer, J. A., J. F. George, and J. S. Valacich (2008). *Modern systems analysis and design,* 5th ed. Upper Saddle River, NJ: Prentice Hall.

Martin, J. (1991). *Rapid application development.* New York: Macmillan Publishing.

McConnell, S. (1996). *Rapid development.* Redmond, WA: Microsoft Press.

McFarlan, F. W., and R. L. Nolan (1995). How to manage an IT outsourcing alliance. *Sloan Management Review* 36(2): 9–24.

McKeen, J. D., T. Guimaraes, and J. C. Wetherbe (1994). A comparative analysis of MIS project selection mechanisms. *Database* 25(2): 43–59.

Nunamaker, J. F., Jr. (1992). Build and learn, evaluate and learn. *Informatica* 1(1): 1–6.

Valacich, J. S., J. F. George, and J. A. Hoffer (2009). *Essentials of systems analysis and design.* Upper Saddle River, NJ: Prentice Hall.

CHAPTER 11

Bielski, Z. (2008, June 21). World unprepared for coming catastrophes, warn experts. *National Post,* Retrieved July 15, 2008, from www.nationalpost.com/most_popular/story.html?id=602830.

Bocij, P. (2004). *Cyberstalking: Harassment in the Internet age and how to protect your family.* Westport, Connecticut: Greenwood.

Burgess-Proctor, A., J. W. Patchin, and S. Hinduja (2008). *Cyberbullying and online harassment: Reconceptualizing the victimization of adolescent girls.* In V. Garcia and J. Clifford, eds. Female crime victims: Reality reconsidered. Upper Saddle River, NJ: Prentice Hall.

Business Software Alliance (2007). The fight for cyber space. Retrieved July 15, 2008, from www.bsa.org/~/media/9CA4C9DFEDE24250AA16F16F0ED297A6.ashx.

Business Software Alliance. (2007). Fifth annual BSA and IDC global software piracy study. Retrieved July 15, 2008, from www.bsa.org/country/~/media/F64F2ABF2A94416EA7BBE12D15984214.ashx.

Chen, H., E. Reid, J. Sinai, A. Sike, and B. Ganor (2008). *Terrorism Informatics: Knowledge Management and Data Mining for Homeland Security.* Berlin: Springer.

Computer Security Institute (2007). CSI Survey 2007: The 12th annual computer crime and security survey. Retrieved July 15, 2008, from i.cmpnet.com/v2.gocsi.com/pdf/CSISurvey2007.pdf.

FBI (2008, October 16). FBI coordinates global effort to nab 'Dark Market' cyber criminals. Retrieved October 22, 2008, from http://www.fbi.gov/pressrel/pressrel08/darkmarket101608.htm

Galbraith, J. K. (1987). The affluent society. New York: Houghton Mifflin.

Geers, K. (2008). A new approach to cyber defense. *Internet Evolution.* Retrieved July 15, 2008, from www.internetevolution.com/author.asp?id=628&doc_id=151762&f_src=flffour.

Kabay, M. E. (2007). How far could cyberware go? *NetworkWorld.* Retrieved July 15, 2008, from www.networkworld.com/newsletters/sec/2007/0723sec2.html.

Mason, R. O. (1986). Four ethical issues for the information age. *MIS Quarterly* (16): 423–433.

Panko, R. (2007). *Corporate computer and network security.* Upper Saddle River, NJ: Prentice Hall.

Salek, N. (2008, June 24). Does cyberterrorism exist? *CRN.com.au.* Retrieved July 15, 2008, from www.crn.com.au/Feature/4652,does-cyberterrorism-exist.aspx.

Sipior, J. C., and B. T. Ward (1995). The ethical and legal quandary of e-mail privacy. *Communications of the ACM* 38(12): 48–54.

US News (2007). Top computer crimes of 2007. *USNEWS.com*. Retrieved July 15, 2008, from www.usnews.com/usnews/news/badguys/070515/top_computer_crimes_of_2007_fi.htm.

Volonino, L., and S. R. Robinson (2004). *Principles and practice of information security*. Upper Saddle River, NJ: Prentice Hall.

Weber, T. (2007, January 25). Criminals 'may overwhelm the web.' *BBC*. Retrieved July 15, 2008, from news.bbc.co.uk/1/hi/business/6298641.stm.

Websense Security Labs (2008). Research highlights Q3-Q4 2007. Retrieved July 15, 2008, from www.websense.com/securitylabs/docs/SecurityLabsReport_Q4_011808.pdf.

Weimann, G. (2006). *Terror on the Internet: The new arena, the new challenges*. Washington, DC: U.S. Institute of Peace Press Books.

Weisband, S. P., and B. A. Reinig (1995). Managing user perceptions of e-mail privacy. *Communications of the ACM* (December): 40–47.

TECHNOLOGY BRIEFING

Aksoy, P., and L. Denardis (2008). *Information technology in theory*. Boston: Course Technology.

Amer, B. (2007). *Computers in our world*, 2nd ed. Boston: Course Technology.

Berghel, H. (1996). U.S. technology policy in the information age. *Communications of the ACM* 39(6): 15–18.

Evans, A., K. Martin, and M. A. Poatsy (2009). *Technology in action, complete*, 5th ed. Upper Saddle River, NJ: Prentice Hall.

FitzGerald, J., and A. Dennis (2007). *Business data communications and networking*, 9th ed. New York: Wiley.

Hoffer, J. A., J. F. George, and J. S. Valacich (2008). *Modern systems analysis and design*, 5th ed. Upper Saddle River, NJ: Prentice Hall.

Hoffer, J., M. Prescott, and H. Topi (2009). *Modern database management*, 9th ed. Upper Saddle River, NJ: Prentice Hall.

Laudon, K. and C. Guerico Traver (2008). *E-commerce: Business, technology, society*, 4th ed. New York: Pearson Addison Wesley.

Panko, R. R. (2009). *Business data networks and telecommunications*, 7th ed. Upper Saddle River, NJ: Prentice Hall.

Te'eni, D., J. M. Carey, and P. Zhang (2007). *Human-computer interaction: Developing effective organizational information systems*. Chichester, UK: John Wiley.

Name Index

A

Adelson, Jay, 245
Adleman, Len, 288
Allen, Paul, 96, 97
Anderson, Chris, 118, 119
Anderson, Tom, 420
Andreessen, Marc, 44–45
Applegate, L.M., 438
Arndt, M., 63
Austin, R.D., 438
Avey, Linda, 439

B

Baatz, E., 396
Baekdal, Thomas, 258
Bakos, J.Y., 112
Bartlett, 71, 73
Barton, Jim, 83
Batra, D., 429
Beckert, Stephan, 272
Berners-Lee, Tim, 243
Bezos, Jeff, 359
Bhasin, Pramod, 54
Biswas, Sanjit, 29
Bragale, Christine Nyirjesy, 68
Brynjolfsson, E., 94
Buffet, Warren, 97
Burns, Larry, 404
Bush, George W., 251, 289
Bushnaq, Firas, 475
Butterfield, Stewart, 469

C

Carr, Nicholas, 29, 251
Cerf, Vinton, 539
Champy, James, 373
Christensen, Clayton, 114
Clark, James H., 44–45
Clinton, Bill, 289
Crook, C.W., 363, 397

D

Darwin, Charles, 450
Del Greco, Kimberly, 450–451
DeWolfe, Chris, 266, 420
Diffie, Matt, 288
Donlin, Kevin, 128
Doz, Y.L., 70
Draper, John, 477
Driscoll, L., 15
Drucker, Peter, 5
Duell, C.H., 111

E

Eminem, 465
Engardio, P., 63

F

Fake, Caterina, 469
Fanning, Shawn, 453
Friedman, Thomas L., 39, 46, 51
Friis, Janus, 289
Fryer, B., 440

G

Galbraith, John Kenneth, 457
Gallupe, R., 15
Gates, Bill, 96, 97
George, J.F., 412, 416, 429, 431, 551

Geschke, Chuck, 345
Ghoshal, 71, 73
Goldratt, Eli, 97
Gutenberg, Johann, 455
Gutierrez, Carlos, 386

H

Hammer, Michael, 373
Harris, S.E., 99
Hector, Hans-Werner, 374
Heichler, 65
Heller, Lisa N., 439
Hitt, M.A., 70
Hoffer, J.A., 412, 416, 429, 431, 550, 551
Hoffman, Reid, 128
Hopp, Dietmar, 374
Hoskisson, R.E, 70
Hubbard, L. Ron, 318

I

Ilbarco Veeder-Rott, 37
Ireland, R.D., 70

J

Jacobs, Jon, 61
Jobs, Steven Paul, 3, 4, 19

K

Kahn, Robert, 539
Kahney, Leander, 19
Katz, J.L., 99
Kawasaki, Guy, 128
Keech, Gail, 66
Kelvin, Lord, 111
Kerkorian, Kirk, 74
King, D., 53
Kiuchi, Kakushi, 121
Koch, C., 396
Kumar, R.L., 363, 397

L

Lee, Hans, 112
Levchin, Max, 80
Loveless, Mark, 280
Lundberg, Abbie, 30

M

Madden, Cynthia, 89
Maddox, Sir John, 107
Magee, David, 74
Maiffret, Marc, 475
Makkula, Mark, 19
Mallaby, S., 55
Martin, K.E., 429
Mason, Richard O., 458
McConnell, S., 429
McFarlan, F.W., 438, 440
McKeen, J., 15
Millar, V., 27, 362, 364, 367
Miraflor, Michael, 104
Mitnick, Kevin, 477
Moore, Gordon, 110
Morris, Robert, 481
Murchu, Liam O., 474

N

Nadkarni, Shirish, 66
Needham, Col, 259
Negroponte, Nicholas, 495, 496

Nilekani, Nandan, 39
Nolan, J.W., 440

O

O'Reilly, Tim, 234
Olsen, Ken, 111

P

Page, Larry, 243
Palin, Sarah, 470
Pascal, Blaise, 516
Perens, Bruce, 449
Pergams, Oliver, 244
Peters, Tom, 9
Plattner, Hasso, 374
Porter, Michael, 27, 99, 100, 111, 362, 364, 367
Prahalad, C.K., 70
Prescott, 550
Price, Jill, 356

R

Ramsay, Mike, 83
Rather, Dan, 251
Raymond, Eric S., 449
Reshef, Eran, 413
Rivest, Ron, 288
Robinson, R.S., 490
Rogers, Everett, 113
Rose, Kevin, 233, 245
Rothfeder, J., 15
Rubin, Howard, 106, 107
Ruffalo, Jr., Robert, 55
Russinovich, Mark, 92

S

Santosus, M., 342
Schmidt, Eric, 244
Schonfeld, E., 257
Sculley, John, 19
Shamir, Adi, 288
Sims-Taylor, Kit, 7
Sipior, J.C., 467
Slater, D., 396
Smith, G., 63
Sprague, R.H., 330
St. John, Mike, 108
Stallings, W., 287
Stanley, Tim, 15
Steinnon, Richard, 275
Surmacz, J., 342

T

Tao, Shi, 28
Tapscott, Don, 30
Taylor, Frederick, 372
Tennebaum, Ehud, 488
Terzopoulous, Demetri, 256
Thiel, Peter, 80
Todd, P., 15
Toffler, Alvin, 454, 455
Topi, 50
Totenberg, Marc, 467
Treacy, M.E., 112
Tschira, Klaus, 374

V

Valacich, J.S., 412, 416, 429, 431, 551
Volonino, L., 490

W

Wagoner, Rick, 404
Ward, B.T., 467
Warner, H.M., 111
Warnock, John, 345
Warrilloe, Emma, 377
Watson, Thomas, 111
Weimann, G., 487
Wellenreuther, Claus, 374
Wells, H.G., 483

Wheeler, B.C., 97
Winter, S.G., 341
Wojicki, Anne, 439
Wolf, Gary, 356
Wozniak, Petro, 356
Wozniak, Stephen, 3, 19
Wynne, Michael W., 485

Y

Yang, Jerry, 28

Z

Zaradic, Patricia, 244
Zennström, Niklas, 289
Zimmerman, Phil, 288
Zuboff, Shoshana, 86

Organization Index

23andMe, 439

A

Accenture, 54, 432
Adobe, 345
Alexa.com, 253
All England Lawn Tennis and Croquet Club, 242
Amazon.com, 30, 109, 359, 360, 466
American Civil Liberties Union (ACLU), 451
Anheuser-Busch, 112
Apache, 450
Apple Computer, 2, 3, 4, 9, 19, 115, 121, 251, 466
AT&T, 14
Atomico, 290
Avon, 464

B

Bank One, 80
Bebo.com, 258
Best Buy, 30
Betamax, 109
BitTorrent, 453, 454
blackplanet.com, 258
Blizzard Entertainment, 61
Blockbuster, 127
Blue Security, 413
BMW, 258, 528
Boeing, 47, 58, 280
British Royal Society, 111
Business Software Alliance (BSA), 312, 478, 479
Business Week, 111

C

Canon, 121
Chrysler, 59
Church of Scientology, 318
Cisco, 28, 30
Citigroup, 23, 30, 80
Classmates.com, 258
Comcast, 119
Compaq Computers, 115
Compete.com, 253
Cover Girl Cosmetics, 99
Crest, 99
Cyworld, 256

D

Daimler, 70
DarkMarket, 473
Dell, 99, 115, 392
Digg.com, 233, 245, 246
Digital Equipment Corporation, 111, 114, 115
Dreamworks SKG, 60

E

eBay, 61, 277, 311, 312, 477
EDS, 432
eEye Digital Security, 475
Eli Lilly, 260
Embraer, 62
Emsense, 112
Enron, 301
Equinix Inc., 245
Ernst & Young, 23
everyblock.com, 239
Expedia, 261

F

Facebook.com, 36, 128, 237, 255, 258, 259–260
FBI, 450–451, 466
FedEx.com, 27, 30, 260
Flickr, 79–80, 128, 248, 469
Ford Motor Company, 74

G

Gamezone, 128
Gap, 464
Garage Technology Ventures, 128
GE, 30
General Motors, 404
Germain, 405
GM, 70
Goodwill Industries International, 68
Google, 28, 37, 46, 51, 235, 243, 265–266

H

Haier, 62
Harrah's Entertainment, 15
Harris Corporation, 386
Herman Miller, 30
Hertz, 464
Hewlett-Packard, 14, 60, 115, 364, 365
Hi5.com, 258
Hotmail, 259

I

IBM, 14, 46, 111, 432
In2Movies, 454
Infosys Technologies Ltd., 39
Intel, 46, 341
International Consumer Electronics Show (CES), 404
Internet Movie Database (IMDb), 259
iTunes, 128

J

Joost, 290
JVC, 109

K

KaZaA, 289–290
Kenmore, 377
Kodak, 121
Konica Minolta Holdings, 121

L

Life Sciences Center of Excellence, 55
LinkedIn, 128, 256, 258
Linux, 450
Live Mocha, 66
Livejournal.com, 258
London-Heathrow Airport, 26–27
Lotus, 335
Ludicorp, 79, 469

M

Mahindra, 62
Marriott, 30
McAfee, 484
McDonald's, 23, 368
Meraki Networks, Inc., 29
Mercedes Benz, 37
Meta Group, 106
Microsoft, 96, 97, 110, 407, 410, 427
MIT, 341
Mosaic Communications Corporation, 44

Motion Picture Association of America, 453
Motorola, 115
Mozilla, 427
MySpace.com, 255, 256, 257, 258, 420
myyearbook.com, 258

N

Napster, 453
Netflix, 127, 128, 355–356
Netscape, 44–45
NeXT Computer, 3, 4, 19
Nike, 49
Nikon, 121
Nintendo, 407
Nissan, 74
Nokia, 46, 115, 513
Nordstrom, 23

O

One Laptop per Child (OLPC), 29, 457, 495
OpenOffice.org, 21, 45
Orbitz, 261

P

Palo Alto Research Center (PARC), 341, 345
PayPal, 45, 80, 128, 277
PepsiCo, 30
Polaroid, 121
Popular Mechanics, 111
Port Authority Terminal, 477
Prentice Hall, 111
Price Waterhouse LLP, 30–31, 110
Pringles, 99
Procter & Gamble, 99
Progressive Casualty Insurance, 30
Project Entropia, 61
Psion, 513

Q

Quantcast.com, 253

R

Recording Industry Association of America (RIAA), 453
Renault, 74
Rent-A-Hacker, 475
Reuters, 468
RIM, 512
RSA, 288
Rush University Medical Center, 255

S

Samsung, 115
SAP, 371, 374
Sears, 114
Second Life, 128, 496
Shockwave, 128
Sky Chefs, 394
Skype, 51, 290
Smith Barney, 23
Sony, 46, 61, 71, 92, 109, 110, 115, 121, 407
Southwest Airlines, 30
Starbucks, 30, 255
Supermemo, 356
Symantec, 60
Symbian, 513

T

Tagged.com, 258
Time Warner, 29

591

TiVo, 83–84
Toshiba, 110
Toyota, 70
Travelocity, 261

U

U.S. Office of Patents, 111
UPS, 49, 50, 292–293

V

Verizon, 29
Virgin Entertainment, 398
Vulcan Inc., 97

W

Wal-Mart, 38, 49, 59, 127
Walt Disney Studios, 19
Warner Brothers, 111, 454
Washington State Cougars, 236
Washington State University, 243, 275
WebMD, 339
Webroot, 275
Western Union, 111
Wikipedia, 46, 47, 247, 248, 266–267
WildCharge, 299
World Economic Forum, 495
World Intellectual Property Organization of the
    United Nations, 464

World of Warcraft, 128, 496
World Security Corporation, 476
WorldCom, 301
Wyeth Pharmaceuticals, 55

X

Xerox Corporation, 14, 405
Xing, 256

Y

Yahoo, 28, 253, 469

Z

Zales Jewelry, 2

Subject Index

A

Active tags, 394
Ad-hoc queries, 321
Advanced Access Content System (AACS), 233
Advanced Research Projects Agency Network (ARPANET), 158
Affiliate marketing, 209
Air Force Cyber Command, 484, 485
Amateurization of journalism, 251
American Standard Code for Information Interchange (ASCII), 502, 503
Analog signals, 539
Anti-Cybersquatting Consumer Protection Act, 464
Applet, 520
Application service provider, 152
Application services, 528
Application software, 150, 514
Architectural value, 106–107
Arithmetic logic unit (ALU), 138
Associations, 548
Asymmetric digital subscriber line (ADSL), 544
Asynchronous collaboration, 254
Asynchronous transfer mode (ATM), 545
Attenuation, 156
Attribute, 167
Audio input, 501
Automating, 85

B

Backbone, 531
Bandwidth, 155
Bar code reader, 501
Basic input/output system (BIOS), 139
Batch data, 135
Batch data, entering, 500
Batch processing, 319
Best practices, 342
Best-cost provider strategy, 87
Bid luring, 216
Bid shielding, 216
Binary codes, 136, 502
Biometric scanner, 501
Bit, 136
Blogging, 249, 250, 251
Blogosphere, 251
Blogs, 247, 249, 250
Bluetooth, 157
Bot, 340
Bot herder, 482
Botnets, 481
Break-even analysis, 102
Brick-and-mortar business strategy, 193
Bricks-and-clicks business strategy, 194
Bridge, 540
Broadband wireless, 545
Brouter, 540
Business case
    presenting, 103–104
Business case arguments, 98–99
Business competency, 18
Business intelligence (BI), 312
    artificial intelligence (AI), 337
    association discovery, 323
    classification, 324
    clickstream data, 324
    clustering, 324
    collaboration systems, 332, 334
    continuous planning process, 314
    data mining, 322–323

data reduction, 323
decision support system (DSS), 330, 331
effective planning, role of, 313–314
executive information systems (EIS), 327–330
executive level, 316
expert system (ES), 338, 339
functional area information system, 331–332
information and knowledge discovery, 321–322
inputs into BI applications, 317
intelligent agent systems, 340
key performance indicators (KPIs), 316
knowledge management systems, 341–344
management information system (MIS), 325–327
managerial level, 315–316
neural network, 338–339
online analytical processing (OLAP), 322
operational level, 314
role of, 312–313
semistructured decisions, 316
sequence discovery, 323
structured decisions, 314–315
text mining, 324
threats and opportunities, responding to, 313
transaction processing system (TPS), 317, 318–320
transactions, 317
unstructured decisions, 316
visual analytics, 346
visualization, 346
web content mining, 324
web mining, 324
web usage mining, 324
Business model, 196
Business process management, 91
Business processes, 86
Business rules, 170
Business-to-business (B2B), 188
Business-to-consumer (B2C), 188
Business-to-employee (B2E), 188
Buyer agent, 340
Bus network, 536
Byte, 136
Bytes per inch (BPI), 504

C

Cable media, 156
Cable modems, 544
Cache, 139, 503
Campus area network (CAN), 156, 526
CAN-SPAM Act of 2003, 464
Carding, 477
Carnivore, 466, 467
Carrier sense multiple access/collision detect, 535
Cathode ray tube, 504
CD-R (compact disc-recordable), 504
CD-ROM, 140
CD-RW (compact disc-rewritable), 504
Cells, 532
Cellular phone technology, 532–533
Censorship, 223
Centralized computing, 523
Central processing unit (CPU), 138
Channel service unit (CSU), 540
Characters per inch (CPI), 504
Chief information officer (CIO), 14
Click fraud, 209
Click-and-mortar business strategy, 194

Click-only business strategy, 193
Click-through rate, 209
Clock speed, 503
Clock tick, 503
Cloning, 477
Coaxial cable, 530
Collaboration, 254
Collaborative computing, 525
Collector, 482
Collocation facility, 101
Combination primary key, 548
Command line interface, 150
Competitive advantage, 27, 88–89
Competitive click fraud, 209
Compiler, 516
Computer access, 470–471
Computer-based information systems, 11
Computer crime, 470
Computer criminals, 476
Computer ethics, 458
Computer fluency, 457
Computer forensics, 473
Computer Fraud and Abuse Act, 284, 472
Computer literacy, 455–457
Computer networking, 153
Computer ports, 506
Computer Security Institute (CSI), 470
Computer Software Copyright Act, 478
Computer-aided design (CAD), 399
Computer-aided engineering (CAE), 399
Computer-aided manufacturing (CAM), 399
Computer-aided software engineering (CASE), 522–523
Computer-assisted auditing tools (CAAT), 301
Concept of time, 65
Connectivity hardware, 539
Connectors, 539
Consulting, 39
Consumer-to-consumer (C2C), 189
Control objectives for information and related technology (COBIT), 301
Control unit, 138
Conversion rate, 209
Convertible tablet PCs, 512
Cookies, 464
Copyrights, 478
Cost–benefit analysis, 102
Crackers, 475, 476, 482
Crowdsourcing, 260–261
Culture, 64
Customer dot mapping, 348
Customer relationship management (CRM), 379
    analytical CRM, 380, 385
    architecture, 380–381
    back-office system, 380
    benefits of, 380
    collaborative CRM, 380, 385–386
    customer interaction center (CIC), 384
    customer service and support (CSS), 384
    developing a strategy, 380
    enterprise marketing management (EMM), 385
    ethical concerns, 386
    front-office system, 380
    operational CRM, 380, 381–382
    overview, 378–379
    sales force automation (SFA), 382
    sales force management systems, 383

Customer Verification Value (CVV2), 212
Customization, 372
Customized software, 408–409
Cyber bullying, 483
Cyber harassment, 482
Cyber stalking, 482
Cybersquatting, 464–465
Cyberterrorism, 485–486, 487, 488
Cyberwar, 484

D
Data, 8, 10
Data cleansing, 175
Data dictionary, 169
Data diddling, 477
Data mart, 176
Data model, 168
Data privacy statements, 463–464
Data type, 169
Data warehouse, 175
Data-mining agents, 340
Database, 166
Database administrator, 170
Database design, 547–548
Database management systems (DBMS), 547
Dedicated grid, 145
Defense Advanced Research Projects Agency
    (DARPA), 158
Density, 506
Desktop versus portable computers, 511
Desktop videoconferencing, 337
Destructive agents, 340
Differentiation strategy, 87
Digital dashboard, 347
Digital divide, 7, 457, 495
Digital rights management (DRM), 465,
    466
Digital signals, 539
Digital subscriber line (DSL), 544
Digital video disks, 504
Digital world
    characteristics of, 7–8
    cultural barriers, 65
    cultural challenges, 64–65
    data-sharing challenges, 58–59
    demographic challenges, 63
    economic welfare challenges, 62
    environmental challenges, 66
    expertise-related challenges, 63
    geoeconomic challenges, 60–61
    governmental challenges, 57–58
    infrastructure-related challenges, 62
    Internet access, and, 60
    political system challenges, 57
    regulatory challenges, 58
    standards, 59
    time zone challenges, 60
Digitizing, 155
Dimensions, 322
Discount rate, 102
Disintermediation, 193
Diskette, 139
Disruptive innovations, 113, 114
Distributed computing, 524
Docking station, 511
Domain name, 161
Domain Name System (DNS), 541
Domestic companies, 69
Dot matrix printer, 142
Dragnet fishing, 467
Drill down, 322
Drill-down reports, 321
Dumpster diving, 477
DVD-ROM (digital versatile disk-read-only
    memory), 504

E
e911, 281
e-auction, 215
e-business, 116
E-Business Innovation Cycle, 116
e-information, 205
e-integration, 205
e-government, 219
e-lancing, 261
e-tailing, 205
e-transaction, 205
e-waste, 68–69
EAN-13 (European Article Number), 59
Eavesdropping, 156
Economic opportunities, 117
Edge computing, 145
Electrically erasable programmable read-
    only memory (EEPROM), 140
Electromagnetic interference (EMI), 156
Electronic bill pay, 215
Electronic commerce (EC), 232
Electronic Communications Privacy Act
    (ECPA), 467, 472
Electronic Data Interchange (EDI), 198
Electronic meeting system (EMS), 336
Electronic paper (e-paper), 505
Embargoes, 58
Embedded system, 150
Enabling technologies, 117
End-user development
    benefits of, 441
    challenges of, 442–443
    definition, 440
    encouragement of, 441–442
Enterprise network, 527
Enterprise resource planning, 370, 375
Enterprise system success, 396–398
Enterprise systems, 361
    administrative activities, 366
    and customer relationship management
        (CRM), 377
    best practices-based software, 372
    business process management (BPM),
        372–373
    business process reengineering (BPR),
        373
    business processes, supporting, 362–363
    choosing an ERP system, 376–378
    continuous process improvement, 373
    conversion, 370
    core activities, 365
    custom applications, 367
    customer service activities, 365–366
    downstream information flow, 367
    externally focused applications, 367
    externally focused systems, 362
    human resource activities, 366
    inbound logistics activities, 365
    infrastructure activities, 366
    integrating data to integrate applications,
        375–376
    internally focused applications, 364–365
    internally focused systems, 362
    interorganizational system (IOS), 363
    legacy systems, 369–370
    marketing and sales activities, 365
    modules, 371
    operations and manufacturing activities, 365
    outbound logistics activities, 365
    overview, 360–361
    packaged applications, 367, 369
    procurement activities, 366–367
    rise of, 367, 369
    stand-alone applications, 369
    support activities, 366
    technology development activities, 366

total quality management, 373
upstream information flow, 367
value system, 367
vanilla versus customized software, 372
Enterprise-wide information system, 361
Entity, 167
Entity-relationship diagram (ERD), 169, 418,
    549–550
Ergonomic keyboards, 499
ERP core components, 376
ERP extended components, 378
Ethernet, 539
Ethics of information systems, 454–455, 468–469
Exception reports, 321
Explicit knowledge assets, 342
Export regulations, 58
Extensible business reporting language
    (XBRL), 393
Extensible markup language (XML), 393
External acquisition, 432–434
External cache, 503
Extraction, Transformation, and Loading
    (ETL), 175
Extranets, 90, 196
Eye-tracking device, 499

F
Facts, 322
Fast Packet Keying, 269
FDA Revitalization Act, 405
Fiber to the home (FTTH), 545
Fiber to the premises (FTTP), 545
Fiber-optic cable, 530–531
Fifth-generation languages (5GLs), 518
File services, 528
Five-forces model of competition, 100, 111
Flash, 522
Flash drive, 140
Flash memory, 140
Flops (floating points operations per second),
    507
Foreign key, 549
Form, 171
Forward auction, 216
Fourth-generation languages (4GLs), 517
Freeconomics, 118
    application in the digital world, 119–120
    freemium approach, 120
    process, 118
    value proposition, 118–119
Fully automated data entry, 319
Fuzzy logic, 338

G
Gateway, 540
Geo-tagging, 248
Geographic information system (GIS), 347,
    349
Global business strategy, 71
Global information dissemination, 191
Global networks, 527
Global Positioning System (GPS), 158
Global workforce, opportunities for a, 55–56
Globalization, 7, 40
    Berlin Wall, fall of the, 41–42
    evolution of, 40
    globalization 1.0, 40–41
    globalization 2.0, 41
    globalization 3.0, 41, 42
    Netscape Web Browser
    phases of, 41
Gopher, 161
Government-to-business (G2B), 220
Government-to-citizen (G2C), 219
Government-to-government (G2G), 220
Graphical user interface, 150

Graphics card, 142
Graphics tablet, 499
Green computing, 146
Grid computing, 144
Groupware, 334

H

Hackers, 269, 474, 475
Hacktivists, 475
Hard data, 327
Hard disk, 139
Hard drive, 139
Hardware, 8
Head crash, 503
High-frequency radio, 156
Home replication strategy, 70–71
Honeypot, 473
HTML editor, 518
Hub, 540
Human intelligence tasks, 260
Human Terrain Teams (HTT), 486
Hyperlink, 161
Hypertext, 161
Hypertext Markup Language (HTML), 161
Hypertext Transfer Protocol (HTTP), 161

I

Identity theft, 459, 460
In-forming, 49–50
In-house systems development, alternatives to, 430–431
In-sourcing, 49
Independent networks, connecting, 541
Individualism/collectivism, 65
Inferencing, 338
Informating, 86
Information, 10
Information accessibility, 466, 467
Information accuracy, 461–462
Information age, 455
Information privacy, 459
Information property, 463–464
Information systems, 12–14
    acceptable use policies, 295–296
    access-control software, 282
    application-level control, 285, 286
    assessing value, 106–107
    audit, 300–301
    audit-control software, 291
    authentication, 281, 286
    backup sites, 294
    backups, 294
    biometrics, 282, 283
    business continuity planning, 297
    career prospects and opportunities, 24–25
    certificate authority, 288
    circuit-level control, 285–286
    closed-circuit television, 294
    cold backup site, 294
    collaboration systems, 21
    collocation facilities, 293
    computer-assisted auditing tools (CAAT), 301
    confidentiality, 286
    controls, 299, 300
    defined, 8
    developing a security plan, 296
    digital signature, 288
    disaster planning, 297
    disaster recovery plan, 297
    downsizing and outsourcing, 24
    drive-by hacking, 283
    dual nature of, 26–27
    early history, 22
    encryption, 286–289
    end-user development, rise and fall of, 22–23

evolution of, 411
facilities, 291–293
firewall architecture, 286, 287
firewalls, 285–286
hot backup site, 294
human safeguards, 294–295
impact on competitive forces, 100
importance of, 29
information systems security plan, 295–297
infrastructure, 133
integrity, 288
internetworking, 20–21
managerial personnel, 15, 16
mirrored, 294
modern system organization, 23
network address translation (NAT), 286
nonrepudiation, 288
office automation systems, 21
offshore outsourcing, 24
packet filtering, 285, 286
physical access restrictions, 281–282
piggy-backing, 284
privacy, 286
professional core competencies, 17
proxy server, 286
public key technology, 288
recovery point objectives, 297
recovery time objectives, 297
redundant data centers, 294
resources, safeguarding, 279–280
Secure Sockets Layer (SSL), 289
service mentality, 23
smart card, 282
symmetric secret key system, 288
systems integration, 20–21
technological safeguards, 281
technology, spread of, 23–24
tunneling, 284, 285
types of, 20–21
uninterruptible power supply (UPS), 294
virtual private network (VPN), 284, 285
virus prevention, 290–**291**
wireless lan control, 283–284
Information systems security
    adware, 275
    Bayesian analysis, 277
    CAPTCHA, 277, 278
    cookies, 278, 289
    cyberthreats, 272
    defined, 270
    denial of service, 273–274, 274
    information modification, 271–272
    phishing, 277
    primary threats, 270–271
    spam, 275, 276
    spam filters, 275
    spim, 277
    spyware, 275
    unauthorized access, 271, 273
    viruses, 272–273, 274
    worms, 272–273
    zombie computers, 273–274
Information technology, 11
Informational system, 175
Infrastructure, 132
Infrared line of sight, 531
Ink-jet printer, 142
Innovations, valuing, 107, 109, 113, 116
Input technologies, 134
Instant messaging, 333
Intangible benefits, 101
Intangible costs, 101
Integrated services digital network (ISDN), 544
Integration, 191
Intellectual property (IP), 478

Intelligent system, 338
Interactive communication, 192
Interactive voice response (IVR), 501
Interexchange carriers (IXC), 545
Interface, 150
Internal cache, 503
International business strategy, 70
International Consumer Electronics Show (CES), 404
Internet, 158, 540
Internet backbone, 542
Internet Corporation for Assigned Names and Numbers (ICANN), 542
Internet hoax, 482
Internet hosts, 546
Internet Movie Database (IMDb), 259
Internet over satellite (IoS), 544
Internet Registry, 541
Internet Service Provider (ISP), 542
Internet Tax Freedom Act, 222
InterNIC, 542
Interpreter, 516
Intranet, 201
IP address, 161
IP convergence, 163
IP datagram, 161
IPv6, 542

J

Java, 520
JavaScript, 521
Joystick, 500

K

Keyboard, 135
Key indicator reports, 321
Knowledge, 11
Knowledge assets, 341–342
Knowledge management, 341
Knowledge management system, 342
Knowledge portals, 343
Knowledge society, 6
Knowledge worker, 5

L

Laser printer, 142
Learning organization, 86
Life focus, 65
Light pen, 500
Liquid crystal displays, 504
Local area network, 525–526
Location-based services, 217
Logic bomb, 481
Long tail, 207
Low-cost leadership strategy, 87
Luddites, 455

M

m-commerce, 217
Machine language, 136
Magnetic ink character recognition (MIRC), 501
Magnetic tape, 139
Mainframes, 142, 509
Making the business case, 91
Malware, 307, 480
Manual data entry, 319
Maquiladoras, 52
Masculinity/femininity, 65
Masquerading, 477
Mass customization, 191
Measures, 322
Media access control, 535
Menu-driven pricing, 205
Mesh network, 536
Message services, 528

Metadata, 249
Metropolitan area networks, 156, 526
Microcomputers, 142, 509–510
Microprocessor, 138
Microsoft.NET, 520
Microwave technology, 533
Microwave transmission, 157
Midrange computers, 142, 509
Mobile wireless, 545
Model, 330
Modem, 539
Monitor, 142
Monitoring and sensing agents, 340
Moore's Law, 139
Motherboard, 502
Mouse, 135, **500**
Multidomestic business strategy, 72
Multiplexer (MUX), 540
Multipurpose Internet Mail Extensions, 503

N

National Science Foundation (NSF), 159
National Science Foundation Network (NSFNET), 159
Nearshoring, 54
Neo-Luddites, 457
Net-present-value analysis, 102
Netbooks, 511
Netcasters, 251
Netcasting, 251
Netcasts, 247, **251**–252
Net neutrality, 223
Network, 155
Network access points (NAPs), 542
Network click fraud, 209
Network computers, 510
Network effect, 257
Network interface card (NIC), 539
Network operating system (NOS), 528
Network services, 528
Network standards and technologies, 535
Network topology, 535
Networking hardware, 540
Neural network system, 340
New economy, 6
Nonrecurring costs, 101
Nonshipment, 216
Nonvolatile memory, 139
Normalization, 551
Notebook computers, 511

O

Object-oriented analysis and design (OOA&D), 429–430
Object-oriented languages, 518, 519
Off-the-shelf software, 409
Offshore outsourcing, 47, 54
Offshoring, 47, 48, 54
OLAP cube, 322
OLAP server, 322
On-demand computing, 144
One Laptop per Child (OLPC), 457
Online banking, 215
Online investing, 215
Online predators, 483
Online privacy, 460–461
Online processing, 319
Online transaction processing (OLTP), 172
Open Source Initiative, 449
Open Systems Interconnection (OSI) model, 537–538
Open-source software, 150, 515
Operating systems, 146, 513
Operational system, 174
Operational value, 107
Optical character recognition (OCR), 501

Optical disks, 140
Optical mark recognition (OMR), 500, 501
Organic light-emitting diodes (OLED), 504
Organizational learning, 86
Organizational strategy, 87
Organizations and information systems, 20
Output technologies, 134
Outsourcing, 39, 47, 48, 52, 53

P

Packet switching, 160
Paid inclusion, 211
Passive tags, 394
Patents, 478
Patriot hackers, 484
Payment failure, 216
Pay-per-click, 209
Peer, 155
Peer-to-peer network, 155
Personal area networks, 156, 527
Personal computers (PCs), 509
Personal digital assistants (PDAs), 512
Petaflop, 507
Phisher, 482
Phishing, 307, **477**
Phreaking, 477
Piggybacking, 477
Plain old telephone service (POTS), 544
Plotter, 142
Podcasting, 251
Podcasts, 251
Pointing device, 135
Portable computers, 510
Power distance, 65
Power line communication, 546
Power supply, 503
Pretty Good Privacy (PGP), 58, 288
Primary key, 548
Primary storage, 139, 503
Print services, 528
Printing-on-demand, 247, **252**–254
Privacy, online, 460–461
Private branch exchange, 156, 525
Processing technologies, 134
Productivity paradox, 93–94
Productivity software, 515
Programmer, 482
Programming languages, 516, 517
Projector, 142
Propagation delay, 534
Protocols, 153, 536–537
Prototyping, 364, **428**–429, 430
Proxy variables, 105
Public switched telephone network, 544

Q

Query, 171
Query by example, 171
Quotas, 58
QWERTY keyboard, 499

R

Radio frequency identification (RFID), 49, 328, **393**–395, 500
Random-access memory (RAM), 139
Rapid application development (RAD), 429, 430
Read-only memory (ROM), 139
Read/write heads, 503
Real Simple Syndication (RSS), 251–252
Record, 167
Recurring costs, 101
Redistribution, 95
Redundant array of independent disks (RAID), 503
Registers, 139
Regulatory and compliance value, 107

Reintermediation, 193
Relational database model, 550–551
Relationships, 548
Removable storage media, 503
Repeater, 540
Report, 171
Report generator, 171
Reproductions, 216
Request for proposal (RFP), 434–436
Revenue model, 196
Reverse auction, 216
Reverse pricing system, 205
RFID tag, 394
Ring network, 536
Risk acceptance, 280, 281
Risk analysis, 280
Risk reduction, 280, 281
Risk transference, 280, 281
Roll up, 322
Router, 160
RSA, 288
Rule, 338

S

Salami slicing, 477
Sarbanes-Oxley Act, 93, 298–299, **301**
Satellite microwave, 157
Satellite technology, 533–534
Scalability, 144
Scanner, 135
Scanning technologies, 500–501
Scheduled reports, 321
Scientific Management, Principles of, 372
Scripting languages, 235, **521**
Search advertising, 211
Search engine optimization (SEO), 211–212
Search marketing, 211
Second Life, 128, 496
Secondary cache, 503
Secondary key, 548
Secondary storage, 139, 503
Selecting and pointing devices, 499–500
Self-publishing, 247
Semiautomated data entry, 319
Server, 155
Server-centric network, 155
Service-oriented architecture (SOA), 397–398
Services, 397
Shipping fraud, 216
Shopping bot, 340
Shoulder-surfing, 477
Silentbanker Trojan, 474
Slate tablet PC, 511
Slicing and dicing, 322
Slingbox, 219
Smart cards, 501
Social engineering, 477
Social network analysis, 343
Social networking, 255–256, 258
Social online communities, 255–256
Soft data, 327
Software, 8
Software as a service (SaaS), 151
Software engineering, 411
Software Forensic Tool Kit, 489
Software licensing
    click-wrap licenses, 436
    enterprise license, 436
    external acquisition by application service providers, 437
    shrink-wrap licenses, 436
    software asset management, 437
    types of software licenses, 437
    volume license, 436
Software piracy, 477, 478, 479
Sound card, 142

Source documents, 319
Spam, 464
Speech recognition, 501
Sponsored search, 211
Spoofing, 477
Spyware, 464
Star network, 536
Stickiness, 324
Storage service provider (SSP), 144
Strategic, 27
Strategic necessity, 94
Strategic planning, 87
Streaming media, 502
Streaming video, 502
Streamlined Sales Tax Project, 223
Structured decision, 314
Structured Query Language (SQL), 171
Structured systems development, 411
Subnotebooks, 511
Supercomputers, **142**, 507–508
Supermemo, 356
Supply chain management (SCM), 388
  architecture, 389–390
  bullwhip effect, 388
  defined, 387
  demand planning and forecasting, 389
  distribution planning, 389
  distribution portals, 392
  emerging trends, 391
  enterprise portals, 391–392
  financial flow, 390
  information flow, 390
  optimization of, 388–389
  overview, 387
  procurement planning, 389
  procurement portals, 392
  product flow, 390
  production scheduling, 389
  supply chain effectiveness, 390–391
  supply chain efficiency, 390
  supply chain execution (SCE), 390
  supply network, 387
  trading exchanges, 392–393
Supply chain planning (SCP), 389
Supply chains, 39, 49
Surface, 410
Symmetric digital subscriber line (SDSL), 544
Synchronous collaboration, 254
System clock, 503
System effectiveness, 94
System efficiency, 94
System unit, 136, 502
Systems analysis and design, 411
Systems analyst, 411
Systems benchmarking, 435
Systems competency, 18
Systems development process
  adaptive maintenance, 426
  alpha testing, 424
  beta testing, 424
  corrective maintenance, 426
  critical success factor (CSF), 416, 417
  data flows, 418
  databases and files, designing, 422
  developmental testing, 424
  evaluation criteria for classifying and ranking projects, 415
  human–computer interface (HCI), 421
  information systems planning, 413–414
  joint application design (JAD), 416
  modeling data, 418
  outsourcing, 437–438, 440
  patch management systems, 426
  perfective maintenance, 426

preventative maintenance, 426
processing and logic, designing, 423
processing logic, 419, 421
psuedocode, 419
requirements collection, 416
software maintenance, 426
sources of systems development projects, 414
systems analysis, 415–416
systems design, 421
systems development life cycle (SDLC), 412–413
systems implementation, 423
systems maintenance, 425
systems planning and selection, 413
user training options, 425
users, role of, 412
Systems software, 146

T

T1 lines, 545
T3 line, 545
Table, 167
Tablet PC, 511
Tacit knowledge assets, 342
Tag, 393
Tagging, 248–249
Tangible benefits, 101
Tangible costs, 101
Tariffs, 58
TCP/IP, 539
Technology, 11
Telecommunications networks, 8
Terminals, 523
Terrestrial microwave, 157
Text recognition software, 500
Thematic mapping, 348, 350
Thin client, 510
Time bombs, 481
Time lags, 94–95
Token passing, 535
Top-level domain, 162
Total cost of ownership (TCO), 101
Touch screen, 500
Trackball, 500
Trade area analysis, 348
Transborder data flows, 58
Transaction support, 192
Transmission Control Protocol/Internet Protocol (TCP/IP), 160
Transmission media, 153
Transnational business strategy, 72–73
Triple convergence, 51
Trojan horses, 480
Twisted pair cable, 156, 529–530

U

Ultra Low Power (ULP) Bluetooth, 157
Ultramobile PCs (UMPCs), 511
Unauthorized computer access, 471
Uncertainty avoidance, 65
Uniform Resource Locator (URL), 161
Universal Product Code (UPC), 59
Uploading, 46
USA PATRIOT Act, 221
User agent, 340
Utilities, 513, 514
Utility computing, 144
Utility programs, 513

V

Value chain, 90
Value chain analysis, 90
Value, assessing, 117
Value-added networks (VANs), 527

Valuing innovations, 107, 109
Vertical market, 392
Video card, 142
Video input, 501
Videoconferencing, 336
Videoconferencing over IP, 164
Viral marketing, 257–258
Virtual company, 193
Virtualization, 146
Virtual machine, 146
Virtual meetings, 254
Virtual reality (VR), 244
Virtual teams, 255, 334
Vishing, 477
Visual programming languages, 518
Voice input, 501
Voice over IP (VOIP), 164
Voice-to-text software, 501
Volatile memory, 139

W

War spamming, 269
Warez, 478
Warez peddling, 478
Watermark, 466
Web 2.0
  capabilities, 236–237
  collaboration software, 240
  collaboration tools, 238–239
  collaboration, enhancing, 254–255
  components, 235–236
  content management systems, 242–243
  defining, 234
  Google Apps, 240–241
  mashups, 238
  Microsoft SharePoint and Groove, 241
  peer-to-peer technology, 235
  semantic Web, 243–244
  Web-based collaboration tools, 239–240, 241
  widgets, 237–238
Web 3.0, **244**, 246
Web analytics, 210
Web browser, 161
Web cam, 337
Web crawlers, 340
Web development languages, 518, 519, 520
Web log, 249
Web page, 161
Web servers, 161
Web services, 237
Web site, 161
Web spiders, 340
Web vandalism, 484
Weblogging, 249
Webroot, 275
Weighted multicriteria analysis, 103
What-if analysis, 330
Wide area network, 156, 526
Wikis, 47, 247, 248
Wikipedia, 247
WiMax, 546
Wired Equivalent Privacy (WEP), 269
Wireless camouflage, 269
Wireless fidelity (Wi-Fi), 157
Wireless local area networks (WLANs), 157
Wireless media, 156, 531, 534
Wisdom, 11
Work flow software, 45, 46
Workstation, 142
World Wide Database, 246
World Wide Web (WWW), 161
Worm, 480

Credits

Cover: Getty Images.

Chapter 1: Page 3, Apple/Splash News\Newscom; 9, Frank Pryor\Apple Computer, Inc.; 19, AP Wide World Photos; 26, Susan Van Etten\PhotoEdit Inc.; 27, Mark Richards\PhotoEdit Inc.

Chapter 2: Page 39, Reuters\Corbis/Bettman; 42, Anthony Suau\Getty Images, Inc–Liaison; 44 (left), AP Wide World Photos; 44 (right) Loudcloud Inc.\AP Wide World Photos; 46, David Young-Wolff\PhotoEdit Inc.; 47 (top), Wikipedia, The Free Encyclopedia; 47 (bottom), Getty Images, Inc.; 48, © Allen Birnbach/Masterfile; 49, AP Wide World Photos; 50, Shutterstock; 52, Getty Images, Inc.; 59, Carol and Mike Werner\Phototake NYC; 67, © Basel Action Network (www.ban.org); 69, Sean Young\Landov Media.

Chapter 3: Page 96, © UW/Mary Levin; 110, Newscom; 120, Copyright ©1984 Water Productions Inc. and Warner Bros. Inc. (All Rights Reserved).

Chapter 4: Page 133, Getty Images, Inc.; 135, Lenovo Group Limited; 138, Intel Corporation Pressroom Photo Archives; 140, Apple / Splash News\Newscom; 143, Jamstec / Earth Simulator Center; 165, Hewlett Packard Imaging & Printing Group.

Chapter 5: Page 187, Copyright 2007, Linden Research, Inc. All Rights Reserved.; 191, Butler Photography; 192, Joshua Lutz\Redux Pictures; 195, Charles Schwab & Company, Inc.; 206, David Young-Wolff\PhotoEdit Inc.; 214, Noah Berger\AP Wide World Photos.

Chapter 6: Page 238, Courtesy of Google. GOOGLE is a trademark of Google Inc.; 245, Jim Wilson/© The New York Times; 250, Corbis Royalty Free, 252, *The New York Times*, 255, Stephen Chernin\Newscom; 257, Stephen Hilger/Bloomberg News\Landov Media.

Chapter 7: Page 269, Wireless Garden, Inc.; 282, Jonathan Drake/Bloomberg News\Landov Media; 283, AP Wide World Photos; 290, Matthew Staver/Bloomberg News/Landov; 293 (top). United Parcel Service; 293 (bottom), Sungard Availablity Services.

Chapter 8: Page 311, Michael J. Ray/These materials have been reproduced with the permission of eBay, Inc. COPYRIGHT © EBAY INC. ALL RIGHTS RESERVED;

335, Lotus Development Corp.; 336, Courtesy of GroupSystems Corporation; 337 (top), Courtesy of TANDBERG; 337 (bottom left), Spencer Platt/Getty Images, Inc.; 337 (bottom right), © 2002 Paramount Pictures/Courtesy: Everett Collection; 339, WebMD Health; 345 (left), Richard Drew\AP Wide World Photos; 345 (right), REUTERS/Larry Downing, 346, NASA Headquarters; 350, Caliper Corporation.

Chapter 9: Page 359, © Jack Kurtz/ The Image Works; 368, Ng Han Guan\AP Wide World Photos; 374, Vario Images/GmbH&Co. KG\Alamy Images; 394, Kruell/laif\Redux Pictures; 395, Courtesy of METRO AG.

Chapter 10: Page 407, istockphoto.com; 410, Courtesy of Microsoft Corporation; 420, Getty Images.

Chapter 11: Page 453, Jeff Christensen/Reuters\CORBIS–NY; 456 (top), Erich Lessing\Art Resource, N.Y.; 456 (bottom), 3M Touch Systems; 457, Jean-Yves Rabeuf\The Image Works; 458 (top), Fuse Project; 459, David Young-Wolff\PhotoEdit Inc.; 460, Pat Wellenbach\AP Wide World Photos; 463, Images.com; 465 (bottom), Agence France Presse/Getty Images; 466, Ron Alston\Getty Images Inc.–Stone Allstock; 469, © Photo by MARTIN KLIMEK/klimekphoto.com; 478, AP Wide World Photos; 485 (top), AP Wide World Photos; 485 (bottom), Courtesy of United States Air Force Cyber Command.

Technology Briefing: Page 499, Martin Meissner\AP Wide World Photos; 500, Andersen/Ross/Brand X\Jupiter Images–PictureArts Corporation/Brand X Pictures Royalty Free; 503, Intel Corporation Pressroom Photo Archives; 508, LBNL\Photo Researchers, Inc.; 509, Courtesy of International Business Machines Corporation. Unauthorized use not permitted; 510 (top), Apple Computer, Inc.; 510 (bottom), Courtesy of Sun Microsystems, Inc.; 511, Apple Computer, Inc.; 512 (top left), Toshiba America Information Systems, Inc.; 511 (top right), Patrick Olear\PhotoEdit Inc.; 512 (bottom), Blackberry Research in Motion Ltd.; 521, Courtesy of Google. GOOGLE is a trademark of Google Inc.; 528, Courtesy of BMW AG Munich; 530 (top left), Courtesy of Belkin Corporation; 530 (top right), Getty Images, Inc.–Photodisc; 530 (bottom), Getty Images, Inc.–Photodisc; 531, Getty Images, Inc.–Photodisc.